# THE
# CAMBRIDGE
# ANCIENT HISTORY

## THIRD EDITION

### VOLUME II
### PART 2

### HISTORY OF THE MIDDLE EAST AND
### THE AEGEAN REGION *c.* 1380–1000 B.C.

*EDITED BY*

**I. E. S. EDWARDS** F.B.A.
*Formerly Keeper of Egyptian Antiquities, The British Museum*

THE LATE **C. J. GADD**

**N. G. L. HAMMOND** F.B.A.
*Professor Emeritus of Greek, University of Bristol*

**E. SOLLBERGER** F.B.A.
*Keeper of Western Asiatic Antiquities, The British Museum*

**CAMBRIDGE**
AT THE UNIVERSITY PRESS
1975

Published by the Syndics of the Cambridge University Press
Bentley House, 200 Euston Road, London NW1 2DB
American Branch: 32 East 57th Street, New York, N.Y. 10022

© Cambridge University Press 1975

Library of Congress Catalogue Card Number: 75–85719

ISBN: 0 521 08691 4

Printed in Great Britain
at the University Printing House, Cambridge
(Euan Phillips, University Printer)

# CONTENTS

CHAPTER XVII

## THE STRUGGLE FOR THE DOMINATION
## OF SYRIA
### (1400–1300 B.C.)

*by the late* A. GOETZE
*Sterling Professor Emeritus of Assyriology
and Babylonian Literature, Yale University*

CHAPTER XVIII

## ASSYRIA AND BABYLON
### *c.* 1370–1300 B.C.

*by the late* C. J. GADD
*Professor Emeritus of Ancient Semitic Languages
and Civilizations, School of Oriental and African
Studies, University of London*

[ v ]

CHAPTER XIX

# EGYPT: THE AMARNA PERIOD AND THE END OF THE EIGHTEENTH DYNASTY

*by* CYRIL ALDRED

*Formerly Keeper of the Department of Art and Archaeology in the Royal Scottish Museum, Edinburgh*

CHAPTER XX

# THE AMARNA LETTERS FROM PALESTINE

*by the late* W. F. ALBRIGHT

*W. W. Spence Professor Emeritus of Semitic Languages in the Johns Hopkins University*

CHAPTER XXI

# (a) ANATOLIA FROM SHUPPILULIUMASH TO THE EGYPTIAN WAR OF MUWATALLISH

*by the late* A. GOETZE

## (b) UGARIT

*by* MARGARET S. DROWER
*Reader in Ancient History in the University of London*

## (c) TROY VII

*by the late* C. W. BLEGEN
*Professor Emeritus of Classical Archaeology in the University of Cincinnati*

CHAPTER XXII

# (a) THE EXPANSION OF THE MYCENAEAN CIVILIZATION

*by* FRANK H. STUBBINGS
*Lecturer in Classics in the University of Cambridge*

## (b) CYPRUS IN THE LATE BRONZE AGE

### by H. W. CATLING
*Director of the British School of Archaeology at Athens*

### CHAPTER XXIII

## EGYPT: FROM THE INCEPTION OF THE NINETEENTH DYNASTY TO THE DEATH OF RAMESSES III

### by R. O. FAULKNER
*Fellow of University College London*

CHAPTER XXIV

# THE HITTITES AND SYRIA (1300–1200 B.C.)

*by the late* A. GOETZE

CHAPTER XXV

# ASSYRIAN MILITARY POWER 1300–1200 B.C.

*by* J. M. MUNN-RANKIN

*Lecturer in Near Eastern History in the University of Cambridge*

CHAPTER XXVI

## PALESTINE IN THE TIME OF THE NINETEENTH DYNASTY

### (a) THE EXODUS AND WANDERINGS

*by the late* O. EISSFELDT
*Professor Emeritus an der Martin Luther-Universität Halle-Wittenberg*

### (b) ARCHAEOLOGICAL EVIDENCE

*by* H. J. FRANKEN
*Rijksuniversiteit te Leiden*

CHAPTER XXVII

## THE RECESSION OF MYCENAEAN CIVILIZATION

*by* FRANK H. STUBBINGS

CHAPTER XXVIII

## THE SEA PEOPLES

*by* R. D. BARNETT

*Formerly Keeper of Western Asiatic Antiquities in The British Museum*

CHAPTER XXIX

## ELAM *c.* 1600–1200 B.C.

*by the late* RENÉ LABAT
*Professeur au Collège de France*

CHAPTER XXX

## PHRYGIA AND THE PEOPLES OF ANATOLIA IN THE IRON AGE

*by* R. D. BARNETT

CHAPTER XXXIII

# SYRIA, THE PHILISTINES, AND PHOENICIA

*by the late* W. F. ALBRIGHT

CHAPTER XXXIV

# THE HEBREW KINGDOM

*by the late* O. EISSFELDT

CHAPTER XXXV

# EGYPT: FROM THE DEATH OF RAMESSES III TO THE END OF THE TWENTY-FIRST DYNASTY

*by the late* J. ČERNÝ
*Professor of Egyptology in the University of Oxford*

CHAPTER XXXVI

# THE END OF MYCENAEAN CIVILIZATION AND THE DARK AGE

## (a) THE ARCHAEOLOGICAL BACKGROUND

### by V. R. D'A. DESBOROUGH
Senior Research Fellow of New College, Oxford

## (b) THE LITERARY TRADITION FOR THE MIGRATIONS

### by N. G. L. HAMMOND
Professor Emeritus of Greek in the University of Bristol

CHAPTER XXXVII

# THE WESTERN MEDITERRANEAN

*by* GLYN DANIEL
*Disney Professsor of Archaeology in the University of Cambridge*

*and* J. D. EVANS
*Director of the Institute of Archaeology in the University of London*

CHAPTER XXXVIII

# GREEK SETTLEMENT IN THE EASTERN AEGEAN AND ASIA MINOR

*by* J. M. COOK
*Professor of Ancient History and Classical Archaeology in the University of Bristol*

CHAPTER XXXIX(*a*)

# THE PREHISTORY OF THE GREEK LANGUAGE

*by* JOHN CHADWICK
*Fellow of Downing College and Reader in Classics in the University of Cambridge*

CHAPTER XXXIX(*b*)

# THE HOMERIC POEMS AS HISTORY

*by* G. S. KIRK

*Professor of Greek in the University of Bristol*

CHAPTER XL

# THE RELIGION AND MYTHOLOGY OF THE GREEKS

*by* W. K. C. GUTHRIE

*Formerly Master of Downing College and Laurence Professor of Ancient Philosophy
in the University of Cambridge*

# BIBLIOGRAPHIES

CONTENTS

# MAPS

# TEXT-FIGURES

# PREFACE

F o r very different reasons the two kings who lived at the beginning of the period to which this part of the *History* is devoted have received more attention in modern times than any of their predecessors or successors on the Egyptian throne: Akhenaten, on account of his religious and artistic innovations, and Tutankhamun, on account of the chance survival of his tomb at Thebes with its fabulous contents untouched since antiquity until its discovery in 1922. Neither of them was accepted as having been a legitimate ruler worthy of inclusion in the king-lists of the Nineteenth Dynasty kings Sethos I and Ramesses II, as recorded in their temples at Abydos. While they and their successors until the end of the Twenty-first Dynasty occupied the throne of Egypt, important events were happening in Western Asia, the course of which is traced in this volume. The long Kassite rule in Babylonia came to an end and the rivalry between Assyria and Babylonia began. The Hittite empire reached its peak, declined and fell, as did the Elamite kingdom in Persia. The Phrygians appeared on the scene for the first time. Along the Mediterranean shores, in Phoenicia and in Ugarit new forms of writing were developed. Palestine emerged from its long period of anonymity with the rise of the Hebrew kingdom culminating in the reign of Solomon. Inevitably some of these events and others too, such as the southern movement of the so-called Sea Peoples, affected Egypt either directly or indirectly and she was fortunate in having on the throne a succession of warrior-kings who were able to ward off the worst of the threats to their country's independence either by military action or by judicious diplomacy. Indecisive battles between the Hittites and the Egyptians under Sethos I and Ramesses II ended with a peace-treaty which was honoured by both nations until the Hittites had ceased to be a power in Western Asia and the Sea Peoples had taken their place as the most serious menace to Egypt. The first clash came in the reign of Merneptah when the Sea Peoples, in alliance with the Libyans, invaded the western Delta but were beaten in a six-hour battle in which they suffered heavy losses. Further battles on land, outside Egyptian territory to the north-east, and in one of the mouths of the Nile, fought by Egypt's last great pharaoh, Ramesses III, proved more conclusive and the danger of invasion from the north was removed. The Libyans, however, in spite of being driven back by Ramesses III, continued to encroach on Egyptian soil and ultimately, under his weak successors of the same name, they set up communities in the Delta and at Heracleopolis, near the entrance to the Faiyūm. Their relations with the native population are not easy to understand. On the one hand Libyan bands are reported as harrying workers in the royal necropolis as far south as Thebes, and on the other hand Libyans served as mercenaries in the Egyptian army. Not very many years after their arrival a descendant of one of the chiefs of the Libyan community at Heracleopolis named Sheshonq was able to establish himself on the throne as king of Egypt, but his reign lies outside the scope of this volume.

The central theme in the Aegean region is the spread of Mycenaean civilization. Although deeply influenced by Minoan culture, the rulers and the upper classes of the Mycenaeans imposed their own pattern upon the outlook and the art of the peoples of the mainland. They built strongly fortified castles, organized their realms into powerful kingdoms and made conquests overseas. In the fourteenth century, when the Mycenaean civilization was at its zenith, the overseas settlements extended from Acragas and Syracuse in Sicily to Miletus in Asia Minor and to Cyprus. At this time when the civilizations of the Near East enjoyed a high level of prosperity and the resources of Europe and the Western Mediterranean were being developed, especially in minerals, the Mycenaeans held the intermediate zone through which most of the seaborne traffic passed between Europe, Africa and Asia. Mycenaean objects and Mycenaean traders reached many distant parts of the world, and the Greek language was enriched by contact with many peoples. Mycenaean experiences were incorporated in the myths which were to be transmitted to the Classical world and to modern times, and the foundations of Greek religion were laid in a Minoan–Mycenaean context which was itself influenced by the other religions of the Near East.

The decline of the Mycenaean civilization was a result of a general deterioration of trade and a dislocation of political conditions, to which the Mycenaean states themselves contributed by attacking one another and by destroying Troy. The Aegean Bronze Age drew to its end with the migrations of less civilized peoples into the Balkan peninsula and Asia Minor, which led in their turn to the migrations of Greek-speaking peoples from the North into Greece and from Mycenaean Greece to Crete, Cyprus,

Asia Minor and other places. It was in this final stage of the Mycenaean world that the expedition of Agamemnon against Troy took its place in Greek legend and provided Homer, centuries later, with the theme of the *Iliad*. The prehistoric cultures of the Western Mediterranean region, including the islands and the coastal lands, are described in Chapter xxxvii, and the account is carried down to the arrival of migrants and colonists from the Eastern Mediterranean in the Early Iron Age.

Four contributors wish to express their gratitude to other scholars for giving them assistance: Dr R. D. Barnett to Dr J. Chadwick, Dr M. and Dr T. Dothan and Professor O. R. Gurney in his revision of Chapter xxviii, and to Professor Gurney, Mr J. D. Hawkins and Dr G. I. Martin in his revision of Chapter xxx; Professor D. J. Wiseman to Professor J. A. Brinkman for generously placing at his disposal the manuscript of his doctoral thesis (see the bibliography to Chapter xxxi, G, 2 and A, 3), and allowing him to use it freely when writing Chapter xxxi; Professor J. M. Cook to Mr R. V. Nicholls; Professor W. K. C. Guthrie and the Editors to Mrs Helen Hughes-Brock for additions to the bibliography of Chapter xl. The Editors are also indebted to Dr Chadwick for the generous help which he has given in matters deriving from the decipherment of Linear Script B.

The task of the Editors has been greatly facilitated by the friendly cooperation which they have received from the staff of the Cambridge University Press and they wish to thank them both for the readiness with which they have given it and for their patience in enduring the delay which has attended the submission of the text to the printer. Several contributors have availed themselves of the invitation of the Syndics to revise their chapters, and they, as well as the Editors, are grateful for the opportunity thus afforded to make use of information which was not available when the chapters appeared in fascicle form.

It is with sadness that the Editors record the deaths of no fewer than seven contributors since the publication of the previous part: Professors W. F. Albright, J. Černý, O. Eissfeldt, C. W. Blegen, A. Goetze, R. Labat and R. de Vaux.

Chapters xxix and xxxii by Professor Labat were originally written in French and were translated into English by Mr D. A. Kennedy of the Centre national de la recherche scientifique, Paris.

I.E.S.E.
N.G.L.H.
E.S.

# CHAPTER XVII

## THE STRUGGLE FOR THE DOMINATION
## OF SYRIA (1400–1300 B.C.)

### I. MITANNIANS AND HITTITES—TUSHRATTA
### AND SHUPPILULIUMASH

SYRIA lies at the crossroads of the Near East between Mesopotamia in the east, Anatolia in the north and Egypt in the south.
Both Mesopotamia and Anatolia are lacking in indispensable raw
materials which they must acquire by trade. For them, then,
Syria means access to world trade. Through Syria pass the overland communications that lead from one to the other. More
significant still, Syria possesses ports where merchandise from
far-away countries is received and exchanged for whatever Asia
has to offer. By land and by sea Syria is also linked to Egypt,
another important centre of ancient civilization. For these reasons
all political development in the Near East tends toward the domination of Syria by its neighbours. In antiquity possession of this
key position assured supremacy in the world as it then existed.
The fourteenth century, a period of intensive interrelations among
all parts of the world, was no exception. In fact, the struggle for
the domination of Syria was never more marked than during this
period.

The efforts of the various powers involved in the struggle were
facilitated by the ethnic and social conditions which they encountered when they invaded Syria. The Amorite rule over the
country had created a large number of small city-states which were
organized along feudalistic lines. This had become more accen-
tuated when the Hurrians, revitalized by Indo-Aryan dynasts,
had expanded from Upper Mesopotamia toward the west. Hurrian knights had then replaced the Amorite princes, taken over
the best parts of the land for themselves and their liegemen
(*mariyanna*), and now formed a caste of their own. Thus the rift
between the rulers and the ruled was not only economic and social,
it was ethnic as well. Anyone who gained the co-operation of the
upper class could easily dominate their countries.

Egyptian power had been omnipotent in Syria in the days of

* An original version of this chapter was published in fascicle 37 in 1965.

the great Tuthmosis III. During the reigns of his successors it
was definitely on the decline, until under Amenophis III (1417–
1379) Egyptian domination was only nominal. The most important source illustrating these conditions is the Amarna letters,
the remnants of the political archives of Amenophis III and IV.
Found in the ruins of Amenophis IV's palace at Amarna they
have given the name 'Amarna Age' to the whole period which
they cover. The Amarna letters consist of the messages, mostly
composed in Akkadian and all of them written in cuneiform script
on clay tablets, which had been sent to the Egyptian court by the
contemporary rulers of the great powers in neighbouring Asia
and by the numerous independent princes of Palestine and Syria.
At the period in question Egyptian officers, appointed to supervise and control the local princes and to collect the tribute which
these had to pay to the pharaoh, still resided in the area. The
Akkadian sources call such an officer *rābiṣu*, literally 'watcher,
observer', the corresponding word in the Semitic vernacular of
the country being *šākinu* (Canaanite *sōkinu*). During our period,
the cities of Kumidu and Ṣumura served as residences for these
'commissioners' or 'regents' of Syria. Both these cities are strategically located. The former blocks the passage through the
Biqāʿ, the narrow plain between the Lebanon in the west and the
Anti-Lebanon and the Hermon in the east; it is close enough to
Damascus to control it as well. The latter is situated on the coastal
highway, near the mouth of the Eleutheros River, and also dominates the road which leads eastward along that river to the Orontes
Valley. Along the coast Egyptian control was firmer than inland.
When roads were disrupted there was always the sea route to
maintain communications with Egypt.

The Mitanni kings ruled in Upper Mesopotamia with their
capital Washshuganni probably near the Upper Khabur River,
and the influence which they exercised upon Syria no doubt
depended on the fact that since the days of the Hurrian expansion many, if not most, of the small states there had passed into
the hands of Hurrian princes. In the days of Egyptian weakness, the Mitannian kings used this circumstance to create a kind
of Hurrian confederacy which was controlled from their capital.
Mitannian power was at its height at the beginning of the fourteenth century.

It had then taken the place of the Hittites as the dominating
factor. With the decline of Egyptian might after the death of
Tuthmosis III the Hittites had, with considerable success, tried
to re-establish themselves in Syria where they had ruled during

their 'Old Kingdom'. But when their homeland on the Anatolian plateau had been attacked from all sides in the times of Tud-khaliash III, they had been forced to withdraw from Syria. Yet their power continued to loom in the background as a factor with which to reckon.

The interplay of all these forces—the Egyptians, the Mitan-nians with their Hurrian partisans and finally the Hittites—determined the fate of Syria in the fourteenth century.

Since the middle of the second millennium the dynasty which called itself 'kings of Mitanni (Maitani)' had become dominant among the Hurrians.[1] From Washshuganni it exercised power eastward over Assyria and the East Tigris regions, northward over the country which later became Armenia, and westward into Syria.

Within the Hurrian realm there existed a rivalry between the kings of Mitanni and those who called themselves 'kings of the Khurri Land'. This must refer to a Khurri Land in the narrower sense of the term. The border dividing this Khurri Land from the Mitanni kingdom apparently ran along the River Mala, i.e. the Euphrates (Murad Su?). It seems that the Khurri Land had been the older of the two, but that Mitanni had overtaken it in power and political importance. Tushratta, the younger son of a Shut-tarna who had been an older contemporary of Amenophis III,[2] had acquired kingship over Mitanni in irregular fashion. Shut-tarna had first been succeeded by his son Artashuwara. He was slain, however, by a certain Utkhi (*UD-ḫi*), a high officer of the state, and Tushratta (*Tuišeratta*), a younger brother, then still a minor, was installed on the throne.[3] Artatama of Khurri apparently did not recognize Tushratta as his overlord; on the contrary he seems to have claimed at least independence if not more. Judgement on the situation is rendered difficult by the circumstance that the earlier relations of the two rivalling states are not known to us. According to the beliefs of the time, the struggle which ensued between Tushratta and Artatama was conceived as a lawsuit between the two opponents pending before the gods.[4]

The date of Tushratta's accession to the throne falls within the reign of Amenophis III (1417–1379), more precisely into its second half. The Amarna archive has yielded seven letters from Tushratta to Amenophis III,[5] an indication that their friendly

[1] See *C.A.H.* ii[3], pt. 1, pp. 422 ff.
[2] EA 17, 21. [For brevity, EA in footnotes to this chapter refers to the Amarna letters (and their lines) as numbered in G, 12.]
[3] *Ibid.* 1–20.          [4] §1, 8, no. 1, obv. 48 f.
[5] EA 17–21; 23 (Amenophis III, year 36); 24.

relationship was maintained over a number of years. We may estimate that Tushratta's reign is to be counted from about 1385.

Whatever territory Artatama of Khurri may have controlled,
Tushratta was able to maintain himself in the Mitanni kingdom
for the time being. This included, in addition to Assyria and the
adjoining provinces in the east, Upper Mesopotamia and parts of
Syria. There, more specifically, the following territories were under
his overlordship. Farthest north, in Cilicia and bordering on the
Mediterranean lay Kizzuwadna.[1] For a long time it had shifted
its allegiance back and forth between Khatti and Mitanni. The
collapse of Hittite power under Tudkhaliash III had driven it
again into the arms of the Mitannians.[2] Something similar may
have happened to Ishuwa, farther east,[3] although nothing precise
is known about it. In Syria proper the kingdoms of Carchemish
and Aleppo were most important; in the circumstances, neither
can have been independent of Mitanni. For the first this is confirmed by the role it played in the later Hittite war of conquest;
for Aleppo there is documentary proof that it once formed part of
the Hurrian system of states.[4] Further to the south were located
the countries of Mukish (with its capital at Alalakh) and Ugarit.
Formal relations with the Mitanni state are assured for the
former;[5] for Ugarit this remains doubtful. Its position on the
coast may well have resulted in conditions different from those
which prevailed inland; under the protection of Egypt, Ugarit
may have maintained a precarious kind of independence. The
Nukhash Lands, between the bend of the Euphrates and the
Orontes, definitely belonged to Tushratta's realm.[6] In the Orontes
valley we find Neya (Ne'a), Arakhtu, and Ukulzat ruled by
Hurrian dynasties[7] which no doubt maintained friendly relations
with the Mitanni king. Finally there are, in the far south of
Syria, Qatna, Kinza (Kidsa = Qadesh on the Orontes), and
Amurru. Here Mitannian influence was counterbalanced by the
Egyptians, and local princes found it necessary to play the dan-
gerous game of aligning themselves on one side or the other, as
circumstances required.

Tushratta at first experienced no unpleasantness in his relations
with the Hittite kingdom. As long as the Hittites remained re-
coiled upon their Anatolian homeland and maintained themselves
with difficulties, there was no opportunity for friction.

---

[1] §1, 4.
[2] §1, 8, no. 7, i, 7, 38.
[3] §1, 8, no. 1, obv. 10 ff.; no. 7, i. 8.
[4] §1, 8, no. 6, obv. 23; cf. §1, 3.
[5] §1, 9, nos. 13 and 14.
[6] §1, 8, no. 3, i, 2 ff.; §1, 6, i, 4 ff.
[7] §1, 8, no. 1, obv. 31 ff

The relations of Mitanni with Egypt were friendly. Friendship with Egypt had been a traditional policy of the Mitanni kings for several generations. A number of marriages had taken place between the royal houses. Artatama, Tushratta's grandfather, had sent one of his daughters to the pharaoh,[1] and Shuttarna, his father, had given his daughter Gilu-Kheba in marriage to Amenophis III[2] (an event which falls into that king's tenth year,[3] i.e. about 1408). Tushratta himself was to continue this policy by sending one of his daughters, Tadu-Kheba, for the pharaoh's harim.[4]

The inactivity of the Egyptians in Syria made it possible for Tushratta to remain on friendly terms with Amenophis III during all of the latter's reign. When it is realized that this was so in spite of the expansionist tendencies of Mitanni in Syria, one is led to assume that a formal understanding must have existed by which the coast of Syria and all of Palestine, including the region of Damascus, was recognized as an Egyptian sphere of influence, the rest of Syria being considered as Mitannian domain. During the later part of Tushratta's reign, good relations with Egypt became more and more a necessity, because a powerful personality had in the meantime ascended the Hittite throne and had initiated a period of Hittite renascence.

Probably not long after the events which brought Tushratta to the throne of Mitanni (c. 1385), a shift of rulership also took place in the Hittite country. Under Tudkhaliash III the previously mighty kingdom had shrunk into insignificance from which it had only partially recovered before the king's death.[5] If some of the lost territory, especially along the eastern border had been regained, this had been due to the military leadership of the king's son, Shuppiluliumash.[6]

Upon his father's death Shuppiluliumash became king as the next in line. In him there came to the throne a powerful man who was destined to restore the might of his country and to secure for it a position second to none. The ambitions which must have spurred Shuppiluliumash from the outset made him cast his eyes almost automatically upon Syria, where earlier Hittite kings had won glory. Hence an armed conflict with Tushratta became inevitable. It was postponed for some time only because Shuppiluliumash had to reorganize his homeland before he could think of embarking on a war of conquest in Syria.

---

[1] EA 24, iii, 52 ff.; 29, 21 ff.      [2] EA 17, 26 ff.; 29, 21 ff.
[3] G, 17, sect. 866.      [4] EA 19, 17 ff.; 22, iv, 43 ff.
[5] G, 4, VI, 28, obv. 6 ff. (cf. §1, 4, 21 ff.).
[6] See below, p. 117.

This was done with comparative ease, for the Hittite system of government was more firmly knit than that of the Mitannians. The ruling class among the Hittites had long since become amalgamated with the Anatolian population. Strong feudalistic tendencies still lingered on, but as a whole the Khatti Land proper was now governed by officials who were appointed by the king, preferably members of the royal family. Around this inner core of the kingdom an outer ring of vassal states had been formed. Their rulers had concluded formal treaties with the 'Great King' and received back their lands from his hands. They had surrendered to him part of their sovereignty, above all the right to conduct an independent foreign policy. There was a marked trend toward assuring the loyalty of these vassals by tying them to the royal house of Khatti by intermarriage.[1]

The accession of Shuppiluliumash to the Hittite throne can be dated only approximately. It falls within the reign of Amenophis III[2] (c. 1417–1379), and probably later than the beginning of Tushratta's reign which was estimated above as having taken place c. 1385. It can be set at approximately 1380.

The first clash between the two adversaries must have occurred soon after Shuppiluliumash ascended the throne. Tushratta, in one of his letters to Amenophis III, tells about a victory in which he claims to have crushed an invading Hittite army.[3] The letter in which the report is contained is very likely the first of the letters directed to that pharaoh which have been preserved. It seems, then, that Shuppiluliumash failed in his early attempts at expansion toward the south. One may well doubt, however, that it was anything more than a testing raid.

The military situation was not yet such as to encourage Shuppiluliumash to conduct operations on a larger scale. At the beginning of his reign, the Khatti Land and the country of Mitanni had only a comparatively short border in common. It became more extended when Shuppiluliumash recovered Ishuwa which his father had lost.[4] But even then, for the larger part of the distance between the Upper Euphrates and the Mediterranean Sea, the two countries were separated by Kizzuwadna. It must have been one of the first tasks of the young king to come to terms with this buffer state. The result of his efforts is contained in the treaty which he concluded with Shunashshura, the king of Kizzuwadna.[5]

[1] G, 22, 99 ff.                          [2] EA 41, 7.
[3] EA 17, 30 ff.; 45.
[4] §1, 8, no. 1, obv. 10 ff.; G, 4, vi, 28, obv. 12 (cf. §1, 4, 21 ff.).
[5] §1, 8, no. 7; cf. §1, 4, 36 ff.

Large parts of an Akkadian version and parts of a parallel Hittite version have survived. The salient fact in the treaty is that Kizzuwadna renounced its affiliation with the Mitanni kingdom and forthwith returned to the Hittite sphere of influence.[1] Shunashshura was treated by Shuppiluliumash with some consideration and granted certain privileges. This does not alter the fact that he had to surrender essential parts of his sovereignty, especially the right to maintain such relations with foreign countries as suited himself. The common frontier was revised.[2]

Shuppiluliumash also reached an agreement with Artatama, the king of the Khurri Land.[3] In view of the enmity that existed between Tushratta and Artatama—their law-suit was still pending before the gods—this must have been comparatively easy. From Artatama's point of view, Tushratta was a rebel and a usurper. The text of the treaty has not come down to us, but there is every reason to believe that Shuppiluliumash treated Artatama as a 'Great King', i.e. his equal; there is certainly no doubt that the treaty was directed against Tushratta. In all likelihood, Artatama promised at least benevolent neutrality in the impending conflict. This relieved Shuppiluliumash of the fear that the Hurrian might try to interfere in favour of the Mitannian; it thus enabled him to concentrate all his might against the latter. No wonder then that Tushratta considered the conclusion of the treaty as a *casus belli*.[4]

The relations of Shuppiluliumash with Egypt at that moment conformed with the diplomatic customs of the time, but were rather cool. The Hittite had good reason for keeping them correct. He had exchanged courteous messages with Amenophis III; we possess the letter which he wrote to Amenophis IV (1379–1362) when the latter assumed kingship.[5] It betrays a certain tension between the two countries. This is easily understandable when it is recalled that family ties existed between the pharaoh and Tushratta, Tadu-Kheba his daughter having been given in marriage to Amenophis III from whose harim she was transferred to that of Amenophis IV. Furthermore, the Egyptians must gradually have grown apprehensive of the Hittite's intentions. One may rather feel surprised that relations between Khatti and Egypt remained as undisturbed as they apparently did for so long. The situation suggests that Amenophis IV had no desire whatever to become involved in what he considered the internal affairs of Syria and to provide Tushratta with more than nominal support. Tushratta may

[1] §1, 8, no. 7, i, 30 ff.     [2] §1, 8, no. 7, iv, 40 ff.
[3] §1, 8, no. 1, obv. 1 ff.     [4] §1, 8, no. 1, obv. 2 f.
[5] EA 41.

have hoped for more active assistance, and, when none was forthcoming, his feelings toward the pharaoh became increasingly cool.
His three extant letters to Amenophis IV[1] show a growing ani-
mosity, and it may well be that after the third the correspondence
was actually discontinued.

## II. THE FIRST SYRIAN WAR
### OF SHUPPILULIUMASH

When the Hittite attack finally came, Tushratta proved unable to
keep his hold on Syria. Shuppiluliumash moved at will, and all the
country between the Euphrates and the Mediterranean Sea as far
south as the Lebanon fell prey to the invader.[2] One may assume
that see-sawing battles took place before a firm frontier was finally
established. As a matter of fact, existing reports—if they belong
here—suggest that Tushratta conducted a counter-campaign in
Syria. He is said to have reached Ṣumura (which had been before,
and was later, an Egyptian stronghold) and to have tried to capture Gubla (Byblos), but to have been forced to retreat by lack of
water.[3] Was this a mere show of force or was it an attempt at
creating a line which made it possible for him to maintain contact
with the Hurrian princes in southern Syria and ultimately with
Egypt? If so, it was of no avail; the Hittite king's might proved
overpowering. The most loyal partisan whom the pharaoh had in
Syria, Rib-Adda of Gubla, sums up the result of the campaign in
the following words:[4] 'The king, my lord, should be advised that
the Hittite king has taken over all the countries affiliated(?) with
the king of the Mita(nni) land, i.e.(?) the king of Nakh(ri)ma'
(probably meaning Naharina, the name under which the Mitanni
country was known in Egypt).

This move had brought Shuppiluliumash right to the border of
the territory over which Egypt not only claimed, but in some
fashion also exercised sovereignty. Shuppiluliumash halted here.
He could not wish to antagonize the pharaoh unnecessarily at a time
when Tushratta was far from completely defeated. To be sure, the
Mitanni king was no longer undisputed ruler of Syria. But he may
still have held open a line of communication with Egypt by way of
Kinza. At any rate, Kinza defied the Hittites for a long time to
come and was considered by them, even after Tushratta's downfall, as part of Egypt's sphere of influence (see below, pp. 15 f.). At

---

[1] EA 27 (Amenophis IV, year 2); 28; 29.
[2] §1, 8, no. 1, obv. 4 ff.       [3] EA 85, 51 ff.; cf. 58, 5 ff.
[4] EA 75, 35 ff.

the present moment Tushratta still ruled over his homeland in Upper Mesopotamia as well as all his eastern provinces.

Moreover, there existed a treaty of long standing between the Hittites and Egypt. It had been concluded when people of the Anatolian town of Kurushtama had been transferred (in a somewhat mysterious way) to Egyptian territory to become subjects of the pharaoh.[1] It is unknown who precisely had been the contractants, but the political situation suggests that on the Egyptian side it must have been one of the pharaohs who still controlled Syria, and on the Hittite side a king who still held at least the Taurus frontier, i.e. a king reigning before the rebellion against Tudkhaliash, father of Shuppiluliumash. It must go back to the time before the Mitannians had come on to the scene and separated the two great western powers. The treaty had almost been forgotten; it acquired new actuality only when conquest reconstituted a common frontier between them.

It is difficult to assign an exact date to this first great success of the Hittite king. It seems clear, however, from the sources that the event took place during the lifetime of 'Abdi-Ashirta of Amurru (see below) whose death occurred late in the reign of Amenophis IV, perhaps about 1365.

The Hittite victory upset the order in Syria; it destroyed Mitannian control, but it did not replace it as yet with an equally firm Hittite rule. Some of the Syrian states became Hittite vassals, a development which made them susceptible to Mitannian vengeance. Others were freed from their old obligations and thus enabled to follow their own particularistic ambitions.

To safeguard access to his Syrian dependencies Shuppiluliumash installed, perhaps at this time, his son Telepinush as the local ruler ('priest') in the holy city of Kumanni (Comana Cappadociae). The pertinent decree has come down to us in the name of the great king, his second queen Khenti, and the crown prince Arnuwandash.[2]

The Syrian states in the north, the territories of which were contiguous with former Hittite possessions, were reduced to vassalage. The most important among them was the state of Aleppo (Khalap). So far we have no direct testimony for a treaty between Shuppiluliumash and the king of Aleppo. We may take it for granted, however, that such a treaty must have existed.[3] The same can be assumed for Mukish (Alalakh).[4] The treaty between Shuppiluliumash and Tunip, remnants of which have survived,[5] may belong

---

[1] §II, 5, 208 ff.; §II, 1; 7; 8; 9; 10.
[2] G, I, XIX, 25 (cf. §I, 4, 12 ff.).       [3] §I, 8, no. 3, ii, 14.
[4] *Ibid.*       [5] §I, 8, no. 10.

to this period. As far as Ugarit on the coast is concerned, it is
unlikely that it submitted at that time. Protected as it is by
mountain ranges toward the plains of the north, it could feel
reasonably safe. There are indications that Ammishtamru remained
true to his obligations toward Egypt.[1] His son Niqmaddu who
later had to submit to Shuppiluliumash still corresponded with
the pharaoh[2] and even seems to have married an Egyptian princess.[3]
A treaty between Shuppiluliumash and the Nukhash Lands, the
territories south of Aleppo, is definitely attested; the ruler of that
region was at that time Sharrupsha.[4]

It goes without saying that Tushratta could not accept without
a fight the loss even of northern Syria. In fact, we know that he
reacted violently. He could not but regard the conclusion of a
treaty with the Hittites on the part of the king of the Nukhash
Lands as a treasonable action. Aided by a local pro-Mitannian
party, an armed invasion of Nukhash by a Mitannian army was
temporarily successful, but was ultimately repulsed.[5]

In other countries, e.g. in Neya and Arakhtu, partisans of the
Mitannians must also have existed. After all, the ruling class was
largely Hurrian in origin. Shuppiluliumash proved his deep mistrust of them when later, after his final conquest, he exiled most of
these families to Anatolia. He probably had experienced difficulties with them. Of course, the position in which these dynasts
found themselves was in no way enviable. They were caught between the three parties to the conflict: Tushratta, Egypt, and now
the Hittites. The bolder among them tried to exploit the situation
for their own ends and avoided commitments and eventual submission to any of the great powers. Such men were to be found
particularly in southern Syria. There Mitannian supremacy had
been broken, Egyptian domination was an empty claim, but Hittite influence was still too weak to demand unquestioned recognition. The princes of Amurru in particular took advantage of the
opportunity that presented itself.

The kings of Amurru, 'Abdi-Ashirta and his son Aziru after
him, were easily the most restive personalities in Syria at this time.
A country Amurru had existed there at least since the Mari Age;
it apparently lay west of the middle Orontes. Reactivated by
Ḥapiru people it now showed a marked tendency to expand toward the Mediterranean coast; gradually it gained a foothold between Ṣumura in the south and Ugarit in the north. This had

---

[1] EA 45 (cf. Nougayrol, J., *Le Palais royal d'Ugarit*, III, p. xxxvii). See below,
pp. 137 ff.    [2] EA 49 (cf. Nougayrol, *loc. cit.*).
[3] G, 16, 164 ff.    [4] §1, 8, no. 3, i, 2 ff.    [5] *Ibid.* 4 ff.

happened before Shuppiluliumash appeared on the scene. Already Amenophis III had had to recognize 'Abdi-Ashirta as the Amurrite chief; he had even tried to use him as a tool of Egyptian policy in order to check Tushratta's Syrian schemes.[1] Rib-Adda of Gubla (Byblos), who was to become the foremost victim of the Amurrite, dates the beginning of his troubles from a visit that Amenophis III had paid to Sidon.[2] The Hittite conquest of northern Syria did not make Rib-Adda's situation any less dangerous. On the contrary it removed every restraint that had held back 'Abdi-Ashirta. Egyptian control had ceased for all practical purposes. Pakhamnate, the Egyptian 'commissioner', had to give up his residence Ṣumura and probably returned to Egypt.[3] 'Abdi-Ashirta stepped into the gap thus created; in doing so he seems to have obtained the official sanction of the pharaoh.[4] He used his enhanced position to expand inland toward Damascus and to get a firmer hold on the coast, to the dismay of Rib-Adda of Gubla. The territory controlled by this tragic champion of Egyptian rule began to dwindle; his ever-repeated complaints and his incessant demands for help were not taken seriously by the pharaoh. Neither did his southern neighbours comply with his calls for help. In consequence, Ṣumura fell.[5] Then the rulers of the town of Irqata and Ambi were murdered at the instigation of 'Abdi-Ashirta, and these places, together with Shigata and Ardata, were taken by the Amurrite.[6] The appointment of Kha'ip (Ḥa'api) as the new Egyptian commissioner[7] did not arrest this development. 'Abdi-Ashirta, Rib-Adda says, acted as though he were the Mitanni king and the Kassite king all in one.[8] Gubla itself was seriously threatened.[9] It was saved at the last moment when, after Bīt-Arkha[10] and Batruna,[11] the last possessions of the prince of Gubla, had fallen, the Egyptian general Amanappa finally appeared with some troops.[12]

Ṣumura and the other towns just mentioned are later in Egyptian hands again.[13] Their recapture perhaps took place in connexion with the events that led to 'Abdi-Ashirta's death. This fierce fighter, whose activities in the interest of Amurru, his country, had been troublesome for many of his contemporaries, was at last slain, no matter in what way.[14] His death did not, however, change the situation materially. After a temporary set-

---

[1] EA 101, 30 f.
[2] EA 85, 69 ff.
[3] EA 62; cf. 67.
[4] EA 101, 30.
[5] EA 83, 11 ff. (cf. 67, 17 f.); 91, 6.
[6] EA 74, 23 ff.; 75, 25 ff.
[7] EA 71, 7 ff.
[8] EA 76, 9 ff. (cf. 104, 19 ff.).
[9] EA 78, 11 ff.
[10] EA 79, 21; 83, 29; 91, 8 f.
[11] EA 87, 18 ff.; 88, 15 f.; 90, 14 ff.
[12] EA 79, 7 ff.; cf. 117, 23.
[13] EA 106; 107; 112.
[14] EA 101, 2 ff.; cf. §1, 5, 27 f.

back, the people of Amurru, now led by Aziru, 'Abdi-Ashirta's son, resumed their activities with renewed vigour. Very soon Irqata, Ambi, Shigata and Ardata were reoccupied by them.[1] Ṣumura did not fall at once; it was besieged and could for some time be reached only by boat.[2] The Egyptians made an effort to hold it, and the commissioner of Ṣumura was killed in the fight.[3] But the Egyptians finally had to evacuate their troops from the city.[4] Rib-Adda, now left alone, faced a hopeless situation, particularly when Zimredda of Sidon allied himself with Aziru.[5] Finally Gubla alone was left in his possession,[6] and it too fell[7] when intrigues compelled Rib-Adda to flee his hometown; he met a—probably violent—death in exile.[8] At the same time Aziru took possession of Neya.[9] All this seems to have taken place shortly before, or at the very beginning of, the second war in Syria.[10]

It is quite likely that already at that time some understanding had been reached between Shuppululiumash and Aziru.[11] It need not necessarily have consisted of a formal treaty. At repeated times Aziru calls the pharaoh's attention to the fact that the Hittite stands in the Nukhash Lands,[12] as though to remind him he might be forced to throw in his lot with the northerners. But, at the height of the threatening crisis, and before Shuppululiumash was able to advance further to the south, the pharaoh called the Amurrite to Egypt.[13] The correct interpretation of this act is probably an attempt at removing from the scene at the decisive moment the potentially most dangerous man. The pharaoh may even have hoped to draw Aziru over to his side, assigning him a role in a scheme for the preservation of Egyptian influence in Syria. Be this as it may, Aziru complied and, once there, played his ambiguous game with political skill and cleverness. His son, left at home, had to listen to accusations that he had sold his father to Egypt.[14] But Aziru eventually returned from the court of the pharaoh unharmed. His treaty with Niqmaddu of Ugarit,[15] which greatly strengthened his position in Syria, may have looked as though inspired by Egypt. It revealed its real import only when

---

[1] EA 98, 10 ff.; 104, 10 ff.; 40 ff.; 140, 14 ff.
[2] EA 98, 12 ff.          [3] EA 106, 22; 132, 45.
[4] EA 103, 11 ff.; 132, 42 f.; 149, 37 ff., 67.
[5] EA 103, 17 ff.; 106, 20; 149, 57 ff.
[6] EA 126, 37 ff.          [7] EA 136–138.
[8] EA 162.          [9] EA 59, 27 f.
[10] EA 126, 51 ff.; 129, 76          [11] §11, 3, no. 1, obv. 2 f.
[12] EA 164, 21 ff.; 165, 18 ff.; 166, 21 ff.; 167, 11 ff.
[13] EA 161, 22 ff.; 164, 20; 165, 14 ff.
[14] EA 169, 17 ff.          [15] G, 15, 284 ff.

shortly thereafter,[1] it seems, he also entered into a formal pact with Shuppiluliumash.[2] Thereby he took finally his place in the Hittite system of states.

At about the same time Shuppiluliumash took another step of a highly political nature: he married a Babylonian princess. Assuming the name Tawannannash, a name which the first queen of the Hittites had borne in the old days, she also became reigning queen.[3] The purpose is clear: in anticipation of the attack on Tushratta of Mitanni, Shuppiluliumash sought protection of his rear. Burnaburiash must then have been king in Babylon.

## III. THE SECOND SYRIAN WAR
## OF SHUPPILULIUMASH

His rival's earlier successes had alerted Tushratta to the things to come. Naturally he had tried to reassert his power. We know of two counter-measures he took. He interfered in the Nukhash Lands deposing Sharrupsha;[4] he also initiated an anti-Hittite action further toward the north in Ishuwa.[5] This gave Shuppiluliumash the pretext for his final attack. He declared that the Nukhash Lands were 'rebels'—neighbouring Mukish and Neya were likewise involved[6]—and that the Mitannian had acted with arrogant presumptuousness.[7]

At the same time he had prepared himself with circumspection. Approaching Ugarit beforehand he proposed a treaty of mutual peace which, in the circumstances, can only have been favourable to the small country where Niqmaddu, the son of Ammishtamru, then reigned.[8] In this way he kept his right flank secure; sending a detachment to the Nukhash Lands,[9] he himself crossed the Euphrates into Ishuwa where Tushratta had threatened him. Having obtained King Antaratal's permission he passed through Alshe and appeared on the north-western border of the Mitanni land proper. Having there captured the forts of Kutmar and Suta, he made a swift stab at Washshuganni, the Mitannian capital. When he reached it, he found, however, that Tushratta had fled.[10]

---

[1] §II, 2, 380 f.
[2] §I, 8, no. 4; §II, 4; cf. §II, 3, no. I. obv. 3 ff.
[3] §II, 6, vol. I, 6 ff.; G, 16, 98 ff.        [4] §I, 8, no. 3, i, 2 ff.
[5] §I, 8, no. 3, i, 14; no. I, obv. 17 ff.
[6] G, 15, dossier II A 3; cf. dossier II A I and 2.
[7] §I, 8, no. I, obv. 17, 45; §II, 7, frgm. 26, ii, 11 ff.
[8] G, 15, II (29 ff.).        [9] §I, 8, no. 3, i, 9.
[10] §I, 8, no. I, obv. 17 ff.; cf. §II, 7, frgm. 26, ii, 21 ff.

He did not bother to pursue him, but turned westward; Syria was of much greater importance to him. He entered it recrossing the Euphrates from east to west, probably south of the strongly fortified Carchemish. Once on Syrian soil, one country after another fell to him. Everywhere he removed the Hurrian city-rulers who had been the mainstay of Mitannian domination and replaced them with men of his own choice. The list of the rebellious countries which Shuppiluliumash gives himself includes Aleppo, Mukish, Neya, Arakhtu, Qatna, Nukhash and Kinza,[1] the sequence most likely indicating the order in which he defeated them. The campaign ended in Apina (Damascus), i.e. in clearly Egyptian territory.[2] The negative fact is noteworthy that the report does not mention Carchemish, Ugarit and Amurru. The first probably remained independent; the two others were already bound by treaty to the Hittites.

This war had profoundly changed the overall political picture. Above all it meant the end of Tushratta and his empire. He himself may have held on for a while after his flight from Washshu-ganni; in the end he was murdered by conspirators among whom was his own son Kurtiwaza.[3] In accordance with the beliefs of the times, his death was interpreted as the final decision of Teshub (the Mitanni Land's highest god) in the long-pending lawsuit between him and the king of the Khurri Land.[4] It was now considered proven that Tushratta had usurped a throne which had not been rightfully his.

To be sure, the immediate advantage of Tushratta's downfall was not Artatama's, but went to Alshe and above all to Assyria. These two countries, freed by the Hittite victory from Mitannian overlordship, divided most of the Mitannian territory between themselves,[5] Alshe taking the north-western part and Assyria the north-eastern. The liberation of Assyria, where Ashur-uballiṭ was then king, was an event which, unwished for and of little consequence at the moment, became of great significance later on. However, the Mitanni kingdom, although greatly reduced in area, did not entirely cease to exist; Kurtiwaza remained its ruler. A serious rival to him arose in the person of Shutatarra (Shuttarna), apparently son and successor of Artatama, who maintained, so it seems, that the Mitanni Land was now a vacant fief of the Khurri king.[6] Kurtiwaza, expelled by Shutatarra (Shuttarna) sought refuge in Kassite Babylonia; finally he appeared at the court of

---

[1] §1, 8, no. 1, obv. 30–43.    [2] §1, 8, no. 1, obv. 43 f.

[3] §1, 8, no. 1, obv. 48.    [4] §1, 8, no. 1, obv. 49 f.

[5] §1, 8, no. 2, obv. 1 ff.    [6] §1, 8, no. 2, obv. 28 ff.

Shupppiluliumash and tried to enlist the help of the Hittite king for the recovery of his throne.[1]

Of greater immediate significance for the Hittites was the new order which Shuppiluliumash, after the destruction of the Mitanni Empire, created in Syria. It was based on the system of vassal states. In northern Syria some treaties already existed, with the successors to the vanquished rebels new ones were concluded. Soon the south was also reorganized. This time Ugarit was firmly included in this system. Niqmaddu came to Alalakh, the capital of Mukish, to pay homage to Shuppiluliumash. He received his country back as a fief, the frontier toward Mukish being regulated in detail, and assumed, as usual in vassal treaties, the duty of furnishing troops in wartime and paying a yearly tribute to his overlord. The documents written out then and handed to Niqmaddu bear the seal of Shuppiluliumash and sometimes that of the Great King and his third queen Tawannannash.[2]

The treaty with Aziru of Amurru was confirmed; parts of a copy have survived.[3] Aziru proved a loyal vassal of the Hittite king for the rest of his life which lasted into the reign of Murshilish, the son of Shuppiluliumash. The treaties no doubt concluded with Mukish and Neya have not come to light. Further inland and in the south the reorganization seems to have taken somewhat longer. At first Shuppiluliumash merely removed the reigning families to Hittite territory, Eventually, however, he brought them back; probably a few years later.

Thus in the Nukhash Lands, where Tushratta had started his last war, he replaced Sharrupsha, who had lost his life in the upheaval, by his grandson Tette. The treaty concluded with him is partly preserved.[4] In Kinza Shuppiluliumash had not wanted to interfere. However, attacked by the local king, Shutatarra, and his son, he had been forced to engage himself. Defeated, they were deported, but the son, Aitakama, was eventually brought back. No doubt a formal treaty, not recovered as yet, was concluded also with him. Abi-milki of Tyre reports to Amenophis IV the fact of his restoration with obvious misgivings;[5] he may have had good reasons. For Aitakama, backed by Hittite power and seconded by Aziru, immediately sought to extend his own borders by attacking the nominally Egyptian territory on his southern frontier.[6] Not far east from Kinza, in Qatna, Aitakama found another target for his attempt at expansion. In a way not clear to

[1] §1, 8, no. 2, obv. 14 ff.      [2] G, 15, 30.
[3] §1, 8, no. 4; §11, 2.      [4] §1, 8, no. 3.
[5] EA 151, 58 ff.      [6] EA 140, 25 ff.

us a certain Akizzi had gained possession of the small kingdom which had been listed only a short while ago as conquered by Shuppiluliumash; this Akizzi, as his letters show,[1] recognized Egyptian overlordship. He reports to the pharaoh that Aitakama had tried to persuade him to take part in an anti-Egyptian conspiracy.[2] He also reports that Aitakama's advances had been more successful with Teuwatti of Lapana and Arzawiya of Ruhhizzi.[3] Indeed, reinforced by Hittite troops, he attacked Qatna,[4] apparently capturing it and compelling Akizzi to flee.[5] Aitakama was even able to attack Apina (Damascus) where Piryawaza, the 'commissioner' of Kumidu, represented the pharaoh.[6]

The advance of Hittite partisans as far south as the Biqā', the valley between Lebanon and Anti-Lebanon, and further east as far as Damascus ought not to have left the Egyptians indifferent; this was undisputed Egyptian territory. However, they either were unwilling or unable to help their friends in southern Syria. The letters of Akizzi—like those of Rib-Adda—are vivid testimony to Egyptian impotence.

A word remains to be said on chronology. The precise date of Tushratta's downfall is not ascertainable. Tushratta once mentions that friendship had prevailed between Amenophis IV and himself for four years.[7] All his letters keep the memory of Amenophis III alive as though he had passed away only a short while ago. On the other hand, all of Aziru's struggle with Rib-Adda of Gubla must fall before the victory of Shuppiluliumash. The latter occurred early in the reign of Ashur-uballit of Assyria and certainly before Kurigalzu became king of Babylon, i.e. during the reign there of Burnaburiash. Therefore, one will be inclined to propose a date about 1360 or a little later.

## IV. THE HURRIAN WAR OF SHUPPILULIUMASH

The summaries of the Hittite conqueror's reign list—allegedly after twenty years of war against the Kaska (Gasga) people[8]—six years of campaigning in the Khurri Lands, i.e. in northern Syria.[9] The combined evidence from various surviving sources makes at least a tentative reconstruction possible.

---

[1] §III, 3, 8 ff.                     [2] EA 53, 1 ff.
[3] EA 53, 35 ff.; 54, 26 ff.; 56, 23 ff.
[4] EA 53, 8 ff., 174–176. See G, 14, 94 f.
[5] EA 55, 40 ff., 56 f.               [6] EA 53, 24 ff., 56 ff.
[7] EA 29, 113.
[8] G, 1, xix, 9, i, 8 ff. (cf. §IV, 4, II/I, 10).
[9] G, 1, xix, 9, i, 7 ff. (cf. §IV, 4, II/I, 10).

The first link in the series of campaigns is probably a Hittite attack on Amqa, the land between Lebanon and Anti-Lebanon which was considered an Egyptian dependency. The attack was commanded not by the king himself, but by one of his generals.[1] The second year of this campaign[2] saw serious fighting on the Euphrates frontier; the main adversary there was Carchemish which—surprisingly—had so far not been conquered. The city must have had helpers from further east. The military leader on the Hittite side was Telepinush, the king's son, who held the position of the 'priest' in Kumanni. His quick success resulted in the submission of the countries of Arziya and Carchemish; only that city itself continued to resist. The victorious army took up winter camp in Khurmuriga (or Murmuriga). When Telepinush had to go home in order to attend to urgent religious duties, the command was entrusted to the general Lupakkish. The prince's departure precipitated an attack of Hurrian troops on Khurmuriga, which was enveloped and besieged. At the same time, Egyptian troops—probably reacting to the Hittite raid on Amqa which had just been mentioned—invaded Kinza. It was probably then that Kinza and Nukhash, as other sources relate, 'revolted' against Shuppiluliumash. Aziru of Amurru, however, remained loyal to his overlord.[3]

Shuppiluliumash prepared his counter-stroke carefully.[4] He gathered a new army in Tegarama and with the arrival of spring (this then is the third year of this series of campaigns) he sent it to Syria under the joint command of the crown-prince Arnuwandash and Zidash, the major-domo. Before he could join this army himself, it defeated the Hurrians and lifted the siege of Khurmuriga. He could at once proceed to laying siege to the city of Carchemish, and still had sufficient troops at hand to send a column under Lupakkish and Tarkhunda-zalmash against the Egyptians. They promptly drove the Egyptians from Kinza and re-entered Amqa, the Egyptian border province.[5]

While Carchemish was under siege and this second army stood in Amqa, news reached Shuppiluliumash that a pharaoh, whom our source calls *Piphururiyaš*, had died. His identity has been much discussed;[6] the publication of a new fragment[7] in which the name

---

[1] §II, 5, 208 ff.  [2] §II, 7, frgm. 28.
[3] §II, 3, no. 1, obv. 3 ff.  [4] Main source again §II, 7, frgm. 28.
[5] Also EA 174, 14 ff.; G, I, xxxi, 121 a, ii, 8 f. (cf. §IV, 4, II/I, 23 ff.; §II, 8, 59 ff.).
[6] Above all §IV, 7; §IV, 2, 14 f.; §IV, 8.
[7] G, 5, xxxiv, 24, 4 (cf. §II, 7, 98, l. 18).

is given as *Niphururiyaš* finally decides the issue in favour of Tutankhamun, Akhenaten's son-in-law. According to the chronology followed in this work his death occurred *c.* 1352. A remarkable message from the pharaoh's widow[1] was conveyed to Shuppiluliumash. It deserves to be quoted here in full: 'My husband has died, and I have no son. They say about you that you have many sons. You might give me one of your sons, and he might become my husband. I would not want to take one of my servants. I am loath to make him my husband.' This offer was so surprising to the Great King that he called together his noblemen into council and decided first to investigate whether the request was sincere. A high official, Khattusha-zitish was sent to Egypt. During his absence in Egypt, Carchemish was taken by storm more quickly than anyone expected.

At the beginning of the following year—the fourth—Khattusha-zitish returned with a second message from the Egyptian queen, who bitterly complained about distrust and hesitancy. She added: 'I have not written to any other country, I have written only to you.... He will be my husband and king in the country of Egypt.' This time Shuppiluliumash complied with her wish. He sent Zannanzash[2] to Egypt, but the prince never reached the goal of his journey. He was murdered on the way,[3] probably by the 'servants' of the queen who did not wish a foreigner to ascend the throne of the pharaohs. Thus, by over-cautious hesitation Shuppiluliumash missed the chance of making one of his sons pharaoh of Egypt. All that he was able to do then was to send Hittite troops on a new expedition against Amqa.[4] This seems to be counted as the fifth campaign in the series. On their return they carried home to the Hittite country a plague which harassed the people for a long time to come.[5]

After the fall of Carchemish Shuppiluliumash reorganized northern Syria: he elevated his two sons Piyashilish and Telepinush (until then 'priest' of Kumanni) to kingship in Carchemish and Aleppo respectively.[6] Thereby he assured firm control of the Taurus and Amanus passes and Hittite domination of the two most important states in northern Syria.

The downfall of Tushratta had set free Assyria, a result which was not altogether desirable from the Hittite point of view. Shup-

---

[1] §IV, 3.    [2] §II, 7, frgm. 31.
[3] §II, 5, 210 f.; §II, 7, frgm. 31; G, I, XIX, 20 (cf. §IV, 4, II/I, 28 ff.).
[4] §II, 5, 210 f.    [5] *Ibid.*
[6] G, 4, VI, 28, obv. 19 ff.; G, I, XIX, 9, i, 17 ff. (cf. §IV, 4, II/I, 10); G, I, XIX, 20 obv. 13 (cf. §IV, 4, II/I, 28 ff.).

piluliumash was not oblivious of the danger inherent in this development. To counteract it, he decided to make use of the presence of Kurtiwaza, the Mitannian prince, at his court. Piyashilish, the new king of Carchemish—now known as Sharre-Kushukh[1]—was entrusted with the task of re-establishing him as king in Washshuganni. This may be counted as the sixth Hurrian campaign; it involved a serious armed expedition. The two princes set out from Carchemish, crossed the Euphrates, and attacked Irrite. The people of this city and the surrounding country, after some fighting, recognized that resistance was useless and surrendered. The next objective was Harran, which was quickly overrun. Further advance toward Washshuganni brought about some interference from the Assyrian, i.e. Ashur-uballiṭ, and from the king of the Khurri Land. But the Hittite troops, acclaimed by the populace, were able to enter the former capital. The advance east of Washshuganni, however, proved to be difficult, mainly for lack of supplies. Nevertheless, the Assyrians did not risk battle and withdrew. Shuttarna retired beyond the Upper Euphrates and only insignificant skirmishing took place beyond that line.[2] It became the north-eastern boundary of Kurtiwaza's new kingdom. The two versions of the treaty which Shuppululiumash concluded with the new king are preserved.[3] By taking one of the overlord's daughters in marriage, Kurtiwaza had previously been made a member of the royal family.

Either simultaneously with this campaign in the Mitanni country or in the following year, Arnuwandash, the crown prince, was sent out against 'Egypt'.[4] Nothing beyond the mere fact is known.

When the reign of Shuppululiumash drew toward its end—he must have died soon afterward, i.e. about 1346, the victim of the plague which Hittite soldiers had imported from Amqa—he was the undisputed master of Syria and wielded more power than any one of his contemporaries. The Egyptians, at the end of the Amarna period, were for internal reasons in no position to challenge the Hittites, and remained unable to do so for the next fifty years. The Assyrians, still in process of reorganization after their liberation from Mitannian overlordship, were not yet ready to oppose them seriously. Thus the struggle for Syria had ended for

---

[1] §II, 7, 120 f.
[2] §I, 8, no. 2, obv. 35 ff.; G, I, VIII, 80+xxiii, 50+G, 2, 21 (cf. in part §IV, 5); G, I, XIX, 9, i, 13 ff. (cf. §IV, 4, II/1, 10); §II, 7, frgm. 34 ff.
[3] §I, 8, nos. 1 and 2.   [4] §II, 7, frgm. 34 ff.

the time being and a balance of power had been established. Despite the efforts of the pharaohs of the Nineteenth Dynasty, and also despite the intermittent resurgence of Assyrian might, this remained essentially unchanged down to the great migrations toward the end of the thirteenth century.

# CHAPTER XVIII

## ASSYRIA AND BABYLON,

### *c.* 1370–1300 B.C.

### I. RECOVERY IN WESTERN ASIA

T H E pages of this history have had little to tell about Assyria or
Babylonia since the reigns of Shamshi-Adad I and of his son
Ishme-Dagan in the former, and since the end of Hammurabi's
last successor in the latter. The intervening space of nearly three
centuries was occupied by the invasions and retarding influences
which affected the whole of Western Asia and Egypt as well, and
had produced a similar dimness in the view of all that vast area.
In Egypt the invaders were the Hyksos,[1] in Syria, Mesopotamia,
and eastward the Hurrians, in Babylonia the Kassites; all of them
peoples of origins as obscure as their cultural levels were generally
low, and all alike destined to lose their individuality, partly by
conquest, but mostly by absorption, before they had attained a
distinctive civilization or much history of their own. For this
dark age modern research has therefore to depend partly upon
survivals and intermittent gleams of the old. The point now
reached in the story is that where the gloom is everywhere receding—it had been dispelled from Egypt with the ejection of the
Hyksos and the counter-invasion of Syria by the kings of the
Eighteenth Dynasty, but these had never approached near
enough to the old seats of the Babylonian culture to exercise a
direct influence there or to break (if such had been the effect) the
deadening spell which still overpowered them. The greatest of
Egyptian conquerors, Tuthmosis III, was indeed able, at the
farthest point of his penetration into Syria, to include among the
spoils of his campaign a tribute from Ashur, which his fame if
not his armies had reached.[2] Little affected by this distant
intruder, and not at all by his successors, the Assyrian nation had
far more to fear and to suffer from the nearer oppression of the
Hurrians, represented by kings of the states called Mitanni and
Khanigalbat, whose history up to the present point has been

---

* An original version of this chapter was published as fascicle 42 in 1965.
[1] See *C.A.H.* II³, pt. 1, pp. 54 ff., 289 ff.
[2] *C.A.H.* II³, pt. 1, pp. 452 f.; G, 28, 227 ff.

related in the foregoing chapters.[1] The Kassites had begun to raid and settle in Babylonia under the son of Hammurabi, and had at length established themselves in the capital, filling the void left after the Hittite raid which ended the Amorite Dynasty there.[2] Yet despite violent interferences the two lands had lost little of their respective identities. Throughout all these years the line of Assyrian kings was never broken, and the invaders of Babylonia had come, like so many of their forerunners, to be accepted as merely a new dynasty in a country seemingly gifted with an inexhaustible capacity of absorbing the most intractable elements and reshaping them in its own mould.

In Assyria the line of kings is preserved unbroken to us only by lists of their names and reigns.[3] Of the thirty-six counted between Ishme-Dagan I and Ashur-uballiṭ several occupied an uneasy throne for a moment only, and the rest have left no more than a few records of local building activity in the city of Ashur,[4] coupled with a genealogical notice. Their inscriptions occupy not half-a-dozen pages in modern books, and where they have told nothing of themselves it is not surprising that the outside world has told, in general, no more. There is no doubt that most of these reigns were passed under the shadow of foreign domination, projected partly from Babylonia, where the equally obscure early Kassite kings seem to have claimed a certain sovereignty over the northern neighbour. But a much more menacing cloud impended from the west, from the various rulers of the Hurrian peoples, who, if they never supplanted the Assyrian kings in their own small domain, at least extended their power and occupied districts which more naturally belonged to the Assyrians, even on the side remote from the principal seats of the Hurrian kingdoms. It chances that we are very amply informed upon the population, the institutions, language, and life of a district centred upon Arrapkha (modern Kirkuk) with an important outlying subsidiary at Nuzi, only a few miles away. The towns were then inhabited by a mostly Hurrian population, which rather awkwardly affected to use the Akkadian language[5] for its legal business and public records, but spoke its own uncouth vernacular[6] and acknowledged the rule of Saustatar, king of Mitanni.[7] The city of Ashur hardly appears at all in these voluminous documents,[8] but Nineveh is

---

[1] *C.A.H.* II³, pt. I, ch. x; and above, ch. xvII.

[2] *C.A.H.* II³, pt. I, pp. 224 f.          [3] *C.A.H.* I³, pt. I, pp. 194 ff.

[4] G, 3, 20 ff; G, 8, 28 ff; G, 22, vol. I, 47–57.

[5] §I, 5; 7; 10, 9 ff.; 20.          [6] §I, 4; 18; 19; 23.

[7] §I, 4, I; §v, 32, 54; §vI, 4, 202.          [8] §I, II, 20.

prominent, especially in personal names,[1] and may probably be considered a Mitannian possession, containing a strong blend of Hurrian inhabitants at this time. Arrapkha, lost to Babylonian rule since the days of Samsuiluna,[2] passed into the domain of the Hurrians, not of the Assyrians, despite its comparative proximity to Ashur; the Nuzi tablets give sufficient indication that the kings of Assyria must, in these generations, have been no more than vassals of the Hurrian monarchs who controlled the country far and wide around the city on the Tigris.[3] In these circumstances it is not surprising that what little is known about Assyria, even in the time which directly preceded her great recovery, is derived incidentally from the history of Mitanni, itself fragmentary and partly dependent upon still other records.

## II. EXTERNAL RELATIONS

The restorer of the power of Assyria was, beyond doubt, Ashur-uballiṭ who was destined to become a leading figure of his day, but he has told us nothing to the purpose about himself. Half-a-dozen short inscriptions[4] concern the repair of two temples and some work upon a well in his city of Ashur, no more than the least distinguished of his predecessors. The Assyrian kings had not yet learned[5] the art of appending to their building-inscriptions those notes of contemporary events which were soon to expand themselves into the detailed annals of later reigns. A first mention of the great king's deeds is made, in his own family, by his great-grandson, looking back over the glories of his line and taking Ashur-uballiṭ as the inaugurator of these.[6] In the general documentation of his age he makes a better appearance, though sometimes anonymously. His own most interesting relics are two letters[7] found in distant Egypt among the celebrated archive of Amarna. These two despatches clearly belong to different periods of his reign and power. The first is addressed 'to the king of Egypt from Ashur-uballiṭ, king of Assyria', and its contents are suitable to this modest beginning—the writer sends his messenger to make contact with the potentate, 'to see you and your land', and to offer a suitable present, a fine chariot, two horses, and a jewel of lapis-lazuli, in lauding which he observes that his father had never sent such gifts, a remark which is amplified in the

---

[1] §I, 4, 106, but the connexion is questioned, *ibid.* 239.   [2] §IV, 2, 54 ff.
[3] §I, 15, 191 ff.        [4] G, 8, 39 ff.; G, 22, vol. I, 58–63; G, 3, 26 ff.
[5] Below, pp. 217 f.; but also pp. 295 ff.
[6] G, 8, 62 ff.; §I, 26; G, 3, 37.   [7] G, 20, nos. 15, 16; §I, 9, 212 ff.; §II, 1, 43.

second letter. This is longer and more interesting; Ashur-uballiṭ, writing later in his reign, has now become 'the king of Assyria, the great king, your brother', and addresses Amenophis by the corresponding titles, including 'my brother'. The gifts are repeated, even increased, but it is made very clear that they are sent strictly upon the understanding *do ut des*, for the writer goes on to say he is informed that 'gold in your land is dust, they pick it up'. So, as he has to sustain the expense of building a new palace, let his brother send all the gold it needs. This is reinforced by an interesting appeal to the past, 'when Ashur-nādin-ahhē my father [second predecessor] sent to Egypt they returned him twenty talents of gold, and when the Khanigalbatian king sent to your father they sent him also twenty talents. Send me as much as to the Khanigalbatian.' In the same ungracious strain he churlishly dismisses the favour already accepted—'(what you have sent) does not even suffice for the expense of my messengers going and coming'. This is, of course, only one example of the greed for Egyptian gold which pervades the letters of the Asiatic princes, who evidently saw nothing unworthy in such bartering of presents. It has been observed[1] that, for uncertain reasons, gold had at this period temporarily replaced silver as a medium of exchange, and that the mutual gifts, massive and carefully inventoried, passing between these courts, may be considered a form of state trading; as gold was the particular export of Egypt so were lapis-lazuli and horses the Asiatic valuables traded in return. In any case, princes had never been restrained in criticizing their correspondents' gifts with unblushing candour.[2] The letter of Ashur-uballiṭ ends with some words about the difficulties of communication, 'we are distant lands, and our messengers must travel thus', subject to hindrances. There had been complaints on both sides about undue retention of messengers; some of the Egyptians had been kept prisoners by the Sutu, the desert nomads, and the Assyrian king writes that he had done everything possible to effect their release. But this misfortune, he adds, is no reason for the Assyrian messengers to be detained as a reprisal—why should they die in a far land? If this brought any advantage to the king, so be it, but since there is none, why not let them go?

There is nothing to show that the pharaoh took all this in particularly ill part—the style was too familiar. But there was another who thought it worth while to send him (or his successor)[3] a sharp protest against these negotiations, the contemporary

---

[1] §II, 3.    [2] §IV, 1, vol. v, no. 20.    [3] §I, 2, 14 f.; §II, 1, 54, 62 ff.; §I, 9, 213.

Kassite king Burnaburiash, the second of that name in the dynasty.[1] This indignant letter[2] recalls that Kurigalzu, his father,[3] had been tempted by the Canaanites to make a league with them for a raid upon Egypt, and Kurigalzu had repulsed these overtures. 'But now the Assyrians, subjects of mine, have I not written to you how their mind is? Why have they come to your country? If you love me, let them accomplish nought of their purpose, but send them away empty.' The ancestors of Burnaburiash may indeed have claimed and even exercised a certain supremacy over the shadow-kings of Ashur, pent in their small domain between the hordes of a nearer oppressor. But not only was there now a man of different temper upon the Assyrian throne; the oppressors had been repulsed and every circumstance changed. Protest from Babylon was in vain, for the pharaoh was too well advised to ignore reality. To be noticed, it would have had to come from another quarter, and there all was silence.

Burnaburiash was a regular correspondent with the Egyptian court, and had much more to write than complaints about the Assyrians. In a first letter[4] to Amenophis IV he was garrulous about his health and his vexation that no condolences had been sent to him; he peevishly enquired whether it was a long way to Egypt and, hearing that it was, he condescended to forgive his 'brother' such neglect. Burnaburiash too wanted much gold,[5] but advised his royal correspondent not to entrust the despatch of this to any knavish official, for the last time when it arrived the weight was short, and on another occasion there was less than a quarter of the due tale.[6] More serious subjects (if there could be any more serious than the gold supply) figured also in these letters: caravans from Babylon to Egypt had been stopped by the lawless Canaanites, some merchants robbed and murdered, others mutilated and enslaved. 'Canaan is your land ... and in your land have I been outraged. Arrest them, therefore, make good the money they plundered, slay those who slew my servants and avenge their blood!'[7] There were also marriage treatments between the two kings; Burnaburiash promised to send a daughter to Egypt, but was not at all disposed to let her go without due attention.[8] He complained that the delegation from Egypt to fetch her had only five carriages, and imagined to himself the comments of his courtiers if a daughter of the great king

---

[1] *C.A.H.* I[3], pt. I, pp. 206 f.; §I, 9, 212 differs.
[2] G, 20, no. 9.
[3] Or grandfather, §I, 9, 201, 213.
[4] G, 20, no. 7; §I, 9, 213.
[5] G, 20, no. 7, ll. 63 ff.; §II, 3, 47.
[6] G, 20, no. 10.
[7] G, 20, no. 8.
[8] G, 20, no. 11.

travelled with such a paltry escort. However, the marriage came to pass in the end, for there are two interminable lists of costly presents[1] which were probably the mutual compliments of the two monarchs upon that occasion.

Nothing of more than such minor interest occurs in the dealings between Babylonia and Egypt at this time. Parted by a distance so great that Burnaburiash had no idea of it, the two kings did not even co-operate in dealing with the menace which afflicted them both alike, the lawless condition of Syria, and they had no other object in common. The most urgent topic in the letters from Babylon was the protest against recognizing the Assyrians, a matter of some weight to Burnaburiash, who saw his nominal supremacy passing rapidly into the real dominance of his rival, Ashur-uballit. The moment of destiny for Assyria in its relation with the Hurrian kingdoms which had long oppressed her was undoubtedly the murder of Tushratta,[2] king of Mitanni, by one of his sons. This wealthy monarch, who had corresponded at great length with Amenophis III, lived to continue the same relation with Amenophis IV,[3] but disappeared soon after the latter's accession. The events of this time are related in some detail by the preambles of two versions of a treaty made between Tushratta's son Kurtiwaza and the great king of the Hittites, whose patronage he obtained and sealed by marriage with a daughter.[4]

At Tushratta's death the throne of Mitanni was occupied by Artatama, the king of the Khurri land, who had long been his opponent and had as such enjoyed support from the Hittite king. But he had other supporters as well, particularly the lands of Assyria and Alshe, and he was accused of dissipating in bribes to these allies the riches gathered in the palace of earlier kings. If such were offered no doubt they were readily enough accepted by the avaricious Assyrian, but he had reasons of defence and ambition which in themselves would have ensured his hostility to Tushratta. When Artatama became king of Mitanni he left his son Shuttarna (called elsewhere Shutatarra) as his successor in the Khurri land (these realms are, however, ill-defined), and the latter completed the surrender to Assyria which his father had begun—this according to the hostile account which alone survives.[5] He destroyed the palace built by Tushratta, broke up the precious vessels stored therein, and gave away these rich materials

---

[1] G, 20, nos. 13, 14.          [2] See above, p. 14.
[3] *Ibid.*          [4] See a full account above, ch. xvii, sects. iii and iv.
[5] §1, 25, 36 ff.

to the Assyrian who had been his father's servant, but had revolted and refused tribute. Above all, Shuttarna restored to Assyria a splendid door of silver and gold which had been carried off by a former king of Mitanni and used to adorn his own palace at his capital Washshuganni. He made the same lavish sacrifices of his paternal wealth to the land of Alshe, he destroyed the houses of his Hurrian subjects, and delivered certain obnoxious nobles to the same enemies, who promptly impaled these hapless captives.

There can be no doubt that the Assyrian king who plays so prominent a part in this account was Ashur-uballit, although he is never named. How humble was his position at the beginning of his reign is proved by the definite claim that he was the tributary servant of the Babylonian king, and hardly less clearly by his own reference to a 'Khanigalbatian king' as, in a sense, his own predecessor.[1] At a favourable moment he cast off allegiance to Mitanni, but instead of incurring punishment, received from his master's successor not only the trophies of earlier conquest, but the wealth, the princes, and even the territory of his former sovereign. The reason for this strange behaviour on the part of Artatama and his son can only be supposed the necessity in which they found themselves to win allies against an external danger, and that danger could be only the Hittites. Nevertheless, this too is strange, for it is clear that upon the death of Tushratta, who had been his enemy, the Hittite king viewed with indulgence the succession of Artatama. Estrangement soon occurred, however, and the Mitannian kings knew they must face the hostility of the powerful Shuppiluliumash, who found ready to his hand an opposition headed by Kurtiwaza, son of the murdered Tushratta. This young man's situation soon became dangerous; he was constrained to flee, first to Babylon, and thence to the Hittite, with whom he threw in his lot and married his daughter. The course of a campaign which Kurtiwaza was now enabled to conduct against the Mitannian, and subsequently the Assyrian, powers has been sketched from available evidence in the preceding chapter.[2]

What happened to Kurtiwaza in the end is not known, but that he finally suffered defeat from the Assyrians may be gathered from the testimony, some fifty years afterwards, of the great-grandson of Ashur-uballit, that the latter 'scattered the hosts of the widespread Subarians'.[3] Yet even if he did so this was no

---

[1] See above, p. 24.　　　　　[2] See above, ch. xvii, sect. iv.
[3] G, 8, 64 f.; §1, 26, 93 ff.

more than a bare victory, for his descendants found a kingdom of Khanigalbat still in existence under the family of Shattuara and of his son Wasashatta,[1] probably related to the old ruling house, and had to wage against these enemies repeated wars, which continued into the reign of Shalmaneser I; as the outcome of these the territory of Khanigalbat was annexed to the Assyrian Empire.[2] In addition to victory over the Subarians in the west, the only other specific conquest attributed to Ashur-uballiṭ is that he 'subdued Muṣri'.[3] If, as some think, Muṣri lay to the east of Assyria, beyond Arrapkha (Kirkuk), or even to the north-east of Nineveh, this claim would be an indication of success upon another front, but there is no certainty where this land was situated,[4] for others would place it in the nearer or farther west of Assyria, and this is perhaps favoured by the discovery near Aleppo of an Aramaic treaty (eighth century B.C.) which proves the existence at that time of a Muṣri[5] in the vicinity of the north Syrian city of Arpad; if this was meant, the conquest of Muṣri would have been no more than a part of Ashur-uballiṭ's campaign against the Subarians.

## III. THE ASSYRIANS IN BABYLONIA

In the south, Ashur-uballiṭ's relations with Babylonia were intimate and dramatic, and are fairly well known. He achieved power in the reign of the Kassite king Burnaburiash II, whom we have seen above complaining bitterly to the Egyptian court of the notice accorded to his presumptuous vassal. No attention having been paid to this, Burnaburiash no doubt nursed his grievance for a time, perhaps for the remainder of his life. But a complete change of policy, spontaneous or forced, set in before long. Muballiṭat-Sherua, daughter of Ashur-uballiṭ, married the king of Babylon, and with the backing of her formidable father and her own spirit, evidently became a leading figure in that country. Owing to discrepancies in the two authorities[6] which have preserved the history of this time it is uncertain whether she married Burnaburiash himself or his son Karakhardash; the

[1] G, 3, 36, 38.          [2] G, 8, 116 ff.; G, 3, 38 f., 57; see below, p. 281.
[3] G, 8, 62 f.; G, 3, 57.
[4] G, 28, 389, n. 13; cf. below, p. 460 and n. 2.          [5] §II, 2, 223 f.
[6] The records of this time, called the 'Synchronistic History' and 'Chronicle P' (on which see *C.A.H.* I³, pt. I, p. 196, n. 5), differ as to the names and order of these Kassite kings, and modern historians differ accordingly; see G, 2, 365 f.; G, 28, 263; G, 19, 242 f.; §I, 9, 201, 212; §I, 22, 4 f.

latter may be thought the more likely. The reign of Karakhardash was short in any case, and he was succeeded (according to the Babylonian version,[1] which is followed here) by Kadashman-Kharbe, his son by his Assyrian queen. This young king[2] undertook a campaign in the desert country of the middle Euphrates against the nomads called Sutu whom he used with great severity. After operating against them over a wide area 'from east to west' he built a fort, dug a well and a cistern, and established there a permanent garrison to pacify the country. Not long afterwards his reign came to a violent end, for his Kassite subjects revolted, murdered him, and exalted to the throne one Nazibugash, otherwise called Shuzigash, a person of common birth. This revolt, the murder of his grandson, and the insult to his house called for the speedy revenge of Ashur-uballiṭ; he marched forthwith into Babylonia, defeated and slew the usurper, and set upon the throne Kurigalzu 'the young', son of Kadashman-Kharbe (according, again, to the more probable Babylonian version), who would thus have been his great-grandson, and doubtless no more than a child.

The jejune accounts of these two chronicles certainly refer to events of great moment at the time, the most dangerous of which was the invasion of the Sutu, or Aramaean tribes, continuing the age-old pressure from the north-west which, as ever, had behind it the remoter outflow of the deserts, and invariably ended in Babylonia. The letters both of Burnaburiash and of Ashur-uballiṭ to the king of Egypt describe lawless molestation of their emissaries by the nomads and townsmen of the upper Euphrates and Syria, too remote from either power to be effectively controlled. The depredations of these robbers account sufficiently for the campaign of Kadashman-Kharbe who, like other Babylonian kings before him, had to take up the hopeless burden of holding an indefensible frontier on the Euphrates. But his operations were certainly instigated and supported by Ashur-uballiṭ, who suffered no less from the Sutu, and a letter found at Dūr-Kurigalzu[3] seems to witness this close touch kept with the Assyrians. Whatever success was obtained (and it could have little lasting effect upon so evasive a foe) the effort was a severe strain for Babylon, for it coincided with other afflictions. The result was public detestation of the Assyrian alliance, concentrated upon its representative Muballiṭat-Sherua, whose prominence in the scanty records of the time leaves no doubt that she was a

---

[1] I.e. 'Chronicle P'.

[2] The following actions have otherwise been ascribed to an earlier Kadashman-Kharbe (I), §I, 9, 210.     [3] §III, 5, 149, no. 12; §I, 9, 252.

masterful and probably hated figure. Her son was struck down as the agent of servitude and disaster, but the rash impulse only brought on the heavier vengeance of the outraged Assyrian mother and grandfather.

In the dearth of historical records for this period, indirect illumination has been sought from two works of literature which seemed to have possible reference to the age of Ashur-uballiṭ. These have the added interest of coming respectively from Assyrian and Babylonian sources, being thus parallel with the two prose-chronicles which have been drawn upon hitherto. The Assyrian poem[1] is very inadequately preserved but its character is fairly clear. It is an epical description of a war between Assyria and Babylonia, written in a spirit of undisguised chauvinism; the Assyrians are acclaimed throughout as righteous victims of aggression and as heroes in battle, fighting with the aid of indignant gods against a faithless and cruel foe, who had set at nought the sanctity of treaties. Their respective leaders were the kings Tukulti-Ninurta of Assyria and Kashtiliash the Kassite. Thus the main part of this action would belong to a time more than a century later. But there is a passing reference to earlier reigns,[2] and although a supposed mention of Ashur-uballiṭ himself does not exist,[3] some very fragmentary evidence survives[4] that the war between Tukulti-Ninurta and Kashtiliash was only the last episode in a series of armed clashes between the powers, in the course of which both Adad-nīrāri I and his father Arik-dēn-ili had opposed Nazimaruttash and, still earlier, Enlil-nīrāri of Assyria had fought with Kurigalzu of Babylon.

A close predecessor of this Kurigalzu 'the young' had led an expedition against the Sutu,[5] and from this a connexion has been inferred with some passages in a composition known to the Babylonians as 'King of all Habitations' and to modern scholars as the 'Epic of the Plague-god Erra'. The general purport of this poem, which is strongly marked by the elaborate and prolix style of the Kassite period, is the affliction brought upon the land at a certain time by the wrath of Erra and the hand of his divine minister Ishum. It is needless to resume here the contents, beyond its description of a raid by the Sutu upon Uruk,[6] and the denunciation of vengeance upon these nomads; one day Akkad, now humbled, will overthrow the proud Sutu.[7] Weakness and

---

[1] §III, 2; §III, 8, 45, no. 39A; see below, pp. 287, 298.
[2] §III, 2, 20 ff., ll. 29–33.     [3] §III, 7, 40.
[4] §III, 9.     [5] See above, p. 11; G, 28, 263.
[6] §III, 4, 28 f., ll. 51 ff.     [7] *Ibid.* 34 f., l. 27.

affliction, depicted in the poem as the present lot of the Babylonians, would not be inappropriate to the days when alien, short-lived, and feeble kings held Babylon under the sway of its northern neighbour, but it is now the general opinion[1] that these attacks of the Sutu and the poem itself belong to a later age.

## IV. ENLIL-NĪRĀRI AND ARIK-DĒN-ILI

The Kurigalzu who was set upon the throne of Babylon by Ashur-uballiṭ was destined to enjoy a long if not always fortunate reign of twenty-two years, not only outliving his benefactor but continuing into the tenure of the next Assyrian king as well. But their relations were soon embroiled, for the national feelings of the southern kingdom could not tolerate equality with a nation which they were accustomed to regard as subject. Before long it came to war between the two countries, in which Assyria under Enlil-nīrāri, the son of Ashur-uballiṭ, was successful, whereby he won fame in the words of a successor[2] as he who 'slew the hosts of the Kassites'. Enlil-nīrāri reigned for ten years, and nothing more is known about him than this general description and a few details of the Babylonian wars given by the chronicles relating to this time. The two principal authorities, which have already differed concerning Kurigalzu's parentage, continue to give divergent accounts of what were clearly the same affairs. The Assyrian document, called the 'Synchronistic History', places this war in the reign of Enlil-nīrāri of Assyria,[3] whereas the Babylonian ('Chronicle P') postpones it until the reign of his second successor Adad-nīrāri I.[4] The former (Assyrian) version is undoubtedly correct here, for Kurigalzu did not in fact survive into the reign of Adad-nīrāri, and other fragments of inscriptions and chronicles[5] confirm that the opponents were indeed Enlil-nīrāri and Kurigalzu. It would appear, in fact, that wars between the Assyrians and Kassite kings lasted indecisively through all these reigns, and were brought to a stop only by the more complete victory of Tukulti-Ninurta I.

As to the course of these conflicts little is known. A recently published fragment reveals[6] that in the time of Enlil-nīrāri and Kurigalzu there occurred a battle at a spot not far from Irbil, and thus close to the Assyrian centre, which indicates that

---

[1] §III, 4, 85 ff.; §III, 3, 164, 176; §III, 6, 398, 400.
[2] G, 8, 62 f.; G, 28, 268; G, 3, 37.     [3] G, 7, pt. 34, pl. 38, 18 ff.
[4] §III, 1, 45, ll. 20 ff.     [5] §III, 9     [6] §III, 9, 115 f.

fortunes were wavering. The two main authorities continue to diverge; the Assyrian claims a victory for its own side, whereas the other seems to ascribe it to Kurigalzu. There is some indication that two battles took place, the last at a place called Sugaga on the Tigris, and they were probably hard-fought without a very decisive issue. The succeeding settlement was in accord with this equilibrium of forces. The 'Synchronistic History' has some obscure phrases which relate, in general significance, that an equal division was made of certain territory stretching from the land of Shubari to Karduniash (Babylonia), and a boundary traced between the shares of the two powers. The Babylonian chronicle precedes its brief mention of this war with a longer account of Kurigalzu's quarrel with a rival, one Khurpatila,[1] whom it calls 'king of Elammat'. The final battle between them at Dūr-Shulgi, in which Kurigalzu prevailed, followed a verbal challenge from Khurpatila which suggested the place of the encounter almost as if it had been a duel between the two kings, a picturesque incident[2] exactly matched many centuries later (A.D. 224), when the last of the Arsacid kings replied to a challenge from the usurping Ardashīr 'I will meet you in a plain which is called Hormizdaghan on the last day of the month of Mihr': if the battlefields were known it might prove that they were less separated by distance than by time.

Enlil-nīrāri of Assyria was succeeded by his son Arik-dēn-ili, whose reign lasted for twelve years. War continued with the Kassites, now under their king Nazimaruttash, whose design, as in the preceding reign, was to mount flank-attacks with the alliance of the eastern hillmen, rather than direct assaults upon the Assyrian centre.[3] Consequently the efforts of Arik-dēn-ili appear more as the usual offensive-defensive operations against the highlands than as moves in a conflict with Kassite Babylonia. In a summary of his father's exploits the next king of Assyria divides his victories into two—the first group was achieved against the districts of Turukku[4] and Nigimti[5] and 'all the chiefs of the mountains and highlands in the broad tracts of the Qutu (Gutians)'. This description makes it clear that the opponents dwelt in the Zagros; the general appellation of 'Gutians' is familiar enough, and Turukku was an old enemy of Hammurabi,[6] as also

---

[1] See below, p. 381.
[2] Ṭabarī, tr. Nöldeke, Th., *Geschichte der Perser und Araber zur Zeit der Sasaniden*, p. 14; *C.A.H.* xii, 109.       [3] §iii, 9, 113, 115.
[4] §iv, 3, 17.                                    [5] G, 8, 52, n. 5.
[6] G, 9, vol. ii, 181, no. 139; §iv, 1, vol. xv, 136.

the neighbour of Assyria with whom, in former days, Ishme-Dagan had confirmed peace by a marriage-alliance.[1] Some further details of this campaign were given by Arik-dēn-ili himself in a document[2] of which very little now remains—it was rather a chronicle than the earliest example of Assyrian annals. According to this fragment the opponent of Arik-dēn-ili in Nigimṭi was Esinu, whose land the Assyrian invaded and burned his harvest. In revenge Esinu attacked a district belonging to Assyria and killed many of the inhabitants. In a second invasion Arik-dēn-ili laid siege to a town named Arnuna, where Esinu was confined among the defenders. Gate and walls were laid in ruins and Esinu surrendered on terms of allegiance to Assyria and of bearing a tribute. The inscription continues with mention of a great victory by the Assyrian king and enormous booty, but it is not clear whether Esinu was again the enemy. Among a number of places named in this campaign is apparently Tarbiṣu, a very short distance north-west of Nineveh itself, from which it appears that serious danger was at one moment threatened to the very centre of the Assyrian kingdom.

The other scene of Arik-dēn-ili's wars, according to the summary of his son,[3] was the land of Katmukh, a district lying on the western side of the upper Tigris, between the river and a line roughly drawn through the present towns of Jazīrah-ibn-'Umar, Nisibis and Mārdīn. Here he encountered the local hillmen, who were in alliance with the Aramaean nomads called Akhlamu and Sutu, and another tribe the Yauru, probably cognate with these but otherwise unknown. The Assyrian was successful in this campaign, much as the Babylonian king Kadashman-Kharbe had been in his against the same elusive foes, but the Assyrian victory was more effectual, conquering 'the picked warriors of the Akhlamu, the Sutu, the Yauru, and their lands', since it apparently halted a direct incursion of the nomads into the lands north of Assyria, and directed their pressure southwards to the Babylonian district where they were to establish themselves gradually as the predominant element. With this episode, at whatever period of his reign, ends our knowledge of Arik-dēn-ili, a worthy maintainer of the great tradition established by his grandfather, though destined to be outshone by the military glory of his son. In the south the throne was occupied by Nazimaruttash, son of Kurigalzu, throughout the reign of his northern neighbour.

[1] §IV, 3, 17, 73.    [2] G, 8, 52 f.; G, 22, vol. I, 68–71; G, 3, 31.
[3] G, 8, 60 f.; G, 28, 269, 390.

## V. SOCIETY IN THE MIDDLE KASSITE PERIOD

Both in the northern and in the southern kingdoms the foreign repressions which had so long stifled their normal development were withdrawn at about the same time, although the processes were different in their outward aspects. Assyria, or rather its innermost core, ceased to suffer the domination of the Hurrians, embodied in the kingdoms of Khanigalbat or Mitanni. These either came to an end or languished, and with them disappeared even so vigorous and highly organized a Hurrian community as that which occupied the neighbouring territory of Arrapkha, the ample documents of which have been found to extend over four or five generations[1] and then stop, doubtless at the end of the Hurrian ascendancy. That the local population changed much is unlikely, but Arrapkha's whole future, from the thirteenth century onward, was to be that of a provincial Assyrian capital, and little more is known about it,[2] for when the Hurrian mainspring was broken it ceased to have a movement of its own. In Babylonia it was not the removal of external pressure so much as the advance of assimilation which now allowed native forces again to become operative and the general pattern of life in the south to be re-established. When this growth becomes visible after the long night of the earlier Kassites what reappears is largely familiar as the old life under the First Dynasty and its contemporary kingdoms. But the changes are significant, and certain influences which induced them can perhaps be traced in resurgent Assyria as well.

It happens that the evidence in both countries lies principally in the domain of law and society; in both there are official enactments and a body of semi-official or private documents. In Babylonia here began the age of the 'boundary-stones', famous since the beginning of modern studies, when their fine preservation, strange symbols, and elaborate inscriptions made them objects of strong and immediate interest.[3] The earliest of these[4] bears the name of Kadashman-Enlil, father of that Burnaburiash (II) who was the contemporary of Ashur-uballit. The inscription of this monument purports to confirm a grant of land already made by Kurigalzu (I) in the preceding generation, which is enough to show that the legal usage consecrated by these stones,

[1] §v, 18, 61.                              [2] G, 9, vol. I, 154.
[3] G, 25, 77; §v, 24; 27; 44; G, 19, 245 ff.; G, 6, vol. II, 896 ff.; G, 12, pl. 71.
[4] §v, 27, Introd. ix and pp. 3 ff.; §v, 44, no. 1; a different position in §I, 9, 253 (no. 181). See Plate 132 (*a*).

and probably the stones themselves, may be traced back at least
so far. The purpose of these monuments was to record and ratify
grants of land made by the king to trusted officers and subjects.
There was nothing new in this, but the process of conveyance
exhibits certain peculiarities which were unknown in the First
Dynasty. The external form of the monuments is novel, and
their most striking peculiarity is the presence of sculptured
religious symbols which represent those gods under whose
protection the grant is placed, whose curse is to be incurred by
any who should presume to violate or question the donations.
This introduction of penalties against offenders has been
regarded[1] as a relic of the recent state of society when insecurity
of life and property was the rule under the barbarian invasions,
but it may be observed that invocation of the divine wrath against
violators of monuments was a much older feature in Babylonian
inscriptions, being especially prominent under the Dynasty of
Agade.[2] What is new is the introduction of civil penalties against
non-observers of the contract or donation. Such penalties consist
usually in a manifold delivery of the goods purported to be sold,[3]
or in a monetary fine (frequently to be paid in gold),[4] but sometimes a cruel physical sanction is menaced—a bronze peg shall
be driven into the mouth of the deceiver.[5] The idea of severe
forfeits is thus common to Babylonia and Assyria at this time,
and physical mutilations had earlier been inflicted by Elamite
justice.[6] Both of these innovations seem therefore to be a sign
of foreign, apparently eastern, customs invading the Babylonian
world at this period. Another mark of this might be seen in the
definition of lands as belonging to certain 'houses' or territorial
districts, defined as the property of tribes. This reveals that great
tracts of land were owned collectively by communities, and it is
natural to see in this the effect of settlement by tribes such as
produced the various 'Houses' found in the history of Sennacherib's wars against Merodach-baladan II.[7] On the other hand
it has been observed[8] that a like system of ownership may appear
already in the ancient Obelisk of Manishtusu, and even earlier,[9]
so that perhaps nothing was new in this tenure except the owners.

Certain other peculiarities which mark the legal practice of the
boundary-stones have been noticed as not only novel in them-

[1] G, 19, 247.          [2] Many examples in §v, 26, 37 ff.
[3] §v, 35, 269.          [4] §ɪɪ, 3, 40; §v, 7, 39 f.          [5] §ɪ, 10, 11.
[6] C.A.H. ɪɪ³, pt. 1, p. 281; §v, 25, 89 f.; §v, 28, 307.
[7] §v, 4, 234; §v, 5, 7 f.     [8] G, 19, 250; §v, 11; G, 21, 75 ff.
[9] C.A.H. ɪ³, pt. 2, pp. 131 and 449; §v, 10, 24 f.

selves but as having parallels in the contemporary practice of the northern country. Thus in one place[1] there is a reference to the practice of official proclamation of the sale of land between private persons, after which, when there had been no objection raised by third parties, the transaction was officially registered and the document placed in the archives. A similar requirement appears in the Assyrian law concerning the sale of land;[2] when the bargain had been arranged between two parties it was necessary for the buyer to employ a crier who had to proclaim three times in a full month, within the city of Ashur, or within any other place where the ground was situated, that the prospective buyer was about to acquire such and such lands, and calling upon any person who conceived himself to have a claim upon, or rights concerning, those lands to produce his written documents of title before the magistrate and town-clerk of Ashur, or before the mayor and elders of another city, within that month. Any claim so substantiated was admitted and the proposed sale thereby voided, but if no claim was made within the appointed period the sale proceeded, the buyer took possession, and the transaction was officially registered. The same custom of public proclamation is at least implied in the Assyrian contracts of this period[3] (i.e. the age of Ashur-uballit) where transfers of land, in order to be absolutely legal, were subject to the issue of a 'valid tablet' by the seller to the buyer, and this could be given only after proof that there had been no appearance of anybody laying rival claims to the land. Furthermore, the custom of public proclamation was well known also at Nuzi and Arrapkha, where it was called by a word meaning 'information', and this procedure was ordained not only in transfers of land but in a variety of other transactions such as sales of slaves, and even in such matters as marriage, divorce, and adoptions.[4] Without needing to discuss here the formal aspects of this requirement, it is sufficient to note the introduction of a peculiar act of legal publicity in the practice both of the south country, of Ashur, and of Arrapkha.

Yet one more common feature has been pointed out in the formalities of the boundary-stones and of the northern peoples; this is the appearance of an accurate survey of the site and especially the mensuration of the properties conveyed by the respective documents concerning land-tenure. In the boundary-stones, when the king was making a grant of estate, the phrase

---

[1] §v, 27, no. III, col. iii, 30 ff.; §v, 35, 270.
[2] §v, 12, 312 ff. (Tablet B, sect. 6).      [3] §I, 10, 80 f.      [4] §I, 10, 77 ff.

ran commonly 'he (the king) measured the field and conferred it upon (the recipient)', or even more explicitly 'the king sent (certain individuals) and these measured the field'.[1] In the Middle-Assyrian contracts for the sale of land the regular form is, after acknowledging receipt of the price, that the seller undertakes to meet any outstanding claims, and then 'he will measure the field with the royal tape and will write a valid tablet before the king'.[2] Since this procedure might seem superfluous between the parties once the bargain had been agreed and the price paid, the subsequent measurement 'with the royal tape' and the writing of a 'valid tablet' must be considered as another act, like the proclamation described above, giving official status to the transaction. All of these changes in the law governing transfers of land mark a notable departure from the practice of the First Dynasty of Babylon, and a distinct growth of officialdom. And since they are shared, in varying degrees, by Babylon under the Kassites, Assyria under isolation in a world of foreigners, and Arrapkha with its alien population, it is necessary to look for some common influence which produced these likenesses. Importation of eastern custom has been suggested, and colour might be given to this possibility by the appearance upon Kassite tablets of nail-marks[3] imprinted by the parties to deeds of sale, hire, loan, and pledge as (apparently) a more personal form of attestation than the traditional seal-impression, a practice virtually unknown to tablets of the First Dynasty in Babylonia, but on the contrary frequent in the legal documents found at Susa, which were contemporary with these.[4] It might seem therefore that the custom had spread from Elam and been adopted thence in Kassite Babylon. But a curious difference appears here in the lands hitherto seen as using similar innovations in legal practice, for the nail-marks are unknown to the Nuzi tablets and to the Middle Assyrian contracts.[5]

The boundary-stones are only one kind of legal document from the Kassite period. Side by side with them exist many less solemnly preserved records and letters, such as have been seen to throw so much light upon the life of the Old Babylonian period. In comparison with those, however, the Kassite tablets[6] seem disappointing, the contents being mostly of a very humdrum tenor. This is due to the fact that nearly all belong to a single find at Nippur, which yielded simply the contents of one administrative office, and consequently they are mainly occupied by a

---

[1] §v, 35, 270 ff.   [2] §1, 10, 68, 73, 80 f.   [3] §v, 3, 210 ff.
[4] §v, 28, 305; §v, 33, 53.   [5] §v, 3, 212.   [6] §v, 6, vol. xiv, 5 ff.

single subject, records of rent from temple estates and lists of wages and allowances to officials. Occasional tablets refer to sales, guarantees, and legal proceedings, and the latter are more frequent in a small find at the city of Dūr-Kurigalzu.[1] These documents from Nippur begin at about the time when this chapter opens, in the reign of Burnaburiash II, and continue through the next seven or eight kings to Kashtiliash IV, a century which may be regarded as the most flourishing of Kassite rule. The Assyrian contracts[2] are somewhat earlier, for, although there is no list of the eponyms by whom they are dated, allusions to the names of kings reveal that they were written under Ashur-nīrāri II, Ashur-bēl-nishēshu, Erība-Adad, Ashur-uballiṭ, and Enlil-nīrāri, a few being even later.[3] These Assyrian documents are more interesting than the Kassite, for their contents are much more varied; there are sales of land, houses, and slaves, the payments for which are made in lead, the usual medium of exchange. Some of the legal practices described in these contracts have been noticed above, and another which is of much juristic interest is the custom for joint heirs of a landed property to sell their portions before the details, especially the position, of their shares in the inheritance had been defined[4]—a mortgage of expectations. The buyer acquired the right to 'choose and take' whichever part of the estate should fall to the lot of the heir in a certain territory. A modification of this was the practice of selling the deed-tablet which gave title to a property, the buyer of such a tablet obtaining the right to 'demand and take possession'. Even princes thus disposed of ground which had become the 'share of the palace'[5] by titles which are unexplained or by confiscation. They also accepted payment for transferring the deed of title to a royal fief from one holder to another.[6] Loans too are common among the Assyrian private documents, the commodities borrowed being usually lead or barley, and after the short period of the loan had elapsed interest was charged if payment was delayed. Meanwhile a pledge had been given by the debtor,[7] either land or slaves, from the use of which the lender might in certain circumstances compensate himself for the lead or barley taken out of his capital. Not only the debtor's house but his own person or his children[8] might serve as security for the loan.

The letters[9] found with the Kassite administrative tablets

---

[1] §vi, 2; §iii, 5.    [2] §v, 8; 13; 14; 15; 17; 29; 49; §i, 3; 10, 6 ff.
[3] §i, 3, 42 ff.    [4] §i, 10, 39 f., 149 f.; §v, 49.
[5] §i, 10, 43 ff.; §v, 41.    [6] §i, 10, 44 f.
[7] §i, 10, 96 ff.    [8] §i, 10, 117 ff.    [9] §v, 36; §v, 34, nos. 15–86.

and covering about the same period of time are of greater interest, though perhaps more often because of their form than their matter, which is frequently difficult of interpretation. They preserve the Old Babylonian (and indeed Sumerian) form of introduction 'to X say, thus Y . . .', assuming that a scribe will read out the contents to a perhaps illiterate recipient. But the salutations which follow this[1] show a characteristic increase of formality over those of the Hammurabi period; one official writing to another adds after his name 'your brother', and the phrase 'be it well with you!' which is ubiquitous in the Amarna and the late Assyrian letters. Not only this, but the greeting is extended 'to your house and your office' and the blessing of the gods who were patrons of the writer's city is added, 'may they protect your life, make your path perfect'. In addressing higher officials or even the king himself the compliments are naturally multiplied— 'to your house, your city, your territory, guards, forts, chariots, cattle, harvests, canals, craftsmen'; an almost fantastic phraseology of submission, indeed of servility, to the great king of Egypt is affected by some of the writers of the Amarna letters. An especially frequent phrase in the Kassite letters to a superior is 'I will go as the substitute of my lord',[2] which expresses the sender's readiness to take upon himself all evil which may threaten his master; this locution, sometimes preceded by 'I cast myself down',[3] is shared by a few Assyrian letters of the same period. The contents of these missives are not frequently of much interest, for many are reports of minor officials to the heads of their departments in the temples of Nippur.

Some topics of interest fall, nevertheless, to be discussed in them, such as weavers and their work, the progress of building operations[4] in a temple or upon an official house for which thousands of bricks have to be prepared,[5] irrigation, reed-cutting for use in canals and buildings, repair of flood damage, and maintenance of watercourses.[6] In the course of these appear complaints against royal commissars who are accused of misusing the city levies of workmen,[7] of giving arbitrary orders for tasks not authorized,[8] and of misappropriating temple property and personnel:[9] there is overt collision between the king's authority and the hardly less powerful interests of the great temples.[10] A highly curious group of letters from the Nippur archives concerns the conduct of a temple hospital or sick-room[11] of a special kind.

---

[1] §v, 36, 18 ff.; §v, 46, 6.    [2] §v, 46, 20 ff.; G, 5, vol. 3, 149.
[3] §v, 43, 369.    [4] §v, 46, 45 f.    [5] Ibid. 66 f.    [6] Ibid. 44 ff.
[7] Ibid. 59.    [8] Ibid. 60.    [9] Ibid. 59.    [10] Ibid. 61.    [11] Ibid. 25 ff.

The patients found in this were all female and belonged to the class of temple-singers, the hospital itself being established in the house of the goddess Gula, the divine physician, in the city of Nippur. About a dozen cases were under treatment at the same time, and frequent reports upon the condition of these were sent off, even at midnight, to a superior who occasionally gave directions himself about the cures to be administered. The prevalent diseases were fevers and coughs with various consequences, and the remedies given were medicinal drugs compounded from the plants which abound in the later medical texts, but also externally oil and bandages were applied. Nothing is heard about that other regular ingredient of healing, the incantation, doubtless because this was the business of a different specialist.

Two documents, of which considerable fragments exist in later copies, throw a baleful light upon the temper and institutions of the Assyrians in the renascence begun under Ashur-uballiṭ I. The 'Middle-Assyrian laws' are only chance survivals of what must have been a larger collection, the legal character of which is not clear.[1] Of the two principal tablets, the first deals with offences generally concerning women, which involve incidentally such subjects as sacrilege, theft, enticement, slander, and murder, as well as rules concerning marriage and the conduct of women in public places, but most of these laws are directed to the punishment of sexual offences. In the other principal tablet the general subject is land-holding, with regulations concerning inheritance, sale, and irrigation-rights. Apart from the wealth of detail which these laws supply upon the life of the period, their cultural interest may be thought to lie in the general impression they give of a hard and primitively-minded society, not at all out of accord with the cruelties wreaked upon public enemies which so disfigure the later Assyrian annals.[2] These laws abound, in almost every section, with heavy fines and convict-labour, superadded to savage beatings and ghastly physical mutilations, inflicted upon men and women alike, to which the death-penalty, also freely awarded, can seem only an alleviation. It must be owned that the insistence upon such barbarities, coupled with the accident that some of the offences concerned are themselves of the more repellent kind morally, makes the 'Assyrian laws' disagreeable reading.

No less unpleasing a picture of a more private life, that of the king, is drawn by a series of regulations,[3] collected in the reign of Tiglath-pileser I, and issued by himself and by eight of his

---

[1] §v, 12, 12 ff.; see below, 475 ff.
[2] See, however, a palliation of these, §v, 37, 154.      [3] §v, 48.

predecessors. These regulations governed the conduct of the royal household in Ashur. Sons and brothers of the royal family dwelt there, but also a troop of courtiers and underlings, and especially the numerous women, pining and quarrelling through the idle days in their own quarters, which they hardly ever quitted, having their own ill-used maidservants, and being more distantly waited upon by eunuchs and royal officials, whose access was jealously measured and spied upon. The whole establishment was under the rule of a major-domo and a hierarchy of subordinates, admission to which was gained by passing a rigorous if undefined examination before a board of higher mandarins, who applied a meticulous test, and made errors or omissions at their peril, for the whole system rested upon a compulsory sycophantism, under which the non-informer suffered as severely as the offender. It is again the despotic spirit, the harsh discipline, the jealous seclusion, enforced by the same unmerciful sanctions, which give their whole tone to these decrees; the Assyrian royal residence was more of a prison than a palace. That a more enlightened régime could exist within the conditions and the mentality of that age is suggested by the almost contemporary instructions for officials among the Hittites.[1] Not only are these much wider in their range of interests, more concerned with the interests of a state than of an individual, but they stress rather the impiety of disloyal acts, and are content to leave their punishment to the offended gods, omitting the abominable man-inflicted cruelties. Shamshi-Adad I, in an earlier generation, had sharply rebuked his son at Mari for not keeping a better rule in his household.[2] It was perhaps only because the old tyrant had found ruling there a temper more humane and civilized than was ever allowed to penetrate the Assyrian court.

In literature the creative power of the Kassite period has been underestimated as compared with others, which pass for more glorious. Babylonian and Assyrian texts as a whole are anonymous, and their age can be determined, if at all, only by internal evidence, making much necessary allowance for alteration in the process of transmission through many centuries.[3] The Old Babylonian period, to which is due the preservation of so great a part of the literature now available certainly did not originate most of that which it committed to writing.[4] The succeeding period of the Kassites has hitherto been reckoned the age of

---

[1] §v, 40, esp. 6 f.
[2] §iv, 1, vol. 1, no. 73. The reproach itself was undeserved, *ibid.* vol. xi, 120 ff.
[3] §v, 42, 17 f.          [4] *C.A.H.* ii³, pt. 1, pp. 210 ff.

collection and arrangement of this literary heritage. Such a contrast does indeed seem to be reflected in the diverse image of scribes belonging to these two epochs. The Old Babylonian scribe, for all his pretensions, is an everyday figure. Emerging from the hurly-burly of his school life, passed under the tutelage and the hands of very human, not to say vulgar, educators, the finished scribe shows little sign of having altered much of his adolescent habits. He was at pains to advertise himself as an adept in all trades, even if he specialized in some.[1] A man of letters indeed, and able to recommend himself to kings,[2] he was more often busied in very ordinary affairs as arbitrator, surveyor, cost-expert, businessman, engineer, and even craftsman, in all of which accomplishments he proclaimed his own merits as loudly as he denounced the ignorance and falsity of his rivals. This stirring and mundane figure seems (to us at least) quite absent from the scene in the Kassite period. It is true that scribes still perused the chequered experiences of their forebears in the pursuit of learning, but now as lesson-books provided with a translation into Akkadian,[3] in which guise they were found in the library of Ashurbanipal. But the Kassite scribes, who begin to take on a degree of individuality, are far different characters. Shadows appear of great names, authors and scholars, whose memory was kept alive and honoured by descendants in the same professions. To such men can be attributed not merely the study, the textual fixation, and the exegesis of traditional works, but more original authorship than can be actually identified with any other age. The 'epic' concerning the wars between Tukulti-Ninurta I of Assyria and Kashtiliash IV of Babylon dates itself to the latter half of the thirteenth century B.C. The epic of Erra, the Plague-god, composed (or, as he affirms, divinely received) by one who appended his own name to the composition is clearly dated by internal evidence and language to a time still later.[4] And finally the Babylonian 'Theodicy', also signed by its author in the acrostic form of its verses, was in one document provided with an actual date, which may be the reign of Adad-apla-iddina (1067–1046 B.C.).[5]

Nevertheless, it is clear both from the material itself and from the above-mentioned tradition of master-scribes that in this period was carried forward with great zeal the collection of classes of literature, the revision of their contents, their arrangement into series of numbered tablets, scarcely begun hitherto, and the translation of Sumerian texts into Akkadian, only half-

---

[1] §v, 19, 31 f.    [2] §v, 19, 37; §v, 20, 261.    [3] §v, 20.
[4] Upon these see above, pp. 30 f.    [5] §v, 31, 66 f., 76.

necessary in the Old Babylonian period, when much of the old language and learning was still living. These labours were accompanied by writing of gloss and comment, designed to expound the meaning of Sumerian originals to a body of students now almost wholly Akkadian-speaking. The desire to extract more refined and more comprehensive significance from the words and names of the tradition led to the common result of some misplaced ingenuity and overstrained etymologies being mingled with genuine interpretation, well exemplified in the often-fanciful commentary upon the 'fifty names of Marduk' which conclude the Creation Epic.[1] At this time began also the arrangement of large works of lexicography and of divination,[2] the supreme science of the Babylonians, into the series which embody the principal subjects of extispicy, astrology, and omens from signs upon earth, as they are found fully shaped and named in the late Assyrian kingdom. Authors and scholars with such accomplishments as these do honour to their age, and are entitled to be regarded as the Alexandrians of Babylonian literature.

Strong influences of culture emanating chiefly from the centres of Babylon and Borsippa undoubtedly began to prevail in Assyria about the time which is the subject of this chapter, and under the influence of Ashur-uballiṭ himself. In his reign occurs the first mention in Assyria of the god of Babylon,[3] who, it is revealed, already had a temple in the city of Ashur itself. The source of this information is a remarkable inscription[4] written by a private, if highly placed, individual named Marduk-nādin-ahhē, who declares himself the blessed of god and king, the favourite, the renowned, who rejoices the heart of his lord. He relates that he was granted the right to build for himself a dwelling 'in the shadow of the house of Marduk my lord'. This private residence is described as built with especial cunning and lasting materials, having a well of cold water and rooms for esoteric uses. Marduk and his divine spouse were besought to make it a place of repose for the builder and continue it as the dwelling of his posterity for evermore; the inscription ends with a cordial blessing upon Ashur-uballiṭ the king 'who loves me'. Nothing more is said of the relation, evidently close, between the Assyrian king and this highly favoured foreigner, but the purport of the inscription suggests that Marduk-nādin-ahhē was a man of particular accomplishments, and that he was in Assyria

[1] §v, 2, 198; §v, 30, 36.  [2] §v, 42, 22, 24. See Plate 132 (c).
[3] §v, 39; §v, 38, 203 f; C.A.H. II³, pt. I, p. 210.
[4] G, 4, 388 ff.; G, 8, 38 ff.; §1, 3, 109.

by special invitation, for the purpose of inaugurating the cult of Marduk; so much is implied by his description of his house as built in the expectation of handing it on as the official residence for the priest of Marduk in each generation. A further interest may be found in the name of this individual, for he was the son of a certain Marduk-uballiṭ, son of Ushshur-ana-Marduk, and these latter names are one identical and the other closely similar to those connected with the writer who has left a curious treatise upon the making of glass.[1] Being dated in the reign of Gulkishar, this tablet is presumably earlier[2] than the age of Ashur-uballiṭ, but it may be that the protégé of the Assyrian king was a person of celebrated skill, the contemporary head of an old and famous family (he refers proudly to his forefathers), attracted to Assyria by its enlightened ruler in order to bring the real and imagined benefits of his Babylonian arts to the capital of the northern kingdom. But doubtless the strongest testimony to the prevailing Babylonian influence in the north, before the time of Ashur-uballiṭ, is found in the tablets of Nuzi already mentioned. There is exhibited the whole legal and official business of a completely foreign and heterophone community couched in the language and writing of Babylon, with a fraternity of native attorneys bearing professional Babylonian names[3] striving to cast their institutions as well as their documents as best they could into the medium solely recognized as the authentic vehicle of culture.

## VI. NEW INFLUENCES IN ART

If in literature and all things of the intellect Babylon was at this time supreme it was not so in the material arts. The antiquities of this age are neither common nor particularly distinguished, but their general characteristic is a strong alien tinge. Apart from the boundary-stones, which display as marked innovations in the use of their sculptures as in legal ideas, the principal remains of this period are buildings and cylinder-seals. As concerns the first, the new Kassite foundation of Dūr-Kurigalzu, so far as it has been explored,[4] does not indeed reveal anything which is out of keeping with the Babylonian scene. But at Uruk there stood, on the north-east side of the great enclosure surrounding the stage-tower, a temple of peculiar form and decoration,[5] identified by brick-inscriptions as the work of a Kassite king Karaindash

---

[1] *C.A.H.* 11³, pt. 1, pt. 227. See Plate 132 (*b*).    [2] §v, 32, 68, n. 174(*d*).
[3] §I, 20; §I, 10, 13.    [4] §vI, 2. See Plate 133(*a*).
[5] G, 17, 1, 30 ff., pls. 11, 15–17.

(*c.* 1420 B.C.). The ruin of this temple was marked by two unusual features, first the form of the sanctuary, which was of the lengthwise shape, having the cult-image at one of the ends, not in the middle of a long wall, as was the custom in Babylonia; and this itself is evidence of some influence from the north or east, where this disposition of the image prevailed.[1]

Still more remarkable than this planning exception was the structure of the burnt-brick walls. As restored by the discoverers[2] (since no part was preserved for more than a few courses high) the walls carried on their outer side a series of deep niches, each the breadth of one whole brick, separated by spaces of the like width at the surface of the walls. The niches were occupied by figures in high relief, moulded on the edges of the bricks in such a way that the figure was wholly withdrawn behind the outer surface of the wall. All of these were divine; they wore low flat caps decorated with the single pair of horns which marked inferior or servant deities. Alternately they were male and female, the males bearded, the females wearing a necklace, and the two differing in the patterns of their skirts which fell full-length to the ground concealing the feet. Both alike held in the right hand, and supported with the left, a round-based vase from which sprang a double stream of water flowing outwards to each side, and combining with the streams from the next figure on either hand so as to fall in regular waves down the fronts of the panels separating the niches. In these figures and the streams which they pour out there is indeed nothing un-Babylonian; both the costume of the gods and their symbolic action of bestowing water[3] had been familiar long before the days of Karaindash. But as with the boundary-stones it was not the figures themselves which were novel but the use made of them. No earlier building is known in which these symbolic figures surround the whole outside, and a further innovation is the use of moulded bricks as a medium for producing a decoration in relief upon the surface of a wall.

If the pattern of this temple's exterior seems to have found little favour afterwards it was otherwise with this moulded brick-work which was destined to achieve great fame and popularity; the vast stately buildings of Nebuchadrezzar in Babylon made impressive use of it, so did the Assyrians, and so did Darius in his palace at Susa, recording that the brickwork was executed by the Babylonians.[4] Of all these monuments notable remains are still

---

[1] §VI, 1, 22 f.; §VI, 8, 304 ff.; §VI, 12.

[2] G, 17, 1, pls. 15, 16; G, 12, 63 f., pl. 70A.; G, 6, vol. IV, 2132 ff.

[3] §VI, 26. See Plate 133 (*c*).     [4] §VI, 13, 142 ff., ll. 28–30. See Plate 133 (*b*).

in existence, resplendent in the coloured glazes of which apparently there was no trace upon the building of Karaindash. It is perhaps significant that the only other such figures in moulded brick relief around a temple wall[1] have been found in pre-Achaemenid Susa. There they adorned a temple dedicated to the principal god In-Shushinak by two kings who reigned successively[2] in the twelfth century B.C. In this case too the figures were alternate, but not withdrawn into niches, as at Uruk. The first was a group of two subjects, the half-man, half-bull, divinity bearded and wearing a crown with multiple horns. His arms reached out to the side and touched the trunk and top of a stiffly fashioned palm with pendent dates. The other figure, less well defined, was apparently a standing goddess clasping her hands before her face in the posture of supplication. Above the figures seems to have run a band of quadruple zig-zag pattern, and inscriptions[3] were carried across the middle. It is not inviting to draw a confident conclusion from these two examples. Since they are at present the only two known it would seem logical to trace the influence from the earlier (at Uruk) to the later (at Susa), remembering the constant dependence of Susa upon Babylonian culture and fashions, and also that there is nothing un-Babylonian, but quite the contrary, in any of the subjects depicted. But as the arrangement and the technique were both novel it has been supposed that the temple walls at Uruk were created by an eastern inspiration due to the Kassite origin.[4] As to this, more evidence is required.

There can be no such doubt of the foreign influences prevailing in the cylinder-seals of this period—indeed, for the first time, the most numerous as well as the most characterized of these were not made in Babylonia at all and have nothing more than certain reminiscences of the land which invented them and by its prestige imposed their use upon foreigners. In the homeland itself the Kassite style was distinctive, but is so well known that it needs no description here.[5] Ornamental gold mounts at each end of the cylinders, if not unknown before,[6] became at least more common,[7] perhaps in consequence of the increased gold supply which was noticeable in this period.[8] The materials preferred for the cylinders were brightly coloured stones, chosen

---

[1] §vi, 25; G, 6, vol. ii, 932 f., but see now §vi, 29, 3.
[2] See below, pp. 437 f.                    [3] §vi, 11, 57, no. 29.
[4] §vi, 1, 22; §vi, 12.
[5] G, 11, 180 ff.; §vi, 23, vol. i, 63; G, 6, vol. ii, 906 f.; §vi, 5; §vi, 19, 126 f., 140.
[6] §vi, 6, 47.                [7] §vi, 5, 267.            [8] See above, p. 24.

doubtless for supposed amuletic virtues,[1] the engraving was often shallow and rough. Single figures were the rule, accompanied by symbolic devices such as the familiar 'Kassite cross'. Another novel introduction was the long Sumerian inscription, filling most of the surface, generally prayers to a tutelary god, and often obscure in expression,[2] which may be regarded as another manifestation of the literary and learned interests of the period. But whereas these seals, apart from the importation of a few secondary motives, remained very much in the exclusive Babylonian tradition, there were flourishing at about the same time two other 'schools' which, since they occupied the geographical area of Assyria, must be noticed here. The first is amply illustrated by cylinders found at Nuzi,[3] and the numerous impressions upon the tablets from that town. The second is that which produced the class of seals called 'middle Assyrian',[4] but the title has a misleading implication, since they were in fact the first cylinders of native Assyrian style, formed in the age of national revival symbolized by the name Ashur-uballiṭ.

Much of the répertoire of the Nuzian artists was taken over by the Assyrians, but upon this material they imprinted a strongly individual stamp.[5] Inscriptions are rare and figures few, but these are chosen and combined with a new effectiveness which makes vigour and physical activity the keynote. Their favourite theme was combat,[6] the usual participants demons and monsters. Thus, two seals which bear the names of the kings Erība-Adad and Ashur-uballiṭ himself[7] represent winged demons of fearful aspect overcoming or dispatching smaller creatures or a lion; such winged apparitions, dragons, griffins, lions, and scorpions, in all postures of struggle, fill the Assyrian seals with a world of fantastic vigour which seems untrammelled with any purpose to tell a story but only to picture the clash of mythological terrors against daemoniac champions of the human kind, for, as their later literature shows, the Assyrians were subject to a gloomy cast of religious thinking, dominated by the fear of devils and the threat of ill omens. The seals often depict, likewise, a human figure probably of divine nature which shoots or slays a raging monster[8] and thus is conceived as protecting the owner of the seal. This idea contrasts strongly with the older Babylonian, where the amuletic virtue of the seal lay in its picture of the

---

[1] §vi, 18, 74, 88; §vi, 10.     [2] §vi, 3; 9; 14.
[3] §vi, 22.     [4] §vi, 5, 266 ff.; §vi, 18.
[5] §vi, 4, 200 ff.     [6] §vi, 4, 209.
[7] §vi, 4, 142 ff., Abb. 2, 17, 22.     [8] §vi, 18, 52 ff.; §vi, 5, 266 ff.

owner being led up to his god and recommended to his blessing, while in Assyria the whole emphasis was upon protection from the assault of hostile powers. The other principal subject of the Middle Assyrian seals is the group of animals or monsters ranged symmetrically on each side of a tree or plant,[1] an effective composition which, in addition to whatever religious significance attached to it, probably owed its favour as much to its artistic effect and to its peculiar suitability for the diminutive spaces which the craftsman had to fill.

The most significant distinction between the seals of this period is into two kinds which have been called the elaborate or well-cut, and the common style.[2] What principally gave rise to the rough execution of the latter was the use of a new material, in place of various kinds of stones. This was frit,[3] a composition of powdered silicious grains fused together and coated with coloured glaze—a substance which could be produced in quantity and shaped in moulds, with designs ready-made. The distribution of such seals in the Near East at this time was very extensive,[4] and evidently corresponded with a demand spreading far beyond the official class which had hitherto possessed them. This demand was both occasioned and supplied by a new technique of glass-working,[5] capable of providing cheap substitutes for the individual products of the stone-engravers, although at the sacrifice, as usual, of quality and design.

[1] §vi, 18, 73 ff.; §vi, 4, 160 f., 210; §vi, 5, 274.
[2] §vi, 22, 12, 107; §vi, 5, 274 ff.
[3] G, 11, 5, 278; §vi, 4, 186, 207; §vi, 23, 139; §vi, 15, 341.
[4] §vi, 5, 274, n. 95.
[5] *C.A.H.* ii[3], pt. 1, p. 227. Yet in Egypt the use of this material for small objects, including seals, was much older, §vi, 15, 342.

# CHAPTER XIX

## EGYPT: THE AMARNA PERIOD AND THE END OF THE EIGHTEENTH DYNASTY

### I. THE PROBLEM OF A CO-REGENCY BETWEEN AMENOPHIS III AND AKHENATEN

LETTERS from Tushratta of Mitanni and Shuppiluliumash of Hatti[1] show that on the death of Amenophis III his eldest surviving son, Neferkheprure Amenhotpe (Amenophis IV), who later in his reign took the name of Akhenaten, was accepted by these foreign princes as the new pharaoh. The problem remains whether he had been recognized by the Egyptians as the co-regent of his father for some time previously. The matter has been much discussed in recent years, one body of opinion maintaining the orthodox view that Amenophis IV acceded only after the death of his father and ruled for his full term of seventeen years alone, the other interpreting ambiguous evidence, much of it recently uncovered, as revealing that the son had ruled with his father for a decade or more. No side has produced conclusive proof to convince the other, and a final decision will have to await the emergence of further evidence, perhaps in the field of comparative chronology.

The scheme of chronology adopted in this History admits of no overlap in the reigns of Amenophis III and his son;[2] a co-regency, however, must allow for a joint rule lasting some eleven years.[3] The independence of the two courts and their officials would permit these alternative interpretations, but adjustments would have to be made in the case of certain events which are treated here as occurring consecutively, whereas they may have been coeval. Thus it should be borne in mind that tendencies in art and religion, for instance, which appear in the reign of Amenophis III and are described as anticipating the innovations of Akhenaten, may in fact be contemporary with them.

---

* An original version of this chapter was published as fascicle 71 in 1971; the present chapter includes revisions made in 1973.

[1] E.A. 27, E.A. 41.

[2] *C.A.H.* II[3], pt. 1, pp. 316 n. 9, 322 nn. 7 and 10. See also §1, 1–21; A, 9.

[3] §1, 4, 110; §1, 5, 29; §1, 10, 37.

## II. THE CHARACTER OF THE AMARNA 'REVOLUTION'

The new king was a pharaoh whose monuments have won for him, among modern scholars, the reputation of being the most remarkable king to have occupied the throne in the history of Egypt. Wide claims have been made for him as a thinker, religious reformer, artistic innovator, revolutionary and individualist.[1] It seems probable, however, that such opinions, based upon inadequate evidence, have led to many ill-founded conclusions about his originality and personal qualities. Few would now maintain that his outlook was any more international than that of other pharaohs whose sandals traditionally trod upon captive figures of the Nine Nations,[2] and who claimed to rule as gods over all that the sun encircled.

Akhenaten has also been credited with modern pacifist principles in his conduct of foreign policy that are difficult to reconcile with the testimony from damaged temple reliefs in which he appears as the conquering king smiting the age-old foes of Egypt.[3] Other scholars have seen him as a social revolutionary who chose his high officials and entourage, not from the old scribal families, but from new men of humble origins, free from hereditary traditions and orthodox habits of thought.[4] In the absence of a system of universal education in Egypt, however, it is doubtful whether the king could have found any trained personnel outside the small hereditary scribal caste who were capable of dealing with the essential paper-work by which the Egyptian bureaucratic machine functioned. Some at least of his high officials were clearly the sons of men who had held like offices during his father's reign, and it is to be suspected that many more affiliations lurk under non-committal names and titles.[5] It was a polite convention during the dynasty that such courtiers should occasionally refer to their king as having advanced them from humble origins. Thus Yuya, who was influential enough to arrange for his infant daughter to be married to Amenophis III when that king was a mere boy, refers to himself as one whom 'the pharaoh promoted and made great'.[6] Such protestations of lowli-

---

[1] G, 2, 356, 292; §II, 13, 207; §VIII, 14, 126–7.
[2] §I, 20, pl. 107B; §IV, 5, vol. I, 119; §VIII, 14, pl. XI.
[3] §II, 5, fig. 19; §VIII, 11, 47, nos. 50–51a; A, 9, 190–1.
[4] G, 6, 223–4; G, 8, 297–8; §II, 13, 207; §VI, 5, 539.
[5] §I, 4, 103–4; §VI, 1, 34.
[6] §II, 6, xv–xvi.

ness, like many official pronouncements in ancient Egypt, need not be taken at their face value.

The most striking of Akhenaten's innovations, and one that has gained for him the most attention in modern times, is a style of art which he instigated and which indeed seems revolutionary in its more bizarre forms, but which on closer examination is seen to be a mere distortion of the traditional manner of representing the royal family. The naturalism or realism that has been claimed for it[1] had already appeared in his father's reign.[2] Its true novelty is rather more subtle and lies in an iconography which was new and was created by artists having a non-traditional conception of spatial relationships.[3]

In only one aspect of his religious thinking is Akhenaten seen to be original—in his insistence on a true monotheism, as distinct from the henotheism of the sun-cult, which he embraced with such fervour as to arouse the strong suspicion that he was a religious fanatic. It is significant that the first great event of his reign should be a decree marshalling all the resources of the land for building temples to his god whom he identified by a didactic name which was his profession of faith—Re-Harakhte who rejoices on the horizon in his aspect of the light which is in the Aten (or Sun-disk).[4] This deity first appeared in the traditional iconic form of Re-Harakhte as a falcon-headed god, but was soon symbolized by the elaborated glyph for sunlight, a disk having a dozen or more rays emanating from it ending in hands, some of which hold the sign of life to the nostrils of the king and queen, but to no one else.[5] At the same time the enhanced divinity of the pharaoh, 'the beautiful child of the Aten',[6] is emphasized by the appointment of his own ritual priest or prophet, by the protestation or abasement of his followers when they are in his presence, and by the fact that prayers can be addressed to the god only through him as intermediary. Figures of the king and his family are substituted for Re-Harakhte at the entrance to the tombs of his officials, as indeed they replace representations of the owners themselves in all the principal scenes.[7] The old gods of burial were banished and Akhenaten's favourites prayed that in

---

[1] *E.g.* §II, 13, 214, 218–19; §III, 37, 33; §VIII, 21, 28.
[2] G, 7, fig. 142; §I, 20, 154, 180 (cf. Cairo Museum No. 33900).
[3] §VIII, 21, 11, 15. See below, sect. VIII.
[4] §III, 6, 209; §III, 24, 176.
[5] §II, 1, 24–5.
[6] G, 6, 228; §II, 13, 223–4; §IV, 17, 28; §IV, 20, 16; §VIII, 19, 91 ff.
[7] §II, 12, 84–5, 89; §III, 14, 35.

death they might rest eternally near him and behold him daily, for he was now the patron of the dead as well as of the living.[1]

In this respect, so far from being revolutionary, Akhenaten was reverting to beliefs current in the Old Kingdom when the dead in their mastaba-tombs were clustered around the pyramids of the sun-kings whom they had served in life. There is a distinct antiquarianism in this return to an earlier and more exalted status for the pharaoh which was already a feature of the preceding reign when the records of the past had been diligently searched in an endeavour to find the tomb of Osiris at Abydos and also to revive the proper ritual for the king's first jubilee.[2] It is perhaps significant in this context that a fragment of a predynastic or early archaic slate palette should survive, reworked on its reverse in the reign of Amenophis III with the name of his chief queen.[3]

This increase in the power and glory of the kingship was the inevitable political concomitant of Akhenaten's religious ideas. Such absolutism might have been effective if the king had busied himself with the *minutiae* of government, but it would seem that, absorbed as he must have been in his religious schemes, he left most of the vastly increased business of state to be carried on by his officials.[4] The introduction of monotheism into Egypt necessarily wrought changes in local affairs. The economy of Egypt was almost wholly dependent upon the utilization of land, and this was cultivated on behalf not only of the Crown and various corporate bodies, such as the royal harims, but also of the great temples of Thebes, Memphis and Heliopolis, and the local temples as well.[5] Even such a modest foundation as that of Khnum at Elephantine enjoyed income from estates which it owned as far afield as the other extremity of the country,[6] and although our information refers to conditions during the twelfth century B.C. there is no reason to believe that they differed essentially in the Eighteenth Dynasty. The dispersal of local priesthoods or the closing of the temples would have had the effect of transferring all their domains to the ownership of the pharaoh,[7] doubtless to the advantage of his deity, the Aten.

The administration of this great accession of property evidently ceased to be in the hands of the many local officials, particularly

---

[1] §II, 13, 223–4; §III, 13, Pt. 1, 46.
[2] §II, 8, 462, ll. 9–10 of inscription; §II, 11, 17.
[3] Brooklyn Mus. No. 66. 175; §II, 3, 1–4.
[4] §II, 7, 156–7.      [5] §II, 9, 9–25.
[6] §II, 10, 61.
[7] *Ibid.* 23; §II, 9, 165–7, 189.

for fiscal purposes, and became the responsibility of the king's high officers of state, who may well have called upon the army as the only source of manpower able to enforce the payment of taxation. Without proper supervision the inevitable malpractices would have obtained a firm hold. Over-centralized government was doubtless to blame for the corruption, arbitrary exactions and mismanagement which Horemheb later had to suppress with a heavy hand in restoring the traditional form of government.[1]

The rapid building of the new capital city at El-Amarna and temples to the new god in every major centre must have drained the land of its labour and economic resources, and the lavish offerings to the Aten that were such a feature of the worship in the Great Temple at El-Amarna,[2] and probably elsewhere also, could only have been made at the expense of other cults. The fiscal system of Egypt had developed over the centuries and, by adjusting the claims of small local shrines, the larger temples and the departments of the Palace, had produced a system that operated without intolerable exploitation. But it must now have been overturned by new arrangements that poured the nation's resources into the coffers of the king and his god. It was doubtless the chaos caused by the economic consequences of Akhenaten's religious reforms that brought about a complete reversal to the old order as soon as he was dead. The recollection of the misery of such times was strong enough to bring upon him the odium of later generations.

## III. THE REIGN OF AKHENATEN

The first important record of the new reign to have survived is a stela hewn on the east bank of the Nile at Gebel es-Silsila showing the (erased) figure of Amenophis IV wearing the Upper Egyptian crown and offering to Amon-Re.[3] The damaged text speaks of the opening of a quarry in the vicinity for extracting stone for the erection of a great benben sanctuary at Karnak for 'Re-Harakhte (who rejoices on the horizon) in his aspect of the sunlight which is in the Disk (Aten)'. For this purpose the king ordered that a muster should be made of all workmen from one end of the country to the other and that the high court officials should be put in charge of the work of cutting and transporting the stone. The quarry was evidently opened in a different place from the region

[1] §II, 7, 157; G, 6, 244–5; §V, 12, 311–18.
[2] §I, 18, 15, pls. VIa, VIb.
[3] G, 11, V, 220; §III, 30, 261 ff.; §VIII, 40, fig. 1.

whence came the large blocks of fine sandstone used for the great
temple of Luxor, which was left unfinished on the death of
Amenophis III.[1] The small size of the new blocks was probably
determined less by the shallow depth of the strata from which
they were prised than by the ease with which they could be
handled by a large, unskilled labour force.

The impressment of workers by *corvée* shows the importance
that the new king placed upon the swift fulfilment of his plans.
The remains of dismantled temples to the Aten recovered from
the interior of several pylons and other parts of the main temple
at Karnak betray distinct signs of the haste with which they were
built, particularly in the often careless and summary cutting of
the reliefs in the somewhat coarse granular stone.[2] The fact that
the stela at Gebel es-Silsila does not bear a date doubtless points
to its being carved in the very first months of the reign. Included
in the king's titulary is the designation 'First Prophet of Re-
Harakhte', but, since the pharaoh was *ex officio* the chief priest of
every god in the land, the special emphasis given to the sacerdotal
office here probably means that he had elected to celebrate the
daily ritual in the temples of the Aten and in no other.

A series of temples was built at Karnak, mostly in sandstone,
but, until their dismantled parts have been studied and published
in detail, it is idle to speculate on the size and nature of these
edifices. While they were doubtless built in a remarkably short
time, their decoration must have taken much longer to complete.
A temple to the Aten apparently existed at Karnak in the time of
Amenophis III, if not earlier, to judge from blocks, much greater
in size than those used in Akhenaten's constructions, which have
been found in the core of the Tenth Pylon.[3]

Early in the reign, perhaps by the second year,[4] the Aten
ceased to appear in the traditional therioanthropic form of Re-
Harakhte and was represented by the symbol of the rayed disk.
At the same time its didactic name was enclosed in cartouches
and it acquired a titulary like a pharaoh's and an epithet to
indicate that it had celebrated a jubilee.[5] Coincident with this
epiphany of a heavenly king is the appearance of a new style of
art which has been described as 'expressionistic' and 'realistic',[6]
but the most prominent feature of which is a grotesque manner of

---

[1] *C.A.H.* II³, pt. 1, pp. 395–6.
[2] §I, 20, 178–9; §III, 16, 113–35; §III, 41, 24 ff.
[3] §III, 38, 28–9; §VIII, 40, pl. 4; §VIII, 46, 114; §I, 20, 179, n. 18.
[4] §II, 1, 24.     [5] §III, 24, 170–2.
[6] §I, 20, 179; §III, 39, 57 ff.; §VIII, 21, 28.

representing the royal family, particularly the king himself, as though he suffered from a malfunctioning of the pituitary system, with an overgrown jaw, receding forehead, prominent collar-bones, pendulous breasts and paunch, inflated thighs and spindle shanks.[1] Such a marked departure from the heroic and idealistic traditions of royal portraiture could only have been taken at the instigation of the king himself, and this is made clear in the inscription of his chief sculptor Bak who claims that he was 'an apprentice whom the king himself instructed'.[2]

Temples to the Aten appear to have been raised in most of the principal towns of Egypt during these early years of the reign;[3] but however vast and numerous they may have been, the Aten could only be a parvenu on sites which had belonged to gods since they had first manifested themselves during the creation of the universe. The next ambition of Amenophis IV, therefore, was to find the 'place of origin' of the Aten and to establish there a great city dedicated to him, an ambition in which he claims to have been directed by 'Father Aten' himself.

The favoured spot selected by the king under this divine guidance proved to be a natural amphitheatre about eight miles in diameter lying on the east bank of the Nile half-way between Memphis and Thebes. To this site the modern name of Tell el-Amarna has been rather loosely applied,[4] and this in turn has been used to describe the period covered by the reign of Akhenaten. The king claimed that when found it was virgin ground which belonged to no god, goddess, prince, princess nor indeed to anyone. This may well have been the case, since no definite traces of earlier occupation have been found at El-Amarna[5] and its previous neglect was probably due to the extreme scantiness of the living that could be scratched from the strip of cultivation that bordered the river. Even today the villages on the site are comparatively recent and among the poorest in Egypt. The City of the Aten had to be sustained from the cultivation on the opposite bank, and doubtless from the rest of Egypt, as its population grew steadily during the reign.

In his fourth regnal year the king, accompanied by Queen Nefertiti and his retinue, paid an official visit to the chosen site and offered a great oblation to Re-Harakhte on the festal day of

---

[1] §III, 3, 305; §III, 2, 60–1; §III, 22, 29 ff; A, 1, fig. 12.
[2] §III, 25, 86.
[3] E.g. G, 11, III, 220, 222, 224; IV, 61, 63, 113, 121, 168, 259; V, 129, 144, 158, 196; VII, 73, 172–4.
[4] §III, 13, Pt. I, 1; §III, 35, 2.          [5] §I, 18, 4.

demarcating Akhetaten, 'the Horizon (seat) of the Aten', as the new township was called. After summoning his courtiers and high officers to him, he showed them the site and declared that it was the Aten alone who had revealed it to him. He then swore a solemn oath that he would make Akhetaten in that place and nowhere else, even though the queen and others might try to persuade him to build it elsewhere. He went on to name the various buildings that he proposed to construct there, among them a House of the Aten, a Mansion of the Aten, a House of Rejoicing for the Aten and palaces for himself and the queen.[1] It seems likely that in this respect he was erecting the counterparts of buildings that had already been raised in Thebes and elsewhere. He also stipulated that a tomb should be cut in the eastern hills for the burial of himself, the queen and the eldest daughter, Merytaten, and that, if any of them should die in another town of Egypt, he or she should be brought to Akhetaten for burial there. The burial of the Mnevis-bull, the sacred animal of the sun-cult, should be made in the eastern hills, thus indicating that Akhetaten was to replace Heliopolis as the chief centre of sun-worship. He then promised that the tombs of his high officials should also be hewn in the same hills and, since this proposal may well have caused consternation among his followers, who would have had to abandon their family burial-grounds, he was at pains to emphasize what an evil thing it would be if they were not interred near their king.[2]

All these declarations are contained in a proclamation, unfortunately imperfectly preserved, inscribed on three heavily damaged stelae hewn into the cliffs at the northern and southern extremities of the site.[3] The royal family paid another state visit to Akhetaten in Year 6 of the reign on the second anniversary of the first demarcation and set up landmarks in the form of additional great stelae on each side of the river, giving the precise dimensions of the township and defining its boundaries, which the king swore he would not go beyond.[4] This oath has been interpreted as indicating that the king shut himself up in his holy city and did not venture beyond its confines again,[5] but this is clearly a misunderstanding and the vow appears to be no more than an affirmation by the king that he would not extend the limits of the town beyond the boundaries he had stipulated, probably for

---

[1] §I, 18, 190.     [2] §VI, 5, 300, n. 7.
[3] §III, 13, Pt. v, pls. XXIX–XXXII.
[4] *Ibid*. pls. XXVI–XXVIII, XXXIII.
[5] *E.g.* G, 3, 64; G, 8, 295; §II, 13, 215.

taxation purposes.[1] The entire area so designated was dedicated to the Aten, together with all its produce including its human inhabitants.

During the two years that had elapsed between the early and later proclamations, much of the central part of Akhetaten had been built and from that moment its occupation by the official classes began, if we are to judge from the incidence of dated dockets inscribed on the many sherds from broken wine-jars found on the site.[2]

The official quarters in the Central City were laid out on a fairly well-planned system, the large estates of the wealthy fronting upon two or three main thoroughfares.[3] Behind them the houses of the lesser officials were built on vacant lots and the hovels of the poor, usually sharing a common courtyard, were squeezed in wherever there was space. No system of drainage is evident and rubbish was dumped in any convenient pit or midden. The city spread northwards as its population grew and was still in process of being built when it was abandoned in the next reign. The South City housed the more important officials and was distinguished by a Maru-Aten[4] or so-called pleasure-palace, gay with a lake and basins and decorated with painted pavements and coloured inlays. Here were the kiosks or 'sunshade temples' dedicated to the daily rejuvenation of the queen and some of the princesses.[5]

The Central City contained the main official buildings such as the Great Palace, which extended for over 750 metres along one side of the principal thoroughfare and ran westwards to a frontage on the river. On its eastern boundary was the Great Temple (the 'House of the Aten') set within a huge enclosure about 750 metres long by 250 metres wide and containing several structures, notably the sanctuary and the 'House of Rejoicing' leading to the 'Gem-Aten' ('Aten is found').[6] Further south rose a smaller temple (the 'Mansion of the Aten') which appears to have been similar in design to the sanctuary of the Great Temple.[7] Both buildings appear to have been elaborations of the primitive sun-temple,[8] being a series of courts, open to the sky, with the focal point as an altar before a stela which took the place of the benben-

---

[1] G, 2, 365; §II, 2, 233–4.  [2] §I, 18, 160.

[3] §I, 16, 35–45; §I, 20, 186–204; §III, 17, 32 ff.

[4] §III, 32, 109–24; §III, 5, 58 ff.

[5] §I, 18, 200–8.

[6] *Ibid.* 5–20.  [7] *Ibid.* 92–100.

[8] §III, 36, 233, 237–8, 240–2.

stone pyramidion, as in the sanctuary of Re at Abu Ghurāb.[1]
The stela, however, was an icon of the king and queen worshipping the Aten and not a sacred object of worship in itself.
Because the Aten was not in tangible form, the daily ritual was of
the simplest kind and centred around the presentation of lavish
offerings.  A later feature of the worship appears to have been the
erection of a dense mass of altars in a vast area lying to the south
of the 'House of Rejoicing'.[2]

Between these two temples lay such official quarters as the
'King's House', with its magazines and gardens connected by a
bridge over the main road to the Great Palace.[3]  Also in the
vicinity were the 'House for the Correspondence of Pharaoh',
where the celebrated Amarna Letters were found,[4] the Office of
Works and the Police Headquarters.  Half a mile downstream
was the North Suburb containing the less pretentious houses of
the merchants and minor officials, standing cheek by jowl with
the slums of the poor.[5] The chief quays of the city appear to have
been situated here and received the produce brought over daily
from the cultivation on the west bank and from elsewhere. Further
downstream at the extremity of the site was the North City, which
has not been fully excavated or published.  It contained other
palaces and official quarters.[6]

The temples and the offices of the Great Palace were built of
limestone, apparently quarried locally, and supplemented in
certain parts with blocks of alabaster, quartzite and granite. All
the domestic building, however, was in mud-brick, sometimes
coated with plaster and painted. The mansions of the wealthy had
stone thresholds, door-jambs, lintels, column-bases and window-
grilles; bathrooms were fitted with stone splash-backs and
lustration slabs.[7]  Columns and doors were of wood.  Such
domestic architecture appears to have differed little in style and
methods of construction from the palace-city of Amenophis III
at Western Thebes,[8] but a novel feature of the Amarna buildings
was the use of inlays of coloured stones, glass and faïence, often
applied in a kind of mosaic.[9]

Particulars of the topography and architecture of Akhetaten

---

[1] §III, 7, vol. I, 7–56.          [2] §I, 18, pl. VIA.          [3] *Ibid.* 86–105.

[4] *Ibid.* 113–30; §III, 35, 23–4; §VII, 5; §VII, 7.

[5] §III, 19, 1–4.

[6] §III, 34, vol. XVII, 240–3, vol. XVIII, 143–5.

[7] §III, 19, 98–100; §I, 20, 198–204; §III, 32, 37–50.

[8] *C.A.H.* II³, pt. I, p. 341 n. 2.

[9] §III, 35, 10–12, 28, pl. VI; G, 8, 288–307.

have been recovered by archaeological missions from Britain, France and Germany,[1] which have dug much of the site in the present century. The tombs of the officials hewn in the cliffs and foothills on the northern and southern flanks of the eastern boundary have, however, been available for study since the days of the early Egyptologists. Their sculptured walls are the main source of our knowledge of events at El-Amarna during the king's reign and of the character of the new teaching of Akhenaten.[2]

The later boundary stelae show that, by the time they were carved in Year 6, the king had changed his *nomen* to Akhenaten, while the name of Queen Nefertiti was inflated to include the epithet Neferneferuaten. The titles of the Aten were also altered to indicate that it had celebrated a further jubilee.[3] Probably all three changes took place at the same moment. The later boundary stelae bear a codicil dated to Year 8 in which it is stated that royalty was again in Akhetaten for the purpose of inspecting the boundaries on the south-eastern frontier of the city. A more explicit reference on two of them repeats the oath of the king in fixing the limits of the city and dedicating the entire region to 'Father Aten'.[4]

At some time between this date and the pharaoh's twelfth regnal year, the didactic name of the Aten was altered from its earlier form so as to remove the last vestiges of the old therioanthropic concept from the idea of the sun as a deity.[5] The falcon-symbol, which had been combined with the hieroglyph of the sun's disk to indicate Re in his aspect of Harakhte (i.e. at his rising and setting on the eastern and western horizons) was replaced by a shepherd's crook, thereby changing the name to an abstract phrase meaning 'Re, the ruler of the horizon'. This change probably coincided with other changes of a similar kind, such as the substitution of phonetic spellings for words like 'truth' and 'mother' which had formerly been determined by hieroglyphs in the shapes of the vulture (the symbol of the goddess Mut) and the figure of a squatting woman with a feather on her head (the symbol of the goddess Maet). The new form of the name of the Aten appears at the same time as changes in its epithets, suggesting that it had celebrated a third jubilee.[6] The exact date when this development occurred is not known with certainty, but

---

[1] §III, 32; §III, 19; §I, 18; §III, 8; §III, 10.
[2] §III, 9; §III, 13.
[3] §III, 24, 172; §II, 1, 24–31.
[4] §III, 13, Pt. v, pl. xxxiii.
[5] §III, 24, 174–6; §III, 6, 208–9.
[6] §II, 1, 30–1.

there appears to be no reason to dispute the conjecture that it was in Year 9.[1]

The later form of the name of the Aten appears in the reliefs of private tombs in the northern group at El-Amarna, which were among the last in the series to be hewn. Two scenes in these tombs give differing versions of the presentation of gifts to the pharaoh and are dated by the text to his twelfth regnal year.[2] The representations show the king and queen being carried in their state palanquins to their thrones set up under a great baldachin at Akhetaten. With their six daughters beside them they receive gifts presented by delegates who, according to the accompanying text, came from 'Syria and Kush (the North and the South), the East and the West, and from the Islands in the Mediterranean, all countries being united for the occasion so that they might receive the king's blessing'. Representations of such ceremonies with similar texts are common in tombs of the Eighteenth Dynasty, and it has been argued that they record an event which took place on the occasion either of the king's accession to the throne or of his jubilee, and not the reception of annual tribute or plunder from successful wars, as has generally been supposed.[3] If this be so, the ceremony of Year 12 at Akhetaten must have marked either Akhenaten's accession to sole rulership or his jubilee. The alternative explanation, that Akhenaten arranged a great parade of tribute from his vassals in order to impress his followers at Akhetaten with the power and influence that he exerted abroad,[4] is difficult to reconcile with the apparent collapse of the Egyptian 'empire' in Asia during his reign.[5]

In about the same year the Queen-Mother Tiy either paid a state visit to Akhetaten with her young daughter Baketaten or took up residence there. Evidence of the visit is provided by pottery jar-dockets found at El-Amarna which mention her house and that of Baketaten.[6] Moreover her steward, Huya, was granted a tomb in the northern group, one of the last to be hewn at El-Amarna.[7] Representations in its chapel show Tiy being given a sunshade temple at Akhetaten by her son, who also furnished her with new burial equipment, perhaps intending that, like her courtiers, she should be buried near him.[8] A fragment of red granite inscribed with her name and with the praenomen

[1] §III, 40, 116; §I, 18, 153.
[2] §III, 13, Pt. III, pl. XIII; Pt. II, pl. XXIX.
[3] §VII, 3, 105–16.
[4] §I, 16, 20–1; §III, 13, Pt. II, 43.
[5] §I, 16, 22–7; G, 2, 389. See, however, below, p. 82 ff.
[6] §I, 18, 164, nos. 4, 14, 200(d), (ii), (iii).
[7] §III, 13, Pt. III, pl. VIII.
[8] §IV, 11, pls. XXVII–XXIX, XXXI, XXXII.

of Amenophis III has been found in the Royal Tomb at El-Amarna, but probably belongs to the shattered sarcophagus of Meketaten.[1]

This tomb, in a wādi among the eastern hills at El-Amarna, was prepared as a family sepulchre in accordance with promises on the early boundary stelae. Some reliefs in the subsidiary rooms show the king and queen mourning over the bier of their second daughter, Meketaten, who died some time after the ceremony of Year 12. The presence of a nursemaid holding a baby in these scenes of poignant grief has provoked the suggestion that the princess died in childbirth,[2] which, if true, appears to indicate that the reliefs could hardly have been carved before Year 14 at the earliest. It was soon after this event that Queen Nefertiti too disappeared from the scene, her place being taken by the eldest of her six daughters, Merytaten. This change in her fortunes has been attributed to her fall from the king's favour. The evidence is largely contained in reliefs from the *maru*-temple in the southern part of the city, where a 'sunshade' dedicated to her originally has had its inscriptions and reliefs re-cut to refer to Merytaten.[3] It seems much more probable, however, that this usurpation followed on the death of Nefertiti soon after Year 14, when her sunshade was adapted to serve the needs of her eldest daughter. If she had been disgraced, much more evidence would have been forthcoming in the wholesale excision or alteration of her name and figure in the many representations of her that have survived.[4] The archaeologists who re-excavated the royal tomb in 1931 found evidence that led them to believe that the main chamber had been prepared for her burial.[5]

The place of the queen was taken for a time by her daughters, first by Merytaten and then by the latter's eldest surviving sister Ankhesenpaaten.[6] These two princesses must have played influential rôles at the court of Akhenaten in the last four years of his reign, the elder being mentioned under a hypocoristicon by foreign correspondents in some of the Amarna Letters.[7]

A notorious incident of the reign, and one that has left its mark on not a few of the standing monuments of Egypt, is the

[1] *Cf.* §IV, 16, 102, n. 2; A. 6.

[2] §III, 9, 21, pls. VII–IX; §VIII, 14, 153; §VI, 7, 208; §III, 31, 229; For other views, see §III, 40, 116; §IV, 28, 174, n. 44.

[3] §III, 32, 154–6; §I, 5, 56–7.      [4] §II, 2, 242.

[5] G, 15, 88–9.

[6] §VII, 1, 191–3; §III, 11, 104–8; §VII, 4, 12.

[7] E.A. 10, 44; E.A. 11, rev. 26; E.A. 155, *passim*.

iconoclastic fury which the king unleashed against other cults, particularly that of the influential Amun of Thebes. His agents were active throughout the land in destroying effigies of the gods and excising their names from objects great and small. Even the cartouche of his father, which bore the hated name of Amun in its composition, did not escape the hammers of these zealots. Some at least of the extensive damage which they wrought was not repaired until the reign of Ramesses II. The precise point in the reign of Akhenaten when this campaign of persecution was instigated is difficult to place. The king's name is still given in its Amenophis form in a letter from Ghurāb dated to Year 5,[1] but on the boundary stelae of Year 6 it has changed to Akhenaten. It has been supposed, therefore, that the excisions were made about the time of the *hijrah* to Akhetaten, and later references to Amun in the reign must represent a compromise in the king's views and a partial recognition of the old proscribed cults.[2] But there is evidence that the iconoclasm may belong to the very last years of his reign.

Among the jewellery found in the vicinity of the royal tomb in 1883 and presumed to have belonged to one of the royal women who was buried there after Year 14 is a finger-ring, bearing on its bezel an inscription 'Mut, Lady of Heaven', which shows no signs of any attempt at alteration or obliteration.[3] Since such small items as scarabs often had the name of Amun excised during this period,[4] it is surprising to find that a finger-ring worn by royalty late in the reign could preserve the name of the equally ostracized Mut.

Another piece of evidence is afforded by the shrine made by Akhenaten for Queen Tiy, which bore the names of the Aten in their late form showing that it was made after Year 9 and most probably after Year 12. The words for 'truth' and 'mother' appear in its inscriptions in those phonetic forms which came into use as Akhenaten's ideas of godhead developed along more abstract and monotheistic lines. Yet it seems that when it was first carved the *nomen* of her husband had appeared on it with the Amun element intact.[5] It had subsequently been excised by the iconoclasts and the praenomen substituted in red paint. This evidence, if reliable, would support the theory that the campaign of excision and suppression took place in the last years of Akhenaten's life.

[1] §iii, 21, 343–5.       [2] *E.g.* §i, 16, 28.
[3] §ii, 2, 3, 156, pl. xii; §iv, 3, 45.       [4] §i, 18, pl. lxxvii, 6.
[5] §iv, 11, 14; §iv, 31.

The latest known date of the reign is Year 17 contained in dockets on jars found at El-Amarna, and this would appear to indicate that he died before the grape-harvest in his 18th regnal year.[1]

## IV. THE IMMEDIATE SUCCESSORS OF AKHENATEN

Who the immediate successor of Akhenaten was presents a problem. In the tomb of Meryre, the Chief Steward of Nefertiti at El-Amarna, there appears a scene sketched in ink on a wall of the main hall showing the owner being rewarded for his services by a king and his queen whose names in cartouches are given as Ankhkheprure Smenkhkare and Merytaten.[2] Since the contiguous wall has an elaborate relief showing the tribute of Year 12 being received by Akhenaten and Nefertiti, the presumption is that soon after that date Smenkhkare was made king and married to the eldest daughter of Akhenaten, by which alliance he strengthened any claim he may have had to the throne. Meryre evidently continued in office as steward under the new queen, though he was unable to complete the decoration of his El-Amarna tomb, probably because the Court moved elsewhere.

A dated graffito scribbled in a tomb at Thebes[3] shows that by his third regnal year Ankhkheprure had adopted the nomen of Neferneferuaten in place of Smenkhkare, or as an alternative to it.[4] This change presumably did not take place until the death of Nefertiti who had previously added this same name to her own by Year 6 of her husband's reign.[5] The graffito also mentions the funerary temple of Neferneferuaten as being in the estate of Amun, indicating that by that date at least the site of the royal tomb had reverted to the necropolis at Thebes. Merytaten certainly played an important rôle at El-Amarna after the death (?) of her mother and is believed to have borne a daughter, Merytaten-tasherit, while still a princess.[6] Since Akhenaten appears to have advanced the next of his surviving daughters, Ankhesenpaaten, to her sister's position of favour before his death,[7] the evidence suggests that Smenkhkare was made co-regent and married to Merytaten before the end of the reign of Akhenaten.[8] Monuments have

---

[1] §III, 18, 108–9.　　　[2] §III, 13, Pt. II, pl. XLI, cf. pls. XXXIII. and XXXVII.
[3] §IV, 18, 10–11.　　　[4] For a contrary opinion see §VI, 8.
[5] See above, p. 59.　　　[6] A, 8, 288.
[7] §III, 11, 104–8; §VII, 4, 12 n. 1; cf. §I, 20, 278 n. 4; A, 8, 289, 4a.
[8] §IV, 23, 3–9.

survived which reinforce this view. An unfinished stela from El-Amarna shows two kings seated on thrones side by side in affectionate intimacy, and another represents a young king pouring wine into an elder king's cup, much as Nefertiti was earlier shown performing that office for her husband.[1] Although the cartouches on both unfinished stelae are not inscribed, it seems clear on stylistic grounds that Akhenaten and a younger co-regent are seen together, as also appears to be the case on a sculptor's model relief excavated at El-Amarna showing differing official portraits of the two kings side by side.[2] A fragmentary stela in London is inscribed with the names of Akhenaten, followed by those of Neferneferuaten, above a scene which may have shown both kings together.[3] A box-lid found in the filling of the tomb of Tutankhamun bears the titularies and names of Akhenaten, Neferneferuaten and Merytaten, suggesting that they were all ruling together.[4] Moreover, Neferneferuaten incorporated into his cartouches epithets to show that he was 'beloved' of Akhenaten, and his assumption of the other name of Nefertiti suggests that he had in some way filled the position formerly occupied by Akhenaten's chief queen.

The evidence is therefore strongly circumstantial that Smenkhkare was specially favoured by Akhenaten and appointed his co-regent. As such he would have dated the years of his rule from the time of his accession.[5] The question remains whether he survived his senior partner or died before him. The recent publication of an inscription from Hermopolis has given grounds for believing that Merytaten predeceased him, whereupon he married the next heiress, her sister Ankhesenpaaten.[6] This has been accepted as warrant for thinking that Akhenaten, who in his time had also taken Ankhesenpaaten as his consort in place of Merytaten, must have died before him.[7] The argument, however, is far from being conclusive. If Smenkhkare enjoyed any independent rule it could have lasted no more than a few months since a docket on a honey-jar from El-Amarna with Year 1 written below a partly expunged Year 17 is against the view that Smenkhkare ruled alone, and most probably belongs to the successor of Akhen-

---

[1] §IV, 23, 7; §VIII, 40, pls. 30, 31; cf. §III, 13, Pt. II, pl. XXXII.
[2] §I, 18, 19, pl. LIX, 1; §III, 34, vol. XIX, 116; §IV, 14, 103; §II, 2, pl. 68.
[3] §I, 18, 231–2; A, 11, 104.          [4] §IV, 23, 5 (Carter Cat. No. 1 K).
[5] §IV, 19, 23.
[6] A, 9, p. 169, 5d (826–VIIA). It should be noted, however, that she is not given a queen's titles; nor is her name enclosed in a cartouche like Merytaten's, which could suggest that she filled a subsidiary role while her elder sister was still chief queen.          [7] A, 3, 16.

aten, who in that case must be the boy-king Tutankhaten.[1]
This view is reinforced by another docket from a wine-jar, excavated from the Central City at El-Amarna, reading 'Year 1,
wine of the house of Smenkhkare, deceased...',[2] which can only
mean that, in the first regnal year of an undisclosed king,
Smenkhkare was dead, although wine from his estate was still being bottled. The king in question must be the same Tutankhaten.

Very few of the monuments of Smenkhkare have survived. No
representation in relief or statuary bears his indisputable name,
and a recent attempt to identify his portraits among the Amarna
sculptures has further complicated the problem by confusing his
features with those of Nefertiti, Tiy, Amenophis III and Akhenaten.[3] The most reliable portrait of this king must be sought in
the canopic coffinettes of Tutankhamun, which were originally
made for Smenkhkare since they were inscribed with his name,
still visible under the cartouches of the later king on the interior
surfaces of their gold shells.[4] In adapting them for his successor,
it is to be presumed that a minimum of alteration was made, and the
portait mask on each coffinette was left untouched. Some items at
least of his burial furniture were not used for his interment and
appear to have been adapted for his successor, Tutankhamun.[5]

This latter king was little more than nine years old at his
accession.[6] Nevertheless he was married, as custom required, to
the heiress Ankhesenpaaten, the third daughter of Nefertiti and
presumably the eldest surviving princess. For a time at least the
pair appear to have resided in a palace in the northern quarter
at El-Amarna,[7] but a decision was soon taken to abandon
Akhetaten as a Residence and to make the palace quarters at
Memphis, which had still been used in the previous reign, their
main seat of government.[8] They evidently also refurbished the old

[1] §1, 18, pl. xcv, no. 279.
[2] *Ibid.* 164, no. 8, pl. lxxxvi, 35; §iv, 27, 55, D, iii, 4.
[3] *Ibid. passim*; A, 1, *passim.*
[4] Roeder's denial (§iv, 27, 71) is unjustified. §1, 7, 1 37, pl. xxiii; §iv, 17, 39; §viii,
20, pl. 46; §iv, 5, vol. iii, pl. liv; §viii, 14, pl. xxxiv; A, 2, no. 9. See Plate 134 (*a*).
[5] §iv, 5, vol. ii, 84–5; §1, 7, 136, 138; §iv, 29, 642 ff.; see also p. 70, n. 5.
[6] This deduction is based on the estimated length of his reign and his age at
death, as revealed by his mummy. See §iv, 5, vol. ii, 158–60.
[7] §iii, 34, vol. xvii, 243; §1, 16, 29.
[8] G, 8, 173–6; §iv, 2, 12 n. 25; §ii, 2, pls. 8, 9; §iv, 23, 8; §vi, 5, 538–9. It
should be noted that this decision appears to have been taken very early in the reign.
Pendlebury found houses in the northern suburbs in process of building at the time
of their abandonment with little or no evidence of stonework inscribed after
Akhenaten. The ring-bezels of post-Akhenaten date were inscribed for Tutankh*amun*
(§iii, 19, 3, 71). *Cf.* G, 6, 236.

palace of Amenophis III at Medinet Habu for use whenever their presence was required at Thebes.[1] The artificial town of Akhetaten with its inflated population of officials, craftsmen, priests and workers and its essential garrison could not be sustained from the local resources alone, and when the Court was moved elsewhere it was inevitable that Akhetaten would no longer be able to support itself, but would dwindle to the status of a mere village. In fact, the evidence uncovered by the spade suggests that the entire area had been deserted by Ramesside times in favour of Hermopolis across the river.

The reign of Nebkheprure Tutankhaten (Tutankhamun) was comparatively short. His ninth regnal year is inscribed on two wine-jars from his tomb, and in addition four other dockets bear a Year 9 which is almost certainly his.[2] Another wine-jar, dated to Year 10, also probably refers to his reign and suggests that he ruled for a full nine years.[3] Despite the finding of his burial, however, with its great wealth of golden treasure virtually intact,[4] the monuments of his reign which yield historical data are regrettably few. The most important of them is the so-called Restoration Stela, found near the Third Pylon of the temple of Amun at Karnak, which had been usurped by Horemheb.[5] It is exceptional in Egyptian annals for its confession of past sins and the frank statement of the situation that faced the young king at his accession, with the temples from one end of the country to the other fallen into neglect and the land in a state of confusion through the indifference of the offended gods. Foreign ventures met with no success and the prayers of suppliants went unanswered. The stela goes on to relate the measures which the king was taking to restore confidence in the nation and to propitiate the gods. These included the fashioning of new statues and sanctuaries of the chief deities in gold and precious stones, the repairing of their neglected shrines, the re-establishment of their daily services and offerings, and the restoration of their sequestered treasure and revenues. New priesthoods were created to re-establish the lapsed rituals, and to these were nominated the sons and daughters of notables who commanded the respect of the local populace. Most of the temple serfs and musicians were appointed from the palace staff and their upkeep was made a charge on the king's revenues. In this we may perceive a complete reversal of the policy which had been pursued by Akhenaten, whereby the local

[1] §I, 10, 177, 242.   [2] §IV, 6, 3, nos. 18–23.   [3] *Ibid.* no. 24; §IV, 7, 39, §3.
[4] §IV, 5; §VIII, 20; §VIII, 14; §IV, 6; §IV, 29; A, 2. See Plate 134 (c).
[5] G, 9, no. 34183; G, 13, 2025 ff.; §IV, 2, 8–15; §V, 12, 128–35, 235–7.

temple revenues had doubtless been diverted into the treasury of the Aten and the pharaoh.

Since the king was still a minor when these decrees were promulgated, it is clear that they were made at the suggestion of his advisers, the most prominent of whom was the vizier and regent Ay, who had served Akhenaten as a Master of the Horse and who must now have counselled a return to traditional policies that had worked well in the past.[1] The reins of government were picked up from the point where they had been dropped by Amenophis III, and a start was made on completing that king's monuments as at Luxor and Sulb.[2] The worship of Amun was restored. The royal pair changed their names so as to honour the god of Thebes, where a tomb was begun or extended for the young king, probably in the western branch of the Valley of the Kings, near the sepulchre of Amenophis III.[3] The mortuary temple on the west bank at Thebes is known from at least one reference[4] and this was probably in the Medīnet Habu area, though its remains have not been identified. The colossal statues destined for this temple were unfinished at the time of the king's death and were usurped by his successors.[5]

The removal of the Court from Akhetaten to Memphis, accompanied by its large retinue of officials and chamberlains, would certainly have been followed by the exodus of most of the remaining professional classes with their valuables and house-fittings.[6] Some activity was still carried on in the town, largely at the faïence- and glass-works attached to the Great Palace.[7] The withdrawal of the town garrison would have invited the looting of the local cemeteries. Those who had died there must in the main have been removed to family burial-grounds in other parts of the country, since no cemeteries, apart from a few poor burials, have been found at El-Amarna.[8] No doubt the royal burials were also transferred elsewhere. In 1907 a small tomb, No. 55, was uncovered in the Valley of the Kings at Thebes, which contained a decayed mummy in an elaborate coffin of the royal type and the remains of funerary furniture, including the dismantled parts of the large gilded wooden shrine made for Queen Tiy by Akhenaten.[9] The burial had been desecrated and the names on the coffin excised before the tomb was re-sealed in antiquity. The mummy has recently been re-examined with the aid of modern techniques by medical experts whose findings leave little room for

---

[1] §IV, 24, 50–2; §V, 19, 58.    [2] §IV, 15, 3–9; §I, 21, 278.
[3] G, 15, 89–90, 92.    [4] G, 7, fig. 191.    [5] §V, 15, 101–5.
[6] §III, 19, 3.    [7] §III, 35, 44.    [8] §III, 32, 95; §III, 8.    [9] §IV, 11.

doubt that it is of Smenkhkare, who died in his twentieth year.[1]
A reappraisal of the objects left in Tomb No. 55 and the circumstances in which they were found has also recently sought to show
that, before desecration, this small tomb-chamber housed the
burials of Queen Tiy, Akhenaten and Smenkhkare, and that it
was under Tutankhamun that their remains were deposited here.[2]
It would seem that from the first there was no intention of burying
Akhenaten in the tomb he had designed for himself at El-Amarna.
Fragments of his alabaster canopic chest, found in the royal tomb,
show no signs of the staining by the sacramental oils that would
have been poured into it if it had ever been used.[3]  It is virtually
certain that other burials of the royal family, including those of
Nefertiti and Meketaten were also transferred to Thebes during
the reign of Tutankhamun, though their heavy stone sarcophagi
were left behind, to be smashed into thousands of fragments and
scattered far and wide in Ramesside times. During the transfer of
the burials from the royal tomb some items of personal jewellery
belonging to one of the royal women were apparently stolen and
hidden nearby, to be found again in 1883 by natives during their
illicit operations in the royal wādi.[4]

Certain objects of no intrinsic value were, however, left behind
at El-Amarna, notably the master-portraits, model reliefs, plaster-
casts and half-completed studies found during this century in the
ruins of several sculptors' studios in the town.[5]  These works
represented defunct persons, particularly members of the royal
family, whose portraits were no longer being carved.  In the
Bureau of the Correspondence of Pharaoh, too, was a mass of
cuneiform tablets, comprising despatches from the great kings
and vassal princes of Asia, which had been received during the
reign and filed away in the archives. These clay tablets, the
famous Amarna Letters,[6] were also not removed, though there is
some evidence that they had been buried in a hole dug beneath
the office floor.[7]  It is to be presumed that the Egyptian clerks did
not trouble to take away these cumbersome and weighty records,
since they would probably have had copies of them written in
Egyptian on easily portable papyrus, according to age-old
Egyptian office procedure.[8]

[1] §III, 27, 95–119.
[2] §II, 2, 140–62; §III, 2, 41–65; §IV, 17, 25–40; §IV, 20, 10–25; §IV, 31, 193–9.
[3] §III, 26, 537.                    [4] §II, 2, 243, pls. XII, 109; §IV, 3, 45.
[5] §I, 18, 34, 80, 81; §IV, 14, 96–101, 106; §III, 8, no. 52; §VIII, 39; §VIII, 13,
pls. 12–19; A, 1, ch. III. See Plate 134 (b).
[6] See below, ch. XX, sect. I.
[7] §I, 18, 114; §III, 35, 23–4; cf. §I, 5, 34, 35.          [8] §II, 2, 203–4.

Tutankhamun did not live long enough to see his policy of a return to the orthodox traditions of his dynasty take full effect. He died in his nineteenth year, perhaps as the result of a wound in the region of his left ear which penetrated the skull and resulted in a cerebral haemorrhage.[1] How this lesion was caused must remain a mystery, but the nature and seat of the injury make it more likely to be the result of a battle wound or an accident than the work of an assassin.

He left no children to succeed him. Two mummified human foetuses found in his tomb in coffins inscribed with his name are generally taken to be his children, born prematurely and subsequently buried with him.[2] It was at his death that his widow, Queen Ankhesenamun, wrote to the Hittite King Shuppiluliumash asking him to send to Egypt one of his sons, whom she would marry and so make him pharaoh. The suspicious Shuppiluliumash hesitated too long, and when at length he despatched Zannanzash the young prince was killed while making his way to Egypt.[3]

The reason for Ankhesenamun's extraordinary request can only be surmised, but it would seem that Tutankhamun was the last male in the line of descent, and with him the family of Amosis, the virtual founder of the Eighteenth Dynasty, came to an end. Whomsoever his widow married would *ipso facto* be the next pharaoh, and in this quandary it is probable that Ankhesenamun and her advisers sought the hand of powerful foreign royalty rather than that of a native commoner, in conformity with the ideas of the age regarding the divinity of kings. There had been a tradition of intermarriage between the ruling houses of Egypt and the Mitanni for the previous three generations at least; since at this time the Hittites were in the process of absorbing the Mitanni (see p. 83 below), perhaps it was thought politic to transfer the marriage alliance to them. The death or murder of Zannanzash, however, put an end to this scheme. The new pharaoh was the Vizier Ay, who is shown in a painting on the wall of the burial chamber of Tutankhamun's tomb officiating as the dutiful successor at the last rites.[4]

Recent attempts to interpret the inscriptions on damaged architraves retrieved from the Third Pylon at Karnak as demonstrating that Ay served for a time as the co-regent of Tutankhamun have been shown to be mistaken; such a joint rule of a young king

[1] *The Times,* Science Report, 25 October 1969: *Nature,* 224 (1969), 325–6.
[2] §IV, 5, vol. III, 88, 167–9.      [3] See above, pp. 17 f.
[4] §IV, 29, 647–8, 659–60, fig. 90, pl. CXVI; §I, 20, 141A.

with an aged co-regent is by its very nature exceedingly improbable.[1] There is some evidence that Ay secured the throne by marrying the royal widow in the same way as was planned for Zannanzash, since a blue glass ring, formerly in the possession of a Cairo dealer and seen by Professor Newberry in 1931, had the cartouches of Ay and Ankhesenamun engraved on its bezel, suggesting the alliance of these two persons.[2] Ankhesenamun, however, disappears from the scene after the death of her husband and the consort who is represented in the Theban tomb of King Ay is that same Tey who had appeared at El-Amarna as his wife and Nefertiti's nurse.[3]

Ay buried Tutankhamun in the main eastern branch of the Valley of the Kings in a small tomb which does not appear to have been the one he was preparing for himself.[4] Nevertheless, the funerary furniture that was crammed into its confined space was exceptionally rich and incorporated some of the equipment prepared for Smenkhkare's burial and evidently part of Akhenaten's also.[5]

The ill-documented reign of the aged Ay, who had served Akhenaten at least twenty years earlier as Master of the Horse, must have been short. Regnal Year 4 is his highest recorded date,[6] and he probably ruled for a little longer if the entry in Josephus for *Harmais* refers to him.[7] He presumably followed the same policy of rehabilitation that he had doubtless persuaded his predecessor to adopt. He built his mortuary temple at Medīnet Habu at the southern end of the row of such structures at western Thebes and incorporated in it a palace used during religious festivities, a feature of subsequent Ramesside mortuary temples, if indeed it had not already been anticipated by Amenophis III.[8] The entire complex was, however, taken over and extended by his successor Horemheb.

Ay prepared a tomb, No. 23, for himself in the western branch of the Valley of the Kings, near that of Amenophis III,[9] but it is

---

[1] §IV, 28, 179; v, 12, 177–8. In a recently published inscription from Hermopolis, Tutankhaten is already described as a king's son before he came to the throne. Cf. I, 15, 317 n. I. See A, 8, pl. 106 (831–VIII–c).      [2] §IV, 24, 50.

[3] §III, 13, Pt. VI, pls. XXXI, XXXVIII, XXXIX. See Plate 135 (*a*).

[4] G, 15, 89; §IV, 28, 179.

[5] See above, p. 65, nn. 4 and 5. According to Gardiner's note *apud* Carter's Catalogue, pectoral No. 261 P(1) [*q.v.* §IV, 30, No. 43] was inscribed for Akhenaten originally.

[6] On a stela in Berlin. G, 11, v, 22.

[7] G, 16, 103.

[8] §v, 15, 75–82; §IV, 10, pls. I, IX, X, XIV.      [9] G, 11, 1², Pt. II, 550–1.

probable that it had originally been started for an earlier pharaoh.[1]
In the sarcophagus chamber is a wall-painting which is unique for
a royal tomb and shows Ay, in company with his wife Tey,
spearing a hippopotamus and fowling in the marshlands.[2] The
names of the royal pair and their figures, however, have been
mutilated, and the red granite sarcophagus, similar in design to
those of Tutankhamun and Horemheb, has been smashed to
pieces.[3] A thorough clearance of the tomb might uncover
evidence to show whether Ay was ever buried there: so far his
mortal remains have not come to light.

## V. THE REIGN OF HOREMHEB

Ay apparently died without living male issue and was succeeded
by the Great Commander of the Army, Horemheb, who had
exercised supreme power as the King's Deputy under Tutankhamun during the latter's minority.[4] It would seem that Horemheb
continued to enjoy high office under Ay, and the 'Weepers
Relief' in Berlin, showing a funerary procession in which the
figure of a King's Scribe, Heir and Commander of the Army
takes precedence over all other high officials, may date to this
period.[5] The Coronation Inscription on the back of a seated dyad
of himself and his wife, Queen Mutnodjme, in the Turin
Museum[6] recounts the steps in his early career up to his appointment as king, and gives the impression of a smooth transfer of
power from his predecessors to himself. But for ambiguous
references to Horus (the ruling king) and Horus of Hnes (his
divine sponsor), a critical passage in the text could be interpreted
to imply that Ay accompanied Horemheb to Karnak in order to
induct him as co-regent, their participation in the Festival of
Southern Ope being made the occasion of obtaining the recognition of the gods.[7] At least the unusual phrase in which he is
referred to as 'the eldest son of Horus' suggests that he had been
appointed the heir of Ay.[8] The fact that Horemheb considered
himself in the proper line of descent and not as a usurper or the
founder of a new dynasty is to be inferred from the formation of

---

[1] G, 15, 92.
[2] §IV, 5, 246–7, pl. XXI; §I, 20, 141 B.
[3] §III, 26, 542, pl. LVI (6); §III, 38, 3–4, pl. I[6, 7]; §VIII, 40, pl. 57.
[4] §V, 23, 1–5; V, 12, 45–9; A, 6, 11–21.
[5] §V, 21, 56–8; §V, 12, 63–4; §V, 19, 59–61; §II, 2, pl. 78; §III, 29, pls. 54–5.
See Plate 135 (b).     [6] §V, 10, 13–51.
  [7] *Ibid.* pl. II, ll. 4, 12–14.     [8] *Ibid.* l. 12; §V, 12, 211 n. 198.

his praenomen with the 'kheperu-re' element, in which he followed the fashion set by nearly all the kings of the Eighteenth Dynasty and certainly by his Amarna predecessors.

The dated documents of the reign are scanty, Years 1, 3, 7 and 8 only having been preserved for certain, so that recently the view has been challenged that Horemheb enjoyed a long rule of between 25 and 30 years,[1] which follows if the date recorded in the inscription of Mes is accepted.[2] A hieratic graffito found at Medīnet Habu and mentioning a Year 27 must be regarded as too ambiguous to be admitted alone to consideration.[3] It has been argued that the absence of any date after the first eight years, which are consistently documented, is significant. The paucity of the monuments of Horemheb which have survived is also taken as an indication of the shortness of his reign. This is not the place to discuss those arguments, which are made largely *ex silentio*; suffice it to say that the chronology followed in this work demands a reign for Horemheb of some 27 years determined by the Mes date.

Horemheb has often been identified with the King's Scribe, Steward, Master of Works and Commander of the Troops of the King (Akhenaten), Paatenemheb, who had started to cut a tomb among the southern group at El-Amarna, but the equation cannot be proved and remains doubtful.[4] Horemheb makes his first unequivocal appearance at the beginning of the reign of Tutankhamun, and, despite the high military rank which he held, he must be classed as a staff officer rather than a field commander.[5] It may have been his organizing ability which first marked him for preferment. In the tomb which he constructed for himself at Memphis as a private person, he makes a passing reference to having accompanied his lord (doubtless the young Tutankhamun) on the battlefield in Asia,[6] which may refer to some parade of force early in the reign in the disaffected areas of Palestine.

Another early inscription on the Zinzinia fragment[7] almost certainly refers to a diplomatic mission that he undertook to secure the allegiance of the Nubian and Kushite native governors at the accession of the same boy-king, rather than to some military expedition in those regions.[8] We are also to infer from his

---

[1] §v, 13, 95–9; cf. §v, 6, 33.        [2] §v, 8, 3; §v, 12, 405–9.

[3] §v, 15, 106–8; §1, 18, 157–8; §v, 12, 354–5; §v, 13, 96.

[4] §v, 12, 35–6, 41; §v, 19, 60; G, 4, 350.

[5] §vi, 4, 43, 78–84; §vi, 5, 371–4, 486–7.

[6] §v, 16, 16. See below, pp. 84–5.

[7] §v, 12, 64–8; §v, 9, 3.

[8] §vii, 3, 108.

Memphite tomb-reliefs that he acted as the mouth-piece of the king in dealings with foreign legates and Egyptian provincial governors alike.[1] On the death of Tutankhamun he appears to have continued in office under Ay, being accepted as the heir apparent and probably being created co-regent in the last years of the reign. During this period he must have played a key rôle in the rehabilitation of the country, for in the Coronation Inscription he claims to have renewed the temples from one end of the land to the other, fashioning statues of the gods and re-establishing their endowments and services, in much the same way as Tutankhamun in his Restoration Stela speaks of his work of reparation a decade or so earlier. It is perhaps significant that Horemheb should in his lifetime have usurped this stela of the king he had once served.[2]

During his sojourn with the court at Memphis he built a tomb in the nearby necropolis decorated with fine reliefs now dispersed among several museums.[3] An uraeus has been added later to the brow of Horemheb in these reliefs, though no alterations to the texts and other figures appear to have been made.[4] A second tomb, however, was cut for him in due course in the royal necropolis at Thebes in which he appears to have been buried, though no part of his human remains has been identified among the débris found there.[5]

As has been mentioned above, his surviving monuments are relatively few having regard to the length of time he is presumed to have ruled; but this is true for all the immediate post-Amarna kings, and the presumption is that they were so fully occupied with the re-building and re-endowment of the temples up and down the country that they had little resources of labour and treasure to expend on new constructions. In this context it is significant to note that in his nine years of rule Tutankhamun was able only to finish the companion to the granite lion of Amenophis III in the temple of Sulb, and it was left to his successor, Ay, to transport it from the quarry to the site.[6] Nevertheless, apart from his restorations, the building enterprises of Horemheb were far from inconsiderable. He enlarged the mortuary temple of Ay for his own use, or their joint cult, until it assumed gigantic proportions,[7] though it has now almost totally disappeared. At

---

[1] §v, 9, 5, 7–8; §v, 10, pl. II, l. 7; §v, 12, 113–14; §vI, 5, 373.
[2] §v, 12, 130.
[3] §v, 12, 69–125; §v, 5, 2 ff.; §vIII, 11, 23–4; §v, 3, 31 ff.; §vIII, 13, 27–31.
[4] §v, 2, 49–50.          [5] §v, 6; G, 15, 92–6.
[6] §IV, 15, 9.          [7] §v, 15, 78.

Karnak he seems to have planned and begun the great Hypostyle
Hall of the Temple of Amun and the Second Pylon, using in their
foundations and cores blocks from the Aten temples of Akhenaten in the vicinity, though it was left to his successors in the
following dynasty to complete these works.[1] He also raised other
pylons, the Ninth and Tenth on the processional way to the south
of the temple, and joined them by walls forming a large court
enclosing on the east side the jubilee temple of Amenophis II.[2]
The towers of these great gateways were also filled with thousands
of small blocks from the dismantled temples of the Aten.[3] Both
pylons were usurped by later kings and are now greatly ruined.
Before them stood a total of six colossi in red quartzite of the
king, with Queen Mutnodjme on a much smaller scale. It is
probable, however, that some at least of these statues were already
lying on the site, but still unfinished, from the days when Amenophis III planned the erection of the Tenth Pylon.[4] The great
avenue of crio-sphinxes that connected this latter gateway to the
temple of Mut also appears to be the work of Horemheb, though
usurped by others.[5]

At Gebel es-Silsila he cut and decorated with fine reliefs a *speos*
in the cliffs on the western bank.[6] A similar rock temple, but on a
smaller scale, was hewn out of the cliffs at Gebel Adda in Nubia
and dedicated to Amun and Thoth.[7] At Memphis he erected
buildings in the precincts of Ptah, as a damaged stela bearing a
version of the Coronation Inscription proclaims, and these
included a temple furnished with the usual cedar flag-poles and
embellished with gold and Asiatic copper.[8] It is also certain that
similar constructions were raised in Heliopolis.[9]

The tomb that the king cut at Thebes is among the largest in
the Valley of the Kings and followed the fashion introduced into
the design of such royal hypogea by Akhenaten at El-Amarna,
being virtually a long corridor driven into the hillside and leading
to the burial vault.[10] It is decorated in those parts which it was
customary to embellish in the Eighteenth Dynasty, but it differs
from earlier examples in having its scenes cut in relief and not
painted on plaster. It also introduces for the first time in a royal

[1] §v, 20, 7 ff.; §v, 12, 329.   [2] G, 11, 11, 59–63; §v, 12, 331–7.
[3] §111, 16; §111, 12; §111, 41; A, 11.
[4] G, 11, 11, 62. It is difficult to see otherwise why the statues of Amenophis son
of Hapu should have been placed here; (but cf. §v, 12, 256–7).
[5] §v, 12, 282–3.   [6] G, 11, v, 208–13; §v, 12, 359–70.
[7] G, 11, vii, 119–21.   [8] §v, 10, 30, 31.
[9] §v, 12, 289–92, 386; §G, 11, iv, 63, 70.
[10] A, 5; §v, 6.

tomb extracts from *The Book of Gates* which are inscribed on the walls of the pillared burial hall.[1] The decoration is almost complete except for some reliefs in the latter chamber which are in various stages of being sketched, carved and painted. It would be rash, however, to draw inferences as to the length of the king's reign from this circumstance. The paintings, for instance, in the tomb of Amenophis III, who had a long reign, are also incomplete.[2] Doubtless all kings depended upon the piety of their successors for finishing off their tombs before they were buried in them. Horemheb was unfortunate in being followed by a king who had the briefest of reigns.[3]

It may well have been that Horemheb did not begin to cut his Theban tomb until his later years. There is some evidence that the workmen's village at Deir el-Medīna, on the west of Thebes,[4] was only being re-established in this reign.[5] The policing of the Valley of the Kings, at all events, appears to have been negligent during his earlier years, for tomb-robbers were active in the Valley at this period and had evidently broken into several tombs including those of Tuthmosis IV and Tutankhamun.[6] It was in his Regnal Year 8 that Horemheb had to renew the burial of the former and it was probably at the same time that the violated tomb of the latter was cleared up. It seems incredible that Horemheb's tomb could have been in process of construction about 150 metres from the spot where another royal tomb was being violated, and the inference is that it had not at that time been started.

This pillaging is but one indication of a general lawlessness that seems to have prevailed since the end of the reign of Akhenaten, and suggests that the disorder referred to by Tutankhamun in his Restoration Stela had by no means been curbed. The great granite stela which Horemheb erected against the north face of the western tower of the Ninth Pylon at Karnak bears other witness to this general unrest.[7] The woefully damaged text which is usually referred to as 'The Edict of Horemheb' appears to be a selection of the ordinances which the king issued 'to seek the welfare of Egypt' by suppressing illegal acts.

[1] G, 15, 94–5; G, 11, 1², Pt. 11, p. 568.
[2] §v, 18, 116.        [3] §v, 1, 102 n. 1; see below, pp. 77, 217 f.
[4] See below, pp. 620 ff.
[5] Verbal communication by the late Prof. Jaroslav Černý.
[6] §v, 4, xxxiii–iv, figs. 7, 8; §v, 12, 393, pl. lx; §iv, 5, vol. i, 54, 93; vol. iii, 85–6.
[7] §v, 12, 302–18; G, i, iii, §§45–67; §v, 17, 260–76; §v, 14, 109–36; §v, 22, 230–8.

It seems clear from this Edict that the central authority of the Crown had grown considerably, presumably at the expense of the religious foundations both local and national, and much of the administration had in consequence fallen into the hands of court officials, notably of the army, so removing any local checks and balances that the former system may have enjoyed. The result had been widespread corruption, the oppression of freemen by fraudulent tax-collectors, and arbitrary exactions and requisitions by an undisciplined soldiery in the name of the king. Both the tax-paying populace and the crown had been cheated by this extortion, and the enactments were designed to protect the interests of both. In his edict Horemheb quotes examples of abuses that had developed, and threatens future transgressors with savage punishments. At the same time he announces that he has appointed reliable men as supreme judges (viziers) in the two capital cities of Memphis and Thebes and has adjured them to hold themselves aloof from other men and not to accept bribes or presents from them. The district tribunals were also re-organized to consist of the headman of the region and functionaries and ritual priests of the local temples. If any member of these councils should be accused of practising injustice, he would have to answer a capital charge. On the other hand, those judges who performed their duties conscientiously were to have the honour of being rewarded periodically by the king in person.

Despite the numerous lacunae in the edict, several facts emerge from its study, such as the organization of the army into two main divisions, one serving in Upper and the other in Lower Egypt, a system which still prevailed when Herodotus visited the land some nine hundred years later and which probably dated from the beginning of the New Kingdom. Nevertheless, the plundering of the inhabitants by a rapacious army implies that a reform of its command was a necessary preliminary to Horemheb's measures to restore justice, and is already implicit in his statement in the Coronation Inscription that the priesthoods had been re-established from the 'pick of the army', presumably referring to its administrators, a rather different method of recruitment from that employed a decade earlier, when they were drawn from the families of local worthies.[1] Remarkable, also, is the return of supreme judicial power to the viziers in Memphis and Thebes, presumably in place of favourites of the king such as the High Stewards and Butlers, to whom royal authority had so often been delegated in the Eighteenth Dynasty from Hatshepsut onwards.

---

[1] §v, 10, pl. II, l. 25, p. 21 n. 3j; §IV, 2, 10, l. 17.

The success of Horemheb's reforms must have owed not a little to the tours of inspection which he claims to have made throughout the length and breadth of Egypt to ensure that his new measures were enacted with vigour, and that fresh abuses had no chance to develop. But whether he acted thus on behalf of the kings he served in his early career or only when he came to the throne is obscure, since the Coronation Inscription does not specifically mention these activities and the edict lacks its critical date.[1]

If Horemheb had any sons by his principal queen, Mutnodjme, they do not appear to have survived him and he was succeeded by a Ramesses whose claim to the throne is uncertain, but whose former identification with the Vizier and deputy, Pramesse, has apparently to be abandoned.[2] Ramesses, the first of that name, evidently hailed from the Delta and was regarded as founding a new dynasty, his praenomen setting a new pattern in royal nomenclature. His reign was too brief to decide whether it was he who instituted the policy which his son and grandson followed of execrating the Amarna pharaohs, destroying their monuments and suppressing their records.[3] He must have been of advanced years when he ascended the throne, for his son, Sethos, was then a man in the full vigour of life. A fragment of a model obelisk giving part of the titularies of Horemheb and Ramesses I suggests that the former king had associated the latter on the throne with him for some years before his death.[4]

## VI. THE ROYAL FAMILY AT THE END OF THE EIGHTEENTH DYNASTY

It is clear that around the kings of the Fourth Dynasty, for instance, there clustered many officials who were closely related to them,[5] but, because our documentation is far less complete for other periods, it is generally assumed that the custom of appointing viziers and other high officers of state from the circle of the royal family was abandoned in the later Old Kingdom. Thus the title 'King's Acquaintance' was not regarded then as signifying that its owner was a relation of the pharaoh.

In the Eighteenth Dynasty, however, sufficient evidence has survived to encourage the view that many of the king's entourage were related to him, either directly or by virtue of some less

---

[1] But cf. §v, 12, 307–8.  [2] §v, 11, 23–9.
[3] §v, 12, 167; §viii, 11, 2; §iii, 2, 59; §v, 13, 96 n. 9.
[4] §v, 1, 100–3.  [5] G, 8, 62.

exalted familial bond.[1] Apart from the junior sons and daughters who all had to be brought up to wear the purple, in case it should fall to their lot, as it so often did, by the premature demise of elder brothers and sisters,[2] there were also collateral descendants from earlier reigns, foster-brothers whose mothers had acted as wet-nurses of the kings[3] and high officials whose daughters had entered the royal harims[4] or who had been honoured by the gift of a wife brought up in such an institution.[5] In exceptional circumstances men who were not in the direct line of descent, such as Tuthmosis I,[6] or even commoners without evidence of royal blood in their veins, such as Ay,[7] might marry the heiress daughter of the pharaoh.

It is difficult to trace such relationships in detail because, for the most part, the officials are extremely reticent in mentioning their connexions with the royal house, but there is little doubt that such kinsmen must have formed veritable dynasties around the dynasties of the kings and queens whom they served, and the ramifications of one or two influential families can be traced to show the interdependence of the ruling caste of Egypt at this period.[8]

A notable case in point is the family of Queen Tiy, the chief wife of Amenophis III, who is usually regarded as a commoner whom the King married as the result of a 'love-match'.[9] As Amenophis III could not have been more than eight years old at his accession, it can be presumed that romantic passion played no part in this alliance and that the infant Tiy must have had influential supporters. Her father Yuya was an experienced officer of chariotry and the Master of the Horse. It is to be suspected that he was related to the Queen Mother, Mutemwiya, and was perhaps the uncle of the young king.[10] He was in any case sufficiently important and well known to have his name and that of his wife mentioned in the rescript of the infant king's accession.[11] He came from the provincial city of Akhmīm, where he and his wife held important and lucrative sacerdotal positions and in the vicinity of which Tiy acquired large estates.[12] One of

---

[1] §vi, 5, 254, 279–80; cf. §vi, 4, 31 n. 2, 66–71; G, 8, 268; §vi, 1, 30–1.
[2] For deceased eldest sons see §vi, 3, 15; C.A.H. ii³, pt. 1, pp. 316 and 320.
[3] C.A.H. ii³, pt. 1, p. 315; §vi, 4, 66–73; §1, 10, 238.
[4] G, 5, 1, no. 127; §vi, 1, 35–6.     [5] §vi, 9. no. 51005 passim.
[6] C.A.H. ii³, pt. 1, p. 315; §vi, 1, 30–1.
[7] Ibid. 35–7.
[8] E.g. §vi, 5, 435(4), 499(8); §vi, 1, 30.
[9] E.g. §vi, 5, 538.                    [10] §ii, 2, 40, 42, 88–9.
[11] §vi, 2, 5, pls. i–ix.               [12] §vi, 13, 23–33.

his sons, Anen, held the office of Second Prophet of Amun in
Thebes and Chief Seer in the temple of Re in Karnak.[1] It is also
likely that Yuya had another son, Ay, who held his father's office
of Master of Horse under Akhenaten and who as king built a
rock-temple to Min in the family seat of Akhmīm at a time when
little new constructional work was undertaken.[2]

Like his father before him, Akhenaten appears to have married
a cousin as his chief wife, for Nefertiti has been identified as the
daughter of Ay.[3] It was probably by virtue of this relationship,
if not some closer ties with the royal house, that Ay eventually
ascended the throne on the extinction of the direct line.

In addition to the many foreign marriages which Amenophis III
made for diplomatic reasons, he also wedded several of his
daughters,[4] a practice which appears to have been followed by
Akhenaten, and although these incestuous unions seem to have
been as much permitted to the pharaohs as to the ancient Hebrews,
for instance,[5] the custom has been dismissed as no more than a
symbolic rite enabling the princesses to act as deputies of the
queen in ceremonies in which she played an essential rôle, even
though they were mere infants.[6] Since Akhenaten's daughters,
however, are known to have had children while they were still
princesses, not having their names enclosed in cartouches, it is
difficult to accept these marriages as purely nominal.[7] The custom
in fact may have been more general than is supposed, our documentation on the subject being a little fuller for this period than
for nearly all other reigns, though it is noteworthy that Ramesses
II also married some of his own daughters.[8]

Some ambiguity exists about the exact relationship of Smenkhkare and Tutankhamun to the ruling house. That they legiti-
mized their claims to the throne by marrying the eldest surviving
heiress queen is certain, but it is to be suspected that they had
strong rights of their own. In the case of the latter king there is
little doubt in the matter, since he was only eight or nine at his
accession, and a newly published inscription from Hermopolis
names him, while still uncrowned, as the son of a king 'of his
loins'.[9] As he had been born at least four years before Smenkhkare came to the throne, his claims would not have been passed
over, young as he was, if his predecessor too had not been the

---

[1] §vi, 1, 32; §i, 19, 137; §i, 21, 275.                    [2] §vi, 1, 33.
[3] §ii, 2, 89–92; §vi, 1, 37–9; §v, 12, 171–4; §v, 1, 105–6.
[4] §vi, 12, 36–54.               [5] Lev. 18, 6ff., 20, 10ff.; Deut. 27, 20ff.
[6] §vi, 6, 24.            [7] §iii, 11, 104–8.            [8] Cf. §iii, 31, 229.
[9] See above, p. 70, n. 1. Cf. §iv, 28, 178, 179.

son of a king. The mortal remains of these two pharaohs have such close physical resemblances that they have long been regarded as brothers, a view that has recently been strengthened by the recognition that they belong to the same blood groups, A₂ and MN.[1]

The problem remains of the identity of the king whose sons these brothers are. Tutankhamun states that Amenophis III is 'his father' (as distinct from 'the father of his father'),[2] but most Egyptologists refuse to accept this claim and dismiss it as merely implying that Amenophis III was his ancestor. If, however, Akhenaten the only other possible claimant was the father of these two princes, Smenkhkare must have been born at the latest soon after he had come to the throne, and more probably three years before. In the latter event, it is doubtful whether Smenkhkare would have taken precedence over a younger brother who had not been born until his father had been consecrated as a pharaoh. If, on the other hand, Akhenaten had fathered both these princes only after he became king,[3] their mother, who would have held an extremely influential position at his Court as the mother of the heirs apparent, has not been disclosed. She is unlikely to have been the Chief Wife Nefertiti, since that queen is never shown as the proud mother of his sons despite her paramount importance and the unprecedented way in which her domestic life with the king and her daughters is frankly depicted. Despite, too, the intimacy in which Smenkhkare is shown with Akhenaten, calling himself 'beloved' of the older king, he never pretends to be his son, which was the closest relationship that it was possible for him to claim. While, therefore, it remains doubtful whether Akhenaten was the father of Smenkhkare and Tutankhamun, the paternity of Amenophis III can only be admitted in their case if there was a long co-regency between him and Akhenaten,[4] since Tutankhamun must have been born in Akhenaten's seventh regnal year at the very earliest.

Ay certainly gained the throne on the death of Tutankhamun, but that he married the royal widow is denied by some historians,[5] the evidence of the ring inscribed with his name and that of Ankhesenamun being considered too flimsy for admission.[6] It seems inevitable, however, that Ay would have confirmed his

---

[1] A, 4, 13. Also see above, p. 69, no. 1.  [2] §IV, 21, 76; §I, 21, 279.

[3] In view of the jar-dockets mentioned above (pp. 64 f.), this is impossible in the case of Smenkhkare since he died in his 20th year and Akhenaten's highest regnal year was 17 (pp. 63, 68).

[4] See above, p. 49.  [5] G, 6, 236; §IV, 28, 180.  [6] See above, p. 70.

shaky right to the throne by the time-honoured custom of marrying the royal heiress, even though in his case she may have been his grand-daughter, since this was to have been the means by which the prince Zannanzash was to be made pharaoh. Ay, the putative father of Nefertiti, almost certainly had other children, including that Mutnodjme who at El-Amarna is described as the 'sister' of Nefertiti.[1] From the early days of Egyptology she has been identified as the woman who later married Horemheb, and as the royal heiress furnished her husband with his right to the throne. Whether Horemheb married her in his early years and by this alliance climbed to a position of influence at the court, or only espoused her on his nomination to the crown is problematic.[2] It is also doubtful whether the family of Ay succeeded in maintaining its position in the next dynasty. A faience knob, however, bearing his cartouche and evidently from a piece of furniture deposited as an heirloom in the tomb of Queen Nefertari-merymut may be not without significance.[3] This queen was the chief wife of Ramesses II during his early years and must have been given to him in marriage on his appointment as co-regent. She bears a name not unknown in the family of Ay, who were devoted to the worship of Mut,[4] and she may therefore have been a connecting link between the two dynasties.

## VII. FOREIGN AFFAIRS

The victory of Megiddo, won by Tuthmosis III in his twenty-third regnal year over a confederation of Asiatic princelings, asserted Egyptian claims in Syria which had been challenged in the earlier years of the Eighteenth Dynasty by the vigorous and rising power of the Mitanni.[5] The successors of Tuthmosis III, however, were unable or unwilling to maintain their pretensions over vassal states in North Syria and came to an understanding with other Great Powers in the Near East to define their spheres of influence.[6] A treaty with the Khatti was arranged early in the career of Tuthmosis III[7] and was apparently still in force during the reign of Amenophis III.[8] Babylonia also had a pact of mutual assistance with Egypt and invoked it to warn the Canaanites from attacking the territory of its ally.[9]

---

[1] §vi, 1, 39, 41; §v, 12, 171–6; §v, 1, 103–6.    [2] §vi, 1, 41; §v, 12, 78, 232.
[3] §vi, 11, 55, 103, fig. 82.
[4] §vi, 1, 33 n. 1; §ii, 2, 88, pl. 66; §vi, 10, 66–8.
[5] *C.A.H.* ii³, pt. 1, p. 671.    [6] *Ibid.*, p. 676.    [7] *Ibid.*, p. 671.
[8] E.A. 41; §vii, 4, 22 n. 1.    [9] E.A. 9; see above, pp. 24–5.

Such treaties were cemented by marriages between the daughters of the royal houses and the pharaoh, the most documented of such alliances being the series of marriages between princesses of the Mitanni and Tuthmosis IV, Amenophis III and Akhenaten.[1] The daughters of less exalted princes, however, also entered the royal harims in Egypt and played their part in the diplomacy of the age.[2]

Within its Asiatic sphere of influence, Egypt hardly exercised any Roman *imperium*, despite some ambiguous indications of its exploitation of the region.[3] The pharaoh as the traditional vanquisher of the Nine Nations was the divine overlord whom vassals in Palestine and Syria addressed as 'my sun', 'my god', 'my lord' and in similar terms of subservience.[4] Apart from this spiritual leadership, however, it is doubtful whether anything like an empire existed[5] and the scenes of foreigners bearing tribute to lay before the mercy-seat of the pharaoh are capable of other interpretations than the mercantile development of the region.[6]

The many vassal states kept up interminable internecine squabbles, their main objective being to preserve their own autonomy, to extend their frontiers and power at the expense of their weaker neighbours and to enlist the military might and resources of their overlord, ostensibly to protect his interests, but actually to advance their own ambitions.[7] They therefore set up a constant clamour for help to preserve the town or state they were so loyally defending, coupled with assurances of their own honesty and fidelity and the treachery and ruthlessness of their rivals.[8]

Despite the remoteness of these quarrels from the centre of government in Egypt, it seems highly probable that the Egyptians, informed by despatches from their own commissioners and garrison commanders, had a good idea of what was afoot and took the action that seemed best to them, though modern observers of the partially revealed scene have not been slow to level charges of supineness and muddle against the Egyptian administration.[9]

The treaties between the Great Powers of the Near East, however, brought a period of comparative calm and stability to

[1] E.A. 17, 26 ff.; E.A. 19, 17 ff.; E.A. 22, iv, 43 ff.; E.A. 24, iii, 9 ff.; E.A. 29, 16 ff.; §vi, 2, pl. xxix.

[2] E.A. 31; E.A. 31 *a*; §vii, 9, 41, 47.    [3] See below, pp. 105–7.

[4] *Cf.* E.A. 60, 1–7; E.A. 76, 1–6; E.A. 176*a*, 1–6; E.A. 270, 1–8.

[5] G, 6, 230; §vii, 3, 111.    [6] *Ibid.* 105–16.

[7] See below, pp. 104–5; §vii, 4, 14.    [8] §vii, 8, 60–3.

[9] G, 2, 379, 385–6; §ii, 13, 207, 230–1.

Palestine and South Syria during the reigns of Tuthmosis IV and Amenophis III, when the Egyptian garrisons in key cities such as Gaza, Beth-shan, Joppa, Sumura, Rehōb and Megiddo were able to reinforce local levies in checking the pretensions of the more turbulent dynasts and in repressing the Shasu bedawin and the Apiru freebooters who posed a constant threat to law and order.[1]

With the accession of Shuppiluliumash to the Hittite throne, however, about the second decade of the reign of Amenophis III,[2] a new actor appeared on the scene who was to remould decisively the political structure of the region during the following century. The struggle that now developed between the Khatti and the Mitanni for supremacy involved the vassal states of Egypt on her borders with these two powers and ultimately led to the wars of attrition between Egypt and the Khatti in the early Nineteenth Dynasty.[3]

The Egyptian records from the death of Amenophis III to the accession of Sethos I are too scanty and incomplete to give any coherent picture of the foreign scene as viewed through Egyptian eyes. The outlines have therefore to be sketched from the cuneiform archives found at El-Amarna and Boğazköy, and the situation prevailing when Sethos I began his Asiatic campaigns in his first regnal year.[4]

The protracted struggle between Tushratta of the Mitanni and Shuppiluliumash of the Khatti is recounted elsewhere.[5] The Egyptians had treaties with both nations and appear to have shown little inclination to intervene, a policy which has been accredited to the neglect by Akhenaten of the affairs of his 'empire' rather than to the preservation of a strict neutrality. It may have been immaterial to the Egyptians which of the two rivals had suzerainty in North Syria, since they themselves were evidently unwilling to exercise any dominion over the region. Their efforts appear to have been reserved for trying to maintain their influence in the coastal area stretching from Byblos in the south to Ugarit in the north. In this policy they found themselves dealing with the astute and turbulent princes of the Amurru, whose domains straddled the region and who found the confusion caused by the wars between the Khatti and the Mitanni congenial to their own expansionist aims.[6]

Abdi-ashirta, the first of these Amurru princes, made a show of

---

[1] *C.A.H.* II³, pt. I, pp. 27–8; see below, pp. 110–16.
[2] See above, pp. 6–7; §VII, 4, 39.   [3] See below, pp. 226–9.
[4] G, 6, 252–5.   [5] See above, pp. 1–16.   [6] *Ibid.*, pp. 10–13.

recognizing Egyptian suzerainty on the North Syrian coast, but
his intrigues eventually exhausted Egyptian patience and he was
slain by a task-force of marines in the last years of Amenophis III
or early in the reign of Akhenaten.[1] His equally troublesome
successor, Aziru, was summoned to the Egyptian court to give an
account of himself and to serve as hostage for the good behaviour
of his state.[2] Though he eventually returned to the Amurru with
the confidence of the pharaoh, the pressure of events left him no
option but to become the faithful vassal of Shuppululiumash.[3]

By the end of the reign of Akhenaten, Egypt had proved a
broken reed in its failure to support the independent states of
South Syria with effective military aid. Qatna, Nukhash, Qadesh
and above all the Amurru passed into Hittite vassalage.[4] It is
doubtless this loss of influence which is referred to in the
Restoration Stela of Tutankhamun when it is admitted with rare
candour that, if in the days of his predecessor an army was sent to
Syria to extend the boundaries of Egypt, it met with no success.[5]
It would appear, however, that some attempt was made during
the reign of Tutankhamun to recover lost ground, a more
aggressive policy being promised to the king's District Commissioners in an inscription in the Memphite tomb of Horemheb,
where the owner is spoken of as 'the guardian of the footsteps of
his lord on the battlefield on this day of smiting Asiatics'.[6] The
cuneiform records reveal that the Hittites raided Amqa between
the Lebanon and Antilebanon, which was a violation of Egyptian-
held territory. As a riposte the Egyptian forces captured Qadesh
on the Orontes and doubtless encouraged the revolt of Nukhash.[7]
Their triumph was shortlived, however, for in the following year
a Hittite force drove the Egyptians from Qadesh and re-entered
Amqa. It was at this point that Tutankhamun died and his widow
petitioned Shuppululiumash to give her one of his sons in marriage.[8]
After the murder of Zannanzash, Shuppululuimash again attacked
Amqa, defeated the Egyptian forces and brought back prisoners
who carried with them a plague which spread among their
captors and became endemic among the Khatti for years afterwards.[9]

Evidently the Hittites realized that by their aggression they
had broken the terms of their treaty with Egypt, a pact which had

---

[1] §vii, 4, 27–8.
[2] E.A. 161, 22 ff.; E.A. 164, 14 ff.
[3] See above, pp. 12–13; §iv, 4, 17–18.
[4] See above, pp. 15–16; §iv, 4, 46.
[5] G, 13, 2025 ff.; §iv, 2, 9, l. 9.
[6] §v, 16, 16; §v, 9, 7.
[7] See above, p. 17; §iv, 4, 47.
[8] See above, p. 69.
[9] §viii, 34, 395.

been sealed by oaths to the gods, probably of both powers,[1] who were now accredited in their anger with visiting the plague upon the violators. Shuppiluliumash himself died of the disease early in the reign of Horemheb and his successor, Murshilish, undertook penances to deflect the wrath of the gods, making restitution and returning prisoners to Amqa.[2] It seems probable therefore that the frontiers of Egypt and of the Khatti were stabilized at the Lebanon throughout the reign of Horemheb and that Egyptian policy was confined to trying to exert the claims over the Amurru and Ugarit which it had exercised in the prosperous days of Amenophis III. In this it appears to have enjoyed some temporary success, but was defeated by the superior skill of Murshilish.[3]

Further south in Palestine the task of the Egyptians in maintaining their influence was simpler, since here they were not opposed by a unified great power commanding trained military forces and enjoying interior lines of communication. This area was also in a constant state of unrest caused by the rivalries and feuds of local princes, whom it was not difficult to divide and rule. In the reign of Akhenaten a more serious threat developed in Central Palestine through the ambitions of the 'Apiru Chief' Labaya of Shechem, who, however, was killed in a skirmish with loyalist forces.[4] He was succeeded by his sons, who proved no less fractious.[5] Towards the end of the reign unrest at Gezer imperilled the whole Egyptian position in Central Palestine, and it would seem that forces and supplies were being marshalled for a more serious campaign which may have been mounted early in the reign of Tutankhamun.[6] Whatever threat may have developed to the Egyptian position here, it had evidently been dispersed by the time Sethos I set out on his first foreign campaign, and there is no reason to doubt that under the successors of Akhenaten Palestine was as firmly held as it had ever been, despite the fissiparous nature of its politics, the constant jockeying for power by its princelings and the disorder caused by the operations of the Shasu and the Apiru.

Nubians and Kushites are represented on the monuments as equally prostrate beneath the feet of pharaoh as the Asiatics or the adoring *rekhyt* populace of Egypt, but during the greater part of the Eighteenth Dynasty the African dependencies were peaceful and well-ordered, being governed through an administration

---

[1] *Cf.* §VII, 6, 197.   [2] §VIII, 34, 396.
[3] See below, pp. 139–40; §IV, 4, 36.   [4] See below, pp. 114–16; §I, 5, 104, 110.
[5] *Ibid.* 103, 109; E.A. 289, 5; E.A. 287, 29–31.   [6] §VII, 8, 63–4.

modelled on that of Egypt itself.[1] Punitive expeditions against
nomad disturbers of the peace on the unsettled borders were
undertaken by the Viceroys of Kush as part of their duties and
were no more than police actions.[2] The processions of manacled
prisoners in some of the representations of the time give a misleading picture of events in Africa, since these captives are often
not prisoners of war, but the traditional 'black ivory' of the
region, captured in slave-raids or trafficked together with the
elephant tusks, ebony logs and gold dust as part of the native
produce. The visit of Heknufer, the Prince of Mi'am (Aniba),
and the Sudani princess with their retinues to the court of
Tutankhamun, presumably at his accession, as represented in the
tomb of the Viceroy Huy,[3] is a peaceful occasion and not a scene
of conquest.[4] Similarly the victory over Kush depicted in the
*speos* of Horemheb at Gebel es-Silsila is doubtless pure bombast,
if it is not merely heraldic, showing the pharaoh as all-conquering
in his southern domains as elsewhere.[5] If it has any basis in
historical reality, it almost certainly refers to slave-raids or police
action undertaken by the viceroys in his name.

The reliefs on the east wall of the court between the Ninth and
Tenth Pylons at Karnak, showing delegates from Punt bringing
gifts to Horemheb,[6] may, however, represent an historical event,
since here the Puntites are hardly likely to represent the southern
peoples in an equipoise of the foreign nations that owed allegiance
to the pharaoh. This scene may therefore indicate that at the end
of the Eighteenth Dynasty trading relations with the mysterious
spice-lands of Punt had once more been re-established.

## VIII. RELIGION, LITERATURE AND ART

A feature of religious thought during the Eighteenth Dynasty is
a preponderance in the influence of the sun-cult, whose centre at
Heliopolis, the Biblical On, was the chief seat of its theologians.
These traditional 'wise men' of Egypt had radically overhauled
their doctrines and re-interpreted old beliefs, perhaps as a result
of seminal ideas from other sun-cults imported from Asia in
Hyksos times.[7] The interpenetration of the new thought can be
seen not only in the solarization of the old cults, which hastened
to add the name of the supreme sun-god Re to the name of their

---

[1] *C.A.H.* II³, pt. I, pp. 348–50; §G, 12, 186 ff.  
[2] *Ibid.* 162–7.  
[3] §IV, 9, pls. XXVII, XXVIII.  
[4] §VII, 3, 115.  
[5] G, II, V, 211 (34)–(36); *cf.* G, 12, 107–8, 163 ff.  
[6] G, II, II, 61 (56).  
[7] §VIII, 8, 113–14.

local divinity, but also in the royal tombs at Thebes where the Pyramid Texts used in the Old and Middle Kingdoms were replaced by extracts from such sacred works as *The Book of What is in the Underworld, The Litany of the Sun* and *The Book of Gates*.[1] In these writings a new interest is revealed in a monotheistic syncretism of ancient beliefs. In them Re becomes the sole god who has made himself for eternity. He is invoked in *The Litany* under his 'seventy-five names which are his bodies, and these bodies are the other gods'.[2] He is hailed as 'the sole god who has made myriads from himself: all gods came into being from him'.[3] He is also invoked as 'he whose active forms are his eternal trans-formations when he assumes the aspect of his Great Disk'.[4] This disk, or *Aten*, which illumines the world of the dead as well as the living, and daily brings both to life from death or sleep,[5] is the constant element in these transformations, and the power immanent in it, Re, is the supreme god of whom the pharaoh is the offspring on earth.

The sun-worship of Akhenaten, which most modern observers have accepted as a new and revolutionary religion, differed from these re-edited doctrines of the Re-cult by a mere nuance, by placing a little more emphasis upon the Aten, or visible mani-festation of godhead, than upon Re, the hidden power that motivated it.[6] It would seem that, as far as theological thought was concerned, there was little to choose between Atenism and the cults that it displaced. Amon-Re, the influential god of the dynasty, for instance, was also a 'hidden' force like Re, who might manifest himself in some tangible form, *e.g.* a ram (*cf.* the Mnevis bull of Re) rather than a remote and celestial body like the sun-disk. But his identification with Re weakened his ancient primal aspect of an ithyphallic god of storm, air and fertility, like his counterpart Min of the Eastern Desert, and he became purely the sun-god under the name of the god of Thebes, sailing over the waters above the earth in a divine bark, contending with the cloud-dragon Apophis and being worshipped as the creator and sustainer of all living things.[7] In Papyrus Bulaq 17, written about the time of Amenophis II,[8] all these aspects are praised in terms which differ little from similar phrases in the Great Hymn to the Aten, and it is doubtful whether a devotee of Amun of Thebes in the reign of Akhenaten would have found anything

---

[1] §VIII, 30, 121–2.        [2] §VIII, 31, 207–8.        [3] *Ibid.* 208 n. 5.
[4] *Ibid.*        [5] §VIII, 16, 21 ff.        [6] §VIII, 31, 218; §IV, 26, 12–13.
[7] §VIII, 18, 49 ff.; §VIII, 29, 7–14; §VIII, 41, 35; §II, 12, 87.
[8] §VIII, 34, 365–7.

heretical in the doctrines being propounded by the new prophet at Akhetaten. In fact there is evidence that the personnel required for staffing the temples of the Aten at Karnak were drawn initially, at least, from the priesthood of Amun.[1]

Kings from the time of Ammenemes I had been spoken of as departing at death to the horizon and uniting with the Aten.[2] In the reign of Amenophis II a symbol of the sun-disk had appeared with a pair of embracing arms,[3] and under Tuthmosis IV the Aten is mentioned on a scarab as a great universal god whose exalted position in the sky entitles it to rule over all that it shines upon.[4] In the reign of Amenophis III it became even more important, being attached to the name of the king's palace, his state-barge and one at least of his children, if not of himself.[5] Under Akhenaten, this deity became the supreme state-god, gradually achieving the position of a heavenly pharaoh who, like his earthly counterpart, had his names inscribed in two cartouches, assumed titles and epithets and celebrated jubilees. Where the Aten of Akhenaten differed from the Re of the new sacred books was that, instead of incorporating all the old deities in a comprehensive henotheism, it rigidly excluded them in an uncompromising monotheism.[6] This is seen as early as the Great Hymn to the Aten inscribed in the tomb of Ay before Year 9.[7] In this work, which has often been compared with Psalm 104, sentiments and phrases are included which can be found in earlier hymns to Amun and Osiris; where it differs from them is in ignoring completely the existence of other deities.

Later in the reign of Akhenaten this passive disregard of the other gods changed to an active antagonism which manifested itself in the excision of their names wherever they appeared, and the changing of the word for 'gods' to its singular form only. Just as remarkable, also, is the complete neglect of the old mortuary cults such as that of Osiris, with whom dead kings had become identified, and which had enjoyed an enormous expansion since the end of the Old Kingdom. The sun-god and his incarnation, the pharaoh, had taken over the care of the dead, and the new eschatology is seen in such features as changes in burial customs and funerary furnishings and the excision of the old

[1] §VIII, 25, 5, 6 n. 1; G, 13, 1935, l. 18; §VI, 5, 390–1.
[2] *Sinuhe*, R, 7; *cf*. G, 13, 54.
[3] §VIII, 27, 53 ff.                    [4] *C.A.H.* II³, pt. I, p. 343.
[5] §I, 10, 179; §III, 13, Pt. III, pl. XVIII; §III, 35, 33; §III, 19, 108; §VI, 2, pls. XXX–XXXI; §I, 18, 164, no. 13.        [6] G, 3, 63; G, 6, 227.
[7] §III, 13, Pt. VI, pl. XXVII; §VIII, 34, 369–71; G, 6, 225–7.

*setem*-priest from the scenes of the last Osirian rites before entombment.[1] It is perhaps significant that special emphasis should have been placed upon the restoration of this scene in the wall-paintings in the tomb of Tutankhamun, where Ay officiates at the burial of his predecessor.[2]

Where Akhenaten's ideas of monotheism came from in a world which widely tolerated so many diverse forms of godhead is unknown, but the inference is that they were his own, the logical outcome of regarding the Aten as a heavenly king, whose son was the pharaoh. Like the latter, he could only be regarded as 'unique, without a peer'. It was, as has already been stated, the insistence by Akhenaten on a rigid monotheism in state affairs which proved disastrous for Egypt, since it destroyed the old system by which the lives of all the populace, from the lowest to the highest, had been regulated. In the world of the Late Bronze Age, religion and government were as inextricably mixed as they had ever been.

On the return to orthodoxy initiated by Akhenaten's successors, the old gods improved their position by the force of reaction, and that 'pagan' delight in the sunlit world of the living was in the ensuing dynasty to be excluded from the scenes painted on the walls of private tomb-chapels.[3] Nevertheless, it is probable that the faith of the mass of the Egyptian people was untouched by Akhenaten's religious reforms. They evidently continued to worship their old gods and godlings in the manner of their ancestors, for references to Bes, Toeris, Shed, Isis and even Amun were found in the workmen's village at El-Amarna.[4] The prayers and appeals of such humble folk, which show that a direct personal relationship was felt to exist between the petitioner and his god, are in marked contrast with the optimistic and complacent utterances of the official religion.[5] This spirit of self-abasement is more Hebraic than Egyptian in its concept of a merciful god who forgives the transgressor, and it may have owed something to the influence of the many Semites who had found an occupation in Egypt during the Eighteenth Dynasty. What has been called 'the religion of the poor' is better known from prayers written by the workmen at Thebes in Ramesside times,[6] but examples exist to show that such humble petitions were already being made as early as the reign of Amenophis III.[7]

---

[1] §VIII, 16, 24–5; §VIII, 22, 21, 24, 58.
[2] See above, p. 69, n. 4.
[3] §I, 20, 226.
[4] §III, 32, 25, 60, 65–6, 95–8.
[5] See below, p. 248.
[6] §VIII, 26, 87 ff.
[7] §VIII, 23, 188 ff.; cf. §IV, 18, 10–11.

Such minor compositions have often by their very unobtrusiveness survived unscathed the passage of time, but it is one of the ironies of chance that the Eighteenth Dynasty, which was one of the most prolific and imaginative periods of Egyptian art, has bequeathed us scarcely anything of its great literature. Hints exist in fragments of a story about the insatiable greed of the sea,[1] a book on the pleasures of marsh sports and a poem on the joys of spring,[2] to suggest that the elegance, good proportions and high technical accomplishment of the plastic arts would have found their counterparts in contemporary writing; if so, it was a style of composition that made little appeal to the schoolboy copyists, or rather their teachers, whose scribbles have bequeathed us almost all that we now possess of earlier Egyptian literature.[3] Nothing original exists, moreover, of the sapiential writings of Amenophis son of Hapu, whose wise sayings were treasured throughout the centuries, though a fragment of the *Instruction of Amonnakhte*[4] shows that this class of wisdom literature was not neglected in the Dynasty.

That literary composition was moulded by the same influences that shaped the progress of the other arts is suggested by the utterances inscribed in the temple of Queen Hatshepsut at Deir el-Bahri accompanying reliefs inspired by Theban models of the early Middle Kingdom, and quoting from the classical *Story of Sinuhe*.[5] As the dynasty wears on and art becomes freer, its lines more flowing and its compositions more adventurous, particularly in such a non-royal genre as the paintings in the private tomb-chapels at Thebes, the language also changes to express a more flexible and vernacular manner of speech. New grammatical tendencies and idioms, foreign words and a different orthography characteristic of Late Egyptian began to replace classical Middle Egyptian about the reign of Tuthmosis III for less formal writings, but at El-Amarna they had already entered the monumental texts.[6]

It is from its official inscriptions, in fact, that any appreciation of the literary achievement of the Eighteenth Dynasty has to be gleaned. The Annals of Tuthmosis III, inscribed on walls adjacent to the innermost shrine of the temple of Amun at Karnak, are remarkable for their terse, methodical record of events, with so little of the bombast that passes for the writing of

---

[1] §VIII, 24, 74 ff.; §VIII, 32, 461 ff.
[2] §VIII, 9, 1–21; §VIII, 17, 252–3; §VIII, 12, pl. LXX.
[3] *Ibid.* 185 ff.
[4] §VIII, 33, 61 ff.
[5] §VIII, 17, 14 n. 4.
[6] *E.g.* §II, 13, 220–1.

history in ancient Egypt that they can be accepted with some confidence.[1] The stelae which describe the Homeric prowess of the pharaohs as sportsmen also, in their vivid hyperbole and the elegance of their diction, are surely indicative of a not unhappy striving on the part of their authors for a literary excellence which would match the marvellous feats of the royal paragons.[2] By the end of the dynasty literary artifice had almost triumphed over clarity of expression, as in the Coronation Inscription of Horemheb, where the historical facts of his accession have been obscured by elaborate flowers of speech.[3] This may, however, be a deliberate glossing over of the means by which the king attained a throne to which he had no strong claim.

Such records are the prose of the period. The poetry has to be sought in the hymns written to Amun of Thebes and the Aten of Akhetaten. The great triumphal hymn celebrating the victorious might of Tuthmosis III, inscribed on a magnificent stela of polished black granite from Karnak,[4] contains an apostrophe by Amun which is clearly cast in a poetical form, the balanced strophes being emphasized by the disposition of the hieroglyphs:

I have come
    that I may cause thee to trample upon the great ones of Phoenicia; that
    I may strew them under thy feet throughout their lands; that I may
    cause them to see thy Majesty as the Lord of Radiance,
        when thou shinest in their sight like my image.

I have come
    that I may cause thee to trample upon them that are in Asia; that thou
    mayest strike the heads of the Asiatics of Syria; that I may cause them to
    see thy Majesty equipped with thy panoply
        when thou seizest the weapons in thy chariot...

This composition was evidently considered a masterpiece, for phrases from it inspired similar triumphal hymns written for later kings.[5] Thus Amenophis III set up a great black granite stela at Medīnet Habu which recounted his achievements based upon a phrase taken from the earlier inscription:

I turn my face towards the south,
    that I may perform a wonder for thee;
    causing the great ones of Kush to
        hasten to thee bearing all their gifts upon their shoulders.

[1]  G, 13, 645–756; G, 1, vol. II, §§407–540.
[2]  §VIII, 34, 243–5; *C.A.H.* II³, pt. I, p. 333
[3]  §V, 10, 21.
[4]  G, 9, no. 34010; G, 13, 610–19; §VIII, 34, 373–5.        [5]  *Ibid.* 373.

I turn my face towards the north,
   that I may perform a wonder for thee;
   causing the nations to come from the ends of Asia,
   bearing their gifts upon their shoulders and giving
   themselves to thee, together with their children,
   that thou mayest grant them in return the breath of life.[1]

The hymn to Amun written on Papyrus Bulaq 17 has already been mentioned as a forerunner of the Great Hymn to the Aten. In it Amun is hailed as a pharaoh and in phrases that recall those of the later hymn is referred to as 'the Solitary One with many hands, the Sole One who made all that exists' and is identified with the Creator 'who made mankind, distinguished their nature and made their life...Who made that on which the fish in the river may live and the birds soaring in the sky...Who gives breath to that which is in the egg and gives life to the offspring of the worm.'[2] The Great Hymn to the Aten, however, is justly praised as the masterpiece of psalmodic writing in the Eighteenth Dynasty, and its unknown author is often identified as Akhenaten himself, though it should be noted that the only known full-length copy appears in the Amarna tomb of Ay.[3] Many of its sentiments can be paralleled in other hymns, as has been mentioned, but the organic succession of its thought and expression demonstrates the difference between the mechanical stringing together of resounding phrases, culled from a corpus of such passages, and the inspired work of a true poet:[4]

Thou it is who causeth women to conceive and maketh seed into man; who giveth life to the child in the womb of its mother; who comforteth him so that he cries not therein, nurse that thou art, even in the womb! Who giveth breath to quicken all that he hath made.

When the child cometh forth from the womb on the day of his birth, then thou openest his mouth completely and thou furnishest his sustenance.

When the chicken in the egg chirps within the shell, thou givest him the breath within it to sustain him. Thou createst for him his proper term within the egg...

How manifold are thy works! They are hidden from the sight of men, O Sole God, like unto whom there is no other!

We shall have occasion to observe the same sensibility at work in the creation of Amarna pictorial art, where a unified composition replaces the old assemblage of diverse parts. Some of the shorter hymns at Amarna also contain passages of poetic beauty,

---

[1] G, 9, no. 34025; §VIII, 34, 375–6.
[2] *Ibid.* 365–7; §VIII, 17, 282–8.      [3] See above, n. 1.      [4] §II, 12, 90.

particularly in their loyal praise of Akhenaten and his queen,[1] and
the same original phraseology is found in the substitutes for the
old Osirian funeral formulae. A notable example of this is the
prayer on the foot-board of the coffin in which Smenkhkare was
buried, but which originally was made for a daughter of Akhenaten,[2] who addresses him thus:

I shall breathe the sweet air that issues from thy mouth. My prayer is that
I may behold thy beauty daily; that I may hear thy sweet voice belonging to
the North Wind; that my body may grow young with life through thy love;
that thou mayest give me thy hands bearing thy sustenance and I receive it
and live by it; and that thou mayest call upon my name for ever and it shall
not fail in thy mouth.

The modernization of Amarna hymnody is here complete.
Instead of the conjuration of the god by his suppliant with
propitiatory praises that had varied little since archaic times, the
relationship of worshipper to deity is one of mutual affection. It is
perhaps significant that this prayer of a faith that spoke much of
love[3] should contain sentiments which find their echo in the
secular love poetry of the following dynasty, though the fragment
from the tomb of Nebamun in the British Museum[4] shows that
some of it could have been composed in the Eighteenth Dynasty.

The same vulgarization is seen in the plastic arts which, during
the reign of Amenophis III, were characterized by the weakening
of the idealism of the official style in favour of a more sensuous
naturalism. The rather prim and precise drawing of the reigns of
Tuthmosis III and Amenophis II is replaced by a more dashing
line and adventurous use of colour, though the craftsmanship is
still meticulous.[5] The change is most marked in the last decade of
the reign, by which time a new generation of artists must have
succeeded their fathers.[6] The sculpture of this period is much
more realistic. The torsos of the king found at Medīnet Habu and
the statuette in New York[7] show him in all the obesity of his later
years, while the little head of Tiy from Sinai is no less frank in
revealing her features as sharp and lined.[8] At the same time
iconography is brought up to date to reveal fashions of dress
that had replaced the traditional garments of both kings and

[1] §III, 13, Pt. I, pl. xxxvi; Pt. II, pl. xxxvi; Pt. III, pl. xxix; Pt. VI, pl. xxv.
[2] §IV, 17, 35–6.          [3] §III, 13, Pt. I, 45; §V, 5, 8.
[4] §VIII, 12, pl. LXX; §VIII, 17, 252–3.
[5] Cf. §VIII, 12, pls. XVII, XXXV, XXXVI, LII, LXI, LXX.
[6] §VIII, 3, 78.          [7] See above, p. 51, n. 2.
[8] §VIII, 2, nos. 83, 84; §II, 2, pls. 21, 22.

commoners. This tendency towards 'modernism' continues unabated in the reign of Akhenaten and is found in such stylistic details as a more natural setting of the eye within its socket, the delineation of the lines that run from the corners of the eyes and nose, the folds in the neck, the large perforations in the ear-lobes and the contemporary modes of dressing the hair.[1] The innovations, however, were not accepted wholesale, and the finished reliefs in the tomb of the vizier Ramose at Thebes and one or two statues of private persons are completely in the style of the preceding reign.[2]

The great departure of Akhenaten's reign, however, and the one that has been responsible for accrediting him with a new 'realism' in Egyptian art, is his choosing to have his family and himself represented as though they suffered from some physical abnormality. Akhenaten's faithful courtiers followed his example in claiming similar diseased physiques, though the common folk were spared such marks of the elect. The distortion that Egyptian drawing now underwent is so gross as to verge on crude caricature in its more extreme and less accomplished examples,[3] but it cannot be denied that the colossal statues from Karnak, presumably the work of his master-sculptor Bak, still have a power to move the spectator by their inner spiritual malaise.[4] This revolutionary style erupts early in his reign, perhaps in his second regnal year, but it becomes more refined with the passage of time, presumably as his artists became more experienced and the less expert among them were replaced.

Apart from this new mannerism, Akhenaten inspired no fundamental change in age-old Egyptian conventions of drawing the human figure, but his artists did introduce a new space-concept in which to represent the new subjects for illustration which he must have specified. We have already remarked that in the Amarna tombs traditional themes for decoration are banished in favour of representations of events in the life of the royal family. During the dynasty there had been a steady growth in the popularity of a trinity consisting of a pair of deities and their male offspring, an idea that appealed particularly to the Egyptian with his strong love of family. This tendency received a considerable stimulus

---

[1] A, 1, chs. iv, v; §viii, 1, 141 ff.; cf. §viii, 21, 29 n. 3. This stela (G, 9, no. 34023), however, is a posthumous representation of Tuthmosis IV belonging to a later period in the dynasty.

[2] §iii, 15, pls. xlvi–xlviii; §viii, 6, 79 ff.; §viii, 7, 167 (reg. no. 69·45).

[3] §viii, 13, 10; §iv, 14, 105.

[4] §ii, 2, pls. 2–4; §viii, 2, nos. 107–9; §iv, 14, pl. 95; §viii, 28, pls. 176, 177.

when the new sun-god could no longer be exhibited in iconic form, and scenes of religious import were replaced by compositions in which his incarnation in the person of the pharaoh with his wife and daughters enacted incidents from their lives—the worship of the Aten,[1] the investiture before the palace balcony,[2] the visit to the temple[3] and so forth.[4] Stelae used like triptychs in the chapels connected with private houses show the royal family in even more intimate scenes with the queen seated in the king's lap, or playing with their children.[5]

There were no precedents in Egyptian religious art for such subjects, and the artists therefore took their inspiration from the vernacular art that had already appeared in the scenes of everyday life in the Theban tomb-paintings. The royal family and the courtiers are now grouped in the same poses that had hitherto been reserved for the lowly and the vulgar.[6] They express emotions of unction, joy, pride and sorrow not by a symbolic gesture, but by pose and facial expression, like the mourners before the tomb-door or the dancers at the feast.[7]

These new subjects are depicted in a novel manner in the Amarna tomb-reliefs. Instead of a selection of standard scenes taken from pattern-books and assembled haphazardly according to the taste of the patron, each wall of the chamber is considered a complete entity and decorated with a single composition. Indeed, in a chamber in the royal tomb, one scene is spread over two adjacent walls.[8] A room in the Northern Palace was decorated apparently with one continuous scene of bird-life among the papyrus thickets.[9] The same readiness to regard space as a totality is revealed in the sarcophagus of Tutankhamun, where the goddesses stand at the corners, each with her spine in alignment with the edge where two adjacent sides meet.[10] The disposition of Nefertiti on a fragment of a corner of a sarcophagus from the royal tomb shows that this pose was an innovation of the preceding reign.[11] That it was felt to be outside the natural instincts of the Egyptian artist is seen in the similar sarcophagi of Ay and Horemheb, where the four goddesses have been so placed

[1] §III, 13, Pt. II, pls. v, vii, viii; Pt. iv, pl. xxxi.
[2] Ibid. Pt. vi, pls. xxix, xlii.        [3] Ibid. Pt. i, pl. xxv; Pt. iii, pl. viii.
[4] E.g. ibid. Pt. i, pl. x; Pt. ii, pls. xviii, xxxvii; Pt. iii, pl. xxxiiA; Pt. iv, pl. vi; Pt. vi, pl. vi.
[5] §III, 35, pl. i, 16; §viii, 13, pls. 8, 9, 11; §viii, 40, pl. 22; §viii, 35, pl. 51.
[6] Cf. §viii, 11, 29; §viii, 28, 147.
[7] §viii, 21, 8, 9; §viii, 10, 11–12.        [8] §III, 9, pl. i.
[9] §viii, 21, 58–9.        [10] §viii, 2, no. 161.
[11] §III, 38, 5; §viii, 40, pl. 56.

that two are fully revealed on each long side, one only of their winged arms being on each short end.[1] Nevertheless, many of the Amarna novelties remained in the repertoire of Egyptian art-forms, such as the 'caryatid' figures of the pharaoh standing against a pillar in the costume of the living[2] and the decoration of Ramesside walls and pylons.[3] In the unified compositions of Amarna art we can see at work the same influences that are manifest in a monotheistic conception of godhead and in the progression of thought in the Great Hymn to the Aten, although such tendencies are already present in the reign of Amenophis III.[4]

The excesses of the earlier Karnak style, still evident in the Boundary Stelae and other reliefs from Amarna, had been modified by the later years of Akhenaten, though the casts found in the sculptors' studios at El-Amarna tend to give an unbalanced view of the 'naturalism' of the period, since for the most part they appear to be portrait studies modelled from the life in wax or clay to catch a likeness and be cast in plaster for working over to an accepted standard.[5] To this period belongs the famous painted bust of Nefertiti modelled in plaster over a limestone core.[6]

This restrained style was more sympathetic to the temper of the post-Amarna age when a return was made to the traditions of Amenophis III, though the artists did not discard all they had been allowed to express under Akhenaten. The statuary of the end of the dynasty is among the finest produced in its noble proportions, high technical excellence and the individualism of its portraiture.[7] A group of sculptors working at Memphis produced reliefs for the private tombs, notably that of Horemheb, which show the same qualities in their lively scenes, splendidly conceived and executed.[8] These are among the last expressions of that delight in the world of the living and pride in worldly success which is the special contribution of the Eighteenth Dynasty to Egyptian art.

The decoration of tomb walls at El-Amarna and Memphis with carved reliefs broke the traditions of the Theban tomb-

[1] §II, 2, pl. III; §V, 6, pls. LXV, LXVIII, LXXIII.

[2] As, for instance, in the first courts of the great temples at Abu Simbel and Medīnet Habu (Ramesses III).    [3] §I, 20, 209, 222–4.

[4] *Cf.* scenes of the owner before his king in Theban tombs nos. 48 and 57, G, 11, 1², Pt. II, p. 88 (4), 89 (7); p. 115 (11), 116 (15).    [5] §VIII, 36, 145 ff.

[6] §VIII, 5; §VIII, 4; §VIII, 13, pls. 13, 14; §II, 2, pls. VIII, 7.

[7] *E.g.* §II, 2, pls. 56, 63–6; §VIII, 13, pls. 7, 24; §VIII, 28, pls. 196–9; §VIII, 2, no. 175.

[8] §VIII, 2, nos. 144–8; §V, 3, pls. V–VII; §VIII, 13, pls. 4, 5, 22, 23, 27–31.

painters and they never recovered the assurance and mastery that they had demonstrated under Amenophis III. The painting in the tomb of Huy and others is often poor in its drawing and proportions and crude in its colouring, and many of the mannerisms of the Ramesside style are already anticipated.[1] The same loss of confidence is seen in the wall-paintings in the tombs of Tutankhamun and Ay.[2]

The Amarna age showed no falling-off in its appetite for exotic objects of great luxury, particularly in gold, glass and polychrome faïence, that had characterized the reign of Amenophis III. The specimens found in the tomb of Tutankhamun give an unparalleled conspectus of the applied arts of the period, and while some of them seem hasty in execution and over-exuberant in taste, certain items may be singled out for their high technical excellence, such as some of the wooden furniture, an ivory bracelet exquisitely carved in coin-like relief with a frieze of horses, and the great head-rest of rich blue glass.[3] A novelty of the age is the gold tinted in tones from pink to purple by a metallurgical process,[4] but as Tushratta of the Mitanni speaks of sending the pharaoh gold ornaments 'through which blood shines',[5] we may presume this to have been an Asiatic invention, like his iron dagger-blade.[6]

---

[1] §IV, 9, 3; §I, 20, 210.          [2] §IV, 25; §IV, 29.
[3] §IV, 5, vol. I, pl. XLIX; §VIII, 14, pls. XII, XLIA, L.
[4] *Ibid.* pl. XXIIA.
[5] E.A. 22, I, ll. 20, 25; II, ll. 8, 15.
[6] E.A. 22, I, l. 32; II, l. 16; III, l. 7; §VIII, 14, pl. XXIB; §IV, 5, vol. II, 135–6.

# CHAPTER XX

## THE AMARNA LETTERS
## FROM PALESTINE

### I. THE TABLETS AND THEIR CHRONOLOGY

In 1887 an Egyptian peasant woman accidently discovered a large collection of tablets at El-Amarna in Middle Egypt; they were dug out by the local inhabitants and sold to various dealers. Eventually more than 350 cuneiform tablets, some complete, some broken, were purchased by various museums and private collectors. More than half of them were acquired by the Berlin Museum. Smaller collections found their way to the British Museum and the Egyptian Museum in Cairo. In 1915 the publication of all then available Amarna Tablets, begun by J. A. Knudtzon in 1907, was completed.[1] Since then another seven important tablets belonging to the original find have been published by F. Thureau-Dangin[2] and G. Dossin,[3] while a dozen additional tablets and fragments were recovered still later by German and British excavators at the same site.[4] These tablets are mostly letters from the royal archives of Amenophis IV or Akhenaten (1379–1362 B.C.) and his father, Amenophis III (1417–1379 B.C.);[5] only about twenty-five of the texts are not epistolary in content. About 150 of the letters either are written directly from or to Palestine, or are so immediately concerned with Palestinian affairs that they fall within the scope of the present survey.

Some similar documents have also been discovered in Palestine. In 1892 F. J. Bliss found a well-preserved tablet of the Amarna Age at Tell el-Ḥesi.[6] So far twelve tablets and fragments have been excavated at Taʿanach, near Megiddo,[7] one at Gezer,[8] two at Shechem,[9] one at Jericho,[10] one at Megiddo,[11] and one at Hazor.[12]

---

* An original version of this chapter was published as fascicle 51 in 1966.

[1] §1, 35.  [2] §1, 50.  [3] §1, 25.
[4] §1, 46; §1, 31. See also A. R. Millard in *P.E.Q.* (1965), 40 ff.
[5] I should prefer to date their reigns *c.* 1365–1348 and *c.* 1401–1365, respectively.
[6] §1, 5.  [7] §1, 9; §1, 44, 490.  [8] §1, 8.  [9] §1, 4; §1, 36, 59, n. 121.
[10] §1, 49, 116 ff. I am inclined to date this piece in the early sixteenth century B.C. (Alalakh VII period).  [11] §1, 30.
[12] Fragments of liver models; see now *I.E.J.* 14 (1964), 201 ff.

Most of these documents from Palestine belong to the period between 1450 and 1350 B.C.; at least nine of them are letters.

The interpretation of the letters concerning Palestine is relatively difficult because the scribes who wrote them were nearly all Canaanites, with a few Egyptians. None had a native command of Akkadian (Babylonian), and most of them had learned their cuneiform from local teachers, who had themselves learned it from other local teachers. This we infer from many facts. The recent discovery of a fragment of the Gilgamesh Epic at Megiddo, written in a local Phoenician hand of the early fourteenth century, demonstrates the existence of a scribal school in that area.[1] A letter written by a teacher to a patrician of Shechem says: 'What is my offence that thou hast not paid me? The boys who are with me continue to learn; their father and their mother every day alike am I.'[2] School texts were found at El-Amarna, and some of these texts show the same lack of familiarity with Akkadian grammar and phonetics which we find in the letters. The Akkadian of the letters contains many archaisms which are no longer to be found in contemporary Babylonia, but do occur in Old Babylonian, especially in the letters written by Amorite scribes of the eighteenth and seventeenth centuries in Syria and Upper Mesopotamia. Most significant is the fact that the letters abound with Canaanitisms in vocabulary, syntax, morphology and phonology, proving a Canaanite substratum in the mind of the scribe.[3] Moreover, many grammatical forms which recur constantly in these letters are neither Akkadian nor Canaanite but a mixture of both, showing a formalizing of mistakes which must themselves have been taught in the schools. In short, the language of the Amarna Letters was a scholastic and diplomatic jargon, the use of which had become acceptable for written communication between Canaanites and foreigners, as well as among Canaanites who did not wish to use either of the native consonantal alphabets which we know to have been current at the time. Because of the nature of this jargon, it is not enough for the would-be interpreter to know Akkadian; he must also be a specialist in Hebrew and Ugaritic, and above all he must be so familiar with all the letters that he knows what to expect from their writers.

The chronology of the Amarna Letters is gradually being cleared up, though it will perhaps never be possible to give each

---

[1] §1, 30.

[2] §1, 4. Contrast §1, 36, 59, n. 121, where the fact is overlooked that in all Canaanite letters voiced and voiceless stops are sharply distinguished.

[3] §1, 7; 5; 6; 14.

letter a date exact to the year.[1] Since all the letters from foreign princes which contain the official name of the reigning pharaoh are addressed either to Amenophis III or to his son, Akhenaten, with the possible exception of one letter that may be addressed to Tutankhamun,[2] it is obvious that they must be limited to a period of little over half a century. Moreover, it is possible to limit them more closely than that. Akhetaten, the new city built by Akhenaten at El-Amarna, was occupied from the fifth to the seventeenth year of Akhenaten, in the first and second years of his successor Smenkhkare, and apparently during the first four years of Tutankhamun, as indicated by hundreds of inscribed portable objects, mostly dated jar-sealings, which were excavated at the site. To what extent the regnal years of Smenkhkare over-lapped the end of Akhenaten's reign, is uncertain. When the royal archives were brought to Amarna they included documents from the latter part of Amenophis III's reign, probably going back at least to the latter's thirty-second year.[3] We may safely allow a minimum chronological scope of twenty-seven years and a maximum of just over thirty for the correspondence—about 1389–1358 B.C.[4]

Inside these limits we can fix the relative chronology of most of the letters within about five years, by relating their contents to external evidence from other sources, mainly Egyptian.[5] The most important group of letters consists of some 67 (or 68) letters from and to Rib-Adda, prince of Byblos. These may be divided into two main groups, EA 68–96 and 102–138,[6] dating from before and after the death of 'Abdi-Ashirta, prince of Amurru. Subdivisions may also be set up within the groups, particularly the second. In Palestine the role of 'Abdi-Ashirta was filled to a certain extent by Labaya (Lab'ayu), prince of Shechem, who was equally involved in happenings in northern and southern, western and eastern Palestine. Fortunately we have a hieratic docket, written in ink on one of Labaya's letters to the pharaoh, which probably mentions the thirty-second year of the king, 1385 B.C.[7] After Labaya's death his place was taken by his sons, who played an even more active part than their father in Palestinian

---

[1] §1, 18.             [2] §1, 18, 49, 53 ff.

[3] §1, 18, 69 ff., 103, 109 n.

[4] I should prefer the dates c. 1375–1344.      [5] §1, 18; 34.

[6] §1, 18, 79 ff. groups them as follows: 71–95 and 68–70; 101–138; 362. (For brevity, EA in footnotes to this chapter refers to the Amarna Letters (and their lines) as numbered in §1, 35.)

[7] c. 1370 in my system of chronology. On the situation of Labaya at that time see below, pp. 114 f.

politics. We have several such local dynastic sequences, which are very helpful in fixing relative chronology; thus Milkilu of Gezer was followed by Iapakhu and Ba'lu-shipti, in uncertain order; Zimredda of Lachish was followed by Shipti-Ba'lu and Iabni-ilu.

Knowledge of the succession of Egyptian commissioners and other high officials involved in Palestinian affairs is also very helpful. The Canaanite Iankhamu, who attained the high rank of 'Feather-Bearer on the Right of the King', figured prominently in the affairs of Byblos and Palestine in the middle period of the Amarna correspondence; his name is rare until after Labaya's death but it is very common for some years thereafter; similarly it does not appear in the earliest or the latest Byblos correspondence. Iankhamu is never mentioned in the latest letters of all from Tyre or Palestine. Since there is no trace of his name among the officials of Akhenaten mentioned in the Egyptian inscriptions from Amarna, and since he is never mentioned together with Egyptian officials belonging to the Aten circle, we may safely infer that he held power during the first years of Amenophis IV, being removed from office after the Aten revolution.[1] Maya followed Iankhamu; his name is never mentioned in a letter of the Iankhamu period, and his official role coincides well with that of a high military officer of Akhenaten bearing the same name. The representation of only three royal princesses in his unfinished tomb at Amarna establishes a date for his *floruit* between the eighth and twelfth years of Akhenaten's reign; we may place his rise after the sixth year and his downfall about the eleventh year. The Amarna references to him would then fall roughly between 1374 and 1368 B.C.[2]

While many more illustrations of the chronological evidence could be given, a single example of combinatory character must suffice. Piryawaza, prince of the region of Damascus, was a contemporary of Akhenaten and of Burnaburiash II, king of Babylon, who complains about him in a letter to the former.[3] He was also contemporary with the sons of Labaya, whose father had written to Egypt in the thirty-second(?) year of Amenophis III.[4] He was, further, still alive and engaged in an otherwise unknown war with Aziru, son of 'Abdi-Ashirta of Amurru, at the very end of Akhenaten's reign, as we know from a letter of Abi-milki of

[1] §1, 18, 90 ff.; §1, 33, 259.
[2] §1, 18, 75 ff., 126 ff.; §1, 33, 260, 266. My date would be between c. 1360 and 1354.
[3] EA 7.　　　　　　　　　[4] See above, p. 100.

Tyre.[1] The relative date of the last-mentioned letter is fixed by the fact that Abi-milki's reign in Tyre came after that of Iapa-Adda, who flourished until late in the reign of Rib-Adda of Byblos, and by the references to Akhenaten's daughter Mayate (Merytaten) as queen (of Smenkhkare) in one of Abi-milki's letters.[2] Piryawaza's correspondence is thus relatively as late as any.

## II. POLITICAL ORGANIZATION OF PALESTINE IN THE AMARNA AGE

During the two centuries of Egyptian occupation of Palestine since the conquest under Amosis and Amenophis I, its political organization had become more or less normalized. As far as practicable the Egyptians had left the local princely houses in control of their own territories, but under the close supervision of Egyptian agents whom we may conveniently designate as 'commissioner' (Akkadian *rābiṣu*, Canaanite *sōkinu*, Hebrew *sōkēn*)[3] and 'envoy' (Egyptian *uputi* [*wpwty*]). These agents were generally Egyptians, but they were not infrequently Canaanites of Semitic stock, as in the case of Iankhamu and Addayu. Sometimes native princes played an important role in Egyptian administration, as in the case of Iapa-Adda, who was probably prince of Tyre,[4] or Piryawaza, prince of the Damascus region. The chief centres of Egyptian administration in Palestine were Gaza and Joppa on the coast;[5] Gaza is mentioned several times as the residence of an Egyptian commissioner in one letter,[6] and it appears already in that role in an earlier letter from Ta'anach.[7] There were also Egyptian outposts at strategic points through the country, such as Beth-shan,[8] where excavations have brought to light a series of Egyptian fortresses from the fifteenth to the twelfth centuries.

In addition to Egyptian commissioners, whose military functions seem to have been subordinated to their administrative duties, there were also military officers, such as the *ākil tarbaṣi*, or 'inspector of the stable',[9] who was a commander of chariotry, and the *wē'u* (Egyptian *w'w*), 'petty officer', often in charge of a detachment of archers (*pitate*, Egyptian *pdtyw*). The contrast

---

[1] EA 151. Cf. §1, 34, 17, 45.    [2] §1, 18, 70 ff.
[3] Gloss in EA 256, 9; 362, 69.
[4] §II, 1, 10 n.; §1, 33, 178, 193; §1, 18, 92 n. The last two favour Berytus.
[5] EA 296, 32 ff. On the Egyptian administration in general see §1, 34, 256 ff.
[6] EA 289.    [7] Ta'anach no. 6, 12 ff.; see §1, 9.
[8] EA 289, 20.    [9] §II, 2, 38; §II, 1, 11.

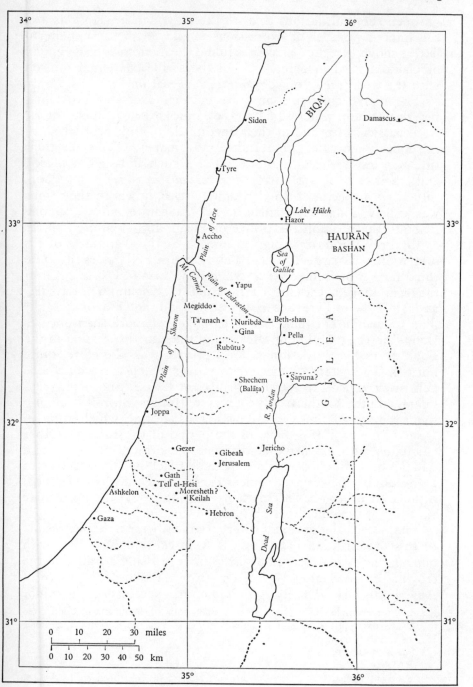

Map 2. Political geography of Palestine, about 1400–1200 B.C.

between the multifarious titles of the Egyptian inscriptions and
the limited number of expressions employed in the cuneiform
letters shows that the Canaanites found the intricacies of Egyptian
officialdom hard to define. Often the scribe contented himself
with the word *rabū*, 'officer' (literally, 'great one').

The native chieftains, in spite of their excessive grovelling
before Pharaoh, which sometimes occupies over half their letters,
were patricians, proud of their ancestry.[1] A high proportion of
the Palestinian chiefs bore Indo-Aryan names.[2] Officially their
title was *awilu*, 'free man', 'chief' (of such-and-such a place),
and their office was that of *haziānu* (*hazānu*), 'governor'
(literally, 'inspector'). In Canaanite circles, however, the prince
was called 'king' (Akkadian *šarru*, Canaanite *milku*); in one
letter to the pharaoh the prince of Hazor forgot himself so far
as to apply the term 'king' to himself at the beginning of his
salutation.[3] Elsewhere, Mut-Baʿal, prince of Pella, does the same
thing farther on in his letter, [4] while Piryawaza of Damascus uses
the term 'king' of the chiefs of Buṣruna and Khalunnu in Bashan,[5]
and Abi-milki of Tyre calls the princes of Sidon and Hazor 'kings'.[6]
The Canaanite chieftains are also spoken of more than once as
'kings' in the plural. The later use of the same expression in the
Book of Joshua to designate local princes was, therefore, quite
normal. The extent of the territory over which these chieftains
held sway varied greatly. The princes of Hazor, Shechem, Jerusalem, and the southern hill-country of Judah controlled among
them almost all the areas of western Palestine which were in
Israelite hands during most of the period of the Judges. Other
chieftains with extensive lands were the princes of Gezer and
Megiddo. Though details are generally lacking, there seems to
be no doubt that certain princes exercised acknowledged feudal
rights over other weaker chieftains; e.g. Tagu was the immediate
suzerain of the chief of Gath (Jett) in Sharon.[7]

The Amarna letters exhibit very frequently the unhappy results
of this organization. The princes were continually at war with
one another; each accused his neighbour of being a traitor to the
crown. In the Tell el-Ḥesi letter, from the end of the reign of
Amenophis III or the beginning of his successor's,[8] a minor

---

[1] Cf., for example, EA 224, 17 from Shamu-Adda of Shamruna in Galilee (so
read). The name of his ancestor Kuzuna is identical with the Ketjun (*Ktwn*) of a
Hyksos scarab (§11, 3, pl. xxiii, 28).

[2] See below, p. 109.

[3] EA 227, 3.

[4] EA 256, 8.

[5] EA 197.

[6] EA 147; 148.

[7] See EA 289, 18 ff., compared with EA 249.

[8] §1, 5. On the date of this letter (EA 333) see also §1, 18, 101, 134.

Egyptian officer, Pa'apu, accuses the prince of Lachish and his brother (who later became prince himself) of disloyalty to the crown. Pa'apu is particularly indignant because Shipti-Ba'lu has had the effrontery to accuse the writer himself of disloyalty to the king. Similarly, 'Abdi-Kheba of Jerusalem accuses his neighbours, Milkilu of Gezer and Shuwardata of the Hebron area, of being traitors and rebels,[1] an accusation which they return with interest.[2] The extraordinary extent of such recrimination in the Amarna letters, which far exceeds anything found in other comparable archives, shows the extent to which Canaanite morale had deteriorated after nearly two centuries of Egyptian domination. The demoralization of Canaanite ethos was, moreover, not much worse than that of Egyptian. Bribery and corruption were rampant among the Egyptian officials of the time, as we learn from contemporary Egyptian documents. Most instructive in this connexion is the edict of Horemheb, which was issued only a few years after the last of the Amarna Letters was written.[3] In it we find the most stringent penalties invoked against corrupt or oppressive officials, and instructions for the complete reorganization of the local *qenbe* (*knbt*) courts by the appointment of well-born and respected priests to judicial posts. Moreover, these judges were thenceforth to receive salaries, evidently in order to make it less necessary for them to take bribes so as to live in proper style.

Additional evidence from Egyptian sources is abundant, but we do not have to go beyond the Amarna Letters themselves to hear of exactions by Egyptian officials, especially by military officers. For example, late in the reign of Akhenaten, Ba'lu-shipti of Gezer complains that Pe'eya, a minor Egyptian official stationed at Joppa,[4] not only appropriates for himself the services of the men of Gezer sent there to work on the *corvée* and to guard the royal granaries, but even holds them for ransom. The prince of Gezer asserts that 'from the mountains people are ransomed for thirty (shekels) of silver, but from Pe'eya for one hundred (shekels) of silver'.[5] In other words, the bandits from the hill-country of Palestine asked as ransom only the conventional price (which was also the normal price of an able-bodied male slave), but the rapacious Egyptian official is said to have demanded over three times as much!

[1] EA 287; 289; 290.    [2] EA 280.
[3] See §II, 4, 260 ff.; §II, 5, Übersetzung zu den Heften 17–22, 416 ff.
[4] §II, I, 19.
[5] EA 292; 294 (assuming that the illegible name of the sender of EA 294 [see §I, 18, 101, n. 73] is a form of *Ba'lu-shipti*).

5

The extent to which both official and irregular exaction went is almost unbelievable. The regular tribute alone must have been a terrific burden. The grain-lands of Megiddo and Sharon were all considered as crown property, and the harvest was stored in royal granaries (Akkadian *maškan[āti]*,[1] Egyptian *šunut [šnwt]*).[2] Thus Biridiya, prince of Megiddo, complains to the pharaoh (about the end of the reign of Amenophis III or early in that of Akhenaten): 'Behold, I am working in the town of Shunama, and I bring men of the *corvée*, but behold, the governors who are with me do not as I (do): they do not work in the town of Shunama, and they do not bring men for the *corvée* from the town of Yapu (Yafa, near Nazareth). They come from Shu[nama], and likewise from the town of Nuribda (Nuris near Zer'in).'[3] The chief of Gath (Jett) in the northern part of Sharon complains bitterly: 'And let (the king) know that my m[en] have gone [to] Mil[kilu]. What have I done to Milkilu (of Gezer) that he oppresses my men because of his subservience to Tagu, his father-in-law, (to whom) he has rendered his service. But what can I do?'[4] In addition to regular tribute and the *corvée* there were also all kinds of exactions for the feeding and clothing of troops and fines for real or imaginary crimes. Levies for the support of troops, especially of garrisons and of armies on their way to Syria, were normal practice; we have a number of copies of letters written from Egypt to local princes demanding supplies of cattle, grain, oil, etc., for the troops. Frequently a local chieftain tries to persuade the central authorities in Egypt that his neighbours should do more than he, for reasons duly set forth. Milkilu of Gezer writes complaining that the Egyptian commissioner Iankh-amu demands two (or three) thousand shekels from him. Until he gets it the luckless Milkilu is to hand over his wife and children as surety, besides being flogged if he cannot scrape the amount together.[5]

The Egyptian garrisons in Palestine and Syria were mainly composed of Egyptian and Nubian archers. In his extant letters, Rib-Adda of Byblos asks at least a dozen times for troops, nearly always specifying equal numbers of Egyptians and Nubians (men of Kashu, biblical Cush, which alternates with Meluhha, an archaic designation for Negro Africa). When they were not provided with rations, owing presumably to official corruption, they resorted to robbery or brigandage. The local chieftains complain bitterly of the depredations of the troops. Even 'Abdi-Kheba,

---

[1] EA 306, 31.   [2] EA 294, 22.   [3] EA 365.
[4] EA 249, 5 ff.   [5] EA 270.

who unceasingly repeats his request for garrison troops, complains that the Nubians almost killed him when they broke into his quarters on the terrace of his palace.[1]

## III. PALESTINE: DEMOGRAPHY AND SOCIETY

The population of Palestine in the Amarna age was small; it was mostly concentrated on the coastal plains and the adjacent low hills, the plain of Esdraelon and the Jordan valley. The hill-country of western Palestine was sparsely settled; its population was mostly concentrated around well-watered centres such as Shechem, Jerusalem and Hebron. Eastern Palestine (Transjordan) was occupied by a sedentary population only in the Jordan valley and the extreme north, between the wooded hills of Gilead and the Syrian desert, just south of Bashan (southern Ḥaurān). Otherwise it was occupied chiefly by nomadic tribes which did not begin settling down until the following century. This situation has been demonstrated by the exhaustive surface surveys of Nelson Glueck, made possible by the fact that there are very few stratified mounds in southern and central Transjordan. Virtually all sites exhibit only one or two superimposed layers of occupation, and many sites which were reoccupied in different periods were never walled, so sherds of different ages may be found either mixed together or in different parts of a given site. His discovery that there was a long period of abandonment in the eighteenth to thirteenth centuries sandwiched between two periods of relatively heavy sedentary population, has been confirmed by the explorations and excavations of others. It is instructive to note that only a single town of all those mentioned in the Amarna Tablets and in the New-Kingdom Egyptian lists of conquered places can be plausibly identified with any site in Transjordan south of latitude 32° 20′ (Pella); this town is Ṣapuna (Zaphon),[2] some 12 miles in a straight line south of Pella (which is mentioned frequently). And both Zaphon and Pella were in the Jordan valley.

By combining evidence from archaeological surveys and excavations with written evidence, we are able to give a rough

---

[1] EA 287 translated in §1, 44, 488. Mention of their breaking through the roof is vividly illustrated by Dame Kathleen Kenyon's excavations, which prove that most of Late Bronze Age Jerusalem was built in terraces rising from the original edge of the Kedron Valley.

[2] §1, 7, 15 ff. The identification of Zaphon with Tell es-Saʿidiyeh, excavated by J. B. Pritchard, seems probable to the writer.

estimate of the population. Archaeological indications point to the contemporary existence in the fourteenth century of not over a score of fortified towns, large and small, in the entire region which later belonged to the kingdom of Judah, but was at this time divided among three major chieftains. Besides these fortified towns, some of which were exceedingly small, there were villages and hamlets at points which were watered by nature (since the technique of lining cisterns with watertight lime plaster had not yet become widely known). The sedentary population cannot have exceeded a rough total of 20,000 and the nomadic population must have been under 5000, since the hills were then densely wooded with scrub timber and bush. Proceeding through the country, district by district, we reach an approximate total of 200,000 for all Palestine, eastern and western. In no case can the population at this time have exceeded a quarter of a million. It is interesting to note that this was the approximate population of the country at the lowest ebb of its prosperity under the Turks, about A.D. 1800. The population of Egypt in about 1800 was also very low, and was estimated at about two millions by the members of the French scientific mission brought out by Napoleon. The same average ratio between the population of Egypt and that of Palestine has been maintained until recently; Egypt first gained proportionately under the *pax Britannica*, and Palestine gained subsequently as a result of British rule and Jewish immigration. In the early fourteenth century B.C. Egypt was enjoying its period of greatest prosperity before Hellenistic times, while Palestine was at a very low ebb. Assuming a ratio of twenty to one as in 1914, when Egypt had been governed by the British for some two decades and Palestine was still ruled by the Turks, we obtain the reasonable figure of four million for the population of Egypt (two-thirds of the probably inflated figure which Diodorus gives for Egypt in the first century B.C.). When we glance through the Amarna letters, we cannot but be impressed with the smallness of the garrisons which were considered adequate by the local princes when clamouring for aid; the prince of Megiddo wants a hundred men,[1] but three other chieftains, including the princes of Gezer and Jerusalem, are satisfied with fifty each.[2] Even the prince of wealthy Byblos, who constantly asks for assistance, is generally satisfied with two hundred to six hundred infantry and twenty to thirty chariots. Piryawaza of the Damascus region also wants two hundred men.[3]

Ethnically Palestine was very mixed, though dialects of

[1] EA 244.　　　　[2] EA 237; 289; 295.　　　　[3] EA 196.

Canaanite or of a closely related Amorite were spoken everywhere, as is proved by the language of the letters.[1] Not a single letter from Palestine shows any trace of the Hurrian substratum which appears everywhere north of the region of Damascus and the Biqā' in central Syria. Nor is there any trace of the Egyptian substratum which characterizes the letters of the scribe of the prince of Tyre.[2] If we turn to the non-Egyptian names in the Amarna letters proper we find the following situation:[3]

| | |
|---|---|
| Clear north-west Semitic names | 32 |
| Certain or probable Indo-Aryan names | 20 |
| Certain or probable Hurrian names | 3 |
| Miscellaneous or uncertain, but not Egyptian | 6 |

In the case of the twelve earlier tablets and fragments from Ta'anach, owing to their broken condition and the defective copies which we have, most of the seventy-five names are incomplete or cannot be read with confidence. Omitting the Egyptian names, we have the following picture:

| | |
|---|---|
| Clear north-west Semitic names | 14 |
| Certain or probable Indo-Aryan names | 5 |
| Certain or probable Hurrian names | 4 |

The two tablets from Shechem contain eight certain or probable north-west Semitic names, two certain or probable Indo-Aryan names and one uncertain name.

Evidently the proportion of Indo-Aryans decreases as we go downward in the social scale (most of the Amarna names belong to native princes, whereas the lists from Ta'anach and Shechem are of miscellaneous persons). Moreover, we find traces of the symbiosis of Hurrians and Indo-Aryans which was already well known from Nuzi, Mitanni and northern Syria. In all these areas the highest-ranking patricians (*mariyanna*) tended to have Indo-Aryan names, while the common people were overwhelmingly Hurrian in name.[4] At Ta'anach two of the five clear Indo-Aryan names are borne by a 'king' and a 'prince' (both carefully labelled as such); Indo-Aryan names are also borne by the princes of Ta'anach and Megiddo mentioned in the Amarna Tablets. The patrician to whom was addressed a letter found at Shechem bore an Indo-Aryan name also known from Nuzi. The Indo-Aryan

---

[1] See above, p. 99.        [2] §III, 1, 196 ff.

[3] There is a certain amount of fluidity in our numbers, since it is often hard to tell whether a given place belongs in northern Palestine or southern Syria. For convenience Ḥaurān has been included.

[4] §I, 43, 56 ff., 149 ff.

ruling class was scattered over northern, central and eastern Syria;
it was particularly strong in the Damascus region and Ḥaurān,
and appears to have been well represented in the plains of Acre
and Esdraelon, where the princes of Accho and Achshaph,
Megiddo and Taʿanach were all Indo-Aryan in name. Indo-
Aryans were also represented at Shechem and in the Hebron
region (Shuwardata). There can be little doubt that they were
bracketed in Hebrew tradition with the Hurrians (Horites).
According to the Septuagint, the prince of Shechem (who was
also called 'father of Shechem') and the Canaanites of Gibeon
were also Horites. Similarly the Boğazköy texts call both Indo-
Aryans and Hurrians by the latter name. Evidently the Indo-
Aryans migrated into south-western Asia in such small numbers
that they became submerged in the Hurrian mass, in spite of
their obvious pride of family and their preservation of Indo-Aryan
names as a token of nobility—much as happened to the Visigoths
in Spain. It is likely that there was a somewhat comparable situation at Jerusalem whose prince, ʿAbdi-Kheba, bore a name formed
with that of a Hurrian goddess, while Araunah the Jebusite, who
is said to have sold the site of the future Solomonic temple to
David, appears to have the same Indo-Aryan name as Ariwana
or Arawana, a prince of the Damascus region in the Amarna age.

The evidence of the Amarna Letters is confirmed by excavations, which show a striking contrast between the spacious, well-
built houses of the patricians and the hovels of the poor during
the Late Bronze Age. The letters from Palestine exhibit little
interest in the downtrodden peasants except as material for *corvées*;
there is no appeal on behalf of an individual of humble origin and
it is doubtful whether a single native outside the patrician class
is ever mentioned by name. The generic Canaanite word for
'peasant' or 'serf' does not appear at all in the letters from
Palestine; it is known from the Byblian correspondence and from
Ugarit to have been *ḫupšu*, Ugaritic *ḫpt*, a word also employed
in Assyria for 'half-free person', or the like. By a very interesting
shift of meaning Hebrew *ḥopšī*, 'free', is derived from it.

There was also a large and apparently increasing class of state-
less and reputedly lawless people in Palestine and Syria to whom
the appellation *ʿApiru* was given. It has now become certain that
they were a class of heterogeneous ethnic origin, and that they
spoke different languages, often alien to the people in whose
documents they appear.[1] The cuneiform spelling *ḫapiru* (formerly
read *ḫabiru*) appears in the letters of ʿAbdi-Kheba, prince of Jeru-

[1] §1, 16; §1, 32; §1, 33, 526 ff.

salem; elsewhere it is always written ideographically as *SA.GAZ* or the like, employing a logogram also used for *ḫabbātu*, 'bandit'. For a long time it remained uncertain whether there was any direct connexion between the two expressions; Hugo Winckler discovered that they were synonymous in Hittite documents of the same general age. Finally, in 1939, Ch. Virolleaud found that the same logogram had the Ugaritic alphabetic reading '-*p-r*, with a medial *p* which had been surmised from Egyptian transcriptions of the word. The problem of the 'Apiru is complex and many different solutions have been suggested; it is rendered even more elusive by the fact that it recurs in cuneiform texts from different parts of Mesopotamia, Syria, Egypt and Asia Minor, all dating between the Dynasty of Agade and the eleventh century B.C. The problem took a new turn with the publication of a triumphal inscription of Amenophis II (1450–1425 B.C.), at the end of which is a list of captives, including especially the following four groups: '3600 'Apiru; 15,200 Shasu; 36,300 Hurrians; 15,070 men from Nukhashshe in northern Syria.'[1] Other entries in the same text include 550 patricians (*mariyanna*), 640 merchants (*Kina'nu* = Canaanites),[2] 217 princes of Syria and Palestine, together with many sons and daughters, wives and concubines, and brothers of the princes. At the end of the second list all the wives (or 'relatives')[3] are mentioned without details. In order to understand the above collocation we turn to a letter of Piryawaza, prince of the Damascus region, who writes: 'Behold, I am in front of the royal archers, together with my troops and my chariots, and together with my brethren, and together with my 'Apiru, and together with my Sutu.'[4] Since the term Sutu is used as a generic term for 'bedawin' in the Amarna Tablets, following Babylonian usage in earlier centuries, we have exactly the same terminology as in the Amenophis text, where the 'Apiru are also followed by the bedawin (Shasu). We must accordingly differentiate sharply between the two groups: both were donkey nomads, but the 'Apiru were less nomadic than the Sutu.[5]

In the Amarna Tablets the 'Apiru generally appear as the foes of both native princes and Egyptian officials, as men who raid and destroy settled areas. Each prince accuses his enemies of being in league with the 'Apiru, and it would seem from a number

---

[1] §I, 39, 9; §II, 5, Übersetzung zu den Heften 17–22, 32 ff.
[2] §I, 39.     [3] §II, 5, Übersetzung zu den Heften 17–22, 40.
[4] EA 195.
[5] See below, p. 112, on the Curse of Agade and on a composition from the reign of Shulgi.

of passages that they sometimes call their most hated enemy by the same opprobrious term. In one passage, a Canaanite chieftain named Dagan-takala begs the king to save him 'from the hand of the 'Apiru, the bandits (*ḫabbātu*), and the bedawin (Sutu)'.[1] This passage again shows that the 'Apiru were distinct from both bandits and bedawin, though obviously similar in some respects to both. One letter says that Zimredda of Lachish had been killed by slaves who had become 'Apiru.[2] Similarly we read in a fifteenth-century text from Alalakh that the king Idrimi found refuge among the 'Apiru, and in thirteenth-century documents from Ugarit we hear of men of Ugarit, including slaves, who had escaped to the 'Apiru in Hittite territory.[3]

There are many sidelights on the background of the 'Apiru now available which were still unknown when Bottéro and Greenberg published their syntheses in 1954–5.[4] It is now virtually certain that *ḫabbātu*, one of the standing equivalents of the logogram *SA.GAZ*, meant originally 'tramp, wanderer, roving agricultural worker, donkey driver', etc., from the verb *ḫabātu*, 'to tramp', 'rove', 'cross over', and that the meaning 'robber', 'bandit', with the derived verbal sense, 'to rob', is secondary.[5] The Neo-Sumerian literary texts confirm this view. In the Lipit-Ishtar code *SA.GAZ* activity obviously refers to smuggling or similar illegal pursuits, since it is carried on by a boat's crew,[6] and in the 'Curse of Agade' the *SA.GAZ* were thrown out of work on the caravan routes when the empire of Agade collapsed.[7] A composition from the reign of Shulgi, towards the end of the third millennium, is even more informative, since we read that 'the rebellious people, the *SA.GAZ*...their men go where they please, their women carry spindle and spinning bowl.[8] They pitch their tents and their camps, they spend their days in the fields, and they do not obey the laws of Shulgi, my king.'[9] Evidently they refused to pay the proper tolls and taxes—in other words

[1] EA 318.          [2] EA 288, 43 ff.

[3] §III, 10, 107, 161 ff. The latter document is otherwise extremely interesting, since it explicitly states that certain men of Siyannu were not the *Ḫapiru* who had smitten a certain fortress.

[4] §I, 16; 32.          [5] See under these words in §III, 5 and §III, 13.

[6] For the original publication see §III, 14.

[7] §III, 9, 62 ff. My translation of the relevant passage is partly based on the obvious fact that when the cities lay in ruins, the caravan roads would be abandoned anyway. See now A. Falkenstein in *Z.A.* 57 (1965), 43 ff.

[8] The Sumerian word is ᴳᶦˢˢKEŠDA. This must surely mean a wooden spinning bowl, which was necessary in spinning, and could be used for many other purposes. On the spinning bowl in the Ancient Near East see §III, 7, 97 ff.

[9] §III, 8, 286.

they engaged in smuggling, as well as in other reprehensible activities. But they were far superior in culture to the nomads of the Arabian desert (the Martu), who are said to have lived in tents, had no houses, eaten their food raw, raised small cattle but no grain, left their dead unburied, and otherwise behaved like savages.[1]

Some of the most instructive passages relating to the 'Apiru come from recently published Old Hittite texts; they date from about 1500 B.C. Here the *SA.GAZ* troops are mentioned together with the Hittite troops and they are given a pledge not to be mistreated. Then are mentioned successively the 'men of the desert tribes' (bedawin)[2], the grooms (literally, 'the dusty men', *LŪ.SAḪAR*),[3] 'the... *SA.GAZ* troops'.[4] Here again they are distinguished sharply from the bedawin and the grooms. They share with the latter, however, the interesting designation 'dusty ones'. It has been pointed out that the word 'Apiru must mean 'dusty one' in north-west Semitic.[5] It has since been observed that the word still appears in Syriac with the same meaning,[6] and that the international pedlars and hucksters of the Middle Ages also bore the name 'dusty feet' (*pies poudres*, which passed into Anglo-Norman law as 'pie-powders').[7] Characteristic of all these terms is the common fact that the bearer of the designation trudges in the dust behind donkeys, mules or chariots. In 1961 I collected the then available archaeological and documentary material bearing on the caravan trade of the twentieth to nineteenth centuries B.C. and the organization of donkey caravans; I found far-reaching correlations with early Patriarchal tradition in Genesis.[8] It became particularly obvious that the previously enigmatic occupational background of Abraham becomes intelligible only when we identify the terms '*Ibrī*, 'Hebrew' (previously '*Abiru*) with '*Apiru*, later '*Abiru*, literally 'person from across or beyond'.

This is not the place for a detailed treatment of the involved question, but it may be observed that after the catastrophic decline of caravan trade at the end of the Dynasty of Agade and again

---

[1] §III, 9, 253, 278, etc.

[2] The word is *līm ṣēri* (*līmu* is a synonym of *kimtu*, 'single family', 'clan'). It corresponds with the usual Akkadian designation *Sutū*.

[3] Akk. *kizū*, W. Sem., *kāziy[u]*, Eg. *kudji* or *kutji* (*kt* and *ktn*).

[4] §III, 11, 216 ff.

[5] §III, 6, 261.

[6] §III, 4, 131. Cf., for example, E. Lipson, *The Economic History of England,* I (The Middle Ages), 221 ff., 250 ff.

[7] This analogy was first suggested to me by Dr P. F. Bloomhardt.

[8] §III, 2, 36 ff. Cf. also §III, 3, 5 ff., 11 ff.

after about 1800 B.C., when there were perhaps even more violent disruptions of caravaneering, the donkey caravaneers were forced into other occupations in order to exist. Among available means of gaining a livelihood were banditry, service as mercenaries, and more peaceful activities such as peddling and viniculture.[1] But donkey caravaneers continued to ply their ancient trade in the Amarna period,[2] and their mode of life is still described in the Song of Deborah from the twelfth century B.C.[3] It is interesting to note in this connexion that in the above-mentioned list of captives[4] there are five or six times as many 'Apiru as Kina'nu, 'merchants', which seems to be a very plausible ratio. It is obvious from the respective contexts that the Kina'nu were much more highly respected than the 'Apiru. Though the 'Apiru were generally just as nameless in the Amarna Letters as other people of the lower classes, we can follow the career of one 'Apiru and his apparently nameless sons. This fortunate exception is Labaya (Lab'ayu) 'the lion man', who controlled the hill country of central Palestine during the first half of the Amarna period. Characteristically, however, he is anonymous in the first letter of Shuwardata which mentions him.[5] In this letter, which probably belongs to the beginning of the reign of Amenophis IV,[6] Shuwardata writes from southern Judaea: 'The 'Apiru chief[7] has risen in arms against the lands which the god of the king, my lord, gave me, but (thy servant) has smitten him. Also let the king, my lord, know that all my brethren have abandoned me and that it is I and 'Abdi-Kheba who fight against the 'Apiru chief. And Zurata, chief of Accho, and Endaruta, chief of Achshaph

---

[1] The first three kinds of activity are well attested in our sources; viniculture as an 'Apiru occupation is known from Egyptian sources (see §III, 12, 1, 5 ff., and G. Posener in §I, 16, 166 ff.). There is additional evidence from the north-eastern Delta and a very striking parallel in Hebrew tradition (see §III, 3, 11 ff.).

[2] §I, 53. See also EA 227, 11, where the prince of Hazor writes to the king that his donkey caravan has escaped intact (§III, 2, 40). Cf. also §III, 10, 176 ff., which mentions 400 donkeys belonging to caravans of merchants which had been seized by the king of Ugarit. From this letter it follows that the current price for a caravan donkey was ten shekels.

[3] §III, 2, 43, 53.

[4] See above, p. 111.

[5] Published in §I, 50, 98 ff., 106, now listed as EA 366. For my translation see §I, 44, 487.

[6] The following excerpt contains several major changes in rendering which are explained briefly in the following notes. See §I, 18, 134 and *passim*.

[7] The expression *awil ḫapiri* must surely mean ''Apiru chief'. That it is not to be taken as collective is certainly suggested by its use twice with the following singular verb.

pretended[1] to come to my help in return for fifty chariots—
I have been robbed (!)[2]—and now they are fighting against me.'
Obviously the area menaced by the 'Apiru chief lay between later
Judaea and the Plain of Acre—which is precisely the territory
held or directly threatened by Labaya. In a later missive[3] Zurata
is again portrayed as a traitor to the king because of his friendship
with Labaya.

That the latter's beginnings were insignificant also appears in
one of the earliest letters from him to the pharaoh,[4] which was
written by a scribe so untutored that he wrote the second half of
the letter in almost pure Canaanite, obviously not knowing enough
Akkadian to translate it even into the strange jargon taught in
the schools. The truculence of Labaya's tone in writing to the
court contrasts oddly with the grovelling subservience of most
Palestinian chieftains. In another semi-literate early letter,
probably written in the 32nd year of Amenophis III,[5] he is
much more conciliatory, ending with a drastic statement of his
obedience to the king.[6] Immediately before, he writes: 'The
king has written about my father-in-law.[7] I did not know that
my father-in-law was continuing to make raids with the 'Apiru.
And truly I have delivered him into the hand of Addayu.' This
statement does not necessarily mean that the unknown father-
in-law—or Labaya himself for that matter—was not originally
an 'Apiru; it may merely be an effort to prevent the bad reputation of the latter among the Egyptian officials and the Canaanite
princes from interfering with his own ambitious plans. We read
in another letter:[8] 'I will resist my foe(s), the men who captured
the "city of god", the despoilers of my father.' The term $āl\ ili$[9]
may well refer to the temenos (sacred enclosure) of Shechem,
excavated by Sellin and Wright,[10] in which case Labaya was presumably a native of the city like Abimelech over two centuries
later. His father may even have been prince of Shechem, in

---

[1] *Šunima* can scarcely be identical with normal Amarna Akkadian *šunu-mi* in this
context, but is probably the same word as Biblical Hebrew *šōnīm* (Prov. xxiv. 21)
which seems to refer to duplicity (i.e. shifting of purpose), as understood in the
Syriac version.  [2] *bazzāku* (Hebrew *bzz*).

[3] EA 245.  [4] EA 252.  [5] EA 254.

[6] See the translation in §1, 44, 486 and Campbell's version in §1, 52, 196 ff.

[7] I see no escape from rendering *i-mu-ia* as father-in-law, corresponding to normal
Middle Babylonian *e-mu-ia*; *imišu*, 'his father-in-law', appears in EA 249 with
reference to Tagu, the father-in-law of Milkilu.

[8] EA 254, 28 ff.

[9] Contrast the renderings of the text in §1, 44, 486 and §1, 52, 196 ff.

[10] See especially §1, 52, 87 ff. and *passim*.

which case he (like Idrimi) presumably joined the 'Apiru after his father's ruin.

By one means or another Labaya was able to extend his control from the Mediterranean to the hills of Gilead and from the plain of Esdraelon to the frontiers of Jerusalem. Milkilu of Gezer and Tagu of Gath in Sharon were more or less faithful allies of his, and he kept the princes of Megiddo and Jerusalem in a perpetual state of apprehension. A son of his (?), Mut-Ba'al, became chief of Pella on the eastern side of Jordan south of Beth-shan.[1] After his violent death early in the reign of Amenophis IV, his sons continued in his footsteps and were just as fervently denounced to the king as their father had been.

Shechem appears in a letter of 'Abdi-Kheba[2] in the following passage:[3] 'And now Jerusalem—if this land does belong to the king, why like the city of Gaza[4] does it [not] concern the king? See, the land of Ginti-kirmil belongs to Tagu and (yet) the men of Gintu (Gath in Sharon) are on garrison duty in Beth-shan.[5]— Or shall we do like Labaya and [his sons who] have given the land of Shechem to the 'Apiru men?—Milkilu (of Gezer) has written to Tagu and the sons of Labaya, "As for you, go on and give all they want to the men of Keilah,[6] and let us break away from the city of Jerusalem".'

It has not infrequently been suggested that the episode apparently referred to here may also be reflected in the tradition of Gen. xxxiv. This is possible, especially since the events alluded to[7] probably include the capture and plundering of the city. And yet we cannot go beyond the possibility of such a connexion. It is clear, however, that the Hebrews of central Palestine gained the upper hand in Shechem about this time and that they still held it at the time of the Israelite conquest, over a century later.[8]

---

[1] §1, 52, 205 ff. Judging from Schroeder's copy of the Berlin original, the reading *La-ab-aya* is virtually certain. [2] EA 289, 14 ff.

[3] For a recent translation see my rendering in §1, 44, 489, and Campbell's still later in §1, 52, 200 ff. The following translation shows a number of significant changes in detail.

[4] Gaza was held by an Egyptian governor and was the administrative capital of Palestine at that time, as we know from the Ta'anach and Amarna letters.

[5] The mound of Beth-shan was then occupied by an Egyptian fortress. 'Abdi-Kheba's point seems to be that the Egyptians trusted Tagu sufficiently to man the fortress with his subjects.

[6] The men of Keilah were followers of Shuwardata, whose capital was probably at Hebron. The use of such an expression for the followers of Shuwardata seems to be rather contemptuous. At the end of line 26 we should read *ṣa-mi at-tu-nu*, 'as for you, go on'.

[7] In EA 254. [8] See §1, 52, 139 ff.

# CHAPTER XXI (*a*)

## ANATOLIA FROM SHUPPILULIUMASH TO THE EGYPTIAN WAR OF MUWATALLISH

### I. THE RESTORATION OF HITTITE POWER

THE condition in which Shuppiluliumash found the Hittite country when he began to take part in state affairs as crown prince and as military leader is summarized by a Hittite historiographer in a dry but impressive enumeration. He states that on every frontier the enemies of Khatti were attacking. The Kaska people (in the north) had invaded the Khatti Land proper and occupied Nenashsha; they had burned down the capital Khattusha itself. The people of Arzawa (in the south-west) had invaded the Lower Land and occupied Tuwanuwa and Uda; the Azzians (in the east) had invaded the Upper Lands and occupied Shamukha. Smaller inroads had been made by raids from Arawanna (in the north-west) and from Ishuwa and Armatana (in the south-east); they had reached respectively the country of Kashshiya and the country of Tegarama and the city of Kizzuwadna (i.e. Comana Cappadociae).[1] In other words, the Hittite realm had been severely trimmed around the edges and reduced to its very core. All the outlying dependencies—not only in Syria but also in Asia Minor—had been lost.

Shuppiluliumash had already as crown prince succeeded in stabilizing the situation during the later part of the reign of Tudkhaliash, his father. He had led the Hittite armies skilfully and successfully and had restored the frontier, particularly in the north and in the east.[2] After his accession to the throne he continued these activities with increasing vigour.

In the east the country of Azzi required close attention.[3] Not only had the relationship of that country (also called Khayasha) to Khatti to be regularized for its own sake, this was also necessary as a preliminary to re-establishing the Hittite position in Syria which must have been in the prince's mind already then. His campaign

---

\* An original version of this chapter was published in fascicle 37 in 1965.

[1] G, 2, VI, 28, obv. 6 ff.; §1, 2, 21 ff.

[2] Above, ch. XVII, sect. IV.

[3] §1, 4, frgms. 10 and 13.

(or campaigns) in the east of Anatolia, the details of which escape us, culminated in the treaty with Khukkanash of Khayasha-Azzi and his chieftains, the text of which has come down to us.[1]

The Kaska people, who, since their first appearance during the Old Kingdom in the days of Khantilish, the son of Murshilish I, had incessantly harassed the districts along the northern border, and who were the most dangerous of the enemies enumerated in the just-quoted text, must have caused the Hittites no small worries. It was fortunate that they were loosely organized and, as is occasionally stated, did not possess the institution of kingship.[2] Being mostly swineherds and weavers[3] they were considered as inferior by the Hittites. Nevertheless, they had seriously interrupted important state-cults, above all in the city of Nerik, cutting off that city from the capital. A prayer of Arnuwandash I and his queen Ashmu-Nikkal, composed about half a century before Shuppiluliumash, vividly shows the inconveniences and distress which this caused the responsible leaders.[4] The capital Khattusha itself was within striking distance of the border and had—as mentioned before—just been raided when Shuppiluliumash began to reign.

The summaries of his achievements which we possess state that it took him twenty years to restore the northern frontier as it had existed before.[5] The length of this 'war' alone illustrates the effort that had to be exerted. There is hardly any doubt that it was guerrilla warfare[6] in which success and failure quickly alternated. The long absence of the king in Syria and the ensuing weakness of the Hittites in their home country aggravated the situation. In the circumstances, it is not surprising that the town of Tumanna had to be abandoned to the Kaska people, and that the Hittite troops in Pala under the command of Khutupiyanzash, the governor of that province, were barely able to hold their own.[7]

The Arzawa Lands—Arzawa in the narrower sense, Mira-Kuwaliya, Khapalla, Shekha-River Land—filling the west of Asia Minor were independent during most of his reign. This is best illustrated by the fact that Tarkhunda-radu of Arzawa corresponded with Amenophis III and could discuss with him marriage questions as they were customary between equals.[8] This, of course, does not mean that Shuppiluliumash did not try to assert his influence in the Arzawa Lands; he certainly did. According to his

[1] §1, 1, vol. 11, 103 ff.    [2] G, 2, 111, 4, iii, 74 f.; §11, 5, 88 f.
[3] G, 1, xxiv, 3, ii, 39; §1, 3, 28 f.    [4] G, 1, xvii, 21 (see G, 6, 399 f.).
[5] See above, p. 16.    [6] §1, 4, frgms. 10–14.
[7] G, 2, v, 8, ii, 8 ff.; §11, 5, 152 ff.    [8] G, 3, 1 = G, 4, 31; §1, 5, 334.

annals he campaigned, probably based on Tuwanuwa, in Kha-palla.[1] In connexion with Wilusa—a country on the (northern) fringes of Arzawa—it is stated that the Arzawa Land (in the nar-rower sense) revolted while Wilusa under Kukkunnish remained loyal. The Arzawa Land was subjugated.[2] It seems obvious, then, that Wilusa had a common border with the Khatti Land and that a treaty regulating the relationship of at least Wilusa with the Hittite king must have existed. In other words, the Hittites were more successful in the north-west than in the south-west.

Toward the end of the Great King's reign, when he was fully occupied with the 'Hurrian War', the Arzawa Lands again re-volted. The southern Arzawa front was then guarded by Khanut-tish, the governor of the Lower Land;[3] on the northern Arzawa front Wilusa again kept true to its obligations.[4] It was probably then that Uhha-zitish of Arzawa—who in the meantime must have replaced Tarkhunda-radu—entered into relations with the country of Ahhiyawa.

The latter, met from now on again and again as a main western adversary of the Hittites, makes at this point its first appearance in history. Its identity has been much discussed with little positive result.[5] The similarity in name with that of the Achaeans is not sufficient reason to seek its capital in Mycenae, as has been done. The texts we possess furnish no valid argument for looking out-side of Asia Minor. If Ahhiyawa, then, is an Anatolian country, the chances are in favour of a location in the north-western part of the peninsula.

Uhha-zitish of Arzawa persuaded the city of Millawanda to make also a bid for independence and to seek likewise the support of Ahhiyawa.[6] The neighbouring country of Mira became, prob-ably at the same time, restive. Mashkhuiluwash of Mira rejected a suggestion on the part of his brothers to join the revolt and as a result had to flee to the Hittite court. He was well received: he married the king's daughter Muwattish and was promised re-instatement in his principality. Shuppiluliumash, however, was too deeply engaged in Syrian affairs to fulfil his promise.[7] In the Shekha-River Land things had developed in a similar manner. Here Manapa-Tattash had been driven into exile by his brothers

[1] §1, 4, frgms. 18–20.  [2] §1, 1, vol. 11, 42 ff. (sect. 3).
[3] G, 1, XIX, 22.  [4] §1, 1, vol. 11, 42 ff. (sect. 4).
[5] Selected bibliography below (pp. 931 f.) as Appendix.
[6] G, 1, XIV, 15, i, 23 ff.; §11, 5, 36 ff.; cf. 232 ff.
[7] G, 1, XIV, 15, iv, 38 ff. (see §11, 5, 72 f.); G, 1, IV, 4, iv, 56 ff. (see §11, 5, 140 ff.; also §1, 1, vol. 1, 95 ff., sect. 2).

and found a refuge in Karkisha where Hittite influence protected
him.[1] He eventually returned to his country. Mashkhuiluwash of
Mira was later used by Murshilish, successor to Shuppiluliumash,
when he reasserted Hittite power in that part of Asia Minor.

There is no doubt that the endless campaigning in Syria, first
against Tushratta and later against the Egyptians, the Assyrians
and whatever other forces tried to resist the Hittite conquest,
taxed the king's resources to the utmost. At the end of his reign,
to be sure, Syria was firmly in his hands, but home affairs, both
political and religious, had been sorely neglected. On the political
side, even the cults of the main goddess of the country 'who
regulated kingship and queenship' were not properly attended to.[2]
When death came to the king, all the outlying countries revolted;
besides Arzawa, the list[3] includes Kizzuwadna (in one copy of the
respective text its name has been erased, however, and, in fact, his
successor held it firmly in his possession), and Mitanni (i.e. the
part of it that had been restored to Kurtiwaza[4] and his descendants),
furthermore Arawana and Kalashma in the north-west of Asia
Minor, Lukka and Pitashsha in its centre, and above all the
Kaska people in the north. To judge from the troubles encountered
by his successor in his attempts at making his empire secure, the
general state of affairs at the king's death was no less serious than
it had been at the time of his accession to the throne.

## II. THE HITTITE EMPIRE UNDER MURSHILISH

Immediate successor to Shuppiluliumash was his son Arnuwandash.[5] The potentially dangerous situation created by the death
of the conqueror was aggravated by the circumstances that the
new king was seriously ill and, therefore, could not demand the
authority which was needed. Syria, on possession of which the
Hittite claim for world leadership rested, was naturally the critical
danger spot. Arnuwandash made haste to confirm his brother
Piyashilish as king of Carchemish and also appointed him to the
position of the *tuḫkantiš* (a high rank in the government).[6] He
was apparently the mainstay of Hittite domination in the provinces
south of the Taurus, and is known from then on by the (Hurrian)
name Sharre-Kushukh.[7] With some justification one may consider
it fortunate that the reign of Arnuwandash was only of short

[1] §1, 1, vol. II, 1 ff. (sect. 1).          [2] G, 2, III, 4, i, 16 ff.; §II, 5, 20 f.
[3] G, 1, XXIV, 4, obv. 17; §1, 3, 28 f.     [4] See above, p. 19.
[5] G, 2, III, 4, i, 3 ff.; §II, 5, 14 f.; G, 2, XII, 33.
[6] G, 2, I, 28; §II, 3, fasc. 1/2, 101.      [7] §1, 4, 120 f.

duration. Murshilish,[1] a younger son of Shuppiluliumash, who now assumed kingship, was still very young but in the full possession of his powers. He proved himself an extremely able and energetic ruler.

When he ascended the throne, the Lower Lands, the province on the Anatolian plateau guarding the frontier toward the Arzawa lands, were administered by Khanuttish.[2] Unfortunately, he also died immediately after the accession of Murshilish. This resulted in a precarious situation on this frontier too; it was counteracted by the despatch of reinforcements to the new governor (whose name remains unknown).[3]

In Syria interference from the side of the Assyrians was feared. One might have expected that Ashur-uballit would choose the change over for an attack. To forestall any untoward developments Murshilish strengthened the hand of Sharre-Kushukh, his brother, the king of Carchemish. He assigned to him another army under the command of Nuwanzash.[4] The Assyrian attack did not materialize, but no doubt the Mitanni state as it had been restored for Kurtiwaza fell into Assyrian hands. The claim of Ashur-uballit that he 'scattered the hosts of the far-flung country of the Subarians' (i.e. the Mitannians)[5] seems quite justified. It was this conquest that entitled him to assume the title of 'Great King'.[6]

Egypt might have made the situation still more embarrassing for the Hittites. However, it never seriously entered the strategic picture. It is safe to assume that it had not sufficiently recovered as yet from the strife that followed after Amenophis IV and the restoration under Horemheb.

The efforts of the first ten years of Murshilish were concentrated upon the reassertion of Hittite power, mainly in Asia Minor. His main object was the subjugation of Arzawa (south-western Asia Minor). But, before he could devote himself to his great task, he had to secure his rear. In other words he had first to punish the unruly and rebellious Kaska people.[7] This was accomplished during the first two years and part of the third year of his reign. Only then Murshilish felt sufficiently prepared for the attack on Arzawa.[8]

His main adversary was Uhha-zitish of Arzawa; he had aligned with himself most of the other Arzawa states: Khapalla, Mira-

---

[1] For the rest of this section see mainly §11, 5.
[2] G, 1, xix, 29, iv, 11 ff.; §11, 5, 19.    [3] G, 1, xix, 22.
[4] G, 1, xiv, 16, i, 13 ff.; §11, 5, 26 f.    [5] §11, 2, 56 f.
[6] G, 4, 16.        [7] §11, 5, 22 ff.    [8] §11, 5, 44 ff.

Kuwaliya, and the Shekha-River Land. Wilusa, it seems, once more
—as under Shuppiluliumash—remained loyal to the Great King.
But Uhha-zitish had previously persuaded the city Millawanda—
apparently an important centre—to desert the Hittites and to seek
the protection of the king of Ahhiyawa. Hence a preliminary step
taken by Murshilish was an expedition against Millawanda; it
was successfully carried through.

In the third year the main expedition could then begin. For it
Sharre-Kushukh, the king of Carchemish, joined Murshilish with
a corps from Syria. The opposing forces of the Arzawa people
were led by Piyama-Inarash, a son of Uhha-zitish; the latter had
entrusted the command to him because of ill health. Murshilish
defeated him in a battle near Walma on the River Ashtarpa.
Pursuing the fleeing enemy he entered Apasha, the capital of
Arzawa. But Uhha-zitish, he found, had fled 'across the Sea'.

This left two centres of resistance to be dealt with: the mountain
fortresses of Arinnanda and of Puranda. The former was captured
before the third year came to a close; the latter had to be left for
the next year. For the time being the Hittite king retreated to the
river Ashtarpa and established camp there for the winter; the
Syrian corps, it seems, went home.

When the season suitable for the resumption of warfare arrived,
the final attack against Puranda was mounted. During the winter
Uhha-zitish of Arzawa had died, but Tapalazanaulish, another of
his sons, had organized resistance. When asked to surrender he
declined, an assault was launched; it resulted soon in the fall of the
fortress. Tapalazanaulish escaped and sought refuge with the king
of Ahhiyawa. It seems that Murshilish demanded his extradition
and that it was granted. If so, we must assume that between the
Hittites and Ahhiyawa a treaty existed which made provisions for
the extradition of fugitives.

Thus Murshilish emerged as the victor over Arzawa. The
princes of the other Arzawa states drew quickly the consequences
and surrendered without further resistance. Both Targashnallish
of Khapalla and Manapa-Tattash of the Shekha-River Land were
generously treated and reinstated as Hittite vassals. The affairs of
Mira, long unattended to, were also settled when Murshilish
passed through on his way home; the new ruler was to be Mashkhuiluwash, who, since his flight to Shuppiluliumash, had fought
on the Hittite side.[1] The treaties which at that time were concluded
with Manapa-Tattash[2] and Targashnallish[3] are preserved. What

[1] §1, 1, vol. 1, 95 ff. (sect. 2 f.).
[2] §1, 1, vol. 11, 1 ff.          [3] §1, 1, vol. 1, 51 ff.

provisions were made with the Arzawa Land proper is unknown; since it is later found in the Hittite camp, the assumption seems safe that a willing member of the Arzawa dynasty swore an oath of allegiance to Murshilish.

The fifth, sixth, and probably also seventh years again required the king's presence on the Kaskean frontier.[1] Beginning with the seventh year, operations shifted to Azzi-Khayasha in the far east of Anatolia.[2] Before Anniya, king there, could be dealt with decisively, grave complications arose. The beginning of the ninth year[3] brought alarming news from Syria: the Nukhash Lands and Kinza had revolted. Suspicion seems justified that Egypt, now firmly reorganized under Horemheb, was behind the unrest. Sharre-Kushukh, the Hittite viceroy in Syria, had to invoke the treaty with Niqmaddu of Ugarit and ask for military help from him.[4] At the same time the enemy from Khayasha had invaded the Upper Land, taken the town Ishtitina and laid siege to Kannuwara. Murshilish himself was obliged to go to Kumanni in order to perform long-delayed religious duties. Sharre-Kushukh was able to restore order in Syria sufficiently so that he could come up and join his brother, the Great King, in Kumanni. However, he fell ill there and died quite unexpectedly. With him Murshilish lost his ablest helper, also the man to whom the task of protecting Syria would naturally have fallen.

His death was the signal for new disturbances in Syria. More serious still, it moved the Assyrians to make an attack on Carchemish. Thus Murshilish was faced with weighty decisions of a military kind. He finally dispatched the general Nuwanzash to take command on the Khayasha front and sent another general Inarash to deal with the Nukhash Lands and with Kinza. He himself went to Ashtata on the Euphrates, and Inarash was ordered to meet him there on his return. They both were then to go together to Aleppo and Carchemish.[5]

Matters went according to plan. The Syrian rebels were punished. It was at that time that Aitakama of Kinza who had played a part in Syrian affairs during the days of Shuppiluliumash[6] met his death. He had revolted, it seems, because he saw a chance for regaining his independence. However, his son Ari-Teshub (*NÍG.BA-Teššub*) opposed his father's step and had him murdered. Ari-Teshub was brought back by the victorious general to face Murshilish, who had in the meantime reached Ashtata; he was

[1] §II, 5, 76 ff.   [2] §II, 5, 96 ff.
[3] §II, 5, 108 ff.   [4] §II, 9, 53 ff.
[5] §II, 5, 110 ff.   [6] See above, pp. 15 f.

reinstalled by the Great King as the prince of Kinza.[1] Murshilish then went to Carchemish and installed there [. . .]-Sharruma, the son of Sharre-Kushukh, his dead brother. At the same time Talmi-Sharruma, a son of Telepinush, was made king in Aleppo.[2] The treaty concluded with the latter has survived.[3] It is noteworthy that Carchemish, at that time, had clearly overtaken Aleppo as the most important centre of Hittite power in Syria. It was the king of Carchemish who played the role of something like a viceroy of Syria.

It was probably then that Murshilish confirmed Niqmepa, the king of Ugarit. He renewed with him the treaty which his father Shuppiluliumash had concluded with Niqmaddu, Niqmepa's father. The new treaty contains a detailed description of the frontier between Ugarit and Mukish.[4]

While Murshilish was in Syria, Nuwanzash in the north had accomplished his mission. The king of Khayasha who had invaded the Upper Land had been forced to retreat and the siege of Kan-nuwara lifted. The way for a campaign against Khayasha was thus free. However, the season was too far advanced for any serious operation in this mountainous region. Therefore, only small raids were executed and a larger campaign prepared for the coming spring.[5] The king's tenth year passed before Khayasha was brought to its knees.[6] Although its actual submission did not take place before his eleventh year, the Great King could consider the task of reasserting himself as completed with the end of the tenth year. The so-called 'Ten-year Annals'[7] depict matters in this light.

It would be untrue to assume that Murshilish was saved the necessity of making incessant efforts through the rest of his reign for maintaining the position he had won. In fact it is known that in his twelfth year a new uprising in the Arzawa lands took place. It was instigated by a man named *É.GAL.KUR* (Hittite reading unknown)[8] about whom nothing further is known, but who may well have been a successor of Uhha-zitish and Piyama-Inarash. Mashkhuiluwash of Mira-Kuwaliya was implicated and had to flee when Murshilish undertook a punitive expedition. Kupanta-Inarash, his adopted son, who, on the occasion of his father's first feoffment, had been designated crown-prince became his successor. The text of the treaty concluded with him is known.[9]

It is very likely that here again, as before,[10] the king of Ahhi-

[1] §II, 5, 120 f.
[2] §II, 5, 124 f.
[3] §II, 11, 80 ff.
[4] §II, 9, 59 ff.
[5] §II, 5, 124 ff.
[6] §II, 5, 130 ff.
[7] G, 1, III, 4; §II, 5, 14 ff.
[8] §I, 1, vol. 1, 128 f.
[9] §I, 1, vol. 1, 95 ff.
[10] See above, p. 119.

yawa played a sinister role in the background. It is certain that he pretended to be an equal of the Great King of the Khatti Land; one also has the impression that the power of Ahhiyawa was on the upswing. This is important for the overall view. For it indicates that the Hittite kings had, from this time on, to be alert to developments in the west also. As though it had not been enough of a strain to keep a constant eye on Egypt and Assyria!

The Euphrates frontier was far from being stable. The pressure from the Assyrians was incessant and their attempts at conquering as much of the former Mitannian territory as they could never slackened. If Murshilish was to continue the role in world politics on which his father had embarked he had no choice but to maintain a firm hold on Syria. As before, much of the burden fell upon the ruler of Carchemish, now Shakhurunuwash, another son of Sharre-Kushukh.

One can also discern a tendency to curtail the power of the Syrian vassals as though the overlord was not entirely certain of their loyalty. The secession of Siyanni from Ugarit, which halved the territory controlled by Niqmepa, was recognized by the Hittite overlord and Shiyanni was placed under supervision from Carchemish.[1] When Abirattash of Barga raised old claims to the city of Yaruwanda against the Nukhash Land, the case was decided in favour of the former. He was thereby rewarded for the support he had given the Hittite king when Nukhash had risen against him.[2] The Hittites adhered, wherever the occasion presented itself, to a policy of *divide et impera*.

Further south Amurru developed into a champion of Hittite domination. The fact that the once so unruly Aziru, now rather advanced in age, had remained true to his oath of loyalty[3] when Nukhash and Kinza revolted, must have been a source of satisfaction to Murshilish. He reaffirmed his friendship with Amurru by installing Aziru's son *DU*-Teshub as his successor and soon thereafter also his grandson Tuppi-Teshub.[4]

It is quite possible, though not specifically attested, that Murshilish undertook himself another campaign in Upper Mesopotamia or at least sent one of his generals there. Muwatallish, his successor on the Hittite throne, counts Mitanni as one of his vassal states. It seems to have been regained from the Assyrians in the preceding reign.

What we possess of annals from the later years of Murshilish—

[1] §II, 9, 71 ff.          [2] §II, 1; §II, 4, 19 ff.; §II, 7.
[3] §I, 1, vol. I, 1 ff.    [4] §I, 1, vol. I, 1 ff. (sect. 3 f.).

it is unfortunately incomplete[1]—does not relate any large-scale military operations anywhere. In quite detailed manner it speaks about never-ending guerrilla warfare on the Kaskean frontier. These expeditions were routine to the king and had the nature of police actions. If considerable space was given to them in the royal annals it seems to indicate that nothing of greater importance was to report. Later on, we find firm military control established all along the Kaskean border, a veritable *limes*.[2] We do not know who first built it, but since from the time of Murshilish onwards the scheme worked with some measure of success, we may infer it was he who initiated it.

In a long reign Murshilish succeeded in firmly organizing the empire which he had inherited from his father. As in the days of Shuppiluliumash it spread from the Lebanon and the Euphrates in the south to the mountains of Pontus in the north and to the western reaches of Asia Minor. It was a continental power in the sense that it only accidentally, so to speak, reached the sea, and certainly did not extend beyond it. The negative fact should be stressed that the island of Cyprus—Alashiya[3] as it was then called —did not form part of the Hittite realm. Its kings had corresponded as independent rulers with Amenophis IV, and it served as asylum for all those who, in danger of their lives, had to flee from the continent.

Little is known about the internal affairs of the Hittite Empire during the reign of Murshilish. Worthy of note is his conflict with Tawannannash, last queen of Shuppiluliumash. She had survived her husband and was reigning queen also during the first part of the following reign. She was accused of various offences, above all of having caused the death of the young king's wife by black magic. The incident is mentioned in prayers which seek to determine the reasons for divine anger and the ensuing misfortune.[4] There seems to have been some doubt as to whether the steps taken against Tawannannash had been entirely legitimate. The affair had political overtones, since Tawannannash was originally a Babylonian princess.[5]

A word remains to be said about the chronology of the reign of Murshilish. Its beginning is approximately fixed by the death of his father Shuppiluliumash, which took place several years after that of Tutankhamun (*c.* 1352), i.e., about 1346.[6] The preserved parts of the annals of Murshilish justify the assumption that his reign covered more—and probably not much more—than twenty-

---

[1] §11, 5, 146 ff.          [2] §11, 10, 36 ff.          [3] G, 4, 33–39.
[4] §11, 6, vol. 1, 12 ff.; §11, 8, 101 ff.     [5] See above, p. 13.     [6] See above, p. 19.

two years.  If we estimate that it lasted about twenty-five years, we come down for its end to about 1320, or a few years before that. The Syrian campaign of the pharaoh Sethos I may fall in the very end of his reign, or when his son Muwatallish had recently succeeded him.

## III. ASIA MINOR UNDER MUWATALLISH

The sources at our disposal for the reign of Muwatallish are rather poor.  Moreover, they are most of them not impartial toward the king.  Much of the little we do know must be culled from the texts of Khattushilish, his younger brother and rival,[1] which make it abundantly clear that he had personal ambitions irreconcilable with the position held by his brother.  The information thus gathered hardly does justice to Muwatallish.  At least it gives a one-sided picture which belittles the king's achievements and unduly stresses those of the younger brother.

At first the relations between the brothers were cordial.  As soon as Muwatallish assumed kingship, he made his brother not only Great Majordomo (*GAL ME-ŠE-DI*) but also field-marshal of the Hittite armies.  In addition he appointed him governor of the Upper Land which included the important town Shamukha.  In this capacity Khattushilish replaced Arma-Tattash, who as the son of Zidash, a former Great Majordomo, was cousin to the late king. The power thus vested in the prince was quite extraordinary.  No wonder then that his enemies—and above all Arma-Tattash and his friends—grew envious and denounced him to the king; they asserted that Khattushilish nursed ambitious plans, in fact aspired himself to the kingship over the Khatti Land.  Whatever truth might have resided in such accusations, Muwatallish trusted his brother and rejected them as malicious slander.

As field-marshal of the Hittite armies Khattushilish claims to have conducted numerous campaigns for his brother, both offensively and defensively.  Nothing specific is known of these military activities, but, as far as we can see, they were limited to the northern frontier area where Khattushilish ruled as governor.  Later in the reign of Muwatallish, when the Great King personally undertook a campaign to the Arzawa Lands, his brother had to concentrate his efforts on the Kaska people.  The king's absence, as was to be expected, provoked serious raids on their part.  Khattushilish speaks of ten years of warfare he had to go through.  There is every reason to believe that the unruly neighbours continued their

[1] §III, 1; 2.

harassment indefinitely, although the territory affected at one and the same time always remained small. The so-called Kaskean War can hardly have been more than an annoying series of small-scale raids and counter-raids.

Neither do we know details of the king's campaign against Arzawa, but we can at least recognize some of its results.[1] At that time the term Arzawa Lands comprised four principalities: Arzawa proper, Mira-Kuwaliya, Khapalla and Wilusa. In the end, it seems, all four of them remained Hittite dependencies, their rulers vassals of the Great King.[2] King of Arzawa was probably Piyama-Inarash, either the same person who had fought against Murshilish or a younger member of the same dynasty. In Mira-Kuwaliya the kingship was still held by Kupanta-Inarash, who had been installed by Murshilish. In Khapalla we find one Ura-Khattushash as ruler. And in Wilusa Muwatallish placed Alakshandush upon the throne; the customary treaty, then concluded, has come down to us.[3] The Shekha-River Land is no longer counted as an Arzawa Land; its legal status must have changed in the meantime. Manapa-Tattash who also had been a vassal of Murshilish was in control there when Muwatallish became king. When he died his son Mashturish succeeded him, and the Great King gave his sister in marriage to him.[4] Thus domination of the most important countries adjacent to Hittite territory was complete.

On the northern frontier, even after the successful conclusion of the Arzawa campaign, conditions remained unsettled. The Kaska must have made dangerous inroads. For Kahha, where Khattushilish, despite depleted forces, claims to have won an important victory over the Kaska people lies far to the south. He was also able, so he says, to repel a dangerous attack which had been launched from the town of Pishkhuru.[5]

While all this was going on, Muwatallish began to prepare for a major war in Syria. As will be pointed out later,[6] war in the south became inevitable when Egypt, reorganized by the pharaohs of the nineteenth dynasty, resumed its traditional policy of domination there. This test, Muwatallish foresaw, would be crucial. Wise strategist that he was, he therefore had to concentrate as many troops as he could possibly muster. With this goal in mind he saw to it that the far-flung system of fortifications which already existed along the Kaskean frontier was strengthened so that he could

---

[1] §1, 1, vol. 11, 42 ff. (sect. 6).     [2] §1, 1, vol. 11, 42 ff. (sect. 17).
[3] §1, 1, vol. 11, 42 ff.
[4] G, 1, xxiii, 3, 1, ii, 14 ff. (see §iii, 3).
[5] §iii, 1, 16 ff.     [6] Below, ch. xxiv, sect. 1.

withdraw most of his troops from the area. As a precautionary measure he moved his capital from Khattusha, which was considered too close to the border, to Tattashsha and had the state deities and also the *manes* of the royal family brought there for safe-keeping. In the north Khattushilish was left in command. To the territory which he had administered so far the whole frontier zone—largely devastated and depopulated—was added, including Palā and Tumanna. Furthermore, he was made king in Khakpish, the territory of which included the important cult centre of Zippalanda, a town holy to a Storm-god who, as the son of the Sun-goddess of Arinna, was highly venerated. The power of Khattushilish, very considerable before, was thus still further increased, and no doubt he was now the most powerful man in the Khatti Land, second only to the Great King himself. After the Syrian campaign, in which Khattushilish took part as a military commander of the army contingent raised in his province for the event, his prestige rose further by his marriage to Pudu-Kheba, the daughter of Bentibsharre, the local king of Lawazantiya.[1]

Khattushilish was doubtless ambitious; the power he had accumulated might have led a lesser man into temptation. Thus a situation had been created which led to internal strife soon afterwards.

[1] §III, 1, 18 ff.

# CHAPTER XXI(*b*)

## UGARIT

### IV. UGARIT IN THE FOURTEENTH AND THIRTEENTH CENTURIES B.C.

In previous chapters, frequent reference has been made to the city of Ugarit, the North Syrian coastal town whose site, the modern Ras Shamra, meaning 'Fennel Cape', is situated some seven miles north of Latakia. More is known about Ugarit during the two centuries before her downfall, in about 1200 B.C., than about any other Syrian city of the second millennium. The reasons are twofold. First, whereas most excavators of ancient mounds in Syria have been forced to concentrate on the central area only, where public buildings were likely to be found, at Ras Shamra over two-thirds of the site have been systematically explored, and the nearby port installation has also been uncovered. Secondly, a wealth of documentary evidence is becoming available with the gradual publication of some thousands of tablets found in private and public buildings in various parts of the city.[1] Some of these tablets are the letters and memoranda of merchants and private individuals, written in the local dialect and script;[2] others deal with matters of domestic administration: lists of towns and country districts, for instance, furnishing contributions to the government in the form of silver, produce or *corvée* labour, lists of bowmen and slingmen, or payrolls and tax receipts. There are diplomatic archives written in Akkadian, the language of international intercourse,[3] and legal texts which are for the most part also in Akkadian. Large tablets in Ugaritic contain mythological and liturgical texts, invaluable for our knowledge of Canaanite[4] religion, and there are lists of offerings and omen texts for the use of priests. Glossaries and lexicographical

---

* An original version of this chapter was published as fascicle 63 in 1968; the present chapter includes revisions made in 1973.

[1] §iv, 30; §iv, 44; §iv, 30; A, 19.

[2] §iv, 11, 63 ff.; *C.A.H.* ii³, pt. 1, pp. 506 ff.      [3] *C.A.H.* ii³, pt. 1, p. 468.

[4] The extension of the term 'Canaanite' to include the North-West Semitic peoples of the Syro-Palestinian littoral in the second millennium B.C. needs no excuse (§v, 44, 16), though it should perhaps more properly be applied to the inhabitants of the Egyptian province Kanaʻan (§iv, 31, 105 f.)

texts for scholastic use, and tablets in Hurrian,[1] Hittite[2] and Cypro-Mycenaean,[3] are also included in the miscellany.

The importance of these archaeological and textual discoveries may, it is hoped, justify the present attempt to trace briefly the part played by one of the richest and most powerful cities in the Near East during the latter part of the Bronze Age, in spite of the fact that in doing so, some repetition of historical narrative becomes inevitable.

The kingdom of Ugarit possessed many natural advantages which her rulers turned to good effect. Augmented, thanks to the good sense and careful diplomacy of King Niqmaddu, by territory in the hinterland taken from Mukish,[4] it included a long stretch of fertile coastal plain, hills clad with olive groves and vine terraces, and thickly wooded mountains; behind, the steppe afforded both grazing and hunting.[5] The thirty odd miles of its coastline contained at least four ports,[6] that of Ugarit itself—the bay today called Mīnet el-Beidha, the 'White Harbour'—being capable of accommodating ships of a considerable size.[7] The most southerly port was probably Shuksi, the modern Tell Sūkās, south of Jebeleh, where a tablet in the Ugaritic script has been found.[8] Ugarit, situated as she was at the intersection of land and sea routes, was destined from the beginning to become a commercial power. Within easy sailing distance of Cyprus and the Cilician coast, and the most northerly of the chain of ports which served coastal traffic to the Lebanon, Palestine and Egypt, she was the natural link between the Aegean world and the Levant. Ships from Beirut and Byblos and Tyre,[9] from Alashiya, and from far-away *Kptr* or Crete (the Biblical Caphtor)[10] and *Ḥkpt*, which is usually associated with it,[11] unloaded their cargoes at her ports. She also commanded the caravan route from the coast through the 'Amūq plain to Aleppo, and thence by way of Emar and Carchemish to join the riverine Euphrates route to Babylonia or the road eastwards to Assyria by way of the Upper Khabur region.[12] Another road ran northwards through the territory of Mukish to the Beilān pass, giving access to central Anatolia.[13]

[1] §IV, 44, vol. 5, 447 ff.    [2] *Ibid.* 769 ff.    [3] *Ibid.* vol. 3, 227 ff.
[4] §IV, 30, vol. 4, 11 ff., 48 ff.; §IV, 10, 261 ff.; A, 4, 398 ff.
[5] §IV, 44, vol. 2, 17; §IV, 30, vol. 2, xxxviii f.    [6] §IV, 7, 255; A, 20, vol. 3, 6 f.
[7] §v, 55, 165; A, 28; §IV, 44, vol. 1, pl. viii. Miss Honor Frost (*ibid.* vol. 6, 235 ff.) estimates, from the size of stone anchors found, that some Ugaritic ships were of at least 200 tons.    [8] §IV, 33, 215; A, 15, 538 no. 502; A, 27, 4.    [9] §IV, 7, 253.
[10] §IV, 30, vol. 3, 107 = *RS.*16.238.
[11] §v, 25, 169; §v, 77, 192 f.; §IV, 30, vol. 2, 162 = *RS.*16.399, l. 26.
[12] *C.A.H.* I³, pt. 2, p. 333.    [13] §IV, 56, 20.

In addition to her activity in middleman trade, Ugarit was herself a centre of considerable industrial activity and exported her products far and wide. Metal workers had their foundries in the port district and in the town,[1] and the fine bronze weapons and vessels they turned out were in more than local demand.[2] Linen and wool, obtained from the large flocks of sheep and goats grazed in the hinterland, were dyed red-purple or blue-violet[3] in the same quarter, where heaps of crushed murex shells were found,[4] and made into bales or finished garments for export.[5] Merchantmen carried grain to Alashiya and Cilicia, and olive oil, produced in commercial quantity in large presses,[6] was shipped abroad in amphorae, some of which were found in the quay warehouses.[7] The wine of Ugarit, too, was exported,[8] and salt from the numerous salt-pans along the coast,[9] while fine woods, such as box and juniper,[10] as well as the coarser pine,[11] were in demand. A flourishing trade in scented oils and cosmetics is attested by the presence in Ras Shamra of locally made containers of ivory and alabaster modelled on Egyptian originals,[12] perhaps because Egypt was the original home of the industry.

Little is known of the early history of the kingdom of Ugarit. The city was already flourishing in the eighteenth century B.C., and on a tablet from the palace,[13] unfortunately much damaged, the names of about thirty of the deified kings of Ugarit are listed in two columns, the first of which ends with YQR, perhaps the 'Yaqaru son of Niqmaddu' whose dynastic seal, in the style of the Old Babylonian period, was treasured by later kings of the dynasty as an heirloom and employed to give ancient authority to their decrees.[14] Either Yaqaru or Niqmaddu may have been the unnamed ruler of Ugarit who wrote to the king of Aleppo expressing his desire to visit Mari in order to see for himself the renowned palace which Zimrilim, the king of Mari, had built.[15] The foundations of a large building, probably a palace, of the Middle

---

[1] §IV, 30, vol. 2, xxxiv ff.  [2] §IV, 7, 253; A, 34.
[3] A, 11, 231 ff.  [4] §IV, 30, vol. 2, xxvi, pl. xiv; §IV, 35, 38; §IV, 36, 2.
[5] §IV, 44, vol. 4, 142 = *RS*. 19.28. See *C.A.H.* II³, pt. 1, pp. 510 f.
[6] §IV, 44, vol. 4, 421, figs. 6, 7; §IV, 30, vol. 5, 117 f. = *RS*.18.42.
[7] §IV, 44, vol. 1, 30 f., pl. IX.  [8] §V, 66, 44.
[9] §IV, 30, vol. 5, 118 f. = *RS*.18.27, 18.30.
[10] EA (the Amarna letters), 126, ll. 4–6; §IV, 26, 126 f.; §IV, 30, vol. 4, 196 = *RS*.17.385 ll. 11 ff.
[11] *C.A.H.* I³, pt, 2, pp. 346 f.
[12] §IV, 44, vol. 1, 31, figs. 21, 22.  [13] §V, 65, 214 f.
[14] §IV, 30, vol. 3, xl ff., pls. XVI, XVIII; §IV, 52, 92 ff.; §V, 63, 260 ff. Plate 136(c).
[15] §IV, 44, vol. 1, 16, n. 2, 15; *C.A.H.* II³, pt. 1, pp. 11 f.

Bronze period, were discovered in 1969;[1] many of the large ashlar blocks from this building had been re-used in the later palace.

After a long lacuna in which even the names of the dynasts are
lost, the history of the royal house of Ugarit begins in the early
fourteenth century with Ammishtamru I.[2] At this time Ugarit
was 'on the water' of Egypt, as the Egyptians themselves would
have phrased it; that is to say, within the Egyptian sphere of influence and almost certainly bound by a treaty to keep her ports
open to Egyptian shipping for both commercial and strategic
purposes. In a previous chapter[3] it has been argued that the
theory that Tuthmosis III or Amenophis II conquered Ugarit is
based on the mistaken identification of the name of an otherwise
unknown town in the Biqā' captured during the latter's return
from North Syria. It is more reasonable to suppose that during
the early part of the fifteenth century Ugarit came for a time
under the protection of Saustatar of Mitanni who, as has been
seen, controlled both Mukish and Kizzuwadna.[4] His successors
were forced to withdraw over the Euphrates, but in that age of
power politics no country could long remain neutral and un-
committed,[5] and early, perhaps, in the reign of Amenophis, or even
sooner, Ugarit must have yielded to diplomatic pressure and joined
the other cities of the east Mediterranean seaboard, some of which
had been under Egyptian control since the 1580s. Egyptian resi-
dents paid homage to the local deities; a treasury official named
Mami, who later dedicated a stele inscribed in hieroglyphics to the
city god, Ba'al S<sup>e</sup>phōn,[6] may have been stationed there to secure the
collection and dispatch of tribute due under the terms of a treaty;
the style of the carving is Ramesside.

One of the letters from Ugarit found among the Amarna correspondence bears the name of Ammishtamru.[7] In it the king
declares himself a loyal vassal of the Sun, Amenophis III, and
asks for Egyptian aid against an enemy who may be either the
neighbouring state of Amurru[8] or else perhaps the Hittite king
Shuppiluliumash,[9] whose intervention in North Syria had already
begun. Other Amarna letters from Ammishtamru or his son, Niqmaddu II, make it clear that during the lifetime of Amenophis
III Ugarit was faithful to her allegiance, a state of affairs which

[1] A, 30, 524 f.      [2] §IV, 26, 23 ff.; §IV, 30, vol. 4, 6 ff., 27 f.
[3] C.A.H. II³, pt. I, pp. 460 f.
[4] C.A.H. II³, pt. I, p. 436.      [5] §IV, 28, 110.
[6] §IV, 44, vol. I, 39 ff., 40, fig. 30; vol. 4, 133 ff. and fig. 101; §IV, 26, 31.
[7] EA 45, ll. 22 ff.; G, 4, 309 ff., 1097 ff.; §IV, 3, 30.
[8] §IV, 26, 24.      [9] §IV, 21, 34 f.; G, 4, 1098.

must go back at least to the earliest years of the pharaoh's reign, since one of the scarabs issued to commemorate his marriage with Queen Tiy in his second year was found at Ras Shamra[1] and the cartouches of the royal pair were on fragments of alabaster vases uncovered in the palace ruins.[2] Akhenaten and Nefertiti sent similar diplomatic gifts in the early years of their reign[3] and Nefertiti must have been the queen of Egypt to whom the Ugaritian queen sent a present of a pot of balm.[4] At about this time, a disaster overtook the city in which at least part of the palace, and quarters of the town, were destroyed by fire. The passage in the letter in which the king of Tyre informed Pharaoh of the news[5] is of doubtful interpretation[6] and leaves it uncertain whether the destruction of the palace was due to enemy action of some kind or whether it was rather, as the excavator himself maintains, the result of a violent earthquake of which signs can be discerned in the masonry.[7] However this may be, the damage was made good and the palace rose again, more splendid than before.[8]

At its greatest extent, in the fourteenth and thirteenth centuries, this palace covered some two and a half acres and must have been one of the largest in western Asia; its fame was great among the Canaanites; according to the king of Byblos, only the palace at Tyre could rival it in size and magnificence.[9] The original building had not been very large: it consisted essentially of an entrance hall and staircase leading to a large courtyard with rooms around it, under one of which was the royal hypogeum with three corbelled vaults.[10] As time went on, and with increasing prosperity, the administration grew more complex and the court more numerous. The palace was accordingly repeatedly enlarged and rebuilt;[11] over ninety rooms have been excavated, and there are eight entrance staircases, each with a pillared portico, and nine interior courtyards. Rooms were panelled with cedar and other precious woods, and flights of stairs led to an upper floor. In the eastern part of the palace was a large walled garden with flower beds and a pavilion,[12] and in one of the courtyards a piped water supply led to an ornamental basin.[13]

[1] §IV, 44, vol. 3, 221 ff., fig. 204.    [2] *Ibid.* vol. 4, 97; §IV, 40, 16; §IV, 37, 112.
[3] §IV, 44, vol. 3, 167, fig. 120; §IV, 38, 41; §IV, 21, 36.
[4] EA 48; G, 4, 315 ff.        [5] EA 151, ll. 55 ff.; G, 4, 625, 1251 ff.
[6] §IV, 26, 28 ff.; §IV, 1, 203; A, 20, vol. 2, 356 ff.
[7] §IV, 44, vol. 1, 35 ff. and fig. 29; §IV, 43, 9; §IV, 42, 7.
[8] §IV, 44, vol. 4, 7 ff.; §IV, 30, vol. 3, xii f.
[9] EA 89, ll. 48 f.; G, 4, 425; §IV, 44, vol. 4, 9; §IV, 4, 164.
[10] §IV, 42, 16 and fig. 8.        [11] §IV, 44, vol. 4, 9 ff. and fig. 21.
[12] *Ibid.* 15 ff.        [13] *Ibid.* 27 ff., 42, fig. 29, 47, fig. 31.

The palace was the centre of great scribal and administrative activity. Here were drawn up the contracts to which the king set his name as witness and affixed his stamp, the dynastic seal of Yaqaru. When written and sealed, the documents were taken to a bell-shaped oven in one of the courtyards for baking;[1] they were then stored, according to their category, in one of several archive rooms in various parts of the palace.[2] Most of the diplomatic correspondence was kept together, and here the scribes who could read and write Babylonian learned their craft[3] with the help of school exercises and glossaries. Some of the more important letters were translated on receipt into Ugaritic for greater convenience.[4]

Craftsmen, too, worked in the palace. Ivory was lavishly used in the decoration of furniture in the royal throne room and private apartments, and an ivory-carvers' workshop contained some fine pieces, perhaps brought for repair, including a series of panels which must have adorned the headpiece of a couch or bed.[5] A circular table-top more than a yard in diameter, elaborately fretted,[6] a carved elephant tusk[7] and a large ivory head from the chryselephantine statue of a queen or deity,[8] with inlaid eyes and curls in silver-and-gold niello work, were also among the objects found in the garden near this workshop.

The spacious houses of the well-to-do, some of them minor palaces for high officials and members of the royal family, lay grouped in large *insulae* to the east and south of the palace; that of Rap'anu, for instance, who held a high position at court, had no less than thirty-four rooms on the ground floor alone; his library contained both private and official correspondence.[9] Most of the houses were provided with bathrooms and lavatories and had a well-planned drainage system.[10] Below each was the family vault, a corbelled chamber with an arched roof in the Mycenaean manner,[11] in which the bodies of successive generations were laid on the flagged floor, surrounded by rich grave-goods—vessels of alabaster and lapis lazuli and metal, and painted pots of Aegean manufacture. Similar tombs were found in the residential quarter of the port,[12] where rich merchants had their houses and warehouses.[13] Smaller houses in the north-eastern and

[1] §IV, 44, vol. 4, 31 ff., 91, figs. 35–39.
[2] *Ibid.* 45 ff.; §IV, 30, vol. 3, xi ff.  [3] §IV, 50; §IV, 30, vol. 3, 211 ff.
[4] §IV, 44, vol 4, 91.  [5] *Ibid.* vol. 4, 17; §IV, 38, pl. VII.
[6] §IV, 44, vol. 4, 30, fig. 22; §IV, 38, 59.
[7] §IV, 38, 62 and fig. 9.  [8] §IV, 44, vol. 4, 25 f., figs. 24–6. Plate 136 (*a*).
[9] §IV, 39, 233 f.  [10] §IV, 44, vol. 4, 30, pl. VI.
[11] §IV, 44, vol. I, 30, figs. 75–80, pls. XVI, XVII; *ibid.* vol. 4, 30, pl. XVI, 2; §IV, 35, 49 ff.  [12] §IV, 44, vol. I, 30 ff. See Plate 137.  [13] §IV, 44, vol. 4, 30 f.

north-western sections of the town were densely grouped on each
side of narrow, winding streets, much like those of the older
quarters of oriental towns today.[1] The artisans' quarter was to the
south: here goldsmiths and silversmiths, seal-cutters, sculptors
and workers in bronze had their dwellings,[2] their houses grouped
around an open square overlooked on the south side by an imposing stone building which had housed a library of texts in
Babylonian cuneiform, some astrological and some literary, perhaps used for teaching purposes.[3] On the highest part of the hill
rose the two main temples, one, dedicated to the god Dagan, very
massively built, that of Ba'al being to the west of it;[4] between them
was the residence of the high priest, in which most of the large
mythological tablets in alphabetic cuneiform were found.[5] The
city was surrounded by a rampart of formidable proportions,
with a postern gate in Hittite style.[6]

Pottery models of huts[7] suggest that some of the houses, perhaps those in the surrounding villages, may have had a conical
'sugar-loaf' roof similar to those in parts of North Syria today.
Judging by the large number of town and village communities
listed for administrative purposes, the kingdom must have been
comparatively densely populated. Many different nationalities
were represented in Ugarit.[8] The official language was a local
dialect of North Canaanite, which was spoken by the largest
group among the population, but for the benefit of the large
Hurrian-speaking minority,[9] many of them soldiers and craftsmen in the king's service,[10] who maintained their identity and
their cult practices, a number of bilingual glossaries were compiled,[11] and one lexicographical tablet from Rap'anu's library contains equivalents in no less than four languages: Hurrian,
Ugaritic, Sumerian and Babylonian.[12] Akkadian legal terms, too,
were translated into Hurrian for administrative purposes.[13] The
presence of Minoan and, at a later date, Mycenaean colonists at
Ugarit has been inferred[14] from the numerous figurines and fine
pottery vessels, some in the Cretan 'palace' style, found in the
tombs together with local imitations of such objects.[15] Tablets in

[1] §IV, 39, 235.     [2] §V, 65, 206 ff.     [3] §IV, 39, 235; §IV, 30, vol. 3, fig. 21.
[4] §V, 64, 154 ff. and pl. 36.     [5] §IV, 11, 63; §IV, 20, 7 ff.
[6] §V, 67, 289 ff., pls. XLII, XLIII, figs. 12, 13. See Plate 104.
[7] §IV, 44, vol. 2, 194 f., fig. 79 and pl. XXX.     [8] A, 16, 4 f.
[9] §IV, 44, vol. 1, 28; vol. 4, 51, 83 f.; §V, 76, 24.     [10] A, 10, 188 ff.
[11] §V, 52; §IV, 44, vol. IV, 87, 136, fig. 119; §IV, 30, vol. III, 311 = RS.13.10.
[12] §IV, 44, vol. 4, 87 = RS.20.123+149.     [13] §IV, 50, 264; §IV, 44, vol. 1, 28 f.
[14] §IV, 44, vol. 1, 53 ff., 67.
[15] Ibid. 77, fig. 68; otherwise §IV, 26, 53 f.; §IV, 6, 354.

the Cypro-Mycenaean script betray the presence of Alashiyans from Cyprus,[1] and large quantities of *bilbil* jars and other characteristic wares found stacked in the sheds of Mīnet el-Beidha suggest that the Cypriots, too, were there for commercial reasons.[2] Hittite and Egyptian merchants and envoys, too, had their residence in Ugarit,[3] and objects of Egyptian and Anatolian workmanship were in demand.[4] Travellers and traders from Tyre, Byblos, Beirut and other neighbouring kingdoms, as well as neighbouring Amurru, frequented the city,[5] and mention in the texts of the Kassite deities, Shuqamuna and Shumalia,[6] and of the Moabite Chemosh[7] suggests that Babylonians and Palestinians from over the Jordan contributed to this cosmopolitan community.

A fragment of an alabaster vase found in the rebuilt palace is incised with a scene of great interest: it depicts an Egyptian lady of noble or royal rank (her name is unfortunately missing), in the presence of 'Niqmad, the king (*wr*) of the land of Ugarit'.[8] The scene has been dated on stylistic grounds to the Amarna or immediately post-Amarna period[9] and the royal marriage which it appears to imply may have been prompted by the desire of Akhenaten or one of his immediate successors to cement the bond which linked Ugarit and Egypt,[10] an alliance not only profitable for commercial reasons but also of great strategic value in the face of Shuppiluliumash's threatening aggression. The Hittite king was even now making preparations for his great offensive in Syria.[11] Niqmaddu, cut off from the help of Egyptian troops stationed at Byblos by the hostile activities of Aziru of Amurru and his brothers,[12] found his kingdom endangered on two fronts. A treaty was accordingly negotiated with Aziru[13] by the terms of which the latter was bribed by a large payment of silver[14] to renounce all claims on Siyanni, Ugarit's most southerly dependency, which the kings of Amurru had long coveted,[15] and to promise help to Ugarit in case she were attacked. The pact between Aziru

[1] §IV, 44, vol. 3, 227 ff., 247; *ibid.* vol. 4, 131 ff., 122, fig. 100.

[2] §IV, 44, vol. 1, 72, figs. 69–74; *ibid.* vol. 3, 227 ff.; *ibid.* vol. 4, 30 f., fig. 20, *cf.* §IV, 7.

[3] E.g. §IV, 30, vol. 4, 103 ff.=*RS*.17.130; *ibid.* vol. 3, 19=*RS*.15.11; *ibid.* 142=*RS*.16.136 (Egyptians); §IV, 41, 199 f. (Hittite merchants).

[4] E.g. §IV, 44, vol. 4, 30 ff.; §IV, 39, 235; §IV, 41, 199.

[5] E.g. §IV, 44, vol. 4, 140=*RS*.19.42.   [6] §V, 30, 88; §IV, 14, vol. 2, 528 ff.

[7] §IV, 54, 96.   [8] §IV, 44, vol. 3, 164 ff., 179 ff., figs. 118, 126.

[9] *Ibid.* 179 ff.   [10] §IV, 21, 34 f.   [11] See above, pp. 13 ff.

[12] EA, 126, ll. 4–13; G, 4, 539.

[13] §IV, 30, vol. 4, 284 ff.=*RS*.19.68; EA 98, ll. 5–9; §IV, 28, 11.

[14] A, 20, vol. 2, 349; but see §IV, 44, vol. 5, 259 ff.

[15] §IV, 26, 33; §IV, 30, vol. 4, 282.

and Shuppiluliumash,[1] however, which must have been negotiated soon after,[2] revealed the policy of the Amorite ruler in a clearer light and Niqmaddu was forced to accede to the pressing demands of the Hittite king: he had first to promise to withhold aid from the 'rebel' kingdoms, Nukhash and Mukish,[3] and subsequently to accept the terms of a treaty imposed upon him by the Great King in Alalakh.[4]

Instead of the rays of the pharaoh, the Egyptian 'Sun', the Sun of Khatti-land now shone upon Ugarit. By the terms of the treaty, Niqmaddu recognized Shuppiluliumash as his overlord; he was required to send large annual tribute, in specified amounts of silver and of blue- and purple-dyed wool and garments,[5] for the Hittite king and queen and various members of their court.[6] In return for his loyalty, the frontiers of his kingdom were delimited and guaranteed,[7] and, contrary to the usual practices of international law,[8] Niqmaddu was accorded the right to retain at his disposal fugitives from the defeated rebel kingdoms, Mukish and Nukhash.[9] The tablets on which the frontier territories are enumerated are somewhat broken, but, judging by the complaints of the people of Mukish,[10] it appears that Ugarit's new frontiers included land taken from both Mukish and Neya, districts which had long been the subject of disputes between the Ugaritians and their neighbours. If the identifications of place-names proposed by one scholar[11] can be accepted, the size of Niqmaddu's territory must have been increased by nearly four times, and his eastern frontier extended beyond Idlib to Afis, 95 miles inland.

Niqmaddu remained faithful to this alliance for the remaining years of his long reign, and when Sharre-Kushukh, the viceroy appointed by Murshilish II to rule at Carchemish,[12] summoned the aid of the Syrian vassals against Tette of Nukhash, who had once more risen in revolt against his Hittite overlord,[13] there is no reason to suppose that the king of Ugarit failed in his obligation. Unlike Alalakh, the city of Ugarit shows no sign of Hittite occupation,[14] but appears to have retained its role as a wealthy port, affording the Hittites an outlet for maritime trade which

---

[1] §IV, 15, 377 ff.; §IV, 26, 36 ff.
[2] §IV, 8, 45; §IV, 22, 456.   [3] §IV, 30, vol. 4, 35 ff. = RS.17.132.
[4] §IV, 30, vol. 4, 40 ff. = RS.17.227 etc.; §IV, 23, 68.
[5] §IV, 30, vol. 4, 37 ff. = RS.17.227 etc.; §IV, 14, vol. 3, 75 ff.; §IV, 17, 128.
[6] §IV, 16.
[7] §IV, 30, vol. 4, 63 ff.; RS.17.340; 17.62, 17.399A; 17.366; §IV, 26, 48 f.
[8] §IV, 22, 456.   [9] §IV, 30, vol. 4, 52 = RS.17.369A.
[10] §IV, 30, vol. 4, 63 ff. = RS.17.237, ll. 3 ff.   [11] A, 4, 399 ff.
[12] See above, pp. 120 f.   [13] §IV, 30, vol. 4, 53 ff. = RS.17.334.   [14] §IV, 32, 54.

they valued too highly to reduce by excessive interference.[1] The reign of Niqmaddu appears to have been a prosperous one in which literary texts were copied[2] and the palace enlarged and embellished.[3] It may even be that the city maintained her position as a commercial intermediary between Egypt and the Hittite empire, for Egyptian influence continued to be strong in his reign and that of his successors. A queen named Sharelli, whose name appears on several documents and on a stele dedicated to the god Dagan,[4] had a seal engraved not in cuneiform but in Egyptian hieroglyphs;[5] though it is tempting to equate her with Niqmaddu's nameless bride,[6] the style of the writing indicates a somewhat later date.[7] It may however be significant that Sharelli appears to be the exact Hurrian equivalent of Akhat-milki, 'sister of the king', which would suggest a title rather than a proper name.[8]

Two of Niqmaddu's sons in turn succeeded to the throne. Ar-Khalba, the elder of the two, reigned for nine troubled years at the most.[9] Sharre-Kushukh was now dead. Syria rose again in revolt against Hittite rule, and so serious was the peril that Murshilish II himself was forced to march against Nukhash and Kinza (Qadesh); even Carchemish itself may for a time have been lost.[10] Ugarit too seems now for a time to have thrown in her lot with the rebels, for a subsequent treaty between Murshilish and Niqmepa, the second son of Niqmaddu,[11] makes it clear that he was set on the throne by the direct intervention of the Hittite king. Ugarit was punished by the loss of two of its most valuable territories, Siyanni and the neighbouring kingdom of Ushnatu, on the south-eastern frontier,[12] both of which were handed over to Carchemish. This reduced the kingdom of Ugarit to two thirds of its former size[13] and must have been a great blow to the country's economy; a fresh assessment of tribute had to be made on the basis of her reduced revenues.[14] The presence in the palace at Ras Shamra of alabaster vases inscribed with the cartouches of

---

[1] §IV, 23, 73.    [2] §IV, 26, 56, n. 111; §V, 72, 31, n. 1; A, 20, vol. 2, 357.
[3] §IV, 44, vol. 4, 13 ff.
[4] §IV, 44, vol. 3, 81; §IV, 30, vol. 2, xix; §IV, 26, 138 f., 30 f. = *RS*.15.08; §V, 43, 117 f.
[5] §IV, 44, vol. 3, 85, fig. 106.    [6] *Ibid.* 168.    [7] *Ibid.* 81, n. 3 (by J. Vandier).
[8] §IV, 44, vol. 5, 261 f.
[9] §IV, 30, vol. 4, 57; §IV, 26, 58, Klengel (A, 20, vol. 2, 359 f.) argues for a reign of not more than two years.    [10] See above, p. 123.
[11] §IV, 30, vol. 4, 84 ff.; A, 20, vol. 2, 362 ff.; §IV, 23, 68 f.
[12] §IV, 30, vol. 4, 16 f., 71 ff. = *RS*.17.335, 17.344 and 17.368; §IV, 26, 75 ff.
[13] §IV, 22, 459.    [14] §IV, 30, vol. 4, 79 ff. = *RS*.17.382 + 380; §IV, 23, 68.

Horemheb,[1] the Egyptian contemporary of Murshilish II, suggests that it may have been the pharaoh who attempted to woo Ugarit away from her Hittite allegiance, since such gifts usually accompanied a diplomatic mission.[2] What happened to Ar-Khalba is not known. He may have had a premonition of disaster, for, in a legal document executed in his name,[3] he willed that, according to the levirate custom, his wife should marry his brother Niqmepa after his death, thereby ensuring the continuance of the hereditary line.[3] The presence at Ugarit of an actual seal of Murshilish II[4] suggests that it was brought here by the Hittite envoy who negotiated the deposition of Ar-Khalba and set Niqmepa on the throne.

Henceforward Ugarit appears to have remained loyal to her Hittite overlord. In common with many of the kingdoms of Anatolia and North Syria, she sent a contingent to the aid of Muwatallish when, in the year 1300, he encountered the army of Ramesses II at Qadesh.[5] At this time, as a later treaty indicates,[6] Amurru had deserted her alliance and was fighting on the Egyptian side. A letter found at Ugarit[7] appears to be a dispatch from a general Simiyanu (or Simitti) operating against Ardata, an important town in Amurru;[8] he speculates on the likelihood of Egyptian intervention, and asks for more troops. This letter may have been written shortly before the battle of Qadesh, when an Egyptian army may have been reconnoitring in the area; after the battle, Amurru surrendered to the Hittites and its king Benteshina was deposed. Other documents from the reign of Niqmepa belong to the period after the accession to the Hittite throne of Khattushilish III.[9] Relations between monarch and vassal appear to have remained cordial: when complaints were received at Khattusha of the overbearing behaviour of Hittite merchants from Ura in Cilicia,[10] a fair compromise was agreed.[11] Another royal edict lays down that fugitives from Ugarit will not be allowed to settle in the land of the *Ḫapiru* of the Hittite king,[12] that is to say, in nomad

[1] §IV, 40, 16.

[2] §IV, 26, 61 f.; §IV, 22, 458. Ugarit appears with Tunip, Qadesh and Qatna in a topographical list of the reign of Horemheb in the temple of Karnak (§IV, 47, 50 ff., no. XII, *a*, 12).			[3] §IV, 17, 130; §IV, 51; A, 22, 108.

[4] §IV, 44, vol. 3, 87 ff., 161 ff., figs. 109–112; §IV, 26, 63 f.

[5] See below, p. 253; A, 20, vol. 2, 369.			[6] *K.U.B.* 23, 1, vs. 1, 28 ff.

[7] §V, 56, 80 ff. = *RS.*20.33; §IV, 28, 119 f.

[8] *C.A.H.* II³, pt. 1, pp. 454 and 459; §IV, 44, vol. 5, 69 ff.			[9] §IV, 26, 80 ff.

[10] §IV, 30, vol. 4, 103 ff. = *RS.*17.130; §IV, 24, 270; §IV, 23, 70.

[11] *C.A.H.* II³, pt. 1, p. 507; A, 20, vol. 2, 370.

[12] §IV, 30, vol. 4, 107 f. = *RS.*17.238.

country,[1] but shall be returned to Niqmepa. When Kadashman-Enlil of Babylonia complained to Khattushilish that merchants of his were being killed in Amurru and Ugarit,[2] the Hittite countered by declaring that such things could not happen in his territory;[3] an argument based on a different understanding of the text, that Khattushilish was denying that Ugarit was within his jurisdiction,[4] must be rejected in view of the overwhelming documentary evidence that, while refraining as far as possible from interference in internal matters, the Hittite kings of the time were the ultimate arbiters of Ugarit's destiny. At the same time, after the peace treaty of 1284 or thereabouts which finally put an end to hostilities between the Hittites and Egypt,[5] there was nothing to prevent the resumption of diplomatic relations between that land and Ugarit, and an alabaster vessel fragment bearing the name of Ramesses II, found at Ras Shamra,[6] may be a witness to the *rapprochement*. A letter,[7] unfortunately fragmentary, hailing the king of Egypt as 'puissant king...master of every land, my master' and couched in the language of a vassal to his overlord, is thought on other grounds to be addressed to Ramesses II. It appears to refer to the settlement of some dispute between people of Canaan—Egyptian territory in southern Syria?—and people of Ugarit.

After a long reign of perhaps more than sixty years,[8] as the vassal of four successive Hittite sovereigns, Niqmepa was succeeded in about 1265 B.C. by his son Ammishtamru, the second of the name.[9] Although he must have been a middle-aged man at the time of his accession, it would appear that the affairs of the state were managed for a short time by the dowager queen Akhat-milki,[10] the daughter of King *DŪ*-Teshub of Amurru. An impressive list of her personal ornaments, vesture and furniture, which she presumably brought with her as her dowry at the time of her marriage to Niqmepa, has survived among the palace archives.[11] As queen of Ugarit, she was the arbitrator in a dispute between her sons, Khishmi-Sharruma and *ARAD*-Sharruma, and

---

[1] §IV, 9, 215; §IV, 5, 70 ff.; §IV, 22, 459, n. 1.
[2] *K.Bo.* 1, 10, vs. ll. 14–25; §IV, 13, 130 ff.
[3] §IV, 44, vol. 1, 41.
[4] §IV, 46, 134, n. 3; §IV, 32, 54 ff., 63, n. 35.
[5] See below, pp. 256 and 258 ff.; A, 20, vol. 2, 373.
[6] §IV, 44, vol. 3, fig. 121; §V, 67, 287 f., fig. 10.
[7] §IV, 44, vol. 5, 110 ff. = *RS*.20.182.
[8] §IV, 26, 67.      [9] *Ibid.* 99 ff.; §IV, 30, vol. 4, 113 ff.
[10] §IV, 26, 99 f.; §IV, 30, vol. 3, 178 ff. See above, p. 139.
[11] §IV, 30, vol. 3, 182 ff. = *RS*.16.146; *ibid.* vol. 4, 10 and 120.

their brother or half-brother, Ammishtamru himself,[1] and her seal appears also on a legal document of the latter's reign.[2] An Assyrian envoy to the Ugaritic court, on receipt of a letter from Ashur, was directed to read it to the Queen.[3]

The renewed *entente cordiale* between Amurru and Ugarit had been strengthened yet again by the marriage of Ammishtamru to the daughter of Bente-shina, the grandson of *DU*-Teshub and nephew of Akhat-milki.[4] The union of the two houses was this time less happy, however, in its outcome, for the Amorite queen, whose name the documents are careful to omit, after having borne her husband a son, was accused of 'having sought evil [? sickness] for Ammishtamru'. A bill of divorcement was accordingly drawn up,[5] the Hittite king, now Tudkhaliash IV, acting as arbitrator, for the matter had the nature of a dispute between vassals. Following the usual custom in divorce proceedings, it was decreed that the woman repudiated was to take her dowry and depart; everything she had acquired at Ugarit since her marriage, however, belonged to her husband and must be left behind.[6] A knotty problem remained to be solved, for her son, Utri-Sharruma, was the heir to the throne of Ugarit. Tudkhaliash gave his decision: if the prince should elect to stay in Ugarit with his father, he might inherit the kingdom; but, if he chose to return to Amurru with his mother, then he forfeited the right to the throne and Ammishtamru must nominate as his heir a son by another wife.[7] This was not the end of Ammishtamru's marital troubles, however, for further divorce proceedings appear to have been taken against another of his wives, called 'the daughter of the noble lady [*rabītu*]';[8] since she, too, came from Amurru it is tempting to identify her with Bente-shina's daughter[9] but there are reasons for supposing that a different wife was involved[10] and that the 'great sin' of which the second was accused was adultery.[11] Condemned to death by Ammishtamru, she fled to Amurru and took refuge with Bente-shina's son and successor, Shaushga-muwash. Hard words and a military exchange between Ugarit and Amurru over this affair led again to the intervention

---

[1] §IV, 30, vol. 4, 121 ff. = *RS*.17.352.
[2] §IV, 30, vol. 3, 150 f. = *RS*.16.197.          [3] §IV, 49.
[4] §IV, 26, 104 f.; A, 20, vol. 2, 307.
[5] §IV, 30, vol. 4, 126 f. = *RS*.17.159 and 127 f. = *RS*. 17.396; §IV, 57.
[6] §IV, 30, vol. 4, 126 f. = *RS*.17.159, ll. 8–18.    [7] *Ibid.* ll. 31–39 and *RS*.17.348.
[8] §IV, 30, vol. 4, 129 ff. = *RS*.16.270, 17.372A + 360A, 17.228.
[9] §IV, 44, vol. 3, 31 f.
[10] §IV, 30, vol. 4, 131; §IV, 26, 108; A, 20, vol. 2, 224 ff., 323.
[11] §IV, 27, 280 (*cf.* Gen. xx. 9); A, 22, 104.

of Tudkhaliash,[1] and it was finally agreed that the erring wife must be returned to her husband; Ammishtamru might carry out the sentence of execution, as was his legal right,[2] but had to pay Shaushga-muwash a large sum of money by way of compensation.[3]

The tablets, sent from Khattusha, which conveyed the decisions of the Great King on these matters of more than domestic importance[4] were sealed with the royal seal of Tudkhaliash himself,[5] but his son, Ini-Teshub, was now viceroy at Carchemish, and as the Hittite governor responsible for affairs in North Syria his name and seal appear frequently on documents of the reign of Ammishtamru and his son Ibiranu.[6] It was he who decided what might be taken by Bente-shina's daughter after her divorce,[7] arbitrated in cases of dispute affecting merchants travelling from kingdom to kingdom in the area under his jurisdiction,[8] and settled claims for compensation made by individuals of one kingdom against those of another. The verdicts appear to have been delivered without bias: in one case a Hittite merchant convicted of theft was condemned to make triple restitution to the Ugaritian from whom he had stolen.[9] Sometimes the disputes were over border incidents between kingdom and kingdom. Ugarit and her neighbour and erstwhile vassal Siyanni quarrelled over relatively unimportant local incidents involving acts of hooliganism, a tower destroyed and vines chopped down, and the smuggling of wine or beer through Ugaritian territory to Beirut;[10] a complaint from the king of neighbouring Ushnatu that Ugaritians had violated his frontiers and captured a town called forth a sharp reproof from the viceroy.[11]

From such documents the figure of Ini-Teshub stands out with dignity. In these latter days, when the Hittite empire was hard pressed and the Great King was often occupied with urgent military matters in the west of his wide realm, it was the Syrian viceroy, resident at Carchemish, to whom the kingdoms of Syria turned for guidance in their affairs[12] and the protection of their commerce. The close contact maintained thus between Hittites

---

[1] §IV, 30, vol. 4, 137 f. = RS.18.06 + 17.365; §IV, 23, 71.

[2] §IV, 26, 109; §IV, 23, 71.

[3] 1400 shekels of gold (RS.17.228, ll. 30 ff.).　　[4] §IV, 28, 115; §IV, 57, 23 f.

[5] §IV, 44, vol. 3, 14 ff.; §IV, 30, vol. 4, 126 = RS.17.159.

[6] §IV, 44, vol. 3, 21 ff., figs. 26–35; §IV, 26, 115 ff.

[7] §IV, 30, vol. 4, 127 f. = RS.17.396; §IV, 57, 26.

[8] E.g. §IV, 30, vol. 4, 169 ff. = RS.17.158; 171 f. = RS.17.42; 172 f. = RS.17.145.

[9] §IV, 30, vol. 4, 179 = RS.17.128.

[10] Ibid. 161 ff. = RS.17.341; §IV, 26, 118 ff.

[11] §IV, 44, vol. 5, 90 f. = RS.20.174A.　　[12] §IV, 23, 74 ff.

and Canaanites resulted in a lasting influence: the rulers of North Syria were known to the Assyrians of the first millennium as 'the kings of Khatti-land'.[1]

Ugarit itself was still enjoying a fair measure of autonomy. A letter addressed to Ammishtamru by Shukur-Teshub, on the latter's installation as Hittite representative in Mukish, assured his new neighbour that his friendly intentions would be cemented by an exchange of gifts.[2] The carved orthostat found in the palace of Alalakh, depicting Tudkhaliash and his queen,[3] is not paralleled by any monument yet found in Ugarit. Commercial contact with Egypt was maintained. Egyptians resident in Ugarit were given land by the king,[4] and a bronze sword engraved with the cartouche of the pharaoh Merneptah, found in a private house at Ras Shamra, was probably commissioned by him but for some reason never delivered.[5] In the emergency produced by the advance of the Assyrian army led by Tukulti-Ninurta I[6] to the Euphrates, however, the vassals in Syria were called upon by Tudkhaliash to show their loyalty and lend assistance. Among them were Ugarit and Amurru, with whose ruler, Shaushgamuwash, the Hittites had recently signed a new treaty.[7] The danger was great, and the war needed costly preparation:[8] while Amurru was called upon to furnish troops, wealthy Ugarit's aid took the form of a heavy monetary contribution in gold;[9] the royal coffers had to be replenished for this purpose by means of a special tax levied on the towns and villages of the realm 'for the tribute of the Sun'.[10]

Ammishtamru's successor on the throne of Ugarit was not his first heir designate, Utri-Sharruma, who had presumably chosen to return with his mother to Amurru, but Ibiranu, a son by another wife.[11] During his reign the close relationship between Carchemish and Ugarit continued, but the judgements which have been preserved are not delivered in the name of Ini-Teshub, the king of Carchemish, or of his son and successor Talmi-

---

[1] E.g. G, 6, 279, 281, 291.

[2] §IV, 28, 115.

[3] §IV, 55, 241 and pl. 48.

[4] §IV, 30, vol. 3, 142.

[5] §IV, 7, 253.

[6] A, 20, vol. 2, 380; §IV, 26, 110 f. M. Nougayrol (§IV, 30, vol. 4, 150) places these events in the reign of Shalmaneser I.

[7] §III, 3, 113 ff.; §IV, 47, 320 f.

[8] The view is expressed below, p. 291, that the Assyrian threat was nothing more serious than a border raid.

[9] §IV, 30, vol. 4, 149 ff. = RS.17.59; §IV, 23, 70.

[10] §IV, 44, vol. 4, 73 = RS.19.17; §IV, 30, vol. v, 75 f.; §v, 66, 42.

[11] §IV, 26, 125 f.; A, 20, vol. 2, 388 ff.

Teshub, but in that of a prince Armaziti;[1] it was he who stabilized the frontiers of Ugarit after some border incident.[2] A certain coolness appears to have sprung up at this time between the court at Boğazköy and that of Ugarit.[3] Ibiranu was sharply reprimanded for not having presented himself at the Hittite capital,[4] perhaps to do homage on his accession, and for sending no messages or presents.[5] Since he had also failed to meet his obligations in sending a contingent of foot soldiers and chariotry when urgently requested to do so, a Hittite officer had to be sent to make a personal inspection. Already, it may be surmised, the Hittite hold on North Syria was weakening.

Ibiranu was a contemporary of Tudkhaliash IV and probably also of his successor Arnuwandash III. The next king of Ugarit, Ibiranu's son Niqmaddu III, can have had only a brief reign;[6] whether 'Ammurapi, who followed him, was of the royal line or no is uncertain, for, contrary to the usual custom, his parentage is nowhere mentioned;[7] he is likely to have been of the same generation as his predecessor.[8] Divorce at this time ended the marriage of an Ugaritic prince, perhaps the son of 'Ammurapi, to a Hittite princess;[9] and Talmi-Teshub, who adjudicated in the affair, allowed her to keep her dowry but ordered her to give up a royal residence which she had, it seems, been reluctant to leave.[10]

Shuppiluliumash II now ascended the Hittite throne and, facing a mounting tide of threatening disaster, found himself relying more and more on the fleet of his most important vassal on the Levant coast. The blow was not long delayed. In the ruins of the latest level of the palace at Ras Shamra, the kiln used for baking tablets was found to be packed full of documents,[11] a batch of about one hundred brought by the scribes when freshly written; many are transcriptions into alphabetic Ugaritic of letters and despatches which must have been received in the weeks—even the days— before the fall of the city: there had been no time to take them from the kiln.[12] The immediacy of the danger facing Ugarit is implicit in the wording and content of some of these and other tablets.[13] The Hittite king asks urgently for

---

[1] §IV, 25, 143; A, 20, vol. 2, 394.   [2] §IV, 30, vol. 4, 188 = RS.17.292.
[3] §IV, 30, vol. 4, 187; §IV, 26, 127 f.   [4] §IV, 30, vol. 4, 191 = RS.17.247.
[5] §IV, 30, vol. 4, 192 = RS.17.289.
[6] §IV, 30, vol. 4, 199 ff.; §IV, 26, 129 ff.; cf. §IV, 44, vol. 5, pp. 102 ff. = RS.20.237.
[7] §IV, 30, vol. 4, 8; §V, 74, 76.
[8] §IV, 22, 461; A, 20, vol. 2, 403.   [9] §IV, 30, vol. 4, 209 f. = RS.17.355.
[10] §IV, 30, vol. 4, 208 = RS.17.355.   [11] §IV, 44, vol. 4, 31 ff., figs. 35–39.
[12] §IV, 30, vol. 5, 81 ff.; §IV, 44, vol. IV, 31 ff.
[13] A, 21, 29 ff.; §IV, 28, 120 f.; §IV, 7, 254 ff.

a ship and a crew to transport grain from Mukish to the Hittite town of Ura in Cilicia, as a 'matter of life and death' since there is famine in the area.[1] In making this demand, the Hittite refers to an act of liberation whereby he has formally released the king of Ugarit (probably 'Ammurapi) from vassalage, but he makes it clear that Ugarit has not yet been absolved from all her obligations towards her former overlord. Famine may also have afflicted Alashiya at this time: a certain Pagan whose letter to the King of Ugarit was one of those found in the kiln, calls the Ugaritian 'my son', perhaps indicating that a dynastic marriage linked their houses; he asks for a ship to be sent with food supplies for the island.[2] In reply,[3] 'Ammurapi informs his 'father', the king of Alashiya, that he has not a ship to spare, since the enemy has plundered his coasts, while his own fleet is in the Lukka lands and his troops in the land of the Hittites.

Only one known situation fits this predicament: the approach of the 'Peoples of the Sea' whose destructive progress by way of Qode (Kizzuwadna), the Khatti-land, Carchemish, Alashiya and Amurru is all too briefly related by Ramesses III in his inscription on the north wall of the temple of Medīnet Habu.[4] At the approach of the enemy, Shuppiluliumash must have summoned his vassals in North Syria to his aid, and Ugarit, loyal to the last, must have sent her whole army. One of the letters found in the kiln[5] appears to be an urgent dispatch sent to the king in Ugarit from the commander of the army in Lawasanda (Lawazantiya) in Cilicia,[6] which his troops had fortified in anticipation of attack. The enemy is nowhere mentioned by name, probably because so motley a horde had no collective name. Their presence in Mukish, only a few dozen miles from Ugaritian territory, is indicated in a letter of Ewir-Sharruma, another of the Ugaritian generals in the field, to the queen or queen-mother,[7] in the absence of the king at the front. Part of the letter is unfortunately damaged, but it sounds the note of extreme urgency and makes reference to Mount Amanus, though a contingent of two thousand horses (equivalent to a thousand chariots, a very formidable force[8]) is apparently still at the king's disposal. Other letters which may well date from this time of crisis tell of looting and burning.[9]

[1] §IV, 44, vol. 5, 105 ff., 323 f. = RS.20.212, 26.158.    [2] §IV, 28, 120.
[3] §IV, 28, 121; §IV, 7, 255 = RS.20.238.
[4] G, 6, 262; see below, pp. 242 ff.
[5] §IV, 30, vol. 5, 90 = RS.18.40; §IV, 7, 256 f.
[6] §IV, 7, 257; see below, p. 514.
[7] §IV, 30, vol. 2, xviii, 25 ff. = RS.16.402.    [8] §IV, 7, 257 f.
[9] E.g. §IV, 30, vol. 5, 137 = RS.19.11.

Of the anxiety of the king and people of Ugarit in the face of impending danger the tablets leave us in no doubt. Whether or not the destruction of the city was due to enemy action is less certain. M. Schaeffer, the excavator of Ras Shamra over more than forty years, who long held the view that the Peoples of the Sea were responsible for the final pillage and burning of Ugarit,[1] has now reached a different conclusion.[2] Ugarit, he suggests, may have come to terms with the invaders and persuaded them to by-pass the city. The letter mentioned earlier,[3] addressed to the king of Ugarit by a general operating in the field near Ardata, was in fact found among the archives of Rap'anu, who held office under the last four kings of Ugarit.[4] 'Half my chariots', he says, 'are drawn up on the shore of the sea, and half at the foot of the Lebanon'; Ardata has been hard pressed; he speculates on the likelihood of the Egyptian king intervening, presumably against Ardata, and complains that he has been awaiting reinforcements for five months. If, as M. Schaeffer now argues,[5] the pharaoh in question is indeed Ramesses III (since he would be the only Egyptian king likely to have been engaged in Amurru during Rap'anu's lifetime) the situation must have been one in which the Egyptian army was preparing for its final decisive action against the Sea Peoples on the coast of Amurru, and a possible reason for the delay of the king of Ugarit in sending troops might be his desire to maintain a neutral attitude and not to provoke either his old friends the Egyptians or his new neighbours and potential enemies. There are however many obscurities in this letter and its interpretation must remain in doubt; moreover in script and language it differs from the other tablets in the archive[6] and its date is therefore problematical.

The excavator attributes the final destruction of Ugarit to natural causes: a terrible earthquake, or series of shocks, which must have overwhelmed the city very shortly after the events mirrored in the tablets from the kiln. The disaster, he thinks, was sudden and complete. Fire swept the city, covering it with a thick layer of ash. The inhabitants had apparently had enough warning to escape, for no skeletons were found in streets or houses other than those buried in the tombs. *Objets d'art* were left half-finished on the workshop benches, others were hidden in walls or beneath floors, in the vain hope that they might one day be recovered.[7]

---

[1] §IV, 44, vol. 1, 45 f.; §IV, 35, 27 f. Schmidtke (§IV, 45) attributes the destruction to the army of Ramesses III.   [2] §IV, 44, vol. 5, 760 f.

[3] See above, p. 140.   [4] §IV, 44, vol. 5, 69.

[5] §IV, 44, vol. v, 666 ff.   [6] *Ibid.* 76 ff.   [7] §v, 65, 206 ff.; §IV, 39, 235.

Pillagers, prowling soon after among the ruins, prised open the family vaults and carried off their treasures, but there was no attempt to rebuild the houses. Fragments of the large, beautifully written mythological tablets were used later in the construction of small walls[1] by a people who had no reverence for, or understanding of, their contents. The alphabetic script of Ugarit was forgotten and the city abandoned by those who could read it. Ugarit's history was ended.

## V. CANAANITE RELIGION AND LITERATURE

Until the discovery of the cuneiform texts of Ras Shamra, little was known of the mythology and religious beliefs of the peoples of Syria–Palestine in times preceding the Iron Age. The *Phoenikikē Historia* attributed to a priest named Sanchuniathon, who was supposed to have lived before the Trojan war and to have derived his knowledge from a perusal of the archives of the temple at Byblos, his native town, was preserved in Greek translation in the works of Philo of Byblos,[2] who wrote in the first century A.D., but the latter's text survives only in an abridged and altered form in the *Praeparatio evangelica* of Eusebius, written three centuries later;[3] moreover, the account of the Phoenician pantheon there given is coloured both by Greek elements (much uncertainty arising, for instance, from the custom common among classical writers on oriental religion of substituting for the names of Semitic deities their imagined equivalents in Greek mythology) and also by the glosses of the Christian commentator.[4] Until recently, therefore, the account was generally dismissed as late and untrustworthy. The publication of the Ugaritic epics, however, has thrown revealing light on Philo's statements, and has rendered the existence of Sanchuniathon himself as a figure of history more probable,[5] though his date is still in dispute.[6]

Similarly, the Phoenician account of the creation of the world, preserved by Damascius from the writings of Mochus of Sidon,[7] has a ring of authenticity,[8] and Lucian of Samosata, writing in the middle of the second century A.D., gives a plausible account of

---

[1] §IV, 11, 31.
[2] §V, 32, 75 ff.; §V, 20, 3 ff.
[3] §V, 34; Eusebius I, 9, 20–1, 10, 28; IV, 16, 11.
[4] §V, 31, 31 ff.; §V, 44, 119.     [5] §V, 19, 77; §V, 33, 68 f.
[6] O. Eissfeldt (§V, 32, 70 f.) suggests *c.* 1000 B.C., but W. F. Albright (§IV, 2, 24) argues for a later date, between 800 and 500 B.C.
[7] §V, 20, 310 ff.     [8] §V, 19, 33 ff.

the cult of one Phoenician deity, the goddess of Hierapolis, the modern Membij.

Apart from these literary sources, the ritual and cult practices of the early Canaanites are known mostly from the polemic directed against them by Old Testament writers[1] and from the material legacy of these rites, the standing stones and altars, incense-burners and similar cult paraphernalia which are found in the majority of archaeological sites in Palestine and Syria, in levels of the later Bronze Age as well as those of the first millennium.[2]

The Canaanite temple of the Late Bronze Age was a simple building in comparison with its grandiose contemporaries in Egypt and Mesopotamia. It consisted essentially of an anteroom, a larger pillared room or open courtyard, and a sanctuary beyond, usually on a higher level reached by a short flight of steps; in this sanctuary was the altar. Storage rooms were sometimes built around, to contain the offerings and the trappings of the cult.[3] The two large temples at Ugarit, on a grander scale than most, as befitted the wealth and size of the city, were similar in plan;[4] built on the highest part of the *tell*, their towers must have dominated the town. The temple of Ba'al had a large forecourt with an altar on which sacrifices must have been offered in the sight of the assembled worshippers.[5] References in the Ugaritic texts[6] to the sacred courtyard (*ḥẓr*), the 'table of gold', and the Holy of Holies suggest that the Solomonic temple built by Tyrian workmen may have followed traditional Canaanite design.[7] The reconstruction of buildings thought to be temples or shrines is, however, often in doubt, and rooms with pillars which were in reality parts of private houses have sometimes been taken to be shrines with *maṣṣēbōt* or standing stones.[8] Such stones were, however, found in the Bronze Age shrine at Hazor;[9] and in one of the temples at Byblos they were a striking feature of the sanctuary.[10]

Many of the technical terms employed in the Old Testament for the different sacrificial rites are found also in the texts from Ras Shamra;[11] it may be assumed that the Israelites adopted much of their ritual of offering from the Canaanites, and also some of

[1] §v, 48, 45 ff.; §v, 44, 15, 119; §v, 2, 158 ff.; §iv, 35, 59.
[2] §v, 11, vol. 2, 375 ff.; §v, 2, 42 ff., 64 ff.
[3] §v, 66, 84 ff.; §v, 11, vol. 2, 355 ff.; §v, 68; §v, 62, 6 ff., pl. vi.
[4] §iv, 44, vol. 1, 15 f.; §v, 62, 1 ff.     [5] §v, 64, 154 ff.     [6] §v, 49.
[7] §v, 11, vol. 2, 436 ff., fig. 348.     [8] §v, 68, 83.
[9] §v, 84, vol. 1, 90 f. and pls. xxviii–xxx; §v, 6, 254 ff.
[10] §v, 24, vol. 2, Atlas, pls. xxii–xxxii; §v, 44, pl. 25.
[11] §v, 48, 63 ff.; §iv, 11, 180 ff.; §v, 47, 143 ff.; §v, 26.

their festivals, for references to seasonal rites in the poems correspond with those performed at early Hebrew festivals such as the
Autumnal Festival[1] (ḥag ḥāāsīp) and the Feast of Weeks.[2] It has
been further suggested that certain of the Ugaritic epics contain
sections of the liturgy accompanying the rites performed at such
festivals,[3] and that one, at least, may even contain the text, with
stage directions, of a religious drama enacted in mime and accompanied by music.[4] Another poem,[5] in which the Kotharoth, the
goddesses of song,[6] appear, has been thought to be a wedding
hymn.[7] The fragmentary nature of many of the tablets, however, and
imperfect understanding of many of the words and phrases used
make the interpretation of the texts a matter of great difficulty.

Similar uncertainty clouds the question whether it is possible
to see, in the Ras Shamra texts, references to the practice of
sacred prostitution and infant sacrifice, both said to have been
characteristic of Phoenician religion at a later date and to have
survived among the Carthaginians. The mention of votaries
(qdšm) of both sexes as members of professional guilds at Ugarit[8]
has been thought to furnish proof that the former practice, against
which the Hebrew prophets of the eighth century B.C. thundered
their denunciations,[9] was an ancient institution in Canaan;[10] there
is, however, no proof that the term qdš, 'sacred', had this particular connotation in the second millennium B.C.[11] Similarly, a
handful of references to the sacrifice called mlk[12] (not, as was once
supposed, to the non-existent god Moloch[13]), contain nothing
which would indicate that the terrible sacrifice of newborn infants
was a Canaanite practice, though this is sometimes assumed.[14]

Priests with various ranks and functions appear frequently in
the administrative texts from Ugarit,[15] and the house of the chief
priest (rb khnm), which lay in the heart of the temple quarter, was
one of the largest and richest in the city.[16] It contained a library
of mythological and religious texts, including some in the Hurrian

[1] §v, 38, 37 ff.; 65 ff.; §v, 36, 72 f.   [2] §v, 38, 232; §v, 48, 58.
[3] §v, 11, vol. 2, 337; §v, 38, 72, 235 ff.; §v, 52, 128 ff.
[4] §v, 36, 49 ff.; §v, 38, 225 f.   [5] §v, 25, 23 ff. ,125 ff.
[6] §v, 21, 81; T. H. Gaster (§v, 37, 37 f.) translates 'swallows'.
[7] §v, 37; §v, 32, 76 f.   [8] §v, 69, 166; §v, 80, 147 ff.
[9] Deut. xxiii. 18.   [10] §v, 5, 234 f.; §v, 11, vol. 2, 341; §v, 69, 168 f.
[11] §iv, 11, 179; §v, 66, 44 f.
[12] §iv, 44, 77 ff.; §v, 75, 67; §v, 76, 168 f.; §iv, 30, vol. 5, 7 =RS.19.15.
[13] §v, 31, 31 ff.; otherwise §v, 22; §v, 2, 163 f.
[14] §v, 65, 44 f.; §v, 2, 75, 179.
[15] §v, 80, 135 ff.; §v, 69; §iv, 30, vol. 5, 75 ff. =RS.19.17; §iv, 11, 76 and 179.
[16] §iv, 44, vol. 1, pl. 24.

language, as well as vocabularies, syllabaries and school exercise tablets, showing that the house also filled the function of a seminary for the training of priestly scribes.[1] Another priest's house, on the southern edge of the city, also contained a library; this man was probably a diviner, for inscribed models were found in it of the lungs and liver of sheep.[2] In common with other peoples of the ancient Near East, the Canaanites evidently set great store by divination; inscribed models of sheep's livers found also at Hazor[3] and Alalakh[4] were used by apprentice diviners to learn the ancient Babylonian science of hepatoscopy, as popular in Syria–Palestine as it was in Anatolia.[5] Other tablets contained medico-magical texts, incantations intended to ward off disease, which also derived from Babylonia.[6]

The Canaanites do not seem to have acquired from the Egyptians belief in the survival of the soul after death. Aqhat, tempted by the goddess 'Anath with promises of immortality, professes disbelief, declaring that death is the lot of all men, and none may escape the grave.[7] Yet few graves were without their complement of grave-goods, and at Ugarit each of the well-to-do houses had its family vault below the floor of the living-room: a vaulted tomb reached by a flight of stone steps and closed by a door, in which successive generations of the family were buried.[8] Not only were the tombs richly furnished, but the dead were thereafter carefully tended by their relatives, for provision was made for their sustenance, in the shape of a baked clay pipe leading vertically down from ground level; through this channel libations could be trickled down into a receptacle or pit in the ground below, to which the dead could have access through a window cut in the wall of the vault.[9] Thus they could be supplied with food and drink. Mention of the *rp'um* in the alphabetic texts[10] has suggested the Rephaim, the ancestral shades of Hebrew tradition,[11] but *rp'um* appear in the administrative texts to be priests,[12] and may have been members of a clan of noble descent with special ritual functions.[13]

Stelae erected in the temples by devotees, and figurines of bronze or terracotta found in a number of sites, appear to depict Canaanite deities with their several attributes. The horned head-

[1] §IV, 20, 5 f.      [2] §V, 77, 94; §IV, 21, 5 f.; §IV, 44, vol. 6, 91 ff., 165 ff.
[3] §V, 83, vol. III–IV, pl. 315; §V, 44, pl. 47.      [4] §IV, 54, 256 ff., pl. LIX 4–c.
[5] §IV, 19, 158 f.; *C.A.H.* II³, pt. I, p. 522. *Cf.* §V, 72, 118.
[6] §V, 57, 41 f.      [7] §V, 25, 55 = *Aqhat*, II, vi, ll. 33 ff.
[8] §IV, 44, vol. I, 77 ff. and pls. XVI, XVII. See Plate 137.
[9] §IV, 35, 49, fig. 11 and pl. 38.
[10] §IV, 18, 161, texts 121–4; §V, 25, 9f., 67 ff.
[11] §IV, 35, 72.      [12] §V, 47, 154.      [13] *Ibid.* 92 f.; §V, 45.

dress worn by some of these figures derives from the tiara of the Mesopotamian gods;[1] others reflect Anatolian influence in their pointed helmets, dagger worn at the waist, or shoes upturned in the Hittite manner.[2] The stance and proportions of many of the figures recall Egyptian prototypes and the elaborate crowns worn by some deities also derive from those worn by Egyptian gods.[3] A few of the stelae were dedicated to Canaanite deities by Egyptians visiting or resident in Syria or Palestine; unlike the purely local stelae, which are usually anepigraphic, these usually bear hieroglyphic inscriptions which identify not only the worshipper but also the deity portrayed; it is thus possible to distinguish the attributes of Resheph, the Syrian war-god, who brandishes a fenestrated axe in one hand and holds shield and spear in the other,[4] and of Mekal, the Annihilator, the local god of Beth-shan,[5] who like Resheph wears the horns of a wild goat on his brow in place of the royal uraeus of Egypt.[6] His tall helmet with streamers and his thick Syrian beard proclaim his nationality, but he proffers the Egyptian symbol of life and prosperity to his worshipper. Similarly, 'Anath, Lady of Heaven, Mistress of all the gods', wears in Beth-shan a typically Egyptian crown of high feathers.[7] The Egyptian royal scribe Mami, 'Overseer of the House of Silver', who at Ugarit dedicated a fine stela to Seth of Sapuna,[8] was a worshipper of the local Ba'al Ṣᵉphōn, the personification of Mount Khazi (Mons Casius),[9] whose peak, thrusting through cloud on the northern horizon, was understandably thought to be the seat of the storm-god.[10]

Ba'al is the central figure of many of the Ugaritic poems, the majority of which concern the loves, rivalries and wars of the various deities of the West Semitic pantheon, called 'the assembly of the children of El'.[11] In spite of difficulties of interpretation such as those already mentioned, the fragmentary nature of many of the tablets, and consequent uncertainty concerning the sequence of fragments (so that the order of episodes in some of the myths cannot with any certainty be established), these poems are in-

---

[1] §IV, 44, vol. 1, 128 ff., pls. 28–30; vol. 2, 83 ff., pl. 20, 121 ff., pls. 23, 24.
[2] §IV, 44, vol. 2, pl. XXII. See Plate 138(a).   [3] E.g. §IV, 44, vol. 2, pl. 22.
[4] §v, 44, pl. 19; §v, 12, 638.   [5] §v, 62, frontispiece.   [6] §v, 44, 52.
[7] Ibid. pl. 23; §v, 62, pl. XXXV, 3.
[8] §IV, 44, vol. 1, 39 ff., 40 fig. 30; §IV, 36, 10 f. and pl. 6. See Plate 101.
[9] The modern Jebel Aqra'.
[10] §IV, 55, 178, 182; §v, 28, 5 ff.; §v, 25, 21, n. 1; §v, 51, vol. 2, 217 ff.; §IV, 41, 203; §IV, 44, vol. 5, 557 ff. = RS.24.245. See §IV, 14, vol. 4, 53 ff. for the theory that Ba'al Ṣᵉphōn was the head of the state pantheon, the counterpart of Amun in Egypt.   [11] §v, 21, 66; Baal, II, ii, 13; IV, i, 3.

comparably rich sources of information about the religious beliefs and ritual practices of the people of Ugarit in the second millennium B.C. They leave the impression, moreover, that the tradition they embody is not exclusively local, but rather one in which the whole of Canaan may at one time or another have participated, since many of the deities who form the *dramatis personae* of the myths are known to have been worshipped in a number of cult centres from Mount Casius in the north to Egypt, from the Mediterranean coast to the banks of the Euphrates.[1]

Chief among these was the god Ba'al himself, whose worship was widespread, indeed universal, in Canaan.[2] In the Ugaritic mythological texts, he appears as a warrior god, 'the Prince, Lord of Earth', and 'the Victor (Aliyan)'. As 'Rider on the Clouds', he is the storm-god of the mountains, manifest in lightning and thunder, who sends rain and snow on the earth[3] and causes the growth of vegetation. His daughters are Mist and Dew,[4] and his father, Dagan, the personification of corn;[5] elsewhere, however, Ba'al is said to be the son of El.[6] A well-cut stela found in the temple of Ba'al at Ras Shamra without doubt depicts the god holding a thunderbolt in one hand and lightning in the other.[7] On his head he wears a horned helmet, symbol of divinity throughout the Near East and, in its peculiar North Syrian form, recalling the bull, the embodiment of male potency, to which Ba'al is often likened.[8] His feet tread the mountain tops. The name Ba'al means 'Lord', and the local gods of individual city states of Canaan were often referred to as 'the Ba'al of City X'. Some had special epithets: Melqart (King of the City), for instance, was the Ba'al of Tyre. As the lord *par excellence* of the early Semitic peoples of North Syria, Hadad the storm-god is identified in the texts with Ba'al,[9] and it has been suggested that the worship of Ba'al may have originated in the old Amorite cult of Hadad centred in Mari, Tirqa and Aleppo.[10]

The high deity of the Ugaritic pantheon, however, was not Ba'al but El, sometimes called *Lutpan*, the 'Kindly One',[11] who

[1] §v, 2, 71 f.; §v, 21, 68 f.; A, 2.   [2] §v, 50; §v, 30, 80 ff.; §v, 27, 362 f.
[3] *Ba'al*, v, i, ll. 6–9; A, 1, 280 f.   [4] *Ba'al*, 1, v, l. 10; 11, i, l. 11.
[5] §v, 25, 154; §v, 27, 364; §v, 23, 746; §v, 2, 74; otherwise §v, 21, 79 f.
[6] *Aqhat*, 11, iv, l. 28; §v, 25, 6, n. 3, 13, n. 2.
[7] §iv, 44, vol. 2, 121 ff., pls. xxiii, xxiv; §iv, 35, 68; A, 32. See Plate 100. A text describing Ba'al's enthronement (A, 13 = RŠ.24.245) calls his sceptre 'the tree of lightning'.
[8] §v, 25, 19, 117, n. 3; §iv, 20, 44; §iv, 44, vol. 4, 45; A, 31.
[9] §v, 25, 10, 71 ff.; §iv, 18, 258.   [10] §v, 50, 136; §iv, 20, 35 f.
[11] §v, 25, 159; §v, 60, 25, 44 f.; A, 24, 15 ff.

is described as an old man with white hair and beard.[1] He was believed to live in or upon a mountain, at a place where 'the two rivers join the two oceans'.[2] His epithets 'creator of creatures' and 'father of mankind' proclaim his function.[3] Most of the other deities are counted among his progeny and he entertains his sons, the seventy gods, at a banquet in his palace.[4] In this creative aspect he is called 'the bull El'.[5] In spite of his pre-eminent position, however, he plays little part in the myths and is a somewhat remote and mysterious figure;[6] he is not invoked in treaties or referred to in texts other than literary, and no priest or temple of his is mentioned in the administrative tablets. El may perhaps be the god represented by a relief, in rather clumsy style, found at Ras Shamra in the level of the fourteenth century B.C., which depicts an elderly bearded figure seated on a throne and footstool of Egyptian type and wearing a crown which derives from the curious crown of horns and feathers worn by Egyptian divinities and known as the *atef*.[7] Over his head, and that of the king who performs a ceremony of offering before him, the winged sun-disc hovers. The central figure in a group of bronze statuettes found together[8] wears a similar *atef* crown; he is an elderly god, seated between two identical youthful Baʿals. The fourth figure of the group is, significantly, that of a bull. The iconography is again Egyptian: the bull wears between his horns a sun-disc engraved with the hieroglyph for 'life' (ʿ*nkh*).

The question of the relationship between Baʿal and El has been much discussed. Baʿal is a youthful, vigorous god, and a considerable part of the cycle of myths concerning him is devoted to the building of his temple, since he alone of the great gods has no fitting abode.[9] Does this point to a comparatively late introduction of the cult of the storm-god from elsewhere?[10] A theory has been put forward that the Ugaritic texts contain hints of a struggle, the account of which may one day be unearthed, between El and Baʿal, a struggle[11] which finally ended in the victory of the young god over the old (just as in Hurrian mythology Kumarbi was replaced by the storm-god, the Babylonian Enlil

---

[1] *Aqhat*, II, i, l. 25; *Baʿal*, II, v. l. 4; etc.

[2] §v, 77, 110 f. Pope, who translates 'the two deeps' (§v, 60, 72 ff.), suggests Afqa at the source of the Adonis river. Cf. A, 24, 106 ff.

[3] *Aqhat*, II, i, l. 25; *Baʿal*, II, ii, l. 11; iii, l. 31; etc.; §IV, 20, 54 ff.; §v, 21, 73 ff.

[4] §IV, 44, vol. 5, 545 ff.; §v, 78, III = *RS*.24.258.

[5] §v, 21, 73; §v, 60, 35 ff.; A, 29; A, 32, 129 f., 161.      [6] §v, 60, 28.

[7] §IV, 35, pl. 31; §v, 65, 213; §v, 60, 46. See Plate 138 (*b*).

[8] A, 31, 1 ff. and pls. 11 f.      [9] §v, 58, 5 ff., 52 ff., 84; A, 7, 58 ff.   [10] §IV, 35, 8.

[11] §v, 50, 75 ff., 86 ff., 130 ff.; §IV, 21, 58 f.

gave place to Marduk, and Kronos was deposed by Zeus),[1] and that El was thereafter banished to the nether world.[2] There is no doubt, however, that, at the time when the majority of the Ugaritic texts were composed, El was still one of the high gods.

It must be admitted that there are reasons for supposing that a gap of some centuries separates the composition of the texts and their copying or redaction in the fourteenth century B.C. The hierarchy of the gods who play the chief roles in the myths which survive does not fully correspond with the pantheon of fourteenth- and thirteenth-century Ugarit as it may be compiled from lists of some fifty or sixty deities drawn up by the priestly scribes for ritual purposes,[3] and from some hundreds of personal names compounded with those of deities, found in the administrative and economic texts.[4] Babylonian and Hurrian deities, who played an important part in the daily life of Ugarit and Alalakh,[5] are absent from the myths. Dagan, who is mentioned in the literary texts only as Baʻal's father,[6] was accorded the honour of having one of the two major temples in the heart of the city dedicated to him.[7] Similarly, the Syrian god Resheph[8] is rarely mentioned in the poems: once, in the legend of Keret, his role as a god of pestilence is emphasized,[9] and in a fragment he is called Resheph the Archer, referring to his warlike character.[10] On the strength of such evidence it has been claimed that the mythological poems of Ugarit are of very ancient origin, some perhaps antedating the second millennium altogether,[11] or at least that they were some hundreds of years old at the time when our copies were made by King Niqmaddu's scribes.[12]

Of the leading position of Baʻal at Ugarit throughout the period covered by the textual and archaeological remains there is, at any rate, no doubt. His was the largest and richest temple in the city;[13] oaths were sworn before the king in his name.[14] In the myth which is called after him, he vanquishes his enemies. One of

[1] §v, 21, 77, n. 4; §v, 60, 29 ff.     [2] §v, 60, 72 ff.
[3] §v, 82, 170; §v, 65, 214; §iv, 18, 132, text 9; §iv, 44, vol. 5, 42 ff.; A, 5; §v, 56, 82 f.=RS.20.24.
[4] §v, 73.     [5] §v, 52, 152 f.; §v, 82, 70; §iv, 18, 139, text 50.
[6] §v, 25, 31, n. 1.     [7] §v, 64, 156 ff., pls. 31, 36; §v, 21, 78 ff.
[8] §v, 54; §v, 21, 84 f.; §v, 46, 28.     [9] §v, 25, 28 f.=Keret, I, i, 1.19.
[10] §iv, 30, vol. 2, 5=RS.15.134, l. 3.     [11] §v, 5, 175; §v, 8, 38.
[12] §v, 25, 115=Baʻal, III, vi, l. 16 ff. See also A, 24, 143 ff. for the view that Baʻal-Hadad was introduced by Amorites in the nineteenth or eighteenth centuries B.C., replacing the Canaanite El.
[13] §v, 64, 154 ff. and pl. 36.
[14] §iv, 30, 84=RS.16.143, l. 27; 76=RS.16.144, l. 9 f.

these enemies is Yam, Beloved of El, the personification of the ocean which loomed understandably large in the myths of sea-bordered Canaan. The taming of the ocean of chaos may be mirrored in Ba'al's defeat of Prince Yam in single combat,[1] and the latter's epithet 'Judge River' perhaps shows him in the role of arbiter of the destiny of human souls[2] and reminds us, too, that the ordeal by water was an accepted form of trial in criminal cases.[3] The same poetic cycle relates Ba'al's struggle with his antithesis Mōt, the god of dryness and death,[4] to whom he is for a time forced to submit, with disastrous consequences to the fertility of earth and its creatures,[5] and his subsequent return from the underworld and reinstatement. Once explained as part of an allegorical drama of the annual death of vegetation and its re-awakening, enacted to ensure the continuation of the cycle of sowing and harvest,[6] the episode perhaps rather emphasizes the function of Ba'al as the rain-god, bringer of fertility;[7] while he is temporarily vanquished by drought,[8] 'Athtar, the god of springs and irrigation waters, attempts to take over, but is too small (inadequate[9]) and Ba'al must be revived by his sister, the virgin 'Anath. In another part of the poem 'Anath appears in the guise of a goddess of battle, familiar from her Egyptian manifestations:[10] like the Indian Kali, she revels in destruction and wades in blood.[11] A fragment tells of her battle with the dragon Tannin.[12] In a milder role, as mother of the child-king, she may be depicted in a striking ivory panel from the palace of Ugarit.[13]

Ba'al's consort 'Athtarat, or 'Ashtoreth, the West Semitic form of Ishtar,[14] appears in various guises at Ugarit and Alalakh. As 'Ashtoreth of the Field,[15] she was, like 'Anath, a goddess of battle, and thus rides on horseback in Egypt, as the patron of horses and chariots.[16] Ishtar of Khurri is invoked in Ugarit[17] and the same aspect of the goddess was paramount at Alalakh.[18] In

[1] §v, 25, 12 ff., 20 f.=*Ba'al*, iii*a; §v, 38, 123; §v, 50, 39 ff.; §v, 47, 71.
[2] §v, 25, n. 7.
[3] §iv, 30, vol. 3, 311 ff.=*RS*.15.10, l. 3; §v, 11, vol. 2, 339; §v, 42, 99; §v, 8, 19 f.
[4] §v, 21, 81 f.; §v, 38, 154 ff.; A, 7, 81 ff.; A, 18; A, 33, 62.
[5] §v, 25, 111 ff.=*Ba'al*, iii, ii, l. 17* ff.; iii, iv, l. 1 ff.; cf. §v, 25, 10, 71 ff.
[6] §v, 49, 17 f.  [7] A, 7, 65 ff.  [8] §v, 43, 3 ff.  [9] §v, 25, 20 ff.; §v, 21, 88 f.
[10] §v, 12, 37 f.; §v, 61, 76 ff.  [11] §v, 25, 14; §v, 17; §v, 74, 183; A, 9.
[12] §v, 78, 187 ff.  [13] §v, 18, 54 ff.; see Plate 136 (*b*).
[14] §v, 21, 87; §v, 1, 246.
[15] §iv, 30, vol. 4, 122 =*RS*.17.352, l. 12; §iv, 26, 104, n. 18.
[16] §v, 12, 55 ff.; A, 3, 116 f.; A, 26; see *C.A.H.* ii³, pt. 1, p. 482.
[17] §iv, 30, vol. 3, 171 =*RS*.16.173, ll. 4–5.
[18] §v, 83, 16 f.; §iv, 30, vol. 4, 52 =*RS*.17.340, l. 20.

her astral form she personified the planet Venus, as did the Baby-lonian Ishtar,[1] and her male counterpart 'Athtar, who, as we have seen, aspired to the kingship during Ba'al's absence, appears in South Arabia later as a stellar deity.[2] He is called the son of another goddess, Athirat, or Asherah, who, as the wife of El and Mistress of the Gods, plays a more important part in the myths than her spouse or her son.[3] Her epithet 'Dame Athirat of the Sea'[4] emphasizes her connexion with the coastal cities: she is called Athirat of Tyre[5] and at Sidon was known as Elat, the female aspect of El.[6] Qadesh, the Holy One, who is depicted on stelae from Egypt[7] and on a pendant from Ras Shamra[8] as a naked goddess standing on the back of a lion, may represent an aspect of one of these goddesses, whose personalities and attributes merged and interchanged against a background of common belief. Which, if any, of them is represented by the numerous crudely formed plaques and pendants found in Syrian and Palestinian sites[9] cannot be determined.[10] The emphasis placed upon the female parts suggests that they were amulets worn by women to aid fertility or protect in childbirth. On a plaque from Alalakh, the nude goddess holds in each hand a dove, symbol in Mesopo-tamia of the goddess Ishtar.[11]

The importance of Horon, god of the underworld, is attested in Canaanite place-names and personal names.[12] In Egyptian texts he is equated with the god Horus, and it is possible that figurines of hawks found at Minet el-Beidha represent this god.[13] His adventures are described in a large mythological text recently dis-covered, in which his home is said to be the City of the East.[14] The chief role in this text, which appears to be an incantation against snake-bite,[15] is played by the goddess Shapash, 'the lamp of the gods',[16] who personified the sun as did her counterpart Yerakh, 'the Illuminator of Heaven', the moon—while Kushukh, their own moon-god, was invoked by the Hurrians in Ugarit.[17] Divine

---

[1] §v, 16, 57.    [2] §v, 21, 85; §v, 15, 57.    [3] §v, 59, 38 f.; §v, 1, 42.
[4] §v, 25, 93 = Ba'al, II, i, l. 19, etc.    [5] §v, 25, 33 = Keret, I, iv, ll. 35, 38.
[6] Ibid. ll. 36, 39.    [7] §v, 12, 362 f.; C.A.H. II³, pt. 1, p. 483.
[8] §IV, 44, vol. 2, 36, fig. 10.
[9] §v, 3; §v, 61; §v, 11, vol. 1, 401, fig. 149; vol. 2, 395.    [10] §v, 30, 79.
[11] §IV, 55, 247, pl. LIV, no. 0; §v, 10, 42.
[12] §v, 2, 81; §v, 21, 82 f.; §v, 35, 61 f.; §IV, 44, vol. 2, vii f.
[13] §IV, 44, vol. 1, 32, fig. 24; §v, 44, 177 f.
[14] §v, 79, 108; §v, 65, 213, Abb. 33.
[15] §IV, 44, vol. 5, 564 ff.; §v, 78, 106 = RS.24.244; A, 6.    [16] §v, 16.
[17] §IV, 30, vol. 3, 316. For the Hurrian pantheon at Ugarit, see E. Laroche in §IV, 44, vol. 5, 518 ff.

pairs such as Dawn and Sunset[1] (or Morning Star and Evening Star[2]) and Mist and Dew[3] bear the stamp of mythopoeic imagination and reflect, too, that deeply rooted love of symmetry which was manifest in literature as well as in art. So, too, some beings have composite names and are treated in the poems sometimes as one deity, and sometimes as two: such are Gupan-and-Ugar, the messenger of the gods, apparently a personification of vineyards and fields,[4] Qodesh-and-Amurr, a compound perhaps of the separate gods of Qadesh and Amurru, by a process of syncretization,[5] and the craftsman god Kathir-and-Khasis, 'Skilful and Clever',[6] who comes to the aid of the gods whenever something is to be fashioned with skill, and was said to hail from far-off Caphtor,[7] an indication that the people of North Syria recognized the debt owed by their craftsmen to the inspiration and techniques of Minoan Crete.[8] He must be the Khusor to whom Philo, quoting Sanchuniathon, ascribes the invention of iron.[9]

The fragmentary text containing the myth of Aqhat, son of King Danel,[10] again contains the theme of dying vegetation.[11] At the instigation of 'Anath, who covets his wonderful bow, Aqhat is murdered and the bow shattered. Drought follows, the crops fail, and Danel rides about his kingdom seeking the cause of the disaster, aided by his daughter Pughat (Perfume):

> 'Hear, O Pughat, who carriest the waters on thy shoulders,
> Who sprinklest the dew on the barley, who knowest
> The courses of the stars; saddle the he-ass,
> Yoke the donkey, put on my trappings of silver,
> My saddle-cover of gold.' . . .
> Forthwith she saddled the he-ass,
> Forthwith she yoked the donkey; forthwith
> She lifted up her father (and) put him on the back of the he-ass,

[1] §v, 25, 22 f., 121 ff.; §v, 21, 91; A, 12, 7 ff.

[2] §v, 36, 70 ff. Cf. A, 5, 281 f.

[3] §v, 25, 85. Sometimes Ba'al has a third daughter, perhaps 'Earth'. Aistleitner (§v, 1, 254) associates *Pdry* rather with the thunderbolt of Ba'al, and Neiman (A, 23) with lightning.     [4] §v, 25, 146, n. 26; *Ba'al*, 11, vii, l. 54.

[5] §v, 1, 26 no. 289, though J. R. Kupper (*L'iconographie du dieu Amurru*, Acad. royale de Belgique, Lettres LV/1, 1961) doubts the authenticity of Amurru as a god of a city or region. Alternatively 'Holy and Blessed' (§v, 30, 787).

[6] §v, 38, 154 ff.; §v, 21, 81 f.; §v, 47, 97.

[7] §v, 25, 91 = *Ba'al*, v, vi, ll. 14–16. He is also said to come from *Ḥkpt* (*Ba'al*, v, vɪ, 13), possibly Egypt (from Egyptian *ḥt-k3-ptḥ*, Memphis; §v, 47, 137), but perhaps rather a name of Crete, or some place in Crete (§v, 25, 169).

[8] §v, 34, vol. 1 = Eusebius, 1, 10, 11.

[9] §v, 25, 12 n. 1 and 169; §v, 47, 95; A, 8, 35 f.

[10] §v, 25, 5 ff.; 48 ff.; §v, 72, 125 ff.; 186 ff.; 217 ff.          [11] §v, 47, 84 ff.

On the fairest part of the back of the donkey.
Danel approached, he went round his parched land(?)
That he might descry green corn in the parched land(?), might descry
Green corn in the scrub, might embrace the green corn
And kiss (it saying): 'May, ah! may green corn shoot up in the parched
    ground(?), may green corn shoot in the scrub
(Blasted) with heat, may the hand of Aqhat the Hero
Gather thee (and) put thee within the granary!'[1]

Aqhat's body is found and mourned for seven years, and Pughat girds on her armour and sets out to avenge her brother. The end of the story, which is lost, must have told of the resurrection of the dead hero and the consequent revival of vegetation upon earth.[2]

Another of the texts, entitled by the scribal copyist 'Of Keret',[3] purports to relate the deeds of a hero or demigod. As the poem opens, Keret, king of 'well-watered Khubur', is bemoaning the loss of his wife, the destruction of his sons and the ruin of his palace. El appears to him in a vision and promises him success. In obedience to the god's instructions, Keret sacrifices to the gods and prepares a great army, which overruns the countryside. On the third day's march he comes to a large shrine where the goddesses of Tyre and Sidon promise him success. The following day he reaches Udum, whose King Pabil[4] attempts to buy him off; the latter insists only that he shall be given Pabil's beautiful daughter Ḥuriya to wife, for El has promised that she will bear him sons. The request is granted, and Keret, with divine blessing, begets seven sons and eight daughters. Later in the tale he falls sick, and at a feast prepared by his queen the nobles of Khubur are bidden to pray for him; bread, wine and oil, which depend on the king's well-being, begin to fail. One of the king's sons, Yaṣṣib, supposing the sickness to be mortal, attempts to seize the throne, but the king is restored by the intervention of El and threatens his rebellious son with the vengeance of the gods.

The latter half of the story follows a familiar pattern but the opening narrative has been interpreted as embodying the memory of some historical invasion of Edom and the Negeb by an army from North Syria.[5] The names Keret and Pabil, however, have not so far been found in any inscription or text and the theory, in whole or in part, has been rejected by most scholars.[6] Alterna-

---

[1] §v, 25, 61 = *Aqhat*, I, ii, ll. 1–5, 8–18.        [2] §v, 25, 8.
[3] §v, 25, 2 ff.; 28 ff.; §v, 39; §v, 41, 142 ff.; §v, 43, 66 ff.; §v, 46; §v, 70; §v, 71.
[4] §v, 25, 5, n. 7.        [5] §v, 70; §v, 51, vol. 2, 105 ff.; §v, 49, 38 ff; §v, 52, 147 f.
[6] §v, 25, 5; §v, 47, 14 f.; §v, 39, 6 ff. Albright (A, 3, 103 and n. 19) suggests that the name Keret may be the Indo-Aryan *Kirta*, the ancestor of the Mitannian royal house.

tively, the story has been interpreted as a social myth pertaining to the rise of the dynasty of Ugarit.[1]

The language of this earliest Canaanite literature is full of metaphor and poetic imagery.[2] Many of the stylistic conventions of later epic poetry are employed.[3] Statements are made twice or three times in parallel terms for greater emphasis:

> Ba'al opened a window in the mansion,
> A lattice in the midst of the palace,
> He opened a skylight in the roof.[4]

The effect of emphasis is frequently achieved by the cumulative use of numbers in progression;[5] the poet thus describes the conquests of Ba'al:

> He did seize six and sixty
> Cities, seven and seventy towns,
> He became lord of eight and eighty,
> Lord of nine and ninety.[6]

Similarly, the countless army of King Keret is described as

> Going by thousands like rain,
> By tens of thousands like drops of rain.[7]

Set phrases recur, as they do in Hebrew literature of the Old Testament[8] and in the Homeric poems.[9] The close similarity between the phraseology of the Ugaritic texts and that used in certain poetic passages of the Pentateuch, the Song of Deborah, for instance, and some Psalms,[10] has led some to suggest an early, perhaps even second millennium, date for the latter.[11] Similarly, there is reason to think that the epics of Homer derive their inspiration, and even part of their text, from an ancient tradition, oral or written, of Mycenaean heroic poetry, a tradition which may go back at least to the fourteenth century B.C.[12] Mycenaean merchants at the court of the kings of Ugarit, must have listened to the priestly musicians singing their lays of Ba'al and of 'Anath and Astarte. Such contacts, in countries throughout the eastern Mediterranean, gave birth to that interchange of forms and themes which was the literary heritage of the Late Bronze Age.[13]

[1] §v, 46, 3 ff.; §v, 47, 14 f.    [2] §iv, 18, 102 ff.; §v, 1, 9 f.; A, 15, 111 ff.
[3] §v, 50, 80 ff.; see below, pp. 566 ff.
[4] §v, 25, 101 = Ba'al, ii, vii, ll. 25–28.    [5] §v, 47, 211 f.; §v, 1, 11; §iv, 18, 104.
[6] §v, 25, 101 = Ba'al, ii, vii, ll. 9–12.    [7] Keret, i, iv, ll. 17–18.
[8] §v, 2, 15 f.; §iv, 18, 108; §v, 47, 189 ff.; §v, 50, 80 ff.; see below, p. 566.
[9] §v, 14, 81 ff., 91 ff.; §v, 42, 102 ff.
[10] §v, 38, 73 ff.; §v, 29, 134 ff.; §iv, 18, 114 f.; §iv, 2, 23.
[11] §v, 7, 27 ff.; §v, 8, 38.    [12] §v, 13, 14, 19 ff., 33; §iv, 80, 37, 66.
[13] A, 8, 44 f.; A, 14.

# CHAPTER XXI (c)

## TROY

### VI. TROY VII

Under this designation Dörpfeld grouped two layers of very different character, and called them VII 1 and VII 2 respectively (our VII*a* and VII*b*). See Fig. 1.

Settlement VII*a* represents a direct continuation after the earthquake of the culture that flourished in Troy VI. The fortress walls were repaired where needed and most of the earlier gateways were re-used. Inside the citadel the old streets were cleared and new houses were erected; they were built in a characteristic masonry that, along with rough unworked material, re-utilized many squared blocks that had obviously been shaken down from the structures of the Sixth Settlement. The houses themselves, for the most part small, were numerous; they were crowded closely together, often with party walls, and they seem to have filled the whole area inside the fortification, where they were superposed over the earlier buildings, as well as the considerable spaces that had previously been left open. Another distinctive feature is the presence in almost every house of large *pithoi* or storage jars: ranging in number from one or two to eight or ten or even twenty, they were sunk deeply beneath the floors so that the mouth, covered by a stone slab, projected only an inch or two above the ground.[1]

The minor objects and pottery clearly attest a continuity in all branches of craftsmanship. Grey Minyan Ware, for the most part indistinguishable from that of Troy VI, occurs in abundance; alongside it are found in large quantities Red and Tan Wares closely resembling those of the preceding period, though the Tan Ware especially is often coated with a distinctive orange-tan glaze. Some changes in the pot shapes may also be noted, though the repertory as a whole conforms to that of Troy VI. Imported Mycenaean pottery in the style of Late Helladic III*a* still occurs, but that of III*b* is much more common, being found along with Cypriote White Slip II Ware. The incidence of Mycenaean imports, however, has fallen off greatly since the time of Troy VI,

* An original version of this chapter was published in fascicle 1 in 1964.
[1] See Plate 139.

[ 161 ]

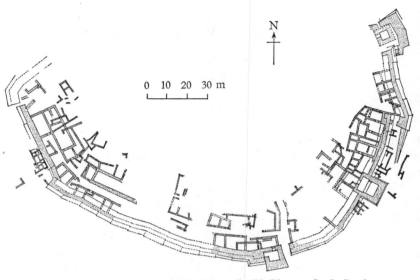

Fig. 1. Buildings of Troy VII. (From C. W. Blegen, C. G. Boulter, J. L. Caskey and M. Rawson, *Troy* IV 1 (Princeton, 1958), fig. 321.)

and the number of imitations in local Trojan fabric has grown proportionately. The evidence seems to indicate that relations with the Aegean had lost much of their intensity and importance. No objects were found that could be identified as importations from Central Anatolia.

The layer of accumulated deposit of Period VII*a* had an average thickness of little more than 0·50 m.; but in streets and certain other places debris from the final destruction was heaped up to a height of 1–1·5 m. In some houses two successive floor levels were noted. One, or at the most two, generations would seem to be a reasonable estimate of the duration of the settlement. It came to its end in a devastating conflagration that swept over the entire citadel and reduced all the houses to ruins. Under the masses of stones that fell into the streets inside the South Gate were found remnants of the skeletons of two human victims of the catastrophe, which has the appearance of the handiwork of man. The crowding together of a great number of small houses within the fortress and the installation of innumerable huge storage jars to lay up a supply of provisions are factors that suggest preparations for a siege, and the final holocaust was the usual accompaniment of the capture, sacking and burning of an ancient town. The general agreement of this evidence with the accounts preserved in Greek tradition cannot safely be disregarded: if a Troy of Priam,

besieged and taken by an Agamemnon, ever actually existed in
fact, it must be identified with the settlement called VII *a*.

The exact date of the capture and destruction of Troy by the
Achaeans has not been definitely fixed in terms of absolute years.
The Greek chronographers, who based their conclusions on com-
putations of genealogies, reached many different results, ranging
from the fourteenth century through the thirteenth and on down
to 1184 B.C., as calculated by Eratosthenes. The latter date has
been more or less tacitly accepted by numerous scholars. Archaeological research has now shown that the event took place at a
time when imported pottery in the style of Mycenaean III b was
in common use on the site, though the style of III a had not yet
been wholly abandoned. The fashion of Mycenaean III c was still
altogether unknown. These observations give a plausible fixed
point in the sequence of ceramic styles, but to convert it into a
specific year B.C. is another matter on which one finds no close
agreement among the specialists. The evidence from contacts
with Egypt is still, particularly for the later Mycenaean phases,
woefully inadequate. There is, however, a fairly general belief
that the style of Mycenaean III a prevailed through most, if not
all, of the fourteenth century, whereas that of III b flourished
during the greater part of the thirteenth century, coming to its end
shortly before 1200 B.C. If this view is approximately right, the
fall of Troy and the end of Settlement VII *a* should be placed
about 1250 B.C.,[1] coinciding with the estimate of Herodotus. In
any event the expedition against Troy must surely have been
carried out about the middle of the ceramic phase III b when
Mycenaean Greece stood at the height of its wealth as well as of
its political and military power.

In Settlement VII *b*, which seems to have been built without an
interval after the fire, two successive strata have been recognized.
The objects recovered from the lower stratum (VII *b* 1) make it
clear that some part of the Trojan population survived the disaster
and in their reconstructed houses they continued to maintain the
same culture that had flourished in Period VII *a*. This is especially
evident in the pottery which in all respects carries on the local
tradition of the past. Grey Minyan, Red-washed and Tan Wares
continue to be made in large quantities and in forms which,
except in small but distinctive variations, can scarcely be differentiated from what had gone before. Exactly how long this phase
lasted has not been determined, but it can hardly have been less
than a generation and may have been more.

[1] For a later date, *c.* 1200 B.C., see *C.A.H.* I³, pt. 1, p. 246.

The pottery found in strata of Troy VII*b* 1 offers a little evidence for sequence dating. The imported Mycenaean ware includes some pieces in the style of Furumark's category IIIb and others that must be assigned to IIIc. It thus appears that the settlement overlapped the phase during which the ceramic change from IIIb to IIIc was working itself out. This carries us down, in accordance with most current views, to a time near the end of the thirteenth century.

The upper stratum of Troy VII*b* reveals an abrupt change in culture which unmistakably signifies the arrival of a new people on the scene. The most conspicuous innovation makes its appearance in the pottery, known as *Buckelkeramik*, or Knobbed Ware, a rude, handmade, black polished fabric in a wholly new repertory of shapes. In broad general lines the closest analogy for this pottery is to be found in the Late Bronze Age in Hungary, and it is from that region that many archaeologists believe the migration to have started which brought the *Buckelkeramik* folk to Asia Minor, probably by way of Thrace. Certainty has not yet been reached regarding details of this problem, nor is the extent of the diffusion, if any, which this rude culture attained in Anatolia yet adequately known.

The minor objects which come from the stratum of VII*b* 2 at Troy also exhibit a break with the past of the site; and the architecture, too, has a stamp of its own. Many small houses were built throughout the citadel, and a fairly consistent feature in the masonry is the setting of rough orthostates along the lower edges of the walls. In some parts at least the old fortification walls seem to have remained standing above ground and were evidently re-used; in other places the settlement now spread out over the earlier walls.

Not all the previous inhabitants were exterminated. Some pottery in Grey Minyan and Tan Wares still continues to be made, and this fact suggests that there were survivors familiar with the old culture.

A few sherds of imported Mycenaean ware of the Granary Class have been found: they indicate that some relations were still maintained with the Aegean, and they also give ground for concluding that Settlement VII*b* 2, following immediately after VII*b* 1, continued to exist for some time, presumably lasting on well into the twelfth century while the pottery style of Mycenaean IIIc prevailed. How much longer the settlement endured has not been ascertained. It was destroyed in a conflagration, perhaps in connexion with the disorders that attended the long and troubled transition from the Late Bronze Age to the Iron Age.

# CHAPTER XXII(a)

## THE EXPANSION OF MYCENAEAN CIVILIZATION

### I. THE ECLIPSE OF THEBES

THE destruction of the Minoan palace centres about 1400 B.C., whatever its cause,[1] left the leadership of the Aegean world thenceforth to Mainland Greece; and for nearly two centuries the Mycenaean civilization was free to develop and enjoy a remarkable prosperity, founded in part on the heritage of Minoan culture which it had already absorbed, in part on new opportunities, vigorously exploited, of commercial and cultural relations with all parts of the eastern Mediterranean. The chronology of the period[2] is based on the typological sequence of Mycenaean pottery styles;[3] and that a reliable dating sequence can be established is due to the remarkable degree of uniformity of style throughout the area in which Mycenaean pottery occurs, a uniformity obviously bound up with the frequent and easy communications that characterize the period. Absolute dating, in turn, depends on the occurrence of Mycenaean pottery in datable contexts in Egypt, Palestine, and Syria, which is evidence of regular traffic with those parts. In these two centuries of maturity Mycenaean Greece becomes, as we shall see, part of a much larger cultural area, comprising the whole eastern Mediterranean, and exists on virtually the same level as the older civilizations in that area. It is, until well into the thirteenth century, a period of prosperity and of peace. There is no observable major event, natural or political, that separates Myc. III a from Myc. III b; the two phases may be treated as a continuum. Some hostile encounters abroad the Mycenaean Greeks must surely have had; but we shall find but little trace of them either in the written history of their neighbours or in the archaeological record. In Crete the destruction of the palaces (oddly, if Mycenaeans were the destroyers) is not followed by any obvious or considerable signs of Mycenaean settlement;

---

* An original version of this chapter was published as fascicle 26 in 1964, the present chapter includes revisions made in 1970.

[1] See *C.A.H.* II[3], pt. 1, pp. 558 and 656.

[2] See *C.A.H.* I[3], pt. 1, p. 245.　　　　　　　[3] See Plate 144.

indeed the divergence between Late Minoan III and Late Helladic III is much greater than between Late Helladic II and the last phase of the palace at Cnossus. In Rhodes, though Trianda may have been destroyed by Mycenaeans, actual Mycenaean settlement[1] had begun before this. At Miletus, however, on the coast of Asia Minor, the first Mycenaean pottery, of III a style, occurs above the destruction by fire of the preceding Minoan settlement;[2] we have here, perhaps, early evidence of the increased freedom and strength of Mycenae.

In the history of events, then, it is primarily the destruction of the Cretan palaces that marks off Late Helladic II from Late Helladic III. Yet the period of maturity was not achieved without some further adjustments at home, some of which involved hostilities between the various kingdoms of Greece, to judge from tradition, though these conflicts are but doubtfully tied to the archaeological data. We have already seen in L.H. II the growth of a united Argolis, with its palace-capital established by Perseus at Mycenae;[3] of Laconia we hear little as yet; Pylus to the southwest is a formidable kingdom, though we cannot be sure for this period where its capital lay: the beehive tombs of Kakovatos imply a palace site in that area,[4] and we know that Messenian Pylus (Ano Englianos) had at least a citadel, and so probably a ruler's palace, by L.H. I;[5] Elis, the home of Pelops and his line, completes the picture of the Peloponnese, for the more rugged areas of Achaea and Arcadia were not sufficiently productive or populous to be of political importance. Attica we may think of as a separate state, shortly to achieve greater prosperity now that it is free of the Minoan yoke.[6]

Further north the most important state is the city of Cadmus, the later Thebes, so important indeed as to be a rival of Mycenae for the supremacy of Greece. Its eminence at this time may need a word of explanation, though the reasons for it are in part the same that were operative in the days of its classical greatness. It is not simply that it lies in a productive territory; it also controls important routes. Obviously it sits in the path between Attica and northern Greece; less obviously, to the modern traveller, it is at the crossing of this route with another which ran by sea from the coasts near Corinth or Sicyon to the north-eastern inlets of the Corinth-

---

[1] See *C.A.H.* II³, pt. 1, p. 644.   [2] §v, 17, vol. 7, 131 f.
[3] See *C.A.H.* II³, pt. 1, p. 650
[4] Cf. *C.A.H.* II³, pt. 1, p. 642.
[5] §1, 2, vol. 64, 156; A, 2, 31–3 and 420.
[6] See *C.A.H.* II³, pt. 1, p. 657.

ian Gulf and so from the later Thisbe or Creusis straight across Boeotia to Chalcis, Euboea, and the Aegean. A Peloponnesian power was as sure to be involved with Thebes in the fifteenth century B.C. as in the fifth. Tradition was well aware that this had been so. The greatness of Thebes in the first heroic age left a wealth of legends which provided the themes of many a classical Greek tragedy; and it was indeed a fit subject for tragedy. Here was a city most remembered for its fall. First there was the great siege which to us is most familiar through the drama of Aeschylus, the *Seven against Thebes*—a siege indecisive in its outcome; then, in the latter age of heroes, the final destruction by the Epigoni, the sons or successors of the Seven. Hesiod mentions the Theban War and the Trojan War in the same breath, as the greatest events of heroic times, and as the most disastrous, by which the race of heroes was brought to an end:

> τοὺς μὲν πόλεμός τε κακὸς καὶ φύλοπις αἰνὴ
> τοὺς μὲν ἐφ᾽ ἑπταπύλῳ Θήβῃ, Καδμηΐδι γαίῃ,
> ὤλεσε, μαρναμένους μήλων ἕνεκ᾽ Οἰδιπόδαο....[1]

Here the occasion of the war is given as the flocks of Oedipus, a characteristic bone of contention among early peoples. To us the version used by the tragedians is more familiar, the quarrel between Polynices and Eteocles who disputed the throne after the death of Oedipus. Eteocles seized the government, and Polynices fled to the court of Adrastus of Argos. It is significant that the Argolid is the natural refuge for a Theban exile. At Argos Polynices was joined by Tydeus, also an exile, from Calydon. (Both the man and the place confirm that this is an event of the first heroic age.) Adrastus espoused their cause, and in due course an army led by these and four other heroes—the famous Seven— marched against Thebes. It was essentially an Argive expedition; the surviving first line of the *Thebaïs*, beginning Ἄργος ἄειδε, θεά..., makes that clear; and the *Iliad* agrees that Mycenae took no part, though invited to do so.[2] This seems, historically, strange; it may be that as with the stories of Danaus and Perseus we have here some distortion resulting from rival traditions.[3] To return to the story, Thebes withstood a long siege, until in the final desperate assault Eteocles and Polynices each fell by the other's hand; the city was saved, and the attackers were obliged to withdraw. A generation later, however, the attack of the Epigoni was more successful, and Thebes was destroyed. Both campaigns were the

---

[1] *Works and Days*, 161 ff.  [2] *Iliad* IV, 376 ff.
[3] See *C.A.H.* II³, pt. I, p. 650.

subject of epics now lost, and are referred to frequently from
Homer[1] onwards; and there is no reason to suppose the tale was
not based on fact. We have noticed Hesiod's allusion to it; and
when, much later in time, Pausanias comments[2] that in his opinion
the Theban War was the most important internal conflict in
Greece in all the heroic period, he is but echoing the general
testimony of antiquity. In Homer, references to the War of the
Seven are linked with the praise of Diomede's father Tydeus, who
had been one of them, and it is cited as an outstanding exploit
of the previous age, an example to live up to. The campaign of
the Epigoni (which the son of Capaneus remarks was a yet greater
exploit, since it was successful) is ascribed to the generation of the
Trojan War heroes. This, as observed before,[3] need not represent
the true chronological interval between the two campaigns; but
if it does not, where are they to be dated?

On the interpretation which we have advanced, the campaign
of the Seven, as an event of the first heroic age, belongs not later
than L.H. II. It need not have left any trace in the archaeological
record. The eventual sack of Thebes, however, should be identifiable by a destruction level on the site. Unfortunately the Mycenaean palace lies most unfavourably for excavation, beneath the
modern town; but such investigation as has been possible[4] when
parts of the site have been cleared for rebuilding showed clearly
that the palace had been a structure of some magnificence, deco
rated with frescoes and carved stonework, and with extensive
store-chambers in which lay wine or oil jars with brief painted
inscriptions in Linear B. Certain place-names in the inscriptions,
together with analysis of the clay, suggest that at least some of the
jars were imports from Crete.[5] Fragments of carved ivory attest
the elegance of the palace furnishing, and a few Linear B tablets
survive from its administrative records. The whole was destroyed
by a fire of unusual intensity, which left a thick burnt layer on
much of the site. What the earlier excavators published of the
pottery found in this burnt stratum consisted largely of plain cups
and *kylikes* (stemmed goblets), which are harder to date than
decorated wares but have usually been ascribed to L.H. III a.[6] The
more recent investigations, however, have distinguished two successive palaces, both destroyed (on the evidence of the pottery)
within the L.H. III b period. A treasure of semi-precious stones
discovered in the later palace includes thirty-nine inscribed

---

[1] *Iliad* IV, 376 ff.; V, 801 ff.; X, 284 ff.
[2] Paus. IX, 9.
[4] §1, 3 and 4; A, 16; 17; 20.

[3] *C.A.H.* II[3], pt. 1, pp. 646 f.
[5] A, 7.  [6] §1, 1, 118.

cylinders of lapis lazuli, of Kassite Babylonian style, which as a possible royal gift raise interesting speculations on Theban contacts with the Near East. They do not, however, assist us with the dating; none of them, nor of other associated cylinder-seals, can be later than the fourteenth century B.C.,[1] and they are therefore older than the L.H. IIIb pottery which gives the destruction date. Without more detailed study it is wiser not to try and translate this into years B.C., though it falls within the thirteenth century. The site lay vacant thereafter right down to Christian times, which agrees with the evidence of Strabo[2] that the Cadmea, the palace-citadel of Thebes, was not rebuilt after the sack. Pausanias similarly records that in the *agora* at Thebes the sometime site of the House of Cadmus was still left as an ἄβατον, a place taboo.[3] It also agrees with the evidence of the Homeric *Catalogue of Ships*, which does not even mention Thebes or Cadmea among the cities of Boeotia, though *Hypothebai* in that list, *Nether Thebes*, was by some ancient authorities interpreted as referring to the unwalled lower town.[4]

The sack of Thebes may then be regarded as one of the certain events of Mycenaean history; and the elimination of this rival has an obvious bearing on the development of the Mycenaean power in the Peloponnese. Perhaps, too, it contributed to the prosperity of Attica in L.H. III, which is archaeologically well attested by a wide distribution of large cemeteries of well-furnished Mycenaean tombs.[5] Whether such prosperity was due to or combined with the political maturity implied by the ascription to Theseus of the συνοικισμός, the political unification of Attica, is not certainly established. Some modern scholars are indeed reluctant to admit that the synoecism could have occurred so early; yet the tradition[6] is unanimous; and there are hints that it may be true in the archaeological remains. The citadel that in L.H. II was the castle of 'Cephalus' at Thoricus seems not to have been occupied in the succeeding period;[7] and at Brauron too the L.H. III remains seem confined to the open lower slopes of the citadel hill.[8] Were these strongholds in fact dismantled voluntarily as part of the scheme of unification that made the Athenian acropolis the citadel of all Attica?

---

[1] A, 18; 19.    [2] Strabo 412.    [3] Paus. IX, 12, 3.
[4] Strabo 412.    [5] §1, 6.
[6] Thuc. II, 15; Plutarch, *Life of Theseus*, 24.
[7] §1, 5; cf. §1, 1, 109.    [8] Personal observation.

## II. THE RISE OF THE PELOPIDS

If the sack of Thebes took place, as the remains imply, within L.H. IIIb, it may or may not have been the work of literally the same generation of men who fought at Troy. But that the Homeric epic does date it in the same generation must at least imply that it belongs in some sense to the same period, a period regarded already as historically separate from the first heroic age. The implication is that for the generation of the Trojan War the campaign of the Seven was already 'past history', matter perhaps for epic; that of the Epigoni was not: it was part of the current era. This break in tradition we probably ought to connect, for Mycenae at least, with the change of dynasty from Perseids to Pelopids which is so firmly attested by the legends.

The coming of Pelops and his establishment in Elis has already been discussed.[1] The acquisition by his descendants of the kingdom of Mycenae itself, and so of the supremacy of Greece, is represented as subsequent to and to some extent consequent upon the death of Heracles and of his rival Eurystheus. Perhaps that is only another way of saying that it marks a new era. Thucydides tells us briefly that on setting out on a campaign against the sons of Heracles in Attica, Eurystheus had entrusted the kingdom of Mycenae to Atreus, being his mother's brother; and when Eurystheus was killed the people of Mycenae invited Atreus to take over the throne permanently.[2] Thus the Pelopids became more powerful than the Perseids. Later versions of the tale[3] are more elaborate, but do not alter the basic facts of the dynastic change, which there seems no reason to doubt. It is noticeable that Attica is represented as an independent territory; this is always so in the legends. The only hint of connexion with the Argolid that we come across is that Aethra, the mother of Theseus, is said to have been of the family of Pelops; and that Theseus was brought up by her on the further side of the Saronic Gulf, at Troezen. It might be plausible to suggest that the tale of Theseus' 'home-coming' to claim his birthright as the heir of the Athenian king Aegeus, killing brigands and monsters in the Megarid as he came, is but a patriotic Athenian disguise for the annexation of Attica by a Peloponnesian prince. But this remains speculation, and if Attica was ever part of the Peloponnesian kingdom in Mycenaean times Athenian tradition has successfully eliminated the record of it. More probably it really was independent.

[1] *C.A.H.* II³, pt. I, pp. 638 f.
[2] Thuc. I, 9, 2.  [3] E.g. Diod. IV, 58; Apollodorus 2, 4, 5, 2 ff.

Accepting the truth of a major change of dynasty at Mycenae we may find in this the crucial event which separates the first heroic age from the second. No other in the traditional records of heroic dynasties bears any comparable importance. The new establishment in the Peloponnese endured to the end of the Bronze Age; it is the descendants of Atreus—Agamemnon at Mycenae and Menelaus at Sparta—who virtually control the Peloponnese at the time of the Trojan War, and therefore lead the expedition. The kingdom of Pylus never came under the Pelopids' rule, but it was well-disposed towards them. Other parts of Greece, though they might like Attica be independently governed, could be rallied to the Mycenaean standard if the interests of Hellas as a whole were at stake. But though the Pelopids had achieved the supremacy, the rival house, the sons and descendants of Heracles, still sought opportunity to regain it. They figure in this role in the legends right down to the end of the heroic age, when they eventually attained their aim with the help of the Dorian Greek tribes. Thus the dynastic change at Mycenae from Perseids to Pelopids was bound up in the Greek memory with inner racial conflict.

When, in terms of our archaeological chronology, the change took place, is difficult to decide. If it is a fact that the people of Mycenae accepted their new ruler voluntarily, we shall not expect to find there any marks of sack and pillage such as might have confirmed or dated a conquest by violence. We do however know that at some time in Mycenaean IIIa much of Mycenae was rebuilt. The palace whose remains lie on the citadel is the successor of earlier Mycenaean II structures;[1] so are some of the large houses outside the citadel.[2] But not enough is known of the earlier buildings to determine when and why they were replaced. In the absence of more particular clues we need assume no more than rebuilding and improvements prompted by growing economic prosperity. But we may reasonably consider this new era to have been as much the creation of the new dynasty as the result of the removal of the Minoan obstacle to expansion. Which of the two came first, the fall of Crete or the establishment of the Pelopids, we cannot surely tell. Within Mainland Greece, however, we may feel fairly confident that the destruction of Thebes was the work of the new masters of Mycenae. Perhaps that is why it is a clear event in the tradition, while the fall of Cnossus is not.

[1] §III, 34, 189 f.; §III, 35, 266 ff.; A, 13, 59.   [2] III, 38.

## III. THE MATERIAL EVIDENCE

### (a) CITADELS AND PALACES

The palaces of the Mycenaean rulers are best known to us from Mycenae, Tiryns, and Pylus, but undoubtedly there were others. That of Thebes has been mentioned already; one has been identified at Iolcus[1] but not fully excavated; the 'House of Erechtheus' on the Athenian acropolis has been completely razed by classical building activity;[2] there must have been one at Sparta, but it awaits discovery. Mycenae[3] is, unfortunately, the least well preserved of the three excavated palaces; landslips, the levelling of part of the site to build a later temple, and to a lesser extent the unrefined technique of early excavation, have all added to the natural decay of millennia. But unlike their Minoan counterparts, the mainland palaces were built on fortified citadel sites; and Mycenae still retains a colossal magnificence in the monolithic entrance gate surmounted by its limestone relief of lions,[4] and approached between high and massive walls. The citadel wall contained a considerable area in addition to that of the palace proper which occupied the main hill-top. West of the Lion Gate it swings out expressly to include the Grave Circle; and when it was built yet further respect was shown for this royal cemetery by terracing it up to form a level precinct, surrounded by a carefully made wall of upright slabs, within which the already ancient grave stelae were reset at the new level.[5] (So, perhaps, Pelopids made themselves acceptable to a city that still remembered the Perseids with pride.)

Ahead of the gate, a broad ramp, partly preserved, zig-zagged up towards the royal residence. Final access by a staircase of at least two flights brought one to a small courtyard, placed high up where it commands a splendid view south-west over the Argive plain, while to the west rise the mountain massifs of Arcadia, and to the north-west lies the route towards the Isthmus of Corinth. On to the courtyard opened the great hall of the palace, what modern scholars, from its analogies in the Homeric epic, have dubbed the *megaron*. This is distinctive of the Mycenaean palaces; descended from a Middle Helladic type (which can be traced yet farther back) it has no true parallel in Minoan arrange-

---

[1] §III, 21: 1956, 43 ff.; 1957, 31 ff.; 1960, 55 ff.; 1961, 55 ff.; §III, 32.

[2] §III, 8; §III, 20.

[3] §III, 27; III, 34; III, 35; III, 37; III, 38; III, 18; III, 19; IV, 1; IV, 2; IV, 5; III, 39, 386 ff.; A, 13, chs. II and III.

[4] See Plate 140 (a).           [5] See Plate 140 (b); A, 13, 15–35.

ments. It is the nucleus and focus of the whole; other parts of the building are subordinated to it and lead up to it.

This is yet more obvious in the plan of the Tiryns[1] citadel. There a long history of building and expansion resulted in a final fortified circuit of dimensions unusual even in Mycenaean times. In Homeric epic τειχιόεσσα is a standard epithet of the town, 'Tiryns with its walls'. The blocks are so huge that tradition ascribed the building to giants, the Cyclopes,[2] specially invited over from Asia Minor, and so gave to such masonry the name of 'Cyclopean', which is still used. That tradition has a particular interest in that the nearest parallels to such fortifications are in fact those of the Hittites, which may well have been known to the Mycenaean builders.[3] The latest defences at Tiryns on east and south are pierced by a series of embrasures linked to each other by a tunnel, corbel-vaulted, within the twenty-foot thickness of the walls. This forbidding mountain of masonry admitted the visitor indirectly, from an exterior ramp through monolithic gateways like that of Mycenae and by a long corridor leading eventually to a more decorative gate, with columns on either side, opening into a courtyard about thirty yards across. From this a second columned gateway opened into the smaller inner court, surrounded by a colonnade, with on the far side the megaron. This consisted of a shallow porch with two columns, an anteroom of similar dimensions, and the main hall, almost square, with a large circular hearth in the middle around which stood four timber columns supporting the roof. On the right, facing the hearth, stood the king's throne. It is a standard plan, repeated at Pylus,[4] and at Mycenae, though in these the courtyard is much smaller, and without continuous colonnades. It is repeated again on a smaller scale within the Mycenae citadel in the House of Columns[5] (east of the palace), which was perhaps the residence of some high officer of state. A smaller megaron at Tiryns, alongside the chief one, known as the 'Queen's megaron' has a parallel, though not on the strict megaron plan, at Pylus. In both cases the secluded siting lends colour to the idea that these are the women's quarters, but this should not be taken to imply an oriental segregation of women in Mycenaean society, for which there is no evidence.

The megaron, rising to the height of two ordinary floors, with its great hearth and throne, was clearly a ceremonial as much as a

---

[1] §III, 17; III, 26; III, 11; III, 33; A, 13, 11–15 and 46–52. See Plate 141 (a).
[2] Paus. II, 16 5; II, 25, 8; Apollodorus 2, 2, 1, 3; Strabo 373.
[3] §III, 15, 193.          [4] §III, 1; III, 2; III, 39, 422 ff.; A, 2. See Plate 141 (b).
[5] §III, 37, 91 ff.; A, 14, 11 ff.

domestic centre. Other living-rooms were perhaps often on an upper level, for many of the ground floor rooms that cluster round the megaron were used only for storage and service. At Pylus there were large separate buildings for storing jars of wine and oil, and the subordinate rooms and corridors were particularly compact and orderly in plan. At Tiryns or Mycenae the irregularity may be due to a longer history of building or to the unevenness of the site.

The basic structure, of stone or unbaked brick, with timber framing, is common to the Aegean Bronze Age; but decorative features and refinements show specifically Minoan origins. From Crete comes the use, and the form, of columns. Though they were of wood we know their appearance from representations in fresco and ivory carving,[1] as well as from stone half-columns in the façade of one or two beehive-tombs.[2] The fresco decoration of the principal rooms is Minoan in technique; but in L.H. III the style and subjects are more peculiar to the mainland. At Mycenae[3] was a battle scene, with warriors storming a building, and a group of armed men with horses; at Tiryns a lively boar-hunt,[4] with spearmen and dappled hounds in pursuit of the wounded beast; at Pylus[5] lions and griffins, a frieze of dogs, a lyre-player, and a fight between Mycenaean warriors and 'barbarians' clad in skins. The decorative use of gypsum or carved stone for the floors and facings of entrances, as we noted earlier,[6] was another Minoan feature. But floors were more often of plaster, which could be painted in chequerboard schemes to imitate decorative flagging. Sometimes, as in the Tiryns megaron and in a smaller room at Pylus, the squares were filled with motifs of octopus or dolphins—Minoan in origin, but unmistakably Mycenaean in their stylized treatment.[7]

Normally the Mycenaean citadel was not merely a royal residence; it was a military stronghold.[8] At both Mycenae and Tiryns the fortified area included a considerable space that was not built on, presumably to provide accommodation in time of danger for extra forces and perhaps cattle and people from the surrounding countryside. In case of siege, protected access to water was provided: both citadels had hidden rock-cut passages

---

[1] E.g. §III, 35, pl. 33; §IV, 2, fig. 73; §III, 38, vol. 49, 241 and pl. 40. See Plate 143 (*b*).

[2] §III, 37, 29 and 36, fig. 51. See Plate 148 (*b*).

[3] §III, 25. See Plate 142 (*a*).      [4] §III, 26, p. 13. See Plate 142 (*b*).

[5] A, 9.                    [6] *C.A.H.* II³, pt. I, p. 644.

[7] §III, 26, 222 ff. and pls. XIX–XXI; §III, 2, vol. 57, 61; vol. 61, 132 and pl. 45. See Plate 142 (*c*).      [8] Cf. §III, 37, 111; §III, 39, 352 and fig. 17.

and stairs leading to a cistern or other supply.[1] But clearly the bulk of the population in peacetime lived outside the citadels, nearer to their fields and their work. At Mycenae the location of their cemeteries suggests several separate groups of dwellings.[2]

## (b) ARTS AND CRAFTS

Few private houses have yet been explored; but remains at Mycenae show that they could be substantial and luxurious.[3] On a smaller scale we find the same building methods, with well-plastered walls and floors, and even fresco decoration, as in the palaces. They too had their cellars of wine and oil, their stores of painted pottery. Movable furniture has perished, leaving little trace; but a scrap or two of carved wood[4] and numerous fragmentary inlays of ivory,[5] carved in relief, show how delicate and sophisticated was the decoration of tables, chairs, or footstools,[6] in these houses, and a fortiori in the palaces. Ivory was used also for carved boxes[7] and the ornamental handles of large mirrors, for parts of lyres,[8] and occasionally for carving in the round, as in an exquisite group of two women and a small boy found at Mycenae.[9] Favourite subjects in ivory carving include griffins and sphinxes, monsters probably borrowed from the repertory of the eastern countries from which the ivory itself came;[10] others, such as the heart-shaped ivy-leaf, and the figure-of-eight shield, are also familiar in Minoan art.

Jars and lamps of carved stone[11] were sometimes used, but not with the figured reliefs such as are known from the preceding age in Crete. Repoussé work in gold and silver, however, was still current, as we can tell from the splendid cup from Dendra (Midea) in the Argolid.[12] So was the technique of metal inlay; Dendra

[1] §III, 10; §III, 33.                    [2] §III, 36, 121 ff.

[3] §III, 38; §IV, 1; §IV, 2; §IV, 5; §III, 22.

[4] §III, 38, vol. 50, 184 and pl. 27; cf. §III, 5, 166 and fig. 164.

[5] §IV, 2, figs. 11–17, 70–3; §III, 38, vol. 48, 8 and pl. 5; vol. 49, 235 ff. and pls. 33–6; 38–40; vol. 50, 182 and pls. 25, 26, 30; vol. 52, 197–9; A, 17. See Plate 143.

[6] §IV, 7, 332–46.        [7] E.g. §III, 13, pl. VII; §III, 29, 283 ff. See Plate 148.

[8] §III, 34, pls. 55–6; §III, 35, 369 f.; pl. 59; cf. §III, 3, 283; and for lyre §III, 13, pl. VIII, 6 and 10.

[9] §III, 37, 83 f., 86, pls. 101–3; §III, 40. See Plate 143 (a).

[10] Cf. §V, 1 and 2.

[11] E.g. §III, 37, fig. 86; §III, 38, vol. 50, 182 f., pls. 23–4; §IV, 2, figs. 18–23; §III, 35, pl. 52a; §III, 24, fig. 77. See Plate 145.

[12] §III, 24, 31 f., 43 f., frontispiece and pls. IX–XI; 33 f., 50 f., pl. XVI; §III, 23, 89 ff., frontispiece and pls. IV, VI. See Plate 146 (a).

again provides a fine example, a silver cup ornamented with bulls' heads (which has a parallel, even more beautiful, from Enkomi in Cyprus); and other pieces are known from Mycenae and the Pylus area.[1]

Vessels of bronze were doubtless common. They are fairly often found in tombs;[2] and a further indication is the frequency with which pottery imitates obviously metallic shapes and finishes.[3] Though less often found, bronze tools must equally have been plentiful. Axes, adzes, saws, chisels, and hammers were essential to the Mycenaean builders, whether working in wood or stone, as were hoes, ploughshares, and sickles to the farmer.[4] Finer tools were needed by carvers of wood and ivory, and by the engravers of signets of semi-precious stone, which the Mycenaean officials, like the Minoans, used to authenticate the sealing of wine or oil or other valuable goods.[5] Weapons and armour too were of bronze. Swords, daggers, and spearheads are reasonably familiar to us from Mycenaean graves;[6] protective arms are less so, but we have several surviving examples of bronze greaves,[7] and one magnificent suit of bronze body armour found in a grave at Dendra.[8] Comparatively few bronze objects of any kind survive, and it is easy to see why; the metal was valuable, and things doubtless went to the smiths as scrap when broken or worn out. But the importance of metal in the everyday life of the Mycenaeans can hardly be exaggerated; all their surviving works attest the need of a large supply, and the Linear B tablets from Pylus fill in some local detail. In them we find at least 270 smiths (*ka-ke-we*) mentioned by name, and allowing for the incompleteness of the records we may suppose there were up to 400 in the two dozen or so towns of the area governed from Pylus. The tablets record the distribution from the palace of over a ton of bronze, in individual lots averaging about seven pounds; but we do not know how frequent such distributions were, and since not all smiths received such allotments there were possibly other channels also for the supply of raw metal. This palace issue may have been for the manufacture

---

[1] §III, 24, 38 and 48 ff., pls I, XII; §III, 39, pl. 36 (*c*); §III, 14, pls. XXXVIII, 196. See Plate 146 (*b*).

[2] E.g. §III, 3, 352 f.; §III, 24, pls. XXX–XXXIII.

[3] Cf. §III, 31, 60 ff.; §III, 24, 135 ff.

[4] §III, 3, 342 ff.; §III, 30, especially p. 296, with references; §III, 16, 152 ff. See Plate 147 (*a*).

[5] Examples in §III, 14, pls. 208–11; §IV, 2, 103 f.

[6] E.g. §III, 3, 330 ff.; §III, 24, pls. XX–XXII.

[7] §III, 4; cf. §III, 39, 505 f., and fig. 55.

[8] §III, 9, 9 f., and figs. 8, 9; A, 17. See Plate 147 (*b*).

of special requirements (perhaps arms), a kind of government contract, perhaps to be associated with certain remissions of tax which the tablets show some smiths enjoyed.[1]

Much the most plentiful Mycenaean product to survive is of course the pottery.[2] Pottery is a staple of the archaeology of most ages, but it has special importance here. It was manufactured in great quantities, and this, together with good communications, made for a standardized style—the Mycenaean *koine* as it has been called. The comparative absence of local variation makes typological study the more valid, and this provides the basis of our relative chronology for the period. L.H. III pottery is interesting, too, as reflecting the general trends of the art and culture of the times. The continuity of both shapes and patterns from L.H. II is readily traceable; but with the removal of Minoan sources of inspiration the decoration becomes increasingly stylized. The use of horizontal stripes (painted mechanically as the pot revolved on the wheel) is very frequent; and motifs that had once been naturalistic became wholly linear, and were used for the construction of new abstract patterns.[3] This is typical of Mycenaean art; it seems not to grow, but to be built; it reflects the high organizing capacity of its producers. Technically, the pottery is of the highest quality. It is a skilful feat to throw on the wheel in one piece either the wholly closed globular or piriform 'stirrup-jar' type, or the tall-stemmed shallow goblet or *kylix*.[4] Yet these are among the commonest and most characteristic of a wide and attractive range of shapes. The clay is excellently refined, and fired at a higher temperature than most ancient pottery, which gives practical as well as aesthetic advantages.[5] As a result, it was traded all round the eastern Mediterranean, and the surviving examples thus give invaluable clues, as will be shown later, for the history of Mycenaean commerce and foreign relations.

### (c) TOMBS

Most of the Mycenaean pottery to be seen in the world's museums has been found not on habitation sites, but in tombs. So well-equipped a world as the Mycenaean was not lightly to be left, and these people took considerable care over their funeral arrangements. Burial was, for ordinary folk, in rock-cut chamber-tombs, many of them already in use in L.H. II, and continuing so, as family vaults, for the remainder of the Bronze Age. Pottery

[1] A, 10.  [2] §III, 6 and 7.  [3] See Plate 144.
[4] See Plate 144, (*c*, *d*, *f*).  [5] §III, 13, especially 109, 119.

vessels, personal ornaments, sometimes tools, weapons, or other metal utensils, were laid with the dead. A farewell toast was drunk outside the tomb door, and the goblet smashed. Yet there seems to have been no thought that the departed would continue to use or need the grave-gifts, and when the tomb was opened for later burials they were often unceremoniously pushed aside, along with the mortal remains.[1]

For the rulers, the stone-built beehive-tomb was their final resting-place and monument; and we can trace, especially at Mycenae, a growing skill and refinement in their construction.[2] The 'Treasury of Atreus' at Mycenae,[3] one of the latest, dating from the fourteenth century, is much the grandest and best-preserved example of Mycenaean architecture. The heavy sawn blocks of conglomerate that line the entrance passage, the doorway sixteen feet high with its hundred-ton lintel, the vast and still perfect stone chamber, nearly fifty feet wide, and as high, are even now awe-inspiring. No stone-roofed building of equal size was constructed between this and the Pantheon at Rome. In its pristine state, it would have impressed by the skilful finish as well as the mass; the entrance was flanked and surmounted by carved columns and relief decoration in stone; great bronze-mounted doors pivoted on the threshold; ornaments of bronze adorned the surface of the vault. The name of 'treasury' that had attached to these structures by the time of Pausanias[4] bears witness to the splendour of the grave-goods that would have accompanied a royal burial; and it is confirmed by the riches of even a much smaller beehive tomb found unplundered at Dendra.[5] Beside the precious objects laid in the actual grave-pit, others were heaped on a pyre and burned within the tomb chamber. Animals too might be sacrificed—dogs or horses: at Marathon[6] two horse skeletons lay stretched outside the tomb door. Sometimes there may even have been human victims; the practice of suttee is suggested by the remains at Dendra, though it cannot be proved. These royal tombs, obviously constructed in the ruler's lifetime, were doubtless in the main intended (unlike the family chamber-tombs) as monuments to individuals. Enormous and extravagant expenditure of time and labour and material went to their construction; they imply an extreme exaltation of the monarch, even to the extent of raising the question, which remains at present

1 §III, 3, ch. VI; §III, 36, 121–46; §III, 37, 14 f. See below, p. 898.
2 §III, 37, 16, 26–46.
3 §III, 37, 28–33; §III, 35, 338 ff. See Plate 148 (b).     4 Paus. II, 16, 6.
5 §III, 24, 1–70.          6 §III, 21, 1958, 23–7.

unsolved, whether more than mortal status was ascribed to him, either in life or after his death.[1] They imply too a remarkable economic prosperity; and it is hardly surprising that they did not continue to be built throughout the Myc. III period; the ordinary tombs remain in uninterrupted use till the twelfth century, but it is doubtful whether any beehive at Mycenae itself can be dated as late even as the thirteenth, though one at Menidi[2] outside Athens belongs to Myc. III b. It may be that in this phase the labour forces available were employed rather on the great works of fortification.

## IV. MYCENAEAN SOCIETY

The high level of social and economic organization that must have prevailed in a society that could construct the beehive tombs is amply confirmed and illustrated by the palace records that survive, scratched in the Linear B script on tablets of unbaked clay.[3] That no such tablets were found in the palace at Mycenae is clearly an accident of time and excavation, for a number have survived in houses outside the citadel.[4] At Pylus the excavators were lucky to find (in their first trial trench) some 600 tablets lying in the ruins of a little office near the palace entrance, and many more have come to light since.[5] They are all administrative records. It is likely, but not provable, that other types of document may have been written on different material; but to judge from the tablets the chief purpose of writing was to record those matters of daily business which in themselves are difficult to remember with accuracy, and concerning which an objective record will obviate dispute and inefficiency. A large proportion are lists of persons, some indicating their duties or occupations, their tenancy of land, or the produce due from them or delivered by them: others the provisions issued to the palace servants and dependants; offerings sent to the sanctuaries of the gods; inventories of domestic chattels or military equipment; the disposition of troops. Above all we get a picture of the palace itself, with hundreds of men, women and children busied over their domestic or administrative tasks.

The palace controls everything; it is the main channel of economic distribution; and the territory of Pylus was conceivably regarded as fundamentally the personal estate of the *wa-na-ka* (king). But two categories of land-holding are referred to, *ki-ti-me-na* and *ke-ke-me-na*, which in effect (though not in etymology) seem to

---

[1] Cf. *C.A.H.* II[3], pt. 2, pp. 35 f.  [2] §III, 13.
[3] §IV, 7; §IV, 4; A, 15.  [4] §IV, 1; §IV, 2; §IV, 5.  [5] §IV, 3.

refer to private and communal lands respectively. It is possible (though no more) that the two categories reflect a dual society, an original distinction between a native population and its conquering overlords; if so, the *ki-ti-me-na* would have been originally the demesnes assigned to individual immigrants. The king's special portion or *te-me-no* of land is presumably that which was farmed for his direct use. Similarly there is a *te-me-no* of the *la-wa-ge-ta*—'leader of the people'—an important office, tentatively explained by some as commander-in-chief of the army, but not necessarily military; he might be a sort of *tribunus plebis*. We can identify too some other grades of society: the *e-qe-ta* ('followers' or 'companions' of the king), whose names are distinguished by patronymics and who seem to have important military duties; and the *qa-si-re-we* ( = βασιλῆες), who are governors of subordinate towns. Other minor offices or ranks also are named. There was a developed specialization of labour: carpenters, masons, shipwrights, bronze-smiths, potters, and goldsmiths, might have been assumed from other archaeological evidence; but the tablets tell also of workers who have left no visible products of their crafts, of spinners, weavers, and fullers, of perfume-makers, doctors, and heralds. The tablets prove also the existence of slaves, some privately owned, but more of them 'slaves' of a god or goddess, a term which may conceal some different status.[1] The gods appear in the tablets only as recipients of offerings; these are business documents, not ritual texts or temple records. The information indirectly provided about Mycenaean religion is, however, important, and will be discussed later in this volume.[2]

We shall not be far wrong in reading into the tablets a system of administration in which members of the ruling class govern and enjoy allotments of territory in return for contributions of produce in kind and of service in war. This pattern is virtually certain for the Pylus area. For Greece or the Peloponnese as a whole we have no similar contemporary evidence; but the tradition of at least a war-time allegiance to Mycenae is strong: Menelaus of Sparta is twin brother of Agamemnon; Nestor of Pylus, though of another lineage, is a willing ally, and so with the other heroic principalities. How far friendly relations between them were maintained when no foreign danger or campaign was afoot, we cannot tell. It seems improbable, however, that Mycenae could have exercised any precise centralized control over the more distant parts even of the Peloponnese, since communication cannot have been easy. Built roads can indeed be traced in the

[1] A, 11.  [2] See below, ch. XL.

immediate vicinity of Mycenae,[1] and within the kingdom of
Pylus,[2] and some of the chariotry listed in the Pylus tablets may
have been available for travel as well as for war; but we have so
far scarcely any evidence of built roads over longer distances,
without which communication in Greece must be on foot or by
pack-animal.

## V. OVERSEAS CONTACTS

Though slow, communication must have been reasonably frequent, or we should surely find fashions of material culture
diverging more from place to place than they do. The island of
Rhodes, for example, in L.H. III a uses pottery which in the main
is hardly distinguishable from that of Mycenae or of Attica.
Yet there is just enough difference for us to conclude that we
have here a local product, not an import from the mainland.[3] So
far as the evidence goes, most of the Aegean islands seem to have
shared the standard Mycenaean fashions, which by L.H. III b, if
not III a, stretched also to the Ionian islands to the west and into
Thessaly. But Mycenaean pottery also spread by trade far beyond
the areas of Greek population. The eastern Mediterranean
markets already occasionally touched in L.H. II[4] were in L.H. III
more fully exploited. In Egypt the new régime of Akhenaten
favoured foreign traders in Egypt, and the neat little red-
striped Mycenaean stirrup-jars and pilgrim flasks (perhaps filled
with scented oil) were familiar in the new-fangled palace at El-
Amarna[5] during its short life from 1379 to 1362. From the
coasts at Askalon and Tell el-'Ajjūl near Gaza they made their way
to inlands sites in Palestine and even beyond the Jordan.[6] Further
north, in Syria, the port of Ugarit (the modern Ras Shamra) was
an entrepôt favourable to Mycenaeans throughout L.H. III a–b;
and from the mouth of the Orontes their pottery reached Alalakh
(Tell Açana) and occasionally (until the southward advance of
the Hittites), to sites like Qatna and Qadesh, well up the valley
beyond Hama.[7] Occasional finds in the Cilician plain[8] may be
indicative of a more frequent trade there than we yet know of;
more exploration is needed.

Perhaps the most important region of all, in this eastward area,
is Cyprus.[9] The flow of Mycenaean pottery to sites on the south

[1] §III, 37, 27, 46 f. See Plate 148 (a).    [2] §IV, 6; A, 12.    [3] §V, 15, ch. II.
[4] See *C.A.H.* II[3], pt. I, p. 645; A, 8, 135 f.
[5] §V, 15, 90 ff., with references.         [6] §V, 15, 64 ff.; A, 8.
[7] §V, 15, 59–63; A, 8.                      [8] §V, 15, 88 f.; §V, 12.
[9] §V, 15, ch. III; §V, 13, 65–73, 205; §V, 6; A, 4, ch. II.

and east coast of the island, which is already substantial by the L.H. III a period, clearly represents a frequent trade, which was probably followed by the permanent establishment of Mycenaean Greeks in these parts. We should envisage them at first as small groups, living as foreigners within the native towns for purposes of trade, rather than establishing their own independent settlements. In Myc. III b, however, we find a growing independence of style in the Mycenaean pottery of Cyprus,[1] and it looks as though there were Greek potters working on the spot, though clay-analyses have raised some doubts about this. Certainly these 'Levanto-Helladic' wares are in this later phase frequently distinguishable among the Mycenaean pottery in Syria and Palestine. This suggests there were Mycenaeans in Cyprus trading on their own account, not merely as agents for mainland Greece; and although their goods did not now penetrate into the Orontes valley they find a wider distribution in the coastal areas further south, from Byblos to the Bay of Acre, areas now restored to greater tranquillity after the settlement between Egyptians and Hittites subsequent to the battle of Qadesh.[2] In the thirteenth century, too, it seems that new openings for Mycenaean traders were developing at Tell Abu Hawwām,[3] outside modern Haifa; for here we find pottery of mainland Greek origin (as opposed to Cypriot Mycenaean), and finds inland seem to hint at a link with caravan routes across the eastward deserts to Mesopotamia.

As we have already suggested, some of these pottery exports perhaps went abroad as containers for oil or perfume, some for their own sake. What Greece imported in return we can only partly deduce. There is no doubt that copper[4] accounts for the Mycenaean interest in Cyprus; it travelled in big ingots,[5] shaped like a dressed ox-hide, such as are known at both Minoan and Mycenaean sites and even as far west as Sardinia; recently some were recovered from the wreck of a Late Bronze Age ship at Cape Gelidonya on the south coast of Turkey.[6] From Egypt may have come gold mined in Nubia; from Syria, ivory, for there is ancient evidence for elephants in those parts, and there was a school of ivory-carving there both in the Bronze Age and later.[7] About other more perishable commodities we can only speculate. The Greek names of various spices and herbs (already current in

[1] But cf. A, 3; A, 5; A, 6. Plate 149 (*a*), (*b*).
[2] §v, 15, 71–87, 106 f.; A, 8, 145–7.
[3] §v, 15, 78 ff.; A, 8, 124 f.     [4] Cf. §v, 13, 202; A, 4.
[5] A, 4, ch. XII. See Plate 149 (*c*).     [6] §v, 5; A, 1, esp. 52–83.
[7] §v, 1; §v, 2, especially p. 5. See Plate 106 (*b*).

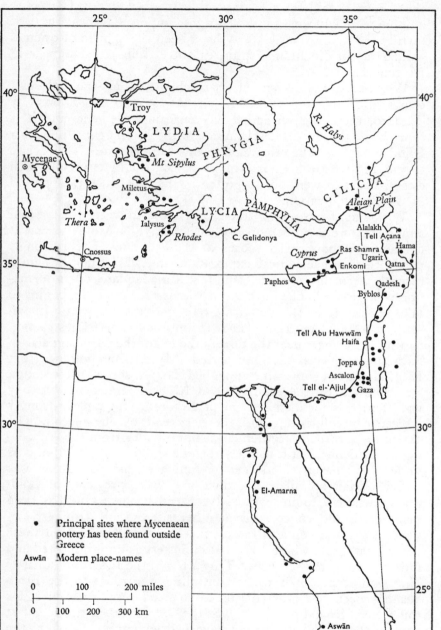

Map 4. The Eastern Mediterranean.

the Linear B tablets) are of Semitic origin;[1] a few Canaanite amphorae at Mycenaean sites suggest imported wines;[2] figured textiles (as well as ivories) may have been the vehicle of oriental animal motifs (including sphinxes and griffins) that appear in Mycenaean art.

Westward, Mycenaean pottery reached as far as Ischia, the east coasts of Sicily, and even Malta.[3] At Scoglio del Tonno, by Taranto, there was an actual Mycenaean settlement, and it is remarkable that in L.H. III a much of the pottery there betrays a Rhodian style.[4] The other side to this western trade is harder to divine, but whatever their primary object, the links became well established and were not forgotten in the great historical period of Greek colonization.

With such far-reaching trade to east and to west, it may seem strange that we have not more evidence than we have for Mycenaean contacts on the eastern shores of the Aegean. The reason is partly that archaeological exploration of Asia Minor has until recently been limited; but though still inadequate, our information is increasing. The history of Miletus,[5] for example, begins to take shape. It had trade with Crete, perhaps received Minoan settlers, from M.M. III to L.M. II, but then suffered destruction by fire, somewhere near the time of the fall of the Minoan palaces. Subsequent levels show imported Mycenaean pottery from L.H. IIIa until some time in L.H IIIb. A second destruction was followed by the rebuilding of Miletus with a mighty city wall, and this fortified settlement endured, still under strongly Mycenaean influence, until the very end of our period. The extent of Mycenaean settlement is not obvious from the archaeological evidence, but it is likely that we should regard Miletus as under Mycenaean rulers, even if much of the population was native Carian. Similar conditions may have prevailed at Colophon,[6] where a tomb of the Mycenaean beehive type has been discovered, and conceivably at other sites. Our strongest evidence for trade contacts (as distinct from settlement) on these coasts is at Troy, where Mycenaean pottery is both imported and imitated down to the sack of Troy VII*a* in the L.H. IIIb phase.[7] The significance of Troy as controlling the route to the Black Sea has been too often discussed to need recapitulation. This route may have brought goods the Mycenaeans wanted, but equally the Troad itself may have had something to offer: the

---

[1] §IV, 7, 221–31.  [2] §V, 7.
[3] §V, 16, 7–9, 54–78, 79 f.  [4] §V, 16, ch. IV.  [5] §V, 17 and 18.
[6] §V, 9, 91; §V, 10, 39.  [7] §V, 4, vol. IV, 8 f., 23, 46 f.

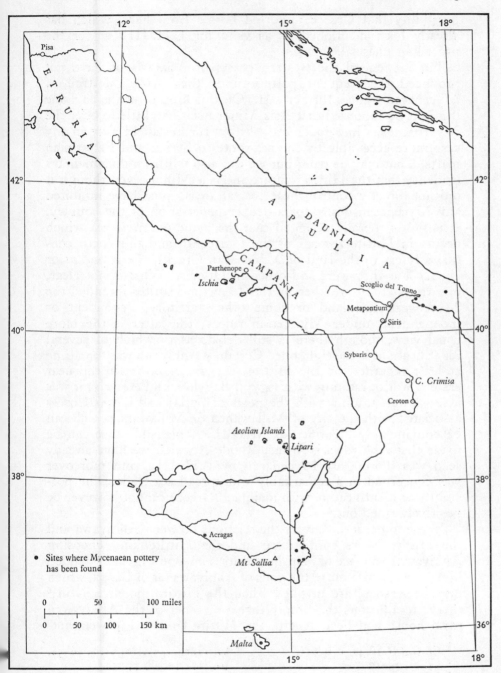

Map 5. South Italy and Sicily.

possibility that Greece imported horses from here, which has already been mentioned, is as valid for L.H. IIIb as for the preceding phases.[1]

But in general the western coasts of Asia Minor have not produced the frequent pottery finds that mark the trail of Mycenaean traders further east. On this kind of evidence alone it might be supposed that Asia Minor itself had little to offer the Mycenaeans, while goods traded from further afield were in any case more accessible by the sea-route to Syrian and Palestinian marts. That may be true; but we can also tell from documentary evidence that the Hittite empire in Asia Minor, even though it did not directly control these coastal areas, must have inhibited any Mycenaean desire for a deeper penetration of the country. It is now generally accepted that the name of *Ahhiyawa* which occurs in Hittite records of the fourteenth and thirteenth centuries refers to the land of Mycenaean Greeks, the *Achaeans* or Ἀχαιϝοὶ as they were still called in Homer.[2] What is not clear, unfortunately, is whether by this term the Hittites intended the Mycenaean mainland or some other territory, dependent or independent, under Mycenaean rulers; the latter is the more usual view, though there is still debate as to which of several identifications is the right one. Certainly Ahhiyawa was for a time at least regarded by the Hittites as a major power in the near eastern world, ranking with Egypt, Babylon, and Assyria; it was a sea-power, trading with the ports of Syria; and it was closely associated with the city of Millawanda or Millawata, which can be convincingly identified as Miletus. A plausible case can be made that Ahhiyawa is in fact Rhodes,[3] which we have already seen was thoroughly Mycenaean by L.H. IIIa, and moreover was concerned in a remarkably widespread sea trade. The possibility of identification with mainland Greece cannot however be positively ruled out.[4]

In the fourteenth century the relations between Ahhiyawa and the Hittites were cordial; we find the Hittite king choosing Ahhiyawa as a place of banishment for someone who has offended him (perhaps his wife);[5] the gods of Ahhiyawa (as of Lazpa, which may be Lesbos) are invoked when the Hittite monarch is ill;[6] there are allusions that imply that a member of the Ahhiyawan royal house had been sent to the Hittite land to learn chariot-

---

[1] Cf. *C.A.H.* ii³, pt. 1, p. 645.     [2] §v, 11, ch. 1; §v, 10; §v, 8, 46–58.
[3] §v, 11, 15–17.     [4] §v, 10, especially pp. 28 f.
[5] §v, 14, 298–306; §v, 10, 5 f.; §v, 8, 46 f.
[6] §v, 14, 275–94; §v, 10, 5; §v, 8, 47.

driving.[1] The famous Tawagalawas letter,[2] however, datable to the late fourteenth or early thirteenth century, shows a less friendly picture. Essentially it is a diplomatic protest by the Hittite king to the king of Ahhiyawa, asking for the extradition of one Piyama-radus who had been using Millawanda as a base for hostilities against the Hittite lands of Lukka (probably equivalent to Lycia). The same letter refers to the somewhat earlier establishment of Tawagalawas, a relative of the king of Ahhiyawa, in part of Lukka, and his claim to be recognized as a vassal of the Hittite king. It seems to be implied that the authority of Ahhiyawa extends, at least nominally, over Millawanda, though that city in fact appears to act with considerable independence. How far the king of Ahhiyawa was really responsible for these infringements of the Hittite sphere of influence our evidence does not show. Possibly we have simply the phenomenon of Mycenaean vassals doing a little empire-building on their own account. What is clear is that at this time the Mycenaeans were a power to be reckoned with and treated with diplomatic respect even by the great Hittite empire. Greeks had made their début on the stage of world history, and in a major role.

[1] §v, 8, 49; §v, 14, 59 ff.
[2] §v, 14, 2–194; §v, 10, 1 f., 17; §v, 11, 10 ff.; §v, 8, 47 ff.

# CHAPTER XXII (b)

## CYPRUS IN THE LATE BRONZE AGE

### INTRODUCTION

In the five hundred years that the Late Bronze Age lasted in Cyprus the island finally entered into full association with her more developed neighbours. This brought not only a share of their greater cultural sophistication and material prosperity but also of the troubles which beset them and the disasters by which they were eventually overwhelmed. When the end of the period was reached, Cypriot material culture had largely lost its special character, which for better or worse had distinguished it in the preceding phases of the Bronze Age, and had assumed a flavour almost entirely compounded of influences from stronger neighbours.

The Late Cypriot period is divided into three main phases, of which L.C. I occupies the years *c.* 1550–1400 B.C., L.C. II the years 1400–1200 B.C. and L.C. III the final stages from 1200–1050 B.C. These main phases have been divided into a number of subphases, which are not of immediate concern.[1] In many respects, L.C. I is an extension of the Middle Bronze Age, and this is strongly reflected in its material culture. L.C. II coincides with the island's high prosperity in the period of intimate trading ties with the Aegean. Material culture shed its homespun quality. The beginning of L.C. III witnessed major convulsions in neighbouring areas, and the arrival in Cyprus of refugee settlers from Greece whose appearance marked the first major step in the Hellenization of the island, including, it is to be presumed, the introduction of the Arcado-Cypriot version of the Greek tongue. There were few survivors of the last disastrous years of L.C. III to usher in the Early Iron Age.

### VI. THE PATTERN OF LATE CYPRIOT SETTLEMENT

The distribution of L.C. sites[2] shows that the period started modestly, even uncertainly. By L.C. II, however, it is clear that

---

* An original version of this chapter was published in fascicle 43 in 1966; the present chapter includes revisions made in 1971.

[1] §VII, 9, 197.       [2] §VI, 1, 142–6.

there had been a great increase in population, which can be deduced from the corresponding increase in the number of occupied settlements and in the overall size of individual sites. In both earlier phases of the Bronze Age, large areas of Cyprus seem not to have been settled; only the Troödos mountains seem to have been shunned in the L.C. period. Comparison of the locations of L.C. sites with their predecessors shows the furtherance of the move to the coast, especially in the area between Cape Pyla and Cape Kiti, which was initiated in M.C. III. The old fears that had concentrated so much settlement inland in the river valleys, on the upland plateaux, and along the foothills of the Kyrenia hills, often under the protection of promontory forts, gave way before an optimistic self-confidence, which encouraged the founding or great expansion of countless sites on or immediately adjoining the coast. Some inland settlements, amongst them Nicosia and Ayios Sozomenos, evidently maintained the importance they had enjoyed in M.C. times, but many of the old centres dwindled to little more than village status, or were abandoned altogether. Thus Dhenia lingered on, a shadow of its former greatness, but the *Vrysis tou Barba* cemetery at Lapithos was deserted. It is very unlikely that even the most prosperous of the inland sites in L.C. could compete in wealth or importance with the coastal settlements. Though north Cyprus seems never to have regained the full importance it had enjoyed in the E.C. period, sites at Vasilia,[1] Lapithos,[2] Kazaphani,[3] Akanthou[4] and Dhavlos[5] suggest that this side of the island must have had some share in the sea traffic. But the richest L.C. sites belong to the south coast. From Palaeopaphos (now Kouklia)[6] in the extreme south-west to Enkomi in Salamis bay on the eastern shore a succession of townships was established on or near the coast. One group merits special mention. This is the concentration that surrounds Larnaka bay;[7] it was based on the sheltered harbours of Citium (mod. Larnaka) and Hala Sultan Tekke. Many of the cemeteries attached to these settlements have been excavated or pillaged;[8] the contents of their graves offer an idea of their material prosperity and the volume of trade goods imported from abroad which their citizens commanded. Only at Enkomi was this level of wealth rivalled.

Insight into the way Cyprus worked in the Late Bronze Age

[1] §vi, 1, 169.   [2] §vi, 1, 165–6.   [3] G, 8 (1964), 335–8.
[4] G, 3 (1962), 374–7; *C.A.H.* ii[3], pt. 1, pp. 172, 174 and n. 9.
[5] §vi, 1, 162.
[6] G, 11, 174; §vi, 1, 165; §xi, 7.   [7] §vi, 3.   [8] G, 10; G, 11, 180–8.

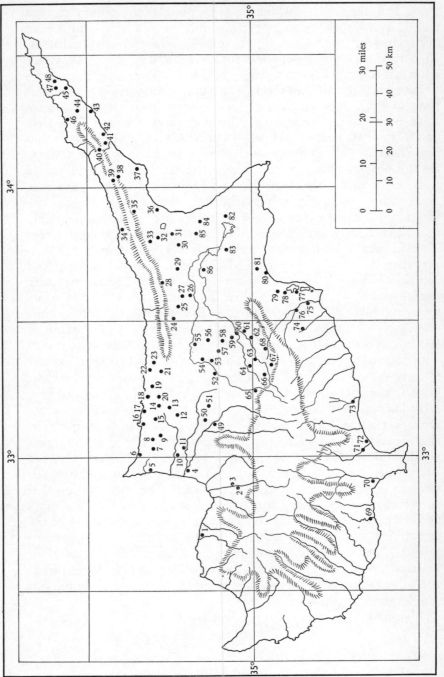

Map 6. Middle Bronze Age Cyprus. (In some cases, several adjacent but separate sites are represented by a single symbol.)

## NUMERICAL KEY

| | | | |
|---|---|---|---|
| 1 Kato Pyrghos | 37 Ayios Theodhoros | 55 Kaimakli | 71 Polemidhia |
| 2 Linou | 38 Livadhia | 56 Leondari Vouno | 72 Limassol |
| 3 Katydhata | 39 Komi Kebir | 57 Laxia | 73 Moni |
| 4 Syrianokhori | 40 Lythrangomi | 58 Yeri | 74 Anglisidhes |
| 5 Ayia Irini | 41 Vasili | 59 Ayios Sozomenos (Nikolidhes) | 75 Arpera |
| 6 Kormakiti | 42 Neta | | 76 Klavidhia |
| 7 Dhiorios | 43 Korovia (Nitovikla) | 60 Ayios Sozomenos (Ambelia) | 77 Hala Sultan Tekke |
| 8 Myrtou (Stephania) | 44 Galinoporni | | 78 Larnaka (Laxia tou Riou) |
| 9 Myrtou | 45 Galinoporni (Trakhonas) | 61 Potamia | |
| 10 Kapouti (Kapnistos) | 46 Ayios Thyrsos | 62 Dhali | 79 Livadhi |
| 11 Kapouti | 47 Rizokarpaso | 63 Kochati | 80 Pyla (Verghin) |
| 12 Skylloura | 48 Rizokarpaso (Sylla) | 64 Margi | 81 Pyla |
| 13 Ayios Ermolaos | 49 Akaki | 65 Politiko | 82 Akhyritou |
| 14 Pileri | 50 Dhenia | 66 Kataliondas | 83 Kalopsidha |
| 15 Larnaka tis Lapithou | 51 Kokkini Trimithia | 67 Lythrodhonda | 84 Enkomi |
| 16 Vasilia | 52 Lakatamia | 68 Alambra | 85 Styllos |
| 17 Lapithos | 53 Strovolos | 69 Evdhimou | 86 Sinda |
| 18 Elea | 54 Nicosia | 70 Episkopi | |
| 19 Karmi | | | |
| 20 Krini | | | |
| 21 Dhikomo (Onisha) | | | |
| 22 Kyrenia | | | |
| 23 Bellapais (Vounous) | | | |
| 24 Kythrea | | | |
| 25 Bey Keuy | | | |
| 26 Angastina | | | |
| 27 Marathovouno | | | |
| 28 Trypimeni | | | |
| 29 Psilatos | | | |
| 30 Milea | | | |
| 31 Lapathos | | | |
| 32 Ayios Iakovos | | | |
| 33 Ayios Iakovos (Melia) | | | |
| 34 Phlamoudhi | | | |
| 35 Ovgoros | | | |
| 36 Trikomo | | | |

## ALPHABETICAL KEY

| | | | | |
|---|---|---|---|---|
| Akaki 49 | Dhali 62 | Katydhata 3 | Linou 2 | Politiko 65 |
| Akhyritou 82 | Dhenia 50 | Klavidhia 76 | Livadhi 79 | Potamia 61 |
| Alambra 68 | Dhikomo (Onisha) 21 | Kokkini Trimithia 51 | Livadhia 38 | Psilatos 29 |
| Angastina 26 | Dhiorios 7 | Komi Kebir 39 | Lythrangomi 40 | Pyla 81 |
| Anglisidhes 74 | Elea 18 | Kormakiti 6 | Lythrodhonda 67 | Pyla (Verghin) 80 |
| Arpera 75 | Enkomi 84 | Korovia (Nitovikla) 43 | Marathovouno 27 | Rizokarpaso 47 |
| Ayia Irini 5 | Episkopi 70 | Kochati 63 | Margi 64 | Rizokarpaso (Sylla) 48 |
| Ayios Ermolaos 13 | Evdhimou 69 | Krini 20 | Milea 30 | Sinda 86 |
| Ayios Iakovos 32 | Galinoporni 44 | Kyrenia 22 | Moni 73 | Skylloura 12 |
| Ayios Iakovos (Melia) 33 | Galinoporni (Trakhonas) 45 | Kythrea 24 | Myrtou 9 | Strovolos 53 |
| Ayios Sozomenos (Ambelia) 60 | Hala Sultan Tekke 77 | Lakatamia 52 | Myrtou (Stephania) 8 | Styllos 85 |
| Ayios Sozomenos (Nikolidhes) 59 | Kaimakli 55 | Lapathos 31 | Neta 42 | Syrianokhori 4 |
| Ayios Theodhoros 37 | Kalopsidha 83 | Lapithos 17 | Nicosia 54 | Trikomo 36 |
| Ayios Thyrsos 46 | Kapouti 11 | Larnaka (Laxia tou Riou) 78 | Ovgoros 35 | Trypimeni 28 |
| Bellapais (Vounous) 23 | Kapouti (Kapnistos) 10 | Larnaka tis Lapithou 15 | Phlamoudhi 34 | Vasili 41 |
| Bey Keuy 25 | Karmi 19 | Laxia 57 | Pileri 14 | Vasilia 16 |
| | Kataliondas 66 | Leondari Vouno 56 | Polemidhia 71 | Yeri 58 |
| | Kato Pyrghos 1 | Limassol 72 | | |

may be had from observing the interrelationship of L.C. settlements, even though the means by which internal administration was managed cannot even be guessed at. Behind the prosperity which so distinctively marks the L.C. II period at the coastal towns undoubtedly lay successful management of the commodities sought by foreign merchants, of which none can have been more profitable than copper. A number of L.C. settlements are so located[1] that copper mining and smelting seem likely to have been their *raison d'être*. Into this category may be put the sites at Katydata,[2] Akhera,[3] Lythrodondas[4] and Kalavassos.[5] They were all well placed on lines of communication by which the raw material produced by their energies could be dispatched to the industrial centres at the coast. It is probably significant that the two most prosperous inland sites, Nicosia and Ayios Sozomenos, were situated athwart the routes by which the consignments of ore or smelted copper travelled from the mining centres to the factories. The towns near Larnaka bay, moreover, may have drawn on an extra ore-body at Troulli[6] little more than 10 miles due north of Larnaka, though Late Bronze Age exploitation of this Troulli copper has not been proved.

In addition to these two types of settlement were the old rural sites, many of them in regions inhabited throughout the Bronze Age, depending on agriculture[7] and stock-rearing for their existence. Such agricultural centres continued to be concentrated around the great springs or along the water courses adjoining light and easily cultivable soils, such as those of the Kormakiti peninsula, the Kyrenia foothills, the Karpass peninsula and the river valleys of the western half of the central plain. Settlement not only continued in these areas, it expanded considerably. Possibly this rural expansion resulted from a conscious agrarian policy dictated by the urban centres in response to the needs of their growing populations, more and more of whom, it may be presumed, were absorbed by the urban trades and skills which developed during the L.C. period. If so, the move into the virgin lands of the Kormakiti peninsula[8] was at the behest of the town site at *Toumba tou Skourou*[9] near the sea in the plain north of Morphou, whose wealth and importance may have matched Enkomi's.

It may be inferred that the L.C. period saw the development of

[1] §VIII, 6, 32.     [2] §VI, 1, 164.     [3] G, 8 (1960), 245, 248; (1961), 310.
[4] §VI, 1, 166.                          [5] §VI, 1, 164.
[6] §VIII, 6, 21; §XIII, 4, 39–40.       [7] G, 5.          [8] §VI, 1, 142; §VI, 2.
[9] G, 8 (1964), 313–14; §VI, 1, 167; *R.D.A.C.* (1936), 115.

a complex internal marketing system, in which the produce of the copper mines was sent to the manufacturing towns, together with surplus agricultural produce from the rural areas. Excavation of the rustic sanctuary at *Pigadhes*, Myrtou,[1] where magazines containing large pithoi were found, suggests that religious centres may have acted as middlemen in such internal trade, and that commercial transactions may have been nominally on behalf of the gods. Return traffic to the inland settlements, both industrial and agricultural, can be seen in the imported trade goods, like Mycenaean pottery, that have been found in their cemeteries; Akhera and Angastina provide clear instances.[2]

There can be no more vivid illustration of the magnitude of the disasters that brought about the end of the Bronze Age than the wholesale desertion of the areas of settlement that took place in the twelfth and eleventh centuries B.C. Even the richest and most powerful sites were not immune from this process. The occupation at Enkomi may have lingered on until the end of the eleventh century;[3] its place was later taken by Salamis. In the coastal area which had been so prosperous only Citium survived of the towns on Larnaka bay. In the long stretch between there and Curium the post-Bronze-Age foundation of Amathus was the only reminder of former prosperity. Only at Palaeopaphos may occupation have continued into historical times without interruption. The same kind of contraction took place inland. The Ayios Sozomenos group of sites was abandoned, though their role and importance were eventually inherited by Idalium (now Dhali) a few miles further up the Yalias valley. The sites at Politiko and Pera survived as did Tamassus, although there was almost certainly an interruption. *Toumba tou Skourou* at Morphou may have survived briefly into the Early Iron Age, but its place was taken by Soli some miles away on the south side of the bay. This change may be explained by a deterioration in the port facilities of the Morphou site due to the silting of the mouths of the Serakhis and Ovgos rivers.

It is difficult to isolate the point at which this calamity took place. But for the flourishing character of material culture at Enkomi, Citium and Palaeopaphos in the twelfth century B.C., a date early in L.C. III would seem probable. Material of this date amongst surface finds from unexcavated L.C. sites is rare, especially in comparison with the mass of sites at which L.C. II material has been collected. Such evidence suggests that the Karpass was deserted by the middle of the twelfth century; so was the

<hr />

[1] §xii, 12.　　　[2] §viii, 22.　　　[3] §x, 7; §xi; 3.

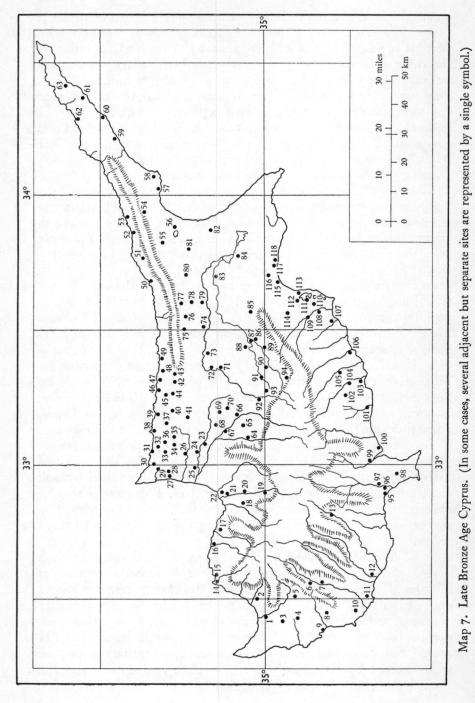

Map 7. Late Bronze Age Cyprus. (In some cases, several adjacent but separate sites are represented by a single symbol.)

## ALPHABETICAL KEY

Kormakiti peninsula.  On the south Kyrenia foothills only
Dhikomo and Palekythro provide certain evidence of continued
occupation.The onset of the Early Iron Age reveals the full
measure of the catastrophe and the nadir of the island's fortunes.
By the end of the eleventh century, the known centres of settlement had dwindled to a mere handful of sites,[1] chiefly known
from the location of their cemeteries.  Lapithos[2] and Karavas[3]
represent the occupation of the north coast, Citium,[4] Amathus,[5]
Curium[6] and Palaeopaphos[7] the south.  In the far west was
Marium[8] (now Polis-tis-Krysokhou); Idalium survived in central
Cyprus.  Cypro-Geometric dawn indeed came on a sombre and
desolate scene.

## VII. EVENTS IN CYPRUS BEFORE THE AEGEAN CONNEXION

The Late Cypriot period emerged from the confines of the
Middle Bronze Age without significant change of population or
break in material culture.  The process took place in the middle
of the sixteenth century B.C., and synchronizes approximately
with the expulsion of the Hyksos from Egypt and the establishment of the Eighteenth Dynasty, which was to bring the pacifica-
tion of the Levantine littoral and the adjoining seas that culminated
under Tuthmosis III.  The touchstone for the new period is the
appearance of a new pottery fabric, Base Ring ware,[9] starting
almost exclusively as a class of small jugs (*bilbils*) for unguents
etc., later developing larger jugs and cups for common use.
White Slip ware[10] came into use almost as soon; both fabrics are
handmade.  Material culture, however, continued in very much
a M.C. mould for many years, so that degenerate versions of the
familiar M.C. fabrics—White Painted, Red-on-Black, Black and
Red Slip wares—outnumber the new goods.  L.C. I metalwork[11]
likewise is exclusively a poor reflection of the simple M.C.
repertory.

Continuity between M.C. III and L.C. I is to be seen in many
ways.  At home the rise of the new towns on the east and south
coasts continued.  At Enkomi[12] to a M.C. III building nucleus

---

[1] §vi, 1, 146.    [2] G, 4(i), 172–265.    [3] *R.D.A.C.* (1964), 114–29.
[4] §xi, 8; §xi, 9; §xi, 10.    [5] G, 4(ii), 1–141.
[6] §xii, 2.    [7] *Liverpool Bulletin*, 2 (1952), 51–2.
[8] G, 4(ii), 181–459.    [9] §vii, 9, 34–43; §vii, 10. See Plate 150(*a*).
[10] *C.A.H.* ii³, pt. 1, pp. 165 f; §vii, 9, 43–50; §vii, 1; §vii, 5; §viii, 12, 39–
42. See Plate 150(*b*)
[11] §viii, 6, 299.    [12] §x, 7.

there was added in L.C. I a fortress block on the north side of
the town. Though it was destroyed soon after its construction, it
was quickly rebuilt, with a modified plan. Part of it was now used
for industrial processes connected with copper-working, an industry which was concentrated in the north half of the city almost
throughout its history.[1]

At Nitovikla[2] the fortress had been destroyed by fire at the end of
M.C. III. It was repaired and recommissioned in L.C. I; it
seems to have been demilitarized, but not entirely abandoned,
before the end of the period. At Nikolidhes, near Ayios Sozomenos, a very robust building first erected in L.C. I has also been
identified as a fortress.[3] It suffered destruction by fire before the
end of L.C. Ia, was quickly rebuilt, but was abandoned before
L.C. Ib was over. It is uncertain whether any of the fortified
sites above the Aloupos valley or on the south Kyrenia foothills[4]
remained in use during L.C. I. It seems probable, however, that
the symptoms of insecurity which applied to the M.C. III period
continued through much of L.C. I. It is not certain, however,
whether the mass-burials which were made in L.C. Ia graves at
Ayios Iakovos,[5] Pendayia[6] and Myrtou, *Stephania*,[7] are to be
attributed to disturbed political conditions or to some natural
misfortune.[8]

The Cypriots continued to enjoy and to develop their trade
links with the Levant and Egypt throughout L.C. I; this is in
sharp contrast with a virtual exclusion from Cilicia (whose local
version of Base Ring ware[9] may have been copied from North
Syria), for which there must be some political explanation. Conceivably those who enjoyed the protection of the Egyptian fleet[10]
did so in return for observing certain economic sanctions. But
Cyprus was free to traffic with North Syria, where Alalakh and
Ugarit received a high proportion of the trade, Palestine, notably
with Gaza (Tell el-ʿAjjūl), and Egypt itself, where Base Ring
ware *bilbils* were particularly popular.[11] Only a minute number
of Cypriot goods travelled to the Aegean in these years; White
Slip and Base Ring pottery have occurred in Rhodes,[12] at Phylakopi
in Melos,[13] in Thera[14] and at Cnossus.[15] Foreign goods reached
Cyprus in some quantity during L.C. I. Especial interest attaches

---

[1] G, 7, 517.   [2] G, 4(i), 371–407.
[3] *C.A.H.* ii³, pt. 1, p. 168; §vii, 19, 11–12.
[4] §vi, 1, 140–1.   [5] G, 4(i), 302–55.
[6] G, 8 (1961), 308–9.   [7] §vi, 2, 52.
[8] §vii, 9, 199.   [9] *C.A.H.* ii³, pt. 1, p. 174.
[10] §vi, 2, 51.   [11] §vii, 9, 151–60; §vii, 3.   [12] §vii, 9, 160.
[13] *Ibid.*   [14] *Ibid.*   [15] *C.A.H.* ii³, pt. 1, p. 173.

to the highly decorative pottery fabric, often embellished with
birds or fish, known as Bichrome wheel-made ware,[1] found on a
number of sites in east Cyprus but most particularly at Milia[2] on
the north side of the Mesaoria. The ware is probably Palestinian;
an important factory was located at Gaza.[3] Of ambiguous origin
are the spindle bottles of Red Lustrous ware[4] which first appear
in L.C. I a grave groups, many having had *graffiti* incised on
their bases before firing. Of the many sources suggested for their
manufacture[5] North Syria is perhaps the least improbable. The
fabric had a very wide currency in contemporary trade, including
the Aegean and Anatolia as well as the Levant and Egypt.

Foreign inspiration must have been responsible for the building at Enkomi in L.C. I a of a small tholos-like tomb[6] within the
area of the settlement. The diameter of the chamber, just under
2·50 m., equalled its height. It was partly set into a pit sunk in
the bed-rock, but the upper part of the corbelled masonry was
probably free-standing, covered by an earth tumulus. Both its
diminutive size and the lack of supporting evidence from the
Aegean at this date make a relationship with Mycenaean tholoi
improbable.[7] A connexion has been suggested with Middle
Bronze Age tombs at Megiddo,[8] which may be significant. No
other tomb of this type has yet been reported in Cyprus.

The duration of L.C. I may be estimated as a century and a
half, between *c.* 1550 B.C. and *c.* 1400 B.C. The atmosphere of
insecurity that was mirrored in the material remains at the start of
the period gave way to one of prosperous stability that Cyprus
owed to and shared with her powerful neighbours. Security in
the east Mediterranean for which Egypt was responsible was
about to invite the active attentions of the Mycenaean Greeks who,
with the destruction of Cnossus accomplished *c.* 1400 B.C., had
become masters of the sea routes to the east.

## VIII. CYPRUS AND THE AEGEAN AREA

Though there are clear indications in Cyprus of contact with
Crete and Greece during the late sixteenth and earlier fifteenth
century B.C.,[9] her relationship with the west during almost the
whole of L.C. I was insignificant; Syria, Palestine and Egypt

---

[1] §VI, 2, 53; §VII, 2.   [2] §VII, 11.   [3] §VII, 2.
[4] §VII, 9, 51–4; §VII, 4.   [5] §VII, 4, 194–6.
[6] G, 4(i), 570–3; §VII, 9, 18–19; §VII, 12.
[7] Cf. *Antiq.* xxxiv (1960), 166–76.
[8] §VII, 9, 147–50.   [9] §VIII, 6, 36; §VIII, 10, 203–15; §VIII, 25, 26–31.

claimed the exclusive attention of her manufacturers and merchants. There had been tenuous links between Cyprus and Crete in E.C. III and M.C. I,[1] but these had lapsed before M.C. III. No L.M. I object has been identified in Cyprus, and L.M. II finds are few and far between.[2] Contemporary Mycenaean pottery has been found in equally small quantities. It is clear that for well over a century after 1550 B.C. the Aegean states were even less interested in Cyprus, or less able to visit her than they had been in the Middle Bronze Age.

A change took place during L.C. Ib (c. 1450–1400 B.C.), when Mycenaean IIb and IIIa I pottery appears in modest, but significant quantities. This material has been found at Milia and Enkomi in east Cyprus,[3] at Nicosia[4] in the centre, and at Maroni, Hala Sultan Tekke and Arpera on the south coast.[5] Its appearance should be associated with similar finds in the Levant and Egypt.[6]

Whatever the historical facts may be that are represented by the sack of Cnossus c. 1400 B.C.,[7] that catastrophe seems to have cleared the way for a great Mycenaean trading expansion into the east Mediterranean, of which Cyprus became the focus. What had been a trickle of Mycenaean trade in the late fifteenth century became a flood during the fourteenth, a flood which was maintained for at least the first half of the thirteenth century. The quantities of Mycenaean IIIa 2 and IIIb pottery from the cemeteries of Cyprus are so enormous that some have been persuaded that Greek colonies were established at a number of Cypriot sites early in the fourteenth century[8] and that Greek craftsmen set up their pottery factories in these colonial towns to produce most of the Mycenaean pottery that has been found in Cyprus. Particular attention has been directed to Mycenaean pictorial pottery,[9] more of which has been found in Cyprus than in the rest of Mycenaean world put together. It has been suggested that the style of the pictorial vases found in Cyprus is different from that in which the vases of mainland provenance are decorated. This has led to a fairly widely held belief that the home of the pictorial style was in the ateliers of colonial Cyprus, and that the pictorial work of the mainland came from derivative schools inspired by eastern artists. Any Mycenaean pictorial vase of this

---

[1] *C.A.H.* II³, pt. I, p. 173.
[2] *Ibid.* p. 174 notes 9 and 10; §VIII, 10, 205–6.
[3] §VIII, 25, 27.                    [4] §VIII, 6, 36.
[5] §VIII, 25, 28–9.                  [6] §VIII, 25, 56–8.
[7] To adopt the traditional date for this event.
[8] G, 2; G, 3; §VII, 9, 92–7; §VIII, 6, 40–4; §VIII, 13; §VIII, 21; §VIII, 25, 25–6.
[9] §VIII, nos. 4; 8; 11; 12; 18. See Plate 151 (a).

alleged eastern school which appears on the Greek mainland is supposed to be an import from the east. Recent laboratory work suggests[1] that the mass of Mycenaean pottery in Cyprus in L.C. II was imported from the Aegean, almost certainly from the Peloponnese. Some, however, particularly in the later thirteenth century B.C., was made by Cypriot potters in imitation of Mycenaean work. Though Cyprus provided a most appreciative market for the work of the pictorial vase-painters, finds in Greece, particularly at Berbati[2] in the Argolid, have shown that the lack of pictorial vases of the so-called Levanto-Helladic type is more apparent than real. It was the repeated visits of Aegean trading ships during L.C. II, not the presence of Aegean colonies, that was responsible for the proliferation of Mycenaean IIIa and IIIb pottery in Cyprus.

The proposal to locate Aegean colonies in Cyprus during the fourteenth and thirteenth centuries B.C. has never surmounted the obstacle of missing evidence.[3] Though Mycenaean pottery is present in such enormous amounts, practically every other characteristic of Mycenaean material culture is missing. An unmistakably Cypriot cultural atmosphere was dominant even at those sites where Aegean pottery has been found in greatest abundance. It is exceptional for a Cypriot tomb group to contain more Mycenaean than Cypriot vases;[4] the tombs themselves are Cypriot in design and burial custom. Fine Mycenaean metalwork in Cyprus is confined to the magnificent silver bowl with inlaid gold and niello bucrania[5] and two other silver vases, all from Enkomi.[6] There is no Mycenaean bronzework in a L.C. II context,[7] while Mycenaean types of stone vases are unknown. No Aegean sealstones have been recorded. Nearly all the characteristic types of Mycenaean jewellery are missing[8] from even the wealthiest Cypriot burials, though the influence of Mycenaean ornament can be seen in some of the work of Cypriot goldsmiths.

Towards the end of the thirteenth century B.C. some kind of recession took place in the trade exchanges between Greece and Cyprus. This happens in the context of the increasing instability on the mainland that is attested by the concentration on military works and by the troubles at Mycenae that resulted in the burning of the houses outside the citadel. This phase is marked in Cyprus

---

[1] §VIII, 5.　　　　　　　　　　　　　　[2] §VIII, 1.

[3] §VIII, 6, 35–54; §VIII, 16; §VIII, 19; §VIII, 24.

[4] E.g. G, 4(i), 546–58.　　　　　　　　[5] §VII, 8, 379–89. See Plate 146(b).

[6] §VIII, 6, 46; §VIII, 23.　　　[7] §VIII, 6, 300–1.　　　[8] §VIII, 6, 45–6.

by an increased output of Cypriot pottery made in the Mycenaean manner, and a corresponding scarcity of the genuine article.[1]

The meaning of the relationship between Cyprus and the Mycenaeans during L.C. II is not difficult to appreciate, particularly if the mass of Mycenaean pottery in Cyprus is accepted as imported. Mycenaean Greece maintained a great demand for Egyptian and Levantine merchandise, and a regular trading association was built up between the two areas. In the process, Aegean merchants learned of the value of the ports of south and east Cyprus both as markets and as bases of operations for their trafficking further afield. The dealings of these Mycenaean merchants can be traced from the 'Amūq plain in north Syria to the Second cataract in Egypt;[2] they are nowhere so much in evidence as in Cyprus. Cyprus proved an appreciative market for their painted pottery and whatever perishable commodities may have been packed in their ubiquitous stirrup jars and pilgrim flasks.[3] The well-to-do evinced an especial liking for the big Mycenaean craters on which processions of chariots or scenes from the bull-ring were depicted.[4] In this they merely foreshadowed the taste for fine Greek pottery shown centuries later by wealthy Etruscans. Though proof is lacking, it can hardly be doubted that copper was bought in Cyprus for Greece. Its importance to the Mycenaean economy is alone sufficient to account for the effort expended on the Cyprus trade.

## IX. THE IDENTIFICATION
## OF CYPRUS WITH ALASHIYA

The evidence of archaeology proves that intimate terms existed between Cyprus and her more powerful and sophisticated neighbours in the Levant and Egypt during the Late Bronze Age. It is natural therefore to try to identify references to Cyprus in contemporary documents; regrettably, her own few texts are still undeciphered. Both in texts found at Boğazköy[5] and in the archives preserved at el-Amarna[6] are references to a kingdom called Alashiya. Although its location has not been definitely established, it is commonly considered to be Cyprus, whether in part or whole.[7] It is even suggested that Alashiya should be more

---

[1] §viii, 5; §viii, 25, 37–44.     [2] §viii, 25.     [3] §viii, 21, pls. 20–2; 30.
[4] Bibliography of Mycenaean pictorial pottery in *B.S.A.* 60 (1965), cf. §viii, 11.
[5] G, 6, 45–7; §ix, 9; §ix, 13.     [6] G, 6, 38–45; §ix, 4; §ix, 14.
[7] G, 6, 36–50, with references, supplemented by *C.A.H.* ii³, pt. 1, p. 174; §ix, 13; §ix, 5.

8

narrowly identified with Enkomi, and that in the Middle Bronze Age the name belonged to Kalopsidha.[1]

Before the identification is accepted, the evidence of the texts themselves should be considered. In Boğazköy texts of *c.* 1400 B.C., Alashiya is represented as within the sphere of Hittite political influence.[2] When Tudkhaliash III was assassinated, his brothers were sent into exile in Alashiya. Apparently, Muwatallish, son of Murshilish II (*c.* 1330–1310 B.C.) confirmed Hittite rule in Alashiya whither, somewhat later, Khattushilish III banished his adversaries.[3] This Hittite suzerainty continued until *c.* 1200 B.C., according to texts of the time of Arnuwandash III (1245–1220 B.C.). About this time one of the king's vassals, a certain Madduwattash, grew so strong that he eventually emerged as the *de facto* ruler of south-west Anatolia, and elected to attack Hittite territory, including Alashiya. Though the text is mutilated[4] it seems that Madduwattash in company with Attarshiyash of Ahhiyawa and a third ally called 'the man of Piggaia' had invaded Alashiya and taken prisoners. Arnuwandash protests that Alashiya is his territory and demands that Madduwattash should return them. In return, Madduwattash professes ignorance that Alashiya was Hittite territory, and undertakes to return the prisoners. More recently discovered Boğazköy documents[5] refer to an action between the Hittite fleet and the ships of Alashiya, including a Hittite victory that resulted in the burning of the ships of Alashiya, at sea. This engagement took place at the end of the thirteenth century B.C.

In Egyptian sources, there are references to Alashiya in the time of Tuthmosis III,[6] apparently in connexion with towns in the neighbourhood of Aleppo and the Euphrates. But the chief Egyptian contexts are the Amarna letters,[7] which include correspondence that was exchanged between the pharaoh, probably Akhenaten, and the king of Alashiya in the second quarter of the fourteenth century. We note that the king of Alashiya writes to his 'brother', making use of the cuneiform script and the Akkadian tongue. Alashiya complains that his territory is annually raided by the Lukki; they plunder his towns. He exchanges emissaries with Egypt—he sends a present of copper, apologizing for its smallness, but misfortune has befallen the land—Nergal (the Babylonian god of battle and death) has slain all his people.

---

[1] *C.A.H.* II³, pt. I, pp. 168 and 169 n. 4.
[2] G, 6, 45.                                  [3] *Ibid.*
[4] §IX, 3, 9; §IX, 10, 97–102.      [5] §IX, 9, 20–3; §IX, 13, 131–4.
[6] §IX, 14, 33.                              [7] §IX, 4, nos. 33–40.

In return, Alashiya asks for gifts of silver, oxen and oil. We hear
of a citizen of Alashiya who has died in Egypt; his king requests
that his property should be sent home for the benefit of his son
and widow. There is a puzzling reference to Alashiya in a communication to the pharaoh from Rib-Adda, governor of Byblus,
in which he explains that in order to please him he had arranged
for an official called Amanmasha to go to Alashiya. Later Egyptian references to Alashiya include mention in an inscription of
the eighth year of Ramesses III which deals with his Northern
War, where it is associated with Kheta, Qode, Carchemish and,
perhaps, Arvad. The last Egyptian mention of Alashiya comes
as late as the eleventh century when, c. 1085 B.C., Wenamun,
emissary of Hrihor, was sent to Phoenicia to acquire wood from
Lebanon. After a number of misadventures, Wenamun was
driven off course to Alashiya, where he narrowly escaped death
at the hands of the local people. He was brought before Hatiba,
the local queen; an interpreter was needed.[1] The document is
incomplete, and the sequel is lost.

Egyptian records mention a territory, Asy,[2] that is also considered to be Cyprus, or part of Cyprus. That Asy appears side
by side with Alashiya in at least one text[3] would in fact compel
identification of the two names as different parts of Cyprus. Asy
was subject to Egypt in the time of Tuthmosis III. In the
Karnak Annals[4] are references to booty from Asy that included
horses, chariots of gold and silver. Tribute levelled on Asy
included copper, unrefined and refined, lead and elephants'
tusks. Asy is mentioned in the Nineteenth Dynasty geographical
lists, under Sethos I and Ramesses II; most of the identifiable
names with which it is coupled are on the mainland, towards the
north. Since there are no other east Mediterranean islands, however, mention of Cyprus in a topographical list would inevitably
place it in juxtaposition with regions which might otherwise
be regarded as inappropriate.[5]

There is mention of Alashiya in sources other than Egyptian
and Hittite. In the Mari archives of c. 1800 B.C. there is a
reference to the export of copper from Alashiya to Mari.[6] Alashiya is also mentioned in eighteenth-century texts from Alalakh,
though there is no specific information.[7] Several Ugaritic texts
contain details of relations between Alashiya and Ugarit. In one,
the king of Ugarit writes to a king who is probably to be identi-

---

[1] G, 6, 44–5.       [2] §IX, 14.       [3] G, 6, 40.
[4] G, 6, 39.       [5] §IX, 14.
[6] C.A.H. II³, pt. I, p. 174.       [7] §IX, 15, 8.

fied as the king of Alashiya, whom he greets as 'my father', to complain of acts of piracy taking place on his unprotected territory.[1] There is also a letter from Eshuwara, High Steward of Alashiya, to the king of Ugarit confirming the latter's suspicions about some of his subjects who have taken advantage of a call at Alashiya to deliver an entire flotilla to the enemy.[2] Yet another document discusses some individuals who have fled from Alashiya to the Hittite kingdom. They were handed over by Khattushilish III to the king of Carchemish who in turn entrusts them to his son Tili-Sharruma.[3] Of considerable interest is the record of a judgement of Ini-Teshub, king of Carchemish, contemporary of Ammishtamru II of Ugarit. Two royal princes, sons of the lady Ahatmilku (brothers of Ammishtamru), have 'sinned'. The queen mother takes them to Alashiya where, in front of Ishtar, they are made to swear that in future they will not ask anything of the king of Ugarit or his son. This may imply some kind of banishment.[4]

Thus, references to Alashiya extend from the eighteenth century B.C. until the eleventh, as a country with its own king which, at various times, has political and economic relationships with the Hittites, the kingdoms of Syria and with Egypt. If Asy is drawn in as well, it was rich enough by the fifteenth century to pay heavy tribute to Egypt. Near the end of the thirteenth century it was important enough to have its own fleet. Early in the twelfth century it was overrun by the Peoples of the Sea.[5] Were Alashiya and Cyprus one and the same? Though there are undoubtedly good grounds for supporting the identification, it is not as certain as some commentators suppose.[6] Hittite imports are confined to the gold tripod *bulla*, said to have been found at Politiko,[7] and Cypriot objects are extremely rare in the Hittite homelands. Though Cyprus was literate in the Late Bronze Age (see below), no traces of the use of cuneiform can be found, and it is not known what language was current before the introduction of Greek. Yet the Alashiya chancellery was fluent in Akkadian and able to use cuneiform. The copper which Alashiya had to send as tribute has been given undue prominence, not only because there were other sources of copper besides Cyprus, but because the items of tribute cannot necessarily be identified as local produce. There were certainly no elephants in Cyprus, but Alashiya had to contribute elephant tusks.

---

[1] §ix, 8, 165–6.     [2] §ix, 8, 166.     [3] §ix, 6, 144; §ix, 7, 108.
[4] §ix, 6, 144; §ix, 7, 120–2.     [5] G, 6, 44.     [6] §ix, nos. 5; 8; 11; 13.
[7] *C.A.H.* ii³, pt. i, p. 167.

Not a little weight has been ascribed to the argument that Cyprus *must* be named in contemporary documents, and that Alashiya is the best candidate. It is doubtful, in fact, whether Cyprus had achieved an appropriate degree of importance by the date of the Amarna letters, which were written near the end of L.C. IIa. The much later dedication to Apollo Alasiotas found at Tamassus[1] is not as decisively in favour of the identification as has been argued.[2] 'Apollo of Alashiya' is at least as likely to be a foreign god whose toponym was retained to distinguish him from local deities as to be indigenous. The effect of these and other difficulties is to suggest that the identification should be regarded as unproven until fresh evidence is available.

## X. LITERACY IN THE LATE CYPRIOT PERIOD

The proposal that Cyprus was already literate in the Early Bronze Age cannot be seriously entertained, despite the occasional use by E.C. potters of a system of pot-marks.[3] From a date early in the Late Bronze Age, however, there began a much more frequent and systematic use of marks on vases and other objects.[4] The forms of these signs were seen to have a general similarity with the syllabary used in Cyprus,[5] chiefly for writing Greek, in the Archaic and Classical periods. A relationship was also proposed with the syllabic writings used in the Aegean Bronze Age; it came to be known, in fact, as the 'Cypro-Minoan script'.[6] No serious progress could be made with its decipherment while texts of only extreme brevity were available.[7] In 1952, the first fragment of a continuous Cypro-Minoan text was found at Enkomi on a clay tablet;[8] three more have since been found to encourage hope that a library or palace archive will eventually come to light.

The earliest of the four tablets was found in a sealed deposit within the L.C. I fortress on the north side of the town, where it was buried *c.* 1500 B.C. It has three lines of text;[9] it has been said of its syllabary that it has 'many specific similarities...with Cretan linear scripts and in particular linear A'. This must be viewed against what is virtually complete lack of contact between Crete and Cyprus at this date.

The three other tablet fragments from Enkomi are some 200

[1] G, 6, 48.                              [2] §vii, 8, 1–10.

[3] *C.A.H.* ii³, pt. i, pp. 605 ff.       [4] §x, 3.

[5] §x, 12.      [6] A. J. Evans, *Scripta Minoa*, i, 69.

[7] §x, 15.      [8] §x, nos. 4; 5; 6; 17.      [9] §x, 6; §x, 7. See Plate 152(*a*).

years later and differ somewhat from the earlier one in both form
and script.[1] They were inscribed on both faces, before firing.
The scribe evidently used a carefully prepared bone stylus,
examples of which have been found at Enkomi[2] and at Kouklia.[3]
The largest fragment belonged to a tablet which must originally
have contained a text of about 200 lines; it may have been a
literary text.[4] These tablets are undeciphered; attempts to read
the longest as a Greek text are not convincing.[5]

With these Cypro-Minoan tablets at Enkomi must be linked a
complete tablet and fragments of others found at Ugarit,[6]
written in an almost identical syllabic script. Their context is
within the thirteenth century. The complete tablet has seven lines
of text on each face. These Ugaritic documents must be connected
with Cyprus, either as copies of letters sent to Cyprus, or communications from a Cypriot town to Ugarit. In either event they
were presumably written by Cypriots to be read by Cypriots;
the presence of a Cypriot community at Ugarit has frequently
been suggested.[7]

Although the Cypro-Minoan syllabary suggests the influence
of the Aegean, this influence is not to be seen in the physical
character of the tablets themselves, which are modelled on the
kiln-baked cushion-type familiar in the Near East, not the sun-
dried leaf-shaped Minoan and Mycenaean documents.[8] None of
the Cypriot tablets suggests the ledger-work that comprises the
bulk of their Aegean contemporaries.

While these tablets are unquestionably the most important
evidence for L.C. literacy, mention must also be made of the large
numbers of objects that bear brief inscriptions. Much the largest
class of inscriptions is that on clay vases, in a series from L.C. I
to L.C. III, the latest instance of which,[9] on a pithos in a late
sanctuary at Enkomi, proves the use of the script as late as the
eleventh century B.C. Signs appear either singly or in small
groups on almost any part of a vase. They were most commonly
scratched on after firing.[10] Many have been found on imported
Mycenaean vases,[11] where they are as likely to be painted as
scratched. They were painted after firing, however, and are
quite unlike the painted inscriptions on coarse Mycenaean stirrup

---

[1] §x, 11, figs. 23–5.          [2] §x, 17.          [3] Unpublished.
[4] G, 9, pl. xx; §x, 18, 61. See Plate 152(*b*)
[5] *Harv. Stud. Class. Phil.*, LXV (1961), 39–107.
[6] §IX, 12.          [7] *C.A.H.* II³, pt. 1, pp. 174 and 491.
[8] §x, nos. 8; 9; 13; 16.                    [9] §XI, 3.
[10] G, 1, 98–107; G, 4(iii), 601–18; §x, nos. 1; 2; 3; 11.
[11] G, 12, 120–1; §VIII, 25, 45–52.

jars found on the mainland. As these Cypro-Minoan inscriptions were painted after firing, they cannot be used to prove a Cypriot origin for the vases on which they are painted.[1] Although the significance of the vase inscriptions can only be guessed at, in all likelihood they define the contents or capacity of the container, or they record their owner's identity or they record a dedication.

Similar inscriptions, amounting in some cases to several signs, occur on bronze objects, particularly tools (flat axes, socketed adzes, ploughshares, socketed sickles),[2] vessels[3] and miniature ingots.[4] The marking of the tools almost certainly indicated ownership, and perhaps suggests the existence of a slave or hired labour force to whom valuable tools were only issued with suitable precaution. No satisfactory explanation had yet been advanced to account for the relatively common clay balls, of diminutive size, on which groups of signs were written with a blunt stylus before they were fired. Nearly all these enigmatic objects have been found at Enkomi,[5] but at least one has come from Hala Sultan Tekke.

While it would be misleading to insist on a general literacy in the L.C. period, so many quite humble objects have inscriptions and are distributed so widely that it can surely be inferred that at least a limited degree of literacy was the prerogative of more than the scribal class alone.

## XI. THE ACHAEAN COLONIZATION OF CYPRUS

At the end of the thirteenth century B.C. many of the Mycenaean homelands were afflicted by disaster, in the course of which Pylus was overwhelmed, Mycenae grievously afflicted. There took place a considerable diaspora of the mainland population, which resulted in the establishment of refugee settlements at widely separated points from the Ionian islands and Achaea in the west[6] to Chios in the east. At least one substantial group of these people fled to Cyprus, where their establishment at a number of sites was an event of incalculable significance for the future history of the island. The main sources of evidence for this Achaean influx are archaeological, consisting of the abrupt appearance at a relatively small number of sites of Mycenaean material of types that had been entirely missing in the two previous centuries of close commercial contact. In consequence of this Aegean irruption into Cyprus, the early part of the L.C. III

[1] §x, 3, 265 f.    [2] §viii, 6, 78–106.    [3] G, 8 (1960), 259; §x, 11, 24c.
[4] §viii, 6, 268–9.    [5] §vii, 8, 397–409; §x, 11, 19–20; §x, 15.    [6] §xi, 4.

period which it inaugurated was a dynamic phase almost without parallel in the island's history. If we may judge from the quality of material objects found in L.C. III contexts, the refugee settlers included many fine craftsmen. So much is clear from the well-known ivories from Enkomi[1] and Kouklia;[2] it is equally applicable to the development of L.C. III bronzework[3] and gem-cutting.[4]

The impact of these Achaean settlers on Cyprus has been most clearly shown by the results of the Enkomi excavations. The L.C. IIc period was brought to a close by a major destruction, in which the whole town was affected.[5] It was quickly rebuilt; at the same time it was enclosed with a massive fortification wall. During the rebuilding numbers of large buildings were erected, in which the architects made much use of fine ashlar masonry.[6] Associated with all these activities were large quantities of Mycenaean III c1 pottery, whose antecedents belong to the Argolid.[7] Never before had so much Mycenaean pottery been encountered in Enkomi occupation deposits; it virtually ousted native Cypriot painted wares. A very similar set of circumstances has been observed at Citium,[8] including the building of a massive fortification.

Though the cause of the destruction at Enkomi at the end of L.C. II is uncertain, it may have been due to an effort to repel the Greek refugees. It had been a common practice at Enkomi in L.C. II for family vaults to be hewn out of the rock below the courtyards of the town houses. In the rebuilding that was the sequel to the L.C. IIc destruction, many of these sepulchres were perforce abandoned as the new constructions encroached on the yards from which they had been entered. This closure applied to one very important tomb in particular, no. 18 of the Swedish excavation,[9] which was last used either shortly before or immediately after the catastrophe. Two of the latest bodies to be buried in this tomb were accompanied the one by a bronze sword,[10] the other by a pair of bronze greaves,[11] the immediate source of both of which can only have been the Mycenaean west. There was no Mycenaean IIIc pottery in the grave, but the IIIb vases in it stand at the very threshold of the transition to the new style. It is tempting to infer from this grave that at least one party of the refugees had arrived before the disaster.

---

[1] G, 10.     [2] G, 9, pl. xli, 1; §xi, 7.     [3] §viii, 6. See Plate 151 (b)
[4] §vii, 8, 72; §viii, 6, 51.     [5] §x, 7, 40.
[6] G, 7, 515–18; §vii, 7; §vii, 8, 239–369; §xii, 5.
[7] §xi, 4, 229.     [8] §xi, 8; §xi, 9; §xi, 10.
[9] G, 4 (i), 546–58; §vii, 8, 318–46.   [10] §vii, 8, 337–41; §xi, 2.   [11] §xi, 1.

It is possible that the Greek refugees established themselves on a virgin site in west Cyprus before they moved east into the urban areas. This is the very short-lived fortified settlement at Maa on the coast 5 miles north-west of modern Ktima,[1] where Mycenaean III c 1 pottery has beeen found. Less certain is a second fortified site at Lara, near Cape Drepanum, a few miles further north.[2] Although Enkomi seems to have been the most important of these Achaean refugee settlements, the presence of the refugees has been recognized at Sinda in the Mesaoria,[3] at Citium[4] and at Kouklia.[5] The Mycenaean III c 1 pottery that has been found in Nicosia[6] and at Ayios Sozomenos[7] is equivocal, and may represent no more than internal trade.

## XII. THE END OF THE BRONZE AGE IN CYPRUS

There is a degree of conflict in the archaeological evidence for the nature of the last century and a half of the LC period. On the one hand, as shown above, there was a terrifying diminution in the population and abandonment of large parts of the island. On the other, at those sites where occupation persisted until the threshold of the Iron Age, there is evidence of reasonable prosperity and a fairly vigorous material culture, in which the native Cypriot elements were heavily overlaid by cultural traits for which the Achaean colonists were responsible. Recent excavation at a number of L.C. III occupation sites has done much to clarify the sequence of events from c. 1200 B.C. until the end of the period c. 1050 B C.

Enkomi had been replanned and rebuilt after the destruction at the end of the thirteenth century B.C., which coincides with the arrival of Achaean colonists from Greece. It cannot have been long afterwards that a fresh catastrophe afflicted the city; for Mycenaean III c 1 pottery has been found in the destruction layer that marks this event.[8] Similar destructions at Citium,[9] Sinda[10] and Maa[11] may well be connected with the calamity at Enkomi; all are possibly to be associated with the attempt of the Peoples of the Sea to overrun the east Mediterranean which was finally frustrated by Ramesses III.[12] Though the synchronisms are very tenuous, this was perhaps the occasion for the final abandonment of many of the sites that had continued in occupation into the

[1] §xi, 4, 198.    [2] *Arch. in Greece* (1954), 54.    [3] §xi, 4, 197–200; §xi, 6.
[4] §xi, 10; §xi, 12.    [5] G, 8 (1961), 288–90.    [6] G, 8 (1959), 354–5.
[7] §viii, 6, 50.    [8] §x, 7, 41.    [9] §xi, 10, 11.
[10] §xi, 6.    [11] §x, 7, 41; §xi, 4, 198.    [12] See below, p. 377.

L.C. III a period, including the sanctuary at *Pigadhes*,[1] the mining settlement at Apliki[2] and the Ayia Irini sanctuary.[3] It is also possible that this was the occasion for the desertion of Ayios Sozomenos and the complementary founding of Idalium in a more defensible position nearby.

The chief historical problem of these episodes in L.C. III a is the part played by the Peoples of the Sea and the relationship of the Achaean colonists with these freebooters. If they were in league, then the destruction at Enkomi and Citium which preceded the period of ashlar construction could be attributed to them. But if they were not associated, then only the second destruction was the work of the Sea Peoples, and a difficulty has been removed by finding agents for an otherwise unaccountable but very widespread catastrophe. The correct solution of this problem is of considerable importance for establishing the date by which Mycenaean III c pottery had been developed. The Sea Peoples' onslaught on Cyprus must have taken place before their defeat at the hand of Ramesses III in 1191 B.C.

In the period following the second destruction at Enkomi, when the ashlar buildings were repaired and reoccupied, there are signs of considerable contact with the opposite coast.[4] These signs may mean the arrival in Cyprus of Levantine refugees, however, rather than the continuation of traditional economic ties. The Sea Peoples had been responsible for widespread destruction in the Levant, from which Ugarit, the city most closely tied to Cyprus, did not recover. Almost certainly the survivors of the original bands of Achaean refugees in Cyprus were joined about this time by fugitives from the opposite coast. To the resulting fusion of Aegean and oriental elements in the island is due much of the ambivalent character of L.C. III material culture, perhaps most clearly seen in ivory work and glyptic.

After the second destruction at Enkomi, the buildings on the north side of the town, adjoining the wall, seem not to have been replaced. Elsewhere, occupation continued without interruption until an advanced date in the eleventh century. Well before this date, however, both in Enkomi[5] and at Citium[6] there had appeared new contingents of fugitives from the Aegean, bringing with them painted pottery with the distinctive 'wavy-band' ornament,[7] which at Mycenae was contemporary with the destruction of the Granary and takes its name from it. The date of the destruction

[1] §XII, 12.    [2] §XII, 10.    [3] G, 4(ii), 642–74.
[4] §XII, 5.    [5] §VII, 8, 346–50; §X, 7, 43.    [6] §XI, 8; §XI, 10.
[7] §XI, 5; §XI, 8, 570–81.

of the Granary is unlikely to have been earlier than 1150 B.C. Fresh trouble came to Enkomi *c.* 1075 B.C., when the town was destroyed by an earthquake,[1] but life continued on the site, probably on a very reduced scale, almost to the end of the eleventh century, and after the start of the Cypro-Geometric period.[2] The final phases are marked by intensive use of at least two sanctuaries dedicated to a male god, in which a cult associated with bulls was intimately connected.[3] Whether either of the two important bronze figures of men in horned headgear found in the sanctuaries represent the god himself, or should be taken as worshippers, is undetermined.[4]

The stratigraphy at Citium, as already suggested, keeps close pace with Enkomi. During L.C. II family tombs had been constructed within the courtyards of individual houses.[5] These continued in use until near the end of the thirteenth century B.C. The site was then completely rearranged architecturally; the old buildings were demolished and replaced by new, in which the use of ashlar masonry was incorporated. The occupation of these buildings was associated with much Mycenaean IIIc 1 pottery. Not long afterwards, when Mycenaean IIIc 1 pottery was still in use, the site was destroyed, perhaps by the Sea Peoples. The next occupation was typified by Granary-style pottery; it was destroyed in the eleventh century by an earthquake, perhaps the same that afflicted Enkomi. The final occupation of Citium can be dated to the beginnings of the Cypro-Geometric period, when most of the houses damaged in the earthquake were levelled and replaced, though others were merely repaired.[6] It was not until the tenth century that the site was finally abandoned.

At the *Bamboula* settlement at Curium[7] four levels of occupation belonged to L.C. III. The evidence for two periods of Achaean settlement is altogether missing, but the pottery shows the site was not abandoned until the end of L.C. IIIb in the middle of the eleventh century. Achaean influence, however, is clearly to be seen in the nearby *Kaloriziki* cemetery,[8] some of whose tombs show all the characteristics of Mycenaean chamber tombs, notably in the use of long, straight *dromoi.* Others have been recorded in the Kastros cemetery at Lapithos on the opposite side of the island.[9] One *Kaloriziki* tomb was probably a royal sepulchre. It contained the well-known Curium sceptre-head[10]—two gold-

[1] §x, 7, 43.          [2] G, 8 (1963), 370–3; §xi, 3.
[3] G, 8 (1964), 353–6; §x, 7.   [4] §viii, 6, 256.   [5] G, 8 (1964), 350; §xi, 10.
[6] §xi, 10.          [7] §xii, 11.          [8] §xii, 2; §xii, 8.
[9] G, 4(i), 172–265.   [10] G, 9, pl. xl; 1 §xii, 8. See Plate 151 (*c*).

and-cloisonné hawks perched on a sphere, covered in cloisonné scale ornament—as well as a rich group of bronzes, including weapons, vessels and tripod stands.[1] Notable are the remains of a shield,[2] which may possibly have resembled one of the varieties represented on the warrior vase at Mycenae.[3] The cremated remains of a woman were found in one of the bronze vessels, with a set of fibulae of relatively advanced type.[4] The burial can be dated c. 1050 B.C. Many features in it, including the fibulae, the appearance of cremation and some of the details of its proto-White-Painted-pottery suggest that the movements of people from Greece to Cyprus continued even after the stage at which Granary-class pottery was introduced to a date contemporary with the earliest burials in the Ceramicus at Athens, but before the appearance of Protogeometric pottery. It may have been these last comers who introduced the Mycenaean chamber tombs at Curium and Lapithos.

Ten miles west of Enkomi at Sinda in the Mesaoria a small fortified settlement was first occupied c. 1300 B.C.[5] It was destroyed by burning at the end of the thirteenth century; its reoccupation immediately afterwards was marked by the same influx of Mycenaean III c 1 pottery already observed at Enkomi and Citium. Not long after there was a second destruction at Sinda, for which the Sea Peoples were perhaps responsible, and there was only a brief and uncertain phase of reoccupation.

Idalium in the Yalias Valley was not founded until L.C. III, yet appears to have stood outside the events in which the Aegean settlers were so heavily involved. The site on the west acropolis[6] was fortified and occupied in L.C. IIIa, and the three Late Cypriot levels continue into L.C. IIIb, but the hill was abandoned before the beginning of the Iron Age. Mycenaean pottery was missing from the occupation.

Though the evidences of the several settlement sites investigated differ in detail, they agree in the broad outline they offer of the L.C. III period. They show the arrival of refugees from the Aegean at the time of the sack of Pylus. The refugees either occupied virgin sites on their first landfall, as at Maa, or fought their way into long-established towns, as at Enkomi and Citium, probably at Palaeopaphos as well. On their arrival at Enkomi and Citium these towns were strongly fortified and largely rebuilt in an architectural style quite novel to Cyprus. Not long

---

[1] §viii, 6, 193–5.    [2] §viii, 6, 142–6.    [3] *Crete and Mycenae*, pl. 233.
[4] §xii, 8, 139.    [5] §xi, 4, 196–201; §xi, 6.
[6] G, 4 (ii), 460–628; §xii, 11.

afterwards much of the island was involved in a great catastrophe, in which it is reasonable to see the work of the Sea Peoples. Many sites were abandoned for good; but others, perhaps with an injection of new blood from Levantine refugees, picked up the pieces and continued on a somewhat reduced scale. The copper industry remained important. Before the end of the twelfth century fresh groups of emigrants from Greece, bringing Granary pottery with them, were absorbed by Enkomi and Citium. This type of pottery was still to be exercising a profound effect in the Early Iron Age. Some sites, of which Curium is the clearest instance, seem to have remained outside the Aegean sphere until the eleventh century. Yet it was to Curium, and probably also to Lapithos, that a third and final group of Greek refugees made their way at a time when the Mycenaean world in Greece was all but dead, the Early Iron Age about to begin. It fell to Cyprus to shelter the remains of Mycenaean civilization, including its political structure, aspects of its language, traces of its writing and much of its visual art long after its complete disappearance from the Greek mainland. This, then, was the first and most radical step in the Hellenization of Cyprus.

## XIII. CYPRUS AND COPPER IN THE LATE BRONZE AGE

Much of the importance of Cyprus in the L.C. period must have been due to her position, both for commercial and military reasons. Yet her role as a source of copper production must be stressed. If the identification of Cyprus with Alashiya were established (see above), there would be documentary evidence to show that Cypriot copper had at various times been exported to Mesopotamia (Mari), Asia Minor (to the Hittites)[1] and Egypt.

Although the location of many ancient slag-heaps[2] has been noted in the ore-bearing regions of Cyprus, none can be certainly attributed to the L.C. period, nor can mine-workings or other industrial sites. Nevertheless, finds connected either with smelting copper or with the making of copper or bronze objects have occurred on many L.C. sites, including Enkomi, Citium,[3] Hala Sultan Tekke, Klavdhia and Lapithos amongst the most important settlements; Apliki, Ayios Sozomenos, Mathiati and Lythrodondas of the sites of secondary importance.[4] The best documented industrial site is Enkomi, where evidence of copper working

[1] §ix, 9, 14.                              [2] §viii, 6, 21.
[3] G, 8 (1964), 350.                        [4] §viii, 6, 21.

appears in buildings on the north side of the town as early as
L.C. I; this area continued its industrial activity throughout the
fourteenth and much of the thirteenth centuries. Other parts of
the site show similar activity during the twelfth century.[1] The
volumes of waste material associated with these operations suggest that the ore was only partly processed in the areas where it
was mined, and that the refining was completed in the big industrial towns. There may be political as well as economic
implications in this arrangement. Though tin-bronze was widely
used in Cyprus throughout the L.C. period, the source of the tin
is unknown; it cannot have been produced in the island itself.

During L.C. III, the copper-founders of Enkomi prepared
their raw copper for marketing and transport in the form of
'ox-hide' ingots, several complete and fragmentary examples of
which have been found on the site.[2] Theories that these ingots
were intended to simulate the flayed hide of an ox, and that they
should be interpreted as units of currency echoing an earlier
situation when wealth was expressed in heads of oxen have now
been discarded.[3] Such ingots have been found in widely separated
parts of the Mediterranean,[4] from Sardinia to the bay of Antalya;
they are also represented in several tribute scenes in Egyptian tombs
of the Eighteenth Dynasty.[5] The earliest ingots lack the prominent
carrying handles which distinguish the later examples.[6] This
variety has been found in Crete, both in a great hoard at Hagia
Triada and more recently in the palatial deposits at Zakro;
others come from the sea off Euboea and from the bay of Antalya.
They occur in fifteenth-century tomb paintings in Egypt, sometimes on the shoulders of 'tribute-bearers' of Aegean aspect.[7]
None have been found in Cyprus.

By 1400 B.C. a new type of ingot with a prominent carrying
handle at each corner had been introduced; it appears as an ideogram on Cnossian linear B texts.[8] There are two varieties, with
only a dubious chronological distinction; both have been found in
Cyprus. The most notable find of handled ingots, however,
comes from the cargo of a wrecked ship recently raised from the
sea off Cape Gelidonya in south-west Asia Minor.[9] Some forty
complete or fragmentary ingots were recovered, together with a
large number of bronze artifacts, particularly tools, of types
familiar in Cyprus in L.C. III,[10] and much scrap besides. There

---

[1] §VII, 8, 27–35.

[2] §VIII, 6, 267–72. See Plate 149 (c)    [3] §XIII, 1.

[4] §VIII, 6, 267–72, §IX, 3.    [5] §VIII, 6, 270.    [6] §VII, 8, 30.

[7] §VIII, 10, 227, fig. 24.    [8] §X, 18, 380.    [9] §XIII, 1.

[10] §VIII, 6, 292–4.

is a strong presumption that this ship was on her way to Greece from some Cypriot port; the voyage should probably be dated in the first half of the twelfth century B.C.

The Mycenaean colonization of Cyprus at the end of the thirteenth century B.C. brought a revolution in the working and management of the metal industry, including the introduction of the 'ox-hide' ingot as a technical and administrative convenience. Though the final history of this ingot type belongs to Cyprus, there is no proof that it originated there.[1] The idea probably was developed in Crete as an administrative measure in the palaces. It will then have been adopted by the Mycenaeans (who borrowed heavily from Minoan metallurgical ideas), who brought it to Cyprus when they fled there at the beginning of L.C. III.

Bronze-founders' hoards of scrap metal became relatively common at Enkomi in L.C. III deposits.[2] They can be linked with somewhat similar hoards in Greece by the cargo of the Cape Gelidonya ship.[3] The most likely explanation for the collection of scrap in a copper-producing country is a breakdown in tin-supplies from abroad, and a consequent enhanced value for tin-bronzes. This would certainly account for the miscellaneous rubbish which the Cape Gelidonya ship was taking to Greece.

## XIV. THE LATE CYPRIOT PERIOD AND THE FOUNDATION LEGENDS

It is now obvious that there is a broad agreement between the traditions preserved in Greek literature[4] concerning the foundation of Cypriot towns from Greece and the archaeological evidence that shows Greek settlers were establishing themselves in Cyprus from the late thirteenth century B.C. until the end of the Late Bronze Age. Since there was no comparable movement in the Iron Age, whatever historical worth these traditions hold belongs to the Bronze Age. This is where their own context places most of the traditions, for they refer to men involved in the Trojan War and the disturbances that followed it. These were the circumstances which brought Agapenor to Paphos, brought Teucer to Salamis and led to the arrival of Pheidippus and his party of Coans.

Nearly every settlement said to have been 'founded' at this time was in fact long established at the time of which the traditions speak. This applies to Paphos, to the Argive foundation

[1] §VIII, 6, 271–2.    [2] §VIII, 6, 278–92.
[3] §VIII, 6, 294–8.    [4] §XIV, 2.

of Curium, Praxandrus at Lapethus and Chytrus at Chytroi. In all likelihood, the Salamis of the Teucer legend must in fact be Enkomi nearby. There is obviously a capricious element in what tradition remembered; for it seems difficult to substantiate the foundation of Chytroi by Chytrus, grandson of Acamas, with an actual Mycenaean IIIc influx, and the same is true at Golgi, said to have been established by Golgus and a party from Sicyon. Yet there are important sites, such as Citium, in whose development the Mycenaean settlers played a dominant role, of which tradition knew nothing.

Some traditions are sufficiently circumstantial to carry conviction, such as that which portrays Agapenor, king of Tegea and leader of the Arcadian contingent at Troy, driven by foul weather to Cyprus after the fall of Troy. He founded Paphos, and established a temple of Aphrodite. Later his daughter Laodice founded a cult of Aphrodite Paphia in Tegea; she also sent a peplos to Tegea as a gift to Athena Alea. There seems to have been a special connexion between Tegea and Cyprus, for Tegea was unique in its cult of Aphrodite Paphia. But if Agapenor founded Paphos, what of Cinyras its king at the time the Trojan expedition was launched? Agapenor cannot be accommodated at Nea Paphos, 10 miles further west, for recent investigation has shown it was not occupied before the classical period.[1] Agapenor and Cinyras must therefore belong to the same town. In one tradition Agamemnon avenged himself upon Cinyras after the Trojan War; such vengeance could be equated with the earliest appearance of Mycenaean IIIc 1 pottery, and Agapenor would then belong to the second colonizing phase, marked by Granary-class Mycenaean pottery.

It is easier to decide that there is a general correspondence between archaeology and the foundation legends than to single out those elements which preserve the true grain of history, those which were retrospective efforts of particular communities to provide themselves with a past that was both politically and emotionally satisfying. But this cannot diminish the importance of the support which archaeology has brought to the traditions.

[1] §xiv, 1, 9–11.

# CHAPTER XXIII

## EGYPT: FROM THE INCEPTION OF THE NINETEENTH DYNASTY TO THE DEATH OF RAMESSES III

### I. THE RISE OF THE NINETEENTH DYNASTY

THE death of Tutankhamun brought about a break in the royal succession; his successors Ay and Horemheb were not of royal blood and neither left an heir of his body. In these circumstances Horemheb appointed his vizier Pramesse[1] to succeed him, so that on the king's death in *c.* 1320 B.C. Pramesse ascended the throne as Ramesses I, thus inaugurating the Nineteenth Dynasty. He was probably well advanced in years when he became king, for no date of his is known higher than Year 2, on a stela from Buhen (Wādi Halfa)[2] which records the dedication and endowment of a temple to Min-Amun. Among the personnel were slaves 'from the captures made by His Majesty'; these 'captures' may well refer to the Asiatic campaign of Year 1 of Sethos I,[3] the son and co-regent of Ramesses who was probably too old for campaigning. The terms of the Abydos stela of Sethos I[4] make it virtually certain that there was in fact a co-regency which may have begun in Ramesses' second year, for duplicating his Buhen stela is another inscription dated in Year 1 of Sethos.[5] Ramesses did not reign long enough to carry out any major building work in Egypt, but a few reliefs from Karnak bear his name.[6] Two stelae of this king at Serābīt el-Khādim[7] testify to activity at the turquoise mines of Sinai, and some faience cartouches of Ramesses were found under the temple of Beth-shan (Beisān),[8] the city which Sethos I had to relieve from hostile attack at the outset of his first campaign. The tomb of Ramesses I, as of all the rest of the dynasty, is in the Valley of the Kings opposite Luxor.[9]

---

\* An original version of this chapter was published as fascicle 52 in 1966.
[1] §I, 2.  [2] G, 1, vol. III, sects. 74 ff.
[3] See below, pp. 218 ff.  [4] §I, 4.
[5] G, 1, vol. III, sects. 157 ff.  [6] G, 8, vol. II, 16 (25–6).
[7] G, 5, nos. 244–5.  [8] §II, 6, 24.  [9] §I, 3.

It may perhaps not be out of place here to refer to the era described by Theon of Alexandria as *apo Menophreōs*,[1] which began in 1321–1317 B.C. An attempt has been made to derive the name from *Mry-n-Pth* 'Beloved of Ptah;[2] an epithet regularly attached to the personal name of Sethos I, but it is more plausible to derive the Greek name from Menpehre, the current form of the praenomen of Ramesses I, which is an exact Egyptian counterpart of *Menophrēs*. This identification of *Menophrēs* with Ramesses I is not new,[3] for it held the field until the less convincing alternative was put forward, and it has recently been revived;[4] chronologically there is nothing against it, for the four-year period 1321–1317 B.C. is enough to cover all the known reign of Ramesses I with a couple of years to spare.

## II. THE FOREIGN WARS OF SETHOS I

To Sethos I, who succeeded to the throne in 1318 B.C., there fell the task of restoring Egypt to the standing of a Great Power, for her prestige had fallen low during the Amarna episode and its sequel. It is true that the old notion of the total loss of all Egyptian influence in Palestine can no longer be held, for certain fortresses, e.g. Beth-shan, Rehob, and probably Megiddo,[5] were held in the Egyptian interest, but many of the Palestinian city-states were hostile to Egypt, and even engaged in warlike operations against towns which were still loyal. That Sethos did in fact look on himself as dedicated to the restoration of his country's fame is witnessed by his motto 'Repeater-of-Birth', i.e. inaugurator of a renaissance, which he took for his Horus name.

The campaigns of Sethos I are recorded in a series of scenes carved on the east and north walls containing the hypostyle hall of the temple of Amun at Karnak, and these reliefs show actions in the field, the submission of defeated chieftains and the presentation of prisoners-of-war to Amun, the national god.[6] The scenes appear to have been arranged in chronological order, and despite the loss of most of the third or uppermost register, we have records of four campaigns, all of which have been subsumed under the date of Year 1, although four successive wars cannot all have been fought in one year. This kind of single dating to cover several expeditions is known also on the Tumbos stela of Tuthmosis I and on the Armant stela of Tuthmosis III. As

[1] See *C.A.H.* 1³, pt. 1, p. 190.  [2] G, 4, 249.
[3] G, 6, 19.  [4] §I, 1.
[5] §II, 1, 36.  [6] G, 9, pls. 34–53; §II, 1.

regards the first campaign of Sethos, information which forms a
valuable supplement to the temple record is provided by a stela
found at Beth-shan,[1] so that it is possible to reconstruct the course
of the war with more detail than usual.

The point of departure from Egypt was the north-eastern
frontier town of Tjel, modern Tell Abu Seifa near El-Qantara,[2]
the starting-point of the military road from Egypt to Palestine.[3]
The distance from Tjel to Raphia (Rafa), the frontier town at the
Asiatic end of the road, is 120 miles, and along this distance there
were nine fortified wells.[4] The scenes at Karnak depict a battle
raging among the wells, so that the fortifications were certainly
necessary; clearly the passage of the Egyptian army along the
desert road was disputed, the enemy being a force of Shasu[5]
probably based on Raphia. This opposition proved unavailing,
and first Raphia and soon afterwards 'the town of the Canaan',
probably Gaza,[6] fell to the Egyptian army.

On his passage from the Canaanite coastal plain into the plain
of Jezreel, Sethos seems to have met with no opposition from the
key fortress of Megiddo, commanding the passage of the Carmel
ridge, for he does not mention that town, so that it is probable
that, like Beth-shan, it was still held for the Egyptians. One of
the first tasks which lay before the king when once he had de-
bouched into the central plain of Palestine was to send a column
to relieve Beth-shan, which together with the neighbouring town
of Rehob, was under attack from an alliance of Hamath and the
trans-Jordan town of Pella (Egyptian *Pḥr*). Beth-shan lay about
15 miles south of the Sea of Galilee and 4 miles west of the Jordan;
Hamath, not to be confused with the Syrian town of that name,
may have lain at the mouth of the Yarmuk valley;[7] and Rehob
seems to have been situated a short distance to the south of
Beth-shan, where it has been identified with Tell es-Sarem.[8]
There was also trouble with the 'Apiru of 'the mountain of Yar-
met' and of Tirka-el, who had made common cause against the
town of Ruhem.[9] The exact situation of these places is not known,
but Tirka-el is named in the Anastasi Papyrus No. 1 in association with Rehob and Beth-shan.[10] In any case, the trouble was
effectively dealt with.

To cope with these disturbances, as well as to prosecute his

---

[1] §II, 6, 24 ff.; pl. 41.  
[2] G, 3, vol. II, 202* ff.  
[3] §II, 3.  
[4] §II, 3, pls. 11–12.  
[5] §II, 3, 100, n. 1.  
[6] G, 9, pl. 39.  
[7] §II, 6, 26, n. 50.  
[8] §II, 4, 20; §II, 6, 26, n. 52.  
[9] §II, 4, 20.  
[10] §II, 2, 24*.

main purpose of advancing northwards, in 'Year 1, 3rd month of Summer, 10th day'[1] Sethos dispatched 'the first army of Amun Mighty-of-Bows' against Hamath, 'the first army of Pre Rich-in-Valour' to Beth-shan, and 'the first army of Sutekh Victorious-of-Bows' against Yenoam, another town of uncertain location which must, however, have been readily accessible from Megiddo, for it is the first-named of the towns which fell to Tuthmosis III after his great victory there.[2] Presumably the relief of Beth-shan automatically brought about the relief of Rehob, since the latter place receives no further mention. We may guess also that it was either the Beth-shan column or the Hamath column which dealt with the trouble at Ruhem. The objectives of this three-pronged operation having been achieved, the army took the sea-ports of Acre and Tyre[3] and advanced into the Lebanon region, taking the town of Qader.[4] Having received the submission of the Lebanese chieftains, on whom he enforced a levy of timber,[5] Sethos returned in triumph to Egypt,[6] having secured the spring-board for his contemplated conquest of Syria. On his return march he crossed the Jordan and chastised Pella[7] for its share in the attack on Beth-shan, and set up a stela at Tell esh-Shiḥāb in the Ḥaurān.[8]

Of the Karnak record of the second campaign there remains only a fragment showing a scene of the assault on Qadesh with the legend 'The ascent which Pharaoh made to destroy the land of Qadesh and the land of Amurru'.[9] Since the reduction of Qadesh-on-Orontes and the coastal strip of Amurru was the essential next stage in the Egyptian advance, it seems probable that the whole of the lost record referred to this campaign, which presumably took place in Year 2; the names of the Amorite towns Ṣumura and Ullaza on a sphinx from El-Qurna[10] show that at least of Amurru was overrun. The conquest of the region of Takhsy, recorded on the same sphinx, may have been an event either of this campaign or of the later Hittite war, according to whether Takhsy is to be located south or north of Qadesh.[11]

On the assumption that the sequence of the scenes at Karnak is chronological,[12] it appears that the third campaign was directed

---

[1] §II, I, 36.
[2] G, I, vol. II, sect. 436.
[3] G, I, vol. III, sect. 114.
[4] G, 9, pl. 35.
[5] *Ibid.*
[6] §II, 3, pl. 11.
[7] G, I, vol. III, sect. 114.
[8] §II, 5.
[9] G, 3, vol. I, 140*.
[10] G, I, vol. III, §114; G, 7, 17.
[11] G, 3, vol. I, 150* ff.
[12] §II, I, 35, 38.

not against the Hittites but against the Libyans,[1] showing that the pressure on the western Delta which was to give later kings so much trouble was already beginning to develop. No localities are named where fighting occurred, but the Egyptians were victorious. The fourth and last campaign was against a Hittite army,[2] presumably somewhere north of Qadesh; again no places are mentioned, but a great slaughter of the enemy is claimed and captives were brought back to Egypt. As a result of this success, Sethos seems to have won temporary control of part of Syria, for he claims Qatna and Tunip[3] among his conquests, but there can be no doubt that ultimately he lost the north, though a failure of this kind would certainly not have been placed on public record; Ramesses II would not have had to fight his famous battle at Qadesh if the Egyptians had still held that town. Although the frontier between the Hittite and the Egyptian spheres of influence was not demarcated on the ground, the effective boundary must have run south of Qadesh;[4] beyond that frontier neither Great Power could expect to maintain itself in the face of determined opposition. In recognition of this fact, Sethos concluded a treaty of peace with Muwatallish, the king of Khatti,[5] but even if his Hittite venture had failed, Sethos had to his credit the solid achievement of having restored Egyptian authority over all Palestine and of having made Egypt once more a power to be reckoned with.

## III. INTERNAL AFFAIRS UNDER SETHOS I

At home in Egypt it was the task of Sethos I to round off the work set on foot by Horemheb in restoring the ravages of the Amarna episode. Lacking extensive written documentation, the best index to the state of the realm is the amount of building activity undertaken by the pharaohs, and the reign of Sethos was not lacking in this respect, so that it would seem that Egypt was well on the road to recovery. The Ramesside line seems to have sprung from a Delta family with a personal devotion to the god Seth of Avaris (most probably the later Djane, Biblical Zoan, Greek Tanis),[6] formerly the capital of the Hyksos invaders; on account of this association with the ancient enemy and of his legendary role as the murderer of Osiris, Seth was unpopular

---

[1] G, 1, vol. III, sects. 120 ff.; G, 9, pl. 50.
[2] G, 1, vol. III, sects. 142 ff.; G, 9, pls. 45 f.
[3] §II, 1, 38.                    [4] See below, ch. XXIV, sect. 1.
[5] §II, 1, 38; G, 1, vol. III, sect. 377.    [6] G, 3, vol. II, 199* ff. See below, p. 225.

elsewhere. Therefore, despite their family connexions and their preference for residences in the north—the Buhen decree of Ramesses I was issued from Memphis[1] and Sethos I had a palace at Qantīr[2]—the Ramesside kings maintained Thebes as the state and religious capital and Amun as the national god, for his influential priesthood had to be propitiated; the Ramessides were an upstart line of rulers, and it was important for them to have the support of the powerful corporation which served the god of Thebes. In the case of Sethos I, however, we get the impression that will marched with necessity, and that he looked on it as a pious duty to restore the monuments of his predecessors, especially in the matter of replacing the name of Amun where it had been hacked out by the Atenist iconoclasts. In such cases he contented himself with the brief added inscription 'Restoration of the monument which King Sethos made'. That in fact a good deal remained to be done to set the land in order is clear from the stela which Sethos set up[3] in the chapel which he built at Abydos for his father Ramesses I,[4] where the king complains of the utterly neglected state of the sacred necropolis of Abydos.

The principal contribution made by Sethos to the great temple of Amun at Thebes was the building of a considerable part of the famous hypostyle hall.[5] Like every other major construction begun by Sethos, it was unfinished at his death, and the work was completed by his son Ramesses II. On the opposite bank of the Nile at El-Qurna Sethos built his funerary temple, setting aside certain rooms in it for his father's rites.[6] His tomb in the Valley of the Kings is the finest of all; over 300 ft. long, it contains coloured scenes and inscriptions of the highest quality.[7] His greatest work, however, was his splendid temple at Abydos.[8] For centuries this locality had been sacred to Osiris and a place of pilgrimage for the devout, and it was here that Sethos erected a temple with the unusual ground-plan of an inverted L, in which the beauty of the scenes and inscriptions in low relief, often with their original colouring, can challenge comparison with any temple now extant in Egypt. The centre and heart of the building is a row of seven chapels, dedicated respectively to Osiris, Isis, Horus, Amun, Ptah, Re-Harakhte and to Sethos himself in his

---

[1] G, 1, vol. III, sect. 77.  [2] §III, 8.
[3] §I, 4.  [4] §III, 11.
[5] See Plate 154(a). The records of his wars cover the outside of the north wall and part of the east wall, see the plan G, 1, vol. III, 39.
[6] G, 8, vol. II, 140 ff.  [7] §III, 9.
[8] §III, 3. See Plate 153(a).

capacity of god on earth. It fell to Ramesses II to complete this temple also, and his coarse incised reliefs and hieroglyphs show a marked contrast with the delicate work of his father's craftsmen. A copy of a decree by Sethos describing the endowment of this temple and safeguarding its staff and property from outside interference is inscribed on a rock at Nauri, a short distance north of the Third Cataract.[1]

A characteristic mood of the Nineteenth Dynasty was a harking back to the past and a consciousness of the long history of Egypt, and as an expression of this mood Sethos set up in his temple at Abydos a list of the most illustrious kings of Egypt from Menes of the First Dynasty down to his own reign,[2] and he and his son Ramesses are depicted making offerings to their predecessors. A duplicate list, of which part is in the British Museum,[3] was originally set up in Ramesses II's own temple at Abydos, while a third list was inscribed in a private tomb at Saqqara.[4] Further, in Turin there is the much more extensive but sadly fragmentary chronicle on papyrus known as the Royal Canon,[5] which once contained not only the names of all the ancient kings known to the chronicler, but also the lengths of their reigns and the totals of years of the dynasties. It must have been on documents such as this that Manetho based his division of the kings of Egypt into thirty dynasties, and even today, after a century and a half of Egyptology, these king-lists are not devoid of value.

Behind his great temple at Abydos, Sethos constructed a subterranean building which has no parallel in Egypt. Once known as 'the Osireion', from the belief of the first excavators that it was intended to represent the tomb of the god Osiris, it has in fact been shown to be a cenotaph for Sethos in the holy ground of Abydos.[6] The lay-out of the central hall appears to represent the sacred hill which rose out of the primeval waters at the creation of the world, while the 'tomb-chamber' contains interesting astronomical and dramatic texts. Here also this construction still lacked the finishing touches when Sethos died, but some scenes and inscriptions were added by his second successor Merneptah.

Any buildings erected by Sethos at the other great sites of Egypt have almost entirely vanished, but the base of a votive model of the sun-temple at Heliopolis which bears his name was

[1] §III, 7; §III, 5.    [2] §III, 10, pl. 1, upper. See Plate 26.
[3] §III, 1, 163.    [4] §III, 10, pl. 1, lower.
[5] §III, 6.    [6] §III, 4.

found at Tell el-Yahūdīya,[1] and from Heliopolis itself come an inscribed door-post and an obelisk,[2] showing that he made some additions to the temple there.

## IV. SINAI, THE EASTERN DESERT AND NUBIA UNDER SETHOS I

The turquoise mines at Serābīt el-Khādim in Sinai were still being exploited, for there have survived from that site two stelae and some small objects bearing the name of Sethos, as well as another stela in the joint names of Sethos I and Ramesses II, indicating a co-regency.[3] The gold mines in the desert of Edfu were worked on behalf of Sethos' great foundation at Abydos, and owing to the shortage of water on the route to the gold-field Sethos sank a well in the Wādi Miāh, an offshoot of the Wādi Abbād, and also cut in the rock wall of the valley a chapel with a built-up portico;[4] an inscription dated in Year 9 records the construction of the well and the chapel. A second inscription offers thanks to the king for the well, while a third consists of curses on anyone, king or commoner, who shall interfere with the supply of gold to Abydos.

The Egyptian hold on Nubia does not seem to have been seriously weakened by the events of the latter part of the Eighteenth Dynasty, and, as noted above, already in Year 2 of Ramesses I and Year 1 of Sethos I a temple at Buhen was dedicated. We learn from a stela of Ramesses II found in the fortress of Qūbān in Lower Nubia[5] that Sethos also drew gold from the region of the Wādi el-Allāqi, but that an attempt to sink a well on the road thither was a failure, though Ramesses was more successful. In Year 11 Sethos dedicated a hall of columns in the temple of Amun at Napata (Gebel Barkal).[6] Yet even in Nubia Sethos had to enforce the *pax Aegyptiaca* with military action against a tribe named Irem,[7] an event to which allusion in very general terms is made in a rock inscription cut in honour of the king at Qasr Ibrīm.[8] In normal circumstances the government of the Nubian provinces was in the hands of the Viceroys of Nubia, the titular Kings' Sons of Kush, and the pharaoh did not appear in person except on ceremonial or military occasions.

[1] §III, 2; G, 1, vol. III, sects. 244 ff.
[2] G, 1, vol. III, sect. 245.
[3] G, 5, nos. 246–50.
[5] G, 1, vol. III, sects. 282 ff.
[7] §IV, 4, 168.

[4] §IV, 1; §IV, 5.
[6] §IV, 3.
[8] §IV, 2.

## V. THE FIRST YEARS OF RAMESSES II

The date of the accession of Ramesses II to sole rule was probably 1304 B.C.,[1] but before that date he was co-regent with his father for an uncertain period.[2] The dates on his monuments, however, refer to his sole rule and do not include the years of the co-regency. As has already been remarked,[3] the royal family preferred to reside in the north, the administrative capital as distinct from the state and religious capital at Thebes being probably Memphis. The first recorded act of Ramesses II was to travel south to Thebes for the great festival of Opet, when the god Amun journeyed in state from Karnak to Luxor. When the festival was over, Ramesses halted at Abydos on his return journey northwards, and in the great inscription dated in Year 1 which he caused to be set up in his father's temple[4] he describes how the temple stood unfinished, with its endowments alienated, and how the tombs of former kings were falling into rack and ruin. Summoning his entourage, Ramesses recounted his appointment as his father's co-regent and declared his intention to complete the great temple and to restore its endowments, which in fact he did. The long and verbose inscription of more than a hundred lines of text ends with Ramesses recounting what he has done and praying to his deceased father to intercede with the gods on his behalf; his father is made to give a favourable response. He also appointed a local ecclesiastic, one Nebunenef, to be a high priest of Amun at Thebes,[5] before continuing his northward journey.

The Delta residence of the pharaohs from the reign of Ramesses II on was known as Per-Ramesse 'House of Ramesses', the Biblical Raamses, but its site is still disputed. Its identity with the great city of Tanis seems the more probable, but a case has also been made out for Qantīr,[6] some 11 miles to the south, where both Sethos I[7] and Ramesses II had palaces. The *literati* of the Nineteenth Dynasty at times became quite lyrical in praise of its beauty and luxury.[8] The situation of the Residence in the eastern half of the Delta was certainly more practical for a ruler concerned with affairs in Palestine and Syria than a capital far to the south; when not abroad with an army the kings of the Nineteenth

---

[1] Cf. *C.A.H.* I[3], pt. 1, p. 189.  
[2] §v, 4.  
[3] See above, p. 222.  
[4] G, 1, vol. III, sects. 258 ff.  
[5] §v, 5. Cf. below, ch. xxxv, sect. iv.  
[6] G, 3, vol. II, 171* ff.; §v, 2.  
[7] §III, 8.  
[8] §v, 1, 73 ff., 153 f.

Dynasty seem to have spent most of their time in either Per-Ramesse or Memphis.

Another enterprise which Ramesses undertook early in his reign was the securing of an adequate water-supply for the gold convoys to and from the Wādi el-Allāqi. The viceroy of Nubia reported to the pharaoh on the losses from thirst on this route and stated that a well dug by Sethos I had failed to reach water. In Year 5 Ramesses ordered that another well be sunk, and water was struck at one-tenth the depth of the dry well sunk by his father.[1]

A problem which first showed itself in the reign of Amenophis III and which by this time was becoming endemic was the defence of the coast of the Delta against the inroads of Sherden pirates, and already in Year 2 a raid of this kind was driven off.[2] That these raids were of fairly frequent occurrence is suggested by the fact that Sherden prisoners were enlisted in the Egyptian army in sufficient numbers to furnish a contingent of their own, as also were Nubian and Libyan captives.[3]

## VI. THE STRUGGLE WITH THE HITTITES

The outstanding feature of the reign of Ramesses II was his long drawn out struggle with the Hittites. Apparently he had to occupy the first three years of his sole reign with setting home affairs in order, for the neglect and corruption that he found ruling at his father's temple at Abydos suggest that during the last years of Sethos I the reins of government had fallen slack. Be this as it may, it was not until Year 4 that we find Ramesses setting up an inscription at the Nahr el-Kalb near Beirut to record his first campaign in Asia.[4] Owing to weathering, except for the date, the inscription is illegible, so we have no information as to the events of this war, though it is possible that some of the names of captured places recorded at Karnak may belong to this first campaign.[5] In year 5 Ramesses used his springboard in northern Palestine and Phoenicia to mount a major attack on the Hittite Empire. No opposition seems to have been met by the Egyptian army during its northward march from Raphia, and at a point on the coast in the south of Amurru Ramesses detached a special task force, presumably to secure the seaport of Ṣumura, whence it was to turn eastward along the Eleutheros valley road to make

---

[1] G, 1, vol. III, sects. 282 ff.
[2] G, 3, vol. I, 194* ff.; §v, 6.
[3] §v, 3, 476.
[4] Cf. below, ch. XXIV, sect. 1.
[5] G, 9, pls. 54 ff.

junction with the main force at Qadesh,[1] the main Hittite bastion of defence in the south. Having dispatched this task force, the Egyptian army, which was organized in four divisions named respectively after the gods Amun, Pre, Ptah and Sutekh, turned inland and marched probably by way of the valley of the river Litani to the valley of the river Orontes, which was crossed from east to west at the ford of Shabtuna nearly 8 miles south of Qadesh. Between this ford and Qadesh lay the wood of Robaui, where once Amenophis II had hunted, and which the army had to traverse. The division of Amun, under the command of Ramesses himself, was the first to cross the river. On its northward march two Hittite spies were taken and questioned. They informed the Egyptians falsely that the Hittite army was at Aleppo, and as this news seemed to be confirmed by the inability of the Egyptian scouts to find any trace of the enemy, Ramesses pressed on and encamped to the west of Qadesh. At this point two more Hittites were captured who on being beaten admitted that the Hittite army, far from being at Aleppo, was concealed behind the city of Qadesh and was standing on the far bank of the Orontes. Ramesses at once sent off messengers to hasten the march of the division of Pre, which was the next in order of march and which was emerging from the wood of Robaui. But before any effective action could be taken the Hittite king launched a heavy chariot charge which took the division of Pre, still in column of route, in the flank and scattered it. The fugitives fled to the camp of the division of Amun, hotly pursued by the Hittites, who broke into the camp. The division of Amun too was stricken with panic and fled, leaving the pharaoh and a body of chariotry completely surrounded by the enemy. At this very opportune moment reinforcements arrived in the shape of the Amurru task force making its rendezvous with the main army. Taking the Hittite chariots in the rear, it joined itself to the hard-pressed band round Ramesses and thus saved the day. The Hittite king Muwatallish sent off a second force of a thousand chariots, but to no avail; in six successive charges the Egyptians drove the Hittite chariots into the Orontes, aided in the last stages of the battle by the van of the newly arrived division of Ptah. The division of Sutekh was too far in the rear to take part in the action.

By this time the day must have been far advanced, and further fighting was impracticable. The Egyptians camped on the

[1] G, 3, vol. I, 188* ff. For the extensive literature of the battle of Qadesh see below, ch. xxiv, sect. i, Bibliography.

stricken field, Ramesses greeting with bitter reproaches the fugitives who now came filtering back, while the Hittite king, who for some reason made no use of his infantry during the battle, kept his remaining forces on the east bank of the Orontes. One Egyptian account states that on the next day the Hittites asked for an armistice, and this may well be true. The Hittite chariot force had been badly mauled, while a quarter of the Egyptian army, the division of Sutekh, had not been engaged, and thus consisted of fresh troops, including chariotry, so that Muwatallish may well have felt that it would be inadvisable to risk another field action. On the other hand, the morale of one half of the Egyptian army must have been at zero, and Ramesses was no doubt only too glad of an excuse to withdraw without loss of face. Although the actual battle was drawn, strategically the result was a defeat for the Egyptians, and they had to retire homeward with nothing to show for their efforts, though Ramesses did not fail to publicize his admittedly gallant stand against odds. With the retreat of the Egyptians from Qadesh, the Hittites advanced southward to Damascus, which was well on the Egyptian side of the frontier.[1]

The result of the campaign of Year 5 afforded the client states of Palestine the spectacle of an unsuccessful Egyptian army marching home, and the consequent loss of prestige had widespread effects. Many of these petty states took the opportunity to throw off the Egyptian yoke, and the revolt must have spread far south, for in Year 6 or 7 Ramesses had to storm Askalon,[2] while in Year 8 he took a number of places in the Galilee region and the town of Dapur in Amurru.[3] In Year 10 Ramesses was again on the Nahr el-Kalb, where he set up another stela, also illegible,[4] and it may have been in the following year that he broke through the Hittite defences and invaded Syria. Certainly Ramesses must have held Tunip for a period, since there was a statue of himself as overlord in the city; it is mentioned incidentally in the account of a Hittite attack which may have been a surprise assault, since the pharaoh went into battle without his corselet.[5] Qatna also was claimed among his

---

[1] Cf. below, ch. xxiv, sect. i.

[2] G, i, vol. iii, sects. 353 ff.; G, 9, pl. 58.

[3] G, i, vol. iii, sects. 356 ff.; G, 3, vol. i, 178* ff., though Gardiner's suggestion that Dapur may have been in the region of Aleppo is surely impossible in view of the military situation prevailing in Year 8.

[4] Cf. below, ch. xxiv, sect. i.

[5] G, i, vol. iii, sect. 365.

conquests,[1] and further to the north-west he invaded Qode,[2] so
that he must have penetrated deeply into Hittite territory.
Nevertheless, as Sethos I found, it was impossible for the
Egyptians to hold indefinitely territories so far from base against
Hittite pressure, and after sixteen years of intermittent hostilities,
a treaty of peace was concluded in Year 21 between Egypt and
Khatti[3] as between two equal Great Powers, and its provisions
were reciprocal. It is clear that a mutual frontier was recognized,
but its position is not stated; probably it was not far removed from
what it had been before hostilities broke out, so that the long
struggle may well have had no other immediate result than to
convince the two Powers that neither could overcome the other.
The most important provisions of the treaty were a mutual
renunciation of further war and a joint defensive pact, while
other sections dealt on a similar mutual basis with the extradition
and treatment of fugitives from one land or the other.

Once the treaty was concluded and peace restored, relations
between Egypt and Khatti became really amicable. Letters on
diplomatic matters were regularly exchanged,[4] and a state visit
of the Hittite king Khattushilish to Egypt was contemplated,
though it is uncertain whether it took place.[5] In Year 34 Ramesses
contracted a diplomatic marriage with the eldest daughter of
Khattushilish,[6] and there is a possibility that a second daughter of
the Hittite king also, at a later date, was married to Ramesses.[7]
Clearly the peace and friendship between the two countries now
rested on a firm foundation.

## VII. THE OTHER WARS OF RAMESSES II

Apart from the years of fighting in Palestine and Syria, Ramesses
II had to wage war elsewhere. His undated expeditions against
Moab, Edom and Negeb[8] may well have been no more than
punitive wars to repress raiders or to punish aid to hostile dynasts
in Palestine, but the menace from Libya was more serious.
Here the tribes known since ancient times as the Tjemehu[9] and
the Tjehenu,[10] and now also their more westerly neighbours the
Meshwesh[11] and the Libu,[12] under the pressure of hunger were

---

[1] G, 1, vol. III, sect. 366.
[2] G, 3, vol. I, 134* ff.; G, 9, pl. 72.
[3] §vi, 3; §vi, 4.
[4] Cf. below, ch. xxiv, sect. III.
[5] G, 1, vol. III, sect. 426; §vi, 1.
[6] §vi, 2.
[7] G, 1, vol. III, sect. 427.
[8] §vii, 3.
[9] G, 3, vol. I, 114* ff.
[10] Ibid. 116* ff.
[11] Ibid. 119* ff.; §vii, 5.
[12] G, 3, vol. I, 121* ff.; §vii, 2.

attempting to invade and settle in the Delta, and the pharaohs from Sethos I onwards had to fight hard to keep them out. Ramesses II has left us a number of general allusions to his Libyan war,[1] but we know no details except that in Year 44 Libyan captives were employed in building the temple of Es-Sebūa in Lower Nubia;[2] it is significant, however, that Ramesses built a string of forts along the western coast road, starting from Rhacotis, the site of the future city of Alexandria, and extending to well beyond El-Alamein,[3] clearly in order to keep the western tribes in check. It has been suggested that the Sherden pirates were making common cause with the Libyans,[4] but this is not certain; the broken inscription in question[5] may be referring to the Libyan war and to a piratical raid by Sherden as separate events, but a Sherden contingent certainly served in the Libyan army in the war of Year 5 of the next reign. Scenes depicting war in Nubia appear in the temples of Abu Simbel, Beit el-Wāli and Ed-Derr, but no details of date or place are recorded, and it is possible that these may be purely conventional depictions without historical value.[6] If there were in fact any fighting, it can have amounted to no more than the driving off of desert raiders or the quelling of local disturbances, for Nubia by now was virtually part of Egypt. Even the undoubted Nubian war of Sethos I was probably only a small-scale affair.[7]

## VIII. THE KINGDOM UNDER RAMESSES II

If the building of temples be an index to the prosperity of the realm, then indeed Egypt was flourishing under Ramesses II, for he surely erected more fanes up and down the land than any pharaoh before or since, though it must be admitted that he was apt to be ruthless in dismantling older shrines and re-using the material. Here it is possible to mention only a few of the most important sites where he erected or enlarged temples. The ruins of Tanis are eloquent of his name,[8] but the great temple which he dedicated to Ptah of Memphis has vanished apart from a few remains of statues, though it is mentioned in a stela of Year 35 at Abu Simbel.[9] At Abydos he built a temple near the famous one

---

[1] G, 1, vol. III, sects. 457, 464 f., 479; see also Anastasi Papyrus No. II, 3, 4.
[2] §VII, I.          [3] §VII, 4, 4.
[4] G, 1, vol. III, sect. 448.   [5] *Ibid.* sect. 491.
[6] §IV, 170 ff.      [7] §IV, 168.
[8] §VIII, 6.
[9] G, 1, vol. III, sects. 412 f.

erected by his father;[1] at Karnak he completed the great hypostyle hall[2] and at Luxor he added a pylon and a court,[3] while in
the western necropolis of Thebes stands his great funerary
temple known as the Ramesseum.[4]  It is Nubia, however, which
possesses the most astonishing construction of this reign, namely
the well-known rock-cut temple of Abu Simbel, dedicated to
Amun, Re-Harakhte, Ptah and the King as god;[5] near it there was
constructed another rock shrine dedicated to the goddess Hathor
and to Queen Nefertiry.[6] To this lady belonged also a splendid
tomb in the Valley of the Queens at Thebes,[7] the first of a series
of burials of royal ladies in the valley. The reign also abounds in
private stelae and inscriptions of which very few yield any
historical information, but which as a whole suggest a fairly
widespread moderate degree of affluence, at least among the
literate classes.

So far as government was concerned, there was no great
change from the system which had long prevailed, the vizier—
or viziers when there was one for each half of the country—
being the highest official in the land, but a new factor was developing in the increasing influence of the high priests of Amun at
Thebes,[8] who in the Twentieth Dynasty were able to make their
office hereditary and who by the end of that dynasty were on terms
of virtual equality with the monarch.[9] An interesting glimpse of
the administration of law during this reign is afforded by a long
inscription in a tomb at Saqqara, where the course of a lawsuit
heard before the vizier and the Great Court is set out in some
detail.[10] Litigation in respect of a parcel of land amounting to
13 arouras had been going on spasmodically for several generations, forcible ejection and the forging of documents being among
the methods employed by one side to the dispute, and the hearing now recorded was the final one in the case. From the legal
point of view it would appear that men and women were on equal
terms both in regard to the ownership of land and in regard to
the right to plead in the courts.

Beyond the boundaries of Egypt proper, the mining of turquoise at Serābīt el-Khādim in Sinai went on and some fragments
of statuary have been found there.[11] The gold mines of the Wādi

[1] G, 8, vol. vi, 33 ff.                    [2] G, 8, vol. ii, 15 ff.
[3] *Ibid.* 100 ff.                          [4] *Ibid.* 149 ff.
[5] G, 8, vol. vii, 95 ff.                    [6] *Ibid.* 111 ff.
[7] For paintings from this tomb see §viii, 1, pls. 91–3.
[8] §viii, 4.                                 [9] See below, ch. xxxv, sect. v.
[10] §viii, 3.                                [11] G, 5, nos. 263–4.

Miāh in the eastern desert[1] and of the Wādi el-Allāqi in Nubia[2] were exploited. The town-site now known as Amāra West, over 100 miles south of Wādi Halfa, which had been founded in the previous dynasty, was given the name of Per-Ramesse-miamun and endowed with a considerable temple, probably becoming the administrative centre of the province of Kush and the seat of the provincial governor.[3]

During the long reign of 67 years[4] vouchsafed to Ramesses he outlived a considerable part of his family. His first and perhaps favourite consort was Nefertiry, to whose temple at Abu Simbel reference has already been made; she is mentioned in a Boğazköy letter in the form Naptera. Her successor was Isinofre, the mother of four princes, one of whom succeeded Ramesses as King Merneptah. A third queen was Maetnefrure, the Egyptian name given to the eldest daughter of the king of the Hittites when she married Ramesses.[5] It is possible that there was a second Hittite marriage, and Ramesses's daughter Bint-'Anath received the title of Great Consort during her father's lifetime, so that it would seem that she filled the office of queen for a while.[6] The pharaoh also had a considerable harim of which the foundations were laid by Sethos I,[7] and he took pride in his family of well over a hundred children.[8] The original Crown Prince was Amenhiwenmaf, but Ramesses outlived him and eleven of his other sons. The pharaoh celebrated his first jubilee (*Heb-Sed*) in Year 30 and thereafter held others at frequent and somewhat irregular intervals;[9] the organization of these festivals down to the fifth in Year 42 was in the hands of the king's eighth son Khaemuast, high priest of Ptah at Memphis, whose reputation as a sage and magician endured into Graeco-Roman times. In Year 55 he was followed in his office by the king's thirteenth son Merneptah,[10] who at his father's death twelve years later succeeded to the throne.

## IX. MERNEPTAH: EGYPT ON THE DEFENSIVE

Merneptah was probably well over fifty years of age when he succeeded to the throne in 1236 B.C., and he inherited a difficult situation, for during his father's old age the vigilance of the

---

[1] §IV, 1, 249.
[2] G, 1, vol. III, sects. 282 ff.
[3] §VIII, 2.
[4] G, 7, 39.
[5] *Ibid.* 34 f., 82 f.
[6] G, 4, 267.
[7] G, 1, vol. III, sect. 267.
[8] G, 7, 35 ff.
[9] *Ibid.* 39; §VIII, 5.
[10] G, 7, 85.

frontier patrols had slackened and the army had fallen into neglect,[1] with the result that, driven by famine in their own land, roving bands of Libyans were raiding into the western Delta[2] and terrorizing the people. With the threat of invasion from the west steadily growing, the first task to which the new king had to set his hand was the reorganization of the army, and the effectiveness of his work was demonstrated when in Year 5 the storm burst.[3] A coalition consisting of Libu, Meshwesh, and Kehek,[4] together with certain 'peoples of the sea',[5] to wit Sherden, Sheklesh,[6] Lukka,[7] Tursha,[8] and Akawasha,[9] led by a prince named Mauroy, overran Tjehenu and advanced on the Delta.[10] These 'Peoples of the Sea' who allied themselves with the invading Libyans seem to have come from the coasts and islands of Asia Minor and the Aegean Sea, and as Gardiner wrote,[11] were 'forerunners of the great migratory movement about to descend on Egypt and Palestine from north and west'. The invaders came with intent to settle in Egypt, for they brought their families and household goods with them.

At the news of this threat Merneptah consulted the oracle of Amun at Thebes. The god expressed his approval of the war, while Ptah of Memphis appeared to the king in a dream, seeming to hand him a scimitar. A fortnight was taken up with the mobilization of the army, which then marched to meet the enemy. Contact was made on the western frontier at an unidentified place named Pi-yer, and after a 6 hour battle the invaders were routed. Over 6000 were killed and many prisoners and much booty were taken. The Libyan prince Mauroy fled alone to his own people, where he was treated with contumely, deposed from his chieftainship, and a brother chosen in his stead.

The principal sources for the Libyan War are a long inscription at Karnak[12] and a stela from Athribis,[13] but there is a third inscription that must be mentioned, the so-called Israel Stela.[14] The information it yields concerning the course of the war adds nothing material to what is known from the other sources, but it expresses at length the intense relief felt by the Egyptians at the defeat of the invaders. A few sentences will be sufficient

[1] G, 1, vol. III, sect. 577.
[2] Ibid. sect. 580.
[3] Ibid. sects. 595, 598.
[4] G, 3, vol. I, 123*.
[5] Ibid. 196*; §IX, 5.
[6] G, 3, vol. I, 196* ff.
[7] Ibid. 127* f.
[8] Ibid. 196* ff.
[9] Perhaps identical with the Ahhiyawa of the Hittite texts.
[10] G, 1, vol. III, sects. 569 ff.
[11] G, 4, 270.
[12] §IX, 2.
[13] §IX, 1.
[14] §IX, 4; see also §v, 3, 376 ff.

to convey the emotion caused by the victory: 'Men come and go with singing, and there is no cry of men in trouble. Towns are populated once again and he who plants his harvest shall eat it. Re has turned himself back to Egypt.'[1] Of even greater interest is a passage which has long been familiar to scholars: 'The chieftains are prostrate, saying "Salaam!", and no one lifts his head among the Nine Bows. Destruction is for Tjehenu, Khatti is at peace, the Canaan is plundered with every evil. Askalon is carried off, Gezer is captured, Yenoam is made non-existent, Israel is waste and has no seed, Khor[2] has become a widow because of Egypt.'[3] In the first place we have here clear evidence of the suppression of a revolt in Palestine, which is confirmed by the epithet 'reducer of Gezer' given to Merneptah in an inscription at Amada.[4] The second point that arises is the mention of Israel, the only instance known from any Egyptian text. Until the discovery of this stela in 1896 the general belief was that Merneptah was the pharaoh of the Exodus, yet here in the middle of his reign we find Israel already settled in Palestine.[5] Discussion of this problem has been endless, but the fact remains that there is no positive evidence relating to the date of the Exodus. A third significant point is the reference to Khatti. Breasted suggested that the Libyan invasion had at least the sympathy, if not the active assistance, of the Hittites, but this seems unlikely. The power of the Hittite kings was diminishing, and Arnuwandash III, the ruler of Khatti contemporary with Merneptah, was too much involved in problems nearer home to wish to embroil himself with Egypt.[6] Against Breasted's suggestion we have the specific statement 'Khatti is at peace', as well as a reference in the great Karnak inscription to the shipping of grain to Khatti at a time of famine.[7] The peace made between Egypt and Khatti half a century before still held.

As might have been expected in his comparatively short reign of ten years,[8] Merneptah did little in the way of erecting new public buildings, though inscriptions of his, including usurpations of older monuments, are not rare.[9] His funerary temple at Thebes, at least partly built of material robbed from the temple of Amenophis III, has been destroyed in its turn, as have his

---

[1] Ll. 24–5.
[2] G, 3, vol. I, 180* ff. In this context presumably Palestine only is meant.
[3] Ll. 26–8.   [4] G, 4, 273.
[5] G, 1, vol. III, sect. 570. See below, ch. XXXIV, sect. III.
[6] See below, ch. XXIV, sect. IV.   [7] G, 1, vol. III, sect. 580; §IX, 6.
[8] §V, 1, 303.   [9] G, 7, 104 ff.

temple and palace at Memphis; he made additions to the temple of Thoth at Hermopolis,[1] but no notable building still standing dates from his reign. A few fragments from Serābīt el-Khādim[2] show that mining operations in Sinai went on. The remains of a stela in the temple of Amada refer to a rebellion in Wawat (Lower Nubia),[3] but nothing further of interest has come to light from this region. From the north-eastern frontier, however, we have extracts from the journal of a border official which have been included in a papyrus consisting of miscellaneous texts collected for educational purposes. Dated in Year 3, two years before the outbreak of the Libyan war, they record over a period of eleven days a continual coming and going of officials and letter-carriers between Egypt and Palestine, one dispatch being addressed to the prince of Tyre.[4] A copy of a letter from a similar source refers to Edomite tribesmen being allowed to pass a frontier fortress by the pharaoh's permission in order to graze their flocks at 'the pools of Pi-Tum'.[5] A curious text on papyrus which probably dates from this reign purports to be a letter from a scribe Hori to his friend Amenemope in which he points out that Amenemope is a failure in all he undertakes.[6] Among other duties the latter claims to be a *maher*, a scribe accustomed to foreign travel who could be sent on errands abroad, and in exposing his friend's incompetence Hori names a number of places to which such messengers might be sent or through which their route might lie; among many others we may mention Byblos, Tyre, Beth-shan and Qadesh. It seems that, while Egyptian suzerainty in Palestine was maintained, there was constant traffic on the roads between Egypt and the Asian principalities.

## X. THE END OF THE NINETEENTH DYNASTY

After the death of Merneptah in 1223 B.C. the Nineteenth Dynasty died out in short reigns and dynastic intrigue, and even the order of succession of its kings is not certain.[7] The names in question are those of Amenmesses, Sethos II, Sekhaenre Ramesses-Siptah,[8] Akhenre-setepenre Merneptah Siptah, and Queen Tewosret. Of these only Sethos II was recognized by Ramesses III as

---

[1] §IX, 3.
[2] G, 5, nos. 266–267 A.
[3] G, 1, vol. III, 259, n. *a*.
[4] §V, 1, 108 f.
[5] §V, i, 293.
[6] Anastasi Papyrus No. 1, cf. §V, 3, 475 ff.
[7] See, for example, §X, 1.
[8] See *C.A.H.* I³, pt. 1, p. 190.

a legitimate king,[1] and it is natural to look on him as the immediate successor of his father Merneptah, while it is now fairly generally accepted that there was only one King Siptah who changed his name during his reign.[2] Since two stelae of Amenmesses at El-Qurna were usurped by Siptah,[3] it appears that the latter came after Amenmesses, while Tewosret, the consort of Sethos II, outlived them all to become queen-regnant at the very end of the dynasty. On the face of it, therefore, it would seem that the order of succession was Sethos II, Amenmesses, Siptah and Queen Tewosret, but there is evidence, quoted below, that Siptah directly succeeded Sethos II, and many scholars believe that Amenmesses preceded Sethos. The reason for this belief is that in a papyrus in the British Museum,[4] which contains many serious accusations extending over a considerable period against one Pneb, it is stated that at one stage in his nefarious career he was accused before the vizier Amenmose, who sentenced him to punishment. Pneb then appealed against his sentence to one Mose, who dismissed the vizier from office. Now the only person who could do this was the pharaoh himself, so that Mose was apparently a nickname of the king then ruling, like Sese for Ramesses II. It is assumed that Mose is an abbreviation of Amenmesses, and since there is reason to think that this episode occurred soon after the death of Merneptah,[5] it is believed that Amenmesses preceded Sethos II on the throne. Unfortunately, it is not yet proved that Mose and Amenmesses are identical, for in the Anastasi Papyrus No. 1 (p. 235), which was probably written in the reign of Merneptah,[6] and which is certainly a copy of a work already extant, there is mention of a name Mose which may also be a nickname for the pharaoh,[7] who in this case could hardly be Amenmesses. If at this time Mose was a current designation of any ruling king—perhaps derived from the name of Ramesses, the king *par excellence*—the identification with Amenmesses in particular would fall to the ground. Another fact that raises a doubt about the proposed position of Amenmesses is that it was Siptah and not Sethos who on the Qurna stelae substituted his name for that of Amenmesses, suggesting that it was Siptah who replaced him. Finally, in Liverpool there was a statue base, now destroyed, which is said to have had originally a cartouche of Sethos II which had been usurped by

---

[1] §x, 1, 43; §x, 4, 70, n. 2.
[2] §x, 11.
[3] §x, 5.
[4] §x, 7.
[5] §x, 1.
[6] G, 4, 274.
[7] §11, 2, 20*.

Amenmesses.[1] This, of course, would be conclusive as to the sequence of the two kings, but the reading of the original name as that of Sethos is open to question.[2] The one piece of incontrovertible evidence that we have is an ostracon in the Cairo Museum,[3] which records the death of Sethos II and the accession of Siptah as consecutive events, showing that Amenmesses cannot have intervened at this point. It is clear therefore, that we must either accept Amenmesses as the immediate successor of Merneptah, which seems unlikely, since Sethos was the legitimate heir, or else intercalate him as a temporary usurper into the reigns of either Sethos II or Siptah. It seems not impossible that the unexplained change in the names of Siptah may have had its origin in an interruption by Amenmesses, Siptah assuming a new form of name on regaining his throne; the substitution of Siptah's name for that of Amenmesses on the Qurna stelae would thus be accounted for. In any case Amenmesses's tenure of the throne was probably very short, for we have no date of his, and the only considerable monument is a tomb in the Valley of Kings. His mother Takhaet may have been a child or grandchild of Ramesses II[4] and so have provided a basis for his claim to be king. His consorts were Baktwerel and possibly Tia. It has been suggested that the latter was the mother of Siptah,[5] but this is speculative.

The reign of Sethos II was short, for he died in Year 6, but in that time he was able to carry out a certain amount of building. Apart from his tomb and a funerary temple now destroyed, he built a small temple at Karnak,[6] made additions to the Karnak temple of the goddess Mut of Ishru,[7] and completed the decoration of the temple of Thoth at Hermopolis which had been begun by Ramesses II and of which the fabric had been completed by Merneptah.[8] Some minor remains of his at Serābīt el-Khādim testify to the continuance of turquoise mining in Sinai.[9] As already remarked, he was the only successor of Merneptah who in later years was regarded as legitimate, and his consort was Tewosret,[10] who apparently was the heiress of the royal line. A son Seti-Merneptah[11] and possibly a daughter[12] both predeceased him, so that he left no heir in the direct line, unless indeed Siptah

---

[1] G, 7, 127.        [2] §x, 5.
[3] No. 25515; §x, 6; cf. §x, 1, 44, n. 6; quoted in §x, 9, 190 ff.
[4] §x, 11.        [5] §x, 1.
[6] §x, 8.        [7] G, 8, vol. ii, 9.
[8] §ix, 3, 320.        [9] G, 5, no. 268.
[10] §x, 11.        [11] §x, 1; §x, 11.
[12] §x, 2.

was his son. Siptah certainly succeeded him directly,[1] but his parentage is uncertain.[2] What does appear evident is that Siptah was set on the throne while yet a boy[3] by Tewosret and the 'Great Chancellor of the entire land' Bay, who is said to have 'established the king on his father's throne'.[4] On the face of it this designates Siptah as the son of Sethos II, but it is possible that 'father' might refer to royal descent rather than to actual parentage. Even if, as seems likely, Siptah was the direct heir of Sethos, the fact that he was a minor may have made it necessary for Tewosret to seek the support of Bay to set her son in his rightful place, especially if there were an adult rival claimant. In the present state of our knowledge, Amenmesses is the only candidate for the role, and an ostensible ground for such a claim may well have been that the heir was a minor. We do not know why Siptah was not regarded later as a legitimate king; his parentage, if he was not the son of Sethos II, his early age, or even the fact that Tewosret and Bay were his supporters may have been the factors which caused his reign to be disregarded; certainly the memory of Tewosret was not in favour with her successor Sethnakhte, the first king of the Twentieth Dynasty.

To have played the role of king-maker Bay must have been a man of immense influence. He claims to have 'banished false-hood and granted truth', as if he were himself royalty, and in a formal hymn of praise to Siptah he says: 'I placed mine eye on thee alone', which may well be an allusion to his king-making activities.[5] In a relief at Aswān[6] and in another at Gebel es-Silsila[7] he is shown standing behind the king. Most significant of all is the fact that, whether by permission or not, he actually hewed for himself a tomb in the Valley of the Kings. There is a suggestion that he was a foreigner, for from the mid-Ramesside period onwards it became quite usual for men of foreign origin to serve in high office at Court, and, like many such men, Bay adopted an Egyptian pseudonym Ramesse-Khamenteru.[8]

A point which favours the view that Siptah was the legitimate heir of Sethos II is the fact that at Siheil at the First Cataract, at Wādi Halfa and at Abu Simbel there is a series of graffiti of prominent officials from the viceroy of Nubia downwards, all perpetuating the name of Siptah and begging his favour.[9] These

---

[1] Cairo Ostracon No. 25515; see above, p. 237.
[2] Cf. §x, 1, but the conclusions reached are open to question.
[3] §x, 4.           [4] §x, 11.                              [5] §x, 11.
[6] G, 1, vol. iii, sect. 647.      [7] *Ibid.* sects. 648 f.           [8] §x, 11.
[9] G, 1, vol. iii, sects. 642 ff.

graffiti range in date from Year 1 to Year 6, and they show that the Nubian administration supported Siptah's claim to the throne; the graffito of Year 6 is the highest date known of this reign. Siptah's tomb is in the Valley of the Kings, where after his death his cartouches were cut out and later replaced.[1] His funerary temple is destroyed and may never have been finished; Bay's name actually appears beside that of the king in its foundation deposits.[2]

On Siptah's death without issue, Queen Tewosret herself ascended the throne, the fourth queen-regnant in Egypt's long history, the others being Nitocris, Sobkneferu and the illustrious Hatshepsut, and she took the throne-name of Sitre 'Daughter of Re'. The length of her reign is not definitely fixed; the latest date known is Year 8,[3] but she may have included Siptah's six years, since in view of his youth she probably acted as regent during his reign, in which case her sole reign would not have greatly exceeded two years. The latter is more likely, for the vizier and the Nubian viceroy under Siptah were still in office under Ramesses III,[4] with the reigns of Tewosret and of Sethnakhte of the Twentieth Dynasty intervening, not to mention any interregnum there may have been. Unless the officials in question both had an unusually long tenure of office, an interval of four to five years, rather than ten or eleven, is the most that can be allowed between the death of Siptah and the accession of Ramesses III. Queen Tewosret's tomb is in the Valley of the Kings, but it was usurped by Sethnakhte, who evicted its rightful owner.[5] Of her funerary temple nothing has survived except the foundation trenches and some foundation deposits, and it is doubtful whether any considerable part of it was ever built. Some objects with her name were found at Serābīt el-Khādim,[6] but nothing else is known of her reign, and with her the Nineteenth Dynasty came to an end.

## XI. THE RISE OF THE TWENTIETH DYNASTY: SETHNAKHTE

The date of the beginning of the new dynasty cannot be fixed with precision, owing in part to the doubt regarding the length of Tewosret's sole reign. Merneptah died in 1223 B.C., and no more

---

[1] G, 4, 278.         [2] §x, 11.

[3] Cairo Ostracon No. 25293, cf. §x, 6.

[4] §x, 12.         [5] §x, 10.

[6] G, 5, no. 270.

than about twenty-three years can be reckoned for the remaining rulers of the Nineteenth Dynasty, even if Tewosret be allowed a total of eight or nine years. There arises also the question of an interregnum following the death of Tewosret before the accession of Sethnakhte, the first king of the Twentieth Dynasty. If there was such an interval it must have been short, perhaps no more than a matter of months; some scholars, probably rightly, do not believe that there was an interregnum,[1] in which case, allowing only two years of sole rule for Tewosret, the accession of Sethnakhte will have taken place in about 1200 B.C.

An important source for the history of the early Twentieth Dynasty is the Great Harris Papyrus in the British Museum.[2] This long and stately document, dated on the day of the death of Ramesses III, represents his claim to enter the company of the gods, and its compilation was ordered by Ramesses IV, who prays that the blessings enjoyed by his father may be vouchsafed to him also. After a brief introduction and a coloured scene of Ramesses III worshipping the Theban triad Amon-Re, Mut and Khons, there comes a detailed list of the benefactions bestowed by the dead king on the temples, which occupies 72 pages, and finally four pages are devoted to the events of his own and his father's reigns,[3] which are almost the only source of information for the reign of Sethnakhte. The first part of this historical summary thus describes the rise of the Twentieth Dynasty:

'The land of Egypt was cast adrift, every man being a law unto himself, and they had had no leader for many years previously until other times when the land of Egypt consisted of magnates and mayors, one man killing his fellow among high and low. Then another time came after it consisting of empty years[4] when Irsu the Asiatic was with them as chief, having put the entire land into subjection before him; each joined with his neighbour in plundering their goods, and they treated the gods as they did men, so that none dedicated offerings in their fanes. But the gods turned themselves to peace so as to put the land in its proper state in accordance with its normal condition, and they established their son who came forth from their flesh as ruler of every land upon their great throne, even User-khaure-setpenre-meryamun, the Son of Re Sethnakhte-meryre-

---

[1] §x, 4.
[2] G, 1, vol. IV, sects. 151 ff.; a convenient hieroglyphic transcription in §xi, 2.
[3] §v, 3, 260 ff.
[4] Probably meaning years of famine.

meryamun'. The text then goes on to describe how Sethnakhte set the land in order, appointed the future Ramesses III to be crown prince, and then died and was buried with full rites.

The above quotation is a good example of Egyptian historical writing, but it need not be assumed that conditions in Egypt were quite as chaotic as this passage suggests; it was a convention when describing the advent of a new era to show the preceding state of affairs in as unfavourable a light as possible. On the other hand, it is inherently probable that during the Siptah–Tewosret régime, when there would appear to have been serious dynastic quarrels, the administration of the country may have deteriorated, and it certainly would seem that Sethnakhte, who from his name may have been a scion of the royal family, was at enmity with Tewosret. It is by no means certain who 'Irsu the Asiatic' was. The name, which appears to mean 'the self-made man', may well have been a pejorative pseudonym such as was sometimes given in state papers to offenders in high places; Černý has made the plausible suggestion that the person in question was the Great Chancellor Bay,[1] who was possibly an Asiatic and who was certainly a power in the land. Little else is known of the reign and even its length is uncertain, though lack of public works, as well as the apparently brief interval between the death of Siptah and the accession of Ramesses III, suggests that it was short, possibly no more than two years;[2] apart from a stela at Serābīt el-Khādim on which the date is now effaced,[3] no dated monuments or documents of this reign are known. Sethnakhte's consort Tiy-merenese was the mother of his successor Ramesses III,[4] the last of the great warrior kings of Egypt.

## XII. THE WARS OF RAMESSES III

Ramesses III came to the throne in *c.* 1198 B.C. Of the first four years of his reign we lack information, but in the period from Year 5 to Year 11 inclusive there were three major wars for which the main sources are the scenes and inscriptions in Ramesses III's funerary temple at Medīnet Habu.[5] The inscriptions contain but a halfpenny-worth of historical fact to an intolerable deal of turgid adulation of the pharaoh, but combining them with the vivid scenes sculptured on the temple walls and the narrative of the Harris Papyrus, which to some extent supplements the

---

[1] G, 4, 282.  
[2] G, 4, 446.  
[3] G, 5, no. 271.  
[4] §xi, 1.  
[5] §xii, 1, vols. i and ii; §xii, 2.

temple record, we can get a fairly clear picture of the course of events. The war of Year 5 was against the Libyans, who in a coalition of Libya, Meshwesh and an unknown tribe named Seped, were again contemplating a descent into Egypt, having recovered from their defeat by Merneptah. The ostensible cause of the war was interference by Ramesses with the succession to the chieftainship of the Tjemehu when he nominated a child to be chief,[1] but the real cause was the continuing desire of the western tribes to take possession of the rich lands of the Delta. Like Merneptah before him, on receipt of the news Ramesses consulted the oracle of Amun at Thebes, and the god handed him a scimitar with which to destroy the enemy.[2] Where the Egyptians encountered the invaders is not known, but the Libyans were utterly defeated.[3] It is not possible to extract from the somewhat unsatisfactory records[4] the number of slain, but it certainly ran into many thousands, while those taken captive were put to servitude in Egypt.

For two years there was peace, and then in Year 8 Egypt had to face an even more serious danger. All the Levant seems to have been in a turmoil of which the repeated Libyan attacks were a symptom, possibly as a result of pressure by nomad races of the steppes driving to the west, and in the words of the Egyptians: 'The foreign countries made a plot in their islands, and the lands were dislodged and scattered by battle all at one time and no land could stand before their arms, Khatti, Qode, Carchemish, Arzawa and Alashiya.'[5] The confederate peoples consisted of Peleset or Philistines,[6] Tjekker,[7] Sheklesh, Sherden, Weshesh[8] and Denyen,[9] probably the Danaoi of the *Iliad*, and having destroyed the Hittite empire they advanced into Amurru and apparently halted for a while to rest and concentrate their forces. Thereafter the confederates continued their march down the Syrian coast with their women and children in ox-carts, for this was an invasion to occupy and settle in the lands overrun, not merely a raid on a large scale, while offshore a considerable fleet escorted the march. To deal with this threat Ramesses mobilized his garrisons in Palestine with orders to bar the way to the advancing horde and hold them as much as possible while

---

[1] §XII, 2, 25.  
[2] §XII, I, vol. I, pl. 13.  
[3] *Ibid.* pls. 18–20.  
[4] §XII, 2, 14–15.  
[5] *Ibid.* 53 ff.  
[6] G, 3, vol. I, 200* ff.  
[7] *Ibid.* 199* f.  
[8] Otherwise unknown.  
[9] G, 3, vol. I, 124* ff.; on the Sea Peoples as a whole see §IX, 5, and below, ch. XXVIII.

he got his main army into action,[1] and in the event the invasion
by land was effectively stopped. Meanwhile the hostile fleet was
trapped by the Egyptian ships in a harbour or an estuary, probably
in one of the mouths of the Nile, and utterly destroyed; the
enemy's ships were capsized or carried by boarding, while any
vessel coming within effective range of the shore was greeted
with a volley of arrows from troops lined up at the water's edge.[2]
The danger from the Peoples of the Sea was thus averted on the
very threshold of Egypt, but at least two of the confederate
peoples remained to settle in Palestine, namely the Peleset or
Philistines and the Tjekker; in the narrative of Wenamun[3]
about a century later the latter people are described as sea-
pirates based on the port of Dor.

This victory was followed by two quiet years and then in
Year 11 the Libyan trouble broke out afresh. The Libu and the
Meshwesh were again the moving spirits, though they were
supported by five other tribes of whom nothing further is known.
From the account in the Harris Papyrus[4] it is clear that they had
achieved some initial success. Peaceful infiltration had apparently
been going on for some years, and that part of the Delta west
of the Canopic branch of the Nile had been occupied from Memphis to the sea; now the western tribes were advancing in force
to overrun the Delta. Ramesses expelled the intruders from
Egyptian soil and met the main shock on the western border
where he had the support of the garrisons of the frontier forts.[5]
Again he achieved a crushing victory; over 2000 were killed and
much booty in prisoners and cattle was taken.[6] Among the captives was Mesher, commander of the Meshwesh, and when his
father Keper came to beg for his release, he was slain together
with his escort.[7]

At Medinet Habu there are also scenes of Ramesses invading
Syria, Khatti and Amurru,[8] but as political entities these had
ceased to exist; the scenes in question are anachronisms copied
from a building of Ramesses II. Yet there may be a substratum of
fact beneath them. The historical portion of the Harris Papyrus
makes no mention of a war in Syria, but it mentions only one
Libyan war and so cannot be trusted entirely, and it seems not
improbable that after the defeat of the Peoples of the Sea Ramesses may have attempted to follow up his success by pushing on

[1] §xii, 1, vol. i, pls. 82 ff.          [2] *Ibid.* pls. 37–9.
[3] G, 4, 306 ff.          [4] G, 1, vol. iv, sect. 405.
[5] §xii, 1, vol. ii, pls. 70–2.          [6] §xii, 2, 67.
[7] *Ibid.* 91–2.          [8] §xii, 1, vol. ii, pls. 87 ff.

into Syria in an attempt to drive the enemy farther away from Egypt; there are scenes of both Syrian and Libyan wars in the small temple which Ramesses built in the precinct of the temple of Mut at Karnak,[1] and the well-known copy of a Syrian *migdōl* at Medīnet Habu has the look of a war memorial.[2] On the other hand, the scenes of a Nubian war at Medīnet Habu[3] are surely only conventional with no historical reality behind them; Nubia by now was entirely Egyptianized, and it is very unlikely that there was any trouble there[4] apart perhaps from an occasional scuffle with desert raiders. A minor campaign mentioned in the Harris Papyrus was against the Edomites of the Mount Seir region,[5] but it was probably no more than a punitive expedition against raiding nomads. The army with which Ramesses fought was of course mainly Egyptian, but, as under his predecessors, there were also contingents of Sherden and Kehek who apparently had no qualms about fighting against their racial kinsmen.

## XIII. THE KINGDOM UNDER RAMESSES III

After the war of Year 11 peace came to Egypt. In the Harris Papyrus the king says: 'I planted the whole land with trees and verdure and I let the people sit in their shade; I caused the woman of Egypt to travel freely to the place where she would, for no foreigner or anyone on the road molested her. I allowed the infantry and the chariotry to settle down in my time, the Sherden and the Kehek lying full-length on their backs in their towns; they had no fear, for there was no destroyer from Nubia or enemy from Palestine, and their bows and their weapons were laid aside in their arsenals.'[6] This idyllic picture was probably largely true for the middle part of the reign, for there seems to have been a good measure of prosperity, though in Ramesses's latter years serious troubles developed. One indication of this prosperity is the temple and palace on the Theban west bank at Medīnet Habu,[7] for such a complex could hardly have been raised by a poverty-stricken people. The palace is ruined, but the temple is by far the best preserved of all the royal funerary temples, with great pylons and columned courts, and its sculptured reliefs are a rich mine for the historian as well as the student of religion. One feature it possesses is unique; in the centre of the eastern side was built a gatehouse which, as already mentioned

---

[1] G, 8, vol. ii, 89 ff.   [2] See Plate 154(*b*).   [3] §xii, 1, vol. i, pls. 9–10.
[4] §iv, 4, 173 ff.   [5] G, 1, vol. iv, §404.
[6] Cf. G, 1, vol. iv, sect. 410.   [7] §xii, 1.

is a copy of a Syrian fortress (*migdōl*), the upper part forming a resort where Ramesses could relax with the ladies of his harim. Apparently the king spent more time at Thebes than at Per-Ramesse in the Delta, as otherwise he would surely not have permitted the massive infiltration of Libyans which preceded the war of Year 11, but he did occasionally reside in the north.[1]

At Karnak Ramesses built a modest temple to the Theban triad across the south wall of the forecourt of the great temple of Amun, with its entrance within the forecourt.[2] Within the temenos of the great temple he founded a temple to the moon-god Khons which was completed under the later Ramessides,[3] and of his temple in the precinct of Mut we have already spoken. According to the Harris Papyrus a temple of Sutekh was built at Per-Ramesse,[4] but we know of no further building enterprises of importance in this reign.

A great event was the dispatch of an expedition to Punt,[5] probably in the region about Cape Guardafui, to exchange the products of Egypt for tropical produce such as myrrh. The ships were taken overland in sections from Koptos to the Red Sea and there assembled for the voyage, and the cargoes travelled to and from Egypt by the same route. Another mission went to Atike, a region otherwise unknown, but possibly in Sinai, to fetch copper,[6] and yet another went to Serābīt el-Khādim to mine turquoise.[7] Ramesses also sank a great well in 'the country of Ayan';[8] this region has not been identified, but the analogy of the well-sinking activities of Sethos I and Ramesses II suggests that the site may have lain in the goldfields of Nubia or the eastern desert.

One feature of the great Harris Papyrus which makes it of unique interest is the detailed record of the possessions of the temples of Egypt and of the donations made to them during the whole of the reign of Ramesses III,[9] which apart from its intrinsic interest is a testimony to the meticulous keeping of records in the administrative offices of Egypt. As might have been expected, the Theban temples are by far the most wealthy; next in order come those of Heliopolis and Memphis, and after them the smaller fanes to as far south as Koptos; why none of the lesser religious centres south of that point have been included

[1] §XIII, 7.
[2] §XIII, 3.
[3] G, 8, vol. II, 75 ff.
[4] G, 1, vol. IV, sect. 362.
[5] *Ibid.* sect. 407.
[6] *Ibid.* sect. 408.
[7] *Ibid.* sect. 409; G, 5, no. 272.
[8] G, 1, vol. IV, sect. 406.
[9] *Ibid.* sects. 156 ff.

is a matter for conjecture. What impresses the modern reader is the immense amount of wealth concentrated in the hands of the great religious corporation of Amun; the later history of the dynasty shows the consequences which arose out of it.

The latter part of the reign was beset with troubles arising from administrative incompetence and from active disloyalty. An unnamed vizier was dismissed from his post and expelled from the town of Athribis;[1] in this reign also we hear of the first workmen's strikes on record.[2] On the site now known as Deir el-Medīna once stood the village of the necropolis workers whose duty it was to excavate the royal tombs, and as state employees they drew their pay in the form of food from the royal storehouses. In Year 29 these supplies failed and the people of the village were reduced to downright need, so that strikes and rioting ensued. An intervention by the vizier put an end to the disturbances, but even he was able to provide no more than half of what was needed. The source of the trouble in this case was probably less positive misconduct than inefficiency or neglect of duty on the part of those whose business it was to keep the supplies in the storehouses up to date and to issue them to the workmen.

Worst of all, however, was a palace conspiracy to assassinate the pharaoh and to set on the throne one of his sons who was not the rightful heir. We know of this because the conspiracy did not succeed and the conspirators were put on trial, an account of the proceedings having by good fortune been preserved.[3] A secondary wife of Ramesses named Tiy plotted to murder the king and to set her son Pentwere on the throne, and she involved in her plot not only the women of the harim but also the major-domo Paibekkamen, the butler Mesedsure and a number of other officials of the harim and the administration, including the butler Pluka ('the Lycian') and the butler Inini, who was a Libyan. One member of the harim involved her brother Be-yenemwast, who was captain of archers of Nubia, writing to him: 'Stir up the people, make enmity and come to make a rebellion against your lord'; an army-commander Paiis was also involved. Actually we have the names of twenty-eight men among the conspirators as well as an uncertain number of women, none of whom are named except Tiy. Among the names of the accused are examples of the pejorative pseudonyms alluded to above,[4] e.g. Mesedsure 'Re hates him'; Beyenemwast 'Evil in Thebes', though by no means all the conspirators are thus disguised. It

---

[1] *Ibid.* sects. 361.  [2] §XIII, 4, 9.
[3] §XIII, 1. 6.  [4] §XI.

seems also that magical practices were employed, including the making of wax puppets,[1] but the conspiracy was discovered and the offenders arrested. A bench of twelve judges consisting of officials of the Court and officers of the army was appointed to try the accused, two of the judges holding the high Court rank of 'butlers' having foreign names and one at least being obviously Asiatic. Of the seventeen accused in the first list, all were found guilty and sentenced, presumably to death; the actual expression used is: 'they (the judges) caused their punishment to overtake them'. Of the seven persons in the second and third lists of accused, including the prince Pentwere, all were found guilty and were condemned to suicide. It is an eloquent commentary on the standards of conduct then current that five of the bench of twelve judges were arrested for carousing with the accused women and one of the male offenders; of the five, one was condemned to suicide, three had their noses and ears cut off and one was severely reprimanded. There is no reason to think that Ramesses was actually murdered or wounded by the conspirators; his mummy in the Cairo Museum shows no signs of injury, and the documents in the case are not dated, so that the affair may have taken place some time before his death.

Ramesses III died in Year 32;[2] by his consort Queen Ese and the women of the harim he had many sons, four or five of whom predeceased him, but one of them succeeded to his father's throne as Ramesses IV.[3] Seven of the latter's successors took the famous name of Ramesses, but with the death of Ramesses III the glory departed, and Egypt was never again an imperial power.

## XIV. RELIGION, ART AND LITERATURE UNDER THE RAMESSIDES

By way of reaction to the Atenist heresy, and under political necessity, the god Amun of Thebes—more fully Amon-Re—attained, as has already been remarked, to greater power than ever before, carrying with him his spouse Mut and his offspring the moon-god Khons, the other members of the Theban triad, so that more and more benefactions were bestowed on the Theban temples until they outstripped in riches all the other sanctuaries of Egypt. Other deities of major rank, though not approaching

---

[1] I am not convinced by Goedicke's negative argument on this point, §xiii, 6.
[2] G, 1, vol. iv, sect. 182; cf., however, §xiii, 2.
[3] On the family of Ramesses III cf. §xi, 1; §xiii, 8; §xiii, 10.

Amun in wealth, were Re-Harakhte the sun-god of Heliopolis and Ptah the creator-god of Memphis, while Seth of Tanis, patron of the royal family, was of considerable local importance, and in his variant form of the war-god Sutekh had clearly attained more than just local worship; the reigning monarch also was worshipped as god on earth.[1] The possessions of both major and minor deities in the reign of Ramesses III are set out in detail in the Harris Papyrus (see above, pp. 245 f.), and it is certain that the nation was being bled white by so much of its wealth going in one direction.

Other phenomena also were becoming prominent in the world of religion. Long-continued intimate contact with Palestine and Syria had brought with it the worship of foreign deities, and among others we meet with Resheph, often identified with Sutekh, and Ba'al, and with the goddesses Astarte (riding on horseback with shield and mace), 'Anath, Qadesh (standing naked on a lion) and Ishtar.[2] Ramesses II must have had a special attachment to 'Anath, for he named one of his daughters Bint-'Anath 'Daughter of 'Anath' and built a temple to the goddess in Per-Ramesse. But beside the state cults and the worship of exotic deities there grew up among humble folk a very personal relationship to the gods and a consciousness of sin which is something new in Egyptian religion.[3] The deities so worshipped and addressed in humble prayer were Amun, Ptah, Haroeris, Thoth, the Moon, Isis, Meretseger the patroness of the Theban necropolis, and the deified king Amenophis I.[4] Amun, for example, is invoked as 'that beloved god who hearkens to humble entreaties, who stretches out his hand to the humble and who saves the wearied', while of Amenophis it is said, 'whoso enters to thee with troubled heart, he comes forth rejoicing and exulting'. Nothing comparable with this personal relationship between deity and worshipper has been noted during other periods of Egyptian history.

In the royal tombs the greatest part of the wall-space was given up to strange scenes and texts relating to the passage of the sun through the Netherworld during the hours of the night, which were carved not only on the walls of the tombs but also on sarcophagi, and copies on papyrus were made for the non-royal

[1] §III, 3, vol. II, pls. 29 ff.; §XIII, 7; §XIV, 16.
[2] §XIV, 4, 126 ff.; §XIV, 5, 149 ff.
[3] §XIV, 8.
[4] See also §XIV, 4, 73 f.; §XIV, 5, 145 f.; §XIV, 17; statue of Amenophis I carried in procession, §VIII, pl. 85.

dead.[1] Another feature which often occurs in the royal tombs is the cult of the stars, stellar diagrams and tables being found in the cenotaph of Sethos I at Abydos and in the tombs of many Ramesside kings;[2] this stellar cult is of great age, references to it occurring in the Pyramid Texts of the Old Kingdom and stellar diagrams being found in the wooden sarcophagi of the Middle Kingdom, while in the Eighteenth Dynasty there is a very fine diagram in the tomb of Senenmut.

An aspect of religion which developed very extensively during the later part of Egyptian history was the use of oracles to decide not only the policy of kings but also the most mundane affairs, such as appointments to a post, the right decision in disputes over property, or the innocence or guilt of an accused person.[3] The image of the god in a portable bark was brought from the temple on the shoulders of priests, the case was laid before him in writing and he would indicate by a motion of his bark his approval or otherwise of the action proposed; in the case of a decision between two alternatives, both were laid before him in writing and the god indicated the correct choice.

The art of the period under discussion is on the whole a picture of decline. At the beginning of the period it produced a few masterpieces such as the temple of Sethos I at Abydos,[4] where the proportions of the design and the craftsmanship of the delicate low raised relief still preserved on many of the walls are alike admirable, while the statue at Turin of Ramesses II as a young man stands comparison with any of Egypt's celebrated portrait statues.[5] Yet even here, despite their grace and beauty there is, especially in the wall-reliefs, a certain languor, a lack of the vigour that characterizes much of the work of the earlier Eighteenth Dynasty; the sculptors seem to have inherited something of the 'softness' of the immediately pre-Amarna work as found, for example, in the Theban tomb of Ramose. On the grand scale, the façade of the great temple at Abu Simbel is an astonishing achievement, but most of the colossal statues of Ramesses II at Thebes and Memphis have survived only in fragments. In architecture generally, the Abydos temple apart, the surviving temple remains are impressive rather than beautiful; the great hypostyle hall at Karnak is an architectural *tour de force*,[6] but it impresses by mass rather than by proportion, and the columned courts at Medīnet Habu can hardly be described as graceful. The scenes of battle and the chase carved in sunk

[1] §III, 9; §XIV, 2; §XIV, 10; §XIV, 15.          [2] §XIV, 13.
[3] §XIV, 1.   [4] See Plate 153(a).   [5] See Plate 153(b).   [6] See Plate 154(a).

relief on temple walls and pylons are often striking in their portrayal of vigorous action, but the coarse and often ill-proportioned hieroglyphs in the temple inscriptions are a sad decline from the grace of earlier work. The mural painting which has survived on temple walls from Abydos to Nubia, while it is skilfully executed and is pleasing to the eye, deals with entirely stereotyped subjects of battle and ritual; for painting as an art it is necessary to turn to the walls of tombs. There is some beautiful work in the tomb of Queen Nefertiry,[1] and in the tomb of the high priest of Amun named Userhet we find good drawing and a wider range of colours than in earlier times,[2] while in the tomb of Nakhtamun there is a pleasing portrait of Ramesses II.[3] In the private tombs the scenes from daily life persist and are often lively and humorous,[4] but the tombs of the sons of Ramesses III in the Valley of the Queens show a sad decline; there is an overall effect of gaudiness in the painting and the hieroglyphs in the inscriptions are not well formed.[5] On the other hand, a meed of praise cannot be witheld from the painted illuminations accompanying the texts in the more elaborate copies of the Book of the Dead.

In contrast with the artistic decline, the period here dealt with showed great activity in the literary field. The masterpieces of the Middle Kingdom were still being copied and read, but there was no lack of new composition. Especially was this the case in the realm of fiction. Here we have historical tales, 'Seqenenre and Apophis',[6] 'The Capture of Joppa';[7] stories with a religious background,'The Tale of the Two Brothers',[8] 'The Contendings of Horus and Seth', an entertaining burlesque of the dispute between Horus and Seth for the kingship of Egypt as tried before the tribunal of the Heliopolitan Ennead;[9] an allegorical story, 'The Blinding of Truth by Falsehood';[10] a folk-tale, 'The Doomed Prince',[11] and a number of other stories of which only fragments remain. Of more serious works, intended for the instruction of boys and young men with regard to conduct, the writing of letters, the learning of geography, the adoption of the profession of scribe and so forth, we have 'The Teaching of

---

[1] §VIII, I, pls. 91 ff.; §XIV, 11, 140, 142–3. See Plate 155 (a).

[2] §VIII, I, pls. 87 ff.; XIV, 11, 132, 135 ff.

[3] §VIII, I, pl. 100.

[4] §VIII, I, pls. 96 ff.; §XIV, 11, 145 ff.

[5] §VIII, I, pl. 103.

[6] §XIV, 9.

[7] §XIV, 14.

[8] §XIV, 6, 150 ff.

[9] §XIV, 7, 8 ff.

[10] §XIV, 3, vol. I, 2 ff.

[11] §XIV, 14.

Anii',[1] the letter of Hori to Amenemope,[2] and the curious medley known today as 'Late Egyptian Miscellanies'.[3] There are many magical or medico-magical compilations, and a work on the interpretation of dreams,[4] while poetry, apart from stereotyped hymns to the gods, is represented by some charming love-songs;[5] also, despite a recent objection, the inscription on the Battle of Qadesh hitherto known as the Poem surely has a right to that title.

[1] §xiv, 6, 234 ff.　　　　　　　[2] §ii, 2.
[3] §v, 1.　　　　　　　　　　　[4] §xiv, 3, vol. i, 9 ff.
[5] §xiv, 7, 27 ff.; §xiv, 12.

# CHAPTER XXIV

## THE HITTITES AND SYRIA
### (1300–1200 B.C.)

### I. THE LATER REIGN OF MUWATALLISH

SINCE the conquest of Shuppiluliumash the Hittites had considered Kinza (Qadesh on the Orontes) and Amurru their southernmost possessions. With the rise of the Nineteenth Dynasty, the Egyptians sought to recover their former Syrian dependencies, in other words to dislodge the Hittites and to drive them as far north as possible. The issue then, seen from the Hittite point of view, was this: which of the two rivals was to dominate Syria and, more specifically, which of them was to control Kinza and Amurru?

The latent rivalry between the Egyptians and the Hittites erupted into open warfare as soon as Amurru, as an immediate result of the successful Syrian campaign of Sethos I (1318–1304) which had brought the pharaoh at least as far north as Kinza (Kidsa, Qadesh),[1] was compelled to abrogate the treaty which bound it to the Hittite king. This was done in a formal way which must have made it clear to the Hittite that Bente-shina, then king of Amurru, had no other alternative.[2] Kinza had likewise been drawn into the Egyptian orbit, the rest of Syria, however, remained in Hittite hands. At that time Muwatallish had ruled over the Khatti Land for only a short time. Conditions induced him to acquiesce temporarily. He doubtless sent the customary message to Ramesses II (1304–1237) upon his accession to the throne of the pharaohs; but he definitely did not consider himself, as Egyptian sources will have it, a subject of the pharaoh.[3] On the contrary, it is obvious that he prepared feverishly for the inevitable trial of strength. It was close at hand when Ramesses in the campaign of his fourth year (1301), reached Beruta and Byblos.[4]

Muwatallish, now fully prepared, accepted the challenge. Lists

---

* An original version of this chapter was published in fascicle 37 in 1965.
[1] §I, 8; §I, 15, 200 ff.; §I, 20, pl. 28 and pp. 19 ff.
[2] G, 6, XXIII, 1, i, 28 ff.; §IV, 12, 114 ff.
[3] Pap. Anastasi, 2, 1 ff. (§III, 16 col., 1878 f.).
[4] §I, 19; G, 9, pl. 9 and pp. 19 ff.

of the contingents composing the Hittite army which he assembled for the impending war have come down to us in Egyptian sources.[1] First of all, these lists state that Muwatallish 'had gathered together all countries from the ends of the sea to the land of Kheta'. Secondly—and this is of particular value—they specifically enumerate these countries; most of them recur in the Hittite texts. Their geographical range gives us a fair idea of the empire of Muwatallish. The first place after Khatti itself is occupied by *Nhrn* and *'Irtw*, i.e. Mitanni and Arzawa; these two are called '*kuirwana* countries' by the Hittites, a term which signifies a preferred status in the Hittite confederacy.[2] Then a group of Anatolian countries follows: *Drdny, Ms, Pds, 'Irwn, Krkš, Lk*. Only the first mentioned remains obscure; the others, in Hittite terms *Maša, Pitašša, Arawanna, Karkiša*, and *Lukka*, can all of them with certainty be localized in the central and western parts of Anatolia. The list concludes with the enumeration of south-eastern and Syrian territories: *Kdwdn, Krkmš, 'Ikrt, Kd, Nwgs, Mwšꝫnt*, and *Kdš*. In Hittite they correspond with *Kizzuwadna, Karkamiš, Ugarit*, (probably) *Halba, Nuhaš*, and *Kinza*; *Mwšꝫnt* is not identified. It is no accident that Amurru is missing; that country had temporarily been taken over by the Egyptians. It goes without saying that the Hittite provinces furnished contingents; we know from other sources that Khattushilish, the king's brother, took part in the campaign as commander of the contingent raised in the provinces under his administration.[3]

Muwatallish assembled his army near Qadesh on the Orontes where the decisive battle was fought.[4] It is better known than most other battles of antiquity, for Ramesses has described it for posterity in wordy compositions and pictured it on the walls of temples which he built.[5] This documentation naturally gives the Egyptian point of view and must be used with caution by the historian.

The Hittite king had chosen his position well. It could be foreseen that the Egyptian army, approaching from the south, had either to use the coastal road or the inland road through Amqa. In either case it would have to strike out for the Orontes valley where the fortified city of Qadesh blocked its advance. Ramesses left the Delta in the spring of his fifth year (1300) and probably followed

---

[1] G, 3, vol. III, sects. 306, 309; §I, 15, 204 ff.     [2] §v, 4, 98 f.
[3] §I, 12, ii, 69 ff.     [4] See generally Bibliography, §I.
[5] G, 10, pls. 16–25 (Abydos); pls. 63–64 (Luxor); pls. 92–95 (Ramesseum 1st courtyard); pls. 96–99 (Ramesseum 1st pylon); pls. 100–106 (Ramesseum 2nd pylon); pls. 169–178 (Abu Simbel).

the coast right to the northern end of the Lebanon mountains. Advancing north-eastward he then marched toward Qadesh. His troops were organized in four divisions. Without precise information as to the whereabouts of the enemy he allowed his columns to stretch out over a long distance. When the advance division, with which the king himself was, had already reached the heights west of Qadesh, where it prepared to pitch camp, the others had fallen behind several miles, the rear division still being on Amurrite territory. In this dangerous situation Ramesses was caught by a surprise attack of the Hittites who had shifted their chariotry from the north to the south of Qadesh. Fording the Orontes they fell upon Ramesses's second division and shattered it. The first was attacked immediately afterwards, while encamping, and was severely mauled. Fierce fighting ensued in which the Egyptians were able to hang on until the third division could be brought up. This took the Hittite charioteers in the rear and threw them back on to and into the river. Ramesses was able to extricate himself from impending disaster and to reconstitute his forces. However, he recognized that further advance was impossible and decided on retreat. The Hittites remained masters of the battle-field.

There is no doubt that they were quite satisfied with the outcome of the campaign. They pursued the retreating Egyptians and were able to penetrate as far south as Apa (= Apina, Upi, i.e. Damascus),[1] that is to say a considerable distance beyond the border as it had existed before the outbreak of the war. That line was fully held. Kinza, which had temporarily fallen into Egyptian hands, remained a Hittite possession; and Amurru, the chief objective of the fighting, had to surrender to the Hittites. Bente-shina, its prince, was deposed by Muwatallish. But the mild treatment that he accorded to the prince of Amurru was a recognition of the fact that the latter could hardly have acted otherwise. Bente-shina was to live in Khakpish for a while under the eyes of Khattushilish; he was later to play his role in the conflict between that prince and his nephew Urkhi-Teshub. For the time being, he was replaced in Amurru by a certain Shapilish.[2]

No Hittite text, either of Muwatallish or of his successors, suggests in any way that the control over Amurru was lost again by the kings of Khatti. On the contrary, the sources leave no doubt that nothing of the kind happened. This means that not even Ramesses II can have had enduring military successes of any

[1] §1, 14, col. 837; §1, 6, 212.
[2] §1, 23, 124 ff. (obv. 11 ff.); G, 6, XXIII, 1, i, 28 ff. (see §IV, 13).

significance in Syria after the battle of Qadesh. His 'war' in Amurru in his eighth year during which *Dpr*—probably in the vicinity of Qadesh—was captured,[1] his raid up to Tunip[2] and his second visit, in his tenth year, to the Dog-River[3] remained episodes.

Muwatallish, in the meantime, renewed the treaty which Murshilish had concluded with Talmi-sharruma, the king of Aleppo.[4] A witness to the treaty was, among others, Shakhurunuwash, the king of Carchemish. As stated before (p. 224), this younger son of Sharre-Kushukh had served since the preceding reign as something like a Hittite vicegerent in Syria, and Syrian kings, such as that of Ugarit, were made responsible to him.

The Syrian War did not pass for the Hittites without serious loss. The Assyrians did not let the preoccupation of Muwatallish in Amurru and Kinza pass without exploiting the opportunities it offered them. Adad-nīrāri, after having been king of Assyria for a comparatively short time, defeated Shattuara, the king of 'Khanigalbat', who must have been one of Kurtiwaza's descendants and successors. He was taken prisoner, carried off to Ashur, but released after having taken an oath of allegiance to Adad-nīrāri.[5] This meant that the Hittite and the Assyrian zones of influence now touched each other at the Euphrates.[6]

On the northern frontier, in Asia Minor, the situation had also markedly deteriorated. The Kaska people had taken advantage of the absence of Khattushilish with the greater part of his forces and had renewed their frontier raids. Even Khakpish, where the governor was exercising the power of a 'king', had been lost and had to be recovered when he returned from the Egyptian war.[7] Furthermore, the absence of the Great King as well as his brother gave personal enemies of Khattushilish an opportunity to work and plot against him. We are told that Arma-Tattash, who years back had been relieved of the governorship of the Upper Land in favour of Khattushilish, employed black magic against his rival. His efforts failed, and the Great King turned the plotter over to his brother; he was sent with his family into exile to Alashiya; only his son, Shippa-zitish, escaped.[8] The incident is of no great importance, but it seems to demonstrate the king's unwavering confidence in his brother's loyalty and good faith. Muwatallish died soon afterwards.

[1] G, 3, vol. III, sects. 356 ff.; §1, 15, 223.
[2] G, 3, vol. III, sects. 364 f.          [3] G, 9.
[4] §1, 23, 80 ff.          [5] §1, 24 (obv. 7 ff.).
[6] G, 4, 58 ff. (ll. 8–14).          [7] §1, 12, iii, 9 ff.
[8] §1, 12 and 13, ii, 74 ff., iii, 14 ff.

The chronology of this reign is dependent on Egyptian synchronisms. The end of the preceding reign, and therefore also the accession of Muwatallish, has been put above at (p. 127) about 1320 or a few years earlier. The main event of the later years of Muwatallish is the battle of Qadesh, which falls in the fifth year of Ramesses II, i.e. 1300 B.C. As we shall see presently, the war between the Egyptians and the Hittites was officially concluded by the peace treaty of the twenty-first year of Ramesses, i.e. 1284. Khattushilish had then been king of the Khatti Land for some time, and before him his nephew Urkhi-Teshub had reigned at least seven years. This places the death of Muwatallish at about 1294 or a few years earlier.

## II. URKHI-TESHUB AND KHATTUSHILISH

Muwatallish died without leaving a legitimate son to succeed him. Hence it was necessary to invoke the 'constitution' of Telepinush which provided that in such a case the eldest son of a royal concubine should be made king. In this manner Urkhi-Teshub was proclaimed king. Khattushilish supported his claims; in his 'apology', our main source for this development, he makes much of it and insists that his attitude toward his nephew is proof of his loyalty and generosity.[1] The internal strife that was to follow, he insists, was exclusively the fault of the young king, who obviously mistrusted him.

Urkhi-Teshub, as Hittite king, assumed the name of Murshilish (III). We know that from his official seal which was found at Ras Shamra.[2] Khattushilish—obviously writing *post factum* and under the influence of the conflict with his nephew—always calls him only Urkhi-Teshub, certainly a sign of contempt.

Khattushilish in the meantime had further increased both his prestige and the territory over which he ruled. Above all, he had succeeded in liberating the holy city of Nerik, which for long years had been in the hands of the Kaska people, who had prevented the important cults of that city from being properly attended to. From then on, Khattushilish was known as the king of Khakpish and Nerik.[3] Urkhi-Teshub may have had valid reason for distrusting his uncle. There are definite indications that, at least since early in his nephew's reign if not before, he had ambitious plans of his own. What else could possibly have been the purpose of seeking the friendship of those who had had quarrels with

---

[1] §1, 12 and 13, iii, 38 ff.     [2] §11, 1; §11, 3.
[3] §1, 12 and 13, iii, 45; see *Bull. A.S.O.R.* 122, 22.

Muwatallish or Urkhi-Teshub? Bente-shina of Amurru is an example of which we have accidentally some knowledge.[1] Another case in point is that of the physician Mitannamuwash.[2] There were probably more like these. Urkhi-Teshub obviously suspected that his uncle might prepare an armed coup, and decided to take anticipatory action. He revoked his uncle's appointment as the governor of the Upper Land, a territory to which Khattushilish had greatly added by his military successes, but allowed him to keep for the time being his 'kingdom' in Khakpish and Nerik. When he took this too away, Khattushilish revolted. An uprising ensued in which the Hittite nobility, dissatisfied with the young king and quite possibly contemptuous of his illegitimate birth, took the uncle's side. Urkhi-Teshub was defeated, finally besieged in Shamukha and taken prisoner. Khattushilish assumed the kingship himself. He sent his nephew into exile, first to northern Syria and later, when there were indications that he might try to escape to Babylonia (or to Egypt), 'across the sea', i.e. to Alashiya (Cyprus).[3]

## III. KHATTUSHILISH AS GREAT KING

The sources for this reign are by no means ample, at least as far as actual historical documents are concerned. In his 'apology' (a kind of autobiography) Khattushilish himself states with considerable pride about his reign:

Those who had been well disposed towards the kings, my predecessors, became well disposed toward me. They kept sending envoys and they kept sending me presents as well. Such presents as they kept sending me they had not sent to any of my fathers and forefathers. Whatever king owed me homage did pay homage to me. The lands that were hostile to me I conquered; I added district after district to the Khatti Lands. Those who had been hostile in the time of my fathers and my forefathers made peace with me.[4]

Whatever the events may have been in detail, it is certain that Khattushilish preserved the power of the empire which he had inherited.

When he became 'Great King' the relationship with Egypt was still tense, although diplomatic relations had probably been resumed. Ramesses seems to have written to the new king a somewhat cool letter on the occasion of his accession to the throne, and Khattushilish replied in an equally cool manner.[5] Be this as it may, Syria certainly required the new king's full attention. The suc-

---

[1] §I, 23, 124 ff. (obv. 11 ff.).          [2] G, 5, IV, 12 (see §I, 12, 40 ff.).
[3] §I, 12, iv, 32 ff.; §II, 2. See above, pp. 201 ff.
[4] §I, 12, iv, 50 ff. (pp. 36 f.).          [5] §III, 9.

cesses which Ramesses had won in Palestine[1] may have contributed to making the situation appear more menacing. The fact that the king of Mira corresponded with the pharaoh[2] is another indication of the tensions that had arisen; if the king of Mira was a Hittite vassal he certainly violated his oath of loyalty by writing to Egypt. Moreover, Khattushilish could never be certain that the Assyrians would not utilize a fresh outbreak of the Hittite–Egyptian war for a simultaneous attack upon the Euphrates frontier.

A revolt of Wasashatta of Mitanni, Shattuara's son, had given Adad-nīrāri I, then king of Ashur, the welcome pretext to incorporate the former Mitannian territory into Assyria.[3] After this victory he had claimed the title of a 'Great King'. The ensuing anger of Khattushilish is plainly evident in a letter rejecting such claims. He writes rather contemptuously:

With respect to brotherhood, . . . about which you speak—what does brotherhood mean? . . . With what justification do you write about brotherhood . . . ? Are not friends those who write to each other about brotherhood? And for what reason should I write to you about brotherhood? Were perhaps you and I born of the same mother? As my [father] and my grandfather did not write to the king of Ashur [about brotherhood], even so must you not write [about brotherhood and] Great-kingship to me.[4]

Such words are not indicative of much love lost; on the contrary, they are suggestive of the apprehension with which Khattushilish watched the Assyrian.

In this situation the Hittite king sought the friendship of the Babylonian king. He concluded a formal treaty of friendship and mutual assistance with the Kassite Kadashman-Turgu. It was the purpose of this treaty to threaten the Assyrian with a retaliatory attack from the south, should he ever think of attacking Syria. The scheme served its purpose for a while and helped to maintain the balance of power. But it did not survive Kadashman-Turgu's death for long. His son and successor Kadashman-Enlil, was still a minor when he ascended the throne, and royal power was actually exercised by his vizier Itti-Marduk-balāṭu. He refused to make the interests of a foreign state the guiding principle of his external policy.[5]

But this setback no longer mattered, for Khattushilish had in the meantime come to terms with Ramesses. In the latter's twenty-first year (i.e. 1284), sixteen years after the battle of Qadesh, the two kings concluded a treaty in which they mutually acknowledged

[1] G, 3, vol. III, sects. 356, 366.          [2] G, 5, 1, 24; §III, 1; §III, 12, 43 f.
[3] §1, 24 (obv. 18 ff.); §1, 25; G, 2, 36 ff.
[4] G, 6, XXIII, 102; §III, 7, vol. 1/2, 246 f.          [5] §III, 8, 24 ff.; §III, 14; §III, 5.

their equal status. Thus the rivalry between the two great opponents came to an end and the frontier between the Egyptian and
the Hittite spheres of influence was stabilized. The treaty, of
which we possess both the Egyptian and the cuneiform versions,[1]
makes no mention at all of territorial claims. This means that the
border remained on the line which the conqueror Shuppiluliumash
had established and which his successors had successfully defended. It implies the final renunciation of the traditional Egyptian claims to Syria. The conclusion of the treaty was accompanied
by a cordial exchange of messages not only between the kings, but
also between the queens;[2] the Egyptian crown prince also joined
in the greetings.[3] Abroad, the event was hailed as one of the
greatest importance. The peace of the world seemed assured for a
long time to come.

During the following years a plan seems to have been conceived to arrange for a personal meeting between Khattushilish
and Ramesses. One talked about a possible journey of the Hittite
king to Palestine.[4] Whether the plan was realized or not, it
certainly testifies to a stability in the political situation such as had
not existed for a long time.

That it was a reality can be shown by the example of Amurru.
The geographic position of that country between the two con-
testants furnishes us with an excellent measuring stick. Khattushilish reinstalled Bente-shina as local king, the same man whom
Muwatallish had deposed; he also made him his son-in-law.[5] We
possess the explicit statement that Bente-shina proved himself
worthy of the confidence lodged in him and remained loyal to the
Khatti Land throughout his lifetime.[6] In other words, Ramesses II
was never again able to encroach upon his territory.

If the Egyptian sources try to give the impression that the
pharaoh later won successes against the Hittites, it has no basis
in fact. It is true that Khattushilish gave his daughter in marriage
to Ramesses, an event which falls into the pharaoh's thirty-fourth
year (c. 1271), i.e. thirty years after the battle of Qadesh.[7] But
this must not be construed as consequence of a new, revised peace
forced upon Khattushilish after defeat. It only testifies to enduring good relations between the two powers; it was one of the
numerous dynastic marriages that were frequently concluded—
certainly for political reasons—during this period.

---

[1] §I, 23, 112 ff.; §III, 13; §III, 15; G, 8, 199 ff.
[2] G, 5, 1, 29; §III, 12, 59; §III, 8, 23.
[3] G, 6, III, 70.     [4] §III, 6.     [5] §I, 23, 124 ff. (obv. 19 f.).
[6] G, 6, xxiii, 1, ii, 45 ff.; §IV, 13.     [7] §III, 3 and 4; §III, 11.

We are ill-informed about the affairs of Asia Minor during this reign. In view of the almost normal restiveness of the Kaska people it is not surprising to hear of continuing conflicts with these mountaineers. Khattushilish, we are told, fought with them for fifteen years, and his son, as major-domo, for at least twelve years more.[1] Perhaps it was at that time when the treaty with the town Tiliura, of which we possess a fragment,[2] was concluded.

In Arzawa Mashturish, the prince of the Shekha-River Land, became one of the king's staunchest partisans.[3] A peculiar light is thrown upon the situation in the other western countries by the fact that the prince of Mira, shortly before the official peace with Egypt, could have asked the pharaoh to intervene in favour of Urkhi-Teshub.[4] It is not known whether and how Khattushilish reacted to this endeavour which, from his point of view, could not have been regarded otherwise than as treasonable; but we have no reason to doubt that he knew how to deal with it. His claim that he maintained the power of his predecessors must be taken as substantially true.

Warfare in the Lukka lands is indicated by the miserable remnants of the annals of this reign.[5] In Tattashsha, situated in the southern mountains, which during the Egyptian war of Muwatallish had served as an alternative capital, Khattushilish established a new 'small' kingdom; Inarash, a member of the royal family, was installed as its ruler.[6] Upon his death it was transferred to Ulmi-Teshub and the treaty renewed with him.[7]

During the whole reign of Khattushilish, his consort Pudu-Kheba, whom he had married as prince when returning from the campaign against Egypt, played a prominent role in all important affairs, more so than any queen before her. Documents of state were usually made out in the name of both the king and the queen. Letters to Egypt, for instance, were written out in two copies, one to the pharaoh in the king's name, the other to the pharaoh's consort in that of the queen.[8] There must be some legal reason for this complicated procedure. That no documentation of the same kind exists for other queens is possibly due to an accident.

The chronology of Khattushilish, like that of Muwatallish, depends mainly on Egyptian synchronisms. The peace treaty with Ramesses falls in the latter's twenty-first year (i.e. 1284); thirteen years later (i.e. 1271) Khattushilish sent his daughter to the Egyptian court. He himself had reigned for some years when he

---

[1] G, 6, xix, 8, iii, 21 ff.      [2] G, 6, xxi, 29 (untranslated).

[3] G, 6, xxiii, ii, 20 ff.; §iv, 13.     [4] G, 5, i, 24; §iii, 12, 44.

[5] G, 6, xxi, 6 and 6a; §iii, 7, fasc. 1/1, 6 ff.; G, 6, xxxi, 19.

[6] §i, 12 and 13, iv, 62 ff.     [7] G, 5, iv, 10; §iii, 10.     [8] §iii, 2.

succeeded in concluding the peace treaty; his reign—it was estimated above—had begun about 1286. At that time he would have been at least forty years old, for his mother, the wife of Mursnilish, had died in that king's ninth year, i.e. about 1326. Both Khattushilish and his son Tudkhaliash were contemporaries of Kacashman-Enlil of Babylon, to whom fifteen years are ascribed. The scn, still reigning when Tukulti-Ninurta became king in Ashur, cannot have assumed kingship over Khatti much later than Shalmaneser I did in Assyria. When he ascended the throne he had been an army leader for at least twelve years, i.e. he was then at least thirty years old. Being the son of Pudu-Kheba he might have been born in 1299 (the year after Qadesh) at the earliest. Considering all circumstances 1265 B.C. seems a reasonable estimate for the death of Khattushilish.

## IV. THE LAST KINGS OF THE KHATTI LAND

Tudkhaliash (IV), the son of Khattushilish and Pudu-Kheba, like his father, had begun his career as a 'priest'[1]—in his case of the 'Ishtar' (i.e. Shaushga) of Shamukha, his father's patroness. It seems that before becoming king he was known under the name of Khishmi-Sharruma.[2]

The new king had to strain the resources of the empire to the utmost. Relations with Egypt were, as far as we can see, friendly during his lifetime. But the renascent Assyria caused new troubles to the Hittites. And in the west there was Ahhiyawa which was intent upon taking advantage of any sign of weakness on the part of the central power. The political problems of the times can be sensed when we consider the list of contemporaneous powers which is contained in a treaty made at this time with Amurru. It includes the names of Egypt, Ashur, Karduniash (i.e. Kassite Babylonia), and—erased again in the draft which is preserved—Ahhiyawa.[3]

In the east, in Syria, Carchemish continued its role as the main Hittite centre. It was now Ini-Teshub, the son of Shakhurunuwash, who represented the Great King here and acted in his name in all Syrian affairs. The sources at our disposal show him dealing with matters concerning Ugarit and Amurru, both vassals of Khatti. In Ugarit the former[4] decision to separate Shiyanni from Ugarit was confirmed by Tudkhaliash.[5]

Ini-Teshub was instrumental in keeping interior peace when

---

[1] §1, 12, iv, 67 ff.    [2] §v, 8, 387 f.; §v, 12, 118 f.
[3] G, 6, XXIII, 1, iv, 1 ff.; §IV, 13; §IV, 12, 320 ff.
[4] See above, p. 125.    [5] G, 7, 290 f.

two brothers revolted against Ammishtamru, the new king. They received the shares in their mother's inheritance to which they were entitled and were sent (as refugees) to Alashiya (Cyprus).[1] Also marital complications among the vassals kept Ini-Teshub busy. There is above all the case of the Amurru princess, daughter of Bente-shina and married to Ammishtamru, who committed adultery, fled to her homeland, but finally on Hittite request had to be extradited, which might have meant death for her.[2]

Amurru was likewise under the supervision of Ini-Teshub. But, of course, the treaty by which Shaushga-muwash (*IŠTAR-muwaš*) was recognized as king of the country was concluded in the name of Tudkhaliash himself.[3] The fact alone that Amurru remained a Hittite vassal in spite of the international situation is worthy of note. The treaty of course envisaged the possibility of war against Egypt, and also against Ashur, but that was theoretical rather than real.

With Ashur the relations of Tudkhaliash must indeed have been tense, to say the least. Although he was still alive under Tukulti-Ninurta I (1244–1208),[4] most of his reign must be assumed to be contemporary with that of Shalmaneser (1274–1245). The latter, like his father Adad-nīrāri, had become heavily engaged in Upper Mesopotamia. Apparently, domination over 'Khanigalbat'—this is what they called the revived Mitanni state—almost assured when Wasashatta had been defeated,[5] had again slipped away from the Assyrians. The local king, another Shattuara, had to be vanquished anew by Shalmaneser and after his downfall the war was carried to the banks of the Euphrates.[6] Ini-Teshub of Carchemish had part in it.[7] It is not by chance either that the treaty with Amurru contains an interesting clause— not duplicated anywhere else—which prohibited commercial relations between Amurru and Ashur.[8] Its purpose patently was to cut off Ashur from the Mediterranean coast and thereby from access to world trade. The success of his defence of Upper Mesopotamia is attested by the fact that Tudkhaliash himself— certainly in defiance of Assyrian claims—adopted the title 'king of the world' (*šar kiššati*).[9]

It has been remarked above that in the Amurru treaty of Tudkhaliash the name of the country Ahhiyawa had been secon-

[1] G, 7, 120 ff.  [2] G, 7, 125 ff.; §IV, 6; §IV, 15. See above, pp. 142 f.
[3] G, 6, XXIII, 1; §IV, 13.  [4] G, 6, III, 74; §IV, 9, 65.
[5] See above, p. 258.  [6] G, 4, 116 ff.
[7] G, 7, 150 f.  [8] G, 6, XXIII, 1, iv, 14 ff.; §IV, 13.
[9] §IV, 8, 74.

darily struck from the list of the great nations of the period. This indicates that Ahhiyawa did not properly belong to them. Nevertheless, it remains remarkable that a court historiographer, if only momentarily, could have thought of the king of Ahhiyawa as equal to the other Great Kings. Hittite kings and the military must have had reason to fear the man of Ahhiyawa. Indeed, he is mentioned as an enemy in the annals of Tudkhaliash.[1] His home was obviously in western Anatolia. The available evidence, fragmentary as it is, allows the observation that at this time the interest of the Hittite kings in the affairs of Anatolia is clearly on the increase.

In this connexion the raids of the Kaska people,[2] eternally repeated routine, do not mean much. But great interest must be attached to the Arzawa war of Tudkhaliash. Its immediate cause was the defection of Kupanta-Inarash, the local king. The sources are rather fragmentary, but there is reason to suspect that once more the king of Ahhiyawa stands behind the revolt.[3] Tudkhaliash gives a long list of Arzawa districts which he says he vanquished,[4] he adds a still longer list of towns in Assuwa.[5] Only in exceptional cases are they mentioned in other Hittite sources. This suggests that Tudkhaliash penetrated westward into regions which earlier kings had not reached. Did he do so in order to ferret out the king of Ahhiyawa?

Another important event may be connected with this trend. As a continental power the Hittite Empire had never shown much concern about Alashiya (Cyprus), the island lying offshore in the north-eastern corner of the Mediterranean. But changes had come about which had enhanced the importance of the island significantly. Not only had it become the foremost source of copper, the metal basic for the civilizations of the Bronze Age; it had also developed into a focal point of civilization through which, by-passing the Hittites, ran the communications between the east and the west, from Egypt and Syria to the Aegean world. As long as this was only a trade route, the Hittites might have acquiesced. But as soon as it assumed political importance—and sooner or later this was inevitable—the Hittites had to intervene; otherwise they were in danger of being cut off from Syria. This stage was reached under Tudkhaliash. He therefore invaded

---

[1] G, 6, XXIII, 13, obv. 5; §IV, 11, 52; §IV, 12, 314 f.
[2] G, 6, XXIII, 11, iii, 9 ff.; §IV, 11, 58 ff.
[3] G, 6, XXIII, 21, ii, 12 ff.; §IV, 2, 156 ff.
[4] G, 6, XXIII, 11, ii, 2 ff.; §IV, 11, 53 f.
[5] G, 6, XXIII, 11, ii, 16 ff.; §IV, 1, 27 ff.; §IV, 11, 54 ff.

Alashiya—probably with the help of his Syrian vassals—and subjected the island by military victory to Hittite domination.[1]

The fateful role played by the king of Ahhiyawa in the further development becomes abundantly clear through the so-called Madduwattash text.[2] This is the bill of indictment in which Madduwattash, prince of Zippashla-Khariyata (in north-western Anatolia), was accused of conspiracy with Attarshiyash, king of Ahhiyā (Ahhiyawa) and of acts hostile to the Great King. The events recorded in the text begin in the reign of Tudkhaliash and continue into that of his son and successor Arnuwandash. Seen in the context of Hittite history it draws a vivid picture of the rise in the west of Anatolia of a strong anti-Hittite coalition. This coalition proceeded step by step to undermine Hittite authority. Slowly advancing toward the south-east it threatened the Empire with slow disintegration.

Madduwattash had been driven from his country by Attarshiyash of Ahhiyā; he had taken refuge with Tudkhaliash and had been reinstated by him. Later Madduwattash had tried to bring the Arzawa Land under his rule, but the local prince, Kupanta-Inarash, had thwarted such efforts. Again it had been the Great King's intervention which saved him, and also provided aid against renewed attacks on the part of Attarshiyash. Madduwattash, nevertheless, persisted in his independent policies. It was clearly his aim to unite the states of western Anatolia and to build up an alliance strong enough to defy the Great King. It may well be that the latter's campaign against Kupanta-Inarash of Arzawa[3] was intended to break up the dangerous coalition in the making. If so, it had the opposite effect; it brought about the reconciliation of the two enemies. From now on they acted in unison.

This was the state of affairs when Arnuwandash succeeded his father as Great King. The increasing tenseness of the situation becomes noticeable in the Syrian sources. Ibiranu of Ugarit, who had just ascended the throne of his father Ammishtamru, had to be reminded by the Hittite—probably Arnuwandash—that he was supposed to appear before his suzerain or at least to send an ambassador.[4] Apparently he was in no great hurry either to fulfil the military obligations of a vassal.[5] These are symptoms of beginning contempt for the overlord.

The position of Arnuwandash soon grew worse. In his days the western alliance of Madduwattash with Ahhiyā and Arzawa took over Khapalla and finally Pitashsha; it was even able to ravage

[1] G, 5, XII, 38, i; §IV, 10, 13.      [2] §IV, 2.
[3] See preceding page.     [4] G, 7, 191.     [5] G, 7, 192.

Alashiya. A climax was reached when Madduwattash came to terms with Attarshiyash of Ahhiyā, his former adversary. Thus the whole west was now united against the central power.

King of Assyria at that time was Tukulti-Ninurta I (1244–1208), who naturally took advantage of the Hittite plight. Once more the Assyrians advanced to the Euphrates, and when Tukulti-Ninurta boasts[1] that he captured and deported thousands of 'Hittites' from across the Euphrates to Assyria this is substantially true although he may have exaggerated their number.

The Egyptian contemporary of Arnuwandash was Merneptah (1236–1223). The two sovereigns remained on good terms with each other. Even Egypt felt in these days an increasing pressure from the north-west. Therefore, it had an interest in keeping the Hittites, who formed a bulwark against the new enemies, as strong as possible. This seems the motivation behind his 'generosity' when, in his second year, he sent grain to the Hittites to alleviate a famine which plagued their land.[2]

Arnuwandash died without offspring[3] after a reign which cannot have been very long. His younger brother *Šuppiluliamaš* (Shuppiluliumash II)[4] took over as the next in line.[5] His name alone, harking back to the days when the Empire was founded, contained a programme. Certainly the new king must have bent every effort to master the menacing situation which he had to face.

In Syria he was, as it had become a tradition, supported by the king of Carchemish. There exist fragments of a treaty which he concluded with Talmi-Teshub, the son of Ini-Teshub.[6] Ugarit remained a vassal of the Hittites until the very end. Talmi-Teshub corresponds in an official capacity with ʿAmmurapi of Ugarit, the last king of that town of whom we have records.[7]

Ugarit was probably the home port of the ships with which Shuppiluliumash conducted naval warfare off Alashiya. Either the people of Alashiya had rebelled or they had been themselves overwhelmed by invaders who had come over the sea. However this may be, Shuppiluliumash was able to sink the Alashiyan fleet and to land on hostile soil. At any rate Alashiya remained in Hittite possession.[8]

The Hittite king even seems to have undertaken a campaign in

[1] §IV, 14, no. 16; G, 2, 82.
[2] G, 3, vol. III, sect. 580.          [3] G, 6, XXVI, 33, ii, 6 ff.
[4] G, 6, XXVI, 32 +XXIII, 44 +XXXI, 106; §IV, 3.
[5] G, 1, 56; G, 5, XII, 38 and 41; §IV, 3. All other reconstructions are disproved.
[6] G, 5, XII, 41 (and Bo. 4839 unpublished); §IV, 16, 17.
[7] G, 7, 205 ff.
[8] G, 5, XII, 38; §IV, 16, 13 ff.; §IV, 7, 166.

Upper Mesopotamia,[1] perhaps to forestall Assyrian action. It is quite possible that Tukulti-Ninurta was still alive. His downfall came too late. The Hittites hardly profited by his murder and the ensuing period of Assyrian weakness. Shuppiluliumash seems not to have been very successful either. Turbulent times lay ahead.

The written sources peter out at this point and finally cease altogether. The archaeological evidence proves that a catastrophe overtook Anatolia and Syria. Wherever excavations have been made they indicate that the Hittite country was ravaged, its cities burned down. When civilization slowly rises again from the ruins, it is no longer Hittite and clearly bears new characteristics.

The catastrophe can be dated to about 1200 B.C. The main fact cannot be denied, but all details are shrouded in mystery. Did Madduwattash and Attarshiyash contribute to the destruction of the mighty Empire which for the last two centuries had dominated the Near East? Were they themselves swept away in the disaster? A firm answer cannot be given to these questions. But certainly the change was brought about, directly or indirectly, by the migrations which engulfed at that time the Aegean world and the eastern Mediterranean; they were stopped, with considerable difficulty at the very gates of Egypt. What the Egyptian chronicler says about the countries attacked by these 'Peoples of the Sea', as he calls them, is true: 'Not one stood before their hands from Khatti on. Qode, Carchemish, Arzawa and Alashiya were crushed.'[2] It was the end of an epoch.

## V. HITTITE CIVILIZATION IN THE EMPIRE PERIOD

The Empire period, from Shuppiluliumash to the catastrophe around 1200 B.C., saw the Hittites at the height of their political power. They ruled supreme over the Anatolian plateau from the western valleys to the headwaters of the Euphrates, and had expanded their domain to include Cilicia and Syria from the Taurus to the Lebanon. It is only natural that over all this territory a unified civilization developed which we call 'Hittite'. The term[3] has often been used in a loose way; it should be limited to the cultural phenomena of the period in question and its preliminary stages which reach back into the early centuries of the second millennium.[4] Specifically, it should not be extended without careful qualifications to the beginning of the first millennium. The

[1] G, 5, IV, 14; §IV, 16, 5 f.
[2] G, 3, vol. IV, sect. 64.
[3] §V, 9.
[4] *C.A.H.* II[3], pt. I, pp. 232 ff.

name 'Hittites' lingers on in northern Syria; however, the civilization of this late period, even though it contains some genuinely Hittite elements, should be kept apart.

In this place no detailed description of Hittite civilization can be given. Only its most striking characteristics can be sketched. When doing so, it must be particularly emphasized that the Hittite civilization (applying the term in the restricted sense just defined) is the result of complicated historical processes. Its foundations are heterogeneous and are only now becoming gradually clearer.[1] The 'Khattians', an eastern people of whose language we know a little, are only one element of many in this mixture. There may have been others in the east, and certainly also in the west and north-west of whom not even the names are known. Only archaeology bears witness of their existence.

Over these 'Asianic' elements in the course of history a younger population was deposited, and it is they who appear to us as the real creators of the 'Hittites'. They spoke languages that are either outright Indo-European or at least related to that linguistic group. We know from the epichorial texts 'Palaic', 'Luwian', and 'Neshian' (which is the language customarily called 'Hittite').

Finally, there are the Hurrians. Originally a people *sui generis* at home in easternmost Anatolia they had spread to Upper Mesopotamia where they had been influenced by the variant of Sumero-Akkadian civilization at home there. At the beginning of the Empire period they expanded into Anatolia[2] and contributed to its civilization. They imparted to it much of that flavour which makes it particularly 'Hittite'.

He who compares the Empire with the preceding periods realizes at once that significant changes have taken place in the meantime. They go deep and concern essential points. Above all the concepts of kingship and state[3] have assumed new aspects. The king is no longer the patriarch he had been in the old days. While he called himself just 'king', he now styles himself 'my Sun'. The new title expresses a change in the king's relationship to the divine world; he is on his way to being translated thither. The texts make him the deputy of the Storm-god, the country's highest god; it is in his stead that he administers the Hittite realm. One has the impression that kingship has gathered into itself divine qualities on every side. Being the mediator between the gods and men, the one who has to see to it that the gods remain on the side of his people, the king is now subject to strict rules designed to assure his ritual purity.[4] He also has become more of an

---

[1] §v, 4, 45 ff.　　[2] §v, 8.　　[3] §v, 4, 85 ff.; §v, 6; §v, 18.　　[4] §v, 4, 89 ff.

absolute monarch; it is taken for granted that his office is inherited by his descendants. In fact the idea of the royal dynasty gains central importance.

When the king dies he himself 'becomes god'; images are erected for him and he becomes the subject of a cult with sacrifices offered daily and festivals regularly celebrated. It is strange to observe that the role of the queen, although sacrifices are likewise due to her after death, preserves more archaic features. Queenship is still an office of its own with functions paralleling those of the king. It is inherited independently of kingship.

As far as political organization[1] is concerned, the Hittite Empire has the appearance of a confederacy. Its structure is feudalistic throughout, and the principles of feudalism are applied at every level. Already during the Old Kingdom tendencies leading toward feudalism were observable. These tendencies were strengthened by the developments in the technique of warfare[2] which mark the middle of the millennium. The horse had been trained to draw a light chariot; horse and chariot together had a revolutionizing effect. Horses capable of drawing chariots had to be bred and trained, the training had to be continued so as to maintain efficiency. This is also valid for the men. A military caste developed, a veritable class of knights, which had to be made economically independent so that it could devote itself to its vocation. The crown (or state) achieved this by placing at their disposal sufficient tracts of land in the form of fiefs. The relationship between the king and those feoffed by him, their obligation to 'protect' him and his descendants (*paḫš-*), becomes a feature of growing concern. The security of the dynasty and the permanence of the state, its ability to withstand its foes depended on this system.

Feudalism soon determined the relationship of the king not only to the military, but also to his civilian officials, it became an instrument of politics. The governors of the provinces, by now 'small' local kings, swore oaths of allegiance and did homage to their overlord at regularly repeated times. Still further out, on the periphery of the Empire, there were the vassals who were bound to the Great King by treaties describing their duties: to send help in times of war, to pay tribute each year, to extradite refugees and fugitives and above all to renounce the right to conduct their own external policy. The Great King acted in their stead. Thus the concept of the *išḫiul* 'bond, obligation, treaty' gains all-embracing significance for the structure of state and society.

The changes described were forced upon the Hittites by the

[1] §v, 4, 109.    [2] §v, 5.

progress of the times, ultimately by technical achievements which nobody could neglect, least of all those who aspired to a leading political role. Otherwise, conservatism is a most characteristic feature of Hittite civilization. Nowhere can it be better observed than in the religion.[1] Here it went so far that cults of the various ethnic layers amalgamated to form the 'Hittite' people were to be conducted in the time-honoured manner, including the use of the original and already half-forgotten languages. In spite of multifarious origins syncretism is avoided; the old gods inherited from preceding periods are carefully kept apart, similar to one another as they may be. One can still recognize that animal worship lay behind certain gods who otherwise had long since acquired human appearance. The Storm-god was originally conceived in the form of a bull, and this idea still lives on in the 'god on the bull' in Roman times. There was a stag god, and a god of the hunt, to whom eagle and hare were sacred.

The exception to this aversion from syncretism is the official cult of the Imperial dynasty as exemplified by the rock sanctuary of Yazilikaya, near the capital Khattusha (Boğazköy), and its reliefs. This requires a special explanation;[2] it is provided by the (very likely) hypothesis that this dynasty was of Hurrian origin and inserted itself into Hittite history in a way the details of which are still unknown. The rocks of Yazilikaya form the open-air courtyard of a sanctuary; on its walls one sees a procession of deities, the goddesses coming from the right, the gods from the left. In the middle where both meet one recognizes the main gods of the Empire, the great Storm-god, the Sun-goddess (of Arinna) and their circle. The astonishing fact here to be stressed is this: to each figure its name is ascribed in so-called 'Hittite' hieroglyphs, and the names so written are linguistically Hurrian names. The mixture well symbolizes the elements which, in the Empire period, had fused into what we call 'Hittite'.

It is interesting to observe that the advanced stage of fusion represented at Yazilikaya is in striking disagreement with the state religion as visible in the great number of surviving texts. Yazilikaya is far ahead of them. Ordinarily the capital united in its temples the cults brought together from the various regions of Asia Minor and Syria. The gods resided there not only in the spirit, but we assume also in the body, namely in the form of images. Many of them had been brought home by conquering kings. Native gods and the new conquered gods were worshipped in the capital according to their accustomed ritual which left nothing to chance.

[1] §v, 4, 130 ff.; §v, 10.     [2] §v, 11.

Ceremonialism and ritualism are the basic religious attitudes; they deserve some additional remarks. At the back of them stands the fundamental notion of cultic purity. It has been observed before that such is essential in the relation of the king to the divine world. Violations of the canon of purity by contamination of any kind, corporeal as uncleanliness or spiritual as 'sin', were believed to cause the wrath of the gods, and thus were the reason for all human misery and suffering. It was the purpose of all cultic actions, for which the king was chiefly responsible, to keep the gods favourably inclined. On their regular and correct observance depended the well-being of state, king and common people.

Unfavourable situations could be prevented from arising by divination. Portents had to be interpreted by experts, and *omina* consulted to recognize dangers that lay ahead. When the gods struck, *omina* made it possible to find out by systematic questioning what was the reason for divine anger, what god was angry and how he could be pacified.

Unfavourable situations when they did arise despite all caution and forbearance could be eliminated by magical means. Man could intervene by staging a magic 'ritual', and thus restore the purity required by the gods. The expert also knew how to foil malicious sorcery performed with the intention to do harm.

Thus magic had a very wide range—so wide that even legislators had to deal with it. White magic, beneficial to him who performs it or has it performed for himself, is the business of an authorized expert, a priest or physician. Black magic which inflicts harm on an enemy is no better than murder and must be punished accordingly.

During the Empire period all regions of the Near East formed part of a power-system that embraced their world. This was first of all a political phenomenon. But the longer it lasted, and the more intimately it operated, the more it was bound to produce parallel intellectual phenomena. In the end these effects appear to the observing historian as more characteristic for these centuries of vivid cultural exchange than the resulting political balance. Within the limited world of those days an international consciousness developed which, despite armed conflict, united its parts, whether they were Mesopotamian, Egyptian or Hittite.

To a large degree the cuneiform system of writing[1] and the clay tablet on which it was inscribed served as a vehicle of this internationalism. Mesopotamia had been its original home. With the

[1] §v, 4, 171 ff.; §v, 17.

expansion of Sumero-Akkadian civilization it spread up to Syria and it is there that the ancestors of the Hittites must have picked it up. The reception of cuneiform must go back to a rather early period; it is certain that in the Old Kingdom Hittite scribes already employed the art of writing. If most of the preserved tablets have been copied or produced during the Empire period, it is a mere accident. Even Egypt had learned scribes who could read and, if need be, write cuneiform and thereby communicate with their contemporaries in the north.

Besides the cuneiform script borrowed from outside, the Hittites also possessed a native 'hieroglyphic' script.[1] It has a long history too but does not play the international role which cuneiform played. A few monumental inscriptions of the Empire age, not sufficiently understood as yet, have come down to us from Anatolia; it was perhaps more widely used for writing documents of daily life on wood. It lived on in the stone inscriptions of post-Empire times, most of them found in the Taurus regions and in northern Syria.

Their familiarity with cuneiform writing and the continuous connexions of scribal schools with Mesopotamian centres of learning enabled the Hittites to take part in the intellectual life of the times. To an appreciable degree the Hurrians of Upper Mesopotamia were the intermediators. In this way, for example, the Gilgamesh Epic became known in Anatolia. We possess not only Hittite but also Hurrian fragments of this literary work which can justly be called the greatest of the Ancient Near East. The Hurrian source of the epic dealing with the generations of gods who succeeded each other in the domination of the world, and of the Kumarbi Epic, is obvious. Both these cycles of mythic tales are at home in a Hurrian milieu.

Of greater importance for our evaluation of Hittite civilization under the Empire are those texts that are not borrowed, but rooted in a genuinely Hittite thought. The practices of religious life gave rise to a great number of ritual and ceremonial texts, not to forget the *omina*; the political customs produced rules and regulations, oaths and treaties. Most characteristic for the Empire are the annals of the kings. These too have their foundation in religious life: the kings had to report their achievements to the gods whom they represented on earth. These reports grew out of the annals of the Old Kingdom, but they assumed a definite literary style only under the Empire. The annals of the Empire can justly be claimed as the oldest examples of true historiography that

[1] §v, 13; §v, 14.

we possess. Events were here reported objectively for their own sake; but at the same time situations resulting from the inter-dependence of various individual facts were artfully described. The author, so to speak, views them in a higher perspective from outside. Fateful complications were followed up to their final dénouement with a definite feeling for the dramatic. A historical style was here created which was later continued and developed by the Assyrians. But there are essential differences: Hittite annals have a quality of realism which is lost in Assyrian historical writing. They impress us by their unspoiled vitality, which tends to petrify into patterns and clichés later on.

The political greatness of the Hittites, who after all in the Empire period were world leaders for two centuries, must, one should suspect, have its counterpart in the field of art. Their in-dividuality and originality in architecture[1] is apparent in all the remnants that have survived. Hittite temples and Hittite palaces would plainly be impossible in any other part of the ancient world; they exhibit characteristics which are specifically Hittite. The foundations of their walls are formed by gigantic blocks which are sometimes adorned with reliefs. Large windows in the outer walls, beginning immediately above the foundations blocks, are particu-larly striking. They open up the buildings toward the outside so that the inner courtyard does not play the centralizing role which it plays in other provinces of the Near East. It now keeps loosely together various groups of rooms which surround it. The house does not have the castle-like aspects it has elsewhere.

The acropolis of Boğazköy (Büyükkale) as it existed during the Empire was a rather impressive group of buildings within the protective ring of fortifications which made skilful use of the natural strength of the location. From the gate a road led upward across open spaces toward and into the public buildings and the residence of the Great King. Behind it and in its substructures were hidden the storerooms and magazines without which the administration of a great empire cannot function.

What is left of the representative art of the Hittites[2] is inti-mately connected with architecture. There are the sculptures still to be seen on the gates of Boğazköy and Hüyük. There is the sanctuary of Iflatun-Pinar. Among the so-called 'rock-sculptures', some like those of Gavur-kalesi belonged to a fortress; those, for example, of Yazilikaya near Boğazköy to a sanctuary. It would be rash, however, to generalize thus. Let us not forget that—to judge by the texts—many works of art, especially the movable ones,

---

[1] §v, 16.    [2] §v, 15; §v, 3; §v, 1; §v, 2.

must have perished. Only few examples, like statuettes,[1] seals[2] and other small pieces escaped destruction. The remnants left give a very inadequate idea of Hittite art, but they justify the statement that it indeed had an individual quality which was worthy of a great nation.

The reliefs which have been recovered excel by soft round modelling, in many cases they become half plastic. They display a forceful monumental style which does not have its equal elsewhere in the Ancient Near East.

In the discussion of Hittite art the problem of its origins has been too much in the foreground of interest. Admittedly this is important, but it should not be allowed, by over-emphasis on terminology, to deny the existence of a genuine Hittite art commensurate with the grandeur of the Empire. We may say that a great art was here in the making, that it did not reach the limits of its potentialities, that its growth was broken off before it became fully mature. Fate interrupted a development full of promise when the catastrophe of 1200 swept the Hittites and their Empire away.

[1] See, for example, Bittel, K., *Boğazköy*, III (1957), pls. 23 ff.; Alp, Sedat, in *Anatolia*, 6 (1961/2), 217 ff.

[2] §v, 7; §v, 11; also Beran, Th. and Otten, H., in *M.D.O.G.* 86 (1953), 87 (1955), 89 (1957), 91 (1958), 93 (1962), *passim*.

# CHAPTER XXV

## ASSYRIAN MILITARY POWER

### 1300–1200 B.C.

## I. THE CAMPAIGNS OF ADAD-NĪRĀRI I

THE reign of Adad-nīrāri I (1307–1275), the son of Arik-dēn-ili, inaugurated a period of rapid expansion. Under his able leadership and that of his immediate successors, Shalmaneser I (1274–1245) and Tukulti-Ninurta I (1244–1208), Assyria in the course of some eighty years greatly extended its territories and eventually emerged as one of the most powerful states of the Near East. Its success must in large part be attributed to its growing economic and military strength, to its political stability, and to the vigorous personalities of its kings, but it was also favoured by the international situation, for the Hittite Empire, faced by more urgent problems, both internal and external, was not in a position to offer a sustained resistance to Assyrian expansion in upper Mesopotamia. The conquests of Assyria, however, outran its capacity to hold and govern all that had been gained and its political decline was as meteoric as its rise. Nevertheless, the empire of the thirteenth century, although ephemeral, laid the foundations of future Assyrian greatness, not only in the political sphere but also in literature and in art.

In the introduction to a number of building inscriptions, Adad-nīrāri boasts that he smote the armies of the Kassites, Quti, Lullume and Shubari, smashed all enemies above and below and harried (lit. 'threshed') their lands from the towns of Lubdu and Rapiqu in northern Babylonia to Elukhat in upper Mesopotamia.[1] More precise information on the war with Babylonia is given by the Synchronistic History.[2] He defeated Nazimaruttash (1323–1298) at the town of Kār-Ishtar in the land of Ugarsallu,

---

* An original version of this chapter was published as fascicle 49 in 1967; the present chapter includes revisions made in 1973.

[1] G, 2, 57; G, 11, 27. Lubdu lay south of Arrapkha, perhaps near modern Tāūq (Dāqūq), for literature see A, 2, 178 f., n. 1096; Rapiqu was on the middle Euphrates, probably near modern Ramādi, *ibid.* 127, n. 748; Elukhat west of the Ṭūr ʿAbdīn, §1, 3, 9 f.

[2] Col. 1, 24–31; G, 14, 60.

plundered his camp and carried off his royal standards.[1] The
Assyro-Babylonian frontier was then realigned to run from Pilasqi,
on the east side of the Tigris,[2] through Arman in Ugarsallu, a
city which lay between the Lesser Zab and the Shaṭṭ el-ʿAdhaim,[3]
to the border of the land of the Lullume (Lullubi). Although the
boundary change was probably of a minor nature, the Assyrians
considered that they had avenged the reverses suffered by Arik-
dēn-ili at Kassite hands and a long epic was composed to celebrate
the exploit.[4] In default of a Babylonian account, it is not certain
that it was as decisive as the Assyrians claimed.[5] It did, however,
restore the state of uneasy equilibrium which had existed between
the two countries in the time of Enlil-nīrāri and Kurigalzu.[6] Indeed, the advantage appears to have shifted from Babylonia to
Assyria. Whereas Kurigalzu met the Assyrian army at Sugagu,
only a day's journey south of Ashur,[7] and at Kilizi, near Erbil,
Adad-nīrāri fought and plundered in the northern borderland of
Babylonia. When he raided Lubdu and Rapiqu is uncertain.
There is no record that he was involved in hostilities with Kadashman-Turgu (1297–1280) and Kadashman-Enlil II (1279–1265).

No details are known of his expeditions against the Lullume and
Qutu. Any permanent pacification of these turbulent Zagros
peoples was as yet out of the question, but by punitive action he
may temporarily have secured a cessation of raids on Assyrian
territory and plundering of caravan traffic at the western end of
the routes to Iran. When giving his genealogy, he records the
defeat by Arik-dēn-ili of Turukku and Nigimṭi, from which it
may be inferred that he retained control of both these eastern
districts. In Katmukhi, in the Tigris valley west of the Judi Daǧ,
he probably suffered a reverse, for his reference to the subjection
of this land by his father is omitted from a number of his inscriptions. There is no record that he campaigned against the other

[1] According to the dates adopted for Nazimaruttash in the chronological scheme
of this *History*, the war must have occurred in the earlier part of the reign of Adad-
nīrāri. A wider margin of variation downward for the last Kassite rulers is proposed
in A, 5, 305 f.
[2] Location unknown, cf. A, 5, 309, n. 96.
[3] For Arman in general, A, 2, 195, n. 1195.
[4] §IV, 20, 113 f. In the epic, Adad-nīrāri says of Arik-dēn-ili: 'My father could
not rectify the calamities inflicted by the army of the king of the Kassite land.' The
war between Adad-nīrāri and Nazimaruttash is also mentioned briefly in the Tukulti-
Ninurta Epic, §IV, 5, col. v, ll. 31–2, corrected to col. II in §IV, 7, 40.
[5] Babylonian Chronicle P, G, 1, 45, ll. 23 f., which may have recorded these
events, breaks off after a reference to Nazimaruttash and an Assyrian king.
[6] See above, pp. 31 f.
[7] A, 5, 313 f.

small states of the upper Tigris valley. Although this area formed part of the land of the Shubari or Subarians, his claim to have defeated these people must refer to his conquest of Mitanni-Khanigalbat.[1]

His main territorial gains were made at the expense of Khanigalbat, which at this period extended from the Ṭūr 'Abdīn westwards across the upper reaches of the Khabur and Balīkh to the Euphrates. For Adad-nīrāri it was both a traditional enemy and a present threat to the security of his country. The earlier subjection of Assyria by the kings of Mitanni and the subsequent attempt of Ashur-uballiṭ to seize control over the land of Mitanni had certainly left a legacy of mutual hatred. Behind it, moreover, lay the power of the Hittite Empire, which, since the time of Shuppiluliumash, had sought to maintain it as a buffer state against Assyria. Hittite influence, lost at the death of Shuppiluliumash, had been re-established, presumably by Murshilish II, since a contingent from Naharain, i.e. Mitanni-Khanigalbat, was among the forces of Muwatallish at the battle of Qadesh. Although the ruler of Khanigalbat was recognized by Muwatallish as an equal[2] there is little doubt that, as in the case of Kurtiwaza of Mitanni, he was a *kuirwana* vassal, accorded a semblance of independence but in fact acknowledging Hittite 'protection'.

According to Adad-nīrāri, his first war with Khanigalbat was caused by the attack of its king, Shattuara I.[3] If the Hurrian was indeed the aggressor, he may have feared that the growing power of Assyria would lead Adad-nīrāri to renew the attempt to overrun his country and so have taken the offensive in the hope of forestalling such a move. Whatever his motives, he had fatally misjudged the strength and temper of his adversary. He was captured and taken to Ashur, but on swearing an oath of allegiance was permitted to retain his kingdom as an Assyrian vassal. He remained loyal to Adad-nīrāri for the rest of his life, sending him tribute year by year.[4]

The war against Shattuara I must be dated after the battle of

---

[1] For the Assyrian use of the term Khanigalbat for Mitanni, see A, 26, 526 f.
[2] §1, 5, 68, col. III, 10 f.   [3] §1, 14.
[4] Weidner suggests that Adad-nīrāri annexed most of Khanigalbat so that Shattuara returned to a diminished kingdom. In consequence he was known, not as king of Khanigalbat, but as king of Shubria (Subartu), A, 26, 523 ff. The text cited, a letter from an Assyrian vassal found in the Boğazköy archive, is difficult to interpret because of its damaged condition. According to the best preserved passage, the king of Shubria had seized the throne of an unidentified land, perhaps that of the writer, and had also secured the return of people who had fled from Khanigalbat during a war with Adad-nīrāri: G, 8, 1, 20; G, 6, 258 f.

Qadesh in the fifth year of Ramesses II (1300), in which Khani-galbat fought as a Hittite ally. That it preceded the accession of Khattushilish III is suggested by a letter from the Hittite to another king, almost certainly Adad-nīrāri.[1] Writing soon after he came to the throne, Khattushilish requested the Assyrian to stop the people of the frontier town of Turira from raiding Carchemish. Since the king of Khanigalbat was claiming Turira it may be inferred that the Hittite was asking Adad-nīrāri to intervene in his capacity as overlord of the Hurrian ruler. As Shattuara apparently received no Hittite assistance, it is a reason-able assumption that his defeat occurred during the troubled years of Urkhi-Teshub.

The advance of Assyrian influence to the Euphrates repre-sented the collapse of the Hittite attempt to maintain Khanigalbat as a buffer state and constituted a potential threat to their control of Syria. It did not, however, lead to an open breach of relations between the two countries. Khattushilish refers in his letter to regular diplomatic exchanges between Adad-nīrāri, Urkhi-Teshub and another Hittite king who must be Muwatallish. He himself appears anxious to placate the Assyrian who had failed to send him the customary gifts of a royal garment and oil at his accession. In neglecting this courtesy, Adad-nīrāri may have wished to mark his displeasure at the treatment of his messengers who, as Khattushilish admits, had had 'sad experiences' in the time of Urkhi-Teshub. Khattushilish also excuses himself for not sending the supplies of iron and iron weapons for which Adad-nīrāri had asked. His conciliatory tone may be explained by his wish to secure Assyrian neutrality in the event of an attack by Ramesses II, a danger which at the time seemed imminent. To strengthen his position against both Egypt and Assyria, Khattushilish entered into a defensive alliance with Kadashman-Turgu of Babylonia who, in fulfilment of its terms, broke off diplomatic relations with Ramesses and promised military aid.[2]

In the event, war with Egypt was avoided but, perhaps while the situation was still critical for the Hittites, developments in Khanigalbat led to a strengthening of the Assyrian position.

___

[1] G, 8, 1, 14; §1, 7, 27 ff.; §1, 10, 3 ff.; *C.A.H.* I³, pt. 1, p. 216.
[2] G, 8, 1, 10; §1, 2; §1, 11, 16 ff.; for a fragmentary letter from Kadashman-Turgu to Khattushilish III, see G, 9, III, 71. If a passage in a letter from Khattu-shilish to Kadashman-Enlil has been correctly restored, the former did not place much reliance on the promises of Kadashman-Turgu: 'They used to call [your father] a king who prepares for war but then stays at home.' See A, 20, 146.

Wasashatta, son of Shattuara I, rebelled and went to Khatti to solicit support.[1] The Hittites accepted his presents but, presumably because of their preoccupation with Egypt, failed to send aid when Adad-nīrāri attacked. Forced westward by the Assyrian advance, Wasashatta made his final stand at Irrite, between Carchemish and Harran, probably the modern town of Ordi. Here he was captured and, together with his palace women, his sons, his daughters and his people, taken in chains to Ashur, where his royal standard was triumphantly set up in the temple of Ishtar. It is probable that Adad-nīrāri abandoned the attempt to rule Khanigalbat through a vassal and annexed it to Assyria. Although this campaign is more fully reported than the earlier war against Shattuara I, there is no reference to the installation of a ruler, and at Taidi, the royal city of Wasashatta between Cizre and Diyārbakr,[2] he rebuilt the palace, doubtless as the residence of an Assyrian governor. In addition to Irrite and Taidi, he captured and looted the towns of (A)masaki, Kakhat, Shuri, Nabula, Khurra, Shudukhu and Ushukanni (Washshuganni). All seven lay in the area of the Khabur triangle but the only one to be certainly located is Kakhat, modern Tell Barrī on the River Jaghjagha.[3] He defines the conquered area as extending from Taidi in the east to Irrite; it included 'Elukhat and the Kashiari mountain (Ṭūr 'Abdīn) in its entirety, and the fortified districts of Suda and Harran up to the bank of the Euphrates'. To celebrate this conquest of upper Mesopotamia he revived the royal title 'king of the totality' (šar kiššati), previously held by Shamsi-Adad I.[4]

He now felt able to treat on equal terms with the Hittites. He informed Khattushilish of his defeat of Wasashatta, claimed the status of 'great king', wrote of 'brotherhood' and proposed himself for a visit to Mount Ammana, the Amanus.[5] While admitting that he was entitled to recognition as a great king, Khattushilish furiously rejected his other demands. 'What is this talk of brotherhood and visiting the Ammana mountain?... Why should I write to you concerning brotherhood? You and I, were we born of one mother?'[6] The request to visit the Amanus has been interpreted as a veiled threat of aggression or a territorial claim, but a more

---

[1] §1, 14; §1, 15; §1, 16.   [2] §1, 9, 59.

[3] On the left bank of the river, 12 km. upstream from Tell Brak, §1, 1. For Elukhat, Khurra, Irrite, Suda and Washshuganni, cf. §1, 3.

[4] The title was accorded to Ashur-uballiṭ by a scribe but is not attested in his official titulary. Cf. A, 24, 308.

[5] G, 9, XXIII, 102; G, 6, 262 f.; §1, 15, 21 f.; §III, 12, 67.   [6] See above, p. 258.

plausible explanation is that Adad-nīrāri had asked for an agreement for Assyrian trade in Amanus timber, hence his 'talk of brotherhood' or a treaty relationship. The violent reaction of Khattushilish is a measure of his fear of Assyrian designs on Syria, a fear which in all probability drove him to compose his quarrel with Egypt and negotiate the treaty with Ramesses II in the latter's twenty-first year (1284). He may have had immediate cause for anxiety. In certain texts Adad-nīrāri claims to have conquered 'as far as Carchemish on the bank of the Euphrates'. While this probably represents no more than the desire of the Assyrian scribe to give precise definition to the Euphrates frontier, the possibility exists that it refers to an Assyrian attack against the city or at least the territory of Carchemish which, since it guarded the principal crossing of the Middle Euphrates, was one of the most strongly held Hittite positions in Syria.

There can, however, be little doubt that Hittite support was in large measure responsible for the success of the rebellion which broke out in Khanigalbat, either late in the reign of Adad-nīrāri or early in that of Shalmaneser. If Muṣri lay south of the Taurus in the plain of Harran,[1] the fact that Adad-nīrāri does not refer to its conquest by Ashur-uballiṭ in all his inscriptions would strongly suggest that at least the western part of Khanigalbat had been lost to Assyria before his death. Less significant is the omission from certain texts of the list of captured towns of Khanigalbat. It could have been left out for the sake of brevity.

## II. SHALMANESER I AND THE CONQUEST OF KHANIGALBAT

Immediately Shalmaneser I succeeded his father he was attacked by Uruaṭri (variant Uratri), the later Urartu, one of a large number of Hurrian principalities in the mountainous regions round Lake Vān and Lake Urmia, known to the Assyrians from the time of Tukulti-Ninurta I as the Nairi lands.[2] Their territory corresponded, at least in part, to that of the Khurri land ruled in the fourteenth century by Artatama, but was now split up into a loose confederation of small political units. Shalmaneser names eight districts of Uruaṭri which may have been situated on the middle or higher reaches of the Greater Zab.[3] Whether it also included the area of Lake Vān, the centre of the later state of Urarṭu, is uncertain. Information on the civilization of the Nairi

---

[1] See above, p. 28 and below, p. 460 and n. 2.
[2] §II, 6, 190 ff.; §II, 8, 13 ff., 150 ff.     [3] §II, 8, 150 ff.

lands is at present derived mainly from textual and archaeological evidence of the ninth to seventh centuries when they had been united in the kingdom of Urarṭu.[1] That their population was Hurrian is evident from personal and place names and the Urarṭian language known from texts of this period, which was a later dialect of the Hurrian spoken in Mitanni in the second millennium.[2] With its rich mountain pastures the country was especially suitable for stockbreeding, and cattle, sheep, goats and pigs were kept in large numbers. Certain areas, notably the Urmia plain, were also important centres of horse breeding. The principal crops were wheat, barley, rye, millet, sesame and flax; and vines were grown extensively for wine. The country also possessed important resources of copper, iron and lead, and the metal industry was, in consequence, highly developed. In warfare the inhabitants were redoubtable fighters, putting into the field armies that were well equipped and strong in chariotry and, at this later date, cavalry. The towns, many of large size, were strongly defended by walls of cyclopean masonry.[3]

Although there is no reference to Uruaṭri in the extant records of his predecessors, Shalmaneser accuses it of rebellion. He conquered its eight lands and their forces, sacked fifty-one (variant forty-one) towns, imposed tribute on the inhabitants and carried off young men to Ashur as hostages. He boasts that he brought the whole land of Uruaṭri into submission at the feet of the god Ashur in three days. Although the eight districts overrun were certainly small and the sack of some fifty towns and villages could have been carried out by a number of columns operating simultaneously, it is difficult to believe that the whole campaign was concluded in so short a time. If his claim is to be taken seriously and not dismissed as a flight of literary fancy,[4] and if, as seems most likely, it refers to the actual fighting, it can only relate to the decisive battles and not to the subsequent reduction and pillage of individual settlements.

His next attack was directed against the strongly defended city of Arini in Muṣri, which he accused of rebellion. It was sacked and razed to the ground, earth from its ruins being taken to Ashur and symbolically scattered in the city gate. The subjection of the whole of Muṣri followed. If this land lay to the west rather than to the east of Assyria, then this expedition must be interpreted as a preliminary move against Khanigalbat, the reconquest of which was achieved in his next campaign.

[1] §II, 5, 70 ff.; §II, 6, 195 ff.; §II, 9, 131 ff.    [2] §II, 2; §II, 6, 193.
[3] §II, 1.    [4] §IV, 2, 56.

In Khanigalbat he was opposed not only by its ruler, Shattuara II, but by a Hittite army which, since it included a contingent of the Akhlamu tribe of the Syrian desert, may have been raised and commanded by the ruler of Carchemish. Well-organized measures had been taken to resist his advance. The passes and watering places on the line of his march had been occupied and in consequence his troops suffered severely from exhaustion and thirst. Nevertheless, there was no wavering in their discipline and morale, and when the opposing forces met in pitched battle Shalmaneser inflicted a crushing defeat on the Hurrians and their allies. Shattuara himself escaped from the field and fled westward but Shalmaneser took 14,400 prisoners, whom he blinded, probably partially, as a reprisal for their rebellion. The reduction of all Khanigalbat followed, nine fortified towns, the royal city of Shattuara II and 180 other places being laid waste. He defines the conquered area in terms similar to those of Adad-nīrāri and like his father gives Carchemish as the western limit.[1]

There is no doubt that on this occasion Khanigalbat was annexed to Assyria. To the reigns of Shalmaneser and Tukulti-Ninurta I belong texts from Ashur mentioning governors of several of its cities[2] and a few legal documents from Tell Fakhari-yah, south of Ras el-'Ain, which are dated by Assyrian eponyms and the Old Assyrian months. All the personal names in the Fakhariyah texts are Assyrian but, since there is no indication of the profession or title of the persons mentioned, it is not possible to say whether they were members of the administration, garrison troops or colonists.[3] One of the urgent problems facing the newly appointed Assyrian officials was the maintenance of those who had fled or been forcibly removed from their homes. Issues of royal grain collected from Amasaki were made to the 'uprooted' people of Shudukhu and Nakhur.[4]

The victory over Shattuara II was the most significant of the thirteenth century. It brought to an end over three hundred years of Hurrian rule in upper Mesopotamia and finally decided the century-old struggle of Assyrian and Hittite for control of the area. It gave Assyria undisputed command of trade-routes leading to Syria and Anatolia, added rich agricultural land and prosperous cities to its territory and placed at the disposal of its military command a large population with long experience in the art of

---

[1] For a letter from a ruler of Khanigalbat to a Hittite king, see §11, 7, where the writer is identified as Shattuara II. A, 26, 253 prefers Wasashatta or, less probably, Shattuara I.

[2] G, 6, 266.     [3] §v, 14, 86 ff.; see now A, 23.     [4] G, 5, 44, n. 8.

war. That the Assyrian skill in chariot fighting owed much to
Hurrian example is shown by the Middle Assyrian version of a
Hurrian treatise on the breaking in and training of horses for
team work.[1] The Assyrian onomasticon of the thirteenth century
also shows a marked increase in Hurrian names, which are borne
by persons in all walks of life. Some held high offices of state,
two indeed being *līmu* officials.[2] For Assyria, limited as it was
in area, population and economic resources, the conquest of
Khanigalbat was an indispensable condition of its rise to the
stature of a major power.

Shalmaneser also had to deal with renewed revolts in Qutium
and Lullume. The Qutu were attacking in the north, between the
Uruaṭrian frontier and Katmukhi. Since a call-up of the general
levy would have involved a dangerous delay he decided, after
obtaining a favourable omen, to hasten north with a third of his
chariotry. The enemy, caught unawares by his swift action,
suffered considerable punishment and their attack was repelled,
but significantly he does not claim to have brought Qutium into
submission. Developments on the north-western frontier are
obscure but it is possible that Shalmaneser reimposed Assyrian
suzerainty on Katmukhi and other Shubari lands in the upper
Tigris area only to lose it again later in his reign, for according
to Tukulti-Ninurta they rebelled against him.

There is no reference in his extant inscriptions to his relations with his Babylonian contemporaries, Kadashman-Enlil II
(1279–1265), Kudur-Enlil (1263–1255) and Shagarakti-Shuriash
(1255–1243), and such information as is available from other
sources throws only a partial light on their nature. Babylonia
was now less of a danger to Assyria, for the recovery of Elam
from its defeat by Kurigalzu II threatened the security of its
eastern border.[3] Probably in the time of Kadashman-Turgu,
Attar-kittakh regained Susa, earlier subjected by Kurigalzu, and
his son, Khumban-numena, further extended the kingdom. If a
broken word in a statue inscription originally read [Ṭup]liash,
then his successor, Untash-(*d*)*GAL*, raided across the Babylonian
border, west of the river Kerkhah.

By the end of Adad-nīrāri's reign the close alliance of Babylonia
and Khatti had also come to an end. Since Kadashman-Enlil II,
son of Kadashman-Turgu, was a minor at his accession the conduct of state affairs was for some years in the hands of the vizier,
Itti-Marduk-balāṭu. He strongly opposed the Hittite connexion,
believing that Khattushilish was attempting to use Babylonia as

[1] §II, 3.  [2] G, 5, 103 f.  [3] See below, pp. 383 ff.

a tool for the furtherance of his own policies and, in particular, seeking to embroil it in his struggle with Assyria. In view of the expansionist activities of Khumban-numena of Elam, it may be surmised that Itti-Marduk-balāṭu considered that the interests of his country would be better served by the adoption of a conciliatory policy towards its northern neighbour. Khattushilish, in fulfilment of his treaty with Kadashman-Turgu, wrote on the latter's death to the Babylonian notables, promising aid should any power attack Babylonia but threatening war if they refused to recognize Kadashman-Enlil as king. Itti-Marduk-balāṭu chose to regard this as a sinister attempt to interfere in the affairs of Babylonia and in his reply accused the Hittite of treating it as his vassal. Later, Kadashman-Enlil complained of Hittite opposition to his resumption of diplomatic relations with Egypt, which had been broken off by his father at the time of the crisis between Ramesses II and Khattushilish. Babylonian messengers were no longer sent regularly to the Hittite court on the pretext that the nomadic Akhlamu were interrupting communications north of Hīt and that Assyria refused them passage through its territory. Writing to Kadashman-Enlil after he attained his majority, Khattushilish was at pains to refute the Babylonian charges made against him and bitterly attacked Itti-Marduk-balāṭu for misrepresenting his actions.[1] His anxiety to placate the Babylonian king and secure him as an ally against Assyria leaps to the eye. Appealing to his pride, he assured him that Assyria was too weak to threaten Babylonia and that as a great king he could compel it to allow his messengers to pass. In another passage, which can only refer to Assyria, he urged him to attack the enemy land. As further evidence of his good will, he promised the settlement of Babylonian claims against two of his Syrian vassals. One concerned the murder of certain Babylonian merchants while on a journey to Amurru and Ugarit. The other involved Bente-shina of Amurru whom Kadashman-Enlil had accused of disturbing his land. Khattushilish reported that when taxed with this offence Bente-shina had advanced a counter-claim for thirty talents of silver against the inhabitants of Akkad. He advised Kadashman-Enlil that he should prosecute his claim; Bente-shina should defend himself in the presence of the Babylonian ambassador; and if Kadashman-Enlil could not conduct the action in person he should send a representative with knowledge of the affair. Bente-shina, concluded Khattushilish, 'is (my) vassal. If he troubles my brother, does he not trouble me?'

[1] G, 8, 1, 10; §1, 2; §1, 4, 24 ff.; §1, 11, 16 ff.; §1, 13, 74 f.; A, 20, 139 ff.

It is not known whether Kadashman-Enlil was persuaded by these blandishments to reverse the policy of his vizier and resume intimate relations with Khatti. That Shalmaneser had trouble with one of his Babylonian contemporaries is, however, suggested by a passage in the Epic of Tukulti-Ninurta, which deals with past conflicts between Assyria and Babylonia. The much damaged passage relating to Shalmaneser describes his defeat of the Shubari[1] and, in a broken context, names the Hittites. The Babylonians do not appear in the extant text but, in view of the subject matter of the section, were presumably involved in some way. It is tempting to connect the war against the Shubari with the defeat of Shattuara II, but so much of the text is lost that speculation as to its date and circumstances can hardly be profitable.

### III. TUKULTI-NINURTA I AND THE CONQUEST OF BABYLONIA

The conquests made by Shalmaneser's son, Tukulti-Ninurta I, during the early part of his reign consolidated and greatly extended those of his predecessors. For much of his first decade his energies were directed to establishing a firmer control over the lands to the east and north than had been achieved by his predecessors. In his accession year he marched against the Qutu, concentrating his attack on the land Uqumeni. Despite the fierce resistance of the inhabitants it was forced into submission, its settlements being laid waste and the corpses of the slain piled up at the gate of the principal city. Its king, Abuli, and his nobles were taken in chains to Ashur but on swearing an oath of allegiance were returned to their land. Control of the Zagros districts through vassal princes, although unsatisfactory, was enforced by the nature of the country. The isolation of the settled valleys, the poor lines of communication and the opportunities for resistance afforded by mountain and forest have throughout history made the administration of this area a task of peculiar difficulty. Direct rule by Assyria would have necessitated the permanent deployment of a large occupying force, the burden of which on the national resources would have been out of all proportion to the advantages gained. The subjugation of the country was more economically attained by the regular dispatch of punitive expeditions and the establishment of military bases at strategic points. Rebellion was endemic, but by the determined prosecution of such measures it could be controlled. Cowed by the defeat and savage treatment

[1] §IV, 5, 20 f., col. v, 33–41.

of Uṭumeni, the inhabitants of Elkhunia submitted without resistance. Nor was opposition apparently encountered when, either
in the same or the following year, the Assyrian army appeared in
Sharnida and Mekhru. In the latter district Tukulti-Ninurta
employed Qutian troops to cut supplies of its much prized timber
for the construction of a palace at Ashur. His reduction of the
Qutian lands although brutal was effective and for many years
they sent tribute regularly to Ashur.

Other campaigns were directed to the restoration of Assyrian
authority over the small Hurrian states of the upper Tigris area
which he refers to collectively as the land of the Shubari. They
are listed as the land of the Papkhi, Katmukhi, Bushe, Mumme,
Alzi, (A)madani, Nikhani, Alaya, Tepurzi and Purukuzzi.[1] According to the fullest account of these wars,[2] his first attack, in
the same year as the expedition to Mekhru, fell on Katmukhi,
which had been plundering Assyrian territory and carrying off
the inhabitants. Five of its main strongholds were attacked and
captured and their people and property taken to Ashur. Returning to the Kashiari mountain, he advanced against the other
Shubari lands which, alerted by the fate of Katmukhi, had formed
a coalition to oppose him, probably under the leadership of Ekhli-
Teshub of Alzi. After seizing the capital of Purukuzzi, he overpowered four towns in Alzi and six in Amadani, the Diyārbakr
district. Ekhli-Teshub thereupon panicked and fled to Nairi with
members of his family and court while his leaderless troops took
to the hills to save their lives. The resistance of Alzi having
collapsed, Tukulti-Ninurta proceeded to devastate it, sacking 180
towns. Certain texts also mention that the land of the Papkhi
resisted and had to be crushed by force.[3] The reduction of the
Shubari lands brought Assyria important economic and strategic
gains, notably access to the rich and easily workable copper deposits at Ergani Maden, and command of the routes leading
across the Euphrates and Murad Su into central and eastern
Anatolia. In a triumphant summing up of these early campaigns,
Tukulti-Ninurta enumerated the conquered territories in approximately geographical order, beginning in the south-east with lands
on the further bank of the Lesser Zab and ending in the north-
west with the land of the Shubari 'as far as the frontier district
of Nairi and the frontier district of Makan to the Euphrates'.
The reference to Makan shows the confused ideas of the Assyrians about countries beyond their immediate ken. The scribes,
having heard of Magan on the Gulf of Oman as a distant land,

[1] §III, 12, Text 5.     [2] §III, 12, Text 1.     [3] §III, 12, Texts 6, 16, 17.

located it in the unknown territory to the west of Nairi.[1] That subsequently they realized their error is suggested by the fact that in later texts of Tukulti-Ninurta the non-committal phrase 'the frontier district of the totality' is substituted for this passage.

The northern frontier had been re-established and strengthened but beyond it lay the Nairi lands which by border raiding or intrigue with dissident elements could imperil its security. Their rich supplies of metal, cattle and horses were an added incentive to conquest. Their subjection led Tukulti-Ninurta into territory unknown to his predecessors, the mountainous nature of which represented a formidable challenge to the military engineers charged with the task of preparing a passage for troops and chariotry. 'Mighty mountains, a narrow *massif*, whose paths no king had known, I traversed in the triumph of my transcendent might, their highlands I widened(?) with bronze axes, their untrodden paths I made broad.' He claims that his conquests extended as far as the shore of the Upper Sea, either Lake Vān or Lake Urmia. Forty Nairi kings who opposed him in battle were heavily defeated and taken to Ashur with copper chains round their necks but were subsequently released to their lands as tributary vassals. In his titulary Tukulti-Ninurta calls himself 'king of the Nairi lands', but neither he nor his successors ever achieved the permanent subjection of these mountain peoples and in the course of the following centuries repeated Assyrian attacks led to their unification in the kingdom of Urarṭu. In certain texts the account of the Nairi war is followed by the statement that he made Azalzi and Shepardi his frontier, but whether these districts lay in Nairi or elsewhere is unknown.

The Nairi war was followed by the greatest military triumph of Tukulti-Ninurta's career, the defeat and occupation of Babylonia. By the time Kashtiliash IV (1242–1235) succeeded his father, Shagarakti-Shuriash, there had been a change of dynasty in Elam and the danger of invasion from this quarter had receded.[2] Possibly while Tukulti-Ninurta was occupied in the distant north against the Nairi lands, Kashtiliash judged the moment opportune to attack Assyria. The war provoked by this ill-advised action and its disastrous consequences for Babylonia are described by Tukulti-Ninurta,[3] Chronicle P,[4] and an Assyrian epic composed soon after the event.[5] According to the first two sources, Tukulti-Ninurta captured Kashtiliash in battle and took him in chains to Ashur.

---

[1] §III, 11, 9.
[2] See below, pp. 383 ff.
[3] §III, 12, Texts 5, 6, 15, 16, 17.
[4] §III, 12, Text 37.
[5] §IV, 5; §IV, 7; §IV, 15, 116 ff.; §IV, 16, 131 ff.

The Chronicle then states that he returned to Babylon, demolished its fortifications, put the inhabitants to the sword, looted Babylon and the temple E-sagila and carried off the statue of Marduk to Assyria. The epic gives a vivid and more detailed account of the war. Responsibility for its outbreak is firmly placed on the Kassite, who by invading Assyrian territory had broken his treaty with Assyria. Before marching against him, Tukulti-Ninurta read out its terms before Shamash, god of the oath, in order to pin the guilt on his adversary and secure divine sanction and support for his counter-attack. Kashtiliash, having failed to obtain a clear omen, realized that the gods had condemned and abandoned him. Urged on by his troops he nevertheless gave battle, only to turn and flee at the first clash of arms. He withdrew to a distant place but eventually stood to fight, after Tukulti-Ninurta had taunted him with cowardice and boasted of his capture and spoliation of Babylonian cities. A great battle ensued in which Kashtiliash was captured. The epic goes on to describe how Tukulti-Ninurta carried off the treasures of the Kassite king, using them to enrich and embellish the temples of his gods.[1] According to this contemporary or near contemporary account, therefore, the final defeat of Kashtiliash in 1235 was accomplished only after considerable fighting and after Tukulti-Ninurta had seized part of Babylonia. It may also be inferred from the Chronicle that the strongly defended city of Babylon either continued to resist after the capture of Kashtiliash or rebelled later, so that a further campaign was needed for its reduction. The subjection of the whole country as far as the Persian Gulf was then completed and its citizens were deported to Assyria in considerable numbers.[2] He removed from the control of Babylonia 38 districts which were of particular strategic and commerical value to Assyria. They included Mari, Khana, Rapiqu and the hill of the Akhlamu, which gave him command of the middle Euphrates, and Arrapkha, terminal of the trade route leading through Sulaimaniyah to Iran. Sikkuri and Sapani lay in the mountains south-east of Assyria, while Turna-suma and Ulaiash were on the Babylonian–Elamite border. The location of the remainder is unknown.

Having occupied Babylonia, Tukulti-Ninurta assumed its royal titulary, styling himself 'king of Karduniash, king of Sumer and Akkad, king of Sippar and Babylon, king of Tilmun and

[1] They included a seal of Shagarakti-Shuriash which was later returned to Babylon, only to be carried off once again by Sennacherib, §III, 12, Text 29. For a list of booty from Babylonia see §III, 10, 123 f.

[2] §III, 10, 121 f.

Meluhha'.[1] Because of ambiguities in the historical sources, however, there is considerable uncertainty as to the duration and character of his administration. According to the Chronicle, he appointed governors and ruled the country for seven years. Afterwards the Akkadian nobles of Babylonia rebelled and placed on the throne Adad-shuma-uṣur,[2] a son of Kashtiliash.[3] However, the name of Tukulti-Ninurta does not appear in the Babylonian King List A, which between Kashtiliash and Adad-shuma-uṣur gives Enlil-nādin-shumi and Kadashman-Kharbe II, both of whom ruled for 'one year six months', and Adad-shuma-iddina, who reigned six years. Thus it appears to assign a total of nine, not seven, years to the interval between Kashtiliash and Adad-shuma-uṣur. Furthermore, the three successors of Kashtiliash can hardly be identified with the governors (*šaknūtu*) of the Chronicle since it is unlikely that kings would have been so designated, and that they actually exercised the kingship is confirmed by documents from Ur dated by the accession years of Kadashman-Kharbe and Adad-shuma-iddina.[4]

This evidence has been interpreted to mean either that the seven-year period of Assyrian rule is omitted from the King List or that it is represented by the three successors of Kashtiliash. According to the first solution, which is that adopted in the chronological scheme of this *History*, Tukulti-Ninurta administered the whole of Babylonia directly through governors for seven years (1234–1228).[5] At the end of this period Enlil-nādin-shumi rebelled and seized the southern part of the country including Nippur, possession of which entitled him to recognition in the royal canon. The Assyrians, however, retained Babylon and the north until they were driven out by the revolt which brought Adad-shuma-uṣur (1218–1189) to power. Therefore their rule, although it weakened and contracted, lasted not seven but sixteen years. Against this reconstruction it may be pointed out that Enlil-nādin-shumi, far from being kept out of Babylon by the Assyrians, is attested there by tablets dated during his reign. Also there is no evidence in the Kassite period or later that possession of Nippur secured recognition in the royal canon.[6] According to the alternative solution, Tukulti-Ninurta governed Babylonia indirectly through vassal rulers who appear in the King List instead of their overlord, presumably because they had been duly invested

---

[1] For Babylonian contacts with Bahrein and Failaka in the Kassite period, see A, 1, *passim*; A, 9.
[2] For the reading of the name, see A, 3, 233 ff.   [3] §III, 1, 151.   [4] §I, 11, 19.
[5] *C.A.H.* I³, pt. I, p. 199; §I, 11, 18 ff.       [6] A, 5, 311, n. 125; 313.

with the kingship. It has to be assumed on this interpretation
that the governors of the Chronicle were Assyrian officials appointed by Tukulti-Ninurta to supervise and control these puppets.
Numerous attempts have been made to resolve the difficulty presented by the apparent discrepancy between the Chronicle and
the Canon as to the duration of Assyrian rule. If the reigns of the
three immediate successors of Kashtiliash were consecutive, so
that they covered a period of nine years, then it is possible that the
Chronicle reckoned the seven years of Assyrian rule not from the
defeat of Kashtiliash but from the occupation of Babylon. The
eighteen-month reign of Enlil-nādin-shumi and the first six
months of that of Kadashman-Kharbe would then fall in the interval between these two events and the latter king, who remained
on the throne after the conquest of Babylon, and also Adad-shuma-
iddina were Assyrian vassals.[1] However, this may be a case in
which reigns listed as consecutive in the royal canon in fact over-
lapped and the seven years of the Chronicle may therefore be a
correct figure for the period between Kashtiliash and Adad-
shuma-uṣur.[2] If so, one possible reconstruction is that Enlil-
nādin-shumi was recognized by Tukulti-Ninurta as his vassal
immediately after the defeat of Kashtiliash. The Kassite, Kadashman-Kharbe, however, continued to resist in the south, being
recognized at Ur, and, when Enlil-nādin-shumi was defeated by
Kidin-Khutran of Elam, instigated a revolt in Babylon. Tukulti-
Ninurta thereupon returned to Babylonia, sacked the capital,
brought the southern districts under his control and installed
Adad-shuma-iddina in the kingship.[3]

Another suggestion is that the 'one year six months' of the
King List is not to be taken literally as 'eighteen months' but is
rather to be understood as 'one year (that is) six months'. If this
meant that the combined reigns of Enlil-nādin-shumi and Kadashman-Kharbe amounted to no more than a year, then the King List
and the Chronicle would be in agreement. However, one would
expect the King List to reckon in official regnal years, and this
would extend the period between Kashtiliash and Adad-shuma-
uṣur to eight years. A further difficulty is that economic texts
from Ur indicate that Kadashman-Kharbe ruled for at least
fourteen months. In fact, since his reign extended into two
Nisans, the King List should have credited him with two regnal
years. It could be that it was defective or that its calculations were
confused by the Elamite removal of Enlil-nādin-shumi or by a

---

[1] §III, 12, 41; §III, 6, 41 f.          [2] §III, 8, 286 f., 356.
[3] For a further discussion of the problem see below, pp. 387 ff.

struggle for the throne between Enlil-nādin-shumi and Kadashman-Kharbe.[1]

Whatever the status of Enlil-nādin-shumi and his two successors, their reigns represent a period of Babylonian weakness of
which the Elamites were able to take advantage. Kidin-Khutran
raided Nippur and Dēr, massacring or deporting the inhabitants,
drove away Enlil-nādin-shumi and ended his rule. Later, in the
time of Adad-shuma-iddina, he captured Isin and advanced as far
as Marad, west of Nippur.

The defeat of Kashtiliash established Tukulti-Ninurta as the
outstanding military leader of the thirteenth century. Ability on
the battlefield, however, is not necessarily matched by political
vision or personal courage by the strength of character to withstand the lure of victory and power. In retrospect his occupation
of Babylonia must be judged to have been against the real interests
of his country. Admittedly the temptation was great. For over
a century the Babylonians had contested the establishment of
Assyrian control over the Zagros area. That, so long as they
remained independent, they would continue to do so was inevitable. From the earliest historical period the eastern hills had
been their main source of supply for the metal, stone and building
timber which they themselves lacked. Assyria, by diverting the
trade of this area to its own markets, was striking at the basis of
their economy and threatening their existence as a political force
of any consequence. This was a situation no Babylonian king
could accept. Nevertheless, Tukulti-Ninurta would have been
better advised to continue the policy of his predecessors who had
held the Babylonians in check by limited campaigns and the
establishment of a favourable southern frontier. The main economic motive underlying Assyrian expansion and determining
its direction was the quest for raw materials. These Babylonia
could not provide and the heavy and continuous military effort
required for its occupation diverted Assyrian energies and resources from the task of securing them elsewhere. Weakened
by over-extension of its forces, Assyria lost Babylonia, suffered
reverses on other fronts, and fell into a condition of internal
disorder.

Between Tukulti-Ninurta and Tudkhaliash IV of Khatti relations were tense and at times deteriorated into open hostility.
The customary letter of congratulation sent by Tudkhaliash to
Tukulti-Ninurta at his accession was conciliatory in tone.[2] After
paying tribute to Shalmaneser, who had become a great king

---

[1] A, 2, 63 ff.        [2] G, 9, XXIII, 92, XXIII, 103; §III, 5.

and defeated great kings, he exhorted him to protect his father's frontiers and offered assistance should any of his subjects rise in rebellion. At the same time he addressed letters to two high Assyrian officials, one being the chancellor, Baba-akha-iddina, who had previously held office under Adad-nīrāri and Shalmaneser.[1] He assured them of his friendship for Tukulti-Ninurta and called on them to protect their lord. News had, however, reached him that Tukulti-Ninurta was planning to attack Papankhi, the land of the Papkhi of the Assyrian records, and he warned the chancellor of the dangers and hazards of an expedition into this mountainous country. This concern for the safety and reputation of the young prince can hardly be taken at its face value but must rather be understood as a polite intimation that Khatti maintained its interest in Papkhi and other lands of the Shubari and that an Assyrian attack in this quarter would be regarded as an unfriendly act.

Not only did Tukulti-Ninurta disregard this warning, since he subdued the lands of the Shubari, including Papkhi; he also crossed the Euphrates and, according to his account, carried off eight *sar* (28,800) Hittite subjects. This raid heads the list of expeditions undertaken in his accession and first regnal years but their order is not necessarily chronological. Even though the number of captives was certainly greatly exaggerated, it appears, as reported, to have been a major operation. However, if this was indeed the case, it is strange that it is mentioned only in inscriptions composed after the conquest of Babylonia, more than a decade after the event. There is no reference to it in the detailed report of the early campaigns. It is possible, therefore, that Tukulti-Ninurta, triumphant and self-confident after his Babylonian victory and infuriated at the hostile actions of the Hittites, of which an example is cited below, for his own self-glorification and the belittlement of his rivals, magnified what had been a relatively minor incident into a major victory. It may well be referred to in a document from Ras Shamra.[2] In this Tudkhaliash absolved Ammishtamru of Ugarit from the obligation to provide soldiers and chariots for a war with Assyria then in progress. This exemption would not have been given if it had been a major conflict and, since Ini-Teshub of Carchemish conveyed the decision of Tudkhaliash to Ammishtamru, it may be inferred that it was a localized frontier clash affecting his territory. Possibly it was provoked by border raiding, a case of which was

---

[1] G, 5, 75 f.; §III, 2, 3 ff.; §III, 13.
[2] §III, 4, 149 ff., see above, p. 144.

the occasion of a letter probably sent by Tukulti-Ninurta to Tud-khaliash.[1] Replying to a complaint by the Hittite that Assyrian subjects were continuously raiding his land, he strenuously denied the charge, asserting that not so much as a length of timber had been removed from Hittite territory. Whether Tudkhaliash was goaded into retaliation by this war, the reconquest of the lands of the Shubari or some other action on the part of Assyria cannot be said, but he determined on a measure which was an open declaration of his hostile intent and a defiance of Assyrian designs on Syria. In a treaty with his vassal, Shaushga-muwash of Amurru, the Syrian was not only called on to furnish aid in the event of an Assyrian attack, but was obliged to institute a trade blockade against Assyria: 'As the king of Assyria is the enemy of My Sun, so may he also be your enemy. Your merchants shall not go to Assyria, you shall not allow his merchants in your land, neither shall they pass through your land. If, however, one of them comes into your land then seize him and send him to My Sun. As soon as the king of Assyria begins war, if then My Sun calls up troops and chariots...so do you call up your troops and chariots and despatch them.'[2] Although direct evidence for Assyrian trade with Syria at this period is slight,[3] access to its commercial centres was certainly of considerable importance and such economic sanctions, if widely applied, must have hit Assyria hard. Since, in another section of the treaty, Tudkhaliash refers to the king of Babylonia as his equal, the treaty was concluded before the defeat and deposition of Kashtiliash.[4]

After the capture of Babylonia an Assyrian bid for control of Syria must have seemed imminent, and the interests most plainly challenged, if that had occurred, would have been those of the Hittite monarch. However, the threat never materialized. Years of strenuous campaigning followed by the occupation of Babylonia had so overtaxed the resources of Assyria that it was incapable of the sustained effort necessary to hold its conquests. The Babylonian wars are the last to be recorded by Tukulti-Ninurta. After he had reigned for another twenty-five years or so, 'Ashur-nāṣir-apli, his son, and the nobles of Assyria, rebelled against him and tore him from his throne. In Kār-Tukulti-Ninurta in a house they shut him up and slew him with the sword.'[5] That military defeats and territorial losses were a

---

[1] G, 9, iii, 73; §iii, 12, Text 36.
[2] G, 9, xxiii, 1; G, 6, 272 f.; §iii, 9, 320 ff.      [3] §iii, 13, 38.
[4] For a dating of this treaty to the time of Shalmaneser I, see above ch. xxiv, sect. iv.      [5] §iii, 12, Text 37; see below, ch. xxxi, sect. iii.

chief cause of this violent deed is certain. Although the only
countries known to have seceded are Babylonia and the small
states of Sikkuri and Sappani in the eastern hills,[1] a prayer of
Tukulti-Ninurta to the god Ashur suggests that revolt was widespread.[2] In it he speaks of the ring of evil with which all the
lands surrounded his city Ashur. Those whom he had helped and
protected threatened Assyria, and his enemies plotted its destruction. It may be assumed that the peoples of the eastern and
northern hills were among the rebels, while one of the enemies
may have been the Hittite, Shuppiluliumash II, who, perhaps
when Tukulti-Ninurta was still alive, seems to have made an
unsuccessful attempt to regain Upper Mesopotamia.[3] It can
hardly be believed that Tukulti-Ninurta abandoned his conquests
without a struggle, and the absence of royal records must be
interpreted as a sign not of inactivity but of military defeat.

Nevertheless, in view of his long reign of thirty-seven years, age
may in time have diminished his energy and impaired his power
of decision, and the hope that under a younger man the fortunes
of Assyria could be retrieved doubtless furnished an additional
motive for his murder. To what extent this was also prompted by
discontent with his internal policy must, in the absence of positive
evidence, remain a matter of speculation. It may well be that the
economic burdens placed on the Assyrian people had become
intolerable. Not only had the needs of the army to be met; men
and materials were also deflected from productive uses for the
grandiose building schemes of the king which culminated after
the defeat of Kashtiliash in the foundation of a new royal city at
Kār-Tukulti-Ninurta, about 3 km. upstream from Ashur on the
left bank of the Tigris. While prisoners of war certainly provided
much of the immense labour force required for these projects and
booty and tribute supplied many of the materials, a heavy contribution was undoubtedly exacted from the Assyrians themselves.[4]
The economic situation must also have been adversely affected
by the political and military reverses. The Syrian markets had

[1] §III, 12, Text 38c.   [2] §IV, 4.
[3] G, 8, IV, 14; §III, 6, 5 f.; the Middle Assyrian occupation at Tell er-Rimah,
13 km. south of Tell 'Afar, may have ended about this time; the latest eponyms attested in the economic texts belong to the early part of the reign of Tukulti-Ninurta.
Since it lay on the edge of the cultivated zone it may have been deserted because of
the inability of the government to provide security against the Bedawin, as happened
in this area under the Ottoman régime. See A, 14, 66, 75; A, 15, 130; A, 16, 71, 91.
[4] After the Babylonian war building work was in progress at Kār-Tukulti-Ninurta
and on the defences of Ashur, the New Palace and the Shalmaneser Palace. For
texts recording large deliveries of bricks see §III, 8, 112.

been closed by Tudkhaliash and if, as seems likely, Tukulti-Ninurta in his later years lost control of the Zagros districts and those on the northern frontier, Assyria was cut off from important sources of raw materials.[1] The further suggestion has been made that, fascinated by the superior civilization of Babylonia, he introduced some of its cult practices into Assyria, gave increased importance to Marduk, and raised Babylonians and Kassites to important state positions, so falling foul of the Assyrian nobility and priesthood.[2] More recent research has indicated that by the fourteenth and thirteenth centuries, Assyria had assimilated many Babylonian cultic elements. There is, however, very little source material for the Middle Assyrian period, and it is therefore difficult to assess the extent to which this trend was intensified by the conquest of the south. The statue of Marduk carried off from Babylon by Tukulti-Ninurta, which had political as well as religious significance, played a central rôle in certain ritual processions in Ashur.[3] The assumption that its possession led to an increase in the importance of the existing local cult of Marduk has, however, been queried on the grounds that an analysis of theophorous names does not show any significant increase in the element 'Marduk' until the twelfth century.[4] It is indeed possible that, in the thirteenth century, the cult of Enlil of Nippur exercised more influence than that of Marduk of Babylon. This is suggested by the fact that in inscriptions referring to his rebuilding of the Ashur temple, many of the names used for the building by Shalmaneser allude to the shrine of Enlil at Nippur.[5] The evidence for the employment of Babylonians in the administration at present rests mainly on a Middle Assyrian eponymous official who bore the Kassite name Kashtiliash.

Whatever hopes for a speedy recovery of national fortunes lay behind the assassination of Tukulti-Ninurta they were not realized, for, although Assyria retained control of Khanigalbat and the districts immediately adjoining the eastern frontier, the decline of its political and military power continued under his immediate successors.

[1] For evidence of trade in tin from Nairi in the latter part of the reign of Shalmaneser and early in that of Tukulti-Ninurta, see A, 21; A, 27.
[2] §III, 10, 109 f.
[3] A, 25, 52 ff.
[4] G, 5, 98 ff.
[5] A, 25, 35, n. 13, 151 f.

## IV. LITERATURE

The military triumphs of the fourteenth and thirteenth centuries acted as a powerful stimulus to Assyrian literary activity. The desire to record and perpetuate the memory of victory and conquest led to the elaboration of campaign reports in the royal inscriptions and to the composition of epics and also, perhaps, of chronicles. At the same time, closer contact with countries with a developed literary tradition, in particular Babylonia, greatly enriched the resources of literature and learning at the command of the Assyrian scribes.

The official inscriptions with historical content revived and developed a literary form which had arisen in north Mesopotamia some five centuries earlier. Its basic scheme was that of the traditional Babylonian building inscription, the chief elements of which consisted of the royal name, titulary and epithets, an account of the building operation, sometimes accompanied by a brief reference to the historical circumstances of the dedication, and finally curses against those who damaged the foundation document. In the nineteenth century this scheme was adapted to include a narrative of military events. In a text of Iakhdunlim of Mari, recording the foundation of a temple to Shamash, the circumstances of the dedication were expanded into a lengthy description of his expedition to the Mediterranean.[1] Although formally part of the introduction to the building report, it constituted the principal feature of the inscription. Whether this type of historical writing first arose in Mari cannot be said, but that it was practised in Assyria is shown by a text of Shamshi-Adad I (1813–1781).[2] Admittedly this is markedly inferior in construction and literary style to that of Iakhdunlim but it may not represent the best of which the Assyrian scribes were capable. Shamshi-Adad, as ruler of Mari after the murder of Iakhdunlim, was certainly acquainted with the achievements of its scribal school and if they were indeed superior to those of Assyria would, one imagines, have sought to emulate them. No historical texts of this type are known for the period between Shamshi-Adad and Enlil-nīrāri (1329–1320). This is hardly surprising since, during the period of Assyrian political decline after Shamshi-Adad, occasions for their composition must have been rare. Nevertheless, the reappearance of this distinctive type of historical writing in the fourteenth century indicates continuity of tradition. If it had indeed died out in the preceding centuries, then the Middle Assyrian kings may have gone back

[1] §IV, 3.  [2] G, 2, 23 ff.; G, 11, 16 f.

for their models to the earlier period of Assyrian greatness under Shamshi-Adad.

In their inscriptions the historical report takes two forms. In the first, which is not attested earlier, the royal epithets are elaborated to describe the king as conqueror of specific peoples, lands or cities, a device which enabled the scribe to summarize, sometimes at considerable length, the results achieved by war. It did not, however, permit a detailed narrative account of campaigns. This required treatment in a separate section, the position of which within the body of the text was still the subject of some experimentation. Whereas Adad-nīrāri, like Iakhdunlim, placed the narrative of his wars against Khanigalbat immediately before the building report,[1] Shalmaneser inserted his historical passage as a parenthesis in the collection of royal epithets.[2] The latter solution, however, was obviously unsatisfactory, for the clear construction of the inscription was lost, and Tukulti-Ninurta reverted to the more logical scheme of his grandfather.

When conquests are summarized in the royal epithets, their order usually appears to be geographical rather than chronological, but in the narrative passages campaigns of different years seem normally to be listed in temporal sequence, although the expeditions of any one year may be given in variant order in different editions. However, at this period no clear distinction was made between the annual campaigns, and precise dating was given only in the case of wars of the accession year or accession and first regnal years.[3] Others which were certainly later in date either follow these directly without any temporal indication or are introduced by vague phrases such as 'afterwards' or 'in those days'. A clear annalistic form was not achieved until the time of Tiglath-pileser I (1115–1077) when, although annual campaigns were not numbered or dated, they were separated by lyrical passages in praise of the king. A fragmentary text listing the wars of Arik-dēn-ili, thought to be the earliest example of an annalistic royal inscription, can now be identified as a chronicle.[4] It is similar in construction to, and perhaps of the same date as, chronicle fragments dealing with the reigns of Enlil-nīrāri and Tiglath-pileser I, which were probably composed shortly after the latter's death.[5] In this type of document the narrative is in the third person and the events recorded are divided by lines into sections which presumably correspond to regnal years. In compiling the record of previous

[1] §1, 14.  [2] G, 2, 110 ff.; G, 11, 25 f.; §IV, 2, 57 f.
[3] §IV, 13, 26 ff.  [4] G, 2, 51 ff.; G, 11, 25 f.; §IV, 11.
[5] §IV, 14, 133 f.; §IV, 19; §IV, 20, 115.

reigns, however, the eleventh-century chronicler must have had earlier historical sources at his disposal and it is therefore possible that chronicles were already being composed in the fourteenth and thirteenth centuries. In view of the discovery of the Iakhdun-lim inscription and the identification of the Arik-dēn-ili text as a chronicle, it may be doubted whether the historical literature of the Hittites exercised any significant influence on that of Assyria. The inclusion of campaign reports in the building inscription represents a revival of an earlier, north Mesopotamian tradition and the origin of the annalistic form may be seen in the tentative attempts of the thirteenth-century scribes to arrange events in temporal sequence.

Considerable progress was made during the thirteenth century towards the development of an appropriate literary style for official inscriptions. Particularly in the adulatory phrases applied to the king and in the narrative passages, the prose was increasingly enriched by the introduction of new expressions and formulae and the use of metaphor and simile. From the time of Shalmaneser the recital of military events was enlivened by descriptive detail of the difficulties encountered and overcome by the army. Other elements, which subsequently became standard in Assyrian royal texts, are found in his reign, notably the emphasis on the religious character of wars, which were undertaken at the command of the gods and won with their aid, and the description of the fearful punishments meted out to those who by rebelling had sinned against the gods. In the royal titulary, increasing emphasis is placed on the monarchical and more secular aspects of kingship. In the Old and Middle Assyrian periods, the formal title most commonly employed was 'vicar of the god Ashur' (*išš(i)ak* ᵈ*Aššur*); only Shamshi-Adad I deviated from the norm by styling himself 'king of the totality'. In the fourteenth century, however, Arik-dēn-ili assumed the titles 'king of Assyria' and 'mighty king'. To these Adad-nīrāri added 'king of the totality'. Military epithets were also introduced during his reign, as was that of 'city founder'. The lauding of the king as conqueror reached its climax under Tukulti-Ninurta. In addition to the titles which refer specifically to his rule over Babylonia, there are numerous more general and grandiose epithets, such as 'king of the four quarters', 'king of kings', 'lord of lords', 'prince of princes', 'sun of all the peoples'. The new developments in the royal titulary during the fourteenth and thirteenth centuries reflect not only the recovery and expansion of Assyrian military power but also a fundamental change in political concepts. The stress is now on the whole land of Ashur, rather than the city. To this period must be attributed the growth of a national consciousness which Assyria was to retain, even during periods of decline, until its destruction in 612 B.C.[1]

A branch of Sumero-Akkadian literature attested for the first time in Assyria is the epic, of which two examples are known, both inspired by wars against Babylonia. The first, of which little survives, celebrated the victory of Adad-nīrāri over Nazimaruttash.[2] The second commemorated the defeat of Kashtiliash IV by Tukulti-Ninurta, by whom it may have been commissioned.[3] When complete it must have consisted of not less than seven hundred lines. It describes in detail the events which led up to the outbreak of hostilities, the course of the struggle and the ultimate triumph of Tukulti-Ninurta. Its central motif is the king as hero. His praises are sung in hymnal passages and his courage, his might and his righteous behaviour are extolled and contrasted with the cowardice and perfidy of his opponent. In the treatment of this heroic theme, the Assyrian scribe shows a sure command of poetic form and narrative style. The attention of the listener is held by a wealth of striking imagery and by variation in the character and pace of the story, lyrical passages, direct speech and graphic accounts of action being skilfully alternated. This composition, as also the prayer of Tukulti-Ninurta, which is bilingual in Akkadian and dialectal Sumerian,[4] attests the growth of a native literature which, although inspired by Babylonian prototypes, was distinctively Assyrian in outlook and style.

According to the epic, Tukulti-Ninurta, like Ashurbanipal, looted the libraries of Babylonia and carried off their tablet collections to enrich those of Assyria, which prior to his reign were probably limited in extent. His booty included incantations, prayers, omens and medical texts, some of which are doubtless among the Babylonian tablets found in the remains of the library of Tiglath-pileser I.[5]

## V. ARCHITECTURE AND THE ARTS

The prosperity of Assyria in the thirteenth century is shown by the greatly increased building activity. New towns were founded at Kalkhu and Kār-Tukulti-Ninurta, and at Ashur there was an impressive amount of new building in addition to the routine

[1] §IV, 2, 26 ff.; A, 24; A, 5, 303 ff.
[2] §IV, 20.      [3] §IV, 5; §IV, 7; §IV, 15, 116 ff.; §IV, 16, 131 ff.; §IV, 17.
[4] §IV, 4, 40 ff.      [5] §IV, 18, 200; see below, pp. 477 f.

maintenance of existing structures. Although excavation has revealed no major architectural innovation there was an interest in building methods employed outside Assyria, for Adad-nīrāri removed the wooden columns of the palace of Nakhur in Khanigalbat to his own residence at Ashur, whence they were later transferred first to the 'New Palace' and then to Kār-Tukulti-Ninurta by his grandson.[1]

The construction of new temples, palaces and defence works at Ashur is recorded in the royal inscriptions and attested by excavation, although in almost every case the walls had been demolished to the foundations by later builders. Both Adad-nīrāri and Tukulti-Ninurta repaired and strengthened the fortifications.[2] On the vulnerable western side of the town, Tukulti-Ninurta excavated a dry ditch beyond the outer wall, making it 20 m. in width and 15 m. in depth, with almost vertical sides. It extended from the Tabira gate at least as far as the beginning of the New Town,[3] and was crossed by ramps leading to the Tabira and west gates. Commanded by the battlements of the outer wall and too wide to be easily spanned by storming ladders, it presented a formidable obstacle to attack. To protect the river bank against erosion, Adad-nīrāri reconstructed the quay wall along the Tigris with massive limestone blocks set in bitumen mortar and faced with baked brick.[4]

The temple of Ashur, rebuilt by Shamshi-Adad I and kept in repair by later kings, including Adad-nīrāri, was destroyed by fire in the time of Shalmaneser. In rebuilding it, he adhered faithfully to the original lay-out but added the south-west court and also made certain alterations in the cult room and elsewhere.[5] A rebuilding of the Sin-Shamash temple is probably to be attributed to Tukulti-Ninurta and here also the earlier shrine was reproduced.[6] However, in a new temple for Ishtar, now called *Aššurītu*, Ishtar of Ashur, Tukulti-Ninurta not only departed from the plan of the archaic sanctuary, which he demolished, but re-sited it slightly to the south-west.[7] The chief innovation was the addition of a subordinate, single-roomed sanctuary dedicated to the goddess Dinītu (= Ishtar). Although joined structurally, there was no communication between the two shrines, each having its own towered entrance and paved processional way. The re-

---

[1] §v, 26; A, 12, 534 f.     [2] §v, 1; §v, 5, 119 ff.; A, 10.
[3] §v, 1, 124 ff.; §v, 5, 120; §iii, 12, commentary on Text 18.
[4] §v, 1, 149 ff.; §v, 5, 119 f.     [5] §v, 11, 37 ff.; §v, 5, 118 f.; A, 25, 15 f.
[6] §v, 11, 82 ff.
[7] §v, 4, 15 ff.; §v, 5, 108 ff.; §iii, 12, Texts 7, 8, 9 and commentary.

mains of this double temple were exceptionally well preserved, the
mud brick superstructure standing in places to a height of over
2 m. It provides welcome information on the appearance and cult
arrangements of religious buildings of the thirteenth century.
The exterior wall faces were ornamented in Babylonian style with
groups of pilasters and stepped niches and on the evidence of
Middle Assyrian seal designs it may be assumed that they terminated in crenelations. The cult room of the Ishtar shrine, entered
through a large chamber, was of imposing dimensions (32·50 m. ×
8·70 m.). Almost half was occupied by a high platform, set against
the short end, with an alcove for the cult statue and an approach
stairway with stepped balustrades. Five limestone slabs set into
the floor in front of the entrance may have supported a cult
emblem and the posts of a baldachin. The numerous intact
foundation deposits from the temple, which include inscribed
tablets of Tukulti-Ninurta, of limestone, lead, gold and silver,
provide valuable information on the ceremony of deposition, to
which allusion is made by Shalmaneser.[1] Tukulti-Ninurta also
completed the temple of (An)nunaittu, begun by his father,
but its location is unknown. At Nineveh the temple of Ishtar,
which had been damaged by an earthquake, was restored by
Shalmaneser and later renovated by Tukulti-Ninurta.

Repairs were effected by all three kings to the 'Old Palace'
of Ashur between the Anu-Adad temple and the great zikkurrat,[2]
but perhaps because it had proved inadequate as the administrative centre of the enlarged kingdom Tukulti-Ninurta early in his
reign began the construction of a royal residence between the
Tabira gate and the Anu-Adad temple.[3] Of this 'New Palace'
only part of the mud-brick terrace and a few foundation walls
remain but its scale may be judged from the fact that the area
cleared and levelled for the platform was c. 40,000 sq. m. in extent.
Between the zikkurrat and the Ashur temple Shalmaneser built
another palace, which was renovated by his son. It is probably
represented by the remains of a monumental building with inscribed paving bricks of both rulers.[4] Its dimensions could not
be determined but in view of the limited area available it must
have been considerably smaller than the 'Old Palace'.[5]

[1] G, 2, 123; G, 11, 41.  [2] §v, 23, 13 f.; §v, 5, 108.
[3] §v, 23, 30 ff.; §v, 5, 115 ff.; §iii, 12, 6, commentary on Text 1.
[4] §v, 23, 28 f.; §iii, 12, 14, commentary on Text 6; A, 25, 13 f.
[5] There was the same close connexion of palace and temple in other Assyrian
cities, e.g., Khorsabad. Annual visits by the gods to the royal palace are mentioned
by Adad-nīrāri and Tukulti-Ninurta; see A, 25, 14, 165.

Adad-nīrāri describes himself as a 'city founder' but it is not known to which town he refers. According to Ashurnaṣirpal II, Kalkhu (O.T. Calah, modern Nimrūd), on the left bank of the Tigris 22 miles south of Nineveh, was founded by Shalmaneser. His choice of site must have been determined by the need for an administrative and possibly also a military base between Ashur and Nineveh but of its character and function at this period nothing is known. There is no reference to it in his extant inscriptions and because of the overburden of the Late Assyrian city it remains virtually unexcavated. Since in the time of Tukulti-Ninurta an official of Kalkhu had command of 350 Kassites deported from Babylonia, building may have continued here after the death of Shalmaneser.[1] Following the victory over Babylonia, however, the interests and energies of his son were undoubtedly concentrated on the construction of Kār-Tukulti-Ninurta. Here he laid out a new town defended by stout mud brick fortifications and dominated by a zikkurrat and temple of Ashur and a royal palace.[2] A canal was dug to bring water to the town, taxes on the use of which provided for the sacrifices in the temple. He describes it as 'a great cult city (*maḥāzu rabû*), the dwelling of my majesty' but the reasons which prompted him to move his residence from Ashur must remain a matter of speculation. Was it simply the desire to give concrete form to his enhanced prestige as king of both Assyria and Babylonia or, in view of the fact that he had already founded a new palace at Ashur, work on which was still in progress, should some additional motive be sought? Had he indeed become 'an incalculable despot, afraid for the safety of his person', and was he driven to leave Ashur because of the hostility of its citizens?[3] That opposition developed in the latter part of his reign is obvious from his assassination, but whether one is justified in assuming that it existed and had assumed dangerous proportions at the time Kār-Tukulti-Ninurta was founded is questionable. To judge from the historical information given in the building inscriptions, work on the town seems to have begun after the defeat of Kashtiliash but before the subjection of the borderlands of Babylonia and possibly even prior to the capture of Babylon, that is to say at a moment when one would expect the prestige, authority and popularity of the king to have stood high. Of earlier unrest there is no evidence.

Although Kār-Tukulti-Ninurta was still inhabited in the eighth century B.C. it lost its importance after the murder of its founder.[4]

[1] §III, 10, 122.  [2] §v, 5, 122 ff.; §III, 12, 24, commentary on Text 15.
[3] §III, 10, 109 ff.  [4] §v, 26, 160, n. 3.

By the time of Tiglath-pileser I its gods had been moved to Ashur and it may be doubted whether any attempt was made to keep its public buildings in repair. Of the royal palace, which stood on a high mud-brick platform near the Tigris, little has survived, but fragments of painted wall plaster show that its interior decoration was elaborate and colourful.[1] The designs, which began at eye level above a bitumen dado and a band of plain red, were composed of rectangular compartments of varying size and shape, containing such motives as gazelles or griffins flanking a stylized tree, a device popular on contemporary seals, the sacred tree, rosettes, palmettes and flowers. The division of the design into compartments, each with a self-contained motive, is similar to that of the wall paintings of the fifteenth-century palace at Nuzi,[2] but although this points to continuity of tradition there is a complete change in the colour scheme: instead of the muted pink, red and grey tones of Nuzi, the predominant colours at Kār-Tukulti-Ninurta were the clear red and blue which remained characteristic of Assyrian mural art. It is possible, as suggested by Andrae,[3] that the designs represented or were inspired by woven wall hangings made up of patterned rectangles, like carpets sculptured in stone at Nineveh and Khorsabad which also have a fringe of buds and flowers, very similar to the border of one of the Kār-Tukulti-Ninurta wall paintings.[4] In this connexion it is of interest that an inventory from Kār-Tukulti-Ninurta describes two woven carpets, on one of which the design included a pomegranate tree and bouquetin, while the other has scenes representing respectively men and animals, towns and towers, and apparently three figures of the king.[5] The design of the first suggests a central panel. On the second the motives could have filled rectangles, as on the tapestry of the fifth century from Pazyryk, or been disposed in borders, as on a carpet from the same site.[6] As in the Anu-Adad temple at Ashur, the zikkurrat and temple of Ashur formed a single complex. The temple lay directly against the eastern face of the tower, into the brickwork of which was set the deep cult niche, so that Ashur in his epiphany issued directly from the mountain. Symbols of the other seven great gods associated with the temple may have stood in wall niches in one of the larger

---

[1] §v, 2, 11 ff.  [2] §v, 25, pls. 128, 129.  [3] §v, 2, 16.
[4] A. H. Layard, *Monuments of Nineveh*, 2nd series, pl. 184; G. Loud and C. B. Altman, *Khorsabad*, II (*O.I.P.* 40), pl. 48.
[5] §v, 12, 307, col. III, 27–38.
[6] R. D. Barnett, 'The World's Oldest Persian Carpet.' In *Ill. Ldn. News*, 14 July 1953, 69 ff., figs. 4, 10.

subsidiary chambers. Whether the statue of Marduk carried off from Babylon was placed in this temple is unknown. As there were no traces of stairs or ramps giving access to the tower it may have been approached by a bridge thrown across from a small structure of curious plan opposite the western face or more probably from the roof of the temple. The number of stages could not be determined but zikkurrats depicted on Middle Assyrian seals have four or five.

The royal palaces and temples were certainly lavishly furnished with the finest and most costly objects which the workshops of Assyria could produce, but of their contents little has survived. The only branch of art adequately represented is the glyptic, known mainly from seal impressions on tablets from Ashur and Tell Fakhariyah in Khanigalbat belonging to the reigns of Shalmaneser and Tukulti-Ninurta.[1] The seal designs show a further development of the specifically Assyrian style which arose at the end of the fifteenth century, and at Ashur, although not at Fakhariyah, Mitannian seals disappear, except for a few re-used earlier pieces. With the possible exception of a ploughing scene, no new themes were introduced but the mythical contest of heroes, animals and demons now predominates. It is depicted either in the old, static heraldic group or in a free spacious composition, the finest examples of which rank among the masterpieces of Assyrian art. This free design, which is also characterized by the introduction of landscape and a realistic treatment of human and animal forms, appears in both Assyria and Babylonia in the fourteenth century and is curiously reminiscent of Akkadian art of the third millennium.

Since no Assyrian seal impressions can be certainly dated to the half century between Ashur-uballit I and Shalmaneser I, it is not possible to say how much progress was made during this period. Babylonian seal designs belonging to the reigns of Kurigalzu II and Nazimaruttash are, however, markedly superior in quality and vitality to those of Ashur-uballit and there may well have been a parallel development in Assyria. As compared to the seals of Ashur-uballit those from the reigns of Shalmaneser and his son show a striking advance in execution and artistic concepts. There is a much surer feeling for balance in design and the basic contest theme is enriched by the introduction of new participants, both actual and imaginary: the horse and winged horse, the ostrich and the winged, human-headed ibex. The hero appears as a hunter, armed with bow, spear, axe or dagger, stalking his quarry, usually

[1] §v, 15; §v, 14, 69 ff.

a cervoid, or fighting lions, griffins and griffin demons, sometimes in defence of their prey. He may be naked but more often is clad in a kilt with pendent tassels, over which he may wear a long robe. Other scenes depict demons and animals engaged in single combat, the predator and his victim, the latter sometimes endeavouring to protect its young or some smaller weaker creature. These contests are set in the open; birds of prey hover in the air and natural surroundings are indicated by the scale-pattern mountain, plants and trees, a bush with a globular crown and crooked trunk being especially characteristic.

In the portrayal of men and animals there is a strong tendency towards realism. Anatomical details, in particular musculature, are finely observed and rendered and the characterization of each animal is both sensitive and forceful. The fighting mare rears up with flaring nostrils and starting eyes, and the whole attitude of the attacking lion, the gaping jaws, spread claws and lashing tail, directly conveys the power and ferocity of the beast. The spacious treatment and realism which distinguish these contests are also found in the attractive designs of single animals moving in a wooded landscape.[1] Here and in the combat scenes the seal-cutter was able to give full play to his imaginative and creative talents. Full of vitality and infused with the excitement of a new and fresh form of artistic expression, they contrast sharply with the formal, traditional compositions of the cult scenes and the antithetical groups of hero and animals or the sacred tree flanked by animals or demons. In view of the rarity of stamp seals in Mesopotamia during the second millennium, an impression from Fakhariyah with a typically Middle Assyrian motive of a pomegranate tree has a particular interest.[2] It proves that such seals were being made in the thirteenth century and that there was therefore an Assyrian precedent for their extensive use in Late Assyrian times.

Other minor arts, in particular jewellery, are represented in a remarkable burial at Ashur, dated approximately to the period of Tukulti-Ninurta.[3] The vaulted brick tomb, which had been in use for a considerable period, contained as its final occupants two bodies, which may have been interred simultaneously. Both wore elaborate and finely wrought jewellery of gold, silver and semi-precious stones: hair ornaments, earrings, multiple necklaces and pendants. Accompanying them were further pieces of jewellery and fine alabaster and ivory vessels. Because of the poor state of preservation of the skeletons their sex could not be determined

[1] See Plate 156 (a)–(c).　　　[2] §v, 14, 81 f., pl. 80, LIII.
[3] §v, 10, 123 ff.

with certainty. One had less jewellery than the other but it is doubtful whether this implies a difference of sex. The richness of the furnishings and the fact that the tomb was in the vicinity of the temple of Ishtar suggest that its occupants may have held some special position in the service of the goddess. It has been thought that they may have acted as substitutes for the king in the sacred marriage and thereafter been put to death, but in view of doubts as to their sex and the fate of such royal substitutes this can only be speculation.

In technique and design the jewellery attests both the high standard of skill and artistry of the thirteenth-century craftsmen and the continuation of a tradition which goes back to the Royal Tombs at Ur of the third millennium.[1] Two of the most popular motives here and in Middle Assyrian graves at Mari[2] were the pomegranate and the double spiral, both ancient fertility symbols. The existence of a native school of ivory carving is shown by a pyxis and a comb from the Ashur tomb engraved in linear style with typical Assyrian scenes.[3] Fragments of ivory inlay found at the foot of the 'New Palace' terrace[4] may, however, be Babylonian rather than Assyrian work, for the frieze includes the mountain god associated with the flowing vase, a theme characteristic of Kassite art but otherwise attested in Assyria only on a relief sculpture which may also be an import from the south.[5] A completely different style of ivory carving is represented by fragments of ornamental inlays of furniture or boxes from Tell Fakhariyah.[6] The themes, stylistic details and execution of these ivories are strikingly paralleled by the Megiddo hoard of the thirteenth century, although their workmanship is inferior. Their iconography also has close connexions with other products of the Canaanite school of art, characteristic of Palestine and Syria in the Late Bronze Age. The co-existence at Tell Fakhariyah of Canaanite ivories and a glyptic art which is typically Assyrian demonstrates the cultural cross-currents affecting north Mesopotamia and the importance of this area as an intermediary between the civilizations of Assyria and the West.

The only examples of Assyrian sculpture securely dated to the thirteenth century are two symbol bases carved in low relief with representations of the king worshipping divine emblems.[7] On one he stands between two men holding sun standards while in

---

[1] §v, 13, 107.       [2] §v, 18, 83 f.
[3] §v, 10, 135 ff.    [4] §v, 23, 30 f.; §v, 5, 116 f.
[5] §v, 3.             [6] §v, 14, 57 ff.
[7] §v, 4, 57 ff.; §v, 5, 112 f.; §v, 16; see Plate 155 (b)–(c).

a narrow register on the plinth men and horses clamber over mountains, a scene which foreshadows the war reliefs of the ninth century. On the other, which was dedicated by Tukulti-Ninurta to the god Nusku, the king appears twice, standing and kneeling, before divine symbols on a base. Since the kneeling posture was prescribed for the Kassite *šigū* prayers it may have been introduced into Assyria from Babylonia.[1] Although the old intimate meeting of worshipper and seated deity continues as a theme of glyptic art, the representation of a god by his symbols, instead of in person, was becoming more common. This tendency, which, as is shown by the *kudurru* sculptures, was shared by the Babylonians, must express a change in theological concepts. The gods were becoming more remote and withdrawn from mankind.

That faience was employed for large-scale statuary is shown by parts of the human body from the Ishtar temple at Ashur. This material was also extensively used for human and animal figurines, human masks, amulets, vases and beads.[2] Small reliefs and roundels of lead occurred in large numbers in the Ishtar temple and on the site of the New Palace.[3] Many of the designs can be paralleled on the cylinder seals and wall paintings, elaborate rosettes being the most common. Their provenance and motives prove that they were connected with the cult of Ishtar. Their function, however, remains uncertain, although the suggestion has been made that the roundels were used as currency.[4]

[1] §v, 17, 475 f.
[2] §v, 4, 76 ff.; §v, 18, 83 f.; A, 7, 49 ff.; A, 14, 74; A, 15, 125.
[3] §v, 4, 102 ff.; §v, 23, 30.          [4] §v, 24.

# CHAPTER XXVI

## PALESTINE IN THE TIME OF THE NINETEENTH DYNASTY

### (a) THE EXODUS AND WANDERINGS

### I. THE LITERARY CHARACTER OF THE PENTATEUCH

THE only historical sources at our disposal recording the settlement of the Israelite patriarchs in Canaan, their stay there, Israel's sojourn in Egypt, the exodus and the wanderings in the Sinai peninsula and east of the 'Arabah and the Dead Sea are the narratives in the Pentateuch. There are isolated and scattered pieces of information from sources outside the Bible—the texts from Mari, which shed new light upon the 'Amorites';[1] the Egyptian evidence as to the Hyksos;[2] the statements of writers of the Hellenistic and Roman periods concerning the connexion of Israel's sojourn in Egypt with the episode of the Hyksos, which are preserved by Josephus;[3] Akkadian and Hittite texts of the first half of the second millennium, thought to refer to military events recorded in Genesis xiv;[4] documents from Nuzi mentioning legal customs which are, or appear, similar to those presupposed in the stories of the patriarchs;[5] the mention of *Ḥabiru* or *Ḥapiru*[6] in the Amarna letters[7] and the other texts of the same period containing this and similar names. But these are so ambiguous in interpretation that they can be adduced only as supplementing the story to be obtained from the Pentateuch narratives; they should not be used as a guide in any attempt to answer the complex questions posed by the biblical account.

The Pentateuch constitutes a combination of several distinct narrative works dealing with the same general subject. These start with the Creation, in the case of L also called J¹, J also called J², and P, or with the first mention of Abraham, as does E, or with the Theophany on Mount Sinai, as does D; in the Pentateuch they are used until the death of Moses in Trans-Jordan, in the sight of

---

* An original version of sections I–VI was published as fascicle 31 in 1965.
[1] See below, pp. 312 f.    [2] See p. 312.    [3] See p. 312.
[4] See p. 313.    [5] See p. 313.    [6] See p. 314.
[7] See p. 314.

the Holy Land, but originally continued to the death of Joshua and perhaps even later. They all arose in the centuries between 1000 and 500 B.C., and manifest divers incongruities in their conceptions of the course of events. But one thing they all have in common: except when the narrative consists of folk-tales or romantic stories which dispense with considerations of time and space, and are therefore useless for historical purposes, the different forms contain correct, historically useful reminiscences of the time they claim to record, while at the same time they reflect back into the older period circumstances and ideas which cannot in reality belong to it, but date from the time at which that form of the narrative was composed.

All the narrative works, even the oldest, share the view that the entity Israel, with its twelve tribes, existed in a germinative stage from the time of Abraham onwards. Consequently, the narratives concerning the period before David always have this entity, Israel, in view. This is an anachronism, with consequences which are not historical. The entity Israel, though probably prepared by a much older national-religious team-spirit of some tribes or tribal groups[1] which later merged into 'Israel', was first created by David, and thereafter continued to exist at least as an ideal, an object of desire for which man strove. In view of this idea, 'all Israel', all those groups and individual personalities of the time before Moses who were remembered thereafter were given enlarged dimensions, quite as a matter of course. They were treated as precursors of the Israel which David created, not simply of particular parts of it. This had widespread effects, one of which was that it became necessary to place these personalities in a genealogical succession. For as each of them represented the entity of Israel, or at any rate the kernel of all Israel as it existed later, they could be thought of only as succeeding one another. In the case of the patriarchs, this results in Abraham, Isaac and Jacob appearing as grandfather, father and son. In other cases the same interpretation of older traditions, as referring to all Israel, forced on the story the arrangement of events as occurring in an itinerary; stories which, in their original form, were intimately connected with a particular district, and confined in their significance to its immediate surroundings and inhabitants, could be made to fit the entity, Israel, only by representing this same united Israel as visiting these districts in its wanderings. This is what happened in the stories about Israel's wanderings in the desert.

The conclusion, then, is that the arrangement of the stories in

[1] See below, pp. 319, 324.

the Pentateuch based on a genealogical order that appears chronological, or in the form of itineraries, has no claim to be in itself truly
historical. On the contrary, each narrative should be examined by
itself and in isolation, to see to which period or which area its
subject belongs.

## II. THE TRADITIONS OF THE PATRIARCHS AND MODERN CRITICISM

Among those who study closely the stories of the Genesis (Abraham's journey from Ur Kasdim by way of Harran to Canaan; the
attribution to him of Ishmael and Isaac as sons, to Isaac of Esau
and Jacob, and to Jacob of his twelve sons; the sale of Jacob's last
son but one, Joseph, to Egypt by his jealous brethren; the subsequent descent of Jacob and the brethren into Egypt during a
famine) there is complete unanimity on one point: these accounts
can be used for historical purposes only after critical examination.
But opinions differ widely as to what can be accepted as reliable
statements in the detail of these stories.

The first cause for disagreement lies in the question whether
the three patriarchs and the twelve sons of Jacob, or at least Joseph,
are to be considered as individuals, or as personifications of tribes,
or as groups and sections of tribes. It is clear that in Israelite
thought the personification of communities was quite common,
and it is practically certain that the twelve sons of Jacob (including
Joseph) are to be so regarded. The patriarchs might be interpreted
in the same way, and many scholars do so. Others, however, see
in the patriarchs and in Joseph real individuals belonging to the
prehistory of Israel. Still others explain the three patriarchs as
former gods of Canaanite origin, bereft of their divine aspects. In
addition to this difference, there is another question still unsettled:
to what period do the patriarchs, whatever their character may be,
belong? Did they actually exist in the time before Moses, as the
tradition affirms, or do they really belong to a later period, simply
having been transferred to an earlier date? Stade[1] and Wellhausen,[2] for example, were inclined to the second assumption,
and thought it difficult to accept anything derived from statements
in the stories of the patriarchs as valid for the period before Moses.
R. Kittel,[3] Th. H. Robinson,[4] A. Alt,[5] W. F. Albright,[6] J. Bright,[7]
A. Parrot[8] and others consider that the patriarchs really belong to

---

[1] G, 26, 9 f.  [2] G, 27, 11 f.  [3] G, 10, 270 ff.
[4] G, 20, vol. 1, 45 ff.  [5] §11, 5, 45 ff.
[6] G, 1, 150 ff.; G, 2, 350; §11, 1; 2; 3.  [7] G, 4, 60 ff.  [8] §11, 50.

the early period before Moses. Eduard Meyer,[1] G. Hölscher[2] and C. A. Simpson[3] derive them from the Canaanite pantheon (or panherôon) and thereby admit their great antiquity.

As to the question whether these figures are individuals or personifications, the individuality of Abraham is the most strongly marked of the three, so that he must be considered a historical personality, while in the cases of Isaac and Jacob it looks rather as if we have to deal with personifications of tribes or tribal groups or sections. This impression finds confirmation in the fact that 'Abraham' is never used as the name of a people, while 'Isaac' can be (Amos vii. 9, 16), and 'Jacob' constantly is (Num. xxiii. 7, 10, 21, 23; xxiv. 5, 17, 19; Exod. xix. 3, etc.). As to the period to which it may be claimed the patriarchs belong, it must be admitted that many of the statements made about Abraham, Isaac and Jacob clearly reflect conditions at the time after the settlement or under the kings of Israel. Isaac's treaty with the king of the Philistines, Abimelech of Gerar, probably belongs here. According to all we know from other sources about the appearance of the Philistines in Palestine they invaded the country only after the settlement of the Israelites,[4] and it seems artificial to suppose that before the invasion by the main body of the Philistines smaller pioneer groups of them had come into the country, enabling Isaac at the time attributed to him—about the sixteenth century B.C.— to negotiate with one of their representatives. The attribution to Abraham (Gen. xii. 16; xxiv. 10) and Jacob (Gen. xxx. 43; xxxii. 8) of camels as transport and riding animals may be looked upon as an anachronism. At the time assumed for these patriarchs, that is the first half of the second millennium B.C., there seem to have been no domesticated camels in Western Asia and Egypt.[5] But we must leave open the possibility that the camel, that is the dromedary (with one hump), was in fact already domesticated about the middle of the second millennium B.C. in Palestine. But the account of Genesis xxvii where Jacob surreptitiously obtains the blessing as the first-born, and makes his father promise that Jacob would become the master of his brothers and that Esau would serve him, almost certainly presupposes the subjection of Edom by David as told in II Samuel viii. 13–14, and in other places. It must also be admitted, in general, that often no sharp line is drawn in the narratives between the final, decisive invasion of Canaan by Israel, almost certainly in the thirteenth century, and the previous stay of individual Israelite heroes or groups in the Holy Land

---

[1] G, 16, 249 ff.   [2] §1, 7, 60 ff.   [3] §1, 16, 455 ff.
[4] G, 4, 73.   [5] §11, nos. 15; 39; 44; 58.

that is claimed in the tradition.[1] Episodes in the land settlement, that is, events of the later period, are attributed to the patriarchs, that is to the earlier time.

Yet it is difficult to suppose that no correct recollections of the period before Moses were current in Israel at all, and that events and persons were simply invented, either through complete self-delusion, or consciously. Some have interpreted the patriarchs as Canaanite gods or heroes adopted as their own by the Israelites and then turned into men. Improbable as this is in view of the sharp opposition to all things Canaanite which is so apparent everywhere else in the Old Testament, it is obviously due to the impression that we have to deal, in these figures, with things really ancient. Some account, then, must be taken of the probability that, before the final settlement of Israel (linked with the names of Moses and Joshua), individual Israelites like Abraham, and tribal groups like Isaac and Jacob, did live for a longer or shorter time in Canaan, especially in those districts with which the tradition brings them into close connexion.

The stories say that Abraham stayed in and around Hebron, Isaac further south at Beersheba and Beerlahairoi, Jacob partly east of Jordan, partly in the neighbourhood of Shechem and Bethel. This connexion of Abraham, Isaac, and Jacob with certain Canaanite places was first of all, according to our tradition, influenced by worship, the patriarchs worshipping the deities living in these places. Abraham gives the tithe to El 'Elyon of Jerusalem and receives the blessing of Melchizedek, high priest of this god (Gen. xiv). Also he worships El Shaddai of Hebron (Gen. xvii. 1) and El 'Olam of Beersheba (Gen. xxi. 33). Hagar, mother of Abraham's son Ishmael, is related to El Roi of Beerlahairoi (Gen. xvi. 14), and this also applies to Isaac (Gen. xxiv. 62). Jacob experiences in Bethel a revelation of El Bethel (Gen. xxviii. 10–22) and erects in Shechem a *maṣṣēḇāh* or an altar for El, god of Israel (Gen. xxxiii. 20). Everywhere we have hypostases of the Canaanite god El.[2] The ancestors of later Israel who, in pre-Mosaic times, stayed in the country of Canaan evidently joined this cult. In most cases this surely meant a renunciation of gods they had brought to Canaan, the 'gods of the fathers' (Gen. xxxv. 4; Joshua xxiv. 2, 14–15).

The various attempts to arrive at a more exact dating of the patriarchs based on chronological dates in the Old Testament itself, and facts known from sources outside the Bible which are of doubtful relevance, must be regarded with extreme caution.

[1] §II, nos. 4; 5; 6.   [1] §II, 17, 73 ff.; §II, 24; §II, 25; §II, 52.

The statements in the Old Testament are self-contradictory. According to I Kings vi. 1[1] the exodus of Israel from Egypt took place 480 years before the commencement of the building of the temple, which may have been about 970 B.C. The exodus then fell about 1450 B.C. In Exodus xii. 40,[2] the length of Israel's sojourn in Egypt is given as 430 years. Israel's movement from Palestine into Egypt would then fall about 1900 B.C., and thus the period of the patriarchs would have to be reckoned as covering the end of the third millennium and the beginning of the second. But the patriarchs are brought much nearer to the exodus from Egypt by another reckoning. Abraham, Isaac, Jacob and Joseph are thought of as four generations in direct descent, averaging about forty years each. According to Exodus i. 8, the oppression of the Israelites by a new pharaoh, which led to their migration from Egypt, began immediately after the death of the pharaoh who befriended Joseph. On this reckoning, if we date the exodus in the thirteenth century B.C., for reasons still to be given, then the time of the patriarchs would seem to be the fourteenth century.

Among the efforts to determine this period with the help of information from sources outside the Bible, the first to demand attention is the attempt to connect the patriarchs with a people attested in the first centuries of the second millennium B.C. in Mesopotamia, Northern Syria, and in other places. These people are called Amorites, Eastern Canaanites, Proto-Aramaeans, or more generally, Western Semites.[3] The personal names of these people greatly resemble the oldest names occurring in the Old Testament; and in sociological and juridical conceptions and customs as well as religion the Old Testament has much in common with this group. Efforts were therefore made to connect the patriarchs with this group and to place them in the first centuries of the second millennium B.C.; consequently the entry of the Israelites into Egypt was considered as part of the conquest of that country by the Hyksos about 1700 B.C.[4] Thus the exodus was connected with the expulsion of the Hyksos about 1570 B.C., so that the statements of certain writers of the Hellenistic and Roman periods[5] were given new currency. But even if we abstain completely from the different nominations of the 'Amorites' which make it difficult to determine them sufficiently, the traits this group and the patriarchs have in common are much too open to

[1] G, 24, 57 ff.                                    [2] *Ibid.*
[3] §II, nos. 8; 19; 27; 37; 42; 43; 47; 48; 49.
[4] §II, 7; §II, 36, 15 ff.; §II, 45; §II, 53.
[5] Cf. Josephus, *Contra Apionem*, I, 26 f. = §§ 227 ff.

various interpretations to allow a clear placing of the patriarchs in it. There is a similar situation with regard to the Nuzi texts,[1] which belong to the middle of the second millennium B.C. These texts contain some ideas and customs presupposed in certain stories of the patriarchs. The Old Testament, that is Genesis, continues to be the chief source for the assignment of the patriarchs, and for determining their characters. This authority connects Abraham with the Mesopotamian Harran and tells us about connexions of Isaac and Jacob with the same place. This may be a genuine memory, though it is also possible that the account is merely expressing the theory that Mesopotamia was the native place of all Semites. Similarly, in Genesis xi. 28–31, Terah, Abraham's father, is connected with Ur-Kasdim.[2] One conjecture which must be considered valid even today is that Terah's wandering from Ur-Kasdim is not a folk-memory of an actual event but reflects the close relationship between the two cult-places of the moon god, at Ur and Harran. On the other hand it is possible that a nomadic or semi-nomadic group which may be placed among the forefathers of Israel came to Ur-Kasdim in their wanderings, and went on to Harran. The question is further complicated by the fact that the Septuagint translates Ur-Kasdim as 'Land of the Chaldeans', and it is not certain that the accepted identification of Ur-Kasdim with the South-Babylonian El-Muqay-yar is in fact correct; we ought perhaps to look for Ur-Kasdim in the area around Harran.

It has proved a delusion to think that the story of the struggle of Amraphel king of Shinar, Arioch king of Ellasar, Chedorlaomer king of Elam, and Tid'al king of the 'nations' or of the land Gōyīm, against five petty kings in the region of the Dead Sea might be a basis for a fixed date for Abraham and therefore for the other patriarchs.[3] Even if it were possible to agree upon the identity of the eastern kings named, it would remain questionable whether the contemporaneity of Abraham with them has any real claim to credibility, owing to the peculiar character of the narrative in Genesis xiv in which Abraham is represented as connected with them. So we must be satisfied with the following facts: the account of Genesis xiv contains genuine folk-memories of historical events as well as of religious conditions (Melchizedek, priest of El 'Elyon[4]) but the details remain obscure.

Finally it was hoped that the Amarna letters of the fourteenth century B.C.[5] would support the historical character of certain

---

[1] §II, nos. 26; 28; 30; 31; 55.   [2] §II, 32; §II, 50, 14 ff.; §II, 54.
[3] §II, 10; §II, 11; §II, 12, 43 ff.   [4] §II, nos. 24; 25; 52.   [5] See above, pp. 98 ff.

features and figures of the biblical narratives. The *Ḥabiru*, who appear very often in these letters and in other documents from the second millennium B.C., have been compared with the *'Ibrīm* of the Old Testament;[1] and attempts have been made to identify Joseph with Iankhamu, an Egyptian ambassador to Syria and Palestine often named in the Amarna letters.[2] But these attempts have in general failed.[3]

So the patriarchs remain figures enshrouded in mists and shadows, and historical conclusions as to their character are hard to reach. No date assigned to them is indisputable. The point of importance for the tradition through which we know them was not their own careers but the future promised them for Israel in the land of Canaan.

The nature of the evidence, with its emphasis on the future of Israel rather than on personal details concerning the patriarchs, does not allow us to draw conclusions about the history of individuals, or about the period in which they lived. Nevertheless we may say that the narratives concerning them point more probably to the two centuries immediately preceding the final land settlement of Israel than to the first half, or rather the first third, of the second millennium or to yet older times. This earlier dating depends, as we have seen, on the figures given in Exodus xii. 40 and I Kings vi. 1, and these are clearly secondary.

## III. THE ISRAELITE SETTLEMENTS BEFORE THE DESCENT INTO EGYPT

Conditions in the North Arabian steppe, arising from its geographical position and climate, permit its inhabitants to maintain their cattle, the basic means of existence, only in the winter during the rainy season. In summer, when the sparse vegetation of the desert dies off, the inhabitants are compelled to move into the neighbouring lands surrounding the desert on the east, north or west. The result has been that Palestine, from the most ancient periods down to the present, has had to accept the presence of tribes from the desert in search of pasture. Nowadays it is generally the nomadic tribes which go there with their herds of camels in summer, and these have their own pasture-areas and watering-places exactly defined. At the end of the second millennium, when the camel was still not used in these parts, there were

[1] §11, nos. 13; 14; 33; 35; 40; 41.
[2] G, 10, 303; G, 21, 162ff., 167, 173, 188f., 191f.
[3] But see below, p. 317, nn. 1, 2.

semi-nomads with their asses, sheep and goats who did the same thing.[1] There are several indications that the patriarchs' sojourn in Canaan was due to the same factor in the mode of living, though it is concealed in the narratives by the religious conception, arising from theology, that Abraham went to Canaan by God's direct command, and that he, Isaac, and Jacob stayed there for a considerable time as recipients of the promise given to Israel for its future in Palestine.

Certain features of the narratives disclose this factor of social economy. There is the dispute between the shepherds of Abraham and Lot as to the pasture and watering-places they were entitled to (Gen. xiii), or that between the shepherds of Abimelech and those of Abraham or Isaac as to the wells belonging to them (Gen. xxi. 22–33 and xxvi. 12–33). It will be shown in detail that actually this necessity for change of pasture plays a considerable part in the entry of Israelite groups into Egypt too, and also in the final land settlement, though the latter now appears in the narratives as a military enterprise of the entity Israel under a unified command. This means that the three periods, the time of the patriarchs, the sojourn in Egypt, and the final land settlement, though they seem separated from one another by clear intervals, belong together as phenomena arising from a single cause. Individual events divided between the three periods are to be treated as constituent parts of a coherent, much larger movement. These events were no doubt spread over a considerable period of time, and their sequence is probably, at any rate speaking generally of the whole story, correctly maintained by the tradition. Nevertheless they must all be much more closely related than the conception to which the extant narratives have been accommodated makes apparent. The stay of the patriarchs in Canaan and the later conquest of the land by an Israel which, according to the tradition, consisted of twelve tribes, are plainly distinguished. In the first case the patriarchs were clearly guests, and no direct consequences were entailed, while in the second the invasion led to permanent supremacy over Canaan. There is this further distinction that, in the case of the patriarchs, disputes with the Canaanites led to fighting only in exceptional cases, whereas the invasion had to be carried through to a large extent by force of arms. That the interval between the two is not so clear-cut can be shown by two or three examples.

The account of Reuben's conduct with his father's concubine Bilhah (Gen. xxxv. 21–2a) at first probably preceded the story

[1] See below, pp. 319, 320.

about Simeon's and Levi's treacherous and violent assault on Shechem[1] the son of Hamor (Gen. xxxiv). It is in all probability one of local origin, connected with a place, perhaps east of Jordan, called Migdal-Edar, while the story about Simeon's and Levi's misdeed is connected with the neighbourhood of Shechem. It is quite conceivable that these stories, like that of the shameless behaviour of 'Ham the father of Canaan', or—since 'Ham the father of' is a later addition to the original story—of Canaan himself to his father, Noah (Gen. ix. 20–7), are to be explained as literary inventions, poetic symbolizations, to account for the fall of those tribes from their former importance into weakness and dissolution as due to misdeeds of the three eponymous ancestors of the tribes. But if that is not so, we probably ought to consider the Genesis stories of Reuben, and of Simeon and Levi, as preceding by a considerable period the land settlement linked with the names of Moses and Joshua. The position in Genesis xxxviii is much the same. The point of the story is to explain the origin of two sections of the tribe of Judah,[2] which was obviously thought of as already settled finally in the area it occupied later.

It may be that the division of the twelve sons of Jacob between two recognized wives and two concubines or slaves[3] is simply poetic invention serving to enliven the narrative. The assumption that the division reflects, at any rate to some extent, the historical facts, is not necessarily correct. If it is, the facts reflected in the stories of Reuben, Simeon, Levi, Judah, Zebulun and Issachar, would concern the common fortunes of these six tribes, that is, presumably, their joint entry into Canaan from the south, from the Sinai peninsula, at a time earlier than the final conquest. In that case the attribution of Reuben, Simeon, Levi and Judah, with Zebulun and Issachar, to the same mother, Leah, would lead to the inference that these tribes were in Palestine for a fairly long time before the final land settlement of Israel. The statements in Numbers xiv. 39–45; xxi. 1–3; Joshua xiv. 6–15; xv. 13–19; Judges i. 1–21, should be considered in this connexion. In their present context these passages form a part of the narrative of the enterprise of the entity Israel, under the command of Moses and Joshua, with the object of gaining possession of Canaan. But in themselves they, or some of them, may refer to the individual fortunes of Simeon, Judah and other groups; that is to their entry into Palestine from the south, from the neighbourhood of Qadesh. But in their present form these narratives link the entry of these six tribes closely in time with the final land settlement.

[1] §III, 4; §III, 7.    [2] §III, 9; §III, 10.    [3] G, 25, 71 ff.; §III, 5.

However, this dating of the events was a necessary consequence of the inclusion of the separate enterprises of these tribes and groups in the general, united attack of the entity Israel under a unified command, the conception embodied in the form of the tradition extant. The impression arising from the narratives in Genesis is to be preferred; the fortunes of the Leah tribes as told in those narratives should be regarded as considerably earlier than the events which, as will be seen in what follows, finally secured Israel's possession of Palestine. But many details, of course, remain hazy and uncertain. It is no longer possible to decide when and how the tribe of Reuben arrived in its habitations east of Jordan where the tribe is found later; the first mention of it there is almost certainly in the song of Deborah, that is about the middle of the twelfth century. We may proceed to assume, recognizing that it is only an assumption, that Simeon and Levi, after incurring heavy losses in the struggle with the city state Shechem, of which Genesis xxxiv and xlix. 5–7 give some hint, returned to the places in the south from which they started, Simeon to the Negeb and Levi still farther south to the neighbourhood of Qadesh. It would appear, however, that Zebulun and Issachar, the Leah tribes which pushed farthest north, to southern Galilee, were able to maintain themselves there for good. It is possible also to derive from the story of Issachar a date, which will serve as a hypothesis, for the occupation of settlements in Palestine by the Leah tribes, which preceded the final land-settlement of Israel. In the first half of the fourteenth century a certain Labaya destroyed the city-state Shunama,[1] the Shunem of Joshua xix. 18; I Samuel xxviii. 4; II Kings iv. 8. It has been shown[2] that there is reason to connect with this event the settlement of the tribe Issachar in the plain of Jezreel, at the sacrifice of its political independence, and therefore to date Issachar's settlement shortly after Labaya's conquest.

This is all that can be said with any degree of probability about the abode of Israelite tribes in Canaan at a time before the descent into, and sojourn in, Egypt. It must therefore remain an unsolved problem, whether the name 'Israel' was (as Gen. xxxii. 29; xxxiii. 20; xxxv. 10, make probable) already applied at that time to these groups or to some particular part of them or whether this first arose as an appellation of their descendants, either in the period between the exodus and the final land settlement, or in the period after that settlement, when the twelve tribes founded an amphictyonic community whose centre, as many think, was

[1] EA 250, 43 ff. See above, pp. 100 f., 114 ff.　　[2] §III, 1.

Shechem.[1] There is the story about the change of Jacob's name to Israel, which occurred at Penuel or Bethel (Gen. xxxii. 29; xxxv. 10), and another story that he gave the name 'El, god of Israel' to an altar erected at Shechem (or rather a sacred stone, *maṣṣēbāh*, as the text, Gen. xxxiii. 20, is perhaps to be corrected). These stories suggest as probable inferences that the name Israel was a local one in Canaan and indigenous there, and was only transferred to the newcomers secondarily. But there can be no certainty about this, for it is also possible that (as Gen. xxxii. 29; xxxiii. 20, seem to show) the name Israel was accepted by the Jacob group in connexion with the acceptance of the worship of El. Unfortunately, even the supposed earliest mention of the name Israel in the triumphal hymn of Merneptah composed about 1230 b.c. does not provide any unambiguous answer to this question.

The Egyptian sojourn was followed by the completion of the conquest, and the land settlement. This conquest, in the revised form that is the tradition, was presented as an enterprise of the entity 'all Israel', consisting of twelve tribes. We shall see that the house of Joseph led this undertaking, and that it included perhaps other tribes as well as those descended from Leah, or at any rate parts of other tribes. It is certain that Manasseh and Ephraim originated through splitting off from the house of Joseph. This is very probably true of Benjamin,[2] though some scholars would trace a connexion between the biblical tribe of Benjamin and the Mesopotamian Benē-Iamina as testified in the Mari texts for the eighteenth century b.c.[3] They suppose that a sub-group of these Benē-Iamina, called Iarikhu, wandered to Canaan, settled in the area of the later tribe of Benjamin, and changed the older name— which we do not know—of its most important town into Jericho, after their own name. As for Dan and Naphtali it is also probable or at least possible that they separated from the 'House of Joseph'. At any rate the tradition which calls their eponymous ancestors sons of Bilhah, slave of Rachel, mother of Joseph, could be understood in this way. On the other hand, as the ancestors of Gad and Asher were regarded as sons of Leah's slave Zilpah, it is at least a matter for consideration whether these tribes did not force their way into Palestine from the south, together with the Leah tribes, and so were already settled there before the advance of the house of Joseph. However, conclusions about the period and manner

[1] G, 25, 10ff.; §iii, 8.
[2] §iii, 3.
[3] §iii, 2; 6; 11. [The 'Benē-Iamina' have now disappeared from the Mari Texts: see *C.A.H.* ii[3], pt. i, p. 25, no. 1. (Ed.)]

of the settlement of these tribes should not be based with much confidence on the attribution of Gad and Asher to one mother, the slave of Leah, and of Dan and Naphtali to another, the slave of Rachel, for this reason. In later times Dan and Naphtali were neighbours, owing to the migration of the tribe Dan to the north.[1] It may be that this later position is the real cause of the ancestors of these two tribes being classed together. At the time of the song of Deborah and thereafter Gad and Asher were not connected by their geographical situation at all. Their abodes were pretty well at the extreme opposite ends of the Israelite settlements, one in the north-west, the other in the south-east. The story of the birth of the sons of Jacob may conceivably have assigned one and the same mother to the eponymous ancestors of these two tribes because their names suggested a similar interpretation, something like 'Good luck'.[2]

The conception that governs the tradition as we have it is that before the sojourn in Egypt, and before the final land settlement of Israel which followed it, the twelve tribes, or at any rate their eponymous ancestors, had already been in Palestine. This cannot, in any circumstances, be correct, but must be revised in the sense that only some of these tribes had forced their way into Palestine from the south in the course of seeking new pastures. Most of the tribes that did so were those which played no conspicuous part later, and some of them maintained themselves in Palestine only for a time that varied in length for each, while others stayed for good. It is unfortunately no longer possible to judge whether tribes already worshipped Yahweh, and if so, in what sense he was their God. It would seem that his cult was not unknown to them, a point still to be discussed,[3] but it also seems clear that Yahweh did not occupy the exceptional position he held later. So far as we can discern the truth, the worship of Yahweh by the tribes already settled in Palestine was first kindled into flame by the advance of the house of Joseph into the land, undertaken as the result, and proof, of the worship of this god.

## IV. THE NATURE OF THE DESCENT INTO EGYPT

The tradition represents the entry of Jacob and his sons with their families into Egypt from Canaan as resulting from a famine arising in Canaan. Thus the impression is created that this was an

---

[1] See below, p. 547 and Map II (p. 542).
[2] See *J. Bibl. Lit.* 82 (1963), 195 ff.    [3] See below, p. 324.

isolated event of a special kind. But there is no lack of indications that immigrations of individuals and of groups from the eastern lands neighbouring on the Nile valley owing to this cause were fairly frequent. Abraham and Isaac are said to have journeyed to Egypt with their wives Sara and Rebecca because a famine made it necessary to do so (Gen. xii. 10; xxvi. 1). A report of Egyptian boundary officers, belonging to the end of the thirteenth century B.C., mentions the fact that bedawin or half-settled nomads had been allowed to cross the border and proceed to the marshes round the city of Pithom, to save their own lives and their herds.[1] This should tend to show that the entry of Israelites into Egypt is to be understood as due to a change of pasture, just like the advance of Israelite tribes from the Sinai peninsula into southern, and then into central and northern Palestine which has been discussed. It is not necessary to assume that there was a clear-cut interval between the first and the second movement. It is possible that the sequence of the two movements claimed in the tradition should be rejected in favour of the view that both were contemporary. While one part of the Israelite tribes which pitched their tents in the Sinai peninsula looked for a change of pasture in Palestine and remained there, another section preferred to take its herds to Egypt during the summer drought, and settled there for a time.

The reason for differing from the traditional view is that the arrangement of the two processes, the movement into Egypt and then into Palestine, is due to the conception that the entity 'all Israel' played a part in both. That this conception is erroneous can be shown by the general considerations already stated. This is confirmed by an analysis of the sagas relating to the entry into Egypt and to the exodus. In these, the importance of the part played by Joseph, the eponymous hero of the tribe, and of the house of Joseph, is so clearly emphasized that a historical interpretation of this characteristic feature of the story is forced on us. Thus there is much reason to believe that it was, in fact, the tribe of Joseph, or perhaps only a part of it, which emigrated to Egypt.

A question that arises is whether we must take account of a stay of individual members of the tribe of Levi in Egypt. According to the tradition it was in fact Moses,[2] born in Egypt of parents belonging to the tribe of Levi,[3] who at the command of Yahweh encouraged Israel to break out of bondage in Egypt and then successfully executed that enterprise. It is conceivable that

---

[1] G, 22, 259; on Pithom see below, pp. 321 f.
[2] §v, nos. 2; 6; 13.　　　　　[3] §v, 9.

the tradition misrepresents the historical facts. It may be that a member of the tribe of Levi, which was settled or had pitched its tents in and around Qadesh, has been wrongly represented as being in Egypt, so that the decisive part in freeing the Israelites from the bondage there could be attributed to him. The purpose of the narrative would be to assign the same importance to the tribe of Levi in earlier times that it unquestionably had for the group which made its way out of Egypt later. But there are really no decisive reasons against believing the tradition that the Levite Moses inspired the movement out of Egypt by his preaching, which invoked a direct order of God, Yahweh. The feature in the tradition which may be unhistorical is that Moses proposed the Holy Land, Palestine, as the goal for the march. In all probability a much nearer and more modest objective would have been sought, at least as a provisional goal, namely reunion with the related tribes staying in and around Qadesh. Perhaps there was also the idea of a pilgrimage to Mount Sinai, the principal abode of the God, Yahweh, who sanctioned or ordered the exodus.

## V. THE HISTORICAL EVIDENCE FOR THE EXODUS

There is no evidence outside the Old Testament for the sojourn of Israel in Egypt or for the exodus. But the statements therein that have to be considered are, in spite of their character as sagas, sufficient warrant for treating what is told as referring to actual events. It is quite inconceivable that a people could have obstinately preserved traditions about a dishonourable bondage of its ancestors in a foreign land, and passed them on from generation to generation, unless it had actually passed through such an experience. Moreover the narratives of the forced labour imposed on the Israelites in Egypt contain features which not only indicate that the Egyptian settlement is historical, but actually correspond quite well with the circumstances prevailing in Egypt at the time to which the Egyptian bondage is to be dated, i.e. the end of the fourteenth and beginning of the thirteenth century B.C. The tradition relates that, after the Israelites had spent a few decades in Egypt, they were compelled by the new pharaoh to do forced labour on the building of the cities Pithom and Ramses which he had ordered. The implication that there was some specially energetic activity in building leads to the assumption that the pharaoh who displayed it was Ramesses II (1304–1237 B.C.), pre-eminent among the rulers of Egypt for his building activities. The mention of the cities Pithom and Ramses makes the conclusion a practical certainty. It is known that Ramesses II undertook very considerable renovations and alterations in building at Pithom, the modern Tell er-Ratāba in the Wādi Tummilāt, and in Ramses, Pi Ramessu, which is the modern Sān el-Hagar on the Tanitic arm of the Nile[1] or perhaps Qantīr[2] fifteen miles to the south. This was soon after his accession, at the beginning of the thirteenth century. If the inclusion of the Israelites among those compelled to do forced labour is to be assigned to the decade 1300–1290 B.C., or thereabouts, then their entry into Egypt must be dated to about the end of the fourteenth century. The exodus will then fall in the second half of the thirteenth century, for the tradition gives the impression that both phases of the Egyptian episode (first the favourable reception by the pharaoh then ruling, and afterwards the forced labour on new building imposed by his successor) lasted only a few decades. General considerations make it possible that this was in fact the course of events.

The tradition of the sojourn of Israelites in Egypt can be corroborated by an argument from the history of their religion. The Israelites, when reflecting on the earliest stages of their worship of God, maintained so firmly that it was connected with a miraculous act by which God saved his people, an act experienced by their ancestors in Egypt, that one is forced to regard their tradition as deserving belief. For this reason it is likely to be true that the Israelites enslaved in Egypt came to choose Yahweh as their God through the agency of Moses. They probably did not know of him, or hardly knew of him, before, though the Midianites and Kenites and some tribes quite closely related to the Israelites sojourning in Egypt had long done so. It was in confident reliance on this God that they ventured the march out of Egypt. When, in doing so, they were saved from a dangerous situation, they could only explain their salvation as due to direct intervention by their God. For that reason they retained the grateful memory of that experience as an indisputable proof of their election to be his people by this God whom they had recently chosen to worship.

The exact course of this historical event, the exodus and the miraculous act of Yahweh, can unfortunately no longer be discerned. In particular, the question of where Yahweh's intervention took place will probably never be answered with certainty.[3] The statements which have to be considered in determining the

---

[1] G, 14, 58; §vi, 2, 15.  [2] §v, 3; §v, 8.
[3] §v, nos. 1; 5; 10.

scene of the event are ambiguous, including the description 'at the sea of reeds' or 'at the sea'. It remains doubtful whether the northern end of the Gulf of Suez, or one of the salt lakes, or the Gulf of 'Aqaba, or the Serbonian Sea is meant. The doubt is the greater because the Old Testament tradition is self-contradictory on this point, and seems to have admitted at least two of these possibilities, namely the salt lakes or the Serbonian Sea. But this uncertainty does not in the least affect the credibility of the tradition in the main, namely that Israelites in flight were saved from destruction on the Egyptian border, and that they attributed this to Yahweh's aid. The position is rather that the tradition on these points is so firmly established that it makes a historical core to the sagas a practical certainty.

As to the nature and size of the group which was in Egypt and took part in the exodus from that land, it has already been said that except for individual members of the house of Levi (including Moses) it consisted probably only of the 'house' of Joseph, and perhaps merely a part of it. An indication of the date of the miracle of the parting of the waters has already been mentioned; it points to the event having taken place in the second third of the thirteenth century b.c.[1]

## VI. THE WANDERINGS

In the narratives of Israel's wanderings in the period between the exodus from Egypt (Exod. xiii) and the death of Moses in sight of the Holy Land (Deut. xxxiv), large sections dealing with laws of later origin have been inserted. Even apart from these, the narratives belong to several different types. There are aetiological sagas and legends intended to explain why certain geographical areas have a peculiar nature, and why places received certain names, or to account for the origin of customs and institutions and religious practices. These are, as such, not of one single period, but of many. Other stories, though they take the form of legends or sagas, clearly retain memories of the period we are here considering, on which reliance can be placed. The latter class, as is immediately evident on closer examination, centres about three geographical points, Qadesh,[2] the modern 'Ain Qadais or 'Ain el-Qudairat, between six and seven miles north-west of 'Ain Qadais, in the Sinai peninsula; Sinai itself,[3] the position of which will have to be discussed; and Trans-Jordan.[4] These groups of narratives

---

[1] §v, nos. 8; 11; 12.     [2] See below, pp. 325f.
[3] See below, pp. 324f.     [4] See below, p. 329.

must be examined to see what their historical content is. For this purpose, no value must be accorded to the position which the stories now have in the account of an itinerary. It is essential to bear in mind that the position in the itinerary must have been a consequence of the conception in which the narratives are enwrapped, since the narratives refer to the entity 'all Israel'.

The Sinai and Qadesh narratives are dovetailed into one another in various ways. The material that relates to Sinai exceeds that connected with Qadesh by a good deal. But on close examination the historically useful results of the Sinai narratives in Exodus xix–Numbers x are reduced to a very small content. The principal portions of the material contained in these chapters are demonstrably laws which are for the most part, at any rate as they stand now, of late date. They originated in the periods just before, during, and just after the Exile, and have, of themselves, nothing to do with Sinai.

That leaves only the account of a march of Israel to the mountain of God, of which the central point is the experience of Yahweh's epiphany, the confirmation of his bond with Israel, and the promise of the land Canaan.[1] What Israelites took part in this march to Sinai cannot be said. If it was only the tribe of Joseph, or merely a part of that tribe, which had ventured to leave Egypt because it trusted the God it had hardly known before, and had formed the belief that it had been saved during the flight by Yahweh's aid, then it is permissible to assume that the horde rescued by a miracle went immediately to the pre-eminent abode and oracle of this God, to Sinai. They wished to manifest the worship and gratitude felt for him, and to assure themselves of his protection and assistance for ever. But there is another conceivable explanation. The worship of Yahweh had long flourished among the Midianites and other tribes, including some like the Levites with whom the people leaving Egypt recognized a close relationship. These worshippers of Yahweh had almost certainly striven to maintain the connexion with the principal abode of their God, Sinai, by regular pilgrimage to it. It would be possible to explain the Sinai narratives as arising from a recollection of this kind of pilgrimage.

The position of Sinai or Horeb,[2] as the mountain of God is called in some narratives, is still disputed. There is a tradition of the Church which can be proved to go back to the fourth century A.D., and is certainly at least two centuries older than that.[3] Ac-

---

[1] G, 24, 79 ff.; §vi, nos. 5; 7; 8; 19.   [2] §vi, nos. 1; 2; 14; 22.
[3] §vi, 11; §vi, 22.

cording to this Sinai is one of the mountains in the southern part of
the Sinai peninsula, which rise to a height of 7500 feet or more;
the heights mentioned in identifications are Jebel Sirbal, Jebel
Mūsa, Jebel Qaterin, and others. Some modern discussions start
from the incorrect assumption that the narratives render it necessary to locate Sinai near Qadesh, and would accordingly identify
it with one of the mountains in the neighbourhood of Qadesh,[1]
say Jebel 'Ara'if. The accounts of Yahweh's epiphany on Sinai
make probable a natural explanation of the phenomenon, a volcanic eruption. The scanty notices of the position of this mountain
available in the Old Testament seem to locate it in the Midianite
area, and the Midianites had their tribal settlements east of the
Gulf of 'Aqaba and, generally speaking, east of the northern end of
the Red Sea.[2] At the time with which we are dealing, the middle of
the thirteenth century B.C., volcanic eruptions did still occur there.
Sinai ought then to be this district. We may therefore believe that
the pilgrimage of those who fled from Egypt had as its objective a
volcano on the eastern side of the Gulf of 'Aqaba, or at the northern
end of the Red Sea.

It seems that when Israel settled in Canaan, it kept up at first
the connexion with this mountain of God. A phrase in the song
of Deborah (Judges v. 4–5) shows that about the middle of the
twelfth century B.C. Yahweh was still thought of as enthroned
there, and hastening from there to aid his people, as they were
still fighting in Canaan. An incident in the story of Elijah
(I Kings xix. 8–18) proves that, if God was really to be approached
in close communion, a pilgrimage to Horeb must still be undertaken even in Elijah's time, about the middle of the ninth century
B.C. But the more firmly Israel, and therefore not only Israel, but
Israel's God Yahweh, was associated exclusively with the land of
Canaan, and the places of worship there, the more vague became
the association with Sinai. The pilgrimages thither ceased, and all
knowledge of the position of the mountain was lost. The identification of Sinai with one of the mountain peaks on the Sinai
peninsula (which is thus incorrectly so named) was first made a
thousand years later and has remained so till the present day.

While the historical content of the Sinai stories amounts to no
more than a pilgrimage of Israel to the outstanding abode of Israel's
God, Sinai, much more results from the Qadesh narratives. These
include, besides Numbers xi. 1–xx. 21, the sagas connected with
other localities in the text as we have it, Exodus xv. 22–xviii. 27.
The neighbourhood of Qadesh is well-watered, for it includes not

---

[1] G, 10, 346ff.          [2] §VI, nos. 22; 26; 27; 28.

only the water at 'Ain Qadais, which lies about ninety miles or so south of Jerusalem, but also the neighbouring water-sources at 'Ain el-Qudairat and 'Ain Qusaimah.[1] The impression given by the narratives is that the horde which left Egypt conquered the owners of this land, the Amalekites (Exod. xvii. 8–13), took their place, stayed in that neighbourhood a fairly long time, and came into touch there with related tribes which had previously pitched their tents there. The most important of these was that of the Levites, to which Moses belonged. This impression seems to be correct, for it is specifically stated in Deuteronomy i. 46—admittedly contradicting ii. 14—that the Israelites camped at Qadesh 'many days'. The hypothesis is clearly justified by the importance of this period in the formation of the religious, moral and legal standards accepted in Israel, and the part played in that process by Moses and his tribal brethren, the Levites, whose special duty was the maintenance of the cult of Yahweh.

The formation of such standards of conduct must have been in the first place, and principally, to the advantage of the horde which left Egypt and regarded Qadesh as the next objective of their flight.[2] But it is hardly possible to suppose that all the stories relating to Qadesh affect only the tribe of Joseph, the people who came thither from Egypt. Even apart from the Levites, there were still other related tribes settled in that neighbourhood who had to do with the holy place of Yahweh at Qadesh. Among these must be reckoned, at any rate partially, those tribes which, as previously explained, had advanced into southern, central and even northern Palestine in search of change of pasture from the Sinai peninsula, and had remained in the new area for a considerable time or even permanently, without breaking the link with Qadesh and the fractions of their groups which stayed there. The tribes dwelling round Qadesh and those which had emigrated thence retained a bond of union with the holy place there, though we have not the means to determine the nature and strength of that bond.[3]

The subsequent course of Israelite history presupposes the existence of a feeling that these and other tribes belonged together. This is exemplified in the combination of several tribes when Israel was threatened by Jabin of Hazor and Sisera of Harosheth ha-Gōyīm, the subject of the narrative (Judges iv) and of the song of Deborah (Judges v).[4] Even the tribes which failed to join the combination should have done so, according to the conception of the song, and are sharply reproached for their failure. It is not

[1] §vi, 1, 295f.; §vi, 22; §vi, 30.  [2] Cf. pp. 17, 25.
[3] G, 25, 10ff.  [4] See below, ch. xxxiv, sect. v.

enough to suppose that the tribe of Joseph, the last to force its way into Palestine, imposed its enthusiastic, but quite recent—and so the more zealous—acceptance of the worship of Yahweh on tribes long settled in Palestine, and thus laid the foundation for the development of Israelite national sentiment, conditioned as it were by religion. The basis for this feeling of unity must have existed at a much earlier period than the political union.[1] The twelve tribes which constituted the later Israelite state recognized that they were related to other tribes like Cain and Jerachmeel, and that they were united with them by a common bond of worship. But Cain and Jerachmeel did not become members of the Israelite state, and parts of them were never settled in Palestine.

The feeling of national unity among the Israelite tribes, based on religion, which made it possible for them to combine first into a coalition, and then into a state, can thus be said to have its original basis in the common relations of the tribes with the holy place at Qadesh and its God, Yahweh, and with his mountain Sinai or Horeb. The proper place for the epiphany of the God worshipped at Qadesh was on Sinai, and pilgrimages thither constituted a substantial part in the cult. To that extent interconnexion of the tribes which had dwelt in and around Qadesh with Sinai can be regarded as the source of the feeling for unity. Perhaps it can even be described as a union of comrades bound by an oath of fidelity to Sinai. But a reservation must be made, for Sinai and its God were holy not merely to those tribes which came to form the entity Israel because of their relations with Qadesh, but also to other tribes. These were the Midianites, who never joined the political unity and at any rate in later periods were actually reckoned as Israel's enemies, and perhaps also the Amalekites who were—as we have seen[2]—expelled from the area of Qadesh by the Israelites. It will therefore be better to abandon the description of the Israelite tribes as a union of comrades bound by an oath of fidelity to Sinai, and to be satisfied with the conclusion that the sense of national unity based on religion was deeply rooted in the connexions of the Israelite tribes with Qadesh and Sinai.

Among the sagas connected with Qadesh is the story in Numbers xiii–xiv of the despatch of agents to Palestine to collect information. Their discouraging report caused the Israelites' refusal to risk a dangerous undertaking, the invasion of the land; they were for that reason condemned to wander for forty years in the wilderness. The result was the advance northwards, undertaken in opposition to Yahweh's command, leading to their dispersal as far north as

[1] G, 25, 10ff.; G, 27, 23.    [2] See above, pp. 325f.

Hormah (Numbers xiv. 40–5). In Numbers xxi. 1–3, there is an account of a victory of Israel over the Canaanites at Hormah. The idea underlying the narratives, that there were enterprises undertaken by the entity 'all Israel', under a single command, is in any case unhistorical; but it would seem that there is reflected in them a memory of actual events about a century or two earlier than the advance of the 'house' of Joseph and the final land settlement by Israel. This hypothesis is supported by the part played in the story, Numbers xiii–xiv, by Caleb the Kenizzite.[1] There are several indications that the Kenizzites, to whom the tribe or clan Caleb belonged (Joshua xiv. 6–15; xv. 15–19; Judges i. 12–15), may have found their way into Palestine with the Leah tribes. There are however arguments that can be urged against so early a date for the narratives of Numbers xiv. 40–5; xxi. 1–3. Judges i. 17, reports that Judah and Simeon, marching southward from the permanent camp at Gilgal, used in common by the Israelites, 'slew the Canaanites who inhabited Zephat and utterly destroyed it; and the city was renamed Hormah'. As we see, the defeat of the Canaanites near Hormah is linked here with the *Landnahme* of the Israelites under the leadership of Joshua. But it is possible that the place of Hormah in Numbers xiv. 40–5; xxi. 1–3 may not be identified with that of Judges i. 17, but is to be sought further in the south, so that the event reported in Numbers xiv. 40–5; xxi. 1–3, and that of Judges i. 17 belong to different times: the event of Numbers xiv. 40–5; xxi. 1–3, to the fourteenth, and that of Judges i. 17 to the thirteenth century B.C.

It remains possible, then, to see in the narratives of the defeat or the victory at Hormah in Numbers xiv. 40–5; xxi. 1–3, a reminiscence of the entry of the Leah tribes into Palestine. On the other hand, the idea that the 'house' of Joseph actually made an effort to force its way from the south before deciding on the advance into Palestine from the east should not be summarily rejected. The allusion to the ark of the covenant,[2] which was in the possession of the Joseph tribe, in Numbers xiv. 44, is perhaps an argument for this thesis. The distinction between the advance of the tribe of Joseph and that of the tribes settled in Palestine before Joseph seems to be that the tribe of Joseph used force, or was at least prepared to use force, from the start, while the Leah tribes reached their areas in the course of a peaceful process, the search for a change of pasture. It was an exception for the Leah tribes to be involved in disputes leading to war, as happened in the case of Simeon and Levi (Gen. xxxiv).

[1] §VI, 10.          [2] G, 25, 56 ff.; §VI, nos. 4; 6; 13; 18; 20.

If the 'house' of Joseph did, in accordance with this hypothesis, advance into Palestine at first from the south, then the attempt in any event failed. In the case of this group, that did not at all mean giving up the objective aimed at; another way soon seemed to be opened up for them, namely the way through Trans-Jordan. The statements about the march of the Israelites from Qadesh to Shittim, which lay east of Jordan opposite Jericho (Num. xx. 22–xxv. 1 and xxxiii. 36–49) have little claim to credibility in detail, and the narratives dealing with the fortunes and deeds of Israel in Trans-Jordan in Numbers xxi. 10–xxxii. 42, are, in type, sagas.[1] Yet there is a good deal to be said for believing that an Israelite horde, the tribe of Joseph, started forcing its way into Palestine from the east, across Jordan, and made its way thither through Trans-Jordan.[2]

It may be that some information reached Qadesh that one of the political units existing in Trans-Jordan was so weak that it would fall before an attack, and thus gave the first impulse to this undertaking. In Judges xvii–xviii something of the sort happened when Laish-Dan fell into the hands of the tribe Dan after such a report. Neither Edom nor Moab can have been the weak element. Archaeological investigations and isolated Egyptian reports are sufficient to prove that both were strongly organized, flourishing states in the thirteenth century B.C.[3] The tradition (Num. xx. 14–21; xxi. 4; Deut. ii; Judges xi. 17–18) implies that Israel treated these states with respect and raised no claims of any kind to their territory; much less, then, did Israel make any move to attack them. But the tradition was able to record Israel's victorious struggle against the Amorite king Sihon of Heshbon and his territory north of Moab, between the Arnon and the Jabbok, against the city state of Jaazer (Khirbet Jazzir) about twenty miles north of Heshbon, and against Og of Bashan, whose kingdom stretched from the Jabbok far to the north-east; and the tradition added that Moses divided these territories between Reuben, Gad and half Manasseh (Num. xxi. 21–35; xxxii; Deut. ii. 26–iii. 22; Joshua xiii. 8–33).

Now there can be no possible doubt that the true explanations of these stories is that, to a great extent, they reflect later events and conditions back into an earlier period. The settlement of Israelites east of Jordan for the most part at least followed the settlement in the west and did not precede it. Thus sections of the tribe Manasseh went into Trans-Jordan from their abodes in the parts west of Jordan (Joshua xvii. 14–15). Further, the twilight

---

[1] §VI, 24.      [2] §VI, nos. 3; 9; 12; 16; 17; 25.
[3] G, 4, 109f.

of myth plays round the figure of Og, as is shown by the remark in Deuteronomy ii. 11: the king belonged to the Rephaim, and his coffin, of superhuman proportions, was kept in the Canaanite city Rabbath. No historical affirmation can be made about such a figure. The case of the Amorite Sihon of Heshbon is different. Serious arguments have been advanced in an attempt to show[1] that the narrative about him in Numbers xxi. 21–30, is in reality an account of a victory over a king of Moab called Sihon won by Israel in the ninth century B.C. The poem attached to the narrative Numbers xxi. 27–30 (the text of which is unfortunately greatly damaged and therefore often interpreted differently) refers in fact, by its nature, to a later Israelite invasion of territory possessed, at the time the poem was written, by Moab, but in the earlier period ruled by the Amorite king Sihon. But it does not follow at all that the narrative itself cannot have preserved a reliable recollection of an event belonging to the time of the land settlement by Israel. On the contrary it is quite possible that a city state surviving from the earlier time, corresponding with the city-states of the pre-Israelite period west of Jordan, maintained itself among the national states that arose during the thirteenth century in the 'Arabah, east of it, and in parts east of Jordan, that is side by side with Edom, Moab and Ammon. The emphatic way in which Sihon is called a king of the Amorites favours this view. Such a state might not be strong enough to resist the attack of the Israelite horde in its fresh enthusiasm.

The victory over Sihon of Heshbon, and therewith the creation of a corridor that made it possible to march from the desert of Trans-Jordan through to the Jordan can, then, be attributed to the horde which left Qadesh, the tribe of Joseph. But another possibility must be reckoned with. The tradition may have attributed a success won by one of the tribes settled in the neighbourhood of Heshbon, that is by Reuben or Gad, either earlier or later than the land settlement, to the advance of the tribe Joseph through Trans-Jordan towards its goal, the land west of Jordan. This would be a use of the narrative meant to lend credibility and colour to the account of Joseph's advance, and would therefore be unhistorical. Even so, this advance of the 'house' of Joseph would still retain its historical credibility for the decisive reason that it is the necessary presupposition for the crossing of the Jordan by this group. That crossing was part of a process that will have to considered at length later.

[1] G, 16, 530.

## (b) ARCHAEOLOGICAL EVIDENCE

### VII. PROBLEMS: THE NATURE OF THE EVIDENCE

In this part of this chapter an attempt is made to answer the question: what is the archaeological contribution towards an elucidation surrounding the origins of the Israelite tribes in Palestine?

The nineteenth Egyptian dynasty covers a period of time which in Palestine may be equated with the Dark Ages following the collapse of the Mycenaean world in Greece. The period 1320–1200 B.C. involves some of the most thorny and complicated problems in the whole of Palestinian history, comprising as it does the date and nature of the Hebrew conquest and settlement; the cultural interrelationship of Canaanite and Hebrew tribes and their place in the Near East as a whole: the historicity of such Old Testament heroes as Joshua and Baraq; the sifting of historical events from folk tales, religious propaganda and certain editorial practices.

Owing to the peculiar position which Palestine holds in respect to three world religions, the reason for and the evolution of excavations in her soil have been somewhat different from those in other parts of the world. The impetus to dig for history in classical lands was stimulated by a combination of romanticism and a familiarity with the literature, philosophy and art of the Greeks and Romans which was shared by all educated people of the Western world. Something of the same romanticism, added to the excitement of discovering that the history of the world was far older than had been supposed, spurred on excavation in Mesopotamia. The discovery of the Assyrian cities and Babylon in turn gave the first firm link with the world of the Old Testament. However, almost from the start, excavations in Palestine took on a slightly different hue from those being made in neighbouring countries. The driving force behind excavations in Palestine may, in the main, have been a desire to write history where none was written, but often subconsciously, and on occasion quite outspokenly, the *raison d'être* of these excavations was to support the biblical text. This is easy to understand and even to condone when it is seen in the context of the late nineteenth century con-

---

* An original version of sections VII–VIII was published as fascicle 67 in 1968.

troversies concerning the unique position of the Bible, brought to a head by Darwinism and liberal German exegesis. There was a great urgency in many circles to put something weighty in the balance against scientific free-thinking, and because archaeology of necessity deals in physical, tangible objects, the results of excavations in Palestine tended to gain an exaggerated significance in the popular public mind. One must not forget that the interpretation of these finds has been and still is largely dependent on the school of biblical exegesis to which the excavator adheres. It is, unfortunately, an inherent characteristic of archaeological evidence that, with the best objective will in mind, it is only too easy to distort it by stressing one aspect of the finds more than another—finds which have come to light not as a controlled scientific experiment, but subject to many different aspects of chance (method of excavation, chemical properties of the soil, climate etc).

With this in mind it seems that for the time being Eggers's *archaeologische These, literarische Antithese,* in which he acknowledged archaeology in its own right, will in Palestinian archaeology of this period have to be changed to *literarische These, archaeologische Antithese.*[1] The literary thesis has been demonstrated in the first part of this chapter, and without this no archaeologist would have had any reason to suppose that the thirteenth century B.C. in Palestine saw the birth of a new nation which came to its fullest development about the end of the eleventh century B.C. With one exception[2] there is no evidence, in the proper sense of the word, that a new ethnic group was taking over power in the land at this time. It is impossible for archaeology, in its present state, to detect new ethnic elements in, or replacing, the population of an area unless, at the time of its arrival, it deposited cultural artifacts of an indestructible nature which differ markedly from those of the established group.

Various distinguishing features of the beginning of the Iron Age, such as the introduction of iron to replace bronze for tools and weapons, and the invention of non-porous plaster for the lining of cisterns, which made settlement less dependent on springs,[3] cannot be attributed to the earliest Israelites in Palestine. Nor, on the whole, can the changing shapes of the pottery repertoire. Albright has suggested[4] that a certain type of storage jar was distinctive for the earliest Israelites but even this 'fossil type' collared rim has been found in Canaanite contexts,[5] and thus

[1] §VII, 6.    [2] See below, p. 335.    [3] §VII, 3, 113.
[4] §VII, 4, 548.                        [5] §VII, 12, 16.

loses its diagnostic value. However, Aharoni has pointed to a cooking-pot with a high rim as distinctive early Israelite ware, and this may prove a fixed point in the search, though it may well prove to be a valid point of recognition for only some of the Hebrew tribes.[1]

A very poor building tradition is frequently taken as an indication of new settlers and on the whole it is assumed that the newcomers largely took over the material culture of the groups which they eventually displaced.[2] However, shabby rebuilding of a flourishing Late Bronze town cannot be taken as proof of the presence of Hebrews. If the population of a town is practically decimated during a destruction (and the cause of this may be accidental fire, earthquake, a local attack from a hostile neighbouring city-state, or a band of marauders or an Egyptian raid), it may take more than one generation before the survivors have even rebuilt their defences.[3] Unless the identity and date of the attackers and destruction can be fixed, the mere destruction of cities cannot be taken as sound archaeological evidence of the arrival of a new ethnic group.

The essential elements for tracing a slow process of penetration of a semi-nomadic folk into urban and agricultural Canaanite populations such as is described as having taken place in Palestine in the first part of this chapter are still lacking, though a beginning has now been made.[4]

The newcomers, being semi-nomadic pastoralists, were unlikely either to have been able or to have wished to build towns for themselves in the pattern of the Canaanite Late Bronze Age inhabitants. Almost all the available archaeological material comes from urban areas, with the exception of some village settlements in Galilee[5] and the temple mound at Deir 'Allā. As it is most likely that the penetrating Hebrew tribes established themselves first of all in the uncultivated areas before attempting either to intermingle peacefully with the established Canaanite population or to take a town by force, it is to be expected that some of their property may be found mixed with Canaanite sherds in the occupation level before the destruction of a town. In order to be able to recognize this material, far more archaeological work will have to be done outside the great tells. Lack of fossil types makes it apparently superfluous to attempt to locate one or other Hebrew tribe outside the borders of Canaan in the period immediately preceding the Settlement. Up till now there

[1] §VII, 2, 220    [2] §VII, 10, 209.
[3] §VII, 7.    [4] See below, p. 335.    [5] §VII, 1.

is no indication, for instance, that any of these tribes had lived for any period in Egypt. The origin of newcomers in any area can be determined only by comparison of their material culture in their new homes with that found outside the new dwelling area.

Those tribes which never left Palestine and were already completely assimilated to Canaanite culture, as, for example, at Shechem, are virtually untraceable archaeologically, when they became part of the Israelite confederation. That it is possible to trace and distinguish nomadic cultures has been demonstrated by Miss Kenyon's work on the E.B.–M.B. tomb groups in Jericho.[1]

The one distinctive element of the culture of the Hebrew tribes of which one may speak with any certainty is their religion, the nature of which was such that during the period in question it remains, archaeologically speaking, an invisible attribute. The culture of the Philistines can be distinguished from the Canaanite not only by its pottery repertoire but by its distinctive burial customs.[2] This is not the case, so far as is yet known, with the incoming Israelites, though the situation may change if more burial grounds of the period are found and excavated.

## VIII. RESULTS

The following are sites where excavation has revealed a destruction which could have been caused by the incoming Hebrew tribes.

Bethel[3] was destroyed in the thirteenth century, but the resettlement did not follow immediately. Tell Beit Mirsim (possibly Debir or Kirjath Sepher) was destroyed c. 1240 B.C., either by Israel[4] or by Merneptah.[5] Tell ed-Duweir (possibly Lachish) was destroyed c. 1230[6] or slightly later, by the Israelites, Merneptah, or the Peoples of the Sea.[7] Of the destruction of the Late Bronze Age cities of Megiddo,[8] c. 1050, Beisan (Beth-shan), c. 1150, Tell Qedaḥ (Hazor),[9] only the last is attributed to the Israelites.

Tell el-Jib (identified by the excavator as Gibeon) has not revealed its origin as an Israelite town, and Tell el-Fūl (Gibeah) apparently developed from its beginning before 1100 B.C., but was, at least in its later stages, in Hellenistic times, an Israelite village.

---

[1] §VII, 8; §VII, 9; §VII, 11.
[3] §VIII, 4, 11 ff.
[5] §VIII, 20, 100; §VIII, 22, 215.
[7] §VII, 10, 209; §VIII, 22, 302.
[9] §VIII, 11, 39; §VIII, 22, 254, 260.

[2] §VII, 5, 151 ff.
[4] §VIII, 1, 38; §VIII, 2, 15 f.
[6] §VIII, 21, 51 f.
[8] *Ibid.*; §VIII, 22, 321.

Key sites for the later history of the Israelite kingdom, such as Jerusalem, Tell Balāṭa (Shechem) and Samaria,[1] throw no light on our problem for various reasons. Jerusalem remained a non-Israelite city until the time of David; Shechem, so far as is known, was never taken by the Israelites; and on the hill of Samaria no traces of settlement have been found which precede the kings of the house of Omri. From other key sites, such as Hebron, Beersheba and Qadesh Barnea, no archaeological evidence is known at all. Jericho seems to have had a slight fourteenth-century occupation but none in the twelfth century,[2] and no site in the Ghor of Jericho stemming from the second half of the Late Bronze Age has been found. Sites once identified with Gilgal bear no traces of occupation earlier than the seventh century B.C.[3] However, an early thirteenth-century occupation was found on the ruins of Et-Tell ('Ai).[4] Aharoni found a 'continuous chain of small settlements' in the southern part of Upper Galilee, which he dates to the beginning of the Iron Age and which seem to be distinctive of a new group of settlers.[5] Although their identity cannot yet be fixed on internal evidence, there seems at least to be no alternative rival identification to that of the Hebrew tribes.

From surface explorations by Nelson Glueck[6] and, more recently, B. Rothenberg,[7] it is argued that the southern and eastern borderlands of Palestine did not have a settled population during the greater part of the Late Bronze Period. The temple at 'Ammān and work at Dhiban have done nothing to upset this picture,[8] though so little has been done on any scale in these border lands that it is too early to draw any firm conclusions on this point. The history of these areas plays an important part in the reconstruction of the arrival of the Hebrew tribes and, in particular, in detecting the closer dating of successive waves of penetration.

An Israelite invasion supposes a settled population and kingdoms. So far, however, there is no archaeological indication of the movement of tribes through these regions, and the fact that some place-names can be identified with certain geographic locations cannot be taken as archaeological evidence.[9] Until such sites are excavated and the archaeological context is seen to fit with a reasonable measure of certainty into the wider geographical context, the traditional identification can only be taken

[1] §VIII, 5.
[2] §VIII, 14, ch. XI.
[3] §VIII, 23, 57 ff.
[4] §VIII, 15.
[5] §VII, 1 and 2.
[6] §VIII, 10.
[7] §VIII, 19.
[8] §VIII, 12, 155 ff.
[9] §VIII, 7, 100.

as an indication. One site in Transjordan—Deir 'Alla—, traditionally taken to be ancient Succoth, has been excavated and can now with some certainty be proved not to be Succoth. This tell has turned out to be an undefended temple mound, without any village occupation throughout the Late Bronze age from *c.* the sixteenth century to the twelfth century B.C.[1] It remained a holy place during the Iron Age until well into the Persian period. One must look for another biblical identification for this important site, and Joshua xxii. 10, 11 may perhaps prove a link here, or one may suppose that a tradition that Jacob founded this sanctuary, which indeed remained independent of Jerusalem right through the history of the Kingdoms and even after the Exile, was suppressed by later biblical redactors. There is no definite proof for either of these suggestions.

Of far greater archaeological importance is the bearing which the Deir 'Allā excavations have on the problems of recognizing the arrival of new population groups. This has been derived from a technical analysis of the pottery; that is to say, from a study of the sherds and vessels based on the way they were made and not only on a typology of form.[2] It can now be proved that the Early Iron Age cooking-pot cannot be a straight descendant of the Late Bronze cooking-pot, as is generally assumed. It is made by potters with a different tradition, not indigenous to Palestine. Occasionally examples of this cooking-pot are found in sites at an earlier date, which indicates contact with a group or groups of nomadic people who had their main centre of activity elsewhere. At Deir 'Allā, at some time in the second half of the thirteenth century B.C., a pottery, totally different technically from the foregoing and generally known Late Bronze repertoire, appears. This can only be taken as an indication that a different population took over the sanctuary. In the first quarter of the twelfth century B.C. the sanctuary was destroyed by earthquake, after which the site was occupied by yet another group or clan, whose pottery once again differs markedly from a technical point of view from the pre-earthquake repertoire, although the shapes of the vessels remain very much the same. Some pottery of Philistine type has been found together with this pottery.

The Deir 'Allā clay tablets do not belong to this period but to the previous one.[3] This phase is followed in the second half of the twelfth century by the building of a village, presumably attached to the sanctuary. This village again exhibits a different pottery

---

[1] §VIII, 9, *passim.*　　　　　　　　　　[2] *Ibid.*
[3] See below, p. 510.

tradition. To sum up: there is evidence for Late Bronze Age semi-nomads living in Trans-Jordan with their religious centre at Deir 'Allā. They are followed by a similar group of nomads who apparently peacefully ousted the earlier group from their place of worship and, by analogy, from the rich grazing grounds in the area of the Jordan valley in which Deir 'Allā is situated. Shortly after 1200 B.C. they in turn move on to make place for a clan of metal-workers who were regular winter and spring visitors at the site, as can be seen archaeologically by the annual deposits in the soil. After another earthquake disaster this group is replaced by a tribe whose cultural orientation is quite definitely eastwards and atypical for the west side of the Jordan. There is as yet nothing by which these ethnic groups can be identified, and although their arrivals and departures can clearly be traced at Deir 'Allā it is still impossible to say where they came from or where they went. A new comprehensive surface survey published in distribution maps might do something to help elucidate this problem, though chance plays a weighty role in such surveys.

As has already been said, the archaeologists would be totally unaware of any important ethnic changes at the end of the Late Bronze Age were it not for the biblical traditions. An analysis of these traditions which in itself tries to conjure up an historically more reliable reconstruction of events can be the only true incentive for the archaeologist to attempt to find relevant traces in the soil. This frequently makes the matter of interpretation even more difficult than when the traditional stories are taken at their face value. Two heavy handicaps rest on the archaeologist of this period: the uncertainty as to the location of territorial boundaries between the tribes and the absence of evidence of close dating. Neither the literary nor the archaeological evidence can be hung on to a firmly fixed chronological peg; both archaeologist and exegete have to deal with the question of whether there ever was a nomadic Israelite invasion and whether this element left the region again after a certain period only to return once more after an unknown period of time. Did the earlier waves of arrivals carry some distinguishing feature which the latter ones did not? And so on. Even inscriptional material lacks the required precision, as can be seen from the Merneptah stele.[1] It is the nature of the archaeological evidence and the almost entire lack of inscriptional material which classify this period as proto-historical. As such it demands a different archaeological approach from that which is generally given to it.

[1] §VIII, 17, 278.

# CHAPTER XXVII

## THE RECESSION OF MYCENAEAN CIVILIZATION

### I. DISTURBANCES IN THE EASTERN MEDITERRANEAN

THE expansion of Mycenaean civilization had been bound up
with a vigorous trading activity in the eastern Mediterranean,
and for the archaeologist the recession of that trade is one of the
most obvious symptoms of the Mycenaean decline. But this
generalization will not get us far in the reconstruction of the
history of the period. Cultural and political history are not the
same thing; and in the L.H. III b phase, when pottery of Mycenaean style found its widest distribution in the east Mediterranean lands, the political decline of the Mycenaean world may
already have begun. We have already noted[1] that at this time the
Mycenaean potters of Cyprus were showing a greater independence of the style of mainland Greece, and that their wares
seem to have captured most of the eastern market, for nearly all
the Mycenaean pottery of L.H. III b style that turns up in
Syrian and Palestinian sites shows Cypriot peculiarities. Cities
such as Alalakh (Tell Açana) and Ugarit (Ras Shamra) continued to import Mycenaean-style pottery[2] until their destruction
in the early twelfth century,[3] but that pottery came in the main
from Cyprus. At the least this must imply that direct trade from
the Aegean was now less frequent, and it is difficult to see why.
Either, one would suppose, something had undermined the commercial vitality of Greece at home, or else the political conditions
in the east Mediterranean had become less favourable to trade.
It may be partly that Mycenaean traders in Cyprus were better
placed, and had therefore become rivals to their homeland; on
these lines we might explain the curious situation at Tell Abu
Hawwām near Haifa, where, quite exceptionally, the Mycenaean
imports at this time do include pots which must have come from
mainland Greece.[4] Perhaps there was here an attempt to by-pass

---

\* An original version of this chapter was published as fascicle 39 in 1965; the
present chapter includes revisions made in 1970.   [1] See above, pp. 182 ff.
  [2] §1, 8, 71 ff., 87; §1, 10, 162.   [3] See below, p. 340.   [4] See above, p. 182 with refs.

Cyprus in the route to the east, though it is difficult to believe that Mycenaean shipping could have reached that far without using some intermediate port of call after leaving the Aegean. In Egypt too it seems likely that a majority of the L.H. IIIb pottery imports were of Cypriot origin;[1] but in any case the quantity of Mycenaean pottery reaching Egypt was comparatively small after the brief Amarna period. Mycenaean merchants from whatever quarter probably met with little encouragement there.

Though archaeology fails to explain the recession of Mycenaean intercourse with the east, one can in this period glean at least some hints of what was going on from the historical records of the Egyptians and the Hittites. It is clear that conditions were becoming less and less favourable to peaceful commerce. In the fifth year of Merneptah (1236–1223 B.C.) Egypt met and successfully repelled an attack by the people of Libya, who were supported by a number of allies from overseas, named as Akawasha, Tursha, Lukka, Sherden, and Sheklesh, 'northerners coming from all lands'.[2] In the debate which has long continued over the identity of these peoples it has often been held that the *Akawasha* 'of the countries of the sea' are 'Αχαιϝοί, Achaeans, or Mycenaean Greeks; but some of the relevant records seem to indicate that the Akawasha warriors were circumcised, which is something not otherwise known of Achaeans.[3] If the Akawasha really were Mycenaeans, we still have no evidence of where they came from, whether from Greece itself, or from, say, Rhodes or some other Mycenaean principality. They need be no more than a band of mercenaries or adventurers. Whether they included Achaeans or not, this wide coalition of presumably maritime allies who assisted the King of Libya is indicative of seriously disturbed conditions in the eastern half of the Mediterranean; and though Merneptah was at this time successful in repelling them the disturbances were to recur in the reign of Ramesses III (1198–1166 B.C.). This time Egypt had to face not only the Libyans, assisted from without as before, but also, a few years later, a combined land and sea invasion by a number of different peoples including Peleset, Tjekker, Sheklesh, Denyen, and Weshesh.[4] Again their identifications are not all clear; but it is agreed that the Peleset are the Philistines, later to settle in Palestine,[5] and the name Denyen may

---

[1] § I, 8, 100 f.    [2] § I, I, vol. III, sects. 569 ff. See above, pp. 233 f.

[3] § I, 6, 21, n. I, with review in *Class. Rev.* II (1961), 9 f.

[4] § I, I, vol. IV, sects. 35–135, esp. 59 ff.; § II, 3, 80 ff.; § I, 2, 237 f. See above, p. 242 n. 8.

[5] See below, p. 372.

perhaps be equivalent to Δαναοί. If so, it appears that Mycenaean Greeks were again involved; and even apart from the name
there is evidence that some of the marauders were of maritime
origin and that they had been operating against the Hittite land
of Arzawa and against Alashiya (probably Cyprus) before they
joined the other forces in Syria. Thence the allies made their way
south, destroying many cities (including Alalakh, Ugarit, and
Tell Abu Hawam, already mentioned) before they were defeated,
in 1191 B.C., on the borders of Egypt.

Such far-reaching operations through territories formerly controlled by the Hittites obviously imply an advanced decay of the
Hittite power; and we can in fact trace darkly in the Hittite
records something of the way events had been turning in the
preceding half-century. Millawanda (Miletus), which had in the
early thirteenth century been at least nominally under the control
of Ahhiyawa, appears in the records later in the century as a
vassal of the Hittites.[1] Archaeology shows that the city was
destroyed some time in the L.H. IIIb period, and rebuilt with
massive fortifications;[2] and there can be little doubt that it was
fortified with Hittite approval, against Ahhiyawa. Mycenaean–
Hittite relations had deteriorated from friendliness and respect
to open hostility, and in the text of a treaty made between the
Hittite Tudkhaliyash IV (c. 1265–1240) and the King of Amurru
(in northern Syria) the name of the King of Ahhiyawa is found
deliberately deleted (though still legible) from a list of kings
reckoned of equal rank to the Hittite emperor. The same text, if
correctly restored, shows it was Hittite policy to prevent ships of
Ahhiyawa trafficking with Syria.[3] Though the Hittites were thus
unwilling to recognize the power of Ahhiyawa, and though their
hostility must have contributed to the decline of Mycenaean trade
eastwards, it is clear that they were not having it all their own way.
For another fragmentary text, probably of the same reign, mentions the King of Ahhiyawa as campaigning in person with both
chariotry and infantry in Asia Minor;[4] and it was also during the
reign of Tudkhaliyash IV that there began the hostilities referred
to in a long text of the succeeding king, Arnuwandash III (c. 1240–
1230), which details the acts of a former Hittite vassal named
Madduwattash.[5] This Madduwattash first appears as seeking

[1] § 1, 7, 198–240; § 1, 4, 50; § 1, 5, 2 f. (no. 3).
[2] § 1, 10, 187, corrected in § 1, 9(b).
[3] § 1, 7, 320–7; § 1, 5, 8 (no. 17); § 1, 8, 110; § 1, 4, 50 f.
[4] § 1, 7, 314–19; § 1, 5, 7 (no. 16); § 1, 4, 51.
[5] § 1, 7, 329–49; § 1, 5, 9 (no. 19); § 1, 3; § 1, 6, 97 ff. See above, pp. 264 f.

Hittite protection from the attacks of a 'man of Ahhiyā' named Attarshiyash. (The name has, notoriously, been equated with *Atreus*; but the phonetic equation is uncertain, and in any case Attarshiyash is not referred to as the *King* of Ahhiyawa.)  Later, Madduwattash throws off all pretence of allegiance to the Hittite empire, seizing for his own the land of Arzawa, formerly a vassal-state of the Hittites, through which they had dominated all the south-west of Asia Minor. Moreover we find him actually in league with Attarshiyash, engaged in raids on Alashiya (most probably to be identified with Cyprus, or a city of Cyprus) which the Hittite emperor claims as his own territory. Such activity by Attarshiyash suggests that he too was endeavouring to profit by the folding up of Hittite power in the south-west.

But this was not the only area of Asia Minor where the recession of the Hittite control was tempting local powers to aggrandisement. Another text[1] tells of rebellion and hostilities against the empire, in the reign of Tudkhaliyash IV, by a league of states headed by the land of Assuwa, which must be located somewhere between Miletus and the Troad. (The name may indeed be the original of *Asia*, which in Roman times was applied to the province in just that area.) As many as twenty-two places are listed as taking part in the rebellion, from Lukka in the south to Taruisa and Wilusa in the north, the names of which have been tentatively identified with the Greek Τροία and Ϝίλιος, though there are some philological difficulties.

In any case these documents are of importance when we consider the story, preserved on the Greek side, of the great Trojan War which marks the beginning of the end of the second heroic age. Here in these undoubtedly historical Hittite texts we find a setting in which that war could well have taken place. Earlier, any major activity in the lands east of the Aegean would have provoked a powerful reaction by the Hittites, as indeed happened in the Miletus area. In the regions between Miletus and Troy there is extremely little evidence of Mycenaean trade, and if this is not due to accidental limitations of archaeological knowledge it may have been the power of Assuwa, backed by the Hittites, that blocked Mycenaean entry. In Troy, however, the Mycenaeans had at least found commercial opportunities, though never any possibility of settlement. Now, in the latter part of the thirteenth century, the changing situation in the hinterland might prompt a more active Mycenaean approach. The Hittite Empire was crumbling; the states to the west which had been a buffer between

[1] § 1, 6, 102 ff.; cf. § 1, 5, 32 ff.

Mycenaeans and Hittites were asserting themselves; and it was almost inevitable that the Greeks should become involved against them, whether as competitors for their territory, now left clear of Hittite influence, and for new trading opportunities, or merely to forestall the dangers that might beset them with fully independent neighbours in western Asia Minor. The Hittite records of the aggrandisement of Madduwattash and the rebellion of Assuwa and its allies show that even now the south-west and west offered no easy field for any Mycenaean aggression. But in the north-west the Troad, where they already had trading access, may have seemed a more practicable approach. Even so they would have to reckon with the other powers of western Asia Minor as allies of Troy.

## II. THE TROJAN WAR

For later Greeks the Trojan War was the best remembered event of the Mycenaean age: it is the central fact of history behind the *Iliad* and *Odyssey*;[1] and it was constantly present to the Greek mind as a turning-point of the heroic age. The two greatest Greek historians both refer to it in the opening chapters of their work: Herodotus recalls it[2] as an earlier conflict of east and west, analogous to that of the Persian Wars; Thucydides speaks of it[3] as the first united foreign enterprise of the Greeks. That it was a united Greek enterprise is a point of some importance. The fame and glory of it were a joint inheritance of all the Greeks, just as the Homeric epics were. But we should be wrong to suggest that it was the Homeric epic that made it so, or that the epic was the sole source of knowledge of the war. It is true that a considered reading of the *Iliad* and the *Odyssey* will give one the outline— that Agamemnon mustered a force of men and ships from all Greece to sail against Troy to avenge the abduction of Helen, wife of his brother Menelaus of Sparta, and that Troy was eventually sacked after a long-drawn-out siege. But Homer does not actually recount these events; rather they are alluded to as though known already, and so no doubt they were. For Homer's poems are nowadays recognized as not the beginnings but the climax of a tradition of epic, in which earlier poems may indeed have been more concerned with the annals of history. But Homer's purpose was to tell a tale of human experience of universal application; and his narratives have the Trojan War for their backcloth because the period of that war and its aftermath was

---

[1] On the Homeric poems as history see below, pp. 820 ff.
[2] Hdt. I, 3.   [3] Thuc. I, 3.

the most momentous in the then remembered past of the Greeks, and was universally recognized as such. Indeed the fact that the Trojan War was accepted as historical by all the ancient Greek world, and that no writer in all that nation of sceptics ever questioned its historicity, is the most compelling evidence that it really did take place.

But though the *Iliad* does not pretend itself to be history, there is incorporated within it what may almost be described as a Mycenaean historical document, the *Catalogue of Ships*[1] in Book II. This list of the contingents (with their leaders and their places of origin) that composed the force attacking Troy represents a political geography quite unlike that of historical Greece.[2] It is not simply that the post-Mycenaean Dorian occupation of Greece is ignored. The cities are grouped in kingdoms with centres such as Mycenae, Tiryns, and Pylus, which are known to have been the focal points of the Mycenaean civilization though unimportant in historical times. Thebes, on the other hand, prominent in early Mycenaean times, is not mentioned; and this too is appropriate, since, as we have seen, the power of Thebes was eclipsed in L.H. III b.[3] This correspondence of the *Catalogue* with the Mycenaean reality extends to more detail. Of nearly 170 places named, over 90 can be pretty certainly identified; and of these a good half can be shown to have been occupied in Mycenaean times, while none of them is known to have been founded later than the Dorian invasion. Further corroboration of the *Catalogue*'s Mycenaean date is to be seen in its inclusion of at least forty places whose very location was no longer identifiable by the classical Greeks.[4]

In view of the good case that can on such grounds as these be made for the authenticity of the *Catalogue*, it will be worth while noting both its general content and, in particular, a few points which, though unexpected and not always corroborated by archaeology, may none the less be historically sound. While Agamemnon, the commander-in-chief, is elsewhere in the *Iliad* (II, 108) spoken of as ruler of 'many islands and of all Argos' (whether *Argos* means the city, the Argolid, or some larger area of Greece), the *Catalogue* defines more narrowly his personal kingdom. This, with its capital at Mycenae, includes only the northern end of Argolis, together with Corinthia and the country between Arcadia and the Corinthian Gulf.[5] The rest of the Argive plain, including the great fortress of Tiryns, is under Diomede, who also rules the

---

[1] Further discussed below, pp. 836 f.   [2] § II, 1; § II, 2; § II, 7, ch. IV.
[3] See above, pp. 168 f.   [4] § II, 7, 121 f.   [5] *Iliad*, II, 569–80.

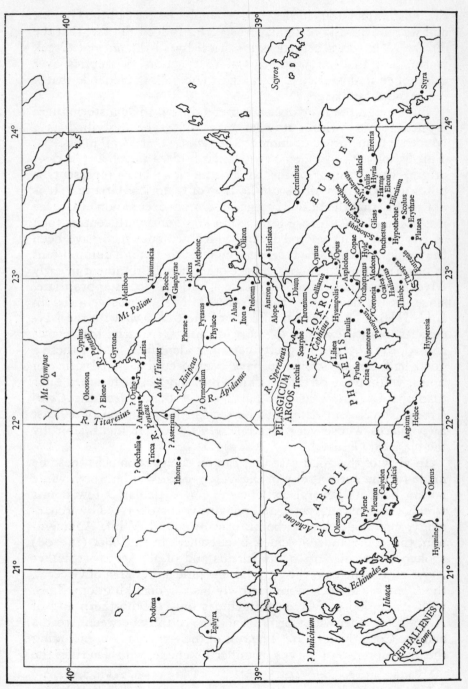

344

Map 8. Homeric geography, I. (Based on Allen and Burr.)

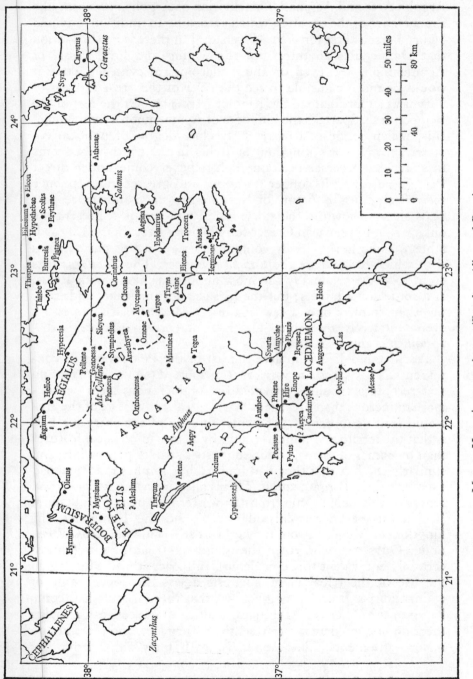

345

Map 9. Homeric geography, 2. (Based on Allen and Burr.)

Argolic Acte and Aegina.[1] This division of Argolis may seem like a recurrence of the situation which according to tradition obtained before Perseus first fortified Mycenae;[2] but there is no suggestion that Diomede is anything but the willing and loyal vassal of Agamemnon, and even on the archaeological evidence alone it would be more plausible to see the ruler of the great fortress of Tiryns as subordinate to the King of Mycenae. Of the rest of the Peloponnese, Sparta is the kingdom of Agamemnon's twin Menelaus, which suggests a particularly close degree of political co-operation. Nestor's kingdom of Pylus in the south-west seems in somewhat freer association; it had never come under direct Pelopid rule, and its longer traditions and greater independence are reflected in the picture of Nestor's great age and the respect he is always shown in the story. The Pylus area is at present the only part of Mycenaean Greece for which we have (in the Linear B tablets) some fairly closely contemporary record of place-names with which to compare the *Catalogue* entries. The *Catalogue* lists eight towns (presumably the most important) along with Pylus, and so do some tablets; but the lists are not the same, and in all the Pylus tablets only a few of these *Catalogue* place-names are even tentatively traceable. The lack of correspondence is disappointing and puzzling.[3]

Arcadia and Elis complete the list of the Peloponnesian contingents. The Arcadian warriors, transported (since they were no seafarers) in sixty ships provided by Agamemnon, seem perhaps more numerous than present archaeological knowledge of the area would lead us to expect. The chief interest of the entry for Elis is that the territory is defined rather by names of physical features than by names of towns, which suggests a sparser population; and similarly the fact that they had four leaders implies that they had a looser political organization. Their collective name is *Epeioi*, and others of this name came from the western islands of Dulichium (which cannot be certainly identified) and the Echinades, the kingdom of Meges. From further west still came the *Kephallenes*, under Odysseus, who ruled the islands of Ithaca, Same (almost certainly equivalent to Cephallenia), and Zacynthos. Here again the use of the tribal name suggests a less developed stage of civilization; and archaeology shows that these islands had come late into the sphere of Mycenaean culture.[4] Mycenaean remains there do not antedate the thirteenth century B.C., and there are no major settlements. The Aetolians, with forty ships from five

---

[1] *Iliad*, II, 559–67.  [2] See *C.A.H.* II[3], pt. I, p. 650.
[3] § II, 8, 141 ff.  [4] § II, 9, ch. XIII (iii).

towns, represent a rather different situation; the fame of the earlier heroes Tydeus and Meleager and the legend of the siege of Calydon[1] imply that Aetolia had once been an important Mycenaean centre, but to judge from the *Catalogue* it had much declined. It is indeed on the fringe of the Mycenaean world, so far as material remains yet tell; and the *Catalogue* equally has nothing to say of the areas to the north-west of it, either the islands of Leucas and Corcyra or the mainland areas of Acarnania, Thesprotia and Epirus. These were peopled, if by Greeks, by rougher, un-Mycenaean Greeks, whose hour had not yet come.

The peoples of central Greece are given by their tribal names, Phokeeis, Lokroi, and Abantes from Euboea, which again is probably indicative of a less advanced political organization than in the Peloponnese.[2] The same probably holds good for Boeotia; for the power of Thebes, which might have led a well-knit state, is a thing of the past, as we have seen, and the Boiotoi are probably newcomers to the Boeotian plain.[3] No less than thirty towns are listed, but their leadership is divided among five commanders. Why the Boeotians should have been given pride of place in the list is now no longer clear; possibly the *Catalogue* was originally composed in Boeotia.[4] Further north also we can recognize a diversity of political development. The people of Achilles, from Pelasgic Argos (probably the Spercheus Valley), from Hellas and from Phthia, go under the names of *Myrmidones* and *Hellenes* and *Achaioi*. *Hellenes* here is still a tribal name, like *Myrmidones*, and like *Hellas* has only a narrow local connotation, though we cannot clearly define it. *Phthia* is still more obscure; nor is it clear in what particular sense this contingent especially are called Achaeans. Only three towns are mentioned, though the contingent comprised fifty ships; but there is nothing incongruous in somewhat undeveloped hill-country producing some of the toughest fighting men in the army. The rich plain of Thessaly is represented in the *Catalogue* by eight small kingdoms with some twenty-five towns between them. This implies a degree of civilization for Thessaly which is only now becoming archaeologically apparent.

Coming south again we are in the area of fullest Mycenaean culture. Finds in Attica have shown that it was as prosperous and populous in L.H. IIIb as any part of Greece; in the *Catalogue* it has fifty ships, yet only the one city, Athens, is mentioned, and the people are named after it, Ἀθηναῖοι. Have we not here further evidence that the political union of Attica was achieved

---

[1] See *C.A.H.* II³, pt. I, pp. 647 f.  
[2] § II, 4, 65 f.  
[3] See Thuc. I, 12.  
[4] § II, 7, 152.

before the Trojan War?[1] Some ancient critics held that the next *Catalogue* entry, referring to Salamis, had been tampered with in the interests of Athenian propaganda; but even so Salamis appears as an independent unit, contributing a dozen ships under the great Ajax.[2]

Crete in the *Catalogue* still bears the epithet ἑκατόμπολις, '(isle of) a hundred cities', which might better have fitted the Minoan than the L.H. III situation; but only seven cities are named, contributing a force of eighty ships under Idomeneus, the grandson of Minos. Cnossus comes first, presumably as the capital, though archaeology shows it never recovered the splendours of the palace period. Phaestus, where too the remains show the palace site reoccupied only on a minor scale, has no distinctive position or comment in the list. Of the other five we can say little enough, except that Gortyn, described as τειχιόεσσα, is not known ever to have merited this epithet in the way that Tiryns did.[3] If the epic tradition is in this particular less soundly based than in some parts of the *Catalogue*, could this be because Crete was, as mentioned earlier,[4] more detached from full Mycenaean culture than most of Greece? That detachment need not have prevented Crete from taking part in the war.

Rhodes is represented by nine ships under Tlepolemus, Syme by three under Nireus and the other islands of the southern Sporades by thirty, led by Pheidippus and Antiphus. Tlepolemus as the *Catalogue* reminds us was a son, and Pheidippus and Antiphus were grandsons, of Heracles—a genealogy which probably reflects the already long-standing traditions of these islands, settled by Mycenaeans as early as L.H. II.[5]

The Cyclades and the northern Sporades find no mention in the list. This is unexpected, since we know that these islands shared the Mycenaean way of life. Probably the simplest explanation is that they did in fact remain neutral in the war. Lesbos and Lemnos in the north-east Aegean were non-Greek, and Lesbos is mentioned elsewhere in Homer[6] as having been conquered by the Achaeans—perhaps as a strategic prelude to the siege of Troy? Excavation has shown that Thermi in Lesbos was actually destroyed at a date which on the evidence of imported Mycenaean pottery must be near that of the fall of Troy.[7]

Agamemnon, king of Mycenae, is throughout the epic recognized as the commander-in-chief of the whole Greek host; but

---

[1] § II, 7, 145 and notes. See above, p. 169.
[2] Strabo, 394.  [3] See above, p. 173.  [4] See above p. 166.
[5] See *C.A.H.* II³, pt. I, p 654.  [6] *Iliad*, IX, 129f.  [7] § II, 6, 72, 213.

there is no special emphasis on his overall kingship in the *Catalogue*, and we are left on the whole with a picture of a temporary union, for the purposes of the war, of a number of diverse and independent kingdoms, rather than of a close-knit Mycenaean Empire. Possibly the ties of political unity were already loosening; or perhaps they had never existed to the degree we tend to imply in talking of 'empire'. Our consideration of the Hittite documents has shown that Mycenaean princes may well have engaged in hostilities abroad without reference to a suzerain in mainland Greece; and even in peace we may suppose that Bronze Age communications would necessitate a fair degree of decentralization in government, and a corresponding independence of local princes. For the Trojan War, however, there is no reason to doubt that the Greeks showed a united front.

The list of Trojan allies[1] in *Iliad* ii is but sketchy compared with the Greek catalogue; and this strengthens our belief in its Mycenaean date. It covers western Asia Minor from the Propontis and the Troad down to Miletus and Lycia, but without detail. It includes only such knowledge of these lands as would have been available in Mycenaean times, and has not been elaborated during the later history of the epic, when Asia Minor was quite familiar to Greeks. It is significant in this connexion that the one coastal city south of the Troad which is named is Miletus, the chief city of the Carians, who are characterized as of foreign speech (βαρβαρόφωνοι). This is precisely the area which archaeology and the Hittite texts show to have been long familiar to the Mycenaeans, and perhaps even, for a time, under Mycenaean rule.[2] Now, however, it is ranged on the enemy side. Furthermore, the Trojan *Catalogue*, like the Greek, mentions some places which were not identifiable by the later Greeks, a sure sign that such references go back to a time before the Ionians settled in Asia Minor.[3]

This Homeric account of the allies of Troy naturally invites comparison with the Assuwan alliance in western Asia Minor which rebelled against the Hittite emperor Tudkhaliyash IV.[4] A certain difference between them is that the Homeric *Catalogue* includes allies of Troy on the European side of the Hellespont— Thracians, Cicones and Paeonians—who are not mentioned in the Assuwan league. On the Asiatic side the difficulty of identification of the names in the Hittite document hampers the inquiry; but we can be fairly sure that *Lukka* and *Karkisha* are the same as

[1] Cf. §ii, 7, 137 ff.   [2] See sect. 1 above and p. 184 above.
[3] §ii, 7, 140 ff.   [4] §ii, 5, 34–7. See above, p. 164.

the Lycians and Carians of the epic. The Assuwan league was defeated, according to the Hittite records, but it nevertheless seems that Hittites did not thereafter intervene in western Asia Minor, and the same or another grouping of states may have recovered and even enlarged itself to meet the Mycenaean aggression. In the present state of knowledge, however, we are reduced to conjecture.

From Troy itself[1] there is good archaeological evidence that the city known as Troy VII a was in fact destroyed by an enemy, after a siege, at a date when L.H. III b pottery was still being used; and there can be no reasonable doubt that this was the event which has echoed through the world's literature ever since. It is the only archaeologically recognizable sack of Troy at all near the period assigned by tradition. But when we inquire more closely after the date of this event,[2] there are difficulties on both sides. Tradition was not unanimous as to an 'absolute' date, though it was agreed[3] that Troy fell from sixty to eighty years (or two generations) before the Return of the Heraclidae, the dynasty ousted from the Peloponnese by the Pelopids. The Return itself was dated through the Spartan royal pedigrees which could be traced back to it. By such rough calculation various dates were arrived at, with the mean at 1203 B.C., in our terminology.[4] Archaeology, in turn, cannot yet date L.H. III b pottery with sufficient precision for us to do any better than place the fall of Troy 'c. 1200 B.C.'. Nor can we place it with any real precision in relation to Hittite chronology, though this has been attempted.[5] It is probably safe to assume that it was later than the texts of the reign of Tudkhaliyash IV referring to the Assuwan alliance, but how much later is by no means certain. There are difficulties, too, in establishing the chronological relation of the sack of Troy to events in Greece itself, attested by archaeology, which must now be considered.

## III. DISTURBANCES WITHIN GREECE: INVASION AND EMIGRATION

The general evidence of the history of Mycenaean settlements, as observed by the archaeologist, shows clearly enough the expansion that took place in the L.H. III b phase. Whereas L.H. III a is represented at some ninety sites, L.H. III b is represented at 143. These figures disregard sites known to have been occupied in

---

[1] See above, pp. 161 ff.
[2] Cf. *C.A.H.* I[3], pt. 1, pp. 246 f., and bibliography thereto.
[3] Cf. Strabo 582, 3; Thuc. I, 12, 3.     [4] §II, 3, ch. IV.     [5] §II, 5, 30–6.

351

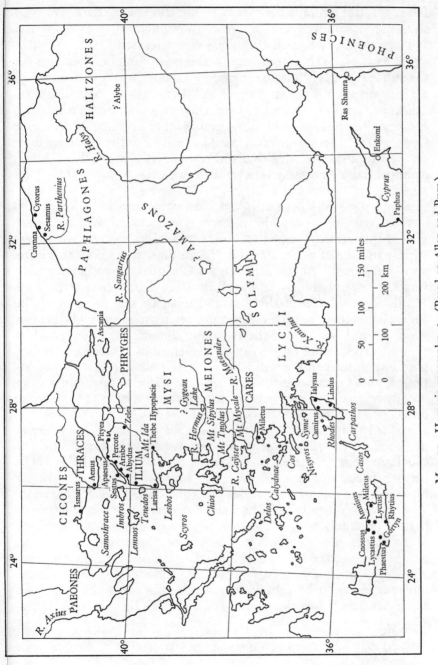

Map 10. Homeric geography, 3. (Based on Allen and Burr.)

L.H. III, but without any preciser indication of the date; yet even so they must imply a great increase in population and prosperity. It is, however, clear that the phase characterized by the archaeologist as L.H. IIIb embraces also the beginnings of decline; for the subsequent IIIc phase is represented only at sixty-four sites—a recession even more striking than the preceding expansion.[1] It might be tempting to deduce from this some single overwhelming catastrophe of invasion and destruction that brought Mycenaean Greece to its knees; but this would be rash. For the evidence does not tell us that the sites that did not survive into L.H. IIIc all disappeared at the same time, nor do we even know that they all perished by sword and pillage.

Some signs of such perils can, however, be traced. The walls of Mycenae appear to have been strengthened and extended within this period,[2] and special care was taken to ensure a water-supply in time of siege. Similar precautions were taken at Tiryns and at Athens.[3] At the Isthmus of Corinth[4] a new fortification was set up, apparently to check invasion from the north. This recalls the tradition of the first and unsuccessful attempt of the Heraclidae[5] to regain their kingdom, when their leader Hyllus was slain in single combat at the Isthmus, and an agreement reached that they should not return for two generations. According to one account,[6] however, they did pass the Isthmus at this earlier attempt, and captured all the cities of the Peloponnese, but had to withdraw again after one year on account of a plague that broke out. This abortive attack occurred before the Trojan War; Pausanias is specific about this, rejecting a view he had held earlier in his work.[7] The archaeologist can only say that the fortification of the Isthmus and the sack of Troy both fell within L.H. IIIb; further precision should some day be obtained from a better knowledge of the pottery styles on which our dates are based.

Also within the L.H. IIIb period occurred the destruction or partial destruction of a number of Mycenaean sites, including some of the most important.[8] South of Corinth the small but prosperous settlement of Zygouries[9] came to a violent end. At Mycenae itself a number of houses outside the citadel were burned, never to be rebuilt.[10] Even within the walls there was some damage,[11] but the citadel continued to be inhabited there-

---

[1] §III, 1, 148–50.   [2] §III, 16, 1959, 93 ff.; §III, 15, 206; A, 2, 31 f.
[3] §III, 19; §III, 8, 355; §III, 6, 422–5.   [4] §III, 9; §III, 7, 299 (plan).
[5] See below, pp. 686 ff.   [6] Apollod. II, 8, 2.
[7] Paus. VIII, 5, and I, 41.   [8] §III, 1, 149.
[9] §III, 5.   [10] §III, 21; §III, 10.   [11] §III, 12; A, 3, 260, with refs.

after. Tiryns too seems to have been attacked; there is considerable evidence of destruction by fire;[1] but here again the citadel did survive. In Laconia, the settlement at the Menelaion[2] was destroyed; in Messenia, the great palace of Nestor at Pylus.[3] Neither was rebuilt. Blegen, the excavator of both Pylus and Troy, can assure us that Pylus was destroyed after Troy,[4] but we do not know just how long after. The sequence of the events at the other sites is less certain. But sites in central Greece tell a similar tale. The huge island fortress of Gla in Boeotia did not outlive L.H. IIIb, but little detail is yet available for this site;[5] its previous history is virtually unknown, but it is possible that its whole existence was short. If so, the very construction of so great a fortification (enclosing ten times the area of Tiryns or Troy) is a symptom of the dangers that now beset Mycenaean Greece. Crisa in Phocis is another site that seems to have come to a violent end at this time.[6] Further north, the final destruction of the palace at Iolcus[7] is obviously another serious disaster for Mycenaean civilization about which the evidence of further excavation will be particularly welcome; it is believed to have occurred at the very end of L.H. IIIb.

What archaeology at present fails to tell us is the order of sequence of these events, and whether they occurred after the Trojan War or not. The traditional history would lead us to expect that they did; for otherwise it would have been a sadly weakened and depopulated Greece that put up the expedition against Troy. Could it indeed have launched its thousand ships? It seems improbable. As events of the post-war period they raise no such question, but rather accord with the traditional picture, in which the nominal success of the taking of Troy is followed by no occupation of the foreign territory, no resultant access of prosperity at home. Honour had been satisfied; and if we believe tradition alone, that was the sole purpose of the expedition. But the historian, however willing to *chercher la femme*, looks for profounder and more substantial interpretations, which at present elude us. The tradition of the Trojan War implies a powerful Greece. The fact of the destruction of sites—and even though the sites are at present few, they are widespread—implies that the Mycenaean glory was departed. We should be perverse not to

[1] §III, 19; §III, 1, 35 f.    [2] §III, 22, 72.
[3] §III, 4, vol. 64, 159; A, 1, 419–22.
[4] §III, 4, vol. 61, 133; A, 1, 422–3.
[5] §III, 16, 1957, 29; 1960, 37 f.; §III, 1, 122 f.
[6] §III, 13; §III, 1, 130 f.    [7] §III, 16, 1956, 49; 1960, 57; §III, 1, 143.

recognize the strong probability that the destructions are to be linked with the Dorian invasion, of which clear and irrefutable accounts have come down to us.[1]

The Dorian invasion and the final break-up of Mycenaean Greece are discussed below, chapter XXXVI; but the Greeks had traditions of events more immediately following upon the Trojan War which also deserve the historian's attention. The heroes had sacked Troy; they shared out the loot and the captives and pointed their ships homeward; but a hard coming they had of it. From Homer onwards the period of the 'homecomings', the *Nostoi*, is a tale of shipwreck and wandering off course, of enforced settlement in distant lands, of return to broken homes and family strife, of consequent emigration to build life afresh in new lands. The story of the *Odyssey* is typical in the picture of difficulties encountered, though not in the hero's ultimate attainment of home and happiness (and even Odysseus, we may recall, was destined to further wandering).[2] Other homeward journeys of heroes presented in the course of the poem have a special interest, in that they are there as background to the main tale, and are therefore presumably intended as a picture of the typical post-war situation. Menelaus, before he reached Sparta, had visited Cyprus, 'Phoinike' (Syria or Palestine) and Egypt; in Egypt he had stayed a considerable time, and accumulated valuable possessions which he brought home with him.[3] Odysseus himself puts over a story of similar wanderings, on occasions when he is at pains to conceal his identity. He claims that after taking part in the Trojan War he had travelled to Egypt, 'Phoinike', and Libya; and more particularly he states in one place that his visit to Egypt was in company with roving pirates—ἅμα ληϊστῆρσι πολυπλάγκτοισι —who got into considerable trouble with the Egyptian forces.[4] These adventures are fiction, even within the framework of the story; but the story demands that they be plausible, the kind of adventures which were typical of the period; and as such both they and Menelaus's wanderings invite comparison with the land and sea raids in the first decade of the twelfth century which we have already noted in the records of Ramesses III. It is not fanciful to see here the poetic record, from the other side, of the same events.

There were current in historical Greece many more such stories, some of them crystallized in the epic *Nostoi* (of which we have now but fragmentary knowledge), others remembered as part of the

---

[1] Discussed below, pp. 694 ff.    [2] *Od.* XI, 128.
[3] *Od.* IV, 81ff., 128ff.    [4] *Od.* XVII, 425ff.

traditional history of individual cities. What survives today is in late authors, but it is clear that they depended on much older sources. The general picture is of Greek heroes emigrating, either direct from Troy, or after a brief return home, to almost every part of the Mediterranean: Apollodorus, for example, mentions Asia Minor, Libya, Italy and Sicily, and even the islands near Iberia.[1] The individual instances which may be collected from the literature are almost innumerable, and a selection must suffice here for illustration.

Teucer, for example, was banished from his home in Salamis and went to found a new Salamis in Cyprus.[2] Agapenor, the Arcadian leader, forced off course on his way from Troy, founded or re-founded Paphus, with its famous temple of Aphrodite.[3] Pheidippus, again, the leader of the Coans, was reputed to have found his way to Cyprus and settled there.[4] For such settlements there is at least some archaeological corroboration. Enkomi, the Bronze Age predecessor of the Cypriot Salamis, had been destroyed at the end of L.H. IIIb, and the people who rebuilt it used L.H. IIIc pottery of a style which is clearly not developed from local antecedents, but from mainland Greek wares.[5] The history of Paphus is less well known at present; but some connexion of the cult there with Arcadia is attested by the fact that in Greece itself the *Paphian* Aphrodite was worshipped only at Tegea.[6]

Equally remarkable is the story of the colonization of Pamphylia and Cilicia by Greeks who left Troy under the leadership of Amphilochus, accompanied by the prophet Calchas. This is mentioned by Herodotus,[7] and Strabo in his several references to it cites Callinus and Hesiod as sources, and indicates that it was known to Sophocles. The migrants apparently proceeded by a coastal route, for Clarus near Colophon is the scene of a picturesque incident between Calchas and another seer, Mopsus, who replaces him and eventually assists in the founding of Mallus in Cilicia. Subsequently, Amphilochus revisited his native Argos, and on returning to Mallus was hostilely received by Mopsus; but despite the tradition that the two killed each other in single combat the names of both were closely associated with the local oracle in later times. The particular interest of this tradition lies in the fact

---

[1] Apollod. epitome, VI, 15.
[2] Schol. on Pindar, *Nem.* IV, 75.    [3] Lycophron, 479ff.; Strabo, 683.
[4] Schol. on Lycophron, 911. Further examples in §III, 11.
[5] See below, p. 660.    [6] Paus. VIII, 5, 2.
[7] Hdt. VII, 91; Strabo, 642, 668, 675–6; Paus. VII, 2, 1.

that Mopsus may plausibly be identified with one Mukshush whom late Hittite kings of this area in the eighth century B.C. claimed as the first of their line.[1] Finds of pottery show that Cilicia had for some time before this (perhaps from L.H. IIIa) been in touch with the Mycenaeans, and the pottery evidence continues into the L.H. IIIc period;[2] but without further excavation of settlements we are not yet able to corroborate by this means the story of the settlement of Amphilochus. For Pamphylia (where some of the migrants made their new home) there is as yet even less archaeological evidence; philological data suggest that Greek settlements there were established at least as early as in Cyprus,[3] but this is not precise enough for our purposes. Certainly the traditions must not be lightly dismissed as unhistorical, especially if we observe how far the tale of this migration through Asia Minor, and of the settlements in Cyprus, seems to echo what the Egyptian records have to say of the movement of peoples in just these areas in the reign of Ramesses III.[4]

For regions to the west of Greece, tradition presents us with a similar picture.[5] The Pylians who sailed away from Troy with Nestor are credited with the foundation of Metapontum on the Gulf of Taranto, and even of Pisa in distant Etruria;[6] Crimisa is said to have been founded by Philoctetes, and the same hero is later associated with the foundation of the more famous colonies of Croton and Sybaris in the same area;[7] Diomede settled in the region of Apulia called Daunia.[8] Most remarkable of all, perhaps, the Rhodians are said to have founded colonies as far off as Spain and the Balearic Islands, besides others on the Italian coasts—at Parthenope in Campania, at Elpia in Daunia (this in conjunction with the Coans), and in the vicinities of Siris and Sybaris on the Gulf of Taranto.[9]

The coasts of southern Italy and Sicily were not of course unknown to the Mycenaeans before this date: pottery and other evidence proves at least trading contact in these parts from L.H. II onwards; and settlement there in the disturbed twelfth century would conform to the same pattern as the migrations to the eastern Mediterranean, which nowhere seem to have opened up wholly new lands or routes. Archaeological support for the traditions is not impressive in either quantity or detail, but it is not

---

[1] §III, 2. See below, pp. 363 ff.  [2] §I, 8, 88f.; §III, 17, 134.
[3] §III, 14.  [4] See above, pp. 339.
[5] §III, 3, ch. IX.  [6] Strabo, 264, 222.
[7] Strabo, 254.  [8] Strabo, 283 f.
[9] Strabo, 654, 264; cf. §III, 3, 61 f. and 348.

wholly wanting. As in the east, there is a falling-off in the pottery evidence at the end of L.H. IIIb. In Sicily no IIIc imports have been discovered, though there are suggestions of IIIc influence in local wares: in the Aeolian Islands it is only at Lipari that IIIc wares appear.[1] But at Scoglio del Tonno, by Taranto, the Mycenaean pottery sequence runs right through into L.H. IIIc; and in Apulia there are local wares which show marked signs of IIIc influence.[2] There is at present no trace of Mycenaeans in Campania or Etruria; but there is nothing unreasonable in the tradition, especially if we recall that Mycenaean sherds of earlier date have been found as far north as Ischia.[3] That Pylus should colonize in the central Mediterranean is likely enough, since it lies on the coasting route up through the Ionian Sea, and there is a further reminder that this was a natural course for shipping in the identification of features in the IIIc pottery from Scoglio del Tonno which derive from Cephallenia.[4] Cephallenia itself seems to have had a fresh access of population in L.H. IIIc;[5] but this movement did not extend northwards to Leucas or Corcyra, which still remained strangely isolated from Mycenaean culture. The superficially improbable tradition of colonization from far-off Rhodes is on examination of the archaeological evidence perhaps the most plausible. Rhodes had been a flourishing corner of the Mycenaean world from L.H. II onwards, and seems not to have suffered as mainland Greece did from the troubles of the IIIb period, but with some others of the Aegean islands continued to enjoy comparative prosperity in IIIc.[6] Moreover, it is clear that Rhodes was a chief participant in the activities of the Mycenaean trading station at Scoglio del Tonno.[7] It would be natural, therefore, that the Rhodians should be foremost in any colonizing that went on in the Gulf of Taranto after the Trojan War. That they went so far as Spain or the Balearics there is as yet no proof; but we shall do well to restrain ourselves from the felicity of incredulity.

The flight from mainland Greece that is represented by all these eastward and westward migrations is not easily explained; and as so often in history, causes and effects seem inextricably tangled. Clearly, conditions at home must have been unsatisfactory, and it is easy to blame the Dorian invasion; but why was Mycenaean Greece unable to resist invasion? Possibly resources had been squandered in the Trojan campaign. But why was the

---

[1] §III, 18, 74 and 47.  [2] §III, 18, 128 ff. and 138 ff.
[3] §III, 18, 7 f.  [4] §III, 18, 132.
[5] See below, pp. 659 f.  [6] See below, p. 663.  [7] §III, 18, 128 ff.

war undertaken? There seems to have been good warning of dangers at home before it began; it was not a moment for aggression in the opposite direction. Perhaps the weakening of the Hittite Empire and the consequent difficulties in east Mediterranean trade had a graver effect on the Mycenaean economy than we can now discern, and the Trojan campaign was a desperate attempt to gain a new opening. Perhaps Greece had burned up her home resources—almost literally, for the consumption of timber in Mycenaean times for building as well as for fuel in the metal and pottery industries must have been enormous. It is not impossible that the first disastrous steps in deforestation, with the inevitable impoverishment that it brings, were taken in Mycenaean times. When the Dorian pirates hove in sight the Mycenaean ship had fought its last fight and was already sinking. There was nothing to do but to take to the boats and row manfully out of reach.

# CHAPTER XXVIII

## THE SEA PEOPLES

### I. ANATOLIANS AT THE BATTLE OF QADESH

The thirteenth century B.C. was an age of increasing turmoil, confusion and obscurity, after which it is largely clear that the civilization of the Age of Bronze in the Levant really tottered to its end. If we wish to obtain a picture of this period of sudden decline and collapse, we have to be content to pick our way through a bewildering tangle of evidence, much of it highly fragmentary, much of it highly conjectural and insecure. The former class is based, it is true, on more or less historically authentic records, partly in cuneiform (but these are sparse), partly in Egyptian hieroglyphic documents (but these suffer greatly in value from the imperfect system of vocalization used in them in transcribing foreign names). In the second group of data, we are driven to fall back on the evidence of Greek legendary traditions. These, though precarious, are clearly not to be ignored. The resultant picture is naturally far from clear, and such objectivity as it may possess has been sometimes brought into doubt by too passionate partisanship on the part of individuals who have sought to win conviction for their possibly justifiable theories by massive over-accumulation of uncertain arguments.[1] The picture drawn here is further incomplete in so far as the publication of several important excavations in Lycia,[2] Syria,[3] Cyprus,[4] and Israel,[5] which, it is to be hoped, may soon throw much light on different aspects, is still awaited.

In the year 1300 B.C., the great clash took place at Qadesh in Syria (modern Tell Nebi Mind on the upper Orontes river) between the young Ramesses II and Muwatallish, the Great King of the Hittites.[6] The list of the Hittites' allies, recorded by the Egyptian scribes,[7] includes a number of peoples of Anatolia and

---

* An original version of this chapter was published as fascicle 68 in 1969; the present chapter includes revisions made in 1973.

[1] §I, 2; §IV, 19; §IV, 20; §IV, 21; §IV, 22.　　[2] §IV, 17.　　[3] §VI, 5.

[4] That of Enkomi by Schaeffer and Dikaios is of particular importance. See now §VI, 2 for a brief account.

[5] See A. Biran and O. Negbi, 'The Stratigraphical Sequence at Tel Sippor', in *I.E.J.* 16 (1966), 160 ff.

[6] §I, 4, vol. III, 125 ff.; §I, 6.　　[7] See above, p. 253.

Syria. This list is of particular importance to us, since it mentions several peoples who all, save the first (*Drdny*), are hitherto already familiar and recognizable from the Hittite imperial records as being the names of peoples of Western and Central Anatolia. The identifications of the remaining names, though necessarily tentative, have been fairly generally accepted among scholars for many years. The list mentions after *Nhrn* (i.e. Mitanni) and *'Irtw* (Arzawa, the Western Anatolian kingdom[1]), the following apparently Western Anatolian names:

| | |
|---|---|
| *Drdny* | usually taken as Δάρδανοι, a Homeric Greek name for Trojans. |
| *Ms* | usually taken as equivalent to *Maša*. |
| *Pds* | usually taken as equivalent to *Pitašša*. |
| *'Irwn* | usually taken as equivalent to *Arawanna*.[2] |
| *Krḳš* (or *Ḳlḳš*?) | usually taken as equivalent to *Karkiša*. |
| *Ṛk* (or *Lk*) | usually taken as equivalent to *Lukka*. |

The Egyptians were on their side aided by *Šrdn* (Sherden)[3] mercenaries, otherwise only once previously mentioned in an Amarna letter *c.* 1375 B.C.[4] The Maša are identified by some with the Μηίονες, or *Μαίονες, an ancient name of the Lydians, but this identification presents difficulties, since, according to some authorities, the Μηίονες invaded Lydia only in the early Iron Age. The mention of *Pds* (*Pitašša*) is of some importance in a later connexion. We do not know exactly where this was, though a place of that name in Western Anatolia was known to the Hittites: in classical times there was a Pedasa near Miletus, and Homer knew very well a Pedasos on the River Satnioeis in the Troad (*Iliad* VI, 35, XX, 92, XXI, 87). Strabo (XIII, 584 and 605) speaks of Pedasos as a city of the Leleges opposite Lesbos. In his second year (1235 B.C.), the pharaoh Merneptah sent a huge gift of corn via Mukish in North Syria through Ura[5] in Western Cilicia to alleviate a severe famine in *Pds* which had formerly fought against Egypt.[6] It is perhaps permissible, with due hesitation, to connect this historical event with legend, and to see in this

---

[1] §IV, 8, 83 ff.; on the correct location of Arzawa, see H. Otten in *J.C.S.* II (1961), 112 f.   [2] See above, p. 253.   [3] §I, 6, vol. I, 194 ff.

[4] §I, 10, I, nos. 81, 122, 123 (*še-ir-da-ni*, *ši-ir-da-nu*), II, pp. 1166 f., 1521 for reference. Cf. W. F. Albright in §VII, 2, 167, who argues that this word is merely a form of a noun *šerdu*, 'servitor'.

[5] See §I, 2, 21, n. 4, on its location (see again below, p. 376). Another Ura in Anatolia is known on the frontiers of Azzi-Khayasha.

[6] §I, 4, vol. III, 244; §IV, 1, 143. A second grave famine in Anatolia occurred some thirty years later; see below, p. 369.

famine, so sore as to become known across the width of the Mediterranean Sea, the grim tribulation which is said by Herodotus[1] to have afflicted Lydia for eighteen years, and finally forced the Etruscans to emigrate from that country. This event is recorded by Herodotus as the Lydians' own version,[2] and is clearly ascribed to a remote antiquity. If it happened at all, it must have taken place before 1000 B.C., for the Etruscans are said to have embarked from the Gulf of Smyrna and they could hardly have done this later without coming into conflict with the Aeolic Greeks who settled, as excavations show,[3] at the head of the bay about this time. It may be noted that an Anatolian origin for the Etruscans was evidently accepted by the Hebrews (or their sources) in the early *mappa mundi* presented in Genesis x, which places Tiras (connected by some with Τυρσηνοί) as a brother of Meshech and Tubal, namely in Phrygia.

The *Arawanna* have sometimes been identified with the Hittite city Arinna[4] and *Karkiša* with Caria.[5] The mention of *Lukka* is of importance since it first raises the question where their home was. According to the Egyptians, they are brigaded closely with the *Ḳrḳš*, and it may be no coincidence that in the Hittite treaty of Muwatallish with Alakshandush of Wilusa, Lukka is placed next to *Karkiša* and *Maša* among Wilusa's allies. The Lukka-lands are often mentioned in Hittite annals as a restless and turbulent area in the west of Anatolia, but we meet some difficulties if, as is often done, we identify the *Lk* mentioned in Egyptian records with the later Lycia—an identification first put forward by de Rougé[6] in 1861—even if we combine the Hittites' *Lukka* with Lycia and even with Lycaonia.

Here archaeology is, for the present, of little help, because no remains of the Late Bronze Age have so far been found or excavated on the Lycian coast, though there are signs that this apparent absence may turn out not to apply to the interior.[7] Perhaps the existence of a common stem *Lu-* in the names of several Anatolian peoples (Lycians, Lydians, Lycaonians, Lulahhi, Luwians) may suggest a common origin. A tribe of 'Inner Lycaones' lived even in Central Phrygia near Pisidian Antioch in Roman times,[8] but the *Lukka* appear to have been a people living on and by the sea, being mentioned in 1375 B.C. as pirates in another Amarna

---

[1] Book I, 94.    [2] *Ibid.*
[3] E. Akurgal, 'Bayrakli Kazisi on Rapor.' In *Ankara Üniversitesi Dil ve Tarih-Coğrafya Fakültesi Dergisi*, 7 (1950).
[4] §IV, 8, 20.    [5] §IV, 6.    [6] §I, 8, 303 ff.    [7] §IV, 17.
[8] A. H. M. Jones, *The Cities of the Eastern Roman Provinces* (1937), 38, 66, 93.

letter.[1] (It has been claimed that the Lukka or *Lk* were present in the Levant from at least the Egyptian Middle Kingdom, on the basis of a reference to a member of that people in an Egyptian hieroglyphic inscription found at Byblos, but this evidence has now been disputed.[2]) The Lycians in later times spoke a dialect descended from Luwian and closely related to Hittite,[3] and preserved it tenaciously into Hellenistic times. It would seem not unreasonable that their historical origins should be traced back to the *Lukka*. According to Greek traditions the Lycians, led by Sarpedon, in the Homeric poem formed part of the allies of Troy.[4] A slight difficulty remains in that we are told that the true name of the Lycians was Termili[5] (Lycian *trm̃ml*), while Lukka was, to the Hittites at least, only a geographical, not a tribal or racial, appellation. Whatever the explanation may be, in the deteriorating state of affairs of the fourteenth to thirteenth centuries B.C. the Lukka certainly played a part, if only that of an irritant.

What was going on in the cultural world of the coast of Western Asia Minor at this time is still largely wrapped in mystery, except for the fitful disclosures of excavation. If Troy and Ilios are correctly identified with *Taruiša* and *Wilušiya*, then Troy formed part of the Hittite Empire,[6] and if Assuwa was Asia[7] we have in this treaty to which we have referred a picture of the Assuwan league in the thirteenth century B.C. Miletus is widely thought to be the Millawanda of the Hittites.[8] At Miletus, though it was a Carian country, a powerful Mycenaean or pro-Mycenaean colony was evidently established from the fifteenth century B.C.[9] At Old Smyrna was a pre-Greek, non-Greek city, but unfortunately the details are largely unpublished.[10] The coastal darkness is only deepened by an occasional discovery such as that at Phaestus in Crete, in a Middle Minoan context *c.* 1500 B.C., of an extraordinary clay disk bearing a spirally written inscription[11] in a strange form of pictographs impressed with movable stamps into the clay while yet soft—a primitive but undeniable anticipation of printing; an invention which remained as far as we know unique in antiquity, and still-born. The forty-five signs used include designs which may represent a ship with a high prow, a house or hut possibly of Lycian type and, most notably, a war-

---

[1] §1, 10, no. 38, 10—*amēlūtu ša (māt)lu-uk-ki*, 'people of Lukki'.
[2] §1, 1.   [3] §IV, 12.   [4] *Iliad*, II, 876; v, 479, etc.
[5] Herodotus, VII, 92.   [6] See *C.A.H.* II³, pt, I, p. 677.
[7] §IV, 2.   [8] §IV, 8, 80 ff.
[9] See above, pp. 340 f.   [10] See above, p. 361, n. 3.
[11] A. Evans, *The Palace of Minos*, fig. 482. See *C.A.H.* II³, pt. I, pp. 595 ff.

rior's head crowned with what appear to be feathers. The discovery in Crete of two allegedly similar, but incised and shorter texts[1] now gives some scholars to think that the Phaestus disk is Cretan, but it may well have some Anatolian affinities or describe some Anatolian business.[2] Does the disk refer, or belong, to some other kindred people? Is it about Lycians?—or are these the σήματα λυγρά carried by Bellerophon to Lycia?[3] Herodotus (VII, 92) mentions that in his day the Lycian sailors wore a 'cap set about with feathers', but we have as yet no illustration of this headgear to compare it with that on the disc and to cause us safely to accept its evidence for a continuity of tribal fashions lasting until a thousand years later. Nor can either of these feather headdresses, whether that of Phaestus, or of the Lycians, even if mutually connected in our view, safely be connected with that of the Philistines to be described below.[4]

## II. MOPSUS AND THE *DNNYM*

The impression of deepening distress and disturbance in Western Anatolia in the thirteenth century B.C., possibly due to climatic changes and famine,[5] amply reflected in Greek legends and the Hittite records, is conveyed more clearly by the affair of the prince of Zippashla, Madduwattash[6] (bearer of a name seemingly of later Lydian type similar to such as Sadyattes or Alyattes) who, in conspiracy with the king of Ahhiyawa, eventually united the western kingdoms of Anatolia against their lawful liege lord, the king of Khatti, and even swallowed up Pitashsha ( = *Pds* of the Egyptians?). In his train came a freebooter named Mukshush, who followed him in some capacity which is left unclear by the fragmentary nature of the text, in which Mukshush is mentioned

---

[1] W. F. Brice, *Inscriptions in the Linear A Script*, 2.

[2] The hut sign (no. 24) has a strange and apparently identical precursor on a sign incised on an Early Bronze Age potsherd found in 1963, suggesting a direct continuity both of the script and of the timber architecture of Lycia. (Machteld J. Mellink, 'Lycian Wooden Huts and Sign 24 of the Phaistos Disk', *Kadmos*, 3, 1, 1964.)

[3] *Iliad*, VI, 168.          [4] See below, p. 372.

[5] The theory that the collapse of the Late Bronze Age world in both Greece and Anatolia alike was due to a vast cyclic climatic change, producing drought and universal famine conditions leading to mass migrations, is powerfully argued in §I, 5. Another theory would attribute it in large part to the great volcanic explosion of Thera and consequent tidal wave, which is ascribed to 1200 B.C. instead of, as hitherto, *c.* 1500 B.C. See Leon Pomerance, *The Final Collapse of Santorini (Thera)* (Studies in Mediterranean Archaeology, vol. XXVI, Göteborg, 1970).

[6] §IV, 9; see also above, pp. 264 f.

only once.[1] The significance of his name was not apparent until
Bossert's brilliant discovery at Karatepe of the bilingual text
where the name of Mukshush is rendered in the Hittite hieroglyphic (i.e. Luwian) version as Muk(a)sas, but in Phoenician
as *Mpš*.[2] It is now accepted that Mukshush, the companion of
Madduwattash, is identical in name with Mopsus, a strange figure
of Greek legend, a seer and prince of Colophon, a city where a
Mycenaean settlement certainly existed, as shown by excavations.[3]
Mopsus, son of Rhakius of Clarus and Manto, daughter of
Teiresias, was reputed to have engaged in a contest of divination
with another seer, Calchas, at Clarus and to have founded the
famous sanctuary of Apollo there.[4] Another version calls him
a Lydian, son of Lydus, and brother of Torrhebus. In Lydian
traditions, Mopsus' name seems to be recorded as Moxus,[5]
a name also met in Greek Linear B tablets as *mo-qo-so*.[6] A year
before the end of the Trojan war (so legend tells) Mopsus set out
southwards with a band of followers, accompanied by Amphilochus and two Lapiths named Leonteus and Polypoetes.[7] Moving
into Pamphylia, Mopsus founded its most notable cities, Aspendus
and Phaselis; then, entering Cilicia, he built the half-Greek cities
of *Mopsou-hestia*, 'Mopsus' hearth' (where there was later a
famous oracle of the hero, clearly in recollection of his prowess in
life as a soothsayer himself), and Mallus, the latter founded
jointly with Amphilochus. Mopsus' name was also commemorated in Cilicia at *Mopsou-krene* ('Mopsus' spring'). Less factually
perhaps, but significantly, he is said to have married Pamphyle,
daughter of Kabderus (a name obviously derived from Caphtor[8]),
an aetiological myth evidently designed to explain how the mixed
population of Aspendus and Phaselis resulted from intermarriage
of Greeks (or half-Greeks) with natives. Whoever those were, it
was agreed by the Greeks that the Pamphylians were a racial
hotch-potch, as their name suggested. From Cilicia Mopsus,
according to the Lydian historian Xanthus,[9] moved on to Askalon, where he threw the statue of the goddess Astarte into her own
lake, and finally died there.

H. Bossert's discovery in 1946[10] of the bilingual inscriptions at
Karatepe in the Ceyhan valley of Cilicia in Southern Turkey,
written in the Phoenician alphabet and in Hittite hieroglyphs
(i.e. Luwian), described above, not only finally solved the riddle

---

[1] §I, 2, 61 ff.                    [2] §IV, I, 142.                    [3] See above, p. 184.
[4] §IV, 2, 54.                                                          [5] §I, 2, 56 ff.
[6] §V, 6, tablets KN X 1497 and PY Sa 774.                             [7] See above, pp. 355 f.
[8] See below, p. 374.          [9] §IV, 25.                            [10] §IV, 4; §IV, 5.

of the reading of the hieroglyphs, but made a historical contribution of unusual importance by transforming for the first time a
figure of Greek legend, Mopsus, into an undeniable historical
personality.[1] In this inscription, King Azitawatas, author of the
Karatepe texts, discloses himself as a lesser chieftain of the
Danuniyim (the exact vocalization of the name is uncertain; these
people of the ninth century B.C. are clearly the same as the Danuna
mentioned in the fourteenth century B.C. in an Amarna letter[2])
who seem to have formed an important kingdom[3] in the fourteenth
century B.C., but whose chief city was probably Pakhri, mentioned by Shalmaneser III[4] and identifiable with Pagrai in the
Amanus mountains. It is of importance that, where the Hittite
hieroglyphic, i.e. Luwian, text describes Azitawatas's overlord
Awarkus[5] (identified usually with a king of Que or Cilicia mentioned in the Assyrian records of Tiglath-pileser III under the
name of Urikki), as 'king of the city of Adana', the Phoenician
text describes him as 'king of the Danuniyim'. The names are
thus virtually identical, the prefixed 'A' of Adana having some
unexplained implication.[6] Further, a connexion is perhaps to be
seen with Greece in the likely identification of Danuniyim–
Danuna with the Greek Danaoi and the family of Danaos, who is
credited in Greek legends with an oriental origin.[7] Possibly these
*Dnnym* may be also the hitherto elusive Hypachaioi, or 'sub-
Achaeans' of Cilicia, mentioned by Herodotus (VII, 91) as a
former name of the Cilicians.[8] Some scholars have seen, somewhat dubiously, a survival of the name of Achaeans ('Αχαιοί) in
the Assyrian name Que (= *Qawa?) for Eastern Cilicia.[9] More
important, Azitawatas states in his inscription that he is of the
house of *Mpš*, or Mopsus, whose name, as we have said, is rendered
in the Luwian version as Muksas by a $p > k$ change for which

---

[1] See below, pp. 679 ff. Since 1969, however, it has been powerfully argued
by Otten (A, 12) and others, on both philological and historical grounds, that the
Madduwattash episode and consequently Mopsus' date have to be put back to the
early fourteenth century B.C. As stated in *C.A.H.* II³, pt. 1, p. 677, the present
*History* cannot take full cognizance of this development and treats these texts in the
traditional way.

[2] §I, 10. The value of the Mopsus legend in history is well discussed in §I, 2, 53 ff.

[3] The considerable extent of their kingdom as far as the Amanus is discussed by
§I, 2.

[4] §I, 2, 2 n. 4.                              [5] '*Wrk* in the Phoenician version.

[6] Since, according to Stephanus, the founder of Adana was called Adanos, M. C.
Astour believes that Adana is derived from a personal name (Adan = lord), §I, 2, 39;
§I, 2, 2.

[7] §I, 2, ch. I.

[8] §IV, 13; §IV, 14.                        [9] §IV, 13.

Lydian gives illustrations.[1] This form of his name (Moxus), which is recorded by Xanthus, adds a city, Moxoupolis, in Southern Phrygia to his list of foundations and connects with him a tribe of Moxianoi in Western Phrygia.

### III. THE CLASH OF SEA AND LAND RAIDERS WITH EGYPT

The *razzia* of Mopsus may be reasonably regarded[2] as part of the downward thrust of the horde of assailants whom the Egyptians called collectively the 'Peoples of the Sea'—who first massed against Egypt from the West via Libya in the reign of the pharaoh Merneptah about 1232 B.C., but were then repulsed and withdrew.[3] These events were known to us largely from the Egyptian accounts, but a casual reference in the Bible to the bloody repulse by Shamgar Ben-Anath of a force of six hundred invading Philistines (Judges iii. 31) may refer to this phase of preliminary probings, and there are some archaeological reasons to think that some settlement by Philistines or other closely related 'Sea Peoples' in Palestine, e.g. at Beth-shan and Tell el-Fār'ah, may start in this period[4] before 1200 B.C. Soon, gathering full strength and benefiting from the overthrow of the Hittite Empire in about 1200 B.C., the Sea Peoples surged down again like a flood through Syria and Palestine, carrying all before them, until they were stayed only at the north-eastern gates of Egypt.

Let us take the earlier onslaught first. In his records at Karnak and Athribis[5] Merneptah (1236–1223 B.C.) boasts that he won his great victory in Libya in his fifth year (1232 B.C.) against an army of Libyans and Meshwesh (the later 'Maxyes'), who were supported by an alliance of northern sea-borne forces. Their names are given as *'Ikwš* (vocalized variously as Akawasha, Akaiwasha, or Ekwesh), *Trš* (Teresh or Tursha), *Lk* (Lukku or Lukka), *Šrdn* (Sherden or Shardana), *Škrš* (Sheklesh or Shakalsha), 'northerners coming from all lands'. These names

---

1 §1, 2, 62: as stated above, p. 364 and n. 6, the *q* is preserved in Mycenaean Greek, i.e. Linear B versions of his name, but paradoxically it is the Phoenician version in the Karatepe text which has followed a Western Anatolian tendency to change *q* to *p*.

2 See now, however, above, p. 365, n. 1.

3 §1, 4, vol. III, 238 ff.; see also above, p. 233.

4 §VII, 25; §VII, 27. At Tell el-Fār'ah, five tombs with multiple burials in the '900' cemetery have been recognized as strongly Mycenaean in type, containing LM IIIb ware, yet otherwise Philistine in their content.

5 §1, 4, vol. III, 240 ff; see also above, pp. 233 f.

include only two which were previously known, namely Lukka
and Sherden.[1] The numbers of prisoners recorded by the
pharaoh's scribes as captured are given as: Sheklesh, 222;
Teresh, 742; Akawasha, 2,201. These figures, though we need
not trust them too blindly, might well imply that the Akawasha
were the strongest element and very probably to some extent the
ringleaders, but the Athribis stela gives the figure of 2,200 as
Teresh, thereby injecting some doubts into our minds about its
accuracy. All these peoples are described as 'of the Sea'.[2] The
ending of their names in -sha has suggested since Maspero
(1897) an Asia Minor ethnic ending; today we might see it as an
Indo-European nominative. Illustrations of several of these
peoples occur in various Egyptian triumphal scenes,[3] and aid us
in identifying them. No illustration exists of Lukka or Akawasha, but we learn with surprise that the Akawasha were circumcised Merneptah, in his victory inscriptions at Karnak and
Athribis,[4] records the number of slain Akawasha, mentioning
that their hands were cut off instead of their genital members as
was done in the case of uncircumcised victims. Since de Rougé's
time, too, Akawasha have been identified with Ἀχαιοί, the
Mycenaean Greeks and, since the recovery of the Hittite records,
by most with the Ahhiyawa.[5] If this is so, it is absolutely out
of keeping with everything that we know about the Greeks,
and therefore about the Akawasha, that they should have been
circumcised, though it was a practice common to both Egyptians
and Semites. The matter remains inexplicable.[6]

The Tursha (or Teresh) and Sheklesh–Shakalsha are shown
bearded alike, the Sheklesh wearing a high headcloth, the Tursha
a smaller type; both sport a pointed kilt with tassels and many
hang a medallion on a cord or thong round their necks—a custom
common in Syria and Anatolia, even in Iran.[7] Their armament
consists of a pair of spears or a khepesh (scimitar); their chests are
protected by bandaging with strips perhaps of linen or leather.
These two races have been identified since Champollion and de
Rougé,[8] though, admittedly, only speculatively, with the Etruscans (the Tyrsenoi of Lydia who bear the ethnic ending in -ēnos,
common in Anatolia) and the Sicels, who are supposed by the

---

[1] See above, pp. 360 f. also p. 233 and below p. 508.
[2] §1, 8, 305 and 318.
[3] §1, 19, pl. 160A and 160B; §1, 19, plate on p. 342.
[4] See above, p. 366 n. 5.                                    [5] §1, 8.
[6] But see §1, 2, 355 ff.
[7] §III, 3, 83 ff. and reference therein; §III, 2.
[8] §1, 8.

advocates of this view to have been on their way westwards to their ultimate Mediterranean home in Sicily.[1] In fact, new-comers are said to appear at this time in Sicily bringing with them a new type of lugged axe; the archaeological evidence in Italy, however, for the arrival of the Etruscans so early is still wanting.

The Sherden, who as mercenaries are known in Egyptian records from the time of Amenophis III, are shown in Egyptian reliefs as beardless and wearing a very distinctive helmet (some-times held under the chin with a chinstrap) with a large knob or disc at its apex, and ornamented with enormous projecting bull's horns.[2] They are armed with a round shield with a handle, and brandish a huge two-edged sword of distinctive type, suitable either for slashing or thrusting. A unique example of it, now in the British Museum, was obtained in 1911 at Beit Dāgān, a Pales-tinian village near the town of Jaffa (it was not from Gaza, as often misstated).[3] The Sherden have been very plausibly identified with the bronze-working population of the Sardinian stone-built towers or *nuraghi*, a race whose remarkably vigorous bronze statuettes (though hitherto known from examples not earlier than the ninth century B.C.) often show them as warriors armed with round shields and wearing horned helmets resembling the Sherden type, but without the central knob or disc very characteristic of Sherden.[4] A further connexion between Corsica and the Sherden is strongly suggested by R. Grosjean's[5] recent observation that menhir-like tombstones still stand in Corsica showing male warriors wearing banded corselets, daggers and formerly horned helmets, the horns having been separately inserted into holes in the stone, but now having long disappeared. That the Sherden were seafarers and pirates is more than likely. It fits the evidence fairly well that the builders of the *nuraghi* appear suddenly in Sardinia between about 1400 and 1200 B.C., though we have no positive indication as to whence they came.[6]. It is likely enough that they immigrated into Sardinia from Cyprus,[7] where they may well have been a native

---

[1] See below, ch. XXXVII, sect. II.    [2] E.g. §I, 19, pl. 160 B.

[3] See R. D. Barnett, *Illustrations of Old Testament History* (London, 1966), 29 and fig. 16. Near Beit Dāgān is the ancient site of Azor, now under excavation, where plentiful Philistine material occurs.

[4] §II, 1, 187 ff.    [5] §II, 2.    [6] §II, 1, 111 and 187 ff.

[7] A significant pointer to contacts between Cyprus and Sardinia in this period is to be seen in the occurrence in Sardinia of copper ingots of the characteristic 4-handled Cypriot shape, derived from a leather hide, now well known from the Cape Gelidonya wreck. (See above, pp. 214 f.; and G. Bass, 'The Cape Gelidonya Wreck' in *A.J.A.* 65 (1961), 267 ff.)

copper-working people. In the earliest Phoenician inscription found in Sardinia, that from Nora, probably of the ninth century B.C., although it is incomplete, the name of the island appears as Shardan (*be-shardan*), and thus the identification of Sardinia with the Sherden seems much strengthened.[1] Another pointer in Sardinia to the former presence of the Sea Peoples lies in the representation in a bronze figure and on the island's coins in Roman times of the eponymous divine ancestor Sardus Pater as a bearded man wearing a stiffly erect headdress,[2] resembling that favoured by Sea Peoples, particularly the Philistines, to be described below.

As we have said, the final assault on Egypt came after the turn of the thirteenth century B.C. The gathering clouds are reflected in the last documents found at Khattusha and Ugarit. Among the tablets from the archives of Rap'anu found at Ras Shamra (Ugarit) during the 20th and 26th seasons of excavations were three letters mentioning a famine in Anatolia (Khatti). Ugarit is asked to send 2,000 measures of grain from Mukish to Ura in Cilicia.[3] In another letter from Ras Shamra[4] the king of Ugarit appeals for help to the king of Alashiya (almost certainly Cyprus), whom he calls 'my father'. A reply (?) found in the oven from one *Ydn* urges him to arm a considerable fleet of 150 ships to resist the enemy. Meanwhile, the king of Ugarit writes: 'Does not my father know that all my forces and chariots are stationed in Khatti Land, and all my ships are in Lukka Land?' [which is thus identifiable as coastal] 'Thus the country is abandoned to itself... seven enemy ships have appeared and inflicted much damage upon us.'[5] Clearly, the combined fleets are massing off Lycia, while the armies are joining up in the West. By the end of the reign of Shuppiluliumash II, the last Hittite king, we find from Hittite sources that Alashiya has changed sides, and its ships are fighting against the Hittites. Finally, a tablet found at Boğazköy in 1961 reports the defeat of the Alashiyan navy.[6] 'I called up arms and soon reached the sea, I, Shuppiluliumash, the Great

[1] C.I.S. I, no. 144, on p. 191; see also W. F. Albright below, ch. xxxiii and *Bull. A.S.O.R.* 83 (1941), 14 ff.
[2] G. Perrot and C. Chipiez, *Histoire de l'Art dans l'Antiquité* (Paris, 1887), vol. IV, fig. 7 on p. 21. He seems however to have been also identified with the Phoenician god of Hunting, Sid; see U. Bianchi, 'Sardus Pater' in *Rendiconti dell'Accademia Nazionale dei Lincei*, ser. VIII, 18 (1963), 97 ff. and S. Moscati, 'Antas: a new Punic site in Sardinia', in *Bull. A.S.O.R.* 196 (Dec. 1964), 23 ff.
[3] J. Nougayrol, *Ugaritica* V (1968), texts 33, 44 and 171. See also §1, 3, 253 ff.
[4] §1, 3, 255.        [5] §IV, 18, 20 ff.
[6] See above, p. 265; §IV, 18.

King, and with me the ships of Alashiya joined battle in the midst of the sea. I destroyed them, catching them and burning them down at sea.' Meanwhile, at Boğazköy, in the royal palace of Büyükkale all the walls were demolished and the flood of invaders poured onwards in a southerly direction perhaps joining hands with the coastal force led by Mopsus and his allies. At about this time the late Mycenaean settlement at Miletus in Caria was burnt. In Cilicia Mersin,[1] with its late Hittite palace, fell, as did Tarsus.[2] So, too, fell Carchemish, the great capital city controlling the crossing of the Euphrates, from which the Hittite Great King's Viceroy had long ruled over the cities of North Syria.[3] Ras Shamra–Ugarit and Tell Sūkās[4] on the Syrian coast were sacked; the former never recovered. Hamath was captured and occupied by the newcomers, who, it seems, after the resettlement were responsible for introducing the rite of cremation burial,[5] as happened at Carchemish,[6] Tell Sūkās,[7] and Açana.[8] This suggests that the Sea Peoples brought it with them. Sidon, too, was destroyed, according to tradition, while its inhabitants fled to Tyre.[9] Tell Abu Hawwām (identified by Mazar with Salmon, a Tyrian colony), a vast site on the Palestinian coast near Haifa, likewise fell.[10] With several of these destructions is associated the discovery of LH III c 1 a pottery, a circumstance which may well indicate the presence or passage of the Akawasha–Achaeans mentioned by Merneptah. The story in Cyprus is similar. Excavations at Kition (Larnaca) since 1962, until then supposed to have been a purely Phoenician foundation of the Iron Age, show that it was a wealthy city in the Bronze Age, comparable with Enkomi,[11] but there are traces of a great catastrophe at the end of the thirteenth century B.C., followed by fresh settlers. These were evidently the first Greek settlers, who built themselves large houses of ashlar masonry, and used LH III c 1 pottery. This settlement was short-lived, being destroyed by the same movement of the Sea Peoples as Enkomi. It was reconstructed before the period of LH III c 2 or 'Granary Style' pottery which was used there in the eleventh century. It was finally abandoned c. 1075 B.C. after a catastrophe, probably an earth-

---

[1] §IV, 7.   [2] §IV, 10.

[3] See E. Laroche, 'Matériaux pour l'étude des relations entre Ugarit et le Hatti', *Ugaritica*, 3, 1956 (ed. C. F. A. Schaeffer).

[4] §I, 15

[5] §I, 16; W. F. Albright in *Bull. A.S.O.R.* 83 (1941), 14 ff.

[6] C. L. Woolley and R. D. Barnett, *Carchemish*, vol. III (London, 1952).

[7] §I, 15.   [8] §I, 18.

[9] Justin, XVIII, 3, 5; cf. Josephus, *Ant. Jud.* VIII, 62.

[10] §VII, 20.   [11] §VI, 3; A, 9.

quake, only later to be recolonized by the Phoenicians. Similarly, at Enkomi[1] in the early twelfth century the 'Close Style' appears, perhaps emanating from Rhodes, which was by now under control of the Achaeans, possibly those known to the Hittites as Ahhiyawa. (This is the point at which the Hittite king Arnuwandash III is complaining to Madduwattash that he has supported Attarshiyash and Piggaya in seizing Cyprus.[2]) The 'aristocratic' quarter on the west side of the city was burnt, probably by Sea Peoples, at the beginning of the twelfth century B.C., but industrial life continued, using debased Levanto-Helladic ware in Levels IV–II. 'Granary Style' then appears in Levels III–II, finally dominating by the time of Level I, together with Cypriot Iron Age I pottery.[3] At Paphos, the city and shrine of Aphrodite was traditionally founded (or refounded) by an Arcadian, Agapenor.[4]

## IV. THE PHILISTINES

In his fifth year (1194 B.C.), Ramesses III found himself involved in a fresh war with the Libyans on his western border, and reports in his triumphal record at Medīnet Habu that already[5] 'the northern countries quivered in their bodies, namely the Peleset, Tjekk[er]... They were cut off [from] their land, coming, their spirit broken. They were thr[6]-warriors on land; another [group] was on the sea...' Three years later, he graphically pictures the collapsing world of the Levant as far as the farthest horizon: 'As for the foreign countries, they made a conspiracy in their isles. Removed and scattered in the fray were the lands at one time. No land could stand before their arms, from Khatti, Qode [ = Cilicia], Carchemish, Yereth [ = Arzawa], and Yeres [Alashiya] on, [but they were] cut off at [one time]. A camp [was set up] in one place in Amor [Amurru]. They desolated its people, and its land was like that which has never come into being. They were coming, while the flame was prepared before them, forward toward Egypt. Their confederation was the Peleset, Tjekker, Sheklesh, Denye[n] and Weshesh lands united.'[7] From

---

[1] §vi, 2; §vi, 4; §vi, 6.
[2] §iv, 9, 157 ff.; §vi, 3; see above, ch. xxiv, sect. iv; but see above, p. 365, n. 1.
[3] §vi, 3.
[4] Strabo, xiv, 6, 3.
[5] §i, 4, vol. iv, 18–26; W. F. Edgerton and J. A. Wilson, *Historical Records of Ramses III*, pp. 30 f.; see below, pp. 507 ff.; above, pp. 241 ff.
[6] A foreign word for chariot-warriors, see §i, 13, 239, n. 3; §i, 7, 40.
[7] Edgerton and Wilson, *op. cit.* p. 53.

the above account it is deducible (though not by any means proved) that the clash took the form of two battles:[1] the first in Syria (Amurru or Zahi) against the Land Raiders, perhaps taking the form of a rearguard action; the second real fight, against the Sea Raiders, taking place in the Delta at the entrance to Egypt itself, though Schaeffer[2] believes that this battle too occurred far north of the frontier, near Arvad. This sea battle is depicted in the sculptures of the exquisite temple at Medīnet Habu with great realism.[3] The Egyptians are aided by Sherden mercenaries. The Peleset are clean-shaven, wearing a very distinctive head-gear made of what seems to be a circle of upright reeds (or possibly leather strips or horsehair not, as often said, feathers) mounted on a close-fitting cap with a horizontal, variously decorated band round the wearer's brow.[4] The whole head-dress was held in place by a chin-strap tied under the chin. On their bodies the Peleset or Philistines, for such they are, wear a panelled kilt, falling in front to a point, usually decorated with tassels (such a tasselled kilt is worn by a Southern Anatolian god on a stele from near Çağdin[5]) and their chests are protected by bandaging with horizontal strips, perhaps of linen, or a ribbed corselet. They carry a pair of spears, sometimes a full-size rapier sword (which, it has been argued, has Caucasian affinities[6]), and a circular shield with a handle like those of the Sherden. On land, they fight in the Hittite manner from a chariot with crews of three, consisting of two warriors and a driver, while their families follow, partially guarded in wooden ox-drawn peasant carts usually of Anatolian type with solid wheels, like those used by the Hittites at the Battle of Qadesh. The draught animals are humped oxen, a breed bred in Anatolia, but not used in the Aegean or Palestine.[7] It is universally agreed that the Peleset are the Philistines of the Bible, of whom these Egyptian records thus form the first explicit historical mention. This people clearly in some respects has a strong connexion with Anatolia—a point supported by their monopoly and expert mastery of metal-working (cf. I Sam. xiii. 19–22 often interpreted as reference to

[1] This is suggested in §1, 13, 260, n. 4.
[2] §VI, 4, 60.
[3] §1, 20, 334–8, 340.
[4] T. Dothan suggests that this decorated band, bearing knobs, zigzag patterns or vertical fluting indicates differences of rank or class (A, 5). It is also worn in this battle by Tjekker and Denyen.
[5] H. T. Bossert, *Altanatolien*, fig. 567.
[6] R. Maxwell-Hyslop, 'Daggers and Swords in Western Asia', in *Iraq*, 8 (1946), 59 f. (type 53).
[7] §1, 10, 338 f.

ironworking) of which the Hittite kings boasted some skill, and which is attested by the actual discovery of increasing amount of artifacts of iron at the Philistine sites in Palestine of 'Ain Shems, Tell Jemmeh, Fā'rah, Azor and Ashdod.[1] Other indications equally, or even more clearly, point to very close connexions with the Mycenaean Greeks (who as Akawasha are in fact quoted by the Egyptians as serving with the Philistines against Egypt in year 5 of Ramesses III). That the Philistines traditionally had a connexion of some kind with Crete is upheld by the fact that part of the Philistine coast was called the 'Cretan' South or *negeb* (I Sam. xxx. 14), and Cretans are sometimes described with Philistines in the Bible (Ezekiel xxv. 16, Zeph. ii. 5).[2] The ships in which the Philistines are shown fighting against the Egyptians in the sea battle are of a most unusual type, powered by sail only, not by oars, with a central mast bearing a crow's nest, a curved keel, a high stern and prow ending in a duck's head; yet such a ship is depicted on a late Helladic III vase[3] from Skyros, and on a Levanto-Helladic Pictorial Style vase from Enkomi.[4] Some scholars have seen significance in two Philistine words preserved in the Hebrew Bible: *kōba'* (I Sam. xvii. 5), for Goliath's helmet, apparently to be derived from the Anatolian word *kupaḫḫi* (helmet); and the Philistines' word for chieftain, preserved in Hebrew as *seren*, which may be connected with the word τύραννος 'lord', itself borrowed by the Greeks from Lydia.[5] Others see in the challenge to single combat between David and the Philistine champion Goliath a typically European, Hellenic idea. An important index is naturally the Philistines' very distinctive pottery (including a rapidly growing group of distinctive cult vessels and figurines),[6] partly Mycenaean in shape, yet unlike Mycenaean ware in being not varnish-painted but matt-painted bichrome ware, decorated in metopes, often with volutes, a common design being a swan with turned-back head. It is connected with LH III c 1 b ware of Greece and Rhodes (the so-called 'Close Style'). This Philistine pottery is not merely found at the sites in Palestine associated with the Philistine invasion, at Megiddo in Levels VII A, VI B and A and in Beth Shemesh in Level III, but also closely

---

[1] §vii, 1; §vii, 6. R. de Vaux considers that the Sea Peoples' ships, apart from prow and poop, basically do not differ from Syrian merchant-ships depicted on Egyptian reliefs (A, 13).

[2] A group of Cretan seals was found near Gaza: V. Kenna, *Cretan Seals* (Oxford, 1960), 65, 78, 151 f.

[3] §v, 7, figs. 43 f. on p. 259.

[4] §vi, 7, fig. 10 (from Tomb 3, no. 2620).

[5] See below, p. 516 and n. 3.     [6] §vii, 5; §vii, 15; §vii, 16.

resembles LH III 1b ware found at Enkomi and Sinda[1] in Cyprus.

We might perhaps hope to find some clues to the Philistines' origins in their religion, but of the Philistines' religion we know almost nothing, since their gods of later times—Dagon, Ashtoreth and Ba'al-z[e]būb—are clearly either Canaanite or adaptations to Canaanite cults. B. Mazar sees in the introduction and spread of the cult of Ba'al-shamem, god of the sky, Philistine influence inspired by the Greek Olympian Zeus.[2] H. Margulies[3] sees in the reference to flies and bees in Philistine cults and legends such as that of Samson allusions to bee-cults and other worships and beliefs of the Greek and Minoan world. Early terracotta figurines illustrating a seated female deity of Mycenaean style have been found in excavations at Ashdod which point clearly to a Mycenaean origin.[4] Philistine burial customs take various forms, including Mycenaean-type chambers with *dromoi* and anthropoid clay coffins at Tell el-Far'ah[5] (probably to be identified with Sharuhen) in the twelfth and early eleventh centuries B.C. and cremations at 'Azor (like those of Hamath) in the eleventh. At Beth-shan in the thirteenth century begin these clay slipper-type sarcophagi with heads crudely modelled in relief.[6] Some of the heads on these sarcophagus lids have the decorated headbands characteristic of the Philistines and in one case a row of vertical strokes indicating the common Sea Peoples' war headdress. Over the dead man's mouth a plate of gold foil was occasionally tied, a custom reminiscent of burials at Mycenae, but also met surviving into the tenth century[7] at Tell Halaf (Gozan), a half-Aramaean city of North Syria, suggesting a remote echo of the passage of the Peoples of the Sea.[8] Hebrew traditions about the origins of the Philistines unanimously agree on their connexion with the Aegean world. In Genesis x. 14 (cf. I Chron. i. 12) they are said to be derived from Caphtor, son of Miṣraim ( = Egypt) brother of Ludim (i.e. the Lydians) and various Egyptian and North African races —a highly possible allusion to the participation of the Peleset in

[1] §vii, 5, 154. Recent discoveries at Ashdod in the earliest Philistine levels have disclosed two things: first, its LH III 1c pottery can be in fact demonstrated by analysis of the clay to have been locally made (A, 4). Next, it is accompanied by the earliest form of Philistine ware, a white wash and bichrome pottery in which several later characteristic Philistine shapes are represented.    [2] §vii, 20.

[3] In an unpublished MS, to which the author kindly allowed me to refer.
[4] §vii, 5.                         [5] §vii, 27; see also above p. 366, n. 4.
[6] §vii, 5; see below, pp. 510 f. I am indebted to Mr E. Oren, who will shortly publish the Beth-shan cemetery, for this information and for his comments.          [7] §vii, 23.            [8] *Ibid.*

the Egyptian wars. But according to Amos (ix. 7), Deut. (ii. 23) and Jeremiah (xlvii. 4) their home was Caphtor, 'an island in the sea', certainly identifiable with the land *Kapturi* or *Kaptara* known from cuneiform texts,[1] and probably correctly identified with Crete, for Egyptians the home of the Keftiu,[2] an Aegean people often depicted in Eighteenth Dynasty tombs as foreigners bearing tribute. It is, however, conceivable, as argued by Wainwright, that Caphtor and the land of the Keftiu were Cilicia;[3] yet if so, how is it that Caphtor–Keftiu is never mentioned by the Hittites? Probably in Egypt and the Levant during the Eighteenth Dynasty Kaphtor became used as a generalized term for the Cretan–Mycenaean world. The word then seems to have gone largely out of use after the fall of Cnossus. The word *kaptōr* remains in Hebrew as a curious vestige that by the time of Exodus (xxv. 31–6, cf. Amos ix. 1) had come to mean for the Hebrews, doubtless borrowing it from the Phoenicians, an ornament perhaps in the form of a lily-flower or palmette, presumably originally of Aegean (Minoan) origin. Other origins, however, have been proposed for the Philistines:[4] Albright[5] returns to the old identification of them with the mysterious pre-Greek population called by the Greeks Pelasgians, assuming this name to be equated somehow with Peleset.

Archaeological finds, on the other hand, suggest that the immigration of the Philistines into Palestine was effected in two or even three stages. First come some settlements represented by tombs at Deir-el-Balaḥ and Beth-shan.[6] Then, about 1200 B.C., comes a period of invasions and burnings, e.g. at Megiddo and Ashdod. To about 1200 B.C. is to be dated the find in a sanctuary at Deir 'Allā of clay tablets bearing inscriptions in an unknown script of very Aegean appearance.[7] (This date is given by a broken faience vase found in the sanctuary bearing the cartouche of Queen Tawosret of Egypt.) After this comes the third stage: the Land and Sea Battles, followed by final Philistine settlements in Palestine to be described. There also seem to be increasing indications of Philistine connexions with some part of Cyprus. In

---

[1] E.g. §I, 12, vol. IV, 107, text 16238, 10. Kaphtor is also known in the Ras Shamra Texts, where it is called the residence of the artificer god, *Ktr-w-Ḫss* (§I, 2, 110). 　　　　　　　　　　 [2] §I, 17, 110 f.

[3] §IV, 19; §IV, 10; §IV, 21; §IV, 22; §IV, 23.

[4] E.g. by M. Müller, §VII, 22. 　　　　 [5] See below, pp. 512 f.

[6] Bronze figures of men wearing feather head-dresses from sites in Syria and Phoenicia, e.g. H. T. Bossert, *Altsyrien* (1951), fig. 584, have been used in discussion of the Sea Peoples but evidently are unconnected with them.

[7] §VII, 11. See below, p. 510; above, p. 336.

the first place we have connexions indicated by the origin of Philistine ware, described above. Above this level were traces of Philistine 'squatters'. Ramesses III (1198–1166 B.C.) mentions among a list of his enemies several towns of Cyprus, *Srmsk* (Salamis), *Ktn* (Kition), *'Imr* (Marion?), *Sr* (Soli), *Rtr* (Idalion). Ramesses III claims to have repulsed the *tk(k)r* (Tjekker),[1] a group identified on Egyptian reliefs as wearing a head-dress of a type described above,[2] commonly accepted as Philistine. One branch of this people certainly settled in strength at points on the coast of Phoenicia and Palestine, at Byblos and Dor, as is shown by the Tale of Wenamun, the Egyptian emissary from Thebes in the time of Smendes (early eleventh century B.C.), who is sent to buy cedar logs but brings back a long tale of woe.[3] But to connect the Tjekker with the Greek hero Teucros or Teucer of Salamis is very tempting. To Teucer is traditionally ascribed the foundation of Olba (Ura?) in Cilicia and Salamis in Cyprus. Tjekker appear to be already present in Enkomi (Salamis) even before its destruction at the turn of the thirteenth to twelfth century B.C., for late thirteenth-century vases from Enkomi Tomb 3 show men wearing what is apparently a headdress of 'Philistine' type, walking or riding in chariots.[4] The ivory gaming-box from Enkomi in the British Museum decorated in Mycenaean style shows a chariot-eering nobleman or king of Syrian type followed by a bearded Tjekker servant with 'Philistine' head-dress holding an axe.[5] In the ruins of the city of Enkomi of the twelfth century B.C., afterwards rebuilt, was found a stone seal engraved with figure of a warrior holding a large shield and again wearing the familiar 'Philistine' head-dress.[6] It may very well be that the Teucrians–Tjekker destroyed, rebuilt and ruled over the new Salamis. Thereafter, we find that in Cyprus the Philistine type of boat, ending in a duck's head, continued in use there till the seventh or sixth century, as depicted on a vase.[7]

The Tjekker were, it would seem, not the only group of Sea Peoples to live, or to gain a foothold, in Cyprus. A splendid bronze statuette of a god wearing a felt or fur helmet with huge horns somewhat resembling the Sherden type was discovered at Enkomi by Dikaios in 1952.[8] In 1963 other statuettes with horned helmets were discovered, one holding a spear and round

---

[1] §1, 4, vol. IV, 24–5 and 75–6.    [2] §VI, 8; §III, 3. See above, pp. 372 f.
[3] §1, 13, 25 ff.    [4] §VI, 7, fig. 19 and fig. 10.
[5] A. S. Murray, A. H. Smith and H. B. Walters, *Excavations in Cyprus* (1900), pl. I.    [6] §VI, 2, fig. 11.
[7] Unpublished, in National Museum, Cyprus.    [8] §VI, 2; A, I.

shield standing on a model of an ingot.[1] Such figures tempt us to suggest not only that the Sherden came to Egypt from Cyprus, but that there were other Sea Peoples there too. In the Great Harris Papyrus, Ramesses III declares:[2] 'I extended all the frontiers of Egypt and overthrew those who had attacked them from their lands. I slew the Denyen [who are] in their islands, while the Tjekker and the Peleset were made ashes. The Sherden and the Weshesh of the Sea were made non-existent, taken captive all together and brought in captivity to Egypt like the sands of the shore. I settled them in strongholds bound in my name. The military classes were as numerous as hundred-thousands. I assigned portions for them all with clothing and provisions from the treasuries and granaries every year.' As for the 'Weshesh of the Sea', there is little to be said. Axos in Crete (spelt *Waxos* on its coinage) and Iasus or Iassos (also spelt Ouassos in inscriptions) in S.W. Caria have been suggested.[3] But this proclamation gives us an explicit clue that the invading Denyen–Danuniyim at least came through the Aegean islands; possibly also through Cyprus, and evidence may be plausibly seen in the Assyrian name for Cyprus in the eighth century B.C.,[4] Yadnana, to be interpreted as 'Ia-danana, 'Isle (or Coast) of the Danana', though no archaeological proof of Danuna settlement in Cyprus has so far been found. Very possibly Aspendus in Pamphylia was an outlying settlement of theirs, since its native name as given on its coins was *Estwedi*, apparently identical with the name of *Azitawata*, king of the city at Karatepe. In Eastern Cilicia, however, their old home, the Denyen lived on, as we have seen, into the ninth century B.C., strong enough to cause alarm to their neighbour across the Amanus, Kalamu of Sam'al,[5] and to be a thorn in his flesh. Whatever their original racial affinities, both groups were by then alike Semitized in speech though largely Anatolian in culture.

The outcome of the war between Egypt and the Sea Raiders is well known. Ramesses III claims to have utterly defeated them and suggestions that he and his successors settled groups of Peleset (Philistine) mercenary garrisons in Beth-shan in Palestine are demonstrated by the finds there of 'Sea People' burials. Others are found at Tell el-Fār'ah. He further seems to have given over to their care the four Canaanite cities of Gaza, Askalon, Ashdod and Dor, occupied by the Tjekker, as is made clear by Wenamon's

---

[1] §vi, 5.      [2] §i, 13, 262.      [3] See §iii, 3, 71, n. 3.
[4] D. D. Luckenbill, *Ancient Records of Assyria and Babylonia*, §§ 54, 70, 80, 82, 92, 96–9, 102, 186, 188 (Sargon II); § 690, 709–10 (Esarhaddon).
[5] §iv, 15.

report. (Two more cities, Gath and Ekron in the plain to the east, were occupied by them and formed with Gaza, Askalon and Ashdod a league of five cities ruled by *seranim*.)[1] One may perhaps wonder if the pharaoh's victory was as crushing as he suggests or whether, as was his wont, he is protesting too much; whether in fact it was not a Pyrrhic victory. The Peleset hordes were indeed prevented from entering Egypt, if such was their intention, but whether by treaty or tacit consent of the pharaoh were able to settle unhindered in the fertile Shephelah or coastal plain of Palestine,[2] to which they have given their name ever since, commanding the 'going out from Egypt', the *Via Maris*, and forcing the pharaohs to abandon their claims—maintained since the Eighteenth Dynasty—to sovereignty over Palestine. Egypt thereupon withdrew upon herself and a new phase of the history of the Near East was begun.

[1] The Egyptian *Onomasticon* of Amenemope, *c.* 1100 B.C. (see §1, 6)—a kind of gazetteer—mentions Shardana, Tjekker and Philistines after naming the cities of Askalon, Ashdod and Gaza.

[2] §7, 26. See also W. F. Albright, 'An Anthropoid Clay Coffin from Sahab in Trans-Jordan', in *A.J.A.* 36 (1932), 295 ff.

# CHAPTER XXIX

## ELAM *c.* 1600–1200 B.C.

### I. REIGNS AND EVENTS

I⊤ is generally admitted that after the end of the First Dynasty in Babylon, and following upon the death of Shamshi-Adad I in Assyria, there begins a period of great obscurity. The former abundance of documents ceases as though some catastrophe had paralysed the ordinary life of these countries. No text reveals the true causes of this overthrow, but we know that, with the beginning of this sterile period, there came a fresh and powerful advance towards Mesopotamia of the mountain peoples which had harassed it so long. By this time the Hurrians had settled about the upper reaches of the Tigris, and Kassites from the Zagros had drifted into the Mesopotamian plain as workers.

Tribal groups of these peoples who dwelt on the mountain border were now driven from behind by a new Indo-European influx coming, this time, from the north and north-east. The Hurrians, mingled with Aryans, spread over the area between the bend of the Euphrates and the district of Nuzi, to the east of Assyria, and advanced southwards into Palestine. At the same time the Kassites descended in force and made themselves masters of Babylonia, carrying with them isolated groups of Hurrians, some of whom settled around Nippur,[1] where they are found afterwards. The irruption of these less civilized highlanders is generally considered to be the reason for the sudden cessation of historical sources and for the evident decline of Mesopotamian culture in this period.

From the native evidence alone it is difficult to estimate the influence these events had on the history of Elam. Undoubtedly there was an abrupt change in the locality of our sources. It is no longer at Mālamīr, in Susiana, but at Liyan, several hundred miles to the south-east, that the next Elamite texts reappear. We have no means of estimating the lapse of time involved here, as the indigenous sources do not indicate a gap of any importance. The later texts which begin with the names of earlier kings do not show a break in the succession of the dynasties.

* An original version of this chapter was published as fascicle 16 in 1963.
[1] Some earlier Hurrian elements were already there in the Sargonic period; see §1, 2, 187 ff.

Elamite chronology depends, however, on Babylonian chronology. We know that Ammiṣaduqa and Kuknashur were contemporary,[1] and that the texts of Mālamīr overlap the end of the First Dynasty of Babylon. Events occurring just before the foundation of the new Elamite dynasty are known to us through the texts of Kurigalzu II. Therefore the interval between these two periods in Elamite history depends on the dates assigned to Ammiṣaduqa and Kurigalzu II and there is little agreement on these dates. Some authors consider that at least four centuries separate the two kings, thereby leaving a blank of over four hundred years in Elamite history, whereas others reduce the gap considerably by lowering the date of Hammurabi and adopting a less rigid chronology for the early Kassite kings. As the documents of Mālamīr and of Susa overlap considerably the end of the First Babylonian Dynasty, the gap between the two periods would be greatly reduced by the latter chronology. The Mālamīr texts show that there were about ten of a dynasty, known by the titles *sukkal* or *sukkalmaḫ*, who ruled in Elam after Kuknashur I, the contemporary of Ammiṣaduqa. It is in this period that the texts of Mālamīr are to be placed.[2] These are more or less homogeneous and date from the same period.[3] To judge from their syllabary, they belong to the time of Tan-Uli or Temti-khalki—that is, according to the chronology here adopted, to the middle of the seventeenth century. And lastly the recent excavations in Susiana would seem to indicate that the intervention of Kurigalzu in Elam occurred very soon after the end of the period of the *sukkalmaḫ*. From this we can deduce that the fading-out of Susa was short,[4] and certainly much shorter than the obscure period in contemporary Mesopotamia.

Despite this, the texts from Mālamīr do not fail to reflect the ethnic changes that were taking place throughout the entire Near East. Even though Babylonian traditions are still prevalent, the proper names bear witness to new elements. Certain of the attested names could be Hurrian, while others could be Kassite, Lullian, Gutian or Subarian. They indicate that Susiana was directly affected by the invaders, and it is likely that there was a considerable Hurrian proportion among these.

Excavations in Iran have not, indeed, as yet discovered the

---

[1] See §1, 8, 2 ff., and *C.A.H.* I³, pt. 1, pp. 218, 234 f.

[2] *Mém. D.P.* 8, 169 ff., nos. 1–16, re-edited in *Mém. D.P.* 22, *passim*.

[3] Except perhaps no. 15 (*Mém. D.P.* 22, 76).

[4] Mlle M. Rutten (*Mém. D.P.* 31, 155 ff. and table, 166) proposes to cancel this gap altogether.

pottery characteristic of sites on the Khabur, which in other places (Alalakh or Ras Shamra), seems to trace an expansion of the Hurrians. But their presence in Elam seems to be proved by certain particularities of the Elamite syllabary shortly after this period,[1] perhaps by the seals,[2] and certainly by the proper names.[3] Moreover, certain native princes already have names with the component -ḫalki,[4] which, whatever its origin,[5] evidently belongs to the Hurrians. The question of these foreign elements, their actual proportion, their influence, and how they arrived in Elam, remains to be answered.

Such information as we possess concerning Elam, from the intermediate period, is of only the slightest importance for history. It concerns an assault upon Elamite territory made by the last king of the Sea-Land, Ea-gamil, who was later defeated by the Kassite Ulamburiash, brother of Kashtiliash.[6] Such a brief allusion certainly does not warrant the hypothesis[7] that Ulamburiash, at this opportunity, took possession of Elam and extended Kassite rule even to the extreme south of the country.

It is not in fact until the time of Kurigalzu II that Elamite history comes to light again. A late Babylonian chronicle tells of a conflict between Kurigalzu II and the contemporary 'king of Elam' Khurpatila.[8] Whatever misgivings we may have about the way the chronicle presents these events, the facts themselves are above suspicion, since the victorious campaign of Kurigalzu II against Susa and Elam is known from other sources.[9] It is rather the figure of his opponent Khurpatila which raises doubts. Neither his name nor his reign are given in later dynastic lists, and the passage in the Chronicle is the only mention we have of

---

[1] In particular the use of *qa* for *ka*, which is characteristic of the Akkado-Hurrian syllabary.

[2] Mlle M. Rutten tells me that there is an unpublished seal from Susa in the Louvre of Hurrian origin or inspiration.

[3] For example, Akkamaneni, *Mém. D.P.* 22, 86, nos. 73, 27.

[4] Ike-khalki, Temti-khalki; and cf. Atta-khalki (*Mém. D.P.* 22, 75, 17; 149, 4, etc.).

[5] For a Hurrian origin: J. Friedrich, *Hethitisches Wörterbuch*, 147; for Indo-European: H. Pedersen, *Hittitisch und die anderen indo-europäischen Sprachen*, 177; E. Laroche in *R.A.* 47 (1953), 41.

[6] See §1, 5, ii, 22 ff.

[7] See G, 6, 331 a.

[8] Chronicle P, iii, 10 ff. (F. Delitzsch, *Die babylonische Chronik*, 45). Khurpatila is there called 'king of Elammat', whereas Elam is written with the ideogram ELAM.MA.KI in the rest of the text. For the name of Khurpatila see recently §1, 1, 54.

[9] *R.A.* 26, 7.

him.[1] However, we have at present no valid reason to reject this evidence. Khurpatila, as his name indicates, might have sprung from one of those groups of Hurrians whose existence in Susiana is revealed by study of the names. It is possible that he was able to create a short-lived kingdom on the western border of Elam, and the fact that he challenged Kurigalzu implies that he had designs on southern Babylonia, perhaps towards Nippur, around which other groups of Hurrians had already settled. Indeed, that city seems to have been somehow the prize at stake, for after his victory Kurigalzu took care to leave there, no less than at Susa, concrete evidence of his success.

Khurpatila did not strike forthwith into Mesopotamia but massed his troops instead at the stronghold of Dūr-Shulgi, on the other side of the Sea-Land, from which position he defied the Kassites to attack. In the ensuing battle he was defeated and his army routed. He then took refuge in Elam but was unable to unite an army powerful enough to oppose the advance of Kurigalzu who, taking advantage of the situation, ravaged Barakhshe and Elam and captured Susa. Khurpatila was forced to surrender. Kurigalzu celebrated his victory in Susa itself by offering an agate scaraboid to the god Ishataran[2] and the pommel of a sceptre to Enlil.[3] On the acropolis of Susa, he dedicated a statuette of himself bearing an inscription recording the different phases of his conquest.[4] When he returned to Babylonia, he brought back from Susa an agate tablet which had once been dedicated to Inanna 'for the life of Shulgi' and presented it to the god Enlil of Nippur[5] with a new dedicatory inscription.

Despite the wide extent of Kurigalzu's victorious campaign and his occupation of Susa, the interior provinces of Elam seem to have escaped this fate, the political conditions of Elam being different from those in Mesopotamia. The geography of Elam does not lend itself to political unity, and as soon as the bond of a firm central authority holding the country together disappears or is relaxed the different provinces tend to separate and to live their own lives. These conditions probably prevailed during the period for which we have no texts and indeed at the time of

---

[1] E. Unger, in *Forsch. u. Fortschr.* 10 (1934), 256, purported to have found the existence of Khurpatila proved by its occurrence upon a business document from Nippur which he believed to be dated by his fourth regnal year as 'king of Babylon'. But F. R. Kraus, in *J.C.S.* 3 (1951), 12, has shown that the reading was wrong, and that there is nothing about Khurpatila in that text.

[2] *Mém. D.P.* 6, 30; 7, 135. The god's name is written KA.DI.

[3] *Mém. D.P.* 14, 32.

[4] *R.A.* 26, 7.         [5] §1, 3, no. 15, no. 73, and p. 31.

Khurpatila himself. This prince of foreign origin could hardly have ruled over more than Susiana and the western borders of the country, notwithstanding his title 'king of Elam', because for the Babylonians 'king of Elam' meant simply the ruler of Susa. Moreover, Kurigalzu's campaign in Elam, other than at Susa, must have passed over Barakhshe and some other districts like a sudden but momentary shock, so we are not surprised that, almost on the morrow of the defeat, there was already a resurgence of nationalism in the interior of the country which would soon, under vigorous leaders, give birth to a new native dynasty. Extending their authority step by step, successive rulers found their own advantage in restoring the unity of Elam, and out of this they created an empire which soon made its weight felt in the balance of powers arrayed in the Near East. This national resurgence was also to be favoured by circumstances, for the Babylonians became uneasy at the fresh aggressive tendencies of Assyria under Arik-dēn-ili (1319–1308) and Adad-nīrāri I (1307–1275) and turned their gaze away from a land which they might think subdued towards frontiers more immediately threatened.

Later native sources attributed the founding of this dynasty to a certain Ike-khalki. Seeing that the dynastic lists name him only as the father of the first two actual kings he was probably a local chieftain who never himself came to the throne. His native country is unknown although certain indications point to the region of Mālamīr. The texts from this place contain several allusions to a person called Attar-kittakh, son of Atta-khalki,[1] and these names seem to belong to the same family descent as those of Ike-khalki and his second son Attar-kittakh. The name of the father, Ike-khalki, might suggest that the new royal family was, as in the case of Khurpatila, closely related to the Hurrians of Elam.

In any case, the real founder of the dynasty was Pakhir-ishshan, a son of Ike-khalki: he ruled probably during the time of Nazimaruttash (1323–1298). He has left no inscriptions of his own but we know from later texts that he was active in the district of Aakhitek[2] (still unlocated), and that he erected some monument in honour of the god In-Shushinak. The stele of dedication was transported to Susa by one of his successors, Shilkhak-In-Shushinak.[3]

---

[1] *Mém. D.P.* 22, 75, 17; 149, 4, etc.

[2] Inscription of Shutruk-Nahhunte, §1, 4, no. 28, line 24. The nature of this activity is still uncertain; the hypothesis of G, 2, 106, n. 6 (transport of valuable timber) is difficult to accept, for the word under discussion can designate only living beings or objects assimilated to these.       [3] §1, 4, no. 49; §1, 6, 26 ff.

Concerning his brother and successor Attar-kittakh, who was probably contemporary with the Babylonian king Kadashman-Turgu (1297–1280), the same later texts show that he extended to Susa the operations which his brother had confined to the province of Aakhitek. Two maces have been found at Susa[1] inscribed with his name. On the first he styles himself 'king of Susa and Anzan'; on the second, an original inscription—'Attar-kittakh, son of Ike-khalki'—is partly covered by a later dedication inscribed at the command of Untash-(d)GAL.

It was during the reign of his son, Khumban-numena (c. 1285–1266), that this Elamite renewal proved itself decisively. The name of this king is frequently mentioned by his successors who, symbolically, attach him to the great royal line issuing from the great and glorious Shilkhakha. Several of his royal inscriptions, in Elamite, are known to us and his titles attest the extent of his personal power.[2] His title in western style—'king of Anzan and Susa'—is here preceded by a series of native titles (merri, katri and halmeni of Elam), which no doubt define the nature of the sovereignty he exercised over the provincial tribes. The epithet 'expander of the empire' is probably more characteristic, as it alludes to the victorious campaigns which allowed him to extend the kingdom that he inherited. Susa was already part of this empire as is indicated by the title 'king of Anzan and Susa', which was also used by his father. A bead inscribed with his name was found in a well of the sixth city of Susa, and the later texts show that he had a temple built in honour of In-Shushinak in Susa. However, it was some four hundred kilometres to the south-east, at Liyan, that his inscriptions were found; they are foundation-deposits celebrating the construction of various sanctuaries. This does not prove that Liyan was the capital of the kingdom, as archaeological evidence discloses that it was a place of little importance, established in an area of backward culture, probably no more than a stronghold designed to protect the southern frontier of the empire. Susa was probably not at that time the real capital of Elam, and the site where Khumban-numena established his capital is as yet unknown, though it may have been in the province of Anzan, the position and extent of which is still a subject of dispute.

Khumban-numena was succeeded by his son, Untash-

---

[1] I am indebted to Mlle M. Rutten for this information.

[2] G, 1, 1, no. 4c ( = Mém. D.P. 15, 42 ff.); Z.D.M.G. 49, 693 ff. and various fragments in Berlin.

(d)GAL[1] who was probably the contemporary of Shalmaneser I of Assyria (1274–1245) and the Babylonians Kadashman-Enlil (1279–1265) and Kudur-Enlil (1263–1255). It was during his reign, which probably lasted some twenty years that the dynasty founded by Ike-khalki reached its apogee. Numerous temples and many stelae and statues are proof of his building activities. Some of these stones were found at Susa[2] but even more at Chogha-Zanbil,[3] 42 kilometres to the south-east, where the city of Dūr-Untash is situated, founded by and named after Untash-(d)GAL. This is confirmed by a foundation-deposit recently discovered in its ruins.[4] A holy city built around a monumental sanctuary, Dūr-Untash was undoubtedly the religious centre of that period and the main residence of Untash-(d)GAL. Despite this Susa was not neglected. It grew continually in importance during his reign and consequently the kingdom opened out more and more towards the west. His predecessors seem to have entertained a fear of their western neighbours and thus refrained from making any show of force along these frontiers, but Untash-(d)GAL, much more confident in his might, did not hesitate to restore to Susa something of its ancient glory. He had, perhaps, always foreseen Susa, as did the ancient kings, as a base for future operations against Babylonia. For the greater part of his reign, however, Elam seems to have been at peace with its neighbours and there is no proof, at present, that the material wealth which he must have possessed for his extensive building projects in the cities of his realm resulted from booty taken in successful wars.

If so, Untash-(d)GAL was biding his time. The reign of Kashtiliash IV and the subsequent apparent weakening of Kassite strength gave him the opportunity of sweeping into Mesopotamia. A mutilated statue of a Babylonian god, brought

[1] The second element of the name Untash-(d)GAL is a logogram meaning 'God-Great'. It is probably the epithet of a major god in the Elamite pantheon. Some scholars (in particular, §1, 4, 95) assert that the god is Khu(m)ban and that therefore the name of the king should read Untash-Khu(m)ban. This is probably true, but not certain (see below, p. 404). Because of this doubt I continue to use the formal writing Untash-(d)GAL and Unpatar-(d)GAL.

[2] Their Elamite inscriptions are collected and transliterated by Hüsing in §1, 4, 44 ff., nos. 5 ff. For their Akkadian inscriptions see below, p. 386, n. 3.

[3] Mém. D.P. 28, 29 ff., nos. 16 f.; Mém. D.P. 32, 19 ff., nos. 3 ff. Since this publication by M. Rutten around twenty new texts have been found in the latest excavations and they will be published in a future volume of Mém. D.P.

[4] Excavations of 1958–9. The inscription on this stone seems to prove that Chogha-Zanbil is actually Dūr-Untash: 'I built the city of Untash-(d)GAL and (its) siyankuk' (for the possible meaning of this term see below, p. 410, n. 2).

back as booty by Untash-(*d*)*GAL*, has been unearthed in the
ruins of Susa,[1] provided with an Akkadian inscription to commemorate its capture. In addition to the name of the god
Immeria (Imerum, a local form of the god Adad), the inscription
mentioned its origin or to whom it belonged. But this name is
broken and only the following can be seen, . . . *li-ia-aš*. It has
been commonly held that it is the end of the name of the Kassite
king Kashtiliash IV and that Imerum was his personal god. This
interpretation is far from being certain, for a reading [Ṭup]liash
(a Babylonian city) is also possible and perhaps preferable.[2] If so,
it would mean that booty was brought back from a victorious
expedition led by the Elamite king against the border province
west of the Uqnû river, the present Kerkhah. Even if this were
only a swift raid without lasting results it proves at least that
Elam had emerged from its long isolation and was not afraid
to confront its western neighbours.

Elam was once again open to Semitic influence. Babylonian
deities formerly worshipped were not excluded from the national
pantheon and the native gods had Akkadian epithets. The
temples were modelled on the massive stepped towers of the holy
cities of Mesopotamia. Many official documents were written
in Akkadian, the international language of the day.[3] If their
syllabary includes a few local variations, their syntax is none the
less classical and shows a high degree of Mesopotamian culture
on the part of the Elamite scribes. This borrowing from a foreign
civilization does not mean that national sentiment weakened. The
native language was preponderant in dedications proclaiming the
piety and greatness of the 'king of Anzan and Susa'.

Untash-(*d*)*GAL* was succeeded by Unpatar-(*d*)*GAL*, who was
not his son. The later dynastic lists give one Pakhir-ishshan as his
father, without indicating whether or not this was the same
person as the like-named grandfather of his predecessor; if so
Unpatar-(*d*)*GAL* would have been the uncle of Untash-(*d*)*GAL*.
This is not impossible but very unlikely, for Kidin-Khutran, the

---

[1] *Mém. D.P.* 10, 85.

[2] This suggestion of Dr E. Reiner was communicated by Dr M. Rowton; see
*C.A.H.* I³, pt. 1, p. 218. A synchronism with Kashtiliash would require the reign of
Untash-(*d*)*GAL* to be lowered in time by some twenty years. The *kudurru* of
Agaptakha may best be dated in this king's reign, as indicated below in relation to
Kidin-Khutran.

[3] *Mém. D.P.* 28, nos. 16, 17, p. 32, nos. A, B, C ( = *Mém. D.P.* 32, I and II).
Since this last publication ten or so Akkadian texts have been found at Chogha-
Zanbil. The inscription of Untash-(*d*)*GAL* on a statue of the god Immeria is also
in Akkadian.

brother and successor of Unpatar-(*d*)*GAL*, would also have been a son of the same Pakhir-ishshan, and the interval seems too long. There is no evidence that dynastic changes were caused by internal upheavals following upon the death of Untash-(*d*)*GAL*, nor is there proof that the queen Napirasu ruled over Elam for a year after the death of her husband. We have only one inscription of hers, upon her bronze statue.[1] Apart from the usual maledictions against profaners, it gives only her name and her title 'wife of Untash-(*d*)*GAL*'.

Whether owing to old age or a short reign, Unpatar-(*d*)*GAL* (*c*. 1245) was not as active as his predecessor. He was incapable of intervention in events taking place even a short distance from his borders. In this period Assyria was forcefully renewing its policy of expansion in the Zagros and towards the Persian Gulf. Tukulti-Ninurta I led a victorious expedition from the mountain Tarsina, on the southern bank of the Lesser Zab, as far as the land of Guti, between the regions Zuqushki and Lallar.[2] He then marched south into Babylon, attacked Kashtiliash and took him prisoner, annexing to his own land a whole series of cities which had been the subject of rival claims by the Babylonians and the Elamites. Elam had to abandon to Assyrian control the cities of Turna-suma, in the region of Me-Turnat, and Ulaiash near the source of Kerkhah, not far from the present-day Mandali.[3] All these events are known to us from Assyrian sources. The only Elamite sources for the reign of Unpatar-(*d*)*GAL*, two texts of a later date, mention only the restoration of a sanctuary of In-Shushinak at Susa, on which work had been done by several previous kings.

On the death of Unpatar-(*d*)*GAL*, his brother Kidin-Khutran came to the throne and ruled for some twenty years (*c*. 1242–1222). Either because he succeeded in rallying the military forces of his kingdom or because he was less faint-hearted than his brother, the new king reverted to the aggressive policy of Untash-(*d*)*GAL* and openly opposed the Assyrian conqueror. Tukulti-Ninurta had installed one of his followers, Enlil-nādin-shumi, on the throne of Babylon after the death of Kashtiliash. Kidin-Khutran, taking advantage of this puppet ruler, swept suddenly into lower Mesopotamia. He crossed the Tigris and, marching towards the centre of the country, seized Nippur and massacred the population; then, turning north, he recrossed the Tigris and sacked Dēr,

---

[1] *Mém. D.P.* 8, 245 ff. and pl. 15; *Mém. D.P.* 5, 1 ff., no. 65; §1, 4, 50, no. 16.
[2] Cf. §1, 9, 1, IV, 25 ff.; 17 ff., etc.
[3] §1, 9, 16, 73 ff., and 27 f., note (ll. 66–82).

destroying the famous temple E-dimgal-kalamma and taking the inhabitants into captivity. The Babylonian king was forced to flee and lost his sovereignty over this whole area.

But the Elamite victory was short-lived. Tukulti-Ninurta took immediate counter-measures and re-established the position in Babylonia to his own advantage. After installing first the Kassite Kadashman-Kharbe, and then, eighteen months later, the Babylonian Adad-shuma-iddina (1224–1219), he kept a constant vigil over this land which he regarded as a kind of Assyrian protectorate. For this reason presumably Kidin-Khutran avoided any further aggressive action. It was only when Adad-shuma-uṣur (1218–1189) had become king in Babylon that he judged the time ripe for a new attempt. On this occasion, encouraged by his previous success, he advanced further, crossed the Tigris, seized Isin and went north as far as Marad, west of Nippur. There alone, it seems, did he meet resistance but he defeated his adversaries and returned to Elam without encountering further resistance.

It was probably during his first or second campaign in Babylonia[1] that he brought back as booty to Susa the *kudurru*[2] on which were inscribed the proprietorial rights to a domain near the city of Padan that Kashtiliash had granted to a certain Agaptakha. We know that this city is to be located between the Turnat (Diyālā) river and the mountain Yalman; that is, on the north-eastern border of Babylonia. Previously the Kassite king Agum-kakrime had asserted his suzerainty over the city by calling himself 'king of Padan and Alman'. But the Elamites had never ceased to claim that this territory was an integral part of greater Elam and in taking this stele the Elamite king was probably reasserting, symbolically, his suzerainty over the territory constantly in dispute between the Babylonians, Assyrians and Elamites.

This reconstruction of the course of events has to be based on Assyrian and Babylonian sources.[3] As yet no contemporary Elamite documents of the time of Kidin-Khutran have been found in the excavations. Some later references mention only the restoration by him of the temple of In-Shushinak at Susa and the temple of Kiririsha at Liyan.[4] If the interpretation of this latter, mutilated,

---

[1] See, however, p. 386, n. 2.
[2] *Mém. D.P.* 2, 95 and pl. 20.
[3] Chronicle P, IV, 14 ff., now in §1, 9, no. 37.
[4] §1, 4, no. 48 (*Mém. D.P.* 5, no. LXXI, 29 f.; §1, 4, no. 48 B (*Mém. D.P.* 5, no. XCVI), 37; §1, 4, Lïyan (?), no. 49 (*Mém. D.P.* 5, no. LXXVI), 12.

text is correct it would tend to prove that Kidin-Khutran had firmly re-established Elam up to its southernmost borders. This would account for the boldness of his enterprises in Babylonia. He challenged, in fact, not merely the Babylonians, whose weakness at this time is well known, but Assyrian power, impelled by Tukulti-Ninurta, whose aim it was to establish his influence as far as the shores of the Persian Gulf. In the clash of these two ambitions, Kidin-Khutran was twice successful, due probably to the advantage of surprise attack, but the issue was finally decided in favour of the Assyrians. Tukulti-Ninurta lost no time in avenging his early setbacks and marched triumphantly 'to the southern shores of the Lower Sea'.

It is possible that this expedition brought Kidin-Khutran's reign to an end, perhaps by giving rise to a revolt in Elam. He disappears, in any case, from the political scene and several years passed before a new king ascended the throne. With him, the Anzanite dynasty founded by Ike-khalki came to an end, in all probability overthrown.

## II. ARCHITECTURE AND THE ARTS

All the information concerning military and political affairs during this period of Elamite history comes, as has been stated, from foreign sources. It is very likely that Elamite kings had accounts of their victorious campaigns inscribed on stelae as their successors did later, and there is mention of several such campaigns in later inscriptions; but so far no such document has been found and only bricks recording the foundation of buildings have been discovered. These enable us to form a fairly precise idea of a different aspect of the rule of these kings—their building activities, an important guide to the development of civilization in the land. Although we know that nearly all the kings of this dynasty built or restored temples at Susa or in the other cities of the empire, the only inscribed bricks found belong to the time of Khumban-numena and Untash-($d$)$GAL$ and they all concern the construction or the repair of religious buildings. The bricks themselves, especially those of Untash-($d$)$GAL$, are beautiful, well-baked and superior in manufacture to those of the period of the *ensi* and *sukkal* rulers.

At Chogha-Zanbil there are whole friezes of these very fine bricks which, inside and outside, follow the contours of the walls. The number of the inscribed bands varies according to the height of the building. They are usually repeated at every ten layers of bricks.[1] The inscription on these bricks is always short and identical, giving the name of the founder, his genealogy, title, and the simple statement 'I have built such and such a building for such a deity and have given it to him'. Sometimes they have curses against anyone who might desecrate the building, an invocation of the god's blessing upon the king's work, or even a prayer for the prosperity of his reign and a long life.

We have several of such documents of Khumban-numena. We learn from them that this king built a sanctuary in the city of Liyan dedicated to the god Khumban (*GAL*) and his consort Kiririsha, and to the Pakhakhutep who were probably old protector-gods of the place. Several later kings, especially Shilkhak-In-Shushinak, refer to this foundation and also mention a chapel built at Liyan by Khumban-numena, dedicated exclusively to Kiririsha, and repairs done at Susa to the temple of In-Shushinak.

The pious works associated with the name of Untash-(*d*)*GAL* were a good deal more numerous. At Susa, if the bricks found there all actually belonged in buildings erected in the city, he built or restored some twenty sanctuaries. As much attention was paid to Babylonian gods, traditionally worshipped in the city— Nabu, Sin, Adad, his consort Shala, *NIN-URU*—as to the Elamite deities—In-Shushinak, Khumban, Nahhunte, Pinikir, Khish-mitik, Rukhuratir, Pelala, Napratep, Shimut, Nazit, Upurkupak, and so forth.[2] For each of them he had a new statue sculptured in stone or cast in metal placed in the appropriate temple. Of these temples about a dozen already existed in the city, for Untash-(*d*)*GAL* states that he had them rebuilt on their original sites. In about an equal number of cases it is not clear whether the inscription records a new foundation or not; but at any rate in the case of the goddess Upurkupak he claims to have been the first to build a temple expressly for her, as there had never been one in the capital, and he made several additions to the temple of In-Shushinak. A certain number of these sanctuaries must have been of modest proportions, built most often of sun-dried brick, sometimes with a glazed-brick façade. Some, indeed, were no more than secondary shrines, small chapels which were part of the interior plan of one of the great temples. Of these the most important was certainly that dedicated to the combined cults of Khumban and In-Shushinak.

---

[1] In the zikkurrat there are seven of these inscribed friezes in place, and three on the walls of another building.

[2] For references, see G, 2, 102 f.

Dominating all of these sacred buildings by its size was the zikkurrat of Susa which stood at that time on the acropolis of the city. It was built along the lines of the zikkurrats of Nippur, Babylon and the other sacred cities of Mesopotamia. The presence of numerous inscribed bricks identical with those that can still be seen in the walls of the zikkurrat at Chogha-Zanbil prove that Untash-(d)GAL built or restored a like structure at Susa. At its top stood the upper temple which the Elamites called *kukunnu*, a name which could also be applied to the whole zikkurrat.[1] This edifice had existed at Susa for a long time before that date. A predecesor, Kuknashur, claimed that he built or restored 'a *kukunnu* of baked bricks on the acropolis of In-Shushinak'.[2] The merit of Untash-(d)GAL was to have replaced this covering of baked bricks by enamelled plaques in iridescent colours.[3] In the upper chapel he had erected, as well as a statue of the god, a statue of himself on the pedestal of which was a bilingual inscription commemorating the restoration of the edifice and consigning any profaners to the wrath of the gods. The acropolis was surrounded by a sacred wall and one of its towers was called, as at Chogha-Zanbil, *nūr kibrāti*, 'light of the (four) regions (of the world)'.

The building activities of the king were not confined to Susa. It would appear in fact that the greater part of his pious pre-occupations were in another important religious centre of his kingdom, at the city that he founded and to which he gave his name, Dūr-Untash, on the site now called Chogha-Zanbil. All of the many bricks found there have his name on them and many of them commemorate the building of the city's monumental stage-tower. As at Susa, it was dedicated to the joint cult of Khumban and In-Shushinak, but each had a private chapel as well. It was this zikkurrat that Untash-(d)GAL described thus: 'I built and dedicated to the gods Khumban and In-Shushinak a *kukunnu* with bricks enamelled in silver and gold, and with white obsidian and alabaster.'[4] In one of the rooms he hung a lyre to which he gave the significant style 'glorification of my name'.[5]

Other bricks from here mention sanctuaries dedicated to the

---

[1] For this Sumerian loanword which corresponds with the Akkadian *gigunû*, cf. C.A.D. 5, 67 ff.

[2] *Mém. D.P.* 6, 28, 5.

[3] Resembling those used at Chogha-Zanbil (*Mém. D.P.* 28, 31, no. 17).

[4] *Mém. D.P.* 28, no. 17 ( = *Mém. D.P.* 32, no. 11; cf. C.A.D. 5, 68 *b* for this text).

[5] *Mém. D.P.* 28, no. 16 ( = *Mém. D.P.* 32, no. 1; cf. W. von Soden, *Assyr. Handwörterbuch*, 98 *b* (lyre or harp).

goddesses Ishme-karab, Kiririsha, Pinikir, Manzat, Inanna and Bēlit; to the gods Napratep, Nabu, Shiashum, Khumban, Sunkir-Risharra, Kilakh-supir, and to the divine partners Khishmitik and Rukhuratir, Shimut and *NIN-URU*, Adad and Shala, Shushmushi and Bēlit.[1] As at Susa, some of these chapels were certainly situated within the big temple. There were also other chapels outside the first wall and especially in front of the north-west side. There, in a conglomeration of ruined buildings, a bronze hoe dedicated to the god Nabu was found, thus indicating the location of this god's sanctuary.[2] Further on, an important building was dedicated to the goddess Kiririsha and an adjoining building of similar importance to the goddess Ishme-karab. This sacred complex formed the acropolis of Dūr-Untash and was undoubtedly called *Siyankuk*.

At Liyan, M. Pézard carried out excavations on a mound where Dr Andreas had previously discovered inscribed foundation bricks in the remains of two walls forming a corner. These walls have since disappeared and the archaeological results were meagre. Apart from traces of pavements consisting of plain slabs, there were only remains of very roughly constructed walls; the building work done there was inferior to that in Susiana. The impression thus conveyed is confirmed by the presence of primitive-looking rows of stones which perhaps once formed the backing for mere banks of rammed earth. In general, the remains point to a provincial or archaic technique, or to the work of a local population not far advanced above the stage of barbarism.[3]

At Susa, bricks of Untash-(*d*)*GAL* were found inserted in the walls and pavements of a later date, contemporary with Shilkhak-In-Shushinak; the positions in which they were found show that they were not serving their original purpose but had been gathered from older buildings when these were demolished to make way for new temples. The foundation levels of buildings put up by Untash-(*d*)*GAL* ought then to be found more or less immediately below the level in which these bricks were placed, but the excavations revealed only insignificant remains at that depth. The most important of these remains was simply a long wall, without inscriptions, 2 metres high, with panels jutting and

[1] A certain number of these names should be added to the list of deities of Chogha-Zanbil published by M. Rutten in *Mém. D.P.* 32, 8–9. The non-existent name *Akkipish is a misinterpretation of *Mém. D.P.* 32, xviii, no. 1, 3 and should be eliminated.

[2] R. de Mecquenem and G. Dossin, 'La marre de Nabu', in *R.A.* 35, 129 ff., and cf. *Mém. D.P.* 33, 56 f. See below, pp. 409 f.

[3] M. Pézard, 'Fouilles de Bender-Boushir (Liyan)', in *Mém. D.P.* 15.

recessed to an extent of 20 centimetres; this may have been the façade of a wall of unbaked brick. The decoration, either within or without, can only have been slight, for the fragments of decorated relief that can be attributed to the time of Untash-(*d*)*GAL* are few and of very little interest. However, it is possible that the other ornamental motifs and the enamelled decorations were, like the inscribed bricks, pulled out and collected for re-use by later kings.

A much more impressive sight, even today, are the ruins of Chogha-Zanbil. Even in Babylonia there are few sites possessing a zikkurrat as grandiose and as well preserved.

The city is located forty-two kilometres south-east of Susa; built on a prominence, it dominates the meandering river Āb-i Diz. The remains, which were found in 1935, at first received only a few superficial soundings. A zikkurrat was identified in the débris of a large mound and along its north-western side a number of other buildings were superficially unearthed. These were later seen to be part of a complex of temples.[1] It was not until 1951 that this site was systematically excavated under the direction of R. Ghirshman. As yet the complete results have not been published but the preliminary reports and articles by R. Ghirshman[2] give us a fairly clear idea of the site. It takes the form of three concentric enclosures. The outer wall, a quadrangle, measures about 1200 by 800 metres and was probably the defensive-wall of the city. Back from this is a square (400 metres square) within which again was the third enclosure which contains the zikkurrat and its surrounding parvis. It is with the zikkurrat that the excavations started and it is completely unearthed today.

It was seen almost immediately that the zikkurrat of Chogha-Zanbil was quite different from the zikkurrats of Mesopotamia.[3] These differences arise both from the method of construction and the planning of certain parts. At Chogha-Zanbil it is an almost perfect square which measures 105 metres each side and it is oriented by its angles. Two storeys and part of the third were uncovered from the surrounding rubble, thus allowing a reconstruction of its original height and showing the stages of its construction. A sort of foundation, 1 metre high and 3 metres wide, encloses the zikkurrat at its base. Solidly constructed, it could be an actual foundation but its real purpose was to protect

---

[1] The results of these first excavations were published by R. de Mecquenem and J. Michalon, 'Recherches à Tchoga-Zembil', in *Mém. D.P.* 33.

[2] See §11, 1; and see Plate 156 (*e*).

[3] Already during the third campaign, cf. R. Ghirshman in *Arts Asiatiques*, I (1954), 83 ff.

the base of the zikkurrat against the infiltration of water. Above
this, in successively receding steps, stood four storeys, the
fourth of which supported the upper platform and the temple
which crowned the edifice. At each storey the base of the wall was
protected by a smaller version of the foundation at the base of the
zikkurrat.

The first storey rises 8 metres above the parvis; the second
11·55 metres, and the third and fourth, which no longer exist,
were probably of the same height.[1] Thus the bottom of the
temple on the summit was about 43 metres above the ground,
and the whole structure must have been about 52·60 metres in
height.[2] The upper storeys were solid masses 8 metres thick,
consisting of a core of crude bricks with a facing of baked bricks.
But the first, the lowest, storey is of a quite different design, and
the discovery of rooms made within the mass has revealed the
different phases in the building of this tower.

Originally the edifice which was to be the first storey was a
quadrilateral built around a courtyard. The north-east side,
thicker than the others (12 metres instead of 8), contained a
double row of rooms, with the inner rooms opening through a
doorway into the courtyard. Another group of rooms lay in the
southern part of the south-east side, and communicated with the
courtyard by another monumental door. Inscribed bricks found
in the walls here show that this group of rooms formed a temple of
the god In-Shushinak. To the east of this side there was another
sanctuary of the god, opening this time not upon the courtyard,
but externally upon the parvis of the zikkurrat. Apart from these
two temples of In-Shushinak the other rooms cannot be identified
and we have no texts concerning them. The other rooms do not
have windows and those which have no doors to the court are
entered by a narrow stairway from above. The walls were white-
washed with great care. Most of the rooms were empty but one had
jars in it and two others, in the north-west corner, were filled with
baked clay objects shaped like mushrooms with glazed heads.

The existence of the temple of In-Shushinak with its façade of
inscribed bricks thus shows that the original construction was
limited to this one storey and that it was not until some time
later that the other storeys were added. When the other storeys
were constructed those rooms that open into the courtyard were

---

[1] See §11, 3, 25.

[2] If the Elamite cubit—deduced from the dimensions and proportions of Chogha-
Zanbil—was in fact 0·526 metre. Thus the zikkurrat should have measured 100 cubits
in height and 200 cubits on each side at the base.

condemned and filled in with unbaked bricks and their doors were closed off by the mass of the zikkurrat.

At its finished height its last storey must have measured 35 metres on each side, which was large enough to accommodate the temple that crowned the construction. Nothing is left today of this upper part of the zikkurrat, but its remains are strewn along the slopes down as far as the parvis where they can be found today.[1] In particular, inscribed bricks from the summit of a special form. have been found, which commemorate the construction of the *kukunnu*.[2] The precious materials of which they speak, bricks of gold and silver, are undoubtedly the bricks glazed with metallic hues, fragments of which were found in the débris. The upper temple was plainly the residence of the god.

Communication between the parvis and the top of the tower was by a series of stairways opened in the zikkurrat. A door was built in each of the four sides. But only the stairway on the south-west side went beyond the first storey, thus giving access to the second storey. The rest of the ascent was probably made alternatively by each of the other sides. This means of ascent differentiates it clearly from the Mesopotamian zikkurrats. There are other but less important differences. For instance, the drainage system depends on a vertical system of gutters at each landing which channel off the rainwater from the zikkurrat; in Babylonia drainage is effected by successive layers of reeds. The clay of the bricks is homogeneous and not reinforced with débris and sherds as in Babylonia. The door arches are constructed in an original manner by an irregular alternation of wedge-shaped bricks and complete bricks.

The zikkurrat is surrounded by large paved parvises of different kinds which are about 20 metres wide. On the north-east side, near the central stairway, there is a ramp between the parvis and the base of the tower. At the northern angle of this ramp there is a circular construction, which can also be found at the north-western and south-western doors. These have four symmetrically placed niches and the whole is decorated by rings of inscribed bricks. The wording of these bricks does not help us to identify their purpose.[3] Another problem is set by the fourteen small square socles, made up of five bricks, one of which forms the top, which

[1] *Mém. D.P.* 32, nos. II, VI–IX.

[2] In the Akkadian inscriptions, at least, this is the word used. The corresponding Elamite word is *ulḫi*, which is applied to the royal residence in the Achaemenid period. It is difficult to say whether these two words have the same meaning.

[3] *Mém. D.P.* 32, no. V.

face the south-east stairway. They are probably too small and too fragile to be used as tables or altars for sacrifices. The zikkurrat and the parvises are surrounded by an enclosure with angular projections. On the north-west and the south-west sides the enclosure wall is double and forms rooms. Between these rooms, where there is a single wall, the resulting opening is like a gallery which faces the ramp rising from the parvis to the second storey.

On the north-west side, starting from the northern angle, three temples as a group break the line of the enclosure and spread out over the parvis. The first, completely outside the enclosure, is a sanctuary of the 'Great God', (*d*)*GAL*; a paved passage runs between it and a large door which opens out on to the parvis. The two others, farther west and straddling the line of the enclosure are large adjoining temples dedicated, respectively, to the deities Ishme-karab and Kiririsha. These two temples are separated by three rooms in the form of a **T**. It was here that the bronze hoe of Nabu was found during the first excavations.[1] These three temples in their simplest form are planned in the same way: a courtyard, on one side of which there is the ante-cella and cella and on the other side a number of annexes. In the temple of Kiririsha, other buildings—probably workshops and storehouses—were added.

Outside the inner enclosure which surrounds the zikkurrat is another area, 130 metres in breadth, which is circumscribed by the second wall. This wall has three gates, one on the north-east line, the second on the south-east side and the third on the south-west side. The latter two, called the 'Royal Way' and the 'Gate of Susa' by the excavator, both have the same inscription which seems to give a list of the various royal foundations in this holy quarter of the city. Towards the south there is a tower with its frieze of inscribed bricks still in place. They seem to indicate that this tower was the 'Light of the Regions'.[2]

The remains of four other temples were found in the eastern corner and their inscriptions allow us to identify the gods to whom they were dedicated. The first is the sanctuary of the goddess Pini-kir; the following two of the divine pair, Adad—Shala and Shimut—*NIN-URU*; and the fourth of a divine group, the Napratep. From the results of the excavations it might be concluded

---

[1] *Mém. D.P.* 33, 57.

[2] *nūr kibrāti.* It is consequently very doubtful whether this term means the zikkurrat, as has been supposed. The text was published in *Mém. D.P.* 32, no. III. The same inscription has been found on bricks at Susa, cf. *Mém. D.P.* 3, no. XVIII and p. 32.

that the area between the two inner walls was reserved for religious buildings.

Between the second wall and the outside enclosure was the site of the city itself or at least this space was reserved for it, for it seems in fact that the city was never finished. In this whole area the only things found were the remains of three palaces, the remains of a private house (near the northern angle of the area) and a few individual or family tombs. These tombs look like a well but they branch off at the bottom into a vaulted room. The first palace (I)[1] was a building of very large dimensions. Its rooms, one of which contained some beautiful ivories, give on to a large courtyard which is partly paved. On the west side, contrary to the usual disposition, the rooms have their long side on the courtyard, and it was under some of these rooms that the most remarkable discovery was made. Several stairways leading into subterranean rooms were found, access to them being very carefully disguised by a filling of baked bricks, the last courses of which were cemented by a thick coat of plaster and bitumen. Six metres below, the stairs lead into vaulted rooms about 17 metres long and 4 metres wide and high. The vault as well as the head of the door are fully arched and made of matching baked bricks which are covered with a layer of plaster. There is a sort of brick funerary couch in one of these tombs on which there was an intact skeleton and the remains of two burnt bodies. In a neighbouring tomb were some small heaps of ashes and bones of carbonized bodies placed directly on the floor in groups of two, four and five. This is the only evidence we have of cremation in Elam.

The other two palaces are in the eastern angle of the area. Although they do not have underground rooms their general aspect indicates that they were much larger than the first. Each one contains two large courtyards around which are situated four suites with several rooms in each. One of these was a bathroom with a low plaster-covered basin, the drains passing out under the walls. Near the third palace a trench containing different-sized and well-preserved alabaster urns was found.

To the south-west of palace I are the remains of the only religious building found in the 'urban' zone. This building, the inscription of which shows that it was dedicated to Nusku, is rather odd in appearance, being built like a T. The bar of the T is a long vestibule while its leg is a paved court with a pedestal of unbaked brick at the far end. It seems, judging from the distance

---

[1] Discovered in 1958–9.

between the walls and the lack of remains, that this building did
not have a roof.

   The outer wall had only one monumental gate, situated near
the eastern angle of the wall, and made up of two gate-houses
which face each other across a large paved square courtyard. In
each gate-house there is a long paved room which was perhaps
the guard room. On large bricks the inscriptions 'gate of the
king', 'great gate' and 'gate of justice' were found. On the
north-west face of the wall there was an ingenious system for
bringing in water; along the outside of the wall was a reservoir
which received water from a nearby canal. A system of small
pipes, in nine steps, brought the water up from the reservoir
under the wall into a basin along the inner side of the wall. The
surface of the reservoir and the basin are at the same level, but
the basin is not as deep as the reservoir. Thus by using the
principle of water seeking its own level they were able to bring up
water from one to the other while leaving any sediment behind.

   The excavations at Chogha-Zanbil have furnished us with
much precious information on Elamite architecture at the time
of Untash-(*d*)*GAL*, on building materials, planning, systems of
measurement, use of the arch and the vault. In the other Elamite
arts of this time it is not always easy to date remarkable examples
of jewellery or figurines found in the excavations, but stone
sculpture and bronze-working reach a high level. The composition and carving of a stele bearing the name of Untash-
(*d*)*GAL*, now in the Louvre, is an example of contemporary
Elamite sculpture in relief. Although it has survived only in a
fragmentary state, it has proved possible to reconstruct the
general scheme. Two long serpents with winding coils form a
frame for several superimposed panels. In the uppermost the
king stands with his hands outstretched to a seated goddess
wearing a head-dress with three pairs of horns. The king is also
represented in the next panel, in company with his queen,
Napirasu. In a lower panel are semi-divine guardians. One of
them preserved in its entirety is a female creature, a sort of siren,
the head adorned with a pair of horns, the scaly lower body
ending in two little fins that serve as feet. She holds against her
breast two streams of flowing water issuing from four vases so
disposed as to frame the subject, two balanced on the back-
turned tips of her tail, the other two at each side of her head in
the upper corners. In the bottom panel is another such semi-
divine creature, with a rectangular beard and hair falling in
tresses at the back; the lower part of the figure is broken off, but

the end of a tail curving backwards shows that it is another type of hybrid, half human, half animal.[1]

Remains of a great many stone figures in the round have been found but so mutilated as not to allow of a just appreciation. Many limestone statues date from the time of Untash-(d)GAL. One of these represents the king, the lower part alone being extant with a bilingual inscription in Akkadian and Elamite; another statue of the king is in diorite.[2]

Elamite mastery of the technique of bronze-working is well illustrated for this period by the celebrated statue of the queen Napirasu.[3] The headless figure stands 1·20 metres high and weighs not less than 1750 kilogrammes. The procedure used for casting such a large figure is not known and we cannot but admire the results obtained. Not having our modern high-temperature furnaces they must have had to use a considerable number of small crucibles in order to pour such a large quantity of molten metal, and it is astonishing that they could maintain a more or less constant temperature for each melting. The interior is not perfect but the exterior is remarkably well done, and this statue is a real masterpiece of ancient metallurgy. The queen stands with crossed hands, clothed in a fine embroidered dress which closely fits her shoulders and breasts. A long skirt wrapped round her waist and hanging to the ground covers the feet. The folds of the material, the embroidery, the bands and the incrustation are executed—like the jewellery on the fingers and the wrists—with great delicacy. On the flounce of the skirt an Elamite inscription invokes the anger of the gods upon anyone who may destroy, mutilate or remove the statue or efface the queen's name.

It will therefore appear that Elam was scarcely inferior in the practice of the arts to Babylonia and Assyria at this period, if the combined evidence of the extant objects and of the texts be considered; this was the prelude to the age of Shilkhak-In-Shushinak, the true apogee of Elamite civilization.

## III. RELIGION

About one other aspect of this civilization the documents, in spite of their terse character, also provide information: the religion.

[1] G, 8, 41, n. 1; *R.A.* 13, 120; *R.A.* 17, 113 ff.; G, 4, col. 932; §iii, 6, 98 and fig. 52.

[2] *Mém. D.P.* 10, 85 pl. x; *Mém. D.P.* 11, 12 and pl. iii, nos. 1–2; G, 8, 64, nos. 61–64.

[3] *Mém. D.P.* 8. 245 ff.; §iii, 2, vol. ii, 914 ff. See Plate 157 (*a*).

All of the bricks from the time of Untash-(*d*)*GAL* and his pre-decessor contained many references to the gods and their sanctuaries, and invocations of the gods in documents of all the Elamite kings are ubiquitous. But while in Babylonia very many rituals, incantations, prayers and the like have been found, in Elam not a single text with this kind of purely religious content is yet known. Almost all that can be done at present is to enumerate the divine names with such explanations as are provided by incidental phrases in the Elamite texts or by Akkadian god-lists and references in Babylonian and Assyrian inscriptions dealing with Elam.

The principal native sources, apart from the inscribed bricks of Khumban-numena and Untash-(*d*)*GAL*, are either earlier or later than this period. A treaty of alliance concluded between Naram-Sin of Agade and a prince of Awan includes a list of deities cited as witnesses and guarantors. In the documents of the time of the *ensi* and *sukkal* rulers there are divine names included in the theophorous personal names, and those invoked in oaths. After the reign of Untash-(*d*)*GAL* the evidence lies in royal inscriptions of the dynasty of Shilkhak-In-Shushinak, of the last native Elamite kings at Susa and at Mālamīr, and in references to Elamite gods occurring in Akkadian literature. In this last class are divine names occurring in the god-lists and in the Babylonian magical series called *šurpu*, as well as the account of the sack of Susa given in Ashurbanipal's annals describing temples and statues which his soldiery plundered or destroyed. As the inscrip-tions of the time of Shilkhak-In-Shushinak are more numerous and more varied in type than previously, it might seem that a general study of the religion should be attempted only for his period; but the pantheon was more or less formed at the time of Untash-(*d*)*GAL* and this period furnishes a good vantage-point to observe the evolution through which, in the course of centuries, this religion passed. When the statements of the different sources are compared, there is a notable divergence between the resulting lists of gods, according to the date or origin of the source.

Historically it appears that the order of the pantheon under-went important changes. Originally the dominating figure seems to have been the great goddess Pinikir, the first name invoked in the Naram-Sin treaty, while In-Shushinak was secondary. This predominance of a supreme goddess is probably a reflexion from the practice of matriarchy which at all times characterized Elamite civilization to a greater or lesser degree. Even when the supre-macy of a male was fully recognized in the pantheon, perhaps under the influence of western ideas, the cults of the goddesses always preserved their popularity in all parts of the empire. Nevertheless the progressive decline of the great goddess in favour of the major gods is one characteristic of religious evolution in Elam. Another, and of no less general significance, is the rise in importance of In-Shushinak the god of Susa; from a purely local god there developed step by step the great national god, who gradually eclipsed the principal ancient deities. In the time of Untash-(d)GAL he was already the equal of the 'Great God', with whom he is frequently associated; a century later, in the time of Shilkhak-In-Shushinak, he supplanted that god completely.

If, again, the documents are studied with regard to their provenance, Awan, Susa, Mālamīr, or Liyan, a clear differentiation of the worship in the different localities can be observed. Apart from certain great gods worshipped throughout the country, most of the deities clearly present provincial features. It would seem that there never was, in Elam, a unity of religious belief worthy of the name. Even in his most formal inscriptions Shilkhak-In-Shushinak invokes 'the gods of Elam', 'the gods of Anzan', 'the gods of Susa', as divine communities fundamentally distinct. Still another group, 'the gods of Aiapir', occurs in other inscriptions, while Tirutir, frequently invoked by Khanni at Mālamīr, appears nowhere else. Yet the name of Shimutta is always followed by the epithet 'god of Elam'. It is perhaps above all in the cults of the goddesses that this geographical differentiation can be observed. Although Kiririsha and Pinikir each had a sanctuary at Chogha-Zanbil, Kiririsha—'the lady of Liyan'—was worshipped more in the south, while Pinikir was worshipped in the north; Parti is essentially the goddess of Mālamīr, although known at Susa also by the name Partikira, according to the annals of Ashurbanipal. The variations of one and the same name are equally revealing as an indication of provincialism; in one place a god is called Lukhuratil, in another Rukhuratir, in one place Manzat, in another Manzit, in one place Khutran, in another Uduran or Duran, and so forth.

These fundamental differences can be explained by the fact that greater Elam was never anything but a political concept realized by a few energetic or ambitious kings. It was always a tribal federation constantly on the verge of breaking up, and with each tribe retaining its own gods. The nationalization of the local cults was one of the means used by the kings of the great dynasties to cement the precarious hold they had on the country. It was with this in mind that they made their capitals—Susa or

Dūr-Untash—into sacred capitals where they tried to group together the provincial gods but avoided attempts at complete assimilation. These cities must have fulfilled much the same purpose as did pre-Islamic Mecca, that of a 'resting place' for the divinities of the different tribes.

Besides regional figures the Elamite pantheon also included gods of peoples who lived in or passed through the Zagros as well as, during the whole of Elamite history, many Babylonian deities. These were worshipped throughout the empire, not in the way that captured deities might be, in that the conqueror sometimes made offerings to such in order to avoid their wrath, but as gods who formed an integral part of the pantheon. Susa, where a large Babylonian colony was established, was always quite open to in-fluence from the west; this would account for the acceptance there of these foreign gods, but the worship of them spread far beyond the area round the city. In the time of Untash-(*d*)*GAL*, for example, certain Babylonian gods had their own shrines in the new sacred city at Chogha-Zanbil. The influence of Babylonia on the religion can be seen also in the use of Akkadian epithets for the deities, in the form of temples, and perhaps in certain ceremonies such as that which seems to bear the Akkadian name, *ṣīt šamši*, the rite at 'sun-rise'. It is almost impossible to discern why some Baby-lonian gods were accepted in Elam while others, no less important, were never admitted. The reasons were probably not political. Formerly the Third Dynasty of Ur and the sovereigns of Akkad exercised a firm sovereignty in Elam and this had a very deep influence on the culture of the country, whereas the cults of Ur and Akkad left only slight traces in Elamite religion. Instead of these Susiana was imbued with the doctrines of the great religious centre at Eridu, the holy city of Ea. Various phenomena might be explained on this assumption; the fantastic half-antelope half-fish or half-human half-fish figures of semi-divine beings on reliefs or seals,[1] the ideograms that are used for some divine appellations such as *A.É.A.LUGAL*, *NUN.LUGAL*, recalling the supreme name of Ea, *ENKI.LUGAL*, or the rites of ablution and lustra-tion to which the many finds of great bowls and ritual basins in the ruins of Susa testify.

Eridu was certainly not the only Mesopotamian sanctuary which influenced Elam, for the goddess Ishtar of Uruk was also of importance. Thus we know of the gift of three richly bedecked white horses sent to her by the king Tammaritu (a contemporary

---

[1] M. Rutten, 'Une cuve décorée provenant de Suse', in *Mém. D.P.* 30, 220 ff.

of Ashurbanipal),[1] and no doubt intended to draw the chariot of the goddess in processions. Nevertheless, the lack of documents prevents our knowing whether this assimilation of foreign ideas penetrated the more distant provinces of the empire. Extensive though it may have been, the influence of Babylonia on Elamite religion is not such as to justify the opinion that the introduction of these new cults ended in the superseding of the old indigenous religion by purely Babylonian beliefs and practices. The fact that divine names are written with logograms borrowed from Mesopotamian divine lists does not mean they should be read as Akkadian gods: in most cases they represent the name of a native god.

One more feature of the Elamite pantheon is shared, no doubt, by other pagan religions in ancient Western Asia, though it seems to be of wider application in Elam than elsewhere; that is the ill-defined character of the individual gods and goddesses. This want of formal distinction is due not merely to a defect of our knowledge but to the ideas that seem to have been current among the Elamites about their deities. Most of them were not only ineffable beings whose real name was either not uttered or was unknown, but also sublime ideas, not to be exactly defined by the human race. This may be the reason why Akkadian scribes experienced obvious difficulty in identifying them with their national gods; Ninurta, according to their account, corresponded with no less than eight members of the pantheon at Susa, Adad with three, and Shamash with two. The names used in the native language also illustrate this position. When Elamite gods are not called simply *napir*, 'the god', *zana, zini, sina*, 'the lady', *temti*, 'the protector', they often bear only an epithet indicating local origin or a particular quality, or else a description containing the elements *nap*, 'god', *zana*, 'lady', *kiri*, 'goddess', or *GAL*, 'the Great'. Even the name of the august Kiririsha means no more than 'the great goddess', while that of In-Shushinak derives from his position of 'lord of Susa'. There were, moreover, groups of gods known only by a collective epithet, such as *napratep, paḥaḥutep, paḥakikip*, or the ancient protecting deities whom Shilkhak-In-Shushinak invokes: *e nap paḥappi aktip nappip*—'O protecting deities, ancient deities'.

These general observations provide the background to any review of the gods and goddesses in the inscriptions of Khumban-numena and Untash-(*d*)*GAL* at this period. The most important deities are unquestionably *GAL*, In-Shushinak and Kiririsha. The god with the simple epithet *GAL*—'the Great'—is frequently

[1] R. F. Harper, *A.B.L.* no. 268.

associated with In-Shushinak and always precedes him in the
enumeration of their names. Their statues were placed side by
side in the same temples, and together they are called 'princes of
the gods'. The reading Khumban has been proposed for the
logogram _GAL_ and this is probably right.[1] There is some doubt,
however, for beside the many mentions of _GAL_ and In-Shushinak,
either together or separately, there is one isolated mention, on a
brick at Chogha-Zanbil,[2] where Khumban is written syllabically.
Despite this, Hüsing's arguments still seem conclusive, until a
more definite reason can be brought against them, that _GAL_ and
Khumban represent one and the same god. This god was, from
the time of the earliest texts, the supreme male god in Elam. It is
not impossible that he was also worshipped by other peoples
more or less related to the Elamites. Even if it be granted that he
was himself originally subject to the supreme power of the great
goddess, his spouse, he displaced her immediately the idea of the
superiority of the female principle began to lose its hold on the
religious ideas of the Elamites. There is evidence that this cult was
practised in all the provinces of the empire. With his name,
Khumban or _GAL_, 'the Great', such epithets as 'the king', 'the
greatest of the gods', 'the great protector', 'the sublime divine
protector', 'the one creating stability', are constantly associated.
The Babylonians treated him as the equivalent of their own
Marduk, the creator, lord of Babylon. Although in certain parts
of the kingdom he gradually yielded place to In-Shushinak,
whose cult continually spread, he never ceased to be the personal
god of the kings of that dynasty. Moreover, although 'the lord
of Susa' displaced him, that god's pre-eminence was due essentially to political events. In the strictly religious aspect Khumban
always kept his proper position in comparison with his rival;
his name is always invoked first, and In-Shushinak, alternately
with the goddess Kiririsha, appears only in the second place.

The prestige of In-Shushinak continually increased as the
centuries passed. His position was closely linked with that of his
city, Susa, which began as a provincial city and ended as the
capital of an empire. In the early treaty with Naram-Sin his
name is mentioned only in seventh place after those of Pinikir,
Pakhakikip, Khupan (Khumban), _A.MAL_, Sit and Nakhiti,

---

[1] §1, 4, 95. See above, p. 385, n. 1.
[2] From this, one could suppose that there was one temple (or several) of _GAL_ and
a temple of Khumban. It should also be noted that in Khumban-numena, Khumban
is always written syllabically whereas in the names of his successors Untash-(_d_)_GAL_
and Unpatar-(_d_)_GAL_, the divine element is always written with the logogram _GAL_.

while in the time of Untash-(d)GAL and his predecessor his cult was already recognized outside the limits of Susiana, for he is mentioned on the inscribed bricks of the temple which Khumban-numena built in the island of Bushire.[1] The extension of his cult reached its maximum in the reign of Shilkhak-In-Shushinak who instituted, or re-instituted, his worship in numerous cities: Susa, Ekallatum, Marrut, Peptar, Shakhan-tallak, and others. A damaged stele with an inscription of this king mentions twenty of his foundations: out of the fourteen still legible, ten are dedicated to In-Shushinak, while Khumban, Pinikir, Sukhsipa and Lakamar are honoured with only one each.

The Assyrians identified 'the divine lord of Susa' with the Babylonian gods Ninurta and Adad, but he was most often invoked as 'god of the king' rather than in his character as a storm-god or fertility-god or war-god. He was, like Khumban, called 'the great god', 'the great protector', but the epithets which are much more indicative of his nature are 'the protector of our city', 'my god, my king, my ancestor', as the kings describe him; they hold their royal authority by his grant, they thank him for the aid he lends in war and in their peaceful enterprises. But this 'protector of the city', this 'god of the king', was for the Elamites a power as mysterious and as concealed as the other deities. In his description of the sack of Susa, Ashurbanipal says: 'I bore In-Shushinak away to Assyria, the god of their mysteries, who dwelt in a secret place, whose divine acts none was ever allowed to see.' In spite of the extension of his worship, In-Shushinak always remained in essence the god of Susa and Chogha-Zanbil. He was never regarded as a 'god of Elam' and the rock inscriptions of Mālamīr do not mention him.

The goddess of the supreme triad at this time was Kiririsha, specially celebrated as 'lady of Liyan' where Khumban-numena erected not only the temple that she shared with Khumban and the protecting deities of the locality, but also a private sanctuary which subsequent kings maintained. Although there is no evidence that Untash-(d)GAL consecrated a temple to her at Susa, it is known that she had a sanctuary at Chogha-Zanbil which she shared with another goddess, Ishme-karab. These buildings seem to have occupied a privileged place in the holy quarter. In his curses on possible violators of his pious works, the king never omitted to invoke her, together with (d)GAL and In-Shushinak. Some have thought that she was essentially a

---

[1] [On the 'island' of Bushire, see now E. Sollberger and J. R. Kupper, *Inscr. royales sum. et akk.*, Paris, 1971, p. 283, n. 1. (Ed.)]

chthonic deity, the ruler of the kingdom of the dead,[1] as they translate an epithet, *Kiririša Liyan laḥakara* by 'Kiririsha of the dead city of Liyan'. But this translation is probably wrong and the epithet means rather 'who dwells at Liyan'. Other texts merely call Kiririsha 'the Great' or 'the divine mother'. Although her name is invoked by Khanni in the inscriptions at Mālamīr, she is not mentioned in the Naram-Sin treaty, or in the documents of the early dynasties at Susa. These facts, combined with the absence of any record of her cult in the inscriptions of Untash-(*d*)*GAL* at Susa seem to be good reason for assuming that she was essentially a deity of the interior, especially the southern provinces of the empire.

In the north, on the other hand, the great goddess was Pinikir, whose cult seems to have been unknown at Mālamīr and Liyan. The primitive importance of this great goddess in the Elamite pantheon has already been mentioned; as the centre of the kingdom gradually shifted southward, she became less important, and gave place to the 'lady of Liyan', Kiririsha. At Susa, however, there was a temple dedicated to her alone at a very early date. Untash-(*d*)*GAL* restored it and added to it another construction called *aštam*.[2] At Chogha-Zanbil he also built her a sanctuary which seems less important than those of Ishme-karab and Kiririsha. The cult of Pinikir was observed throughout the centuries in Susiana, for Shutur-Nahhunte still invoked her as 'sovereign of the gods' and Ashurbanipal names her among the deities whose temples he destroyed. Assyrian lists of his time identify her with Ishtar, the supreme goddess of the Babylonians and Assyrians.

At least two other local goddesses were particularly honoured in the time of Untash-(*d*)*GAL*, called Upurkupak and Ishme-karab, but little is known of either of them. Upurkupak must be a provincial goddess, for the king boasted of having built a temple for her at Susa where none had been in the time of his predecessors. At a much later date Khutelutush-In-Shushinak seems to have been particularly devoted to this goddess, for he built a sanctuary for her in the town Shalulikki where her cult had not previously been observed. Ishme-karab, on the other hand, had been worshipped at Susa since the time of the *sukkal*-rulers. Yet it was not at Susa, but at Chogha-Zanbil, that Untash-(*d*)*GAL* dedicated a temple to her. Next to the temple of Kiririsha it occupied, as we have seen, a privileged place directly on the enclosure around the

---

[1] §1, 7, 101 ff.

[2] It would not seem at present that the Elamite word *aštam* is to be identified with the Akkadian *bīt aštamme*.

zikkurrat. Later, Shilkhak-In-Shushinak restored one or two of her sanctuaries, but the broken text recording them does not allow of our knowing where.

To another important member of the pantheon, the god Nahhunte, Untash-(d)GAL built a new temple at Susa[1] and Chogha-Zanbil,[2] in which he placed a statue to thank the god for having heard his prayers and performed his desires. This god, like Shamash, with whom the Babylonians compared him, was the Elamite god of justice, the Sun. His cult was always a flourishing one in Elam and at Susa his temple was among the most ancient sanctuaries. Some kings call themselves 'servants of Nahhunte' and invoke him as their 'protector' and their 'ancestor'. The kings of the dynasty of Shilkhak-In-Shushinak devoted special attention to him as is shown by his appearance in several personal names of this house. This sun-god is invoked for a specific reason in the curses on possible violators: 'May Nahhunte...deprive him of descendants.'

Other gods whose names occur on inscribed bricks of this period are less known and less important; such are the divine Shimut and his consort, the two associated gods Khishmitik and Rukhuratir, Pelala, Nazit, Shiashum, Sunkir-Risharra, Kilakh-supir, Shushmushi[3] and the Napratep. Shimut, although expressly called 'god of Elam', is known to have been worshipped at Susa, Mālamīr and Awan. If an Assyrian text which mentions a star of the same name can be relied upon, he was perhaps an astral deity; his cult was much in favour in Elam, and never ceased throughout the centuries. In the Naram-Sin treaty he was invoked immediately after In-Shushinak. In the personal name of a *sukkal* called Shimut-wartash he has the character of a tutelary god. He had a temple on the acropolis at Susa before the reign of Untash-(d)GAL and that king, not content with restoring this traditional sanctuary, built another for him at Chogha-Zanbil. When, a century later, the temple at Susa had again fallen into ruin, Shilkhak-In-Shushinak, one of whose brothers was called Shimut-nikatash, rebuilt it completely of more durable material. It survived till the days when the destructive fury of Ashurbanipal's soldiery reduced it to ashes.

[1] *Mém. D.P.* 3, no. xiv.

[2] A brick like *Mém. D.P.* 3, no. xiv, was found at Chogha-Zanbil during the excavations of 1958–9.

[3] These last two gods are mentioned on bricks that were found since the publication of the list of deities given by M. Rutten in *Mém. D.P.* 32, 8 f. The non-existent *Akkipish should be removed as it is the result of a misreading of *Mém. D.P.* 32, xviii, no. i, 3.

In all these sanctuaries Shimut was worshipped with his divine spouse. At Susa and Chogha-Zanbil she was called at this period *NIN.URU*, 'lady of the city'. It is not certain whether this logogram is to be read in Akkadian, Bēlit-āli, or whether this is simply an epithet of Manzat, who is later constantly associated with Shimut as his spouse. Manzat, 'the great lady', was a very ancient deity whose name is found on a business document of the Agade dynasty, and it occurs several times in personal names of the Third Dynasty of Ur. Likened to a leonine Ishtar by the Akkadian scribes she was worshipped not only in Susiana but also, as Manzit, at Mālamīr. She certainly had a sanctuary at Chogha-Zanbil[1] and at Susa, her temple, or perhaps the chapel she occupied in the sanctuary of Shimut, was restored first by Shutruk-Nahhunte and then by Khutelutush-In-Shushinak. She probably had another temple as well not far from Chogha-Zanbil on the other side of the Āb-i Diz on the unexplored mound now called Deh-i Now.[2] A brick found on this site states that a temple of Manzat stood there at the time of Shutruk-Nahhunte.

The two deities Khishmitik and Rukhuratir shared, both at Susa and at Chogha-Zanbil, a common temple built for them by Untash-(*d*)*GAL*. Khishmitik, also written Ishmitik, is known only from inscribed bricks of that king, but Rukhuratir is found more often. His cult existed at all periods, and must have been widespread in the country, as shown by various spellings of his name. In the contracts from Mālamīr he is joined with Shamash as a god before whom oaths were sworn. Assyrian scribes regarded him, together with In-Shushinak, as identical with the god Ninurta, and he appears in the series of incantations *šurpu* as potent to protect against witchcraft.

Of other individual gods little is known. Pelala is named in the contracts from Mālamīr and in the annals of Ashurbanipal, but we are left without information as to the part he played in the Elamite pantheon. The personality of Nazit is equally obscure. His chapel at Susa, mentioned on an inscribed brick of Untash-(*d*)*GAL* may have been part of the joint temple of *GAL* and In-Shushinak, for these two are invoked in this dedication. Only on bricks from Chogha-Zanbil are found the deities Shiashum,

---

[1] The brick mentioning this was found after the publication of *Mém. D.P.* 32, 8 f.

[2] This site was certainly occupied for a long time as bricks dating from the Third Dynasty of Ur to the times of Shutruk-Nahhunte and Shilkhak-In-Shushinak were found there.

Sunkir-Risharra, Kilakh-supir and Shushmushi, of whom nothing more is known than their names, although the first is mentioned in the Naram-Sin treaty. The name of the second is simply an epithet, 'the great king'. All we know about the last, Shushmushi, is that he was coupled with a *bēlit*, a 'lady', who is otherwise unknown. As for the Napratep, worshipped both at Susa and Chogha-Zanbil, we know only that they constituted a group, for the form is plural, as in Pakhakhutep, gods to whom Khumban-numena dedicated a great temple at Liyan. It is not clear whether the former, like the latter, were old, more or less anonymous, protecting deities, or whether it was a generic for several known gods such as the Igigi or Anunnaki of the Babylonian pantheon. The first element means simply 'god' but the second, *ratep*, cannot be interpreted although it formed part of the personal name of a prince of Awan, Khishep-ratep.

In addition to these indigenous gods, the Elamite documents of this period mention many Babylonian deities for whom Untash-(d)GAL had temples built both at Susa and at Chogha-Zanbil. They are Nabu, Sin, Adad and Shala, Inanna and Nusku. Earlier inscriptions show that a number of Babylonian gods had long been worshipped in Susiana, but it is worthy of note that these cults, adopted from the west, remained in existence at this time when the country took an independent course and displayed a certain chauvinism in the persistent struggle for a national policy and an internal development of civilization. Since many names such as Sin and Adad were written with logograms the question arises whether these should not be interpreted in the same way as the logogram, *UTU*, to be read Nahhunte, that is to say, as true Elamite names. Assyrian lists in fact inform us that Sin was called Dakdadra in Elam, and that Adad corresponded to both Shunnukushsha and Sihhash, as well as In-Shushinak. But Sin and Adad are so well attested in Elam in other periods that there is no *a priori* reason for excluding them from the Elamite pantheon of this time. That Adad and Shala were worshipped in their own names is proved by syllabic writing, and this is another reason for maintaining that the other Akkadian names were used.

It is a pertinent question whether these Babylonian deities preserved in this foreign land the characteristics and qualities which they had in their own country. A votive hoe has been found at Chogha-Zanbil, with its handle in the form of a serpent and bearing the inscription '*marru* of Nabu'. The *marru*, probably borrowed from the symbols of Marduk, is not an emblem of his cult-centre Borsippa, whereas the serpent, on the other hand, seems to indicate that in Susiana Nabu was connected with the chthonic powers which that reptile symbolizes. Again, the goddess Shala was in Babylonia the traditional spouse of Adad. Her cult appeared in Elam immediately after its adoption in Babylonia by the Semites of the Amorite dynasty; but in the contracts of Susa she appears independent of Adad as one of the gods before whom oaths were taken.[1] It was not until later, in Susa as in Chogha-Zanbil, that she was closely associated with the cult of Adad. However this may be, in the dedicatory inscriptions of Untash-(*d*)*GAL*, no distinction seems to be made between the foreign and Elamite gods. They were all 'gods of Siyankuk'[2] whom the king implores to accept his pious works and bless his kingship in exactly the same terms. The foreign, like the native, gods receive the tribute of new statues in the restored temples. And to these Babylonian gods, fully accepted in Elam, there is no doubt that Bēltia, 'my lady', should be added. She occurs in the inscription on the statue of Napirasu and it is certain that she was the Ishtar of Babylon, for one of the successors of Untash-(*d*)*GAL* describes her as *zana Tentar*, 'the lady of Babylon'.

In spite, then, of the brevity and monotony of the formulae on the bricks of the kings of this dynasty, a broad reconstruction of the Elamite pantheon in this period is possible, but it would be an exaggeration to treat the list as exhaustive. The excavations of Chogha-Zanbil and Susa have not as yet revealed all there is to know about these two cities. Other cities and other temples are still hidden under the débris of unexplored mounds. Moreover, there were certainly other temples, at Susa and elsewhere, which did not need repairs at that time, and consequently do not appear in the kings' inscriptions, Khutran is a case in point; he was an ancient deity of the national pantheon, closely associated with the divine pair Khumban and Kiririsha, perhaps their son, if an invocation of Shilkhak-In-Shushinak, which calls him 'the chosen descendant' of these two, can be said to prove that. A tutelary god, his name occurs frequently in personal names such as Khutran-temti, Kidin-Khutran and the like. Although his cult

---

[1] It is doubtful whether the personal name Shala on the tablets of Mālamīr refers to this goddess. The name is never preceded by the divine determinative and once (*Mém. D.P.* 8, 16 = *Mém. D.P.* 22, 76) instead of Shala we find the personal name Tepti-akhar, which is also on a tablet from Susa (*Mém. D.P.* 23, 248, 18).

[2] According to the brick cited above for the identification of Chogha-Zanbil with Dūr-Untash, it seems that *siyankuk*, in which there is the word *siyan* 'temple', designated a part of the holy city, probably the group, temples and zikkurrat, within the two inner enclosures. It seems to have the same meaning at Susa.

originated perhaps in Awan, he had a temple at Susa which Ashurbanipal was to destroy in the sack of that city. Two other native
divinities, Lakamar and Narundi, as well as the Babylonian gods
Nergal, Shamash, and Nin-khursag, are in the same situation; no
texts from this period mention them, but there is no reason to
suppose that their cults fell into disuse at this time, for they
occur both earlier and later. It may be that they are disguised
under names given to many gods as yet unidentified.

The results of this review of Elamite religion sufficiently
demonstrate the inadequacy of our sources. An enumeration of
the deities worshipped by a people is not a sufficient guide to the
true substance of the religion. We do, however, have other evidence
than the dedicatory inscriptions and god lists. There are the
monuments, reliefs and sculpture as well as the seals from
Elam. Despite the fact that they are difficult to interpret because
of their particular symbolism, some of them may illustrate certain
fundamental ideas of Elamite religion. The archaic seal impressions[1] seem to show that Susa and Mesopotamia had the same
primitive concepts about the gods. Each city-state worshipped a
patron god who was partnered by his consort, either one being
pre-eminent. A pantheon, even regional, does not seem to
exist until pre-Sargonic times. There is seen also the king-
priest standing beside a temple with a high terrace.[2] According
to similar pieces from Uruk these motifs seem to be related to the
neo-Sumerian concept of the divine king. Another seal, slightly
earlier than the dynasty of Agade, illustrates a feature which we
consider distinctly Elamite: the multiplicity and the eminent
position of goddesses. A very curious sort of feminine pantheon
is evoked by a line of goddesses taking part in a mythological
drama which seems concerned with vegetation.[3]

There has already been occasion to mention rites of ablution,
which were perhaps due to the influence of the cult of Ea on
Elamite religion. These rites are known through the discovery at
Susa of many containers and basins, one at least of which is
decorated with the representation of an intertwined cord, the
symbol of the flowing waters, and with the half-antelope, half-
fish figures. Other such rites are illustrated by the votive bronze
model called *ṣīt šamši*; two naked figures, perhaps a priest and his
acolyte, kneel face to face before a temple and, presumably at

---

[1] Period of Uruk V–III. As well as a style similar to that of Uruk, there was an
original style which shows that Elamite art was not simply a borrowing from Mesopotamia, cf. §II, 2, 105 ff. For the documents of Uruk cf. §III, 8.
[2] See §III, 1, 41.　　　　　[3] §III, 3, 1, pl. 45, 11–12 (S. 462), and p. 57.

dawn, are about to commence ritual ablutions with the water contained in a vase of a form not unlike the *agubbu*, the vessel containing holy fluid, used by the Babylonians.[1]

These two objects are later in date than the time of Untash-(d)GAL but the stele carved in relief that bears his name provides other religious motifs that are no less instructive. The flowing streams recur on this stele and the gesture of prayer is shown, a deity is replaced by a symbol, and the Elamite belief in fantastic creatures half man, half animal is illustrated, together with the religious importance of the serpent. Most of these features can also be found in a rock relief at Kūrangān,[2] between Susa and Persepolis. This depicts seated deities, groups of worshippers, the flowing streams, the serpent figure. In this religious scene there is a theme which adds to the interest, the advance of a procession towards the 'high place' where the divine pair sit.[3] The worshippers, marching in a column, hold their hands out towards the god, the gesture of prayer, which does not differ from the Babylonian act of adoration. The supernatural character of the gods is symbolized as in Babylonia by the triple row of horns on the head-dress; even semi-divine beings or demons are sometimes so distinguished, but in their case a single pair of horns for their leaders is usual. One detail, however, which may also be found on certain North Syrian reliefs of the 'Hittite' style, distinguishes these representations of the gods from the Babylonian tradition: whether the god's head is in full face or profile, the horns are always full face. But the motif of the flowing streams leads us back again to the direct Babylonian influence. On the stele these have the appearance of two long wavy tresses crossing one another, which join heaven and earth; in the middle they are held by a semi-divine being, half human, half fish, who holds them tight against his chest. At Kūrangān, on the other hand, it is the god himself who lifts in his right hand a bellied vase from which the two streams flow; the water, curving backwards and forwards, falls on two groups of worshippers. The comparison with the frequent use of this *motif* in Babylonia shows a close connexion with fertility rites.

---

[1] This bronze model is studied in detail below, pp. 496 f.   [2] See Plate 53 (*b*)–(*c*).
[3] See the end of this chapter, and also compare *C.A.H.* I³, pt. 2, pp. 673 f. N. C. Debevoise, 'The Rock Reliefs of Ancient Iran', in *J.N.E.S.* 1, 72, dates this relief in the third millennium, but § III, 2, iv, 2139 prefers the middle of the second. Neither of these dates is certain. It could also be dated to the neo-Sumerian period by comparing it with a seal-impression found in the Ur III level (*Mém. D.P.* 25, 233, fig. 53) and with the different representations on the seals of Susa B (see *R.A.* 50, 135, no. 4).

The form taken by the semi-divine creatures likewise belongs to a common set of ideas. In the earliest periods of Elamite civilization these supernatural beings had the strangest forms— half human, half plant; half human, half serpent; half human, half goat; and so forth. This was probably common to Elam and Babylonia, but the Elamites seem to have been much more imaginative. They created the griffon, as a temple guard, which was unknown to the Sumerians.[1] Contrariwise, the nude hero 'Gilgamesh', the usual acolyte of the god Ea, was unknown in the glyptic art of Susa.[2] Later, Babylonian influence restricted and regularized the types; to an upper body in human form there was added either the tail end of a fish or the hind quarters of a bull. They are thus represented either in the midst of the interlacing streams, or beside a palm-tree, or on either side of a stylized 'tree of life'. Themselves producing and protecting the fertility of the land, these creatures were also, in Elam as elsewhere, the guardians of sacred buildings. Ashurbanipal mentioned in his annals the *šēdū* and *lamassū* which guarded the temples at Susa and the figures of wild bulls which watched over the gates. There is no doubt that the Elamites believed in the existence of evil demons as well as of these beneficent deities. Their Babylonian neighbours in fact regarded Elam as specially the land of witches and of demoniac creatures; the typical demoness Lamashtu herself, though often called 'the Sutian',[3] is just as often named 'the Elamite'. Even if it cannot be denied that Babylonia exercised a controlling influence on Elamite art in the representation of semi-divine beings, it is none the less certain that many of these fantastic creatures were directly due to Elamite imagination.

As well as good and evil demons the Elamite engravers also invented others which seem to personify cosmic ideas and have nothing to do with the notions of good or evil. The scenes that they depicted, most often in a style of caricature, are more probably taken from myth than from stories or fables. There are not only animals parodying men,[4] but Atlas-figures holding up the world,[5] and successions of gigantic animals, perhaps symbolizing

---

[1] This is later found in Egypt; see § III, 1, 42, and fig. 5.

[2] This is the more curious in that the seals of an older period (Susa I) display figures of conquering heroes who anticipate 'Gilgamesh'.

[3] I.e. one who haunts the Syrian desert.

[4] Dog-ploughmen or farmers (*Mém. D.P.* 16, nos. 196, 260, etc.); antelope holding a bow and arrows (§ III, 5, no. 775), etc. Cf. the statuettes from Susa showing drinking and sitting animals (*Mém. D.P.* 13, pl. xxxix, 2–3); cf. M. Rutten in *Rev. ét. sém.* (1938), 97 ff.

[5] *Mém. D.P.* 16, 266, 267, etc.; P. Amiet in *R.A.* 50 (1956), 125 f.

natural cycles, victorious over each other alternately in strict order.[1] These themes conjure up a 'land of fable' from which man is absent, and mysterious domains where the cosmic balance is in operation.

The most important motif in Elamite religious art is the serpent.[2] Our attention has already been drawn to this recurring theme by the two long serpents which frame the stele of Untash-(*d*)*GAL*. Actually the serpent appears on very ancient objects, notably on seals that belong to the time of the Third Dynasty of Ur. It is represented on the stele of Puzur-Shushinak, in the rock relief of Kūrangān, and in another relief cut in the rock at Naqsh-i Rustam. It is the essential theme on the celebrated 'altar with serpents', a masterpiece of Elamite metal work dating from the period after Untash-(*d*)*GAL*, and bodies of reptiles frequently form the butt of votive sceptres or the handle of a *marru* dedicated to the god Nabu.

All these examples, together with many others that need not be quoted here, whether the serpent is depicted naturally or as a symbol, are simply representations of a very ancient deity, the serpent god, or rather, a god of which the serpent is the symbol, the captive, and the guardian of his subterranean realm. Undoubtedly the theme of the serpent was popular in Mesopotamia at different times, and even had an influence on Elamite tradition. Thus, during the dynasty of Agade, Susa as well as Babylonia[3] used on their seals a representation of the serpent-god that had been worked out by Agadean artists. In the same way the serpent on the stele of Untash-(*d*)*GAL* can be compared with similar representations on several Kassite *kudurru*.[4] But the serpent was always more important in Elam than in Mesopotamia, and the Elamite artists created a type of human-headed serpent that was typically Elamite.[5] This originality is of special importance from a religious point of view, as it shows a deification of the

---

[1] *Mém. D.P.* 16, no. 330. (An enormous bull mastering two small lions is counterpoised with an enormous lion subduing two small bulls.) Another seal, now lost, shows two antithetic scenes: a lion theatening a kneeling bull with his bow and the same bull, this time standing, holding a club over the head of the now crouching lion. The same kind of alternation and balancing of forces can be seen in the document *Mém.D.P.* 16, 335, studied by E. Porada, 'A Leonine Figure...', in *J.A.O.S.* 70 (1950), 225.

[2] P. Toscanne, 'Études sur le serpent...dans l'antiquité élamite', in *Mém. D.P.* 12, 153 ff. and 25, 183 ff., 232 f.; and cf. §III, 7, 53 ff.

[3] Cf. *R.A.* 44 (1950), 172, nos. 30, 31.

[4] See §III, 4, pl. I, pl. LXVIII, 1; pl. LXXXIII, 1.

[5] See §III, 3, 1 S. 105; *R.A.* 19 (1922), 148, no. 11.

serpent little known in Mesopotamia. This deity tends to become less and less animal. Sometimes it has the head and shoulders of a man and from the torso downwards the body becomes the winding coils of a serpent. Sometimes, however, the serpent is no more than an attribute of the deity, as in the relief of Kūrangān, where the god, entirely human in form, holds the head of the serpent in his left hand while its body, folded coil upon coil, serves as his seat. This serpent-god, the origin of whose cult is lost in the mists of time, is rather a mysterious figure, a symbol perhaps of all those dark powers that are hidden in the depths of the earth, or spring up from the ground, sometimes beneficent, sometimes terrifying, bringing sometimes fertility, sometimes destruction. It is thus not surprising that many representations of serpents have been found in foundation deposits. Heads or bodies of these reptiles were a common form for ex-votos, buried to secure the protection of the chthonic deities for the foundations which descend into their dark realm.

One other religious motif in the relief at Kūrangān deserves special notice. On the rock surface to the left, slightly overhanging the face with the principal relief, where the god with the serpent and the seated goddess beside him form the central group, the procession represented seems to be moving towards the divine pair. Such long files may be seen recurring on the rocks of Kul-i Fir'aun, at Mālamīr, in the rock reliefs carved in honour of Khanni, the ruler of Aiapir.[1] The custom of religious processions, with their trains of priests and worshippers, was common in Mesopotamia from a very early date. Certain of these processions, in particular those of the New Year, even left the environs of the temple and filed out into the surrounding country. But here the worshippers did not accompany their god but came from afar to pay homage. The scene is more reminiscent of a pilgrimage than of a procession, and this form of worship is very rarely known in Mesopotamia. On the other hand, the fact that their goal was a high place, the seat of chthonic deities, rather recalls certain aspects of Anatolian cults, where may also be found these three features: a high place, a procession, and chthonic deities.[2]

It will be apparent from these remarks on Elamite religion that it is still difficult for us to form any precise idea of this

[1] The seals only seldom depict religious ceremonies. The most striking example is the amusing scene which shows a line of sedan-chairs and standard-bearers on the document in *Mém. D.P.* 29, 20, fig. 16 (12). Unfortunately this scene, like many others, is difficult to interpret.

[2] See § III, 2, iv, 2139.

people's beliefs. Certainly we know the name and often the nature of the greater proportion of their gods, certainly also their beliefs contained ideas common to most of the primitive religions of the Near East, together with obvious influence from Mesopotamian cults. But the original bases of the native religion still escape our knowledge. Until future excavations have put at our disposal specifically religious documents, especially prayers and rituals, it will be impossible to attempt a comprehensive account of Elamite religion.

# CHAPTER XXX

## PHRYGIA AND THE PEOPLES
## OF ANATOLIA IN THE
## IRON AGE

T H E Hittite Empire collapsed in ruins in about 1200 B.C., at the hands of the invaders, among whom their traditional enemies on the eastern frontier, the Kaska peoples, were surely numbered, and a horde or series of hordes flooded over the land; excavation has revealed a level of destruction by fire in the east, at the Hittite capital of Boğazköy, at Alaca and at Ališar.[1] Written records of the Hittites, hitherto our most important source of historical information concerning Anatolia, cease abruptly with the reign of Shuppiluliumash II. At Ališar there was a brief occupation by a people who, it is thought, may have been the Luwians and who may have played an important part in the destruction. When the curtain rises again, central Anatolia is ruled (or at least, occupied) by an invading people, a horse-rearing military aristocracy called the Phrygians (as they were known in the West to the Greeks through Homer), or the Mushki and Tabal (as they were known to the Assyrians in the East). According to the traditions preserved among the Macedonians, says Herodotus (III. 73), the Phrygians crossed the straits into Anatolia from Macedonia and Thrace, where they had until then been known as Bryges or Briges. The Greeks in general believed that this event took place before the Trojan War, enshrining it in legend; though Xanthus, a Lydian historian, held it took place after that event, in a joint invasion with the Mysians.[2] According to one such Greek tradition, the royal house of Priam was connected with Phrygia by marriage, since Hecuba was daughter of the River Sangarius.[3] Another tale (*Iliad*, III. 184 ff.) tells how Priam, king of Troy, fought as an ally of the Phrygian leaders Otreus and Mygdon when they battled against the Amazones on the River Sangarius.

---

\* An original version of this chapter was published as fascicle 56 in 1967; the present chapter includes revisions made in 1973.

[1] Boğazköy (Büyükkale): §III, 7, 27, 67 ff.; Ališar, §III, 24, esp. 289 (destruction in Level 5 M); Alaca, §III, 18, 179.

[2] Xanthus: F. Jacoby, *Frag. Hist. Graec.* 765 F14.

[3] Schol. on Homer, *Il.* XVI. 718.

Some scholars see in this battle that which Tudkhaliash IV fought against twenty-two states in the 'Land of the city of Assuwa'.[1] This assumes that the Amazons were the Hittites[2] (which is nothing but a guess) and, what is perhaps more likely, that Assuwa is 'Asia', i.e. north-west Asia Minor.[3] In fact, if the memory of the Amazons refers at all to a historical people, they are more likely to have been one of the peripheral peoples of the Hittite Empire nearer to the Greeks: Luwians or other races of Arzawa, e.g. Mira, Kuwaliya, Kaballa, who acted as buffer states between Hittites and Greeks; perhaps they were the armed priestesses of some goddess of war such as Ma of Comana. It would be a mistake to base much in any direction on these legendary Greek traditions (though they may well contain a germ of fact), unless and until they are confirmed by some new discovery. However, recent excavation in Troy VII b has revealed the introduction, after a destruction of the city by fire,[4] of a new population using a coarse ware apparently of central European origin, and this may reasonably be held to mark the passage of the Phrygians and Mysians. At Gordion, hand-made black pottery suddenly appears at a corresponding level, then disappears as if its makers had been absorbed.[5] In fact, the area in which the Mygdones, the tribe of the eponymous Phrygian hero Mygdon, traditionally lived was round Lake Ascania, by Nicea, close by the last curve of the River Sangarius: and this may very well mark the earliest Phrygian area of settlement, while the Mysians occupied the Troad and Propontis. Within a short time, presumably during the twelfth century B.C., the Phrygians flowed over most of the western Anatolian plateau, isolating the Luwians of the western plateau (who had withstood them, to form the kingdoms of Lydia and Lycia), perhaps driving others before them to safety beyond the Taurus and absorbing the rest. At Beycesultan[6] the city was destroyed about 1000 B.C. It has recently been suggested that the newcomers were at least partly nomadic in their way of life; and this may account for the interruption in the life of the central plateau which seems now to occur over a long period of at least a century or more.[7]

[1] But for a much earlier dating of this episode see *C.A.H.* 11², pt. 1, pp. 677 f.

[2] See article 'Amazones' in *P.W.* 1 (1894). It is noteworthy that, as Akurgal points out (*Späthethitische Bildkunst*, Ankara, 1949, p. 14 and n. 107), on the frieze of the Hellenistic Temple of Hecate at Lagina, Amazons are represented wearing helmets of the type worn by Hittite soldiers at Carchemish.

[3] §1, 3, ch. 1, 'Asia, Isj.j, Assuwa'.          [4] §III, 9.

[5] M. J. Mellink, review of §III, 9 in *Bi.Or.* 5/6 (1960), 251.

[6] §III, 20, 94.          [7] G, 5, 64; §II, 9, 52; §III, 16.

## I. GEOGRAPHY

In Greek times, the Phrygians' most north-westerly settlement, according to Xenophon,[1] was Keramon Agora, where a branch of the Royal Road left Lydia to strike northwards. The southern limit of the Phrygians' conquests is obscure, but it is worth noting that another Lake Ascania is found in Pisidia near Sagalassus, north of which was located the tomb of Mygdon, on the road running south towards Lycia; while the inland area beside the River Caÿster, through which ran south-west the road to Iconium and Barata, was later called the Phrygian Paroreia.

But the area which was especially sacred to them, where we find their principal religious monuments, is the hilly area, still well forested today (in Hellenistic times called Phrygia Epictetus or Little Phrygia), rising to four thousand feet above sea level, between modern Eskişehir and Afyon Karahisar, where rise several rivers sacred in myth and religion, such as Parthenius, Tembris, Sangarius, Rhyndacus,[2] and which includes the sacred city of Pessinus and that today called after its most notable inscribed monument 'Midas City' (evidently called in antiquity Metropolis, the 'City of the Mother', because dedicated to the mother goddess, Cybele).[3] On the east adjoined the areas of the Sangarius and the ancient (western) capital Gordion, around which are still to be seen as many as eighty great tumuli, once containing the rich burials of the Phrygian nobility and associated with the names of famous Phrygian kings, Gordius and Midas. Another important area of Phrygian settlement lay still further east around Ancyra (mod. Ankara), where typical Phrygian burial tumuli and temples and other remains of the eighth to sixth centuries have been found,[4] linking the westerly settlements with other Phrygian centres further east beyond the Halys, at Pteria (by some identified with Boğazköy, the former Hittite capital),[5] Pazarlı,[6] Alişar,[7] Alaca[8] and Kültepe.[9] In fact, pottery associated with Phrygians is found at a number of points all over the plateau.[10]

[1] *Anab.* I, ii, 11.

[2] §III, 4; G, 7.

[3] §III, 13, 14; §IV, 4; 14. The identification of Metropolis with Midas City is not accepted by all scholars. See Plate 157(*b*).

[4] §III, 1.                         [5] §III, 3, 7; 6, 52; 7, 78, 120; 8, 6.

[6] §III, 19.                       [7] §III, 24.

[8] §III, 3; 18.                    [9] §III, 25.

[10] Find-spots of Phrygian pottery marked on G, 1, Map 6; §III, 6, pl. 4; §IV, 8.

## II. THE NEWCOMERS AND THE
## CLASH WITH ASSYRIA

Assyrian sources name as the occupants of this area, in particular that east of the Halys, in the Iron Age from the twelfth century B.C., not Phrygians but Mushki.[1] The Assyrians sometimes speak of the Mushki and Tabal as if linked with Kashku, i.e. the Kaska peoples, formerly the great enemies of the Hittite kings on the latter's east and north-east frontiers, and this alone suggests that the Mushki may have been allied with them in some way, joining them in finally overthrowing the Hittite Empire. It is possible, too, that the mention in the latest records of the Hittite Empire of an unfriendly prince named Mita of Pakhuwa[2] (a city tentatively located west of the upper Euphrates, probably near Divriği), may point to a Phrygo-Mushkian thrust already then developing on that easterly frontier under an early bearer of an afterwards famous royal Phrygian name. It is tempting, in any event, to connect the Mushki on the one hand with the Georgian tribe of Mes'chi (known from about the fifth century A.D. around Lake Çildir beside the present Russo-Turkish frontier), and on the other, perhaps more plausibly, with the tribes recorded by the Greeks as Moschi and Tibarani, who dwelt beside the iron-working Chalybes, near the Black Sea coast around Cerasus, between Themiscyra, the reputed home of the Amazones, and the 'Moschian Mountains'. These Moschians and Tibaranians were still brigaded together in Xerxes' army. We assume that these tribes swarmed southwards from the direction of the eastern Pontus over the central plateau into the Halys bend, joining hands with the Phrygians advancing from the north-west. From the Assyrian royal annals[3] we learn that about 1160 B.C. a great army of Mushki swept on southwards through the Taurus Mountains and settled in the provinces of Alzi and Purukuzzi, 'where no man had vanquished them in battle', but acknowledged Assyrian overlordship by paying tribute. Fifty years later, the Assyrian king Tiglath-pileser I (1115–1077) accused the Mushki of having wantonly invaded the province of Katmukhi[4] with an army of twenty thousand men, i.e. implying that they were moving south-east threateningly. He may of course have been, and probably was, simply picking on their action of fifty years

---

[1] §II, 3, vol. I, §§220, 221.     [2] §I, 4; 5.
[3] §II, 3, vol. I, §221.
[4] The identification of Katmukhi and Kummukh (Commagene), formerly proposed by some, is impossible.

before as a *casus belli* to justify an attack on them. In any event he attacked, and defeated them in a pitched battle, annexed Alzi–Purukuzzi as a province and carried off six thousand Mushki as captives to a district,[1] probably in north-east Syria, where in Strabo's time they were still known as 'the Mygdones around Nisibis'.[2] Strabo's allusion, if it is to be trusted, is particularly interesting as implying that the original deep south-eastern thrust included also western Phrygian elements (Mygdones).

As the number of captive Mushki claimed is about one third the number of those who were said to have invaded the area, it may be accepted as possible. We are, however, told that the Mushkian army was led by five kings, implying that their horde consisted of at least five tribes; and it is likely that the ultimate Phrygian Empire as a whole was a federation or coalition of several tribes or elements. In this confederation the Phrygians seem to have represented the western element, with their capital at Gordion; the eastern was formed by Mushki with their capital at Mazaca (later Caesarea Mazaca, modern Kayseri), 'said to be derived from Mosoch, the ancestor of the Cappadocians', (Eusebius),[3] and Tabal. Tabal formed a neo-Hittite state, called by the Assyrians Bīt-Burutash, lying east of Niğde and Kayseri. Mushki and Tabal correspond with the names of Meshech and Tubal, two of the sons of Japheth, symbolizing Anatolian origins to Biblical writers (Gen. x. 2; Ezek. xxvii. 13, and xxxii; Ps. cxx. 5). This Anatolian figure of myth, Japheth, is most probably the same as that preserved in Greek legend as Iapetus, one of the Titans.

The eastern group of Mushki in the Euphrates valley seems to have been under partly Hurrian leadership, as the Katmukhian king's name, Kili-Teshub, son of Kali-Teshub, shows (he is also called Irrupi, Hurrian for 'my lord');[4] but possibly they were also partly Indo-Iranian, for kings of Katmukhi, presumably descended from the invaders of 1160 B.C., bear such names as Kundashpi or Kushtashpi still in the ninth and eighth centuries B.C.[5] (Or are we to interpret this ethnic element as a pre-existent Iranian native element, perhaps deriving from Mitanni, which survived the Mushki pressure?) Certainly in Hellenistic times the kingdom of Commagene represented a deeply conservative western

---

[1] §II, 3, vol. I, §221; see below, pp. 457 f.
[2] Strabo, XI. 14. 527; XVI. 1. 23.
[3] *Hist. Eccles.* IX. 12; §I, 7, 303.
[4] G, 4, 91, 178.
[5] §II, 3, vol. I, §§610, 769, 772, 797, 801,

outpost of Iranian religion, albeit in a mixed form,[1] under a diadochic dynasty claiming Achaemenid origins, but possibly with
much older roots.

Though at this point the chronological limit of the present
volume of this *History* has been reached, it is convenient to continue summarily the history of the Phrygian Empire to its end.

Between the twelfth and ninth centuries B.C. the empire of the
Phrygians, Mushki and Tabal spread southwards over the whole
of the vast Anatolian plateau. Tabal seems to represent the older
Luwian elements that survived the Hittite collapse north of the
Taurus, and to have been the new name particularly adapted for
the area formerly called 'Lower Land' by the Hittites. This is the
later Lycaonia and Cappadocia, the area south of the Halys river
as far as the barrier of the Taurus. Here the Tabalians were confronted and held back by the kingdom of Que or Khilakku
(Cilicia) in the eighth century B.C.,[2] while further east a coalition
of small Hittite principalities was formed called 'Land of Khatti',
centred around the old Hittite fortress of Carchemish on the
Euphrates. Til-garimmu (Hebrew, Togarmah; modern Gürün,
classical Gauraina) marked the eastern frontier of Tabal.[3] The
south-eastern limit of Tabal seems, however, to have been at
some time in part pushed by some tribes even beyond the Taurus,
for in the time of the proconsulate of Cicero (51 B.C.) the minor
passes of the Taurus were held by fiercely independent brigand
tribes called Eleutherokilikes ('Free Cilicians'), with a capital
at Pindenissus, controlling some of the Taurus passes, while their
allies the Tibarani (i.e. Tabalians) held the Amanus route. Cicero
soon disposed of their pretensions.[4] Yet it is astonishing how long
such groups preserved their identity, for in the seventh century
A.D., the Mardaites, or *Jarajīma*, apparently preserving the name
of Gurgum (a north Syrian mountain principality of the ninth
century B.C. located at Maraş in the Amanus Range[5]), were still
renowned as fighters in early Muslim times. The Mushki remained
in contact with Assyria, being invaded by Tukulti-Ninurta II
and acknowledging the authority of Ashurnaṣirpal II by sending
him gifts of copper vessels, cattle and wine in about 883 B.C.[6]
But the latter's son and successor, Shalmaneser III, took a more

---

[1] For Nimrud Dağ, see K. Humann and O. Puchstein: *Reise in Kleinasien und
Nord-syrien* (Berlin, 1890).

[2] §II, 3, vol. 2, §349.                    [3] *Ibid.* §§290, 349.

[4] Cicero: *Ad Fam.* xv, 4.

[5] H. J. Lammens, *La Syrie* (1921), pp. 81 ff.  See now U. B. Alkım in *Anadolu
Araştırmaları*, 1965.           [6] §II, 3, vol. 1, §442.

active line, sending an army in his twenty-second year (836 B.C.)
as far as Mount Tunni, 'the copper mountain', perhaps the site of
Tunna located near Bulgar Maden[1] and Mount Mulī, 'the marble
mountain'. Whereas Mushki was previously described as being
under five kings, he records now that Tabal was made up of
twenty-four 'kingdoms', which submitted to him, sending him
tribute in his twenty-second and twenty-third years;[2] the surrender of the cities of Perria (perhaps modern Peri near the
Euphrates) and Shitiuarria and twenty-two others is mentioned.
After that we hear nothing of the history of inner Anatolia for
fifty years.

The Tabalian princes, however, owed only reluctant allegiance
to the Assyrians, preferring the protection of the kings of Urarṭu,
and willingly forming part of the latter's sphere of influence. In
fact we find in the eighth century B.C. Urarṭian influence steadily
encroaching upon Eastern Anatolia. The Urarṭian king Menuas
(c. 810–785) claims to have conquered the principality of Malatya
as far as the modern Murad-Çay, and to have made its ruler Sule-
hawali or Sulumel[3] his vassal. At the same time he also attacked
Khilaruada, 'king of Khate'. Menuas's successor, Argishtis I,
claims in his third year c. 775 B.C. the conquest of a descendant of
Tuate, king of Malatya, possibly the same as King Tuwatis
mentioned in Hittite hieroglyphs, whose authority extended as
far west as Topada near Nevşehir.[4] Sarduris III of Urarṭu c. 750
claimed as his vassals Kummukh (Commagene) and Tabal, and
attacked Khilaruada, son of Sakhu king of Malatya, capturing his
capital, Sasi, and annexing nine of his fortresses along the line
of the Upper Euphrates. Their names are given as: Khazani,
Ugarakhi, Tumeiski, Asini, Maninu, Arusi, Qulbitarri, Tase,
Queraitase, Meluiani.[5] As a proof of this expansion of Urarṭian
influence into Syria south of the Taurus we see in the sculptured
doorways of palaces at both Zincirli and Sakçagözü figures of
lions and reliefs which suddenly appear in a purely Urarṭian style.
Further north, recent discoveries indicate that an Urarṭian principality, probably Dayaeni, extended its control into the Anatolian
plateau westwards in the eighth and seventh centuries as far as
Altıntepe, between Erzincan and Erzurum.[6]

---

[1] See below, p. 424, n. 6.  [2] §II, 3, vol. I, §§579, 580.
[3] §II, 4, no. 25 (Palu Inscription); §II, I, 153.
[4] §II, 4, no. 803 (Van Annals); §II, 2, 161 ff.; §VII, 24, xxix and 114. An earlier
Tuate, spelt Tuatti, is mentioned as king of Tabal by Shalmaneser III; cf. J. Læssøe,
*Iraq* 21 (1959), 155.  [5] §II, 4, nos. 102, 104 (Izolu Inscription); §II, I, 176.
[6] G, 4, *passim*; §III, 26.

When, about 770 B.C., we look into the history of Carchemish, the key position at the crossing of the Euphrates, we find that a new dynasty is installed under one Araras as prince of Carchemish, and from his own inscriptions it is clear that he was a usurper who claimed some authority over Mushkians and even Lydians (of the latter this is the first contemporary mention).[1] It is a fair inference that he was established with Urartian help, to subdue the Tabalian league. Kamanas (*c.* 750), the son of Araras, is explicitly stated to be the vassal of Sasturas, apparently to be identified with Sarduris of Urartu in an inscription found at Cekke between Aleppo and Carchemish.[2] An uneasy balance of power on the Anatolian plateau lasted until the accession in 745 B.C. of Tiglath-pileser III of Assyria, who in his conflict with Urartu found himself steadily drawn forward into Anatolia. After inflicting a severe defeat on Urartu and accepting the consequent submission of Pisiris of Carchemish in 738 B.C. Tiglath-pileser III found his advance into Asia Minor barred by an alliance of four Tabalian kings, Ushkhitti of Tunna, Urpalla of Tukhana, Urimme of Khupishna, and lastly Tukhamme of Ishtunda, with their allies Urikki of Que, Sulumel of Melid and Dad-ilu of Kaska.[3] The domains of these four major rulers evidently consisted of the valleys descending to the north from the principal passes of the Taurus, which they controlled. Urpalla's Tukhana is Tyana; his portrait, showing him worshipping his god Tarkhundas, with his inscriptions in Hittite hieroglyphic script, survives carved on the rock at Ivriz; other texts mentioning him are found at Bor, at Bulgar Maden in the Taurus, and on a stone found at Andaval near Niğde.[4] His was the central position, controlling the road through the Cilician Gates. Tunna is identified with Zeyve-hüyük near Bulgar Maden[5] but Khupishna is most probably Cabissus in the Saros valley (not, as often proposed, Cybistra), while Ishtunda or Ishtuanda is apparently just the Assyrians' spelling of the name of Azitawatas. This city, named after its founder Azatiwatas, Tukhamme's predecessor of the ninth century B.C., has been discovered and excavated at Karatepe, in the Ceyhan (Pyramus) valley.[6]

All four kings, Ushkhitti, Urpalla, Urimme and Tukhamme, acknowledged allegiance to Wassurme ( = Wasu-Sarma) 'great

---

[1] §III, 15c, 262 ff.
[2] §III, 15, Part III, 262 ff.; §II, 8; §VII, 6; A, 5, 105.    [3] §II, 3, vol. I, §772.
[4] Andaval, Bulgar Maden, Bor, §VII, 24, xxi, xxii, xxiii.    [5] By H. Bossert, §VII, 7.
[6] See above, pp. 364 ff. The identification of the city of Azitawatas with Ishtunda was first made by Landsberger and Bossert, §III, 11, part 2, 30.

king' of Tabal, the son of Tuatis mentioned above, who, while remaining in the background, is discernible as the Assyrians' real opponent, and who is mentioned in hieroglyphic Hittite inscriptions at Topada, Çiftlik and Suvasa, south of the Halys, at Kayseri (Sultan Han) and Kululu near Kültepe, probably Wassurme's capital, the name of which is given as Bīt-Burutash or -Burutish.[1] In about 730 B.C. Tiglath-pileser deposed the hostile Wassurme, replacing him as king of Tabal by one Khulli, 'son of nobody', who provided in return a vast tribute of ten talents of gold and one thousand of silver.[2] Khulli, however, after reigning some years, likewise defected from the Assyrian side. On the death of Tiglath-pileser III, there was a shift once more in the balance of power on the unstable Anatolian frontier. Trouble was caused by a princeling of Tabal named Kiakki of Shinukhti, who seems to have alienated Khulli from his loyalties to Assyria. He was joined by Pisiris, king of Carchemish, and a new figure, Mita of Mushki, otherwise Midas the Phrygian of Greek legend, all three making a formidable coalition.[3] Two years later (718), Sargon's army marched against the city of Kiakki, which was given to Matti of Tunna.[4] Mita advanced into Que (Cilicia) and seized three of its towns: but in 717 Sargon II's army marched against Carchemish and deposed Pisiris, carrying him off as a prisoner, and making Carchemish an Assyrian province. Khullu was deposed as king of Bīt-Burutash and replaced by his son named Ambaris (or Amris or Ambaridi—the name is variously written) who stood in high favour with Sargon at Nineveh. Ambaris was given an Assyrian royal princess named Akhatabisha to wife, with Khilakku (a part of Tabal immediately north of the Taurus) for dowry.

But a dramatic turn of fortune's wheel now took place. In 714, the Cimmerians, the Biblical Gomer, from beyond the Caucasus, a horde of fierce barbarians from south Russia, suddenly bore down on the confines of Urarṭu, driven out, according to Greek tradition,[5] by the Scythian tribes down the central passes of the Caucasus, the ancient military road. Rusas of Urarṭu met them at Uesi (probably Baş-Kale), was decisively defeated, and committed suicide, while in 714 Sargon marched through the now defence-

---

[1] §VII, 24, xx–xxiii; for Bīt-Burutash see §II, 3, vol. 2, §§24, 25, 92, 118. For excavations at Kululu, see T. Özgüç, *Kültepe and its vicinity in the Iron Age* (Ankara, 1971).     [2] §II, 3, vol. 1, §802.

    [3] G, 6.         [4] §II, 3, vol. 2, §§24, 25, 55, 118, 137.

    [5] Herodotus, IV. 9; for a discussion of Cimmerian remains in Anatolia see G, 2, 53 ff.

less country and sacked Muṣaṣir.[1] In 713 it was Ambaris' turn; he, too, was accused of playing Assyria false and, in order to strengthen himself, of having sought alliance with Rusas of Urarṭu (now dead) on the east and Mita of Mushki on the west, and 'conspiring to seize Assyrian territory'. Ambaris and his family and court were carried off to Assyria as prisoners and the Assyrian frontier was advanced once more to make Tabal an Assyrian province; the fortresses of Usi, Usian and Uargin were set up on the Mushkian frontier,[2] and Ellibir and Shindarara (Shalmaneser's Shitiuarria?) and ten other fortresses were seized from Meliddu. Midas made an offer of treaty with which Sargon played and temporized.[3] Tabal was made into a province; Khilakku and Que, respectively north and south of the Taurus, into another.

From Urarṭu, the Cimmerians appear to have turned westwards against the Urarṭians' allies, the Phrygians, whose ruler Midas, like Rusas, is also said to have committed suicide. The great tumulus at Gordion, excavated by the Americans in 1957,[4] produced a burial rich in gifts, surrounding the body of a small elderly man of over sixty years of age. None of the gifts included gold which, it has been ingeniously suggested, had all been surrendered to the invaders. At the same period the Phrygian city appears to have been violently burnt, though it revived. The Cimmerians are reputed to have ravaged Ionia, probably attacking Smyrna and Miletus and other cities such as Sinope (Herodotus IV. 12) and Antandrus, but the chief effect of their invasion which terrorized Asia Minor for eighty years was to destroy the Phrygian Empire, the heart of which they appear to have occupied. In 679 B.C., under their king Teushpa, they were defeated by Esarhaddon and thrown back from the Taurus after a pitched battle at Khupishna.[5]

## III. PHRYGIAN ART AND ARCHAEOLOGY

The earlier history of the Phrygian state is lost in darkness, but it is evident that, in spite of great interruptions, it eventually gathered up and preserved much of the arts and culture of the

[1] §II, 6.

[2] P. Meriggi, 'Una prima attestazione epicorica dei Moschi in Frigia', in *Athenaeum* 42 (Pavia, 1964), 52 ff., reading the name of the Mushki in the Hittite hieroglyphic rock-inscription of Kızıldağ near Konya, identifies this site and that of Karadağ nearby with two fortresses of Midas.

[3] See M. E. L. Mallowan, *Nimrud and its Remains*, 1, 205, and cf. now A, 10, 21 ff.          [4] §III, 28.          [5] II, 3, vol. 2, §516.

older Hittite world, having been partly built on the ruins of the kingdom of Arzawa and its smaller neighbours.

The Phrygians, while they superposed a new society in the form of a social order of horse-rearing aristocrats ruling over the older natives, became associated with a vast and powerful land-owning priesthood such as that of Pessinus,[1] of a conservative type, having pre-Phrygian origins. Gordion took the place of a Hittite township, the cemetery of which has been found.[2] Phrygian pottery, though not derived from that of the Hittites, is basically Anatolian in inspiration and derivation. It is of two main kinds: east of a line drawn from the Sangarius through the centre of the Konya Plain to the Taurus, it is polychrome, with geometric animals and designs—a style, called Ališar IV from the type-site, employing a technique which has very ancient roots in Central Anatolia; to the west, it is mainly grey or red monochrome (*bucchero*), a type which can also be followed back to the Bronze Age. Some gaily decorated plastic vases of polychrome ware were also found at Gordion and are particularly notable. It has been suggested that these are imports, and that the polychrome style belongs to Tabal and the Luwians of the east, while the grey *bucchero* alone is purely Phrygian.[3]

The Tabalian campaign of Tiglath-pileser III (conducted by his *rab šāqê*, a high-ranking military officer) is apparently depicted both in reliefs from Tiglath-pileser's palace at Nimrūd[4] and in polychrome frescoes from the governor's palace at Tell Aḥmar (Til-Barsib in North Syria).[5] These show us the earliest representations of the Eastern Phrygians or Moscho-Tabalians; they are men with fine, somewhat Greek features and black or sometimes red curly hair and close beards, wearing earrings of Lydian type,[6] long shirts with horizontal coloured bands and tassels at the corners, and high buskins identical with those typical both of Phrygians and Paphlagonians, 'reaching to the middle of the calf', as described by Herodotus (VII. 72, 73). In his day, Phrygian military equipment was completed by plaited helmets, small spears, and shields common to other central Anatolian tribes. Such is the armament of the Phrygian soldiers depicted on the coloured clay tiles found at the early sixth-century East Phrygian site of Pazarlı.[7] The women shown at Til-Barsib are unveiled and wear

---

[1] §I, 6, 39 ff.                                    [2] §III, 21.

[3] §VI, 8, including a distribution map. See Plate 158(*a*).

[4] §II, 2, xx–xxiii and pls. XLV–LV.

[5] §II, 7, pl. XLIX; §IV, 12, frontispiece, XV–XVII, pls. I, 109–20, 266, 336–48.

[6] §III, 10, figs. 157–8; §VII, 2, 17, 18, 23.          [7] §III, 19, pls. LIV, LV.

long shirts, gaily striped horizontally, and short coats similar to those of the men, with bell-shaped tassels. A sculptured stone figure wearing a dress of this type was found near Maraş.[1] To secure their dress, Phrygian men used a large ornate fibula of bronze, the best illustration of which is that worn by Urpalla in the relief at Ivriz.[2] A hundred and forty-five of these fibulae were found at Gordion in the Great Tumulus.[3] On the reliefs of Sargon,[4] Phrygian tributaries are represented wearing this large bow-shaped fibula on their long dresses; the fashion spread both southwards and eastwards to Maraş,[5] Zincirli[6] and Carchemish.[7]

The rise to power of Midas's kingdom in western Phrygia is the most significant event in the later eighth century in Anatolia. Midas, son of Gordius, perhaps a usurper, was a legendary figure of such wealth, in the memory of the Greeks, that he was popularly thought by them to have possessed the power of turning all he touched to gold. By the late eighth century, Phrygia was supreme over the ancient kingdom of Lydia, through which roads (forerunners of the Persian Royal Road)[8] ran from the interior to the Greek cities and ports of the Ionian coast. Midas is said both to have taken to wife the daughter of Agamemnon, the king of Cyme in Aeolis (a valuable testimony to the importance of the city at that time) and to have been the first of the 'barbarians' to make an offering at the great shrine of Apollo at Delphi, presenting nothing less than his royal throne (Herodotus, I. 14). This is only one example of a close interchange of goods and cultural influences which took place at this period between the two countries. But the excavators of Gordion have also found evidence of contacts with North Syria and Urarṭu.[9] 'Cups of Tabal with ears of gold' and 'censers of Tabal' were exported as far as Muṣaṣir.[10] It is evident that Midas was bidding for the support of the Greek cities as well as of Urarṭu in his trial of strength with the Assyrians.

Phrygian ring-handled bowls[11] were exported to the Ionian cities, and *phialai mesomphaloi*, bowls with a central thumb-hold used in Anatolia for making libations especially in the cult of the Great Mother, were carried to the mainland of Greece.[12] Remains of great wine-mixing bowls decorated with 'bird-women' set on

---

[1] §IV, 11, fig. 63.
[2] §III, 10, fig. 796. See Plate 159(*a*).
[3] §III, 28; §IV, 10. See Plate 158(*b*).
[4] §IV, 2, pl. 106 *bis*. See Plate 159(*b*).
[5] §III, 10, fig. 805.
[6] §III, 10, fig. 953; §IV, 7, vol. IV, pl. LIV.
[7] §III, 15, part III, pl. B, 64C.
[8] §I, 10.
[9] §IV, 10.
[10] §II, 6, lines 358, 361.
[11] See Plate 158(*c*).
[12] §IV, 13.

tripod stands[1] have been found in many Greek shrines. Although these bowls and stands originated in Urarṭu, it is likely that the Phrygians helped to convey them to Greece. The earliest Greek object found at Gordion as yet is a 'bird bowl' of East Greek ware, to be dated *c.* 650 B.C., but Phrygian objects of the eighth century B.C. have been recognized at Delphi, Olympia, Perachora, the Argive Heraeum, Aëtos (Ithaca), the Temples of Aphaea (Aegina) and Orthia (Sparta), Mitylene, Rhodes and Ephesus.[2]

Phrygian architecture was well developed. Vitruvius (II. 1, 68) describes their houses as built of wooden logs laid in a trench excavated in a mound and then covered with reeds, brushwood and earth; this exactly recalls the construction of the funerary tumuli excavated at Gordion. That such log huts were not just made to be buried in tumuli but were also built as habitations is as yet otherwise unattested, but it seems perfectly possible. Houses of the late eighth century at Gordion were built sometimes of stone, sometimes of crude brick, using a half-timber structure, and the walls were sometimes bedded on parallel logs. As to ground plans, excavations at Gordion have revealed the existence in the pre-Cimmerian levels of a building of *megaron* type, a plan of great antiquity in Anatolia; the Gordion *megaron*, which may have been a palace, possessed an upper floor or gallery. Floors were covered with pebble mosaics as early as 750 B.C. at Gordion. Simple wall frescoes were attempted.[3] The appearance of Phrygian houses may be gauged from the carved rocks representing the façades of elaborate buildings, probably temples, and illustrating them in stone at Arslankaya, Bahşayiş, Demirkale or Midas City.[4] These and some valuable, if childlike, 'doodlings' scratched at Gordion[5] confirm that the Phrygians' houses possessed pitched roofs (known also in Urarṭu) of a type made of a framework of wooden beams supporting a covering of reeds and clay. Their gables were crowned by large horn-shaped finials, a stone example of which has been found at Gordion, but which were perhaps more usually of wood. As houses with friezes supported on dentils and similar, though simpler, finials are also depicted in Lycian house-shaped tombs,[6] it may be inferred that these types of timber dwelling in both localities go back to a common original parent, a type of Western Anatolian (Luwian) house of the late Bronze Age that still awaits discovery. The doorways of Phrygian houses, to judge from the rock-cut

[1] §III, 23.
[2] §IV, 10; §I, 2, 186; §IV, 13, pls. 52–5; §IV, 5.
[3] §IV, 16, parts 1 and 2.
[4] §III, 10, figs. 1026–31, 1033; §IV, 14.
[5] §IV, 16, part 1.
[6] §III, 10, figs. 232, 242, 244.

façades, seem to have been hidden under, or at least flanked, by a large geometrically patterned screen, perhaps formed of wood-work employing marquetry, perhaps formed by a hanging carpet; in both these crafts the Phrygians were traditionally most skilled. By the sixth century such screens on buildings were replaced at Gordion, Pazarli[1] and elsewhere by ornamented revet-ments fixed to the *antae* and made of baked clay tiles, moulded in low relief; they are painted in gay polychrome with figures of men or animals, and are obviously related both to Greek and to Oriental art. It is perhaps not insignificant that tradition ascribed the invention of the frieze (Latin: *phrygium*) to the Phrygians.

No city plan has yet been excavated, but remains of a massive city wall of crude brick have been found at Gordion, forming part of an entire fortified citadel dating from the eighth century B.C.[2] Its gateway was built of hewn stone with a slight inward batter and was placed diagonally to the line of the streets. An Assyrian bas-relief depicting an Anatolian town[3] suggests that a star-shaped city plan formed with re-entrants and pointed pro-jecting bastions may have already existed, thus anticipating Vauban. Clearly this great Phrygian architectural tradition, like Phrygian skills displayed in other fields, could not have failed to exert great influence on the archaic Greek cities of the littoral. These and many other powerful cities were built along trade routes connecting, as we have said above, Phrygia with Greece and the west on the one hand and Assyria, Urartu and Iran on the other. To Greece brazen Urartian cauldrons with their tripod supports and ornamented handles were exported, their handles shaped in the likeness of woman-headed birds overlooking the rim inwards, fabulous creations which may have suggested to the Greeks the story of the unhappy Phineus and the Harpies.[4]

## IV. PHRYGIAN LIFE AND CULTURE

The best known feature of Central Anatolia was the so-called 'Royal Road', established by the Persian Kings, running from Ephesus to the Cilician Gates and thus on to Susa, being divided in Lydia and Phrygia into 'twenty σταθμοί (stations)' within a distance of ninety-four and a half parasangs (Herodotus, v. 52). But there was certainly an equally important parallel line farther north running through Smyrna.[5] The 'Royal Road' crossed the Halys by a bridge (Herodotus, i. 75) made of rough stonework,

---

[1] §III, 17; 19.    [2] See Plate 160.    [3] §II, 2, pls. XLV, XLVI.
[4] §IV, 17; §VI, I.    [5] §I, 7, 27 ff.; §I, 10.

remains of which still exist at Çeşnir Köprü.[1] It was really a trade-route of immemorial antiquity going back to Hittite Imperial times. At Pteria (Boğazköy) it met a cross artery that ran northwards to the sea at Sinope, or southwards through Mazaca and through the Taurus to the Euphrates and Syria. A section of it, surfaced with cut stones, leading from Gordion to Ancyra, has been uncovered near Gordion by the American excavators.[2] These ancient trade-routes lent Phrygia a particular importance to her neighbours, because of her natural assets. Of these, the first was the quality of her grasslands, which supported large flocks of fine sheep. The Anatolian sheep bore the best wool, and Aristagoras remarked on the Phrygians' wealth in sheep (Herodotus, v. 49). Even today the Ankara goat's wool, known as mohair, is world-famous. The conversion of these fleeces into textiles, tapestries and carpets was a traditional craft. Patterned or embroidered textiles may be seen in the fine dress of Urpalla of Tyana depicted at Ivriz.[3] Timber was also an important economic factor. The neighbourhood of Midas City still harbours valuable forests. At Gordion, the following woods have been noted by the excavators as used in building, cabinet-making and inlaying of furniture: cedar and Syrian juniper (logs), pear, box, maple, poplar, black pine, pine, and yew. Some of these woods still grow in the vicinity of the site.[4] Lastly, by the time of the Early Iron Age the mineral deposits of Anatolia had already been famous for one thousand years, having been exploited since the times of the Assyrian merchants of Kültepe. The ancient silver and lead mines of Bulgar Maden, and haematite, were important natural resources. Crystal, onyx,[5] mica came from Phrygia. *Miltos*, red earth or ochre used for paint, was obtained from Cappadocia, but, being exported through Sinope, was called 'Sinopic earth'.[6] Sinope also produced red lead; bronzes and slaves were exported from Meshech and Tubal, and horses and mules from Togarmah (the Assyrian Til-garimmu) according to Ezekiel (xxvii. 13 f.)

The excavations at Gordion conducted by the Körte brothers in 1901 and since 1950 by the University of Pennsylvania[7] showed from actual finds that the Phrygians had reached considerable mastery in several crafts, whether as bronze-workers accomplished in both casting and raising, or as expert cabinet-makers and weavers, as workers in ivory, as makers of woollen felt

---

[1] §IV, 6, 2.　　[2] §I, 10.　　[3] See Plate 159(a).　　[4] §IV, 16, part 1.
[5] K. Kannanberg, *Kleinasiens Natürschätze* (Berlin, 1897), p. 207.
[6] §I, 7, 28.　　[7] §III, 17 and 28.

or as weavers of linen, hemp, mohair, and perhaps also tapestry.[1] Phrygian carpets (τάπητες), direct ancestors of the Turkish carpet, were famous—the word is still preserved in the French *tapis*.[2] The influence of their designs and techniques, especially in woodwork, textiles and tapestry, was certainly carried far afield and influenced early Greek art, Phrygian patterns being clearly recognizable in East Greek painted pottery of the seventh century.[3] Embroidery, especially in gold threads, is said to have been a Phrygian invention, the Latin word for an embroiderer being *phrygio*. Fragments of a woven garment, evidently a royal robe, made of woven threads strung with tiny gold beads were found at Carchemish.[4] Many of the craftsmen practising these arts clustered round the royal palace, being organized very closely into craft-guilds of great antiquity.

Throughout the Phrygians' art, great play in ornament is made with interlacing or isolated geometric patterns, and swastikas, maeanders, mazes, lozenges—with this was doubtless connected their interest in Maze games,[5] the *ludus Troianus*. But their human figures are weak: their animals with stylized muscles, their limbs often bordered by rows of dots, but influenced by Mesopotamian, Urartian and Phoenician ideas of art, are more effective.

The Phrygians also appear, however, to have preserved a tradition of free-standing sculpture, though the earliest surviving example (at Palanga) is not earlier than the seventh century;[6] it bears inscriptions in late Hittite hieroglyphs. At Boğazköy, in the gateway, was found a remarkable statue of the goddess Cybele wearing a high headdress and holding her nude breasts, but clad in a skirt. She is flanked by two youths who play the chief musical instruments of her cult, the double *aulos* and lyre respectively, the *aulos*-player's cheeks being comically puffed out—these are the very instruments on which Marsyas and Apollo vied with each other before Midas as the unlucky spectator. This remarkable group is attributed to the sixth century B.C.[7] A fragmentary torso representing the goddess Agdistis was also found at Midas City.[8]

---

[1] §III, 5.

[2] O. Bloch and W. von Wartburg, *Dictionnaire étymologique de la langue française* (Paris, 1950), p. 595.

[3] §VII, 2, n. 50; §III, 2, fig. 67.        [4] §III, 15, part III, 250 ff., pl. 63.

[5] W. F. J. Knight, 'Maze Symbolism and the Trojan Game', in *Antiquity*, 6 (1932), 445 ff.

[6] §III, 10, fig. 786.

[7] §IV, 3. G. Neumann, *Nachr. Göttingen*, 1959, 101 ff., has suggested that the flanking figures represent two Daktyloi, Titias and Kyllenos. See Plate 159(c).

[8] §III, 10, figs. 1108–9.

In some of these works the human body is columnar in appearance, even basically resembling a cylinder, and one has the feeling that this school of human sculpture is created from a tree-trunk, not, as in the East, from a cube of stone. Such works afterwards obviously were connected with, or perhaps moulded, the ideas of some early Ionic Greek sculptors such as those of Samos and Naxos, where the dedicator of a well-known cult statue of the goddess Hera bears a purely Asiatic name, Cheramyes.

The Phrygians' skill in rock-carving, inherited from the stone-masons of the Bronze Age, enabled them to carve the representations of architectural house- or temple-façades which have been already mentioned. Smaller works, too, exist in the form of shrines showing the goddess Cybele from Ankara;[1] but a series of slabs of red andesite showing heraldic animals, now in the Ankara Museum, betray North Syrian influence, and may be by North Syrian or Urartian artists.[2] They were found scattered but come from some Phrygian palace or shrine, probably at Yalincak, 15 km. from Ankara. The Phrygians even seem to have been gardeners, for Midas is said to have 'discovered' roses and to have possessed a rose-garden on the Phrygian Mount Olympus.

Proofs of the Phrygians' accomplishments in the more abstract and intellectual arts are inevitably intangible and harder to show. But here the Phrygians were also evidently of importance, being reputedly great musicians, the inventors of the mode which bears their name. The Phrygians are credited by Greek tradition with the invention of cymbals, flutes, the triangle and syrinx, though this need mean no more than that they inherited some of these from their Hittite predecessors and taught their uses to the Greeks. But in the Bible (Gen. iv. 22) Tubal-Cain, i.e. 'Tubal-the-Smith', who bears the name of the Tabalians, is the brother of Jubal, inventor of lyre-playing and flute-playing. Some of these claims may be partly factual. At Boğazköy, as mentioned above, a fine Phrygian sculpture of the Mother Goddess was found, accompanied by two figures, a double-clarinet (*aulos*) player and a lyre (*cithara*) player. In the diffusion of the alphabet to the west, however, usually attributed to the Phoenicians, the Phrygians certainly played a most important role. One of the bronze vessels found in the Great Tumulus at Gordion, which must be dated before 700 B.C., bears in wax a short inscription in the Phrygian language, written in the Phrygian form of the alphabet. This use of wax for inscribing messages suggests that wax-covered writing tablets were already in use here as in Assyria. It is common know-

[1] §IV, 15. See Plate 159(*d*).　　[2] §III, 10, figs. 1053–6.

ledge that the Phrygian alphabet, no less than the Ionic and other Greek alphabets, is derived from the Phoenician. But that the Phrygian letters most closely resemble both the earliest Greek examples as yet known—those from Crete, and those on Late Geometric vases found in Attica—has aroused little attention. The system of writing lines in alternate directions, called *boustrophēdon* ('as the ox turns in the plough'), which is used in early Greek scripts, is apparently derived through Phrygia from the Hittite hieroglyphs. A Phrygian inscription mentioning Mita (Midas) was found as far east as Tyana;[1] another occurs at Midas City on a rock façade, and it seems that the mixing of races and cultures at Midas's court permitted the evolution there of a script more flexible than the cumbrous Hittite hieroglyphs used elsewhere in Anatolia.[2] Inscriptions in the Phoenician alphabet were written and read no farther away than at Karatepe in the Taurus. In short, the Phrygian alphabet may well prove to be a parent of those of Greece, and Gordion the place of its invention in the mid-eighth century B.C.[3] The relation of the Phrygian script to other Anatolian alphabets such as those of Lydia, Lycia, and Pamphylia has scarcely been studied, but must be close. Though the surviving examples of these scripts are not earlier than the fifth century B.C., their origins must go back much farther. As yet, the Phrygian inscriptions cannot really be understood, as the material is too scanty; that the Phrygians possessed a literature is unprovable, but a precious Greek tradition, which declared Aesop to be a Phrygian, ascribed to them the invention of the animal fable, a form of folk-literature of great antiquity in the East and usually unwritten. The home of the animal-fable, in which the normal roles are reversed and animals play the parts of men, is, *par excellence*, India; but traces of it can be detected in Sumer in the third millennium B.C. in the Royal Graves of Ur in the scenes decorating a lyre, and in a relief at Tell Halaf in North Syria in the tenth century B.C., in the motif of the 'Animal Orchestra', a theme which lived on into modern times to enter into the Grimm Brothers' tales in the form of the *Musicians of Bremen*. Similar satirical animal fables are depicted in New Kingdom Egypt, but have not yet been found in Hittite sources. These might still, however, prove to have been the missing medium of transmission of such stories from Sumer to the Phrygians.

[1] See J. Garstang, *The Hittite Empire* (1929), pl. IV and p. 14.
[2] A, 15.
[3] See A, 15, but *contra*, J. Naveh, *A.J.A.* 77 (1973), 1 ff., who argues that the Greeks borrowed their alphabet direct from the Proto-Canaanite script, *c.* 1100 B.C.

## V. THE PHRYGIAN LANGUAGE

The Phrygians' origins remain something of a mystery, and so does their language. In the eastern half of the plateau chiefly, the Hittite hieroglyphs were used to write the Luwian tongue but from the late eighth to fifth century B.C. a handful of very short Phrygian texts survives which, as they are written in their alphabet of Greek type, can be read though they cannot be understood.[1] Lexicographers and other writers have preserved for us the alleged meanings of some hundred Phrygian words, but all this is hardly enough to permit the re-creation of even the most rudimentary grammar or syntax. In fact, survivals of the Phrygian language linger into Roman times, occurring in bilingual form with Greek translations on tombstone inscriptions from the region south of the thirty-ninth parallel. These are called 'Late Phrygian' texts in contrast to the earlier group known as 'archaic'.[2] But their value as aids in interpreting those texts of nine hundred years before is naturally debatable. The opinions of scholars, therefore, as to the affinities of the archaic Phrygian language are, not surprisingly, divided: some have claimed it as an Indo-European language of the *satəm* branch and have declared it closest to Armenian; and this would consort well with, and is perhaps influenced by, the dictum of Herodotus who calls the Armenians ἄποικοι τῶν Φρυγῶν.[3] But this view is now rejected by scholars[4] who have shown that Phrygian is not a *satəm* speech but basically an Anatolian language, connected with Hittite or, it may yet be shown, with Luwian.[5] If this is so, it will imply that the true original, native tongue of the Phrygian invaders has probably been absorbed into a patois of their subjects—a by no means improbable conclusion.

## VI. PHRYGIAN RELIGION

The Phrygians' religion clearly consisted of at least two strata: primitive Anatolian and Indo-European.

The oldest, most basic and characteristic worship of Phrygia was the cult of the Great Mother of Nature, called Kubaba by the Luwians east of the Halys, Kybele or Kybebe by the Lydians, *Kubile* or *Matar Kubile* in Phrygia, Cybele by the Greeks; she was

---

[1] §v, 3, 7, 8, 14; G, 7.        [2] §v, 1, 12, 13.        [3] §v, 5, 11.
[4] §v, 4; §vII, 13, 123 ff.; §vII, 29, 6, 7. See also A, 14.
[5] §v, 6; *C.A.H.* I³, pt. I, pp. 142 f.; but see O. Szemerényi, in *J.R.A.S.* (1965), pp. 134 ff.

also called Agdistis ('she of the rock', from *agdos*, meaning 'rock' in Phrygian) by the Phrygians. She and her youthful male consort were evidently worshipped from primeval antiquity in Anatolia, at least from the Neolithic Period, as is shown by finds of the seventh millennium B.C. of clay statuettes of the goddess seated with her lions (or perhaps leopards), at Hacılar near Lake Burdur.[1] Her worship (as a bisexual figure) appears to have spread far east and south through Anatolia and north-west Syria, where it appears at an early date in Bambyce-Hierapolis as Kombabos or in the Legend of Gilgamesh Khumbaba.[2] In Roman times one of her great shrines was at Pessinus, where one version of the story of Agdistis–Cybele was told and recorded by Arnobius. Her worship there was sufficiently important for her cult figure, a black stone, to be transferred from there to Rome under the title of 'Bona Dea' in 204 B.C. The latter is perhaps again an illustration of religious continuity in Anatolia, for a deity called the 'Black Goddess' was worshipped by the Hittites.[3]

Several myths were current concerning the Great Goddess of Nature and her lover-consort Attis, and formed the ἱερὸς λόγος which explained or justified the enactment of an annual cycle of ritual. According to one version, Agdistis was a bisexual monster who fell in love with the beautiful Attis, son-in-law of the king of Pessinus, destroyed him and his city and castrated itself, thus becoming female.[4] Such barbarous themes of monstrous gods born from a rock, of gods and demigods mutilating or slaying one another, or their own parents or offspring, are found in Hittite texts of the Bronze Age such as the 'Song of Ullikummi'. A milder version of the story, much abbreviated, describes Agdistis's love for Attis who, in the flower of his youth and beauty, is killed in a boar-hunt. But by dint of his worshippers enacting an annual spring ritual of passionate lamentation, including self-mutilation, he is annually resuscitated, thus reviving the flagging forces of nature. In the course of the ritual, excitement rose to such a pitch that the most fervent devotees of the goddess castrated themselves in honour of her and of Attis, and became his and her priests, as described in a moving poem of Catullus. This ferocious cult of the goddess, for whose sake her handsome lover suffers and dies, filtered early westwards to Ionia, but was reflected in a softer and, indeed, more romantic form in various Greek myths connected with Asia Minor. In these recurs a theme of a youth beloved by a goddess, who brings misfortune on him by her love; such is that of the Moon and Endymion on Mount

Latmus or that of Aphrodite and Anchises on Ida.[1] These themes appear to be derived from aspects of the worship of an ultimately bisexual deity.[2]

Being a fierce and implacable goddess of the rocks, Cybele's centres of worship were most often located on mountains after which her local cults were commonly named (e.g. the Berecynthian, the Dindymene, Sipylene or Lobrine Mother). At her sanctuary on Sipylus near Smyrna was a rock-carved statue of the goddess, which still survives; it was interpreted by the Greeks as a figure of Niobe weeping for her children, slain by Apollo and Artemis; it has been identified as the central feature of a possibly Bronze Age water-sanctuary.[3] In fact, Cybele was regularly believed to issue from bare cliffs beside which fresh water rose, and between the eighth and sixth centuries B.C. great façades representing her temples were carved on such rock faces in the specially sacred plateau between Eskişehir and Afyon Karahisar, where the sacred Phrygian rivers rise. These façades, the most famous of which bears an inscription containing the name of Midas, are to-day among the most remarkable antiquities of Anatolia.[4] That at Arslankaya shows the goddess herself, represented standing facing frontally, in a niche between rampant lions—an association of the goddess with lions which is repeated throughout antiquity in her cult. Other rock carvings merely show a house or temple front, decorated with elaborate geometrical patterns representing a carpet or tapestry.

According to some ancient authorities the cult of the Kabeiroi, which included that of Dionysus, son of Zeus Sabazius and Semele, was introduced to Miletus and other Greek cities from Phrygia.[5] There are good arguments for thinking that the worship of the Kabeiroi derives from the world of the Hittites. To the Indo-European stratum in the religion of the Phrygians, we may assign a cult of Zeus called Mazeus (cf. the Iranian *Mazda*), also called Bagaios (Iranian *baga*='god') or Papas ('Father')—a general term equally applicable to Attis or other gods;[6] also that of Mēn, an equestrian male Moon god. These, however, might perhaps be explained as relics of the Achaemenid Persian rule.

Some other figures are little more than names, but imply some degree of cult. Aristaeus, another fertility figure, in reality (in the writer's opinion) may be but a form of *Agdistaeos (*d* and *r* being

---

[1] §vi, 1; §vii, 4.
[2] The variations on this theme and its origins are explained in full in §vii, 4, 217 ff. [3] §iii, 4.
[4] §iii, 10, 1023–33; §iii, 13; §iv, 4, 14. See Plate 157(*b*). [5] §vi, 9. [6] G, 6.

to some extent interchangeable in Hittite hieroglyphs), meaning
'he who belongs to Agdistis';[1] Marsyas was a river god, inventor
of the *syrinx*, who, after failing in a music contest with Apollo,[2] was
slain, presumably to revive; Lityerses was a rather ferocious form
of John Barleycorn, slain by Heracles and annually lamented by
the reapers. A hero, Tyris or Tyrimnus, is also mentioned but
really appears to belong to Lydia, where he is equated with
Apollo–Helius. Ascanius, or Ascaēnus, is identified with Mēn.
Telesphorus is a dwarf-like, hooded figure who appears first in
Hellenistic times.

The Phrygian pantheon, as envisaged in Roman times at least,
is depicted on a rustic rock-relief at Asi Yozgat, about sixty kilometres east of Ankara. It consists of Cybele on her lion, Heracles,
a seated figure (Attis?), Asclepius, Telesphorus, and finally a
figure in a shrine with an eagle who represents either Cronus or
Zeus. A goat (Amalthea or perhaps the goat which suckled Attis)
is also represented[3] in the group.

There were Phrygian 'mysteries' of Attis, involving initia-
tions, at least in late times. Of them we know virtually nothing.[4]
In short, the Phrygians' religion, like their empire, remains vague,
amorphous, barbaric and mysterious.


## VII. THE NEIGHBOURS OF THE PHRYGIANS

But Anatolia did not consist only of Phrygians. What do we
know of their neighbours in the west during this dark period?
From historical sources, very little; nor is there any great prospect
of increasing our information, save by fortunate archaeological
excavation. We find the western slopes descending from the
plateau along the Maeander River valley inhabited by the
Lydians, alias Mēïoi, Māïoi or Maiones, whose origins and
early history are lost in legend. Perhaps these may be the same as
a people called by the Hittites Masha, whose name may, it has
been suggested, be reflected in that of the ancient Lydian eponymous hero Masnes.[5]

The Heraclid (otherwise Tylonid) Dynasty, ending with
Myrsilus, *c.* 700 B.C., was said to have reigned for 505 years; this
brings us to a date *c.* 1205 B.C., shortly before the fall of the
Hittite Empire. The Lydians' surviving inscriptions are relatively
late; but they are partly bilingual and seem to show a relation
between their language and Hittite, or perhaps Palaic.[6] Their

---

[1] §VII, 4.    [2] See above, p. 432 n. 7.    [3] §VI, 1.    [4] §VII, 17.
[5] §VII, 17.    [6] (Lydian and Palaite) §VII, 8, 13, 26, 27.

chief goddess is called by them *Artimu*, in Greek Artemis, and was identified by them with the Luwian Kubaba (Herodotus, v. 102). Her world-famous shrine at Ephesus was traditionally founded by the Amazones; it is clearly pre-Greek. The cult of Dionysus, god of wine, appears also to have been largely native to Lydia under the name of Bacchus, and to have been imported from there to Greece.[1] Local Lydian worships disclose, otherwise, principally the adoration of a triad, the Mother Goddess, a male god often equated with Zeus, and Mēn—the equestrian Moon god.[2]

No early Lydian settlements, and until now no Lydian works of art earlier than the seventh century B.C., have as yet been identified, though discoveries may reasonably be hoped for in the excavations now in progress at the site of Sardis. But it seems that the Lydians preserved a direct tradition of civilization more or less unbroken from the Late Bronze Age (although backward tribal communities remained in some areas until Hellenistic times). This is hinted at by Herodotus who carries back the pedigree of the ruling family to Heracles, or even Atys son of Manes (Masnes), i.e. to a dim heroic age; the last member of the dynasty bore a name, Myrsilus, which closely resembles the Hittite name of Murshilish. Hittite rock-carvings accompanied by Hittite hieroglyphs, belonging to the Hittite Empire, exist at Karabel (Nymphi) and Sipylus, both being well known in antiquity. To the Greek mind the Lydians were aliens, depraved Orientals; nevertheless, the Lydians were famous as horsemen, musicians, traders, and bankers, who used the natural wealth of their land in precious metals and the gold washings of Pactolus for their momentous gift to mankind, the invention of coinage.[3]

Of the Carians and Lelegians, almost nothing specific is known except that the Carians made good soldiers and left their graffiti in Egypt, where they served as mercenaries in the seventh and sixth centuries B.C.[4] The Carians, like the Pamphylians, had a script and language of their own; it is partly legible but cannot be understood at present. It is possibly Hittito-Luwian in origin.[5] The Carians claimed to be autochthonous inhabitants of Anatolia, and to be related to the Lydians and Mysians. Their custom of

---

[1] §vi, 1.        [2] §vii, 22.        [3] See A, 4, 310 ff.

[4] §v, 3; §vii, 9; A, 7. An important addition to the corpus of Carian inscriptions from Egypt is the group of Carian–Egyptian tomb-stones found at Memphis by W. B. Emery; see *J.E.A.* 56 (1970), 6 ff., pls. x, xv.

[5] §vii, 13; A, 11.

having queens to rule over them recalls the important place given to women among the Lycians. According to Thucydides, in the Late Bronze Age they were active pirates and colonists of the adjacent Aegean islands, repressed by Minos of Crete, but of this there is no archaeological confirmation whatsoever. But at Müskebi, on the Halicarnassus peninsula, a rich Mycenaean cemetery has been found, while at Dirmil another cemetery of the Protogeometric Age has been uncovered, showing that Greek penetration of this area certainly took place in the Late Bronze Age and survived into that of Iron.[1]

With Lycia we fare a little better, although over the origins of the Lycians the greatest obscurity still hangs. But it is now certain that they were an Anatolian people of great antiquity, also related to the Hittites, and thus can trace their history in Asia Minor back into the Bronze Age. This much is clear from their language, with examples of which in inscriptions, some bilingual, albeit no earlier in date than the fourth century B.C., we are fortunate enough to be provided.[2] As a result, it has recently been identified successfully as a dialect of the Luwian language, known (though poorly) from cuneiform texts found in the library of the Hittite kings, and Luwian deities can be identified in Lycian personal names.[3] It is assumed too (plausibly enough) that the Lycians were descended from the people called Lukka, who are mentioned in the Late Bronze Age and figure among the Sea Raiders of Egypt. In the Iron Age the Lycians' chief cities were Xanthus, Pinara, Myra, Phellus and Antiphellus, but as yet no notable remains of occupation have been found, either in the recent French excavations at Xanthus or elsewhere along the rocky Lycian coasts, to occur earlier than the eighth century B.C. But recent finds near Elmalı further inland strongly point to early Lycian settlement there in the Early Bronze Age.[4] Like that of Caria, Lycian society was organized to give an important place to women, through whom inheritance seems to have been reckoned on a matrilinear basis.[5] The Lycians appear to have preserved a spirit of national organization from the Heroic Age sufficiently strong to resist any Greek settlements being planted in Lycia, and to enable them to retain their national script and language till the fourth century B.C.

Other traces of Luwian speech surviving into Roman times

---

[1] §VII, 33.    [2] §VII, 13, 21. See also A, 8.

[3] §VII, 19; cf. §VII, 27, 29, 31, 32.

[4] M. J. Mellink, 'Excavations at Karataş-Semayük in Lycia, 1963', in *A.J.A.* 68 (1964).

[5] See now S. Pembroke in *J.E.S.H.O.* 8 (1965), 217 ff.

have also been found in Cilicia Aspera.[1] A native language also survived in Pamphylia, to be recorded in a peculiar script at Side in the fourth century B.C., but it is as yet not sufficiently clearly understood to be identified. But in the period of the Phrygian Empire, the most important Luwian-speaking area was clearly south-eastern Anatolia where, as mentioned above, a cluster of principalities, called 'Land of Khatti' by the Assyrians, survived the collapse of the Hittite Empire. These principalities, the most important of which were Kammanu (Malatya), Gurgum (Maraş), Kummukh (Commagene) and Unqi (the 'Amūq), spoke a Luwian dialect, and wrote it in Hittite hieroglyphs.[2] They were allied with the Phrygians, and guarded the mountain roads of the Taurus which led from North Syria to the Anatolian plateau. Beyond them lay Carchemish; this great site was partly excavated by a British expedition before 1914.[3] Its period of importance thereby disclosed seemed to be late Hittite, but it is now seen from documents found at Ras Shamra to have been the seat, in the Late Bronze Age, of the viceroy of the Hittite Emperor, from which he ruled over most of the states of Syria. Carchemish was rightly considered by the Assyrians as the chief of the Hittite states, controlling the great road and ford across the Euphrates leading to Mesopotamia.

To help us form a picture of these diadochic principalities, we may note their actual pedigrees. That of the kings of Gurgum, recorded in their Hittite hieroglyphic inscriptions, can be traced back to one LA+ī−mas; that of Carchemish to Sukhis I (formerly read as Lukhas), both *c.* 950 B.C. Beyond these names are to be placed some obscure kings known at Carchemish from single references, probably to be assigned to the period 1200–1000 B.C.; at Malatya they go back to the eleventh century B.C., to which date the fine sculptured palace gateway at Malatya belongs.[4] It is clear that these Luwian principalities dated their independence from a time following soon after the collapse of the Hittite Empire. Until then, they had been for some centuries dominated by the kings of Khattusha; but when the storm passed, they revived and carried on into the Iron Age the customs, arts, cults, and traditions of the Hittite Empire of which they were the veritable heirs.

But their position in south-eastern Anatolia was not uncontested. Towards the vital centres of the Amanus and Taurus passes thrust other national groups. A figure known to Greek mythology as Mopsus, king of Colophon, possibly the same as a person of the fourteenth century B.C. known in Hittite records as

---

[1] §VII, 19.    [2] §VII, 24.    [3] §III, 15.    [4] §III, 12.

Mukshush, a western freebooter, appears to have led his followers through Pamphylia to settle finally on the slopes south of the Taurus at Ishtunda, and establish there his dynasty as the kings of the Danuniyim or Danuna, i.e. the Danaoi, with their capital at Adana;[1] their existence is disclosed by the finds at Karatepe and Domuz Tepe.[2] Mopsus was perhaps a Lydian or a half-Greek; in any event, he is the first figure of Greek mythology to emerge into historic reality. The Danuniyim were clients of the kings of Que (Cilicia). At Sam'al (Zincirli) on Mount Amanus was installed the Aramaean dynasty of Gabar, which claims to have been in conflict with the Danuniyim in the ninth century.[3] This dynasty goes back probably to the tenth century, about 900 B.C., giving us the earliest indication of the most northerly thrust of the Aramaean people. Excavations at Zincirli by the German Oriental Society before the First World War have thrown much light on the importance of this site, where they found a series of palaces. Phoenician cultural influence was very powerful in this area and probably radiated from some local colony not yet discovered.

These principalities, then, were the actors who played out their roles on the stage of history in the Dark Age of Anatolia, from the Bronze into the Iron Age. Though little chronicled, we can now see that these roles were dramatic and important. Surviving the collapse of the Hittite Empire and the blows of the Land and Sea Raiders, their kings made terms with the immigrant Phrygians and other tribes, stood firm on the Taurus and Amanus line, and succeeded in passing on to the West the tradition of Anatolian arts and culture until they were successively pressed back, then finally defeated, destroyed and obliterated by the Assyrians, whose custom, as was later said of the Romans, was 'to make a desert and call it peace'.

[1] §VII, 3; see also below, ch. XXXVIII, sect. III.
[2] §III, 11; §VII, 5.        [3] §IV, 7; §VII, 25.

# CHAPTER XXXI

## ASSYRIA AND BABYLONIA,
### c. 1200–1000 B.C.

## I. THE END OF THE KASSITE DOMINATION

WHEN Tukulti-Ninurta I had abducted Kashtiliash in fetters to Ashur the way was open once again for direct Assyrian control of Babylonian affairs. Resistance, however, continued and Babylon itself was surrounded, the city-wall being breached by siege-apparatus. Entry was resolutely opposed until the troops had robbed the temples and city treasury. Yet the greatest blow to Babylonian morale was the removal of the statue of Marduk to Ashur as a mark of the complete subjugation of the country to Assyria. According to the Chronicle P 'Tukulti-Ninurta installed his governors in the land of Babylon and for seven years he gave orders to Babylonia (Karduniash)'. This source lists as the next ruler Adad-shuma-uṣur whom the Babylonian nobles 'seated on his father's throne' after a country-wide rising against their Assyrian overlords.[1] On the other hand, the King List A follows Kashtiliash by three names; Enlil-nādin-shumi, to whom a reign of '1 year 6 months' is ascribed; Kadashman-Kharbe (one year six months) and Adad-shuma-iddina (six years).[2] From this it has been assumed that these were vassal-kings who followed an Assyrian interregnum of seven years for which Tukulti-Ninurta's name was not given for political reasons. However, if the chronological entries are to be interpreted as '1 year (that is of) 6 months (only)' then these rulers comprised the seven years of Tukulti-Ninurta on whose behalf they exercised power.[3] On this theory the Babylonian chronicler, not wishing to acknowledge the Assyrian domination, entered the names of his puppet rulers, much as was later done for Kandalanu and other Babylonians who held similar positions under northern masters.

It is possible that Enlil-nādin-shumi represented only one party in the capital. When the Elamite Kidin-Khutran raided

---

* An original version of this chapter was published as fascicle 41 in 1965; the present chapter includes revisions made in 1973.

[1] §I, 10, 96 (Chron. P, IV, 6–8); G, 6, 46.     [2] G, 22, 41, nr. 37, 7 ff.
[3] G, 2, 79; cf. A, 3, 77, 86; §I, 12, 137; §II, 7, 73 ff.

lower Mesopotamia, seizing Nippur and sacking E-dimgal-kalamma, the temple of Ishataran at Dēr, his aim was to restrict the hold of Babylon over the East Tigris area and to challenge the Assyrian in the Diyālā region by looting Padan[1] and removing a stela.[2] The Elamites seem to have supported the pro-Kassite Babylonians, one of whom, Kadashman-Kharbe II, claimed descent from Kashtiliash. He may well have gained control as a result of the Elamite action and have been a rival and contemporary claimant to the throne in Babylon.[3]

When Adad-shuma-iddina gained the ascendancy it would seem that once again a Babylonian, to judge by the name, held the reins of government. He may, however, have been pro-Assyrian, for after six years he was killed, or taken prisoner, in another Elamite raid.[4] This time their objective was the city of Isin which was seized, perhaps in an attempt to reinstate Enlil-nādin-shumi, who reappeared with the attackers in Babylonia when they crossed the Tigris and advanced on a wide front as far as Nippur.

Loyalty to the local Kassites was by no means dimmed, for the nobles of Akkad and of Babylon chose this critical time to initiate a widespread agitation to seat Adad-shuma-uṣur on his father's throne. As the popularly elected son of Kashtiliash IV and installed with Elamite approval, his long rule of thirty years (1218–1189) and the absence of further Elamite raids enabled the king to gain firm hold of Babylonia. The revolt was possible and successful only because Assyria was weakened through the court intrigues which marked the closing years of Tukulti-Ninurta's reign. After that king's death the Babylonian court tried to intervene in Assyrian affairs but faced with some disaster, plague or fire in their camp, Adad-shuma-uṣur's forces were forced to withdraw to Babylonia after a battle with Enlil-kudurri-uṣur.[5] There is no certain evidence that this action was taken in fulfilment of treaty obligations.[6]

At home, such few indications as remain show the country to be at peace within its borders. At Nippur, this king restored the inner wall of the zikkurrat in the rebuilding of E-kur,[7] while a fragmentary *kudurru*-inscription tells of a royal grant of land near Daban in the Dullum region.[8]

The same Kassite family continued to hold the country firmly in its power in the person of Meli-Shikhu,[9] 'son' of Kurigalzu,

---

[1] See above, pp. 387 f.     [2] G, 15, 2, 95 and pl. 20.     [3] G, 20, 287.
[4] Cf. A, 3, 87, n. 451.     [5] §1, 12, 131.     [6] G, 20, 238.
[7] §1, 7, 81, 34.     [8] G, 15, 2, 97; §1, 8, no. 4, 17; §1, 11, nr. 156.
[9] For this reading against Meli-Shipak see §1, 1, 70 and 114; but cf. A, 4, 238 f.

during the next fifteen years (1188–1174).[1] The absence of records mentioning external affairs may give a false impression of the internal harmony conveyed by the references to this ruler in contemporary economic documents. On one *kudurru* the king is shown introducing his daughter Khunnubat-Nanā to the goddess Nanā, probably on the occasion of her installation as a priestess.[2] The king farmed royal estates outside Babylon and granted fields from his own irrigated lands in Shaluluni,[3] by the royal-canal at Agade and in the provinces of Bīt-Marduk[4] and Bīt-Piri'-Amurri (attested by the governor of the Sealands and the high-priestess of Agade).[5] The continuity in the recognition and rule of law is most clearly seen in a complicated legal case which came before the king concerning an estate, Bīt-Takil-ana-ilishu, near Nippur. The original owner had died in the reign of Adad-shuma-iddina and the estate passed to an adopted son whose title had been upheld before Adad-shuma-uṣur. Copies of attested documents from these reigns were now produced as evidence in quashing the claim of the descendants of disappointed rivals.[6]

Marduk-apla-iddina I, son of Meli-Shikhu, claimed, like his father, descent from Kurigalzu. Indeed, he seems to have kept court in Dūr-Kurigalzu itself, for tablets found in the fire-blackened ruins of the Tell-el-Abyaḍ quarter (Level I A), which marked the later Elamite destruction of the city, are dated in the first two of his thirteen-year reign (1173–1161).[7] These indicate normal economic relations with Babylonia's western and eastern neighbours, Subarians and Elamites, whose singers entertained the royal household.[8] Thus a field, on the Elamite border, east of the Tigris near Khudada, which Meli-Shikhu had left un-recorded was now disposed of freely, as were other plots near the river Radanu.[9] Allocations of land in the district of Kār-Bēlit between the Euphrates and the Shum-ili canal and at Dūr-Napshati in the province of E-ugur-Ishtar on the Tigris[10] and reconstruction work at E-zida of Borsippa show that royal lands were maintained and held in north Babylonia throughout this reign.

[1] G, 21, 70 f. (Assur 14616c, 11).
[2] G, 15, 10, pls. 10 ff., pp. 87 ff. See Plate 161(*a*).
[3] G, 12, no. IV, pls. xxiii ff.
[4] §1, 11, nos. 38, 57; see also 47.      [5] G, 12, no. III, v, 20 f.
[6] G, 12, pls. v ff., pp. 7 ff.
[7] G, 18, 272 (King List A, ii, 13); §1, 9, 260 ff.; §1, 5, 54.
[8] §1, 3, 9; §1, 4, 89; §1, 6, 89 (another text).
[9] G, 15, 6, 6–11; §1, 8, nr. 10 f.; §1, 11, 62, 49.
[10] G, 12, 24 ff., pls. xxxi f.; §1, 9, 261.

This apparently peaceful situation was radically altered in the accession year of the succeeding Zababa-shuma-iddina (1160). His brief reign is recorded only in King Lists[1] but the Synchronistic Chronicle tells how the Assyrian, Ashur-dan, marched from Ashur across the Lesser Zab to capture the towns of Zaban, Irria and Ugarsallu and remove the loot to his capital. This raid was in continuance of the Assyrian policy to maintain control of the trade-routes linking the Diyālā river-plain and the Iranian plateau. His failure to press into the Lower Diyālā itself was the signal for Shutruk-Nahhunte, who had by now brought together the forces of Elam, to make a move for the control of this same disputed border region. The Elamites crossed the Ulai river and moved through Mara and Eshnunna to loot the north Babylonian cities of Sippar, Dūr-Kurigalzu, Dūr-Shar[rukēn], Opis and perhaps Agade. From Eshnunna two statues, one of Manishtusu, and from Sippar the stela of Narām-Sin recounting his victory over the Lullubi and a stela bearing a copy of the laws of Hammurabi were added to the spoils of war taken to mark the supremacy of Elam's own deity.[2]

The resistance of the Kassites was not yet at an end. One Enlil-nādin-akhi was claimed as 'king of Sumer and Akkad' and maintained the struggle against the Elamites for a further three years (1159–1157).[3] By this time Kutir-Nahhunte, the eldest son of Shutruk-Nahhunte, had been installed as Elamite overlord of North Babylonia, unrecognized as such by the Babylonian Chronicler as by the inhabitants of the south. The struggle was long and fierce. Finally the Elamites met the Babylonians in battle by the Tigris pursuing them via Khuṣṣi to the Euphrates[4] and Nippur. They then robbed the capital and other cult-centres and, in an act of impiety never forgotten or forgiven by the Babylonians, Kutir-Nahhunte removed the statue of Marduk from E-sagila to Elam. Though this sacrilege had been committed by the Hittites and the Assyrians it was now 'far greater than that of his forefathers, his guilt exceeded even theirs'.[5] The statue of Nanā of Uruk was also among the loot taken to Susa to await its release by Ashurbanipal's arms more than five hundred years later. Many of the nobles were taken captive to Elam with the king. With the death in exile of Enlil-nādin-akhi there ended

---

[1] G, 18, 273 (King List A and Assur 14616c, ii, 10′); A, 4, 245.

[2] See below, p. 486.      [3] §1, 12, 137; cf. A, 4, 245 f.

[4] Some assign this attack to a later year of Shilkhak-In-Shushinak (see below, pp. 447 and 492).

[5] §1, 12, 137 f.

an enlightened and, on the whole, successful régime whose thirty-six kings had maintained authority for 576 years and 9 months.

That the Kassites strengthened and continued the ancient Babylonian customs and culture cannot be denied, though the extent of their influence on Babylon and Assyria, apart from the political adroitness of the ruling family is much debated.[1] Long after they had lost political control the Kassites remained a strong foreign element in Babylonia and provided the chief element in the Babylonian armed forces till the ninth century.[2]

## II. THE SECOND ISIN DYNASTY

Except for one possible raid to the Euphrates by Shilkhak-In-Shushinak,[3] the successor of Kutir-Nahhunte, the Elamites now turned their attention again to their border with Assyria in the Upper Diyālā. In a series of campaigns they aimed to gain control of the area between the Tigris and the Zagros and to open the way to trade and influence further north. One expedition to the Kirkuk area to win the mountain passes may have been influential in stimulating the revolt that ended the reign of Ashur-dan.[4]

This failure to follow up the Elamite control of territory normally held to lie in north-east Babylonia enabled the peoples of the south to rally round the nobles of Isin whose influence had already been extended to support one of the rival claimants to the Assyrian throne on the death of Ashur-dan I.[5] Marduk-kabit-ahhēshu of Isin who, according to Babylonian tradition followed Enlil-nādin-akhi without any Elamite interregnum, founded a new dynasty in which eleven members of the line were to rule Babylonia for 132 years and 6 months.[6] For eighteen years (1156–1139—King List C)[7] or seventeen (according to the less contemporary King List A which may omit the accession year)[8] this new contender for Babylonian independence held sway. Isin was an influential city, judging both by the preferential references to governors of the city as witnesses to kudurru-inscriptions at this time, and by the fact that the King List names the dynasty after it.[9] The absence of contemporary records does not necessarily imply, as has been argued, that the economic state of the country following the Kassite régime was such that the ruler had to devote

---

[1] G, 9, 109.　　　[2] G, 20, 295.　　　[3] See above, p. 446.
[4] §1, 13, 7; see below, pp. 491 f.　　　[5] §1, 13, 7.
[6] §1, 15, 146 (C.T. 36, 4); G, 18, 273 (King List A, iii, 5).
[7] §11, 6, 3.　　　[8] C.A.H. i³, pt. 1, pp. 198 f.　　　[9] G, 2, 113.

attention exclusively to internal affairs during his early years. Marduk-kabit-ahhēshu is named by his son Itti-Marduk-balāṭu who, in true Babylonian fashion, styled himself 'king of kings, viceroy of Babylon' and king of two cities the names of which are now lost (though one was presumably Isin).[1] *Kudurru*-inscriptions of this reign record the sale of plots of land in Bīt-Udashi, Bīt-Sapri and Bīt-Naniauti, probably to be located near Babylon. Business documents show that provisions were distributed from the royal stables at Dūr-Sumulael on the Imgur-Ishtar canal near Babylon. Grain was received and slaves hired in the king's first year.[2] It is likely therefore that Babylon was occupied as the capital without a break after this reign.

According to the reading proposed for an Ashur text,[3] now lost, the name of Itti-Marduk-balāṭu was inserted after that of Marduk-nādin-ahhē, the sixth king of the dynasty. This reading has never been verified.[4] Such a position would identify the person of this name with the father of Adad-apla-iddina as listed in the Babylonian Chronicle.[5] The order of names in the Chronicle C is to be preferred. This allots Itti-Marduk-balāṭu eight years (1138–1131) before he was succeeded by Ninurta-nādin-shumi, whose relation to his predecessor is unknown. According to one King List he ruled for six years (1130–1125).[6] So far had the Babylonian fortunes revived that they were once again strong enough to challenge Assyria for the disputed border districts east of the Tigris. He led the Babylonian troops as far north as the vicinity of Irbil only to withdraw on the approach of Assyrian shock-troops who were supported by chariots.[7] This incursion was yet one more attempt to master the disputed upper Diyālā border region. A bronze dagger, inscribed with the name of Ninurta-nādin-shumi, bears the claim to sovereignty over all Babylonia.[8] Like the many daggers, spear- and arrow-heads bearing brief royal inscriptions of this period, it was probably a votive offering originally dedicated to a temple in Babylon as a thank-offering for safety, if not always of success, in battle.[9] If, as has been suggested, the raid by the Elamite Shilkhak-In-Shushinak on Nimitti-Marduk is to be dated to this time as a reprisal for such Babylonian audacity, then it shows the Babylonians were

---

[1] The title 'king of kings' was in use at least a generation earlier by Tukulti-Ninurta I (G, 22, 18, i, 3).  [2] §11, 1, 49 ff.
[3] G, 21, 70; G, 18, 273 (Assur 14616c, ii, 18′); §vi, 15, 216.
[4] §11, 8, 383, n. 1; cf. G, 21, 70; A, 3, 41.  [5] G, 13, 11, 59.
[6] §11, 6, 3.  [7] G, 22, 58 (nr. 70).
[8] §11, 2, 151, n. 2.  [9] §11, 5, 95.

by now strong enough to resist the last attempt by this non-native dynasty to interfere in their affairs.[1]

In a fragmentary letter written by a Babylonian king he chides his Assyrian counterpart with failure to meet him as arranged at the border town of Zaqqu.[2] The writer implies that the Assyrian is not in full control of his court and threatens to reinstate on the throne Ninurta-tukulti-Ashur, whom his father had welcomed as an exile, if relations between the states do not improve. The deportation of the Assyrian had taken place in the reign of Mutakkil-Nusku,[3] but it seems unlikely that the letter was written to him as co-regent of Ashur-dan or early in the reign of Ashur-rēsha-ishi before the clash at Irbil. If the writer was Ninurta-nādin-shumi it would imply that he was in the direct line of succession, a fact otherwise unknown. On the other hand, if the writer was his son, Nebuchadrezzar I, this would explain the confident tone in which the challenge is couched. At the same time, if such a hypothesis is accepted, it emphasizes the independent position and power of the Babylonians in Ninurta-nādin-shumi's day. The evidence would therefore seem to fit best if Ashur-rēsha-ishi is considered the recipient.[4]

## III. DYNASTIC TROUBLES IN ASSYRIA

While the Babylonians were defending themselves against the Elamites and the new ruling house of Isin was establishing control over the southern tribes, the Assyrian court was the scene of intrigues which detracted from its ability to play a leading role in Mesopotamian affairs at this critical juncture. Tukulti-Ninurta I had been murdered by a son in his residence at Kār-Tukulti-Ninurta, a town of his own creation upstream from the ancient capital of Ashur. If a stela at Ashur can be attributed to him the assassin was Ashur-nāṣir-apli who had only a brief reign, giving his name as eponymn to a single year.[5] If this name stood in the Synchronistic Chronicle it is now broken away,[6] though it is certainly omitted in another list. It may be that his name was deliberately erased from a royal stela after he had been acclaimed by only a few followers who were soon crushed,[7] or, less likely, that his name is a scribal error for another son, Ashur-nādin-apli,

---

[1] See below, pp. 492 f.
[2] §I, 13, 2 ff.; §II, 2, 149 f.; G, 22, 53; cf. below, p. 456.
[3] G, 10, 218 f. (iii, 34–6).                    [4] §I, 12, 136 and 140.
[5] §III, 1, no. 10; G, 19, 487 ff.; cf. below, p. 469, n. 11.
[6] G, 20, 391; §III, 7, 71; §I, 10, 99.        [7] §III, 1, 18 ff.

who may have been the murderer.[1] The latter ruled for four years
(1207–1204 B.C.) claiming, as son of Tukulti-Ninurta, the full
royal titles as 'king of all peoples, king of kings'. He repaired
the royal treasury at Ashur[2] and erected a statue on the river
bank outside the vulnerable north-east corner of the city, that
the gods might for ever look upon it and protect the city from
flood-damage. This was in answer to his prayer to Ashur and
Shamash for help when, in the eponymate of Erība-Sin, the Tigris
had swept away 600 acres of rich fields around the city.[3] This
may indicate that the foundation of Kār-Tukulti-Ninurta had
been in part dictated by the unpredictable manner in which the
river was wont to alter its course outside the walls of Ashur, which
depended on its flow for water-supplies.

Ashur-nādin-apli was succeeded by his son Ashur-nīrāri III
who, according to the Babylonian Chronicle, ruled for six years
(1203–1198). The only glimpse of him is afforded by a letter
written by the Babylonian Adad-shuma-uṣur who addresses him
and Ili-khadda as 'kings of Assyria'.[4] The latter, as a descendant of
Erība-Adad I, represented a family whose claims at Ashur were
later actively supported by Babylon. He was formerly a vizier
and ruler of the province of Khanigalbat.[5] The peremptory note
in this letter is, of itself, insufficient evidence for the assertion that
Assyria was now a vassal-state of Babylon. Had she been this, the
return of the statue of Marduk would surely have been claimed.

Enlil-kudurri-uṣur, another son of Tukulti-Ninurta, next had
sufficient backing to hold the throne unmolested for five years
(1197–1193 B.C.). At the end of this time he clashed with the
Babylonians in a battle in which he was heavily defeated by Adad-
shuma-uṣur. Meanwhile, Ninurta-apil-Ekur, a son of Ili-khadda
who, as co-regent or claimant to the throne had earlier been
defeated by his rival, had fled for refuge to the Babylonian court.
He now took the opportunity to re-enter Assyria, rally his many
adherents and seize the throne.[6] Enlil-kudurri-uṣur was killed
in his stronghold, perhaps Ashur itself, since the city was captured
in the uprising.[7] Though Ninurta-apil-Ekur claimed to have
'guarded all the people of Assyria, with wings like an eagle
spread out over his country',[8] he doubtless owed his continued

---

[1] G, 14, 1, §206.                                [2] G, 16, nr. 62.
[3] §III, 9, no. 71; G, 22, 46 f.; §III, 17; §I, 14, 116 for date.
[4] Or, Ilu-ikhadda (G, 1, 99), a name formerly read as Nabu-daian (G, 10, 211,
cf. G, 19, 56 ff.).       [5] G, 22, 50 (nr. 48); §III, 1, 129.       [6] G, 22, nr. 44.
[7] Not in battle with Adad-shuma-uṣur as was previously assumed (§I, 12, 131).
[8] G, 4, 94 (vii, 55–9).

position to the support of his southern neighbours. For thirteen years (or three if the variant of Chronicle B is accepted) he carried on the ancient royal traditions.[1] His daughter Muballitat-Sherua? was dedicated as high-priestess with gifts of inscribed vases, gold and lapis-lazuli chains and other ornaments from the palace treasures to the main temple.[2] Once again, the dearth of sources may give us an imperfect picture of events. Already the pressure of the nomadic tribes towards the Euphrates in the west and in the north was being felt, as in their turn they were forced out of their former grounds by the movement of peoples following the disintegration of the Hittite power. The loss of trading-facilities, combined with poor harvests, was to bring Assyria and Babylonia to one of their weakest states in a long history. At this same critical time Elam again threatened the trade-routes through the Zagros and Diyālā. Ashur-dan, the next holder of the Assyrian throne, made the first move to forestall the Elamites on his south-eastern frontier during the brief reign of Zababa-shuma-iddina of Babylon. He marched c. 1160 B.C. towards the Diyālā capturing Zaban, Irria and Ugarsallu, deporting the inhabitants to Assyria.[3] These unfortunates would have been replaced by other deportees, loyal to the Assyrians amid their alien surroundings, who could be relied upon to warn of any encroachments on their territory, for such was the policy of later Assyrian militarists. If a statue dedicated for the life of Ashur-dan by the scribe Shamshi-Bēl in Irbil refers to this king rather than a later monarch of the same name it would imply that he paid close attention to the needs of this frontier.[4] His descendant, Tiglath-pileser I, writing sixty years later, says that Ashur-dan pulled down the Anu-Adad temple at Ashur but did not rebuild it.[5] This incident may have occurred towards the end of the long reign of forty-six years attributed to him both by the Babylonian Chronicle and by his heirs. There is no proof that he failed to show the customary respect to the cult-centres for he undertook other constructional work at Ashur[6] and probably at Nineveh, where early in his reign an earthquake had destroyed part of the Ishtar temple.[7] There are also records of weapons dedicated at other temples.[8]

---

[1] Note the number of royal edicts extant from this reign (§viii, 14, 277 f.).
[2] §i, 14, 127, n. 3; G, 22, 51 (nr. 49); G, 16, ii, 76.
[3] G, 22, 51.     [4] G, 1, 100.
[5] G, 22, no. 60.     [6] §iii, 16, 209.
[7] §iii, 11, 99; §iii, 12, 97.
[8] §iii, 18, 326; §iii, 4, 91 ff., and 145; §iii, 15, 133.

The closing years of Ashur-dan's long tenure of the throne are obscure.[1] Ninurta-tukulti-Ashur,[2] his son, who may have been co-regent in the last years of his father's reign, 'exercised the kingship for his *ṭuppu*'. This term has been variously interpreted. It may denote an unspecified period of time[3] or the reign of a king who did not hold, and therefore give his name to, the office of eponym, that is one who did not hold the throne for longer than twelve months. Such reigns were therefore marked but accorded zero years in length.[4] Alternatively it may denote a precise twelve-month reign.[5] This last view finds support in official documents and memoranda from Ashur of this reign, some bearing the seal of Ninurta-tukulti-Ashur and of his wife Rimeni, dated by eponyms who cover a full twelve months. These tablets show that tribute and offerings in large quantities were rendered to Ninurta-tukulti-Ashur, perhaps while he acted as regent for his aged, and perhaps sick, father towards the end of his long reign.[6] He is nowhere given the title of king in these texts. Since it is clear that subordinate officials in Ashur controlled an area from Nisibis to the Zagros mountains, and Sutu to the west is a discernible administrative district in these texts, there is no evidence that Ninurta-tukulti-Ashur held an insignificant position.[7] That he was a usurper has long been contradicted, and the Khorsabad King List states that he was son of Ashur-dan who, after 'exercising kingship for a *ṭuppu*', was defeated by his brother, Mutakkil-Nusku, who in his turn held the throne for a *ṭuppu* before disappearing.[8] If the *ṭuppu* were an indeterminate length of reign it would be necessary to suppose that the chroniclers suppressed the length of the reign of the two royal brothers out of a sense of shame at the strife, a motive not observable elsewhere in the same text. When Mutakkil-Nusku overpowered his brother it would seem that the latter fled as an exile to Babylon rather than reached there as a deportee.[9] According to a broken Babylonian prism Ninurta-tukulti-Ashur restored the temple of Erragal in Sirara, reinstating the statue of the deity which had been removed by Tukulti-Ninurta I.[10] He was evidently in sufficient accord with the Isin dynasty at Babylon both to receive a welcome and to be supported as a potential reclaimant of the

[1] G, 22, 51 (nr. 50).    [2] On the name see G, 19, 2, 66 f.
[3] *C.A.H.* I³, pt. 1, p. 203; §III, 4, 265 ff.    [4] G, 22, 52; §I, 13, 9 ff.
[5] §I, 13, 10; G, 9, 90.    [6] G, 9, 92 f.
[7] §I, 13, 22; G, 19, 2, 62.
[8] G, 19, 2, 63; no inscriptions from the latter reign are known (G, 1, 102). Cf. p. 453, n. 2.
[9] G, 19, 2, 63; G, 13, 218 f.    [10] §III, 9, no. 80; G, 1, 100 ff.

Assyrian throne.[1] Although only a few administrative documents from this reign have been recovered as yet, they imply a steady and careful administration which, as marked later by his grandson, paved the way for the long reign of his son Ashur-rēsha-ishi I (1133–1116), who followed the brief rule of his father Mutakkil-Nusku,[2] and led to a restoration of Assyrian prestige.

Ashur-rēsha-ishi claimed, as 'avenger of Assyria', to have shattered the wide-ranging groups of Akhlamu to the north and west of the country.[3] These were primarily semi-nomadic raiders from Sukhi to Carchemish on the Euphrates who, pressing eastwards, now intensified the incursions into the Tigris valley which were to become an important factor in the next reign.[4] Changes in military equipment and technique, in this era of the development of iron, had by now affected the strategy and employment of both Assyrian and Babylonian armies. These were able to build on the military experiences of Shalmaneser I and Tukulti-Ninurta, and now adapted their warfare to combat better-armed opponents whether in the desert or mountain, in the open or in siege-warfare.[5]

Experience would now seem to have led the Assyrians to develop a strategic plan, at first directed to maintaining their existing borders but soon to be extended in offensive operations to control all the main routes into their home lands and to maintain the border along defensible terrain.[6] Fortresses were strengthened to withstand attacks by powerful siege-engines. In the north Ashur-rēsha-ishi improved the defences of Apku, west of Mosul,[7] to maintain control of the district of Khanigalbat and to meet the growing menace from the well-armed Mushki tribe and their confederates in the northern hills. In addition to the construction of a royal residence here, the king undertook a programme of restoration work at Nineveh itself where a new palace was built with an extensive armoury (*bīt kutalli*), storehouses and other depot facilities and repairs made to the Great

---

[1] See above, p. 449.

[2] This king seems to have reigned long enough to undertake constructional work on a palace at Nineveh (§III, 11, 100).

[3] G, 4, 19, l. 6.

[4] See below, p. 460. For the earlier history of nomadic groups in the area see *C.A.H.* II³, pt. 1, pp. 24 ff.

[5] §III, 8, 137 ff.

[6] §III, 8, 141.

[7] G, 20, 297; located at Tell Bumariya (§III, 2, 5) or Abu Mariya (§III, 6, 135). Excavations at Tell er-Rimah in 1965–8 show that the area further west was abandoned by *c.* 1200 B.C. See A, 12, 71; A, 13, 2.

Gate of the Ishtar temple.[1] The temple of Ishtar, severely damaged by earthquakes in the time of Shalmaneser I and of Ashur-dan, was the object of much care, the great court and its gate-towers being restored. Apart from the fulfilment of religious obligations, this was doubtless part of the plan to provide a firm base for operations in the north-eastern hills. The Lullubi (or Lullumi) and Quti were raided and their subjugation claimed. It may be that Nineveh was also the base from which the king called out his élite troops (ḫurādu) to march to Irbil as the first stage of a renewed offensive in the disputed Zagros hills. This action roused Babylonian opposition, for Ninurta-nādin-shumi (or -shumāti) mustered his own forces.[2] The broken text implies a defeat for the southerners who, under Nebuchadrezzar I, were destined to renew their hostility with Assyria and thus divert their forces at a time of crisis due to increasing pressures from the west. However, at first Ashur-rēsha-ishi was able, by the despatch of a mixed group of chariots and infantry, to force Nebuchadrezzar to withdraw from Zaqqu with the loss of valuable siege equipment which he had to set on fire. A later Babylonian attack, this time with a more mobile force, was beaten off at Idu (Hīt?) by a similar Assyrian column which captured the Babylonian general and his baggage-train.[3] With the defeat of Nebuchadrezzar, some time after the end of Ashur-rēsha-ishi's eighteenth year of office (1116 B.C.), military conflict between the neighbours ceased.

## IV. NEBUCHADREZZAR I

By this time the control of Babylonia was firmly in the hands of one ruling family who were to hold the throne for over fifty years. Nebuchadrezzar, whose very name implies the continuance of the line, succeeded Ninurta-nādin-shumi and was to rule for twenty-two years (1124–1103).[4] With the backing of a majority of the tribes he was in a position to avenge the humiliating defeat inflicted by the Elamites when Kutir-Nahhunte had sacked the larger northern cities and removed the statue of Marduk from E-sagila at the close of the Kassite period. This act of sacrilege was long remembered as one of the greatest defeats Babylon had ever suffered. Yet the Elamites still raided the fertile regions east of the Tigris, perhaps in support of a few remaining adherents of the old régime which Nebuchadrezzar, as 'spoiler of the

---

[1] §III, 13, 100; §III, 12, 114; §III, 11, 100.    [2] G, 22, 70.
[3] G, 22, 71; G, 4, 216.    [4] §II, 6 (King List C), 4.

Kassites', claims to have crushed finally.[1] An early counter-raid by Nebuchadrezzar failed when his troops were smitten by plague and the king himself only narrowly escaped death in the headlong retreat which followed.[2] Another account, which may refer to this same event, relates a battle near the river Kerkhah in which the Babylonian troops were forced to retreat to Dūr-Apil-Sin, implying that the Elamites no longer controlled the west bank of the Tigris.[3] This episode may date from the earlier Isin kings though it fits well into this contemporary situation. It was certainly later in his reign that Nebuchadrezzar received favourable omens, in response to repeated appeals to the gods, to launch a further attack.[4] This he did in the month of Tammuz, high summer, when 'the axes (held in the hand) burned like fire and the road-surfaces were scorching like flame. There was no water in the wells and drinking supplies were unavailable. The strength of the powerful horses slackened and the legs of even the strongest man weakened.'[5] The march lay through difficult country for 30 bēru (c. 320 km.) south-east of Dēr before the Elamites were encountered on the banks of the Ulai (River Eulaeus, modern Kārūn) near Susa. Although the Babylonians may have had the benefit of the element of surprise, the battle was hotly contested, the dust of the affray blotting out the sun. The Elamite Khutelu-tush-In-Shushinak fled and soon thereafter died. According to the account by Lakti-Marduk,[6] the shaikh of Bīt-Karziabku, the action which decided the day was that of the chariotry on the right wing. For this their commander was rewarded with a generous grant of land and freedom from local taxes and labour-service in the province of Nawar[7] and thus formed, like the similar colonies of deportees in Assyria, a pro-Babylonian nucleus on the disputed border.

The outcome of the battle was of greater significance for Babylonian morale than for any political or territorial gain. Nevertheless, it marked the end of Elamite domination and of their raids into the plain for many years. Above all, the cult statue of Marduk was restored to E-sagila amid much popular rejoicing

---

[1] G, 12, 96 ff.

[2] This reconstruction of events follows G, 2, 132 f. Cf. A, 3, 105 f.

[3] See below, pp. 501 f.; A, 3, 106.

[4] §IV, 1, 44; §IV, 4, ii, 4 f., dates this to the sixteenth regnal year.

[5] G, 12, 29 f., no. 6, i, 16 ff.

[6] G, 12, 32, i, 35. On the name formerly read 'Ritti-Marduk' see below, p. 502, n. 1, and A, 3, 107 where a possible reading Shitti-Marduk is suggested. See Plate 161(b).

[7] G, 12, 32 f. (i, 36–ii, 10).

and elaborate ceremonies.[1] It may be at this time too, rather than in a separate campaign, that the statue of a lesser deity, Eriya of Dīn-sharri on the same border, was brought first to Babylon and then settled in Khuṣṣi near Bīt-Sin-asharēdu.[2] The priests, Shamua and his son Shamaia, were endowed with land sufficient to maintain the cult in an area less exposed to Elamite marauders. Succeeding generations were to laud Nebuchadrezzar as a national victor and hero. He was the subject both of heroic poetry and of historically based omens, one astrological series of the seventh century being entitled 'when Nebuchadrezzar crushed Elam'.[3] It is possible that this notable event played a decisive part in the elevation of Marduk to be the supreme national deity of Babylon.[4] Subsequently one Neo-Babylonian ruler and two short-lived insurgents who were faced with the prospect of the domination of Babylonia by their eastern (then Persian) rivals, were to adopt this honoured throne-name.

Nebuchadrezzar was less successful in his relations with Assyria, but it is the Assyrian account of events between them which alone survives. If Nebuchadrezzar was the author of the letter to Ashur-rēsha-ishi threatening to reinstate Ninurta-tukulti-Ashur[5] then he would seem to have followed up with an attack on Zaqqu, at which border-crossing his rival had failed to meet him for discussions. His defeat here and later at Idu (Hīt?)[6] may indicate action against invading Amorites whose subjugation Nebuchadrezzar claims. A complaint by a semi-nomad, Kharbi-Shikhu, a frontier-official, that the king's envoys only waited for him a day in Zaqqu territory, is answered by reference to the need for care and mediation between Babylonia and Assyria. The letter is broken and the part played by a certain Ashur-shum-lishir in these events cannot now be understood.[7] There is no reason to doubt the explanation given for this defeat by the Assyrian-biased Synchronistic History as a repulse by the Assyrians of Babylonian border raids.

The Babylonians, like the Assyrians, claim victories over the Lullubi in the disputed Zagros mountains. This may be no mere desire to repeat the activities, or claim the titles, of illustrious predecessors but may be a historical reference to a campaign on the north-eastern border of which no record has survived. Within Babylon, the royal residence, the king refurbished E-sagila, now

---

[1] §IV, 4, 339 ff.; §IX, 17, 10.  
[3] §IV, 8, 542 f.  
[5] See above, p. 449.  
[7] G, 20, 295; §VI, 11, 59 ff.; §IV, 7.  

[2] G, 12, 96 f. (no. 24, 14 ff.).  
[4] §IX, 17, 9.  
[6] G, 22, 59.

restored to its primary place as the seat of Marduk. A dagger
bearing his name and titles may originally have been part of the
endowment.[1] In the western city a shrine of Adad, E-kidur-
khegal-tila, was restored following one successful expedition.[2] At
Nippur care was bestowed on the E-kur temple, the chief priest
of Enlil being granted an adequate revenue from land in adjacent
Bit-Sin-shemi.[3] This 'pious prince' followed the custom of
dedicating objects of gold and silver to the Sin-temple at Ur[4]
where a stela of an *ēntu*-priestess from the sacred cloister, recovered
by Nabonidus more than five hundred years later, may imply that
a royal princess had been installed in that office.[5] Moreover, this
may but reflect other activity in the south noted by the scribe
who counted this reign as falling 696 years after that of Gulkishar,
king of the first Dynasty of the Sealand.[6] Inaccurate though
this computation may be, Nebuchadrezzar left his mark as a
heroic leader, 'king of Sumer and Akkad', who could claim to be
'the sun rising over the land as in a new day'.[7]

## V. TIGLATH-PILESER I

It was as well that the Babylonians had neutralized the Elamites and
taken a part in controlling the raiders both from the Lullubi
tribes in the eastern hills and from the nomadic tribes of the
western desert. Tiglath-pileser I (Tukulti-apil-Esharra of Assyria)
(1115–1077) was thus free to face the growing storm clouds
in the north in his accession year. Although the annals and
historical records afford only summaries of his campaigns on all
fronts it would seem that he at least developed and followed an
overall strategic plan for dealing with his enemies and extending
Assyrian influence.[8] His attention was first directed to the north
where the Mushki—perhaps to be identified with the Phrygians,
and linked with the Kaska (Gasga) peoples who had broken up
the Hittite empire[9]—had crossed the Taurus with a large army
('20,000 men') and were making their way down the Tigris
valley towards Nineveh. The threat of the loss of fine agricultural
land and the copper-mines paying annual dues to Ashur was
serious. For fifty years the Mushki had controlled the rich valleys
of Alzi and Purukuzzi, former tributaries of Ashur. They now

---

[1] §II, 2, 152 (no. 4).
[2] §IV, 1, 43.
[3] §I, 8, ii, 2 ff.
[4] §IV, 3, 143.
[5] §IV, 2, 45.
[6] §I, 7, 83.
[7] G, 12, 31, i, 4.
[8] §III, 8, 141. See Plate 162(*b*).
[9] See above, p. 420.

raided beyond Katmukhi and dominated the countryside west of the upper Tigris fomenting revolt. Tiglath-pileser resolutely met the tribesmen, headed by five chiefs, in the plain beyond the Kashiari hills (Ṭūr 'Abdīn).[1]

The Assyrians adopted their old practice of displaying the hands of the vanquished at the city-gates and of plundering the rebel towns and villages which had sided with the attackers. More than 6000 prisoners and much booty were carried off. Since many of the tribesmen had fled north-east to Sherishe on the east bank of the Tigris, the Assyrians mounted a punitive expedition. Pioneering a track across the mountains for the passage of their chariots, they captured the city and dispersed the Papkhi who had come to the help of Kummukh. In a series of clashes in the mountains Kili-Teshub, son of Kali-Teshub, and possibly descendant of a Hurrian family, who also bore the native name of Irrupi, was captured with his family and much loot.[2] News of the Assyrian advance north-eastward caused the people of Urraṭinash on Mount Panari to take to more distant hills while their ruler Shadi-Teshub, son of Khattukhe, came to make terms with the Assyrian leader. In accordance with ancient practice the suppliant was made a vassal; his sons were taken as hostages to Ashur together with an initial payment of tribute, more than 60 large bronze vessels, 120 slaves and many head of cattle. The bronzes were dedicated to Adad in gratitude for divine favour in this campaign.

In the following year Assyria won back Subartu. The army, equipped with 120 chariots with teams of yoked horses in the Hittite manner, marched through Alzi and Purukuzzi which were again laid under tribute. These tribes were now weak and without help from the Mushki. The force moved up the Tigris valley and across mountainous terrain between Mounts Idni and Aia to invade Kharia and meet rebels from the Kaska (Gasga) who had formerly defeated the Hittites but were now aiding a coalition of the Papkhi tribes. Whether with the same force or another column moving eastward, the Assyrians broke up the opposition at Mount Azu and fired villages in the foothills towards the Zab river. Men of Adaush submitted but those of Saradaush and Ammaush on resisting were defeated at Mount Aruma, at Isua (previously Ishua) and Dara. Another force, led by the king in person, marched up the Zab to engage the more easterly

---

[1] G, 4, 35 f., i, 62 ff.

[2] G, 4, 40, ii, 25 f. The second name may have been an Assyrian misunderstanding of the Hurrian 'lord' (§v, 3, 177).

tribes. Murattash was captured and burnt in a dawn attack as the troops pressed through Saradaush in the Asaniu and Atunu hills to reach the Sugi district of Khabkhi.[1] Here the Assyrians were checked for a time by a stand on Mount Khirikhu of 6000 men from five of the tribes of eastern Papkhi (Khime, Lukhi, Anirgi, Alamun and Nimni). In the event Sugi was finally made a vassal state, the statues of twenty-five of the local deities being carried off as hostages to stand beneath the eye of Ashur in his temple.[2]

With the dominance of the Mushki and Papkhi over the smaller tribes now broken Tiglath-pileser was free in the next year (third campaign) to make a drive north against the Nairi hill-folks west of Lake Vān. His route lay through regions which he claims, probably justly, had never been traversed by his predecessors. Sixteen mountain ridges were crossed as he moved via Mount Amadana, near Diyārbakr, to bridge the Upper Euphrates near its source. Despite abundant geographical detail given in the royal annals the precise route cannot yet be determined. It would seem that the Assyrians marched by Tunube (Turubun) east of the Tigris to the south-west of Lake Vān.[3] A coalition of 23 Nairi chiefs was defeated, 120 of their armoured chariots being taken and 60 other tribal groups chased northwards.[4] The decisive battle took place to the north and north-west of Lake Vān. At the point farthest north on this expedition, Melazgirt, Tiglath-pileser had an inscribed victory stela set up.[5] Once again hostages were taken and an annual tribute of 12,000 horses and 2,000 head of cattle imposed on the conquered tribes. Sieni of Daieni, the leader who refused to submit, was brought as a captive to Assyria. It was in the westerly course of this campaign that the rebel stronghold of Milidia was visited and made to produce an annual due payable in lead-lumps. This is almost certainly to be identified with modern Malatya. Tribute was claimed from Milidia and from neighbouring Enzate and Sukhme. Thus, by the end of three campaigns Tiglath-pileser had carried Assyrian arms further into the Anatolian hills, and laid more of the hill-tribes under duress, than had any of his predecessors. Most of his opponents in the extensive lands of the Nairi from Tumme to

[1] Rather than Kirkhi, see G, 16, II, 83, v, 6; §I, 13, 20.
[2] G, 4, 41 ff. (cols. ii, 36–iv, 39).
[3] §v, 3, 170.
[4] The 'Upper Sea' must here be the Black Sea, a term used as a designation of general direction northward.
[5] §v, 3, 171.

Dazaeni, Khimua, Paiteri and Khabkhi,[1] who now owed allegiance and taxes, are only to be encountered in the annals of this reign. While pressure on the sources of raw materials and the trade-routes which linked them was at least temporarily alleviated, and the internal economy strengthened by the new sources of revenue, the seeds of future dissension were being sown. On these hill frontiers especially the peoples, by nature and location independent, would henceforth be forced to group into larger defensive units. In times of weakness in Assyria they would harass the plain and, five hundred years later, play a decisive part in the overthrow of the southern state. Further, a course had been set from which no subsequent ruler could afford to turn back. Yet the periodic incursions needed to control the tribes and recoup overdue taxes would severely drain the sources of manpower and wealth of the very country they were intended to strengthen.

Tiglath-pileser now aimed to extend his jurisdiction to the trans-Tigridian country of Muṣri.[2] Since Muṣri had received help from the land of Qumani, the Assyrian laid siege to the city of Arini, at the foot of Mount Aisa. The siege was raised on promise of submission and regular tribute-payments. By this means, and because in the second campaign the men of Urumma and Apishal[3] had been defeated, the route westwards was now possible. Moreover, Tiglath-pileser had taken bold action against the Akhlamu —an Aramaean tribe or group dominating the Euphrates between Carchemish and Sutium which often raided to the Tigris. In a single day, so he claims,[4] he raided their territory penetrating beyond the Euphrates, which had been crossed on inflated skin rafts (*keleks*), to the Bishrī hills where six of their villages were burned out. This was but the first action against the semi-nomads of Syria which necessitated the Assyrian army repeating the Euphrates crossing no less than twenty-eight times, twice in one single year. Such constant pressure gives substance to the Assyrian claim to have subdued the Akhlamu—forerunners of the coming Aramaean raiders—from Tadmor (Palmyra) to 'Anah and even as far south as Rapiqu on the frontier with Babylonia. In Sukhi itself the island towns of Sapinata ('Boats') and Khindanu were sacked and ruined by the destruction of their palm-groves. The statues of the local deities were carried off to Ashur as a final disgrace and to mark their reduction to impotence.

---

[1] The tribes here enumerated occupied lands between Erzurum and Lake Urmia.

[2] For the location of Muṣri, see now A, 16, 145 f.          [3] §v, 1, 71.

[4] This is probably to be interpreted as 'at one time', in a single expedition.

With the intervening tribes under close surveillance Assyria could now aim to control the main trade-route to the Mediterranean itself. Tiglath-pileser directed his march to Amurru, which at this time extended from Tadmor to Ṣamuri and included Byblos and Sidon.[1] His march lay to the coast at Armad (Arvad). Here the king embarked on a ship to sail up the Mediterranean littoral to Ṣamuri. On this journey of three *bēru* (*c*. 20 kms.), he hunted a narwhal (*nāḫiru*).[2] The first Assyrian king to venture across the Lebanon in force was brought gifts by the neighbouring rulers of Byblos and Sidon, while the Egyptian king sent him a crocodile as a present. Before turning homewards Tiglath-pileser had massive cedars cut down for use in his renovation of the Anu-Adad temple at Ashur. An annual tax requiring further supplies of timber was imposed on Ini-Teshub, king of Khatti (N. Syria), who paid homage at this time. Thus by the end of his fifth regnal year Tiglath-pileser was able to boast of his conquest of forty-two lands and their rulers between the Lesser Zab and the Euphrates and along the northern hills as far as the Mediterranean.[3] This wide-ranging activity was possible because all was quiet on the southern borders. It was not until well on in the reign of this long-lived Assyrian monarch that Marduk-nādin-ahhē[4] of Babylon raided across the Lesser Zab and carried off the gods Adad and Shala from Ekallate, a royal city not far from Ashur itself.[5]

Owing to preoccupation with the west it was at least a decade before the Assyrian was able to strike back. According to the Synchronistic Chronicle there were two actions involving Assyrian chariotry.[6] The first crossed the Lesser Zab to ravage Arman in the district of Ugarsallu[7] and marched via Lubdi (south of Arrapkha) and over the Radanu river (Shaṭṭ el-'Adhaim) to plunder villages at the foot of the Kamulla and Kashtilia hills. This was a continuation of the struggle for mastery of the upper Diyālā route, now firmly in the hands of the Babylonians. The second force was directed to northern Babylonia itself and, marching along the customary route taken by such raiders down the eastern Tigris bank through Marritu,[8] it crossed to Dūr-

---

[1] G, 16, II, 68, 71. The area to the north of this, bounded on the east by Araziq and Carchemish on the Euphrates, was now included in Khatti.

[2] §v, 10, 355 f.     [3] G, 4, 82 f. (vi, 39 ff.).

[4] See Plate 162(*c*).

[5] The location is disputed. Adad and Shala had a shrine at Kalkhu (Nimrūd).

[6] §v, 10, 351.

[7] Or the 'irrigated district of Saluna'.

[8] Or Gurmarritu. It has been suggested that this may be Sāmarrā, usually written Surmarrāti (see §v, 11, 309).

Kurigalzu ('Aqarqūf), Opis and Sippar of Shamash (Abu Ḥabbah) and of Anunitum to reach Babylon. The cult centres were overrun despite attempts by the Babylonian cavalry to divert the enemy advance. The Assyrians claimed an outright victory setting fire to the royal palaces of Babylon before withdrawing.[1] Marduk-nādin-ahhē remained in control of Babylon and still held the captured statues of the Assyrian deities, presumably having removed them for safety to Nippur or the south.[2] There is no evidence that Assyria either intended or gained any lasting hold over northern Babylonia at this time. Indeed, a fragmentary Assyrian chronicle which records the death of Marduk-nādin-ahhē describes a dire famine in an area usually thought to be in Assyria itself, when Aramaean invaders drove the Assyrians into the northern hills round Kirruria. If this does not refer to events outside the Assyrian home-land or to the Assyrian attack on the north-eastern Babylonian province of Irria,[3] then it would imply that in the closing years of the reign of Tiglath-pileser, who is still named in the text after this event, the Aramaeans were now strong enough to turn on their Assyrian conquerors despite having been so frequently raided. The same text would then imply that Tiglath-pileser outlived Marduk-nādin-ahhē.[4]

Whatever the reasons which led to the retreat of the Assyrian invaders their failure to follow up a military operation was a grave weakness displayed in several campaigns of this reign. The initial successes achieved in constant expeditions over a wide front were only rarely exploited. Tributes and taxes were imposed but not regularly collected. Prisoners do not appear to have been used in major building or resettlement projects as was done by later Assyrian leaders. Nor were they settled to replace rebellious inhabitants at other parts of the dominion. Although the transportation of conquered people is mentioned in the annals it was probably no innovation and there is no sign of the establishment of a system of control of newly overrun areas such as followed the later setting up of provinces and administrative districts. The very scale of Assyrian success therefore paved the way for a swift denial of the Assyrian overlordship and thus for the loss of the hard-won territories if ever the central government was weak. The new trade-routes opened into Syria and the mineral wealth of Anatolia brought an immediate if passing economic advantage. The new weapons and tactics, contrived in imitation of, and

---

[1] §v, 10, 351 (ll. 48 f.). A, 3, 125 interprets this as a mere raid.
[2] Unless the Ekallate raid was itself a later reprisal for this attack, see p. 464.
[3] §viii, 1, 235, n. 2.          [4] G, 2, 133 f.; A, 3, 75.

reaction to, those of their powerful neighbours, had been well
tried in an age of technological innovation. The personal exploits
of Tiglath-pileser, like those of his contemporary Nebuchadrezzar, were to be long remembered and imitated.

The king showed much prowess in battle and skill in hunting.
During campaigns in the Khabur valley, near Harrān and at
Araziq on the Euphrates the jungle provided much sport. He
slew four wild aurochs, four bull elephants and no less than 920
lions, more than a hundred of which were hunted on foot with
the bow or the newly invented iron spear.[1] This claim, especially
of elephants, is small compared with that of Tuthmosis III in the
same area, and may indicate that already their numbers were
declining owing to the predatory activities of the Akhlamu. But
these hunts were not without other purposes. Horns, tusks and
hides contributed to the economy, live animals and birds stocked
the zoological gardens where they were bred for the chase and so
that their young could be offered in sacrifice. The first Assyrian
to include such details in the royal annals, this king sought to
prove his superiority over wild beasts and so demonstrate the
unique power granted him by the god of war to overcome any
evil or enemy in the field. Such a ritual hunt is attested elsewhere
in the Near East at this time. The king was also the first to
record the institution of botanical gardens stocked with specimens
collected during his widespread expeditions.

The more unusual victims of the hunt, such as the narwhal
harpooned off the Mediterranean coast or the wild bull caught
in the Lumash Mountains, were reproduced in bas reliefs to
decorate the entrances to the restored royal palaces at Ashur.[2]
Here, according to many inscriptions, the Anu-Adad temple
with its adjacent twin zikkurrats was restored, the temple being
re-roofed with Lebanon cedars, the terrace resurfaced and the
associated cult buildings (*bīt šaḫuru* and *bīt labbuni*)[3] enlarged
and repanelled with cedar and pistachio woods. This work of
building the temple, according to Tiglath-pileser, had not been
completed; though sixty years earlier Ashur-dan had relaid the
foundations of a building first constructed by Shamshi-Adad (III),
the son of Ishme-Dagan (II), 641 years earlier.[4] Of similar
chronological interest is the claim that the walls of the new city,
built by Puzur-Ashur III (*c.* 1500 B.C.), had been neglected for
about two centuries since the time of Ashur-nādin-ahhē I (1452–
1433). These were now reinforced by a great earth rampart

[1] G, 4, 85.            [2] §v, 10, 356 f.
[3] *Ibid.* 354 f.        [4] G, 4, 95 (vii, 60 ff.); G, 19, 1, 303; G, 20, 359.

between the Tigris Gate and the inner town.[1] In Nineveh
Tiglath-pileser had work carried out on the city walls, which were
reinforced with stone, and on the royal palace built by his father
between the Ishtar and Nabu temples to which attention was now
also given. Water was diverted from the River Khosr both to
the city and to a newly set out park.[2] Similar work was carried
out at other cities and there is every indication that, despite the
irony that Tiglath-pileser is best known from the accounts of
his wars, his claim at the end of his reign to have 'made good
the condition of my people and caused them to dwell in peaceful
habitations' was justified. He left behind also a legacy of literature collected in what must be one of the oldest extant libraries.[3]

## VI. PRESSURES FROM THE WEST

Meanwhile in Babylonia, according to the King List,[4] Nebuchadrezzar I had been succeeded by a son, Enlil-nādin-apli who reigned
for four years (1102–1099). Little is known of his activities
though in his fourth year he ordered the governors of the
provinces of Bīt-Sin-māgir and the Sealand to investigate a dispute of title to some land,[5] an indication that the central government still controlled the southern tribes. While the reason for the
change is at present unknown he was succeeded by his uncle
Marduk-nādin-ahhē, son of Ninurta-nādin-shumi and a younger
brother of Nebuchadrezzar.[6] Thus the gains of the previous years
were initially consolidated in a stable government with power
held within the same family. His rule was recognized at Nippur
and at Ur, where he undertook a considerable building programme, restoring the E-(ga)nun-makh and neighbouring buildings.[7] However, it was in the north that the vigour of the
southerners was seen. According to Sennacherib 'Marduk-nādin-
ahhē, king of Akkad had captured the gods of Ekallate, Adad
and Shala, in the time of Tiglath-pileser, king of Assyria, and
carried them off to Babylonia. 418 years later I removed them
from Babylon and restored them to their shrines in Ekallate.'[8]
This implies a date of 1105 B.C.[9] but the exact year when the raid
on Ekallate took place within this reign is uncertain.[10] Sennacherib's calculation is to be taken as an error since it would clash

[1] §v, 10, 344 (ll. 34 ff.).    [2] §v, 7, 142 f.; §III, 11, 100; §v, 5, 122.
[3] See below, p. 477.    [4] §II, 6, 3 (King List C, 5).
[5] §I, 7, 83.    [6] §II, 6, 3 (King List C, 6); §II, 3, 309, n. 3.
[7] §vI, 3, no. 306; §vI, 16, no. 101 (pl. xxv); A, 3, 330 ff.
[8] §vI, 9, 83 (ll. 48 ff.).    [9] A, 3, 83 ff. Cf. G, 20, 354.    [10] A, 3, 124 ff.

with the synchronism Ashur-rēsha-ishi–Ninurta-nādin-shumi.[1]
The economic texts imply that the Babylonian king controlled the
border up to the Lesser Zab until his thirteenth year and a *kudurru-
inscription* of his tenth year refers to a defeat of Assyria and a
grant of land at Irria, east of the Tigris.[2] The carefully planned
expedition would seem to have taken place perhaps in the ninth
or tenth regnal year when Tiglath-pileser was preoccupied with
the west, and unable to retaliate. The Babylonian clash with the
Assyrians at Rapiqu earlier in the reign may have been caused
by some anxiety over the mastery of the Euphrates around the
valuable bitumen deposits of Hīt and the control of the waters
at the border. It is unlikely that these Babylonian expeditions
took place after Tiglath-pileser's raid on Upper Babylonia, for
no permanent results followed from them[3] and Marduk-nādin-
ahhē remained in control though the economy was much
weakened. In his eighteenth year severe famine struck Babylonia
and the inhabitants of the cities were reduced to eating human
flesh. Aramaean semi-nomads pressed in from the desert and
the Babylonian ruler 'finally disappeared', no detail being known
of the manner of his death or retirement after a reign of eighteen
years (1098–1081). This Aramaean invasion may have been
part of the same incursion which distressed Assyria towards the
end of Tiglath-pileser's reign and after the death of Marduk-
nādin-ahhē.[4] An attempt has been made to identify five unnamed
kings in an Akkadian prophecy with Marduk-nādin-ahhē and his
four successors[5] but this is very doubtful.[6]

Marduk-shāpik-zēri, who ruled for thirteen years (1080–
1068),[7] came to the throne in circumstances which are still
obscure and his relation to his predecessor is uncertain. A later
commentator compares his accession with that of Esarhaddon so
that he might have been a younger son of Nebuchadrezzar or of
Marduk-nādin-ahhē who gained the throne after a struggle.[8]
That he was contemporary with Ashur-bēl-kala of Assyria in the
opening years of the latter's rule is certain from the Assyrian
Synchronistic History which records that 'Marduk-shāpik-zēri
pledged mutual peace and good will. At the time of Ashur-bēl-
kala Marduk-shāpik-zēri finally disappeared.'[9] The New Baby-

---

[1] See above, p. 454; G, 2, 149.     [2] G, 12, 45 (no. VIII, ii, 27).
[3] See above, p. 462; also Ashur-bēl-kala had to attack Dūr-Kurigalzu again (G, 4, 133).
[4] §II, 8, 384, 2'; §I, 12, 133 f. A, 3, 125 implies that he disappeared during the invasion.     [5] A, 9, 231 f.; A, 1, 118; A, 8, 9.
[6] A, 3, 129, n. 762.     [7] §II, 6 (King List C, 7); A, 3, 6 f.
[8] §II, 8, 384.     [9] G, 18, 272 (King List A).

lonian Chronicle, after an obscure reference to 'heavy spoil', says that 'Marduk-shāpik-zēri established friendly relations (i.e. a treaty) with Ashur-bēl-kala of Assyria'.[1] It appears to indicate that the Babylonian took the initiative after he had built a defended place, the name of which is now lost, or had won a victory, perhaps over the Aramaeans, for the presence of 105 chiefs or rulers at special (treaty) celebrations is noted. On the other hand, the Chronicle continues, 'at that time the king came from Assyria to Sippar'. This might imply that Marduk-shāpik-zēri had gone to Assyria to establish the international agreement or to receive support for his claim to the throne. This act of reconciliation was probably forced on the parties by their mutual desire to present a united front against the desert tribes. It is possible that it was the Assyrian who came to Sippar, rather than to Babylon which had so recently been the scene of invasion, though Sippar was not necessarily the capital at this time.[2] Extensive repairs to the city-walls and city-gates at Babylon were being undertaken.[3] The temple of E-zida at Borsippa was restored and gifts made to the temples at Ur,[4] Nippur,[5] and other cult-centres.[6] The normal legal procedures for establishing the ownership of land and a list of prices current in the twelfth year of this reign do not indicate any political disturbance at this time.[7] This has, however, to be deduced from the seizure of the throne by an Aramaean usurper, Adad-apla-iddina, which brought the long control of Babylonia by a distinguished family to an end. That the new ruler was to hold the throne for twenty-two years (1067–1046)[8] and himself to be the object of Aramaean attacks makes it unlikely that he was a victorious Aramaean invader.

Adad-apla-iddina styled himself 'King of Babylon, son of Nin-Isinna and son-in-law of Nanna'[9], to assert his divine title to the throne. The Synchronistic History claims that someone, whose name is now lost, 'appointed Adad-apla-iddina, son of Esagil-shaduni, son of a nobody, to rule over them'.[10] While this may mean no more than that he was a native of Babylonia but of non-royal stock, the New Babylonian Chronicle calls him 'son of

---

[1] G, 13, 11, 58 f., 4 ff.      [2] G, 13, 1, 191; G, 2, 159.

[3] §1, 7, pt. 11, 148.      [4] A, 5, 334.

[5] A, 6, 16 (no. 56).      [6] §iv, 3, 143, 15; §vi, 10, 7 f.; A, 2, 247.

[7] G, 12, 80 f.      [8] §11, 7, 86 f.; §11, 6, 20.

[9] §vi, 3, 166 f., 1–5; the first title may not be a divine ascription since the name of Nin-Isinna is given before that of his divine father. See §vi, 2, 27 f. and *contra* §vi, 13, 103; cf. also A, 3, 136 f.

[10] G, 3, 90 (King List A, ii, 31–32); G, 2, 161, n. 222, thinks this was Ashur-bēl-kala. Cf. A, 3, 136.

Itti-Marduk-balāṭu, an Aramaean, a usurper'.[1] This ancestral name is common and need not refer to the second ruler of the Isin Dynasty; if such was his forebear the conservative Babylonian chronicler would scarcely have classed him as an Aramaean. That he usurped the throne is almost certain, but that he was opposed in this is unlikely since he continued his predecessor's policy of close ties with the Assyrian king, to whom he had married his daughter. The initial goodwill did not last. The Babylonian devoted himself energetically to the now traditional endowment of the principal religious foundations. Nabu's statue at Borsippa was ornamented, and the shrines of E-meteursag at Kish and E-kishnugal at Ur restored.[2] The Imgur–Enlil wall at Babylon was repaired as was the outer city-wall of Nippur.[3] However, relationships with powerful neighbours soon deteriorated and Ashur-bēl-kala, perhaps sensing Babylonian support for his rebel brother, attacked northern Babylonia. If the so-called 'Broken Obelisk' is assigned to this reign, then Dūr-Kurigalzu was attacked and its governor, Kadashman-Buriash, taken captive.[4] Once again this district was laid open to incursions from the desert, the Aramaean tribe of Sutu sacking Sippar and causing the regular services in the temple to cease for more than a century.[5] If the Era Epic reflects this disturbed period then there was civil war in Babylon and the Sutu joined in the raid on Dūr-Kurigalzu and Dēr.[6]

As so often after a long and distinguished reign, there would seem to have been family controversy on the death of Tiglath-pileser I. Asharēd-apil-Ekur reigned only two years (1076–5).[7] The reading of the Synchronistic Chronicle (Assur 14616c) which held him to be a contemporary of Itti-Marduk-balāṭu[8] has been disproved.[9] His origin, accession, and end are obscure since no contemporary records have survived. He did not commence his reign until after the accession year of Marduk-shāpik-zēri of Babylon, who reigned for thirteen years.[10] This synchronism, subject to a margin of error of only three years either way, makes it probable that Ashur-bēl-kala who succeeded him came to the throne about the seventh year of Marduk-shāpik-zēri.[11]

According to his annals, Ashur-bēl-kala had first to campaign

---

[1] G, 13, II, 59, l. 8.
[2] §VI, 2, 30; §VI, 7, 65; §VI, 3, 166.
[3] §VI, 12, II, 308; A, 3, 140.
[4] §VI, 5, 209 f.; G, 1, 135.
[5] G, 12, 121, i, 1 ff.
[6] §VI, 6, 398; A, 3, 285 f.
[7] §VI, 15, 21, III, 13–15.
[8] G, 18, 273; G, 21, 70 f.
[9] A, 3, 41.
[10] §VI, 14, 21.
[11] C.A.H. I³, pt. 1, pp. 204 f.; cf. A, 3, 75 f.

in Uruaṭri which was itself being troubled by the Aramaeans who by now had reached the Tigris north and north-west of Ashur.[1] The campaigns form the principal subject of the 'Broken Obelisk' from Nineveh which also includes some of the exploits of Tiglath-pileser I.[2] There have been many theories as to the date and ascription of this monument in which the name of the king, who must have reigned for at least five years, is now missing.[3] That it is to be attributed to this reign rather than that of Tiglath-pileser I is evident from the progress made by the Aramaeans who had hitherto been largely confined to the west of the Euphrates. It would seem from the text that Ashur-bēl-kala, if this assignation is correct, began to take vigorous action against the Aramaeans in his fourth or fifth year. Two campaigns were directed against these tribes, now called *Arime*, in Ṣaṣiri. A further expedition reconquered Turmitta in Muṣri, deporting dissident tribesmen, and fought Aramaeans in Pausa at the foot of the Ṭūr ʿAbdīn; at Nabula, north-east of Nisibis, at a place [. . .]tibua on the Tigris, in Lishur-sala-Ashur (Sinamu district), and Murarir, all places north and north-west of Ashur between Erishu of Khabkhi and Harrān.[4] This prepared the way for a thrust further west in the following year to Makrisi, near the junction of the Khabur and Kharmish rivers by the Yari hills.[5] Once more Assyrian arms crossed the Euphrates[6] and pressed beyond into the Khani territory where Gulguli was captured.[7] If this Broken Obelisk is a description of Ashur-bēl-kala's campaigns, then he claimed to have reached the Mediterranean and emulated his father's hunting adventures both on land and sea.[8] It may be that it was in thankfulness for help in averting the Aramaean danger at this time that the king dedicated a statue of a nude female, perhaps of some captured goddess, at Nineveh. His inscription ends with a curse, that the gods of the West Land might smash anyone who should damage it.[9] Part of the obelisk inscription is devoted to the building activities of the king and his numerous works of renovation in Ashur. The great terrace of Ashur-nādin-aḫḫē, the canal of Ashur-dan which had been waterless for thirty years and the quay-wall erected by Adad-nīrāri all received attention. Finally, the king completed the

[1] §v, 6, 75 f.
[2] G, 4, 128 ff.; G, 14, 1, 118 ff.; §ix, 10, 123. See Plate 162(*a*).
[3] Summarized in §vi, 5, 206, n. 1; 208.
[4] §vi, 5, 211 f.                                    [5] §vi, 5, 212.
[6] At the conjunction with the Sajur: A, 11, 169.    [7] G, 4, 137.
[8] G, 8, 1, pl. 33*a*.                        [9] G, 4, 152; G, 14, 1, 340.

Apku palace begun by Ashur-rēsha-ishi and a palace-terrace of Tukulti-Ninurta.[1] On his death the king was ceremonially buried in the capital to which he had devoted so much attention and had kept free from invasion.[2] As on the death of his illustrious grandfather, there would seem to have been some confusion at the end of Ashur-bēl-kala's reign. An Aramaean Tukulti-Mer, a king of Khana and Mari, son of Ilu-iqīsha, claims in his inscriptions to be king of Assyria and to have campaigned against the Papkhi.[3] Whether this claimant was active at the death of Tiglath-pileser or Ashur-bēl-kala must remain uncertain, though the latter is more likely. An inscribed stone mace dedicated to Shamash of Sippar might imply that he was an Aramaean leader who moved into Babylonia as did the Sutu towards the end of the life of Ashur-bēl-kala and during the long reign of a fellow Aramaean Adad-apla-iddina.[4]

Another claimant to the Assyrian throne at this time was Erība-Adad II, whose broken inscriptions also imply intense military activity along similar lines to those followed by Tiglath-pileser.[5] He restored the temple of E-khursag-kurkurra[6] and continued the religious traditions.[7] However, another son of Ashur-bēl-kala, Shamshi-Adad IV, came up from Babylon and with the support of the Aramaean usurper there, Adad-apla-iddina, deposed him and held the throne for four years (1054–1051).[8] He claimed the title of 'great king' though nothing is known of his political activities.[9] At Nineveh the Ishtar temple was once more renovated according to building and other dedicatory inscriptions, while at Ashur the gate-tower (*bīt nāmeru*) received similar treatment.[10]

The line of Tiglath-pileser continued to dominate Assyrian affairs in the son of Shamshi-Adad, Ashur-nāṣir-apli (Ashurnaṣirpal I) who ruled for nineteen years according to the King and Eponym Lists.[11] Regrettably, only a brief brick-inscription records the residence of the king in the palace which lay between the south-west front of the zikkurrat and the Anu-Adad temple in Ashur.[12] For him as for his predecessors, royal hymns were

---

[1] §vi, 5, 206.       [2] §vi, 4, 177; G, 8, 1, Tf. 33.
[3] G, 20, 308 and pl. xviii.
[4] G, 16, ii, 77.       [5] G, 1, 145.       [6] G, 14, 1, §344b.
[7] §vi, 8, 323.       [8] G, 10, 220.       [9] G, 1, 145.
[10] G, 4, 150 f.; G, 14, 1, §343; §iii, 12, 98 (no. 222); G, 16, ii, 79.
[11] G, 17, 9. If the Ashurnaṣirpal who may have been the murderer of Tukulti-Ninurta is counted as holding the throne (see above, p. 449), then this was the second ruler of Assyria to bear this name. §vi, 15, 21, iv, 4.
[12] G, 8, 1, 214; G, 14, 1, §345.

composed. One of these implies that he had been born in exile
and suffered from some dire disease for which he implored the
help and healing of Ishtar of Nineveh.[1] If the historical allusions
in these later compositions may be trusted the land had been
subject to invasion and the cult overthrown only to be restored
by this king who duly gives thanks to his protecting goddess. If
a much defaced 'white obelisk' is attributed to this Ashurnaṣirpal,
rather than to the later Assyrian ruler of the same name, it would
be proof of vigorous and successful military activity on a wide
front, aimed to restore the border in the eastern hills. But
this ascription has been doubted.[2] The succession of his son,
Shalmaneser II, who ruled for twelve years,[3] supports the view
that at this time the régime was not only strong enough to withstand outside pressures but was already able to take the first steps
to make Assyria once more a dominant power. This is seen more
clearly when their descendant Adad-nīrāri II and his successors
defeated the Amorites and reopened the traditional trade-routes;
but at present all this can only be surmised from the unbroken
line of rulers known from the official lists, but of whom few, if
any, other records remain. Shalmaneser himself tells of work
done on the temple of Anu and the temple of Adad at Ashur.[4]
He was followed by Ashur-nīrāri IV (1019–1014),[5] Ashurrabi
II (1013–973),[6] Ashur-rēsha-ishi II (972–968)[7] and Tiglath-
pileser II (967–935).[8]

Meanwhile in Babylonia the equally long-lived Isin dynasty
was coming to an end. In this, according to the King List
tradition, eleven kings ruled for a total of $132\frac{1}{2}$ years. This is
itself a testimony of stability in an age when no single major
power dominated the political scene throughout the Near East.
The activities of the last two kings of this line are little attested.
Marduk-ahhē-erība, whose name implies that he was not the
eldest son, ruled for a year and six months (1046–1045) as a
contemporary, according to the Synchronistic Chronicle, of
Ashur-bēl-kala of Assyria.[9] His relationship with his predecessor
and successor is undefined in the solitary *kudurru*-inscription
which simply calls him 'king'. He gave instructions to district
governors in the north-eastern province of Bīt-Piri'-Amurri which

[1] G, 16, II, 109; §IX, 7, 107, 358; §VI, II, 72 ff.
[2] §IX, 10, 243, n. 16. [See now E. Sollberger in *Iraq* 36 (1974), 231 ff. (Ed.)]
[3] G, 14, 1, §346 f.; G, 16, II, 80 f.    [4] §III, 1, 23 f. (nr. 14); G, 19, 1, 303.
[5] G, 21, 71; G, 17, 9 (ll. 21); §VI, 15, 21 (iv, 18 ff.).    [6] G, 17, 10, 17.
[7] G, 17, 10 (ll. 25 f.); §III, 1, 22 (nr. 12); G, 14, 1, §348.    [8] §III, 1, nr. 11.
[9] G, 18, 273 (Assur 14616c, ii, 22'; cf. King List A, iii, 2').

was thus still under firm Babylonian control.[1] For his successors we have but the evidence of the King Lists; Marduk-zēr-[x] who ruled for twelve years (1044–1033)[2] and was in his turn succeeded for eight years by Nabu-shumu-libur whose name and titles are also found on an inscribed duck-weight.[3]

## VII. THE SECOND SEALAND AND BAZI DYNASTIES

The ruling house which followed the Second Dynasty of Isin is designated 'ruling succession of the Sealand' in the King List A. This comprised three chiefs who held the throne of Babylon for 21 years and 5 months.[4] It is common to designate this the Second Sealand Dynasty to distinguish it from the earlier family, sprung from the same Persian Gulf tribes, who under Gulkishar had dominated the whole of Babylonia.[5] The Sealand was the title of an administrative province which had owed a loyal, if loose, allegiance to Babylon for more than a century and a half.[6]

Simbar-Shikhu, founder of the Dynasty reigned for eighteen years (1024–1007).[7] It is unlikely that his name can imply a Kassite renaissance for he was the son of Erība-Sin, a military captain who as 'a man of the ruling-line of Damiq-ilishu' may have claimed remote descent from the First Isin Dynasty.[8] According to Nabu-apla-iddina this predecessor had searched in vain for the reliefs and insignia of the deity among the ruins of E-babbar, the temple of Shamash at Sippar, which had been sacked by the Sutu raiders. This would seem to imply that the temple-furnishings were thought not to have been looted. He tells how Simbar-Shikhu, failing to rediscover the earlier cult-statue, built a new enclosure and re-established regular offerings and ceremonies under a priest Ekur-shuma-ushabshi.[9] He also dedicated a throne for Enlil (Marduk) in E-kur at Nippur.[10] As would be expected he continued to hold the Gulf area and this is shown by an inscription of his twelfth year dated at the town of

---

[1] §IV, 2, 149; §IV, 5, 188 f.
[2] A, 3, 146; G, 21, ii, 23'; G, 18, 273 (King List A, iii, 3').
[3] G, 21, 66 f. (14616c, ii, 24'); cf. G, 18, 272 (King List A, iii, 4'); A, 3, 147.
[4] G, 18, 272 (King List A, iii, 9).  [5] §I, 7, 83, 6; cf. G, 13, II, 22, r. 11.
[6] G, 18, 272 (King List A, iii, 6); G, 13, II, 61, l. 12; §VII, 2, 30.
[7] The reading '18' as opposed to '19' is supported by recent collation of the text (G, 3, 92, n. 12).
[8] G, 13, II, 61 (Religious Chronicle, i, 16'); §VII, 2, 28 f. See now A, 3, 151.
[9] G, 12, 121 f., ll. 1–23.  [10] A, 7, 122; G, 13, II, 61, 13'.

Sakhritu in the marshes when a private transaction for land was witnessed, among others by a tax-collector from Kissik and Ea-mukīn-zēri, son of Belani, a priest from Eridu.[1] Two texts, if rightly assigned to this reign, would give glimpses of far different activities. Ashurnaṣirpal II of Assyria, campaigning against Zamua 250 years later tells how he restored the town of Atlila which had been razed by one 'Sibir, king of Karduniash'. If this should be this Simbar-Shikhu, rather than a ruler of the little-known eighth dynasty, it would seem that he must have continued the strategy of his predecessors to contain the hill tribes to the north-east.[2] The Religious Chronicle records an eclipse of the sun associated with abnormal floods and incursions of wild animals on the twenty-sixth day of Siwan of the seventh year of an unnamed king who ruled at least seventeen years.[3] Calculations point to this reign as a possibility (9 May 1012 B.C.), but absence of other supporting evidence makes it a tentative rather than fixed chronological point in the history.[4] Simbar-Shikhu died by the sword and 'was buried in the Palace of Sargon' which phrase may indicate an honourable funeral at the royal mauso-leum.[5] It was probably the act of an assassin, since his successor Ea-mukīn-zēri is called a usurper from Bīt-Khashmar.[6] He was buried in the swamps of his native country after a brief reign of three or five months.[7] Since his home was probably in the south his identity with the priest of Eridu named six years earlier is not improbable, as is the view that he may have met his death in the suppression of a rising.[8] His tenure of office appears to have been too brief for notice in the Ashur chronicle.

Kashshu-nādin-akhi, son of Sappaia, may have led the oppo-sition to Ea-mukīn-zēri and, since he was given a royal burial after a three-year reign (1006–1004), it may be presumed that he was of the ruling family. This may be supported by the refer-ence to him by Nabu-apla-idinna, over a century later, when describing the varying fortunes of E-babbar of Sippar. 'During the distress and famine under Kashshu-nādin-akhi those regular food-offerings were discontinued and the drink-offerings ceased' until restored by E-ulmash-shākin-shumi, his successor (1003–987).[9]

The new family to direct the fortunes of Babylonia for the next

---

[1] G, 12, 101 f.

[2] G, 4, 325; cf. G, 11, 258, n. 2; A, 3, 154.    [3] G, 13, 1, 213, 11, 70 f.

[4] §vii, 4, 106; G, 11, 237, n. 3; A, 3, 68, n. 345.    [5] G, 2, 187, ii, 5′–6′.

[6] This must differ from the Khash(i)mar located in the north-east of Babylonia (§1, 1, 94). On the name of Ea-mukīn-zēri (not -shumi), see G, 8, 11, 259.

[7] G, 18, 272 (King List A, iii, 7); cf. G, 13, 11, 52 (Dynastic Chronicle).

[8] G, 2, 187, n. 338.    [9] G, 12, 122, i, 24–ii, 17.

twenty years and three months came from Bīt-Bazi, which lay east of the Tigris, perhaps to the north-east in Lullu territory.[1] Members of this family had held high office under Marduk-nādin-ahhē.[2] The days were again marked by civil disturbances, perhaps due to famine and the consequent incursions by the neighbouring tribes from the deserts. With the conflicting statements of the King List A and Dynastic Chronicles which allot a span of seventeen and fifteen years respectively, the reign of E-ulmash-shākin-shumi is shrouded in obscurity. Nevertheless, he claimed to be 'king of the world', which formerly implied wide territorial assertions.[3] The religious devotion marked by his restoration of worship at Sippar seems to be tempered by the cryptic notes of the New Babylonian Chronicle—'within the shrine'—probably an indication of the failure to hold the New Year festival in Babylon in his fifth and fourteenth years.[4] This interruption in the ritual was usually the result of political instability. The king was buried in the palace at Kār-Marduk, which may have been the family seat since his successor, a member of the same tribe, held sway there.[5] Ninurta-kudurri-uṣur ruled for two full years as a contemporary of Ashur-rabi IV of Assyria.[6] He maintained the traditional practices of dedications to the main temples.[7] A later *kudurru*-text recounts a lawsuit in the second year of this king, in which he had awarded seven female slaves to Burusha, a jeweller, as recompense for the murder of one of his own slaves.[8]

Shirikti-Shuqamuna of Bazi 'exercised the kingship for three months', a time confirmed by a later extract Chronicle which, however, described him as brother of Nabu-kudurri-uṣur, probably an error for Ninurta-kudurri-uṣur whom he succeeded.[9] The Ashur Chronicle makes him the last king of the Bazi line and a contemporary of Ashur-rabi II of Assyria (1013–973).[10] The king was given a royal burial. Only brief references tell of his successor Mar-bīti-apla-uṣur. From them it appears that he was descendant of an Elamite family who ruled six years before

---

[1] For the location see G, 20, 208; cf. G, 2, 191. For the King List see G, 18, 272 (A, iii, 10); G, 13, 55 (Dynastic Chronicle, r. ii, 9 ff.).

[2] G, 12, 44, i, 30; A, 3, 160.

[3] The name is also written Ul-mash-shākin-shumi, see §VII, 1, 29; §II, 3, 160.

[4] G, 13, II, 61 f; A, 3, 611.          [5] G, 12, 58, 23 f.

[6] G, 18, 272 (King List A, iii, 11'), 273 (Synchronistic Chronicle, iii, 6); G, 13, II, 54 (Dynastic Chronicle, r. ii, 10'–11').

[7] As evidenced by the inscribed arrow heads (G, 3, 93; §II, 2, 160).

[8] G, 12, 57, 1–12.          [9] §VII, 3, 30.

[10] G, 18, 273 (Synchronistic Chronicle, iii, 7).

being 'buried in the Palace of Sargon'. Though there is no
evidence that he was also ruler of Elam at this time, it seems an
irony of fate that a person of such a race should be in control of
the country which for two centuries had striven to maintain its
independence of its eastern neighbours. In Nisan of his fourth
year some unspecified event occurred which, like that noted for
previous kings, may be a mark of the failure to maintain the New
Year festival.[1] With his passing the period of uncertainty and of
brief reigns, indicative of internal dissensions, gave way to the
stable rule of Nabu-mukīn-apli (977–942) who inaugurated the
'eighth' Dynasty at Babylon. Despite continuing pressures from
Aramaean raiders the new government in Babylon was strong
enough to maintain order among the southern tribes, as had the
preceding régimes. This stability in the southern state in turn
left Assyria free to rebuild her own forces, to regain her hold over
western Asia, and later to attempt to assert control over Babylon
itself and her neighbouring sacred cities.

## VIII. LAW AND ADMINISTRATION

The few surviving Babylonian administrative documents, mainly
*kudurru*-inscriptions, confirm this general picture of the country
unified under the king during the twelfth and eleventh centuries.
As with the language, religion and customs, so the administrative
machinery continued unchanged between the Kassite and Isin
régimes. The land was divided into at least twenty small districts
or provinces (*pāḫatu*), each with a local government responsible
directly to the king in Babylon. The areas were named after the
principal city within them (Babylon, Dūr-Kurigalzu, Isin, Nippur)
or after hereditary tribal lands (Bīt-Piri'-Amurri, Bīt-Sin-māgir)
and the provinces stretched from the Persian Gulf (Sealand) to
the Lesser Zab (Namar, Irria and Bīt-Ada). Since the majority
lay to the north of Nippur it would seem that the southern marshes
were sparsely inhabited as in later times.

The governor (*šaknu*) could be posted at the king's direction
and was the normal channel for royal commands reaching his
secretary or the lesser officials responsible for law and order, the
collection of taxes and control of public works, mainly irrigation.[2]
In the remoter regions and on the border with Elam tribal chiefs
made nominal acknowledgement of the royal suzerainty and held
office as independent governors. The king, the final authority

[1] G, 13, 1, 185 f. (New Babylonian Chronicle).
[2] §VIII, 1, 328 lists these functionaries and the older designations now obsolete.

and court of appeal, made frequent grants of land. If crown-land
it might be used to reward outstanding service in battle or
endow a temple and its officials. Such grants were made by
charter or by instruments drawn up locally on the instructions of
the king. The land was carefully surveyed and recorded, and,
though usually granted in perpetuity, private land could revert
to the crown.[1] Land was also owned by individual temples,
cities, villages, and tribes as well as by private individuals, and
if the king wished to grant such land he had first to purchase it.
The king personally heard litigants and ordered investigations
into the precedents of each case. From Ur to the Lesser Zab and
from Rapiqu in the west to the mountains in the north-east there
was stable government broken only by the relatively infrequent
incursions of the enemy across the border.[2]

Similarly, economic texts of the eponym year of Sin-Sheya show
that in the reign of Ninurta-tukulti-Ashur the Assyrian king
controlled affairs through the central government at his royal
palace in Ashur. At Nineveh Iqīshanni collected provisions from
neighbouring towns (Khalahhi and Isana) and dispatched them
to the capital.[3] The *abarakku*-intendant of Amasaki, south of the
Ṭūr 'Abdīn, and the town-governors of Nakhur,[4] Arbail and
Arrapkha also sent supplies from their predominantly agricultural
communities.[5] While there is yet no evidence of the elaborate
provincial organization which was the basis of the later Assyrian
economy and colonial expansion this now existed in embryo,
since Shalmaneser I had incorporated Khanigalbat into Assyrian
home territory. Frontier posts were established and the governors
on whom fell responsibility for the imposition and collection
of taxes and the disposition of prisoners of war were responsible
to the king as in the days of Tukulti-Ninurta.

Royal edicts formulated since the time of Ashur-uballiṭ were
collected by Tiglath-pileser I and, with regulations for the harim
and court at Ashur, show a long tradition found also among the
Hittites. The king as overseer of the royal household held
authority over his subordinates in written agreements. Tiglath-
pileser also continued and copied the legal traditions of the preceding centuries, and it would seem that he was no legal reformer
or innovator.[6] A series of laws and legal decisions compiled in
his reign show that as the ultimate authority his 'word' was
final. The laws which relate in particular to the status, rights and

[1] §I, 7, 83, i, 15.      [2] §VIII, I, 236.
[3] E. F. Weidner, *Arch. f. O.* 10 (1935–6), 15.
[4] §VIII, 5, 109, 10.      [5] §I, 13, 16 f.      [6] §VIII, 14, 258.

duties of women and land tenure applied to the city of Ashur and its environs and to 'Assyrian' men and women. This compilation, incorporating earlier material, shows marked contrasts with the laws of Hammurabi, which were also copied by the scribes of this period.[1] In addition to the usual form of marriage by which a woman left her father's for her husband's family there was an *erebu*-marriage by which a woman could remain with her own tribe or family to be visited there by her husband.[2] This non-Semitic custom reflects the mixed population and customs in Assyria at this time, as does the levirate type of marriage, known from the Hurrians of Nuzi in the fifteenth century and practised on a more extensive scale in Assyria than among the Hebrews during these same centuries. By this, after the death of her husband or fiancé, a woman would be given in marriage by her father-in-law to another of his sons or family. Other customs, including the right of the first-born to a double share of the inheritance, as evidenced in the west at Alalakh and Mari, still survived, as did the old Babylonian class distinctions of freeman, state-dependent and slave.[3] Semi-free men (*ḫupšu*) were required to engage in the militia and their personal names attest the continued virility of this social group in Assyria as in the west with its Semitic or non-Semitic elements.

In general the laws, like the few surviving administrative texts, imply a period of stable government over a predominantly agricultural community. Penalties, apart from death, trial by river ordeal and physical mutilation already enforced in old Babylonian days, included hard labour for the State and payment of heavy fines. The latter were payable in tin or lead, at this time a more common means of exchange than silver or gold. This emphasizes the importance of the campaigns directed to safeguard the trade-routes to the north.[4] If the stamped roundels bearing an Ishtar-symbol found at Ashur were used for this purpose they would be the forerunners of a more highly advanced form of currency.[5]

Until the reign of Ninurta-tukulti-Ashur the old Assyrian calendar was in general use, but by this time the omission of intercalated months, the lack of reference to month subdivisions or *ḫamuštum*-periods of five or ten days and the commencement of the new eponymy coinciding with the beginning of the month

---

[1] §VIII, 2, 4 f.; G, 2c, 319.
[2] [For a contrary view, see now G. Cardascia, *Les Lois assyriennes* (Paris, 1969), 63 ff. (Ed.)]
[3] §VIII, 13, 122.
[4] G, 20, 324 and pl. XIV *d*.
[5] §VIII, 10, 4 f.

Sippu, led to obvious calendric confusion.[1] The Assyrian year, like that of the Babylonians, now began at the spring equinox and their calendars coincided. By the time of Tiglath-pileser I the old month names were already virtually displaced by those of the Babylonian (Nippur) calendar,[2] whether as a conscious innovation by the Assyrians or owing to the gradual insistence of traders and Babylonian-trained scribes is not known.

The Assyrians continued without interruption to date their years by the name and style of leading officials in rotation.[3] In this eponym-system the king gave his name to the first full year of his administration and, if still occupying the throne, again in his thirtieth year (as did Tiglath-pileser II).[4] This may imply, as in Egypt, a periodical renewal of kingship.

In Babylonia also, these centuries are marked by a continuity of legal tradition, despite changes in the ruling houses. No collections of laws or legal decisions have survived,[5] but the few indications of the Middle Babylonian legal procedure seem to imply the same general tradition as revealed by the laws of Hammurabi, as when Nebuchadrezzar I claimed the title of 'upright king who passes just judgments'. Practices and penalties varied with local circumstances though decisions made by one king could be upheld by successors even though they were of a different family.[6]

## IX. LITERATURE, RELIGION AND THE ARTS

In literature, as in law, the Assyrians continued older traditional forms. Babylonian influence predominated and there were few innovations. The Kassites had given a new impetus to historical inquiry and literary composition in what has been described as the last great creative period of Babylonian literature. Throughout the fourteenth and thirteenth centuries the Assyrians continued to employ scribes trained in Babylonia.[7] Tukulti-Ninurta I had used the occasion of his sack of Babylon to increase the small number of original texts of the Hammurabi–Kassite period in his possession.[8] These, supplemented by collections of omens, hymns, prayers and lexicographical texts made in the earlier reign of Shalmaneser I, were the basis of the library built up in the Ashur temple at Ashur by Tiglath-pileser I while crown-prince,

[1] §i, 13, 28; G, 9, 92, n. 18.    [2] §i, 13, 27; §viii, 7, 46.
[3] §v, 9, 283.    [4] §viii, 11, 456; C.A.H. i³, pt. 1, p. 199.
[5] The 'seisachtheia' (§viii, 6) being now dated to the Old Babylonian period. Government by royal edict, however, continued.
[6] G, 12, 29 f. (i, 6').    [7] G, 9, 109.    [8] §v, 8, 199.

with accessions during his later successful career.[1] Among the literary works were copies of the tales of Tukulti-Ninurta, the 'Babylonian Job' (*ludlul bēl nēmeqi*), the Etana myth, and other classical epics which had been composed under the Kassites or their contemporaries. This literary activity may have been occasioned by some desire to preserve the different traditions at other temple-schools which were now dominated by Babylon itself. The 'authors' were royal scribes, some of whom claimed descent from the learned Arad-Ea who flourished at Babylon in the fourteenth century or earlier.[2] The 'Babylonian Theodicy', in which a sufferer and his friend discuss current oppression is a document of social interest. It may reflect a conflict of political and religious ideologies caused by the times of economic stress resulting from the Aramaean incursions. There is evidence that this text, in its present form, was composed by Saggil-kinam-ubbib, a scholar of Babylon contemporary with the Aramaean usurper Adad-apla-iddina.[3] Since few literary works of this period have survived, the tendency is to hail them, being of high merit, as a literary revival. Certainly the account of Nebuchad-rezzar I's victories over Elam and the highly poetic descriptions in his royal inscriptions and *kudurru* are noteworthy.[4] Although not strictly in the same genre as the royal hymns of the Third Ur and First Babylonian dynasties, the recrudescence of hymnography in the time of Nebuchadrezzar I,[5] Ashur-bēl-kala and Ashur-naṣirpal I may similarly have served to clarify separate traditions at Babylon and Ashur.[6]

The political and geographical history underlines the fact that Assyria more than Babylonia was the meeting-place of various traditions. How far the literature, as art, was given a new life by intercourse with the Hittites is hard to judge. Assyrian epigraphy shows that the large and distinctive square hand of the north and west is now refining under Babylonian influence. From at least the reign of Arik-dēn-ili the accumulation of personal details was the first step to prose writing in historical annals.[7] In the military and hunting narratives this development was taken further by Tiglath-pileser I, who was in this respect closely followed by Ashur-bēl-kala.[8] This style has often been attributed to the Hittites, but is as likely to be Babylonian, since the Chronicles presuppose the existence of detailed and continuous

[1] §v, 8, 197.                                    [2] §ix, 14, 2, 9 f., 112.
[3] §ix, 16, 14, 1; §ix, 15, 71; A, 3, 141: (Esagil-kini-ubba).
[4] E.g. G, 12, no. 6.        [5] §ix, 7, nos. 107, 358.        [6] §ix, 12, 113.
[7] G, 20, 335.                              [8] G, 1, 125; §viii, 8, 169 f.

historical records. The Assyrian royal inscriptions would seem to have preserved for us the style of the Babylonian court and scribal schools.[1] This too may mean that the Assyrian court relied upon Babylonian scribes or Assyrian scribes who wrote in a local dialect of Middle Babylonian.

As with literature new religious, as distinct from traditional, trends are hard to judge in the absence of dated religious texts from this period. The onomastic material in the Middle Assyrian contracts may reflect the rise and fall of different members of the pantheon in the northern kingdom. This shows a growing cosmopolitanism accompanying the renewed expansion of the Assyrian Empire. While Ashur as supreme national god supplants the Babylonian Marduk in the local version of the Epic of Creation, Adad as the god of conquest with universal affiliations (like the Hurrian Teshub) appears side by side with him in the twelfth-century texts.[2] Hurrian influences became more pronounced in the thirteenth–twelfth centuries than in the preceding period and Hurrian names are held by persons in all walks of life. Babylonian influence too may be seen in that names compounded with the moon-god Sin are more popular than those with the sun-deity Shamash.[3] This may reflect Babylonian religious and magical ceremonies which were practised in the north without interruption despite hostilities.[4] The New Year festival honouring Marduk at Ashur was no slavish copy of its Babylonian counterpart but an adaptation to local feeling.[5]

In Babylonia, following the Kassites who had accepted the local Babylonian language, religion and customs, Kassite local deities, as Erriya and Shuqamuna and Shimaliya—the creator gods—and Tishpak of Dēr were invoked alongside native Mesopotamian deities. There is some evidence of a gradual change to a monotheistic tendency with the rise to national supremacy of a local southern deity, Marduk. Adad-shuma-uṣur nominated Marduk to second place after Anu and Enlil from a position among the lower group of deities in the official pantheon. Marduk-apla-idinna I, who rebuilt E-zida in Borsippa, was followed by at least six kings who bore this divine name. This shows that even before the unusual popularity accorded to Marduk after his restoration by Nebuchadrezzar I to E-sagila in Babylon from captivity in Elam he had been an influential god.[6] It is in the official documents of Nebuchadrezzar I that Marduk's kingship over the gods and exaltation over Enlil, reflected in the editions of the

---

[1] §VIII, 9, 159.   [2] G, 9, 103.   [3] G, 9, 105.
[4] §IX, 8, vol. 20, 399 ff.   [5] §IX, 13, 192.   [6] §IX, 17, 8, 10.

literary epics composed in these centuries, are clearest seen.[1]  It is, however, likely that a tendency to view gods as remote from men had been present for some time, for at the end of the Old Babylonian period cylinder seals sometimes omit any representation of the deity, as does the altar of Tukulti-Ninurta I. In Middle Assyrian art gods, when rarely represented, are set on a pedestal or, as Ashur, partly invisible in the clouds of his heavenly winged-disk. A distinction was made between the deity himself and his statue. Art and literature combine to emphasize the numinous in religion, and symbols have again particular importance and attraction especially in their protective value, enhancing the traditional curses against anyone who should violate the agreements recorded on the *kudurru*-stones.[2]

The architecture of these centuries also illustrates the new religious tendency. In the temples the gods were set on high niches or platforms approached by steps from a long cella entered from the side, emphasizing their remoteness from human affairs. Tiglath-pileser I restored both the Old Palace and a New Palace, founded by Tukulti-Ninurta I who used the material and human booty of his numerous campaigns, the triumphs of which were thus permanently enshrined. In the doorways representations of victories in the hunting of unusual creatures as well as of bull-colossi show the development of an early Babylonian trend which was to become more common in the Neo-Assyrian palaces. The mainly decorative murals from the palace of Kār-Tukulti-Ninurta—scenes of the hunt and of war in mountainous terrain, the small reliefs of the 'Broken Obelisk', depicting the king and his vanquished foes, like those on the earlier altar of Tukulti-Ninurta I—these already show a distinctive Assyrian style.[3] This was, in part, a development from earlier Hurrian *motifs*, perhaps inspired by renewed contacts with these northern peoples and their descendants. Since their art-forms are often akin to those of the more easterly Kassites it is difficult to attribute the sources of influence with any certainty. This also applies to the locally adapted technique of lead-glazed pottery, glazing, painted and glazed bricks used for façades at this time. This may be of Hurrian origin[4] but, like the contemporary Kassite examples in Babylonia which were imitated during these centuries, both may be but local offshoots from a single and earlier development.

In sculpture the fine modelling of the figures on the Tukulti-

[1] §IX, 16, 4 f.; §IX, 17, 6.    [2] G, 12, viii.    [3] See Plates 155, 162(*a*).
[4] Less likely Egyptian or Cypriote (G, 20, 332).

Ninurta socket as on the better examples of the Babylonian *kudurrus* would point to no diminution in skill following the renaissance of art, as of literature and architecture, which began with that Assyrian king.[1] The rare examples of the glyptic art on dated documents of the period show, however, that Assyria continued to be the home of mixed traditions. The formally presented bearded figures between borders and long dedicatory inscriptions were common in Babylonia in Kassite times. Other seals continued the thirteenth-century styles of contest scenes, mostly of single combat, originally derived from Mitannian glyptic. Babylonian influences can be seen in the full-faced sphinxes and heroes holding lions.[2] By this time figures were carefully modelled with that emphasis on the muscles which was to remain an abiding feature of Assyrian art.[3] The incidental elements, as for example the trees, are transformed into landscapes giving the effect of relief—a realistic tendency found in the contemporary art of Egypt and the Aegean. In the twelfth century the remnant of the earlier Akkadian and Kassite styles gradually gave way to larger seals on which the taller figures and heavier modelling led to the omission of detail and loss of the landscape effect.[4]

The favourite scenes of the period are those of animal life or of the hunt as on the seal of Ninurta-tukulti-Ashur.[5] This may reflect renewed interest in the royal ritual and hunt and, since they are set in mountainous country which was the scene of the major campaigns, in the national fortunes. Court scenes also reappear as do other examples of earlier styles, the Early Dynastic 'textile friezes',[6] Mitannian stylized trees and eagle-headed men fighting bulls or centaurs.[7] Alongside the modelled style shallow, yet precisely, cut seals were in use. Few seals can be definitely assigned to Babylonia in these two centuries, but the dated *kudurru* show unmistakably that in the southern kingdom the arts must have flourished as vigorously as among their northern neighbours. If this long period is still little known, there is sufficient evidence extant to show that, despite occasional internal dissension or pressure from outside, the natural vigour of the inhabitants of Assyria and Babylonia was unabated. Politically, economically and culturally the way was already being prepared for that expansion of territory and influence which was to mark the high point of Assyrian civilization in the following three centuries.

[1] See Plate 155(c).  [2] §IX, 18, 50 ff.; §IX, 19, 23 f.
[3] G, 20, 330, pl. XXXI.  [4] §IX, 22, 67. See Plate 156(a)–(c).
[5] §IX, 21, 49. See Plate 156(d).  [6] §IX, 9, 191.  [7] §IX, 19, 25.

# CHAPTER XXXII

## ELAM AND WESTERN PERSIA,
### *c.* 1200–1000 B.C.

### I. SHUTRUK-NAHHUNTE AND KUTIR-NAHHUNTE

WITH the disappearance of Kidin-Khutran the internal history of Elam seems to have witnessed several political disturbances. The later native sources mention, after him, a certain Khallutush-In-Shushinak not as the successor of Kidin-Khutran but as the father of the king Shutruk-Nahhunte. As no reference is made to any parental ties between this Khallutush-In-Shushinak and one of the sovereigns of the preceding dynasty, nor to his own reign, there is no reason to suppose that he belongs to the royal line or that he ever held power. We are therefore obliged to admit a break in the dynastic line between Kidin-Khutran and Shutruk-Nahhunte. This break can be explained only by supposing that a new line of princes took control, aided by internal troubles of the times. Whence came this family? This cannot be decided from the texts. The only hint we have is onomastic. Whereas the names of sovereigns of the previous dynasty were particularly devoted to Khumban and Khutran, the name of Khallutush-In-Shushinak and those of at least two of his successors were placed under the patronage of the god of Susa. One can suppose that this choice of In-Shushinak as patron god perhaps indicates that this new royal house was somehow linked with Susiana.

However this may be, one thing is certain—with the reign of Shutruk-Nahhunte begins one of the most glorious periods in Elamite history. During a space of almost seventy years five kings succeed to the throne: Shutruk-Nahhunte, Kutir-Nahhunte, Shilkhak-In-Shushinak, Khutelutush-In-Shushinak and Silkhina-khamru-Lakamar; the first three of these at least were destined to win fame. Their personal qualities were to make Elam one of the greatest military powers in the Middle East for a period lasting over fifty years. This Elamite renaissance was aided by a fortunate juncture of international conditions. With the tragic death of Tukulti-Ninurta I (1208) came a

---

\* An original version of this chapter was published as fascicle 23 in 1964.

sudden decline in Assyrian military power, and the country was torn by internal troubles. For several years two kings, each supported by his own faction, struggled for mastery. These struggles continued after them, and were exploited by the Babylonians, whose king Adad-shuma-uṣur (1218–1189) laid siege to Ashur and fought against the Assyrian king Enlil-kudurri-uṣur (1197–1193). During these hostilities another Assyrian prince Ninurta-apil-Ekur (1192–1180), until that time an exile in Babylon, seized the Assyrian throne[1] and reigned with the support of the Babylonian king, who had made Assyria into a kind of protectorate. The Assyrians at that time had not—nor had the Babylonians—leisure to take any interest in Elam. The western frontier of Assyria was threatened by the Mushki, and the Aramaean danger in Upper Mesopotamia was becoming more and more pressing.

It was not until 1160 that the new king of Assyria, Ashur-dan I, thought that Assyria was strong enough to take up an aggressive foreign policy again. He threw off Babylonian domination by a raid on Babylonia which was not revenged by its king Zababa-shuma-iddina. But the Assyrian had counted too much upon his strength, for he was unable to push back the Mushki who had crossed the frontiers and installed themselves on the upper Tigris. The weakness of Babylonia and Assyria was thus revealed. Elam under the leadership of capable and energetic kings could take advantage of this situation, first to establish their new strength, and then to wait for a favourable time when they could intervene decisively in Mesopotamia.

Our sources from Mesopotamia at this period are a fragmentary chronicle, a detail from a letter and a few other texts which must be used with caution. These do, however, give us several important synchronisms. We know hereby that Shutruk-Nahhunte was the contemporary of the Babylonian kings Zababa-shuma-iddina (1160) and Enlil-nādin-akhi (1159–1157) as well as the Assyrian king Ashur-dan I (1179–1134). They also inform us that the last years of Khutelutush-In-Shushinak coincide with the beginning of the reign of Nebuchadrezzar I (1124–1103).

The native sources from Elam are more numerous and more varied in nature than those of earlier periods. To the foundation bricks can be added not only the inscriptions engraved on numerous war trophies that the Elamite conquerors brought back to Susa, but the detailed inscriptions engraved on stelae, which enumerate their peaceful operations as well as lists of foreign

[1] §1, 7, 131.

countries and cities which they conquered  It is unfortunate that our knowledge of the Elamite language, still very imperfect, does not allow us fully to understand these texts.

For the few years preceding the reign of Shutruk-Nahhunte we know practically nothing about the happenings in Elam, but can suppose that the Elamites were not satisfied with being simple spectators of a drama preluded by the violent death of Tukulti-Ninurta I. It is not possible to say whether the Elamites instigated or had anything to do with the plot that Ashur-nādin-apli, with part of the Assyrian nobility, laid against his father, depriving him first of liberty and then of life.

However this may be, the Babylonians, when Shutruk-Nah-hunte ascended the throne, were looking for means of profiting from the state of affairs in Assyria and were not, therefore, much interested in Elam. It was during this calm period that he estab-lished his authority and made Susa the recognized capital of the new empire. Probably with this in mind he brought to Susa various stelae left in different parts of the kingdom by his pre-decessors, and solemnly dedicated them to his god In-Shushinak. One of the stelae, the work of Untash-(d)GÁL, probably came from Chogha-Zanbil.[1] Another, which came from Anzan where it had been set up by a king whose name he admits not to have known, had its itinerary minutely described in another inscription. The following stages in the journey are mentioned: perhaps the districts (?) of Kutkin and Nakhutir, and certainly the cities Dūr-Untash, on the river Khitkhite, and Tikni.[2] Another docu-ment of special importance mentions a third stele which was brought from Aia.[3] The collecting of these, until then dispersed, monuments of Elamite history seems to show the centralist tendencies of Shutruk-Nahhunte and his desire to make the city of In-Shushinak the political and religious centre of the kingdom. Despite this he had temples built in all the principal cities of the kingdom.

He constantly excited, in all respects, Elamite nationalism by pointing out the unity of the empire as well as its lasting tradition. It was undoubtedly this desire that caused him, when he restored the temple of the goddess Manzat, to collect and place next to his own the foundation-bricks of his predecessors who had already done work on this sanctuary.[4] Parallel to this, in the political sphere, he carried on his work of unification and pacifica-tion. He imposed his authority even in the far-removed parts of

[1] G, 8, 52, no. 21.                    [2] G, 8, 52, no. 20.
[3] G, 8, 54, no. 28.                    [4] G, 1, no. 42; G, 8, 86, no. 63; §1, 2.

the kingdom; he was able to subjugate the semi-nomads and obliged them to give back any booty they had taken. And he was no doubt justified in claiming to have been present and active in places where formerly Siwe-palar-khuppak, Pala-ishshan, Pakhir-ishshan and Attar-kittakh had left their marks, as well as in remote districts which none of his predecessors had known, and where his own name had not till then penetrated—such as Shali, Mimurasi, Lappuni, and others.[1]

Towards the south along the Persian Gulf his empire extended into the southernmost parts of Elam. At Liyan, on the island of Bushire,[2] one of his inscribed bricks has been found. In this inscription he boasts of having restored an ancient sanctuary dedicated to the goddess Kiririsha.[3] Susa, as would be expected, had a large share in his religious works. Besides the temple of Manzat he restored a temple dedicated to In-Shushinak which he decorated with baked bricks and possibly a hypostyle room. He offered stone basins for the cult of Sukhsipa as well as In-Shushinak.[4]

Having restored and consolidated the might of Elam, Shutruk-Nahhunte was ready to play an important part on the international scene. He had not to wait long. In Babylon Zababa-shuma-iddina (1160) had succeeded Marduk-apla-iddina on the throne. The new king was a weakling, incapable of maintaining Babylonian domination in Assyria. The Assyrian king, Ashur-dan I, had taken—as we have seen—Zaban, on the Lesser Zab, Irria and Ugarsallu from the Babylonians in 1160. This ineffectual victory which showed the weakness of both sides could only encourage the Elamite. He was all the more tempted because the lower Zab and the Diyālā represented a crucial zone for Elam itself. North and south of the Diyālā pass two important caravan roads which link the Mesopotamian plain to the Iranian plateau.

At the head of a large army Shutruk-Nahhunte and his son Kutir-Nahhunte invaded Mesopotamia. Several stelae, unfortunately in bad condition, record in Elamite the extent and the success of this campaign, as well as details about the tribute extracted from the conquered cities. A fragment of a stele[5] states that after having crossed the Kārūn river (the ancient Ulai) and stopped at Eli he captured many settlements, 700 before arriving at Mara, which is perhaps to be identified with Marriti,[6] and several hundreds more on the other side of Mara. Another fragment[7] gives a list of tributes which several large captured cities were

---

[1] G, 8, 54 f., no. 28; G, 2, 106, n. 26; G, 9, 332 b.    [2] See above, p. 405, n. 1.
[3] G, 8, 51, no. 19.        [4] §1, 5.        [5] G, 8, 56, no. 28 a.
[6] G, 16, 393.            [7] G, 8, 88, no. 67.

obliged to pay to the conqueror. It speaks of great sums paid in *minas* or talents of gold and silver, as well as deliveries of bricks and stone. The following places are mentioned: Eshnunna, Dūr-Kurigalzu, Sippar, Dūr-Shar[....], Opis and perhaps Agade, the name of which is partly broken.

To this evidence we can add other information derived from inscriptions upon spoils of war.[1] Shutruk-Nahhunte removed from Eshnunna two royal statues, one of which represented Manishtusu. From Sippar he took the fine sandstone stele celebrating Naram-Sin's victory over the Lullubi, and perhaps together with it the famous monument inscribed with the laws of Hammurabi. From the country called Karindash, probably the present Karind on the caravan-road from Baghdad to Kirmān-shāh, came a statue of the Kassite king Meli-Shikhu (1188–1174).[2] From another place, the name of which is lost—perhaps Kish—he took the obelisk of Manishtusu, and from Agade two statues of the same king.

Although the above information is probably incomplete it gives a fairly good picture of the zone in which Shutruk-Nah-hunte operated. The mention of Karindash, Eshnunna, Dūr-Kurigalzu, Opis and Dūr-Sharrukīn is very significant as they show that his attention was above all directed towards the lower Diyālā and the passes that commanded the area. He separated Babylonia from the north by cutting across the isthmus between the Tigris and the Euphrates near Sippar. After descending on Kish he had only to bring his campaign to a logical conclusion by the capturing of Babylon. He apparently did not encounter any important resistance despite his destructive progress. Even at Babylon he had no difficulty in bringing the one-year reign of Zababa-shuma-iddina (1160) to an abrupt end.

The collapse of Babylon now seemed irremediable, for Shu-truk-Nahhunte, unlike his predecessors, was not content with booty and prisoners, but decided to establish his authority in the country. To this end he set up his son Kutir-Nahhunte as gover-nor of the province he had conquered in Mesopotamia, and then went back to Susa where he dedicated the booty to his god In-Shushinak. It is probable that he died shortly afterwards, as he did not have time to complete all of the dedications that were to be inscribed on the various captured trophies. A vacant space hammered out on the stele of the Hammurabi laws still awaits the victor's inscription.

[1] G, 8, 52 f., nos. 22–7.
[2] On the reading of the name, see above, p. 444, n. 9.

Despite his successes Shutruk-Nahhunte left his work in Babylonia unfinished. National resistance, which Zababa-shuma-iddina had failed to head, soon took shape under a Kassite leader named Enlil-nādin-akhi, afterwards entitled 'king of Babylon' by the chroniclers who refused to recognize the Elamite usurper. It took Kutir-Nahhunte three years to overcome this opponent, and the struggle was so violent that it lived long in the memory of the vanquished. A later Babylonian ruler was thus to sum up the misdeeds of the intruder: 'His crimes were greater and his grievous sins worse than all his fathers had committed...like a deluge he laid low all the peoples of Akkad, and cast in ruins Babylon and all the noblest cities of sanctity.'[1]

This resistance lasted only for three years, at which time Kutir-Nahhunte captured Enlil-nādin-akhi and exiled him to Elam[2] where he probably died. The Kassite dynasty which had ruled for so many years came to an end with the death of Enlil-nādin-akhi. Babylonia became the vassal of Elam. After having deported[3] much of the population the Elamite imposed upon the country a governor who was not of native stock and detested the local gods.[4]

Marduk[5] and Nanā of Uruk, who were also victims of this defeat, were themselves deported to Susa. Marduk stayed in Elam only until the reign of Nebuchadrezzar I (1124–1103), but Nanā had to wait the victorious armies of Ashurbanipal.

When Shutruk-Nahhunte died, Kutir-Nahhunte succeeded him. It is possible that he exercised some part of the power with his father. We know that before succeeding to the throne he was responsible for the installation of decorative panels in the temple of In-Shushinak.[6] These panels,[7] forming a dado with recurring pattern, represent a monstrous figure, half-man half-bull, standing beside a stylized palm-tree, and the narrow outline of a woman with a thin triangular face; the scene is topped by a frieze. The general aspect of this[8] is reminiscent of the wall of the temple of Inanna at Uruk which was built during the fifteenth century by the Kassite king Karaindash.[9]

As king, Kutir-Nahhunte continued the decoration of his capital. One of his main occupations was the temple of In-

[1] §1, 7, 137 (K. 2660), obv. 4 ff.    [2] *Ibid.* obv. 12 f.
[3] *Ibid.* obv. 8.    [4] *Ibid.* obv. 14.
[5] *Ibid.* obv. 10.    [6] G, 8, 57, no. 29.
[7] This type of panel is known from other sites; see §1, 3, 123 ff.
[8] The difficult art of moulding these panels was possibly brought into Elam by Babylonian prisoners. The glazed bricks of Darius at Susa are in the same tradition.
[9] §1, 1, plates 15–17.

Shushinak wherein he had a statue of himself placed. These works were not finished during his reign and it was his successor who was to complete them. He did have time to restore a chapel dedicated to the goddess Lakamar at Susa, and a chapel dedicated to Kiririsha by Khumban-numena was restored at Liyan. The inscription relating the restoration asks the goddess to bless his life as well as that of his wife, Nahhunte-Utu, and his descendants.[1] When he died, *c.* 1140, he left a strong state with borders extending to Bandar-Bushire in the south and into the Mesopotamian plain on the west. But not all of Babylonia was his vassal, for to the south there were still some independent zones. At Isin a local chief was called king of Babylon and it was around him that the resistance to the Elamite invader formed.

## II. SHILKHAK-IN-SHUSHINAK

Shilkhak-In-Shushinak followed his brother Kutir-Nahhunte on the throne, and this reign was to be one of the most glorious periods in the history of Elam. His military expeditions to the north-west which went far beyond any of those of his predecessors, collected large quantities of booty. This flow of material and prisoners brought much wealth to Elam. With this Shilkhak-In-Shushinak was to begin a period of construction in Susa and the other cities of the country which surpassed anything done until that time. Local art was encouraged and flourished to a remarkable degree.

His authority was unquestioned and extended over the whole country. The desire to make himself the symbol of Elamite power and unity was more marked in him than any of the other kings. Although he was a fervent devotee of his personal god, In-Shushinak, he always invoked the gods of Susa, Anzan and Elam, as well as the unnamed hundreds of local protector-gods, with the same piety. He wanted his reign to be the culmination of Elamite history and himself to be the legitimate inheritor and continuer of all the dynasties, whether of Simash, Susa, Elam or Anzan. Whenever he restored a sanctuary he was very careful to add to his dedications the names of his predecessors who had restored the sanctuary before adding his own. The historical importance of these 'genealogical' inscriptions is evident.

It was above all in respect of his brother and immediate predecessor, Kutir-Nahhunte, that Shilkhak-In-Shushinak carried out his ideas on the continuation of Elamite tradition and royalty. He married his brother's widow, Nahhunte-Utu, to whom he ever

[1] G, 8, 57, nos. 29–31.

paid respect. With each of his pious works he asked the gods to bless her, and she, their children, and her children from her former marriage, were united in his prayers. He carried on the work started by his brother on the temple of In-Shushinak, and after finishing the temple he replaced in it the statue of his brother to which he added a special inscription.[1]

It is difficult to say whether his peaceful works or his victorious campaigns brought him the more renown, for he was both a great builder and a warrior. Thanks to several stelae inscribed in Elamite we know that there were many military campaigns during his reign; one inscription relates at least eight of these.[2] Although in bad condition, this is very important, for it lists the different cities and villages taken by Shilkhak-In-Shushinak and the different districts that he invaded. In the mutilated text only about a hundred of these names are left but in its original state the list must have contained nearly twice as many.

His first four campaigns must have been in a Semitic district to judge by the names of the villages captured. These are of the type *Sha-barbarē*, '(place) of the wolves', or *Bīt-nappaḫḫē*, 'house of the blacksmiths'. The only township which can perhaps be located is Bīt-Nakiru, which is possibly derived from the name of the tribe Nakri against which Tiglath-pileser III of Assyria later campaigned.

The next part of the text is in good condition. This campaign took him into the district of Ukarsilla-Epekh, probably made up of Ugarsallu, which Ashur-dan had just taken from his Babylonian rival, and the region around the mountain Ebekh, modern Jebel Ḥamrīn, which is not far from the point where the upper Diyālā is joined by its higher tributaries. Shilkhak-In-Shushinak captured thirty-one localities in this district, of which only the following names remain: Bīt-lassi, Bīt-Sin-shemi, Bīt-Etelli, Matka, Sha-khalla, Appi-sini-piti, Sha-arad-ekalli and Kiprat. A few villages cited before this paragraph possibly belong to the same district; they are, to list a few: Sellam, Tunni, Matku, Bīt-Sin-eriba and Bīt-Kadashman. These names are mostly Semitic with a few Kassite components.

The next campaign took Shilkhak-In-Shushinak further to the north-west. The name of the district is partially broken and only ...*tilla* is left. The Hurrian aspect of this suffix should be enough in itself to locate the district, but the mention of Arrapkha and Nuzu removes any doubt about where it is—the area around modern Kirkuk. Some of the other names are also known from

---

[1] G, 8, 63, no. 43.                    [2] G, 8, 74, no. 54.

other texts: Khanbati, Sha-nishē, Titurru-sha-... ('Bridge of ...'). As he took only eleven localities one may suppose that he did not want to spend too much time in an area so far removed from his home bases.

Next came an expedition on a larger scale, directed against four districts: Durun (Turnat), Ebekh, Shatrak-... and Yalman (Ḥulwan). He captured forty-one places the names of which are in part Kassite (Sha-purna-mashkhum) and in part Semitic (Bīt-Ishtar, Bīt-redūti—('small' and 'large'). Certain of the names indicate a cult of Babylonian deities (Bīt-Ishtar, Ishertu-sha-Adad, Bīt-rigim-Adad, ...ten-Sin). The name Reshu which is mentioned in this list is perhaps to be identified with the Aramaic tribe Rashi in the district of the Upper Karkhah which is mentioned later in a text of Sargon II.[1]

His following campaign was also very extended and traversed at least five districts. The names of these are completely lost except Yalman (Ḥulwan), which shows that the Elamite army went once again over a road it had already travelled. Some fifty townships were captured by the Elamites, and certain of these, known from other texts, allow us to trace various stages of this campaign: Murattash, which is located south of the Lesser Zab and between the mountains Asaniu and Atuma: also Tukhupuna, which is to the south of the river Turnat (Diyālā) and the mountains of Yalman. This area seems to have been inhabited by a rather mixed population, but its civilization was markedly Semitic. Many names of place begin with the Semitic *ša* 'of' or *bīt* 'house (of)', and the second element may indicate settlements purely Babylonian, such as Sha-Balikhu, Bīt-Sin-ishmanni, Bīt-barbarē, Bīt-khuppani, Bīt-Lakipu, or communities probably Kassite such as Bīt-Nashumalia, Bīt-Milshikhu, Bīt-tasak-*ESSANA*,[2] Bīt-Burra-khutta. Here and there, besides these, are grouped heterogeneous colonies in localities such as Nakhish-bararu, Sha-kattar-zakh, Anakhuttash, etc. Near the end of the list mention is made of Bīt-rigim-Adad, which had been captured during a previous campaign.

The name of the country next invaded cannot be determined but the village-names are clearly Semitic. All that remains of the district itself is ...-*uk*? -*li*? -*lir-kattar*. The last element of this name might recall the middle element of the name Sha-kattar-zakh

---

[1] If this identification is correct it is important for the history of the Aramaeans.

[2] The last element is the logogram 'king'; in what language should it be read? For the comparison of this name with *Bīt-Tassaki* of the annals of Tiglath-pileser III, see G, 5, 52 *b*.

in the previous list. The Elamites captured more than twenty places of which the following can be read with certainty: Bīt-nankari Tan-silam, Bīt-kunsu-pati, Pukhutu, Nakapu and Bīt-rapiku.

The following campaign also took place in a district which cannot be located as all that remains of the names is *Shi-*.... None of the twenty-six villages captured is known from other sources. Only a few of the names can be read with certainty: Kitan-Kharap, Bīt-[...]-kimil-Adad. Some of the others begin with *Bīt-* and one with *Nār-*, 'river'.

With the remains of a last list, where only *Kulāna* and a few others beginning with *Bīt-* can be read, end the victorious campaigns of Shilkhak-In-Shushinak beyond his borders, according to this account. These, however, were not his only campaigns, for new fragments of stelae mention others, in one of which the district of Khalman-Niri[puni?] was captured. This conquest was followed by another campaign during which the Elamites took fourteen localities, in a country the name of which is lost. Two other campaigns can also be discerned; one was in a region which included the district of Niripuni-Shurutukha and the other mentions the capture of the villages Makshia, Shakutu, Assie, Shakilka, Kishshimu and Talzana.[1]

Even a simple list of these geographical names is enough to show the intense military activity of Shilkhak-In-Shushinak. Guided by the localities that can be located we are able to see the strategy behind the king's military campaigns. He evidently wished to control the country between the Tigris and the Zagros which touched his northern borders. His capture of the upper Diyālā, the area around the Jebel Ḥamrīn and around Ḥulwan shows very clearly that he wished to control the route along which Elam could be invaded from the west. It is on this line that the modern Sharābān, Khānaqīn, Ḥulwan, Karind and Kirmānshāh are located.

After having neutralized the Aramaean tribes along the western bank of the Tigris he penetrated even further north. Here he followed another route which ran northward through the high country from Kifri by Kirkuk and Altın-Köprü towards Irbil. It is possible that one of the expeditions was designed to gain control of the Kirkuk area which was a sort of turn-table. Of the different routes that go out from this point the most important is the one leading into the heart of Assyria; but from a strategic point of view that leading through the mountains towards modern

[1] G, 8, 78 f., nos. 54*a* and *b*.

Sulaimaniyyah was even more important. The fact that he should push on as far as the lower Zab shows his desire to bring pressure to bear on Assyria; from this vantage-point the capital Ashur would be only a few days march away. We do not know whether or not the Elamites actually threatened Ashur, but the fact that a revolt, followed by troubles, brought to an end the long reign of Ashur-dan I (1134) seems to suggest that the presence of the Elamites near by was of some consequence in these events.

The one thing certain is that the region of the upper Diyālā was the centre of Elamite attention. It is therefore surprising to find that on another stele there seems to be mention of an expedition directed towards Babylonia.[1] It seemed that Babylonia had been crushed or at least neutralized by Shutruk-Nahhunte and Kutir-Nahhunte and that it was precisely this condition which allowed Shilkhak-In-Shushinak to concentrate his efforts on lands in which Assyria might have been his rival. This seems to show that in a few years there had occurred a noticeable change in Babylonia. Preoccupied with assuring his hold on the region between the Tigris and the Zagros, Shilkhak-In-Shushinak inevitably lost control of the Euphrates. As we have seen, the campaigns of Shutruk-Nahhunte and Kutir-Nahhunte succeeded in controlling only Agade and its immediate surroundings, not lower Mesopotamia. At Isin a new state came into being. This must have grown rapidly in power, for it was strong enough to interfere in Assyria[2] on behalf of one of the sons of Ashur-dan I when the latter died. One can imagine that this attempt to profit, without striking a blow, from the victories of the Elamites was not favourably received by Shilkhak-In-Shushinak, and that the campaign related on this stele was perhaps a reprisal against the Babylonians for their interference in Assyria.

He therefore crossed the Tigris and crushed the first Babylonian resistance on the other bank. Then after capturing the town of Khussi he swept on to the Euphrates, and marched up the river until he reached Nimitti-Marduk, which was perhaps one of the walled fortifications that protected the southern approaches to Babylon. Despite his boast of having once again defeated the enemy, he probably did not capture the city, as it is not mentioned again in the text. His return to Elam brings to an end all Elamite pretensions in Babylonia.

He was now faced by new, although less important, problems on his own borders. The Zagros was inhabited by tribes of warlike plunderers whose raids had to be chastised from time to time.

---

[1] G, 8, 79, no. 54*c*.　　　　　　　　　　　　[2] §II, 7.

Thus the tribe of Palakhutep had raided Elamite territory and carried off booty and prisoners. This tribe is later joined with the tribe Lallarippe in an inscription of the neo-Elamite king Temti-Khuban-In-Shushinak. If the name Lallarippe is derived from the name of the river Lallar, their homeland should be looked for somewhere in the country of Zamua, and that of the Palakhutep was perhaps in the same general area. Shilkhak-In-Shushinak immediately set out in pursuit of them. After having passed via Eli and Susa(?) he cut across Anzan and camped at Ulan and Sha-purna-mashkum. A break in the text does not allow us to follow the rest of the expedition but we know that the booty which the tribe had taken was brought back to Susa and dedicated to the god In-Shushinak.[1]

These expeditions, as well as others mentioned in fragments, come to a large number. The reign of Shilkhak-In-Shushinak must have been long if one considers that the number of campaigns conducted was at least twelve. It is however possible that not all of these were separate, some being perhaps only episodes in wider campaigns. One of the texts mentions the capture of Sha-purna-mashkum, which occurs again in the raid against the tribe Palakhutep. This could also be the case in the campaign where Bīt-rapiqu and KUN-Subbati were captured. If we allow that the former is identical with the Rapiqu mentioned in Assyrian texts as being just to the north of Babylon, and the latter as meaning the KUN of the Euphrates, then we could suppose that this text actually refers to the campaign against Babylonia.

Because of all of these campaigns, and despite the recession of Elamite power in Babylonia, Shilkhak-In-Shushinak merited the ancient title 'enlarger of the empire' of which he boasted in his inscriptions. His kingdom, which was well protected along the borders of the Zagros and in the north-west, extended beyond Anzan and Susiana to the eastern shores of the Persian Gulf. The important works undertaken by the king on the island of Bushire[2] show that his rule in this distant province was well established. That he controlled the inland areas as well as the coast can be seen by the material remains found in the fertile mountain plain between Rāmuz and Shīrāz.[3] Bricks with the name of Shilkhak-In-Shushinak were also found in the remains of a building on the plateau of the Mamasenni Lurs. But it is doubtful whether the Elamites ever went beyond this point on the plateau where later on Persepolis was to be built.[4]

[1] G, 8, 66, no. 46; cf. §II, 5, 18 ff., col. III, 9–22.  [2] See above, p. 405, n. I.
[3] §II, 4; §II, 3, 114.  [4] §II, 2; §II, I, 21 a; G, 9, 333 b.

### III. ELAMITE CIVILIZATION, *c.* 1125 B.C.

All of these territories, despite their cultural differences, were solidly held in hand by Shilkhak-In-Shushinak, as can be seen by the extensive building that he undertook in all parts of his empire. One stele records that temples to In-Shushinak were restored in Tettu, Shattamitik, Ekallatum, Perraperra, Bīt-tumurni, Sha-attata-ekal-likrub, Marrut and Shakhan-tallak; that a sanctuary of Lakamar was restored at Bīt-Khulki; and that a temple of Khumban was rebuilt at Peptar-sian-sit.[1] This list shows that his activities were not confined to Susiana and Anzan but extended even to northern Babylonia, the Sea-Land and probably the provinces of central Elam. In order to conduct such a widespread programme a 'pax Elamitica' was necessary. We should not conclude from the number of references to In-Shushinak that the king was trying to force his personal god on the country as part of his programme of centralization, for all of the above-mentioned temples existed before his time and Shilkhak-In-Shushinak only restored them using a more durable material. But it must be admitted that the list does show a predilection for the god of Susa.

This stele, in which only the peaceful aspect of this 'man of war' is revealed, rightly draws our attention to a very important activity of the king—as a builder. Susa owes much of its splendour to Shilkhak-In-Shushinak. We have many texts which commemorate the foundation or restoration of temples at Susa:[2] there are the traditional foundation bricks inserted in the walls, stelae, votive vases, divine symbols, door sockets, enamelled decorative cones. These texts which are often very long give the name of the deity to whom the temple was dedicated and, if we were able to translate the whole inscription, details about the temple itself. They are also valuable from another point of view, for they give the list of gods venerated by Shilkhak-In-Shushinak, the genealogical line of the ancient kings who had founded or restored the temple, the names of the royal family whom he blesses as well as the text of older bricks which he carefully looked for and had copied at the beginning of his own inscription.[3]

Naturally it is the god In-Shushinak who is the most often invoked. Bricks, stelae and enamelled pommels speak of the

---

[1] §ɪɪ, 6, no. ʟxxɪ; G, 8, 69, no. 48; §ɪɪ, 5, 29 ff.

[2] G, 8, 58 ff.

[3] §ɪɪ, 6, no. ʟxxvɪɪɪ, pl. 9; G, 8, 60, no. 38; cf. §ɪ, 6.

restoration of the great temple of In-Shushinak at Susa. It was entirely reconstructed with baked bricks by the king. The interior was very richly decorated and on a copper pedestal he placed an altar decorated with the same metal; to this were added vases and other objects in copper which were to be used for the cult. Facing the altar was his own statue, beside which were the statues of his father, his brother, his wife and his children. A long bronze cylinder was placed in front of the altar, and bas-reliefs of enamelled bricks and sculptured panels of bronze ran around the walls. Other masterpieces of Elamite metal-workers, as votive offerings, contributed to the embellishing of this holy place. Another temple, which In-Shushinak shared with Lakamar, was also rebuilt. It had been founded by an ancient king whose name was unknown, despite the efforts of Shilkhak-In-Shushinak to find the original foundation brick.

Despite this preference for In-Shushinak, the others gods were not neglected. A temple was rebuilt for Khumban of baked brick and a stele of alabaster and sacred ornaments were placed inside. The temple or sanctuary of Manzat and Shimut, Sukhsipa, Pinikir, Ishme-karab, and Tapmikir were restored. The chapel of Beltia, the Lady of Babylon, was also restored and the interior made somewhat like the temple of In-Shushinak. At Liyan he entirely reconstructed with baked bricks the ancient sanctuary of Kiririsha, and also the temple which this goddess shared with the god Khumban. The restorer took this opportunity to honour the ancient founder Khumban-numena, and to invoke the protection of the goddess upon himself and his family.

One is struck by the ostentatious way in which the king describes how he had these temples, formerly built of crude brick, restored with baked brick. He could well take pride in this, even if the baked bricks were used only as a facing of the walls, for the large-scale use of this material is an act of munificence in itself. The clay is a natural product and cheap enough but the baking is very expensive. The necessary combustibles are not common in the country and what forests there are near Susa supply only a brushwood that flares quickly without giving much heat. The manufacture of baked bricks, therefore, necessitated a large number of workers to cut, collect, transport, and tend the fires, as well as the masons and artists who decorated the outward faces.

Another sumptuous feature of these constructions was the wealth of panels and enamelled motifs as well as the large number of copper and bronze objects with which the buildings were

decorated.  One thinks of the admiration they caused to the
Assyrian conquerers when some centuries later they saw 'the
zikkurrat of Susa which was covered with lapis-lazuli' and its
summit 'which was adorned with shining bronze'.[1] Elam had
always produced excellent artisans in bronze but at this period they
were pre-eminent.  Excavations have brought to light the very
fine bronze bas-relief known as the _bronze aux guerriers_, which
probably decorated the temple of In-Shushinak[2] (as we have
already said).  It is composed of three scenes: the top has now
almost completely disappeared; the lowest, a scene representing
trees and birds, was only partly finished; but the middle register
is executed with incontestable mastery.  The seven warriors are
shown with helmets and a short tunic divided in front.  The left
hand, kept down beside the body, holds a bow and the right
hand brandishes above the head a broad curved dagger.  This line
of warriors, caught by the artist in the same sculptured attitude,
is most striking.

Besides the bronze cylinder, which was more than four metres
long and cast in one piece,[3] numerous other products of Elamite
metallurgy were found in the ruins of Susa.  There is for instance
the remarkable 'serpent-altar' which, despite its damaged state,
is one of the more beautiful examples of this art.  The table, which
was supported by five figures, of which only the upper part of the
torso and the arms are left, has two snakes encircling it.  There
are also channels on the table for draining away liquids, and the
whole is very well modelled.[4]

If we cannot date this object with exactitude to the reign of
Shilkhak-In-Shushinak there is another which is so dated by its
inscription.  This is the curious bronze tray known as the _şīt_
_šamši_, 'sunrise',[5] which merits more than passing attention.  An
adoration-scene is depicted—two nude figures with shaven heads
squat facing each other before an ablution vessel.  On either side
of the figures are stage-towers, the larger of which has three storeys
and is very complicated in design.  The other, simpler and smaller,
is made up of a central section higher than its width, flanked on
either side by two lower cubes.  There is also a table for offerings,
two round pillars the top of which is incurved to support an

---

[1] G, 12, vol. II, sect. 810. 'Lapis-lazuli' refers only to the blue colour of the
enamelled bricks covering the walls of the temple; cf. G, 16, 387, n. 9.

[2] §III, 4, 86; G, 4, 932 f.; G, 8, 62, no. 42.

[3] §v, 2, 37; §II, 6, 39 ff.; G, 8, 64, no. 45; G, 4, 933 f.

[4] G, 4, 933; §III, 3, 164, plate XII.

[5] §III, 2, 143 ff.; §III, 1, 84 ff.; G, 4, 932 f.; G, 8, 81, no. 56; § III, 5, 144 ff.

impost, two rectangular vats, a stele on a platform, two rows of little conical heaps which possibly represent cereal offerings. Finally there are four tree-trunks, their foliage of thin metal almost completely destroyed by oxidization; these probably represented a sacred grove. It was cast in two parts, one in the round together with the tray; the other parts were made separately and then riveted into place.

The interest of this object goes beyond the fact that it represents a remarkable example of native art or that it shows us certain ablution rites, for it is probably a model of the acropolis of Susa, with two of its temples, their appurtenances, their ornaments and sacred grove, at the time of Shilkhak-In-Shushinak. This allows us to complete, to a certain extent, the information we have from the excavations concerning the topography of Susa.

## IV. THE TOPOGRAPHY OF SUSA

In the northern part of the mound certain remains of buildings seem by their orientation to correspond with the smaller of the two temples, which appear on the bronze tray. A tablet from the time of Shulgi identifies this as being, at least in earlier days, the shrine of the goddess Nin-khursag. Rebuilt from age to age this temple carried on the cult of the 'Lady of the Mountain' down to the reign of Shilkhak-In-Shushinak, when she perhaps bore a native name. The temple was built on a platform nearly square, 25 metres each side, cut off by a trench more than one metre in depth. The sanctuary can be located by four brick boxes at each corner containing votive offerings. It measured 16 by 8 metres, and rooms of various dimensions gave off from this space. Four more deposits of offerings marked out the 'holy of holies', 6 metres square, at the western end of a wide passage—here was found the statue of the queen Napirasu.[1] Remains of paving indicate the courtyard, and rectangular basins were built into the east and west inside walls, a brick-built channel leading into one of them. On the north side, where the entrance probably stood, lay fragments of statuettes, vases, pedestals, and various objects, among them especially figures of Puzur-In-Shushinak and a stele of Manish-tusu. Still further to the north some Elamite stelae were unearthed.[2]

At the west of the mound, where according to the bronze model the three-storeyed building of complicated design was located, stood in fact the great temple of In-Shushinak.[3] Its limits again were marked by eight deposits of votive offerings. To judge from

[1] See Plate 157 (*a*).     [2] §IV, 3, 70 ff.     [3] §IV, 3, 67 ff.

what was unearthed during the excavations, the temple had greatly altered during the years. Votive objects of Shulgi and inscribed bricks of Untash-(_d_)_GAL_ and Shilkhak-In-Shushinak were found here and there in the walls and among the paving stones. The building was constructed at the edge of the tell. It measures 40 by 20 metres and was surrounded by a moat 3 metres in depth. The walls on the longer sides still exist and the eastern, which is in a better state of preservation, was built of baked bricks. It was probably the facing of a thick wall of unbaked clay. The temple proper was delimited by four deposits of votive offerings and measured 20·70 by 8·50 metres. It was separated from the secondary buildings, towards the south, by a large paved area which measured 19 by 4 metres and extended towards the west where it touched the enclosure. Inside the temple against the eastern wall the inner temple, which measures about 8 by 5 metres, was delimited by four more deposits of votive offerings. Here and there other pavements were found but being at different levels they were rather difficult to interpret. It seems that there was a large court or parvis on the eastern side and the entrance was probably located here. The parade on which these buildings stood was surrounded by a wall decorated with bas-reliefs and Elamite stelae placed at intervals. Columns of brick or bronze and lion-figures of stone or glazed earthenware were found in the southern part of the area.

Even if the temples of Nin-khursag and In-Shushinak are actually those in miniature on the bronze tray the complete acropolis is not shown there, for the excavations have found remains of several other religious buildings at other places on the mound.[1] A small sanctuary, oriented in a different direction, measuring 4·50 metres on each side, lay to the south of the temple of Nin-khursag, and not far from this was discovered a white marble statue of Puzur-In-Shushinak. Still further towards the south was another building of rather large dimensions. Its long wall was at least 15 metres in length and 1 metre thick. The long covered stairway of at least 120 steps which goes into the mass of the mound between two walls of rammed earth was possibly an element of this building. Towards the east there was another structure of modest proportions, 5 metres square, decorated with glazed bricks. Its entrance, more than 2 metres wide, faced the west, and the far end of the room was paved, where probably had been an altar or a divine statue. A building facing the temple of In-Shushinak towards the south-west was probably of consider-

[1] §IV, 3, 78 ff.

able size. It is difficult to judge its disposition from what remains, but the obelisk of Manishtusu, the victory-stele of Naram-Sin, boundary-stones and pedestals of statues, which were found in this area, suggest that it was a very important temple on the acropolis. In various parts of the site bases of baked-brick columns were found. They were made in a variety of shapes, round, oval and square, and came from a number of buildings on the site, but only those from the temples of In-Shushinak and Nin-khursag could be identified by their inscriptions.

What is left on the acropolis does not give us a complete picture of what Susa must have been in all her glory. The devastating fury of the Assyrian armies, some five hundred years later, and the ravages of time have reduced its buildings to heaps of ruins. At least the bronze tray (*ṣīt šamši*) gives some idea of the splendour that was once the acropolis of Susa. Ashurbanipal was later to describe the shining façade of the great temple of Susa with its wall glazed in blue, its statues of kings and gods, its protective genii of awe-inspiring aspect who guarded the holy places and, finally, its mausoleums of former kings, whose bones and ashes the Assyrian king scattered to the four winds in his desire for revenge on this race of conquerers.

Fountains and woods added to the beauty of the architecture. The many basins and numerous other remains show that there must have been a complex drainage and irrigation system.[1] It was used for the collection of rain-water, as well as for raising water from the canal up to the acropolis itself. This installation supplied water to the sacred groves which protected the acropolis from the burning sun of Susiana. Planting of trees near temples, attested symbolically by the *ṣīt šamši*, was not unknown in Babylonia and Assyria, for references to trees in the vicinity of temples[2] are not to be understood as indicating only artificial imitations.[3] Ashurbanipal in his annals makes this allusion to the trees at Susa: 'Their sacred groves into which no stranger (ever) penetrates, whose borders he never (over)steps—into these my soldiers entered, saw their mysteries, and set them on fire.'[4] Discoveries and texts thus agree in proclaiming the prestige and prosperity of Susa at the time of Shilkhak-In-Shushinak.

[1] §IV, 3, 73 ff. and figs. 34–7.    [2] §IV, 1, 16A f.; §IV, 2, nos. 65, 366.
[3] §I, 3, 26.    [4] G, 12, vol. II, sect. 810.

## V. KHUTELUTUSH-IN-SHUSHINAK

To maintain Elamite power Shilkhak-In-Shushinak needed a successor who would be worthy of himself. This, unfortunately, was not the case with his son and successor Khutelutush-In-Shushinak. The royal protocol shows two symptoms of his weakness. In his genealogy he speaks of himself as not only the chosen son of his father but of his uncle, Kutir-Nahhunte, and his grandfather, Shutruk-Nahhunte, as well. This seems to be an attempt to support his authority by the use of the ancient Elamite matriarchal concept,[1] if we admit that his mother, who had been married to the two brothers, was also the daughter of Shutruk-Nahhunte. In any case this desire to identify himself as being of the same blood as these three kings and his desire to affirm the legitimacy of the bonds between him and his brothers and sisters seem to show a lack of confidence in himself, which appears even in his titles. Although he called himself 'enlarger of the empire', perhaps only for traditional reasons, he did not take the title *sunkir* 'king' which had been used by his predecessors, but merely called himself '*menir* of Anzan and Susa'. This brings to mind one of the titles, '*ḥal-menir* of Elam', used by Khumban-numena, and it refers to a feudal power rather than power based on divine right.

If we compare the very small number of inscriptions left by Khutelutush-In-Shushinak[2] with those of Shilkhak-In-Shushinak they appear lifeless. There were no longer trophies taken from the enemy nor victory stelae. A few texts refer to peaceful pursuits, and these were probably on a smaller scale than those undertaken by his father. At the beginning of his reign, when his mother is still mentioned in the final prayer, he probably had work done on the temples of Manzat and Shimutta and a votive inscription was placed on a door socket in honour of Manzat for the occasion. Later, in the city of Shalulikki, he inaugurated a new temple of baked brick in honour of the goddess Upurkupak, for his life and the life of his brothers. Later again a temple was rebuilt at Kipu, in Elam, for the goddess Ishme-karab from whom he asked blessings upon his children, his brothers and himself. He also had a chapel, constructed of flat green-glazed bricks, founded in honour of his father Shilkhak-In-Shushinak. This building has recently been excavated but it cannot be dated.[3] There is also a fragment of a stele from his reign, invoking the gods of Elam and the gods of Anzan, and of these In-Shushinak, Nahhunte, Upurkupak, Khumban(?), and Manzat are named.

[1] §v, 4; §v, 5.    [2] G, 8, 84 ff. nos. 60–5.    [3] §v, 2, 38.

In the absence of historical texts we can glean some politically important information from these dedication inscriptions. The mention of Shalulikki shows that the Elamite king still controlled a part of lower Mesopotamia, or at least the Sealand. It is probable that the distant province of Liyan was no longer held by the king, as none of the bricks from this site mention him; but Elam, Anzan and Susiana remained under his control and their gods are always named in his inscriptions.

There was a certain coherence in the realm. Shilkhak-In-Shushinak had built up a military power which survived him, but his son was unable to take advantage of this inheritance. This state of affairs was greatly aggravated by the energy and ambition of his adversaries in Assyria and Babylonia. The former, under Ashur-rēsha-ishi (1133–1116), awoke from its lethargy. This king began a policy of expansion and conquest that was to be taken even further by his successor Tiglath-pileser I. Babylonia under Nebuchadrezzar I (1124–1103) had also come to life. Unfortunately Khutelutush-In-Shushinak was not the one who could maintain the position of Elam before two such rivals. As he was to show on two occasions, he did not lack courage, but it was his lack of decision and foresight that was to be his undoing. Instead of moving his armies into the plains and mountains along his borders he allowed Nebuchadrezzar to take the initiative, and the Babylonian king was able to carry out a violent and successful attack against Elam.[1] This might have been preceded by an unsuccessful attempt, for a fragment of a chronicle relates an attack against Elam but the names of the kings involved are missing; it may have involved Nebuchadrezzar or one of his immediate predecessors.[2] This Babylonian king, after having sworn that he would rescue his god Marduk from Susa or die in the attempt, gathered his troops at Babylon and then launched a violent attack through the Zagros towards the upper Karkhah. The Elamite counter-attack, although late, was of equal violence. The Babylonian army was forced to retreat and, after an attempt to take refuge in the city of Dūr-Apil-Sin, the Babylonian king and his army were driven out of the country. The text ends with a lamentation of the defeated king.

That the Babylonians could advance as far as the Karkhah, only 150 kilometres above Susa, reveals that the Elamites had already lost control of the western bank of the Tigris. It was certainly so in the time of Khutelutush-In-Shushinak, but probably

---

[1] §1, 7, 138 f.
[2] *Ibid.* 137.

too at the end of his father's reign, so that the unsuccessful attack recorded by the chronicle may have been made by one of the earliest kings of the Isin dynasty rather than by Nebuchadrezzar himself. But if by the latter, he had learned his lesson, and before launching the attack which was to succeed he made sure of the help of effective allies. By promising Lakti-Marduk[1] of Bīt-Karziabku to free his land of all taxes, statute-labour and service, he was aided by the chariots of this chief. He also welcomed two important persons from the Elamite city Dīn-sharri, Shamua and his son Shamaia, a priest of the god Ria,[2] undertaking to rescue their god and to secure him important privileges. Thus prepared, he began his campaign from Dēr, the modern Badrah,[3] whence an almost impracticable route followed the Gawi river into the Elamite province called Khalekhasta at a later date. The line of attack was now farther south, thus menacing Susa much more than the previous campaign. The aggressor wished also to spring a surprise attack upon the Elamites and therefore, despite the heat of summer and the lack of water, he force-marched his army in a veritable leap to the river Ulai (the modern Kārūn) near to Susa. Here the Elamites counter-attacked, and according to the inscription of Lakti-Marduk the chariots commanded by him saved the day. The Babylonian victory was decisive and the defeated Elamite king fled and died shortly afterwards.[4] All resistance ceased, and the Babylonian was able to conquer the rest of Elam without striking another blow. After pillaging Elam he returned in triumph with his booty as well as the statues of the gods Ria and Marduk, released after so many years captivity in Susa. He then rewarded his allies as he had promised; the income of several cities and villages was given for maintenance of the god Ria, who had been taken from Babylon to the city of Khuṣṣi by Shamua and his son on the order of the Babylonian king.[5]

This Babylonian victory and the death of Khutelutush-In-Shushinak brought Elamite power to an end. A text[6] from a later

---

[1] §v, 1 proposed the reading *Lakti-Shipak* instead of the usual reading *Ritti-Marduk.* This is correct as to the first part of the name, for the signs *rit* and *lak* are easily distinguished at that date. See, however, above, p. 455, n. 6.

[2] [Or Eriya: see above, p. 456, and cf. bibliography to ch. xxxi, A, 3, 108 (Ed.)]

[3] §vi, 10, 47; §v, 7.

[4] This victory was so decisive that it was remembered in succeeding ages, and had its place among the historical references of the astrologers: §v, 8, no. 200, rev. 5; §v, 10, 176.

[5] §v, 11, 534 ff.; §v, 3, nos. vi and xxiv, and see also §v, 9 and §v, 6, 147 ff.

[6] A brick of Shutruk-Nahhunte II, G, 14, 5, 63 ff., no. 84.

period tells us that the successor was *sunkir* 'king' and that he reconstructed a sanctuary of In-Shushinak at Susa. But as a political power Elam was finished. This period was followed by a dark age of three centuries, during which there are no native texts nor are there allusions to Elam in the Mesopotamian sources. Undoubtedly broken up internally, Elam was not to be mentioned again until 821 when Elamite, Chaldaean and Aramaean troops were defeated by the Assyrian king Shamshi-Adad V.[1]

## VI. THE POLITICAL GEOGRAPHY OF WESTERN PERSIA

The elimination of Elam as a major power did not, however, bring peace to the Zagros. The kings of Babylonia and above all the kings of Assyria continued to make war in the region between Lake Urmīyah and northern Elam. Later this was to become one of the principal theatres of operations for the Assyrians. As these became more and more powerful, they were obliged to get a foothold in the mountainous districts along their borders from which they could push their military expeditions much further towards the east.

The Assyrian interest in these high lands went beyond the strategic advantage of allowing them to cut off any invasions that might come through these trails and valleys. Economically they were also very important, for the Zagros and the western approaches to the Iranian plateau were not uniformly poor. The inner plains and some of the valleys were fertile, and there were oases which were highly cultivated or grazing lands with large numbers of horses as well as flocks and herds. They were also an important source of minerals, having metallurgical centres which manufactured bronze, copper, and afterwards iron. Through these regions moved vast quantities of precious stones, copper ore and manufactured copper.

This strategic and economic importance explains the increasing interest of the Assyrians in these regions. To these reasons was soon to be added another; certain movements and migrations of peoples brought a double menace to bear on Mesopotamia, the threat of cutting off supplies, and of possible invasion.

To understand better the changes that were afterwards to take place in this area we must give a short account of its former populations. The sources of our knowledge about this country—texts from Mesopotamia—show that it was inhabited for a long time

---

[1] G, 12, vol. I, sect. 726; G, 15, 156 ff.

by four major ethnic groups: the Subarians, the Hurrians, the Lullubi and the Guti. The two latter groups were native to the area. The Subarians and the Hurrians lived mostly in the plains and only a few of their numbers actually in the Zagros.

The Subarians[1] lived in the mountains to the east of the Tigris between Barakhshe, near the Diyālā, and southern Anatolia. They were neighbours of Anzan and Eshnunna. Hammurabi who had defeated them along with the Guti and Elam put them among those countries whose 'mountains are distant and the languages are complicated'.[2] They had a much fairer skin than the Mesopotamians, to whom they long provided an ample supply of slaves. It was also to the east of the Tigris that the Hurrians first appeared. They entered very early into Mesopotamia but some of them stayed in the area to the south and west of Lake Vān, to the east of Irbil and Altın-Köprü or in the Zagros. Of the latter group some went into Elam and others moved towards the Caspian Sea.[3]

The Lullubi and the Guti stayed in the mountains from where they constantly menaced Mesopotamia. Although the Lullubi (Lullu, Lullubu, Lullumi) may be mentioned as early as in the archaic tablets of Fārah their actual homeland is not revealed until the Agade period, when inscriptions were found in their territory. Those of Naram-Sin are at Darband-i Gawr, south of Sulai-maniyyah, and at Darband-i Ramkan, near the plain of Rania,[4] and commemorate his wars against this people. Others are the work of the Lullubi, celebrating a victory of their king Annu-banini. These inscriptions are engraved on rocks at Sar-i pul, in the district of Ḥulwan, some 30 kilometres to the south of Qaṣr-i Shīrīn.[5] This is much further south than those above mentioned, and is probably the southernmost point reached by the Lullubi in their attempt to control and cut off the commercial route which runs through southern Kurdistān from the Iranian plateau to the Mesopotamian plain. At a later date, the date-formulae of Shulgi[6] seem to indicate that the Lullubi homeland began in the area immediately to the east of Irbil and Altın-Köprü with its centre at Rania, which undoubtedly remained the focus of their culture in later years.[7] Thanks to the rock inscrip-

---

[1] §vi, nos. 11, 12, and 38.     [2] G, 6, no. 146, col. iv.
[3] §vi, 11 and 12; §vi, 15, 31 ff.; §vi, 16, 61 ff.
[4] §vi, 6; §vi, 20, 184.     [5] §vi, 40, 98 ff. and 187 (bibliography).
[6] For the 26th, 45th and 46th years; see G, 5, 141 f. Lullubum is conjoined with Urbillum and Simurrum.
[7] §vi, 23, 77, 24–5.

tions of Annubanini and the victory stele of Naram-Sin we have some idea of the physical aspect of these warlike mountaineers. Dressed in light tunics or kilts, an animal skin over the shoulders, short beards and braided hair they appear to be of Mediterranean rather than of Armenoid stock. The mention of their 'numerous kings' shows that they had not a centralized state but were divided into small clans directed by independent chiefs, and were united only in times of emergency.

The Gutians, or Qutu, also lived in southern Kurdistān. After their expulsion from Mesopotamia,[1] where they had established a barbarian rule, texts written during the First Dynasty of Babylon define with some clearness their habitation in the Zagros. It was delimited by the boundaries of Subartu, Turukku, Eshnunna, Barakhshe and Idamaraz.[2] Some of them also lived in the region of Rania.[3] Later on it becomes more difficult to localize them, as the Akkadians grouped all of the autochthonous groups under the general heading of Gutians. Because of this such locations as 'the city of Karkhar is situated in front of the Gutian country'[4] are very misleading. From what little we know of their social structure, during the period when they occupied Mesopotamia, we can see that they formed a sort of tribal confederation of rough and simple people. They were led by a military aristocracy which elected a 'king' for a fixed, but short, period of time.

From what has been said above two conclusions follow: we know the western limits of these various ethnic groups but nothing of their eastward extent—the Mesopotamians themselves knew little of these distant regions. We also find that they had no particular territory of their own, but often overlapped one another. This is very clear in the Rania plain at the time of Sham-shi-Adad I. There the principal city Shusharra (modern Shem-shāra) was under Assyrian control,[5] but the majority of its population was Hurrian. Others of the inhabitants were Lullubi,[6] and more warlike elements of these lived in the vicinity, maintaining economic relations with the city but holding over it a threat of insecurity.[7] The district was also disturbed by raids of Turukkians,[8] and not far away were Gutians, themselves under a Hurrian chief,[9] and also in relation with the city. Out of this hotch-potch

---

[1] By Utu-khegal, prince of Uruk; §VI, 35 and 36; §VI, 43.
[2] Date-formulae for the 30th, 32nd and 37th years of Hammurabi; G, 5, 180 f.; §VI, 1, vol. IV, 25; §VI, 22, 83, n. 1; §VI, 27, 241.
[3] §VI, 23, 32 ff.
[4] §VI, 28, 12, no. 6, line 7.
[5] §VI, 23, 75.
[6] *Ibid.* 80, lines 45 f.
[7] *Ibid.* 77 ff., lines 24–36.
[8] §VI, 1, vol. IV, 25.
[9] §VI, 23, 36, no. 8.

of peoples arose a kind of common culture throughout the mountain region, and the evidence of names proves that it extended even into Elam.[1]

The Kassites were soon to enter into this community. We do not know whether they migrated thither or whether they originated in the region at the source of the Elamite rivers. In any case they appear on the scene at a time when the more western approaches of the Iranian plateau were in a period of social and economic change. A new type of pottery appears; cities and townships begin to put up walls; small stock becomes more numerous, perhaps to the detriment of cattle; and the problem of moving the flocks and renewing pasture-lands becomes more urgent. We know that the Kassites invaded Babylonia in very large numbers at the time of the First Dynasty and that they settled down in this new land. But certain groups stayed in the Zagros, and these, along with the Lullubi and the Gutians, were the important elements in the Zagros down to the end of the second millennium.

It is these people that Nebuchadrezzar I (1124–1103) and his contemporary Ashur-rēsha-ishi (1134–1116), king of Assyria, met during their military expeditions in the Zagros. The former boasted of having subdued 'the powerful Lullubi' and raided the Kassites; the latter claimed that he subdued 'the Lullume, all of the Gutians, and the whole mountainous region where they live'.[2] It was settlements of Kassites, mixed with Semites and Hurrians, that the Elamite king Shilkhak-In-Shushinak at the same period listed among his conquests to the north of his country. Linguistically, the geographical names show that the Subarian language was predominant in the region of the Tigris and the Diyālā, and the Lullubian south of the Lesser Zab.[3] The personal and the divine names show interpenetration among these different ethnic groups. Some of the gods that the Akkadians considered as Gutian were in fact Hurrian. Certain Kassite words, such as the word for 'king', were known as far away as the district of the lakes.

This situation in the Zagros was, at the end of the second millennium, on the eve of profound changes, although nothing of these had yet appeared. Gutians and Lullubians continued, indeed, to be named in the annals of Assyrian kings, and scattered groups of Kassites survived into the classical age on the east and northeast of Babylonia.[4] But from the outset of the first millennium there was to begin a complete refashioning of the political geography in these lands.

[1] §vi, 33.                                    [2] G, 12, vol. I, sect. 209.
[3] G, 12, vol. I, sect. 449 and 457; §vi, 37, 5, line 11.          [4] G, 18.

# CHAPTER XXXIII

## SYRIA, THE PHILISTINES, AND PHOENICIA

### I. THE SEA PEOPLES IN PALESTINE

I N the early twelfth century B.C. Syria and Palestine were flooded by an irruption of peoples from the coasts and islands of the northern Mediterranean. Unfortunately, we cannot fix the exact date of this invasion, since our chief pertinent sources are the reliefs and accompanying inscriptions of Ramesses III at Medīnet Habu; the former are schematic and undated, while the latter consist almost exclusively of triumphal poems in a stereotyped and bombastic style.[1] Moreover, the date of the reign of Ramesses III is uncertain within a possible range of a generation and a probable range of a decade, but the earliest and latest possible dates for his accession are now considered to have been about 1205 and 1180, respectively. To judge from the monuments, it would appear that the first attack[2] on Egypt came by sea and land not long before the sixth year of the king. The first land onslaught is said to have been beaten back in Phoenicia (*Djahy*). The great triumphal inscription of the eighth year was composed in glorification of the second naval victory; land operations are also mentioned, but it is not clear how successful they really were.[3]

While the inscription of the eighth year makes it certain that the Egyptians connected this migration with the movement which had brought an abrupt end to the Hittite Empire, it seems evident that they were both part of a greater upheaval. The Hittite Empire was overthrown by land peoples who struck deep into the heart of Anatolia and are said in the inscriptions of the Assyrian king Tiglath-pileser I to have reached south-western Armenia about 1165 B.C. The migration with which we are concerned here included five different peoples, at least two of whom are represented as fighting in ships, some manned by warriors with feathered helmets[4] while others have only warriors with low, horned helmets.

---

* An original version of this chapter was published as fascicle 51 in 1966.
[1] §1, 39, 24 ff.  [2] See above, pp. 241 f.
[3] §1, 14, 53 ff. The phrase *iryw šdt m nȝysn iww* should probably be rendered: '(As for the foreign countries,) they were making a (plundering) raid from their islands'—see G, 5, vol. 4, 561.  [4] See, however, above, p. 372.

All of the warriors in the scenes of land-fighting wear feathered helmets. The land-forces of the invaders employ chariots for fighting and heavy two-wheeled carts drawn by humped oxen for women and children. The use of carts suggests a long overland journey but by no means proves it, since they may have been constructed after arrival in Palestine by sea.[1]

The identification of the five peoples listed in the texts of Ramesses III has long been vigorously debated. In the order of importance indicated by the number and character of the allusions to them, they are the Peleset (*Pr/lst*), the Tjekker (*Tjik[k]al/r*), the Sheklesh (*Shekr/lushe*), the Denyen (*Danuna*), and the Weshesh (*Washeshe*).[2] The first people is undoubtedly to be identified with the biblical Philistines, of whom more below. The second is perhaps to be identified with the Teucrians (or less probably with the Homeric Sikeloi, who occupied Sicily and gave their name to the island).[3] The third seems to be unknown otherwise; all proposed identifications are dubious. The fourth is unquestionably to be identified somehow with the land Danuna of a letter of Abi-milki, prince of Tyre in the Amarna period; the name later appears in Cyprus as the *Yad(a)nana* of the Assyrians[4] and in Cilicia as the land of the *Dnnym*.[5] The Washeshe are unknown unless their name is connected with Carian Ouassos. That all these peoples came from somewhere in the Aegean orbit appears reasonably certain. It is significant that the two distinctive types of helmet at Medīnet Habu appear at about the same time on the so-called warrior-vase from Mycenae.[6] On the vase are two processions of five warriors each; one group wears feathered helmets and the other horned helmets. However, the horned helmet is high, with plumes floating from the crest; it is different from both the low horned helmet of the Mediterranean allies at Medīnet Habu and from the crested, horned helmet worn by the Sherden (Shardina), i.e. Sardinian, corps of the Egyptian army itself (shown at Medīnet Habu only when joining with the Egyptians in land operations).

[1] The account in §1, 14, 53 ff. is insufficiently detailed to allow any clear reconstruction of the sequence of events.

[2] For the vocalization see §1, 4, *passim*, and §1, 23, 240 ff.

[3] The vocalization *Tjikar* agrees very well with *Teukr-*; cf. Hebrew *s[u]ran-* (which would be written approximately *\*tju-ra-n* in New Egyptian) and its later Greek equivalent *turann-*. Teucrians are said in Greek sources to have settled at Salamis in Cyprus after the Trojan War. See above, pp. 276 f.

[4] §1, 5, 171 ff.      [5] *Ibid.* 172. See above, pp. 363 ff.

[6] §1, 8, figs. 265 ff. The differences in shape seem largely to be the result of artistic conventions.

Our knowledge of the archaeological and historical background of Philistine culture is now substantial. It is quite certain that the highly distinctive 'Philistine' pottery found in such quantities in Philistine sites as well as in the towns of the adjacent lowland country (Shephelah) of Judah in deposits of the twelfth and eleventh centuries B.C. has been correctly identified. It springs directly from the LH III c 1 ware of the Aegean basin, and its manufacture seems to have been brought from Cyprus to Palestine not later than the early twelfth century, judging from the remarkable likeness of specifically Philistine pottery to pieces found by A. Furumark at Sinda and by C. F. A. Schaeffer and P. Dikaios at Enkomi, both in north-eastern Cyprus near Salamis.[1] This ware has been called by Furumark LH III c 1 b and assigned to the period between c. 1225 and 1175 B.C. It shows Cypriot influence, so there is good reason to reject the view that it was brought by the Philistines directly from their Aegean home.

Since the inscriptions of Ramesses III repeatedly speak of using captives as troops in his own army and since some of the Sea Peoples (especially the Sherden) had been used as mercenaries or as slave troops during the reign of Ramesses II, many scholars now agree that the Philistines were first settled in Palestine as garrison troops. This has been demonstrated on the basis of the virtual identity of weapons, anthropoid clay sarcophagi, and other artifacts in garrison sites from Beth-shan in the northern Jordan valley to Tell el-Fār'ah in the Negeb of western Palestine, as well as at Tell Nebesha in the Delta and Anība in Nubia.[2] In Philistia proper both Ashdod and Gath have been shown by recent excavations to have been originally fortresses of the *Zwingburg* type; Gath is still most probably to be found at the traditional site of Tel Gat (Tell esh-Sheikh el-'Areini) despite the excavator's doubts, for the alternative site (Tell en-Nejīleh) has yielded no Late Bronze remains, and Ashdod was a similar large fortress in early Philistine times. Another fortress may have been the third Philistine inland town, Ekron.[3] Gaza, and Askalon were already, by contrast, important seaports before the Philistine occupation began.

Evidence for the date of the original establishment of the

---

[1] §1, 11, 209 f.; for the best previous study see §1, 24, and cf. §1, 7 (1954 and later editions), 114 f. Since some Philistines had probably settled in eastern Cyprus several decades before their occupation of the Pentapolis, this chronological situation would be expected.

[2] §1, 12; 13.

[3] J. Naveh's identification (§1, 28) of Ekron with the large (but poorly fortified) site of Khirbet al-Muqanna' is impossible for a number of reasons, and the site of 'Aqir again becomes highly probable.

Philistines in key fortresses was uncovered by Petrie and Starkey (1927–30) at Tell el-Fār'ah (Sharuhen), and still more important clues have more recently been found by H. J. Franken at Tell Deir 'Allā (Succoth) some 24 miles south of Beth-shan in the Jordan valley. At Sharuhen the fortified 'Residency' yielded early Philistine pottery in a structure first built by Sethos II (1216–1210 B.C.), as demonstrated by the find of four very large and heavy sherds belonging to a massive jar inscribed in well-carved hieroglyphs with the name of Sethos II.[1] Since these sherds, though found in different places in the 'Residency', fit together, it seems clear that the original jar dates from the foundation of the fortress by Sethos II, who is known from other sources to have built such fortresses in the region between the Delta and southern Palestine. It follows that the Philistines were settled here as garrison troops at some time between the foundation of this Egyptian fortress and its destruction in the latter part of the twelfth century.

The Deir 'Allā finds are much more remarkable, though not entirely unexpected.[2] On the floor of a sanctuary from the end of the Late Bronze Age, about 1200 B.C., was found a broken faience bowl inscribed with the cartouche of Queen Tewosret, who reigned in the last decade of the thirteenth century B.C. In the same occupation level, 8 m. east of the sanctuary, were found (in 1964) three inscribed tablets and a discarded fourth tablet in two rooms containing the same kinds of pottery.[3] Though the sanctuary is said to have been destroyed by an earthquake, Philistine pottery is reported to have been found in the same stratum and, according to information, is to be dated immediately after the time of the tablets.[4] These contain over fifty characters, grouped into some fifteen words separated by vertical strokes; they resemble elongated Minoan Linear A and B tablets, and some of the characters closely resemble signs of Minoan Linear A though simplified in form and reduced in number. Apparently we have to do with a purely phonetic syllabary, analogous to the Cypriot and in part to the Carian. That the tablets are very early Philistine texts is highly probable, though they might represent the script of some other Sea People.

Decisive evidence has now been found identifying the occupants of the anthropoid sarcophagi of Beth-shan with the

---

[1] §1, 36, 28 and §1, 32, 18 (which Starkey seems to have overlooked).
[2] §1, 7, 185 (1954 ed.).
[3] §III, 19.
[4] See above, p. 336.

Philistines of the Medīnet Habu reliefs of Ramesses III.[1] The faces moulded on the cover pieces of the Beth-shan coffins are surmounted by feathered helmets of the same types as we find attributed to the Philistines at Medīnet Habu, with identical decoration around the lower part of the helmets: (1) a horizontal strip with a single row of little circular projections; (2) a horizontal strip with two similar rows of circular projections; (3) a similar strip with a row of chevrons or zigzag decoration above and a row of circular projections below. A fourth modification appears at Medīnet Habu but not at Beth-shan (where the material is incomparably more limited in amount): a strip with a single row of zigzag or chevron decoration. In view of the way in which the pre-Hellenic and early Hellenic peoples were subdivided into three or more tribes (e.g. the Rhodians were divided into three tribes according to the Homeric Catalogue of Ships) we may rest assured that the insignia in question indicate tribal ties, not military rank. In other words, they correspond very roughly with the *wusūm* marks of the Arabs, but they undoubtedly reflect a much higher level of socio-political organization.

The foregoing data establish the fact that there was an early phase of military garrisons manned by Philistines (and quite possibly by other Sea Peoples), which was followed by a large-scale invasion by sea and land, repulsed by Ramesses III early in the twelfth century. The Philistines and their allies were driven back from Egypt proper but were allowed to settle in Palestine as Egyptian vassals. The Philistines occupied the coastal plain from south of Gaza to north of Ekron; south of them there may have been a Cretan colony,[2] and in northern Sharon the Tjekker were settled, as we know from the Wenamun report. Other groups may have been settled in southern Sharon (the 'Auja valley and Joppa) and the plain of Acre, all of which passed under Philistine control before the second half of the eleventh century B.C. The methodical way in which the Sea Peoples appear to have divided up the coast of Palestine is clear from even a superficial geographical analysis of their division. The Philistines themselves, being the dominant group in the confederation, took the best territory. Though only about 40 miles long and averaging little over 15 miles in width, the Philistine Pentapolis had approximately the same area as the whole of Attica; moreover, most of its land was cultivable, producing splendid crops of grain in normal seasons. In due course they absorbed their Cretan neighbours to the south and expanded northwards to dominate the

[1] §1, 12, 57 and much more briefly §1, 13, 156 ff.   [2] §1, 1 and §1, 2, 136 ff.

plain of Sharon. The report of Wenamun, from the early eleventh century B.C., tells us that the Tjekker were then occupying Dor, which probably included not less than 30 miles of sea coast just south of Carmel. This tract, however, is so much narrower and less adapted to agriculture than the Philistine plain that one is scarcely surprised to learn that the Tjekker were still noted for piracy a century or more after their settlement. Between these two areas of settlement is a shorter zone around Joppa and Apollonia (Arsuf), only some 30 by 15 miles in extent, but extraordinarily rich and well watered; we do not know which of the Sea Peoples settled there at first, but it later passed under Philistine control. Nor do we know which people was allotted the rich plain of Acre, or whether any of them settled still farther north on the Syrian coast.

Who were the Philistines originally? Biblical tradition, clearly derived from Philistine sources, brings them from Caphtor (Akkadian *Kaptara*, Crete) and this tradition is supported by the appellation *Minoa* given to Gaza. Just south of Gaza was a Cretan settlement,[1] and David employed 'light-armed' Cretans as mercenaries.[2] As noted above, the Deir 'Allā tablets are written in a script with clear affinities to Minoan A (though greatly evolved and simplified), and the Phaestus disk from a sixteenth-century Cretan palace has a frequently appearing character portraying a male head with feathered headdress. On the other hand, the Lydian tradition as reported by the native historian Xanthus (a contemporary of Herodotus) claims that the Philistines were colonists from Lydia.[3] This conflict of opinion presumably arose from considerations of prestige; the Philistines themselves, before Gyges made Lydia world-famous, claimed Cretan origin, while the Lydians claimed the Philistines as former colonists of theirs.

In 1950–1 a new element was introduced into this previously insoluble debate; the old equation of Philistines and Pelasgians was taken up again,[4] and good evidence was presented for an

---

[1] See preceding note.

[2] Hebrew *Kᵉrētī u-pᵉlētī*, 'Cherethites and Pelethites', is the common designation of David's favourite bodyguard. Since the Lucianic recension of the Septuagint (now known from Qumrān Cave 4 to be exceptionally reliable) offers a reading *pheltei*, we may be justified in treating the expression as a typical Semitic hendiadys, in which case the second word *\*peltī* might be derived from the Aegean source of later Greek *peltē*, 'light shield' (from which comes *peltastēs*, 'light-armed warrior'). The Cretans were known as archers in classical times.

[3] G, 11, 81, n. 1.

[4] See §III, 6, 4; and V. Georgiev in *Jahrbuch für kleinasiatische Forschung*, I (1951), 136 ff.

ancient variant *Pelastikon*, etc., for *Pelasgikon*, both of which presumably went back to an older form with a consonant found by the Hellenes difficult to pronounce. Unfortunately, Greek tradition about the Pelasgians is so confused that Eduard Meyer was inclined to reject it almost entirely.[1] This goes much too far, and we have some evidence from Greek sources which seems relatively accurate. According to Homer (Iliad II, 840) the southern Troad was inhabited by 'spear-brandishing Pelasgians', and Herodotus, who was a native of Halicarnassus in Caria, traces both the Ionians and the Aeolians to Pelasgian origins. It is more than likely that his 'Coastal Pelasgians' actually preceded the Ionians in Ionia, not in the Peloponnesus as he states.[2] There is also much confusion in our sources between the Tyrrhenians (Tursha in the lists of Sea Peoples) of Lemnos in the Aegean and the Pelasgians.[3] However this may be, we have onomastic data which confirm the derivation of the Philistines from the general area of south-western Asia Minor. The only certain Philistine names until recently were Goliath (*Golyaṯ*) and Achish (correctly *Ekaush*, or the like), but we also have three names of Philistine chieftains or merchant princes in the Wenamun report: Waraktir (*Wr/lktr/l*), Waret (*Wr/lt*) and Makamar (*Mkmr/l*).[4] It was suggested in 1951 that their names were South-west Anatolian (i.e. Luwian),[5] and this suggestion was confirmed independently in 1962.[6] Perhaps the details should be slightly modified and the names be explained tentatively as *Warkat/dara*, *Ward/ta* and *Mag/kamola*, all with excellent equivalents in the daughter dialects of Luwian (Lycian, Carian, Pisidian, Pamphylian and Cilician, etc.).[7] Heb. *Golyaṯ* was long ago identified with Lydian *Alyattes*, older *Walwatta*; the reciprocal dissimilation offers no problems, and the element *walwi* as well as the formation *walwatta* are both well illustrated in Luwian.[8] In short, the Philistines may be identified with Pelasgians of some kind, and their language was a Luwian dialect.[9]

---

[1] E.g. G, 11, 237, n. 1.   [2] Herodotus, VII, 94.   [3] Most recently §1, 19, 224.

[4] Only the consonants are known with certainty, since the syllabic orthography had become hopelessly confused by the eleventh century B.C.

[5] §1, 6.                        [6] §1, 20, 50, n. 25.

[7] On the Luwian daughter-dialects see §1, 37, and on Lydian and its relationship to Luwian see §1, 10.

[8] §1, 20, 49; cf. such pairs as *muwa* and *Muwatta* as well as Lydian *walwes* (*ibid.*, n. 21).

[9] An obvious further deduction would be that these Pelasgians spoke a Luwian dialect, but we do not know enough about the Pelasgians to make such a facile generalization—they may have been a multilingual federation for all we know.

As already indicated, the occupation of the coastland of Palestine by the Sea Peoples was attended by much destruction of Canaanite towns. Ramesses III tells us that Canaanite princes and patrician charioteers (*mryn*, *mariyanna*) joined the Egyptian commanders in resisting the foes. It appears that there were successive raids during the generation or more (possibly as much as fifty years) which preceded the mass invasion in the eighth year of Ramesses III. The excavators of Ashdod are inclined to date the destruction of the Late Bronze town about the same time as the Israelite conquest of the Shephelah.[1] Askalon shows clear remains of a destruction level between Canaanite and Philistine levels. Gath (Tell Gat) and Tell el-Qasīleh on the Yarqōn river were not founded until after the irruption of the Sea Peoples, and Dor seems to exhibit the same picture that we find at Askalon. Much farther north Ugarit was destroyed soon after the beginning of the Mediterranean raids. Publication of the documents from the Tablet Oven,[2] excavated in 1954, provides a solid basis for dating the fall of Ugarit, which must have occurred within a very short time after the tablets were placed in the oven. Two letters are particularly important: RS 18.38 and RS 18.40. The former contains the text (or translation) of a message sent to 'Ammurapi, last king of Ugarit, from his Hittite suzerain (probably Tudkhaliash IV). It states that 'The enemy has come up against me, the As[syr]ian', using the familiar Ugaritic and Aramaic consonantal spelling of the name. The second letter, written by an Ugaritic official to the king of Ugarit, says that he is in Lawasanda (Lawazantiya),[3] watching the approaches from the east together with the king of Siannu.[4] The latter 'has fled and...was killed'.

The events mentioned in these letters correspond with happenings in the first full year of Tukulti-Ninurta I of Assyria, whose troops crossed the Euphrates and carried off '28,800 men of Khatti' as captives. Since the destruction of Ugarit did not occur until after the accession of Merneptah, we must fix the accession of his father, Ramesses II, in 1304 instead of in 1290, but at the same time we must date the Assyrian invasion of Syria in 1234 instead of in 1244. The fall of Ugarit then took place in 1234— probably a few months after the victory of Merneptah over the

---

[1] Personal information.

[2] In Ch. Virolleaud, *Textes en cunéiformes alphabétiques des Archives Sud, Sud-Ouest, et du Petit Palais* (*Le Palais royal d'Ugarit V = Mission de Ras Shamra XI*). Paris, 1965.

[3] As identified by Mr M. Astour.

[4] So clearly to be read on a photograph supplied by M. Schaeffer.

Libyans and Sea Peoples in the spring of 1234, possibly in 1233 or 1232. The city was not destroyed by an Assyrian army but probably by a sudden raid of the Sea Peoples at a time when the Ugaritic navy had been sent by the Hittites to another area— perhaps Lycia, as explicitly stated in one tablet.

The destruction of Tyre is presupposed by tradition and that of Sidon (at the hands of a king of Askalon) is explicitly mentioned.[1] In the Shephelah of Judah (especially at Beth-shemesh and Tell Beit Mirsim) there is a gap of a generation or more between the latest imports of Mycenaean pottery (which immediately preceded the disruption of trade by the Sea Peoples during the reign of Merneptah) and the introduction of Philistine pottery from the Coastal Plain.

After the death of Ramesses III the Philistines and their congeners appear to have concentrated on sea and land trade. A century later, not long before the Philistine conquest of Palestine, the Tjekker were still more powerful at sea than the prince of Byblos, and the Philistine prince Waraktir (Warkatara) was in trade alliance (*khubūr*) with Sidon.[2] Since there is no good evidence of any Phoenician overseas colonization before the tenth century B.C., it is practically certain that the Philistines and other Sea Peoples of Palestine controlled the waters of the south-eastern Mediterranean until their defeat by the combined forces of Israel and Tyre early in the same century. Land trade was greatly facilitated by the fact that the Philistines already occupied a number of strategic points in the plain of Esdraelon and the Jordan valley (especially Beth-shan and Succoth) in the period immediately preceding the mass invasion under Ramesses III. The influence of the Philistines on desert trade is illustrated by the discovery at Saḥāb, east of 'Ammān, of an Early Iron Age tomb containing a typical anthropoid clay coffin.[3] The conquest of Israel by the Philistines about the middle of the eleventh century was perhaps dictated mainly by the increasing need of protection for caravans from the desert. It must be remembered that this was less than a century after the great Midianite raids, in which camel-riding raiders appeared for the first known time in the history of south-western Asia. Soon after these raids we find

---

[1] G, 11, 79 ff.

[2] §1, 6, 229 ff., and B. Maisler (Mazar) in *Bull. A.S.O.R.* 102 (1946), 9 ff. See also §11, 5, 359, n. 80. It may be observed that 'partnership' is *ment-shbēr* in Coptic; *shbēr* is the normal Coptic equivalent of Eg. *ḥbr* (*khubūr*), itself a loan-word from Semitic.

[3] See W. F. Albright in *A.J.A.* 36 (1932), 295 ff.

the state of Ammon beginning to make forays into Israelite territory.[1] The very existence of Ammon was dependent on caravan
trade with the desert, and the ethnic composition of the Ammonites in the following centuries, as known from proper names on
seals, etc., was partly north-west Semitic, partly Arab.[2]

The organization of the Philistine 'empire' was also clearly
dictated by the interests of a trading confederacy. So far as we
know, the Philistines were always governed by their five 'lords',
meeting in council; the word is found in Hebrew only in the
plural, *sᵉrānīm*[3] or *sarney Pᵉlishtīm* (which is usually identified
with pre-Hellenic *turan(nos)*, 'tyrant', and compared with Tyr-
rhenian *turan*, 'lady'). The coastal members of the larger confederation marshalled their forces at Aphek above the source of
the 'Auja river north-east of Joppa; this well-watered base of
operations, midway between Philistine and Tjekker territory, was
admirably suited for the purpose and again illustrates the autonomy of the different Sea Peoples about the middle and just before
the close of the eleventh century. Two other items may be cited
to illustrate the nature of the Philistine 'empire'. It has been
pointed out that the solidly and symmetrically constructed late-
eleventh century fortress at Gibeah of Benjamin must be attributed to the Philistines, who had actually built a fortress at Gibeah
according to 1 Sam. x. 5.[4] The existence of such fortresses constructed at key points along trade-routes would naturally indicate
a high degree of organization. The establishment of an iron monopoly in Palestine (1 Sam. xiii. 19–22), after the earlier Hittite
model, served the double purpose of limiting Israelite use of iron
weapons and increasing industrial profits. Apparently the Philistine smiths were organized into a guild, like the earlier guilds of
Ugarit.[5]

## II. THE CANAANITE REVIVAL IN PHOENICIA

Between the late thirteenth and the end of the twelfth century B.C.,
the territory occupied by the Canaanites was vastly reduced. In

[1] On the early history of Ammon see W. F. Albright in *Miscellanea Biblica B. Ubach* (Montserrat, 1954), 131 ff.; and §1, 25, 66 ff.

[2] In addition to the material already mentioned, cf. my note in *Bull. A.S.O.R.* 160 (1960), 41, n. 25 a.

[3] The original Hebrew vowel of the first syllable is quite unknown and may just as well have been *u* as *a*; *sarney* is a secondary formation.

[4] See §1, 27, 13, n. 19 and G, 2, 50. See also L. A. Sinclair, in *Bi. Ar.* 27 (1964), 56.

[5] See §1, 27, 10 and 13, and for other details concerning the Philistines §1, 7, 114 ff. See above, p. 136.

the Late Bronze Age the entire coast of Syria from Mount Casius to the Egyptian frontier had been inhabited by a mixed people sharing a common language (with minor dialectal differences) and a common culture and religion. Inland this was also true to varying degrees; the narrowest belts of 'Canaanite' territory were in Ugarit and Palestine, and the widest eastward extension was in Phoenicia proper, where it stretched across Lebanon at least as far as Anti-Lebanon. First came the Israelites, occupying practically all the hill-country of western Palestine and much of Bashan (Ḥaurān).[1] The Sea Peoples then occupied the coast of Palestine and possibly coastal areas north of Phoenicia. About the same time came the Aramaeans, sweeping over eastern and northern Syria to establish a culture oriented northward and eastward rather than southward and westward. As a result the Canaanites suffered the loss of half their coast and virtually the entire hinterland except for Lebanon, where almost impenetrable mountain forests blocked aggression from the east. In all they must have lost a good three-fourths of their territory and at least nine-tenths of their grain land.

However, there were compensations for these losses. The coast of Phoenicia proper was ideally prepared by nature to become the home of a maritime people. It is true that there were few harbours like that of Berytus, but in those simple days small natural or artificial breakwaters were sufficient to protect most ships against storms. Two of the five leading Phoenician cities, Tyre and Aradus (Arvad), were on islands; they were thus impregnable fortresses as long as they controlled the sea. The remaining three, Sidon, Berytus and Byblos, were on the mainland; it is scarcely an accident that none of the three had the political significance in the middle centuries of the Iron Age that was possessed by Tyre and Aradus. In the Late Bronze Age, as we know from the Amarna Letters and Papyrus Anastasi No. 1,[2] Tyre was dependent on the mainland for its supply of fresh water. From the twelfth century onwards this dependence was greatly reduced; the rapid spread of watertight cisterns about the beginning of the Iron Age[3] explains not only the sudden expansion of settlement throughout the hill-country of Palestine in early Israelite times, but also the similar development of settlement over Mount Lebanon in the same period. This consequent increase in native population provided a substantial part of the

---

[1] Data mentioned above, pp. 514 f., make it probable that the critical phase of the Israelite conquest was nearly contemporary with the beginning of the Philistine raids.

[2] *C.A.H.* II¹, 326.

[3] §II, 5, 341 and 358, n. 72.

personnel needed to man the merchant fleets and colonize the Phoenician trading settlements in the Mediterranean.[1]

Another factor of great importance in the development of Phoenician maritime power was the destruction of the Hittite Empire in the late thirteenth century B.C.,[2] which ended any serious threat from Anatolia to the growth of Phoenician enterprise. After the death of Ramesses III, Egypt soon ceased to be either an actual or a potential danger. During most of the twelfth century Assyria was unable to expand west of the Euphrates. The brief interlude of expansion under Tiglath-pileser I and his sons, at the end of the twelfth and during the first decades of the eleventh century, can scarcely have constituted a direct threat to southern Phoenicia; in any case it soon passed and it was two centuries before Assyrian power again menaced Phoenicia. Moreover, the collapse of Mycenaean sea power during the late thirteenth century relieved the Phoenicians of any serious threat from the west except the perpetual menace of piratic attacks from the Sea Peoples.

Still another factor contributing to Phoenician maritime expansion may be mentioned: the rapid spread of iron after the fall of the Hittite Empire, which had monopolized it. In the sixth century Babylonian economic texts mention iron from Mount Lebanon, and it seems likely that the Phoenicians had long before discovered these deposits, traces of which still remain. Through trade with Asia Minor it soon became easy to obtain iron, which came into use for ordinary tools in the course of the eleventh century. Iron was far better adapted than copper or bronze for making axe-heads, adze-heads, saws and sledge-hammers; it was also much cheaper, once the markets were opened and the arts of smelting and forging iron had been developed. With the new tools came a great expansion in the use of the fine timber of Lebanon for ship construction. Larger beams and boards could now be manufactured much more cheaply.[3]

The devastation of the Phoenician coast by the Sea Peoples in the late thirteenth and early twelfth centuries B.C. must have virtually ended normal economic development. The Sidonians and the Byblians were the first to recover. The ancient rivalry

---

[1] For early Israelite participation in Phoenician shipping see e.g. Judg. v. 17 (twelfth century), Gen. xlix. 13 (eleventh century), 2 Kings x. 22 ff. (tenth century), etc.

[2] It is now virtually certain that this event took place much earlier than is commonly supposed.

[3] §III, 16, on the early development of the Phoenician merchant marine.

between Tyre and Sidon had been brought to a temporary halt
by the destruction of both cities, followed by the rebuilding of
Tyre as a Sidonian town.[1] Thenceforward, until the late eighth
century, we find 'Sidonian' used in the Bible, the Homeric Epics,
and native inscriptions as a term covering the South Phoenicians
in general.[2] Ittoba'al I of Tyre (c. 887–856) appears in the Bible
as 'king of the Sidonians'; over a century later Hiram II of Tyre
(so entitled in the Assyrian inscriptions) is called 'king of the
Sidonians' in a native inscription dedicated to Ba'al-Lebanon;
Elulaeus (c. 701) is called 'king of Tyre' by Menander, but 'king
of Sidon' in the Assyrian inscriptions (which say, however, that
his residence was in Tyre, while Menander says that Sidon was
separated from Tyre by the Assyrians). In late Sidonian coins
Sidon receives the Phoenician appellation 'mother of Kambe
(Carthage), Hippo, Citium and Tyre,' which sufficiently attests
the fact that Sidon claimed Tyre and its chief colonies as its own
daughters. From these and other data it appears certain that Tyre
and Sidon formed part of a single Sidonian state in the twelfth to
tenth centuries. Similarly, it is probable that Berytus, which is
never mentioned in the Bible or the Assyrian inscriptions, was
part of the Byblian state.

After more than a hundred years of complete darkness, the
report of Wenamun casts a bright light on Phoenicia at the end of
the Twentieth Dynasty under Ramesses XI (1100–1085 B.C.).[3]
The Egyptian threat to Asia had ceased, as the king of Byblos
delighted in reminding the unfortunate Egyptian envoy. The
Tjekker, who had settled in Dor (see above), were feared as
pirates. The southern coast of Cyprus, far from being under
Phoenician domination, was ruled by an independent queen,
whose subjects were allegedly about to put Wenamun and his
Byblian sailors to death when the extant portion of the narrative
comes to an end. Most illuminating is the description of the
organization of Phoenician shipping at that time. Zakarba'al,
king of Byblos, says to Wenamun, after scolding him for coming
in a second-rate ship with an unreliable captain: 'There are twenty
*mns*[4] ships here in my harbour which are in trading association[5]
with Smendes (the first Tanite pharaoh), and even in Sidon, which
you passed, there must be fifty *br* ships[6] which are in association

---

[1] G, 11, 79 ff.  [2] §11, 5, 347 ff.
[3] §1, 6. The Wenamun report is 'a real report', not a literary work as formerly
believed; see §11, 11, 41, n. 8 and §11, 12, 22. See below, pp. 641 ff.
[4] §1, 14, 54, n. 206.  [5] See above, p. 515, n. 2.
[6] §1, 14, 54, n. 206. See also §1, 27, 3 ff.

with Waraktir (Warkatara)[1] and are carrying (freight) to his residence.' Here again the reference to Sidon evidently includes Tyre and other ports of the Sidonians, since Tyre itself was mentioned in passing earlier in the same narrative. It follows from the words of Zakarba'al that it was then customary to organize syndicates of trading vessels under the protection of powerful foreign princes, such as Smendes of Tanis and Waraktir (Warkatara, of Askalon?), with whom profits were shared. The reason for such organization of shipping is not far to seek; the syndicates provided both the necessary capital with which to build and fit out trading fleets and the protection against piracy without which they could not have plied their trade. Centuries later the same expression was employed in Hebrew in connexion with the formation of syndicates and trading guilds.

That the word 'Phoenician' (Greek *Phoinix*) was derived from *phoinix*, 'red purple dye', was well known in antiquity, though it has often been denied in modern times. It has been deduced from fifteenth-century documents found at Nuzi that the word 'Canaan' is also derived from an older word for 'purple dye',[2] after which it was shown that the Hebrew word $k^e na'an\bar{\imath}$, 'merchant', was already used in this sense as early as the fifteenth century B.C. and that 'Canaanite' meant properly 'dealer in purple dye', i.e. 'textile merchant'.[3] As late as the time of Job (probably seventh century B.C.) the word $habb\bar{a}r$, 'member of a trading association' ($hub\bar{u}r$), still appears as a synonym of $k^e na'an\bar{\imath}$, 'merchant'. These facts illustrate the basic importance of trade in the Phoenician economy, an importance which was interrupted only temporarily by the crises of the late thirteenth and early twelfth centuries B.C.

It is characteristic of Phoenician as well as of Philistine organization that the power of the king tended to be kept in check by the 'elders', who met as a kind of senate in order to consider matters of importance to the state. In the Amarna Tablets we already have a council of elders ($\check{s}\bar{\imath}b\bar{u}tu$) at Arce (Irqata) in central Phoenicia.[4] In the Wenamun report Zakarba'al of Byblos called the state council (here designated by the well-known Hebrew term $m\bar{o}'\bar{e}\underline{d}$)[5] in order to consider the demand of the Tjekker envoys for the extradition of Wenamun. In later times the council of state still formed an integral part of the constitutions of Tyre, Byblos

[1] See above, pp. 513, 515.
[2] *Language*, 12, 121 ff.
[3] B. Maisler in *Bull. A.S.O.R.* 102 (1946), 7 ff. Cf. §II, 5, 356, n. 50.
[4] Amarna tablet 100, 4. My collation has confirmed this reading.
[5] See A. J. Wilson in *J.N.E.S.* 4 (1945), 245.

and Carthage, as we know from Assyrian, Hebrew and Greek sources of the seventh to third centuries B.C.

Epigraphic material throwing light on Phoenician history is relatively plentiful during the Late Bronze Age, but after the fall of Ugarit in the late thirteenth century it becomes very scanty indeed. The earliest of these texts (aside from a few names and the word *ḥeṣ*, 'luck', 'fortune', on javelin heads)[1] belongs to Ahiram (later Hiram), who was king of Byblos in the early tenth century; his sarcophagus is expressly said to have been made for him by his son Ittoba'al, and cannot be dated in the thirteenth century B.C.[2] Such an early date is disproved both by the character of the script and by the explicit statement of the text. On the other hand, it is quite true that the representations which cover the sarcophagus carry on the artistic tradition of the thirteenth century in many details, though the execution seems to be much inferior. To the tenth and early ninth centuries belong a number of inscriptions from Byblos written in substantially the same script as that on the Ahiram sarcophagus; all are datable by filiation and epigraphic sequence dating. Since two were inscribed on statues of the Bubastite kings Sheshonq (*c.* 935–914 B.C.) and Osorkon I (*c.* 914–874 B.C.), they may be arranged in the following order:

Ahiram *c.* 1000                   Abiba'al (son of Yehimilk?)
Ittoba'al, son of Ahiram          Eliba'al, son of Yehimilk
Yehimilk *c.* 950                   Shipitba'al I, son of Eliba'al[3]

Ahiram was on the throne within half a century or so after the reign of Zakarba'al, Wenamun's contemporary.

It is evident from the inscriptions on the statues of Sheshonq and Osorkon that Abiba'al and Eliba'al regarded themselves as vassals of the first two Bubastite pharaohs. Since there is no hint in Sheshonq's own inscriptions of any penetration beyond the plain of Esdraelon, it does not seem probable that he subjugated any part of Phoenicia by military occupation. The most natural explanation of the Byblian data is that Byblos had voluntarily accepted Egyptian suzerainty in order to protect itself from Sidonian encroachment. There is some Greek and Cypriot[4] evidence for limited Byblian competition with the Sidonians in colonizing the eastern Mediterranean, and Menander of Ephesus

[1] See S. Iwry in *J.A.O.S.* 81 (1961), 30 ff.
[2] §III, 20 *passim*. (For specific references see my criticism of this opinion in §II, 4, 2* ff. notes 4 ff.).
[3] For details see §II, 2 and for the list of kings p. 160.
[4] An unpublished study by William R. Lane suggests dialectal peculiarities of probable Byblian origin in certain Phoenician inscriptions from Cyprus.

tells us that Botrys, north of Byblos, was settled by Ittoba'al of Tyre (*c.* 887–856 B.C.)—a statement which presupposes a preceding defeat of Byblos by Tyre.

New evidence proves that the raids of the Sea Peoples on the coast of Palestine and Syria began several decades before the massive invasion in the eighth year of Ramesses III. This in turn supports the date *c.* 1191 B.C. given by Menander of Ephesus, following generally reliable native Tyrian records, for the foundation of Tyre by the Sidonians (after its previous destruction, on which see above).[1] If the Tyrian date is correct, it means that Tyre and Sidon were among the first Syrian seaports to have been destroyed by the Sea Peoples, and that Tyre was rebuilt under Sidonian auspices not long before the final Philistine irruption. By the time of Wenamun, as we have seen, Sidon was still much less important than Byblos, and Tyre is mentioned only in passing. Since Byblos was still inferior in power to the Tjekker, it follows that the dates given from the fourth century B.C. (at least) onward for the foundation of Utica near Carthage (*c.* 1101 B.C.) and of Gades (Cadiz) in Spain (shortly after the Trojan War) are impossible.

But the obvious impossibility of such high dates does not free us from the necessity of examining their basis. Two points must be borne in mind. First, the Phoenicians and Carthaginians reckoned the passage of time, in the absence of fixed written tradition, by generations of forty years, like the Israelites between the thirteenth and the seventh centuries B.C. and like Hecataeus among Greek historians;[2] in earlier times both Israelites and Greeks (Hesiod) had employed a lifetime as chronological unit.[3] Pityusa (Ibiza) was settled by the Carthaginians 160 years, or four generations, after the foundation of Carthage, according to Diodorus; Arganthonius, king of Tartessus in the sixth century B.C., was said to have lived for 120 years, with his life divided into three periods of a generation each, like the life of Moses. From Carthage we have some long genealogical lists; the longest has seventeen generations of a priestly family.[4] This particular list is undoubtedly historical in substance and probably in detail; most

---

[1] P. 519 and G, 11, 79, n. 2.

[2] On Greek genealogical calculations and their inflationary tendency, see especially §1, 9, and §11, 35.

[3] Well known from Etruria and not so well from Greece (for Hesiod, see §11, 35, 15). For earlier Assyria and Israel see *Bull. A.S.O.R.* 163 (1961), 50 ff.

[4] *Corpus Inscr. Semit.* no. 3778; §11, 26, 305 and Plate 31. Harden dates the stele in the late fourth or early third century B.C., in which case the chronology should extend back to the eighth century soon after the foundation of Carthage.

of the names are otherwise attested and a number of them are hypocoristica. The dedicator's great-great-grandfather bore the good Egyptian name *Pnūfe*, and the earliest ancestor named was called simply *Miṣrī*, 'The Egyptian'. Turning back to the date of the foundation of Utica, which is particularly well attested, we may reckon with an original chronological span calculated on the basis of an exact multiple of forty years, ending at 1101 B.C. Since under the special conditions of colonial adventure we are likely to find some exceptionally long generations, we cannot be far wrong in allowing an average of between twenty-five and thirty years. Being restricted to multiples of forty with a strong probability favouring a whole number of generations, and assuming a starting point between *c.* 600 and 400 B.C., we quickly find that most possibilities cluster about the tenth century B.C. This calculation does not constitute proof, but it fits together with many otherwise known facts to establish a clear pattern.

Thanks to the accumulation of datable epigraphs from different parts of the north-west Semitic world, it is now possible to fix the approximate dates of the earliest known inscriptions from the Phoenician colonies, which include two fairly long texts from Nora in Sardinia and from Cyprus,[1] as well as two small fragments from Nora and Bosa in Sardinia. Both script and language are good Phoenician of ninth-century type; attempts to assign them dates below the early eighth century at latest are quite impossible. The contention that the Nora text was not a complete funerary text but part of a decree which must have covered the face of several stones[2] was rejected by many scholars, but was confirmed and further developed by B. Mazar during a visit to Sardinia in 1962,[3] and he has also shown that the text originally extended farther to the right as well as to the left than had been proposed. The now certain date of the inscriptions in question proves that the beginning of Phoenician colonization in Cyprus and Sardinia cannot well be placed later than the tenth century and that a date after the ninth century is impossible.

A striking confirmation of the early date of the painted pottery in the lowest level of the Tanit Precinct at Carthage, has been obtained by comparison of the published material with similar

[1] §II, 1; and A. M. Honeyman in *Iraq*, 6 (1939), 106 ff.

[2] That it is part of a decree is made probable by the words of the text as well as the relatively huge size of the characters, which would be singularly inappropriate for a funerary stele. In the Mediterranean world we are accustomed to the laws of Gortyn in Crete, dating in their present form from the fifth century B.C. Parallels elsewhere are too numerous to mention.

[3] See provisionally §1, 27, 17 ff., and the excellent photograph published as Fig. 9.

painted ware from Megiddo (which was at the time wholly in the orbit of Sidonian material culture).[1] The Megiddo ware in question is almost all attributed to Stratum V by the excavators, but it is not clear whether this refers to VB (early tenth century) or to VA+IVB (a single stratum of Solomonic date from the second half of the tenth century).[2] If the ware continued into IVA it is even possible that the latest pieces (no longer characteristic) may date well down into the ninth century. We must, of course, assume that this ware was brought to North Africa not later than the late tenth or the early ninth century B.C., and that it continued to be manufactured until the eighth century, some time after it had disappeared in Phoenicia. Such phenomena are exceedingly common.

Art-historical data are also accumulating steadily, even though rather slowly. The finds at Aliseda near Cáceres in western Spain, about half-way up the Portuguese border, carry us back definitely to the seventh and eighth centuries B.C.[3] Much more important are the ivories from Carmona in the Guadalquivir valley near Seville, which have long been known,[4] but are now being dated much too late, after years in which they were accidentally dated correctly—at least in principle. These ivories do not resemble any late ivories from the eastern Mediterranean, but are intermediate in type between the Megiddo ivories (dated by Egyptian inscriptions and stratigraphy between c. 1300 and 1150 B.C.) and the Syro-Phoenician ivories of the ninth and eighth centuries, now known so well from different sites.[5] This intermediate date is particularly obvious when one compares the combs from Megiddo and Carmona, and then compares the Carmona combs with imported pieces from the sanctuary of Artemis Orthia in Sparta, dating roughly between 750 and 650 B.C.[6] The Carmona plaque D 513 has a griffin of Mycenaean type[7] and a warrior with spiked helmet, spear and shield like the well-known figures on the back of the warrior vase of Mycenae (about the end of the thirteenth century B.C.).[8] The coat of mail is Asiatic and the drawing of the head in profile is characteristically Egyptian in style. The last piece suggests a Cypriot prototype. That the Carmona ivories are not of local manufacture is shown by the discovery at Carthage of an ivory comb in precisely the same style, but with the addition of a bull and a female sphinx. In the writer's opinion there is only

---

[1] See provisionally §1, 5, 175 and note.
[2] §1, 5, 175; §11, 4, 5*; §11, 5, 346 ff.
[3] See especially A. Freijeiro in *Archivo Español de Arqueología*, 30 (1956), 3 ff.
[4] §11, 9.   [5] §11, 6; §11, 7; §11, 34, etc.   [6] §11, 16, 222 ff. and Plates cxxix ff.
[7] The late A. J. B. Wace first called my attention to this.   [8] §1, 8, fig. 265.

one reasonable conclusion, that they were made for export in quantity and that they belong to the very beginning of Phoenician trade with Spain in the tenth and ninth centuries B.C. If this is the case it would explain the complete absence of comparable material in western sites known to belong to about the seventh century B.C., as well as the apparent fact that no other foreign imports are known to have been recovered from the Iberian tumuli near Carmona where the ivories were found.

If we relate the evidence described in the preceding paragraphs to Sidonian history, it becomes obvious that it was quite impossible for Sidon and Tyre to expand their sea-trade in the Mediterranean until after the elimination of the Philistine sea and land 'empire' which lasted from the conquest of Palestine c. 1050 B.C. until the destruction of Philistine power by David during the first quarter of the tenth century B.C. (probably about 975). Our information about the succession of Sidonian kings of Tyre begins with Hiram's father Abiba'al at the beginning of the tenth century. It was probably Abiba'al who established Phoenician power in Cyprus,[1] and his son Hiram I (c. 969–936 B.C.), who was closely allied with both David and Solomon, may have continued the search for copper by initiating the serious exploitation of the mineral wealth of Sardinia. Utica also, near Carthage, was probably founded about this time. Before the end of the tenth century the Phoenicians had probably founded Gades, which bears the good Phoenician name *Ha-gader*, 'the walled enclosure'. Whether the Phoenicians or the native Iberians organized the trading caravans which travelled up the Guadalquivir valley past Seville and Carmona, branched off northward toward Cáceres and continued on into north-western Spain we shall not know until there have been systematic excavations along the route taken by these caravans.[2]

The Hebrew designation 'Tarshish ships' for the sea-faring vessels of Hiram's navy probably refers to ore-carrying ships, or perhaps to ships which were sufficiently large and strong to carry loads of copper ingots, like the thirteenth-century ship recently excavated off the southern coast of Anatolia.[3] Such refinery ships seem to have been called *kry* in Ugaritic and Egyptian (plural).[4] There is no direct reference to voyages to Tarshish (originally

[1] §II, 5, 348 and 361; §I, 27, 15.
[2] This route was first proposed by B. Mazar in 1957; see §II, 5, 347.
[3] §II, 8, 2 ff.
[4] These words are presumably derived from common Semitic *kūr*, 'smelting furnace'. Ugaritic *wry* should be read *kry*. The Eg. sing. is both *kr* and *ḳr*.

Tharros in Sardinia?)[1] in the narratives about Solomon's reign, but the expeditions sent out jointly by Hiram and Solomon, following the old trade association tradition, into the Indian Ocean certainly required just as large and strong vessels. There is no reason to locate Ophir anywhere except in the region extending from Eritrea to Somalia and possibly beyond it. In this region (Egyptian Punt) were to be obtained the gold, silver, ivory, ebony and two kinds of monkeys which are listed as the principal imports.[2] Excavations at Tell el-Kheleifeh near 'Aqaba make it virtually certain that this is the Ezion-geber which was the expedition's base of operations.[3]

The tenth century was, in any case, the golden age of Phoenician wealth and power, before the entire hinterland was overrun by the armies of the Aramaeans and the Assyrians. Little as we know directly about Phoenicia at that time, our indirect evidence is considerable; we have sketched only certain aspects of it.

## III. THE SYRO-HITTITE STATES

After the Hittite Empire had been destroyed by the barbarian hordes from the north-west, towards the end of the thirteenth century B.C., the Phrygians and other Indo-European peoples occupied the central plateau of Anatolia. In the mountainous south-eastern provinces (later Cataonia, Melitene and Commagene), the native population seems to have resisted so strongly that it was allowed to go its own way. Syria was protected by the Taurus range and the tough fibre of the northern mountaineers. The Hittites had established several vassal states in northern Syria during the initial period of their occupation in the fourteenth century B.C. At least two of them, Carchemish and Aleppo, were ruled by princes of the imperial Hittite dynasty. In a third state, Khattina, the reigning princes still bore names derived from imperial Hittite history as late as the ninth century B.C., and the imperial name Mutallu was borne by two kings of Gurgum and one of Commagene who are mentioned in the Assyrian records. In the century immediately following the collapse of the Hittite Empire there seems to have been some tendency to bring the various Hittite states together. The inscriptions of Tiglath-

---

[1] §II, 15, 280 ff.; §II, 5, 361, n. 103.
[2] Both the *qōpīm* and the TKYM (1 Kings x. 22) bear Egyptian names; cf. T. O. Lambdin, in *J.A.O.S.* 73 (1953), 154, and W. F. Albright in G, 9, II, 252a, s.v., 'Fauna: Primates'.
[3] §II, 25, 89 ff.

pileser I (1115–1077) repeatedly mention 'great Khatti', whose king, Ini-Teshub,[1] was defeated by the Assyrians. Since this name was borne by a king of Carchemish in the thirteenth century, he probably ruled there also, but Melid (modern Malatya) is said to belong to 'the great land of Khatti' under a local prince with a Hittite imperial name.[2]

Through surface finds and excavations in Syria many Hittite reliefs and hieroglyphic inscriptions have come to light. The first such finds were made at Hamath in 1871; in 1879 A. H. Sayce pointed out that the script on these monuments was identical with the writing on several Anatolian monuments and correctly applied the term 'Hittite' to them. Early Hittite monuments have since been found by the Germans at Zincirli, by the British at Carchemish, and by the French at Malatya on the border of Syria and Anatolia; later sculptures have also been found at many other sites.[3] Thanks to careful stylistic analysis of the pictured reliefs, it is possible to divide them roughly into three groups: (1) monuments showing clear affinities with the art of the great Hittite Empire (fourteenth and thirteenth centuries); (2) transitional monuments showing less true Hittite and Hurrian tradition and more affected by contemporary Phoenician and Aramaean art; (3) monuments influenced directly by Assyrian art.[4] This sequence has been best preserved at Malatya, where the monuments of the Lion Gate may safely be dated to the eleventh century and may in part be still earlier.[5] At Carchemish a much fuller chronological series has been admirably demonstrated.[6]

In 1930 Piero Meriggi published the important discovery that certain groups of characters in the Hittite hieroglyphic monuments represented words for 'son' and 'grandson'. The successful decipherment of the script of these monuments began almost immediately after this discovery and has since been carried to a point where most of the syllabic signs can be read.[7] By combining study of the order of royal names with stylistic analysis of the inscribed monuments, system has been brought out of chaos. Of course, there are dangers: little is yet known about palaeography; the same name may be repeated several times in the course of several

[1] Formerly read *Ili-Teshub*, but the name is identical with the thirteenth-century *Ini-Teshub*, transcribed into Egyptian as well as into cuneiform; cf. §III, 2, 154.
[2] *Ibid.*
[3] See especially §III, 7; 11.
[4] §III, 2 with the bibliographic indications in the footnotes.
[5] §III, 1; 2, 153 ff.
[6] §III, 44, *passim*. See also §III, 2, 155 ff.
[7] §III, 28; 35.

centuries; uninscribed monuments may be wrongly attributed. The union of the two methods brings assured results only in the case of monuments which are stylistically of the latest Assyrianizing type and bear royal names attested by Assyrian inscriptions: e.g. Warpalawas (Assyrian Urpalla) of Tyana. Thanks to figured monuments with Aramaic or Canaanite inscriptions, we know that the critical phase of the shift from pre-Assyrian to Assyrianizing art came in northern Syria west of the Euphrates between *c.* 850 and 825 B.C.[1] If we date the transitional group of monuments between the middle decades of the tenth and the third quarter of the ninth century we can scarcely be far wrong; the archaic group best illustrated by the Lion Gate at Malatya will fall between the late twelfth century and the middle of the tenth.

At Carchemish, thanks to the careful analysis of Barnett, it is possible to distinguish between the sculptures of the Water Gate, which are badly damaged but seem to be roughly contemporary with the Sulumeli reliefs of the Lion Gate at Malatya, and the reliefs of the Sukhis Dynasty in the late tenth or early ninth century B.C.[2] The sculptures of the Water Gate at Carchemish belong to the same general age as the inscriptions of the kings whose names were read provisionally as 'Pa-ī-da' and his son 'GREAT-pa';[3] both are called 'king of Carchemish', 'great king', and may go back to the time of Tiglath-pileser I of Assyria or a little later.[4] The following Sukhis dynasty closed with a king named Katuwas, not long before the time of Sankaras (Sangara of the Assyrian monuments, attested before 866 and until 848 B.C.).

Since it is now possible to analyse the increasing influence of neo-Assyrian art on the West, as the Assyrian arms advanced westward, a few observations on areas just outside of Syria proper will help to illuminate the situation in Syria itself. In the first place neo-Assyrian influence had not yet affected known specimens of Aramaean art in the Euphrates valley in 886 (the stele of Tell 'Asharah south of the confluence of the Euphrates and Khabur) and *c.* 875 (the slightly later steles of Tell Ahmar, south of Carchemish).[5] Similarly, it appears certain that the reliefs of Tell Halaf (Gozan), from the time of Kapara, precede the Assyrian occupation of the district in 894 B.C., since none of them show any neo-Assyrian influence whatever.[6] A date about the second

---

[1] §III, 2, *passim*.

[2] §III, 2, 157 (after R. D. Barnett in §III, 44, 260 ff.). See above p. 441.

[3] These names are now read *x-pa-zitis* and GREAT THUNDER (= Ura-Tarhundas). See J. D. Hawkins in *Iraq* 36 (1974), p. 71. (Ed.)

[4] §III, 44, 259.     [5] §III, 2, 147 ff. and 156 ff.     [6] §III, 2, 150 ff.; §III, 3.

half of the tenth century for most of the reliefs of Gozan is, therefore, clear. Turning to eastern Cilicia, just outside Syria on the
north-west, there is absolutely no sign of neo-Assyrian influence
on the sculptures of Karatepe, which must, accordingly, date from
the ninth century, as it has been observed.[1] They cannot reasonably be dated in the eighth century—much less in the seventh
(as recently attempted by a few classical archaeologists, accustomed
to reducing Iron Age chronology as much as possible). It is true
that the Phoenician script of the bilingual texts has been dated
in the third quarter of the eighth century, but examination of the
photographs shows that several late forms of letters do not actually
occur on the original; a date about 800 B.C. is highly probable.
A substantial lag between the neo-Assyrian style of Kilamuwa in
neighbouring Sam'al (Zincirli) and the nearly contemporaneous
sculptures of Karatepe may be explained geographically. A date
for the sculptures of Karatepe earlier in the ninth century remains,
however, possible. The recurrence of the royal name '*Wrk* (*Urikki*)
in both the ninth and the eighth centuries offers no problem.

In the present state of our evidence, it seems clear that the
refusal of an earlier authority to recognize the existence of any
monumental art or architecture in the neo-Hittite states of
northern Syria between 1200 and 850 B.C. was entirely wrong.[2]
In fact it is now becoming increasingly clear that the eleventh
and tenth centuries were the golden age of Syro-Hittite art and
architecture. By the end of the tenth century most of the small
states of northern Syria had become Aramaized, even though some
of them continued to give their kings royal names of imperial
Hittite or Luwian (in Sham'al and Gurgum) or mixed character.


## IV. EMERGENCE OF THE ARAMAEANS

Aramaean origins are elusive, in spite of the fact that we have much
scattered information about early Aramaean political history; the
less said about supposed occurrences of the name *Aram* in cuneiform texts of the late third and early second millennium the better.
And yet within four centuries of the time when they are first
mentioned as a people in contemporary inscriptions, Aramaic had
become the *lingua franca* of south-western Asia. We are, however,
faced with serious difficulties in trying to locate the region where
the Aramaic language—and presumably its original speakers—
became differentiated from a common Semitic background. We

---

[1] From oral information given the writer by Dr R. D. Barnett in October 1964.
[2] §III, 20, 164 ff., and against it §III, 2, and §II, 4.

first meet with Aramaeans in the Syrian Desert in the reign of Tiglath-pileser I (1115–1077); they were then called by the Assyrians 'Aramaean bedawin' (*Aḥlamē Armāya*). The earliest inscriptions containing more than a word or two belong to Bar-hadad and Hazael of Damascus; the former dates from about 850 and the latter from somewhere between *c.* 840 and 800. Both are in standard Old Aramaic, and so are the Zakir inscriptions from Hamath (before *c.* 750 B.C.) and the Sefire treaties from the neighbourhood of Aleppo (*c.* 750 B.C.). On the other hand, the two long eighth-century inscriptions of Panammu from Zincirli (Sam'al) are composed in an Aramaic dialect with Canaanite affinities, which has been termed 'Yaudic'.[1] Panammu's son wrote his own inscriptions in standard Aramaic. In the light of this situation it seems to be reasonably certain that standard Aramaic was originally the language of the kingdom of Damascus, called simply 'Aram' in native inscriptions and Old Testament literature.

Analysis of the relation between Aramaic and the older north-west-Semitic language of the second millennium shows clearly that the former is not a derivative of South Canaanite (Phoenician) or of North Canaanite (Ugaritic) or Amorite, though it has more in common with the two latter than with the former. In sibilant shift it differs from the other three; in the use of *n* dual and plural it agrees with Amorite. In verbal structure it is rather more closely related to Amorite than to the other two. Early Aramaic was strongly influenced by Phoenician in vocabulary and morphology; from the seventh century onwards Assyro-Babylonian influence dominated, as we can easily see from its sentence structure, as well as from hundreds of loan-words. The superficial difference in sound between Aramaic and Hebrew is largely due to the fact that the forward shift of the accent, common to all known north-west-Semitic tongues after the thirteenth century B.C., reached its climax in Aramaic and was extended to include the article (*h*)*a*, which was attached to the end of the noun (just as in Romanian among the Romance languages). In brief, examination of the linguistic situation confirms our first impression that Aramaic developed somewhere in eastern Syria, possibly growing out of Sutu dialects spoken there in the Late Bronze Age.[2]

[1] G, 6, 153 ff.
[2] Aramaic is not a direct offshoot of 'Amorite', as sometimes thought, but is rather intermediate in type between it and the proto-Arabic dialects of north Arabia. The relation must, however, have been complex, and later Aramaic was strongly influenced by Phoenician (south Canaanite) and by Assyro-Babylonian (Akkadian).

If we turn to Hebrew and Israelite tradition, we gain some idea of the complex tribal relation which presumably existed. The Aramaean stock must have been so mixed that tradition became hopelessly divergent. In Gen. x. 22–3, Aram is one of the principal Semitic peoples, along with Elam, Ashur, and Arphaxad (the putative non-Semitic ancestor of the Hebrews); its principal subdivisions are listed as Uz, Hul, Gether and Mash.[1] Since the nucleus of the list in Genesis X probably goes back to the tenth century B.C.,[2] these names ought to be very instructive; unhappily only Uz and Mash are otherwise known. In a somewhat later(?) passage, Gen. xxii. 20–4, Aram appears as the offshoot of Kemuel, one of the eight sons of Abraham's brother Nahor. Nahor is now known to have been the eponym of the town by that name, probably east of Harran; Nahor (*Naḫur*) appears frequently in Bronze Age documents from Mari and elsewhere, and is mentioned explicitly as a town in Gen. xxiv. 10. Unfortunately, again, most of the eight names are otherwise unknown: Uz reappears elsewhere in the Bible; Chesed is the eponym of the Chaldaeans; Hazo and Buz are Assyrian Khazu and Bazu, in central or eastern Arabia; Bethuel is the traditional father of Rebecca. Nahor's secondary wife, Reumah, is credited with being the mother of Tebah (Tubikhu of Zobah, in central Syria), Tahash (Takhshu, a district north of the region of Damascus), Gaham and Maachah (west of the region of Damascus). The name of Aram's father Kemuel is archaic in formation,[3] but is otherwise unknown. If we add to these two divergent traditions the fact that in the Patriarchal narratives the family of Abraham is represented as closely related to the Aramaeans of the Harran district, and that the Deuteronomic source speaks of Abraham as a 'wandering Aramaean' (Deut. xxvi. 5),[4] the problem becomes still more intricate. Finally, Amos ix. 7 says that the Aramaeans came from some land called Kir, just as the Israelites came from Egypt and the Philistines from Caphtor;[5] Kir is elsewhere stated to be a region near Elam to which the Aramaeans were exiled!

[1] §III, 4, 2 ff.

[2] Most of Gen. x has been attributed by documentary critics to J, which is now increasingly recognized as the chief source of E and partly of P (Noth, Mowinckel, etc.), and is dated by more and more scholars (e.g. the Baltimore school) in the tenth century.

[3] Probably revocalized in Hebrew tradition and actually derived from an original *[Yaq]qim-el* ('May El Be His Champion').

[4] Since '*RMY* meant 'travelling trader' in early South Arabic (Qatabanian), the phrase may possibly have meant 'wandering trader'; cf. G, 7, 34 ff., and *Bull. A.S.O.R.* 163 (1961), 44 ff. and 164, 28.          [5] See above, p. 512.

From the preceding survey of the evidence it is clear that we have to do with a complex process, which may be provisionally sketched as follows. The original speakers of Aramaic were nomads of mixed origin, who began settling down on the fringes of the Syrian Desert in the third quarter of the second millennium. They may then have headed a confederation of tribes which took advantage of the collapse of the Hittite and Egyptian empires, followed by the break-up of the Assyrian empire of Tukulti-Ninurta I, to invade *en masse* already tilled lands. The tribesmen pushed westward into Syria and eastward into the valleys of the Euphrates and its tributaries. Settling wherever possible in the fertile river valleys, they combined sheep-herding with agriculture and probably with caravan trade, after the introduction of camels had given them an extraordinary advantage over donkey caravaneers.[1] Their prestige was such that other nomad tribes joined them from southern Babylonia to the Upper Euphrates, and Aramaic rapidly displaced related dialects, at first for tribal intercommunication and eventually for all purposes. The descendants of the Amorites became Aramaean, a process doubtless facilitated by close dialectal similarities. This process was still at work in Babylonia in the eighth century B.C.; it has been shown that the nomad 'Aramaean' tribes of Babylonia at that time were mostly Arabs who had become assimilated to the Aramaeans.[2]

The original name of the Aramaeans was *Aram* (with two short *a* vowels and the accent on the first syllable), as may be shown by comparing the derived forms in different Semitic languages. The early Assyrian shift between nominative *Arumu*, genitive *Arimi*, and gentilic *Armāyu* resulted from the operation of Assyrian dialectal vowel harmony; it has nothing to do with the original pronunciation of the name. We cannot tell whether the name was at first personal or geographical; the suggestion, sometimes made, that it already appears in Old Akkadian or other early Babylonian texts is improbable.

As already noted, we first meet the Aramaeans in the contemporary documents of Tiglath-pileser I (1115–1077 B.C.). In his fourth year (1112) he launched a simultaneous attack on Aramaean settlements in different parts of the Euphrates valley, from the land of Shuah (Assyrian Sukhu), north-west of Babylonia, as far as Carchemish. Crossing the Euphrates in pursuit of the Aramaeans he burned six 'towns' at the foot of Mount Bishrī (*Bišrī*), that is, in Palmyrēnē. In a later, undated inscription the

---

[1] For recent bibliography see *Bull. A.S.O.R.* 163 (1962), 38, n. 9.

[2] §III, 37.

king claims to have crossed the Euphrates for the twenty-eighth time (twice in one year) in order to pursue the Aramaean bedawin. Here he specifies that the Aramaeans were routed from Tadmor (Palmyra) itself to Anath ('Ānah) in Shuah and even to Rapiqu on the Babylonian frontier. The struggle with the Aramaeans continued under the following kings. If the attribution of a fragmentary unpublished text to Ashur-bēl-kala is correct,[1] that king fought against Aram (*mat Arime*) in 1070. About 1062 Adad-apla-iddina, a usurper who is said by a cuneiform chronicle to have been an Aramaean, gained the throne of Babylonia. Contemporary records now come to an almost complete end in Mesopotamia, but later Assyrian inscriptions give us valuable data. Thus Ashur-dan II (934–912) informs us that the Aramaeans had occupied part of the region between the Lesser Zab and the Ḥamrīn mountains, in the East-Tigris country between Assyria and Babylonia, during the reign of Ashur-rabi II (1013–973 B.C.). Under the same king, according to an inscription of Shalmaneser III (858–824 B.C.), an Aramaean king had stormed the Assyrian stronghold of Mutkinu on the Upper Euphrates, opposite the Hittite town of Pitru (Pethor). Mutkinu had been in Assyrian hands since the time of Tiglath-pileser I, according to this same inscription; its loss evidently made a great impression on the Assyrians. Since Ashur-rabi II was an older contemporary of David, we may safely connect the Aramaean triumph with the situation presupposed in 2 Sam. vii. 3 and x. 16. According to this early source, Hadadezer, king of the Aramaeans of Zobah, was fighting at the Euphrates when David attacked him from the south, between 990 and 980 B.C. It seems only natural to suppose that the Assyrians had a share in turning David's attention to the Aramaeans, since the former were fighting for their lifeline to Syria and might reasonably be expected to look for allies wherever they were available.[2]

The Israelites seem to have first come into hostile contact with the Aramaeans towards the end of the eleventh century in the reign of Saul, who is said to have fought with 'the kings of Zobah' (1 Sam. xiv. 47). When we hear next of Zobah in the reign of David it was ruled by Hadadezer of Beth-rehob,[3] who controlled all eastern Syria from southern Ḥaurān to the Euphrates. Zobah appears as Ṣubatu (Ṣubutu, Ṣubiti) in Assyrian documents of the

---

[1] §III, 43, 84 f.

[2] §III, 15, 25 ff.; §III, 42, 42 ff.; §III, 31, 82 ff.; §III, 32, 102 ff.

[3] Beth-rehob (inferred from *ben Reḥōb*) was probably not Riḥāb north of Jerash, as thought by H. Guthe, but an unknown place of the same name in eastern Syria.

eighth and seventh centuries; it was then a province of greater Damascus, located in eastern Syria. From the account of David's war against Zobah we learn that the chief cities of Hadadezer at that time were Tebah (Late Bronze Tubikhu), Chun (Late Bronze Kunu, Roman Conna) and Berothai (perhaps Bereitan south of Ba'albek).[1] Though all three towns are in the Biqā', between Lebanon and Antilebanon, there can be no reasonable doubt that the land of Zobah proper lay east and north of Antilebanon, and was roughly equivalent to Bronze-Age Takhshu (Tahash, Gen. xxii. 24). Hadadezer was evidently the most important Aramaean ruler of his day; it may well have been he who stormed the Assyrian fortress of Mutkinu on the Upper Euphrates;[2] 2 Sam. viii. 10 (1 Chron. xviii. 10) states that he and Toi (Tou), king of Hamath, had been at war with one another. According to one account of David's war with Hadadezer, the latter began hostilities by sending aid to the Ammonites, who had provoked David into attacking them. In the course of the resulting war, the Aramaean confederation was roundly defeated; we hear of the Aramaeans of Beth-rehob, Geshur (later Gaulanitis, north of Gilead), Maachah (the district around Hermon, west and south-west of Damascus), Ish-tob[3] and Damascus, as well as of auxiliary forces from beyond the Euphrates. The two accounts in 2 Sam. viii and x are too fragmentary to enable us to reconstruct the course of events in detail. The outcome was decisive; Israelite garrisons were placed in Hadadezer's territory, especially in Damascus, and great booty was seized, including gold, silver and especially copper. Thenceforward, until the death of Solomon, the further rise of the Aramaeans in Syria was effectually checked; but the growth of their power in Mesopotamia became correspondingly accelerated.

During the period of obscurity which settled over Assyria under the two weak kings who succeeded Ashur-rabi II, the Aramaeans gained ground very rapidly. By the reign of the *roi fainéant* Tiglath-pileser II (967–935 B.C.) they had occupied Gidara in the region of Nisibis, half-way from the upper Khabur River to the frontiers of Assyria itself. To the second half of the tenth century belong the palace and reliefs of the Aramaean king Kapara[4] at Guzana (Tell Halaf, Gozan in 2 Kings xvii. 6) at the source of the Khabur river. Kapara calls himself 'son of Khadianu,' the Aramaic form of the name which appears as Hezion in

---

[1] In no case Berytus!  　　　　　　[2] See preceding page.
[3] Still enigmatic, though a plausible suggestion connects it with Golan = Gaulanitis east of the Sea of Galilee.
[4] See above, p. 528.

1 Kings xv. 18; the men (or clans) by the name were in any case contemporary. The Aramaean tribe which occupied the territory of Gozan was called Bakhianu (Aramaic *Baḥyān*); its chief was Abisalamu (Absalom) at the beginning of the ninth century.[1]

An inscription of Ashur-dan II (934–912), with whom the Assyrian revival began, mentions the Aramaeans in connexion with campaigns in the west and south-east of Assyria, but it is difficult to form a clear picture. Under his son Adad-nīrāri II (911–891) we have a well-preserved account of the operations against the Aramaeans which occupied much of the king's reign. It is significant, however, that there is no mention of a campaign against the Aramaeans of northern Mesopotamia until about his eleventh year. From then until the end of his reign the Assyrians directed campaign after campaign against the Aramaeans, mentioning particularly various chiefs of the large tribe of Teman[2] which had occupied the region of Nisibis. The military culmination of his reign was reached in 892, when Gozan was captured and the settlements of the Khabur Valley capitulated, one after another. In 877 we have the first mention of the Aramaean state of Bīt-Adini (Biblical Beth-eden), which occupied both banks of the Upper Euphrates below Carchemish.

Meanwhile Solomon had died and Damascus had made good its independence, under an otherwise unknown Aramaean chieftain named Rezon. The latter can scarcely have remained in power long, since early in the ninth century we find Ben-hadad I on the throne; Ben-hadad is said to have been son of a Tabrimmon and grandson of a Hezion, that is, perhaps, member of the clan of Hezion (Khadianu in cuneiform).[3] The new state took over the domination of the northern part of the Syrian desert as political heir of Hadadezer of Zobah; in an inscription from the latter part of Ben-hadad's reign, about 850 B.C., the latter calls himself 'king of Aram', in accord with the practice frequently attested in the Bible and also found in the inscription of Zakir, king of Hamath. It is probably not accidental that the king's personal name was also Hadadezer, like that of his predecessor on the throne of Zobah a century earlier. We may perhaps compare the title 'king of Aram', borne by the princes of Damascus, with

---

[1] §III, 3, 82.

[2] Probably not derived from north Arabic *Teimā* (Babylonian *Tema*, biblical and Qumrān *Tēmān*). The name means simply 'southerner'.

[3] The writer's decipherment of the same names in the Ben-hadad inscription from near Aleppo (in *Bull. A.S.O.R.* 87 (1942), 27 ff.) is disputed, but nothing cogent has been proposed in their place.

the title 'king of all the Arabs', borne by 'Amru 'l-Qais in the inscription of an-Namarah (A.D. 328).

The climax of Aramaean political domination in Mesopotamia may thus be dated between about 950 and 900 B.C.; its climax in Syria did not come until the ninth century, owing partly to the lag caused by the triumph of David over Hadadezer. The remarkable accumulation of wealth in the hands of these Aramaean chieftains, attested in both Hebrew and Assyrian records, was undoubtedly in large part the result of commercial activity. We have already noted that the Aramaeans introduced the use of camels in the caravan trade of Syria and northern Mesopotamia. In keeping with the new importance of the camel, we find representations of riding camels in the late tenth century at both Gozan and Carchemish; references to camels became common in Assyrian inscriptions of the ninth century.

The art of the Aramaeans in the tenth century was still almost purely Syro-Hittite, as we know from the older monuments of Zincirli, Hamath and Gozan. It would be a mistake to assume that the bearers of this Syro-Hittite art were still prevailingly non-Semitic. An excellent illustration is the Melcarth stele of Ben-hadad I, found near Aleppo;[1] though dating from about the middle of the ninth century and inscribed in pure Aramaic, the figure of the god which adorns it does not yet show any clear influence from Assyrian or contemporary Phoenician art; it is still Syro-Hittite. At Hamath we know that Hittite inscriptions continued to be carved under Urkhilina (Irkhulina) as late as the middle of the ninth century, but a century earlier Hadoram, son of Tou, had borne a characteristically Semitic name. We have already noted above that the Aramaeans were actually the dominant people in Sham'al, Gurgum and other old Hittite states at least from the ninth century on and probably still earlier. It was not long before the enterprise of the Aramaeans freed them completely from the dead hand of the Hittite past. This does not mean, however, that the Hittites simply disappeared from this region. There is, in fact, very strong reason to derive the Armenians[2] (who occupied the whole country from Cilicia through Armenia Major until the times of the Arab, Kurdish, and Turkish irruptions) both physically and linguistically from the Hittites.

---

[1] See preceding note.                     [2] §III, 5.

# CHAPTER XXXIV

## THE HEBREW KINGDOM

### I. THE LITERARY CHARACTER OF THE OLD TESTAMENT HISTORICAL BOOKS

T H E sources available for the period between Israel's settlement in Palestine and the division of the kingdom 'all Israel' into two kingdoms, Israel in the north and Judah in the south, are principally the books of Joshua, Judges, Samuel and the first twelve chapters of I Kings. Of these, the book of Joshua[1] certainly presents a combination of narrative elements that are parallel to one another, in exactly the same way as the Pentateuch does. Indeed, exactly the same 'sources' can be found in this book as are found in the Pentateuch, that is L or J[1], J or J[2], E and P. In addition to these, there is a series of isolated passages in Joshua which belong to the 'Deuteronomist' school.

Possibly the books of Judges,[2] Samuel[3] and Kings[4] ought to be analysed in the same way, that is as a combination of several narrative elements that are parallel to one another. But P disappears, for that source certainly ended with the book of Joshua. In the book of Kings the material to be attributed to one or more of the 'Deuteronomist' schools is much more considerable than in the preceding books. Still, it is not possible to be nearly as certain in attributing material to the various parallel lines of narrative in the books of Judges to I Kings as it is in the Pentateuch and the Book of Joshua, and other analyses accordingly remain equally possible. Such a one is Martin Noth's theory of a Deuteronomistic historical work by an author of the sixth century B.C., composed under the influence of the Deuteronomium.[5]

The doubts about the correct analysis are, however, of little consequence for the historical evaluation of these books, as can be shown from two examples. Judges i. 1–ii. 5,[6] and isolated passages of Joshua such as xv. 14–19, contain an account of the

---

\* An original version of this chapter was published as fascicle 32 in 1965.

[1] §1, nos. 1; 9; 13; 15; 23.  [2] §1, nos. 3; 5; 11; 12; 16; 17; 20; 21; §11, 1.
[3] §1, nos. 3; 4; 6; 11; 12; 17; 18.  [4] §1, nos. 2; 8; 10; 12; 17; 22.
[5] §1, 14.  [6] §1, nos. 7; 23.

beginning by individual tribes of the conquest of the land west of Jordan after Joshua's death. From the historical point of view it is of little consequence whether this account is attributed to the 'L source' and the main narrative of the book of Joshua to the 'sources J and E', or whether it is assumed that there were two or three independent narratives, not to be connected with any of the named 'sources'. It is certain that the view represented by Judges i. 1–ii. 5 corresponds more closely with the actual course of events than does the main narrative in the book of Joshua. The same may be said of the narratives of the origin of kingship in Israel in I Samuel vii–xiv.[1] The account in I Samuel ix. 1–x. 16; xi; xiii–xiv, ought perhaps to be subdivided again into two lines of narrative, a point that can be neglected for the present purpose; but this account is undoubtedly more reliable than that of I Samuel vii–viii; x. 17–21 (27); xii. It is a matter of indifference, then, so far as the historical purpose is concerned, whether one attributes the first set of passages mentioned to L and J, and the latter set to E, or not.

## II. THE TRADITIONAL HISTORY AND MODERN CRITICISM

What has already been said about the conquest of the land and the creation of a kingdom of Israel indicates the course of modern criticism, which has pointed out the contradictions in the narratives and has rendered the conception of history presented by the tradition incredible. That conception depended on the main narrative about the conquest,[2] neglecting Judges i. 1–ii. 5, and on the narrative of the creation of the kingdom in I Samuel vii–viii; x. 17–21 (27); xii, leaving I Samuel ix. 1–x. 16; xiii–xiv on one side.[3] Thus it attributed the conquest of the land west of Jordan to 'all Israel', led by Joshua, and to Israel's victories at Gibeon (Joshua x. 1–14) and the waters of Merom (Joshua xi. 1–9). It also derived the origin of the kingdom from a capricious obstinacy of the people, of which Samuel, and Yahweh, disapproved.

The same has happened in other cases too. In the conception of the judges presented by the tradition, they are thought of as having authority over 'all Israel', and were like kings without the title; they were accordingly supposed to have ruled the people in succession. The dangers from hostile attack from which they freed the people were always caused, the tradition ran, by the

---

[1] §1, 19.  [2] §III, nos. 14; 15; 41.  [3] §II, nos. 2; 3.

people's idolatry, while the raising of the judges to bring help was due to the contrite people's cry to Yahweh for assistance. More exact analysis of the book shows, however, that the old stories of the individual judges do not represent these men as rulers of 'all Israel' at all, but only as men who aided their tribes, and perhaps one or more of the neighbouring tribes. The conception of the judges as ruling 'all Israel' presented in parts of the book written at a later date led to their treatment as succeeding one another.[1] That must, at any rate in certain cases, be corrected;[2] some of these judges may have been contemporaries.

Criticism has also shown that only in the late element of the book of Judges is the people's idolatry given as the cause of their dangerous situation, and their contrition as the reason for divine aid being granted. There is no such explanation of the dangers, and of the aid given, in the older narratives; they represented Yahweh rather as a God who regards the enemies of his people as naturally his enemies too, and is therefore intent, of his own will, on Israel's salvation.

The narratives in I Samuel xvi–xxxi[3] concerning the breach between Saul and David, and their struggles against each other, give the general impression that Saul was rejected by Yahweh, for which reason he ruled without success, and ought not in reality to be recognized as legitimate king at all; his coronation was followed immediately by his dethronement in favour of David, anointed by Samuel when still a boy. But there is no lack of indications that Saul exercised a strong and successful rule, and that his fall was not due to his sinful behaviour but had all the elements of a personal tragedy.

Thus modern criticism has isolated from their present context older narratives, or groups of narratives, which are undoubtedly nearer to the truth than the later literary developments in which they have been wrapped. But that does not imply that they can be regarded as historically authoritative without careful, detailed examination of the subject-matter. It is true of these older narratives in Judges and Samuel that they have all the character-istic features of legend, and that therefore the historical content must be extracted from them. Nevertheless, narratives such as that of Abimelech's success and death in Judges ix, and of Saul's victory over the Philistines in I Samuel xiii–xiv, may be fairly close to the truth. The narrative of David's rise in II Samuel i–vii,[4] which closes with an enumeration of his victories, in the style of a catalogue, and the list of his court officials

[1] §v, 9.     [2] §v, 23.     [3] §ii, 5, 132 ff.     [4] §ii, 5, 47 ff. and 133.

(ch. viii) are completely trustworthy, and so is the account of the deaths of his sons who were nominated his successors (II Sam. ix–xx; I Kings i–ii).[1] The history of Solomon given in I Kings iii–x contains the sagas and stories of Solomon's judgement, iii. 16–28, and of the visit of the Queen of Sheba to Solomon, x. 1–10, 13,[2] where the historical substance is wrapped in a thick cover of poetry. Other parts are, in type, simply documents, and therefore historical sources of the very best kind,[3] in spite of the often corrupt text; such are the lists of Solomon's court officials and district governors, iv. 1–6, 7–19, the list of the victuals for Solomon's kitchen, iv. 22–3, which has a parallel in an Ugaritic tablet from the fourteenth century B.C.,[4] and the accounts of the construction of the palace and temple, vi–viii; x. 16–20.[5]

The biblical sources for the time of the patriarchs, for the sojourn of Israel in Egypt, for the exodus and the settlement in Canaan, can be used for a historical account only when subjected to exact study and criticism. This is also true of those books which deal with the period of the judges and of the first three kings, Saul, David and Solomon. But these latter sources nevertheless contain a greater amount of historically reliable material than scholars were inclined to admit in the early years of the twentieth century. It is now completely impossible to believe that David was not a historical person at all, but the ultimate degenerate form of a Moabite god or the like. The contradictions in the accounts of several events or in the opinions concerning them (e.g. as to the course of the conquest or the beginning of Saul's reign) at one time led to the conclusion that these events were not historical, or that at any rate the truth was not ascertainable. These same contradictions have now to be regarded in quite a contrary way, as clearly recognizable witness of historical truth. In such cases, where there are two or even more, separate testimonies to an event, the true character of the event can be the better judged. In the pages that follow there is given, with due regard for the critical caution required, an account of the land settlement and of the three centuries after Israel's settlement in Canaan, recording the deeds of the judges and the personalities and works of the first three kings. The positive form intentionally avoids that resigned scepticism which found expression in the first edition of this *History*.[6]

---

[1] §II, 5, 82 ff.          [2] See below, p. 593.          [3] §II, 4.
[4] Virolleaud, C., *Le Palais Royal d'Ugarit*, II (1957), 163 f., no. 128.
[5] See below, pp. 594 ff.          [6] *C.A.H.* II[1], pp. 405 f.

## III. THE LAND SETTLEMENT

The oldest literary tradition concerning the conquest of Canaan by Israel is, as we have seen, preserved in Judges i. 1–ii. 5.[1] According to that account, after Joshua's death the individual tribes set out from Gilgal, situated near Jericho, to take possession of the districts west of Jordan allocated to them by lot. There is clearly an underlying preconception, that 'all Israel' had previously been under Joshua's command, that Joshua had therefore led all the twelve tribes, or at any rate those later settled west of Jordan, across the Jordan, and captured Jericho with them. The question immediately arises, whether this preconception corresponds with the historical facts.

If it did, the crossing of the Jordan and the capture of Jericho[2] would be regarded as deeds of 'all Israel', even if that did not apply to the subjugation of the whole land west of Jordan. Reasons have already been given for the view that some tribes, namely the Leah tribes, penetrated into Palestine from the south in the process of seeking change of pasture, and that only the 'house' of Joseph entered and then left Egypt. According to that view, only this 'house', after a fairly long stay in Qadesh,[3] forced its way into the districts opposite Jericho, east of Jordan. If this is correct, only a negative answer to the question arising from Judges i. 1–ii. 5 is possible; the crossing of the Jordan and the securing of a bridge-head west of the river, were in fact acts of the 'house' of Joseph only. They came to be attributed to 'all Israel' owing to a secondary development of the tradition.

Despite this, confidence can still be felt in the tradition that Joshua was leader of the 'house' of Joseph in these undertakings.[4] His connexion with this 'house' is clearly established by the information, Joshua xxiv. 30, that he was buried 'in the border of his inheritance', in Timnath-serah of Mt Ephraim, modern Khirbet Tibneh. Although for this purpose no reliance can be placed on the stories of the captures of Jericho[5] and 'Ai,[6] the advance into lands west of Jordan no doubt entailed military action, and in those engagements the ark of Yahweh, the ancient shrine of this tribe, wandering or at war,[7] undoubtedly played its part. The narratives of the abode of the patriarchs in Canaan, Genesis xii–xxxvi, of the entry of Jacob and his sons into Egypt, Genesis xxxvii; xxxix–l, of the commencement of Simeon's

---

[1] §II, 1; §III, 31, 167 ff.  [2] See below, p. 546.
[3] See below, p. 545; cf. above, pp. 328 ff.  [4] §III, 4.
[5] §III, nos. 11; 17.  [6] §III, nos. 12; 18; 21; 24; 34.  [7] §III, nos. 7; 8; 13; 30; 40.

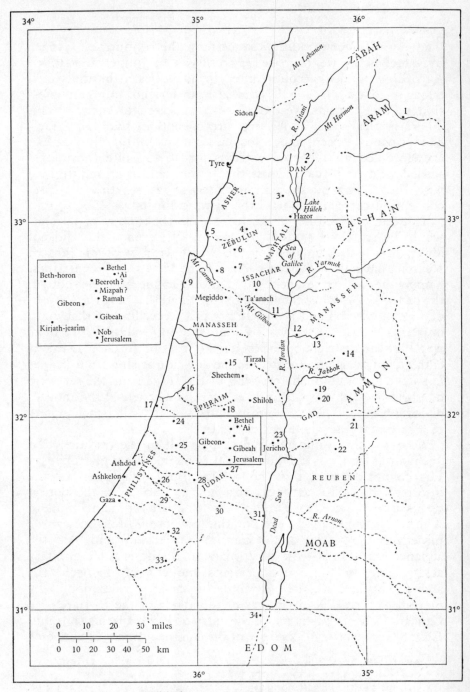

Map 11. Political geography of Palestine, about 1000 B.C.

## NUMERICAL KEY

| | | | | | |
|---|---|---|---|---|---|
| 1 | Damascus | 13 | Mahanaim? | 24 | Lod |
| 2 | Dan | 14 | Gerasa | 25 | Gezer |
| 3 | Qadesh | 15 | Samaria | 26 | Gath |
| 4 | Beth-anath? | 16 | Aphek | 27 | Bethlehem |
| 5 | Accho | 17 | Joppa | 28 | Adullam |
| 6 | Cabul | 18 | Timnath-serah | 29 | Lachish |
| 7 | Bethlehem | 19 | Mizpah | 30 | Hebron |
| 8 | Harosheth? | 20 | Gilead | 31 | 'En-gedi |
| 9 | Dor | 21 | Rabbath-Ammon | 32 | Ziklag? |
| 10 | Jezreel | 22 | Heshbon | 33 | Beer-sheba |
| 11 | Beth-shan | 23 | Gilgal | 34 | Tamar |
| 12 | Jabesh-Gilead | | | | |

## ALPHABETICAL KEY

| | | |
|---|---|---|
| Accho  5 | 'En-gedi  31 | Joppa  17 |
| Adullam  28 | Gath  26 | Lachish  29 |
| Aphek  16 | Gerasa  14 | Lod  24 |
| Beer-sheba  33 | Gezer  25 | Mahanaim?  13 |
| Beth-anath?  4 | Gilead  20 | Mizpah  19 |
| Bethlehem  7 and 27 | Gilgal  23 | Qadesh  3 |
| Beth-shan  11 | Harosheth?  8 | Rabbath-Ammon  21 |
| Cabul  6 | Hebron  30 | Samaria  15 |
| Damascus  1 | Heshbon  22 | Tamar  34 |
| Dan  2 | Jabesh-Gilead  12 | Timnath-serah  18 |
| Dor  9 | Jezreel  10 | Ziklag?  32 |

and Levi's relations with Shechem the son of Hamor, Genesis xxxiii. 19; xxxiv. 1–24, and of Judah's relations with the Canaanites, Genesis xxxviii, emphasize the peaceful character of the proceedings in that period, so that the explanation of the events as arising from the custom of seeking change of pasture is natural.[1] The emphasis in the sagas of the crossing of the Jordan and the early advance of Israel in the parts west of Jordan is on events the reverse of peaceful. They are clearly marked as tales of war, and it can hardly be assumed that reliable historical memories do not underlie the stories in this respect.

The conclusion will, then, be that the entry of the 'house' of Joseph into the districts west of Jordan, and the beginnings of its settlement there were accomplished mostly in the course of a war, probably under the leadership of Joshua. That conclusion may perhaps also be supported by the information from an Egyptian source which would at the same time determine the period of this entry of the 'house' of Joseph into these lands. The poem on the victories of Merneptah,[2] composed in about 1230 B.C., contains admittedly a reference to Israel in a context which must refer to Palestine, but leaves—alas!—some uncertainty on the precise part of the country there meant.[3] It states that 'Israel' is destroyed and has no more seed. In this text the determinative used for this name is that meaning 'foreign people', or 'foreign tribe', not that for 'foreign land'. That can be interpreted to mean that though this people already lived in Palestine, it had not yet settled there. This would fit the 'house' of Joseph and its advance in the parts west of Jordan about 1230 B.C. But this combination may not be relied upon, as, according to Genesis xxxii. 24–32; xxxiii. 20, a group named Israel seems to have existed in the land west of Jordan before the entry of the 'house' of Joseph, and the Israel of the Merneptah inscription might mean this older group.[4] The evidence of this inscription is thus equivocal. But archaeological findings[5] seem to mark a deep rupture probably caused by the entry of the 'house' of Joseph. Canaanite Bethel,[6] which was in the area occupied by the 'house' of Joseph, was destroyed in the last third of the thirteenth century, and resettled from about 1200 B.C. onwards; the conquerors and new settlers can only be supposed to be members of

---

[1] §III, nos. 3; 23.
[2] G, 16, no. 109; G, 15, 20 ff.; G, 30, nos. 342 f.; G. 29, 376 ff.; G, 36, 137 ff. pl. VIII.　　　[3] G, 26, XIV, 86. See above, p. 318.
[4] §III, nos. 9; 10.　　　[5] G, 4, 86 ff.; §III, nos. 1; 27; 35; 36; §V, 28.
[6] §III, nos. 2; 16; 24.

the 'house' of Joseph. Further, it has been possible to show that the hill area belonging to the Joseph tribe was much more densely populated at this time than previously; the construction of the new settlements must in this case too be attributed to members of the 'house' of Joseph, penetrating into that area at the end of the thirteenth century.[1]

The conception prevalent in the book of Joshua, then, that he, after leading 'all Israel' across the Jordan, broke the military power of the Canaanites in two great battles and so made possible the distribution of the land west of the Jordan amongst the nine and a half tribes, is unhistorical and must be corrected. Joshua's command was limited to the 'house' of Joseph and, as Judges i.1 says, he died in Gilgal soon after the crossing of the Jordan by the 'house' of Joseph. On the other hand it is quite likely that the successful progress of the 'house' of Joseph, just penetrating into Palestine, strengthened the Hebrew tribes long settled there, which were closely bound to Joseph through the common national traditions based on a religion linked with Qadesh[2] and Sinai. These may accordingly have proceeded to capture Canaanite positions within their reach. If Albright's assumption that Lachish (Tell ed-Duweir) fell into Israelite hands about 1230 B.C., or shortly after, is correct, it may be that the tribe Judah, which had previously lived in agreement with the Canaanites, as a guest in their midst, had now begun to increase its holding by force. Similar procedures may have been begun by other Hebrew tribes already settled for some time in Palestine, owing to the successes of the 'house' of Joseph.

It is certain in any case that in course of time all the Hebrew tribes did come to take military action against their Canaanite neighbours. These wars lasted a long time, and came to an end only when the tribes were united into the political unity created by Saul and David. The consequence of the union was that many of the tasks left unfinished by the tribes, including the conversion into Israelite areas of those Canaanite enclaves which remained in existence, had to be passed on to the kingdom to complete. It is easy to understand how many of the successes of individual Israelite tribes against Canaanite fortresses in their areas could come to be dated back and attributed to 'all Israel', thought of as being then under Joshua's command. In one or two instances it can be shown that probably this did occur. Joshua xi ascribes the defeat of Jabin, the king of Hazor,[3] and the capture of this

---

[1] G, 4, 87 ff.         [2] See above, pp. 325 and 541.
[3] §III, nos. 19; 42; 43; 44; 45.  See below, p. 554.

city by Joshua, while in Judges iv it is Baraq who overcame Jabin. It is at least possible that both accounts refer to the same event, and if that is so Baraq's deed has perhaps been transferred to Joshua. The excavations of Hazor do not yet admit a clear answer to this question, although they allow the assumption that the destruction of the Canaanite Hazor dates from about 1200 B.C. A similar case may be seen in the victory over five Amorite kings at Gibeon,[1] attributed in Joshua x to Joshua. In this case, too, an event which was really later may have been dated back to the time of the conquest. Similarly the victory over Sihon of Heshbon, attributed in Numbers xxi. 21–31, to 'all Israel' under the command of Moses[2] may in fact represent an enterprise of the tribes Reuben or Gad,[3] later settled in that district, which was wrongly attributed to the period of the conquest.

But we must also consider certain narratives concerned not so much with specific events as with striking phenomena of the later period explained as deriving from the past; these stories are aetiological in purpose. Good examples of this type are the stories of the capture of Jericho, the stoning of Achan, and the battle against 'Ai, in Joshua vi–viii. The first explains the deserted condition of Jericho as it was found by the Israelites advancing west of Jordan. That the city had once been a Canaanite stronghold was shown by the impressive ruins of the walls. The explanation given was, that Yahweh had caused these walls to fall before the Israelites. The second story undertakes to answer the question of the origin of a remarkable heap of stones near Jericho, and why this neighbourhood was called the valley of Achor. The third gives an explanation of the ruins of the place called then *hā-'Ai*, as it is now called Et-Tell, situated about two miles south-east of Bethel. In the last case, the impression given by the narrative itself is of an aetiological saga, and that is confirmed by archaeology.[4] Excavations have proved that 'Ai was inhabited till about 2000 B.C. and was fortified, but was then deserted and remained so until about the end of the second millennium B.C. There was, then, no fortress that Joshua could have destroyed. It is possible that there has been a confusion of Bethel and 'Ai, the narrative of Joshua vii. 2–5 and viii. 1–29 having originally referred to Bethel.[5]

The conception suggested by the book of Joshua that the land west of Jordan was rapidly occupied by 'all Israel' under command

---

[1] §III, nos. 20; 28; 29.  
[2] See above, p. 329.  
[3] G, 28, 69; §III, 22, 81.  
[4] §III, 27.  
[5] G, 4, 88.

of a single leader is therefore not historical. Rather, various exploits were carried out by various groups over a long period, for in all probability parts of the Israelite tribes were already in the land when the 'house' of Joseph penetrated there. On the other hand there is explicit evidence in the Old Testament that certain tribes came to their area of permanent settlement some considerable time after the settlement of the tribe of Joseph in the land west of Jordan. A particularly clear case is that of Dan. In Judges xvii–xviii we learn that this tribe, which perhaps belonged to the 'house' of Joseph and came into Palestine with the other tribes of that 'house', settled first west of Jerusalem, but later changed its area for the sources of the Jordan and the city Laish, renamed Dan by the tribe.

But it seems also to be true of Benjamin that it came into existence as a tribe only after the *Landnahme*. Some think that the Israelite tribe of Benjamin was connected with the Benjaminites mentioned in the Mari-texts of the eighteenth century B.C.[1] and had invaded the land west of Jordan long before the 'house' of Joseph came there. But the narrative (Judges xix–xxi) makes this assumption improbable. This seems to have no other basis than the successful effort of the 'southern province' (for this is the meaning of Benjamin) of the 'house' of Joseph to make itself into an independent tribe, in spite of the extreme measures taken to prevent this by the tribe of Joseph.[2] In the extant form of the story Benjamin was opposed to, and condemned by, 'all Israel'. Here again matters which concerned only the 'house' of Joseph in actual fact have been given wider import and become the concern of 'all Israel'. But in this case the leadership is not attributed to Joshua, and the reason is apparent—a correct recollection of the circumstances had been maintained. This event was later than most of those recorded in the book of Joshua, and so it was attributed (Judges xx. 28) to the generation following that of Joshua and his contemporary Eleazar. Like Benjamin, other tribes too arose only after the conquest and the settlement by the 'house' of Joseph. Such are Machir[3] (mentioned in the song of Deborah), Manasseh and Ephraim; like Benjamin, they split off from the 'house' of Joseph.

Clear traces of the same process remain in the evidence concerning the Israelite settlement in Trans-Jordan.[4] According to the principal account in the tradition (Num. xxxii and Joshua xiii. 8–33; xxii) this was already arranged by Moses. The terms

[1] §III, nos. 5; 39. [See, however, above, p. 318 n. 3. (Ed.)]
[2] §III, 6; cf. §III, 32.    [3] §V, 23, 190 ff.    [4] §III, nos. 25; 26; 33; 38.

of the agreement are actually given. Men of the two tribes Reuben and Gad and the half-tribe Manasseh already settled there undertook the obligation of supporting the other nine and a half tribes in arms in the struggle for the land west of Jordan. This promise was kept. But still there are traces of evidence showing that the process of settlement there continued during rather long periods, and ended only after the settlement of the 'house' of Joseph west of Jordan. In the account given in Joshua xvii. 14–18, the men of Joseph complained to Joshua that the land allotted to them was too small for a tribe of that size. They were instructed by him to cut down the wood 'in the land of the Perizzites and Rephaim'. The fact envisaged is clearly that in some cases the Israelite settlement in 'Ajlūn, that is in the parts of Trans-Jordan between the Jabbok and the Yarmuk, and in El-Belqā south of the Jabbok, started from west of Jordan. The process must certainly have taken a long time. Another trace of the settlement east of Jordan by Israelites from west of the river seems to be found in II Samuel xviii. 6. According to this a part of 'Ajlūn bore the name 'wood of Ephraim', which is most easily explained if men of Ephraim from west of Jordan transferred their habitation to this district and named it after themselves. Many parts of the land east of Jordan, especially 'Ajlūn, have always been a no-man's land and a centre for disorderly elements who take their refuge there owing to geographical conditions; the migrations of Israelites from the west to the east of the Jordan may in many cases have been caused by political or economic troubles of many kinds. These examples give us the right to assume that in other cases too Israelites migrated from west to east of Jordan. One of these is Joshua xv. 6; xviii. 17, where a place called Bohan[1] after Reuben's son is mentioned as on the border of Judah, though Reuben was settled finally east of Jordan. The place actually lies south of Jericho. It may be concluded that the tribe of Reuben reached its later habitations east of Jordan from the west.

## IV. THE TWELVE TRIBES

The idea of the land west of Jordan being occupied by an Israel of twelve tribes under a single leader needs to be rectified in the sense indicated above, and the question arises when the community consisting of twelve tribes came into being, either as an historical entity or as an ideal, and how its origin is to be

[1] G, 28, 62.

explained. In connexion with that question, we must examine whether, and if so how, the stories in Genesis xxix–xxx concerning the birth of Jacob's sons from the fully legal wives, Leah and Rachel,[1] and two concubines, Zilpah and Bilhah, reflect a historical situation, and so can be used in the enquiry as to the origin of the community consisting of twelve tribes.

This question is only part of a far greater problem: what value ought to be ascribed to these Genesis narratives which reflect events or situations in the history of the people or the tribes, but are clothed in the shape of novelistic family stories. It seems clear that the tribal and ethnic history are the primary elements in these narratives, and the novelistic way of telling them the secondary. The absolutely necessary narrative addition to the historical account—which consists mainly of genealogical notices—is the introduction of mothers, if we consider the basic conception of all these stories: that all human societies, and the tribes and peoples as well, descend from fathers. An example for such a genealogy may be found in the list of the twelve descendants of Nahor, Genesis xxii. 20–4, which allots eight of these sons to his chief wife, Milcah, and four to his concubine, Reumah, the distribution into two groups surely reflecting a historical fact. Perhaps the attribution of the greater group to his first wife, and the smaller to his concubine may be supposed to be historical too, as such difference was meant to point to the relative importance of both groups. The mothers ought not to be explained historically, but looked upon as a purely novelistic addition. Therefore they have been given customary names and probably could have been named otherwise. Whereas in Genesis xxii. 20–4 the narrative addition to the historical facts is restricted to a minimum, in Genesis xxix–xxx the historical facts in the account of the birth of Jacob's sons are greatly obscured. This makes it difficult to find them out at all, and various efforts to do so differ very much.[2] But careful examination enables us to recognize the historical substance clearly enough, even in this narrative so greatly altered by novelistic additions.

According to many statements in the Old Testament two groups of Jacob's sons ought to be put more closely together: Reuben, Simeon, Levi and Judah, the first four of the sons of Leah, on the one hand, and on the other Joseph and Benjamin, the sons of Rachel. These two groups (the second being the 'house' of Joseph) were in existence before the *Landnahme*, as is proved by the narratives in Genesis xxv–xxxvi, which deal with

---

[1] §IV, 5.        [2] §III, 37; §IV, nos. 3; 5; 6; 7.

Jacob and Esau and with Jacob and Laban in separate tales, not originally dependent upon each other. For these narratives presume clearly two Jacob-groups camping separately, one of them in the south of Palestine with Esau as its neighbour, the other in the middle of Palestine and east of the Jordan, in touch with the Aramaean Laban; the first of these two groups is identical with Reuben, Simeon, Levi and Judah, and the second with the 'house' of Joseph. This scheme of six or (if Joseph was alone at first) five Jacob-sons from Jacob's two wives, similar to that of the Nahor-sons in Genesis xxii. 20–4, is the basic fact to be evaluated historically, and has been altered in a tradition of centuries by narrative additions, till it took the shape we find in Genesis xxix–xxx. It is not always possible to define what ought to be regarded as purely poetic and what is a reflection of historical facts. The competition between the wives for the birth of sons is surely a purely narrative element, and the same may be said of the introduction of the maids Bilhah and Zilpah. That Gad and Asher were born of the same mother, the one immediately after the other, ought also to be so regarded for both names mean something like 'Good luck!'[1] Other traits may be historical, e.g. the collective naming of Issachar and Zebulun and of Naphtali and Dan. The latter pair being named together shows that the migration of the tribe of Dan from its first residence west of Jerusalem to the area of the Jordan sources (Judges xvii–xviii) is presumed here. Benjamin's birth from Rachel in Canaan is told in Genesis xxxv. 16–20. Is this a purely narrative element or does it reflect the fact that an independent tribe of Benjamin was founded only after the *Landnahme* in Canaan, as mentioned above?[2] The latter is more probable. Then Judges xix–xxi attests in the same manner as Judges xvii–xviii events of the twelfth century B.C. In general the story of the birth of Jacob's sons cannot be held to prove the existence of an Israel consisting of twelve tribes before the *Landnahme*. The supposed list of clans belonging to the twelve tribes in the desert (Numbers xxvi) which certainly contains later material, may be regarded as a similar case.[3]

To seek the origin of the community consisting of twelve tribes, it is best to begin with the document which contains the oldest extant list of Israelite tribes. It is the song of Deborah (Judges v) which was composed in about 1100 B.C.[4]—a date which can be fixed with fair certainty—and it is undoubtedly 'genuine'. This

---

[1] §IV, 2.  
[2] See above, p. 547.  
[3] §IV, 5, 140 ff.  
[4] §V, nos. 2; 5; 12; 17; 20; 27.

mentions ten tribes in this order: Ephraim, Benjamin, Machir, Zebulun, Issachar, Reuben, Gilead, Dan, Asher, Naphtali. Of these, Ephraim, Benjamin, Machir, Zebulun, Issachar and Naphtali took part in the fight and are praised, while Reuben, Gilead, Dan and Asher kept away, and are blamed. This means that some bond of union between the ten tribes mentioned in the song is pre-supposed, whatever the nature of the bond. Simeon, Levi, Judah and—if Gilead in Judges v. 17 is not identical with Gad, but with the Ephraimites east of the Jordan—also Gad are not mentioned at all. It does not necessarily follow that these tribes[1] were not considered to be related, but it does show that they were not expected to take part in the battle, perhaps because of the situation of their settlements; for that reason their abstention might not be felt as a denial of common relationship.[2] It is, then, conceivable that at the time of the composition of the song of Deborah the political institution, an Israel consisting of twelve or of about twelve tribes, or the ideal union of them, already existed. But the song in no way constitutes a proof of its existence.

The lack of literary evidence from the earlier period for a united people does not show that the institution, or the idea, of a community of twelve tribes cannot be older than the evidence available. But when this possibility is more closely examined, it soon appears that the traditional list of twelve tribes cannot have arisen long before the formation of the Israelite kingdom. There are two forms of the list. One includes Levi and accordingly reckons Ephraim and Manasseh with the tribe Joseph, the other leaves out Levi, and accordingly gives Manasseh and Ephraim or Ephraim and Manasseh in place of Joseph. A number of tribes mentioned in both forms of the list either certainly or probably came into existence only after the 'house' of Joseph penetrated into the land west of Jordan and settled there. It is pretty generally assumed, rightly, that Manasseh, for which Machir presumably stands in the song of Deborah, originated by splitting off from Joseph after the conquest. Probably this is also true of Benjamin,[3] and it is by no means impossible that in addition to these, one or other of the twelve tribes was formed only after the land settlement of the 'house' of Joseph.

There is then no unambiguous evidence for the existence of the institution, or the ideal, of an Israelite community consisting of exactly twelve tribes in the period before the formation of the Israelite state, that is before the time of Saul and David. But before that a fair number of Israelite tribes, though no actual

[1] See below, p. 562.      [2] §v, 5.      [3] See above, pp. 547, 550.

figures can be given, did acknowledge fairly near relationship to one another, and a fairly close union of a national type based on religion. These include some tribes not mentioned in the song and not named in the regular list of twelve tribes, namely Cain, Kenaz and Jerachmeel, and particularly the first. When Saul attacked Amalek, he warned the tribe of Cain (Kenites) to go to some safe place, and gave as reason for this act of mercy the good relations between Cain and Israel (I Sam. xv. 6) known to us from other passages. When David went on a raid really directed against the Amalekites and other enemies of Israel, he pretended to his suzerain, Achish of Gath, that he had attacked the Kenites and others, and accordingly brought himself into ill repute with the Israelites because they were related to the Kenites (I Sam. xxvii. 10); and he sent a share of the booty taken from the Amalekites to the Kenites as well as to the Jerachmeelites (I Sam. xxx. 29). The reason for Cain not appearing in the list of the twelve tribes in spite of his relationship is clearly that it kept out of the union when Israel became a state.

Even before the union a community of twelve (or about twelve) tribes may have existed as a sort of federation, however loosely organized. This seems to follow from the voluntary recognition by the tribes that Saul, of the tribe Benjamin, had been granted leadership by God's grace. Not only did the northern tribes acknowledge him, but also Judah; and Judah remained loyal to him even during his struggle with David, a member of their own tribe. On this recognition the foundation of the Israelite kingdom was based. That is surely conceivable only if some feeling existed uniting the tribes that were merged into Saul's kingdom.

There remains the question whether this union was an institution, or purely an ideal. Scholars of the older generation[1] thought it was an institution, and A. Alt[2] has formulated this assumption. M. Noth[3] has developed it and many have adopted it, W. F. Albright[4] and John Bright[5] among them. Their opinion was that Joshua, as leader of the 'house' of Joseph, the last Israelites to invade the lands west of Jordan, organized a kind of amphictyony of twelve tribes, centred upon either Shechem or Shiloh, which created laws binding upon all its members, and thus prepared the ground for the kingdoms of Saul and David. But this theory, although it has had great attrac-

[1] §IV, 6, 47.  [2] §V, 4, 300 f. and 327; §V, 7, 938.
[3] §IV, 6; cf. also G, 27, 88 ff.; G, 28, 60 and 85.
[4] G, 1, 215; G, 2, 353; G, 3, 103 ff., 108, 119, 138.  [5] G, 8.

tion,[1] rests mainly upon two passages, Joshua xxiv and Judges xix-xxi, which are too weak to support it. Many narratives in the books of Joshua, Judges and I Samuel, as we have seen,[2] tell of events really affecting only the 'house' of Joseph, or even only Benjamin, but give these a general national complexion. It is not easy to see why this extension should not have taken place in Joshua xxiv and Judges xix-xxi too, for weighty arguments exist in favour of this explanation.

The tribes that were, theoretically, rather closely united before Israel became a state numbered in reality sometimes more, sometimes less, than twelve, but always about that number. They were accordingly reckoned conventionally as twelve, a number much used all over the world in this way. The Old Testament contains other such groups of twelve, for example the sons of Nahor (Gen. xxii. 20-4), of Ishmael (Gen. xxv. 13-17) and the tribes of Edom (Gen. xxxvi. 10-14). The assumption that in every case these represent regular amphictyonies with twelve members must seem artificial. But there did exist a theoretical community of some sort, consisting of about twelve tribes, before Israel became a state, and this was acknowledged, as the song of Deborah shows, so that Saul's creation of a state had, in fact, a preliminary basis.

## V. THE PERIOD OF THE JUDGES

The time of the judges was the two centuries between the concluding stages of the land settlement and the rise of the kingdom, that is about 1200–1000 B.C.[3] In these the Israelite tribes, settled west or east of Jordan, each acting independently, even though they remained conscious of the bond between them, had to defend and protect their possessions on two sides. On the one hand attacks by the neighbouring states on all the borders had to be warded off, as well as raids by bedawin of the desert, riding camels which were just being introduced into Syria and Palestine.[4] On the other hand, the Canaanite enclaves west and east of Jordan often constituted a threat to Israel's domains. In the Old Testament, or more strictly in Judges iii. 7–xvi. 31, the Israelite tribes are represented as being always on the defensive, but sometimes Israel was certainly the attacking party, not so much against external enemies, but against those Canaanites who remained within their territory, or on its borders. The Israelite

---

[1] §IV, 8; §V, nos. 9; 11; 13; 14; 15; 18; 24; 25.
[2] See above, pp. 545 f., 548.          [3] §V, 19.          [4] §V, 26.

tribes took advantage of favourable opportunities for rounding out and enlarging their areas.

External enemies assailing the Israelite tribes were beaten off under the leadership of saviours raised for this purpose, as they themselves and their followers believed, by God. One of these, Othniel, of the tribe of Kenaz, conquered 'Cushan-rishathaim, king of Aram Naharaim' (Judges iii. 7–11),[1] but it is impossible to make any precise historical statement about this enemy. The others mentioned are historical. Eglon of Moab was murdered by Ehud, of the tribe of Benjamin (iii. 12–30). The Philistines were defeated by Shamgar Ben-Anath (iii. 31)[2] and were given a good deal of trouble by Samson (xiii–xvi), but finally overcame him. Midianite and Amalekite bedawin, repeatedly attacking the northern districts to the west of Jordan in order to plunder the garnered harvest, were defeated by Gideon, a member of the family Abiezer, of the tribe of Manasseh. This success resulted in Gideon being put into the position of ruler, an arrangement meant to be permanent, which might have led to the founding of a dynasty, had it not been that Gideon's son by a concubine, Abimelech, disgraced his house completely, so that it lost all authority (vi–ix). The men of Ammon and perhaps of Moab[3] were driven back within their own borders by Jephthah (x. 6–xii. 7). But only one Canaanite enemy is mentioned in the Book of Judges (chs. iv–v). That enemy was Jabin, king of Canaan, who lived in Hazor,[4] the modern Tell Qedaḥ or Tell Waqqāṣ, whose general was Sisera, dwelling in 'Harosheth of the Gentiles', modern Tell el-'Amr.[5] The prophetess Deborah, at Yahweh's command, summoned Baraq of the tribe of Naphtali, who defeated Sisera and freed Israel from the yoke of Jabin; Sisera was murdered in flight by Jael. Probably two different sets of events have been combined into a single story,[6] one that concerning the reduction of the city Hazor, ruled by Jabin, and the other the victory over Sisera, an independent king living in 'Harosheth of the Gentiles'.

These stories are so arranged that Deborah and Baraq (iv–v), who conquered Jabin and Sisera, are introduced into the series of victors over external enemies between Shamgar (iii. 31) and Gideon (vi–ix). Besides the heroes who helped their tribes against external enemies or Canaanite resistances, there is mention of a series of other judges, in x. 1–5 between Abimelech, the son of Gideon, and Jephthah, and in xii. 8–15 between Jephthah and

---

[1] §v, nos. 16; 22; 29.     [2] See below, p. 558.     [3] See below, p. 558.
[4] See above, pp. 545f., and below, p. 559.     [5] §v, 1, 21 f.     [6] G, 6, 122, n. 83.

Samson. All that is known about them is that they held the office of 'judge', the length of time they held it, their place of burial, and the number of their children, and even the last item is not given in every case; no success of theirs over an enemy is recorded. The names are Tola of Mt Ephraim, Jair of Gilead, Ibzan of Bethlehem, probably the town of that name in Zebulun (Joshua xix. 15), the modern Bēt Laḥm, Elon of Zebulun and Abdon of Ephraim; we commonly call them 'the minor judges'. In xii. 7 the formula: 'He judged Israel . . . years, etc.' which is used only for them except in this one case is applied also to Jephthah. On this evidence Jephthah belongs to both series, that of the heroes who saved their tribe when attacked by enemies and that of the persons who acted as judges of Israel for a definite period. That there was thought to be a continuous succession of all these 'great' and 'minor' judges, is underlined by the figure given for their period. The number of years of oppression preceding, and years of peace secured by, their victory is given, with the single exception of Shamgar, who in this respect is left unrelated. The total number of years for the whole period is in round figures 400, but no credit should be given to this figure. It can safely be assumed that the authority of these heroes was in each case restricted to a section of the Israelite tribes; they were not successors but partial contemporaries. Only the 'minor judges' at most have to be considered as a succession; they may possibly have been contemporary with this or that tribal hero, just as the tribal heroes were partly contemporary with one another. The question is, whether the 'minor judges' really followed one another.

The assumption that they actually did follow one another would be proved correct if it were really the case that the 'minor judges' were 'an unbroken succession of members of prominent families in different tribes, holding an office which attended to legal administration'.[1] This is the hypothesis of A. Alt, developed by O. Grether[2] and M. Noth,[3] while F. C. Fensham[4] and A. van Selms[5] think that the 'minor judges' too had been both judges and rulers. Alt says that the judges' office 'dealt with the handing on of tradition, and the maintenance of the Canaanite law which had been adopted'.[6] The total of years assigned to the 'minor judges' is 70 or, if Jephthah is included, 76. This could be only a part of the interval between the entry of the 'house' of Joseph into the land west of Jordan and the rise of the Kingdom,

[1] §v, 4, 300.    [2] §v, 11.    [3] §1, 14, 21 ff. and 47 ff.
[4] §v, 10.    [5] §v, 21.    [6] §v, 4, 300.

altogether about 200 years, from the end of the thirteenth to the end of the eleventh centuries B.C. Nevertheless, their terms of office—23, 22, 6, 7, 10 and 8 years—do not look like invented figures, but would seem to be sound tradition. On the other hand, the notes concerning the 'minor judges' reveal a number of features which belong in the realm of saga rather than in that of historical statement. One of them, the Gileadite Jair, is quite clearly not an individual person at all but the personification of a group. For it is obvious that the Gileadite Jair of Judges x. 3–5, from whose thirty sons the tent villages of Jair have derived their names, is identical with Jair the son of Manasseh, of whom it is related in Numbers xxxii. 41 that he conquered the tent villages of the Amorites and named them 'the tent villages of Jair'. Thus the notes concerning the 'minor judges', including the numbers of years mentioned as the periods of their activity, are probably to be explained as more or less confused recollections of persons or groups which played some role in Israelite tribes or areas, and of the places at which they were actually or supposedly buried.

Leaving Othniel out of account, and dealing with Shamgar later, we are told the following details about the oppressions and deliverances of the Israelite tribes: Eglon, king of Moab, supported by men of Ammon and the Amalekites, extended his boundaries at the expense of Israel, and actually took Jericho which was in Benjamin's territory. This implies that he brought under his rule territory east of Jordan belonging to Israel (or more exactly, to Reuben and Gad) as far as the northern end of the Dead Sea. Ehud, of the tribe of Benjamin was in Jericho to offer tribute to Eglon. However, he contrived to murder Eglon and then drove the Moabites out of the areas west of the Jordan, with the help of a levy of the men of Ephraim (iii. 12–30). There is nothing to fix the exact period of this event.

The next report tells of Gideon's victory over the Midianites and Amalekites. They were continually raiding west of the Jordan and harrying the people there, especially the clan of Manasseh called Abiezer, which was settled in, or had its border on, the fruitful plain of Beth-shan; but they were a plague to be dreaded by neighbouring tribes too. Gideon at first, it appears, commanded only a small detachment of the tribesmen belonging to Abiezer. After a successful encounter with the raiders in the northern defiles of Mt Gilboa (modern Jebel Fuqūʻah), Gideon received support not only from the remainder of Manasseh but also from the neighbouring tribes, Asher, Zebulun and Naphtali, so that on receiving further reinforcements, detachments from Ephraim, he was able to break the enemy's forces completely. Thereupon, according to the tradition, the 'men of Israel', i.e. probably those representing the coalition of tribes which took part in the struggle, offered Gideon the position of ruler as founder of a dynasty, but failed to get his consent.[1] However in his own district of Abiezer, and indeed in all Manasseh with the autonomous city Shechem, Gideon acted as ruler throughout his lifetime (vi–viii).

After his death it was thought natural that his authority should pass to one of his sons. But it was apparently the least worthy of these, Abimelech, born of a concubine from Shechem, who succeeded in getting rid of all the other heirs of Gideon and imposing himself as the successor. He was an incapable ruler and the inheritance was soon lost. His tactless and challenging behaviour caused Shechem and other places in the area he ruled to revolt, and Abimelech met his death in seeking to suppress one of these revolts, that in Thebez, Ṭūbās ten miles north-east of Shechem (ix). Once again, it is impossible to fix the period of these events, either Gideon's victory or the short autocratic rule of his son Abimelech, which lasted three years.

The same is true of the hero Jephthah (x. 6–xii. 7), a leader of mercenaries who had emigrated to an Aramaean land lying north of Gilead, called Tob. The men of Ammon had brought the Israelites of Manasseh living in Gilead into subjection and also, according to Judges x. 9, had made an attack on Judah, Benjamin and Ephraim that put them to straits. Jephthah, when he returned from Tob, inflicted a defeat on Ammon between Gilead (Khirbet Jel'ād) and Mizpeh (Rashuni, a few miles north-west of Jel'ād), that is just west of the northern part of the territory of Ammon.[2] The victory was won at the cost of his only child's life, if the account in Judges xi. 30–1, 34–40 is really historical and does not represent the story of a ritual myth arising from a vegetation cult. Jephthah's victory over the men of Ammon had one ill consequence—the tribe of Ephraim claimed something like a perpetual right to supreme command over the levy of the Israelite tribes in central Palestine. They had, indeed, done the same thing after Gideon's victory over the Midianites and Amalekites, but without such bad results (viii. 1–3). Jealous of Jephthah's success, the Ephraimites tried to call him to account for acting independently; but Jephthah gathered the Gileadites round him and cut down the Ephraimites (xii. 1–6). According to Judges xi. 12–28 (32–3a), the king of Ammon demanded

---

[1] But cf. §v, 8.     [2] See above, p. 554.

from Jephthah the return of the territory between the Arnon and the northern end of the Dead Sea which Israel had once, according to Numbers xxi. 21–31, captured from Sihon king of Heshbon.[1] When Jephthah refused, the king of Ammon tried to seize it by force of arms. If the narrative is correct in the form we have it, then it must be assumed that this district, at other times a source of dissension between Israel and Moab, had been occupied for a while by Ammon. Noth believed that the narrative attributed conditions of a much later period to the time of Jephthah.[2] It is possible that in the original tradition Jephthah was credited with a victory not only over Ammon but also over the king of Moab, and this too might be factual.

Finally, the Philistines are mentioned among the foreign peoples who bitterly attacked the tribes when they settled in Palestine. At the beginning of the twelfth century the Philistines had penetrated into the coastal strip of Palestine between Gaza in the south and Jaffa in the north, and were continually engaged in the effort to extend their rule to the north and east at the expense of the tribes dwelling there. Judges iii. 31 reports that Shamgar ben-Anath slew 600 Philistines with an ox goad and thus saved Israel. This record seems to be historical, but there are many questions left open. The Hebrew Ben-'Anath 'Son of Anath' is, as many think, an abbreviation of Ben-Beth-'Anath, 'Citizen or king of the town Beth-'Anath'. They then identify this Beth-'Anath with the town Beth-'Anath in Naphtali (Joshua xix. 38; Judges i. 33), the modern El-Eb'ēneh, and are of the opinion that Shamgar was king of this city-state.[3] It seems absolutely clear that Shamgar was no Israelite, but it is possible too that Ben-'Anath means 'Son of the war-goddess 'Anath', i.e. a brave hero.[4] Further it is not certain whether he was a Canaanite or belonged to the 'Sea Peoples', perhaps to the Tjekker who came with the Philistines to Palestine, had possibly skirmished with them and occupied the territory round Dor, modern El-Burj north of Ṭanṭurah. In Judges v. 6 Shamgar appears as an oppressor of Israel. The reason why Shamgar was erroneously included among the saviours of Israel was simply because he was, like Israel, a recognized enemy of the Philistines.

The Samson stories, anecdotes with the character of sagas, give a fair picture of the pressure exercised by the Philistines. They were pushing through the foothills eastwards into the

---

[1] See above, p. 546.
[2] §III, 25 (1941), 53, n. 4 and 66, n. 1; cf. G, 27, 158, n. 1.
[3] §v, 1, 19 ff.; §v, 3.       [4] G, 12, 151, n. 2; G, 13, 162, n. 1.

mountains, against the territory occupied there by the tribes of Dan and Judah. In this case something can be said as to the period of this event. Since the narratives imply that the tribe of Dan was still in its original territory west of Benjamin the events recorded must have taken place shortly after the arrival of the Philistines in Palestine, and in any case before the migration of the tribe of Dan northwards, narrated in Judges xvii–xviii. They should, however, be earlier than the victory of Israel over Sisera celebrated in the song of Deborah (Judges v), since the song seems to imply that the men of Dan were already living at the sources of the Jordan. Besides the limitation caused by the Amorites to the territory of Dan when the tribe dwelt west of Benjamin (Judges i. 34), there was another reason for the migration northwards, the pressure of the Philistines upon this tribe.

At the same time as the Israelite tribes were constantly warding off the attacks of enemies on territory they held or claimed, constant battles went on against the Canaanites who still lived in the land, especially against their fortified cities. Most of these contests were of importance only for the tribes immediately concerned, or even for only a part of them, for which reason the tradition does not contain exact records of them, but only a general memory. This finds expression in the list of places not captured (Judges i. 18, 21, 27–33), where it is stated that individual Israelite tribes had to leave a large number of forti-fied Canaanite cities alone, and that they could impose forced labour on them only gradually. These disputes of the Israelite tribes with their Canaanite enclaves continued into the time of Saul and David; it was only then that the last remnants of inde-pendent Canaanites disappeared. The disputes were conducted not only by negotiation, but also by force of arms. Side by side with these minor issues were operations against Canaanite rulers who threatened to become dangerous to the existence of whole groups of tribes, thus making it essential for these tribes to unite in resistance. Information has been preserved about two such affairs, that against Jabin of Hazor, Tell Qedah or Tell Waqqāṣ, about three miles west of the southern end of Baḥret el-Khēt (Lake Ḥūleh) and that against Sisera, whose residence was 'Harosheth of the Gentiles', Tell el-'Amr, half-way between Nazareth and Haifa. For the narrative as it stands in Judges iv–v, culminating in the song of Deborah,[1] which makes Sisera into the general of king Jabin, is probably to be divided into two

---

[1] §v, nos. 2; 5; 6; 12; 20; 27.

independent narratives, as we have seen;[1] the first had as subject the attack on Jabin, the other the battle with Sisera.

Baraq of Naphtali, roused by Deborah, was certainly the leader in the battle against Sisera, as is shown by the song of Deborah. He probably gained the victory over Jabin too; in any case that would be the easiest explanation of the combination of two distinct events into one in the narrative. In the battle with Jabin, Zebulun and Naphtali bore the burden of the struggle between them, clearly because they had suffered most from Jabin's military autocracy. But Sisera's sphere of influence was much greater; it included nearly all the tribes of the Galilaean and Samaritan hills as well as the plain between—Issachar, Machir, Benjamin and Ephraim besides Zebulun and Naphtali. There is little information upon the course of the two wars; as to the first, practically nothing, as to the second, a few details only, with some emphasis on the murder of Sisera by Jael. Yet the song of Deborah makes the great importance of the second victory absolutely clear, and shows how high it must have raised the self-respect of the tribes which took part in it. The period in which the two battles fell can be deduced from the song, as shown above.

## VI. CANAAN AND ISRAEL

The Israelites should not be thought of as completely isolated from the civilized and settled lands bordering on the desert, even before their settlement in Canaan. Rather they were in continual contact owing to the constant change of pasturage by several of their tribal groups, and thus they came to possess some of the products of the settled dwellers in those lands. Nevertheless, the final land settlement began a change in their manner of living and thinking which ultimately led to basic alterations. The development thus started continued through centuries, and was never fully completed, in that some sense of opposition between the 'desert ideal' and the actual circumstances in the land where Israel settled was always felt so long as this people remained in Palestine. Naturally the period of about two hundred years considered in the preceding sections, was of quite peculiar importance for Israel's relations with Canaanite civilization. Before the course of political development is followed further by considering the wars with the Philistines and the choice of a king, some account may now be given of the influence of their new environment on the Israelites when they settled in Canaan.

[1] See above, p. 554.

In Deuteronomy vi. 10–11, Moses says that Yahweh will give his people 'great and goodly cities which thou buildedst not, and houses full of all good things which thou filledst not, . . . vineyards and olive trees which thou plantedst not'. In Joshua xxiv. 13, Joshua attributes to Yahweh this statement to his people: 'I have given you a land for which ye did not labour, and cities which ye built not, that ye might dwell therein, of vineyards and oliveyards which ye planted not do ye eat.' The results of excavations confirm these words and also the accounts given in the books of Joshua and Judges which inform us of the activities of the Israelites as conquerors and occupiers of Canaanite settlements and agricultural lands. Excavations show a clear distinction between Canaanite and Israelite levels of occupation; while the intruders were at first inferior in the arts of building and pottery, they were able to maintain the general level already attained in these.[1]

At the beginning the Israelites were not themselves capable of work demanding a high level of skill, but long remained dependent upon craftsmen belonging to the earlier settled population of Canaan and of the neighbouring lands, especially Phoenicia, as expressly stated in accounts of the reigns of David and Solomon. But they were quick to learn how to appreciate and use what such artists produced, and to preserve the standards attained by their predecessors. In one craft, ivory-working, this is especially clear, not only from the texts (I Kings x. 18, xxii. 39) but also through abundant material from excavations. The collection of ivories, dating from the twelfth century, found at ancient Megiddo in 1937,[2] was once certainly the property of a Canaanite ruler. If these be compared with those found a few years before at Samaria,[3] dating from an Israelite level of the ninth century, continuity in the choice of motifs—sphinxes, lions, palmettes, lotus-patterns, and the like—is as easily recognized as is the similarity of technical execution. Comparison of bronzes, of seals and gems, of the Canaanite period with those of the later Israelite centuries leads to the same conclusion.[4]

The Israelites adopted not only the material civilization of the conquered inhabitants, but also ideas and practical arrangements in social and legal affairs. It is of course true that in many respects the Israelites retained their tribal constitution as the primary element long after the settlement. Until the creation of the kingship and of the Israelite state formed thereby, there was

---

[1] G, 1, 194 and 212; G, 3, 102; G, 9, 65, 76 ff., 124 f.
[2] §vi, 53.       [3] §vi, 20.       [4] §vi, nos. 9; 10; 11; 22; 29; 58.

no higher political unit superior to the tribes, apart from con-
federations formed by several tribes, limited in duration because
they owed their existence to particular occasions when alliance
was necessary, as in the time of Deborah and Baraq. Even if
there really was, as some scholars have supposed, an amphictyony
of the twelve tribes, based on religion and ritual observance,
grouped round the sanctuary at Shechem or Shiloh in the period
before the kingship,[1] its political importance can only have been
slight. In such matters as defence, administration and legal
edicts, a league of this kind would have been ineffective. Indeed,
a considerable part of these powers was not even in the hands of
the tribes, but was claimed by the clans and families, or, after the
conquest, by the provincial and local communities which gradually usurped the position of the clans and families.[2] The political
autonomy of the individual tribes can be as clearly deduced
from the blessing of Jacob (Gen. xlix), the blessing of Moses
(Deut. xxxiii) and the song of Deborah (Judges v), as from
the narratives in the Book of Judges. But in these sources there
are other features equally perceptible.

The tribes, though they were not by their nature closely
associated with the soil or with the particular district occupied,
came to be more and more closely identified with these. The
original basis of communal consciousness, real or theoretical
blood relationship, began to be replaced by attachment to the
land, the common home. In the blessing of Jacob the sayings that
deal with Zebulun, Issachar, Dan, Gad[3] and Asher refer to the
localities these tribes inhabited. In the blessing of Moses the
same is true of the sayings about Benjamin, Zebulun, Issachar,
Gad, Dan, Naphtali and Asher. In the song of Deborah the
tribes Levi, Simeon and Judah are not mentioned at all, because
of their geographical position, far from the scene of action, so
consideration of them can be omitted here. Reuben, Gad—
called, very instructively, by the name of the locality it inhabited,
'Gilead'—Dan and Asher did not obey the call to take part in
the coalition of related tribes against the pillaging attacks of
bedawin into the lands west of Jordan. This was because the
geographical position of their districts, and the working conditions arising from that position, took their undivided attention,
and in their own opinion must necessarily do so.[4] According
to the assumption that has been favoured previously,[5] when
Benjamin first settled in the land, this tribe was the southernmost

---

[1] See above, pp. 552f.    [2] §v, 4, 314 f.; §iv, 4.    [3] See above, p. 551.
[4] §vi, 31.              [5] See above, pp. 547, 550.

part of the coalition constituted by the Joseph stock; it separated off and established its independence only after the conquest. If this is correct, then it is an eloquent instance of how the peculiar conditions arising from geographical position came to be more important for the individual tribes and their sections than the traditional conception of a community of elements related by blood.[1]

This course of development is similar to that found in southern Arabia. When the history of the tribes there begins to be known to us from the documents, in the first third of the first millennium B.C., they have already come to be thought of as intimately connected with certain localities.[2] It is self-evident that this development necessitated some reconstitution of the Israelite communities, and this reconstitution must have been in accord with the pattern set by institutions which had existed all over Palestine for many centuries. It is moreover possible to trace this reconstitution and even to give detailed documentary evidence for it as regards at least two aspects of social life.

The first of these two aspects is that of law. It is unfortunately true that as yet no laws of the Canaanites themselves are known to us, so that there is no direct proof of their influence on Israelite legal practice. But ample indirect proof is provided by the laws of the Sumerians, Babylonians, Assyrians and Hittites, found within the last generation, which in parts show remarkable similarity to certain laws in the Old Testament, especially to a section of the book of the Covenant, Exodus xx. 22–xxiii. 13. It is generally agreed that Israel took over the laws in question from their neighbours in the ancient Oriental world,[3] and it is natural to regard the Canaanites as intermediaries passing on the regulations which are common to the laws of Israel and those of their neighbours. This is confirmed by due regard to a section of this part of the book of the Covenant, Exodus xxi. 1–xxii. 16, which is headed *mišpāṭīm* 'judgements'. The rules laid down in this section are mostly concerned with farming, pasturing of cattle, agriculture, construction of reservoirs, and can therefore have become of any importance for Israel only after the conquest. They must, then, have been borrowed by Israel from the Canaanites. They take generally a particular stylistic form, based on the conditional clause, which corresponds with that generally employed in the ancient oriental collections of laws already mentioned. In this respect they can be clearly differentiated from

---

[1] G, 22, 391 ff.      [2] §vɪ, 74, 117 ff.; §vɪ, 76.
[3] G, 15, 390 ff.; G, 29, 159 ff.; G, 36, 27 ff.; §vɪ, nos. 47; 73; 79.

other legal regulations of the Old Testament which are framed
as commands and seem, although not exclusively, to have been
used by the Hebrews before their settlement in Canaan.[1] There
are also regulations as to law and custom in the Old Testament,
apart from the book of the Covenant, which are clearly to be
associated with local conditions in Canaan, and must have been
adopted after Israel entered the land. Thus the instruction given
in Leviticus xix. 23–5 to leave the fruit of recently planted trees
hanging unused for three years, to dedicate that of the fourth
year to Yahweh, and to begin ordinary consumption in the fifth
year, is stated in the text to have come into force on the entry
into Canaan.

The regulation just mentioned is in part connected with
religious observance, and is thus a transition between the purely
legal regulations and the mass of ideas, orders and customs
arising from religion and rites which naturally sprang from
Canaanite soil and accordingly came to be observed by Israel.
Canaanite influences on the practices of sacrifice in Israel, though
obviously considerable, may be omitted because they cannot in
every case be distinguished from practices long known to the
immigrants.[2] But there are three principal Israelite festivals
celebrated by Jews and Christians down to the present day which,
though of course they have in general lost, to a very large extent,
all trace of their origin, were first observed on Canaanite soil.
They are the feast of unleavened bread, *maṣṣōt*, at the barley
harvest celebrated at the beginning of the year; the wheat harvest
festival, *qāṣīr*, about seven weeks later; and the fruit (including
grape) harvest festival, *'āsīp*, or *sukkōt*, in the autumn. These
are by nature agricultural and, as such, of Canaanite origin.[3]
Judges xxi. 19–23 tells of the dance of the maidens in the vineyards at Shiloh at the festival of Yahweh; that is the autumn
festival. In I Samuel i. 1–3 Elkanah goes yearly from Ephraim
to Shiloh, obviously at the autumn festival, to bring his annual
offering to Yahweh. These passages show that at the end of the
second millennium B.C. the celebration of this festival was the
general custom, at any rate in the part of Israel concerned.

Another deduction can be drawn from I Samuel i–iii. There was
a temple at Shiloh built of stones, with a forecourt surrounded by
rooms, with one interior room, and indeed several such rooms,
intended for the symbol of Yahweh, the Ark and perhaps its
cover the tent (cf. I Samuel ii. 22), and for the use of the priests.

---

[1] §v, 4, 296 ff.          [2] G, 1, 179; §vi, 27; §vi, 28, 178 ff.
[3] G, 22, 101 f. and 289 ff.; G, 39, 80 ff.; §vi, 70, 148 f.

This temple was regarded as the dwelling of Yahweh and the seat of his oracle. In Shiloh, then, the tent, the sanctuary recognized by the Israelites before the conquest, had either been deposited in or replaced by a temple of the kind usual among the Canaanites for many centuries. Another change was that in Shiloh Yahweh accepts the epithet Sabaoth,[1] 'God of hosts', meaning The Omnipotent, that the Ark was combined with a throne, supported by cherubim and that the name God Sabaoth was amplified by 'throned above the cherubim', so that his complete name was 'Yahweh God of hosts throned above the cherubim' (II Sam. vi. 2; cf. I Sam. i. 3, 11; iv. 4). Solomon may be supposed to have followed this example at Shiloh in his arrangement for the position of the ark which his father David had brought to Jerusalem, as in other points in the temple which he built.[2]

The Israelites not only copied Canaanite cult practices and institutions, including their music;[3] they, or at any rate certain groups among them, were only too inclined to admit even Canaanite divinities as objects of worship, as the Old Testament continually bears witness. According to statements in the book of Judges, it was especially during the two centuries after Israel's conquest that a continuous series of secessions to the 'Baals and Astartes' took place; the intervals between these secessions, caused by the punishments inflicted by Yahweh, were very short. However little reliance is placed upon the details, the general description must be true; actually at that time the permeation of the worship of Yahweh by Canaanite elements was particularly marked. It was then also, towards the end of the Judges' period that a religious movement based upon ecstatic experience, the raving excitement of persons peculiarly susceptible to such a condition, the 'prophets' and their following, penetrated from the Canaanite area into Israel, where it soon underwent a complete change; there arose men of a spiritual elevation and of personal influence previously unknown, a Samuel, an Elijah, an Amos, an Isaiah.[4] This subject of cult-practice affects also the influence of the Canaanite language; it will be shown that in the religious poetry of Israel there are Canaanite elements of various kinds.

We are fairly well acquainted with the indigenous language or rather with the manifold 'Amorite' or 'Canaanite' dialects

[1] §III, nos. 7; 8; 40.      [2] See below, pp. 599 f.
[3] G, 3, 127 and 210; §VI, 78.
[4] §VI, nos. 38; 39; 41; 48; 51; 52; 55; 56; 62; 75.

spoken in Syria and Palestine before the invasion of the Israelites, through documentary evidence dating from the second millennium. The most important elements are the 'Amorite' words, phrases and names in the Mari-texts,[1] dating back to the eighteenth century B.C., the 'Canaanite' glosses of the Amarna letters[2] in the first half of the fourteenth century, and the almost contemporary Canaanite texts from Ras Shamra, the ancient Ugarit. But on the other side we are reduced to mere suppositions about the language the Israelites brought with them. Our uncertainty is the greater because there must have been differences in speech of various kinds among the Israelite invaders, who were not, as we have seen, a united group that arose in one particular period or area. Nevertheless, one result of researches[3] during the last fifty years can be recorded as relatively assured. The Hebrew spoken by the Israelites after the settlement in Canaan, the language found in the Old Testament, probably represents a mixture of the 'Canaanite' used by the earlier inhabitants of the land, and of the language brought in by the Israelites. This was perhaps a near relative of Aramaic, at least so far as part of the invaders was concerned. But it is quite impossible to define the kind of degree of this mixture.

In contrast with the uncertainty of the extent of the influence the Canaanite languages had upon that of the invaders, in point of vocabulary and accidence (particularly of the verb), stands the certainty that in syntax, style and metre Hebrew literature closely followed Canaanite models. The inference could already be drawn from the relation of several Canaanite glosses and expressions in the Amarna letters to specific turns of speech in the Old Testament. It is absolutely apparent in the many points in common between the Old Testament wording and the 'Canaanite' texts of Ras Shamra. In most cases, at any rate, these can be explained only by assuming that the Israelites used the 'Canaanite' literature as a model. Much in the Old Testament that closely resembles Egyptian and Akkadian literature is also probably derived from the Canaanites, in that they were the natural intermediaries.

But in the case of elements derived from Akkadian sources (for example the Creation epic and the Flood legend) it is possible that these could have passed into Israelite tradition through direct contact with Akkadian civilization. This would have taken place before the foundation of 'Israel' through those ancestors

---

[1] §VI, nos. 34; 67; 68.          [2] §VI, nos. 15; 16; 23; 30.
[3] G, I, 181 f.; §VI, nos. 4; 12; 14; 40; 46; 81.

who derived from Mesopotamia. Some emphasis has recently been put on the possibility of this explanation.[1] Even if so, Canaanite influence on the songs and singers of Israel remains very considerable.[2] Both in the Old Testament and in texts from Ras Shamra, 'dew of heaven' and 'fat of earth' are parallel expressions,[3] so are 'wine' and 'blood of trees'.[4] This must be due to the influence of Canaanite idiom on Israelite speech, because such expressions refer to circumstances in the cultivable land, and can have acquired a meaning for Israel only after the settlement in Canaan. Other features common to both Israelite and Canaanite poetry are probably to be explained as borrowings by Israel. These include the expressions such as 'Leviathan the swift (or gliding or fleeing) serpent', 'Leviathan the crooked (or winding) serpent',[5] and 'to plead the cause of the widow, to do justice to the orphan'.[6] The same may be said of the numerous metrical peculiarities which Israelite poetry shares with Canaanite, as exemplified in the texts from Ras Shamra. There is, for example, the phenomenon of the use of synonyms as metrical ballast. In two parallel verses or half-verses the second, which contains fewer meaningful words than the first, contains as substitutes for either one or two of the words in the first, expressions which are parallel, but longer, as for instance *yāmīn*, 'the right hand' for *yād*, 'the hand', or *nᵉhārōṯ*, 'the streams' for *yām*, 'the sea'. The effect can be felt in such a passage of the Old Testament as:

> I will set his hand on the sea
> and his right hand on the streams (Ps. lxxxix. 26)

or this from the Ras Shamra texts:

> Behold their number is in my mouth,
> the tale of them on both my lips.

where *špty*, 'both my lips', has one more syllable than *py*, 'my mouth', and *hn*, 'behold', of the first half-verse is not repeated in the second.[7]

Although the influence of Canaanite models is not so clear in the prose literature, examples are still not lacking. Long ago the Amarna letters indicated a relationship between them and the style of Israelite letters, and this likeness now appears again in

---

[1] G, 1, 180 f.; §vi, nos. 1; 4.      [2] §vi, nos. 37; 44; 82.

[3] §vi, 36, 187, col. ii, 39, cf. Genesis xxvii. 28.

[4] §vi, 36, 141, col. ii, 37 f., cf. Genesis xlix. 11.

[5] §vi, 36, 148, text 67, 1: Isaiah xxvii. 1.

[6] §vi, 36, 182, col. ii, 8: Isaiah i. 17.      [7] §vi, 4; §vi, 36, 106.

letters found at Ras Shamra, including some written in the
alphabetic script and the 'Canaanite' language. Unfortunately
we have no early Israelite letters in their original wording,[1] but
two of the oldest mentions of letters in Israel show that the model
of these in early Israelite correspondence resembles the Canaanite
in one significant detail.[2] II Kings x. 1–3 mentions a letter of
Jehu to the rulers and elders of Samaria, and II Kings v. 5–6 a
letter of the Aramaean king to the king of Israel in the time of
Elisha. Now the 'Canaanite' letters from Ras Shamra, as well as
the Akkadian letters found there, and similarly the Amarna
letters, have a peculiarity which can be traced down to the
Aramaic letter-style of the fifth century and even later. After the
names of the writer and of the receiver, and a clause devoted to
salutations, the words 'and now!', $we^{\epsilon}att\bar{a}h$ introduce the subject-
matter. This formal 'and now!' is preserved in both II Kings v. 6
and x. 2, and can be claimed to be a sure proof that Israelite
letters were in other respects also completely like, or at least
similar to, Canaanite.

In other literary forms the lack of 'Canaanite' examples
reduces us for the time being to the mere assumption that Israel
learnt from the Canaanites. For instance, this is probably true
of the forms known as 'proverbs',[3] 'cult song',[4] 'love song'[5] and
'laws',[6] for it is to be assumed on general grounds that, since
these literary types were known to Canaan's neighbours, the
Egyptians, Babylonians and Hittites, they existed also in Canaan.
As to 'proverbs' there is, in addition, the fact that there are at
any rate traces of extensive use in extant Canaanite material.[7]
Many of the Old Testament Psalms which belong to the type
'cult song' display so many points that recall the poetry of Ras
Shamra (e.g. Ps. 29) or Egyptian hymns (e.g. Ps. 104), that the
assumption of an influence originally from these sources through
Canaanite mediation, is forced upon us.[8] The Egyptian love
songs[9] confirm that the types of love songs represented in the
Song of Songs derive their form in the main from Canaanite
models which are themselves due to Egyptian influence.[10] The

---

[1] The so-called 'letter from Yavne' of the seventh century B.C., found in 1960, is
properly not a real letter but a judicial petition; see J. Naveh, 'A Hebrew Letter from
the Seventh Century B.C.', in *I.E.J.* 10 (1960), 129 ff.; S. Yeivin, 'The Judicial
Petition from Mezad Ḥashavyahu', in *Bi. Or.* 19 (1962), 3 ff.    [2] §VI, 57.

[3] §VI, nos. 6; 8; 13; 21; 33; 71; 80.    [4] §VI, nos. 62; 64; 69; 72; 78.

[5] §VI, nos. 7; 65; 77.    [6] §VI, nos. 17; 42; 45; 59.

[7] G, 1, 135 ff., and 253 f.; G, 3, 15 and 30 f.; §VI, 3.

[8] G, 3, 15; §VI, 2, 338 f. and 345 f.    [9] §VI, nos. 35; 65; 77.

[10] G, 3, 21 f. and 132; §VI, 7.

dependence of Israelite laws, or rather of one particular type of them, on Canaanite laws which themselves owed their form to contemporary laws in the ancient Oriental world, can be shown to be extremely probable.[1]

These Canaanite models must have been known to the Israelites for the greater part through oral communication. But side by side with this a not inconsiderable part must have been played by the adaptation and imitation of models in the form of written documents. At the time of Israel's settlement the use of writing in Canaan was already fairly extensive, and it was no longer principally the Babylonian writing and language as it had been two or three centuries earlier. The Canaanites had now their own forms of writing. There are about a dozen inscriptions which have turned up in Palestine, dating from about 1700 to 1200 B.C., written in Canaanite characters, the predecessors of Phoenician and therefore of the earliest Hebrew, and in the Canaanite language. These prove that at the time of Israel's settlement the use of this writing was no longer rare; the adoption of its use by the immigrants was almost compulsory.[2] When to this is added the fact that about twenty-five of the inscriptions found in Serābīt el-Khādim in the south-western part of the Sinai peninsula, dating from the fifteenth century B.C., are in the 'Canaanite' writing and language and probably owe their existence to Canaanite slave labour or prisoners of war who were employed by the Egyptians in the turquoise-workings at Serābīt el-Khādim, it is quite clear that at that time knowledge and use of Canaanite writing must already have been fairly widespread.[3] It goes without saying that the Israelites must also have adopted from the Canaanites the means of writing, the chisel, stylus, feather pen, ink, colour, and also the materials used for writing, stone, metal, wood, potsherds, leather and papyrus.[4] All in all, the Canaanites handed on to the Israelites a rich heritage. We can understand that thereby Israel might be in danger of surrendering its individuality and of becoming indistinguishable from its neighbours in its new surroundings.

[1] See above, pp. 563 f.  [2] G, 9, 180 ff.; §vi, 2, 333 ff.
[3] §vi, nos. 5; 18; 19; 24; 25; 26; 60; 61.  [4] G, 11, 460 ff.; §vi, 43.

## VII. WARS WITH THE PHILISTINES
## AND CHOICE OF A KING

From the beginning of the thirteenth century the Egyptian
supremacy over Syria and Palestine that had been exercised
continuously from the middle of the sixteenth century grew
rapidly weaker and then finally ceased.[1] For this reason Israel's
fate during the period of the judges turned on the people's own
endeavours. This is the background to Israel's struggles with the
Philistines which led to the rise of the kingship. In the circumstances of the time only Egypt could possibly have interfered;
but as far as we can see no foreign power at all took part in either
of these two developments. The probability is rather that in
dealing with, and removing, the danger threatening them from
the Philistines, and in the constitution of a kingship connected
with that effort, the Israelites were able to act quite independently.

The political unity established by the kingship meant the
achievement of an aim which had already been the goal of efforts
during the preceding decades. Once before it had looked as if
the danger to Israel, or at any rate to a great part of the tribes
belonging to Israel, when threatened by a foreign foe, the
Midianites, would have led to the appointment of the hero Gideon
as a permanent ruler. That this did not result was probably due
less to the incompetence of Abimelech, who seized his father's
position on Gideon's death, than to the individual tribes being
too intent on independence; the external danger threatening them
was still too slight and too evanescent. Before the necessity for
creating such a political unity could be recognized there had first
to arise an enemy whose power was so considerable and enduring
that only a united Israelite state, organized under a single strong
leader, could have any prospect of successful resistance. The
Philistines[2] proved themselves more and more to be just such an
enemy. They were superior to the Israelites not only in equipment,
but also in their stricter military organization. The Israelites,
poorly armed, depended on the general levy of the individual
tribes, called up for fairly short periods, and for that reason
rarely summoned. The Philistines possessed a professional
military class, well-armed, thoroughly trained, under a unified
command.[3] They were thus in a position to attain their object of
extending their overlordship over all Palestine, or at any rate

[1] G, 1, 155; G, 3, 110 f.
[2] §vii, nos. 5; 10; 32.
[3] §iv, 1, 26 f.; §vii, 30.

over central Palestine west of Jordan. Moreover they probably understood how to justify their claims to hegemony on legal grounds. For not only the Boğazköy treaties but also the dispute between Jephthah and the king of Ammon or perhaps of Moab[1] in Judges xi. 12–28 show that these matters of international law were acutely argued in the ancient Near East. Since the Philistines were masters of the coastal plain of southern Palestine, once held by the Egyptians, they could proclaim themselves the heirs and legal successors of the Egyptians and thus consider Palestine as an area subject to themselves.[2]

About a hundred years after the friction between the Philistines and their Israelite neighbours in Dan and Judah, the Philistines undertook a large-scale movement against the hill-lands of Ephraim. The date, about 1050 B.C., is approximately fixed because at the time a great-grandson of Moses, Eli, was the chief priest at Shiloh.[3] There was a battle between the Philistines and the Israelite tribes threatened by them, that is Manasseh, Ephraim and Benjamin, east of Aphek (modern Ras el-'Ain, 15 km. east of Jaffa) at Eben-ezer, perhaps Migdal Yaba. The Israelites were, in the end, defeated. The bringing-up of the Ark, that ancient shrine of the tribe of Joseph in the wanderings, failed to change the fortune of war. The second encounter ended in a still more severe defeat for Israel than the first, and also in the loss of the Ark to the Philistines, its bearers Hophni and Phinehas, the sons of Eli, being slain.

The whole land west of Jordan, especially the hill-country round Samaria, lay open to the Philistines, and they sacked it, while leaving Galilee and the land east of Jordan untouched[4] (I Sam. iv–v). As to the manner and extent of the overlordship exercised by the Philistines, there are only accounts of isolated events to guide us: the destruction of Shiloh[5] (Jer. vii. 14; xxvi. 6), the appointment of military governors (I Sam. x. 5 and II Sam. xxiii. 14),[6] ruthless disarming of the conquered including the prohibition forbidding the procuring or working of iron (I Sam. xiii. 19–22),[7] despatch of small punitive expeditions to collect tribute and to keep down any desire for revolt (I Sam. xiii. 16–18 and xxiii. 1–5). Yet these references suffice to give an impression of the severe repressive measures imposed on Israel.[8]

---

[1] See above, pp. 557f.   [2] §iv, 1, 3 and 8 f.; §vii, 3, 254 f.; §vii, 12; §vii, 13.
[3] G, 3, 104, 108, 220; §iii, 7; §vii, 26.
[4] §iv, 1, 8 f.                    [5] G, 3, 103 f. and 202; §vi, 49; 50.
[6] Perhaps also I Samuel x. 14–16; cf. §vii, 6.
[7] §vii, 31.                   [8] §iv, 1, 8 ff.

It was Benjamin which suffered the most under this; it is accordingly not surprising that the movement to be rid of the Philistines started in that tribal area.

When Baraq was called by an act of grace to save Israel he was strengthened and supported in his consciousness of the call by a prophetess, Deborah. In the same way a prophet, Samuel, was ordered by God to give Saul, of the tribe of Benjamin, encouragement to save Israel from the Philistines. The king of Ammon, Nahash, was besieging the city Jabesh-Gilead,[1] the modern Tell Abu Kharaz, 40 km. south of the southern end of the lake of Gennesareth, 5 km. east of Jordan. This town was clearly closely connected, to judge from Judges xxi. 5–14,[2] with Saul's home, Gibeah of Benjamin, the modern Tell el-Fūl, 5 km. north of Jerusalem. According to the account in I Samuel xi, xiii–xiv, which is probably reliable as to the main fact, it was by relieving this city that Saul drew such attention in his own tribe and also, probably, in the neighbouring tribes to himself that they were willing to proclaim him king. By means of the authority thus gained he and his son Jonathan, already of age, knew how to make good use of a favourable opportunity. They dispersed between Michmash (Mukhmas) and Geba' (Jeba') a detachment of Philistines acting as a punitive expedition, pursued them to Aijalon (Yalo) and thus freed Israel from the overlordship of the Philistines, though they were not of course able to invade the Philistines' own territory or bring any part of it into subjection.

It is unfortunately impossible to make any positive statement as to the exact point of time at which Saul became king owing to the way in which the extant sources relate the event.[3] There is a tradition, represented by I Samuel vii–viii; x. 17–21; xii; xv; in which the success is claimed to be due to Samuel, and therefore no connexion is admitted between the rescue of Israel from the Philistines and the enthronement of Saul. Apart from these passages, the extant accounts are in agreement on one point: Saul began the struggle against the Philistines when he had already been chosen king. That is probably correct. It was probably the deliverance of the city Jabesh-Gilead from the siege by the Ammonites which opened the eyes first of his own tribe, Benjamin, and then of the neighbouring tribes, to the fact that Saul had been chosen by Yahweh as saviour of his people. To the divine will thus expressed they were induced to add the human act, legitimation, by proclaiming Saul king. In any case

---

[1] §vii, 23.      [2] See above, p. 564.      [3] §vii, nos. 7; 8; 9.

it was Saul's consciousness that the choice of himself was an act of God's grace, and the deed which arose from that consciousness, which made the people willing to proclaim the *nāgīd* designated by Yahweh (I Sam. ix. 16) as *melek*, king.[1]

This basis in the act of grace constitutes the peculiar characteristic of Saul's kingship, and distinguishes it from the type of kingship existing in the kingdoms surrounding Israel, both in the city-states of Canaan as well as among the neighbouring peoples Ammon, Moab and Edom, and even more completely from that in Egypt, Babylonia or Assyria. In Egypt the king was a god. The Babylonians and Assyrians regarded the kingship as an institution essential not merely for political but also for cosmic order, and therefore divinely sanctioned. But the events that had preceded the institution of the kingship over Israel, the exodus, the revelation at Sinai, the land settlement, were decisive in the people's history, and were always regarded so in all subsequent periods. For that reason the kingship could never attain the significance attributed to it in Egypt, in Babylonia or in Assyria. Israel's kingship represented a gift granted by Israel's God at a time of sore peril, provided in advance with specific provisions to guard against degeneration into autocracy, and to provide just and honourable treatment of subjects.[2] Because it was a gift of that kind from God, it was held in great respect, but of course only so long as the reigning king remained conscious of this origin of his office, and performed the duties of his office accordingly. As soon as he forgot that he had received his appointment from God, or appeared to his people to have forgotten it, the foundation on which his authority rested began to shake. If confidence can be felt in the tradition as we know it— a point which must be further considered[3]—this actually occurred as early as the time of Saul himself.

God's choice, then, formed the theoretic foundation of Saul's kingship; but the factual basis was the Israelite levy, the right to call up the men of military age in all the Israelite tribes. This is shown for example in the 'court list' (I Sam. xiv. 49–52) where the only holder of executive authority mentioned beside the king is the commander of the Israelite levy, Saul's cousin Abner. The development was similar to that found in the constitution of the Sabaean kingdom, when it became the predominant power in southern Arabia. There too the power to call out the levy was originally the prerogative of the individual tribes, but was

---

[1] §IV, 1, 22 f.  [2] §VI, 63, 66; §VII, 1, 14, 16 17, 18.
[3] See below, p. 577.

finally exercised by the supreme king.[1] When the Hebrew kingdom took its constitutional form under Saul, this power passed to him; but there is room to doubt whether Saul's right to this power was extended to Judah or remained limited to Israel in the narrower sense. Even though Judah, or the community of tribes grouped round Judah, was unquestionably included in Saul's dominion, as will be shown, yet this incorporation can have been only of a comparatively loose kind, which assured to Judah a special position like that which David had to allow. Even at the beginning of the Israelite kingdom, then, the discord between south and north may be observed thus far, though the details can hardly be recognized. After the death of the third king, Solomon, this led to the division of the united kingdom.

It is by no means clear whether, when the Israelite tribes proclaimed Saul king, they granted him still other powers besides the supreme command in military defence. In this respect we are much less well informed than in the case of the old South Arabian states, for in these the inscriptions throw some light on the functions of the kingship. Though varying conditions are reflected in them, it is established that a tribal assembly, in both a more representative and a more restricted form, existed in the kingdoms of Qatabān and Saba', and was summoned by the king for the enactment of laws, the issue of administrative decrees, and the decision of legal rights.[2] It is stated in I Samuel x. 25 that after the election of Saul Samuel announced the 'law of the kingdom' and deposited it before Yahweh in Gilgal. But nothing is said about the content of this 'law of the kingdom', that is, of the powers transferred to the new king by the tribes or their representatives, and it is not legitimate to attribute positive meaning to this purely formal assertion by connecting with it I Samuel viii. 11–18. For the account there given of Samuel's effort to divert the people from its desire for a king, by enumerating the many calls and services a king would impose, does not represent a historical record of facts but a tendentious distortion of the truth. Thus there is no more to be said than that the tribes surrendered the right they had previously exercised of calling out the military levy to the new king they had proclaimed. Thereafter the position in Israel was the same as that in the neighbouring states, Edom in the south, Moab and Ammon in the east, and the Aramaean kingdoms in the north, where kingship had been introduced earlier than in Israel; the

[1] §vi, 54; §vi, 74, 123; §vii, 27; §viii, 27; §ix, nos. 8; 30; 35.
[2] §vi, 74, 125 ff.

calling up of the levy constituted the true source of royal power.

But the military constitution of the Philistines, and of the Canaanite city states still existing within the area of Philistine overlordship, was of another kind, and was not quite without influence on Israel in the time of Saul. Far from this, in imitation of the standing Philistine army which consisted partly of men doing feudal service and partly of mercenaries, Saul began to gather round himself a corps of professional soldiers and mercenaries. Thus David came to Saul's court not as a member of the military levy, but as a professional soldier (I Sam. xiv. 52; xvi. 14–20; xxii. 6–20) and began his career there, to rise continually.[1] In this way a development was introduced which progressed further under David, and under Solomon led to the old levy being almost entirely replaced by the professional army.[2]

In the case of Saul, as in others, the tradition as we have it is more concerned with the rise of a hero than with his later life.[3] In consequence, after the account of Saul's acknowledgement as king and his early successes, attention is immediately turned to the rise of his successor David, and very little can be said about Saul's reign. Even its duration cannot be fixed, for the notice in I Samuel xiii. 1 that his reign was of two years is probably wrong, and should be altered into twelve or even better twenty years. The only unambiguous statement is that David spent one year and four months in the land of the Philistines (I Sam. xxvii. 7); i.e. sixteen months passed between David's joining the Philistines and Saul's death. The year of Saul's reign when David came to court, how long he had Saul's favour, and how long he was an independent freebooter in Judah before going to the Philistines, can only be estimated. If the division of the kingdom is taken as about 930 B.C. and the combined reigns of David and Solomon reckoned as about seventy years, with Saul reigning about twenty years, his date would fall about 1020–1000 B.C., which is probably not far wrong.

It is equally impossible to give an exact definition of the extent of his kingdom. In II Samuel ii. 9 his son is said to have been made king over the remainder of Saul's kingdom, namely Gilead, Asher, Jezreel, Ephraim and Benjamin; these territories then certainly belonged to it. But his rule extended beyond the borders of these, and certainly included Galilee. Moreover, there can be no doubt that Saul had some power over Judah. The

[1] G, 1, 156; §iv, 1, 23 ff.; §vii, 20.    [2] See below, pp. 589 ff.
[3] §vii, nos. 19; 28; 29.

campaign against the Amalekites reported in I Samuel xiv. 48;
xv, was in fact conducted with a view to protecting Judah from
the raids of these bedawin tribes; the prior condition of such
action must have been that Saul felt bound in duty to protect
this territory by reason of his overlordship. After the break
with Saul, David, who was after all a man of Judah, did not
see how to secure his own safety in Judah, or that of his parents
(I Sam. xxii. 3–5), and therefore fled with them to the land of
the Moabites. When he returned thence to Judah he had cause
to fear that the men of Judah would deliver him up to Saul,
who was pursuing him (I Sam. xxiii. 12–13, 14–28). In the end,
he could think of no other plan than to leave his home and
migrate to the territory of the national enemy, the Philistines
(I Sam. xxvii. 1). All these events testify to the loyalty and great
influence Saul must have enjoyed in Judah.[1]

Apart from the campaign against the Amalekites already
mentioned, and further struggles with the Philistines, the last
of which, ending in his death, will be considered later, we learn
that, in taking measures against foreign powers, Saul fought with
success against Moab, the Ammonites, Edom and the Aramaean
kings of Zobah (I Sam. xiv. 47–8).[2] The kingdom of Zobah lay
on the plateau between Lebanon and Antilebanon, El-Biqāʿ, and
included the Antilebanon and its eastern approach. There is no
reason to consider these victories paltry.

As Saul, by the defence of Israelite territory, which must on
occasion have been combined with aggressive attacks of his own,
preserved the inheritance of his predecessors the judges, so also
he followed their example in the struggle with those Canaanite
enclaves that still remained in the territory claimed by Israel. In
II Samuel iv. 2–3, the brief statement that Beeroth also was
reckoned as lying in the territory of Benjamin is combined with
the fact that the former inhabitants of this place fled to Gittaim,[3]
to live there as sojourners. Beeroth lay on the mountain-side
between Jerusalem and Bethel, and is probably to be found at
Ras et-Taḥūneh; Gittaim is then to be located at Tell Ras Abu-
Ḥamīd, 5 km. south of Lydda.[4] This permits the certain inference
that Saul had made Beeroth, formerly Canaanite, into an Israelite
possession. This is the more certain because, immediately after
the statement, there follows the account of the murder of Saul's
grandson and successor, Ish-baal, by two officers who came from

[1] §III, 3, 116 ff.
[2] G, 3, 130 f.; §VII, 11, 26; §VII, 15, 134 f.; §VII, nos. 21; 22; 24; §VII, 25, 127.
[3] §VII, 4.    [4] G, 23, 127.

Beeroth. That is certainly to be understood as an act of vengeance for what Saul had done to Beeroth. In the case of Gibeon, the modern El-Jib,[1] it is still clearer that Saul, pursuing his policy of incorporating Canaanite enclaves, took from that city its autonomy, previously recognized by the Israelites (II Sam. xxi. 1–14). In both these cases the information is given incidentally and only in connexion with other matters. It is legitimate to assume with some confidence that many another Canaanite enclave previously independent was included in Saul's kingdom by force in accordance with his nationalistic policy.

To judge from all this, many successes of benefit to his people can be attributed to Saul's reign. Yet as a whole it was beclouded by a tragedy pregnant with ill results. Apparently there were several reasons for this. The immediate effect of the breach between Saul and David, who was much favoured among the people, did Saul harm. Even among those who did not join David, but remained in Saul's service, David had many followers. Moreover, according to the tradition as we have it, it would appear as though not only Samuel and the community of prophets but also the priesthood, at any rate the priests of the court sanctuary at Nob, took the side of David. It is no longer possible to discern their reasons. Perhaps, in the zealous pursuit of aims important to the state, Saul did not pay sufficient attention to matters of interest to the prophets and priests. Some hints in the accounts we have point to this assumption; the questions at issue were sometimes serious ethical or religious principles.[2] But not the least important reason was undoubtedly that some lamentable change took place in Saul himself, and he was subject to fits of suspicion and depression which could lead to frenzied acts of violence, and thus to loss of that self-confidence which is essential to success. It was accordingly not surprising that he had to meet defeat in a battle when his enemy held the material advantage. But before more can be said of this a glance must be cast at David's relationship with Saul, the breach between them and its results for both.

David came to Saul's court as an experienced soldier, though where he gained this experience it is impossible to say. He then became leader of some kind of troop of mercenaries or police[3] (not of the military levy commanded by Abner) in the continual border fights with the Philistines, and gained such successes as

---

[1] Excavated by J. B. Pritchard. See his *Gibeon, where the sun stood still*, Princeton, 1962.

[2] §VII, 28.          [3] §IV, 1, 26 f. and 38 f.

to win him high esteem, so that he came to be considered a suitable match for Saul's daughter Michal. In this Saul concurred either because he wished to promote the younger man or so as to obtain a hold over him. Moreover, a close friendship united David and the king's son Jonathan. But Saul's fear that David might outstrip his son in popular favour and thus imperil Jonathan's succession was perhaps not wholly without foundation. His personal jealousy of the successful and universally beloved young officer added to this fear, and led to the originally good relations between Saul and David growing weaker and weaker, till finally they were completely broken. David had to seek safety in flight. After a meteoric appearance at Adullam in Judah, the modern Tell esh-Sheikh-Madkūr, 20 km. southwest of Bethlehem, where a band of desperate men gathered round him, he went and stayed for a short time in Moab, taking his parents with him. Afterwards he gained a livelihood as the leader of a volunteer corps numbering about four hundred, in various parts of Judah; but he found that he was nowhere safe from Saul and had to join Achish, king of Gath (perhaps ʿArāq el-Menshiyeh or Tell Sheikh el-ʿAreini, about 30 km. west of Hebron) with his corps now increased to 600 men. Achish accepted him as a vassal of the Philistines and assigned to him the city-state Ziklag (probably Tell el-Khuweilfeh, 20 km. north of Beersheba) in the south-eastern corner of the territory controlled by the Philistines, with instructions to guard the border against raids by nomads[1] and to be ready for disposal by his feudal lord in military duties (I Sam. xxii. 1–xxvii. 2). Achish intended that David should take part in this capacity in the final war against Saul undertaken by five Philistine princes: David was spared this task owing to the mistrust felt by the other Philistine princes for the turncoat (II Sam. xxix).

We do not know the immediate cause of the great struggle between Israel and the Philistines which cost Saul and three of his sons their lives, but it is clear that the Philistines were the aggressors. As they were informed of Saul's weakened position, they obviously considered the occasion favourable for regaining the overlordship they had held in Palestine before Saul's intervention. They assembled their contingents in the valley of Bethshan (the modern Tell el-Ḥuṣn), at that time perhaps Philistine territory or at any rate subject to Philistine overlordship,[2] without any hindrance from Saul, and then compelled him to offer them battle there. As might be expected as a result of Philistine

[1] §IV, 1, 39.    [2] §VII, 3; §VII, 26, 38 ff.

military superiority, and greater efficiency in such terrain, Saul lost the battle and his life (I Sam. xxxi; II Sam. i).

David, who had certainly long cherished the aim of succeeding Saul in the rule over Israel, could now take an important step towards achieving his purpose, even though adherence to Saul's dynasty was firmly rooted enough to allow of Saul's grandson Ish-baal holding part of his father's dominion. In this Abner acted rather as Ish-baal's guardian than as his supporter. Ish-baal managed to maintain his rule from his residence in the land east of Jordan, Mahanaim (perhaps the modern Khirbet Maḥnah, 20 km. east of Jordan, north-west of Jerash), not only over the land east of Jordan, but also over western Galilee, that is Jezreel (modern Zer'in, lying on the range which separates the valley of Beth-shan and the plateau of Jezreel), including at least a part of the tribal territory of Issachar[1] and the hill territory round Samaria. Even so, the prospects for David were unquestionably improved. Hearing of Saul's death, while keeping secret the ultimate object of his desire, he transferred his residence from Ziklag to Hebron, in agreement with the Philistines, or at least with their permission. There he received the elders of Judah, or rather of the coalition of tribes led by Judah, and so called summarily by that name;[2] by these he was anointed king of Judah (II Sam. ii. 1–4). At the same time he sent a message to the inhabitants of Jabesh-Gilead, who had buried Saul's remains with the due ceremonies, and this message clearly implied that he aimed at ruling more than Judah. He then quietly awaited the course of events.[3]

These soon turned in his favour. Abner took advantage of a personal grievance to drop Ish-baal, whom he had protected, and joined David's party. This led to Abner's murder by the dagger of Joab, David's captain, who was jealous of him. Not long after, Ish-baal himself was murdered (II Sam. iv. 2–12), and the way for David to rule over all Israel was completely clear. The elders of Israel, that is of the northern tribes, offered him the throne, and after he had made a covenant with them, anointed him king of Israel. Unfortunately we learn as little about the content of these agreements as about the previous negotiations between the elders of Israel and Saul,[4] or about the conditions accepted by David when he was made king over Judah (II Sam. ii. 4). Certainly the primary agreement concerned the transfer of the command over the armed forces to the king, that is the right granted him by the representatives of Israel to call up the military

---

[1] §III, 3, 116.  
[2] §IV, 1, 40 f.  
[3] §VIII, nos. 8; 9.  
[4] See above, p. 574.

levies of the tribes. There is nothing to inform us whether other dispositions were also made, and David was allowed certain absolute powers pertaining to administration, legal decisions and even perhaps religious observance. The powers granted to the king in these respects were certainly not extensive. It is more probable that the tribes, or the two tribal communities of north and south, were able to preserve their independence as to these matters. For David's kingdom was not a co-ordinated unity, but a combination of two kingdoms united under his rule, dependent on his person.

As a third element of a peculiar kind, Jerusalem itself was shortly added to those two kingdoms. David captured the city by force of arms, and elevated it to the rank of political capital and religious centre. It was the personal possession of David and his successors, and remained, as such, outside the dual monarchies, Judah and Israel.

Thus David had actually attained the object of which he had dreamed as early, it may be, as the time when he was still in Saul's service; he was now Saul's successor, king over all Israel. But the nature of his kingship, the basic conception on which his right was founded, differed most markedly from his predecessor's. In the case of Saul, the determining factor was the designation by Yahweh, and that grant of power by the grace of God was followed by the acclamation of the people. The transfer of the throne to David, first by the representatives of Judah and then also by those of Israel, meant that on the one hand the position of military and political power David had already won for himself by his own efforts was admitted, and that on the other hand David was willing to take upon himself the offered dignity and its burden. His kingship was not, then, conditioned by an act of grace of God, but by a human estimate of the real factors of power. Yet this act was soon transfigured by the religious conception: Yaweh, it was thought, had concluded an eternal covenant with David and assured him of the perpetuity of his dynasty (II Sam. vii; xxiii. 5).[1]

## VIII. DAVID

According to II Samuel v. 5 (cf. ii. 1) David ruled over Judah from Hebron for seven and a half years, and then, after capturing Jerusalem and making it his residence, was king of Israel and Judah for thirty-three years. David must, then, have undertaken the conquest of Jerusalem shortly before being anointed king of

[1] §IV, 1, 39 ff.

Israel. Till then it had been a Jebusite fortress, and an independent city. The account of the capture (II Sam. v. 6–8) is unfortunately complicated by all sorts of textual difficulties, so that the course of events is to some extent obscure. But a topographical investigation of the sites, and more recent archaeological work make it possible to discern something about the nature and extent of the old Jebusite walls, and to see how David made the fortress still stronger after its capture. Nothing however can be learned about the means by which he reduced it.

First, it is certain that the Jebusite fortress occupied the south-eastern hill and was limited to it, but included the eastern slope of this hill with the Gihon spring and the shaft leading to it. This has been established by the recent excavations of Kathleen M. Kenyon,[1] correcting the older results of R. Weill[2] in 1913–14 and 1923–4, of R. A. S. Macalister and J. G. Duncan[3] in 1923–5, and of J. W. Crowfoot and G. M. FitzGerald[4] in 1927. The Jebusite town captured by David was much greater than previously supposed. It was surrounded by a very thick wall, which David repaired and completed. The palace which David ordered to be built with the help of Tyrian craftsmen, according to II Samuel v. 11, will probably have been situated in the northern part of the Jebusite city, henceforth renamed the 'city of David'. Perhaps the actual site was the place called in II Samuel v. 9, *millō*', literally 'filling', a term perhaps meaning a platform created by an artificial rubble construction. In any case it was to the south of the area later used by Solomon for the construction of his palace and temple, the modern Haram esh-Sherīf, which in David's time was not built upon; the only construction that can have stood there then was the altar for burnt and peace offerings set up by David (II Sam. xxiv. 18–25).[5] There is therefore proof that David, after conquering Jerusalem, made it the capital of his united kingdom; it was soon raised to the rank of 'metropolis', the centre of the religious cult, by the introduction of the Ark, the object of ancient religious observance, a ritual act the hymn of which was probably Psalm xxiv. 8–10. Jerusalem remained the political capital as long as, and whenever, there was an Israelite or Jewish state, whether that state was quite independent or only partially so. Its spiritual and religious significance, quite independent of its political position, has been maintained till the present day.[6]

---

[1] §viii, nos. 3; 14; 15.         [2] §viii, nos. 30; 31.
[3] §viii, 18.                     [4] §viii, 6; cf. also §viii, 32.
[5] G, 11, 297 ff.; G, 38, vol. 1, 85 ff.; §viii, 16.         [6] §viii, nos. 1; 21.

Until the capture of Jerusalem the Philistines were, it appears, either on terms of good understanding, or at any rate of peaceful neutrality, with David. But they believed that his removal from Hebron to Jerusalem must be regarded as a rising against their supremacy, or at least as the commencement of an attempt on David's part to free himself from it. David had been able to accept sovereignty over Judah only with the consent of his Philistine feudal lords, and accordingly still remained, as king of Judah, in the position of a vassal of the Philistines, at any rate to all appearances. They could only have been pleased when Saul's kingdom was split into two parts, the territory of Ish-baal and that of David; they therefore willingly allowed David to manage his own affairs as the rival of Saul's grandson and heir almost independently (II Sam. ii–iv). But the position was completely changed when David, chosen king not only of Judah but also of Israel immediately after Ish-baal's death, gained control of the Jebusite fortress and moved his residence there, thus with-drawing from the area under Philistine control (II Sam. v. 1–16).[1] They accordingly attempted to reverse the course of events, by attacking their erstwhile vassal in his new capital, and by creating a movement there against the city's new ruler as a result of their devastating the districts south and north-west of it, which were the city's granary. But David defeated them with such loss that they retired home, and he was able to undertake the equip-ment of Jerusalem as the civil and religious capital (II Sam. v. 17–25).

Approximately the first half of David's reign over the united kingdom, that is roughly the first twenty years of the tenth century, was occupied in waging great wars with the aim not merely of securing the borders but of conquering a considerable territory. The tradition we have is scanty, for, as in the case of Saul, though the rise of the hero is narrated in detail, he is no longer the centre of interest thereafter; the narrative turns to his successor. The result of this is that we are very ill-informed about David's wars of conquest in II Samuel viii; x–xii; I Kings xi. 15–25, though they were of considerable importance. The Philistines appear to have maintained their position best. They had, however, to put up with the loss of their supremacy over Palestine, and probably to agree to pay all sorts of imposts exacted by David. These presumably concerned specially the important trade routes through the Palestine territory.

There was a net-work of these trade routes. A route from

[1] §VIII, 28.

Egypt leads northward to the Mediterranean littoral. This is joined by another leading from west to east at Gaza, connecting up with the caravan route from southern Arabia. This runs past the northern end of the Gulf of 'Aqaba, on the eastern side of the Wādi 'Arabah and of the Jordan up to Damascus. There it joins routes to northern Syria and Asia Minor and the desert road by Palmyra to Mesopotamia. Ever since the third millennium B.C. not the least important object of the wars between the great powers bordering on Syria and Palestine, that is Egypt on the one side and Babylonia and Assyria and the Hittites on the other, had been the control and usufruct of goods carried on those routes. David's campaigns of conquest undoubtedly pursued this aim too. Though the sources for his time do not call attention to this, it can be deduced with certainty from the period that follows, even as early as the days of Solomon, when it becomes at any rate partially clear.[1] The Philistines must, then, have had to grant to David a right of supervision over the caravan routes passing through their land, and a share in the revenue from the road-tolls. In other matters they were apparently able to maintain their autonomy in their own national area (II Sam. viii. 1).[2]

Moab, Ammon, Edom, Aram-Zobah[3] and Aram-Damascus[4] fared worse; they lost their political independence, had to pay a heavy tribute, and were degraded to vassalage status by the Israelites (II Sam. viii. 2–14). The right of supervision over the caravan routes leading through their territories probably passed completely into David's hands. The most severe, and the most considerable, of these wars of conquest, it would appear, was that against Aram-Zobah, for this was at that time the strongest military power in Syria, and had even been able, by attacks on Mesopotamia, to wrest territory from the Assyrians. Unfortunately we learn nothing of the way in which the lands incorporated in David's empire were administered; not even the borders of the enlarged Israelite territory thus created are known to us. The line of the northern border is especially uncertain. But as Toi of Hamath sent a gift of salutation to David after his victory over the king of Zobah (II Sam. viii. 9–10) and mention is made there of wars between Hamath and Zobah, it may be assumed that the northern border of Aram-Zobah, somewhere about the latitude of Riblah on the Orontes, also formed the northern border of David's empire.

[1] G, 3, 130 ff.; §vi, 74, 109 ff.; §vi, 76; §viii, 10, 10 ff., 15 f., 35, 145, 155.
[2] G, 3, 137 and 213 f.; §iv, 1, 49 f.; §vii, 12.
[3] See above, p. 576.          [4] §viii, 13.

The accounts at our disposal of David's successes abroad are
scanty, but nothing at all is told of the annexation of the Canaanite
enclaves which survived till his time. The only recourse is to
draw, as in the case of Saul,[1] inferences from the situation later.
In so far as the cities mentioned in Judges i. 19–21, 27–35 and
II Samuel xxiv. 7 as having remained at first unconquered by
Israel were not subjected by Saul, they must have been embodied
by David in the Israelite kingdom, or rather in the two kingdoms, Israel and Judah, united by his personal rule. The division
of Israel into twelve districts, which, as will be seen later,[2] was
effected by Solomon, presumes this incorporation, for the second,
third, fourth and fifth of these districts include areas which had
belonged to the former Canaanite city states. It cannot be
decided whether David had to use force in these annexations or
whether the Canaanite enclaves still surviving fell into his hands
inevitably when, Philistine supremacy over Palestine being
broken, they lost the support which maintained their independence. Probably the latter view is the more correct.[3] It is also
uncertain whether David's annexations extended to Phoenician
territory too, as Alt is inclined to infer from Judges i. 31 (Sidon),
and II Samuel xxiv. 6–7 (Sidon the fortress of Tyre).[4] In view
of the amicable relations existing between the king of Tyre, the
leading city in Phoenicia at the time, and David (II Sam. v. 11;
I Kings v. 15) it is improbable.[5] Policy would lead David, as it
later led Solomon, to maintain good relations with the Phoenicians,
for otherwise the share in the revenue from the route leading
from south to north through Gaza,[6] which he had won through
his victory over the Philistines, would have been nugatory, since
the northern continuation ran through territory in Phoenician
hands.

The extension of the Israelite kingdom by David naturally led
to the employment of a considerably larger number of officials
than were needed in the time of Saul. Whereas the leader of the
military levy, Abner, alone had executive authority beside Saul,
the list of David's court (II Sam. viii. 16–18; xx. 23–6) mentions,
in addition to the leader of the levy, Joab, and the chiefs of the
priesthood, several high officers. There was a commandant of
the mercenary troops, Benaiah, a superintendent of the *corvée*,
Adoram, a 'remembrancer' or chancellor, Jehoshaphat, and a

---

[1] See above, pp. 576 f.          [2] See below, pp. 591 f.
[3] G, 3, 120 ff.; §iv, 1, 49 ff.; §v, 6, 83 f.
[4] §viii, 2, 140 f. and 144 f.          [5] G, 3, 131 f.; §vi, 2, 347 f.
[6] See above, p. 583.

scribe, Seia or Seraiah. Two of these, the remembrancer, *mazkīr*, and the scribe, *sōpēr*, seem to be imitations of officers at the Egyptian court, for the *mazkīr* corresponds perhaps to the Egyptian *wḥmw*, 'announcer, speaker', and *sōpēr* to the Egyptian *sš*, 'scribe'. Of these the first, the *wḥmw*, united the functions of a master of the ceremonies and foreign minister and other duties also, while the second, the *sš*, was the personal secretary of the pharaoh and his *chef de bureau*.[1] Just as in these cases and also in that of 'the king's friend' (II Sam. xv. 37; xvi. 16; I Kings iv. 5)[2] the offices in David's government were influenced by the example of a great foreign power, so the appointment of the special officer for the mercenary and professional troops represents an assimilation, in this case partly due to Saul,[3] to common custom outside Israel, and a departure from the old Israelite tradition which recognized only the military levy. The same might be said of the office of the superintendent of the *corvée* or 'minister of public works', if it was really introduced by David and not, as has been thought, by Solomon.[4]

It is, then, permissible to imagine that many other features of David's court were copied from the court ceremonial of neighbouring states which reflected an old tradition, especially from that of Egypt and Assyria. Isolated statements such as those about David's harim (II Sam. xv. 16; xvi. 21-2; xx. 3) or about singers, both men and women, at his court (II Sam. xix. 35 (36)) point in this direction. It was also owing to such imitation that —if the 'god' in Psalm xlv. 7 really means the king—the king came to be spoken of as 'god' in a manner completely contrary to ancient Israelite custom.[5] It is apparent that David had much at heart all arrangements for the cult ceremonies in the worship of Yahweh, particularly for a more ample musical form; in this point too he must have been following foreign inspiration to a large extent.[6]

The incorporation into Israel's own territory of many an independent city with a high standard of material civilization, and with important and prosperous industries, and the extension of rule over large and rich neighbouring lands through which passed a lively caravan trade, involved a sudden rapid increase in Israel's prosperity. But the results of this prosperity remained confined to a comparatively small social class, to the court and the

[1] G, 3, 120; G, 37, 251; §VIII, nos. 4; 26; 29.
[2] §VIII, 7.       [3] See above, p. 575.
[4] G, 1, 155; §VIII, nos. 22; 23.
[5] §VI, 63; §VII, 16; §VIII, 11, 1 ff.; §VIII, 12, 150 ff.       [6] G, 3, 125 ff.

officials, to the military leaders and the merchants. The great
mass of the people were subject to the military levy and had to
bear the principal part in the burden caused by David's wars of
conquest. Having to neglect or even quite abandon their own
gainful occupations, most often, that is, their farming, these
could feel only the disadvantages of David's policy with its many
remote aims.[1] Thus in the course of time there accumulated
amongst the masses much discontent with David's government.
Absalom, an ambitious man, eager for power, was of the kind
to find it easy to be borne on this tide of discontent, and he
deposed his father from the royal throne at any rate for a few
weeks (II Sam. xv–xviii). While Absalom's rebellion started in
the city of his birth, Hebron of Judah, it is nevertheless not
necessary to assume that the real cause of this rising is to be found
in the tension between Israel and Judah, though this was always
latent.[2] In this case it was Judah's discontent, arising perhaps
from some feeling that David favoured Israel. A sufficient
explanation can more probably be found in the widespread
resentment felt everywhere in David's kingdom, in the north as
well as in the south, of the great sacrifices imposed by his policy
of aggression. This is even more probable if, as Albright was
inclined to assume,[3] there was a re-awakening of the separatist
tendencies in the tribes against the centralizing tendency of the
monarchy.

Yet this view of Absalom's rebellion renders it still more clear
that the rising against David provoked by Sheba, of the tribe
of Benjamin (II Sam. xx. 1–22) after David's victory over
Absalom, owed its motive power to the opposition between
north and south. David was able to quell both these rebellions
quickly, the second more quickly than the first. But no good
augury for the future could be drawn from either, if a strong hand
like David's were lacking. For the time being, however, the
authority of David and of his choice in the dynastic succession
was so firmly based that a series of other dangers could be safely
overcome. No less than three of the princes who might have
been regarded as having claims to the succession, Amnon,
Absalom, and Adonijah (II Sam. xiii–xx; I Kings i–ii), died
violent deaths prematurely, without the transference of David's
throne to the chosen successor being in doubt for a moment. The
transference was, on the contrary, reckoned a matter of course.
David's decision was even respected and followed at a time when
he was no longer completely in possession of his mental faculties

[1] §iv, 1, 56 ff.          [2] See above, pp. 574, 580.          [3] G, 3, 158.

and his dispositions had quite clearly been determined by court
intrigues (I Kings i–ii). No small part of this preservation of the
succession within David's family must have been due to the
religious ideal, the conception of an assurance given to David by
Yahweh as to the duration of his dynasty.[1]

## IX. SOLOMON

Solomon[2] was able to overcome all attempts at internal opposition
to his accession quickly and decisively, thanks to the soundly
based authority David had won for his dynasty. He was far from
equally successful in maintaining the results of his father's
great expansion abroad. Aram-Damascus and Edom, though it is
true they were unable to recover complete independence, did at
least, shortly after David's death, abate the strictness of Israelite
supremacy (I Kings xi. 14–25). How far the abatement went in
detail cannot be recognized, but it is certain that Solomon kept
exclusive rights at any rate over the caravan routes passing
through the territories of Aram-Damascus and of Edom, otherwise his ambitious commercial policy[3] would have been impossible. More particularly, the fortification of Ezion-Geber (Tell
el-Kheleifeh) situated at the northern end of the Gulf of 'Aqaba,
the construction of a big storehouse and perhaps also the institution of a large foundry for metal-working there, and the
despatch of a merchant fleet thence to Ophir,[4] require the
assumption that Solomon could use the route running northwards through Edomite territory without hindrance.

While the relaxation of Israelite supremacy over Aram-
Damascus and Edom concerns territories which David had but
recently attached to his kingdom, the cession to Tyre of a part of
Galilee named Cabul, on the border of Phoenicia and Israel,
granted by Solomon in payment for the materials delivered to
him for his buildings by the king of Tyre (I Kings ix. 10–14)
represents the abandonment, no doubt painful, of an area which
had long been Israelite, for it belonged to the tribe Asher. On
the other hand, Solomon's marriage to an Egyptian princess
brought him possession of the independent Canaanite city
Gezer (Tell Jezer, 30 km. west of Jerusalem), which had previously recognized Egyptian supremacy, for this city was the
princess's dowry (I Kings iii. 1; ix. 15–16).[5] Though the gain of
Gezer constitutes an extension of Solomon's kingdom, yet the

[1] §VIII, nos. 5; 17; 19; 25.    [2] §IX, 18; §IX, 41.    [3] See below, p. 592.
[4] See below, p. 594.    [5] G, 14, 20, 133 f.; §IX, nos. 21; 48; 50.

manner in which this gain was secured is a sign that Egypt, which
had hardly been able to take any interest in Palestine for a century and a half, had begun to pay attention again at this time to
conditions there. It is therefore possible that, as Malamat thinks,
the pharaoh, probably Siamun, conquered Gezer after a victory
over the Philistines and ceded it to Solomon as a territorial
concession in the guise of a dowry.[1] The re-awakening of
Egyptian interest in Palestine is attested by two other events of
this time; the Edomite prince Hadad, who was able, after
David's death, to recover some of the independence lost by his
country (I Kings xi. 14–25), found refuge and support in
Egypt. The same was true of Jeroboam ben-Nebat, who was made
king of the north when it seceded from the dynasty of David
after Solomon's death (I Kings xi. 26–40). But Israel began to
feel the impact of this Egyptian interest only after the division
of the kingdom (I Kings xiv. 25–8; II Chron. xii. 1–14).
Solomon himself, as David and Saul had done before him, was
able, generally, to act with complete independence both towards
Egypt and towards the power of Assyria in the east, then only a
rather feeble kingdom.

The tradition at our disposal (I Kings iii–xi) concerning
Solomon is of a kind which makes it impossible to review his
reign in chronological order. It is necessary, therefore, to consider its peculiar historical character under individual aspects.
There are five characteristic features of this reign. The first is
a very thorough-going change in Israel's military organization,
namely the introduction of chariotry as the essential, decisive arm
in war. The second is the creation of new administrative districts,
which had to provide victuals and fodder for Solomon's court and
the garrisons of chariotry which he created and posted in various
parts; this probably affected only the northern part of his kingdom, Israel in the stricter sense, not Judah too.[2] The third is the
creation of commercial monopolies, and the extension of the
existing institution of customs and excise taxes on the traffic
passing along routes through territory under the imperial power
of Israel. The fourth is the activity in building on an ample, even
luxurious, scale. One part of this was devoted to the construction
of Solomon's palace, to which the temple of Yahweh belonged,
the other part was conditioned by the change in military methods,
that is by the necessity of building fortified barracks for garrisons
from the newly created corps of chariotry. The fifth is the refinement of court procedure on the model of the neighbouring

---

[1] See below, pp. 656 f.; §VIII, 20, 11 f.    [2] See below, p. 591.

countries, which had in this matter a long tradition behind them, and the maintenance of diplomatic, commercial and cultural relations with other courts.

## SOLOMON'S MILITARY ORGANIZATION

Solomon cannot be compared with his father in military ability in the remotest degree. Nevertheless he recognized quite clearly the necessity of equipping Israel with a defence that would meet the improvements in military methods being introduced, or already introduced; and he carried through the changes in the striking force of his kingdom required by the adoption of an arm new to Israel, chariotry. How radical the change was can be seen from II Samuel viii. 4. There we are told that when David conquered the king of Aram-Zobah and took from him several hundred teams of horses, he ordered that the majority of them should be houghed (that is rendered unfit for further war service). The reason, of course, was that he himself had no chariots at his disposal. David, then, considered the introduction of the chariot unnecessary, though it had long been in use in Egyptian armies, and also in those of the Canaanite city-states once subject to Egypt. In spite of his decision, David must have learnt from his own experience what great service this military arm rendered the Aramaean states in their defensive wars with him. It was probably very soon after his succession that Solomon introduced the change, and made this arm his principal military force. Perhaps the immediate cause was the success of Aram-Damascus in regaining, shortly after David's death, a part of the independence previously lost to David,[1] for Aram-Damascus now constituted a continual threat to Israel, in that it was able to rely on chariotry, long in use there.

The statements in several passages of the chapters I Kings v–xi concerning the number of chariots at Solomon's disposal are not in agreement, but render it probable that an average of 1400, with 4000 horses can be assumed.[2] In the case of some of the barracks built, according to I Kings ix. 19; x. 26, for the chariotry corps, including Megiddo, the foundations of the stables for horses and chariots have been excavated together with remains of the interior construction.[3] The stables in Megiddo would suffice for the accommodation of about 150 chariots and 450 horses.[4] The change to the use of chariotry

[1] See above, p. 583.       [2] G, 3, 135 f.
[3] G, 9, 127 ff.; G, 38, vol. 1, 87 f.; §ix, 51.
[4] G, 1, 223; G, 3, 66 and 135 f.; G, 38, vol. 1, 67 f., figs. 80, 81.

involved reducing in importance the military levy, previously the decisive factor. The charioteer had to be given a long and thorough training, and remain in the service while fit, or at least for several years; that is, he had to become a professional soldier. Since the number of charioteers was of course limited, and presumably a considerable number of mercenaries was attracted to this service from abroad, only a small number of Israelites liable to military duties could become professional soldiers. This did not mean that men previously liable to be called up for the levy were now completely freed from their obligations. On the contrary, when they were not required to serve as infantry in wars, they were now put to building barracks for the chariotry and to undertaking their share in Solomon's other building enterprises. Thus the *corvée*—it would be better to call it the service of public works intended for the creation and maintenance of constructions for defence—developed out of the service in the levy. There is a story (I Kings xv. 16–22) which, though it refers to events some twenty years after Solomon's death, enables us to see the nature of this service on public works. After Baasha, ruler of the northern kingdom, had built a fortress on the southern border of his land, at Ramah (modern Er-Rām, 6 km. north of Jerusalem) as a threat to the southern kingdom, he had to leave it unoccupied owing to an attack by the Aramaeans on his own territory. Then Asa, ruler of the southern kingdom, called up the whole levy of Judah in order to use the stones and timber in Baasha's building for constructing fortresses at Geba' (modern Jeba', 3 km. east of Ramah) and at Mizpeh (probably Tell en-Naṣbeh, 3 km. north of Ramah) intended for defending the south against the north.

Men under the obligation of service for public works in Solomon's time were called up according to a settled rota, reducing to the utmost any interference with their usual occupation, generally, that is, with farming or manufacture, and so inflicting as little loss as possible on their means of gaining a livelihood (I Kings iv. 6; v. 27–30; ix. 20–3; xi. 26–8). Superintendence of all this service was entrusted to a minister specially appointed for the purpose, named Adoniram (I Kings iv. 6; v. 28; xii. 18), who had already held the same office under David, if the statement in II Samuel xx. 24 is really to be trusted.[1] Subordinates of this minister were appointed directors of the service for fairly large districts. We do not know how many of these there were; but the 'house of Joseph', that is, probably,

[1] See above, pp. 584 f.

the territory of the tribes Manasseh, Ephraim, and Benjamin, certainly formed such a district in this system. The head there was Jeroboam ben-Nebat, of Ephraim, who quarrelled with Solomon, fled to Egypt, and became the first ruler of the northern kingdom when it renounced the dynasty of David after Solomon's death (I Kings xi. 26–40; xii). It is moreover uncertain whether Solomon imposed equality on both his kingdoms, Israel and Judah, in this service of public works, or made special regulations for Judah which could be regarded as unfair to Israel. The narrative of the division of the kingdom (I Kings xii) permits, and even renders probable, the view that Israel had to bear greater burdens in this service than Judah. A similar question arises in considering the twelve districts formed by Solomon for administration or taxation to provide for his court and garrisons, as in that case too it is disputable whether Judah was included in this organization or was subjected to services for the same purpose in some different way. It seems certain that Judah provided some services.

### THE ADMINISTRATIVE DISTRICTS

The chariotry garrisons instituted by Solomon had to be provided regularly with victuals for the soldiers and fodder for the horses. There had to be additional deliveries for the maintenance of the court too, which could no longer be provided out of the royal lands as in the time of Saul or of David,[1] for Solomon's palace arrangements were on a much larger scale than theirs. The provision for these requirements had to come from administrative districts created by Solomon for the purpose of taxation (I Kings iv. 7–19; v. 7–8). These were twelve in number and were partly identical with the old tribal divisions, and partly covered the territories of the formerly independent Canaanite city-states which had been recently annexed.

The size of each district was determined with the view that they should be about equal in productive capacity and accordingly be able in turn to supply the materials required by the court and the garrisons for a month each. The head of each district was a high official, $n^e \dot{s} \bar{\imath} b$, and two of them married daughters of Solomon. As in the list of the twelve districts already mentioned Judah is not named, it is legitimate to assume that Judah was subjected to the kind of service imposed on the twelve districts of Israel in some special way;[2] for it is most unlikely that Judah could have been left quite free of any obligations in this respect.

[1] Cf. II Samuel ix. 9 f.; xiii, 23; xvi, 1 ff.; xix, 25 ff.
[2] G, 3, 140 ff.; §ix, nos. 2; 4; 5.

But it is probable that some special ruling applying to Judah was felt by Israel to be preferential treatment and played a part in bringing about Israel's separation from the dynasty of David after Solomon's death.

## COMMERCE AND TAXATION

Solomon has with some justice been called the enthroned merchant. Commercial undertakings on a large scale, treated as royal monopolies, constitute in fact a particularly characteristic trait of his rule. Even the corps of chariotry he created served to promote trade, when not actually employed in defence of the borders. This can be very clearly recognized in one special case. In I Kings ix. 18, among the cities Solomon 'built' (that is fortified), the consonantal text, the *Keṯib*, mentions 'Tamar', while the vocalization of the word, the *Qerī*, is 'Tamor'. This vocalization requires the reading 'Tadmor', and in II Chronicles viii. 4, which is the parallel text to I Kings ix. 18, the consonantal text also has 'Tadmor', thus assuming this reading in the earlier version. 'Tamar' might be located at or near the modern 'Ain el-'Arūs, situated about 5 km. south of the southern end of the Dead Sea, whereas Tadmor corresponds with the later Palmyra, the town about half-way along the caravan route leading from Damascus in a north-easterly direction to the Euphrates, which is known to have been of importance from the beginning of the second millennium.[1] On the basis of purely textual criticism 'Tadmor' is to be preferred as the better reading. This conclusion is reinforced by the fact that Tadmor appears in II Chronicles viii. 4, in a context relating the historical event. The clause 'and he built Tadmor in the wilderness' is preceded by 'and Solomon went to Hamath-Zobah and prevailed against it', and followed by 'and all the store-cities which he built in Hamath'. The reference in I Kings ix. 19 to buildings in the Lebanon attributed to Solomon might be to those in Aram-Zobah, if the term 'Lebanon' is used in this passage in a wide sense to include the Anti-Lebanon and its approaches. All in all, the fortifications of Tadmor can be regarded as one section of a larger enterprise, devoted to the maintenance of commercial intercourse rather than to securing political supremacy over the territories concerned. Zobah, as we have seen, included the Antilebanon and the plateau formed by its western approach, and the interior east-

---

[1] Cf. G. Eisser and J. Lewy, *Die Altassyrischen Rechtsurkunden von Kültepe*, 3. und 4. Teil (*M.V.Ae.G.* 35, 3) (Leipzig, 1935), 18–21, no. 303, B 2, 3, *kunuk Puzur-Ištar Ta-ad-mu-ri-im*, 'Seal of Puzur-Ištar of Tadmor (Palmyra)'.

wards, reaching probably as far as Tadmor. Solomon's aim in this direction was to keep the route through Zobah and its capital Hamath open for his own trading operations.[1]

Just as the mention of Hamath-Zobah in connexion with Solomon's commercial policy shows that his caravan trade reached the north, that is Syria and Asia Minor, and the east, that is Mesopotamia and Babylon, so the story of the visit of the Queen of Sheba in south-western Arabia (Yemen) to Solomon permits one certain conclusion, even though the story has become a legend in other respects. Solomon had some part in the caravan trade between southern Arabia and Syria which must have been in existence in his time, although it can be traced in other sources only from a slightly later date onwards. The visit was certainly not a mere act of courtesy, and the conversations between the king and queen on abstract questions, to be considered later,[2] cannot have been the only or the real purpose of the visit, which must have had something to do with commercial policy. The queen may not have been the actual monarch of her country, but it was she who came on the visit, and from this may be deduced that it was she who desired a commercial arrangement with Solomon.[3] Perhaps this was a frontier organization for the conduct of caravans, such as that described by Theophrastus[4] for the sale of incense in the main temple of the Sabaeans. Ezion-Geber, the starting-point for Solomon's fleet,[5] was also an important halt on the caravan route from southern Arabia through the 'Arabah and east of Jordan to Syria, connected by the branch route to Gaza with the coast route from Egypt to Syria. That route also must have been of interest to Solomon.

Not the least significant of the imports by land routes were the horses obtained by Solomon from Cilicia[6] and the chariots from Egypt, a traffic in which he secured a virtual monopoly. A fairly precise statement about this is to be found in I Kings x. 28–9, not only as to the sources from which these goods were obtained but also as to the purchasers, namely 'all the kings of the Hittites and the kings of Aram', that is the neighbouring Syrian states. The prices are given; a chariot cost 600 shekels of silver, roughly 8·80 kg., a horse 150 shekels of silver, roughly 2·20 kg., so that the horse was reckoned at a quarter of the value of a chariot.[7]

---

[1] G, 3, 132 f.; §vii, 15; §vii, 24.  [2] See below, pp. 602 f.
[3] G, 3, 124; §viii, 10, 85; §ix, 29.  [4] *Hist. Plant.* ix, iv, 5–6.
[5] See below, p. 594.  [6] §ix, 40.
[7] G, 3, 135.

The caravan traffic produced revenue for Solomon not only in so far as he himself controlled it, but also because he extended the collection of transit taxes, already instituted by his father.[1] Unfortunately no details about these are known, but it can at least be inferred from the first half of I Kings x. 15, in spite of textual corruption, that mention was there made of considerable imposts collected by Solomon from this source.

More is said in the texts about Solomon's trading by sea[2] than about his part in the caravan trade, and recent excavations have given substance and colour to what is stated in the book of Kings. According to I Kings ix. 26–7; x. 11, 22, Solomon, with the help of Hiram king of Tyre,[3] had ships built and manned at Ezion-Geber, at the north-east end of the Gulf of 'Aqaba.[4] From there he despatched them to Ophir, that is, probably, to southern Arabia, to bring back gold,[5] precious stones, a rare kind of timber, silver and other goods. Nothing is said in these texts as to what cargoes the ships carried on the voyage out. Yet it is probably right to think that these expeditions were part of an exchange trade, though due account must be taken of the possibility that occasionally the produce was obtained rather by freebooting than by exchange, as Goethe's lines warn us:

> On voyages I could not start,
> for commerce, war and piracy
> are three in one that none can part.[6]

The successful excavations undertaken by Nelson Glueck at the site of Ezion-Geber, combined with isolated *sondages* at several places in the Western 'Arabah, have shown that Solomon quarried copper and iron deposits there and constructed foundries in the 'Arabah and in the Negeb and perhaps also in Ezion-Geber.[7] Possibly it was the copper and iron thus obtained which the ships sent from Ezion-Geber carried as trade goods to be exchanged for the products to be brought from Ophir.

### SOLOMON'S BUILDINGS

Though Solomon may deserve the appellation 'enthroned merchant', the stories which have become folklore just as rightly treat him as the master builder, the creator of buildings of royal

[1] See above, pp. 582 f.     [2] §IX, 37.     [3] §IX, 20.     [4] See above, p. 587.
[5] Near Tel Aviv there was found an ostracon with the inscription from between 900 and 800 B.C. 'Gold of Ophir for Beth Horon' (*Syria*, XXVI (1949), 157); cf. also §IX, 23, 266 f., pl. XI.
[6] *Faust*, Part II, Act 5, ll. 144–6.
[7] G, 3, 133 ff.; §VIII, 10, 89 ff.; §IX, nos. 1; 24; 32; 49.

proportions. Great buildings scattered over the Near East are attributed to him, even though they lie far beyond the borders of his actual sphere of influence, and the remains of them are called 'Solomon's throne',[1] or the like. Solomon did in fact display great activity in building. Mention has already been made of his construction of barracks for the corps of chariotry, called in I Kings ix. 19 'cities for the chariots' and 'cities for the horses'. In addition to these there is mention in the same passage of 'store-cities' or 'depots', which, as it is impossible to draw a sharp distinction between these two terms, may be thought of as depositories of victuals and provender meant to provide both for garrisons and for commercial traffic; for it is apparent that the 'depot cities' in the area of Hamath-Zobah mentioned in II Chronicles viii. 4 served both purposes. The places fortified in this way, beside Megiddo, Tadmor, Hamath-Zobah, and Jerusalem, were Hazor, Tell Qedaḥ or Tell Waqqāṣ, 5 km. south-west of Lake Ḥūleh; Gezer, the modern Tell Jezer;[2] the nether Beth-Horon, now Bēt 'Ur et-Taḥta, 12 km. north-west of Jerusalem; and Baalath, the exact position of which is not fixed but must in any case be west of Jerusalem. In some of these towns excavations have revealed remains of Solomon's building activities. No mention is made in the book of Kings of the fortification of Ezion-Geber by Solomon, but it is probable that the fine fortification there found in excavations by Nelson Glueck, already mentioned, goes back to this time, and the same is true of Qadesh Barneah (probably Khirbet el-Qudairat).[3] These fortifications, combined with the remains of Solomon's buildings at Megiddo, provide a very welcome supplement to the accounts of Solomon's fortresses in the texts.

Naturally, while building was undertaken at many places in various parts of the land, the capital, Jerusalem, would not be neglected. We are, in addition to the main undertaking of Solomon, actually informed about two works only in I Kings ix. 15, 24; xi. 27. He built *millō'*, and the walls of Jerusalem. These statements give no exact idea of the nature and extent of these constructions, owing to their brevity. But the account of Solomon's palace buildings, to which the Temple of Yahweh belonged,

---

[1] R. Naumann and others, 'Takht-i-Suleiman und Zendan-i-Suleiman. Vorläufiger Bericht über die Ausgrabungen im Jahre 1960', in *Archäol. Anzeiger 1961* (1962), 28 ff., 4 pls.; H. H. von der Osten(†) and R. Naumann (eds.), 'Takht-i-Suleiman. Vorläufiger Bericht über die Ausgrabungen 1959' (*Teheraner Forschungen*, 1) (Berlin, 1961).

[2] See above, pp. 587 f.    [3] G, 4, 86 ff.; §IX, 1, 295 f.; §IX, 31; §IX, 43.

is very detailed, and of course contains a good description of the Temple. This arises from the pronounced preference in the book of Kings given to everything concerning religion and the cult, which in many cases leads to incomplete statements on matters and events of more importance historically to us. The secular buildings in the palace, which must have been by far the more extensive, are treated rather summarily.

Israel itself could provide no architects and craftsmen suited to the task. Solomon accordingly had to send to Phoenicia for skilled men, as indeed his father David had done before him (II Sam. v. 11). He had to apply to the same land for the supply of building materials too, especially for timber. Thus the buildings put up in Jerusalem would be in the style commonly adopted in Phoenicia, and Phoenician buildings themselves were in many respects copies of foreign models. The actual effect of this is a matter of hypothesis, because no remains have been excavated and the reports on the building fragmentarily preserved in I Kings vi–vii are ambiguous in many ways. There is the additional difficulty that the account of the secular buildings in the palace in I Kings vii. 1–12 is only summary. Little more is given than a list of the individual buildings which, with the Temple,[1] formed a complex surrounded by an outer wall enclosing the whole. We can attempt a reconstruction by comparison with known monuments or representations on objects from lands connected with Israel, some being neighbouring lands and some quite distant.

The rock terrace on which the palace stood, called 'Mount Moriah' (II Chron. iii. 1) obtained by levelling, was extended in one part by a sub-structure or rubble filling, *millō*'. In the first court there were three elements. 'The house of the forest of Lebanon' was certainly used as an arsenal for weapons (I Kings x. 16–17) and perhaps at the same time as a treasury (I Kings x. 17, 21) possibly also as a mews; the name was due to the three or four rows of pillars made of cedars of Lebanon. The 'hall of pillars' served some unknown purpose. The royal audience chamber was used not only for court ceremonies but also as a court of justice, and contained the magnificent throne described in I Kings x. 18–20. Immediately west of this court was a second, enclosed by a separating wall, in which lay the dwelling quarters proper, the royal palace and the harim. To the north of this, on a raised platform also surrounded by a special wall, was the Temple, with the altar for burnt sacrifices in front of it.

[1] See below, pp. 598 ff.

Perhaps two comparisons may be of use in reconstructing the general lay-out of the secular buildings of Solomon's palace, as Watzinger has suggested.[1] In Sargon II's palace at Khorsabad the rooms accessible to public entry and those reserved for the king and his household were separated from one another and grouped round separate inner courts, in a manner similar to Solomon's palace. At Zincirli there was a hall with columns, with an entrance hall in front, the roof supported by columns; the entrance lay on the long side, and the façade was in the Syrian style. The audience chamber at Jerusalem may have been similar to that in the palace at Tell Halaf, as K. Galling thinks.[2] An attempt to reconstruct the 'house of the forest of Lebanon', by K. Möhlenbrink, on the model of the stables excavated at Megiddo,[3] deserves careful consideration. Firmer ground can be found by comparing the written account of the methods of building with what is known from archaeological research. This applies especially to the wall surrounding the courts, where a layer of beams was interposed between each three course of stone (I Kings vi. 36; vii. 11–12). Building in this style has been found at several contemporary sites in Western Asia, as for example Zincirli.[4]

It is comparatively easy to visualize the throne of gold and ivory, with its six steps, which stood in the audience chamber as it is described in I Kings x. 18–20. Artistic influences of several different kinds which contributed to its creation can be recognized. The lavish use of gold can be compared without hesitation with the wonderfully well-preserved chair of Tutankhamun, and with the thrones of Syrian and Palestinian type represented on the coffin of Aḥiram of Byblos and on the ivory plaque found at Megiddo;[5] these may be considered as partly made of gold. Parallels can be found too for the individual motifs represented on Solomon's throne, the bulls' heads attached to the back and the lions standing under the arms and beside the steps.[6] There are elements of various origins, Egyptian, Assyrian and particularly Syrian and Palestinian, as well as others, in this case, and we shall meet the same feature in the bronze figures cast for the Temple and in the carvings and in the inlays with which the doors and walls of the Temple were decorated.

As already indicated[7] there is a comparatively detailed account

---

[1] G, 38, vol. I, 96.    [2] G, 11, 411 f.    [3] §IX, 26, 18.
[4] G, 38, vol. I, 97; §IX, 39.    [5] §VI, 53, pl. 4; cf. below, pp. 600 f.
[6] G, 11, 520 f.; G, 16, nos. 82–4 and 290; G, 30, nos. 332, 416 f., 456, 458, 460, 525.    [7] See above, p. 596.

of Solomon's Temple[1] in I Kings vi, and it is supplemented by the vision of the new Temple described in Ezekiel xl–xliv. Its plan can be restored with fair certainty, and something can be said both about its external appearance and its internal arrangement. The building was entered from a short side, measuring 20 cubits, and the long side, of 60 cubits, was orientated east-west. The height of the main building was 30 cubits, but that of the adyton only 20 cubits. In every case the cubit should be treated as belonging to the shorter standard. On the east side, in front of the entrance-hall, stood the altar for burnt offerings. Against the walls on the north, west and east sides there were three stories, each containing thirty rooms, of all shapes, which served as stores and the like. Looking from east to west, there was first the entrance-hall, 'ūlām, 10 cubits deep, before which stood the two free columns, Jachin and Boaz, each 23 cubits high, then the *cella*, called *hēkāl*, 40 cubits long, and last the shrine at the back, *dᵉbīr*, 20 cubits long, where the Ark was deposited. The *dᵉbīr* differed in height from the 'ūlām and the *hēkāl* in that it was only 20 cubits high, thus having a cube shape. The cause of this may be connected with the fact that it stood over the holy Rock, and its base was accordingly higher than that of the 'ūlām and *hēkāl*.[2]

It has been said that as Phoenician architects and master-builders advised upon the building of the Temple as well as of the remaining parts of Solomon's palace, it is to be inferred that there were Phoenician models for it. How far, or indeed whether, these Phoenician models were themselves influenced from abroad must remain an open question. That there was a Phoenician model for the Temple is particularly suggested by Josephus.[3] He was excerpting from the historians Menander and Dios, who themselves used the annals of Tyre as a source, and therefore appear reliable. Josephus, then, relates that Solomon's friend and ally, Hiram of Tyre, was engaged in building even beyond the normal measure, and was specially active in the construction or repair of temples. It is true that this supposition is not in itself much help in reconstruction because no trace remains of Hiram's temples, or rather, if there are any such remains still to be found, they have not been excavated. All that we learn from Josephus is that Hiram built temples, not anything about their appearance. Quite apart from Tyre there were, until quite recently, no

[1] §IX, nos. 15; 16; 26; 27; 28; §IX, 44, 373 ff.; §IX, nos. 45; 46; 47.
[2] §IX, 36, see below, p. 599.
[3] *Antiquities*, VIII, 5, 3 = §§144–7; *Contra Apionem*, I, 17, 18 = §§113–19.

examples of temples in the whole of Syria and Palestine belonging to the period concerned. In attempting to arrive at some reconstruction of the general type represented by Solomon's Temple based on buildings actually excavated, it seemed as if the only thing to do was to compare parallels from lands rather distant from Palestine. All Phoenician art, as is well known, is of a syncretistic and eclectic kind. The hypothesis that perhaps Egyptian or Assyrian temples had served as models for the Phoenicians, and so through them for the Solomonic building, seemed thoroughly justified.

But in 1936 the position changed considerably. For in that year a temple was excavated at Tell Ta'īnāt, in the 'Amuq plain in North Syria. This temple corresponds absolutely in lay-out with the Solomonic Temple, though it is two-thirds as large again. It consists, like Solomon's, of an entrance-hall with two pillars in front, a *cella*, and a raised shrine.[1] This temple, which belongs to the ninth century B.C., clearly embodies the normal form of temple in Syria at the beginning of the first millennium B.C. We must accordingly assume that the Phoenician temple which served as a model for Solomon's, and therefore the Solomonic Temple itself, corresponded with that normal form. Similarly, the temple in Shiloh was also probably of this type.[2] This assumption is doubly justified by the following observation. Two Egyptian-Canaanite temples at Beth-shan, modern Tell el-Ḥuṣn, dating from as early as the fourteenth to the twelfth centuries, had just such a shrine.[3] A good many temples of the Hellenistic and Roman periods are preserved which also have a shrine of this kind, and these are situated not only in Syria and Palestine but also far west and east of these lands. Clearly the many features of religious cult which are known to have spread over the civilized world in these periods from Syria and Palestine included this peculiarity in temple construction, and this accounts for its wide dissemination.[4]

The book of Kings is more explicit about the interior architecture and the furnishing with bronze work of all kinds than it is about the exterior of the Temple. In both respects it can be seen even more clearly that all kinds of influence from abroad were at work. Thus the wood panelling on the walls mentioned in the report corresponds with a practice quite general in Syria[5] of covering the inner walls of the palace and temple buildings

[1] G, 3, 42 and 142 f.; §IX, 22; §IX, 47.     [2] See above, pp. 564 f.
[3] §VII, 26, 19 and 24, pls. 24, 56.
[4] G, 3, 105 and 202; §IX, nos. 6; 12; 13; 19, 173 f.     [5] G, 3, 143.

above the orthostats with wood. The motifs of the decoration on the panelling and on the carved and inlaid work applied to the doors, namely cherubs, palms, bunches of flowers, correspond with those used very liberally on all sorts of artistic and manufactured products, especially on the ivory carvings which have been discovered not only at many places in Western Asia but also in the west, in the Mediterranean regions which came under the influence of Phoenicia and Syria. These motifs are everywhere a motley mixture of Egyptian, Babylonian, Assyrian, Aegean and specifically Syrian-Phoenician elements.[1] The same applies to the bronze works of art and the gear with which the Tyrian craftsman Hiram furnished the Temple; to the two colossal pillars[2] set in the pronaos, Jachin and Boaz,[3] which consisted of a base with roll ornament, a shaft, a roll-capital covered with an ornament of pomegranates, net-wise, and a bowl or globe with palm-leaf decoration set above; to the 'bronze sea', a great bronze water-holder for the temple fore-court, carried by twelve colossal oxen, and to the laver on wheels, also for use in the fore-court; similarly to the small vessels and implements for sacrifice, the knives, bowls, cauldrons and the like. The 'bronze sea' has its parallel in the colossal clay-basin of Amathus, the 'Vasque d'Amathonte' in the Musée du Louvre,[4] the handles of which have sculptured bulls. The wheeled laver, decorated according to I Kings vii. 36 with lions, cherubs and palms, can be clearly recognized as a form widely used in Western Asia. Bronze basins on wheels, of the period about 1000 B.C., have been found in Cyprus, very like that made for Solomon by Hiram of Tyre.[5]

Finally, not the least important case in which foreign models influenced the forms of objects in the Temple is that of the two cherubs. These, according to I Kings vi. 23–8, stood in the shrine, were made of olive wood overlaid with gold, and were 10 cubits high, with a total wing-span of 10 cubits. In this case the influence can be ascribed with some certainty to a specifically Canaanite-Phoenician origin. For by *cherubim* are meant fantastic

---

[1] §VI, nos. 11; 22; 29; 32; 57.          [2] §IX, nos. 3; 25; 38; 52.

[3] The giving of names to parts of buildings was practised not only in Babylonia, Assyria, and Egypt, but also in southern Arabia; G. Ryckmans, 'Inscriptions du Yemen relevées par M. Ahmad Fakhry', in *Muséon*, 61 (1948), 227 ff., mentions (p. 239) *knt* (*kawnat*, 'stabilité, fermeté') on one of the pillars of the propylaeum of a temple at Ṣirwāḥ.

[4] A. Parrot, *Le Musée du Louvre* (*Cahiers d'archéologie biblique*, no. 9, Paris, 1957), p. 82, n. 2.

[5] G, 3, 152 ff.; G, 11, 342; G, 38, vol. 1, 105 f.

composite figures with a lion's body, human head and bird's wings. Such figures appear as supporters of the throne represented on the coffin of Ahiram of Byblos, and on the ivory plaque from Megiddo, and also on a small ivory model of a throne, likewise from Megiddo.[1] It has already been pointed out[2] that in setting up these *cherubim* in the shrine of his Temple, and in placing the Ark beneath their wings, Solomon was clearly copying the manner in which the Ark was placed in the temple at Shiloh.[3] Very probably that temple, destroyed by the Philistines more than a century before the building of Solomon's Temple, may have been considered by Solomon as determining certain features in his own building, for the foundations must still have been visible, and a good deal was still known about its appearance before the destruction.

### THE COURT

In Solomon's buildings may be recognized a willingness to accept foreign models, from any country. So also his whole conduct, both in his daily life and in his administration, shows a marked acceptance of the civilized international standards of the time. In imitating the practices usual at foreign courts, Solomon inevitably spent sums on the maintenance of his state greatly exceeding the level set by David. The legend of the visit of the Queen of Sheba, in spite of its character, contains certain features that we may regard as trustworthy. Thus it reflects the truth when it reports that the queen expressed her astonishment at the magnificence and luxury in which Solomon kept his court, for all her expectations, though they had been raised high, had been far exceeded (I Kings x. 4–8). We can understand, then, why Solomon had to increase the number of his chief officers by appointing a chamberlain over the household (I Kings iv. 6). Not the least important result of the adoption of foreign, or rather international, standards was the inclusion of foreign women in his harim, beside the Egyptian princess already mentioned,[4] who was his principal wife. Even if the number of these women, given in I Kings xi. 3, as 700 wives ranking as princesses, and 300 concubines, is certainly an exaggeration, there were a good many of these foreigners, Moabite, Ammonite, Edomite, Phoenician and 'Hittite', that is North Syrian.

One contributory cause which led to life at Solomon's court having an international aspect was his extensive connexions with

---

[1] G, 3, 148 and 216; §vi, 32; §vi, 53, pl. 4, nos. 2, 3.    [2] See above, pp. 565, 599.
[3] §ix, 14. See above, p. 565.                               [4] See above, pp. 587f., 596.

other countries through trade. The most characteristic effect was the cultivation of an educated taste, the willing response to every stimulus from abroad. It is clear that Solomon himself had literary gifts. His father David had also possessed such a gift, but in his case it was lyrical. This is shown by his song on the death of Saul and Jonathan (II Sam. i), by the psalms which may probably be ascribed to him as actual author, and by the attribution to him of many others. The taste and ability of Solomon lay in another direction, that of 'wisdom' literature, and perhaps of erotic poetry, if any trust at all can be put in the attribution to him of the Song of Songs. That he himself contributed to 'wisdom' literature can be regarded as certain from I Kings iv. 29–34, where 3000 proverbs and 1005 songs are attributed to him. The remarks there made as to the contents of these show that the kind of poetry meant is of the learned, instructional kind, productions which though they take a verse form can be regarded at the same time as the beginnings of botanical and zoological studies. In connexion with the statement about Solomon's writings, the biblical text adds that he was wiser than all the famous sages in the east and in the west, and that 'there came of all peoples to hear' his wisdom and to be instructed by him; an intelligible statement reflecting the fact that didactic literature at all times has a peculiarly international character.

An instructive account of the kind of polite literary talk which went on at Solomon's court on the subjects mentioned is given in the story of the Queen of Sheba's visit,[1] and on this point too that story may be reliable. The queen came, it is said, 'to prove Solomon with riddles', and Solomon 'answered all the questions'. This is clearly a correct picture of the pursuit of polite learning, of an international character, practised at Solomon's court. The questions and answers meant must have covered many different subjects; not a few of them were no doubt concerned with the subject-matter of the proverbs and songs of Solomon recorded in I Kings v. 13: 'the trees, from the cedar that is in Lebanon to the hyssop that springeth out of the wall, and the beasts and the fowl and the creeping things and the fishes'. One of the riddles posed by the queen may well have run: 'Which is the largest and which is the smallest plant?', to which the correct reply would have been 'The cedar that is in Lebanon and the hyssop in the wall'. Josephus[2] has a story to the effect that Solomon had such

---

[1] §IX, nos. 11; 29; 42.
[2] *Antiquities*, VIII, 5, 3 = §§143, 148–9: *Contra Apionem*, I, 17, 18 = §§111, 114–15.

a contest in the posing and solving of riddles with Hiram king of Tyre, in which at first Hiram was the loser; but afterwards Solomon lost, for he was no match for Hiram's representative, Abdemon.

When the sources at our disposal for the reign of Solomon are regarded as a whole, they give the impression that his reign was unusually glorious and successful. It is natural, then, that throughout subsequent periods he was regarded as the king whose supreme power and magnificence were never exceeded, indeed never rivalled, by any successor. It is probably true that owing to his wise and determined development of trade a wealth of goods did in fact flow into Israel's territory, to an extent previously unknown. But there is a reverse side to the medal. This new wealth profited only a very small class in the nation besides the king himself: the court officials, the officers and the merchants. The great masses not only gained nothing, but had to bear on their shoulders the heavy burdens which were requisite to meet the expense of the military measures taken to support and protect trade, and to maintain the court. Thus a contrast was beginning to make itself felt between rich and poor such as had not existed to an even approximate degree when the national economy had depended substantially on agriculture and cattle-raising. In this period may be found the beginnings of those conditions which were the subject of such sharp condemnation by men like Amos and Isaiah two centuries later.[1]

The Yahweh cult was one of the chief institutions to benefit from Solomon's taste for magnificence, particularly the Temple at Jerusalem, now the centre of all the religious observances in a way previously without a parallel. The worship of Yahweh was certainly promoted thereby in no common measure, and its superiority emphasized as against the worship of those other gods still enjoying the support of many circles among the people. Henceforth all affairs that concerned the whole nation, or even only large parts of it, were subjects for religious celebrations at festivals in the Temple at Jerusalem and were thus placed under Yahweh's guidance and care (cf. I Kings viii. 27–53); this must have had a considerable effect. On the other hand, the rites conducted in Jerusalem contained many features which ran counter to Israelite feeling, or at any rate did not originate in old Israelite tradition. The Temple itself was built in a fashion belonging to Canaan. The voices of those who had warned David against the plan to build a temple of stone for Yahweh by

[1] §VIII, 24.

appealing to the authority of old Israelite custom (II Sam. vii)[1] were certainly not unheard in Solomon's time. Moreover, the adaptation of the ritual of the worship of Yahweh to suit the recently erected Temple obviously accelerated the adoption of Canaanite practices, a process which had been long at work. If Zadok was originally, as A. Bentzen,[2] H. H. Rowley,[3] C. E. Hauer[4] and others have shown to be likely, a member of the old Jebusite priesthood, a further assumption would follow. Zadok was admitted to the priesthood of Yahweh by David, and is likely to have introduced many elements known to him from Canaanite ritual practice. When his rival Abiathar, a member of an old priestly family, with Moses and Eli as his predecessors, was once deposed by Solomon, the new priest would act with much less restraint than before. It is even possible that the separation of Israel from the dynasty of David, due primarily to political and social causes, was also conditioned by religious differences, Israel claiming to uphold the true tradition, in opposition to the worship practised in the temple at Jerusalem. At any rate such a motive was adduced later, as is shown by the refounding of the holy places in Bethel and Dan, thus linking up with old Israelite traditions.

There are, then, these two points which must not be forgotten while admitting that Solomon's trade policy led to a substantial improvement in the prosperity of Israel, and that the construction of the Temple promoted the worship of Yahweh. A social development was introduced which was to have dire consequences later. There were dangers for religion in the changes resulting from the existence of the Temple. When we turn to consider Solomon's internal rule in Israel itself, it is immediately apparent that it was misconceived. This is especially true of his division of the burdens, caused by the administration of the whole empire, between the two kingdoms of Israel and Judah, which were united only in allegiance to his own person. Obviously he was unable to find a solution just to both kingdoms when distributing the incidence of taxes in kind that had to be delivered for the court and the garrisons, or in the arrangement of the service of public works. Even in Solomon's lifetime there was one outburst of Israel's dissatisfaction with the representative of David's dynasty, the rebellion of Jeroboam ben-Nebat.[5] That event, it is

---

[1] See above, p. 580.　　[2] §IX, 9; §IX, 10.　　[3] §IX, 33; §IX, 34.
[4] §IX, 17. This opinion is opposed by E. Auerbach (§IX, 7), who sees in Zadok a priest of the Tent of Meeting in Gibeon, and by W. F. Albright (G, 3, 110), who regards Zadok as a descendant of Aaron.
[5] See above, p. 591.

true, had no great significance. Solomon's authority and power were sufficient to quell such a rebellion while brewing, with the result that the rebel had to flee to Egypt. But when Solomon's eyes were closed in death, the breach came with his son Rehoboam, who lacked not only the power, but also the caution, of his father. Israel rid itself of the dynasty of David, which was thereafter limited to the rule of Judah, including the territory which had once been the tribal area of Benjamin. The two kingdoms thus formed, mere sections, were from that time on generally hostile to one another.

Thus the empire which David created and Solomon maintained split up. But the religious history of the nation still continued on its course in the later period, both north and south, Israel and Judah, contributing alike to its development. For the religion of Israel survived not only the collapse of David's empire, but even the suppression of the two sectional kingdoms, that of Israel in 721, that of Judah in 587 B.C. That survival was due as much to such men of God as Elijah and Hosea in the north as to men like Amos and Isaiah in the south.

# CHAPTER XXXV

## EGYPT: FROM THE DEATH
## OF RAMESSES III TO THE END OF
## THE TWENTY-FIRST DYNASTY

### I. THE LAST RAMESSIDES

W H E N Ramesses III died on the fifteenth day of the third month
of the summer season, not quite two months after he had begun
the thirty-second year of his reign,[1] no one could have imagined
that the last great pharaoh had gone and that Egypt would never
again have a native ruler whose power would at least approach
that of the mighty kings of the Egyptian empire: that, in fact,
the days of this empire were over. On the contrary, the community of workmen, engaged in hewing out the royal tombs in the
rocks of the Valley of the Kings, to whom Mentmose, the chief
of the Medjay-police, brought the news on the next day that the
falcon had flown to heaven, 'spent the day rejoicing until the sunset'. For Mentmose also brought the news that 'King Usermare-
setepenamun, the son of Ramesses-meryamun, the ruler, sat upon
the throne of Re in his stead'.[2] They could, therefore, soon expect
an order to start working on the tomb of the new king, and with
it the customary extra rations and gifts to whet their zeal.

The new king, called Ramesses IV by modern historians and on
his own assertion a son of Ramesses III,[3] initiated a succession of
kings all called Ramesses, though each bore a distinctive praenomen. They were probably all related to Ramesses III, but the
exact degree of this relationship is still in dispute.[4] The historian
Manetho recorded them all, together with the length of each
reign. His excerptors, however, finding it too laborious to catalogue a set of kings all called Ramesses apart from Sethnakhte the
first king of the dynasty, summarized the Twentieth Dynasty as
twelve kings omitting their names.[5] After deducting Sethnakhte
and Ramesses III this total would leave ten kings for the rest of

---

* An original version of this chapter was published as fascicle 27 in 1965.
[1] §1, 7. See also §1, 47.
[2] Pap. Turin Cat. 1949 + 1946 in §1, 7. Later the king changed his name to
Hikmare-setepenamun.
[3] §1, 19, 96–7.    [4] See, for instance, §1, 9, and §1, 48.    [5] §1, 53, 152–3.

the dynasty, but Egyptian documents mention only eight additional kings who can be ascribed to it, Ramesses IV to Ramesses XI. Except for Ramesses IV the length of their reigns is unknown; the highest known dates total 105 years[1] for the whole dynasty, which is far short of the figures preserved by Manetho's excerptors, 135 years by Africanus and 178 years by Eusebius.

During the first two months of Ramesses IV's reign preparations were taking place for his father's burial. On the fourth day of the first month of the inundation season the funerary equipment was brought to the tomb[2] and on the twenty-fourth day of the same month the funeral itself took place, exactly seventy days after the death of the king, if the intervening epagomenal days at the end of the civil year are disregarded.[3] This delay of seventy days for the mummification was customary, but it is of some interest to have it confirmed for this period in Egyptian history, since the interval between the death and burial will be seen to have importance in the discussion of the burial of Ramesses V.[4]

The workmen of the king's tomb were not disappointed in their expectation of benefit or in their hopes in connexion with the change of reign. Four days after the burial of Ramesses III 'high officials came to hand over to the gang of workmen their silver'[5] and about a month later a scribe brought special rewards for the gang.[6] It was, however, only in the second year of Ramesses IV, on the eighteenth day of the second month of the inundation season, that the Vizier Neferronpe and two King's Butlers, Hori and Amenkha, came and 'went up to the Valley of the Kings to search for a place for cutting a tomb for Usermare-setepen-[amun]'.[7] The king seems to have been determined to have a large tomb made in a short time, for about a month later he gave the order to increase the number of workmen to one hundred and twenty, thus doubling their previous strength.[8] The increase in number will prove of importance later in determining the date of an historical event. Despite the large-scale planning, however, the king's tomb (no. 2 in the Valley of the Kings) is only of average size. More than for its dimensions and decoration it has become famous for a drawing of its plan by a scribe who super-

---

[1] §1, 40. In the table, p. 73, add '7 years at least' for Ramesses VI from §1, 52, pl. LXVIII and p. 22, and delete 'Renaissance 6 years at least', these being concurrent with the reign of Ramesses XI (see below, p. 639).

[2] §1, 6, 1, no. 40, line 2 (pl. 22).  [3] *Loc. cit.* no. 40, line 15 (pl. 22).

[4] See below, p. 612.  [5] §1, 6, 1, no. 40, verso 5–6 (pl. 23).

[6] *Loc. cit.* 1, no. 41, verso 10 (pl. 25).

[7] *Loc. cit.* 1, no. 45, lines 15–17 (pl. 34).

[8] §1, 44, pl. XLIX, 1–5.

vised the construction. This plan has come down to us in a papyrus preserved in the Turin museum.[1]

Even more ambitious were Ramesses IV's schemes for new buildings and for providing buildings already in existence with new statues and other monuments. The greywacke quarries in the Wādi Hammāmāt[2] show signs of great activity during the first three years of his reign, activity on a scale seldom equalled in preceding ages, and not to be repeated for many centuries to come. As early as year 1 two expeditions left their records on the rocks of the quarry. One was led by the High Priest of Harsiese, Usermarenakhte, to 'bring large statues of *bekhen*-stone',[3] as the local stone was called, while the other was led by the High-Priest of Mont, Turo.[4] Both were in quest of material for monuments for the local temples at Koptos and Armant. Another expedition in year 2 is said to have extracted 'this monument for the Seat of Eternity' exactly at the place indicated to his officials by the pharaoh, to whom the god himself had revealed it.[5] Finally, no less than three expeditions worked at Wādi Hammāmāt in year 3 of the reign, one in each of the first three months of the summer season.[6] The expedition of the second month of the summer season was the principal and indeed one of the largest ever led to these quarries.[7] It consisted of 8368 men. Among them were two thousand soldiers commanded by a Deputy of the Army; the majority of the rest were quarrymen, sculptors, and conscripts whose task it was to drag the detached blocks through the desert to the Nile and who were in the charge of the Overseer of the Treasury, that is, of the Minister of Finance. But the High Priest of Amun Ramessenakhte as Overseer of Works and two King's Butlers as the king's trusted delegates were also present. The presence of Ramessenakhte indicates that the 'wonderful monuments' acquired were destined chiefly for Thebes, especially for the 'Place-of-Truth' there.

In this instance the 'Place-of-Truth' can hardly refer to the

---

[1] §1, 5.     [2] For the name of the stone and its nature, see §1, 28, 78–81.

[3] §1, 26, no. 89, pp. 103–6 and pl. xxix.

[4] §1, 11, 64, no. 86, and pl. xix; §1, 15.

[5] §1, 11, 112–13, no. 240 and pl. xl; cf. also §1, 22, 162. The same date is given by the hieratic inscription no. 231, evidently contemporaneous with nos. 232–6, of which no. 235 (pl. xliv) seems to give the dimensions of the 'monument': $5\frac{4}{7} \times 2\frac{3}{7} \times 2\frac{1}{7}$ cubits. This could hardly be anything other than a block for a statue.

[6] §1, 11, no. 223 (pl. xl), 222 (pl. xliii), contemporaneous with no. 12 (pl. iv), and a fragment of a stela from Koptos, §1, 17, 91–2.

[7] Discussed in §1, 14, and §1, 37; certain points previously misunderstood. §1, 22, 162–3.

tomb of the reigning king, though this is its more general meaning. Heavy greywacke monuments were not the type of object which would be placed in a royal tomb. An ancient Egyptian map of the region of Wādi Hammāmāt preserved on another papyrus in the Turin museum,[1] and almost certainly dating from the reign of Ramesses IV, speaks of a portrait-statue of *bekhen*-stone brought to Egypt and deposited in the 'Place-of-Truth' beside the Mansion of Usermare-setepenre, that is, beside the Ramesseum.[2] From other evidence also it is known that there was a place to the west of Thebes called the 'Place-of-Truth' where people condemned to forced labour were occasionally sent to work stone blocks,[3] and this must have been a kind of masons' workshop. Combining these two pieces of information it is tempting to look for the 'Place-of-Truth' in a workshop where stones were dressed for a grandiose edifice devised by Ramesses IV at the valley end of the causeway leading to the temple of King Mentuhotpe at Deir el-Bahri. At this site, not far distant from the Ramesseum, seven foundation deposits were discovered, all containing objects inscribed with the name of Ramesses IV. They marked important points in the plan of a building closely following in its conception the great temple of Ramesses IV's father at Medīnet Habu, but half as large again. For some centuries this building served as a convenient quarry for ready-worked stone blocks and it has, in consequence, almost completely disappeared, but a sufficient number of stones have remained in position to allow an approximate reconstruction of its plan to be drawn. Many of these stones had been extracted from earlier buildings near-by and bore cartouches of previous kings: some small chips however were inscribed with parts of the names of two of Ramesses IV's immediate successors. No trace of Ramesses IV's name was found among the fragments of the superstructure, so that it is doubtful whether he was ever able to do more than lay the foundations.[4] The same fate of complete destruction met another edifice of Ramesses IV laid out further north at the valley end of the Hatshepsut causeway.[5] Nothing suggests that either building had progressed far enough during the reign of Ramesses IV to serve as his mortuary temple. This temple—two priests of which are mentioned in inscriptions[6] and the property

---

[1] See §1, 27, for the latest discussion.  [2] §1, 27, 341.
[3] Unpublished hieratic ostracon Berlin P. 12654, 10–11.
[4] §1, 54, 9–13; §1, 32, 6–9; §1, 29, II, 371–2.
[5] For its foundation deposit, see §1, 4, 48 and pl. XL, and §1, 33, 8.
[6] §1, 38, 114.

of which is frequently mentioned in the following reign[1]—is rather to be sought in a modest construction much nearer Medīnet Habu, not yet excavated but thought to have been carried away almost entirely when the neighbouring sanctuary of the sage Amenophis, son of Hapu, was being enlarged during the Twenty-first Dynasty.[2]

The name of Ramesses IV is found on a number of monuments extending from the turquoise mines at Serābīt el-Khādim in the Sinai peninsula, in the north, to the fortress of Buhen, at the frontier of the Sudan, in the south. In many places he only added his name to work done by his predecessors, but elsewhere he restored and continued unfinished work (as in the temple of Khons at Karnak) or built afresh.[3] On the whole, his building activity was considerable, it being the only way to ensure full general employment, and the king felt entitled to insert the following request into his prayer to Osiris on his stela of year 4 found at Abydos.[4] 'And thou shalt show grace to the land of Egypt, thy land, in my time and double for me the great age and the long reign of the King Usermare-setepenre (i.e. Ramesses II), the great god. For, far more numerous are the beneficent things which I have done to thy house in order to increase thy offerings, to seek every excellent thing and every kind of benefaction to accomplish them daily for thy temple forecourt in these four years than that which King Usermare-setepenre, the great god, did for thee during his sixty-seven years. And thou shalt give me the great age with a long reign which thou didst give to Horus . . ., thy son, on whose throne I am sitting. For it is thou who didst say so with thy own mouth.' Nevertheless, Osiris gave Ramesses IV less than one-tenth of the reign of his long-lived predecessor; we know for certain that he did not reign for more than six years. This useful information has been transmitted to us in a long papyrus[5] which, though written in the reign of Ramesses IV's successor and probably his son, Usermare-sekheperenre (i.e. Ramesses V), throws some rather unfavourable light on the reign of both kings.

The document in question is a long indictment listing the misdeeds, most of them thefts and embezzlements, of a certain

---

[1] §1, 23, vol. II, 133, section 60.    [2] §1, 46.
[3] A full enumeration of monuments of Ramesses IV will be found in §1, 13. See also §1, 12, for Ramesses IV's activity at Memphis.
[4] Cairo stela J. 48876, lines 21–5 (bibliography in §1, 45, v, 44; translation in §1, 3, IV, sects. 470–1).
[5] §1, 44, pls. LI–LX; transcribed in §1, 21, 73–82; translated in §1, 42. For the date of the papyrus and the length of the reign of Ramesses IV, see §1, 42, 119.

Penanuqe, *weeb*-priest in the temple of Khnum at Elephantine.
The earliest crime recorded was committed in the year 28 of
Ramesses III, but the majority occurred in the ten years between
the beginning of the reign of Ramesses IV and the year 4 of
Ramesses V. There can hardly be any doubt that if the papyrus
ever reached the proper authority the culprit must have received
well-deserved punishment, but the fact that his activities could
have gone on for so many years, and have been tolerated, must
necessarily throw an unfavourable light on the administration and
on justice during the two reigns even if it is assumed that an event
of this type was an exception rather than a common phenomenon.

From the reign of Ramesses V another remarkable document,
the Wilbour Papyrus, has been preserved.[1] A little over ten
metres long, it contains in 127 columns or pages totalling more
than 5200 lines the measurement and assessment of fields taken
in a restricted part of the country between the present Medīnet
el-Faiyūm and El-Minya in Middle Egypt. Since not only the
position, size, and calculated yield of each plot of land are given,
but also the holder and land-owner (in most cases a temple or the
crown), this papyrus, as the only extant specimen of its kind, must
form the basis of any inquiry into the land-property and land-
taxation of the Ramesside period in particular and indeed of
pharaonic Egypt in general. The date of its compilation is the
year 4 of a king who on internal evidence must be Ramesses V,
in all probability the last year of his reign. From another source
it is known that in the same year an alabaster monument reached
Thebes, evidently destined for the tomb of the king.[2] This,
together with an ostracon[3] which refers to some deliveries 'in
year 3, third month of inundation, of Sekheperenre, and again
(in) year 1 of Nebmare (i.e. Ramesses VI)', seems to indicate that
the interval between these two dates was short and that Ramesses V
died in the fourth year of his reign. If the observations made on
his mummy are correct he died fairly young and probably of
smallpox.[4]

The king who succeeded him on the throne was Nebmare-
meryamun (Ramesses VI). That he was a son of Ramesses III
seems certain; doubtful, however, is the reason for the grudge
which he apparently bore against his two immediate predecessors.
More than once he had the name of Ramesses IV obliterated[5]

---

[1] §1, 23.                                    [2] §1, 10, pl. LV, 2.
[3] §1, 8, p. 57* and pl. L, no. 25598, verso A, lines 1–4.
[4] §1, 49, no. 61085, pp. 90–2.
[5] Examples in §1, 48, 194, note 29, and in §1, 12, 24–7.

and his own name substituted for it, and he simply usurped the tomb of Ramesses V.[1] It is, indeed, a mystery where Ramesses VI buried his predecessor; the mummy of Ramesses V was found where it had been deposited with others at a later date in the tomb of Amenophis II. In connexion with the burial of Ramesses V another problem remains unsolved, that of its date. A date is given in a hieratic ostracon found in the Valley of the Kings[2] on which a scribe noted down: 'year 2, second month of the inundation season, day 1. On that day Sekheperenre reached the west of Ne being in burial.[3] The doors of his tomb were made by carpenters in the second month of the inundation season, day 2.' This probably means that Ramesses V was first placed in his original tomb and that the tomb was usurped only later. But why was he buried there in the second year of the reign of his successor instead of after the seventy days mentioned above as the usual interval between death and burial? The end of the customary seventy days would necessarily have fallen within the first year of Ramesses VI. It is possible to suggest that the tomb was not yet ready and that the burial had to be postponed, but this is unlikely since the work in royal tombs used to progress fairly quickly and in the fourth year of a king's reign the king's tomb ought to have been fit to receive its royal occupant. Another possibility is that Ramesses V was buried seventy days after his death, but that he died in the reign of his successor. In that case it would seem to follow as a corollary that Ramesses VI deposed his predecessor and, while holding Ramesses V in captivity, counted his own regnal years from the day of his usurpation of the throne.

In the reign of either Ramesses V or Ramesses VI must have happened the strange events alluded to in a journal kept by a scribe of the king's tomb in year 1 of an unnamed king.[4] On one side of the document, among other records, is a list of men required to drag a large quantity of stones for some building on the west bank of Thebes. Since the number of the gang of workmen of the king's tomb is given as '120 men' the reign of Ramesses IV is excluded, for it was only in the second year of this pharaoh that the gang was increased to this unprecedented strength. The other side of the papyrus mentions first that on the tenth and eleventh

---

[1] §1, 34, III, 201–2.

[2] §1, 16, p. 66, pl. LIV, no. 25254; previously in transcription in §1, 50, 13, no. IV.

[3] The reading *m ḳrs* is certain. Daressy also read it thus, while Spiegelberg read incorrectly *m ḳni* and translated (§1, 50, p. 7) 'in a litter (?)'.

[4] Unpublished hieratic Pap. Turin, Cat. 2044.

days of the first month of the winter season the gang '[was idle from fear] of the enemy'. The date of the thirteenth day is followed by a more elaborate entry: 'Being idle from fear of the enemy. The two chiefs of the Medjay-police came saying: "The people who are enemies came and reached Per-nebyt. They destroyed everything which was there and burned its people, so it is rumoured. And the High Priest of Amun told us to bring the Medjay-police of Per-nebyt together with those who were in the south and those of the king's tomb and to let them stand here and watch the king's tomb." A few days later (the date is damaged) '[came] the Chief of the Medjay-police Mentmose and said to the foremen of the king's tomb: "Do not go up (to the Valley of the Kings to work) until you see what has happened. I will go to have a look for you and to hear what they say, and I myself will come to tell you to go up." Only one more date is preserved, that of the seventeenth or twenty-seventh day, when the gang was still 'idle from fear of the enemy'.

That these are allusions to a civil war seems indubitable. 'The people who are enemies' are evidently Egyptians: if it were a foreign enemy the scribe would have chosen the proper designation, as other scribes did when Libyans were concerned. The position of Per-nebyt is not known, but since the police from the region south of Thebes were summoned, which implies that they were not required in the south, the attack must have come from the north. Pending further information, which may be expected when the work on reassembling the papyrus fragments at Turin is resumed, it is possible to conjecture provisionally that we are dealing here with hostilities initiated by a political party which disapproved of the new king. If this king was Ramesses V, the party would be likely to be the followers of the future Ramesses VI who was seeking the throne; if the events took place in the reign of Ramesses VI the enemy were the supporters of the dethroned Ramesses V.

Ramesses VI, having found a tomb ready for himself, is most probably the king in the second year of whose reign the gang working on the king's tomb was reduced to its former numbers. A note of this event has come to us:[1] 'So says the Vizier: Leave these sixty men here in the gang, whomsoever you choose, and send the rest away. Order that they should become conscript labour who carry (supplies) for you.' This too would limit the civil war to the reign of Ramesses V or the reign of Ramesses VI.

Considering the antagonism between Ramesses IV and

[1] Unpublished hieratic ostracon Berlin P. 12654, verso.

Ramesses V on the one hand and between Ramesses V and Ramesses VI on the other, and considering the internal strife which seems to have occurred at the change of reign in each case, it is rather surprising that certain high officials kept their positions during all three reigns following the death of Ramesses III. Thus the Vizier Neferronpe, first safely attested in the second year of Ramesses IV, still acted as vizier under Ramesses VI.[1] The Finance Minister Mentemtowy was Overseer of the Treasury from the end of the reign of Ramesses III[2] until at least as late as year 1 of Ramesses VI,[3] and the same period of office was enjoyed at the court by the King's Butler Qedren,[4] who, judging by his name, was of foreign extraction.[5] Such a continuity, hardly conceivable in an oriental monarchy, can probably only be explained by assuming that these dignitaries, since they had been chosen or approved by Ramesses III, could not be ousted by his two successors, but that they abandoned Ramesses V to side with Ramesses VI and gain his favour.

Evidence of the building activity of Ramesses V and Ramesses VI is scarce. A stela of Ramesses V at Gebel es-Silsila[6] suggests that stones were extracted in the sandstone quarries during his reign, and indeed his name, as well as that of Ramesses VI, was found on fragments of the vast temple founded by Ramesses IV at Deir el-Bahri. The stones, the transport of which is reported in the Turin papyrus mentioned above, may have been destined for this construction. The building was probably considered in the reign of Ramesses V as his funerary temple; in any case, no other place can be suggested for 'the Mansion of Millions of Years of the King of Upper and Lower Egypt Usermare-sekheperenre on the estate of Amun' referred to in the Wilbour Papyrus.[7] No funerary temple of Ramesses VI is mentioned in contemporary documents. It is fairly safe to assume that if he had such a temple it was usurped together with his tomb from his predecessor.

After the death of Ramesses III there is no clear proof that Egypt retained her dependencies in Palestine or Syria. Scarabs of Ramesses IV and VI have been found in three places,[8] but

---

[1] §1, 12, 28–37.  [2] §1, 31, 518–19, no. 30.

[3] Unpublished hieratic Pap. Bibliothèque Nationale, Paris, no. 237, 'carton I'.

[4] Attested in §1, 18, pl. 1, col. 11, 2 (end of reign of Ramesses III) and hieratic Pap. Bibl. Nat., Paris, no. 237, 'carton I' (year 3 of Ramesses VI).

[5] On foreign origin of many of King's Butlers, see §1, 30, 50–1.

[6] Bibliography given in §1, 45, v, 213.

[7] §1, 23, 11 (Commentary), 132.

[8] Ramesses IV at Tell eṣ-Ṣāfī and Tell Zakarīya (§1, 45, vii, 372) and at Tell Jazari (Gezer; §1, 45, vii, 375); Ramesses VI at Alalakh (§1, 45, vii, 395).

the presence of these small objects, widely negotiated all over the eastern Mediterranean, has no significance. The same may be said of the base of a bronze statue of Ramesses VI discovered in Megiddo.[1] More significant is the fact that the name of Ramesses VI is the latest to be found at the site of the turquoise mines at Serābīt el-Khādim,[2] so that it is practically certain that the Egyptian temple and settlement there were abandoned very soon after his reign and the mines were never again the aim of an Egyptian expedition. The frontier of Egypt to the east probably coincided with the shortest line from the Mediterranean to the Red Sea, a line fortified from time immemorial.

The reign of Ramesses VI was followed by those of Ramesses VII and VIII, reigns more obscure than any others. A few monuments of the former, Usermare-meryamun-setepenre, have come to light;[3] his tomb in the Valley of the Kings (no. 1) lies open with the sarcophagus, now empty, still in its burial chamber. No tomb, however, is known for Ramesses VIII, Usermare-akhenamun, and if such a tomb ever existed it may still be lying undiscovered under the rubble of the valley. Indeed, the very existence of this pharaoh is assured almost solely by his inclusion in the list of princes in the temple of Medīnet Habu,[4] which seems to imply that both he and Ramesses VII were sons of Ramesses VI.[5] It is, therefore, not surprising that even the relative sequence of the two kings has been doubted and the inverse order has been proposed,[6] probably justly, since in the Medīnet Habu list no other king is named between Ramesses VI and Ramesses VIII so that Ramesses VII could only follow the latter.

The probability of this order is not disproved by a passage in a Turin papyrus[7] which, while confirming that Ramesses VII was a successor of Ramesses VI, seemed to necessitate an assumption of a minimum reign of seven years for Ramesses VII. The passage was considerably damaged when it was first examined and the need to ascribe seven years to Ramesses VII gave rise to understandable mistrust.[8] A new fragment, has, however, since been added to the papyrus and the passage now reads quite clearly: 'Given to him from year..., ...month of..., day 1, of the

[1] Bibliography given in §1, 45, VII, 381.

[2] §1, 24, II, 192, nos. 290–3.

[3] §1, 25, 202–4; §1, 51.

[4] §1, 36, pls. 250 and 299–302. For the indubitable monuments of Ramesses VIII, see §1, 55.

[5] §1, 48, 203.          [6] §1, 1, 87; §1, 20, 446, n. 4.

[7] Hieratic Pap. Turin Cat. 1907/1908, discussed in §1, 43, and §1, 40, 60.

[8] §1, 20, 446, n. 5.

King Nebmare-meryamun, the great god, up to year 7, third month of summer, day 26, of the king of Upper and Lower Egypt Usermare-meryamun-setepenre (i.e. Ramesses VII), our good lord, amounting to ...years...'. The year 7 of Ramesses VII is therefore assured, but the passage does not exclude the possibility of a reign—which could have been only a very short one—between Ramesses VI and VII. In other words, it leaves room for the king whom we number as Ramesses VIII. It is regrettable that both the opening year of Ramesses VI and the total of years at the end of the summary are lost, for we should have obtained the number of years from the accession to the throne of Ramesses VI to the year 7 of Ramesses VII; in the present circumstances we must be content with a minimum of seven years for Ramesses VI[1] and with the same figure for Ramesses VII.

It is not known who succeeded Ramesses VII and VIII and a reign or even two reigns, of which we are totally unaware, may have occurred before we reach the last three Ramessides. The order of these is beyond doubt;[2] there is, however, no precise information about the length of their respective reigns. They probably did not reign much longer than the highest dates attested for each of them: seventeen years for Neferkare-setepenre (Ramesses IX),[3] three years for Khepermare-setepenre (Ramesses X)[4] and twenty-seven years for Menmare-setepenptah (Ramesses XI).[5]

## II. INCURSIONS OF THE LIBYANS AND THEIR SETTLEMENT IN EGYPT

From reading the boastful account of Ramesses III's victories over the attacking Libyan tribes the impression is gained that the crushing defeat turned them for ever back from the Egyptian frontier. This is, however, no more true than that the earlier victories of Merneptah had saved Egypt permanently from Libyan invasions. It is, therefore, not surprising that in about the middle of the Twentieth Dynasty references are repeatedly made in Egyptian texts to incursions by Libyans, and as before it is the

---

[1] This is supplied by the stela in §1, 52, pl. LXVIII and p. 22.

[2] §1, 40, 61–4.

[3] Hieratic Pap. Brit. Museum 10068, 1, 1, compared with IV, 1 (§1, 41, pls. IX and XI); Pap. Brit. Mus. 10C53, 1, 1–2 (§1, 41, pl. XVII).

[4] §1, 2, pl. 58, 1, compared with pl. 63 e. A reign of ten years has been conjectured in §1, 39.

[5] Stela from Abydos, §1, 35, II, pl. 62 a, and §1, 25, 221, VI.

two tribes of the Libu and the Meshwesh who are expressly mentioned.[1] That we learn about these events at all is due to the fact that this time the invaders penetrated as far as Upper Egypt and made frequent appearances in the region of Thebes. Fear of them was thought by the workmen engaged in constructing the king's tomb in the Valley of the Kings to be a justifiable excuse for staying away from work and keeping safe within the walls of their village.

The earliest mention of the invaders is found in a fragmentary diary of their work dated in the year 10 of a king whose name is lost.[2] At a certain date it is reported that 'the desert-dwellers descended into the town of Smen' situated at the modern Rizeiqāt, some twenty-five kilometres south of Thebes. Consequently on four following dates 'the gang of workmen was idle through fear of the desert-dwellers' and their fears were fully justified, since two days later 'the desert-dwellers descended to the west [of Thebes]'. This took place on the first epagomenal day of the year and the dates on the verso can be assigned to the beginning of the next calendar year. Here the invaders, who so far have been vaguely referred to as 'desert-dwellers' (ḫ3styw), are at last referred to precisely, for we are told that 'the gang was idle through fear of the Meshwesh' and again spent at least five days idle 'in this place', undoubtedly at home in the village. An exactly similar reference to the 'desert-dwellers' appears in a small fragment[3] which probably belongs to the same papyrus, but dates from year 11.

A piece of another diary[4] also from the end of one and the beginning of another calendar year but dated in the thirteenth regnal year contains further information, without, however, being very instructive. This time the workmen were idle because the grain ration was two months in arrears and they 'were hungry'. This was 'though there were no desert-dwellers' or 'though the desert-dwellers were not here'. On two dates we are told who these desert-dwellers were: twice the remark reads 'though there were no Libu here'.

A fragment of a third diary,[5] this time of a year 15, also mentions the Libu. They seem to be crossing the river south of

---

[1] Some of the evidence from Turin papyri has been already quoted in §ii, 5, 258.

[2] Pap. Turin, Cat. 2071/224 [140], unpublished.

[3] Pap. Turin, fragment without number, unpublished.

[4] §i, 2, pls. 4 and 5.

[5] Pap. Turin, Cat. 2071/224 + 1960, unpublished.

some place and the Meshwesh too are reported to be 'in Ne', that is at Thebes on the eastern bank of the Nile.

There is also a small fragment[1] with the regnal year lost, but perhaps belonging to one of the three quoted above. Here too glimpses are caught of a similar state of affairs: twice it is said 'there were no desert-dwellers' and once 'the Meshwesh descended'. On the verso, the desert-dwellers seem to be present and 'the Ethiopians (Kush) [came] to Ne', that is, Thebes. The part played by these latter is quite obscure; they may have been troops arriving from Nubia.

The name of the king under whom these events took place is nowhere given or preserved. We are, however, perfectly justified in assigning the regnal years 10 to 15 to Ramesses IX since, among the rulers of the Twentieth Dynasty, none except Ramesses IX (apart from Ramesses III and XI who are excluded on palaeographical and other grounds) is known to have reigned ten years and longer.

The last time the 'desert-dwellers' are heard of is in a diary which has preserved the only regnal year known of Ramesses X, his year 3. In that year the gang of workmen was idle practically the whole of the 'third month of the winter season'. Fear of desert-dwellers is given as a reason on days 6, 9, 11, 12, 18, 21, and 24 of that month.[2]

The presence or danger of these 'desert-dwellers', specified as the Meshwesh or the Libu, is, therefore, reported intermittently over at least ten years. They were evidently roaming through Upper Egypt and though they were frightening the peaceful and and unarmed gang of workmen of the king's tomb, it is perhaps significant that no actual clashes, violence, or military intervention are ever mentioned. Moreover, on other days in close proximity to the dates when the danger of their presence was imminent life on the west of Thebes seems to have been quite normal.

These roamings of the Meshwesh and the Libu in Upper Egypt were but a ramification of a large scale penetration of Libyan tribes in the north, in the Delta, and below Memphis at Heracleopolis. This penetration was probably on the whole peaceful and resulted in the occupation of the western Delta where Libyans, under their chiefs, founded a number of principalities each with an important town as its centre.[3] The character

---

[1] Pap. Turin, fragment without number, unpublished.

[2] §1, 2, pls. 50 and 51.

[3] This can be safely deduced from the conditions in the Delta under the Twenty-second and later dynasties; see § 11, 6.

of these princedoms was military, and it is probable that the Egyptians, unable to oppose the penetration, engaged these Libyans as mercenaries in the Egyptian army. By doing so they only followed the example of the pharaohs of the Nineteenth Dynasty in dealing with invaders. The Meshwesh themselves had served in the Egyptian army as early as the reign of Ramesses II,[1] though dangerous fighting with the Meshwesh was to come later under Merneptah and especially under Ramesses III. The same method had been adopted for the Sherden of the Mediterranean islands. These foreigners are attested in the Egyptian army from the time of the Eighteenth Dynasty,[2] and are found in the reign of Ramesses V in the Twentieth Dynasty as peaceful settlers and plot-holding cultivators in many places in Middle and Upper Egypt.[3]

References to the Meshwesh in documents dating from the end of the Twentieth Dynasty, though infrequent and obscure, do not give the impression that they were then enemies. In a trial under Ramesses XI a brewer from the west of Thebes declares that he had acquired some silver from the Meshwesh, presumably as a result of trading.[4] About the same time a commander of the army gives an urgent order that the same people who used to give bread to the Meshwesh should supply it to them again at once.[5] This sounds very much like supplying a detachment of the army. On the other hand the vizier asks in a letter to a recipient whose name and title are lost that all the Medjay-police who are in the town of Pi-eḥbō, now Behbēt el-Hagar, in the Delta should be dispatched to him, adding 'and you will come after having taken a very thorough cognizance of how the Meshwesh fare' (or perhaps 'behave').[6] It is not known for what purpose the vizier was in such urgent need of the police of Pi-eḥbō, but the recipient evidently was in that town and the Meshwesh were settled or staying near that town. If so, they were in the middle of the Delta. It looks as if the recipient was supposed to leave to join the vizier only after having persuaded himself that there was nothing to be feared from the Meshwesh. Another group of the Meshwesh were establishing themselves, perhaps a little later, at Heracleopolis, not far from the entrance to the Faiyūm. It was a descendant of a chief of these who eventually seized the throne of the pharaohs as Sheshonq I, the founder of the Twenty-second Dynasty.

[1] §II, 2, I, 120*.　　　[2] §II, 2, I, 194*.
[3] §I, 23, II, 80.　　　[4] Pap. Mayer A, 8, 14 (in §II, 4).
[5] §II, I, 35.
[6] Pap. Louvre 3169, 7 (§II, 3, 110–11 and unnumbered Plate).

## III. WORKMEN OF THE KING'S TOMB

A considerable part of the information now available about the Twentieth Dynasty is derived from documents which were written for the group of workmen who constructed the tombs of the kings of the New Kingdom in the Valley of the Kings and the tombs of their queens in the Valley of the Queens at Thebes. While, however, their royal employers often remain no more than mere names to us, it is possible to piece together a picture of the organization and lives of the workmen from these documents, both papyri and ostraca. In addition to the actual results of their work and the documents referring to their affairs, both the ruins of the village in which they lived and the tombs in which they were buried have been preserved.

The workmen formed a gang[1] for which the same term was used as for the crew of a ship, in all probability because the organization of the gang was copied from that of a boat. The gang was divided into two 'sides', the 'right' and the 'left', each placed under the orders of a foreman ('great one of the crew'). Both foreman had one 'deputy' each to help them. The number of workmen in the gang varied. Usually they numbered about sixty, though at the beginning of the reign of Ramesses IV the number was raised for a short time to 120 (see above, p. 607).

The division into right and left sides was not only administrative, but also applied in the work; presumably the two 'sides' worked respectively on the right and left side of the tomb. The number of workmen in the two sides was not always equal; only rarely did a man change from one side to the other. A few of the workmen were engaged in cutting the rock, while others cleared away the stones and débris in baskets, throwing the rubbish away outside the entrance of the tomb. The two foremen and a scribe supervised the work. They saw to it that the work was done according to the directions on the plan with which they were provided. Two plans of this kind have been preserved: the plan of the tomb of Ramesses IV on a Turin papyrus[2] and that of the tomb of Ramesses IX on an ostracon in Cairo.[3] The progress of the work was carefully noted by the scribe, the number of baskets carried away was counted, and from time to time the progress made was measured with a cubit.

---

[1] §1, 41, 1 (Text), 13–15.
[2] §1, 5. See above, pp. 607–8.
[3] §1, 16, pl. xxxii, no. 25184; §iii, 6.

The scribe kept a diary of the work,[1] noting every day the names of the workmen who were absent, together with the reasons for their absence. Anything else of importance that occurred in connexion with the work was also included. He regularly submitted reports on all these matters to the office of the vizier, who, as the highest official after the king, was the ultimate superior of the workmen. The vizier, or a king's butler from the court, often visited the tomb to see how the work had advanced and whether the workmen had any complaints or requests.

The work[2] went on the whole year, in winter as well as in summer. The tenth, twentieth and thirtieth days of each month were the regular days of rest, the Egyptian month being composed of three periods of ten days each. Apart from these days, the workmen often had time off on the occasion of the great festivals of the principal gods. These festivals mostly involved a holiday of several consecutive days.

The workmen used copper tools which were issued to them and withdrawn when blunt for recasting by the coppersmith. Copper being a valuable metal careful notes were made of these transactions and when a tool was issued to a workman a stone of exactly the same weight, suitably labelled, was retained in the scribe's office as evidence.

When tunnelling had advanced beyond the reach of daylight work on the tomb was continued by the light of lamps. These lamps were ordinary bowls of baked clay filled with vegetable oil, in each of which was placed a wick. These wicks, made of old rags, were provided by the Pharaoh's Storehouse which was situated near the tomb. From time to time wicks were brought to the tomb and the scribe made a careful note of the number issued to the right and the left sides each day; sometimes the numbers issued in the morning and afternoon were separately recorded. The numbers varied from as few as four to as many as forty. From these accounts it may be reasonably inferred that the working day was divided into two parts of equal length with a break for a meal and a rest. It would seem that the normal working day was of eight hours. The lamps would have produced a considerable amount of smoke, but as the tomb walls have remained white we must suppose that the Egyptians put some ingredient into the oil to eliminate the smoke; it has been suggested that common salt was used for the purpose.

[1] Three diaries of scribes have been published in §1, 2.
[2] Most of the following is based on information supplied by hieratic ostraca some of them published in: §1, 8; §1, 6; §111, 8 and §1, 10.

The work itself was not very hard as the limestone of the Theban rock is fairly soft and is easily broken up; difficulty occurred only when the veins of flint, which ran in layers through the limestone, were encountered.

After the tomb had been hollowed out of the rock the walls, which had been left fairly smooth, were overlaid with plaster. They were then ready to receive the decorations, pictures and inscriptions, executed by draughtsmen first in red, and, after revision, in black outlines. The 'chisel-bearer' next turned these outlines into reliefs *en creux*, after which they were coloured by draughtsmen with colours supplied by Pharaoh's Storehouse.

The actual cutting of the tomb never seems to have occupied more than a couple of years; decorating took much longer and most tombs were still unfinished when the pharaoh died. During the rest of the reign the workmen were employed elsewhere: either in the Valley of the Queens preparing the tombs of the king's wives or in other parts of the Theban necropolis preparing the tombs of those of the high officials to whom the king lent his workmen as a mark of his favour. There is also some evidence that they worked in quarries, obtaining stones for constructions undertaken by their royal employer.

Between working days the men spent the nights in the Valley of the Kings in simple huts, several groups of which have been found not far from the tombs where the men worked. The workmen returned to their village only for the regular day of rest at the end of the ten-day week or for a series of festival days.

The preparation of the king's tomb took, therefore, a certain time, and a number of people knew the site. The burial, too, was undoubtedly a grand ceremony in which many people participated. The suggestions that the king employed prisoners of war, that the work was done at night so that no one knew the situation of the tomb, and that the king was buried by night and the workmen were then killed are sheer fantasy unsupported by any evidence. It is true, however, that the entrance to the tomb was surrounded by walls—five walls are spoken of—when the work was in progress. Besides the porter at the gate, the king's tomb also had its own police, two 'chiefs of Medjay', each at the head of three Medjay-policemen.

For their labours the workmen were paid in kind. The larger part of their wages was grain, wheat (emmer) and barley, rations of which were supplied by the royal granaries, in normal times at least, on the twenty-eighth day of the month[1] for the following

[1] §III, 9.

month. There were times, however, when the royal granaries were empty or very short of grain, and the workmen received their rations only after considerable delay. This grain was derived from taxes paid by the peasants of the neighbourhood of Thebes, and in the reign of Ramesses XI the Scribe of the King's Tomb himself had to collect these taxes in the village.[1]

It is interesting to note that the ration of emmer was considerably higher than that of barley; they were used respectively for making bread and beer, the staple Egyptian diet. The rations[2] of foreman and scribe vary little, the normal being $5\frac{1}{2}$ khar[3] of emmer and 2 khar of barley for the foreman and $2\frac{3}{4}$ khar of emmer and 1 khar of barley for the scribe. The payments to the ordinary workmen show a considerable variation which can be ascribed to several reasons, but again the most normal quantities are 4 khar of emmer and $1\frac{1}{2}$ khar of barley. The rations of the 'guardian' of the storehouse of the king's tomb and of the 'porter' of the tomb were 2 khar of emmer and $\frac{1}{2}$ khar of barley for the former and 1 khar of emmer and $\frac{1}{2}$ khar of barley for the latter. The king supplied not only the grain, but also the labour to grind it into flour, for which purpose a few slave women were attached to the gang.

Besides grain the workmen regularly received vegetables, fish, and (as fuel) wood; each workman also had a claim to a certain amount of water, for both the village and the place of work were situated in the desert. The people who were entrusted with providing these commodities belonged to a special group of serfs (smdt) conscripted from among the peasants of the plain between the Theban necropolis and the Nile. From time to time fats and oil, as well as clothing, were distributed to the workmen. Washermen washed their laundry and potters supplied vessels which seem to have been subjected to an unusual rate of breakage. The 'water-carriers' used donkeys for transport. These were lent to them by the workmen, but each water-carrier was responsible for a donkey while it was in his charge.

The fish supplied by the fisherman are sometimes noted so meticulously that even the name of the fish and its condition— whether fresh, dried or cut up—are indicated. The 'right side' and the 'left side' each had their fisherman, and, to simplify the verification of the weight, two stone weights, suitably inscribed,

---

[1] §III, 7, in particular pp. 22–37.

[2] Details in §III, 5, particularly pp. 916 ff.

[3] Ḥꜣr, a measure of capacity, was equal to 76·56 litres. See C.A.H. II³, pt. I, pp. 382 f.

were kept in the office. The weights corresponded with the quantity of fish to which each side was entitled. The quantity required of a fisherman seems to have been 200 *deben*[1] of fish for ten days, while the wood-cutter was expected to supply 500 pieces of wood for the same period.

Over and above the regular provisions, the workmen received from time to time as well as on special occasions, certain extras ('rewards') from the pharaoh, which included wine, salt ground or in cakes, natron (used instead of soap), imported Asiatic beer, meat, and similar luxuries.

Complaints about rations and supplies in arrears were not infrequently made during the Twentieth Dynasty. When these had no results the workmen left their work and went on strike. The strike in the twenty-ninth year of Ramesses III caused considerable alarm; shorter strikes are reported in subsequent reigns,[2] one being as late as the year 3 of Ramesses X.[3]

The workmen's village was situated in a valley at a place now called Deir el-Medīna.[4] It was surrounded by a thick wall of unbaked bricks, all stamped with the name of King Tuthmosis I, which proves that the village dates from the beginning of the Eighteenth Dynasty. The organization of the gang of workmen of the king's tomb may, however, have originated in the reign of Amenophis I, which would account for the popularity of the cult of this king among the inhabitants of the west of Thebes in general and among the workmen of the king's tomb in particular.

The village contains about seventy houses and is divided into two more or less equal parts by a fairly wide street running from north to south. The houses are all in blocks; no space is left between them, and two adjoining houses have a party wall. Several houses were built outside the village wall to the north.

Disputes among the villagers were heard and settled by a tribunal (*knbt*) the composition of which changed according to rules unknown to us. All the members of the tribunal were people from the village, usually a foreman or a scribe or both, and some workmen or their wives, probably the oldest among them. The village tribunal decided on the guilt of a person and on

---

[1] *Deben*, a weight of 91 grammes.

[2] Ostracon Berlin 12631, 15 (unpublished) in year 1 of Ramesses iv; Ostr. Deir el-Medīna 571 (in §iii, 8, pl. ii) in a 'year 9'; Ostr. Cairo Cat. 25533, verso 10 (in §i, 8, p. 31*); repeatedly in §i, 44, pl. 98–9.

[3] §i, 2, pl. 52, 12; 55, 23 ff.

[4] Excavated and published by B. Bruyère in §iii, 1 (1934–5), 3rd part, Cairo, 1939.

his or her punishment, but capital punishment required the decision of the vizier. It was also the vizier who pardoned.

The employment connected with the king's tomb was hereditary and passed on to the eldest son, though formal approval of the vizier was probably required. It can often be observed how a post was handed down from father to son through several generations. Thus the post of scribe was in the hands of one family for practically the whole of the Twentieth Dynasty, six members holding it successively.[1] Two or more scribes were attached to the gang to attend to administrative and private documents.

The cemetery of the workmen is situated near the village, to the west, on the slope of the mountain of Thebes.[2] The majority of the tombs, some quite impressive in their size and decoration, were built during the apogee of the community under the Nineteenth Dynasty; by the time of the Twentieth Dynasty they had been turned into family tombs in which the descendants of the original owners were buried. Apart from the addition of another subterranean burial chamber, little alteration was made.

Just outside the village, to the west and north, were small sanctuaries[3] of the deities popular among the workmen and of deceased kings whom the gang had served. Particularly large and decorated was a sanctuary to the goddess Hathor on the site of which the temple of Deir el-Medîna was built later, in Ptolemaic times. The chapels of Tuthmosis IV and Sethos I can still be identified, but others must remain anonymous for lack of inscriptions, among them the sanctuary of Amenophis I.[4] In his honour several festivals were celebrated in the year; the festival of the seventh month of the civil year gave the month the name Pamenhotep, which, as the name of the corresponding Coptic month Baremhāt, has survived until today.

The workmen themselves played the part of priests, as the god's 'servants' at the religious service held in the chapels and as *weeb*-priests ('pure ones') during processions in which the image of the god in his shrine was carried round by the *weeb*-priests on a barque. It was during such festival appearances that oracular consultations were practised. Questions were submitted in writing and the statue answered 'yes' or 'no' by making the carriers of the barque move towards, or recede from, the petitioner.[5]

---

[1] §III, 4.
[2] B. Bruyère's systematic excavation has been published in §III, 1.
[3] §III, 1 (1935–40), three parts, Cairo 1948 and 1952.
[4] On his cult among the workmen of the king's tomb see §III, 2.
[5] §III, 3, 44–5.

The small community of the king's workmen thus enjoyed a remarkable degree of self-government in both civil and religious matters, an interesting feature in a monarchy governed by a highly developed officialdom and an economically strong priestly class.

## IV. HIGH PRIESTS OF AMUN AND VICEROYS OF NUBIA

The Great Papyrus Harris, which enumerates the generous donations to various Egyptian temples made by Ramesses III during his reign of more than thirty years, permits us to form an idea of the enormous extent of the property of these religious institutions. It has been calculated that at the end of his reign the temples owned about one-fifth of the inhabitants of the country and about a third of its cultivable land. Of this property some three-quarters belonged to the estate of the god Amon-Re of Thebes.[1] It is not difficult to understand the power and influence which this material backing gave to the High Priest of Amon-Re, the First God's Servant of Amon-Re, King of the Gods, who stood at the head of the god's estate, the more so since the god's land was exempt from royal taxation and its dependants from military service and compulsory work for the crown.

In the Nineteenth Dynasty Ramesses II had caused Nebunenef, a politically and financially insignificant High Priest of Osiris of This to be appointed as the High Priest of Amon-Re, though the appointment was adroitly presented as the god's own choice.[2] It would be interesting to know the exact degree of influence Ramesses III was able to exercise on the appointment, in his reign, of the high priest to the enormous wealth and power which the king himself had so considerably increased. In the twenty-sixth year of his reign we find, only once, and quite by chance, a casual mention of Usermarenakhte as high priest.[3] He must, however, have died between the twenty-sixth year and the king's death in the thirty-second year, for ten months after his successor's accession to the throne we meet for the first time a new high priest, Ramessenakhte,[4] in all probability Usermarenakhte's brother.[5]

---

[1] §iv, 9, 67.          [2] §iv, 11.

[3] §i, 6, ii, pl. 22, no. 148, recto, 13. The regnal year is actually lost, but for the dating to year 26 of Ramesses III see §i, 30, 35.

[4] §i, 6, ii, pl. 37, no. 161, line 4, completed by the unpublished hieratic ostracon Strassburg H 82

[5] One of Ramessenakhte's sons was also called Usermarenakhte (see below, p. 628) and was probably so named after his paternal uncle.

If not with Usermarenakhte, then certainly with Ramessenakhte the high-priesthood came into the hands of a powerful family of officials who made this ecclesiastical post, and indeed all the key posts of Amon-Re's clergy, their domain.[1] Ramessenakhte's father, Merybaste, was a native of Hermopolis, where he held the post of chief priest of all the gods of that town, but besides this he was also steward of the king's mortuary foundation at Medīnet Habu, and the chief taxing-master. These two posts commanded the two most important financial institutions of the country. It is probable that it was due to his influence that Ramessenakhte became High Priest of Amon-Re, holding this post through the reigns of Ramesses IV, V, and VI,[2] and probably somewhat longer. While Usermarenakhte is met with only once in our documentation, Ramessenakhte appears not infrequently.

That he led the great expedition to the quarries of Wādi Hammāmāt in the year 3 of Ramesses IV[3] is undoubtedly due to the fact that most, if not all, of the blocks to be extracted were destined for buildings at Thebes, the city of Amun;[4] the presence of the High Priest of Amon-Re at such an expedition was quite unprecedented. Although the king's workmen ought to have been paid entirely by the king's treasury, as they had always been before, it is significant that from the very beginning of the reign of Ramesses IV Ramessenakhte repeatedly attends the distribution of grain and other supplies to the workmen of the king's tomb or acts as intermediary between them and the king. Here also the participation of the high priest is without precedent. Thus at a certain date in year 1 'the High Priest Ramessenakhte came to the entrance (of the king's tomb) with another letter for the gang' and two days later he came again 'to take the despatches to the place where the pharaoh was'.[5] In year 3 he distributed together with the vizier and the Chief of the Treasury Mentemtowy clothes, oil, fish and salt,[6] and again in year 4 with the same officials some liquid, probably oil or honey.[7] In year 1 of some subsequent reign he attended with the vizier and other notables the transport of the king's granite sarcophagus to the tomb.[8] In a year 6 he received 'in the great hall of the house of Amon-Re', presumably at Karnak, a large sum of copper (600 *deben*) from

---

[1] For the following see §iv, 4, 123 f.
[2] Latest occurrence on a stela dated in year 7 of Ramesses VI; §1, 52, pl. LXVIII.
[3] §1, 11, nos. 12 and 223.     [4] See above, p. 608.
[5] See reference in note 4, p. 626 above, lines 3 and 4.
[6] Unpublished hieratic papyrus from Deir el-Medīna, no. 24, line 3.
[7] §1, 16, no. 25271.     [8] §1, 44, pl. cv, 13.

the foremen and the scribe of the King's Tomb,[1] the nature and reason for the payment being quite obscure. It may, however, be the weight of blunted tools with which he seems to be concerned on another occasion.[2] All this can only be explained by the fact that the high priest had assumed new rights and duties, because the wages of the royal workmen had to be paid, or at least supplemented, from the finances of Amon-Re. As high priest, Ramessenakhte was the supreme authority over the domains of this god which he administered through the Steward of Amun Usermarenakhte, who was none other than his own son, named after Ramessenahkte's predecessor (p. 626). The Wilbour taxation papyrus, however, reveals that Usermarenakhte was at the same time the most extensive administrator of royal lands, at any rate in Middle Egypt, and the chief taxing-master.[3] The father and son had the finances of both the chief god Amon-Re and the pharaoh firmly in their hands. Another son of Ramessenakhte, Merybaste, was also a God's Father of Amun, and his daughter Adjeshere married Amenemope, the third priest of Amun,[4] himself a son of the second priest of Amun Tjanofer. In other words the two now related families held between them the highest posts in the hierarchy of Amon-Re.

No wonder, therefore, that two of Ramessenakhte's sons, Nesamun and Amenhotpe, probably in that order, succeeded their father in the high-priesthood. Nesamun, known only from the inscriptions on a statue which he set up in memory of his father,[5] may have been for a short time high priest under Ramesses VII or VIII or at the beginning of the reign of Ramesses IX. In the year 10 of the reign of Ramesses IX the high priest was already Amenhotpe.[6]

On the 'nineteenth day of the third month of inundation' of that year Amenhotpe received 'many favours, numerous rewards in fine gold and silver and millions of all good things' from the king 'on account of many perfect monuments which he had made in the House of Amon-Re, King of the Gods, in the name of the good god', that is, the king. The presentation took place in the great courtyard of Amun at Karnak, and Amenhotpe was there ceremonially saluted by three of the king's courtiers, the Chief of the Treasury of Pharaoh among them. The 'favours' consisted of a golden collar and other jewels totalling 10 *deben* of gold, and

---

[1] Unpublished continuation of §1, 44, pl. xxxiii, line 16.
[2] §1, 16, no. 25311.
[3] §1, 23, II, 131, sect. 52; 150, sects. 200, 201.
[4] §IV, 5, 265.     [5] §IV, 5, 266–7.     [6] §IV, 6, 63.

various silver vessels, in all 30 *deben* of silver, besides various delicacies of food, drink and perfumes.

All this represented a very handsome sum and Amenhotpe had the scene sculptured in relief on a wall of the temple of Karnak.[1] He stands with uplifted arms before the king, as if he had been present in person. The 'favours' are pictured piled up between them, while two of the king's courtiers have just hung a wide collar on the high priest's neck. But while these latter are represented as just about half the high priest's size, Amenhotpe himself is exactly equal in size to the king, though a false impression of the king's size is given by the high helmet which he wears and the low pedestal on which he is standing. The same equality between the king and the high priest can also be observed in another relief where the high priest presents a bouquet of the god Mont to the pharaoh.[2]

Before this time a subject of the pharaoh would never have dared to represent himself as equal in stature to his royal master. The two reliefs of Amenhotpe are therefore eloquent testimony to the high degree of power to which the high priest had attained by then, and to the low ebb to which the king's divinity had sunk. Except for their titles the king and the high priest were for all practical purposes equals.

Exactly how long Amenhotpe enjoyed his exalted position is not known. At the time of the great trials of tomb-robbers in the years 16 and 17 of Ramesses IX he was still in office, and appears as a member of the high-court as second only to the Vizier Khaemuast;[3] the administration seems to have preferred the old order in which it was the vizier who stood next to the king.

Unfortunately, after the seventeenth year of Ramesses IX there is a long gap in our documentation concerning the high priests of Amon-Re. In the year 3 of Ramesses X the high priest is several times referred to,[4] always in connexion with the workmen of the king's tomb, but never named. There is, however, considerable likelihood that it was still Amenhotpe.

When another great trial of tomb-robbers, from which a number

---

[1] §iv, 6, pl. ii. See Plate 163 (*a*).

[2] §iv, 7, iii, 237 *e* ( = §i, 45, ii, 56, [31], adding §iv, 6, 47–50).

[3] Pap. Abbott 7, 3 ( = §i, 41, pl. iv) and Pap. Leopold ii, 3, 8; 4, 1 ( = §iv, i, pls. iii and iv), both of year 16; Pap. Brit. Mus. 10053, 1, 5 and 10068, 1, 6 ( = §i, 41, pls. xvii and ix), both of year 17.

[4] §i, 2, pl. 52, 13; 53, 15. 17. 21; 55, 24; 60, 2. In the unpublished Pap. Turin Cat. 1932 + 1939, verso, i, 3, of an early year of Ramesses X (probably year 2) the name of the high priest is damaged, but the extant beginning 'A...' suits excellently the name Amenhotpe.

of documents recording the interrogation of actual or suspected thieves have come down to us, was taking place at Thebes, the high priest is again mentioned several times, though not by name, but he can no longer have been Amenhotpe. The documents of the trial in question are dated in the year 1 of the 'Repeating-of-birth', an era which will later be shown to have been concurrent with the reign of Ramesses XI from his nineteenth year onwards, by which time the high priesthood of Amenhotpe already belonged to the past. This is clear from the deposition of a certain Ahautinofer, a porter who had been accused of having taken part in the robbery of a gilded portable chest kept in the temple of Medīnet Habu, 'the Mansion of Usermare-meryamun' or 'the Mansion' as it was then called for short. Ahautinofer defended himself by trying to show that he was away at the time of the robbery. He said: 'The foreigners came and seized the Mansion while I was in charge of some donkeys belonging to my father. Peheti, a foreigner, seized me and took me to Epep when Amenhotpe, who was (then) High Priest of Amun, had been suppressed for six months. It so chanced that I returned (only) after nine whole months of the suppression of Amenhotpe, who was High Priest of Amun, when this portable chest had already been damaged and set on fire. Now when order was restored the mayor of the West of Thebes and the Scribe of the Treasury Amennakhte and the Scribe of the Army Qashuty said: "Let us collect the wood so that the store-men may not burn it." So they brought in what was left and placed a seal on it, and it is intact this day.'[1] And a woman stated about someone else: 'After the war of the high priest had taken place (lit. 'had been made') this man stole property belonging to my father.'[2]

There had been, therefore, prior to year 19 of Ramesses XI a 'war' or 'suppression' ('transgression' is the literal rendering) directed against the High Priest Amenhotpe. In the sixth month of the war the enemy, 'the foreigners', stormed the fortified temple of Medīnet Habu, and Ahautinofer who had evidently taken refuge in the fortress along with other inhabitants of the West of Thebes, was taken away by one of the victorious foreigners as a servant or a slave to Epep, a village on the other side of the Nile. The war continued for at least another three months, but presumably not much longer than that, for Ahautinofer was able to return home.

[1] Pap. Mayer A 6, 4–12 (in §II, 4). The details of the translation are discussed in §IV, 10, and §II, 5.

[2] Pap. Brit. Mus. 10052, 13, 24–5 ( = §I, 41, pl. XXXIII).

Further interesting details which cannot but be related to this war are supplied by the deposition of a certain slave: 'When Pinehas destroyed Hardai, a young Nubian Butehamun bought me and a foreigner Pentsekhen bought me from him giving for me two *deben* of silver. And when he was killed the gardener Karo bought me for my price.'[1] It is reasonable to deduce that both the Nubian and the 'foreigner' belonged to the army of Pinehas which destroyed the town of Hardai, the later Cynopolis, at or near the modern Esh-Sheikh Fadl, about 335 miles down the river from Thebes.[2] The captured inhabitants were sold and resold among the victorious soldiers; the prices of slaves, however, were low owing to the plentiful supply. Two *deben* of silver was about half the current price.[3] The fighting continued even after the capture of Hardai; it was then that the foreigner Pentsekhen was killed.

On the other hand it is said of some thieves that they had been 'killed in the war in the northern country',[4] that is, in the Delta, and of others that Pinehas killed them,[5] and these may have belonged to the Theban conscripts mobilized by Amenhotpe against Pinehas.

'I came out from the house of the Pharaoh when Pinehas came and suppressed my superior though there was no fault with him', said yet another man interrogated;[6] his identity is uncertain, but it is likely that the 'superior' here is again the High Priest of Amon-Re. The last witness still to be quoted explained how it came about that valuables had been taken from his house, for he was absent: 'I left from fear of the *mdwt-ʿn* when Pinehas made the *mdwt-ʿn*.'[7] The exact nature of these *mdwt-ʿn* is obscure; in any case they were some hostile actions[8] which caused people to flee from their homes.

It now remains only to establish the identity of Pinehas and to find the date of the 'suppression' of Amenhotpe. When that is done an attempt can be made to present a coherent account of the disconnected information collected from the tomb-robbery papyri. Such an attempt, it is true, has already been made,[9] but the results were vitiated by the incorrect dating of the documents from which the information was obtained. There can be hardly

---

[1] Pap. Brit. Mus. 10052, 10, 18–20 ( = 1, 41, pl. XXXI).    [2] §II, 2, II, 98*.

[3] About the same time 4 *deben* of silver is paid for a slave woman (Pap. Mayer A, 8, 12–13, in §II, 4), in the Nineteenth Dynasty $4\frac{1}{10}$ *deben* (§IV, 3, pl. XIII, 13).

[4] Pap. Mayer A 13 B, 2 (in §II, 4).    [5] Pap. Mayer A 13 B, 3 (in §II, 4).

[6] Pap. Brit. Mus. 10383, 2, 5 ( = §I, 41, pl. XXII).

[7] Pap. Mayer A 4, 5 (in §II, 4).    [8] §I, 40, 68.

[9] §II, 5, and §I, 40, 67 f.

any doubt that the Pinehas referred to on various occasions was none other than the Viceroy of Ethiopia 'King's Son of Kush' Pinehas. Before reconstructing his story, however, some account of the province of Ethiopia and its viceroys during our period must be given.

Unlike the dependencies in Asia which seem to have been lost at, or soon after, the death of Ramesses III, Ethiopia, or Kush, as it was then called, together with Nubia, called Wawat, remained firmly in Egyptian hands throughout practically the whole of the Twentieth Dynasty. They were by then largely colonized and Egyptianized, and extended from the southern frontier of Egypt at Elephantine as far south as Napata (now Gebel Barkal). While at Gebel Barkal itself only a fragment of a statuette with the name of Ramesses IX has been found,[1] there is further north sufficient proof of Egyptian domination during the latter part of the Twentieth Dynasty. Thus the name of Ramesses IV has been found at Buhen[2] and Gerf Husein,[3] of Ramesses V at Buhen,[4] of Ramesses VI at Aniba,[5] Amāra West[6] and Kawa,[7] of Ramesses IX at Amāra West[8] besides the fragment at Gebel Barkal, of Ramesses X at Qūbān[9] and Aniba,[10] of Ramesses XI at Buhen.[11]

The territory, besides giving access for trade to enter the countries further south, was important for its own products, especially for gold from the mines east of the Nile. The supreme god of Egypt whose cult was introduced to various places in Nubia and Ethiopia particularly to the 'Holy Mountain' at Gebel Barkal, claimed these lands for himself as the 'Gold Lands of Amun'. The Overseer of these lands and head of the administration was a viceroy[12] who bore two high titles, 'Feather-Bearer on the Right of the King' and 'King's Son of Kush'. The first corresponded with reality, for the viceroy certainly carried an ostrich feather when walking beside the king, while the second title did not, for he was not the king's son.

The Viceroy Pinehas is reliably dated to the reign of Ramesses XI by two documents. The first is a letter from the king's chancellery to him which bears the date of year 17;[13] the second is a taxation

[1] §IV, 8, 54.
[2] §I, 45, VII, 133–4 (5 S), 134 (12).
[3] §I, 45, VII, 37.
[4] §I, 45, VII, 134 (12).
[5] §I, 45, VII, 76–7.
[6] §I, 45, VII, 159 and 161.
[7] §I, 45, VII, 181.
[8] §I, 45, VII, 159 (14), 161 (19), 163.
[9] §I, 45, VII, 82.
[10] §I, 45, VII, 81.
[11] §I, 45, VII, 130 (5).
[12] On Viceroys of Ethiopia in general see §IV, 8; for the most recent list of viceroys of the Twentieth Dynasty see §IV, 2, especially p. 74.
[13] §I, 44, pls. LXVI–LXVII.

papyrus of the year 12 which records collecting grain taxes in the region south of Thebes for the sustenance of the workmen of the king's tomb.[1] This latter papyrus is headed as follows: 'Documents of receipts of corn of *khato*-land of pharaoh from the hand of the prophets [of the temples of Upper Egypt which (?)] the Feather-Bearer on the Right of the King, the King's Scribe, the General, the Overseer of the Granaries of [Pharaoh, the King's Son of] Kush, the Commander of Southern Lands, the leader of the troops [of pharaoh] Pinehas [ordered to be delivered (?)]'.[2] Though the correctness of the restoration, especially at the end of the heading, is subject to some doubt, several unusual, indeed exceptional, features stand out clearly. On the one hand it is the first time that a King's Son of Kush bears the titles of General and Overseer of the Granaries of Pharaoh, while on the other his presence and command at Thebes, far away from the territory which he administered, is unparalleled and unexpected. It can only be explained by assuming that Pinehas with his army had intervened against the High Priest of Amun, occupied Thebes and its neighbourhood and was claiming the supreme command of the army and agricultural resources of that part of the country. The 'foreigners' and 'Nubians' referred to later during the tomb-robbery trials were clearly his troops levied in his Ethiopian province; at one time they advanced as far as Middle Egypt and probably even farther north in the pursuit of the high priest and his forces. The dating of the taxation papyrus suggests that these events and the 'suppression' of Amenhotpe took place not later than year 12. It is clear that Ramesses XI was recognized during Pinehas's occupation of Thebes and that therefore his intervention was directed not against both the king and the high priest, but against the latter alone. Perhaps the high priest, encouraged by the enormous growth of his power in Egypt, claimed more authority over Ethiopia and its riches than Pinehas was prepared to concede. The king, whether he liked Pinehas's intervention or not, had to accept it; it is, however, equally possible that Ramesses XI himself resorted to Pinehas as the only factor capable of restraining or removing Amenhotpe. Whether Amenhotpe survived the 'suppression' it is impossible to know; there is, however, no evidence that he was ever again High Priest of Amon-Re. Pinehas established himself at Thebes. In the taxation papyrus of the year 12 a number of 'foreigners' are recorded as paying grain tax in the

---

[1] Hieroglyphic transcription in §I, 21, 35–44; translation and commentary §III, 7, 22–37.

[2] §I, 21, 36, 3–5; translated §III, 7, 23.

southern neighbourhood of Thebes;[1] Pinehas, therefore, had followed the old practice and distributed fields among the troops whom he had brought. Seven years later during the trials 'foreigners' with various occupations still appeared as both accused and witnesses;[2] they remained settled at Thebes after Pinehas himself had left.

It is not clear where Pinehas was when the king's letter was addressed to him in the year 17. Its appearance shows that it is the original itself and not a mere copy. Though its provenance is unknown, it is unlikely that it was found anywhere in Nubia; Thebes is the most probable place of its discovery. We can consider one of two possibilities to account for this: either Pinehas was then still at Thebes, or he was back in Nubia and the letter could not be delivered to him and remained at Thebes. The former explanation is perhaps less likely, since the letter is an urgent request from the pharaoh to Pinehas to co-operate with the pharaoh's envoy to the 'southern country', the Steward and Butler of the Pharaoh Yenes,[3] and to send by boat to the pharaoh's residence the 'litter of the great goddess' together with various precious stones and flowers. The stones and flowers are Nubian products, but Nubia was controlled by Pinehas and these might have been ordered from Nubia by Pinehas even if he was at Thebes. On the other hand, by the 'southern country' is usually meant Upper Egypt, so that on balance it seems that Pinehas was still at Thebes in the year 17. He was, however, certainly no longer there in year 19, since on three occasions[4] when his name is referred to in the tomb-robbery trials of that year it is provided with a determinative which classifies the word which it accompanies as something deadly, hostile, or detrimental. Pinehas was then a public enemy and someone far away, belonging to the past. At the same time the High Priest of Amon-Re is mentioned again and again, and though his name is never given in the tomb-robbery papyri, it is almost certain that this was the new High Priest Hrihor.

---

[1] §1, 21, 37, 13; 38, 1. 7. 16; 41, 7. 10; 42, 6; 43, 3 ff.

[2] Pap. Abbott, verso, A 6, 16, 17, 25; B 6, 7, 8, 9, 10, 16 (in §1, 41, pls. xxiii–xxiv); Pap. Mayer A 1, 8. 12. 21; 2, 1.4.9; 6, 5. 20. 21; 9, 3. 15. 20; 12, 24 (in §ii, 4); Pap. Vienna no. 30, 2. 12 (in §1, 41, pl. xxxviii).

[3] Yenes appears in three documents (§1, 40, 70) as member of a tribunal in tomb-robbery trials in years 1 and 2 of the 'Repeating-of-Birth' which are concurrent with years 19 and 20 of Ramesses XI (see below, p. 639). The spelling of his name shows clearly that he was of foreign origin as these King's Butlers often, if not mostly, were.

[4] Pap. Mayer A 13, B 3 (in §ii, 4); Pap. Brit. Mus. 10052, 10, 18 and Pap. Brit. Mus. 10383, 2, 5 (§1, 41, pls. xxxi and xxii).

## V. HRIHOR AND RAMESSES XI

Nothing is known about Hrihor's origin and early career. Wherever he appears in inscriptions he is already 'First Prophet of Amon-Re'. He never names his parents, not even his father, in striking contrast with his predecessors in high priesthood and with the practice of his own descendants. This reticence alone would suggest a relatively humble origin and his name Hrihor ('Horus is a chief') points in the same direction: the name is very rare, only two other bearers of it, both quite obscure persons, being known.[1] That he was an army officer before he became high priest and that his early career was purely military[2] cannot be strictly proved, but it is nevertheless very likely. Even his most elaborate titularies entirely omit any mention of any other priestly office, though it would be expected that he would have had many such titles to offer if he had previously held priestly offices which had eventually led to the high priesthood. Their absence is very conspicuous in comparison with the titularies of his predecessors, Amenhotpe and Ramessenakhte, in the earlier part of the Twentieth Dynasty. On a stela in the Leiden Museum[3] which preserves perhaps the earliest known occurrence of his name, Hrihor's titulary consists of only two titles, Commander of the Army and First Prophet of Amon-Re, King of the Gods, while an ostracon containing a draft of a letter to Hrihor[4] adds another military title, Captain who is at the Head of the Army of the whole of Egypt. Hrihor held the two military titles until he handed over the command of the army to his son Piankh. The titles are also borne by all his descendants and successors in the high priesthood until the extinction of the line. This seems to be a clear indication that the command of the army was the origin of Hrihor's power, and that of his successors.

Hrihor's wife Nodjme, who follows him on the Leiden stela, was the Greatest among the Concubines of Amon-Re, King of the Gods, which is the customary title of the wives of the high-priests of Amun. It is also in his company that she is depicted in two scenes in one of her two funerary papyri. One of these, the hieroglyphic, is now in three separate portions which are in, respectively, the British Museum, the Louvre, and Munich.[5] While this

---

[1] §v, 16, 98 ( = §I, 34, v, 89 [lower]) and 113.　　　　[2] §v, 6.
[3] Leiden V. 65; published in §v, 1, pl. xxviii, and §v, 12, 3rd series, xxxviii–xxxix.　　　　[4] §I, 8, p. 90*, no. 25744.
[5] Pap. Brit. Mus., no. 10541, §v, 14, 14–15, and the Louvre portion, see §v, 10, 29, and §v, 13, II, 131ff. The Munich section is only briefly mentioned in §v, 17, 531.

papyrus does not reveal her parentage, the second papyrus, written in hieratic,[1] gives in several passages the name of her mother Hrere.[2] The name, though not uncommon as the word for 'flower', is unusual enough to make it almost certain that this Hrere is the same as the 'Greatest of Concubines of Amon-Re, King of the Gods, Hrere' mentioned in two letters of the late Twentieth Dynasty.[3] There she gives an order to the 'Chief of the Bowmen Psagai' to issue rations of corn to the workmen of the king's tomb; this authority and her title show that Hrere was the wife of a High Priest of Amon-Re and, since no high priest is known between Amenhotpe and Hrihor, Hrere's husband was in all probability Amenhotpe himself. In other words Hrihor was Amenhotpe's son-in-law and could claim the right above anyone else to succeed him in the high priesthood, there being also the possibility that, after having seized the vacant office of high priest, he sought by marrying Nodjme to acquire some additional claim to it. It seems thus almost certain that the fall of Amenhotpe was due not to Hrihor but solely to Pinehas.

It is not possible to establish the exact date when Hrihor became high priest. All that may be safely assumed is that the event took place some time between the occupation of Thebes by Pinehas, probably shortly before the year 12 of Ramesses XI,[4] and the nineteenth year of this same pharaoh, since the unnamed high priest of the contemporary tomb-robbery papyri[5] must have been Hrihor.

Soon after the seventeenth year[6] Hrihor must have made a further step towards extending his power by claiming Pinehas's titles and offices as King's Son of Kush and Overseer of the Southern Countries. With this rank Hrihor became automatically Feather-Bearer on the Right of the King, King's Scribe and Overseer of the Two Granaries of Pharaoh. Since Akhenaten's time no high priest of Amun, indeed no priest at all, had been invested with the office of feather-bearer, probably because the attendance on the king which the title implied was considered incompatible with a priestly function.[7] It now only remained for

---

[1] Also in Brit. Mus., no. 10490, published §v, 2.

[2] Col. I ( = §v, 2, pl. 1) twice; col. II ( = §v, 2) and pl. 5.

[3] §II, 1, 60, 9, and 61, 2; probably also 3, 8. [See, however, *J.N.E.S.* 32 (1973), 311 (Ed.).]

[4] This being the date of the Turin papyrus recording the collection of grain tax by Pinehas, §I, 21, 36, 1–5.

[5] E.g. Pap. Mayer A 3, 15; 4, 12. 21 (in §II, 4).

[6] In this year the 'King's son of Kush' is still Pinehas, §I, 44, pls. LXVI–LXVII.

[7] §IV, 8, 81–2.

Hrihor to take over the civilian administration of Egypt by having the title of Overseer of the City and Vizier conferred upon him. This could hardly have happened before the Vizier Nebmare-nakhte died, was transferred to the viziership of the Delta, or was otherwise released from his duties in Upper Egypt.

The only direct evidence bearing on the development and nature of the relationship between Hrihor and Ramesses XI is to be found in the temple of Khons at Karnak. Judging from the wall-reliefs and inscriptions, the back part, that is the sanctuary and the store-rooms, was built by Ramesses III and IV. To this original building a hypostyle hall and a forecourt were added in the time of Ramesses XI and Hrihor.

The decoration of the hypostyle is their joint work.[1] In most of the scenes, all religious, into which the wall-reliefs are divided, the protagonist is Ramesses XI. Side by side with these reliefs are six scenes with Hrihor. In these scenes he is called only high priest, great commander, and captain, but never vizier or King's Son of Kush. In two scenes it is Hrihor who burns incense before the barque of Amon-Re; the god, however, speaks not to him but to Ramesses XI 'My son, Lord of the two lands, Menmare-setepenptah, I see this beautiful, pure and excellent monument which thou hast made for me', etc.[2] In another scene Hrihor brings offerings but the purpose, explained in a horizontal line behind him, is 'in order that the King Ramesses XI should be given life like Re forever'.[3] The dedication, in a horizontal line at the base of the wall, names on the one side the king and the high priest, and on the other Hrihor alone. From these representations it can be seen that Hrihor had taken up the high priest-hood where Amenhotpe had left it: he retains the right of being represented in the temple as high priest along with the king (though never in one and the same scene with him) and in the same size as Ramesses XI. Though the king's subject he is almost equal to the sovereign.

The jambs of the door leading from the hypostyle to the sanctuary show perhaps the transitional stage from the Hrihor of the hypostyle to the Hrihor of the forecourt.[4] In every one of six scenes the titles and the name of Hrihor are enclosed in two cartouches: First Prophet of Amun in the first, Son of Amun, Hrihor,

---

[1] For the following consult §1, 45, ii, 77–83, with plan on p. 76 supplemented by the plan in §1, 34, iii, 54.

[2] §v, 8, 651.

[3] §v, 8, 652.

[4] §1, 45, ii, 82, (65) and (66); §v, 8, 653.

in the second. Except for the epithets Good God and Son of Re no other royal title is prefixed to the cartouches in any of the six instances.

In the forecourt, however, everything is done by Hrihor in his name only.[1] Here he bears a full royal titulary consisting of the traditional five names. The first three, the so-called Horus-name, Nebty-name and Golden-Horus-name, appear each in two different forms and seem to have been somewhat fluid, but the last two, the praenomen and nomen, are the same as those on the door-jambs of the hypostyle, First Prophet of Amun and Son of Amun, Hrihor; now, however, they are introduced by the customary titles King of Upper and Lower Egypt and Son of Re respectively, often expanded by others like Good God, Lord of Strength, Lord of the Two Lands and Lord of Appearances, once even by the uncommon Great Ruler of Egypt.[2] By adopting as the first part of his Horus-name the epithet Victorious Bull Hrihor conformed with the tradition which made this epithet the first constituent of the Horus-name of every pharaoh from Tuthmosis I onwards. By a further addition to it of Son of Amun, prefixed also to his own name in the second cartouche (Son of Amun, Hrihor), he claimed divine descent, though in doing so he seems to betray the need of stressing this more than a king with royal ancestry would have done. The most revealing feature of his royal titulary is, however, his first cartouche, the praenomen which a king chose on ascending the throne. If for this Hrihor could find nothing more fitting than his priestly title First Prophet of Amun, it is evident that he claimed royalty chiefly on the strength of his priesthood. It was this office which he thought entitled him to the divine position held by an Egyptian king. He was king because and in so far as he was High Priest of Amon-Re.

From the evidence of the Khons temple it used to be concluded that Hrihor usurped the throne at the death of Ramesses XI, or even that he deposed the king and seized the crown. Such an interpretation can hardly be upheld now; on the contrary, there are solid grounds for assuming that Hrihor not only died before Ramesses XI, but that he never dispossessed that pharaoh. He ruled Upper Egypt, with Thebes as his residence, like the king whose titles he appropriated in the inscriptions of the temple of Khons, though always under the supremacy of Ramesses XI, who, however slight might have been his power and influence, had not ceased to be the pharaoh.

[1] §1, 45, II, 79–80.
[2] §1, 25, III, 234, XII. See Plate 163 (b).

This modification of the former view is borne out by a relief and inscription at Karnak dated in the 'year 7 of "Repeating-of-Birth" under the Majesty of the King of Upper and Lower Egypt Menmare-setepenamun', that is, Ramesses XI.[1] The purport of the inscription and the relief is the commemoration of an oracle issued in connexion with the appointment of a temple official. The questioner of the oracle is Piankh, the son of Hrihor.[2] Though described as Commander of the Army in the vertical lines under the oracle scene, Piankh was presumably acting in his capacity of High Priest of Amun, for only as such could he possibly have been concerned with the appointment to a temple office, while his appearance would be inexplicable if he had been only a Commander of the Army. In fact in the top right-hand corner of the scene the titles accompanying the figure of Piankh are 'Feather-Bearer [on] the Right of the King, King's Son of Kush, First Prophet of Amon-Re, King of the Gods, Commander of the Army, Captain Piankh, true of voice'. A point worth consideration is the possibility that the representation of Piankh in the corner of the scene was secondary and added later at the time when Piankh had become also high priest. There is, however, nothing in the style or execution of the relief to support such an assumption. It has already been pointed out that Hrihor and his descendants attributed great value to, and laid great stress on, their title of Commander of the Army, a feature which is quite comprehensible in view of the likely military origin of the family. It is therefore natural that the title Commander of the Army alone was applied to Piankh in the vertical lines of the inscription where there was not space enough for the lengthy full titulary.

If then this interpretation is correct Piankh besides being commander was also high priest in the year 7 of the 'Repeating-of-Birth' which, according to the inscription, fell in the reign of Ramesses XI. This year 7 must have been identical with the twenty-fifth regnal year of Ramesses XI, since some tomb-robbers interrogated in trials of year 1 of the 'Repeating-of-Birth' are listed in a papyrus, and this time the date is expressed as 'year 1 corresponding to year 19'.[3] It is clear therefore that years 19 to 25 of Ramesses XI were identical with years 1 to 7 of the 'Repeating-of-Birth'. Ramesses XI reigned for at least two more years since a stela is dated in the twenty-seventh year of his

---

[1] §v, 11, 158. The importance of this inscription for fixing the exact position of the 'Repeating-of-Birth' is discussed—though not quite accurately—in §v, 3, 389.

[2] He heads as the eldest the list of Hrihor's children, §1, 25, III, 237, XIX.

[3] Pap. Abbott, verso, A 1 and 19 ( = §1, 41, pl. XXIII).

reign.[1] If it be admitted that Piankh besides being commander of the army was also high priest of Amun in the twenty-fifth regnal year of Ramesses XI, it at once becomes almost certain that Hrihor was no longer alive at that time and that he, consequently, died before Ramesses XI. For Piankh could assume the title of high priest only as heir to his father, who always bore that title; even in the inscriptions in which he called himself king he adopted 'High Priest of Amun' for his first cartouche. There is no evidence whatsoever that Hrihor was ever king without being at the same time High Priest of Amun.

The conclusion that Hrihor was dead in the year 25 of Ramesses XI postulates that the dates of the three dated occurrences of Hrihor should fall before that year. They are the report of Hrihor's envoy Wenamun on his journey to Syria, dated in a year 5, and the dockets, both of a year 6, on the coffins of Sethos I and Ramesses II, which record a reburial of the mummies of the two kings by Hrihor's order. These two years 5 and 6 cannot be those of Ramesses XI, for they would fall before the fight against the High Priest Amenhotpe which has been shown to have taken place shortly before year 12. There is therefore, no alternative but to assign them to the era of 'Repeating-of-Birth'. We have several documents with dates falling within the first eighteen years of Ramesses XI; they all mention the king's name wherever the part containing the date is preserved. It is only with year 19 that the dates begin to be designated as those of the 'Repeating-of-Birth' without the king's name being mentioned. Before that year Ramesses XI's sovereignty was unchallenged.

It is significant that both in year 1 and year 7 of the 'Repeating-of-Birth' reference was also made either to the regnal year of Ramesses XI or to his name, and one is justified in concluding that these were the first and the last years of the 'Repeating-of-Birth'. This was then a period lasting seven years during which Ramesses XI suffered a diminution of his political power, though perhaps not from its very start. It appears, rather, that during the first two years, at least, the king still took an important part in the conduct of affairs of state. In a papyrus dated in a 'year 2' which can only be that of this period, it is still the pharaoh to whom a report on some thefts was made[2] and it is the pharaoh who commissions three high officials to carry out the investigation.[3] In the

---

[1] §1, 35, 11, pl. 62 a.     [2] Pap. Brit. Mus. 10383, 1, 2. 5 ( = §1, 41, pl. xxii).
[3] Pap. Brit. Mus. 10383, 1, 2 ff. ( = §1, 41, pl. xxii). The document is dated in a 'year 2' and the commission consists of exactly the same persons as another in year 2 of the 'Repeating-of-Birth' in Pap. Mayer A 1, 6–7 ( = §11, 4).

same document the appointment of a priestly official by the pharaoh is also alluded to,[1] and this would be an important testimony to the pharaoh's influence if the event were one of not too remote a past; unfortunately it is not stated how long before the date of the document the appointment took place.

A proof that Hrihor was already high priest while he still recognized the supremacy of the pharaoh is supplied by the badly damaged stela in the temple of Khons[2] recording an oracle of Khons confirmed by another of Amon-Re: Hrihor, bearing the titles of High Priest of Amon-Re, King's Son of Kush and Chief of the Granaries of Pharaoh, is the chief actor. The year-date is lost and there is no agreement among the editors of the inscription as to the reading of the preserved part of the pharaoh's second cartouche. The traces, now visible can, however, be reconciled with the end of the nomen of Ramesses XI. The inscription must, of course, be posterior to year 17, because in that year the King's Son of Kush was still Pinehas. Reference is repeatedly made to 'twenty years' which Amon-Re gave to Hrihor, but so little is preserved of the inscription that no chronological conclusions can possibly be drawn from it. It is, however, tempting to see in the oracle of Amon-Re here recorded the very inauguration of Hrihor's rule over Upper Egypt and the introduction of the era of 'Repeating-of-Birth'. The name of the latter seems to express the expectation of a turn towards a prosperous and affluent stage in the history of the country, a period of *Renaissance*, as it had done previously when the first years of the reign of Sethos I were so called, or when the founder of the Twelfth Dynasty, Ammenemes I, assumed 'Repeater-of-Births' as his Horus-name.

It is significant that in none of the three hieratic documents mentioning Hrihor[3] is the name of the latter enclosed in a cartouche, nor is he there given the title of king. This confirms our suspicion that his kingship was a fiction and was restricted to the inscriptions of the Khons temple built and decorated by Hrihor, though with funds provided by the estate of the god. Outside the Theban temple area, and particularly in the eyes of the administration, Hrihor remained merely the High Priest of Amon-Re; even for Wenamun, the Elder of the Portal of the Estate of Amun refers to Hrihor as

---

[1] Pap. Brit. Mus. 10383, I, 10 ( = §1, 41, pl. xxii).

[2] Complete bibliography in §1, 45, II, 80 (39); translated in §1, 3, IV, sects. 614–18; discussed §v, 9, 495–6.

[3] Docket on the coffin of Ramesses II (§v, 8, 557 and fig. 5), docket on the coffin of Sethos I (§v, 8, 553, and pl. x, B) and the report of Wenamun (for which see the next footnote).

his 'lord'. The report of Wenamun[1] also supplies vital information about the state of affairs in Lower Egypt. After having left Thebes on the instruction of Amon-Re and his high priest to travel to Byblos and Syria to buy cedar wood for the second barque of Amon-Re, Wenamun's first stop was at Tanis, near the eastern border of the Delta. There he handed over his letters of recommendation to Nesbenebded and Tentamun[2] and they dispatched him to Syria on board a Syrian ship. Later, when he had been robbed of his money by a member of the ship's crew and, being without means, was unable to pay for the timber he sought, in Byblos they lent him money to be repaid on his return to Thebes.[3] Wenamun gives no title to Nesbenebded, a man, and Tentamun, a woman. In one passage of his report, however, he calls them 'the foundations[4] whom Amun has given to the north of his land'. Clearly Nesbenebded and Tentamun, undoubtedly man and wife, though Wenamun never says so, ruled the Delta, as Hrihor did in Upper Egypt, and resided at Tanis, which had previously been Per-Ramesse, the Delta residence of the Ramesside kings. The name of Nesbenebded, 'he who belongs to the ram of Ded', points rather to Mendes as his native town; it is not known how he rose to power, but from Wenamun's words we can deduce that the fiction was upheld that Amun himself had divided Egypt between Hrihor and Nesbenebded. The two potentates, though rivals, lived therefore on friendly terms. The profitable trade with Asia lay in Nesbenebded's hands, though he had to rely chiefly or solely on Syrian ships and crews.[5]

Wenamun's report affords eloquent testimony that Egypt's political prestige in Syria was at its lowest ebb, especially at Byblos, a town which had been since time immemorial in trade relationship with Egypt. Its king refused categorically to supply timber without being paid in cash, though he recognized the might of Amun and was aware of the fact that the cradle of civilization was in Egypt and that it was from there that craftsmanship and learning had reached Syria.[6] This powerlessness of Egypt in Syria was not a recent development, for it transpires from the

---

[1] §v, 5, 61–76; photographs in §v, 7; the latest and almost complete translation in §1, 20, 306–13.

[2] Wenamun 1, 4 ( = §v, 5, 61, 4–5).

[3] Wenamun 2, 35–6 ( = §v, 5, 70, 9–12) and 2, 39–42 ( = §v, 5, 71, 1–6).

[4] Wenamun 2, 35 ( = §v, 5, 70, 10). The word spelt *snntytyw-t3* has been commonly translated as 'officers', but is clearly a late writing of the word *snt-t3*, foundation', see the spellings of the latter in §v, 4, IV, 178, 19.

[5] Wenamun 1, 7 ( = §v, 5, 61, 9) and 1,58 – 2,2 ( = §v, 5, 67, 3–8).

[6] Wenamun 2, 20–2 ( = §v, 5, 69, 1–4).

narrative that some time previously Egyptian envoys had been kept in Byblos for seventeen years without being allowed to return home, with the result that they had died there.[1] Khaemuast, who had sent them, seems to be the well-known vizier of Ramesses IX.

While the rule in Egypt was clearly divided between Hrihor and Nesbenebded it is difficult to guess the whereabouts of the pharaoh during the era of the 'Repeating-of-Birth'. Among the possible residences Memphis seems to be the most likely place for him to have waited until the death of Hrihor allowed him to regain some of his pre-eminence. In Wenamun's report the pharaoh is mentioned only once[2] during his stay in Byblos. When he stood so close to the king of Byblos that the shadow of the king's umbrella fell upon him, a courtier said to Wenamun: 'The shadow of the pharaoh, your lord, has fallen on you.' Since the king rebuked the courtier, saying 'Leave him alone!' his words must have been either a mockery or a bad joke.

The war which Hrihor's son Piankh as Commander of the Army waged against Pinehas evidently resulted in a complete loss of the province of Nubia, for had there been any success the title of the 'King's Son of Kush' would not have for ever disappeared from Egyptian administration.[3] This and the fact that Pinehas' tomb at Miam (at or near the present Aniba) contained the name of the owner untouched[4] prove that Pinehas died unconquered in his province which henceforward plays no part in Egyptian history.

## VI. THE TWENTY-FIRST DYNASTY

The Twenty-first Dynasty is, still, a particularly obscure period of Egyptian history. According to the excerpts from Manetho it consisted of seven kings called Tanites,[5] Tanis being perhaps the town of their residence rather than their place of origin. Of these seven kings only five can be safely identified with the kings known from monuments, while the monuments supply one royal name which it seems impossible to equate with either of the two remaining Manethonian names. The activities of these kings were evidently limited to the northern part of the country, where their

---

[1] Wenamun 2, 51–2 ( = §v, 5, 72, 5–7).

[2] Wenamun 2, 46 ( = §v, 5, 71, 13).

[3] It is found only in the titulary of Neskhons, wife of the High Priest of Amun Pinudjem II, at the time of the Twenty-first Dynasty (§iv, 8, 53), and was clearly in this case only honorary.

[4] §v, 15, ii, 240–1.          [5] §i, 53, 154–7.

monuments have been almost completely obliterated by the damper climate and by the hand of man. No information is forthcoming from the monuments as to the length of the reigns, which according to Manetho totalled 130 years, and little evidence can be adduced concerning their mutual relationship. There are grave doubts even about the correctness of the order in which they appear in Manetho's list, though the evidence in this respect seems to be contradictory. In these circumstances it is advisable to turn first to Upper Egypt, particularly to Thebes, where owing to the dry climate conditions for the preservation of monuments are far more favourable.

While the kings of the Twenty-first Dynasty ruled from Tanis generations of high priests of Amun, descendants of Hrihor, were in power at Thebes. In so far as each high priest succeeded either his father or his brother in the office, the seven high priests form a dynasty. Piankh, son of Hrihor, has already been discussed in the preceding section. He was followed by his son Pinudjem,[1] whom we shall refer to as Pinudjem I to distinguish him from a later namesake. He, in turn, was succeeded by his two sons Masahert and Menkheperre, apparently in that order.[2] Two sons of Menkheperre became high priests in due course,[3] namely Nesbenenbded,[4] followed by his brother Pinudjem II.[5] The dynasty of high priests closed with Psusennes, son of Pinudjem II.[6]

The name of Manetho's first Tanite king, Smendes, is but a late pronunciation of the name Nesbenebded,[7] and he is evidently identical with the king Hedjkheperre-setepenre Nesbenebded-meryamun of the monuments, and with the Nesbenebded with whom Wenamun had been in contact as ruler of Tanis and Lower Egypt in the reign of Ramesses XI. It was therefore Nesbenebded who, after the death of the last Ramesside king, became the

---

[1] Proofs of the filiation are numerous (see §1, 25, III, 242, n. 2). It suffices to quote §IV, 7, III, 250 c [right] and III, 251 a ( = §VI, 7, II, 212); §VI, 7, II, 217; §VI, 15, 32, LII.

[2] For Masahert being a son of Pinudjem, see the coffin of Masahert (§VI, 10, 77–8, no. 61027); §VI, 33, 133–4; docket on the coffin of Amenophis I (§V, 8, 537). For the filiation of Menkheperre, cf. §1, 34, III, 62 = §VI, 7, 225 = §VI, 2, 50; §VI, 9, 22; Cairo stela, Prov. no. 3. 12. 24. 2 (§1, 25, 265, v).

[3] The existence as high priest of a third son of Pinudjem I, Djedkhonsefonkh, remains somewhat doubtful (C. Torr in *The Academy*, 24 Sept. 1892, p. 270, and *Memphis and Mycenae* [Cambridge, 1896], p. 63 and note d).

[4] Called son of Menkheperre on bracelets nos. 600 and 601 from Tanis (§VI, 37, 149, fig. 54, and pl. cxxii), son of Esemkhebe (wife of Menkheperre) (§VI, 33, 135, and Z.A.S. 21 (1883), 73).

[5] §VI, 9, 24, no. 38, etc.    [6] §1, 25, 285.

[7] First recognized by Daressy in §VI, 8, 138.

pharaoh and the founder of a new dynasty. His hold over Upper Egypt is confirmed by an inscription in the quarry at Ed-Dibābīya, opposite Gebelein, on the right bank of the Nile south of Thebes,[1] recording an expedition sent by the king to extract stones to repair a colonnade of Tuthmosis III at Luxor which had been damaged by flood. The inscription presents Nesbenebded as dwelling at Memphis, but his regular residence was undoubtedly Tanis. That he was also buried in this latter town is suggested by a canopic jar[2] of the king acquired in the neighbourhood of Tanis.

The second king in Manetho's list of the dynasty is Psusennes. This was the pronunciation in Manetho's time of the name of King Psibkhaemne, in full form Akheperre-setepenamun Psibkhaemne-meryamun. To us he is Psusennes I, to distinguish him from the homonymous last king of the dynasty. Judging from the number of monuments bearing his name which have come down to us, he must have been the most prominent king of the dynasty, and we shall refer to him more than once.

Manetho's third king, Nepherkheres, was for a long time a puzzle, and though it was always clear that the name should correspond with a Neferkare, no such royal name was known in this period. Eventually, however, his name was found on two golden caps serving to protect the ends of a bow.[3] The king here appears closely associated with Psibkhaemne I and the complete form of the king's name is revealed to be Neferkare-hikwast Amenemnisu-meryamun.[4]

There has never been any doubt about the fourth king: Amenophthis of Manetho is clearly Amenemope, or more precisely Usermare-setepenamun Amenemope-meryamun.

Osokhor and Psinakhes, the two kings who, according to Manetho, followed Amenophthis, constitute a difficulty. It is impossible to guess with which Egyptian names these transcriptions correspond,[5] nor are there two kings who might remotely resemble Osokhor and Psinakhes and fit this place. Monuments,

---

[1] §vi, 8, 135–6 ( = §i, 45, v, 170).     [2] §vi, 24.

[3] §vi, 37, 105, nos. 413 and 414; 108, fig. 44.

[4] There is some doubt whether the first part of the second name is to be read Amenemnisu(t), 'Amun is a king', or Amenemsu(t), 'Amun is in the (Upper Egyptian) lily,' and objections can be raised against both interpretations.

[5] Osokhor strongly recalls Osorthon or Osorcho, the name of several kings of the Twenty-second and Twenty-third Dynasties; and it is not impossible that this name, of which the most correct Greek transcription would be *Osorchon, has by some mistake in a slightly different form been introduced into the Twenty-first Dynasty by the author of the excerpts from Manetho.

however, supply a king Nutekheperre-setepenamun Siamun-meryamun, and this Siamun, according to all the evidence, must have reigned at this time.[1]

Manetho's last king of the dynasty is another Psusennes, whom we can unhesitatingly equate with Titkheprure-setepenamun Psibkhaemne-meryamun, or Psusennes II. A hieratic graffito in the temple of Sethos I at Abydos[2] calls him 'King of Upper and Lower Egypt, Lord of the Two Lands Titkheperre, chosen of Amon-Re, King of the Gods, the High Priest of Amon-Re, King of the Gods, Son of Re, Lord of Appearances, the First One, Psusennes, who is at the head of the army', and again immediately below, 'High Priest of Amon-Re, King of the Gods, who sets the good laws of Egypt, the First One of the Pharaoh, Psusennes'. This king at the end of the Tanite dynasty bears the same name as the high priest, son of Pinudjem II, the last known descendant of Hrihor's dynasty of high priests at Thebes, and indeed there can hardly be any doubt that both names represent one and the same person. Psusennes, at first only high priest at Thebes, assumed sovereignty over the whole country on the death of a Tanite king, presumably Siamun, and moved his residence to Tanis and was therefore included by Manetho in his Twenty-first Dynasty. The title 'the First One of the Pharaoh' of the Abydos graffito is a remnant of his titulary from the time before he became king.

Manetho's total of 130 years for the whole dynasty bridges tolerably well the gap between the death of Ramesses XI (*c.* 1085 B.C.) and the accession of Sheshonq I, the founder of the Twenty-second Dynasty, placed generally at about 945 B.C.[3] Individually, however, Manetho's figures disagree with the scanty dates of the documents. For Nesbenebded no regnal dates are attested at all and nothing supports Manetho's attribution of nine years to Neferkare Amenemnisu. A Twenty-second Dynasty stela[4] speaks of 'the register of Pharaoh Psusennes, the great god, (in) year 19', meaning presumably the reign of Psusennes I, who receives forty-one years in Manetho. According to him Amenemope reigned only nine years, but a mummy-bandage of one of his contemporaries is dated to the 'year 49' of his reign.[5] The enigmatic Osokhor and Psinakhes are credited by Manetho with

[1] See above, p. 588.
[2] §vi, 16, 10; §vi, 38, pl. 21. Collated with the original.    [3] §vi, 41, 152.
[4] Dakhla stela, l. 11 (§vi, 19, 22, and pl. vi).
[5] §vi, 11, 78. With this high regnal year agrees the observation made on the king's mummy that he 'reached a considerable age', §vi, 18, 149.

six and nine years respectively; for Siamun whom the monuments seem to substitute for these two kings we know of a 'year 17'.[1]

The order of the kings as preserved in the extracts from Manetho's work does not seem to be quite correct.[2] An unknown priest of the Twenty-second Dynasty states[3] that his fifteenth ancestor lived 'at the time of King Amenemnisu', while the fourteenth lived under King Akheperre-setepena[mun] (i.e. Psusennes I) and the thirteenth and twelfth under King Psusennes, by whom he perhaps means Psusennes II. This clearly implies that the reign of Neferkare Amenemnisu preceded that of Psusennes I instead of following it, as recorded in Manetho's excerpts, and this earlier testimony is at least as good as, and probably more trustworthy than, that of Manetho.

Two of the Theban high priests claimed the title of king at some later stage of high priesthood. Pinudjem I, in the inscriptions on the front of the pylon of the Khons temple at Karnak which he entirely decorated, calls himself, almost throughout, only High Priest of Amun Pinudjem, son of Piankh, but he becomes 'Osiris King of Upper Egypt Pinudjem' on his coffin[4] usurped from Tuthmosis I. His son Menkheperre whenever he indicates his parentage calls himself the son of King Pinudjem-meryamum, enclosing his father's name in a cartouche,[5] a practice also followed by Pinudjem's other son Masahert.[6] There are inscriptions of various dates between year 1[7] and year 15[8] in which Pinudjem I is given merely the title of high priest; only one inscription refers to him as king in his lifetime, and that in year 8.[9] It seems almost certain that the regnal years mentioned in the records of the high priests of Amun who were contemporaries of the kings of the Twenty-first Dynasty refer to the reigns of the

---

[1] Sandstone block from Karnak, now at Cairo J. 36495 (§vi, 26, 53–4, and *Rec. trav.* 30, 87); graffito in a quarry near Abydos (§vi, 13, 286; §i, 25, 295; §i, 45, 78).

[2] §vi, 23, 211.

[3] Berlin relief 23673; §vi, 1, pl. 2a.

[4] §vi, 10, no. 61025 (pp. 51, 53, 54, 55, 57, 60, not less than fourteen times).

[5] Stela of banishment (§vi, 4, pl. xxii); Cairo J. 36495, face A ( = §vi, 26); Cairo stela, Prov. no. 3. 12. 24. 2 (= § i, 25, 265, v); inscription at Bīga (§vi, 7, i, 161); inscription in Luxor temple (§v, 8, 702); etc.

[6] Hieratic inscription on the coffin of Amenophis I (§v, 8, 537), in an inscription at Karnak (§vi, 33, 133–4) and on his coffin (§vi, 10, 77 and 78).

[7] On a bandage of Queen Nodjme (§i, 49, 97).

[8] Hieratic inscription on the mummy of Ramesses II (§v, 8, 560 and fig. 18).

[9] Hieratic inscription on the mummy of Amosis (§v, 8, 534 and fig. 7). The same date on the mummy of Prince Siamun, but Pinudjem is not named (§v, 8, 538 and fig. 9).

Tanite pharaoh even if the high priest is given the title of king,[1] and therefore the dates from year 1 to 15 and that of year 8 would belong to two different Tanite pharaohs, perhaps to Psusennes I and Amenemope respectively. Pinudjem I's tenure of office would consequently have lasted at least $19 + 8$,[2] that is, 27 years. In his claim to a royal titulary Pinudjem went so far as to assume a special praenomen, Kheperkhare-setepenamun,[3] and a Horus-name (with less originality) Strong Bull appearing in Wast (i.e. Thebes)[4] which had served several famous occupants of the throne of the pharaohs.[5] Previously, however, he had favoured a different, less pretentious, Horus-name: Strong Bull, beloved of Amun.[6]

Pinudjem I's son Menkheperre seems to have made but a timid claim to kingship, since his name is found enclosed in a cartouche only rarely, and then preceded merely by the title of High Priest of Amun. They occur on leather braces which, at the time of the Twenty-first Dynasty, were placed on the shoulders of the mummies of priests.[7] To the ends of the braces were attached tabs with embossed inscriptions and figures of the high priest of the time. In one instance[8] Menkheperre is shown with a bull's tail attached to his belt, and in another with, apparently, a uraeus on his forehead, both the bull's tail and the uraeus being common royal insignia.[9] Two examples of his name in a cartouche are found in the funerary papyrus of his daughter, Gasoshen,[10] and his name and the title of high priest are sometimes stamped in cartouches on bricks mainly from El-Ḥība in Middle Egypt; on some his name is coupled with that of his wife Esemkhebe, also in a cartouche.[11] In one case a second cartouche encloses only the

---

[1] See especially §1, 1, 98 and note 530.

[2] 19 years being the minimum length of the reign of Psusennes I, see above, p. 646, n. 4.

[3] §1, 25, 250–2.    [4] §1, 25, 250, xxiv ( = §vi, 28, 210).

[5] Tuthmosis III, Amenophis II, Sethos I and Ramesses IX.

[6] §1, 25, 246, xi, d.

[7] For the only account and discussion of this category of objects, see §vi, 43, 275–7.

[8] §vi, 9, 22, from mummy no. 11, the other pair §vi, 9, 27 (mummy no. 64). The braces are now in the Cairo Museum and have been collated. See also §1, 25, 268, xx.

[9] Two braces stated by Daressy to bear the name of Menkheperre without a cartouche (§vi, 9, 31, no. 109, and 32, no. 115) could not be found in the Cairo Museum so that it is doubtful whether they were of this particular type; nor was it possible to find the braces on which Menkheperre's son Pinudjem II provided his father's name with a cartouche (§vi, 9, 31, no. 113); this may be a misreading.

[10] §vi, 40, pls. i and lxv, against two occurrences without cartouche (loc. cit. pl. i, title, and pl. ii, line 2).    [11] §vi, 42, pl. xxiii, 6 and 7.

title of King of Upper and Lower Egypt, the one clear occurrence of his claim to be king.[1]

The pretensions of Pinudjem I and Menkheperre to kingship led their contemporaries, the Tanite kings Psusennes I and Amenemope, to adopt the title of High Priest of Amun. Amenemope does so only once,[2] but Psusennes employs the title almost as often as not, either outside his cartouche, immediately after the title of King of Upper and Lower Egypt[3] and of Son of Re, Lord of Appearances,[4] or within it prefixed to the name Psusennes;[5] once it occupies the whole of his second cartouche.[6] According to Egyptian belief the sole intermediary between man and god was the pharaoh; the priest acted only on his behalf and in his stead. The pharaoh could therefore also claim the function and title of High Priest of Amun, but no king had ever done so previously; Psusennes I and Amenemope clearly did so to assert their supremacy over Thebes.

Despite these rival claims relations between the two halves of the country continued to be good, and even friendly, throughout the Twenty-first Dynasty, as indeed they had been at the time of Wenamun's journey. The religious impact of Thebes on Tanis was now very strong; the god Setekh and the Asiatic goddess Anath, in fashion in Tanis under the Nineteenth Dynasty, were completely eliminated and the Theban triad of Amun, Mut and Khons were the principal, if not the only, deities of the northern capital. With this Theban religious supremacy agrees the fact that the names of all Nesbenebded's successors are of Theban origin or display Theban associations: Amenemnisu means 'Amun is (now) the king', Psusennes (Psibkhaemne) is 'the star that has appeared at Ne (i.e. Thebes)', Amenemope is an old name 'Amun is in Ope (i.e. Luxor)', and Siamun is 'son of Amun'.

The good relations between Tanis and Thebes were fostered by princesses sent from Tanis to become the wives of the high priests. At the time of Pinudjem I two women thus played a considerable part at Thebes, and appear together in Pinudjem's company in reliefs. They are Henttowy and Makare.[7]

[1] §vi, 42, pl. xxiii, 5.
[2] On a statuette of Horus of lapis-lazuli from the tomb of prince Hornakhte at Tanis, §vi, 36, 30–1 and fig. 21.
[3] §vi, 37, 16, fig. 4; 17, fig. 5; 98, fig. 39; 149, fig. 54.
[4] §vi, 37, 149, fig. 54.
[5] §vi, 37, 98, figs. 39 and 40; 99, fig. 41; 101, fig. 42; 137, fig. 52; 152, figs. 56 and 57; 170, fig. 63.          [6] §vi, 37, 16, fig. 4.
[7] §iv, 7, 250a = §i, 34, iii, 56 = §vi, 7, 218 (Karnak, temple of Khons); §vi, 15, 32, lii (Luxor temple).

Henttowy's mummy, coffin and funerary papyrus have survived and their inscriptions supply a number of titles which give some information about her origin and position. Her name, always preceded by the title of Mistress of the Two Lands, is almost without exception[1] accompanied by the epithet Adoratrice of Hathor, so much so that this is even included in the cartouche with her name. The cartouche she owes to the fact that she was the 'beloved king's daughter of his body' and according to her papyrus 'born of king's wife Tentamun'.[2] This Tentamun is clearly the wife of Nesbenebded known from Wenamun's account of his voyage. At Thebes, Henttowy became the First Great One of the Concubines of Amon-Re,[3] which was the regular title of the wives of the high priests. Her husband is nowhere expressly named, but it seems that it must have been Piankh. She was therefore the mother of Pinudjem I, with whom she appears represented in reliefs.[4] That she is not infrequently called King's Mother[5] is not surprising since her son Pinudjem eventually claimed the throne. It is, however, probably not quite appropriate if she is given also the title of King's Wife or even First and Great King's Wife of His Majesty[6] for her husband Piankh is not known ever to have assumed the title of king. She must have married very young for even at her death during the high priesthood of her son she was still a young adult.[7]

The princess Mistress of the Two Lands Makare[8] was still a child when depicted with Henttowy and Pinudjem. Her name is invariably enclosed in a cartouche, for by her origin she too was the 'beloved king's daughter of his body', her father evidently being the Pharaoh Nesbenebded. At Thebes her rank was that of God's Adoratrice and God's Wife of Amun[9] representing for the cult the earthly spouse of the supreme god, as many queens and princesses had done before her from the beginning of the New

---

[1] §vi, 15, 32, lii; §vi, 37, 99, fig. 41; §vi, 31, iii, pl. 16.

[2] §vi, 31, iii, pls. 13, 16, 17.

[3] On a gold plate found on her mummy, Cairo Cat. 61090; §1, 49, 102. Also §vi, 37, 99, fig. 41.

[4] Pinudjem's mother was named in a graffito at Luxor (§vi, 12, 185). Of her name Daressy saw only the initial $H$, but a careful examination revealed fairly certain traces of $Hnwt$.... [See, however, M. L. Bierbrier, *J.N.E.S.* 32 (1973), 311. (Ed.)]

[5] For example on her coffin, §vi, 10, no. 61026 (p. 65, three times), besides 'mother of the high priest of Amun', §vi, 31, iii, pl. 19.

[6] §vi, 10, 65.         [7] §1, 49, 104.

[8] Gardiner (§vi, 20, 48) has justified this previous reading of the name against Kamare of Naville and Sethe.

[9] Often on her coffin (§vi, 10, 82–95) and in her funerary papyrus §vi, 40, vol. i.

Kingdom.[1] On her coffin, however, she is twice given[2] the title of Great King's Wife so that, unless it is an oversight, she must eventually have married, and it is difficult to see who her husband could have been but one of the high priests of Amun who claimed the title of king. It is now generally accepted[3] that her husband was Pinudjem I. She died during the high priesthood of Pinudjem's son and second successor Menkheperre, whose name is embossed on the leather pendants found on Makare's mummy.[4] Her marriage with Pinudjem satisfactorily explains the occasional titles of Pinudjem's mother Henttowy as Mother of Great King's Wife and Mother of God's Adoratrice of Amun;[5] they refer to Makare whose mother-in-law (as well as elder sister) she was.

A golden bowl from the tomb of Psusennes I at Tanis bears, besides his name, the name of a 'king's daughter Esemkhebe'. The name is enclosed in a cartouche, and the girl was undoubtedly his daughter.[6] This princess also married the high-priest Pinudjem I with whom her name occurs on bricks of the town-wall at El-Hība;[7] it also appears later with the name of the high priest Menkheperre who is clearly her son.[8] One of Menkheperre's daughters was called Esemkhebe after her grandmother.[9]

From Pinudjem I onwards the high priests were, therefore, through their mothers, descendants of Tanite kings. Pinudjem II, though he was a son of the high priest Menkheperre and lived in the reign of the king Amenemope, assumed the honorific title of Son of Psusennes or Son of King Psusennes—beloved of Amun. This is proved beyond any doubt by objects found on mummies of some priests buried in a common hiding place at Deir el-Bahri.

[1] § vi, 44, 5–8.

[2] § vi, 10, 88 and 94.

[3] Following § v, 8, 698 and § vi, 40, 1, 7. This view is also criticized in § vi, 21, 68–9, but no satisfactory solution is offered.

[4] § i, 49, 100 (then illegible, but since cleaned). [Recent examination has shown that a mummy buried with her was that of a baboon and not that of a child, as was formerly supposed (see J. E. Harris and Kent R. Weeks, *X-Raying the Pharaohs*, London, 1973, 174–5). (Ed.)]

[5] § vi, 10, 65; § vi, 31, iii, pls. 12, 19, 20.

[6] Bowl no. 403 in § vi, 37, 101, fig. 42.

[7] § i, 34, ii, 45, nos. 1 ( = § iv, 7, iii, 251 *h*) and 2.

[8] § i, 34, ii, 45, nos. 3–5. Lepsius observed (*loc. cit.*, 46) that Menkheperre's bricks lay over those of Pinudjem and were therefore posterior.

[9] It is to this Esemkhebe, daughter of Menkheperre, that the two coffins found in the *cachette royale* belonged (§ vi, 10, no. 61030, p. 125; no. 61031, p. 147); also the mummy (§ i, 49, no. 61093), and probably the heart scarab, § vi, 17.

No less than five of them[1] were provided with leather braces and pendants on some of which Pinudjem bears one of these two titles, while on others he is qualified as 'son of Menkheperre'. The king Psusennes in question can of course only be Psusennes I, since the second king of this name was Pinudjem II's own son, later both high priest and king.

The building activity of the high priests was but small, even if we discount the ravages of time, and this is surely an indication of the relative poverty of the Theban priestly state. Pinudjem I may have finished the pylon of the temple of Khons begun by his grandfather Hrihor; at all events he covered its outer and inner face with his own reliefs.[2] It is not certain that he built the chapel of Osiris-Nebankh at Karnak, though his reliefs and names are seen above one of its doors,[3] because elsewhere he seems only to have placed his name on the monuments already in existence.[4] A contemporary inscription, however, mentions that he 'brought the ram-headed sphinxes to the House of Amun'.[5] The activity of Masahert and Pinudjem II was even more insignificant.[6]

Menkheperre built 'a very great brick wall north of Karnak from the hall ($d\jmath d\jmath$) of Amun to the northern treasury of the House of Amun'[7] and bricks stamped with his name were found at Karnak.[8] The most conspicuous achievement of Pinudjem I and Menkheperre, was, however, a massive town-wall near the modern village of El-Hība in Middle Egypt on the east bank of the Nile; as a result its name was changed from Pohe ('[Military] Camp') to Dehne-wer-nakhte ('Crag, great of strength'), or Teudjoy ('Their wall') as it was henceforth also called. This latter name perhaps refers to the builders, the two high priests.[9] Menkheperre was also the builder of a watch-tower a little south

---

[1] Mummy no. 81 (§ vi, 9, 28), 113 (*loc. cit.* 31), 119 (*loc. cit.* 32), 120 (*loc. cit.* 32) and 127 (*loc. cit.* 33, where 'Pinudjem-meryamun' is Daressy's misreading for 'Psibkhaemne-meryamun' as correctly reproduced in § vi, 11, 76).

[2] References in § i, 45, ii, 77–9.   [3] § vi, 28, 210.

[4] So at Karnak in the temple of Amun (§ i, 45, ii, 9) and of Mut (§ i, 45, ii, 91, (10)), at Luxor (§ i, 45, ii, 102 (29)) and at Medīnet Habu (§ i, 45, ii, 167, (1)–(2); 171, (72)–(75); 192).

[5] § vi, 7, ii, 264 = § iv, 7, iii, 249 f.

[6] For Masahert at Karnak see § vi, 33, 133–4; for Pinudjem II, § vi, 39.

[7] Cairo stela Prov. no. 3. 12. 24. 2, mentioned by Legrain in *Arch. Report of the Egypt Exploration Fund for 1906–1907*, pp. 21–2. A restoration text of his at Luxor in § v, 8, 702.

[8] § vi, 14, 63–4.

[9] For the stamped bricks of the site, see above p. 648, n. 11; p. 649, n. 1; p. 651, nn. 7 and 8, and their bibliography § i, 45, iv, 124; on the names of the fortress, see § vi, 45, 1–4.

of El-Hība, near the modern village of Nazlat esh-Shurāfa.[1] The fortress of El-Hība evidently marked the extent of the territory of the Theban high priests in the north and was intended to protect the frontier. Wenamun's report on his journey is said to have been found here; if this is correct, he composed it as soon as he reached Theban territory.

It seems that the real purpose of this stronghold was to protect Upper Egypt not against the Delta, with which relations were constantly friendly, but against the growing power of local chiefs of Libyan mercenaries settled at Heracleopolis on the opposite (west) bank some thirty-two kilometres to the north.[2] These were the real rivals and it was against them that the high priests proclaimed their military power by the title Great Commander of the Army of Upper and Lower Egypt, or of the Whole Land.[3] Hrihor and Piankh claimed this position against the rebellious viceroy of Ethiopia, but the danger from the south must have completely disappeared by the time of their successors. A group of fragmentary letters discovered at the site of El-Hība confirms that the fortress was the residence of Menkheperre and Esemkhebe. Both are named in the letters[4] and one papyrus is a petition submitted to the local god 'Amun of Pohe' for the recovery from an illness of Masahert, in all probability the high priest of Amun. The petitioner calls Masahert his brother, and is therefore Menkheperre, his brother and probable successor in the high priesthood.[5]

To turn now to the building activities of the Tanite kings, this was equally insignificant outside their place of residence. The inscription already mentioned,[6] according to which Nesbenebded quarried stone near Gebelein for a building at Thebes, is the only witness to the existence of a construction by a Twenty-first Dynasty king in Upper Egypt. Psusennes and Amenemope built a small temple to Isis east of Cheops's pyramid at Giza[7] and one single block is all that has survived of Amenemope's work at Memphis.[8] More extensive are the remains of a temple built at Memphis by Siamun.[9]

---

[1] §vi, 6, 223, iv; §vi, 46, 76 ff.       [2] §vi, 46, 82 ff.

[3] Pinudjem I: §vi, 15, 32, liii; Masahert: §vi, 10, 67, 68, 70, 74, 80; Menkheperre: §vi, 4, pl. 22; Nesbenebded: §vi, 25, pl. xiii; Pinudjem II: §vi, 10, 96; Psusennes II: §vi, 38, pl. 21 ('first officer who is at the head of the armies').

[4] Menkheperre in the unpublished Pap. Berlin 8527, Esemkhebe in Pap. Strassburg no. 22, 1 (§vi, 45, 15).

[5] Pap. Strassburg no. 21 (§vi, 45, pls. v–vi, and pp. 13–14).

[6] See above, p. 645, n. 1.       [7] Bibliography in §1, 45, iii, 5.

[8] §vi, 22, 204–5.       [9] Bibliography in §1, 45, iii, 225.

At their residence at Tanis Psusennes I and Siamun seem to have conducted building operations on a considerable scale, though its exact extent is difficult to judge owing to the utter destruction of the site. The former built a massive brick wall around the great temple, now of Amon-Re, reducing considerably the area of the original sacred precinct as defined by the walls of Ramesses II.[1] Siamun's wall encircled the smaller temple, originally devoted to the Asiatic goddess Anath.[2] Only isolated blocks survive of the temple walls erected by the two kings; enough, however, to show that the material used had been taken from the earlier constructions of Ramesses II. Psusennes I caused the reliefs and inscriptions of the granite blocks of his predecessor to be overlaid with plaster and cut his own decoration in the new surface. In this way the walls, though built of granite, assumed the appearance of white limestone.[3]

In a corner between the great temple and the brick wall lay the tomb of Psusennes, a rectangular limestone construction sunk into the ground.[4] It contained two burial chambers lined with granite blocks, one being for the king himself and the other for his queen, Mutnodjme. The stone sarcophagi had been lowered into the chambers before the limestone slabs forming the ceiling had been placed in position—this sequence was evident because the shaft to the antechamber was too narrow for the passage of the sarcophagi. Later one of Psusennes's successors removed the mummy and funerary equipment of the queen and substituted for them the mummy and equipment of king Amenemope, these having been transferred from an adjacent separate tomb. The burial site of Psusennes I was found intact by P. Montet in 1940. Both the external red granite sarcophagus and the internal one of black granite had been usurped, the first having belonged originally to King Merneptah of the Nineteenth Dynasty and the second to an unknown owner—a proof of the scarcity of good hard stone in the Delta. Like the construction of the tomb itself, which is in sharp contrast to the rock-hewn corridor tombs of the New Kingdom kings at Thebes, the funerary equipment of Psusennes I differs completely from that which could be expected at Thebes, an intact example of which was preserved in the tomb of Tutankhamun. The jewellery of the mummy of Psusennes I is approximately of the same character, but the rest of the equipment

---

[1] §vi, 35, 21–3; §vi, 37, 10–14.    [2] §vi, 35, 25–7.

[3] §vi, 35, 31–2. More details on the traces of cartouches of Psusennes I in §vi, 37, 14–18.

[4] For the following, see §vi, 37, *passim*.

is almost entirely restricted to gold and silver vessels of simple and graceful form.  Perishable material of any kind was carefully avoided, evidently because experience had taught the Egyptians that it would not long resist the damp climate of the Delta. This is an interesting example of the extent to which religious custom could be modified and adapted to suit the natural conditions of the country.

The royal tombs at Thebes had all been pillaged by this time and the high priests of Amun, in whose domain the tombs lay, felt it their duty to undertake the reburial of the desecrated mummies of their pharaonic predecessors.  Hieratic dockets jotted on the coffins and on the linen wrappings of some of these kings show that Hrihor and Pinudjem I gave orders at various times for the re-burial of royal mummies to protect them against further attacks by robbers.[1]  In so doing they clearly did not meet with much success and pillaging continued until Pinudjem II, in the year 5 of Siamun, removed the mummies of the kings and some of the members of their families from their resting places and deposited them, with such of their funerary equipment as still remained, in the tomb of his wife Neskhons.  For her burial an old tomb of Queen Inhapy had been chosen, lying below the cliffs in a small valley south of Deir el-Bahri. The last mummies, those of Ramesses I, Sethos I and Ramesses II, were added in the year 10 of Siamun, and in the same year the mummy of Pinudjem II himself was taken to the tomb of his wife.[2]  From that time onwards the mummies of the high priest, his wife, and all the kings, lay undisturbed until the tomb was discovered by the modern inhabitants of the village of El-Qurna.  In 1881 all the mummies and their equipment were transferred to the Cairo Museum.[3]

Of the high priests of the Twenty-first Dynasty apart from Pinudjem II the royal cachette contained only the mummy and coffin of Masahert.[4]  All the others were missing, though the coffin of Pinudjem I usurped from Tuthmosis I,[5] and the mummies and coffins of Nodjme,[6] Henttowy,[7] and Makare,[8] as well as those of Neskhons, were present.  Since no objects which might have formed part of the funerary equipment of the missing high

---

[1] §v, 8, 530 ff.
[2] On the chronology of these burials, see §vi, 5.
[3] The whole find is described in detail in §v, 8.
[4] Mummy: §i, 49, no. 61092; coffin: §vi, 10, no. 61027.
[5] §vi, 10, no. 61025.
[6] Mummy: §i, 49, no. 61087; coffin: §vi, 10, no. 61024.
[7] Mummy: §i, 49, no. 61090; coffin: §vi, 10, no. 61026.
[8] Mummy: §i, 49, no. 61088; coffin: §vi, 10, no. 61028.

priests have ever come to light, it is virtually certain that their tombs still lie undisturbed in cracks in the rocks of some out of the way parts of the Theban mountain, these well-hidden places having been chosen in preference to the spacious decorated tombs in a well-known and frequently visited part of the necropolis such as the Valley of the Kings and the Valley of the Queens.

Little is known of the relations between Egypt and the outside world during the Twenty-first Dynasty. No allusion is made to hostilities in the south between Ethiopia and the sacerdotal state after the time of Piankh. In the north Nesbenebded maintained friendly trade relations with Palestinian and Syrian coastal towns during the lifetime of Ramesses XI, as Wenamun's report clearly shows, and timber from Lebanon through Byblos was imported even by the Theban state. There are no reasons for supposing that this state of affairs changed later in the dynasty. Syria and Palestine were politically independent, a fact which is confirmed by the biblical tradition of the rise of the kingdom of Israel. An unnamed pharaoh of the Twenty-first Dynasty, however, gave asylum to Hadad, the young prince of Edom, when King David seized his country,[1] and later gave him in marriage to the sister of his queen.[2] Hadad's son Genubath was brought up at the court with the pharaoh's sons. After David's death and in spite of the pharaoh's objections Hadad returned to his own country as Solomon's bitter enemy. The identity of the pharaoh is uncertain.

It is equally uncertain which king of the Twenty-first Dynasty was on such friendly terms with Solomon that he sent his daughter to Jerusalem to become one of Solomon's wives.[3] Perhaps, however, there is some clue to the identity of the Egyptian king in the dowry which the princess brought to Solomon. It was the Palestinian town of Gezer which the pharaoh took by assault, burnt down and gave to his daughter.[4] The gift was very precious, for the Israelites had never succeeded in dislodging the Canaanites from the town, and this remained a thorn in their flesh. A fragment of a relief found at Tanis shows king Siamun smiting an enemy kneeling before him.[5] This, indeed, is the traditional scene in which even the least warlike Egyptian king might be repre-

---

[1] I Kings xi. 14–22.

[2] The queen's name Takhpenes, however, is (according to §vi, 23, 211–16) to be emended into Takhemnes, which is but a transcription of the Egyptian title 'the King's wife' (*t3 ḥmt-nsw*) and not a proper name.

[3] I Kings iii. 1.                                        [4] I Kings ix. 16.

[5] §vi, 34, 196, fig. 58, and photograph in P. Montet, *La nécropole royale de Tanis* I (Paris, 1947), pl. ix, A.

sented, but in this particular case the enemy seems to be holding in his hand, as the characteristic weapon of his people, a double-axe.[1] Such an axe is of Aegean origin, but was adopted by the 'Peoples of the Sea' who after their defeat by Ramesses III settled in Palestine. It seems therefore that the relief commemorates a real invasion by the Egyptians in this direction and Gezer would be an obvious target. Solomon's father-in-law would, if this were the case, be Siamun.

While everything shows that the relations between the two halves of Egypt were friendly and peaceful, there is at least one event which points to internal strife within the Theban state, though its exact nature is obscure owing to the veiled style of the inscription which has preserved its record.[2] When Menkheperre, after the death of the high priest Masahert, his brother, arrived in Thebes from the north—presumably from his residence in the fortress of El-Hība—he was hailed by the population and Amon-Re himself as the new high priest. He found that some people had been banished to the oasis, that is, the oasis of El-Khārga, which even in modern times is the place of banishment for political prisoners, and he obtained from Amon-Re their release and the assurance that no one would ever be sent there again. There can be hardly any doubt that the banished men were members of an opposition party. The incident is also an example of the current practice in Thebes of submitting all decisions of any consequence to the god, that is to the statue of Amon-Re carried in a procession, an oracular decision of the deity being obtained. In this way the fiction was upheld that the god himself ruled the Theban state.

[1] §VI, 34, 196.
[2] Stela Louvre C 256 ('Stela of the banishment'), published §VI, 3, pl. XXII and §VI, 4, pl. XXII; translation in §I, 3, IV, sect. 652 f.

# CHAPTER XXXVI

## THE END OF MYCENAEAN CIVILIZATION AND THE DARK AGE

## (a) THE ARCHAEOLOGICAL BACKGROUND

### I. THE END OF THE MYCENAEAN WORLD

#### (a) DISASTER AND PARTIAL RECOVERY

THE evidence of archaeology shows that in the period known as Late Helladic IIIb, roughly the thirteenth century B.C., there was a remarkable material uniformity throughout the Mycenaean world. As a man travelled from district to district, each centred on its palace, he would find the same kind of architecture and would use the same kind of pottery, apart from some minor local variations; he would find that the men favoured similar weapons, and that the women used the same variety of ornaments to adorn their dress. He would notice other general tendencies: the same types of tomb for burial, inhumation the general custom, with many burials in each family tomb. The little terracotta 'goddess' figurines would suggest some conformity in worship as well. He would find the standard of life reasonably high, and many districts fairly thickly populated.

This Mycenaean world was one of considerable extent: it included the whole Peloponnese, though the western and north-western areas, as also the islands to the west, were not strongly settled; the area from the isthmus of Corinth to the mountains of Phocis; much of Thessaly; all the islands of the central and south Aegean with the exception of Crete, which though possibly under Mycenaean sway nevertheless retained its own characteristics (see below, pp. 675 ff.); even a settlement at Miletus on the coast of Asia Minor. The whole area is to be identified with that kingdom of Ahhiyawa which was so well known to the Hittites. It would then have been a powerful state, embracing lesser kingdoms, whose rulers acknowledged a single overlord. Enjoying wide-spread overseas connexions, it prospered, apparently secure.

* An original version of this chapter was published as fascicle 13 in 1962; the present chapter includes revisions made in 1970 and 1972.

The events of the second half of the thirteenth century show the weakening of the foundations of this security, and perhaps indicate that the foundations themselves were not very strong. A campaign in Asia Minor[1] (during which it is probable that Troy was overthrown), whether a success or not, diminished the military resources of the Mycenaeans. At home, Mycenae itself was attacked, and the defenders were unable to prevent serious damage being done to the outer city.[2] The ensuing alarm resulted in the strengthening of Mycenae's fortifications,[3] and in the construction of a defensive wall at the isthmus of Corinth.[4]

There was indeed good cause for alarm, for the archaeological record reveals, at about the end of the century, a series of catastrophes in the central and southern mainland of Greece, affecting the heart of the Mycenaean world. Zygouries[5] in Corinthia, Mycenae[6] and Tiryns[7] in the Argolid, Pylus[8] and probably other sites in southern Peloponnese—all these suffered total or partial destruction. Crisa[9] in Phocis and Gla[10] in Boeotia as well may have been destroyed at this time. Many settlements were abandoned throughout the southern mainland. Only the islands of the Aegean, and probably Thessaly, remained unaffected.

The principal results of these catastrophes were the break-up of the central political power, and a flight from the affected areas to districts of greater security. Archaeological evidence of the first of these results is to be found in a change of the style of pottery, and in the loss of its uniformity. The new style which appears, Late Helladic IIIc (L.H. IIIc), is a multiple style— there are many regional variations. Evidence of the second is seen in the peopling of districts not previously much favoured by the Mycenaeans; many cemeteries in Achaea[11] and Cephallenia[12] began to be used only at the beginning of L.H. IIIc; the great cemetery of Perati,[13] on the east coast of Attica, is of similar date and contrasts with the insignificance of our evidence for L.H. IIIc in western Attica;[14] the settlement of Lefkandi[15] in Euboea was at its most flourishing in the twelfth century. There are signs of a move to Crete[16] very early in L.H. IIIc. Finally, there was a migration to the east Mediterranean at this time: the pottery of those who settled in the ruins of the Hittite town of Tarsus[17] in Cilicia is a blend of L.H. IIIb and L.H. IIIc; but above all, there was a massive and probably aggressive move to Cyprus, from the

[1] §I, 29.    [2] §I, 59.    [3] A, 35.    [4] §I, 9.    [5] §I, 5.
[6] §I, 50.    [7] §I, 54.    [8] A, 6.    [9] §I, 37.    [10] §I, 52.
[11] §I, 55.    [12] §I, 39.    [13] §I, 30; A, 25.    [14] §I, 8.    [15] A, 39.
[16] A, 38.    [17] §I, 25.

evidence of Enkomi,[1] Sinda[2] and Kition,[3] all of which suffered some destruction at this time, and other sites. Other places of refuge may have been sought, within existing Mycenaean communities, but of such nothing is known.

The events recorded may be used to shed some light on the causes of disaster. On the one hand there is destruction in Phocis, Boeotia, Corinthia, the Argolid, coastal Achaea and Messenia, and clear signs of dismay in Athens; on the other hand there is subsequent migration to Achaea and Cephallenia, probably to Crete and certainly to the east Mediterranean, and a strong concentration in east Attica and in Euboea. With this goes the negative evidence of peaceful continuity in the islands of the Aegean, at Miletus,[4] and probably also in Thessaly: no catastrophe had yet touched these districts. It seems unlikely that internal upheaval was responsible for the disasters, because of their approximate contemporaneity and widespread extent, and because of the consequent complete desertion of many sites and general depopulation. There is much to attract in the theory of natural causes, especially in view of recently published evidence from Ugarit,[5] and a case has been made for a change of climate, leading to prolonged drought and all the ills consequent on this,[6] but as yet the archaeological material from the Mycenaean world does not seem to support it. The third, and perhaps the most likely, explanation (but not necessarily ruling out the other two as contributory factors) is that of invasion from outside, and the pattern of evidence, bearing in mind which areas suffered, which were untouched, and whither the refugees fled, strongly suggests that it came overland, starting from the mountainous district of north-west Greece, then either moving with a single impetus through central Greece and right on down to the southernmost part of the Peloponnese, or to be visualized as a twofold attack, the one affecting Phocis and Boeotia only, the other directed towards the Peloponnese.

If such an invasion took place, there might seem no objection to an immediate link with later tradition, in its equation, at least so far as concerns the Peloponnese, with that of the Dorians.

There should in this case, however, be evidence not only of invasion but also of invaders. Some new element should appear somewhere in the south mainland of Greece, whether of architecture, pottery, burial custom, dress ornament, weapons, or even religious observance. At present the archaeologist can point to two artefacts only as introduced at about this time—the cut-and-

| | | |
|---|---|---|
| [1] A, 20. | [2] A, 22. | [3] A, 26. |
| [4] §1, 61. | [5] A, 42. | [6] A, 8. |

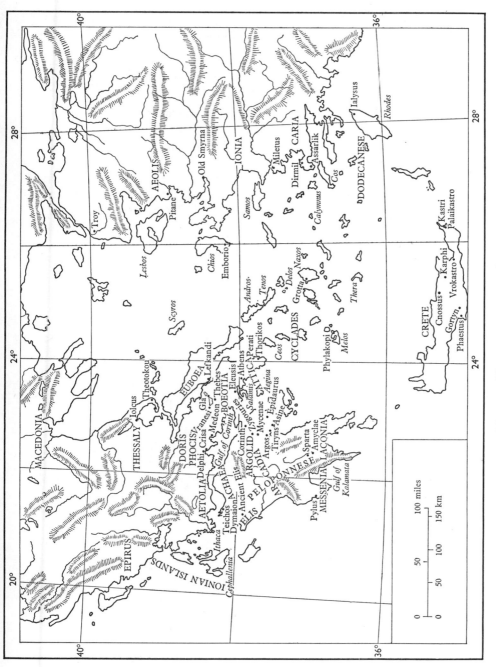

Map. 12. The Aegean area and Crete.

thrust sword (Naue II type) and the violin-bow fibula;[1] the context of both, however, shows that they were used by Mycenaeans and not by invaders. It might be argued that some one of the variations of the new pottery style should belong to newcomers, and this is not impossible, though it is not provable, as in each district L.H. IIIc pottery seems to be clearly linked at the outset with the preceding style. It is true that the tombs of Cephallenia have individual characteristics, and that a native ware appears alongside the Mycenaean vases, at least the latter point indicating a mixture of population; but it would be unsafe to conclude that any invaders were represented here.

If it is true that the invaders moved steadily southwards through the Peloponnese, it would be reasonable to suppose that they settled in Laconia and Messenia. In both areas, excavation and surface investigation indicate the abandonment of many sites at or before the end of L.H. IIIb, but the situation following on this is, precisely in these areas, obscure.[2] A settlement of newcomers perhaps is not out of the question, though the finds at Amyclae[3] prove the continuance of connexions with the Argolid, and the general archaeological picture is unfavourable to such a settlement.

Even if invaders did not occupy the southern Peloponnese, might they not have occupied more northerly districts? For Arcadia and Elis the evidence is far too slender for any judgement to be made, but it is clear that the inhabitants of the Argolid and Corinthia showed no aberration from the previous Mycenaean way of life, and kept in contact with the refugees of Achaea, with Attica, and with the unaffected areas of the Aegean. It is particularly notable that the finest manifestation of L.H. IIIc pottery, the Close Style, was created in the Argolid.[4] Although the wide diffusion of this pottery does not signify any political prominence, its existence suggests some measure of recovery from disaster, even though the simpler Granary class pottery accompanied it, and in time outlived it.

It may be supposed, then, that the north Peloponnese, including of course Achaea, survived disaster and remained fully Mycenaean in character; and a similar conclusion is possible for Attica, for what is known of Boeotia, and probably for some of Thessaly. The catastrophes had nevertheless produced weakening and loss of cohesion, and the centre of Mycenaean civilization now shifts to the Aegean.

[1] See Plate 164(a)–(b).    [2] §1, 40 (Messenia); §1, 60 (Laconia).
[3] §1, 56.    [4] See Plate 165.

It was already evident from earlier excavation that the islands of the Dodecanese[1] continued to thrive. L.H. IIIc pottery was of excellent quality, and the 'octopus' stirrup jars[2] (imitated from Cretan originals, but developing strong local characteristics) had a wider distribution than any other Mycenaean vase shape—north to Aeolis at Pitane, across the Aegean to Attica and the Peloponnese, west to south Italy, east to Tarsus. Also, the objects other than pottery were of high quality, and indicated contacts with the east Mediterranean.

Recent discoveries have now shown that the island of Naxos[3] was no less thriving and had close contacts with the Dodecanese. Furthermore, the settlement of Perati in Attica, on the east coast and relatively isolated from the western area, was equally prosperous, and had close links with Naxos, and through it with the Dodecanese; and once again, objects have been found proving contact with the east Mediterranean, including Egypt. This site, to judge from its pottery, also maintained close communication with the Argolid, but it looked rather to the Aegean than to the mainland, an interesting additional proof of which is the occasional practice of cremation, associated with inhumations in chamber tombs, paralleled only on Rhodes and Cos at this time.

So in the early stages of L.H. IIIc Mycenaean civilization persisted over much of the area it had formerly occupied. In the south Peloponnese it virtually disappeared; the north Peloponnese, Attica and Boeotia survived though shaken, and there was an extension, though of a refugee nature, to Achaea and Cephallenia; there is no sign of a break yet in Thessaly, though the position is not clear, and the district could have been partially isolated from the south; the central Aegean pursued its life untouched by the calamities of the mainland, and it may be at this time that a community of Mycenaeans settled at Emborio on Chios, an island previously outside the Mycenaean sphere.[4]

### (b) FINAL DISASTER

The earlier stage of the L.H. IIIc period was one of partial recovery after disaster: the late stage, a complex one, saw the final disintegration of Mycenaean civilization, marked in certain areas by the survival of Mycenaean settlements until their total or partial desertion, whether as a result of destruction or for some other

---

[1] §1, 31 and 38 (Ialysus); A, 33 (Cos).
[2] See Plate 166(b).  [3] §1, 14; A, 54.
[4] Grateful acknowledgement is made to the Managing Committee of the British School at Athens and to Mr M. S. F. Hood for permission to include this statement.

reason, and in central mainland Greece by the introduction of new factors which, even though in some aspects based on the old, may be said to constitute the beginning of the Dark Age. The sequence of events is extremely unclear, and it will be best to take the central mainland area first, where the later stage may be said to be inaugurated by a final destruction at Mycenae[1]—though still not involving any total desertion.

The pottery current at the time of this destruction had already lost much of the earlier panache, and its decoration was becoming increasingly simple. From it, and exhibiting signs of further decline, there shortly arose the style known as sub-Mycenaean.[2] The principal area of its distribution[3] included the communities of the Argolid, the sites of Ancient Elis, Corinth, Athens and Thebes, a cemetery on Salamis and, during the latter phase of the style, Lefkandi[4] in Euboea.

From it in turn developed the Protogeometric style of Athens (see pp. 671 ff.), and the all-essential continuity was thereby provided. Its special importance, however, is that, except for a few chamber tombs at Argos,[5] it was associated with a change in burial customs over the whole area, the family chamber tombs being discontinued, giving way to single or double burials in slab-lined cist tombs or in pit graves, which on some sites overlay earlier Mycenaean settlements. There were other changes, too: the normal pattern of Mycenaean objects other than pottery deposited with the dead was replaced by a new one, of which arched fibulae and long dress pins[6] are the main elements; and where one can establish the fact, as at Argos,[7] the area of settlement did not coincide with that of the Mycenaeans.

These changes are substantial, and involved a virtual rejection of the Mycenaean way of life. It may be that they were the result of a decision on the part of the existing communities, or else of some previously submerged section of these (though one must remember that most of the communities will have been extremely small), since cist tombs and pit graves, though rare in the preceding century, were by no means unknown to the Mycenaean world.[8] An alternative explanation is that newcomers from the north-west imposed the changes on the Mycenaean survivors.[9] Possible arguments in favour of this are the prevalence of cist tombs in Epirus at this time and earlier, and the presence of a number of objects of northern origin, but there are still difficulties,

[1] §1, 58 and A, 35.    [2] See Plate 167.    [3] A, 44.
[4] A, 39.    [5] A, 19.    [6] See Plate 164 (c)–(d).
[7] A, 14 and 15.    [8] A, 1.    [9] A, 18.

and the intervening gap between Epirus and central mainland Greece remains to be closed.

Whether a local development or the result of migration, the new Dark Age culture was characteristic of this part of the Greek world, but we do not yet know whether it appeared simultaneously everywhere within it. At the close of this stage there came the fresh ceramic development of the Protogeometric style in Athens, but this, it should be noted, was closely preceded by a brief period during which the influence of Cyprus made itself temporarily felt in two ways, over the pottery and in the introduction to the Aegean of the technique of working in iron.

It is now possible to turn to the situation in other areas of the Mycenaean world, which involves serious problems of relative chronology, partly due to the difficulty of establishing cross-references either with central mainland Greece or between the remaining districts themselves, and partly due to the fact that in so many cases no continuity with the succeeding period is observable either in the few settlements or in the cemeteries.

The testimony of Cephallenia reveals that contact was maintained with the Argolid until the time of Mycenae's destruction, but thereafter one cannot be certain. Pottery of L.H. IIIc type was still current when the cemeteries—no settlement has yet been identified—fell into disuse, and it is not known what then happened on this island. Fortunately, continuity is demonstrable from the settlements of the adjoining island of Ithaca;[1] less fortunately, the evidence also shows that culturally this district seems to have been isolated from the rest of the Greek world for well over a century.

The whole of south and south-west Peloponnese has to go by default; the desertion of the countryside had been on so considerable a scale that what traces of habitation have so far been recovered are insufficient for even a provisional analysis of the situation. In Achaea the coastal citadel of Teichos Dymaion[2] was destroyed, and the site abandoned, at a time when L.H. IIIc pottery was in complete decadence (and it is likely that the few settlements of the opposite coastline of Aetolia were abandoned at this time or before), but it is not yet possible to say when this happened. The remainder of the Achaean sites are known from tomb evidence only, and these cemeteries also fell into disuse while their own peculiar but characteristic Mycenaean culture still prevailed. In this case, however, one or two features—especially the duck vases found on two of the sites—make it extremely likely that at least a few Mycenaean settlements survived until very shortly before the

[1] §1, 3, 4 and 27.          [2] A, 29.

end of this period and the emergence of the Protogeometric style in Athens.[1]

The position is equally unclear in northern Greece. The contents of a single tomb at Delphi suggest that the Mycenaean remnants kept contact with the central area up to some point during the final phase. In Thessaly, there is now evidence of a move of people from north-west Greece into the western inland regions;[2] in the north-east there was a movement from Macedonia,[3] probably refugees forced southwards by northern incursions into their own territory, but this is unlikely to have taken place before the Protogeometric period. Principal interest centres on the coast, and chiefly on the site of Iolcus.[4] As it was undoubtedly the Mycenaean capital of the region, its evidence will be of vital importance; so far, however, it is known only that it was abandoned at some undetermined date in L.H. IIIc, and that the earliest reoccupation consisted of no fewer than four Protogeometric levels, the pottery of which is said to have a strong local character and to develop from the preceding Mycenaean. One other site deserves mention, that of Theotokou,[5] on the Magnesian promontory and rather isolated from the rest of Thessaly, where the oldest of a group of three cist tombs contained objects which may precede the Protogeometric period by a short time—but there is no evidence of any earlier occupation here.

South of Thessaly, in Euboea, the history of the important settlement at Lefkandi[6] shows that after a time of revival in the mid-twelfth century, marked by the fantastic style of pottery then current,[7] there followed, as in other areas of the Mycenaean world, a progressive deterioration, and the site was eventually probably abandoned. This desertion is to be placed before the end of the stage under discussion, for the earliest subsequent material, that of a nearby cemetery apparently unconnected with the settlement, is clearly related, from its pottery and its objects of iron, to the concluding phase of the sub-Mycenaean culture in the central mainland area. This cemetery, it may be noted, was one of cist tombs, but the dead were burnt (a custom rapidly gaining ground at this time in Athens).

So one comes to the central Aegean group, extending from Perati in east Attica to the Dodecanese and to Miletus in west Asia Minor. This area, as has been seen, had become the main repository of Mycenaean culture after the disasters on the mainland, and it seems to have remained reasonably prosperous, with

[1] §I, 55.       [2] A, 47.       [3] §II, 14.       [4] §I, 51.
[5] §II, 21.      [6] A, 39.       [7] See Plate 168(a).

wide trade or other contacts, during much of L.H. III c. Then, however, some calamity overtook those who lived in the east. The settlement of Emborio[1] on Chios was destroyed, and the site not again occupied till *c.* 800 B.C. More important, the town of Miletus[2] was also destroyed; it is not known precisely when this occurred, but it must have been before the end of this period, as the earliest reoccupation pottery reflects the period of transition in Athens from sub-Mycenaean to Protogeometric. The date of this reoccupation is also of importance with regard to Greek tradition, as the new occupiers could have formed the spearhead of the Ionian migration.

No destruction is recorded of the Mycenaean settlement of Seraglio on Cos;[3] nevertheless, the abandonment of the chamber-tomb cemeteries both of this island, and of Rhodes and Calymnos, provides evidence of the end of Mycenaean civilization as such and, as in many other areas, no immediate successor has been identified. It may be suggested that the end came before the appearance of Cypriot-type pottery in the central mainland area as noted above.

Further west, the settlement of Phylakopi[4] on Melos was abandoned before the end of L.H. III c, and not reoccupied. At Grotta on Naxos, however, it is entirely possible that there was almost complete continuity into the succeeding period, but as the finds have not yet been published, one is unable to reconstruct the course of events. What is relevant, however, is that the adjacent chamber tomb cemetery was still in use after the establishment of the Dark Age culture on the mainland, as a vase of sub-Mycenaean type was found therein. A similar conclusion may be arrived at for Perati (a vast cemetery with no known successor), but in this instance because of the presence of arched fibulae, a particular feature of the sub-Mycenaean culture.

Something may then be said of most areas, but there is a notable loss of precision so far as concerns relative chronology. One point, however, may be stressed: it had previously been held that all sub-Mycenaean pottery, the characteristic ware of the central mainland region during much of the final stage, and almost invariably associated with individual burials, was later than any pottery known as L.H. III c. This view seems no longer to be valid for some of the communities outside this area, notably those of Achaea, Naxos and Perati, and probably Lefkandi as well.

Before summing up, the contemporary situation in the east Mediterranean, and especially in Cyprus, may be considered.

[1] A, 17.    [2] §1, 61.    [3] §1, 41.    [4] §1, 19.

Brief mention has already been made of the arrival of refugees, possibly from the Argolid, in Cyprus at the beginning of L.H. IIIc. In the second half of this period it is evident that further groups made their way there; a move from Crete will be discussed later (p. 676), but a slightly earlier one may also have originated in the Argolid, as the pottery introduced was of the Granary class, very similar to that in use at the time of and after the last destruction at Mycenae. These, no doubt, were also refugees, and it is likely that, as with their predecessors, they came to play an important role in the island, one reason for their being able to do so being that Cyprus had itself suffered further disaster not long before this migration, and the existing population must have been much weakened.

This destruction in Cyprus was earlier than that of the Granary at Mycenae, and will not have come long after the previous one of the island, which is marked by the current L.H. IIIb pottery giving way to early L.H. IIIc in subsequent settlements. These two destructions in Cyprus, or rather the causes of them, are important in that they provide an opportunity for discussing the question of absolute dating. From other evidence it is clear that L.H. IIIb was still current in the late thirteenth century, but the time of its end, as well as the period covered by L.H. IIIc is less definite. There is, however, one well-dated historical event which we may be able to relate to events in Cyprus, if not in the Aegean as well, namely the great invasion which Ramesses III crushed on the borders of Egypt in 1191 B.C.[1] For it appears from the historical account that the seaborne section of the invaders could have been operating somewhere in the Aegean before they made their way to Syria, wreaking destruction, as they passed, in the land of Alasia, which is probably to be identified with Cyprus. It is therefore likely that the invaders of the 1190s were responsible for one of the two destructions mentioned above, and if we could establish which, we should then have a vital point of absolute chronology, to say nothing of further possible complications for Aegean history. The answer may be provided by one of the groups of the invaders, the Philistines,[2] for in their new settlements in south Palestine, which they occupied very soon after their defeat, they are found to be using pottery which is a variation of an early stage of L.H. IIIc. What is not certain is whether they brought this pottery with them, or whether they adopted it after (but surely not long after) they settled. In the writer's opinion, this and other evidence suggests that the L.H. IIIc period commenced

[1] §1, 7.    [2] A, 17 and 21. See above, pp. 242 f. and 373 f.

*c.* 1200 B.C., and that the first destruction in Cyprus may be attributed to the sea invaders.

Valuable information is also to be obtained from Cyprus concerning the end of the period. It has been estimated that the transition from Late Cypriot III to Cypro-Geometric occurred *c.* 1050 B.C.[1] It is during the decade or two immediately before this that pottery of Cypriot type influenced the Athenian potters, during the latest phase there of the sub-Mycenaean style, shortly before the local development of the Protogeometric style (which was not reflected in Cypro-Geometric pottery). It therefore seems most likely that the end of the sub-Mycenaean period, and therefore of the final stage under discussion, ended *c.* 1050 B.C., and one can say that Mycenaean civilization had almost everywhere passed away by this time. It may finally be suggested that the last destruction at Mycenae took place *c.* 1130 B.C., but this can be no more than a calculated guess.

To sum up, then, the disasters on the mainland at the end of L.H. IIIb resulted in widespread flight, and a temporary and partial recovery was succeeded by more calamities, both on the mainland and in the Aegean, and there were further group movements to the east Mediterranean, and perhaps to Crete as well (see p. 676). During the concluding stage a new culture established itself in the central mainland area, of local origin or originated by newcomers from north-west Greece. Outside this area those communities who retained the Mycenaean culture gradually faded away, no doubt at different times in different places. No precise term can be given for the end of most of these communities, as in most cases they had no recognizable successors —the lack of continuity is in fact one of the remarkable features of the period, which came to an end *c.* 1050 B.C.

### (c) LOSSES AND SURVIVALS

To what extent was Mycenaean civilization completely obliterated? First of all, the central political control was broken, and misfortunes in other parts of the Mycenaean world weakened the control of the lesser kings. Then, the elaborate social and economic system, to which the tablets bear witness, must have disintegrated. There is no indication that the art of writing survived the destruction of the main centres. It cannot be proved that the art was lost, especially since so much of the later evidence comes from tombs, where writing is not to be expected, but it is exceedingly probable.

[1] A, 4.

Particularly on the mainland, a progressive deterioration in craftsmanship is certain. The workers in stone either dispersed (many perhaps to Cyprus) or else found no scope for their activities. There was no rebuilding of major sites in L.H. IIIc, and new buildings of any sort were rare; tombs, also, tended to be re-used rather than built afresh. The minor arts were neglected. The deterioration of the pottery, especially in the concluding stages, was rapid, and work in metal or ivory or precious stones, except in the central Aegean, more or less came to a standstill.

On the other hand, Mycenaean pottery left its mark on the succeeding style in some districts: clearly so in Ithaca, the Argolid, Corinthia and Attica, and very probably in coastal Thessaly and in Naxos, where further publication of material is awaited. Other districts may yet be found to present the same picture. The survival of the Mycenaean potter's craft may, however, be due not only to his descendants but also to the assimilation of this craft by newcomers. Similarly, the tholos tombs occasionally found in later use may have housed newcomers as well as those of Mycenaean stock. In general, even if there were numerous survivors in many districts, the whole fabric of the Mycenaean system collapsed. The spirit was no longer there.

If anywhere, survival should manifest itself in religious practices, for sacred places are the last to be abandoned. There are indeed several instances of later sanctuaries or cults occupying sites known to have been sacred to the Mycenaeans. At Mycenae itself, the temple of historic times overlay the sanctuary attached to the palace;[1] the archaic sanctuary of Apollo Maleatas,[2] near Epidaurus, was preceded by a Mycenaean cult place; both at Amyclae[3] and at Delphi[4] there is evidence of Mycenaean worship in the votive offerings of human and animal figurines; an L.H. III building, which perhaps had a religious purpose, underlay the archaic Telesterion at Eleusis.[5] In no case is there any archaeological evidence of continuous use from Mycenaean times onwards, but it must be stressed that this is an aspect where archaeology may present less than the true picture, since at Amyclae, for example, there is undeniable literary evidence that the pre-Greek deity Hyakinthos was still worshipped in historical times alongside Apollo. Even on archaeological grounds, however, a reasonable claim for continuity can occasionally be made, as for the Artemisium on Delos,[6] for the shrine of Dionysus on Ceos,[7] where the earliest cult evidence belongs to the fifteenth century B.C., and

---

[1] §1, 57.    [2] §1, 44.    [3] §1, 56.    [4] §1, 36.
[5] §1, 42.    [6] §1, 23.    [7] A, 9.

perhaps for the Heraeum on Samos,[1] on the basis of the types of figurine dedicated.

The innovations of this period are few, as has been seen, but important, especially when associated with the disappearance of typically Mycenaean features, and mostly confined to the concluding phase and to central mainland Greece. Some were introduced from outside: from the north, objects such as the Tiryns helmet,[2] and possibly the custom of individual burial; from the east, the knowledge of working iron. For other matters, such as the growing popularity in certain areas of the practice of cremation, and objects as for example the arched fibulae (as opposed to the earlier violin-bow type) and the long pins, which very likely mean a new type of dress, the origin is uncertain, and could have been local.

Finally, it must be stressed that this troubled period did not lead to complete isolation, though some areas, such as that of Achaea, may have been relatively out of touch. There was intercommunication at least throughout the south Aegean and from there to the east Mediterranean.

## II. THE PROTOGEOMETRIC PERIOD

The following period, lasting from about the middle of the eleventh century to the end of the tenth, is not inaugurated by any catastrophe or invasion; there is movement of population during its course, but it is a time rather of settling down and resumption of peaceful communication. The material comes for the most part from tombs, evidence for house construction being extremely meagre, and equally slight for sanctuaries or cult objects, except in Crete, where the emphasis is on the previous Minoan tradition. As before, certain areas are better known than others, and some are almost entirely unknown; in general, this period is less well documented than that which preceded it.

The period is named Protogeometric because much of Greece and the Aegean is dominated by pottery of this style, though certain districts are still relatively untouched. It so happens that the greatest quantity of Protogeometric pottery, and the clearest evidence for its origin, development and transition to the succeeding Geometric style has been observed in Athens.[3] The theory that, in other parts of Greece where this pottery appears, such appearance is due to direct or indirect influence from Athens is that which at present holds the field. The autochthonous origin

[1] A, 36.     [2] A, 50 and see Plate 168(*b*).     [3] §II, 8 and 10.

of the Athenian Protogeometric style is almost certain, but the possibility must remain that local styles of a type similar to the Athenian may have arisen independently in areas where present knowledge is still slight, and this should be borne in mind in the following discussion.

The Athenian style is based on the preceding sub-Mycenaean in the sense that most of the shapes, and some of the decorative motives, can be traced back to this earlier style; there is continuity.[1] On the other hand there is much that is new in Protogeometric which justifies its claim to be a distinct style. There are marked advances in technique: a faster wheel was used, and the contours are more taut and elegant; for the fashioning of the characteristic circles and semicircles there was a further technical advance in the use of compasses combined with a multiple brush. Furthermore, the whole conception of decoration, as an integral and harmonious part of the vase, is new—or rediscovered. This is a creative and dynamic style, and suggests a fresh approach to life after the previous stagnation; it contains elements both of simplicity and elaboration, though on the whole simplicity predominates: it may be described as both sober and conventional, always adhering to the principle of harmony, and it is only rarely that the potter goes outside his repertory of geometric motives. Finally, the style is singularly free from outside influences, though there may be borrowings from the Argolid and connexions with Cyprus are visible in the very earliest and latest phases.

Considerable space has been devoted to the pottery as a whole, and to the pottery of Athens in particular, since one has to depend on it very largely in establishing the interconnexions that permit a reasonably general analysis of Greece and the Aegean during this period. Before embarking on this, however, other aspects may be noted briefly.

As a large proportion of our evidence comes from cemeteries, it might be hoped that an analysis of burial customs would yield useful results. What emerges, however, is a remarkable variety of such customs, so varied indeed that it is virtually impossible to demonstrate links of any sort between one community and another on the basis of this type of evidence. The practice of individual burial spread over most of the Greek world, generally cist tombs and pit graves, with pithos burials also used in the later stages, especially in western Peloponnese[2] and Aetolia.[3] These, however, involve a number of idiosyncrasies in form and detail of usage, for example the differentiation made between child and adult in cer-

---

[1] See Plate 169.     [2] A, 17.     [3] A, 30.

tain communities, the manner of laying out the dead, and the occasional depositing of vases outside the tomb instead of (or as well as) within it. Multiple burial in tholos tombs was revived in certain parts of Thessaly[1] and Messenia,[2] but not as an exclusive practice—one gets this only in Crete, where the use of both chamber tombs and tholos tombs was retained from the preceding period. While inhumation was customary in most districts, a few communities practised cremation. The fact that Athens,[3] Lefkandi[4] in Euboea, Vranesi[5] in Boeotia and Medeon[6] in Phocis make up the total (with the exception of Crete[7] and Caria[8]) suggests a possible cohesive geographical pattern, but there is no uniformity in the subsidiary details of the rite. Nor can any plausible reason be given for the adoption of this custom, so rare in Mycenaean times (see above p. 663 for L.H. IIIc cremations).

Developments in metal working were on the whole confined to the communities within the orbit of the Aegean, and of these the chief one is the more common use of iron, as might be expected—indeed, in Attica, the Argolid and Euboea it replaced bronze almost entirely, whether as a utility or an ornamental metal, until near the end of the period. Objects of gold are almost entirely absent, except in Crete and the Dodecanese. Silver artifacts are even more rare; and it is thus a matter of some surprise that we should have evidence, from Argos[9] at the beginning of the period and from Thorikos[10] in Attica at its end, of the use of the cupellation process for extracting this metal.

To return to the pottery: on the basis of this Greece and the Aegean may be divided roughly into four areas, one of which is Crete, which will be dealt with later. The first of these is that over which the Athenian style had the strongest influence. In spite of extremely scanty evidence, one can assume that the whole of Attica comes into this category, as well as the islands of Aegina[11] and Ceos;[12] so also do the central Cyclades[13] and the island of Samos.[14] On the coast of Asia Minor particular interest attaches to Miletus,[15] whose earliest reoccupation pottery shows close links with that of Athens, at the time of transition from sub-Mycenaean to Protogeometric, and perhaps continuously thereafter, though the community developed its own local style. Protogeometric sherds have been reported on other Ionian sites as well.[16] The geographical connexion between this pottery and the area of the Ionian migra-

[1] §I, 53; §II, 7.  [2] A, 11.  [3] A, 44.  [4] A, 38.
[5] G, 1.  [6] A, 49.  [7] §III, 2 and 4.  [8] §II, 13.
[9] A, 14.  [10] A, 5.  [11] §II, 9.  [12] A, 9.
[13] G, 1.  [14] A, 52.  [15] §I, 61.  [16] §II, 4.

tion is clear, and it also indicates the probable time and place of its origin, namely Attica at the beginning of the Protogeometric period or even slightly earlier. In the Halicarnassian peninsula, furthermore, the pottery of Assarlik[1] is similar to that of Athens, and the vases of a tomb at Dirmil[2] reflect later developments. In the Dodecanese, however, and especially on Cos,[3] where the material, unfortunately, can in no case be dated with certainty earlier than *c.* 950 B.C., the links with Athens are less evident; the potters were evidently familiar with Ionia, and contact with Cyprus is clear, but the main connexion could have been with the Argolid. The mention of this last area brings us back across the Aegean, and in fact it too may be included in the first area, on the basis of gradually increasing influence from Athens, though it had a quite distinct style of its own. Finally, what is known of Corinthian and Boeotian pottery of this period indicates close links with the Attic style, though the material is too sparse for more than provisional inferences.

The second area, which forms a cohesive group of its own, is that which extends from coastal Thessaly through Euboea and Scyrus to the northern Cyclades. The local style of pottery was hardly influenced at all by that of Athens during the early stages, but in the tenth century there was considerable borrowing which led to radical modifications, though on these the potters created a style of their own which in some ways differed completely from the Athenian. There are two outstanding sites in this area. The first is Iolcus,[4] certainly a flourishing town, in view of the four successive levels of the Protogeometric settlement, which provide one of the rare instances of good stone-built rectangular houses of this period (so does the settlement of Grotta[5] on Naxos, but it is not clear whether the island belongs to this area). The second is Lefkandi[6] in Euboea, whose cemeteries provide evidence for almost complete continuity from late sub-Mycenaean into the Geometric period—settlement material is so far lacking, though the earliest reoccupation of the abandoned Mycenaean site could belong to the last years of the Protogeometric period.

This area, then, developed along its own lines, and retained its characteristics after the appearance of Geometric pottery in Attica. It is also of great importance in its outside contacts. Its pottery spread northwards, both into north central Thessaly, and also to some extent into Macedonia, whose inhabitants tended to prefer handmade pottery. It could have been from somewhere within

[1] §II, 13.    [2] A, 3.    [3] G, 1; §II, 12.
[4] A, 46.    [5] §I, 14; A, 13.    [6] A, 39 and see Plate 170(*b*).

the region that migrants made their way across the Aegean to Old Smyrna,[1] where they joined forces with the native community already in occupation. Finally, it may be noted that vases from this area were the first we know of to penetrate the eastern Mediterranean.[2]

The third area is that of southern and western Peloponnese, the adjacent islands and coastal Aetolia. Interesting ceramic inter-connexions are observable at the very end of the period,[3] but material for the earlier stage is extremely slight, except in Ithaca. So far as one can tell, the influence of Athenian pottery, or of any style indebted to it, was minimal, with the interesting exception of Messenian sites facing on the gulf of Kalamata.[4] No doubt there was some communication with other areas, but cultural links were very few, and there is here a sense of separateness such as is not found in the Aegean.

In sum, it may be said of this long period—probably about a hundred and fifty years—that it was a time of solid achieve-ment. There will no doubt have been a fair amount of sporadic warfare, but this did not impede peaceful development. The fact and range of the influence of Attic pottery indicates normal, and mainly seaborne, communication. The general improvement of the potter's art, and that of other craftsmen, argues a time of greater stability and leisure. The southern and western Pelopon-nese may have kept out of the main stream, but there was no absolute isolation. There was no reversion towards the conditions of the Mycenaean world; instead, there was a progressive move-ment towards the conditions under which the independent city-state developed.

## III. CRETE[5]

The island of Crete is here dealt with as a separate unit; for in spite of its very close connexions with the Mycenaean world, of which it is in many ways a part, it exhibits individual character-istics which place it, in other ways, outside the Mycenaean *koine*.

At the time when disaster swept the mainland of Greece, at the end of L.H. IIIb, Crete was in decline after the catastrophes at the end of the Palace period; settlements were restricted, and the population may have been relatively small. The island may have come under the domination of Mycenae, but in many respects it remained un-Mycenaean—in its pottery, its architecture, its

[1] §II, 3.  [2] A, 16.  [3] A, 12.  [4] A, 11 and 45.
[5] It must be stressed that the conclusions of this section are based on very in-complete evidence.

tombs, and particularly in its cults (from the evidence both of sanctuaries and of objects of religious significance). It is probable that it escaped neither the direct nor, at any rate, the indirect effects of the general turmoil in Greece and the east Mediterranean: the abandonment of certain sites can plausibly be assigned to this period; and there is evidence that some refugees from other districts made their way to Crete—a conclusion based mainly on the pottery.[1] What effect these newcomers had on the internal situation is by no means clear, but it is perhaps significant that now or soon afterwards a number of new settlements were founded or old ones reoccupied, both in the centre and in the east of Crete (there is as yet not sufficient detailed information from excavations in west Crete to tell what happened there). Such are to be found at Phaestus[2] and Gortyn,[3] Vrokastro,[4] Kastri[5] replacing Palaikastro in the east, and the remarkable mountain city of Karphi[6] rather later than the rest. All, whether on the coast or in the interior, were in varying degrees in easily defensible positions, and it is reasonable to conclude that conditions were unsettled.

However that may be, a revival took place similar to that experienced in the Aegean and on the mainland. The pottery now current was Late Minoan IIIc (L.M. IIIc), a characteristic feature of it being the elaborate Fringed Style, found widely over much of Crete. It was an uninhibited style, and what is of great interest is that one particular shape, the stirrup jar with octopus decoration, a development from the preceding L.M. IIIb style, was enthusiastically adopted by the communities of the central Aegean and the Dodecanese. It is clear that for a while the Cretans were outward-looking, and involved in Aegean affairs; and they were also probably in touch with Cyprus.

The revival gave way, probably in the second half of the twelfth century, to a progressive deterioration and simplification, at least in the pottery; in other words, the sequence seems to have been much as in the rest of the Aegean, and presumably reflects the recurrence of unrest. It is likely that Crete was subjected to further intrusions of a refugee kind,[7] and this could have led to internal disturbance; whatever the truth of this, there seems no doubt that a group of migrant Cretans made their way to Cyprus at the end of the century, to judge from the distinctive Minoan clay goddesses with upraised arms found there; and there are a number of ceramic links as well.[8] From this time onwards it is extremely likely that there was no break in mutual communication

[1] A, 38.    [2] §iii, 7.    [3] §iii, 6 and A, 40.    [4] §iii, 4.    [5] A, 41.
[6] §iii, 8 and 11, and see Plate 170(a).    [7] A, 17.    [8] A, 27.

between the two islands, even during the rather depressed period in Crete known as sub-Minoan,[1] which persisted throughout most of the eleventh century. Contacts with the Aegean, on the other hand, both during this time and for a while before, are unclear. Crete had lost touch with the central Aegean communities, but that may only mean that the latter were themselves in a desperately weakened state. We know that two of the characteristic developments of the sub-Mycenaean culture, arched fibulae, and long dress pins, made their appearance in Crete, but quite how or when —or indeed why—one does not know. Particularly deserving of attention are two pins from Cnossus,[2] whose closest counterparts are in Argos; but that does not mean that all known pins from Crete arrived from the north.

The tenth century is marked by the resumption of contact with Athens, in the sense that the Athenian Protogeometric style had its customary effect on the local potters, and from the presence of a number of vases imported from Athens.[3] What is remarkable, however, is that the impact was felt only in central Crete; in eastern Crete (we still know nothing of the west) the effect was negligible, and this may mean a genuine division between the two regions, perhaps originating in the early twelfth century when, while those of the centre continued to bury in chamber tombs, the inhabitants of the east reverted to tholos tombs. The relatively large number of weapons in tombs of the period may be an indication of at least a lack of sympathy between the two; but one should tread warily, as evidence of intercommunication is by no means absent. There was certainly no internal isolation.

Cremation, it may be noted, was now widely (but not exclusively) practised in central Crete, much less so in the east. It is tempting to infer from this an extension of the custom of Protogeometric Athens, but there are differences in detail, and also there are occasional earlier examples of the rite in Crete itself.

In one aspect, the Cretans enjoyed an advantage apparently denied to the rest of the Greek world, except the Dodecanese, until the final years of the tenth century—their contacts with Cyprus. Numerous objects, both ornamental and useful, and even a particular type of weapon (an iron pike) certainly or probably came from that island.[4] From this, as well as other, evidence it is clear that many communities were not only stable but flourishing. However, it must be stressed that this did not result in the Cretans taking any active interest in affairs outside their island: people came to Crete from elsewhere, but there is no evidence of any reciprocation.

[1] See Plate 171.    [2] §III, 5.    [3] §III, 2 and see Plate 172.    [4] §III, 2.

## (b) THE LITERARY TRADITION
## FOR THE MIGRATIONS

### I. THE NATURE OF THE LITERARY EVIDENCE

ARCHAEOLOGICAL discovery affects our attitude to literary tradition in two ways. At first there is a tendency to dismiss the literary tradition as imprecise and faulty in comparison with the actual physical remains, from which a past civilization can be reconstructed upon precise foundations but within restricted limits. Then, when the material outlines of such a civilization grow firm, our knowledge of material conditions can be used to test the accuracy of details in the literary tradition. This stage has been reached for part at least of the Mycenaean period, and the literary tradition has been confirmed at many points. Thucydides was certainly correct in believing that Mycenae was a centre of importance, that its rulers spoke Greek for several generations before the Trojan War, and that the power of Mycenae finally overthrew that of Troy. The Homeric Epics, no less than the even more remarkable *Epic of Gilgamesh*, have merged into the world of fact and become historical documents. The *Iliad* provides in the Catalogue of Ships a political map of Mycenaean Greece to which excavation has added little but confirmation,[1] and the poem tells us more of Mycenaean ideas and aspirations than the walls of the citadel can do. But the literary tradition contains much which can never be confirmed or refuted by archaeological discovery, and here we must rely on our own criteria for confidence or distrust.

Continuity of tradition was certainly maintained between the Mycenaean period and the archaic Greek period by the recitation of epic lays which were transmitted orally for several centuries, especially in central Greece, Ionia and Cyprus. Our general faith in their historical accuracy has been strengthened by particular archaeological discoveries. But when Thucydides studied the origins of Agamemnon's power before the Trojan War, he turned to the oral tradition in the Peloponnese (1, 9, 2), probably in the Argolid, and he drew from it an outline of events which had occurred some eight centuries before his own time. It is unlikely that this oral tradition was in epic verse, of which traces are few in the Peloponnese, and the chief centres of transmission were

---

[1] G, 9, 27 (see the bibliography to chapter xxxvi (*b*)), 'The Homeric catalogues are a remarkable tribute to the accuracy of oral epic'; G, 6, 63 f; (*b*) A, 6, 153 ff.

evidently religious shrines, such as the Heraeum of Argos. In particular the founder of a shrine or of a settlement was often honoured in a local cult, and his acts were recited or re-enacted year after year. The information which came down through this channel and was sometimes reinforced by family traditions was of great value, as Herodotus and Thucydides realized in their researches into early Greek history. We are less fortunately placed, because our knowledge of such information is often due to the writings of late authors, whose historical judgement was faulty or capricious; but we can in many cases discern the elements of genuine tradition if we know that these authors were drawing upon epic lays or local cults.

We have an interesting example, and one relevant to our period, in the legend of Mopsus.[1] It is recorded mainly by authors of the Roman period. When Thebes was sacked by the Epigoni, Teiresias was killed at Haliartus and his daughter, Manto, led refugees to Colophon and founded a shrine of Apollo at Clarus (Pausanias vii, 3, 1–2 and ix, 18, 4). Her son, Mopsus, born at Colophon, led 'the peoples' across Mt Taurus into Pamphylia, where some settled, while others scattered to Cilicia, Syria and Phoenicia (Strabo 668; cf. Hdt. vii, 91 and Xanthus, *F.Gr.H.* 765 F17). He was worshipped at Sillyum in Pamphylia, as we know from an inscription of Roman times (*J.H.S.* 78, 1958, 57). Fragments from earlier sources are preserved by Strabo. At chapter 668 he cites Callinus, a seventh-century poet of Ephesus, for a journey of Mopsus into Pamphylia, and at chapter 642 he quotes Hesiod, fr. 278 from the *Melampodia* (ed. Merkelbach), for a contest in divination at Colophon between Mopsus, son of Manto, daughter of Teiresias, and Calchas who was accompanied by Amphilochus, son of Amphiaraus, on the return from Troy. The coming of Calchas to Colophon was mentioned also in Hagias, *Nostoi*. As some warriors fought both at the sack of Thebes and in the Trojan War (*Il.* iv, 406), and as Mopsus was born after the sack of Thebes, he came to maturity towards the end of the Trojan War (in which Dictys Cretensis says he took part) or after its conclusion. It is likely therefore that he led the people into Pamphylia, whence they scattered into Cilicia, Syria and Phoenicia, in the years after the Trojan War. He was believed to have founded Aspendus in Pamphylia and Mallus in Cilicia (Str. 675). If we put the fall of Troy *c.* 1200 B.C., his exploits fell in the 1190's and 1180's. The memory of them was no doubt preserved at the shrine of Apollo at Clarus and in local

[1] G, 1; G, 9, 20; (*a*) §1, 29, 25, 39, 45.

cults of the founder at Aspendus, Mallus and Sillyum, and some of the legend found its way into epic lays of the eighth or seventh century.

Although the literary tradition about Mopsus is no better than that about other heroes of the period, it has been strikingly confirmed by a bilingual inscription from Karatepe in Cilicia, which mentions the house of Mukshush in Hittite and of Mupsh in Phoenician, that is the house of Mopsus. It is concerned with the activities of Azitawatas, a descendant of Mopsus, in the eighth century B.C. As the names Azitawatas and Aspendus are similar, it has been suggested that both the man and the place were named after a son of Mopsus who was called Azitawadda. At any rate the Azitawatas of the inscription is styled 'king of the city of Adana' in Hittite and 'king of the Danuniyim' in Phoenician, and the words Adana and Danuniyim suggest descent from the Danaoi, under which name the Greeks of the Trojan War were known to Homer and Thucydides (1, 3, 3). The migration of Mopsus and his Greek followers to Cilicia is thus revealed by a Hittite record, which was independent of the Greek tradition. A clue to the chronological setting of Mopsus is given by a Hittite tablet from Boğazköy, which mentions Mukshush in connexion with Attarshiyash 'the man from Ahhiyawa' and Madduwattash, a rebellious subject of the Hittite king Arnuwandash III.[1] The tablet itself is dated to the reign of this king. All we know, unfortunately, is that his predecessor was still on the throne in 1245 B.C., and we can only infer with probability that the reign of Arnuwandash III and one of the actions of Mopsus lay within a period not longer than 1245–1230 B.C.[2] This piece of independent Hittite chronology is compatible with that which is inferred from the Greek account of Mopsus.[3]

The legend of Mopsus is typical of the disturbances and migrations which marked the decline of the Mycenaean world. The sack of Thebes, which has been confirmed by excavation, and the migration led by Manto, on the advice of the oracle at Delphi as we learn from a fragment of the epic lay *Epigoni*, afford an insight into the troubled years before the expedition to Troy. Other examples are more firmly attested in the Catalogue of Ships. Thus Tlepolemus and 'much people' migrated to Rhodes (*Il.* 11, 653 f.), and we learn from Diodorus Siculus that he was sent on the advice of an oracle (probably Delphi) to conduct 'some peoples'

[1] See above, p. 264.  [2] See above, pp. 261 ff.
[3] As R. D. Barnett says on p. 442 above, Mopsus 'is the first figure of Greek mythology to emerge into historic reality'.

to Rhodes in the years preceding the Trojan War and was himself killed in the course of that war (v, 59, 5; cf. iv, 58, 7). The channel of transmission was evidently a local shrine in Rhodes, since Tlepolemus was worshipped there and games were held in his honour (Pi. O. vii, 77f.; Schol. Lyc. 911; S.I.G. iii, 1067, 5). He himself was a son of Heracles by Asytocheia (Il. ii, 653f. and v, 639), and Heracles had carried her off 'from Ephyra by the river Selleeis', which was probably in Thesprotia (compare Il. xv, 531 with D.S. iv, 36, and see p. 686 below).[1] Other descendants of Heracles—the sons of Thessalus, son of Heracles—led immigrants to the adjacent islands of Cos, Carpathos, Casos, Nisyros and Calydnae and took part in the Trojan War (Il. ii, 676).[2] It would be rash to deny that these migrations occurred and that they were led by members of that important clan, the Heracleidae.

## II. THE TRADITIONS OF THE DORIANS AND THE HERACLEIDAE PRIOR TO THE TROJAN WAR

The Dorians of classical Greece claimed to be descended from one tribal group. Its movements during the Mycenaean period are briefly told by Herodotus in a famous passage at i, 56.[3] 'In the reign of Deucalion the tribe occupied Phthiotis; in that of Dorus, Hellen's son, the territory below Ossa and Olympus which is called Histiaeotis; on being expelled thence by Cadmeans it lived in Pindus and was called Makednon. From there again the tribe removed to Dryopis, and it was on coming from Dryopis to the Peloponnese that it was called Dorikon.' This account evidently came to Herodotus either from Delphi (as the context i, 56 may imply) or from a Dorian source, probably Sparta, with whose early history he was particularly conversant; at any rate the legend was so well known at Sparta in the seventh century that Tyrtaeus could mention without further explanation that the ancestors of the Spartans 'departed from windy Erineus' (fr. 2), which is a small place in Doris. Other Dorian peoples in the Peloponnese—those of Corinth, Sicyon, Epidaurus and Troezen—were grouped together with the Spartans by Herodotus viii, 43 as being of 'the Dorian and Macednan tribe, whose last point of departure was Erineus, Pindus and Dryopis'. In this passage Pindus was probably a village in Doris, and Dryopis was a small district thereof, between Malis and Phocis; and Doris itself was described as

[1] G, 5, 172, 179; G, 14, 4f.   [2] G, 5, ibid.; G, 9, 23.
[3] G, 5, 151f.; G, 16, 526f.

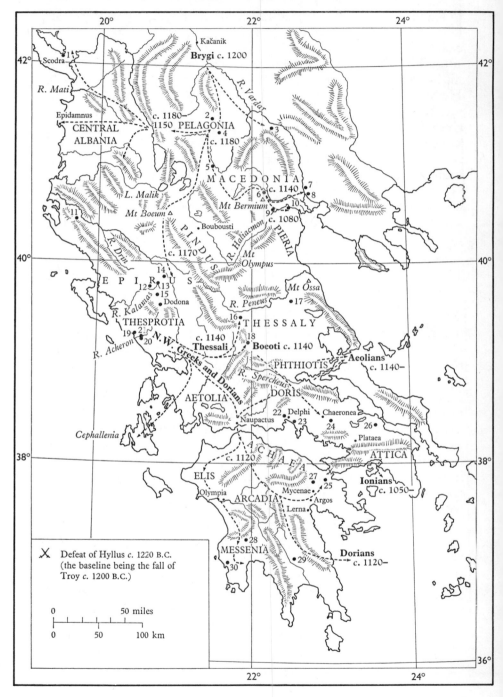

Kačanik

Scodra
**Brygi** *c.* 1200

*R. Mati*

Epidamnus    *c.* 1180–
CENTRAL    1150   PELAGONIA
ALBANIA      *c.* 1180

*R. Vardar*

MACEDONIA    *c.* 1140
*L. Malik*    *Mt Bermium*    *c.* 1080
*Mt Boeum*    PIERIA
.Boubousti
PINDUS
*R. Drin*    *c.* 1170    *Mt Olympus*
*R. Haliacmon*

EPIRUS    *Mt Ossa*
*R. Kalamas* .Dodona    *R. Peneus*
THESPROTIA    THESSALY
N.W. Greeks and Dorians    *c.* 1140
*R. Acheron*    **Thessali**    **Boeoti** *c.* 1140    **Aeolians** *c.* 1140–

PHTHIOTIS
*R. Spercheus*
AETOLIA    DORIS

Naupactus    Delphi    .Chaeronea
*Cephallenia*    ACHAEA    .Plataea
*c.* 1120    ATTICA
ELIS    **Ionians** *c.* 1050–
Olympia    Mycenae    ARCADIA    .Argos
.Lerna

MESSENIA    **Dorians** *c.* 1120–

X    Defeat of Hyllus *c.* 1220 B.C.
(the baseline being the fall of
Troy *c.* 1200 B.C.)

0          50 miles
0    50    100 km

## NUMERICAL KEY

| | | | | | |
|---|---|---|---|---|---|
| 1 | Gajtan | 11 | Vayzë | 21 | Ephyra |
| 2 | Cydrae | 12 | Mazaraki | 22 | Cirrha |
| 3 | Demir Kapu | 13 | Kalbaki | 23 | Crisa |
| 4 | Prilep | 14 | Elaphotopos | 24 | Coroneia |
| 5 | Saraj | 15 | Ioannina | 25 | Solygeius |
| 6 | Scydra | 16 | Hexalophos | 26 | Gla |
| 7 | Vardina | 17 | Larisa | 27 | Zygouries |
| 8 | Vardarophtsa | 18 | Arne | 28 | Stenyclarus |
| 9 | Beroea | 19 | Kiperi | 29 | Amyclae |
| 10 | Vergina | 20 | Nekyomanteion | 30 | Epáno Englíanos |

## ALPHABETICAL KEY

| | | |
|---|---|---|
| Amyclae   29 | Ephyra   21 | Prilep   4 |
| Arne   18 | Gajtan   1 | Saraj   5 |
| Beroea   9 | Gla   26 | Scydra   6 |
| Cirrha   22 | Hexalophos   16 | Solygeius   25 |
| Coroneia   24 | Ioannina   15 | Stenyclarus   28 |
| Crisa   23 | Kalbaki   13 | Vardarophtsa   8 |
| Cydrae   2 | Kiperi   19 | Vardina   7 |
| Demir Kapu   3 | Larisa   17 | Vayzë   11 |
| Elaphotopos   14 | Mazaraki   12 | Vergina   10 |
| Epáno Englíanos   30 | Nekyomanteion   20 | Zygouries   27 |

Map 13. The migrations on the Greek mainland at the end of the Mycenaean Age. (The migrating peoples are shown in bold type, and the dates refer to the time of a movement starting.)

'the metropolis' of the Dorians in the Peloponnese by Herodotus (VIII, 31) and of the Lacedaemonians by Thucydides (1, 107, 2). The penultimate stage 'in Pindus' (after being expelled from Histiaeotis) was evidently in the Pindus range (so too Pi. P. 1, 65 'the Dorians issuing from Pindus took Amyclae'), which is described by Herodotus VII, 129 as enclosing Thessaly on the west side. When the tribe was driven out from the area below Ossa and Olympus, it presumably went through Pieria and the middle Haliacmon valley to reach the northern end of the Pindus range; for according to Hesiod (*Eoeae* fr. 7) and Thucydides (II, 99, 3) this area was the home of the 'Macedonian' name, to which the 'Macednan' name must be related. There is a considerable gap between the northern end of the Pindus range and their next area of settlement, the canton of Doris. It cannot be filled by assuming that they passed again through Thessaly, which would then have been mentioned again, or that they followed the spine of Pindus, which is uninhabitable in winter. The gap must therefore be filled by assuming that they moved through the interior of Epirus, then an anonymous area, which left no name in the tradition and even to Aeschylus was simply 'the district beyond Pindus' (*Supp.* 253). The two stages before that in Histiaeotis and Phthiotis call for no comment, as the regions are close to one another.

The wanderings of this tribal group covered several generations. The genealogy Deucalion–Hellen–Dorus, which Herodotus gives, is not specifically Dorian. It is a general one, which was used for defining the earlier times of Greek prehistory, and it is found already in Hesiod, *Eoeae* fr. 9. In the present case the reign of Deucalion means little more than some remote time in Greek lands. The expulsion by the Cadmeans from Histiaeotis may have occurred by Herodotus' reckoning (V, 59) at any time between Cadmus' arrival and the Trojan War, a span of six generations. The final position in Dryopis was probably reached during the generation before the Trojan War, because we learn that the Dorians were then serving against the Mycenaean peoples under Hyllus, a son of Heracles, and they are likely to have been already on the fringe of the Mycenaean world (Hdt. IX, 26; Paus. VIII, 5). The tradition that a single combat was fought between Hyllus and Echemus of Arcadia and on the death of Hyllus the Heraclids promised not to return for 100 years (not 50 years as given by D.S. IV, 58, following a source rejected by Paus. VIII, 5, 1) has come down to us from the Tegean side and ultimately from a Mycenaean source in the Peloponnese, where the grave of Echemus was revered (Paus.

VIII, 53, 10); and the fragments of Hesiod about Echemus and his wife (frs. 23a, 176) appear to derive from a similar source.

The movements of this group which was later called 'Dorian' are all anterior to the so-called Dorian invasion. They afford some insight into the way of life of these primitive people. All the areas which they held at different times were suited primarily to the rearing of sheep, and they are so used to this day by the Vlachs and the Koutsovlachs. Summer pasture is found only at high altitudes, and winter pasture is available in the lowlands; therefore in early spring the flocks move to the highlands of Ossa, Olympus and Pindus and descend to the lowlands in the autumn. During the migration of the sheep in early spring and autumn the plains of Dodona and Phthia are rich in sheep, as they were in ancient times (Hesiod, frs. 211 and 240). There is no doubt that the ancestors of the Dorians were a pastoral people during their wanderings, and that Doris itself, while suitable for sheep, was only an advanced point of their pastures in south Epirus and north Aetolia. Pastoral people of this kind leave little for the archaeologist. The ancestors of the Dorians, like the Vlachs, must have used skins and wooden or metal vessels in preference to pottery, and they would have had little use for fine pottery in their nomadic life. Yet some traces of them may have been found. A people of crude culture came c. 1300 B.C. from Thessaly and settled at Boubousti near Servia in the middle Haliacmon valley. It has been suggested by the excavator of the site at Boubousti that the people there were a group of 'Macednans' who were later called 'Dorians'.[1] The settlements of this period in central and south Epirus are small shepherd encampments without any Mycenaean pottery, and their rough domestic ware resembles that of west Macedonia.[2]

The north-western area, through which the ancestors of the Dorians moved on their way eventually to south Epirus and Doris, was remarkable for a fine ware of pottery painted with a variety of geometric designs.[3] It appeared first towards the end of the Middle Helladic period in a rich settlement at Malik, high up in good pastureland and close to a once important Vlach centre called Voskopol, and it spread from there to most parts of Central Albania and to the region of Lake Ochrid. In L.H. IIIb it appeared in the upper Haliacmon valley, especially at Boubousti, and in northern and central Epirus. During L.H. IIIb and L.H. IIIc this pottery being in use throughout this large north-western

[1] G, 8, 177.    [2] G, 5, 131 f.; (b) A, 4, 304 f. and 389 f.
[3] (b) A, 4, 295 ff.; (b) A, 9 with Plates I, II, V and VI.

area deserved the name given to it by S. I. Dakares 'north-western Geometric'. The makers of this pottery, which in its artistic principles foreshadows some of the characteristics of the post-invasion Protogeometric and Geometric styles of the Greek main-land, were probably speakers of the North-west-Greek dialect who were to accompany the Dorians in their successful invasion of the Peloponnese.

When the ancestors of the Dorians reached Doris, they became the immediate neighbours of the Mycenaean peoples. Led by the Heracleidae, they pressed strongly upon central Greece in the latter half of the thirteenth century. Tradition records that the Heracleidae and the Athenians defeated and killed Eurystheus, king of Mycenae (Hdt. ix, 27, 2 and Thuc. i, 9, 2), that the Boeoti occupied Cadmeïs, the later Boeotia, after the sack of Thebes by the Epigoni and before the Trojan War (Thuc. i. 12. 3), and that Hyllus at the head of the Dorians advanced in strength to the Isthmus of Corinth (Hdt. ix, 26, 2). It was per-haps this danger from the north that inspired the Mycenaeans of the Peloponnese to build a wall at least part of the way across the Isthmus in the latter part of L.H. III b.[1] It was here, according to Pausanias i, 44, 10, that the Heraclid Hyllus was killed by the Arcadian Echemus. The tide turned at last. According to the literary tradition, the Dorians did not threaten the Mycenaean control of the Peloponnese for a hundred years, that is on the chronology followed here from c. 1220 to c. 1120 B.C.

The Heracleidae were not even a tribe but merely a clan of persons descended from Heracles, 'sons and grandsons of Heracles' as Homer calls them (Il. ii, 666), and they were and remained Achaeans who claimed descent from Perseus, king of Mycenae (cf. Hdt. v, 72, 3). The connexion between the Hera-cleidae and the ancestors of the Dorians is said to have begun when Heracles helped them in Thessaly against the Lapiths and when Aegimius, son of Dorus, repaid a promise to Heracles by giving a third of his land to the Heracleidae (D.S. iv, 37, 3; iv, 58, 6). Although any story about Heracles is likely to have been embellished, the fact remains that the Heracleidae commanded the ancestors of the Dorians before and after the Trojan War. Only two sons of Heracles are mentioned in the Iliad: Tlepole-mus, whose mother came from Ephyra by the river Selleeis, which is probably in Thesprotia; and Thessalus, who bears the name of a tribe which is not mentioned by Homer but is said to have come from Thesprotia (Hdt. vii, 176). It seems likely then that

[1] G, 4, 34 and (b) A, 1.

the Heracleidae were in Epirus, where we believe that the ancestors of the Dorians were not long before the Trojan war. Tlepolemus himself 'built ships quickly, collected much people and fled
overseas after killing his mother's brother, Licymnius; for the
other sons and grandsons of mighty Heracles threatened him'
(*Il.* ii, 661 f.). So far as the run of the narrative is an indication,
Tlepolemus fled to Rhodes from Ephyra.[1] Later, however,
Tlepolemus' killing of Licymnius was located at Tiryns (e.g. by
Pindar, *O.* vii, 29), probably because Argos had a hand in the
later colonizing of Rhodes and, wishing to advance a claim to the
earlier foundation also, did so through Tiryns (Str. 653), where
the name of the acropolis, Licymnia, provided an aetiological
motif for a new account. But it is most unlikely that Tlepolemus
and Licymnius and the Heracleidae who threatened Tlepolemus
were ever acceptable in the Argolid, let alone after the undertaking made by the Heracleidae to Echemus, and that the Argives
permitted Tlepolemus to build ships and collect much folk for the
voyage to Rhodes. Whether they did or not, the Heracleidae as a
clan must have been living somewhere on the mainland outside
the area covered by the Achaean Catalogue, that is somewhere
north of the line drawn through Leucas, southern Aetolia, Phocis,
Thessaly and most of coastal Macedonia; for if so famous a clan
had been resident in a Mycenaean area of the mainland (see
Thucydides 1, 9 for its earlier importance), it would certainly
have received a mention in the Achaean Catalogue. In short,
then, the Dorians' memory of their early wanderings, the origins
of Tlepolemus and Thessalus, and the absence of any Heracleidae
on the mainland in the Catalogue converge to the same conclusion
that the Heracleidae and the ancestors of the Dorians were living
in southern Epirus during the generation before the Trojan War.

Although the surface of Epirus is almost equal to that of the
Peloponnese, places in Epirus are rarely mentioned by Homer.
Zeus of wintry Dodona 'dwelling afar off' is invoked only by
Achilles (*Il.* xvi, 233); his priests the Selli, sleeping on the ground
with unwashed feet (like many Vlach and Koutsovlach shepherds
today), and Hellopia, the plain rich in sheep by Dodona, have
names which are clearly akin to the river Selleeis, by which the
mother of Tlepolemus lived. One group in the Catalogue comes
from Epirus: the Enienes who pitched their dwellings round
wintry Dodona (*Il.* ii, 750); but they served with the Perhaebi
who lived by the Titaressus, in north Thessaly. The *Odyssey*, of
which the dramatic date is later and the background is the north-

---

[1] G, 9, 23.

western area, has rather more information to offer. The river
Acheron is mentioned as leading to Hades (x, 512 f.), which
suggests that the famous Nekyomanteion already existed at
Ephyra, a place where deadly poisons were sold perhaps by the
priests or priestesses of the oracle of the dead. Thesprotia appears
not only as a country through which one travels to Dodona but
also as a kingdom with sea-going ships and some power (XIV, 335;
XVI, 426). Thesprotia's nearest neighbours on the mainland, the
Cephallenes, are followers of Odysseus and well within the
Mycenaean world (*Il.* II, 635; *Od.* XXIV, 377). It is of interest
that the Enienes and the Cephallenes, together with the Hellenes
of Achilles, are the only peoples in Homer's Mycenaean world
with an ethnic ending in -enes (see pp. 701 f. below).

Two groups of people who were within the Mycenaean mainland at the time of the Trojan War had probably entered it from
the north-west, those with Achilles whom Thucydides I, 3, 3
described as the first Hellenes, and the Boeotians then settled in
Cadmeïs (later renamed Boeotia). The Dorians of classical times
were regarded as particularly 'Hellenic' (Hdt. I, 56, 2), and
therefore their ancestors in Doris were related to the Hellenes
over whom Achilles ruled. A connexion between Achilles and
Epirus is indicated by Achilles' prayer to Zeus of Dodona, the
worship of Achilles in Epirus as Aspetus, the visit of his son
Neoptolemus to the Molossi there (Hagias, *Nostoi*), and the claim
of the Molossian royal house to be descended from Neoptolemus.
Indeed Aristotle believed that the original Hellas, the home of the
Hellenes, was in the area round Dodona (*Mete.* I, 14, 352 a). The
Boeotians who figure in the Catalogue (*Il.* II, 494) were regarded
by Thucydides I, 12, 3 as an offshoot of the main group of
Boeotians, which had not yet invaded the area later known as
Thessaly. The origin of the name and the people is probably in
Doris and Epirus; for Boeum is the name of a town in Doris and
also of a high part of the Pindus range, a second wave of Boeotians came from the west into south-west Thessaly, there was a
cult of Achilles and probably Tlepolemus at Tanagra in Boeotia
(Plu. *G.Q.* 37), and Thebes and Dodona were closely connected
as we know from Pindar's privileged position at Dodona and
from the 'tripod song' (Proclus, *Chrestomathia*, Phot. Bibl. cod.
239, p. 990; cf. Str. 402).

The origin of the name 'Dorians' is uncertain. It seems
probable that Herodotus I, 56, 2 is correct in implying that the
tribal group which moved from Phthiotis and ended up in Dryopis
in Doris received its name on each occasion from the territories

in which it settled, at least in two instances—the Macednan name from the Pindus area or 'high'-land (which is probably the meaning of μακεδνός)[1] and the Dorian name from Doris. Both names will then have been given to the tribal group by its neighbours. On the other hand the names of the three individual tribes which made up this group—Hylleis, Pamphyli and Dymanes—seem to have been original and were not subject to change during the migrations. The first occasion on which the Dorian name is likely to have become attached to this group is the first great incursion into the Mycenaean world, when Hyllus was killed by Echemus at the Isthmus. Thus when Herodotus I, 56, 2 says the Dorian name was received 'on coming to Peloponnese' (ἐς Πελοπόννησον ἐλθόν) he may be referring to the first attack of the Heracleidae 'returning to Peloponnese' (κατιόντες ἐς Πελοπόννησον IX, 26). If this is so, we can see that the reference to Dorians in the *Odyssey* XIX, 177 as resident in Crete, presumably in East Crete (cf. Str. 475), may not be anachronistic in the use of the name.[2] These Dorians in Crete were adjacent to the followers of the Heraclids, Tlepolemus and the sons of Thessalus, who had seized Casos, Carpathos, Rhodes, Nisyros, Calydnae and Cos before the Trojan War; they may have come to Crete when the Heraclids came to the Dodecanese, or they may have come earlier in the thirteenth century from Thessaly as some traditions suggest and received the name later (*F.Gr.H.* 10 F 16 Andron, 269 F 12 Staphylus; Hdt. VII, 171, 1; D.S. IV, 60, 1 and V, 80, 2). It is probable that there were Dorians not only in Crete but also in Rhodes. For the system of three tribes which made up the Dorian group offers the best explanation for Homer's epithet τριχάϊκες for the Dorians in Crete and for his description of Tlepolemus' followers settling in Rhodes τριχθὰ καταφυλαδόν 'in three parts by tribe'. As Hesiod, fr. 233 implies, members of the three tribes probably took their parcels of land in tribal groups in Crete and Rhodes. In the latter island the new settlement of Dorians did not displace the earlier and much larger groups of populations, which were already based on the three towns of Lindus, Ialysus and Camirus (*Il.* II, 655–6 διὰ τρίχα, κτλ.).[3]

[1] See A. B. Daskalakis, Ὁ Ἑλληνισμὸς τῆς ἀρχαίας Μακεδονίας (Athens, 1960), 35 f.

[2] G, 9, 24; G, 12, 64; G, 16, 528.

[3] G, 9, 23; G, 12, 63; G, 16, 529. For other interpretations of these passages see p. 348 above, and pp. 790 f. and 844 below.

## III. TRADITIONS OF THE DORIANS AND THE HERACLEIDAE BETWEEN THE TROJAN WAR AND THEIR ENTRY INTO THE PELOPONNESE

Thucydides 1, 12 gives a clear account of the migrations on the Greek mainland soon after the Trojan War. First, Thessalians drove some Boeotians out of Arne (in south-west Thessaly); second, these Boeotians occupied Cadmeïs (where some earlier Boeotians had settled before the war) and renamed it Boeotia, this being sixty years after the fall of Troy; third, 'Dorians together with Heracleidae took the Peloponnese eighty years after the fall of Troy'. It is unlikely that these were the only invasions, or that Thucydides thought they were (for he talks of a long period of migrations), but they were the three chief incursions which occurred before the thorough diaspora of the Mycenaean peoples. As the chronological indications are tied to the Trojan War, in which neither the Dorians nor the Heracleidae were concerned, it is likely that Thucydides owed his information ultimately not to Dorian but to Mycenaean sources; and the other chronological datum, the hundred years between the death of Hyllus and the return of the Heracleidae, was also due to a Mycenaean source, as we have seen. The Mycenaean chronology then runs as follows, if we assume a date c. 1200 B.C. for the fall of Troy: the first Dorian attack c. 1220 B.C., the migration of the Thessalians and the Boeotians c. 1140 B.C., and the Dorian capture of the Peloponnese c. 1120 B.C. The last date fits in with Thucydides' remark (v, 112, 2) that in 416 B.C. Melos had been occupied for 700 years by Dorians, that is since c. 1116 B.C.; for the interval between the Dorian invasion of Laconia and the seizure of Thera was a short one in the tradition, and Melos, which lies between Laconia and Thera, is likely to have been occupied at the same time (see p. 695 below).

The invaders came from the north-west: the Thessalians from Thesprotia (Hdt. VII, 176, 4), the Boeotians having entered Arne earlier from somewhere west of the Pindus range, and the Dorians from Doris and its hinterland. Wherever this wave of peoples broke through the fringe of the Mycenaean world, it carried other tribes ahead of it and deposited them like driftwood.[1] The Enienes, or Aenianes as they called themselves, were around Dodona at the start of the Trojan War; later they are found some on the southern side of the Spercheus valley and others at Cirrha

[1] G, 5, 156f.

(Plu. *G.Q.* 13). The Dolopes, who lived in the upper Spercheus valley in *Iliad* IX, 484, were later pushed some northwards to the upper Achelous valley (Thuc. II, 102, 2) and others overseas to Scyros. The Dryopes, who in earlier times had given their name to south Epirus (Dicaearchus V, 30 p. 459 ed. Fuhr; cf. Pliny, *N.H.* IV, 1), to Mt Tymphrestus, to a part of Doris and to a part of Mt Parnassus, were driven forward some to Styra and Carystus in Euboea and others to Hermione and Asine in the Peloponnese. Two of these tribes remembered their wanderings, rather as the Dorians did, and they maintained contact with their past through religious observances. The Aenianes sent an ox annually to Cassopaea in south Epirus in memory of their stay there, honoured Neoptolemus the son of Achilles at each Pythian festival at Delphi and claimed to be truly Ἑλληνικόν (Plu. *G.Q.* 26; Arist. *Mirab. Auscult.* 133; Heliod. II, 34). The Dryopes commemorated their stay under Parnassus by sending sacrifices each year to a shrine of Apollo there (Paus. IV, 34, 9). The Aenianes, the Dolopes and the Dorians were members of the Delphic Amphictyony. They probably obtained their membership at a time when they lived in larger numbers near Anthela and Delphi than was the case after the Dorian invasion of the Peloponnese.

The route which the Thessali took from Thesprotia to Thessaly can be defined. They did not proceed through the Peneus valley, because the Aethices and the Perhaebi remained in their Homeric habitats. The Thessali therefore used the passes from Ambracia, one to Gomphi in south-west Thessaly and the other to the Spercheus valley, where the displacement of tribes from their Homeric situation has been mentioned. The Thessali were led by a family of Heracleidae, later prominent as the Aleuadae of Larisa (Pi. *P.* x, 1 f.). We do not know who commanded the Boeotians; but there was a bond between them and the Spartans in a famous clan, the Aegeidae, who later helped their kinsmen at Sparta (Pi. *I.* VII, 12 f.). The Boeotian wedge of invasion probably split the Locrians into the two groups of later times (they were a single people opposite Euboea in *Il.* II, 527 f.). The Dorians 'came not through the Isthmus of Corinth, as three generations earlier, but they returned to the Peloponnese by ship, putting in at Rhium' (Paus. VIII, 5, 6). They were commanded by Heraclids, and they were guided by Oxylus, who brought many people from Aetolia. He had advised them to sail from Naupactus to Molycrium. Thence he led them not towards Elis (which had been promised to him) but through Arcadia, which was now on friendly terms because a Heraclid Cresphontes, one of the sons of Aristomachus, had married a daughter of the Arcadian king, Cypselus. The commanders of the Dorians were not interested in Arcadia itself but they were intent on seizing control of the Argolid, which was the chief centre of Mycenaean power (Paus. v, 3, 6 f.; cf. Str. 357, citing Ephorus).

The ultimate source of these accounts is likely to be Mycenaean. They give the points of entry into the Mycenaean sphere and not the earlier stages of the invaders' movements (such as occur in the Dorian account of their previous migrations); they regard Oxylus and other helpers of the Dorians as traitors; and there are several jibes at the primitive Dorians which may be Mycenaean or later and are certainly not Dorian (*e.g.* Paus. v, 3, 5 the triophthalmic man, and iv, 3, 5 the faked lottery with the melting tablet). Intervals of time are not given in terms of generations as we might expect of backward people such as the Dorians, but in terms of 100 years between two attacks, 60 years after the Trojan War and 80 years after it, periods which cannot be forced into one hypothetical pattern of reckoning by generations; for if the 100 years is taken as three generations of $33\frac{1}{3}$ years each (as in Paus. viii, 5, 6), then 60 and 80 are not multiples of a generation. The Mycenaeans on the other hand were conversant with figures, and they kept full statistical records of their treasures and supplies. There can be no doubt that they had an annual system of reckoning, like their civilized neighbours in the east, and we owe these intervals of time in years to them. The accounts of the invasions give no background of geography or of institutions for the invaders; for instance, the Dorians cross from Naupactus to Rhium without any explanation of the places whence they came or the preparations which they had made for an operation by sea, and there are only a few meagre hints about the leadership under which they served. This is what we should expect from a Mycenaean source but not from a Dorian source. It is indeed doubtful if a Dorian account of the invasion survived. Some have supposed that the *Aegimius* of Hesiod was based on a Dorian epic, but the testimonia and the fragments (294–301) give little or no support to the supposition.[1] The complete collapse of culture which the Dorians brought about on the mainland implies rather that they had no epic and no knowledge of writing.

The reason for the Dorians coming by sea to Rhium was presumably that the Isthmus was too strongly held by the Mycenaeans (as on later occasions by the Peloponnesians), and that the Dorians had sufficient seapower to make a crossing in strength

[1] G, 16, 526 f.; G, 17, 59 f.

and to maintain a large force. The traditions of the decades prior to the Trojan War show that invasions were launched through the Isthmus from the Peloponnese into central Greece by the Seven against Thebes, by Eurystheus against the Heracleidae and by the Epigoni but not in the opposite direction, and the towers on the north face of the Mycenaean wall across the southern part of the Isthmus indicate that it was intended to defend the Peloponnese from attack from the north.[1] Where did the Dorians become seamen or acquire seapower? The supporters of Tlepolemus and the sons of Thessalus and the Dorians who went to east Crete were evidently good seamen, and the Boeotians who sailed to Troy had vessels which carried more men than those of any other contingent. They cannot have learnt the art of seafaring in the Gulf of Corinth, which was in Mycenaean hands at the time of the Trojan War. They and their successors must have learnt their seamanship in the Gulf of Ambracia (not mentioned by Homer) and in Thesprotia, which had sea-going ships in the *Odyssey*. The choice of Rhium for the landing was an admirable one. It was easy to ferry supplies and men over from Aetolia, whence many of Oxylus's supporters came (Paus. v, 1, 3); Rhium was remote from the main centres of Mycenaean strength and was probably undefended; and the Mycenaean kings of Pylus, Sparta and Argos would hesitate to concentrate their forces at any one point, because they could not tell where the Dorians would make their main attack.

The successive waves of invaders were doubtless inspired by a desire for loot and for land more fertile than that which they had in Epirus, Aetolia and Doris. But as they came intending to settle with their families and as they displaced lesser tribes such as the Aenianes, Dolopes and Dryopes from their path, they were perhaps impelled by overpopulation (for they came from a country which was then heavily wooded) and by pressure from Balkan peoples behind them (see pp. 707 f. below). One factor which encouraged the invaders was the decline of Mycenaean power. We are reminded of the decline of Greece in the fourth century B.C. by Thucydides' description of the years between the Trojan war and the invasions (1, 12, 1–2). 'After the Trojan War Greece was still the scene of displacement and resettlement of peoples, so that it did not obtain tranquillity for growth. The long delayed return of the Greeks from Troy caused many revolutions. There were for the great part *staseis* in the states, and it was the exiles from them who founded the (new) states.' Thucydides derived

[1] (*b*) A, 1.

his knowledge from a considerable body of epic material which survived from this period and of which we have only the *Nostoi* in a summarized form. But excavation has confirmed that the picture drawn by Thucydides is correct. For at the end of Mycenaean III b Crisa, Gla, Zygouries, Tiryns, the palace at Epáno Englíanos and the 'Citadel House' at Mycenae suffered destruction.

## IV. THE CONQUEST OF THE PELOPONNESE, THERA AND MELOS

The few details of the conquest which survive were probably derived from Mycenaean sources, whether in the form of epic or folk-memory, and some were preserved in local cults. When the invaders landed at Rhium, they came to terms at once with Arcadia. Cresphontes, one of the Heraclid commanders, made a marriage alliance with a daughter of Cypselus, king of Arcadia, which became 'free of fear' (Paus. viii, 5, 6). The invaders then split. Oxylus and his followers invaded Elis, and the Dorians marched through the hills of Arcadia. The division of forces may have been due less to greed than to strategy; for it must have tended to keep Pylus and Sparta on the defensive. The Dorians were in fact bound for the strongholds of the Argolid. This became clear only when they turned eastwards to Lerna. Between there and Argos, near Nauplia, the leader Temenus 'captured and fortified a place in the campaign with the Dorians against Tisamenus and the Achaeans' (Paus. ii, 38, 1).[1] At this place, 'Temenium', as it was later called, honours were paid to Temenus by the Dorians of Argos. The invasion of Laconia was carried out under the leadership of the twin sons of Aristodemus, Eurysthenes and Procles; the Dorians' victory over the Achaeans was celebrated, together with a later victory over Amyclae, in the shrine of Zeus Tropaeus (Paus. iii, 12, 9). Messenia fell to Cresphontes, who divided the land between his followers and the Achaeans and made his own headquarters at Stenyclarus (Paus. iv, 3, 3). These conquests were made rapidly. The palace-citadels of the Mycenaean kings were attacked one by one in isolation, and the assaults were made probably by the combined forces of the Dorian commanders. In the words of Pindar (*P.* v, 69) 'Apollo planted the valiant descendants of Heracles and Aegimius in Lacedaemon, Argos and sacred Pylus'.

Immediately after this initial success bands of Dorians went

[1] Not to be confused with the actions of his grandson Deiphontes (Polyaen. ii, 12), as in G, 12, 58.

overseas. One, led by Theras, who was an uncle of the twins Eurysthenes and Procles, went from Sparta to Thera, where he was later the recipient of annual sacrifices (Hdt. IV, 147; Paus. III, 1, 8). Melos, which lies between Sparta and Thera, was doubtless occupied *en route* by forces from Sparta; the Mycenaean site there at Phylakopi was abandoned shortly before the end of Mycenaean III c, and the Spartan occupation was dated *c.* 1116 B.C. by Thucydides (V, 112, 2). The early seizure of Melos and Thera shows that the Dorians were seafarers, whether they had brought their ships with them or had acquired those of the defeated Mycenaeans. They chose to attack Melos and Thera first, presumably because these islands were on the way to their friends in east Crete, Rhodes and the Dodecanese and also because they held important positions on the trade routes to the Levant.

The capture of the citadels from which the Mycenaean kings had directed affairs was spectacular in itself and crippling to the Achaeans' organization,[1] but it was only the first stage of the conquest. A long period followed in which the Dorians gained control of the countryside, put down insurrections, acquired land and serfs and also fought against one another. In Messenia the land was divided between the existing inhabitants and the Dorians, but a rebellion ousted the latter; eventually the Spartan kings and the Argive king, a son of Temenus, came to the rescue and restored the Dorians (Paus. IV, 3, 8 f.). In Laconia Amyclae, a town a few miles to the south of Sparta and blocking her passage to the sea, was captured only with the help of the Aegeidae of Thebes after a long resistance (Pi. *I.* VII, 14; Paus. III, 2, 6); thereafter the Spartans underwent a very long period of turmoil and internal strife, which lasted until the reform which is associated with the name of Lycurgus (Hdt. I, 65; Thuc. I, 18, 1). In and around the Argolid the Temenids fared better. The towns of the Argive plain were taken by the grandsons of Temenus. Dorian centres were founded outside the Argolid at Sicyon, Phlius, Epidaurus, Hermione, Troezen and Aegina. The occupation of Corinth was achieved by a Heraclid, Aletes, who was not of the Temenid line, and Dorian Corinth tended subsequently to be at enmity with Dorian Argos. Thucydides IV, 42, 2 mentions that a hill called Solygeius on the coast of the Saronic Gulf was used as a base by the Dorians in their attack on the citizens of Corinth—no doubt when led by Aletes. The latest acquisition of the Dorians on the mainland was the Megarid.[2] The Dorians launched a concerted attack on Attica, failed to take Athens, but

---

[1] G, 4, 25.          [2] G, 7, 18 f.

annexed the territory which became known as Megaris; it provided a corridor to their friends in Boeotia, and it ensured Dorian control of the Isthmus. Settlers came from the Dorian communities of Messenia, Corinthia and elsewhere, and a number of Dorians who had taken part in the campaign led bands overseas which settled in central Crete, Rhodes and the Dodecanese and at Halicarnassus and Cnidus on the opposite mainland (Str. 653). The Dorian invasion had at last run its full and undefeated course.

## V. THE INSTITUTIONS OF THE DORIANS

On the eve of the invasion the Dorian group was ruled by three Heraclid kings, the sons of Aristomachus, in order of age Temenus, Cresphontes and Aristodemus, whose twin sons succeeded on his early death. Pausanias IV, 3, 3 retails the traditional legend that Temenus was given Argos 'by the Dorians' and that Cresphontes asked for Messenia, on the grounds that he too was older than Aristodemus; but at the request of Theras, who represented the twin sons of Aristodemus, the matter was referred to the drawing of lots, and Cresphontes did in fact obtain Messenia. In this legend there is a clash between the principle of primogeniture among the brothers and the principle of equality between the three kings; and the verdict is in favour of equality. The meaning of this clash was forgotten later, and the absurd story was introduced that the lottery was prearranged by Temenus who filled an urn with water, had the tablet for Cresphontes made of baked clay and that for the twins made of sun-dried clay, immersed both in the urn and pulled out the tablet which had not melted. But the clash of principles is probably historical. We can now pose the two questions which arise from this situation: why were the Dorians ruled by Heraclids and why were there three rulers and not one?

The Dorian tradition was that Aegimius, a Dorian king, adopted as his son Hyllus, a son of Heracles, at a time when the sons of Heracles were with the Dorians (*F.Gr.H.* 70 F 15 Ephorus). The adoption was made in fulfilment of a promise by Aegimius to Heracles that, in return for his help against the Lapiths of Mt Olympus, he would give Heracles 'a third of the land and a third of the kingship' (D.S. IV, 37, 3; IV, 58, 6; Str. 427 put the scene in Doris). The first part of the promise was honoured; for a third of the land was left in trust with Aegimius for Heracles' descendants. A third of the kingship was a different matter; it makes sense only if there were three kings and Heracles was to be one of them (for a man could not be king on each third day). This is in fact what happened, except that it was not Heracles but his son Hyllus who became king. For Aegimius was succeeded by his adopted son Hyllus and by two sons of his own. Thus we have three kings at a time before the first invasion and also on the occasion of the second invasion. The explanation is, of course, that the kings were φυλοβασιλεῖς 'tribal kings' of the three tribes which made up the Dorian group (just as the four Ionic tribes which made up the Athenian group had 'tribal kings'); and, to remove any shadow of doubt, the three sons of Aegimius were Hyllus, Pamphylus and Dymas, who bear the eponymous names of the three tribes—Hylleis, Pamphyli and Dymanes. It is true that Pamphylus and Dymas look like genealogical figureheads, but Hyllus has some historical substance as the hero who killed Eurystheus and was himself killed by Echemus. Perhaps Hyllus was so named at birth as a compliment to the Dorians (Hesiod, fr. 135, l. 19 records his name at birth as Hyllus), or else he may have been renamed Hyllus on his adoption by Aegimius. A parallel case is another son of Heracles, Thessalus, who bore the eponymous name of the Thessalians (as did a son of the tyrant Peisistratus centuries later). After his adoption by Aegimius Hyllus became king of the Hylleis. The two other tribal kings were then not Heraclids. On the eve of the second invasion all three tribal kings were Heraclids and direct descendants of Hyllus and brothers of one another (Hdt. vii, 204). At the same time all three kings were descended from Aegimius through the adoption of Hyllus, their great-grandfather. Thus Pindar was correct in calling them 'the valiant descendants of Heracles and Aegimius' (P. v, 69).

We can now understand the dispute between the brothers and the recourse to the use of the lot. Cresphontes argued that as an elder brother he had priority of choice over Aristodemus or his heirs, but the claim made by Theras was that as tribal kings the three brothers were equal, just as the tribes themselves were equal, and this claim was upheld, presumably by the Dorians as a group. The three tribes were separate entities at the time; for they are represented as fighting separately in a campaign which the present writer dates to the time of the invasion,[1] but which many scholars date to the seventh century B.C. (Tyrtaeus, fr. 1, 12). When the three tribes joined forces, they formed a group τὸ Δωρικόν, which had three kings and could take such action as the conferring of conquered territory on one of the kings, namely of

[1] In *J.H.S.* 70 (1950), 50.

the Argolid on Temenus (Paus. IV, 3, 3). This group presumably sat in judgement to decide any disputes which arose between the three kings, because otherwise joint action could not have been achieved. We should think therefore of τὸ Δωρικόν as a tribal state of a primitive kind.

While the allocation of the chief Mycenaean kingdoms of the Peloponnese was of great importance to the three kings, it was even more vital for the rank and file to decide how the conquered lands were to be divided. The accounts of Pausanias and Strabo, as well as the regulations made later for the early Dorian colonies, lay much emphasis upon the division and allocation of land. Should each tribe take over one territory, so that the Hylleis held the Argolid or the Dymanes Messenia? The decision is apparent from Herodotus IV, 148, where Theras led the expedition to Thera 'having people from the tribes', that is from the three Dorian tribes. This decision may have been taken when the kings were arguing about the allocation of the kingdoms. At any rate the decision was binding upon all forms of settlement thereafter, whether in the Peloponnese or overseas, and we find from the evidence of inscriptions and other documents that there were in fact members of all three tribes in almost all Dorian communities. For this reason Pindar was able to call the Spartans 'descendants of Pamphylus and the Heracleidae' (*P.* I, 62) and the founders of Aegina 'the Dorian host of Hyllus and Aegimius' (*I.* fr. 1); for the mixed communities claimed descent from all three eponymous tribal ancestors, Hyllus, Pamphylus and Dymas, and they all lived 'under the ordinances of Aegimius and Hyllus', who seem to have been regarded as founders of the Dorian Group or state (Pi. *I.* fr. 1; *P.* I, 62 and 64, where Hyllus and Aegimius are mentioned separately but not in contrast).[1]

The narratives of Hyllus and Aegimius and of the conquest reveal some features of the Dorian form of kingship. Since Aegimius promised a third of the Dorians' land to Heracles and gave it to Heracles' descendants, it is clear that he owned the land; as king he was able to grant it to whom he wished. The concept of the king also owning any lands won by the spear is implicit in the story of the kings contending for Laconia and Messenia and of Temenus being given the Argolid. The limits of the territory which the kings acquired in the Peloponnese were presumably the limits of the Mycenaean kingdoms of Argos, Sparta and Pylus. Thus Eurysthenes and Procles, on occupying the citadel of Sparta, claimed the traditional kingdom of 'hollow Lacedaemon'

[1] G, 16, 527.

(*Il.* 11, 581 f.), much as Alexander the Great claimed the traditional kingdom of the Achaemenids. In order to substantiate the claim, Eurysthenes and Procles appointed six kings to conquer and administer six districts of the Mycenaean Kingdom and to settle them with colonies of Dorians (Str. 364, citing Ephorus), but they themselves were the kings of Lacedaemon and of the Lacedaemonians, to whom they granted the tenure of their lands. As the dark age descended, the central control in Lacedaemon ceased to be effective, and it was not reasserted until the eighth century B.C. Something similar happened in the kingdoms of Temenus and Cresphontes; for when they emerged from the dark age there were many independent Dorian settlements. After the initial stages of the conquest the liaison seems to have broken down between the three Dorian kingdoms, and then the whole system of administration and communication within each kingdom collapsed in the hands of the Dorian kings. The unit of the dark age was not the kingdom but the village (*kome* or *damos*).

The Dorians regarded Zeus as their special god. It was Zeus who gave Sparta to the Heraclids (Tyrtaeus, fr. 2), and Zeus Tropaeus was worshipped at Sparta. They may have brought their worship of Zeus from Dodona in Epirus, which was the particular shrine of Zeus until the Eleans instituted the worship of Zeus at Olympia. Their other special god was Apollo of Pytho 'who planted the valiant descendants of Heracles and Aegimius in Lacedaemon, Argos and sacred Pylus'. The attachment to Apollo was evidently developed during the century before the invasion, when the Dorians, being on the fringe of central Greece were probably members of the Delphic Amphictyony. After the invasion the Spartan kings kept contact with Delphi regularly through special representatives called Pythii. The worship of Apollo Carneius, which all Dorian peoples observed, represented the god as a ram and belonged to the pastoral background of their earlier wanderings.

## VI. THE THESSALIAN, BOEOTIAN AND ELEAN INVADERS

Much less is known about the invaders who were not Dorians, probably because they attacked Mycenaean areas which were less well organized than the kingdoms in the Peloponnese and indeed in the case of Cadmeis had already disintegrated. The Thessali were led by Heraclids who were probably descended from Thessalus, son of Heracles, just as the Dorian leaders were descended

from Hyllus, son of Heracles. These Heraclids were probably
responsible for introducing serfdom in Thessaly, because it appears only here and in the Dorian parts of the Peloponnese, and
for founding the tradition of a single ruler in Thessaly, the *tagus*.
They swept away the Mycenaean system of nine realms as it
appears in the Achaean Catalogue (Iolcus, for instance, being
destroyed in the Mycenaean IIIc period), and they established
four large baronies, of which the rulers set up their own dynasties.
The Boeotians entered the area which later became known as
Boeotia from the north, and they settled Chaeronea and Coronea
first (Str. 411). They made slow progress; they never mastered
Orchomenus completely, and generations passed before they
occupied Plataea on the slopes of Mt Cithaeron (Thuc. III, 61, 2).
The unity of the invaders was commemorated in a religious
festival, the Pamboeotia. In the early stages at least there was a
'king of the Boeotians'. It is possible that he made his capital
at Thebes, as kings in the Mycenaean period had done, and that
his position there inspired the claim of Thebes to command the
Boeotians in war (Thuc. III, 61, 2; Str. 393). The limit of the
Boeotian invasion was reached at the borders of Attica, where
their king was killed in single combat with Melanthus. Fortunately for Attica this attack occurred a generation before the
Dorian attack from the south. The followers of Oxylus the Aeto-
lian were content with the conquest of the rich countryside of
Elis and the lower Alpheus valley. The Oxylidae became the
leading clan in Elis and served later as *Hellanodikai* (judges of the
Hellenes) at the Olympic games (Pi. O. III, 12). At Olympia the
Eleans founded the worship of Zeus and Hera, which had similarities with the worship of Zeus and Dione at Dodona, but this
happened later; for during the dark age the Eleans split up into
independent village communities (*damoi*).

In addition to these invaders there were others who pressed on
in their rear. In the west they occupied Aetolia and Acarnania,
driving the Cephallenes of Mycenaean times into the island which
took its name from them, and in the east they occupied the
Spercheus valley and Phocis; to the south they filled the lands
between Aetolia and Phocis, and they occupied Achaea in the
Peloponnese. The relationship between all these invaders and the
Dorians is best known through the distribution of dialects in the
classical period, which is so clearly marked that 'even if there
were no tradition of a Dorian invasion such a movement would
have to be assumed'.[1] The dialect of Greek which was spoken by

[1] C. D. Buck in *Class. Phil.* 21 (1926), 18.

the invaders apart from the Dorians was one common dialect which we call Northwest-Greek, and it was spoken in all the areas we have mentioned from Acarnania to Elis and from Thessaly to Achaea. They spoke a common dialect, because they had come from one area, namely the north-west mainland of which Epirus was the major part, and perhaps from western Macedonia, which in climate and geography has much in common with Epirus. On the other hand the Doric dialect was distinct from Northwest-Greek, and this fact supports the Dorian account of their wanderings, because the Dorians spent only a part of their time in Epirus and were already a tribal entity of their own before they entered Epirus. The Doric dialect was spoken wherever the Dorians settled—from Messenia to Cnidus and from Aegina to Crete. As Northwest-Greek and Doric are more closely related to one another than to other Greek dialects, they form a single group called West-Greek. Their relationship can only be explained if the two groups of people who spoke them were in close proximity to one another for some time before they invaded central Greece and the Peloponnese. Such conditions are supplied by the Dorian account of their wanderings when they lived in southern Macedonia and central Epirus. Further, as the West-Greek group is related to the Mycenaean dialect or dialects, the speakers of both groups of Greek must have been in proximity before the Mycenaeans gained control of the mainland.

One feature which the Dorians and the western wing of the invasion shared is the ethnic termination in -anes (-enes in the Ionic dialect).[1] We noted that in the Achaean Catalogue the only tribes with this termination were the Enienes, later Aenianes, Cephallenes and Hellenes, and that they all had then or probably had had in the past connexions with Epirus. Further, one of the three Dorian tribes, the Dymanes, had this termination and resided for a time anyhow in Epirus. When the invasions were over, we find Acarnanes in the place once held by the Cephallenes, and Eurytanes and Eitanes in Aetolia. This ethnic termination was therefore typical of many invading peoples who came from the north-west area. In addition it was found in classical times in Epirus, where there were tribes called Athamanes, Atintanes, Arctanes and Talaeanes, and the earliest names of districts in Epirus—Adania and Cammania (Steph. Byz. s.v.) —are related to such ethnic forms. It therefore follows that the group of peoples from whom the invaders came was not drained

---

[1] G, 5, 156f. For a possible example of this ethnic on a tablet from Pylus see E. Risch in *Mus. Helv.* 14 (1957), 63 n. 1.

completely, and that the tribes of classical times in Epirus with the termination -anes were either of Greek blood or at least of Greek dialect at the time when the invasion was launched.

Other affinities between the invaders (particularly the Dorians) and the north-western tribes emerged later in the fourth century B.C. Then the Molossian tribal state, which included members also of the Thesprotian and Chaonian tribes, is the closest analogy we have for the Dorian tribal state at the time of the invasion.[1] And the Macedonian kingship, as we know it during the reigns of Philip II and Alexander the Great, is very similar to the Dorian type of kingship; for in both the king owned the land and any further land won by the spear, and the king claimed authority also over the outer districts. These likenesses may be explained either by long-lasting traditions which the Dorians left behind them, or by the hypothesis that related Greek peoples living under similar conditions evolved similar institutions.

## VII. THE EFFECT OF THE INVASIONS ON THE MYCENAEAN GREEKS

The only area in the Peloponnese which maintained its independence was Arcadia, at first by coming to terms and later by waging continuous warfare, which extended into Laconia and Messenia (Paus. III, 2, 5; IV, 3, 7). There the Arcadian dialect was preserved; elsewhere it was spoken in classical times only in Cyprus, which it had reached probably c. 1350 B.C. In districts which were occupied by the invaders traces of Mycenaean dialects survived among the population, which suggests that some Mycenaean Greeks were absorbed by the invaders; for instance, Aeolic forms appear in the dialect of Elis and some Corinthian colonies, which implies an admixture of Aeolic in the early dialect of Dorian Corinth, and Arcadian forms survived in south Laconia and in Pisa.

The defence of the Argolid and then of Laconia against the Dorians was organized by Tisamenus, son of Orestes, who finally led his defeated followers—Achaeans as they are called in the tradition—into the area then occupied by Ionians but later known as Achaea, which is situated in the northern Peloponnese with Arcadia lying along its flank (Paus. II, 18, 6f.; VI, 38, 1). Here Tisamenus was killed. His bones were removed much later to Sparta, where honour was paid to his memory. After his death the Achaeans occupied the area. They drove out the Ionians who

[1] (b) A, 4, 531.

took refuge in Attica (Hdt. I, 145; Paus. VII, I, 7). The Achaeans in turn were either ousted or overlaid by speakers of North-west-Greek, whose origins and identity are not known.

Outside the Peloponnese the Boeotians met with steady resistance from the Aeolic-speaking population, and classical Boeotia was an area of mixed dialect and mixed population. In Thessaly most of the Mycenaean population was driven out of Thessaliotis, the south-western part of Thessaly, but there were Aeolic-speaking groups in the other districts of Thessaly, where the invaders settled in smaller numbers. Attica lay off the route of all the invasions. It therefore became a haven for refugees from Mycenaean districts (Thuc. I, 2, 6), and, thus reinforced, was able to halt the advance first of the Boeotians and then of the Dorians.

The shock of the first invasion, launched by the Thessali *c.* 1140 B.C., started off the first wave of the Aeolian migration. It was commanded by Penthilus, son of Orestes. Further waves of Aeolic-speaking peoples from the eastern areas of central Greece followed during the next two generations at least (Str. 582, 622; Paus. III, 2, 1). The pressure on the Peloponnese caused first some Messenians from Pylus, including the royal house, the Neleidae, and then the Ionian inhabitants of what became Achaea to take flight from the Peloponnese and seek refuge in Attica. If we put the Dorian invasion *c.* 1120 B.C. and the capture of Pylus within the next few years, then the Neleidae came to Athens *c.* 1110 B.C.; and as Tisamenus fell fighting, we can hardly put his death later than *c.* 1080 B.C. and the coming of the first refugees from Achaea to Athens about the same time. The loss of what became the Megarid and had hitherto been part of Attica must have increased the congestion of the native Athenians and of the refugees, who were themselves granted the citizenship. At this stage the Ionian migration was launched from Attica (Thuc. I, 2, 6). The departure of the emigrants marked the beginning of settled conditions upon the mainland of Greece (Thuc. I, 12, 4).

The details of the Aeolian and Ionian migrations are described in chapter XXXVIII, and all that need be discussed here is the source of our information and the dating of the migrations from literary sources. It is clear that the traditions of Tisamenus, of Penthilus and his descendants, and of Melanthus, Codrus and the Codridae were preserved initially by Mycenaean peoples and then by their descendants. Also some of the colonies had cults of their founder and accounts of their foundation. These traditions and accounts are likely to be correct in their main features, but not necessarily in respect of any elaborate details. This is particularly so because the Mycenaean and sub-Mycenaean periods were an age in which the royal or leading families had an extraordinary influence—Pelopidae, Perseidae, Heracleidae, Opheltiadae, Aleuadae, Oxylidae, Neleidae, Codridae and so on. The nearest parallel in later Greece came in the Frankish period, and in England in the Norman conquest. Such leading families remembered their own history and were remembered by the ordinary people. They held the sceptre of authority, they conducted religious ceremonial, and they had wide powers of patronage. The bulk of Greek mythology in the Mycenaean period and later was based upon the doings and sufferings of the great families. The *Oresteia* of Aeschylus, for example, is a historical play; Agamemnon did spend ten years at Troy, he was murdered by Clytemnestra, their son Orestes, saved by his nurse, did return as a grown man to kill his mother and so on. The traditions of the leaders of the Aeolian and the Ionian migrations belong to the same cycle or type of legend and have an initial claim on our belief.[1]

The chronology of the migrations stems mainly from these same traditions. For instance Tisamenus, who opposed the Dorians in the Peloponnese, and Penthilus, who led the first group of Aeolians to the Thracian coast, were both sons of Orestes, so that their activities fell within the same generation. As the Thessalians invaded Thessaly twenty years before the Dorians invaded the Peloponnese, and as the Thessalian attack set the Aeolian migration under way, we can date the beginning of the migration approximately to 1130 B.C. (Str. 582 dates it to 'about the return of the Heracleidae' and gives a shorter interval after the Trojan War than Thucydides does). His son, Archelaus or Echelas, led Aeolians across the straits to the area by Dascylium, which later became the territory of Cyzicus. His youngest son, Gras, a grandson of Penthilus, moved on to Lesbos, and thereafter Lesbos and Cyme founded other towns (Str. 582, 662, being preferable to Paus. III, 2, 1). Gras was joined by some Lacedaemonians; their king then was Agis, a grandson of Aristodemus, who was a contemporary of Penthilus, and the Lacedaemonians had just been taking part in the founding of Patrae in Achaea by a grandson of Tisamenus (Paus. III, 2, 1 and VII, 6, 2). Meanwhile the Dorian invasion was driving refugees to Athens. When Cresphontes captured Pylus, the Neleidae fled to Athens. One of them, Melanthus, became king of Athens later (Paus. II, 18, 9). When the

[1] G, 2, 478, 'It is remarkable how chronologically consistent the account of these early kings is'.

Neleidae fled to Athens, Tisamenus and his Achaeans made their attack on the Ionians, and they spent at least two generations in expelling the Ionians, if we may judge by the foundation of Patrae. The Ionians fled during these two generations to Attica; some arrived when Melanthus was still king of Athens (Paus. VII, 1, 9), but others probably arrived during the reign of his son, Codrus. This Codrus was king of Athens when the Dorians made their attack on Attica and annexed the territory which was later called Megaris; and his younger sons, Neleus and Androclus, led the first wave of the Ionian migration (*F.Gr.H.* 4 F 125, Hellanicus; 3 F 155, Pherecydes).[1] At the same time a group of Dorians was led to Crete by Althaemenes, a grandson of Temenus, who was a contemporary of Neleus, a grandson of Melanthus (Str. 653). Finally, Strabo (582) remarks that the Aeolian migration started four generations earlier than the Ionian migration (he included in his reckoning Orestes, who was great-grandfather of Gras), and that it lasted over a longer period. On the other hand, Pausanias VII, 2, 2 is obviously wrong in saying that Theras, a contemporary of Temenus, founded Thera one generation before the Ionians sailed from Athens. For, if we follow Strabo, we find that the grandsons of Temenus, Aristodemus, Penthilus, Tisamenus and Melanthus were all involved one with another in contemporary actions.

These genealogies were not invented or made to synchronize by a later historian such as Hecataeus or Ephorus. No one could have imposed them on Argos, Sparta, Aeolis in Asia, Achaea and Athens. Their synchronization is due to the fact that they are historically correct. The problem for us is to interpret them in terms of chronology, because with the collapse of Mycenaean civilization annual dating seems to have disappeared. The length of a generation in a genealogy is the difference between the ages of father and son; this difference depends most on the age at which a man marries, and this is likely to vary, especially in royal families, as times are settled or unsettled. In practice the average generation in the Spartan royal houses was thirty-three years and in the Macedonian royal house twenty-seven years. It is therefore sound for the troubled times of the invasions and migrations to estimate an average generation at thirty years. Thus if Agamemnon was in his prime *c.* 1200 B.C., Orestes *floruit c.* 1170, Penthilus *c.* 1140, Archelaus *c.* 1110 and Gras *c.* 1080; but if the *floruit* is put at the age of thirty-five to forty, each man may (if he survives) have another thirty years of activity. We should therefore think of

[1] G, 14, 37 f.

Orestes being active 1170–1140, Penthilus 1140–1110, Archelaus 1110–1080 and Gras 1080–1050. We may then date the Aeolian migration approximately within the period 1140 to 1050 B.C. If we turn to Melanthus, we may put his *floruit c.* 1110, because he was expelled from Messenia about that time and became king at Athens later; then the *floruit* of Codrus is *c.* 1080 and of Neleus and Androclus *c.* 1050, and the period of the activity of Codrus *c.* 1080–1050 and of his sons *c.* 1050–1020. As Temenus was the eldest son of Aristomachus, we may put his *floruit* at *c.* 1120 and that of his grandson Althaemenes *c.* 1060, and the activity of Althaemenes *c.* 1060–1030. The Dorian attack on Athens, in which Codrus was killed and Althaemenes made his name, may be dated then *c.* 1050 B.C.; the departure of Althaemenes for Crete and the first phase of the Ionian migration under Neleus and Androclus both occurred shortly after 1050 B.C.

## VIII. THE LITERARY TRADITION AND THE ARCHAEOLOGICAL EVIDENCE

The co-ordination of the archaeological results with the main stream of the literary tradition is particularly difficult when there are few fixed points of chronology, and when some peoples, such as the Dorians, have as yet no distinguishing feature in terms of archaeological remains. Even our attempts to date the sack of Troy depend mainly on the Egyptian records which place the Sea Raids in the 1190's and 1180's. As Dr Stubbings has shown (*C.A.H.* I[3], pt. 1, p. 246), pottery found in areas which the Sea Raids affected indicates that the period known as Mycenaean III b ended not sooner than 1180 B.C. The last contacts which Troy had before the sack with the Mycenaean world, so far as they are revealed by pottery, belong to the middle of Mycenaean III b, of which we cannot date the beginning with any precision. Therefore it is only an approximation to say that the Trojan War covered one of the late decades of the thirteenth century. But if we accept the general tradition that some of the Greeks, returning from Troy over a number of years, founded settlements in southern Asia Minor, for instance at Tarsus, and if we place their activities in the period of Sea Raids when penetration of this area by roaming bands was possible, then we may attribute their activities to the last phase of Mycenaean III b (to which the earliest Mycenaean pottery from Tarsus belongs) and date the fall of Troy not more than some twenty years earlier by virtue of the literary tradition. As we have shown, a date such as *c.* 1200 B.C.

for the fall of Troy is compatible with the archaeological evidence, with the Hittite records about Mopsus and Madduwattash,[1] and with the chronological indications given by Thucydides.

There were troubles enough in Mycenaean Greece from *c.* 1250 B.C. onwards to the Trojan War. The literary tradition tells us of strife between Perseids and Pelopids, Heracles and Nestor, Eurystheus and Heracleidae, the war of the Seven against Thebes, the sack of Thebes by the Epigoni, the attempt of Hyllus against the Peloponnese and other acts of war. The expedition against Troy resembles the expedition against Syracuse in that it occurred after much warfare on the mainland of Greece. But the period after the Trojan War was no less troubled. It was concisely described by Thucydides I, 12, 2 as a revolutionary period with *stasis* rampant in the Mycenaean states for the most part and with the foundation of new states by the refugees. Excavation in Greece has confirmed his description, because the last phase of Mycenaean III b is marked by scattered examples of destruction in the Peloponnese at Epáno Englíanos, Tiryns, Mycenae and Zygouries and in central Greece at Crisa near Delphi and at Gla in Boeotia.[2] According to the literary tradition this period of internal strife was followed by a period of invasions, which began sixty years after the fall of Troy, that is in the course of Mycenaean III c and on our dating *c.* 1140 B.C. The century or so from 1250 to 1140 B.C. is very similar to the period from 460 to 350 B.C., when *stasis* and inter-state wars so weakened the city-states that less civilized peoples from the north were able to press southwards with success.

When we turn to the north, we see that new peoples who came ultimately from Central Europe were entering north-western Macedonia and northern Epirus (by which I mean the district in Epirus north of the Acheron valley and the plain of Ioannina). Their culture may be labelled 'Lausitz', with the proviso that it contained some elements not specifically Lausitz. Their ornaments, appearing now for the first time in the southern Balkans, are finger-rings of bronze band with spiralling ends, armlets of bronze wire and of bronze band with spiralling ends, and finger-rings and armlets of bronze band with grooved or incised decoration. They have been found in slab-lined cist graves at Prilep and

---

[1] See also G. E. Mylonas in *Hesperia*, 33 (1964), 366; and pp. 209 f. and 215 above for the broad agreement in Cyprus between archaeological evidence and foundation legends, with the fall of Troy *c.* 1200 B.C.

[2] The suggestion of V. R. d'A. Desborough on p. 660 above, that these examples of destruction were due to invaders, is not supported by the literary tradition.

at Saraj in Grave xi, both places being in Pelagonia;[1] in a slab-lined cist grave for a child near Demir Kapu in the Upper Vardar Valley;[2] in slab-lined cist graves at Kalbaki, Elaphotopos and Mazaraki on the upper Kalamas in northern Epirus;[3] and also as offerings at Dodona in southern Epirus.[4] The Kalamas group is securely dated by other objects in the graves to the period extending from the last decades of L.H. III b to early L.H. III c, i.e. c. 1200–1150 B.C. on the chronology followed here. As the graves in Pelagonia contained a Peschiera fibula and arched fibulae, they are to be dated probably within the twelfth century; and the grave at Demir Kapu likewise, as it contained an arched fibula of the same kind. Amber beads were found in the graves at Prilep, Kalbaki, Elaphotopos and Mazaraki. Amber came probably via the Adriatic Sea; for amber was the material most in use for beads in the tumulus-burials of the Mati valley in Central Albania.[5]

Few only of these cist graves contained pottery, but a number of one-handled curving-bottomed cups from Elaphotopos had two or sometimes three nipple-shaped knobs on the body. Such knobs are typical of the distinctive Lausitz pottery called *Buckelkeramik* or 'Knobbed Ware'. Another type of *Buckelkeramik* is remarkable for grooved or fluted decoration, which imitates the decoration of metal work, as in the armlets mentioned above. Considerable quantities of this type of pottery have been found at the following places: in a settlement at Gajtan near Scodra, probably in the Late Bronze Age and extending into the Early Iron Age;[6] in tumulus-burials of the Mati valley, where some pottery is dated by the excavators to L.B.A. on the basis of shape and the rest to the Early Iron Age;[7] in settlements at Vardarophtsa and Vardina in Central Macedonia, appearing first c. 1150 B.C. together with Mycenaean 'Granary' pottery and lasting until perhaps 1080 B.C.;[8] and in tumulus-burials at Vergina on the lower Haliacmon from c. 1100 to c. 900 B.C. or perhaps later.[9] Weapons of a northern kind, but not specific to the Lausitz culture, made their appearance just before and during the twelfth century at several sites in Epirus, sometimes in cist graves in a tumulus, sometimes in cist graves without a tumulus, and some-

[1] (b) A, 7 and (b) A, 10; cf. *Archaeologia Iugoslavica*, 5 (1964), 71 ff.

[2] (b) A, 14, 243.          [3] (a) §1, 17, 116 ff.; (b) A, 13.

[4] (b) A, 3, 242 nos. 124–7, Pl. 22b 2, 3, 15 and 16.

[5] (b) A, 7, 137 and 8.

[6] (b) A, 11 (cf. (b) A, 5, 103); (b) A, 9, Pl. iii and Pl. v, 1–4.

[7] (b) A, 8, 103 and Pl. xvi, 8–11.

[8] (a) §1, 26, 39, 96 n. 5, 125. Also at Strumsko by the lower Strymon; see *Археология* 1970, 2, 81.          [9] (a) A, 2, 185 ff.

times as chance finds: curving-backed knives, bored battle-axes of three kinds (not found in graves), slashing swords of Naue II type, leaf-shaped spearheads, and flame-shaped spearheads, all of bronze.[1]

This archaeological evidence puts the Lausitz invasion of the southern Balkans in a clear perspective. The Lausitz invaders and their associates seem to have followed the same routes as the Goths under Theodimund. Descending from the pass of Kačanik they moved forward into the middle Vardar Valley and into Pelagonia, and then into Central Albania as far as Epidamnus and into some parts of northern Epirus. This initial phase fell in the period c. 1200–1150 B.C. The next stage, beginning c. 1150 B.C., saw the conquest of Central Macedonia from the west via Edessa and perhaps from the middle Vardar valley via Kilindir. A recession occurred c. 1080 B.C. when they lost their two important bases east of the Vardar at Vardarophtsa and Vardina, but they expanded at about the same time to the south bank of the lower Haliacmon valley. In the period after 1080 B.C. they held most of Macedonia west of the Vardar, and also Pelagonia and Central Albania. With such a pattern of settlement it is clear that the economic centre of the invaders' realms lay in the western part of the central Macedonian plain.

The literary tradition enables us to put an ancient name to the Lausitz invaders. In the summary of Eugammon's *Telegony*, which was composed in the sixth century but drew upon traditional epic material, we learn that Odysseus commanded the Thesprotians at first unsuccessfully against the Brygi, after he had returned to Ithaca, i.e. in the decade c. 1180–1170 B.C. In the foundation legend of Epidamnus, in which the pre-Corinthian occupants are enumerated (Appian, *BC* ii, 39), the Briges held the site after Heracles and before the Taulantii, 'an Illyrian tribe'. The Briges were evidently regarded as not Illyrian. The early history of the Briges in Macedonia was well known, if we may judge from the incidental remarks made by Herodotus (vii, 73 and viii, 138, 2–3), that they lived next to the Macedones and had their capital below Mt Bermium, that is in the region between Edessa and Beroea, until they migrated to Asia. Even after the migration there were some Briges still inland of Epidamnus (Ps.-Scymnus 434) and in northern Pelagonia, where one of their cities was called Brygae (St. Byz. s.vv. *Brygias* and *Bryx*). These Briges of Europe were certainly related to the Phryges of Asia; indeed

[1] (*b*) A, 4, 318 ff., 328 ff., 331 ff. and 336 ff.; for spearheads also (*b*) A, 13, 196 ff., and *A.D.* 23 (1968), 293.

the similarities between the twelfth-century Lausitz pottery of Macedonia and that of Troy VII *b* are very marked.[1] The place-name Edessa is derived from the Phrygian word for water; and if the name Kydrara is Phrygian (Hdt. vii, 30), we have as names of Phrygian origin not only Scodra near Gajtan in Central Albania but also Cydrae in Pelagonia and Scydra near Edessa.[2]

In Southern Epirus the Thesprotian realm which Odysseus helped to defend against the Brygi is indicated archaeologically by the tholos tomb at Kiperi and, at a few kilometres' distance, the Mycenaean citadel above the Nekyomanteion in the Acheron valley. Dodona and the plain of Ioannina, where Mycenaean pottery has also been found, belonged to a separate Mycenaean realm in the epic saga. A particularly favourite weapon in both realms was the Mycenaean short sword of the kind known as Class F ii,[3] and Mycenaean knives and European spearheads were in use. In northern Epirus the European types of weapon predominated, and Mycenaean objects were rare. There the methods of burial were also different. Burials in cist graves in tumuli were made at Vajzë (inland of Valona) and at four places in the valley of the Drin and its tributary, the Kseria. It is mainly in these tumulus-burials, rather than in southern Epirus, that those objects have been found which have been associated with the final downfall of Mycenaean power: slashing swords of the Naue II type, long bronze pins, leaf-shaped spearheads, shield bosses (sometimes worn by women too as ornaments), and perhaps early weapons of iron (for instance an iron knife with a bronze rivet).[4]

When we relate the invasion of Macedonia by the Briges to the invasions of Mycenaean Greece in L.H. III b and III c, we see that the short-lived advance by Hyllus to the Isthmus *c.* 1220 B.C. in L.H. III b cannot have been due to pressure from the Briges who had not yet reached Macedonia. On the other hand, at the start of L.H. III c Odysseus faced the Briges in Epirus *c.* 1180/70 B.C. It was the pressure of the Briges on Western Macedonia and Epirus in the following decades which seems to have been an important factor in starting the Thessali and the Dorians on their invasions, *c.* 1140 B.C. and *c.* 1120 B.C. respectively, and in encouraging others to follow in their wake for another fifty years or so.

---

[1] For a detailed comparison see the author's *Macedonia* i (Oxford, 1972), 318 ff.

[2] See O. Haas, *Die phrygischen Sprachdenkmäler* (Sofia, 1966), 20 and 71 on Kydrara.

[3] (*b*) A, 2, 33 ff. and *A.D.* 23 (1968), 291, 294 and Pl. 235 b.

[4] (*b*) A, 4, 354 ff.

The opening stage of these latter invasions has left little trace archaeologically except for the destruction of some citadels, including Mycenae, but in recent years two significant discoveries have been made. A large, low tumulus has been partially excavated at Hexalophos, twelve kilometres west of Trikkala in Thessaly, and two slab-lined cist tombs in it were dated by the excavator, in view of their contents, to within the half-century *c.* 1150–1100 B.C.[1] Burial in cist-tombs within a tumulus was as novel in Thessaly as it was common in northern Epirus, and the contents of the tombs included a short sword of Class F ii, a knife, a leaf-shaped javelin-head, a finger-ring of bronze band with spiralling ends, bits of a shield boss, a two-handled pot with a knob, such as are common in Macedonia (e.g. at Vergina),[2] and high-footed *kylikes* of an inferior quality, such as have been found in southern Epirus. At Mycenae inside the citadel, in the burnt layer of the final destruction, late in L.H. IIIc, a cist grave has been found which contained a bronze finger-ring with spiralling ends, long bronze pins, and arched fibulae.[3] Most of the objects in these burials were new to Mycenaean Greece and familiar in Epirus. They point unequivocally to Epirus and to its hinterland, namely Central Albania and Pelagonia, as the centre of diffusion from which the first invading forces came, and they underline the dating of the first successful waves of invasion to well within L.H. IIIc, that is *c.* 1140–20 B.C.

The period of *stasis* and the period of invasions are kept separate and distinct in the literary tradition. When Thucydides mentioned the invasions by the Thessalians, Boeotians and Dorians, he probably selected those invasions which resulted in the permanent settlement of new peoples. The aim of these invaders was rather to destroy the centres of resistance in the royal citadels than to lay waste the territories they intended to occupy; and the literary tradition indicates that the invaders captured the citadels of Mycenae, Lacedaemon and Pylus. The citadel of Mycenae fell early in the invasion some 80 years after the fall of Troy, that is *c.* 1120 B.C., which was certainly in the latter half of the archaeological period Mycenaean IIIc, when the Granary within the citadel was in fact destroyed. Certainly Mycenae ceased soon afterwards to be an important centre. There is no doubt that this and similar disasters marked the collapse of the Mycenaean

---

[1] (*a*) A, 47.

[2] Compare *A.D.* 23, B2 (1968), Pl. 201 b with Andronikos, *Vergina* i, Plates 31 and 36, also from tumulus-burials.

[3] (*a*) A, 18, Pl. xxxiii d–e.

system on the mainland and the seizure of the Peloponnese by the
Dorians. A difficulty remains in the case of the site at Epáno
Englíanos which has been identified with the Homeric Pylus.
This open, and then unfortified,[1] palace was destroyed and
abandoned at the end of Mycenaean III b and not in the latter half
of III c. The explanation may well be that the centre of the Pylian
kingdom was moved after the destruction of the palace to a different and stronger site, which eventually fell to the Dorian invaders not by force but by agreement as Pausania's iv, 3, 6 implies.[2]

The end of Mycenaean III c, including the sub-Mycenaean
phase, probably varied in date from place to place. At Melos,
where Phylakopi was abandoned before the end of Mycenaean
III c, the Thucydidean date c. 1116 b.c. for the seizure of the
island is clearly acceptable. The cemeteries of Kerameikos at
Athens were used probably by refugees over a period of two
generations which may fall between 1110 and 1050 b.c., and the
excavations at Old Smyrna date the Ionian settlement in that
region at the latest to c. 1000 b.c. Between 1050 and 1000 b.c.
the literary evidence, as we have seen, puts the Dorian occupation
of the Megarid and the beginning of the Ionian migration from
Attica, the home of the Protogeometric pottery which was carried
by the migrants to the east Aegean area. Here, however, we have
to co-ordinate two very loose systems of dating, which hinge upon
the sequence of pottery styles and the length of generations in
genealogies, and either system has an elasticity of some 50 years.
Nevertheless, enough important sites have been excavated to give
the preliminary assurance that in general terms the literary tradition for the sack of Troy, for *stasis* on the mainland and settlements overseas in the *Nostoi* period, for the leading facts of the
Dorian invasion, for the Dorian expansion to Melos and for the
Ionian expansion to Ionia rests upon a fairly accurate foundation
of folk memory and literary tradition and is correctly interpreted
by Thucydides and some other historians.

[1] (a) A, 6, 8.
[2] See G. E. Mylonas in *Hesperia*, 33 (1964), 366 ff. for an explanation on
similar lines.

# CHAPTER XXXVII

## THE WESTERN MEDITERRANEAN

### I. ITALY

THE Italian Peninsula was the home of human groups from the Lower Palaeolithic onward. During the Quaternary geological period, changes in sea level exposed now more, now less of the low-lying parts of Italy but this had very little effect on the earliest inhabitants. Their area of occupation was in any case limited to the limestone masses of the Apennines, which furnished them with suitable firm terrain, caves to live in, and a supply of flint and chert. The active vulcanicity of certain areas and the glaciers which covered the higher slopes during the cold phases probably affected them much more.[1] The earliest deposits contain hand-axes of Abbevillian type, which in time gradually developed into the more refined Acheulean ones.[2] The latest of these are found associated with types proper to the Middle Palaeolithic Mousterian industry, which flourished long in Italy. This industry is associated with the Neanderthal physical type, of which remains have been found at the caves of Saccopastore and Monte Circeo.[3]

The cultures of the Upper Palaeolithic, which were created by men of modern type who had a much more varied and specialized tool-kit than their predecessors though their economy remained a hunting and gathering one, are well represented in Italy. The flint industry is usually a variant of the Perigordian of France, often called Grimaldian in its late stages. Important evidence for this period has been found in the caves of Liguria, particularly those of Grimaldi, with their ceremonial burials of men and women,[4] and in the Grotta Romanelli in the extreme south-east, where artistic representations of animals, related to those of the 'Franco-Cantabrian' groups of France and Spain, though less accomplished, have been found engraved on the walls and on loose blocks, along with abstract geometric patterns, and what perhaps are stylized human beings.[5] Recently similar things have

---

* An original version of this chapter was published as fascicle 57 in 1967; the present chapter was revised in 1971.

[1] §I, 62; G, 13, 370–544; G, 6, 103–50.

[2] §I, 60; G, 16, 42–70; §I, 51, esp. pls. I–XI.

[3] §I, 12; §I, 13; §I, 31.

[4] §I, 61, II, I, 3–48; §I, 25.

[5] §I, 10; §I, 11.

begun to turn up in a number of other caves, including some of the Ligurian ones, and more will undoubtedly be found. Two small figurines in the round, resembling the 'Venus' figures from Upper Palaeolithic sites elsewhere in Europe have also been found in Northern Italy, but unfortunately both without context.

The radiocarbon date of 9970 ± 580 B.C., which has been obtained for the upper levels at Romanelli, shows that the Perigordian lasted to the end of the period in Italy,[1] but Upper Palaeolithic traditions of flint-working seem to have lingered on even longer, up to the beginning of the Neolithic several thousand years later. Alongside this 'Epipalaeolithic' tradition we find groups with modified flint industries which can be called Mesolithic.[2] Changing environmental conditions at the end of the last Ice Age brought about a shift, in Italy as elsewhere in Europe, from an economy based on hunting big game to one based on small game, fowling, fishing and strand-looping. A few of these Mesolithic groups painted simple designs on pebbles, as did the Azilians of France and Spain, or engraved them on rock-faces. They were probably full of significance to their makers but we cannot interpret them.

The first Neolithic societies with a mixed farming economy have so far been found in quantity only in the south-east and in Liguria, though traces are beginning to turn up in Calabria also. Their most characteristic product is dark-faced pottery decorated with incisions or impressions made in the clay before firing. It is difficult to say how far these economic and other changes were due to groups of immigrant farmers looking for new land, and how far to the adoption of new ideas by the older inhabitants through contact with other cultures. Both processes probably played a part. The impressed pottery of South-east Italy and the Tremiti islands exhibits such close similarities to the impressed wares found on the opposite shores of the Adriatic, particularly those which have been found at Smilčić in Dalmatia and on the island of Hvar, that it is impossible to explain them unless there was some traffic across that narrow sea. The Ligurian impressed wares, separated from the Apulian ones by a considerable area in which no finds have been made, are closely related to those of South France and North-east Spain.[3] On the other hand, at the Arene Candide cave, in Liguria, the flint industry associated with the impressed pottery was directly descended from that found in the Mesolithic levels in the same

---

[1] §I, 5.     [2] §I, 50.
[3] §I, 56; §I, 8, 159–98; §I, 6; §I, 7; §I, 2.

cave, and the lowest level of the Coppa Nevigata settlement on the Gulf of Manfredonia contained impressed pottery associated with remains which indicated a community whose economy was still chiefly, if not entirely, based on gathering, particularly molluscs; indeed they had developed a special flint instrument for opening the shells.[1] The few radiocarbon dates so far obtained suggest that groups making impressed pottery must have been present in Italy already in the earlier part of the fifth millennium B.C., if not earlier.[2]

The Early Neolithic people of South-east Italy inhabited both caves and open villages, but in the succeeding, Middle Neolithic, phase a special type of settlement appeared there. It was usually located on or near good farming land and was surrounded by one or more ditches. These often divided the settlement into a smaller habitation area and a larger area which may have contained the cultivated land, cattle-pens etc. Settlements vary in size from small 'homesteads' with a single 'compound' to large villages with up to a hundred. The 'compounds' are themselves delimited by circular ditches within which, presumably, huts or tents were erected, though little is known as yet about these. The density of occurrence of these ditched settlements, as revealed by air photography, in such areas of good farming land as the Foggia plain suggests that the system of agriculture practised may have necessitated the shifting of a settlement from time to time as the land became exhausted.[3]

The inhabitants of these villages used a variety of pottery, much of it made of refined clay and gaily painted. Simple painted decoration by broad bands of red paint may already have been in use before the end of the previous phase but now there were also pots with more complex patterns built up of narrow lines of paint, and two-colour wares with patterns in red or orange outlined in dark brown and black, like those found in the first settlement on the Lipari Acropolis, though the patterns used are somewhat different and so is the paste of the pottery. Imitations of the old impressed patterns were also used sometimes in combination with painted decoration, and a new self-colour ware, decorated with patterns scratched after firing, became popular, especially in the far south. Later still, wares identical with the Serra d'Alto pottery of Lipari were used, though the range of shapes seems to have differed somewhat. A northern outpost of painted pottery, centred on the Vibrata valley, is known as the Ripoli culture. Painted pottery has also been found recently on sites in Campania

[1] §1, 48.  [2] G, 14; §1, 23.  [3] §1, 16; 14; 15.

and Calabria, thus linking the south-eastern painted pottery geographically with that found in Capri, the Lipari islands and Sicily. The inspiration which led to the production of painted pottery came evidently from the opposite shores of the Adriatic, where painted pottery was used from the Peloponnese to Dalmatia. There are many similarities between the Italian painted pottery and Greek and Yugoslav types of the later Neolithic, but their implications have not yet been worked out in detail.[1]

In Liguria the earliest Neolithic people were followed, at Arene Candide and elsewhere, by people whose equipment included small clay figurines of women, decorated clay stamps, and dark-faced polished pottery, often decorated with geometric or ladder patterns scratched after firing. Many of the vases had square or quadrilobate mouths. This 'square-mouthed vase' culture is also known from village sites and cemeteries of crouched inhumations in cist or earth graves in the Po valley and neighbouring areas, where it is known as the Chiozza culture.[2] In these areas there seems also to have been an earlier Neolithic phase, known as Fiorano, with similar settlements and cemeteries, but with pottery decorated before firing and without the square-mouthed pots, stamps and figurines.[3] True handles were common on the pottery, as they were in the succeeding Chiozza phase. The connexions of both these cultures seem to lie eastwards, round the head of the Adriatic, with the Middle Neolithic cultures of Yugoslavia, and perhaps also of East-central Europe.

The Late Neolithic culture most characteristic of Northern Italy, however, had its centre in the north-west, and represents a developed stage of the Cortaillod culture which is best known from the lakeside settlements of western Switzerland and eastern France. This is characterized by plain, highly polished pottery with rounded or carinated profiles, and the Italian *facies* is called the Lagozza culture. Handles were not used and string-hole lugs were the normal provision for manipulating the pots. They include multiple ones, both simple and of the so-called 'pan-pipe' variety. Other finds include a microlithic flint industry, probably connected with hunting small game and birds, and spinning and weaving equipment, such as weaving-combs, loom-weights and spindle-whorls.[4]

In the south, the Late Neolithic is characterized, as in Sicily and Lipari, by the red monochrome pottery of Diana type (some-

---

[1] §1, 56; §1, 52; §1, 27, 166–7; §1, 41.
[2] §1, 8, 66–113, 199–218.    [3] §1, 34.
[4] §1, 30; §1, 8, 117–38, 219–51; §1, 21.

times called Bellavista on the mainland). It is found in open villages, caves and cemeteries of cist graves. This pottery has been found very far north, for example in the Pescara district, and in a village of huts at Norcia in Umbria, where it was associated with pottery of Lagozza type, showing these two cultures to have flourished contemporaneously, probably in the earlier part of the third millennium B.C.[1]

Trade was well established in the Neolithic period, particularly the Middle and Late Neolithic. This is shown by the occasional occurrence of potsherds in contexts far removed from their normal ones, and by the wide distribution of obsidian throughout the Peninsula. That found in the south seems to have come, as might be expected, mostly from Lipari, but that found on northern sites seems to be Sardinian.[2] At the end of the period, however, metal was already becoming known and scoriae of copper have been found, for instance, in Diana levels in Lipari.

The onset of the Copper Age was marked, in mainland Italy as in Sicily, by far-reaching changes in the cultural pattern. But the dichotomy between the north, the Po valley and adjacent regions, and the rest of peninsular Italy remains. In the northern area the chief influences were those of the cultures of continental Europe, in the rest those of the Aegean.

The Copper Age of South Italy is not as yet fully understood, but there are traces of the Piano Conte culture, with its grey pottery decorated with shallow fluting, in Apulia and at Ariano Irpino at the watershed of the Apennines between Apulia and Campania.[3] In Campania itself a remarkable culture has been found in cemeteries of rock-cut tombs at Gaudo near Paestum and at Mirabella Eclano in the Avellino district.[4] The Gaudo group used pottery which points strongly to close connexion with the Aegean cultures of the beginning of the Bronze Age. Shapes included jugs, covers, double vases and askoi, sometimes with applied or incised decoration. Two copper daggers likewise find their best parallels in the Aegean, as also does the type of tomb. Tanged arrowheads of flint and flint imitations of metal daggers are, however, shared with other Italian Copper Age cultures. They also, surprisingly, used trapezoidal microliths, probably as transverse arrowheads. Further north, between the Tiber and the Arno, we have abundant evidence of another culture, called Rinaldone.[5] This group used the same form of tomb (along with cist graves at times), but their pottery, though similar technically, was much less

[1] §I, 18.          [2] G, 8; 5.          [3] §I, 59, fig. 12c.
[4] §I, 55; 42.      [5] §I, 29; 59.

varied. There were long-necked flasks, usually with two horizontal tubular handles or vertical tunnel-handles, which were
occasionally decorated with applied pellets or cordons, and tronco-
conic cups, sometimes with burnish decoration. Flint arrow- and
lance-heads were common, and battle-axes and mace-heads of
igneous stone were used. Stone beads and pendants also occur.
These people controlled the mineral resources of Tuscany, so it is
not surprising to find copper daggers, axes and awls among their
equipment. More unusual are the two V-perforated conical
buttons of antimony found with other objects in the cave on
Monte Bradoni.[1]

Liguria seems to have been a somewhat backward area during
the Bronze and Iron Ages, but the Po valley, constantly in close
touch with Central Europe across the Alps and, to a lesser extent,
with the Aegean via the Adriatic, was one of the most tech-
nologically advanced areas of Italy and remained so throughout
prehistoric times. The Remedello culture, which ushers in the
Copper Age in this region, is known principally from cemeteries
of crouched inhumations in earth graves.[2] One type of copper
dagger seems to copy an Early Minoan type, but most of the metal
goods, chiefly daggers, axes, pins and ornaments, approximate to
Central and East-central European types, and these connexions
are underlined by other features of the equipment. Pottery is
relatively rare in the tombs and usually coarse in fabric. The
shapes were confined to single-handled pots with a short neck,
biconical pots and tronco-conic cups. Decoration was limited to
bosses and horizontal and vertical grooving. Pottery of bell-
beaker type is, however, also found in Remedello contexts and
serves, along with the metal types, to date the Remedello culture
to the late third and beginning of the second millennium B.C.

By the latest phase of the Remedello culture the Early Bronze
Age had already begun. From then on for several centuries the
technological lead of the Po valley cultures over those of the rest
of Italy became more and more marked. Metal was scarcely
used at all in the rest of peninsular Italy during the Early and
Middle Bronze Ages, but the cultures of the Po valley and those
of the Alpine valleys to the north kept parity with developments in
Central Europe. In the settlements around the Alpine lakes the
Polada culture, characterized by coarse pottery with a limited
range of simple shapes fitted with ring, strap and sometimes
nose-bridge handles, and by a considerable use of bone, antler
and wood (often preserved in the lake-mud), carried many of the

[1] §1, 19.                    [2] §1, 29, 59; §1, 43.

features of the Lagozza and Remedello cultures on into the
Early Bronze Age.[1] In the Po valley itself a large number of
villages of rectangular timber-framed huts are known, whose
occupation generally began in the Early Bronze Age but continued much later. These villages have become known as *terremare* because of the intense blackness of the deposit through the
decay of food-refuse, and the material remains found in them as the
Terramara culture.[2] The inhabitants of these villages were
agriculturalists and stock-breeders, who also did a certain amount
of hunting. They used much pottery, of very varied types, but
characterized especially by a decoration of grooving, dimples and
bosses, and by crescentic, horned or axe-like appendages set
above the handles. Bronze objects were plentiful, and fragments
of moulds attest the working of metal in at least some of the
villages. The earliest types present were those current in the
advanced Early Bronze Age of Central Europe, followed by an
array of characteristic Central European Middle Bronze types,
including socketed spearheads, waisted axes, wheel-headed pins
etc. One type, however, the 'Peschiera' dagger, with flanged tang,
seems to imitate Mycenaean daggers, and may have been developed in Northern Italy. Parallel with the Terramara culture ran
the Peschiera culture of the Alpine valleys and lakeside settlements, sharing the same kinds of bronzes, but having its own
local traditions of potting, which contrasted with imported
Terramara pieces. Throughout the Bronze Age some of these
groups made a habit of carving 'statues-menhirs' and engraving
on glacier-smoothed rocks scenes which give us a unique insight
into their way of life at various times.[3] Rather similar rock-
engravings occur in the Maritime Alps of Liguria, where the
numerous representations of bronze objects contrast with the
scarcity of actual examples.[4] The richness in metal of the cultures
of the Alpine area and the Po valley during the Bronze Age may
be accounted for in part by their geographical position on the
transcontinental 'amber' route, along which amber and doubtless
other products were traded between central and northern
Europe and the Aegean civilizations. The final 'leg' of this route
was by sea down the Adriatic.

During this time peninsular Italy came to be inhabited by
people whose fairly uniform way of life was expressed in their
relatively uniform material equipment. Since they were centred on
the Apennine range and the lowlands which fringe it to east and

---

[1] §1, 28; 4; 63.  
[3] §1, 3; 44; 1.  
[2] §1, 54.  
[4] §1, 9; 36.

west these groups have been classed together as the Apennine culture.[1] The Apennines were, in fact, of great importance in their way of life since the economy of many of them seems to have centred on stock-breeding. The summer migrations of these transhuming people to the high pastures are reflected in the occurrence of sites of the culture as high as 6000 ft. above sea level. Their pastoral interests are also reflected by the presence of pottery cheese-strainers and milk-boilers in their settlements. As might be expected, many elements seem to have been fused in the making of this culture, of which an initial proto-Apennine or Conelle phase has recently been recognized. Among them the Aegean element is strong, especially in the south-east, as exemplified in the finding of a bossed bone object in a rock-tomb at Altamura near Bari identical with one found in an early Middle Helladic context at Lerna.[2] The pottery found in the tomb is classed as proto-Apennine, but some fragments are remarkably like Middle Helladic wares. The characteristic incised decoration of the Apennine culture which is present already in the Conelle phase, and which includes spiral and meander patterns and dotted or dot-filled bands, has many resemblances to the incised decoration of pottery of Vinča tradition in Yugoslavia.

The remains of the Apennine culture are normally found in village settlements consisting of light huts, sometimes on defensible heights. Sometimes also remains are found in caves and rock-shelters, and there were also temporary camps in the open. Burial customs are not so well known, but earth graves were used as well as rock-tombs and, in the area between Bari and Taranto, a kind of megalithic gallery grave.[3] Fully developed Apennine pottery was imported into the Lipari islands, where it was found in Milazzese contexts along with L.H. IIIa imported pottery. It has also been found associated with L.H. II and L.H. IIIa pottery on the island of Ischia.[4]

The beginning of the Late Bronze Age in Central Europe early in the thirteenth century had an immediate effect on Northeast Italy. A range of new metal types, such as winged axes, violin-bow fibulae and swords, appeared. Part of a mould for a winged axe of just this type was found in the House of the Oil Merchant at Mycenae with pottery datable to the thirteenth century and attests the continuing contact between Greece and the lands at the head of the Adriatic, presumably by sea.[5] Bronzes

---

[1] §I, 58; 49.        [2] §I, 47.        [3] §I, 24.
[4] §II, 8, 125 and fig. 23; §I, 17.
[5] §I, 20.

of the kinds found in the *terremare* of this period are also found on sites of the Apennine culture, particularly those on the coast, such as Coppa Nevigata and Taranto, and it seems certain that they were distributed by seaborne trade around the coast.[1] Mycenaean pottery of L.H. IIIa and later phases is also found on some of these sites, but its exact correlation with the bronzes and indigenous pottery is not sufficiently clear to be of use for chronological purposes.[2]

In their later phases some of the Terramara settlements which were low-lying seem to have been raised on piles, to protect them against floodwater (which was perhaps becoming a greater hazard with the deterioration of the climate at this time), and some were surrounded with a bank and a ditch. The latter do not seem usually to have had a defensive function, but to have been a further measure of protection against flooding. There is some reason to believe that there was an influx of new people from East-central Europe into the Po valley at the beginning of the Late Bronze Age, who brought with them new types of pottery, domesticated horses and perhaps wheeled vehicles. The pottery and the antler cheek-pieces of horse-bits are found in the Terramara settlements, and some representations of chariots and four-wheeled carts on the rock-faces of the Alps may be as early as this.[3] The newcomers seem to have mingled with the older inhabitants.

At a somewhat later date, about 1100 B.C., groups of Urnfield people from Central Europe invaded Italy. They seem to have been small and fast-moving, for they swept rapidly through the whole country, settling at various points from the Po valley in the north to Calabria in the far south. This episode ushers in the final phase of the Bronze Age in Italy, and is also the prelude to the Iron Age. The Urnfield groups may have occupied some of the Terramara villages in the north, for their cemeteries are found near some of them. Elsewhere, they made settlements on high ground and sometimes fortified them with walls. But as yet we know them mainly from their cremation cemeteries. The ashes were placed in urns, which are always variants on the biconical urns of Central Europe. The variation in the shape and decoration of the urns from cemetery to cemetery suggests that the different groups had somewhat different areas of origin in their original homeland.[4] The bronzes found in some of these graves and also separately in hoards include, as well as developed violin-

[1] §1, 58, 184–8.
[2] §1, 57.
[3] §1, 54, 236–40; §1, 1, 43.
[4] §1, 26.

bow fibulae, more elaborate types with arc-shaped, serpentine or leaf-shaped bow, and often with spiral foot, and many other Central European Urnfield types, such as pins, wavy-bladed knives and sheet-bronze work, particularly cups with bossed decoration, as represented in the Coste del Marano hoard.[1]

The urns were sometimes placed simply in the earth, sometimes in a specially dug pit or within a box made of small slabs of stone. One of the cemeteries, that of Pianello, in the Marche, was laid out in the ruins of a village of the Apennine culture.[2] This does not mean that the Apennine culture had come to an end, however. The Urnfielders were a small minority, and in the following centuries the native traditions reasserted themselves more or less strongly in different parts of the Peninsula.

The Italian Iron Age began about the middle of the tenth century B.C. A number of regional groups with strongly individual characteristics can be distinguished in the various geographical regions. The rite of cremation in urnfields was preserved in the north, but in the central and southern parts inhumation in various kinds of tomb was the normal practice. In the eastern Alpine area the Golasecca culture flourished, and is known from its rich urnfield cemeteries. Three phases have been distinguished, lasting down to the Romanization of the area.[3] Further south lay the territory of the Villanovan culture, with two distinct provinces, a northern, centred on the area of Bologna in the Po valley, and a southern, in Tuscany and northern Latium, with outliers to the east in the Marche and to the south in the Salerno region.[4] The Villanovan people were basically agriculturalists, but some, particularly those of the Po valley around Bologna and Este, contained communities of specialist smiths who developed a tradition of fine metalwork of the highest quality.[5] Besides tools, weapons, fibulae, etc., their products included vases, buckets and armour made of sheet bronze and decorated with elaborate *repoussé* work.[6] In Tuscany and Latium the Villanovan cemeteries are found near the later Etruscan cemeteries, and they obviously provided the basic population which went to the making of the Etruscan civilization.

South of the Tiber, Latium was the home of a group which practised mainly inhumation burial but also sometimes cremation, when the ashes were placed in an urn shaped like an oval hut and put into a pit, along with other grave goods.[7] Campania and

[1] §1, 39; §1, 38, 30–98.  [2] §1, 26, 369; §1, 46.
[3] §1, 30, 119–200; §1, 53.  [4] §1, 32; §1, 45, 89–94.
[5] See Plate 176(*d*).  [6] §1, 33, 5–60.  [7] §1, 40.

Calabria developed an important local culture which has become known as the 'fossa grave' culture from the prevailing burial custom of inhumation in a trench grave, though in Calabria rock-tombs with rectangular chambers were also used by these people.[1] Their metal weapons and ornaments are of the prevailing Italian types but their pottery shows Urnfield and native Apennine influences. However, they came early under strong influence from Greek traders, whose painted geometric pottery they tried to imitate. Greek colonization put an end to the coastal *facies* of this culture in the later eighth century B.C., but it continued to flourish inland under strong Greek influence for some time.

On the eastern side of the Apennines also there were vigorous local groups. In the Marche and the Abruzzi the remains of these Iron Age groups are found in cemeteries of crouched inhumations in trench graves.[2] Their pottery was predominantly of native tradition, and they showed a marked liking for elaborate bronze ornaments. In Apulia similar crouched inhumations are found under tumuli. The contents of these graves show that the local inhabitants had developed an elaborate painted pottery, doubtless inspired by Greek geometric wares, but elaborating on older native shapes to the point of fantasy.[3] This culture survived late in the regions which were not touched by Greek colonization.

## II. SICILY AND MALTA

The earliest traces of man so far identified in Sicily belong to the Upper Palaeolithic period, and the distribution of the sites is predominantly coastal. These first inhabitants must have come to Sicily from the mainland of Italy. Apart from one site, which may be a little older than the rest, the deposits of this age in Sicily have a flint industry of Gravettian type.[4]

The men who made these tools are as yet known only from a few burials found recently in a cave on the north coast of the island. One skeleton had a necklace of pierced deer's teeth, and all were covered with red ochre. They have left lively representations of themselves and of the animals they hunted engraved on the walls of the caves. One, on the small island of Levanzo, near the west coast of Sicily, has naturalistic figures of red deer, oxen and equids, and simpler, but still vivid, engravings of men.[5] At Addaura, near Palermo, there are scenes incorporating several

---

[1] §I, 33, 160–210; §I, 37.
[2] §I, 33, 105–48; §I, 22.
[3] §I, 33, 211–43; §I, 35.
[4] §II, 8; §I, 60; §II, 34.
[5] §II, 19, 1–43; §II, 20.

engraved human figures, who appear to be taking part in dances and rituals of various kinds, as well as isolated figures and representations of animals.[1]

These engravings are probably not all of exactly the same date. Different styles can be distinguished, some probably of the Mesolithic period. Relatively few Mesolithic remains have yet been found in Sicily and it is not always easy to distinguish them from those of the Upper Palaeolithic. The climatic changes which followed the retreat of the ice at the end of the Pleistocene affected Sicily less than other parts of Europe, so there was less need to change the material culture. The microlithic industries which are characteristic of so many European Mesolithic cultures have so far certainly appeared in Sicily only at two sites.[2] In both the Mesolithic industry was the earliest deposit, and it persisted in later levels, but mingled with potsherds and obsidian which show that Neolithic cultures were by then present in Sicily.

Despite the mingling of Neolithic and Mesolithic elements at these two sites, the introduction of a farming economy seems to have been due to the arrival of new people rather than to the adaptation of the older inhabitants to the new way of life. The flint industry of the new people was quite different from the older industries of the island, and their pottery belonged to a tradition which was widespread in both the eastern and western Mediterranean. Characterized by decoration impressed on the surface before firing with the aid of a variety of simple instruments, this pottery generally accompanies the earliest Neolithic culture in any region in which it appears. People using this pottery came to Sicily by sea, probably in the fifth millennium B.C., or earlier, and quickly established themselves all over the island. Their culture has been called after the site of Stentinello, near Syracuse.[3]

The Stentinello people lived in villages in the open, though they also used caves, as did most later cultures, for various purposes. Stentinello itself was a typical village, surrounded by an oval rock-cut ditch which was backed by a stone rampart. In some cases, as at Matrensa, the ditch was discontinuous and may not have been defensive.[4] Little is known, unfortunately, about what dwellings existed in these villages. On some sites the Stentinello pottery is found mixed with painted wares which do not appear in the earliest stage of the Neolithic in South Italy.[5] Moreover, some of the Stentinello pottery has more elaborate decoration than is usual on similar wares elsewhere, including patterns made

---

[1] §II, 22; 23.   [2] §II, 3; 4.   [3] §II, 24; §II, 8, 38–46.
[4] §II, 7, 42.   [5] §II, 25.

by the use of stamps, and representations of the human face, so that it seems that the impressed pottery survived longer in Sicily than in some other areas.

The later development of the Neolithic in Sicily itself is still somewhat obscure, but some light is thrown on it by what is known of the Neolithic sequence in two smaller island-groups, one to the north and one to the south of it. These are the Lipari, or Aeolian, islands and the Maltese islands. Neither of these groups has so far produced any trace of human occupation during the Palaeolithic or Mesolithic period, and their sequences both begin with the arrival, in the Neolithic, of men closely allied in material equipment to those who brought the Stentinello pottery to Sicily. The impressed decoration was not so complex as that of the most elaborate Stentinello pottery, but very much in the same tradition.

In Lipari this impressed pottery is found with early types of painted pottery at Castellaro Vecchio and it is not possible to be certain that there was a phase without painted pottery.[1] The rest of the culture-sequence in the islands is admirably clear owing to the splendid series of stratified deposits found beneath the old citadel of Lipari, which represent occupation from the Neolithic until medieval times. Here the first stratum was characterized by finely levigated, light-coloured pottery decorated with flame-like patterns in orange bordered with black, or rectilinear patterns made with thin lines of red paint. There was also a black ware which sometimes had decoration scratched after firing. In the next period the painted wares reached the acme of their development. Made of fine clay with a greenish tinge, the pots were covered with small designs in dark paint, which were often based on the spiral and meander. The pots had intricate handles, often built up of spiral rolls of clay. There were also incised wares with meander patterns.[2] Eventually these elaborately decorated pots seem to have palled, and the pottery of the final phase of the Neolithic was a monochrome red ware, with simple shapes and trumpet handles, but with clear traces of derivation from the painted ware of the preceding phase.[3] This last phase of the Aeolian Neolithic seems to have been long, prosperous and peaceful. The pottery shows a clear typological development, which has been confirmed stratigraphically. The population seem mainly to have lived, not on the defensible citadel site, but on the Diana plain behind, which has given its name to the culture.

The importance and prosperity of the Lipari islands were

[1] §II, 11, 5–18.    [2] §II, 10, 18–28; §II, 8, 46–57.    [3] §II, 12.

founded on their deposits of obsidian, which was traded widely
from the beginning of the Neolithic, particularly to Southern
Italy and Sicily.[1] This trade probably reached its apogee in the
Diana phase. The population of the islands must have been
drawn initially from South Italy and Sicily. Since there was no clay
available there, pottery, or the raw material for making it, must
have been imported. The impressed pottery is more like that of
Sicily than that of the mainland, but styles of painting corresponding to the second and third phases are found on the mainland,
mostly, so far, in Apulia. The Diana pottery occurs widely in
peninsular Italy, but it is also very widespread in Sicily.

The Maltese islands were rather differently situated. As they
have no comparable natural resources, their prosperity must have
depended mainly on the products of farming, though their
inhabitants seem to have traded widely at all times. The earliest
Maltese culture is called after a cave, Ghar Dalam, where pottery
similar to that of Stentinello, but lacking such things as stamp
decoration, was first found. It is now known also from a number
of sites in Malta and Gozo, which, though mostly later occupied
by megalithic temples, seem at this time to have been open
villages.[2] A second phase in Malta is characterized by pottery
which, though generally undecorated, seems to have evolved from
the impressed Ghar Dalam ware. It has been named after the
newly excavated site of Skorba, which has given a great deal of
new information about the early stages of settlement in Malta.[3]
The earliest Skorba pottery is grey in colour, usually undecorated,
with few shapes, mainly open bowls and footed vessels. Later a
red surface became fashionable, together with new shapes and
more elaborate handles. Trumpet lugs were common in both
these phases, and the red Skorba greatly resembles the Diana
ware of the Aeolian islands, which also makes great use of trumpet
lugs. Among imports to the islands in these earliest phases,
obsidian with a greenish tinge, apparently from Pantellaria, is of
particular interest. There were some traces of oval huts of this
phase at Skorba.

The next period was marked by far-reaching cultural changes
everywhere, possibly connected with the beginning of the Aegean
Bronze Age. The equipment of the inhabitants of Sicily and the
Aeolian islands, particularly the pottery, points to strong con-
tacts with the Late Neolithic and Early Helladic groups of the
Greek mainland, and in Malta, too, Aegean contacts are indicated.

[1] G, 8; 5.     [2] §II, 18, 41, 44; §II, 29, 300; §II, 31, 11 August 1962.
[3] §II, 29, 33.

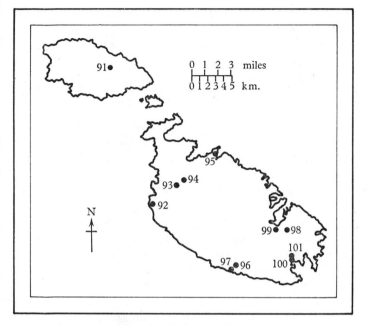

Map 15. Malta and Gozo.

NUMERICAL KEY

| | | | | | |
|---|---|---|---|---|---|
| 91 | Ġgantija | 95 | Buġibba | 99 | Hal Saflieni |
| 92 | Baħrija | 96 | Ħaġar Qim | 100 | Borġ in-Nadur |
| 93 | Ta Ħaġrat | 97 | Mnajdra | 101 | Għar Dalam |
| 94 | Skorba | 98 | Tarxien | | |

ALPHABETICAL KEY

| | | | | | |
|---|---|---|---|---|---|
| Baħrija | 92 | Għar Dalam | 101 | Skorba | 94 |
| Borġ in-Nadur | 100 | Ħaġar Qim | 96 | Ta Ħaġrat | 93 |
| Buġibba | 95 | Hal Saflieni | 99 | Tarxien | 98 |
| Ġgantija | 91 | Mnajdra | 97 | | |

This period is called the Copper Age, though metal is scarce or absent on sites.

In Lipari the Piano Conte culture, which was the immediate successor of Diana, had grey burnished pottery of simple shapes decorated with shallow fluting.[1] Similar pottery has been found on the Italian mainland. Clearer Aegean affinities are found in the Piano Quartara culture which followed.[2] The burnished wares of this culture exhibit many peculiarities found also in pottery from Poliochni, Troy I, Tigani in Samos, and sites in mainland Greece,

[1] §II, 11, 34–49 and figs. 14–27.   [2] §II, 10, 38–41; §II, 14, 329–35.

such as nose-bridge handles, small triangular 'ears' on the rim, etc. Cups with an oval mouth were common.

The picture in Sicily is much more complex.[1] At the beginning of the period a self-coloured ware with incised decoration, which includes dimples and lines of dots among its regular repertoire, seems to have been in use all over the island. The relationship of the San Cono/Piano Notaro ware to the earlier Stentinello pottery is still dubious, but it is difficult to see any ancestry for this type of pottery in the Aegean, though individual shapes can be paralleled. It seems to represent the strong survival of an indigenous element. There was also a painted fabric called Conzo ware which was rather coarse, with a yellow, unburnished surface, decorated with patterns in thin lines of dark brown or black paint, often filled with an orange-red paint, a technique resembling that of Neolithic painted pottery, or in thin black lines on a red wash. It is perhaps significant that the patterns on the painted Conzo wares are often very similar to the incised San Cono/Piano Notaro decorations.

Later a new type of painted pottery, named after the site of Serraferlicchio, near Agrigento, appeared and has been found with material of the two types already described.[2] The most characteristic pieces are painted in matt black on a red-slipped buff surface, a technique which is paralleled in Late Neolithic Greece. Some polychrome ware painted in black and white is also found and red and black monochrome wares are common. The clay 'horns' which begin to appear in Sicily at this period are also Aegean in origin. They closely resemble schematized human figurines of the same material found in Late Neolithic contexts in Greece.

The Serraferlicchio pottery continued in use into the later Copper Age, after the disappearance of the San Cono and Conzo styles, and a new painted fabric known as Sant' Ippolito ware appeared. The dominating ware of this phase, however, was a type of red monochrome ware named after the site of Malpasso. These pots had many features in common with the Piano Quartara wares of Lipari, including the prevalence of oval mouths (though usually on two-handled jars rather than cups), 'ears' on the rim, two-handled bowls, and peaked handles; and they must be contemporary with that culture. The painted and brightly coloured wares of eastern and southern Sicily did not have a great vogue in the north-west, where self-coloured incised pottery stemming from the San Cono/Piano Notaro tradition was de-

[1] §II, 27.        [2] §II, I.

veloped further under a variety of external influences.[1] Shapes
and decorative patterns show Aegean influences, which may have
come via the 'Aegeanizing' cultures of eastern Sicily, Lipari and
perhaps the Italian mainland. The rite of single or multiple
inhumation in rock-cut chamber tombs entered from a pit, often
thought to be Aegean in origin, was well established in this part
of Sicily from the beginning of the Copper Age, but there is only
one equally early example from eastern Sicily, where, as in the
south, burials seem to have been more often in natural caves at
this time.

In Malta the same influences were felt, but the new period
began rather obscurely. The Red Skorba pottery was replaced by
a quite different ware which has been named after a group of tombs
near the village of Zebbuġ.[2] It is a self-coloured ware with incised
decoration, which includes dimples and lines of dots. The patterns
were filled with white or red paste. This pottery is quite different
from Red Skorba ware. On the other hand it has striking resemblances to the San Cono/Piano Notaro wares of Sicily, not
only in the decoration, but also in the shapes. Jars with strong
lug-handles at the widest point are paralleled in the Conzo painted
wares. In Malta, too, painted wares occur in this phase, the paint
being normally in red on a yellow ground, and the patterns often
reproduce those on the incised pots.

At the type-site the pottery was found in five small collective
tombs, which, when excavated, were simply shallow oval hollows in
the rock, but may originally have been real chamber tombs, like
the North-west Sicilian ones. One of these tombs contained a very
crudely carved human head of limestone, which may have been
part of a stela marking one of the graves (it is broken off at the
shoulder). The carving, though crude, has a distinct resemblance
to a crude carving found in the first city of Troy, while the
treatment of the mouth is paralleled in clay figurines of Early
Bronze date from Cyprus.[3] Zebbuġ pottery has also been found
in quantity in habitation levels below several of the megalithic
temples in Malta.[4]

The Zebbuġ culture stands at the head of an unbroken development in the Maltese islands which leads to the splendid
temple culture of the late third millennium B.C. The Zebbuġ
style of pottery was succeeded by the Mġarr style,[5] in which the
decoration consisted of broad bands cut out of the surface of the
vase and subsequently filled with white paste. This pottery had

[1] §II, 21.　　[2] §II, 2; §II, 18, 54–62.　　[3] §II, 15, 79 and n. 2.
[4] §II, 29.　　[5] §II, 18, 48–54; §II, 29, 302.

been found in chamber tombs at Xemxija and in settlement levels
of other sites. The first megalithic buildings seem to belong to the
following phase.[1] The most primitive of these are the two monuments at Ta Ḥaġrat, Mġarr, the smallest of which very closely
resembles a rock-cut chamber tomb of Xemxija type in plan,
though there is nothing to show that it was ever used for burial.
The larger building was already a temple with a clover-leaf plan
and a monumental façade and forecourt.[2]

Later developments are simply elaborations of this basic form.
The Skorba temple is a larger version, and at the Ġgantija in
Gozo there was an even larger one, to which two further semi-
circular rooms were later added to produce the basic five-lobed
form of the later Maltese temple. The pottery found in these early
temples was decorated with curvilinear and rectilinear patterns
scratched on the surface after firing, and subsequently overlaid.
This pottery is known as Ġgantija ware, and is also abundant in the
Xemxija tombs and the earlier rooms of the rock-cut catacomb
known as the Hypogeum (where there is also some pottery of
of Mġarr type and a little of Zebbuġ type). Huts of the Ġgantija
phase at Skorba were oval, and mud-brick was employed in their
construction.[3]

In Malta the temple culture entered its most flourishing period
during two later phases, called respectively Saflieni and Tarxien.
Scratched decoration continued to be popular in both. The patterns of the Saflieni phase were closely related to Ġgantija types,
but in the Tarxien phase these were replaced by graceful flowing
patterns. New techniques of decoration, which include jabbing
and applied studs combined with white paste, and scale patterns
in relief for storage jars, were taken over from neighbouring lands,
especially mainland Italy, Sardinia and South France.[4]

Life centred more and more about the elaborate cult carried on
in the temples, which were built, extended and rebuilt with the
utmost energy and adorned with the greatest skill. The cult
concerned the dead buried in the rock-tombs and the Hypogeum,
but also involved one or more divine figures of indeterminate sex,
whose unattractive effigies, seated or standing,[5] were carved in
stone and placed in the temples and great funerary catacomb
called the Hypogeum. We have evidence for soothsaying and a
healing cult, while statuettes of women reclining on beds from the
Hypogeum may be evidence of the practice of incubation. There
was a regular priesthood; animal sacrifice is well attested, and

[1] §II, 28, 4.  [2] §II, 18, fig. 13.  [3] §II, 31, 23 March 1963, and 14 Sept. 1963.
[4] §II, 15, 84.  [5] See Plate 176(a).

there is some evidence that food-offerings and libations were a part of the cult. The inner halls of the Hypogeum were carved and painted in imitation of megalithic architecture, and were used for religious ceremonies, probably attended only by a few priests or initiates. Carved screens which separate off certain rooms in the temples also point to a distinction between priests and people.[1]

The architectural techniques used in the building of the temples, as well as the carvings and sculptures, and even the pottery found in them, point to imitation of Aegean models, though there are no direct imports from these cultures and few foreign objects of any kind in the Maltese temples and tombs.

Relief carvings of sacrificial animals in the temples seem to be in a purely Maltese style, but abstract paintings and reliefs, particularly of running spirals,[2] have good Aegean parallels. Some of the modelling and sculpture is in a very individual style, but the standing 'divine' figures in stone were ultimately derived from Early Cycladic marble statuettes. A recent find of a very Cycladic-looking head in a Ġgantija context at Skorba suggests that the beginnings of this style may go back to contacts with Early Cycladic traders during this phase.[3]

A series of carbon-14 dates recently obtained on samples from various levels of the Skorba site gives an unexpectedly high dating and long duration to the phases from Żebbuġ to Tarxien in Malta.[4] According to these results the Żebbuġ phase would have begun already by 3000 B.C., while the Tarxien phase at the lower end of the sequence would occupy the last few centuries of the third millennium B.C., with a probable survival into the beginning of the second millennium. In view of the close relationship of the Skorba pottery which precedes Żebbuġ with the Diana wares of Sicily and Lipari, this would seem to imply an equally early start and long duration for the cultures of the Sicilian Copper Age.

The Early Bronze Age, which covers most of the first half of the second millennium B.C., saw the development and intensification of Aegean influences in the central Mediterranean. In Lipari and Sicily new cultures appeared whose roots were in mainland Greece, while the activity of Aegean traders increased continually and left its mark everywhere. In Lipari the Piano Quartara pottery was succeeded by Capo Graziano ware, which displays a mixture of Early and Middle Helladic features. Very similar pottery has been found in Middle Helladic contexts in south-

---

[1] §II, 18, 139.
[2] See Plate 173 (a)–(b).
[3] §II, 31, 30 Dec. 1961, 1144 and fig. 10.
[4] §II, 32, 302–3; §II, 31, passim.

western Greece, for instance at Olympia.[1] The users of Capo Graziano ware inhabited well-defended sites, such as the Acropolis of Lipari and the type-site itself in Filicudi, where they built circular or oval huts with stone foundations. A communal burial ground was found in the island of Filicudi, where bodies and grave goods had been placed in a cleft in the rock. The Capo Graziano culture may have begun as early as about 1800 B.C., and its duration is shown by the variety of sherds of imported Aegean pottery found in its villages. They range from late Middle Helladic matt-painted (a few only) to L.H. IIIa1 and perhaps IIIa2, which implies survival until at least 1400 B.C.[2] It seems certain that Aegean traders maintained a trading-post on the islands from the sixteenth century B.C. onwards.

The Castelluccio culture of Sicily is in many respects a parallel phenomenon.[3] There is no doubt that this represents a colonization of eastern Sicily by a group or groups of people using pottery clearly derived from the matt-painted wares of Middle Helladic Greece. They spread quickly, perhaps mixing with the older inhabitants, until they occupied a good part of the island, excepting the north-west, where the local culture entered what is known as the Moarda phase. The north-east is still little known, but the evidence suggests a local culture with elements derived from both Castelluccio and Moarda groups. It has been identified at several sites, including Tindari, on the north coast opposite the Lipari islands.

The Castelluccio people inhabited small hill-top villages and buried their dead collectively in small cemeteries of up to thirty rock-cut chamber tombs, a form of burial not characteristic of Middle Helladic Greece. One or two of these tombs have elaborately carved façades[4] but most are quite simple. Curious bossed bone objects found in some of the tombs are similar, though not identical, to one found in the earliest Middle Helladic layer at Lerna, and to others which were found by Schliemann in rather vague contexts at Troy.[5] Apart from the vase mentioned above, no objects directly imported from the Aegean have been found in Early Bronze Age contexts in Sicily. Metal was still scarce during this period in Lipari and Sicily; copper trinkets are sometimes found in Castelluccio tombs, but larger objects are limited to two daggers and a fragment of a sword. Stone continued to be a basic material for tools, and flint was mined on an industrial scale.

---

[1] §II, 14, 319–46.        [2] §II, 8, 103–8; §I, 57, 47–52.
[3] §II, 8, 109–19.    [4] See Plate 173 (c).    [5] §II, 16, 80–93.

At the peak of its development the Maltese temple culture suddenly came to a mysterious end. Conquest, pestilence, famine and drought all seem possible explanations, but only the fact of its complete disappearance is certain. Malta was soon afterwards occupied by new people whose strongest cultural affinities in the west are with the Capo Graziano culture of Lipari. It seems likely that the relationship is indirect, both cultures being ultimately derived from the Middle Helladic of South-west Greece. The newcomers are known principally from a cremation cemetery which they established in the ruins of the Tarxien temples, though their pottery has been found on a number of other sites, including small stone cairns and 'dolmens'. Similar 'dolmens' occur near Otranto, which may indicate a stage in the movement which ultimately brought them to Malta. Simple copper daggers, flat and flanged axes, and awls were found among the grave goods, and are the earliest metal objects known from Malta.[1]

These 'Tarxien Cemetery' people were probably contemporary in Malta with the Castelluccio culture in Sicily and the Capo Graziano culture in Lipari. A necklace of mixed shell and faience disk beads from one of the urns at Tarxien is identical with an example from a fifteenth-century Mycenaean tholos tomb in Greece, and there is one sherd from the cemetery which may be a fragment of Castelluccio painted ware. However, the radio-carbon dates now suggest that the Tarxien Cemetery culture must have begun at latest by 1800 B.C. The small quantity of material found to represent these four centuries suggests that the population must have been very small, if there was really continuous occupation during this period.

About a century later further cultural changes took place simultaneously in Lipari, Eastern Sicily and Malta, and were probably all connected. They mark the beginning of the Middle Bronze Age, which lasted from about 1400 to about 1200 B.C. and marked the highest point of Mycenaean influence in the central Mediterranean. In Lipari the Capo Graziano culture was succeeded by the Milazzese people whose way of life was similar though their equipment differed. Milazzese villages were also sited defensively, sometimes on promontories, and consisted of circular or oval one-roomed huts.[2] At the type-site a single rectangular hut, perhaps the chief's house, was found to contain large quantities of Mycenaean sherds, as well as the local grey wares. Mycenaean pottery was common in settlements of this

[1] §II, 18, 168–88; §II, 17.  [2] §II, 8, 122–8; §II, 13, 9–14; §II, 5. See Plate 174(a).

phase; a necklace with faience beads, probably brought by Mycenaean traders, was found in one, and a fragment of a Mycenaean terracotta idol in another. The intensity of the contact is highlighted by the frequent occurrence, on local pottery, of incised signs, probably potters' marks, which often resemble signs in the Minoan–Mycenaean linear scripts.[1] Contacts with mainland Italy are shown by the occurrence of pottery of Apennine type from time to time.

The same culture is found on the Sicilian mainland. A cemetery of inhumation burials in large jars was found at Milazzo on the north coast, and other traces at Tindari and elsewhere.[2] A similar culture appeared in the south-east of Sicily, where it superseded Castelluccio. This must be a southward expansion, though the incoming culture took over some customs from the earlier people, notably burial in rock-cut tombs. The cemeteries are large, having up to several hundred tombs, and one of them, Thapsos, has given its name to this *facies*. They are all the necropoleis of coastal towns or villages, of which little or nothing is known, but Mycenaean pottery is often found in the tombs, and bronze weapons and implements, which are fairly common, have Mycenaean parallels. Necklaces of faience beads have also been found. Traces of the same culture have been found inland, and at Caldare, near Agrigento, where a rock-tomb contained some near-Thapsos pottery, two bronze daggers and two big sheet-bronze basins, probably Mycenaean imports.[3]

Besides grey pottery and Mycenaean imports the tombs of the Thapsos culture also produced some distinctive buff ware with a red slip. Identical pottery characterized a culture which supplanted the Tarxien Cemetery people in Malta at about this time.[4] Probably it came from Central Sicily, where red-slipped pottery went back to the Copper Age. The movement may have been connected with pressures set up by the expansion of the Milazzese–Thapsos people. Sites are hilltop or promontory villages of oval huts, sometimes strengthened by a massive defensive wall. The best preserved is Borġ in-Nadur, after which the culture has been named.

The Mycenaean pottery found on Milazzese–Thapsos sites is mostly L.H. IIIa with a little L.H. IIIb indicating survival into the thirteenth century B.C. The Late Bronze Age began about 1250 B.C. In Lipari the change was violent and sudden. The Milazzese villages were burnt by invaders from mainland Italy,

---

[1] §II, 6.       [2] §II, 10, 59–60 and fig. 38.
[3] §II, 8, 129–35.       [4] §II, 15, 69–73; §II, 30, 253–62.

whose pottery belongs to an advanced phase of the Apennine culture. Professor Bernabò Brea has connected this invasion with the legendary one of Liparos, son of Auson, king of the Ausonians, and hence named the new culture Ausonian.[1] It endured in Lipari for at least 400 years and two phases can be distinguished. Some survival of the older population is indicated by the occurrence in a cemetery of inhumations in large jars, but this was gradually superseded by cremation, the ashes being placed in smaller situlae. A related cremation necropolis found at Milazzo indicates the penetration of mainlanders into North-east Sicily.[2] Though unique for the moment, this may have a bearing on the problem of the legendary Sicel invasion of the island from the mainland of Italy.

In the rest of Sicily insular traditions survived and developed, though with many changes. The Thapsos culture disappeared and with it the intense Aegean trading connexions came to an end. The remains of the succeeding Pantalica culture are found further inland, in a few large hilltop towns and huge cemeteries of thousands of rock-tombs, which honeycombed the cliff-faces below them.[3] The earliest tombs have some bronzes which seem to be Mycenaean imports of a slightly earlier date. Mycenaean echoes are frequent in the earlier pottery, and even in architecture (e.g. the so-called Palace at Pantalica), but there was little direct contact with the latest phases of the Mycenaean civilization. Four phases have been distinguished in the Pantalica culture. In the second of these, contacts with the east Mediterranean are again attested, but now with Cyprus and the Levant more than with the Aegean, which may well reflect the rise of Phoenician mercantile enterprise after 1000 B.C. The third phase is contemporary with the exploratory phase of Greek trading in the West, ending with the establishment of the first colonies in the later eighth century, and the fourth represents the survival of native culture alongside that of the colonists.

The Pantalica culture was marked by a reappearance of the tradition of red-slipped pottery with a fine glossy surface along with painted and some incised wares. Some of the shapes continued Thapsos ones, others were clearly taken over from the Mycenaean repertoire and later the Greek. Bronze was common, as in Lipari. Red-slipped wares also dominated in the San Angelo Muxaro culture of Central Sicily,[4] though here they were not polished and were in shape and finish much more like those of the Borġ in-Nadur culture.

[1] §II, 8, 137.    [2] §II, 9, 149–64.    [3] §II, 8, 149–62.    [4] §II, 8, 177–9.

In Malta the latter continued to flourish and was still in existence when the island was colonized by the Carthaginians in the eighth century. One site in Malta, Baħrija, has produced black pottery with different shapes and a more elaborate decoration which makes use of meander patterns and excised zig zags. The makers were clearly under strong influence from the Iron Age groups of South Italy. Baħrija is a hilltop village of the usual Borġ in-Nadur type, and the Baħrija pottery is closely related technically to that of Borġ in-Nadur, which is also found in quantity on the site. It is the only site of this period in Malta which has so far produced a fair quantity of bronze objects.[1]

## III. SARDINIA AND CORSICA

The earliest Phoenician settlements in Sardinia, such as Sulcis, Caralis, Nora, and Tharros, date from the eighth century B.C. Here our concern is with the indigenous culture which the Phoenicians, the Carthaginians and the Romans met, and conquered, and the evolution of that culture in the millennia before the arrival of named historical peoples on the shores of Sardinia.[2] Sardinia is a large island, 150 miles long from north to south and 75 miles from east to west; and it is situated right in the middle of the west Mediterranean. We have said millennia deliberately because, although there is no direct evidence at the moment that the first peopling of Sardinia took place before 2000 B.C., the radiocarbon dates for the first Neolithic settlement of North Africa and Southern France and the dates of megalithic structures in Malta suggest strongly that we should be prepared to find the first peasant-village Neolithic settlers in Sardinia in the third or even the late fourth millennium B.C.[3]

We can usefully divide the story of pre-Phoenician Sardinia into two main phases. The first is that of the first settlers, the Ozieri and associated folk; and the second is that of the *nuraghi* folk, the people who built the large stone towers which are such a feature of Sardinia, and who made the votive bronze figures which are such a well-known feature of Sardinian prehistory. In very general archaeological terms, the pre-Nuraghic phase is the Neolithic and Chalcolithic of the old terminology, and the Nuraghic phase is that of the Bronze Age. While using this phrase 'Bronze Age' for the Nuraghic civilization it should be remem-

[1] §II, 26; §II, 15, 73–6, 90–1; §II, 30, 258, 261–2.
[2] G, 12; G, 19; G, 3; §III, 25; §III, 24.
[3] §III, 14; §III, 32; §III, 15; §III, 31; G, 6.

bered that the indigenous population of the island was not exterminated by Phoenicians or Romans, but lived on; the late
*nuraghi* are contemporary with Punic and Roman settlements
and belong, formally, to the Early Iron Age.

From our present knowledge it would appear that the first
settlers of Sardinia were the people responsible for the Ozieri
culture, and also those represented by cist graves at Limuri near
Arzachena in the Gallura district of north Sardinia. These latter
may well represent settlers from the east Mediterranean. The
Ozieri culture is known from caves, villages, and rock-cut tombs.
The most famous cave sites are San Michele outside Ozieri, and
San Bartolomeo near Cagliari, while the most famous group of
rock-cut tombs is that of Anghelu Ruju near Alghero.

The material equipment of the Ozieri people consisted of
decorated and undecorated pottery, polished stone axeheads and
maceheads, querns and grain-rubbers, spindle-whorls and loom-
weights. They were farmers and their domesticated animals
included sheep, oxen, pigs, and goats as well as dogs. They had
limited access to copper, but metal played a very small part in
their economy.

There are well over a thousand rock-cut tombs in Sardinia;
they occur either in groups, like Anghelu Ruju, which had 35,
or Su Crucifissu Mannu, which had 19, or singly. These rock-cut
tombs (the *domus di gianas*, or witches' houses, as they are called
locally) are collective tombs and the normal rite is inhumation.
Of the skeletons recovered from Anghelu Ruju 53 were doli-
chocephalic and 10 were brachycephalic. One of the tombs
(S. Andrea Priu) shows very clearly in the decoration of its roof
skeuomorphic features reminiscent of a timber-roofed building.[1]
Some of the tombs have decoration in relief and in paint. At
Anghelu Ruju there are carved bulls' heads outlined in red ochre;
Pimental near Cagliari has carved symbols emphasized in red,
including double-looped spirals and long boat-shaped signs. The
stone closing the tomb of Is Araus (San Veromilis), between
Cagliari and Oristano, has carved on it two pairs of breasts and
the possible representation of a face, and here we may have a
mural form of the Earth Mother Goddess of early Mediterranean
religion.[2]

The religious life of the Ozieri people can be deduced from
these rock-cut tombs with their decorated designs, from the
sacred site of Monte d'Accoddi (an extraordinary truncated
pyramid of earth and stones revetted with blocks of limestone

[1] §III, 14, pl. 17.     [2] §III, 14, 57.

and forming some kind of sacred altar or high place), and about twenty small idols of Cycladic appearance, of which the most famous and the best preserved are those of marble from Senorbi and Portoferro.[1]

The Ozieri people had cultural relations with the Pyrenees, South France, Malta, Italy and Corsica. Pottery of Chassey and Fontbouïsse types, which are characteristic of the Neolithic and Chalcolithic in southern France, occur, and also about a dozen beakers and about the same number of tripod bowls. These Beaker wares are all from burials in caves or rock-cut tombs except for one from Nuraxinieddu near Oritano, which was found in a rectangular slab-lined stone grave. In the cave of San Bartolomeo there are burials associated with Beakers stratified above an Ozieri habitation level. The pre-Nuraghic culture of Sardinia is therefore to be seen as a pre-Beaker settlement of people from the east Mediterranean which developed in contact with other West Mediterranean cultures during what some would still think is the first half of the second millennium B.C. but which now seems to us to be probably at least as early as 3000 B.C. The rock-cut tombs with their East Mediterranean motifs and the Cycladic idols hardly allow any other explanation of origins. The accumulation of carbon-14 dates for Mediterranean and Western European contexts scarcely permits a date as late as 2000 B.C. for the beginning of the Ozieri phase.[2]

In their analysis of pre-Nuraghic Sardinia archaeologists now distinguish, in addition to the Ozieri culture, the Monte Claro and Bonnanaro cultural *facies*. The pottery of the Monte Claro *facies* is better than that of Bonnanaro: it consists of large brownish red or brown pots, and smaller, finer pots, yellow in colour, painted with red ochre and burnished with a spatula. Monte Claro itself was a rock-cut tomb found near Cagliari in 1904. Its characteristic pottery is also known from other sites such as the villages of San Gemiliano (Sestu), Monte Olladiri near Monastir, and Enna Pruna near Mogoro, and from early Nuraghic sites. Bonnanaro ware was found stratified at San Bartolomeo in the same levels as Beaker ware, in natural caves in the Iglesiente, and mainly up the western half of the island. Bonnanaro ware is plain, brownish in colour, and the shapes of the pots include simple hemispherical or cylindrical bowls: another common form is the tripod dish with flared sides and rectangular-sectioned legs. This ware was either evolved locally or introduced from outside at a time when Beakers were still current.

[1] §III, 14, pls. 5 and 6.  [2] §III, 6; §III, 1; §II, 17; §II, 8; §II, 26.

Without doubt the most impressive monuments of prehistoric Sardinia are the *nuraghi*—great stone towers looking
from the distance like monumental versions of the sandcastles
made by tipping out the contents of children's buckets.[1] There
are between 6500 and 7000 *nuraghi* surviving in Sardinia; they
vary in height, the highest being 60 feet in height. About 30 feet
in diameter, they decrease in size as the walls ascend. The *nuraghi*
have often been compared with the brochs of Scotland; but, while
the brochs are hollow towers, there are inside the *nuraghi* a cen-
trally roofed chamber and a staircase in the walls leading to a
second chamber. In rare cases there is a third chamber above. The
walls are built of large stones, sometimes 2 ft. high, arranged in
fairly regular courses but set without mortar. The roof of the
central chamber is usually done by corbelling. The Cyclopean
masonry of the walls is reminiscent of Tiryns and Mycenae, as
the corbelling is reminiscent of the *tholoi* of Mycenaean Greece.

The Nuraghic towers or fortresses are often part of a village.
They constitute the strong point of a community, and one must
envisage the great stone fortress surrounded by the *capanne*, the
small corbelled stone huts of the peasants, made in a simple
style still used in the west Mediterranean and southern France.
The famous *nuraghe* of Barumini, for example, had a village
around it which was enlarged between the mid eighth and the
late sixth centuries B.C. to include between 200 and 300 people
living there.[2]

There has been much speculation on the date of the *nuraghi*
and the whole Nuraghic culture. Some have thought to put its
beginnings early in the second millennium B.C., but by general
consent at the present day it seems difficult to argue in favour of
any date before 1500 or 1400 B.C. A radiocarbon test for the
earliest nucleus of the *nuraghe* of Barumini gave a date of 1470 ±
200 B.C. (K. 151). Copper ingots of East Mediterranean origin
were found near the *nuraghi* of Serra Illixi and at Assemini.
Schaeffer[3] dated these from 1200 to 1050 B.C., but Lilliu argues
for a date of 1400 B.C. Buchholz says 1200 B.C., and the recent
excavations of the Philadelphia Museum at Cape Gelidonya also
suggest this date.[4]

We know of the culture of the Nuraghic people not only from
their fortified settlements, but also from their religious sites and
tombs. Their religious sites include sacred wells and springs, and
rectangular temples such as Serra Orrios and Esterzili. The tombs
of the Nuraghic period are known in folk parlance as the giants'

[1] §III, 16; 23; 17. See Plate 174(*b*).  [2] §III, 17.  [3] §III, 28.  [4] §III, 2; 3.

tombs—*tombe di giganti*: there are a great number of these in Sardinia and a very considerable literature has grown up about them.[1] They are rectangular tombs often walled with megalithic slabs, and roofed over by corbelling, set in long cairns of large stones, with the entrance sometimes on to a straight wall (giving an elongated D-shape to the plan of the cairn), at others on to a curving wall, and in very many examples on to a semi-circular forecourt with the ends of the semi-circle prolonged to form two horns: hence the name for many of these monuments, 'the horned cairns of Sardinia'. Often the entrance to the tomb is defined by a large stone sculptured into panels with a small opening at the base like the entrance to a dog's kennel.

These *tombe di giganti* are the burial places of the families or clans inhabiting the *nuraghi*: the number of the dead buried varies from about thirty to sixty. It is only in the last decade that the date of the *tombe di giganti* has become established. They were at one time thought to be early in the second millennium B.C. or, for that matter, even earlier, and they have often been compared with the horned cairns of northern Ireland and south-western Scotland, some authors going so far as to derive the Irish and Scottish cairns of the Clyde–Carlingford culture from Sardinia. We now see that these resemblances are superficial, and that the tombs around the Irish Channel and those in Sardinia provide us with an interesting example of parallel development in funerary architecture in different parts of prehistoric Europe at different times in prehistory.[2] It would now appear that the floruit of the Sardinian giants' graves was from 1500 to 500 B.C.: they belong to the Early and Full Nuraghic periods, whereas most of the Irish and Scottish 'horned cairns', together with the other chambered long barrows of the British Isles, date well before 1500 B.C., indeed many of them over a thousand years before then.

The origin of the *tombe di giganti* has aroused a great deal of discussion.[3] A widely accepted view at present is that they developed out of the Sardinian 'dolmens'. The word 'dolmen', originally a folk Breton name for megalithic tombs, is a difficult one to use exactly in archaeology: it is applied in a wide variety of ways, for example to all megalithic tombs (the current French usage), to ruined monuments, or to single rectangular or polygonal chambers (as in Sweden and Denmark, the *dös/dysse* terminology). It is in this last sense that the word is used in Sardinia, and the Sardinian 'dolmens' are rectangular or polygonal chambers. There are no more than forty of them. Mrs

[1] §III, 14, ch. 7; §III, 19; §III, 20.    [2] §III, 26; §IV, 14, 196; G, 9.    [3] §III, 7.

Guido, following Duncan Mackenzie's earlier analysis, suggests that the 'dolmen-builders' landed at the mouth of the river Tirso, not long after (but perhaps just before) the middle of the second millennium B.C., and there gradually evolved their tombs into the elaborate *tombe di giganti*.[1] Bray takes a different view and sees the Sardinian 'dolmens' as late and degenerate versions of the Giants' Graves.[2] It seems to us that too little is still known about these small Sardinian megalithic tombs to be certain about their ancestry. They may well all be contemporary with the *tombe di giganti*, or impoverished versions of them—the Giants' Graves themselves being surface versions of the rock-cut tombs of the pre-Nuraghic Ozieri culture.

The bronzes of the Nuraghic culture are well known and more than four hundred of them survive.[3] They vary in height from 2 to 40 cm. and date mainly from the eighth to the sixth centuries B.C. The subjects vary from warriors, shepherds, musicians with pipes and horns, to cripples and model ships. Some of the figures have very interesting head-dresses, perhaps of Punic ancestry. One of these Sardinian model ships was found in the Etruscan tomb of Tombe del Duce in Vetulonia dating from well after the beginning of the seventh century B.C.; another was found at Populonia with a carp's-tongue sword of the type Hencken would date to the seventh/sixth centuries B.C.[4]

From all the information now at our disposal it would appear that the Nuraghic period of Sardinia began *c.* 1400 B.C. It can conveniently be divided into the Archaic Nuraghic period 1400 to 900 B.C., the Full or Middle Nuraghic period 900–500 B.C., and the Late Nuraghic period after 500 B.C. Most of the bronzes belong to the Middle Nuraghic period.

We must now refer to the vexed problem of the Sherden. Among the 'peoples of the sea' who made raids on the coasts of the Mediterranean and against Egypt in the period 1400 to 1190 B.C. and who were employed as mercenaries in the Egyptian army soon after the middle of the second millennium B.C. were a people calling themselves Sherden. They are mentioned in the Tell el-Amarna letters of *c.* 1370 B.C. and also in the time of Ramesses II (1304–1237). The great invasion of the Western Delta *c.* 1191 B.C. in the time of Ramesses III (1198–1166), which was led by the Philistines, included the Sherden. There are two main views about the origin of these people. One is that they came from Sardinia itself, in a word that they are Nuraghic heroes campaigning in the east Mediterranean, already well

[1] §III, 14; 19; 20.   [2] §III, 5 *passim*.   [3] See Plate 175 (*a*)–(*b*).   [4] §III, 18; 23.

known to them by trade. The other view is that they came from the region of Hermus in Asia Minor, east of the island of Chios—indeed from Sardis and the Sardinian plain. This second view would appear to be the more likely.

We can then see in the period 1400–1190 B.C. groups of people led by warlike chieftains, themselves expert sailors and with a knowledge of the routes between the east Mediterranean and the west, setting out from some such area as Sardis and, after periods of harassing Egypt, ending up in the island of the west Mediterranean which was eventually called after them, Sardinia. They provided in the island a dynastic kingship and a group of wealthy chieftains, as well as new crafts, particularly in building and in bronze-working. These people were a powerful agent in reinforcing relations between east and west Mediterranean. Indeed the Sherden may well provide us with a historical glimpse of the invaders who have been postulated on archaeological grounds as the originators of the Nuraghic culture. When the Phoenicians established Sulcis, Nora, Caralis and Tharros they may have been dealing with East Mediterranean chiefs of a lineage which had been established there six hundred years before, and they may have been ruling over an indigenous population which was still in a Late Bronze Age state of culture.[1]

Whereas a very great deal of work has been done on the prehistoric archaeology of Sardinia, and the *nuraghi*, the *domus di gianas*, and the *tombe di giganti* have been known about and discussed for a long time, the island of Corsica, about 6 miles north of Sardinia, has been neglected until the last decade. A department of France, it was visited by Prosper Mérimée in 1839 when Inspector General of Prehistoric Monuments. He gives an account of his travels in his *Notes d'un voyage en Corse* (1840) and mentions some of the island's megalithic monuments including two of the statues-menhirs for which Corsica is now famous, although he was at a loss to decide whether they were 'Roman or African'. A. de Mortillet made a general survey of the megalithic monuments of the island and Commandant Octobon included an account of five statues-menhirs in his general survey of these sculptured standing stones.[2]

It is, however, only since the end of the Second World War that a campaign of research has been mounted in Corsica under the auspices of the Centre National de la Recherche Scientifique with Roger Grosjean in charge of excavation and field-survey. Since 1954 Grosjean's work has enormously extended our knowledge of

---

[1] §III, 14, ch. 6; §III, 4; §III, 22; §III, 29; §III, 30; §III, 27.    [2] §III, 21; §IV, 37.

early Corsica; and while we still have no complete picture, at least we can now say something sensible about the prehistory of the island. Grosjean divides prehistoric Corsica into two phases, which, chronologically, if not culturally, correspond to the Ozieri (and pre-Nuraghic) and Nuraghic phases of Sardinian prehistory. These two phases in Corsica he calls the *megalithic* and the *torréen*, the latter after the round towers or *torri* which are a special feature of the island.[1] Already publicists, anxious to encourage tourism in Corsica, have baptized these two phases as representing *la Corse virgilienne* and *la Corse homérique*.

Grosjean dates the megalithic phase of Corsican prehistory before 1500 B.C., and sees it shown by 'dolmens', by alignments, and most of all by the statues-menhirs, of which by now over fifty have been found in Corsica. His latest account would divide this period of megalith-builders into three phases, characterized respectively by small stone cists, by 'dolmens' and the first statues-menhirs, and by the fine statues-menhirs. He sees the statues as representations of friends, vassals, or enemies of the chief buried in the megalithic tomb or as recounting the exploits of the chief. Around 1500 B.C. (and the date of the beginning of this phase has been confirmed by carbon-14 dating) Grosjean sees this phase as representing an invasion of the island by warriors with bronze swords, axes, and spearheads, and wearing bronze cuirasses, who conquered and dominated the pre-Bronze megalithic people, who were Neolithic and Chalcolithic stock-rearers and agriculturists. These Bronze Age invaders built circular citadels or *torri*, and this is why Grosjean gives the name *torréen* to their culture. The most celebrated of these *torri* are Filitosa, Cucuruzzu, Torre, Cecciu, Foce, Balestra and Tappu, and it is reasonable to see these *torre* and their builders as parallel in many ways to the *nuraghi* of Sardinia, the *sesi* of Pantelleria, and the *talayots* of the Balearics.

There are now over fifty statues-menhirs known from Corsica, and they, with the *torri*, form the most interesting and exciting aspect of prehistoric Corsica. They vary in size, but their average dimensions are 7 ft. 6 in. high. The heads of the statues are generally fully three-dimensional, and the neck and shoulders clearly demarcated. Sometimes the breasts are shown. The backs of these statues have indications of shoulder-blades; sometimes the back-bone is shown and, in some examples, the ribs. Many of these statues are shown with weapons, and an analysis of these weapons would suggest a date of about 1500–1400 B.C.

[1] §III, 11; 8; 13; 12.

R. Lantier had at first thought that the Corsican statues-menhirs were *protohistoriques ou historiques*. Many have sought to compare the figures with those from Easter Island, but most have kept their comparisons within the field of known statues-menhirs in the western Mediterranean and France. Yet while the Corsican figures have superficial affinities with some of the known statues-menhirs, on the whole they seem to us to be *sui generis*. In his analysis of Filitosa, the most important and exciting of the sites recently discovered and excavated in Corsica, Grosjean distinguished two phases, one which belongs to the full flowering of the megaliths and megalithic art of Corsica, and the second that of the *torre*-builders who re-used the statues-menhirs, often after having broken them. If this is really true, and there is no reason why it should not be, we are presented with a dramatic archaeological demonstration of a conflict between invader and indigene. Years of research built on the fine beginning of the last decade are required to bring completeness and detail into our picture of Corsican prehistory. But already Corsica is no longer a blank, and fits into the story of prehistoric Sardinia and the Balearics.

## IV. SOUTHERN FRANCE

Until recently the prehistory, and protohistory, of Southern France would have been set out according to the subdivisions of the three-age system of Stone, Bronze and Iron first developed as an archaeological system by C. J. Thomsen and J. J. A. Worsaae in Denmark, and elaborated in France by men such as Gabriel de Mortillet and Joseph Déchelette.[1] And indeed in a recent publication written by A. Leroi-Gourhan, J.-J. Hatt and P.-M. Duval we learn that the Neolithic or New Stone Age began in France at 4000 B.C. and lasted until 1600 B.C. (being divided into *Néolithique ancien*, 4000 to 2500 B.C.; *Néolithique moyen*, 2500 to 1800 B.C.; *Néolithique récent*, 1800 to 1600 B.C.); that the Bronze Age lasted from 1600 to 750 B.C. (divided into *Bronze ancien*, 1600 to 1400 B.C.; *Bronze moyen*, 1400 to 1200 B.C.; *Bronze final I*, 1200 to 900 B.C.; and *Bronze final II*, 900 to 750 B.C.); and the Iron Age from 750 to 50 B.C. (divided into the Hallstatt period from 750 to 500 B.C., and the La Tène period from 500 to 50 B.C.).[2]

This classification of the archaeology of France in prehistoric and protohistoric times, with its nine labelled periods between 4000 B.C. and the Roman conquest of Gaul, is a useful pigeon-

[1] §IV, 34; 35; 36; 18.          [2] §IV, 30.

holing system for the archaeological material, but is rapidly becoming itself a fossil for two reasons. In the first place many archaeological categories, and the people whose life and thought we attempt to describe by studying these archaeological types and the persistent groups of types that are called cultures in English and *civilisations* in French, span in time many of the nine pigeon-holes. Thus the great megalithic tombs, of which there are over six thousand in the whole of France and at least three thousand in southern France, occur from the *Néolithique ancien* to at least the *Bronze moyen*, and probably to the *Bronze final I*. Secondly, the development of radiocarbon-dating is producing every year approximate dates for the various phases of pre-Roman and pre-Greek France, so that we can begin to abandon the old three-age pigeon-hole system and attempt to write the early past of France in dated and historical terms.

At the end of the fifth millennium B.C. South France was occupied by small semi-nomadic groups of hunters and fishers and collectors technically known as Mesolithic people. There can have been very few people in France at this time, and, judged by its surviving remains, their culture is unexciting.[1] The remarkable floruit of art which characterized some of the cultures of the Upper Palaeolithic in southern France and northern Spain[2] was over. It has often been suggested that some of the painted symbols on the pebbles of the Azilian culture of the Pyrenees may be some form of writing, but this view is not now seriously held, and the idea that the Upper Palaeolithic cultures of southern France themselves generated a Neolithic peasant village society which then itself developed into an urban literate society before the arrival of Greek colonists in Provence is now seen to be a pardonable and misguided form of archaeological chauvinism which flourished when the palpable forgeries of Glozel were eagerly accepted as authentic by scholars and others anxious to decry *le mirage oriental*.[3]

It now seems certain that the higher arts and crafts which constitute what Gordon Childe called the 'Neolithic Revolution' originated, as far as Europe is concerned, in the Near East region of South-west Asia, and were diffused by settlers, individuals and traders to Western Europe via the shores and seas of the Mediterranean, and the river valleys of the Balkans and eastern Europe. The Danube was one such route of river-valley penetration, and peasant-village farmers from the Danubian region with their characteristic *Bandkeramik* were in the Low Countries well

[1] §IV, 45.  [2] G, 4; G, 11.  [3] §IV, 15; 42.

before 4000 B.C. and are attested in the Paris basin by the middle of the fourth millennium.[1] In the south of France the settlers from Italy, Spain and North Africa who introduced agriculture and the use of domesticated animals are characterized, archaeologically, by their pottery. Their pottery was generally of simple, rounded shapes with round bases and with lugs perforated for string-holes rather than for use as handles; it is either quite plain or decorated by rough impressions before firing. These impressed decorations are made by fingernails or, most often, by the edge of a Cardium shell—so much so that this oldest pottery of the west Mediterranean and southern France is usually referred to as cardial ware.[2]

The cardial wares are restricted in distribution in South France to the littoral and extend a short way up the Rhone valley. This first and oldest South French Neolithic culture has been called the Châteauneuf culture by Piggott[3] after the type-site of Châteauneuf-les-Martigues;[4] it is the Montserratian of Arnal's analysis.[5] At the site of Roucadour, Thémines (Lot), the lowest strata with impressed pottery produced a carbon-14 date of 3980 ± 150 B.C.[6] It therefore seems reasonable to suppose that the Neolithic impressed ware began in the south of France between 4500 and 4000 B.C.

While impressed wares continued in use for a very long time in Southern France, they were generally succeeded by the main French Neolithic culture, the Chasséen, named after the Camp de Chassey near Mâcon. This culture, with its characteristic, largely unornamented pottery, has close affinities with the Lagozza of northern Italy, the Cortaillod of Switzerland and the Windmill Hill culture of southern Britain. While the Chassey pottery is largely undecorated, decorated pots do occur, the decoration done by scratching with a fine point after firing. The designs are rectangles, diamonds and triangles done in outline or filled with diagonal or criss-cross lines. Arnal has argued that the Chassey culture can be divided into two phases, an earlier, A, with decorated wares, and a later, B, with undecorated wares, but we do not consider that this division has yet been proved. The Chassey culture is found in defended sites or camps (like the type-site of the Camp de Chassey), and in caves such as the Grotte de Bize near Narbonne, the Grotte de la Madeleine (Hérault). The earliest dates yet obtained for the Chassey culture in Southern France are 3270 ± 230 B.C. from La Madeleine[7] and 3230 ±

[1] §IV, 6.  [2] §IV, 10.  [3] §IV, 41.
[4] §IV, 19.  [5] §IV, 5.  [6] §IV, 38; 39.  [7] §IV, 2.

140 B.C. from the layer overlying the impressed ware at Rouca-dour.[1] It seems reasonable then to suppose that the Chassey folk began in southern France perhaps around 3500 B.C.; their culture survives until the end of the third millennium B.C.

But during the third millennium various other groups of people are distinguished in Southern France, of which the two best known are the Peu-Richard group in south-western France and the Fontbouïsse group in Provence. The Peu-Richard group in the Gironde and Saintonge and Charente is characteristically represented by ware decorated in a channelling technique with tunnel handles, the channelling and tunnelling often combining to produce *oculi* designs like the *Symbol-Keramik* of southern Spain, and is mainly found in defended settlement sites like the name-site of the Camp de Peu-Richard near Saintes. Recent excavation in two of these Peu-Richard sites has provided carbon-14 dates: the Neolithic camp of Les Matignons, Juillac-le-Coq (Charente), gave a mean date of $2615 \pm 160$ B.C. for two samples from a burnt layer indicating the end of the occupation of the site by its Chasséen builders, and the site of Biard, Segonzac (Charente), gave an occupation date of $2391 \pm 137$ B.C.[2]

On the plateaux of the Languedoc Louis distinguished a late Neolithic and Chalcolithic group which he termed *les pasteurs des plateaux*.[3] They also are distinguished by channelled wares, but never wares with the *oculi* designs of the Peu-Richard group. The *pasteurs des plateaux* have been divided by Arnal into the *Ferreriens* from the site of Les Ferrières and the *Fontbuxiens* from the site of Fontbouïsse. A remarkable settlement site of the Fontbouïsse culture has been excavated recently; it is Lébous, St-Mathieu-de-Tréviers (Hérault), and has been described as 'a prehistoric castle'. It is a fortified enclosure with bastions or towers and reminds one of the Iberian settlement sites of Los Millares and Vilanova de São Pedro; a carbon-14 dating for its occupation gives $1920 \pm 250$ B.C.[4]

France is very rich in megalithic monuments but those who have visited only Brittany and seen the great *alignements* at Carnac, the *grand menhir brisé* at Locmariaquer, and the stone tombs of Kercado, Tables des Marchands, and Gavrinis may be pardoned for not realizing that over half the megalithic tombs of France are in the south. There are no great stone rows and no tall menhirs in southern France, but it has over 3000 megalithic tombs and, as well, a special feature of the megalithic civilization, statues-menhirs which are famous throughout prehistoric Europe.

[1] §IV, 38; 39.  [2] §IV, 12; 13.  [3] §IV, 31; 32.  [4] §IV, 3.

It is important to realize how rich southern France is in megalithic tombs; the department of the Aveyron, for example, has
over six hundred of these prehistoric stone tombs—over twice as
many as exist in England and Wales. These megalithic tombs in
southern France are mainly to be found in the foothills of the
Pyrenees, in the country from Narbonne to Toulouse on both
sides of the Carcassonne Gap, and in the *causses* country to the
south of the Massif Central. There is also a small group in south-
eastern France in the department of the Var, and one of these
tombs, La Bouissière, Cabasse, in the Var, gave carbon-14 dates
based on charcoal under the paving of the monument of 2020 ±
130 B.C.[1]

At the mouth of the Rhône, and near Arles, is a group of five
collective tombs generally known as the Arles–Fontvieille group.
One of this group is entirely megalithic in construction, three (the
famous Grotto Arnaud-Castellet, the Grotte de la Source, and the
Grotte Bounias), are rock-cut but with roofs made of megalithic
capstones, and the fifth—the Grotte des Fées or the Epée de
Roland, on the Montagne de Cordes—is entirely rock-cut. The
artifacts from these tombs suggest that they were first in use by
the Chassey folk, and although, as with all collective tombs, we
must realize that they could have been and were used over a very
long period of time, it seems likely that the rock-cut tombs of the
Rhône delta were first used somewhere between 3500 and
3000 B.C.[2]

The Fontvieille tombs are only one of many groups of collective tombs that can be distinguished in southern France. Other
groups that may conveniently be distinguished are the Passage
Graves of the Hérault, the tombs of the eastern Provence area
and especially the Var, the tombs on the *causses* country, the
Gallery Graves between Narbonne and Bordeaux and in south-
western France, and the tombs in Roussillon and the foothills of
the Pyrenees.

The Passage Graves of the Hérault, which have been made the
special object of a detailed and painstaking study by Jean Arnal,[3]
may well be the tombs of some of the *pasteurs des plateaux*, and
Lébous may be the settlement site of people who buried their
dead in tombs like Lamalou. These Passage Graves have special
features which suggest that their builders came from south-
eastern Spain. They were probably metal prospectors; and although there are no metal objects in their tombs, there are flint
copies of metal daggers. The Gallery Graves that extend on either

[1] §IV, 9.          [2] §IV, 17.          [3] §IV, I.

side of the Carcassonne gap from Narbonne to south-west France and are found again in the Bordeaux region are long stone tombs, often with portholes and set in the eastern end of long mounds. It seems likely that they represent a spread from the mouth of the Rhône to south-western France, and perhaps ultimately to the British Isles, where tombs closely resembling these South French tombs are found dating from around 3000 B.C.

The very great number of megalithic tombs on the *causses* country are to be explained either as versions and late developments of the Hérault Passage Graves or as varieties which have evolved from the Arles–Fontvieille rock-tombs and the Narbonne–Carcassonne Gallery Graves in long mounds. Certainly in the *causses* these tombs were used right up to 1000 B.C., if not later, and may well have been constructed up to this date. The megalithic tombs of the Pyrenean foothills are closely linked on formal and general grounds with the tombs in the Spanish Basque and Catalonian areas, and are unlikely to be very early; certainly some of them were used, if not constructed, up to the end of the second millennium B.C.

There is no general agreement about the origins of the great stone tombs of southern France. Those in the Pyrenean foothills are closely connected with the Spanish megaliths of Catalonia.[1] The Hérault Passage Graves have their closest parallels in south-eastern Spain and may be the tombs of metal prospectors working the copper of that part of southern France. The Gallery Graves in long mounds of the Aude and their counterparts in south-western France have been held to be surface versions of the Arles–Fontvieille rock-cut tombs, and these themselves to be connected with the rock-cut tombs of other parts of the west Mediterranean;[2] but it has also been argued that they represent a spread from the coasts of South-west France to the Rhône delta, and that the Arles–Fontvieille tombs are rock-cut versions of the surface tombs like Boun Marcou, Pépieux, and St-Eugène.[3] We need many more carbon-14 dates before this issue can be resolved.

While, with one or two unimportant exceptions, the megalithic tombs of southern France have no surviving decoration, and there is nothing to be found like the magnificent mural art of New Grange and Gavrinis or the magnificent mobiliary art of the south Iberian tombs, South France is rich in statues-menhirs. These occur in two areas, the first comprising the departments of Aveyron, Tarn-et-Garonne and Lozère, the second the Rhône delta and to the east of the delta. These sculptured stones

[1] §v, 42.  [2] §IV, 17; 21.  [3] §III, 5.

are the oldest examples of statuary in Western Europe; from Palaeolithic times we have only sculpture in low relief: now in these South French figures we have sculpture in the round. These figures vary in size from 3 to 5 ft. and are not naturally done or representational; they are stylized and include in their stylization a face motif, necklace, breasts, hands and feet, and often a girdle and what French archaeologists have for long referred to as '*l'objet*', a dagger or cult object of some kind. Most of these statues-menhirs occur alone and were free-standing. A few, however, are associated with datable monuments; two incorporated as roofing stones in Collorgues probably date from early in the second millennium.[1] The inspiration of these statues-menhirs is without any doubt in the mural and mobiliary art of the Iberian collective tombs, which itself derives from the religious art of the third and fourth millennia B.C. of the east Mediterranean.

The relations of the builders of the megalithic tombs to other groups in southern France in the third and second millennia B.C. is not clear, but the builders of the Hérault Passage Graves may be one and the same people as the people of Fontbouïsse and Lébous; the *pasteurs des plateaux* are surely some of the people who occupied the *causses* country perhaps seasonally and by transhumance, and built the many megalithic tombs of Aveyron and neighbouring departments; it is difficult to divide the people of the *camps* of Peu-Richard and Les Matignons from the builders of tombs in the neighbourhood like Availles-sur-Chizé and the cemetery at Bougon.

It used to be asked whether the megaliths of France belonged to the Neolithic Age or to the Bronze Age, or, to put the question in a more modern form, whether the megalith-builders were metal-using. The answer to this question is now simple: the earliest megalith-builders were not metal-using but they soon became so, although very little metal is buried in their tombs. It is from the amalgam of the late Neolithic societies in the years around 2000 B.C. in southern France—Chassey, Peu-Richard, megalith-builders, *pasteurs des plateaux*—that bronze-working is first found.

Metal first appears in southern France associated with Beaker pottery, and the first metal objects are flat axes, tanged daggers, biconic beads, rings, spirals and pendants of copper (sometimes beads and rings of silver and gold). The beginning of metal-working in southern France does not seem to have involved any great ethnic changes and the Bronze phase of second-millennium

[1] §IV, 40.

southern France is merely a technical change in existing societies.[1] The role of 'the Beaker people', if there were such people in the sense of a large ethnic group, in culture changes and the beginnings of metallurgy is still a matter for discussion. If we accept Sangmeister's modern interpretation of the nature of Beaker pottery, it represents a tradition which started in Spain and Portugal, spread to Central Europe, and then came back to South-western Europe crossed with cord-ornamented beaker traditions and much modified. This return of a modified Beaker tradition is his 'reflux', and it is well seen in the valley of the Rhône and in sites in the Aude. Whatever we may think of the nature of the movements associated with the spread of Beaker pottery or various forms, there can be little doubt that the movements that certainly occurred were those that brought Southern France into the orbit of Central European metallurgy.[2]

In her study of *Bronze Age Cultures of France*[3] Miss N. K. Sandars redefines the Rhône culture usually described as of the Early Bronze and perhaps dating from 1800 to 1500 B.C. This culture extends from Burgundy and the Jura eastwards into Switzerland and south to the mouth of the Rhône. It is essentially a continental and central European and not a Mediterranean bronze-using culture, with types that reflect the Straubing culture. Archaeologically some of its characteristics are the pottery (big pots nearly always decorated with cordons, often finger-printed) and metal types such as the Rhône dagger and trefoil pins. There are some sherds of this Rhône-type pottery from the Camp de Chassey, and two trefoil pins occur at La Liquisse in the Aveyron, but it is interesting to note that, while the characteristic Rhône culture graves are stone cists or trench graves, these Aveyron trefoil pins come from the Dolmen de la Liquisse, a typical south French *causses* megalith. Miss Sandars sees no evidence in pottery parallels that are sometimes adduced for an extension of the Rhône culture to Provence and Languedoc. Here another and Mediterranean tradition of metal-working had developed by 1500 B.C.[4]

This Mediterranean tradition seems to have developed on the Mediterranean coast in close contact with the Polada culture of northern Italy; pottery is decorated by excision sometimes in a native style or sometimes in the *Kerbschnitt* or chip-carving style found in eastern France and south-western Germany. Another bronze industry developed from 1500 B.C. onwards in southern

[1] §IV, 11; G, 15.   [2] *Ibid.*
[3] §IV, 43.   [4] §IV, 17, 184 and pl. xxviii; §IV, 14.

France, centred around the estuary of the Gironde and characterized by an elongated straight-sided flanged axe. This Médoc type of flanged axe occurs in large hoards and frequently in association with palstaves, a type which, Savory argues, was spread from eastern France by routes skirting the Massif Central on the north. This flourishing Médoc culture must indicate the importance of the estuary of the Gironde as a focal point; to quote Savory, 'the coastal regions of France form one of the geographical bases for a persistent dualism of metallurgical tradition in this country, which is the master-key to the regionalism so often encountered'.[1]

We know far less about the other coastal region of southern France—the Rhône delta and Provençal littoral—than we should. In many ways the period from 1250 to 750 B.C. is the darkest in the prehistory of southern France. That there were contacts with the Mycenaean world of the east Mediterranean is shown by the finds of faience beads at Treille, the Grotte du Ruisseau, the Grotte de Monier and Font-Blanco,[2] and light has been thrown on the nature of these contacts by the discovery in 1964 off the Cap d'Agde, near Béziers, of a ship dated to between 1300 and 1000 B.C., and claimed to be the oldest wreck yet found off the coasts of France. It has been reported that a considerable cargo has been discovered including about 300 bars of copper and bronze, 80 axes of various kinds, some 50 decorated bracelets, arrows, spears and javelins.[3]

The transition from the Middle Bronze Age to the Late Bronze Age of the older systematists in Europe is marked by great movements of people, and the newcomers are characterized archaeologically by their custom of burying their dead in urnfields. These urnfield folk got to southern France before 700 B.C. The second quarter of the first millennium B.C. saw two different and archaeologically intrusive groups moving into southern France from the north: the first group is the urnfield group, and then come, later, a group burying their dead in barrows. Together they must have transformed the prehistory of the whole area; for a Mediterranean tradition, which had dominated the area from the fourth millennium (apart from Sangmeister's reflux Beakers and the southward extension of the Rhône culture), is replaced by, or overlaid by, a northern and central European tradition. These two groups give historical continuity with Celtic-speaking peoples, and they may certainly be called Celts, although they may not have been the first Indo-European-

[1] §IV, 44.      [2] §IV, 16; §IV, 17, 201 and fig. 74.      [3] §IV, 4.

speaking peoples in South French prehistory. The labels Celto-
Ligurian and Celtiberian attached to them and their descendants
in later times may mask their real affinities, or on the other hand
be a realistic appreciation of the fact that they mingled with the
South French autochthonous population of the Middle Bronze
Age. The population of France in the south that came into contact with the Greeks in the seventh century was, we may
surmise, a fusion of the Middle Bronze Age autochthones and the
Late Bronze Age/Early Iron Age invaders—a medley of south
and north.[1]

The key site for the study of the south French urnfield culture
is Cayla de Mailhac near Biz in the Aude,[2] and Kimmig has proposed a division of the Mailhac urnfields into Mailhac I (700 to
600 B.C.), Mailhac II (600 to 550 B.C.), and Mailhac III (550 to
475 B.C.).[3] There was, outside this key site, evidence of a pre-
Mailhac urnfield phase comparable with Maluquer's Group B in
Catalonia. These earliest urnfield folk came from various sources,
and in part from Miss Sandars's Sassenay group of the Lower
Saône.[4] Bernabò Brea has argued that the changes in the archaeological record in southern France around 750 to 700 B.C. could be
due merely to the arrival of a new religion, but we feel with
Sandars, Kimmig, Hodson and others that, with Mailhac I, and
the arrival of a completely new range of pottery and metal types,
and a new burial rite, we are in the presence of an invasion—a
direct influx of Urnfield peoples from somewhere in the north or
the west Alpine region.[5]

Mailhac I is a flourishing local urnfield culture best represented
at Cayla de Mailhac itself and at Agullan where it is Malaquer's
Group C. These and other sites are west of the Hérault. There are
no real urnfields known in southern France east of the Hérault;
here we find Hallstatt tumulus-builders. The expansion of the
Late Bronze urnfield people across the Rhône and down into
Catalonia had hardly got going before the people responsible
were overtaken by the metal styles and forms of ornament emanating from the new Hallstatt/Early Iron Age culture.

This Hallstatt culture of southern France established itself in
the highlands behind the coastal plains of the Hautes-Alpes,
Ardèche, and parts of the Rhône valley, towards the end of the
seventh century B.C., and is closely related to the classical Hallstatt
groups of Burgundy, the Franche-Comté, and south Germany.
It was characterized by burial in barrows, a knowledge of iron,

[1] §IV, 23.　　　　[2] §IV, 33, 58–60.　　　　[3] §IV, 27; 28.
[4] §IV, 43.　　　　[5] §IV, 10.

and a range of new metal types (long Hallstatt swords, crescentic razors, toilet sets, bronze bowls, certain types of bracelet) and pottery decorated in the *Kerbschnitt* style. Their burial rite was mixed and they even re-used for burial older megalithic structures. These people had certainly arrived before the end of Mailhac I, and certainly flourished into the middle of the sixth century.

What were they and what was their relationship with the Mailhac–Agullana Urnfielders? They may have been a powerful minority—a chieftainship group; or they may represent whole tribes. They seem to occupy pasture land, whereas the Mailhac–Agullana folk seem firmly based on agriculture. It would, however, be a mistake, as Hodson points out, to suggest a dichotomy in southern France in the second quarter of the first millennium B.C. between agricultural Urnfielders and pastoral Hallstatt tumulus-builders.[1] A real dichtomy did, however, come into existence during this quarter-millennium and persisted into the third quarter of the first millennium, for Greek colonies were established on the coast of South France and now barbarian Celt and civilized Greek were in direct contact.

The traditional date for the settlement of Massalia by the Phocaeans is 600 B.C. but little survives of the early colony or indeed of Greek Marseilles at all, which has been properly called 'la cité antique sans antiquité'.[2] It has been suggested that the Greeks were in southern France before 600 B.C. in the course of the early Ionian voyages to the west Mediterranean and Spain, but the number of well-attested Greek imports before 600 B.C. is negligible. Even so, it may well be that St-Rémy-Glanum and St-Blaise-Mastramela were Ionian precursors of Phocaean Marseilles. However that may be, certainly from 600 B.C. the Celts, Celto-Ligurians and Celtiberians of the shores of the Gulf of Lions were in touch with the Greeks at Massalia, Agde, Nice, Antibes, Monaco, Ampurias and Rosas. They were also directly in touch with the Etruscans in the sixth century B.C.; an Etruscan wreck was found off the coast near Antibes, Etruscan bucchero ware is found in southern France and at Ampurias, and there are clay imitations of beaked flagons at Les Pennes.

Greek influence penetrated up the Rhône-Saône valley and also up the Isère; grey bucchero (Phocaean) pottery is found in the Hautes-Alpes and further north at Lons-le-Saunier and Salins, small three-winged bronze Greek arrowheads can be traced up the river valleys and into northern France, and amphorae with coarse mica tempering, originating in Marseilles, occur at Mont Lassois

---

[1] §IV, 23.    [2] §IV, 20; G, 3; G, 19; G, 1; G, 10.

in Burgundy and in the Heuneberg. The influence of Greece reached Central Europe not only by the Rhône but over the Alpine passes from the head of the Adriatic and the plain of Lombardy. It was an influence inspired by trade and prospecting: the Greeks were collecting salt, slaves, textiles, and metals—and the tin trade route from southern France to south-western Britain is part of this Greek penetration.[1] The Greeks themselves traded wine and containers for wine. The extent and the nature of this trade can be guessed at from the magnificent princess's grave from Vix near Châtillon-sur-Seine with its great krater and the gold diadem.[2]

From these Greek and Etruscan contacts in the late sixth and early fifth centuries b.c. was created in eastern France and south-western Germany the La Tène culture, destined to spread later over most of Europe, with its very remarkable art—the so-called Early Celtic art.[3] In the south of France at Malpas, near Valence and Le Pègue, north of Nyons, are groups of classic La Tène material, and examples of classic Early Celtic metalwork do occur in southern France, such as the mask in the museum at Tarbes dating from the third or second century b.c.[4]

Contact between the Greeks and the autochthones in southern France is attested by such things as the wine flagon and cup at Pertuis, but perhaps in the first colonial phase the natives were kept away or kept themselves away. Gradually there was created, however, in the centuries following the fifth century b.c., what has been called the Entremont culture after the site of Entremont near Aix-en-Provence. The people of this culture lived in caves and isolated farmsteads, but are known best from village sites like Les Pennes and from towns or oppida like Entremont, La Cour-tine and St-Estère. These large sites were permanently occupied. They were barbarian townships, and it is not improper in speaking of Entremont to distinguish among its inhabitants a knightly aristocracy. Trade with Marseilles existed from the sixth century but was most brisk from the end of the third. It was mainly trade in pottery and wine; Massilian and imitation Massilian coinage circulated. The Entremont culture was not a Gallia Graeca; the people were quite illiterate and the local pottery manufacturer was unindustrialized. The Entremont barbarians learnt much from the Greeks—new types of quern, currency, how to grow and process olives, the technique of making mosaics, and not least the idea of monumental sculpture in stone.[5]

[1] §iv, 22.          [2] §iv, 26.          [3] §iv, 37; §iv, 8; §iv, 24.
[4] §iv, 46; §iv, 29, pl. 36.               [5] §iv, 25; 23.

The Celto-Ligurian sculptures from Entremont itself, and from other sites like Roquepertuse, Grézan, Russan and Noves are most remarkable: unlike anything else in the Celtic or classical world, they are remarkable for their style and their subjects —especially the *tête coupée*.[1] At Entremont and Roquepertuse there is great emphasis on the decapitated head, and no doubt that these barbarians had shrines in which these *têtes coupées*, perhaps trophies of war or heads of ancestors, were stored and displayed.[2]

The Entremont people were basically the Urnfield population of the seventh century B.C. overlaid by Hallstatt chieftains and subjected to the influence of Greece. They appear to be the Saluvii whom Classical writers describe as extending from the Rhône to the Var. To the north of them were the Cavari (centred on Cavaillon). When in 121 B.C. they seized Marseilles, the Romans came to the aid of the Phocaean Greeks and drove the Celts away to the valley of the Isère, appropriating the Mediterranean coast. Provence was born from the Roman *provincia*: Aix-en-Provence (*Aquae Sextiae*) replaced Entremont, and prehistory ended in that part of Southern France.

## V. SPAIN AND PORTUGAL

The old land mass which forms the core of the Iberian peninsula has always, in human history, performed the contradictory functions of a link and a barrier between Europe and Africa, between the Mediterranean and the Atlantic world.[3] It has also generally been an important centre of culture in its own right.[4] Already at the beginning of the Lower Palaeolithic human groups were established in all parts of the Peninsula, though they were confined, for the most part, to favourable habitats such as river valleys and ancient shore lines.[5] An exception is the site of Torralba in Soria, where Lower Palaeolithic implements were found along with bones of elephant, rhinoceros, horse, aurochs and deer, on the shore of an ancient lagoon at a height of 1112 m. above sea level. The hunters had probably followed game which retreated to these heights to avoid the effects of the hot and waterless summers in the lowlands to the east.

The men of the Lower Palaeolithic probably came to Spain from Africa across the Straits of Gibraltar. Whether there was a complete land bridge or not, which is still a matter of controversy, the

---

[1] See Plate 175 (*d*).
[2] §IV, 7; 23.
[3] G, 18, 86–118; G, 13, 164–368; G, 6, 231–43.
[4] §V, 16; 38; 43; 4.
[5] G, 16, 71–99.

strait must have been at least much narrower than it is now. The stone industries are predominantly core industries, with hand-axes, which have their home in Africa. Industries of Abbevillian type and of the more advanced Acheulean type, which continued the same tradition, are found. No human remains have yet been found with any of these in the Iberian Peninsula, but some were recently found with similar bifacial tools at Ternifine in Morocco.[1] They were those of a primitive type of man who has been christened Atlanthropus.

The Middle Palaeolithic is represented in the Iberian Peninsula by remains of the Mousterian culture, probably the creation of Neanderthal men, remains of a number of whom have been found in Spain. They appear to fall into two types, which may represent two races, one which resembles the type found at Saccopastore in Italy, and which has been called Mediterranean Neanderthal, and another which resembles the classic Neanderthal of the rest of Europe. The Mousterian industries belong partly to an Interglacial phase and partly to the beginning of the last Glacial, after which they disappear, giving place to the Upper Palaeolithic industries which were the products of men of modern type.

The Upper Palaeolithic of Spain and Portugal covered the last period of the last Glacial and its cultures were extremely rich and varied. Broadly speaking, the flint and bone industries of these cultures correspond to contemporary ones elsewhere in Western Europe. All the main phases of the classic French sequence are represented in Spain and the cultures are known by the French names. As yet a complete sequence is only known for the Cantabrian region, which formed part of a cultural province which had its centre in South-west France. The first phase, known as the Aurignacian, had a flint industry based on blades, instead of cores or irregular flakes, which facilitated the manufacture of a greater variety of small tools than hitherto. The true Aurignacian has been found only in Cantabria, but a Mediterranean variant known as the Perigordian is very common all over the rest of the Peninsula.

The next phase is marked by the appearance of the Solutrean culture, which seems to be intrusive into the Peninsula, but from which direction is still a matter of considerable doubt.[2] The Solutrean, though basically a blade industry, is characterized by implements made in a way quite different from that normal in European Upper Palaeolithic industries. Their most typical implements are made from flakes of flint carefully worked on both faces. Examples are the fine points, known from their shape as

[1] §v, 10.          [2] §v, 23.

'laurel leaves', which are found on every Solutrean site. The
origins of this culture are obscure, but there seems little doubt
that the flint work represents a development and refinement of
Acheulean and Mousterian techniques of the Lower and Middle
Palaeolithic, contrasting with the revolutionary blade technique
of other Upper Palaeolithic cultures. Two separate groups can be
distinguished among the Spanish Solutreans: one centred on the
Cantabrian area, though also found in Catalonia, Central Spain
and Portugal, and more or less identical with the French Solutrean; the other found only in the eastern and south-eastern
coastal regions and characterized by special types, such as
the anachronistic-looking tanged and barbed points first found
at Parpalló.[1]

Wherever this culture came from (and neither North Africa
nor Central Europe seems very likely as a homeland, though
both have been suggested), it was only an episode in the Iberian
Upper Palaeolithic. Levels with a Perigordian industry have been
found above as well as below Solutrean ones in the caves, and the
Magdalenian culture, which flourished in many parts of Iberia
in the last part of the Upper Palaeolithic, represents a further
development of this kind of blade industry.

A remarkable development of artistic activity is characteristic
of all the cultures of the Iberian Upper Palaeolithic.[2] This expressed itself chiefly in engravings and paintings of animals,
conventional signs and, more rarely, schematized human figures
done on the walls of deep caves, but similar representations were
also sometimes engraved on movable objects. This art reached a
peak of technical accomplishment in the Magdalenian, illustrated
by the magnificent polychrome paintings of animals at Altamira,
though many other masterpieces can be pointed to in other phases
and in other parts of Spain. The Solutrean was relatively poor in
works of art compared with the other phases, though not as poor
as is sometimes supposed. These pictures, like the comparable
ones from France, probably had a ritual or magical function, but
their technical excellence implies the existence of specialists whose
skill was the result of training and long practice, and this in turn
seems to imply that game was fairly abundant and that a relatively
high standard of living prevailed among these tribes. This is
fully confirmed by other evidence.

The end of the last Glaciation, about 8000 B.C., resulted in
sweeping ecological changes which brought about drastic alterations in the pattern of life in the Peninsula, as elsewhere. The

[1] §v, 40, pls. VIII–X.            [2] G, 4; G, 11; §v, 2.

Mesolithic people were still food-gatherers, but different groups can be recognized who reacted in different ways to the new limitations and possibilities. Descendants of the Magdalenians are clearly recognizable in the Azilians of the Cantabrian area, both physically, and in their economy. The high Cantabrian mountains and the Pyrenees preserved something of the rich Arctic game which had flourished in the preceding period, but the Azilian culture was poor compared with its parent, and showed a progressive degeneration as the climatic improvement became more and more marked. In the Mediterranean part of Spain and the highlands of the interior, descendants of the Upper Palaeolithic people developed a markedly successful hunting and gathering economy, fully adapted to the new conditions. These folk also developed a new and vigorous style of art with which they recorded their activities of hunting and collecting, fighting and dancing, in vivid scenes which they painted on the walls of rock-shelters in the mountainous areas.[1] Other groups adapted themselves to a rather poor sort of life based on the products of the coastal waters and the shores, particularly shellfish. The large shell middens of the Tagus valley are the visible monuments of some of these people. Though widely distributed around the coasts they probably formed only a small part of the Mesolithic population.

The process by which a food-producing economy was finally introduced into the Peninsula is still far from clear. It was probably slow and gradual, involving the transformation by acculturation of the Mesolithic population and their adoption of the techniques of animal husbandry and agriculture. Some of the more schematized, and therefore probably later, rock-paintings show people leading apparently domesticated animals by means of halters.[2] Pottery was also adopted, at first in the form of simple wares with impressed or cordoned decoration. This perhaps points to the immigration of at least some fully Neolithic groups from the south or the north-west, or both, though it has been found in contexts which show a strong continuity with earlier Mesolithic cultures, for example at the Cueva de la Cocina.[3] The date of this development in Spain and Portugal is still very obscure, but the radiocarbon dates available for the Italian Neolithic would suggest that it happened before 4000 B.C.

The settlements and burials of the users of impressed pottery are normally found in caves, at first mainly in the mountains of the coastal ranges of Spain and Portugal, though later they seem to

[1] §v, 2; 8.  [2] §v, 2, fig. 390.  [3] §v, 41.

have penetrated into the central meseta as well.[1] In the plains, and particularly near the coast, somewhat different cultures appeared with more predominantly agricultural interests. The impressed-ware people, on the other hand, seem to have concentrated on the stock-breeding appropriate to their favourite terrain. Both groups at first still betrayed strong Mesolithic traits, particularly in their flint work. The agriculturalists are known from the open villages, such as that of El Garcel,[2] which sometimes have silos for grain storage as, well as traces of dwellings, and from their tombs, which were usually monumental. In the south-east, they were cists of slabs, or circular chambers enclosed in a small round mound; in Portugal, chambers made of large rough slabs, or 'dolmens'.[3] Some of these were for single burials, others accommodated up to half a dozen bodies. In Catalonia there was a group which was under strong influence from the Chiozza culture of North Italy, and which interred its dead in small cemeteries of earth graves.[4] All these groups used almost exclusively plain pottery, with simple, baggy shapes.

Further developments in the Iberian Peninsula during the Neolithic and the earlier part of the Copper Age affected chiefly the lowland groups, although the impressed-ware people survived, continuing their own way of life, and may have played a very important part in the events of the later Copper Age.[5]

At this point the mineral resources of the Peninsula became an important factor in determining its future development. By the beginning of the third millennium B.C. the cultures of the Aegean had become metal-using, and because of the poverty in ores of their homelands they were on the lookout for sources of raw metal abroad. Somehow, through deliberate or accidental explorations, they became aware of the riches of the Iberian Peninsula in copper, silver, gold, lead and, ultimately, tin. It now seems virtually certain that some of these Aegean communities, perhaps the daring seafarers of some of the Cycladic islands, established colonies in the coastal regions of southern Spain and Portugal with a view to the exploitation of these resources. Remains of townships of strongly Aegean aspect have been found in both these regions which covered areas of up to $12\frac{1}{2}$ acres and were defended by massive walls with semicircular bastions, like those at Chalandriani, in Syros, or at Lerna on the Greek mainland.[6] At Los Millares in Almería these defences were further strengthened by a series of four detached forts set on the surrounding hills.[7]

[1] §v, 49, 18.  [2] §v, 54; 20.  [3] §v, 25, pls. I–IV; 26, pls. I–IV.
[4] §v, 53.  [5] See below, p. 762.  [6] §v, 14; 11; 47.  [7] §v, 9.

Circular, oval and rectangular houses have been found within these settlements, and the equipment of the inhabitants differed in many respects from that of the earlier people of the lowlands. At Almizaraque, a settlement site in Almería near to the silver deposits of Herrerías, slags show that copper, silver and lead were smelted.[1] Some of the metal was probably sent back east by sea, but some copper was used for making tools and weapons, which were sometimes cast in two valve moulds. Besides metal pins, awls, daggers, knives and axes, they used elaborately worked flint arrowheads of various forms, and flint daggers, and had a great range of ornaments and toilet articles, including unguent containers of ivory and limestone, and bone and ivory combs. Along with pottery in the old tradition we find new types, including pyxides resembling Cycladic ones, with grooved decoration, vases incised and sometimes painted with symbolic patterns,[2] and plaster vases imitating ostrich-egg shells.

Most striking is the sudden appearance of a range of ritual equipment, including owl-eyed figurines incised or painted on stone or ivory cylinders, phalanges of cattle or flat plaques of schist. Flat stone figurines seem to have been known already in Neolithic times and perhaps date back to the earliest contacts with the East. Many of these ritual objects have been found in the collective tombs of the 'colonial' settlers, which were beehive-shaped chambers, roofed by corbelling, set in a circular mound and entered through a stone passage. About a hundred of them are scattered on the level ground just outside the defences at Los Millares, and many others are known elsewhere in South Spain and Portugal, both singly and in groups. In Portugal they were sometimes replaced by rock-cut tombs of similar form, as in the necropoleis of Palmella and Alapraia. This new funerary architecture, perhaps influenced by the family tombs of the Aegean Early Bronze Age, had a notable effect on the indigenous tomb-building in Iberia, and the native cists and dolmens were developed into massive megalithic tombs of various kinds. The tradition of building monumental tombs seems to have lasted long in some parts of the Peninsula.[3] Radiocarbon dates so far indicate that some were in use, and perhaps were built or altered, after 2000 B.C.[4]

In the last centuries of the third millennium B.C. a new culture made its appearance in the Iberian Peninsula, that of the users of Bell Beakers. They seem to have penetrated into or taken over

[1] §v, 7; 48.     [2] See Plate 176(b)–(c).
[3] §v, 25; 26; 27; 42; 44.     [4] §v, 28, 359–66.

entirely the 'colonial' settlements, and their burials are found in many of the Iberian collective tombs, though they had their own characteristic burial rite of single inhumation in trench graves, exemplified in the cemetery of Ciempozuelos, near Madrid. At the fortified settlement of Vilanova de São Pedro, north of Lisbon, their remains are clearly stratified above those of the 'colonists'.[1] The same situation was found at Ghar Cahal, a stratified cave site[2] on the Moroccan coast opposite Gibraltar, and their burials can often be seen to be late in the series in collective tombs, even in some cases unconnected with the primary use of the tomb. They used metal, but their casting techniques do not seem to have been as advanced as those of the earlier 'colonial' communities, since all their products could have been made in simple open moulds.

The Bell Beaker people, whose chief hallmark is their bell-shaped drinking cup, usually of red polished ware, with incised decoration arranged in zones or panels, are found in many parts of western and central Europe at this time. Their origin, if indeed they were a unitary people, has been much debated. Many prehistorians have favoured the Iberian Peninsula as their homeland though it has never been possible to produce conclusive proof of this. The most recent theory, propounded by Sangmeister, sees them as descendants of the pastoral impressed-ware communities, who came to dominate the lowland communities and the colonists, and learned metallurgy from the latter, though they did not attain the same level of skill. They would then have spread rapidly up into Central Europe, where they met, and were influenced by, other groups, including warlike pastoral people who decorated their somewhat similar drinking vessels with the impressions of twisted cords. The subsequent southward 'reflux' movement of certain types of beakers and characteristic associated material to the Mediterranean is well documented, but the first part of the theory cannot yet be counted as more than an ingenious hypothesis, though admittedly no better alternative has so far been provided.[3]

A radiocarbon date of $2345 \pm 85$ B.C. has been obtained from a sample found beneath a collapsed defensive wall at Los Millares, which should represent a late stage of the life, if not the end, of that settlement.[4] The Bell Beaker culture was probably already in existence by this time; for other radiocarbon dates from temperate Europe seem to show that it was present there only about a century later. Its duration, counting in the late groups certainly derived from Central Europe, probably amounted to several

[1] §v, 39.                                    [2] §v, 55.
[3] §v, 24, 11–15, 19–22; G, 15.               [4] §v, 5.

centuries. However, it was never the sole existing culture in any part of the Iberian Peninsula. Other traditions, such as those of the collective tomb-builders and, in some areas at least, those of the impressed-ware people, survived until the beginning of the Bronze Age, and even formed a noticeable element in the Bronze Age population.

Copper Age traditions lingered long in many parts of the Peninsula. In the Balearic islands the earliest finds, collective burials in natural caves, seem to belong to a later phase of this period, and the material shows a close similarity, as might be expected, with that found in Catalonia.[1] In certain areas of the Peninsula, however, groups with a new look and a truly Bronze Age equipment began to emerge in the second quarter of the second millennium B.C. South-east Spain became the centre of the El Argar culture, which combined traits derived from many divergent sources, and whose customs and equipment contrasted sharply with those of the earlier cultures.[2] The settlements of this culture are found almost always in inaccessible and easily defensible spots, such as steep mountainsides or hilltops. They consist of groups of houses with rectangular rooms built of unworked stones, and are sometimes strengthened by defensive walls of larger rough stones. The dead were inhumed in stone cists or large jars, usually within the houses, but sometimes also outside the settlements altogether.

The equipment of the El Argar people is marked by the disappearance of the elaborate ritual paraphernalia of the collective tomb people and also of the fine flintwork which had characterized the Copper Age. There was also a great increase in the use of metal tools and weapons, about 50 per cent of which were of bronze. The metal types were mostly versions of tools and weapons current in the late Copper and Early Bronze Ages in Central Europe but include rare examples of swords with broad flat blades. Some elements, such as stone wrist-guards, seem to connect them with the movement which brought developed Bell Beaker types from Central Europe to Spain,[3] while others suggest the survival of some at least of the earlier population in a changed environment. However, there were also very strong features in the El Argar culture which must be due to renewed influence from the east Mediterranean. Some of these, such as the metallic qualities of the pottery, and certain shapes, such as the high-footed chalice, can be explained as the result of superficial contacts, but the adoption of the Anatolian and Aegean rite of pithos burial

---

[1] §v, 30.  [2] §v, 54.  [3] §v, 15; 51.

argues a stronger link.[1] The probability of this is strengthened by the recent finding of some Argaric 'circle graves' resembling Middle Helladic ones found in Leucas.

The Argaric culture undoubtedly lasted for a long time and it is beginning to be possible to recognize different phases in the material. The segmented faience beads found at Fuente Álamo probably belong to a relatively late phase, as perhaps also do the rare swords, if their origin lies in western Europe. If it is eastern, however, as has recently been claimed, they could be earlier. A group of rock-cut tombs at Alcaide, which are said to have contained Argaric material, have many features which are found in Mycenaean rock-tombs, and they are almost identical in all respects with the tombs of Thapsos type in Sicily.[2] The Thapsos parallel might suggest a date after 1400 B.C., but the still unpublished contents have been said to be of early type.

From its centre the El Argar culture spread eastwards towards Granada and northwards to Murcia and Valencia, though losing some traits on the way. Eventually we meet it, in an attenuated form, even on the central meseta near Madrid. An independent group, very closely resembling the El Argar people of the southeast, was established in the south of Portugal, centred on the Algarve province. In the Balearic islands, people were buried in cemeteries of collective rock-cut tombs, at first simple, but later more elaborate and carefully finished, with pots and other material which somewhat resemble El Argar types, especially those of the Valencia area. To some parts of the Peninsula groups of Argaric character never really penetrated. In central and northern Portugal, north-west Spain, the Pyrenean region and Catalonia old-established cultures went their own way under a variety of external influences without violent change.

The period immediately following that of the El Argar culture, comprising the last few centuries of the second millennium B.C. and the beginning of the first, are the most obscure in the prehistory of the Peninsula. From the scattered finds which exist it is extremely difficult to piece together an intelligible picture of life during this middle part of the Bronze Age. In north-west Spain and northern Portugal, regions whose riches in metal ores gave them an important place in the economy of Bronze Age Western Europe, and ensured contact with the countries of the Atlantic coastline, objects of European Middle Bronze Age type, such as palstaves, are found.[3] Cemeteries of cist graves with the so-called 'hat-bowl' pottery in Portugal probably belong to this phase.[4]

[1] §v, 18.        [2] §v, 19.        [3] §v, 29, 64–6.        [4] §v, 13.

In the south-east the El Argar culture with its Early Bronze Age repertoire of metal types may have continued to exist for a very long time, and the same may be true of its Balearic *facies*. Throughout the rest of the Peninsula pottery which continued Copper Age and even Neolithic traditions constitutes the bulk of the remains from this period. It is found in caves, sometimes stratified above late Beaker material, as at Toralla, in Navarre, and sometimes also on open sites.[1]

The next event of major importance in the prehistory of the Peninsula was the beginning, in the ninth or eighth century B.C., of the infiltration of groups of people from South France into Catalonia and thence into Aragon and the central parts of Spain. These people had a culture of Urnfield type which originated ultimately in Central Europe. They represent the beginning of a long-drawn-out folk movement which ultimately also brought people with equipment of Hallstatt type to Spain.[2] The latter were certainly of Celtic speech, and it is probable that the earlier immigrants were so too. At first only the north-eastern parts of Spain were strongly affected by this influx, but gradually the centre and the west were also transformed. The south and east were never so strongly affected; for though the newcomers established political domination in some parts, the population was not radically altered, speech was not transformed, and other influences, Phoenician, Punic and Greek, were also strong in these parts.

In the western parts of the Peninsula, where contacts with the Atlantic coasts of France and southern Britain had always been strong, a local Late Bronze Age developed which is closely related to that which emerged contemporaneously in the western, non-urnfield, part of France, and whose types are also found in Britain.[3] Its most characteristic bronzes are single- and double-looped palstaves and the 'carp's tongue' sword, which combines features of Central European Urnfield swords with a reduction in the width of the blade near the point, a feature which is also found commonly on swords and daggers of the early first millennium in Italy.[4] The close links between the coasts of Atlantic Europe may well have been fostered by the activities of Phoenician traders, and it is no accident that a cargo of bronzes carried by a ship of this period which sank in Huelva[5] harbour should have included, as well as 'carp's tongue' swords, a spearhead of Irish type and stilted fibulae derived from a type which seems to have originated in the Levant in the tenth century B.C.,

---

[1] §v, 31, 17.  [2] §v, 3; 17.
[3] §v, 50.  [4] §v, 22.  [5] §v, 1.

and which is found in Sicily in the Pantalica II phase.[1] These
fibulae have been found also in Atlantic France,[2] while bronze
'carp's tongue' swords have been found also in Sardinia.[3]

In the extreme east the Balearic islands also continued to
develop in their own way, evolving a remarkable local civilization
which in its essentials survived right into Roman times. The inhabitants of Majorca and Minorca had begun to inhabit villages
of stone-built houses which were girt with massive stone defensive
walls, whose gates were both monumental and easily defensible.
Each of these villages possessed a number of strong points in the
form of massive stone towers, known as 'talayots', which contained
beehive chambers roofed by corbelling and spiral stairways leading from one storey to the next. Sometimes burials were made in
these towers, but they were not primarily burial places. There
were also cult places within the villages, which included, in
Minorca only, the strange 'taulas', horseshoe-shaped enclosures
containing, as the central feature, a T-shaped erection made of two
huge slabs. The dead were normally buried collectively outside
the settlements in built tombs, which are called 'navetas' because
they resemble upturned boats. The chambers within are very
similar in shape to those of the developed rock-tombs of the preceding phase.[4]

In general the *talayot* culture resembles the roughly contemporary cultures of Sardinia and Corsica with their complexes of
*nuraghi* and *torri*, but some features, such as the *taulas* of Minorca
and the so-called 'hypostyle halls', are unique to the *talayot*
settlement of the Balearics. The chief subsistence activity of the
*talayot* people was probably agriculture, but they were undoubtedly
a turbulent and warlike people, warriors on land and pirates at
sea. It was this milieu which produced the Balearic slingers, so
famous as mercenaries in classical times.

The Iron Age communities of the mainland were no less warlike. Already in the Late Bronze Age the tombstones of warriors
in Extremadura were engraved with representations of the complete panoply of the occupant.[5] In Celtic society everywhere
warfare was endemic, and the groups which came to Spain were
no exception. The massive hill forts which sprang up all over the
Celtic parts of the Peninsula testify to the introduction of the
normal Celtic pattern of attack and defence. Hill forts were not
normally for permanent occupation; and for the record of their
everyday lives we have to look to their settlements, such as

[1] §II, 8, 154–6; §v, 36.          [2] §v, 21, fig. 4.
[3] §v, 56; §III, 13, 167–9.         [4] §v, 30, 717–51.          [5] §v, 46.

Cortes de Navarra in Navarre, which lasted from the beginning of the eighth to the fourth century B.C., and whose rectangular-roomed, mud-brick houses were several times rebuilt. The walls of some rooms were plastered and decorated with simple geometric patterns in red paint and in one instance with a schematized human figure.[1]

Pottery was often plain, or decorated with excised or applied decoration, but fine pottery might be decorated by painting. The finest achievements of Celtic art in Spain and Portugal, however, were in the sphere of fine metalwork, weapons, ornaments and jewellery, which are normally found in graves and chance finds of hidden treasure rather than in settlements. The Celts continued to cremate their dead, but interred the dead person's personal possessions with the ashes.[2]

The intensive character of the Celtic occupation of the central meseta, which contrasts so strongly with the scanty remains of earlier occupation there, has been explained by the climatic deterioration during the first half of the first millennium B.C., whose effect, so detrimental in northern Europe, was thoroughly beneficial to the arid plateau of central Spain.

Though Celtic influence in the southern and eastern parts of the Peninsula was considerably more important than had been supposed until recently, the basic Mediterranean population of these parts survived to create, under strong Punic and Greek, as well as Celtic, influence, the distinctive culture which is called Iberian.[3] Iberian settlements are on hilltops or hillsides, often defended with walls and towers. Their houses were rectangular stone structures, and their coarse pottery at any rate seems to be directly descended from Argaric ware, though of course made on the wheel. The fine wares were painted, and the influence here was predominantly Punic at first, though later there was some Celtic and finally strong Greek influence. The finest Iberian painted pottery is probably very late, dating from the third and second centuries B.C., but it is aesthetically very satisfying and gives us some vivid sidelights on Iberian life. Sculpture was developed for religious purposes and sometimes attained high quality. Statues and statuettes represent divinities, worshippers with offerings, and priestesses (of which the best known is the famous Dama de Elche[4]). Exquisite jewellery was made, some of which has been found in hoards or 'treasures', and which is represented as being worn by some of the sculptured priestesses.[5]

[1] §v, 32.      [2] §v, 34; 52.      [3] §v, 45; 12.
[4] See Plate 175 (c).      [5] §v, 37; 35; 38, part 3, fig. 489.

This jewellery was until recently thought of as Punic, but has now been recognized as a distinctive Iberian style developed under Oriental influence, whose original centre of production was probably in south-west Spain, the area of Tartessus. With other material, this jewellery seems to constitute evidence of a distinctive Iberian orientalizing style, comparable to the contemporary Greek and Early Etruscan ones.

The Iberians buried their dead in a variety of ways. The rite of cremation was predominant, though inhumation in jars was known in the south. The tombs themselves range from elaborate chamber tombs surmounted by a tumulus, common in the cemeteries of Andalucía (which also provide evidence of the differing treatment of people of varying social importance), to the simpler, more egalitarian cemeteries of the Levant, where the ashes were placed in a small stone cist, a pottery urn, or simply a hole in the ground. Personal possessions were buried with the ashes, arms with the men, and ornaments and spinning equipment with the women. We have little idea of the religion of the Iberians though a number of sanctuaries are known in which offerings were made to deities, particularly statuettes of metal or terracotta representing the worshipper.

The Iberians were formidable fighters, with an excellent armament. Their chief weapon, a kind of falchion or sabre, was borrowed from the Greeks, and in the finest examples the hilt was elaborately moulded and damascened with silver. Daggers and knives and a variety of spears and javelins were used, as well as the bow and arrow and the sling. Several of their weapons were later adopted by the Romans, good judges in these matters.

Finally, a word must be said about the legendary kingdom of Tartessus, about which traditions were preserved by Greek writers, and which may be the same as the Tarshish mentioned several times in the Bible, and once also by Esarhaddon of Assyria (though not all scholars would accept this identification). This rich and ancient state was situated in modern Andalucía, where, also according to legend, the Phoenician colony of Gades (modern Cádiz) was founded in 1100 B.C. If this were so, the 'ships of Tarshish' referred to in the Biblical account of the reign of Solomon could indeed, manned by Phoenician sailors, have been carrying back the silver and tin of the West to the Levant in the tenth century B.C. Unfortunately, the earliest archaeological evidence so far found for the presence of Phoenicians in Spain belongs at best to the eighth century B.C. There has been very little systematic excavation of Iberian settlements in this area but recent work by Spanish scholars seems to indicate that the vague, yet persistent, traditions about the civilized and learned Tartessians may still prove to be in some measure justified.[1]

## VI. NORTH AFRICA

The south shores of the west Mediterranean are markedly dissimilar in later prehistoric times from the rest of the Mediterranean and this must surely be due to the desiccation of the Sahara and the inhospitable hinterland which the southern shore of the Mediterranean had in the four millennia before the Christian era. Here we find no great flourishing of Late Neolithic and Bronze Age cultures, nothing to compare with Los Millares and El Argar, with the Nuraghic civilization of Sardinia and the Torrean civilization of Corsica; no developments such as produced the great megalithic temples of Malta and Gozo. The story on the northern shores of Africa west of Egypt is rather one of the spread of basic and early Neolithic culture, and this spread, perhaps in the sixth and fifth millennia B.C., seems to have happened in a different climate, preceding the onset of the desiccation which produced the Sahara. The sharp contrast between the abundance of early Neolithic remains in the desert areas of North Africa and the present-day aridity surely proves the existence of wetter climatic conditions.[2]

The spread of the basic early Neolithic cultures to western and north-western Africa seems to have occurred from two separate areas, Egypt and the Sudan. In Egypt, food-producing communities had been in existence from the middle of the fifth millennium B.C., and this is no longer an archaeological guess based on calculations back from the beginning of dynastic Egypt. In the south, near Khartūm, the Shaheinab settlement gave a carbon-14 date of 3110 B.C. (C-753). From these two centres, Egypt and the Sudan, prehistoric agriculture could have spread to North-west Africa and the shores of the south Mediterranean, first from Egypt along the coasts to Cyrenaica, Tripolitania and beyond, and second across the Libyan Sand Sea to the central Sahara.[3]

This is the generally accepted view of the diffusion of Neolithic culture in North Africa, but there exist scholars who suggest that two separate and independent Neolithic and agricultural origins should be considered in North Africa, one involving the

[1] §v, 33.
[2] §vi, 3; 9; G, 16; §vi, 1; 5; 13; 11; 4; 2.
[3] G, 7.

domestication of cattle in Abyssinia, and the other the invention of agriculture based on sorghum, rice, and *blé dur* in the southern Sahara.[1] However this may be, what we do know is that in the Hoggar region a number of sites have revealed a Mediterranean type of vegetation there between 4000 and 3000 B.C., with a remarkable culture based on domestic cattle. Four of these early sites have yielded carbon-14 dates as follows: Jabbaren, 3520 B.C. (Sa-55), Hassi Meniet, 3450 (Sa-59), Adrar Bouss III, 3190 (Sa-100), and Sefar 3080 (Sa-62). We also know that Dr Charles McBurney's excavations in the cave of Haua Fteah in Libya, on the coast of Cyrenaica, showed an early Neolithic with the first domestic animals on the coast of North Africa as from the fifth millennium B.C.[2] The earliest Neolithic in Libya and in the Hoggar is based on domestic cattle. The change from hunter-gatherer to self-supporting food-producer in North-west Africa is first a change to a pastoral economy; agriculture comes later. And the pastoral economy was first based on cattle: sheep and goats came later, and the camel of course very much later.

From our point of view here, the most interesting area is the Maghreb. This was the name which the Arabic-speaking geographers of the Middle Ages applied to North Africa lying to the west of Egypt; it was, in fact, what the word means, 'the western land'. But this phrase has been modified in the course of time and nowadays the Maghreb does not include Cyrenaica and Tripolitania: it is now Tunisia, Algeria and Morocco—the Barbary of old writers and the Africa Minor of modern German geographers. In the Maghreb the earliest Neolithic is simply a phase in which the Mesolithic cultures of Oranian and Upper Capsian tradition persist with domesticated animals and new tools. Vaufrey considered the Oranian as simply a different *facies* of the Upper Capsian, and so does Leakey, and the story seems to be an acculturation of Upper Palaeolithic (or Mesolithic) indigenes and invaders from the east or south; this translation into the Neolithic took place, as Breuil said, 'par pénétration progressive. . . des éléments industriels nouveaux'. The Capsian/Oranian Neolithic (or the Ibéro-maurusien, if you prefer this phrase) is characterized partly by microlithic flint types and partly by non-microlithic types (such as scrapers, blades, backed blades, notched blades, transverse arrowheads, tanged points), polished stone axes and adzes, stone vessels, grain-rubbers and querns, bone points, needles, knives and spatulas, and containers made of ostrich-egg shells. Ostrich shells were also used for making beads.

[1] §VI, 4.    [2] G, 14; §VI, 12.

The pottery is mainly conical-based but there are also round-bottomed pots. The normal burial practice seems to have been to bury the body, inhumed and sometimes treated with red ochre, in a simple trench in the caves of open sites occupied by these early Neolithic people.[1]

While some writers see the Neolithic of the Maghreb as a unitary phase, others would wish to divide it into two phases, the earlier or *Néolithique ancien* of French writers (which is the Capsian/Oranian or Ibéro-maurusien we have been describing) and a later phase or *Néolithique récent* such as appears in the Grotte d'Achakar and Dar-es-Soltan in Morocco. This later Neolithic is characterized by polished axes, grooved axes, red burnished pottery, pots with spherical or ovoid bodies and everted necks and decorated with cord and *Cardium* shells. Sherds closely resembling the Beaker pottery of Iberia appear in these contexts. It would seem that there is a recent or second Neolithic in the Maghreb though its interrelationships with the Neolithic and Chalcolithic cultures of Iberia have not yet been worked out. Some have too readily seen the origin of all European Beakers in the few sherds from North-west Africa.

In the last few years the rock paintings of the Sahara and North-west Africa have received much attention, but they do not affect the Mediterranean littoral which is our concern here. Suffice it to say that while it would appear that some of the Saharan rock sculptures and paintings go back to a pre-Neolithic phase, though perhaps not to a phase contemporary with the Franco-Cantabrian art of the Upper Palaeolithic in other parts of the west Mediterranean, most of them are Neolithic, and reflect the mixed hunting and pastoral economy of the Saharan Neolithic.[2]

The story of protohistoric North Africa is, then, that of Neolithic pastoralists lasting through until the first millennium B.C., when they met the Phoenicians and the Greeks. One final matter needs our attention—the position of the megalithic monuments, or stone-built surface tombs, of which there are many thousands in North-west Africa. They have often been dated to the Neolithic and described as contemporary with the megaliths of Europe.[3] Perhaps more strange things have been written about the megaliths of Africa than about other aspects of African prehistory or other aspects of megalith study. Even as recently as 1957 Professor Alimen wrote as follows: 'Those great currents of megalithic culture that swirled around such a vast area in the

[1] §vi, 6; 7; 8; 15; 18; 17.    [2] §vi, 16; 10.
[3] §vi, 7; 1; 14.

Old World also reached Africa. The megalithic stream took its course from the Atlantic coasts of Europe to the Pacific shores of Asia and again from Scandinavia to southern Africa.'[1] There was no megalithic culture and no great megalithic stream. Different people in different parts of the world built in what is called the megalithic style and produced as a result vaguely comparable monuments. Gsell first argued that the 'megaliths' of North Africa date from the centuries immediately preceding and following the beginning of the Christian era, and this is Reygasse's view. It is just possible that the late flowering of some megalithic tombs in southern France in the beginning of the first millennium B.C. could have influenced the Late Neolithic peoples of North Africa, but we think Gsell and Reygasse were right and that the megaliths of the Maghreb date from between 300 B.C. and 500 A.D.

[1] §VI, I, 407.

# CHAPTER XXXVIII

## GREEK SETTLEMENT IN THE EASTERN AEGEAN AND ASIA MINOR

THE great kingdoms of the earth crumbled or fell in the century or two before the close of the second millennium. The Hittite empire in Asia Minor vanished. Scarcely even a memory remained of its central power; and the western principalities, such as Arzawa, Assuwa and the Shekha River Territory, passed into so total an oblivion that fifty years of research on the imperial archive of Khattusha has not availed to fix their positions with certainty on the map of ancient Anatolia. Theirs was an age of which the moralist might have said, 'Omnes quae usquam rerum potiuntur urbes quaeque alienorum imperiorum magna sunt decora, ubi fuerint, aliquando quaeretur.'

In the Aegean the following centuries constitute the Dark Age that preceded the Greek Renascence of the later eighth century. On the west coast of Asia Minor the people that set the pace was the Greeks. Seeking new lands, they crossed the Aegean; and settling on a coast which was probably underpopulated and certainly lacking in political organization, they cherished their old traditions and invented new modes of rational thought, urban civilization and poetry. It was not till the seventh century, long after they had consolidated their possession of the coastlands, that the Greeks of Asia began to meet opposition to their inland penetration. The beginnings of their settlements lie beyond the threshold of recorded history. The knowledge of writing had been lost in this quarter of the ancient world; and the main Greek prose traditions of the migrations, though they may enshrine historical fact, constitute a schematic tableau coloured by the sentimental attachments or political pretensions of a subsequent age. The local historians of the individual cities may here and there have preserved genuine memories of early times; though not immune from prejudice, they could record without the same need to systematize and co-ordinate. But their works are almost totally lost. Beyond this, modern study of ancient cults and institutions and of the Greek dialects may indicate connexions and, to some

* An original version of this chapter was published as fascicle 7 in 1961; the present chapter includes revisions made in 1970.

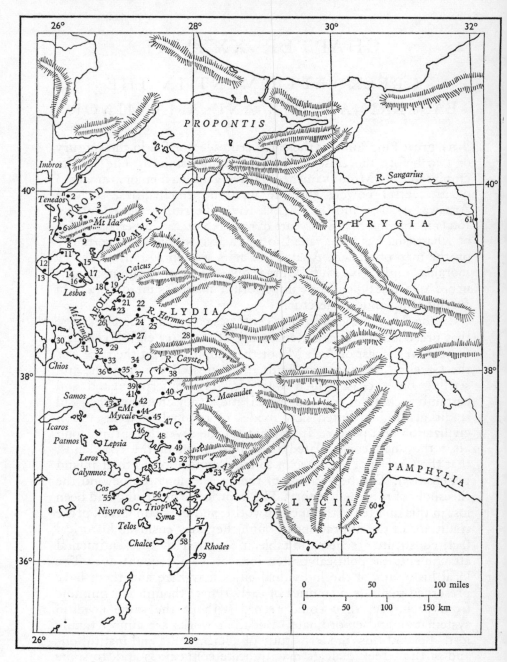

Map 16. Greek settlement in the Eastern Aegean and Asia Minor.

## NUMERICAL KEY

| | | | | | |
|---|---|---|---|---|---|
| 1 | Abydus | 22 | Aegae | 42 | Panionium |
| 2 | Ilium | 23 | Cyme | 43 | Samos |
| 3 | Scepsis | 24 | Tamnos | 44 | Priene |
| 4 | Cebren | 25 | Magnesia | 45 | Myus |
| 5 | Colone | 26 | Phocaea | 46 | Miletus |
| 6 | Larisa | 27 | Smyrna | 47 | Latmus |
| 7 | Hamaxitus | 28 | Sardis | 48 | Iasus |
| 8 | Assus | 29 | Clazomenae | 49 | Mylasa |
| 9 | Gargara | 30 | Chios | 50 | Cindya |
| 10 | Adramyttium | 31 | Erythrae | 51 | Halicarnassus |
| 11 | Methymna | 32 | Aerae | 52 | Ceramus |
| 12 | Antissa | 33 | Teos | 53 | Cedreae |
| 13 | Eresus | 34 | Colophon | 54 | Meropis |
| 14 | Messon | 35 | Lebedus | 55 | Astypalaea |
| 15 | Thermi | 36 | Myonnesus | 56 | Cnidus |
| 16 | Yera | 37 | Clarus | 57 | Ialysus |
| 17 | Mitylene | 38 | Larisa | 58 | Camirus |
| 18 | Canae | 39 | Ephesus | 59 | Lindus |
| 19 | Pitane | 40 | Magnesia | 60 | Phaselis |
| 20 | Gryneion | 41 | Pygela | 61 | Gordium |
| 21 | Myrina | | | | |

## ALPHABETICAL KEY

| | | |
|---|---|---|
| Abydus 1 | Ephesus 39 | Miletus 46 |
| Adramyttium 10 | Eresus 13 | Mitylene 17 |
| Aegae 22 | Erythrae 31 | Mylasa 49 |
| Aerae 32 | Gargara 9 | Myonnesus 36 |
| Antissa 12 | Gordium 61 | Myrina 21 |
| Assus 8 | Gryneion 20 | Myus 45 |
| Astypalaea 55 | Halicarnassus 51 | Panionium 42 |
| Camirus 58 | Hamaxitus 7 | Phaselis 60 |
| Canae 18 | Ialysus 57 | Phocaea 26 |
| Cebren 4 | Iasus 48 | Pitane 19 |
| Cedreae 53 | Ilium 2 | Priene 44 |
| Ceramus 52 | Larisa 6 | Pygela 41 |
| Chios 30 | Larisa 38 | Samos 43 |
| Cindya 50 | Latmus 47 | Sardis 28 |
| Clarus 37 | Lebedus 35 | Scepsis 3 |
| Clazomenae 29 | Lindus 59 | Smyrna 27 |
| Cnidus 56 | Magnesia 25, 40 | Tamnos 24 |
| Colone 5 | Meropis 54 | Teos 33 |
| Colophon 34 | Messon 14 | Thermi 15 |
| Cyme 23 | Methymna 11 | Yera 16 |

extent, origins. But the application of these studies to the prehistory of the Greeks of Asia depends overmuch on inference
from speculative theories; and, in the absence of contemporary
documents, these studies can only be regarded as ancillary branches
of historical inquiry. Archaeology is a more serviceable instrument; for its testimony, though easily misinterpreted, is objective.
Within well-defined limits excavation can project the most certain
historical light. But, like a hand-torch, it can only direct its beam
within a narrow compass, and much closer field research must be
undertaken before the Dark Age can receive a general illumination.
Archaeology is concerned with material remains; it is capable—or
potentially so—of answering specific questions about the extent, the
processes and the duration of the migrations to the East Aegean,
and about the material civilization that was developed there. But
it cannot illuminate the spiritual forces and vicissitudes of that
epoch, except in so far as it may help us to a better understanding of the world into which Homer was born; and it cannot
relieve our ignorance of the constitutional history of these early
settlements.

## I. AEOLIC SETTLEMENT IN LESBOS AND THE ADJACENT COASTLANDS

The island of Lesbos is large by Aegean standards (665 square
miles), and it is fertile in its eastern half. A dozen Bronze Age
sites are known, and no doubt more await discovery. Though the
known ones are not all contemporary, it is clear that in the time
of Troy I and again in the Late Bronze Age the settlements in the
island were numerous and flourishing. In historical times, under
the conditions of archaic Greek settlement, the island was too large
to be ruled by a single city; in the fifth century B.C. there were five
independent cities (Mytilene, Methymna, Antissa, Eresus and
Pyrrha), and a sixth city (Arisba) was known to have been enslaved
at some previous time by Methymna. The Elder Pliny adds the
names of two dead cities (Hiera and Agamede); he does not
disclose the source of his information, but, as it stands, his mention
of these two cities can only relate to pre-classical times (and indeed
before the time of Alcaeus). So far as the inadequate archaeological exploration of the island permits a judgement, the Bronze
Age site near the modern village of Thermi (on the east coast of
Lesbos at the focal point of road communication)[1] may in its time
have been the biggest inhabited centre in the island; and if we

1 §1, 4.

wish to infer from Homer that there was a single city of Lesbos, the one at Thermi could have been the seat of a dynasty ruling the whole island in the Late Bronze Age; but there is another similar unexplored Late Bronze Age site at Yera (Hiera) on the other side of Mytilene. For our present purpose the significant histori- cal fact is that the old settlements at Thermi and Hiera seem to have died out by the beginning of the Dark Age, and that Mytilene became the mistress of the whole eastern end of the island.

In the days of our forefathers and from the history books it is reported of this island that in ancient times it was ruled by sons of Nemrud—and then came an infidel ruler named Qataluza (in whose name it is easy to recognize the Genoese dynasty of Gattilusi). Such is the history of Lesbos in the marine guide which Piri Re'is composed in A.D. 1520 to prepare the way for Suleiman the Magnificent's expedition to Rhodes. The modern scholar is left wondering how long the wild asses stamped their feet in Lesbos before the infidel came. The Greek antiquarians constructed history differently. They had a *horror vacui*. Seven generations before the Flood came Xanthus, king of the Pelasgians, and settled the island. In the wake of the deluge Macareus came from Achaea, and in the next generation a grandson of Aeolus called Lesbus, who married the king's daughter and called his own daughters by the names subsequently borne by the cities of Lesbos. Stories like this were duly translated into a chrono- logical system, so that the Elder Pliny knew that Mytilene was *annis MD potens*. With such mythical fabrications we shall not be concerned in this chapter. But the literary reconstructions of Dark Age migrations cannot be wholly ignored; for here some continuity of memory may have existed among the settlers.

The schematic prose traditions of the migrations to the East Aegean after the Trojan War seem in general to have been compil- ations of the fifth century B.C. Aeolic expeditions to Lesbos and the Aeolis are recorded, under the leadership of sons and descendants of Orestes; and priority is thus given, in prestige as well as time, to the Aeolic settlement as against the Ionic further south. The connexion with Orestes, which alone gives a precise dating, carries no conviction. But the names—as opposed to the genea- logies—of the founders may have some basis in local traditions; and there is at present no good ground for disputing the belief that the Greek cities of the Southern Aeolis (on the Asiatic mainland) were foundations of the Dark Age. In later times the dialect of Lesbos and the Aeolis bore a close resemblance to Thessalian and Boeotian, and in the fifth century B.C. the Aeolians of Lesbos and

Cyme recognized a kinship with the Boeotians. The new settlers may well have come mainly from these regions.

In Lesbos itself the problem of Greek origins is more complex. The eighth-century Ionic poetic tradition, in which no mention of Greek settlement in Ionia was tolerated, seems to have recognized Greek occupation of Lesbos before the time of the Trojan War; and in the hymn to Delian Apollo—itself most Homeric in diction and background—this occupation is represented as Aeolic (Μάκαρος ἕδος Αἰολίωνος). We therefore cannot confidently assume that the Dark Age migrations represent the first Greek or Aeolic settlement in Lesbos. The site at Thermi has been extensively excavated. The place evidently ceased to be occupied well before the end of the Bronze Age; and the disappearance of this city and of that at Hiera may most naturally be interpreted as evidence of the expansion of Mytilene in the east of the island—matched in the Dark Age by the further extension of Mytilenaean supremacy to the adjacent coast of the Troad. If this interpretation is correct, Mytilene must already have been flourishing in the Late Bronze Age (Mycenaean sherds are said to have been found there); and this continuous expansion is most naturally to be explained as the work of Aeolians. The persistence of the local tradition of monochrome pottery in the island (in preference to both Mycenaean and painted Geometric wares) would fit with the view that there was no general cultural break at the end of the Bronze Age; but, on the other hand, at the excavated site of Antissa on the north coast[1] it is not quite certain that the grey wares of the Dark Age derive without interruption from the Late Bronze Age monochromes. Unfortunately, the other ancient city sites have not been investigated.

The situation of Mytilene was distinguished by a little island almost touching the Lesbian coast. At Antissa, where the continuous occupation dates from the fourteenth century B.C., there was a similar island which had already become linked to the coast. These two sites are of a sort that attracted immigrants from overseas, and the other classical cities of Lesbos (except perhaps Arisba) stood on headlands or coastal heights. But the prehistoric inhabitants of Lesbos seem also to have preferred coastal sites; so the criterion of geographical siting, though not by any means to be neglected, cannot be very effectively used to distinguish Aeolic from native settlement here. The problem of Greek beginnings in Lesbos thus seems to be insoluble without fuller archaeological evidence; and indeed, to be quite honest, we can only say

---

[1] §1, 5.

that the Greek settlement there is not likely to have begun before
2300 B.C. or later than 1000 B.C.

The territory of Mytilene was extensive and fertile; so also was
that of the Methymnaeans after they had annexed Arisba. Vines
flourished, along with cults of Dionysus; the consumption of
wine, in historical times at least, was notoriously great; and if the
grey-fired standard containers found in Smyrna and Athens are
Lesbian, the export of wine goes back at least to the seventh
century. Life was probably easy in the rich lands of Mytilene
and Methymna; and though the Lesbians do not seem to have
been backward in their forms of constitutional government in the
seventh century, the sites of their citadels show little sign of
regular urban concentration, even in classical times. No doubt
agriculture was the principal occupation of the Lesbians in the
Dark Age, and music their principal relaxation. The cities of the
island formed some sort of amphictyony in early times; for they
had a common sanctuary furnished with altars of their *makares*—
Zeus Antiaos, the Aeolian goddess (perhaps Hera), and Dionysus
Omestes. It was there that the poet Alcaeus appears to have taken
refuge, and presumably there also that he was a witness of the
annual beauty competition of the Lesbian maidens. This place
of meeting was most probably by the land-locked gulf now appro-
priately called Kallone, either at Messon, where there was a
sanctuary of some federal significance in Hellenistic times, or on
the west horn of the gulf at the archaic sanctuary terrace near
Makara, which bears the modern name of Καλὸν τεῖχος.[1]

After his long digression on the Ionians Herodotus (1, 149)
turns briefly to the Aeolic cities of the Asiatic mainland. Like the
Ionic cities they were twelve in number (Cyme called Phriconis,
Larisa, Neon Teichos, Tamnos, Cilla, Notium, Aegiroessa, Pitane,
Aegae, Myrina, Gryneion, and Smyrna which fell into the hands
of Ionians). These places cannot all be placed with certainty on
the map; and, in particular, Cilla, Notium and Aegiroessa are
virtually unknown apart from this one mention of them. But it is
clear that the general area which the twelve cities occupied is that
bounded by the Gulf of Smyrna on the south and the Caicus plain
on the north; the cities under Ida are expressly distinguished by
Herodotus. The country of the twelve cities is therefore only the
southern part of what was later known as the Aeolis. Excavation
at Smyrna seems to show that the city there had become almost
completely Ionic in character before the eighth century, and that,

[1] A, 5.

if Smyrna was originally Aeolic (as we should in any case infer
from the abundant grey ware in the earliest Greek strata on the
site), the Aeolic settlement there must go back to about 1000 B.C.[1]
If therefore Herodotus is to be believed when he implies that these
twelve cities formed a dodecapolis before Smyrna was lost, Aeolic
settlement in the Southern Aeolis must be dated relatively early
in the Dark Age. The objection that on the excavated site which
is conjecturally identified as Larisa the earliest datable Greek
pottery is almost without exception of the seventh century cannot
invalidate this conclusion—Greek pottery of an earlier date can
be picked up on the surface on unexcavated sites here, such as
Cyme, Gryneion and Tamnos; it serves rather to cast doubt on the
identification of the site of Larisa.

The most important of these cities was Cyme. It was said to
have been founded by settlers from Locris in Central Greece, who
began by reducing the Pelasgian citadel of Larisa near the river
Hermus; and it subsequently ranked, with Lesbos, as the metropolis of some thirty Aeolic towns in the region. In later times the
Cymaeans were ridiculed as a people who had lived on the coast for
three hundred years before they noticed the presence of the sea
and exacted harbour dues; but it was from there that Hesiod's
father sailed across the Aegean to Boeotia. Of the other towns of
the Southern Aeolis little is known before Hellenistic times.
Planted on small peninsulas or hilltop citadels, they formed a
fringe along the Elaitic Gulf from Cyme to Pitane and inland from
Cyme up the Hermus valley. Magnesia under Sipylus, a city of
uncertain origins in the western Lydian plain, formed the terminal
of this advance. One Aeolic city, Aegae, was founded up-country
in a mountain valley east of the Elaitic Gulf, and this uninviting
mountainland may in due course have come under Aeolic control.
But in general the Aeolic settlement here seems to have lacked
depth. The cities of the Southern Aeolis occupied a belt of good
land with rough mountains at the back; and, unlike the Ionic
cities, they had no commerce in products or ideas with native
peoples inland. Thus isolated, they made no contribution to the
history of western Asia Minor; and the great universal historian
from Cyme, Ephorus, was reduced to punctuating his narrative of
Greek history with the recurring observation that in the meantime
his fellow-countrymen kept the peace.

From the Black Mount of Canae northward to the confines of
Adramyttium the coast was in native hands. Its inhabitants, the
Mysians, were aborigines with no taste for Greek culture and little

[1] §II, 4, 10 ff.

interest in urban life until the Emperor Hadrian collected them into new inland cities that he founded among their wooded mountains. They are known to us through the lone Mysian in the Ten Thousand, who covered the rearguard above Trebizond by staging a counter-ambush in the scrub and then, when the time came to slip away, lost his head and ran yelling down the path—fortunately he survived to dance a one-man duel and produce a cabaret at the gala day among the Paphlagonians. At some time before 546 B.C. Chios acquired a mainland territory (*peraea*) at Atarneus in the corner of the Caicus plain, and further north a little Aeolic town on Poroselene Island (Nasos) encroached on the mainland coast. But it was probably not before the fourth century B.C. that the Mysians of this shore withdrew inland and the Mytilenaeans planted their villages up the long coastal stretch facing their own beaches.

In the Troad the earliest Aeolic settlements were probably those on the west coast, where archaeological research seems to indicate Greek occupation at least as early as the eighth century. The Aeolic towns here seem to have been dependencies of Mytilene until 427 B.C.; and being founded on crests that rise directly from the sea, they give the impression that the initial settlement here was only skin-deep. A gap in the towns on this shore above Colonae seems to indicate that the little island-city of Tenedos—*male fida carinis*, and yet in later times the friend of imperial powers concerned in shipping corn through the Dardanelles—was already taking possession of the coast that lay opposite. Before 700 B.C. the Mytilenaean Acte had reached as far north as Ilion (Troy), and it was probably about this time that the European shore of the Dardanelles received Aeolic settlers. These Mytilenaean towns of the coast were farming communities; and they were evidently small, since the plain of Troy was divided between three or four of them. The Bronze Age cultures in the Troad seem to have been maritime in their origins, for the great majority of the sites are coastal. Troy itself is thought to have been unoccupied when the Lesbians came to settle there; in the lack of excavation it is not known whether the other Mytilenaean town-sites were also unoccupied at this time—it looks as though some (but not all) of them may have had prehistoric settlement. Inland, the big wool-cities of the Scamander basin (Cebren and Scepsis), which in historical times were fully independent and bit deep into the interior, may not have been founded until the seventh century. On the south coast of the Troad were two daughter-cities of Methymna set on towering heights (Assus and Gargara); they lived a self-contained life, enjoying a sufficient competence from the cultivation of the sheltered, fertile valleys down which the springs of Ida discharge. A notable feature of these Aeolic coasts is the prevalence of old cults of Apollo; presumably the region lay outside the sphere of the Anatolian mother-goddess.

## II. THE IONIC MIGRATIONS

In historical times Ionia was divided between the twelve cities of the Panionic league. Two of them were island-states: SAMOS, which, as the terminal of the all-weather crossing of the Aegean, was the key-point of Aegean naval strategy down to the Byzantine era and itself at times wielded sea-power, and CHIOS, the greatest financial centre of the north. Under the lee of Samos lay the Milesian Gulf with the long fertile plain of the river reaching far inland between high mountain walls. MILETUS itself lay on a peninsula at the south entry point of the gulf, little MYUS at the head of the gulf, and PRIENE, home of agriculturalists, on the north shore by the Maeander mouth. North of the headland of Mycale was the sanctuary of Panionium; but no Panionic city stood on the thirty miles of shore that forms the southern coast of the Central Ionic gulf. In the orchard terrain by the Cayster mouth lay EPHESUS, commanding the entry to the river valley and the Colophonian plain. COLOPHON itself was situated inland on the edge of the great plain that reaches almost to Smyrna on the north; but it had outlets to the sea by defiles leading down to Clarus and to the coast further west, and at some date before the fifth century it planted its southern fort (Notium) on the promontory above the roadstead of Clarus. Further up the coast lay LEBEDOS, with the mountain at its back, and placid TEOS with rolling sheep country behind. Across the isthmus on the Gulf of Smyrna was turbulent CLAZOMENAE. Facing Chios, ERYTHRAE controlled the peninsula of Mt Mimas, where the vines were immune from pest and the young goats maintained life by snuffing the sea breezes; the Erythraean territory dispensed abundant grazing and over a hundred miles of rugged circuitous coastline. And, finally, at the north entry point of the gulf, PHOCAEA won her bread from the seas. These constituted the Ionic dodecapolis. At the head of the gulf, Smyrna at an early date became Ionic; and, in the south, Magnesia, non-Ionic like her namesake under Sipylus and claiming a Thessalian origin (by a conveniently devious route that secured her a *concordia amicabilis* with the Cretan pirates of Hellenistic times), formed the outpost of Greek advance up the Maeander valley. The geography of Ionia was in general favourable to Greek initiative; a great extent of territory lay between the heads of the gulfs, and, with their broad flat bottoms, the deep-carved river valleys invited settlement further inland. Later, they delivered Ionia into the hand of the native power of the interior.

Our two main ancient sources for the foundations in Ionia are Strabo (xiv, 632–3) and Pausanias (vii, 2–4). Strabo says that (according to Pherecydes) Androclus, the son of the Athenian king Codrus, led the Ionic colonization and was the founder of Ephesus—hence the institution of the kingship of the Ionians there; he goes on to name Neleus, the founder of Miletus, who was of Pylian origin, and the founders of the other Ionic cities, of whom two are of Pylian origin and three are sons of Codrus. Pausanias, in a more circumstantial account, makes Neleus (whom he calls Neileus) the second son of Codrus and, together with his younger brothers, the leader of the Ionians in their overseas migration; with the exception of Clazomenae and Phocaea, all the mainland cities had sons of Codrus as founders (a grandson at Priene). Apart from the rival claims of the houses of Miletus and Ephesus to the leadership and from some minor discrepancies—of which the most serious concerns the Codrid founders of Colophon—the two accounts are tolerably consistent; and in general they seem to represent the reconstructions of the history of Ionic settlement that were current in the fifth century B.C. The underlying assumption in the surviving literary testimonies is that, except perhaps in the extreme north of Ionia, the colonization was a single organized act and issued from Athens, where refugees from other parts of Greece had collected. Herodotus (i, 142–8) and other ancient writers found an anomaly in the presence of Pylians and others as leaders and the intrusion of Boeotians, Euboeans and a variety of non-Ionic peoples into a main body of Ionic settlers; but they do not seem to have doubted that Athens was the principal focus of the emigration.

The anomaly of the non-Ionians need not detain us. The classical Greeks were concerned to systematize their racial origins, and their theory required that these Ionians should have been a distinct branch of the Greek people with their eponymous ancestor and their own ancient homeland (generally held to be in the north Peloponnese), from which of necessity they had been expelled before the colonization of Ionia took place; being thus distinct, for instance, from the inhabitants of Boeotia and Pylus, these Ionians proper must have formed a hard core to which the extraneous elements attached themselves. This 'hard core' of Ionians, which provided the rank and file but never by any chance a leader or an act taken on its own initiative, is a myth. We may say—without defining the connotations of the term in dialect and customs—that some of the emigrants may have been less 'Ionic' than others; but, generally speaking, the Ionism of the twelve cities was the sum of its various components.

Two historical problems can be considered in the light of ancient literary sources. The first—that of the original homes of the settlers—may some day be illuminated a little by fuller excavation on the sites of the Ionic cities. But there can be little doubt that the diversity of origin claimed in the traditions had some historical basis. Thus, in the seventh century, Mimnermus possessed certain knowledge that his Colophonian ancestors were of Pylian origin; and at Priene, where Pausanias expressly records that Thebans took part, there are undeniable connexions with Boeotia in historical names and cults. The second problem is the general belief that Athens was the main focus of emigration. Many modern scholars have contended that this claim was invented by the Athenians in the sixth century, or even when Athens assumed the leadership of the Ionians after the Persian Wars; and Mimnermus is cited as declaring (as he appears to do, but in a historical narrative of unique compression) that his Colophonians sailed to their beloved Asia direct from Pylus. But this view presents great difficulties. The belief in Athens as the metropolis of the Ionians was generally conceded by fifth-century writers, and the leadership of the Codrid Neleus was accepted by Panyassis, the epic poet of Halicarnassus, in the early part of that century. It seems unlikely that an Athenian political fiction could have won such immediate and universal acceptance. Literary and epigraphical evidences combine to indicate that in historical times Athens and the cities of Ionia had in common the essentials of their calendar, a number of old festivals and cults (such as the Apaturia and the worship of Eleusinian Demeter), and, basically, the four 'Ionic' tribes (Aegicoreis, Argadeis, Geleontes and Hopletes). It is true that few of these Ionic institutions were exclusively Athenian; and they cannot therefore constitute direct proof that Athens wielded the dominant influence in the migrations. But their widespread diffusion in Ionia is consistent with the tradition of Athenian leadership; and certainly, if we do not believe in a 'hard core' of Ionians among the emigrants as distinct from Pylians and others, and if at the same time we believe, for instance, that Mimnermus' Pylians sailed from their old home to Ionia without first concentrating in Athens, the strength of the common Attic-Ionic institutions in Ionia cannot easily be explained. Finally, in so far as the early painted pottery of Ionia is evidence of outward connexions, it is Athens that seems to have exerted the principal influence on Ionia. The history of Greek colonization after the Dark Age shows clearly that waves of emigration to a particular region tended to be organized by a single city whose sea-captains were familiar with routes and local conditions; and in the present instance Athens alone seems capable of having fulfilled such a role.

There are three questions to which archaeological research may ultimately give unequivocal answers: (i) When did the Ionic migrations commence? (ii) How long did the process last? (iii) How many original settlements were there? A fourth question, which in the opinion of some scholars renders the first three nugatory, is that of the evidences for earlier Greek settlement in Ionia; but that will be considered last. Question (ii) can be set aside at once; only substantial excavation on a number of Ionic sites will provide the comparative data required for a satisfactory answer. To question (i) a provisional answer can be given. Painted pottery of Protogeometric character has been found in bulk in excavated strata on the sites of Miletus and Smyrna, is reported in excavation at Phocaea, and has come to light at Clazomenae and several minor sites on the coast.[1] These finds seem to indicate widespread Ionic settlement as early as the tenth century. At Smyrna the deposit is deep, and painted Protogeometric pottery may be considered to have made its appearance somewhere around 1000 B.C. by current archaeological reckoning (in absolute terms, between 1050 and 950 B.C.).[2] At that time Smyrna may have ranked as an Aeolic city, and in fact abundant monochrome pottery of Aeolic type has also come to light in the Protogeometric and earlier Geometric strata on the site; but, so far as can be judged, the painted ware displays Ionic characteristics, and it must be either Ionic production or a direct reflexion of Ionic production in this region.[3] Ionic settlement in the region should therefore go back at least to about 1000 B.C., and perhaps still earlier at Miletus.

A satisfactory answer to question (iii) will depend primarily on the search for Protogeometric deposits on Ionic sites; and it is not possible at present to give more than an interim statement. Protogeometric pottery has come to light on several of the twelve city-sites; but bits of such pottery have also been noted on several settlement-sites that were not of Panionic status, both on the

---

[1] §II, 2, 40 f., 48.            [2] §II, 4, 10.
[3] A large fragment of a characteristically Ionic Geometric vase is illustrated on Plate 177.

extensive coastline that in historical times belonged to Erythrae
and on the long shore between Ephesus and Mt Mycale.[1] On the
latter stretch there existed in antiquity several small towns which
did not achieve Panionic status and were believed to have been
absorbed by their more powerful neighbours at the time when
the league was formed at Panionium (see below, p. 803). If pottery
of Protogeometric character is to be accepted as the archaeological
recognition symbol of original migration settlements, we may
expect evidence of a plurality of original settlements which failed
to achieve Panionic status; and the total number of such settlements could well have equalled the ten successful ones which ultimately apportioned the coast among themselves. Some of the
cities on the Ionic and Aeolic coastline were founded on small
peninsulas which can hardly have accommodated more than a few
dozen families; and we may think of them as being in appearance
nothing more than villages. If this view of the original pattern of
Ionic settlement is well founded, the supply of sons of a historical
king Codrus could not credibly have sufficed to provide leaders
for the majority of these groups of settlers; and we may therefore
conclude that for the most part the title of 'son of Codrus' is a
posthumous distinction conferred, where the tradition permitted,
on the founders of those cities which had achieved Panionic status.
With this certificate of simultaneous foundation removed, the
belief in a single act of colonization has no longer any secure
foundation.

We must now consider the condition of Ionia before the Ionic
migrations. In the main, the ancient traditions give Carian habitation (or rather, Carians in the south with Lelegians in the north)
as the core of the pre-existing population; but there are individual
notices of settlements prior to the Ionic colonization—Cretans
and their associates at Miletus, Samos, Chios and Erythrae,
Minyans of Orchomenus at Teos, and the sanctuary of Apollo at
Clarus has its own private prehistory. To turn to the archaeological evidence, Ionia is still very inadequately explored at the
present day; but in general it seems that prehistoric sites are not
infrequent there, and that a number of the Ionic settlements were
founded on sites that had been occupied in the preceding epoch.
In the north the dominant pottery of that epoch is monochrome
ware of native character; but in the south of Chios, in Samos, at
Ephesus, and apparently at Colophon, some Mycenaean pottery
has been found, and at Miletus there is the one certain Cretan and
Mycenaean settlement of the mainland coast. Some scholars

[1] §II, 2, 40.

maintain that this Mycenaean pottery testifies to partial or total occupation of Ionia by Greeks in the Late Bronze Age, and therefore argue either that the Greek settlement was already far advanced before the time of the Ionic migrations or that the Ionic migration itself commenced as early as the fifteenth century B.C.[1] For Miletus, where the Cretan pottery seems to have given way to Mycenaean in the fifteenth century, we have unique documentary evidence in the Hittite archives (assuming that the Millawanda or Milawata of the texts is to be identified with Miletus): in the second half of the fourteenth century it was a dependency of the Achaean king, but subsequently it was held by a vassal of the Hittite. This testimony could be held to confirm the claim that the Mycenaean remains at Miletus represent Greek settlement. But there is no certainty that on the fringes of the Mycenaean world Mycenaean pottery necessarily betokens a Greek population; for, without literary confirmation, the equation of cultural phenomena with race is hazardous. It is at least worth bearing in mind that, viewed in terms of geographical spread, the sphere of Mycenaean influence or settlement in south-west Asia Minor and the adjacent islands corresponds almost exactly with the region which in ancient Greek tradition was occupied by the Carians at the time of the Ionic colonization; and we have no ground for supposing that the maritime Carians did not belong to the Cretan and Mycenaean cultural sphere.

In this dilemma we may turn to the Homeric poems, which evidently reflect with considerable fidelity the beliefs current among the Dark Age Ionians about the geographical situation of the Greek peoples before the collapse of the Achaean kingdoms. In Homer, as in the Hittite texts and the archaeological record, Miletus is unique; it is the only place mentioned on the whole Ionic coast. But it is Carian, not Greek. Apart from this, there is no mention of inhabitants of the Ionic coast, nor indeed, in the whole of the *Iliad*, is there any other mention of the west coast of Asia Minor south of the Troad except for the simile of the migrating birds that settle on the Cayster flats. This seems to be proof that in the Dark Age the Ionians knew that their settlements were post-heroic; and the absence of Achaean legends relating to cities of Ionia seems equally to indicate that the early Ionic poets had no knowledge of any previous stages of Greek settlement in Ionia. For this reason, in the present state of knowledge, we do not appear to be justified in rejecting the established belief that the Ionic migrations of the Dark Age constituted the primary Greek

[1] §II, 2, 39 f.; A, 6.

settlement of Ionia. It may be that there had been limited Achaean penetration of this region in Mycenaean times, of which virtually all memory had vanished before the Dark Age. What is clear is that the Dark Age migrations were not a reinforcement of already existing Greek settlements.

Herodotus (I, 142) remarks that in the cities of Ionia four distinct forms of the Ionic dialect were spoken, and that in this respect the grouping was (i) the cities in Caria (Miletus, Myus, Priene), (ii) the cities in Lydia (Ephesus, Colophon, Lebedos, Teos, Clazomenae, Phocaea), (iii) Chios and Erythrae, and (iv) Samos. There is no evidence of differences in the literary dialect, and no doubt Herodotus was referring to the colloquial idiom, which may well have been subject to Carian and Lydian influences—there is no lack of native words in the work of the Ephesian poet Hipponax. The dialect of Chios and Erythrae could have been less influenced by Lydian and more akin to the neighbouring Aeolic; but if that were so, we should expect that Phocaea—founded on the tip of Aeolic territory at the greatest possible distance from Lydia, and akin to the Aeolians in culture (for monochrome pottery is reported to be abundant in the Dark Age level on the site)—would have been included in this group. The peculiarity of the Samian dialect might be due to the traditional Argolic origin of the settlers there; but it might mean simply that the Samian dialect was uncontaminated. And in any case the Samians would be different—their φιλότιμον would not permit them to be otherwise. Whatever the value of Herodotus' testimony may be, it can hardly connote general distinctions in the origin of the Ionians of the coast. Similarly, the differences of temperament that distinguished the Ionic cities in historical times are to be attributed in the main to geographical circumstance, and not to ethnic diversity.

Some of the local traditions of individual cities may contain a kernel of historical fact.[1] Pausanias (VII, 3, 5) relates that the settlers of Clazomenae were mainly refugees from Cleonae and Phlius who obtained from Colophon a leader called Parphorus and made abortive settlements under Mt Ida and on Colophonian territory at Skuppion before finally coming to rest at Clazomenae; the attempt under Ida and the implication that Colophon was already well established might suggest that Clazomenae was a late foundation, but Protogeometric sherds have in fact been found there. In the same passage the settlers at Phocaea are said to have been natives of Phocis who crossed to Asia with Athenian leaders

---

[1] For these stories see A, 11.

and occupied their headland by courtesy of the Cymaeans; but the claim to Phocian origin may depend on nothing more than the common name. Pausanias also states that the sites of these two cities were uninhabited before the Ionians came, and the lack of traditions about them agrees with this. Of Phocaea it may be true, for the only pre-Greek pottery yet found on the site is of the Early Bronze Age; but at Clazomenae monochrome potsherds of late prehistoric types can be picked up by the end of the later causeway and a few Mycenaean sherds are claimed as having been found. Smyrna was an Aeolic city and was captured by refugees from Colophon, who (according to Herodotus I, 150) watched until the inhabitants had left the town to celebrate a festival of Dionysus and then closed the gates against them; coming to an agreement, they handed over the furniture but kept the town. On the evidence of the pottery found in the excavations it appears that Smyrna became increasingly Ionic during the first two centuries of its existence, but there is no point in the sequence where a very sudden change occurs; if the substance of the story is true, we must suppose that Ionians had been establishing themselves in Smyrna for several generations before the dispossession of the Aeolians (which will then probably have occurred about 800 B.C.).

Various stories show Androclus of Ephesus as especially active: he expelled the Leleges and Lydians from the upper city but came to terms with the suppliants and Amazons who lived around the Artemisium—archaeologists have found no trace of these pre-Greek settlements; crossing to Samos, he expelled the Samians for plotting with the Carians and held the island for ten years; finally he died fighting to establish Ionic Priene. A revolution against his sons was said to have resulted in the introduction to Ephesus of new settlers from Teos and Carene, and a similar insurrection against the sons of Neleus at Miletus resulted in a secession to Myus that ended with a love story. A son of Neleus brought reinforcements to Iasus when it was depleted by losses in war with the Carians, and a romantic legend has a youth of the royal family at Halicarnassus held as a hostage by the rulers of Miletus. At Miletus itself the women would not eat with their husbands or address them by name because the Ionic settlers had killed the male Carians and taken the women as their wives. To Erythrae, where there was a veritable consortium of races, the Codrid founder, Cleopus (or Cnopus), brought reinforcements from all the cities of Ionia; according to the local antiquary Hippias, his effeminate murderers, with a bodyguard from Chios, established a tyranny, drove the inhabitants out of the fortification, and had the streets cleaned—a climax of tyrannical behaviour which can hardly be the invention of a Hellenistic writer. In later times, tombs and altars of founders were pointed out in or near various of the cities; these, together with the stories about the families of Neleus and Androclus, are likely to be pious accretions to famous names. The local traditions could be more satisfactorily analysed if they were not reduced to scattered fragments and could be read in their proper contexts; thus, the mention in Vitruvius' architectural handbook of a city of Melite, which was destroyed by the united action of the Ionic cities because of the arrogance of its people, could scarcely engage the serious attention of scholars until a detailed account of the partitioning of this Melite (or rather, Melie), resting on the authority of eight classical historians, was discovered on an inscription of Priene (see below, p. 803).

## III. THE TRIOPIAN DORIANS AND THE CARIAN COAST

'Cnidus and Halicarnassus did not exist at that time; but Rhodes existed, and Cos.' This is Strabo's remark (xiv, 653) on the state of settlement in the south-eastern Aegean before the Doric colonization; and, being based on knowledge of Homer, it is correct. There are perhaps some faint traces of early prehistoric settlement on the horns of Halicarnassus harbour, and primitive marble idols have been excavated at the extremity of the Cnidian peninsula; but in the epoch that preceded the foundation of these two Greek cities there does not seem to have been regular settlement on either of their sites. The position in the offshore islands was quite different. Here the traditions speak of aboriginal, Cretan, and Carian settlement, followed by the rule of the immigrant descendants of Heracles who are named in the *Iliad* (Tlepolemus in Rhodes, two sons of Thessalus in Cos); and, as though in confirmation of this, Mycenaean remains are abundant. In Rhodes, Mycenaean finds are widespread; at Ialysus the Mycenaean was superimposed on Cretan settlement and began in the fifteenth century. On Cos, Mycenaean tombs have come to light in several places, and excavations at Meropis in the east end of the island revealed a Mycenaean settlement dating from the fifteenth or fourteenth century. Further, Mycenaean cemeteries have been found on the Carian island of Calymna, which lies to the north of Cos. The early Ionic poetic tradition recognized Achaean rule in Rhodes and Cos; and—whether we prefer to regard Mycenaean settlement in the south-east Aegean as pure Achaean or basically Carian—there is no reason to doubt the existence of late Achaean principalities there.

The Doric settlement presumably occurred during the Dark Age. In Cos, on the site of Meropis (that of the Hellenistic city and the modern town), the excavations have shown that Dark Age settlement, attested by graves containing Protogeometric pottery, followed the Mycenaean. If it were certain that this signifies new settlers, the inference would be that the Dorians arrived in the tenth century; and this may be correct. But the settlement at Meropis seems to have faded away before the end of the Dark Age, and in historical times (until the removal in 366 B.C.) the Dorian capital of Cos was at Astypalaea near the other end of the island; it is therefore equally possible that the archaeological evidence of the Dorian conquest is to be sought at Astypalaea, and that the dwindling city at Meropis—the Cos of the Homeric tradition— was a pre-Dorian centre.[1] Thus the Dorian settlement may date to either the tenth or the ninth century. The sites of the Rhodian cities have yielded some late Protogeometric; this is probably to be regarded as evidence that Doric settlement on the island dates at least as early as 900 B.C. Calymna ranked as Doric in later times; but its archaic remains have a Carian complexion, and there is at present nothing to suggest that the island became Greek in the Dark Age.[2]

The ancient literary tradition of this Doric colonization is fragmentary. It was apparently systematized (along with the Doric settlement of Crete) and scheduled as occurring after the defeat of the Dorians by the Athenian king Codrus—thus being made contemporary with the Ionic colonization; in late times the Dorian hero Althaemenes was claimed as a founder by the Rhodians and honoured at Camirus, but he was primarily associated with Crete in Greek tradition. Diodorus (v, 53) refers the Greek settlement of the little island of Syme (near Cnidus) to a late stage in the activity of an Armada of the Lacedaemonians and Argives, which was cruising in these waters and (as his narrative implies) had already colonized Rhodes and Cnidus. In his historical scheme this Doric *stolos* was presumably envisaged as a counterpart to the Ionic *apoikia* and the Aeolic *stratia*. But in itself it looks no more than a paper fleet. The mention of Lacedaemonians is, of course, required by the local tradition of Cnidus; for the Cnidians, according to Herodotus (1, 174), claimed to be of Lacedaemonian descent, and their actions show them to have

[1] §III, 4, 120 ff.　　　　　　[2] §III, 4, 129.

been the most faithful of Sparta's allies in the Aegean after 413 B.C. For the remainder of the Doric settlements here Argolic origin was the standard tradition, and it may well be the fact; their Greek cults in historical times betray Argive associations, with little sign of a Spartan connexion except on Cnidian territory.

Cnidus was the strongest Doric city on the Asiatic mainland in early times. Before it was removed to the western cape in the fourth century, the city lay on a broad sheltered bay at the waist of the narrow, forty-mile-long peninsula that comprised the Cnidian home territory. Its park-like setting consorts strangely with the sheer serrated crest of the high Triopian ridge to the west and the forbidding mountain chain that binds it to the Carian mainland on the east. In a long strath under the high western ridge the old settlement of Triopium, annexed by the Cnidians, formed the meeting point of the cities which jointly celebrated the Dorian games in honour of Triopian Apollo. In the fifth century these cities were five in number—Cnidus, Cos, and the three cities of Rhodes (Lindus, Ialysus and Camirus); but Herodotus insists that his own native city of Halicarnassus had participated in the festival until a victor from there flouted convention by taking home his prize (I, 144). The Chersonese opposite Rhodes, which forms the south-western corner of Caria, was the home of a number of little communities and healing cults; most celebrated among the latter was the pilgrimage shrine of Hemithea at Castabus, where the taboo against pork and wine was ascribed to an accident that occurred when the heroine was guarding her father's barrel. This Chersonese, which was Rhodian from the fourth century B.C., may previously have belonged to Cnidus; it seems to have been more Greek than Carian in historical times. The old site of Cnidus has not yet been explored; stray finds indicate that there, as also at Halicarnassus, Greek occupation must go back at least to the eighth century, but the foundations may well be older than that.

The settlements of the Triopian Dorians defy a common characterization. The citadels of Lindus and Cnidus rose over the calm waters; and these two cities maintained an interest in seafaring. Coan Astypalaea and Ialysus were set on inland heights, while Camirus occupied a lower crest. In the old cities of Rhodes the habitation seems to have straggled over the countryside, and we should perhaps imagine the Dorians of the islands as stolid proprietors of farms in the fair acres—in contrast to the volatile, city-dwelling Ionians. It was only after the collapse of the

Athenian empire that the Triopian Dorians came to perceive the advantages of organized civic life and built themselves new planned cities in dominant commercial and strategic situations on the main thoroughfares of seaborne traffic.

Halicarnassus lay on the sultry south coast of the main western peninsula of Caria. The original settlement was probably on the 'island'—a small rocky peninsula (at times divided from the mainland by an artificial canal) which, together with the spit of Salmacis, enclosed a capacious harbour. It faced towards Cnidus and Cos. Though excluded from the Triopian festival, the Halicarnassians claimed to be Dorians, with Argive Troezen as their mother-city. Their institutions were partly Doric in later times; but their speech was throughout Ionic—even in their public documents they made no appreciable headway with the Doric *koine*; and a long list of householders of Halicarnassus (with their patronymics) on a mid-fifth-century inscription permits the calculation that at the time when Herodotus lived there Carian names were as numerous as Greek.[1] We have here an example of a Greek city which absorbed a considerable native population without suffering a diminution of its Hellenism. To the outside observer classical Halicarnassus appears an Ionic city. If we ask why Samos ranked as Ionic and Halicarnassus did not, the answer may be that the emigration to Halicarnassus occurred at a later date and that adventurous or discontented Dorians may have played a substantial part in its foundation. Halicarnassus itself possessed little territory. Until the fourth century B.C. it was hemmed in by a group of little townships which (according to Callisthenes) were inhabited by a fragment of the non-Greek population of the Aegean called Leleges, but its economic strength and hellenizing power were probably not confined within narrow territorial limits.

Philip of Theangela asserted that the Leleges were used by the Carians as domestic slaves, and the native dynasts from these towns of the Halicarnassus peninsula pass as Carians in the pages of Herodotus; so we are not in a position to distinguish between Carians and Leleges here. On the archaeological evidence, the inhabitants of these townships seem to have been established in their hilltop citadels in the Dark Age and to have subsisted mainly by tending their flocks in the gnarled mountains.[2] When Mausolus compelled the Carians to adopt city life about 360 B.C., two cities of up-to-date Greek design came reluctantly into being here—new Myndus and Theangela; and they apparently received courteous recognition as ancient colonies of Troezen, the mother-

[1] §III, 7, 96.          [2] §III, 7, 116 ff., 167 f.

city of Halicarnassus. Here we seem in all likelihood to have evidence of one genuine old Greek foundation (Halicarnassus) and of two late and fictitious accretions to the Doric colonial tradition.

Further east the position is very obscure. In the Iasic Gulf, Iasus had a Greek cult of Zeus Megistus in the fifth century; but Bargylia, the mushroom city of the fourth century that supplanted dynastic Cindya, had no stronger claim to a Greek origin than a blow from the hoof of Pegasus. At the point where the Ceramic Gulf contracts to a blue, silent canyon, Ceramus—the stifling basin that traps the midday heat, or perhaps the 'jug' that is easily reached downwind but difficult to escape from—possessed a temple of Zeus whose crumbling foundations now disgorge relics of archaic Ionic statues. There is some ground for supposing that both Ceramus and Iasus claimed descent from Troezen, which might imply that they lacked traditions of their own; but it seems likely that both places had a substantial Greek element in their population from quite early times. Cedreae, a small town of the Ceramic canyon whose population Xenophon called 'mixobarbarous' (*H.G.* II, I, I5), was perhaps a Carian community that welcomed Greek cultivators and industry; so also, perhaps— before the fourth century when it blossomed as a Greek city under the name of Heraclea—the native town of Latmus on the granite and marble mountain at the head of the Latmic fiord. There was probably no essential difference between these and many other little places on the Carian coast which were enrolled among the Athenian allies by Cimon; Caryanda, the home of the explorer Scylax, is expressly mentioned in the fourth-century periplus as being inhabited by Carians, but probably the object was not to contrast it with 'mixobarbarous' settlements so much as to distinguish it from the larger islands, which had regular Greek settlement. The headland of Salmacis at Halicarnassus was pointed out as the scene of the first fraternization when a Greek settler built a tavern which the natives learnt to frequent. This building will hardly have been erected by human hands. But the story must have been in harmony with existing beliefs; and the evident mixture of Greeks and Carians on the fringes of the Carian gulfs constitutes evidence of friendly relations between the two peoples in the early days of Greek settlement. The excavations which are now commencing at Iasus may help to clarify these problems.[1]

The origin of the Carians is archaeologically inscrutable.[2] At

<hr />

[1] See A, 7.          [2] See above, pp. 439 ff.

Miletus a Mycenaean settlement has been discovered; and, south of this, late Mycenaean finds have been reported near Mylasa. But otherwise this coast is almost blank on the map of the second millennium B.C., and the interior of Caria seems to have been virtually uninhabited throughout prehistoric times. In the main, the Carians cannot then have been occupying Caria. In Greek tradition they were an aboriginal people of the Aegean. But they themselves claimed to be native to Asia Minor, and some scholars are now inclined to recognize them as a people of the Luwian language-group who descended to occupy south-west Asia Minor about the end of the Bronze Age. This view of course conflicts with the Greek traditions; and, involving as it must the assumption that Carian belonged to an Indo-European language-group, it is liable to the serious objection that the known Carian proper names seem to be devoid of Indo-European characteristics. The early Carians seem—admittedly on evidence that should not be pressed very far—to have been a people of maritime inclinations; not only names but also cults that seem to be of Carian origin flourished in the islands in historical times; and Dark Age chambered tumuli, reminiscent of Mycenaean built tombs, are found alongside settlements that in historical times ranked as Carian and Lelegian towns. At Termera, opposite Cos, Sub-mycenaean pottery even has been found in the earliest graves of the cemetery.[1] Unfortunately there has been no excavation of hilltop settlements of the Carian interior, and consequently no critical assessment of early Carian culture can be made. But, in the present state of our knowledge, the more convenient hypothesis is the one which, following the Greek traditions, regards the Carians as a people of the Cretan and Achaean world who moved into Caria under pressure of Greek expansion. It was only in the fourth century that the Carians began to adopt the Greek way of life in its totality. But in western Caria at least they had long been in close contact with the Greeks, and especially under the cultural influence of Miletus; they had been associated with the Ionians in mercenary service overseas, and perhaps in voyages to the west.

The coast of Asia, Isocrates remarked, was inhabited by Greeks from Sinope to Cnidus. The implication that the south coast of Asia Minor was not inhabited at all by Greeks might well have been disputed in the fourth century. But from about the eighth century the mountainous bulge east of Caria was firmly possessed

[1] §III, 7, 118. Cf. also A, 6.

by the Lycians, who in historical times were more receptive of Greek art and architecture than of Greek settlers. And further east, in Pamphylia and Cilicia, the Achaean settlements, which are associated in Greek legend with Amphilochus and the ubiquitous Mopsus and in recent archaeological discoveries with the Sea Raids and the late Mycenaean Diaspora, seem to have left no legacy of Greek institutions or language in Hellenic times. So there is no ground for supposing that Greeks were installed on this coast in the period under consideration. It is true that Doric Phaselis was one of the cities that shared in the foundation of the Hellenium at Naucratis before the end of the seventh century, and other cities in later times claimed to be colonies of old Greek cities. But it is not clear that we are dealing here with regular Greek colonies (as opposed to Greek communities in native towns); and in any case it is doubtful whether any of these settlements received a Hellenic population before the expansion that followed the Dark Age.

## IV. THE IONIC CITIES IN THE DARK AGE

The discussion of the settlement of Ionia in an earlier part of this chapter was concerned with the problems of the migrations; and it still remains to consider the historical development of Ionia in the Dark Age. Of history as a pageant of memorable deeds and personalities deployed for the instruction or entertainment of the general reader there is nothing to tell here. The instruments of historical reconstruction are inference from the beliefs and institutions of a later age and the impersonal data provided by archaeological research in the field; only in a limited sphere of social environment, human intercourse and intellectual propensities can we draw upon written texts—the *Iliad* and the *Odyssey*—and then only with discretion. Nevertheless it is clear that the Ionic development had a depth and complexity that is lacking in the other sectors of the coast and that justifies the special treatment which Ionia will now receive in the concluding pages of this chapter.

The majority of the original Ionic settlements were planted on peninsulas on the coast. Some of these, like Phocaea, Aerae, Myonnesus and Pygela, were natural islands which became joined to the mainland by deposits of sand or deliberately constructed causeways; others, as Myus and Lebedos, were linked to the mainland by a rocky isthmus or low neck. These peninsulas were to some extent protected from the hot blast and choking dust of the winds that blow overland during summer gales; and they provided sheltered anchorage for people who had come to Asia in ships and did not fear piracy at the hands of others. With their narrow approach from the mainland, they were also conveniently situated for defence against potentially hostile natives; and this, though not necessarily the principal governing factor in the choice of such sites, was an important consideration in their subsequent development: thus the peninsular site of Smyrna, as excavation has shown, was enclosed by a stout fortification wall in the ninth century, and even on their desolate island 'far from the traffic of mankind' Homer's Phaeacians are depicted as having chosen such a peninsula for their new migration settlement and equipped it with strong defences.

In their earliest stages these Ionic settlements probably lacked any coherent planning. There may be traces of Dark Age buildings at Miletus, both on the peninsula where the Mycenaean town had stood and on the citadel hill (Kalabaktepe) a few hundred yards inland; but they cannot be clearly distinguished as yet, and the archaic house-foundations recently discovered in the clearing of a small town in the south of Chios—with scattered megaron-type buildings on the slope under a little hilltop citadel, and with a small cult down below at the harbour head where there had formerly been late Mycenaean settlement—hardly reach back into the Dark Age.[1] The best evidence is that of Smyrna,[2] though it may have been a bit backward by the late eighth century. There, the earliest Greek house discovered in the excavation was a small single-room cottage, oval in plan and with its door at the end; it was built of mud brick laid on a damp-course of small stones, and had evidently been covered by a thatched roof supported by internal poles—comparable to Achilles' barrack in the *Iliad* or the temple that the priest of Apollo roofed at Chryse (xxiv, 448–56; I, 39). This mud-brick dwelling dates from about the end of the tenth century. Its foundations stood isolated in the sector of the excavation, and it would seem that Smyrna was not at all densely populated in the first century or so of its existence as a Greek city. In the later eighth century, however, the houses—of similar construction, though sometimes with an open porch at the front— jostled one another uncomfortably; and it requires no strong effort of imagination to picture the Homeric simile (*Il.* xvii, 737–9) of a sudden conflagration sweeping through a town so that 'the houses crumple in a big blaze and the whistling wind makes it roar' (see Fig. 2). Houses had their fenced yard at the front, in which no doubt an animal or two could be kept, and in one or two of them

[1] A, 9.          [2] §IV, 4; A, 1, 8 ff.; A, 2, 30 ff.

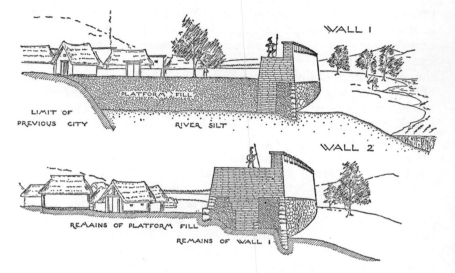

Fig. 2. A semi-diagrammatic reconstruction of the fortifications, together with contemporary houses, at Old Smyrna in the ninth and eighth centuries B.C. (From R. V. Nicholls, 'Old Smyrna', *Annual of the British School of Archaeology at Athens*, 53–54, p. 51, fig. 7.)

stone-lined *tholoi* (circular sunk granaries) have been found; it was no doubt round the peak of such a granary roof that Homer made Telemachus sling his line to hang the shameless maidservants (*Od.* xxii, 465–7). Of temples there is no trace in Ionia before the eighth-century hecatompedon of Hera in Samos,[1] and we may assume that before that time simple open-air cult spots sufficed; only with the dedication of cult statues and expensive offerings will a roofed building have become necessary.

Some of the Ionic cities, like Phocaea, Lebedos and Priene, were hemmed in by powerful neighbours; and to the end these remained small. Erythrae had a great peninsula to absorb; and Chios and Samos had to digest their islands before they started to nibble at the mainland coast. The task of penetration inland from the coast thus fell to Colophon and Ephesus, together with non-Ionic Magnesia. Colophon was situated on the edge of a wide interior plain and was the home of famous cavalrymen. It evidently had access to the plain of Smyrna on the north before the eighth century, and it was apparently concerned in the foundation of Clazomenae; its territory may also have extended in early times to march with Ephesus on the south. Ephesian penetration up the

[1] §IV, 3.

Cayster valley seems to have reached twenty-five miles inland to Larisa before the rise of the Lydian kingdom, and it is not surprising if in historical times Ephesus showed more native influence than the other cities. The third great Ionic city of the mainland, Miletus, was on a cape accessible only by mountain routes from the interior; apart from the highlands of Grion, which bordered the Milesian home territory, its expansion can only have proceeded by water. It acquired land on Mt Mycale, and probably in the eighth century was beginning to lay its hand on the neighbouring islands of Leros, Lepsia, Patmos and Icaros. At the same time, it must also have been at an early date that the Milesians crossed the gulf to annex the lower end of the Maeander plain; for otherwise they could hardly have advanced to Magnesia after that city fell to the Cimmerians in the seventh century. By then, however, Miletus was devoting all her energies to colonization beyond the Dardanelles; with the rise of the Lydian kingdom Ionia was in need of more living space and, like the Euboean cities and Corinth two generations earlier, planted new settlements overseas.

Of the condition of Lydia nothing is known before the new kingdom arose under the Mermnad dynasty in the early seventh century. But we are now once again in a position to say, as Hogarth did forty or fifty years ago in the predecessor of this chapter,[1] that the earlier Asiatic culture of Lydia 'is being tapped by the American excavation of Sardis'; and the report of Greek Protogeometric potsherds in a low level there may indicate early relations with the Ionic settlements. Mycenaean sherds are also reported. In the eighth century the main power in the interior of Anatolia seems to have been that of the Phrygians on the plateau; but it lay far off to the east. Excavation has thrown light on the early centres of their power around the River Halys, and is now illuminating their capital city of Gordium on the Sangarius, where an advanced civilization (with a skilled bronze manufacture, fine furniture and ivory craft, mosaics, and developed architecture) flourished in the second half of the eighth century. The Phrygian king Midas is known in Greek legend and was believed to have dedicated his judgement seat to Apollo at Delphi; and it may have been through Ionia that the Phrygians acquired their alphabet, which is attested by writing on bees-wax from the great royal tomb of this era at Gordium. But the excavations seem to show that there was no exchange of manufactured objects or artistic motifs between Phrygians and Greeks before the seventh century; and though the rulers of Gordium were evidently in touch with

[1] *C.A.H.* ıı[1], p. 558.

the powers of Assyria and Urartu in the late eighth century, there is still no solid foundation for the long-established modern belief in a caravan route leading from the Near East through Phrygia to the cities of the Ionic coast. In general, such traffic passed to Greece by sea from the North Syrian ports.[1] The capital of Midas fell before the onslaught of a wave of Cimmerians about the beginning of the seventh century; and while Gordium itself quickly revived, the political domination passed to the Lydian rulers of Sardis. The Cimmerian raids seem to have rocked the Greek cities also; and it is possible—though no more than possible—that the archaeological evidences of severe damage at Smyrna and Miletus about the beginning of the seventh century may be further indications of the devastation caused by these invaders. But the destruction that the Cimmerians caused did not retard the progress of Ionic civilization. Altogether more momentous was the transference of political power to Sardis, which lay only two or three days' march from the Greek cities and controlled the routes to the different sectors of the coast. There could thenceforward be no common defence of the Ionic cities against attacks from the interior power.

Of the population of the Greek cities at the end of the Dark Age the excavation at Smyrna alone permits a calculation. Here there may perhaps have been four or five hundred houses in the crowded peninsular city of the late eighth century, and this would give an overall figure of two thousand free Greeks living in the city, to which may conjecturally be added another thousand or so living outside. At Miletus the inhabited city may have been larger, but not enormously so. The Greek population of Ionia was evidently small, and it is remarkable that these cities were able to contribute so much to early Greek civilization and thought. The reason for this is perhaps to be sought in their relationship with the native population. At Miletus and elsewhere, to judge by references in later Greek writers, there appears to have been a native element which may have worked the land for Greek masters; and in his *Politics* (1290b) Aristotle remarks that at Colophon the majority of the citizens were wealthy and possessed extensive properties (in land) before the Lydian war—since they were the majority they cannot have had citizen labour to work their land. We are therefore justified in concluding that it was by exploiting native labour on the land that the Ionians gained the leisure required for cultural pursuits, and we may offer this as the explanation of the great contributions that they were able to make to Greek civiliza-

[1] See, however, A, 3, 42 f.

tion and city life. From our reading of Homer we gain the impression that in early Ionia women enjoyed a higher status and a freer life than was accorded to them in classical Athens. Of crafts in Dark Age Ionia we know little.[1] Carpenters, smiths and potters there must have been; but building and quarrying may not have become skilled occupations before the seventh century. Leather working and the manufacture of textiles are likely to have been carried out in the home, and there is no evidence of shop-keepers. The most skilled craft was that of the *aoidoi*, who developed an art-form of extraordinary complexity in the Dark Age. The visual arts, on the other hand, seem to have been cultivated less assiduously than in mainland Greece. Writing does not seem to have come into general use in Ionia before the seventh century; but considerable evidence for Aegean trade is found in late eighth-century levels at Smyrna, where not only Corinthian pottery but fragments of standard containers of Chian wine and Attic oil have been recovered.

Our conception of human behaviour and qualities of mind in eighth-century Ionia is of necessity formed from reading Homer. The social code that prevails there is in many respects traditional. Achilles has much that is barbaric in him, Agamemnon nurses his grievances even beyond the tomb, and Menelaus is made to display a pettiness that at times borders on the contemptible. But these qualities are not admired; and Homer's nobler characters command a deeper respect. The opening lines of the *Odyssey* remind the audience of the leader's responsibility to his men, and throughout the poems humanity demands care for the weak and sympathy for the unfortunate. Some of the finer speeches display tact and comprehension of a sort that even in a more sophisticated age would help to make this vale of tears a pleasanter place to pass through; and in the person of Odysseus the Ionic *aoidos* created a balanced ideal of the complete man that the poets of classical Greece were not fully capable of understanding. The ability to find a way of dealing with any situation was perhaps most admired. In the knowledge of the Greek world and the sea routes, and in the curiosity about the cities and mentality of other peoples which betrays itself in the first sentence of the *Odyssey*, we may detect the beginnings of geographical and anthropological study and the Ionic learning that later matured in the academic atmosphere of Miletus. Finally, Homer's age was one of enlightenment. Standards of morality could be improved because they were not burdened by any deadweight of divinity but could keep pace with

[1] §IV, 2, 36 f.

human reason and man's own better nature or his regard for public opinion (*aidōs*). For us Homer is the first flowering of Ionic humanism, and indeed the first witness to it.

Ionia and the East forms no topic for consideration in this chapter. The archaeological evidence seems to indicate that the cities of Ionia were not in contact with the Orient in the Dark Age; and the eighth-century sea route to the North Syrian coast seems to have had its Aegean terminals in Ionic Euboea and in Corinth; in eastern Ionia the Levant routes touched only at Samos, and that hardly before the seventh century. We are thus confronted with the paradox that the cities of Eastern Greece were less influenced by the East at the end of the Dark Age than the leading centres of Old Greece. As against this, they were more concerned in developing their traditional heritage and a new interest in city life; and their ways of thought and evaluation of man's potentialities thus seem to have been singularly little affected by oriental ideas and imagery. By a natural reaction among scholars it has become fashionable in recent years to deny that there were essential differences between the Doric and the Ionic temperament in antiquity; and certainly the differences, which are not negligible in Greece even at the present day, are more easily sensed than demonstrated by specific proofs. Our knowledge of the Dark Age is not of a sort to indicate to what extent the Ionians were already distinguished by their qualities of individualism and opportunism; but it can hardly be doubted that they were much further removed from communal barbarism than the Dorians who had occupied the prostrate Mycenaean kingdoms. The Ionians of the twelve cities were of course members of a larger Ionic world of the Aegean, whose unity at the end of the Dark Age finds its clearest expression in the supremely Homeric hymn sung by the blind *aoidos* from Chios at the festival of Apollo on Delos. There the Ionians assemble in their trailing robes with their modest wives and their children, and entertain the god with boxing and dancing and song. Anyone who came upon them when they were thus gathered together would think that they were immortal and ageless, such is the charm of the men and girdled women and their caiques and all their belongings (one thinks of rugs and painted water jars, and a hen or two in a basket)—and not least the wonder of the Delian maidens who can sing in imitation of the accents and chatter of everyone, and who must not forget the blind singer as he continues his travels from city to city (*Hymn. Hom.* III, 146–78).

The narrow exclusiveness of the Ionic dodecapolis, about which Herodotus complained in the fifth century, must have been the outcome of a hardening of feeling that gradually developed after the institution of the Panionic league with its common festival of Poseidon Heliconius. It cannot have been very strongly felt before the seventh century; although the worship of Poseidon Heliconius is mentioned in one of the similes of the *Iliad* (xx, 403–5), no hymn in the Homeric tradition was composed for his festival or for any common festival of the twelve cities.

The Panionic league itself was a religious union, comprising the twelve cities and centred on this cult of Poseidon on the north coast of Mt Mycale. The individual cities that participated in it were completely autonomous in historical times. But some modern scholars maintain that this was not their original condition and that the historical league of Panionium was the relic of a primitive quasi-feudal kingdom ruled by a king of the Ionians.[1] It is true that in documents of the Ionic federation in Roman times a title of 'King of the Ionians' is found. But there is no evidence that it had any authentic historical basis; and there are serious difficulties in this interpretation of Panionium. The site of Panionium was at the old city of Melie, to which the sanctuary had belonged; and Vitruvius records (iv, 1) that this old city, which had been one of the *thirteen* Ionic cities, was destroyed *propter civium adrogantiam* by common action of the other cities. To this testimony may be added that of a Hellenistic inscription recording the arbitration of a frontier dispute between Priene and Samos.[2] In this mutilated document eight classical historians are cited as authorities for the division of the territory of Melie (and apparently also the apportioning of Pygela, Marathesium, Anaea, and Thebes on Mt Mycale); these events were recognized as having taken place at some time prior to the Cimmerian raid under Lygdamis (Dugdamme), and Ephesus, Priene, Samos, Miletus and perhaps Colophon appear to be named as gaining (or in some cases exchanging or ceding) territory. On this evidence the natural assumption is that the institution of the league and common festival at Panionium resulted from the common action taken in the Meliac War; and in the foundation of Panionium, which may have occurred about 700 B.C.,[3] we may see the conclusion of the process of elimination of the weaker Ionic cities and the bond of ratification of the exclusive annexation of the whole coast by the league cities. The inclusion of the northern Ionic cities and the completion of the canon of twelve may in that case have occurred in the years that followed the Meliac War.

[1] §iv, 8 (Roebuck); iv, 2, 28 ff.     [2] No. 37 in *Inschriften von Priene*.
[3] A, 10.

The later Greek literary traditions indicate that kingship was a universal institution in the Ionic cities in the generation or two after they were founded; and families of Basilidae survived in a number of the cities long after kingship itself had lapsed. Aristotle even mentions an oligarchy of the Basilidae at Erythrae 'in ancient times', which was deposed, not for misgovernment (for it governed providently), but because the demos objected in principle to the rule of a few (*Pol.* 1305 b). Tyrants are also mentioned as having seized power in some of the cities; but where their activity is set in the early years of the settlement, the word cannot be regarded as evidence of a change of constitution—it seems rather to denote temporarily successful claimants to the royal power. Oligarchy, in the sense of concentration of power in the hands of a wealthy minority of the citizens, was undoubtedly present or latent in most of the Ionic cities in classical times. But it is dangerous to project such a condition back into Dark Age Ionia; in Colophon, at least, the majority of the citizens are said to have possessed extensive estates in early times, and we have no evidence of the existence of a poor or oppressed demos in early Ionia before land became scarce. The excavation at Smyrna has shown that in the early seventh century the peninsular city was laid out afresh on an axial plan with well-built, commodious houses of a sort that are not likely to have belonged to a poor or depressed class. The inhabitants of the city would seem rather to have formed a well-to-do urban community.

The absence of clans (*gene*) in Homer is probably a reflexion of the evolution of city life in Ionia; the city commanded the citizen's loyalty, and every citizen had his share in the state. Council (*boule*) and assembly (*agora*) were no doubt essential organs of government; but there is no means of ascertaining the pattern of the civic organization that functioned in Smyrna when the peninsular city was remodelled in the seventh century and the citizens received new ground plots (some in the old city and others in the new suburb across the isthmus). The material aspects of civic development cannot be discussed in this chapter; for they belong to the Ionic Renascence rather than the Dark Age. But the political conception which the material evidence necessarily implies is of fundamental significance for the study of ancient history. It is the first certain and unambiguous apparition of the organized Hellenic polis.

# CHAPTER XXXIX (*a*)

# THE PREHISTORY
# OF THE GREEK LANGUAGE

## I. THE IDENTIFICATION OF GREEK

T HE nature of the Greek language during the prehistoric period is, for obvious reasons, hard to determine, so that most statements about it must be qualified as probable rather than certain. There are three sources from which we can obtain information about it: by working backwards from the classical dialects, especially those recorded by inscriptions earlier than the fourth century B.C.; from the documents of the Mycenaean age written in the Linear B script, which can now be interpreted as Greek;[1] and by the comparison of Greek with the related languages which we trace back to a common, hypothetical origin known as Indo-European. The combination of all three sources allows us to make some deductions with fair certainty. In many cases, however, one of our sources may fail us; a word may be attested by Mycenaean and classical Greek, but have no certain cognates elsewhere; many features are known from both comparative and classical evidence, but are either absent from the scanty Mycenaean material or attested ambiguously by it; and a few rest upon comparative and Mycenaean evidence unsupported by historic Greek. Satisfactory deductions about the prehistoric period are impossible without at least two sources.

Historic Greek may be defined as the language as it is known from texts and monuments from the eighth century B.C. onwards. Homeric Greek should be reckoned as historic, though it is known to include much linguistic material of prehistoric date. The prehistoric period therefore runs from the creation of a separate Indo-European idiom recognizable as Greek, which at the lowest estimate must be well before 1500 B.C., down to the eighth century.

All Greek dialects exhibit certain features in common, and these are numerous and particular enough for us to be able to

---

\* An original version of this chapter was published as fascicle 15 in 1963; the present chapter includes revisions made in 1970.

[1] §III, 22.

presume a common origin for them; we can thus distinguish Greek from related Indo-European languages, even those in the closest contact with it, such as Phrygian or Macedonian. The list of these features is in effect the highest common factor of all the dialects; but their identification is fraught with difficulties and dangers, which must be observed even if they cannot always be avoided.

The dialects are all, with the exception of Attic, imperfectly known and recorded. Any idiom no longer spoken is of course imperfectly known, but where sufficient records exist in a reasonably accurate notation, we may feel satisfied with our knowledge. Some dialects, such as Pamphylian, are attested by little more than a single inscription, and almost all are only adequately recorded in the fifth century B.C. or later. But it was precisely at this period that mutual influence between the dialects, already strong, became overwhelming, so that they were tending to converge—a process which in the Hellenistic age rapidly eliminated the local dialects as the speech of the educated classes in favour of the Attic-based κοινή. In general terms, the greater the intercourse between speakers of different dialects, the faster their language will approximate to a norm; and this factor was clearly increasing from the eighth to the fourth centuries B.C. Thus any feature shared by the classical dialects may be due to convergence rather than descent from a common ancestor, and we can only eliminate this source of error if we are able to establish an accurate date for its introduction. For instance, we can attribute Attic κυναγέτης to a relatively recent borrowing by Attic from a non-Ionic dialect, because of the retention of ā (cf. ἡγοῦμαι).

Secondly, independent innovations in scattered dialects may produce a misleading appearance of relationship; such a shared feature, or isogloss, is the vocalization of -ν- to -ι- in the groups -ανσ-, -ονσ-, which occurs in varying conditions in Lesbian, Elean and Cyrenaean. There can be little doubt that these three dialects, which were geographically remote and show little evidence otherwise of significant isoglosses, are not to be regarded as belonging together and deriving from a common origin more specialized than that which unites all Greek dialects. This shared feature must have arisen much later than any period at which the ancestors of these peoples were in especially close contact.

Thirdly, the inheritance of an ancient form is of less significance than a shared innovation. The presence or absence of F depends much more on the date of an inscription than the dialect group to which it belongs, but its total elimination from even the earliest Ionic inscriptions is a fact of some significance. The modification of -τι to -σι in East Greek (Attic, Ionic, Lesbian, Arcadian, Cypriot) is a fact of major importance in establishing the relationships of these dialects.

The ideal conditions are provided by a word which shows wide divergence in form in the dialects. For instance, Attic κόρη answers to Ionic κούρη; Aeolic κόρα; West Greek κώρα; Arcadian (archaic) κόρϜα: all these forms can be traced back to regular modifications by the various dialects of an original κόρϜα, and we can therefore be sure that the word was known to the common ancestor of all the dialects in this form.[1]

The lists of Common Greek features which have been compiled[2] need now to be revised in the light of our knowledge of the Mycenaean texts, which reveal imperfectly and often ambiguously the state of one branch of the Greek language about the fourteenth to thirteenth centuries B.C. Few differences are discernible through the medium of the syllabic script between the dialects of Mycenae, Pylus and Cnossus, although the last may be as much as 200 years earlier than the rest.[3]

The following list is necessarily incomplete, but will give some indication of the features which distinguished Greek from the other languages of the Indo-European family in the second millennium B.C. (In what follows, forms prefixed by an asterisk are theoretical reconstructions not directly attested. The symbols i̯ and u̯ represent the semi-vowels (English *y* and *w*); ə represents a short vowel of obscure quality.)

## (I) PHONOLOGY

(a) Initial *i̯- is replaced by an aspirate: ὅς = Skt. *yaḥ* (cf. Myc. *o-*, *jo-*, verbal prefixes which are parts of the relative pronoun or more likely a relative adverb equivalent to ὡς[4]); but in certain words a 'reinforced' *i̯- has a different reflex, namely classical ζ-, as ζυγόν = Skt. *yugám* = Lat. *iugum*, and Myc. *z-*, the exact value of which is still obscure: *ze-u-ke-si* dat. plur. of ζεῦγος.[5] Intervocalic -i̯- is lost in historic Greek: Cret. τρέες, Att. τρεῖς = Skt. *tráyaḥ* < *treies; the Mycenaean evidence is obscure.

(b) i̯ following a stop provokes palatalization and consequent modification; the details are complex and vary in the dialects, but it is likely that the process had begun in the Common Greek period. The Mycenaean evidence is hard to interpret, since although we may know the ultimate origins of the sounds noted

[1] §II, 2, 50.  [2] §I, 5, 71.  [3] §III, 22, 75.  [4] §III, 22, 125.  [5] §III, 22, 47.

by such graphs as Myc. *s* or *z*, we cannot be sure of the sounds actually pronounced in the Mycenaean period. Examples: *pi̯* > πτ: κλέπτω < *κλεπ-ι̯ω (cf. κλοπ-ή). *ti̯* and *ki̯* both > *ts* > σσ (Att. and Boeot. ττ): ἐρέσσω < *ἐρετ-ι̯ω (cf. ἐρέτ-ης), φυλάσσω < *φυλακ-ι̯ω (cf. φύλαξ); Myc. fem. adjectives in -*we-sa* = -*wessa* < *-*wn̥t-i̯a* with analogical *e*; *totios* has a special history, Myc. *to-so*, classical τόσος or τόσσος. *di̯* and *gi̯* > *dz* > zd (the fifth-century Attic value of ζ) later developing to zz or in some dialects to *dd*: πεζός < *ped-i̯os*, Myc. (in compounds) -*pe-za*; μέζων (Att. μείζων) < *meĝ-i̯ō-n*, Myc. *me-zo*. The Mycenaean forms confirm some development in this direction in view of the like reflexes of *ti̯* and *ki̯*, *di̯* and *gi̯*, but it is impossible to say how far this development had gone.

(*c*) Voiced aspirated stops (*bh*, *dh*, *gh*), which are maintained intact by Sanskrit, become unvoiced, yielding φ, θ and χ: θυμός = Skt. *dhūmáḥ*; φέρ-ω = Skt. *bhár-āmi* (with different endings); ὀμίχλη, cf. Skt. *mēghάḥ*. The development affects equally the voiced aspirated labio-velar (*gᵘh*): θερμός, cf. Skt. *gharmáḥ* 'heat'. It can be demonstrated for Mycenaean only for the dental series, since all other voiced stops are not distinguished by the script from unvoiced ones: *e-re-u-te-ro* = ἐλεύθερος; *e-ru-ta-ra* = ἐρυθρά.

(*d*) Initial prevocalic *s* and intervocalic *s* become *h* and are subsequently lost: ὁ, ἡ = Skt. *sá*, *sā́*; εἷς < *sem-s* (cf. Lat. *sem-el*), Myc. *e-me* dat. sing. masc. = ἑνί; Ion. gen. γένεος < *ĝenes-os* = Skt. *janasaḥ*; Myc. neut. plur. of adj. *no-pe-re-a₂* = νωφελέα (Att. ἀνωφελῆ). The absence of any means of noting *h* in the Mycenaean script makes it impossible to establish the chronology of the second stage;[1] -*h*- was in any case lost earlier in the intervocalic than in initial position, where it survived as the *spiritus asper* down to classical times. This change applies only to original *s*, and does not affect σ developed by secondary sound-changes: σάκος ( < *ti̯u-), πᾶσα ( < *παντ-ι̯α), γένεσι ( < *γενεσ-σι), etc.

(*e*) Labio-velar stops in contact with *u* lose their labial element and appear as κ, χ or γ: λύκος, εὔχομαι, γυνή; Mycenaean man's name *ru-ko-wo-ro* = Λυκοῦρος, *e-u-ke-to* = εὔχεται, *ku-na-ja* = γυναία.

(*f*) Final consonants other than -ν, -ρ, -ς are eliminated; final -κ only occurs in two words (ἐκ, οὐκ) and is due to special secondary developments with a following word. Similarly final -τ, -π, etc. in apocopated forms of prepositions (ἄπ, κάτ) occur

[1] §III, 22, 48.

only in combination. The absence of any notation for final consonants in Mycenaean script prevents verification of the date of this change, but it is universal in the historic dialects.

(*g*) Prothetic vowels, probably in some cases the remnants of so-called 'laryngeal' consonants, appear at the beginning of certain roots, which in other languages (except Armenian) begin with consonants: ἐρυθρός, Skt. *rudhiraḥ*, Lat. *ruber*; ἀμέλγω, Lat. *mulgeo*, Skt. *mṛj*- 'wipe'; Myc. *e-ne-wo-* = ἐννεα-, Lat. *nouem*.

(*h*) The syllabic nasals \*-*ṃ* as acc. sing. termination of consonant-stems and \**ṇ*- as negative prefix appear as -*a*, ἀ(ν)-: Myc. *pe-re-u-ro-na-de* = Πλευρῶνα-δε 'to Pleuron'; *a-ta-ra-si-jo* = \*ἀταλάσιοι 'having no ταλασία'; *a-no-we* = \*ἀνοϝες 'having no handles'. It seems unwise to make this treatment of syllabic nasals a general rule, since in a number of dialects their reflex is o in certain words (e.g. Arc. δέκο, cf. Lat. *decem*), but the conditions are obscure. The differences in the treatment of syllabic \**ṛ* by the dialects (αρ, ρα : ορ, ρο) suggest that this development is not Common Greek.

### (2) MORPHOLOGY AND SYNTAX

(*a*) The formation of superlatives with the suffix -τατος is exclusively Greek.

(*b*) The genitive of masc. a-stems is in -ᾱο: Myc. *ta-ra-ma-ta-o* = Θαλαμάταο; Hom. Ἀτρείδαο. The Attic form in -ου is not original.

(*c*) The infinitive active of the thematic verb is in \*-εεν: Myc. *e-ke-e* = ἔχεεν, Att. ἔχειν, West Greek, etc. ἔχην. A shorter form in \*-ν is found in some dialects: e.g. Arc. ἔχεν.

(*d*) The medio-passive participle is in -μενος: Myc. *ki-ti-me-na* = κτιμένα; *de-de-me-no* = δεδεμένῳ; cf. Skt. -*mānaḥ*.

(*e*) The form of the numeral 'one': εἷς < \**sem-s*, μία < \**sm-iə*; Myc. *e-me* = ἑνί. The replacement of μ by ν in the declension of masculine and neuter is post-Mycenaean.

(*f*) It is possible that the syncretism which reduced the eight (or more) cases of Indo-European to five had begun, but unlikely that the classical pattern had already emerged. Mycenaean may have preserved the ablative, at least in certain usages, but it was probably already syncretized with the instrumental (which in the plural of consonant- and a-stems was marked by the suffix -*pi* = -φι), and the locative and dative may also have begun to coalesce (for example, in the plural of consonant stems with the termination -*si* = -σι, originally a locative).

## (3) VOCABULARY

It is impossible to detail all the words characteristic of all forms of Greek but not paralleled in other Indo-European languages. The paucity of our material imposes a severe restriction, and it is much easier for one dialect to borrow a word from another dialect than a sound-change or a grammatical form. None the less Greek can be shown to possess a large stock of well-distributed common words which have no exact cognates in other languages, some of them attested in Mycenaean: e.g. ἄρτος (Myc. in compound *a-to-po-qo* = ἀρτοκόπος), βασιλεύς (Myc. *qa-si-re-u*), κῆρυξ (Myc. dat. *ka-ru-ke*), ξένος (Myc. *ke-se-nu-wi-ja* = ξένια), ξύν (Myc. *ku-su*), οὐ (Myc. *o-u-*), ποιέω. Moreover, even words belonging to known Indo-European roots adopt characteristic forms in Greek: e.g. ἀμφιφορεύς or shortened ἀμφορεύς (Myc. plur. *a-pi-po-re-we*, *a-po-re-we*); ἀνδρίας (Myc. dat. *a-di-ri-ja-te*); ἄνθρωπος (Myc. *a-to-ro-qo*); ἄργυρος (Myc. *a-ku-ro*); δῆμος (Myc. *da-mo*); ἱερός (Myc. gen. *i-je-ro-jo*); ἵππος (Myc. *i-qo*; the first vowel is *i* in Mycenaean as in classical Greek in place of the expected *e*, cf. Lat. *equos*). The large class of nouns in -εύς (fem. -ειἄ) is typical of Greek; these are especially common in Mycenaean (e.g. *i-je-re-u* = ἱερεύς, fem. *i-je-re-ja* = ἱέρεια). The pronoun οὗτος (Myc. neut. sing. *to-to*) is not found elsewhere.

These lists could be extended almost indefinitely, especially if presumed borrowings from pre-hellenic languages are included (e.g. θάλασσα, κυπάρισσος, τερέβινθος). There is also a large class of inherited words which have acquired specialized meanings in Greek (e.g. θυμός, the cognates of which mean 'smoke' or 'vapour').

## II. THE CLASSIFICATION OF THE DIALECTS

The classification of the historical dialects is generally agreed, though the reconstruction of dialect prehistory is disputed. The ancients divided the dialects into Doric, Ionic and Aeolic, and this pattern, with some subdivision and refinement, is followed by modern scholars. The chief alteration is the substitution of Achaean for Aeolic, thus allowing Aeolic in a stricter sense and Arcado-Cypriot to form sub-groups of Achaean.

Colonies of historical date normally preserved the dialect of the mother city. They can therefore be disregarded in any investigation into prehistoric conditions, though they occasionally allow interesting deductions. For instance, most of the peculiarities of classical Laconian can be shown to be relatively late developments, since they are not shared by the dialect of Heraclea in South Italy, which was an offshoot of the eighth-century Laconian colony of Tarentum.

The Doric dialects are now generally known as West Greek, because in historical times they lay mainly to the west of a line running north and south down the centre of the northern mainland, and then turning east so as to leave the Isthmus, including Megara, and the Peloponnese to the west. Arcadia, however, is an enclave within this West Greek area. Overseas the West Greek group includes the islands of Crete, Melos, Thera, Rhodes and Cos, together with the adjacent coast of Caria. This represents a prehistoric colonizing movement. A sub-group of West Greek is that known as North-west Greek. This comprises the West Greek dialects north of the Corinthian gulf, which are very little known in early times apart from Phocis and Locris, and Elean on the southern shore, which, as its geographical position suggests, forms a bridge between North-west Greek and Peloponnesian Doric.

The remaining dialects can be classified by opposition as East Greek; but the position of the Aeolic group is somewhat ambiguous, and this is a much looser group than West Greek. The two main branches, omitting Aeolic, are Arcado-Cypriot and Attic-Ionic. Arcadian and Cypriot display an astonishing similarity, for at the time they are recorded (fifth to fourth centuries B.C.) they had certainly been out of touch for at least five centuries. Cypriot retained a syllabic script, ultimately related to the Mycenaean, and in some details it is impossible to reconstruct exactly the spoken form. Both dialects use κάς in place of καί (though this is rare in Arcadian), πός in place of πρός; they construe the prepositions ἀπύ and ἐξ with the dative; and they share the sound-shifts visible in ἰν for ἐν and middle endings -τυ, -ντυ for -το, -ντο. Certain Arcado-Cypriot features are also found in the poorly recorded dialect of Pamphylia. Historically these facts are only explicable if these two dialects are the remnants of a widespread dialect which was elsewhere displaced by West Greek; this implies that Mycenaean Greek should also belong to the same group, and the decipherment of the Linear B script has shown this to be true, though Mycenaean does not show all the features shared by Arcadian and Cypriot.

The second division of East Greek is made up of Attic and Ionic; these dialects are so closely akin that they are commonly treated together under the name Attic-Ionic, implying that, if they could be traced back before the historical period, they would be found to have a common ancestor at no very remote date. This is in keeping with ancient tradition and archaeology, which date the Ionian colonization of the Asiatic coast to the Dark Age (roughly eleventh to ninth centuries B.C.). Ionic changes all original instances of $\bar{a}$ to $\eta$; Attic retains $\bar{a}$ after $\rho$, $\epsilon$ or $\iota$; the process of vowel contraction differs, and the loss of the digamma has sometimes different consequences. Some differences of Ionic, such as the use of $\sigma\sigma$ for $\tau\tau$, may be due to a normalization of the dialect ($\tau\tau$ being rare outside Attica and Boeotia) resulting from the mixture of populations common in colonial enterprises (cf. Herodotus 1, 146).

The Aeolic dialects are Lesbian, Thessalian and Boeotian. Although they share some fundamental characteristics, such as the tendency to develop labio-velar stops in all positions to labials (e.g. $\pi\epsilon\mu\pi\epsilon$ for $\pi\epsilon\nu\tau\epsilon$), they also exhibit considerable diversity, a fact which is generally ascribed to West Greek influence on Thessalian and Boeotian. Without denying the fact of this influence, it is none the less important not to overrate its significance; East Thessalian is less influenced than West Thessalian and probably represents the pure Aeolic type much better than Lesbian, which has been modified by contact with its Ionic neighbour.[1]

## III. HISTORICAL RECONSTRUCTION

As a statement of the distribution of the dialects as they existed in historical times, the outline given above is unexceptionable. But there has been a tendency to regard these synchronous divisions as corresponding to facts of prehistory, though it is obviously perilous to project backwards in time the concepts or conditions of a particular period. The growth and development of a dialect is a long and complex process, for rarely does it take place in isolation; it is continually subject to outside influences, which may vary from time to time in accordance with political or economic circumstances.

It has, however, been customary to regard the three main dialect groups, Doric, Ionic and Achaean, as corresponding to three separate waves of invaders, who brought to Greece their distinct dialects of the Greek language.[2] On this theory the Ionians were probably the first to arrive, since there are numerous references in ancient literature to Ionian occupation of parts of central Greece and the Peloponnese.[3] The Ionians were later

[1] §II, 4, 154; §II, 5, 71.　　[2] §III, 2.　　[3] §III, 20.

displaced everywhere except in Attica by a wave of Achaeans; these soon split into South Achaeans, whose descendants we find in classical Arcadia and Cyprus, and North Achaeans, the ancestors of the Aeolic peoples. Finally the irruption of Dorians again disturbed the linguistic pattern, and Doric dialects ousted Achaean from almost all the Peloponnese.

This theory is clearly correct as regards the Dorians. Their entry into southern Greece was remembered in historical times in the form of a legendary 'return of the Heraclidae'. The details are probably fictitious, but folk-memory preserved tales of how conquerors coming from north-western Greece made themselves masters of the principal towns of the Peloponnese, and colonized Crete and Rhodes. Two facts in this story need to be emphasized. It is generally agreed that the Dorian invaders came from the north shore of the Corinthian gulf, the hinterland of which comprises some of the most difficult and inhospitable parts of the Greek mainland. If the attacks were mounted overland from Aetolia, Acarnania and even Epirus, we may reasonably inquire why. No tribe immigrating into the Balkan peninsula from the north is likely to have chosen to advance by the west coast rather than the east; either they must have been repulsed from the East, or they came from the North-west because they were already established there.

Secondly, the pattern of Dorian expansion overseas is significant. Once in control of the coasts of the Peloponnese, the route across the Aegean lay open. Yet instead of advancing through the Cyclades, they pursued a southerly route via Crete to the Dodecanese, taking in only Melos and Thera. Lack of interest will hardly account for their failure to extend northwards; the central Cyclades must have remained secure only because some power existed strong enough to defend them and inhibit Dorian expansion in the Aegean.

Nor must it be assumed that each wave of invaders entirely replaced the earlier inhabitants. Athens totally destroyed the dialects of Aegina and Melos in the fifth century; but wholesale removals of populations are rare in Greek history. Much more often a conqueror is numerically weak, and the former population either survives as a subject class (like the Helots in Laconia) or is gradually assimilated by the new rulers (an example may be the fourth tribe alongside the three Dorian ones at Sicyon). In either case, but more particularly in the latter case, the speech of the subject population influences that of the ruling class. Evidence of this process can be seen in certain West Greek dialects which show curious East Greek features. The Laconian form of the name of the god Poseidon is akin to the Arcadian and must have come from a pre-Dorian or Achaean source; in Crete the nominative plural masculine and feminine of the article follow the East rather than the West Greek type. Thus the process of invasion must be regarded linguistically as leading to fusion rather than replacement.

There are, however, no legends which tell of the coming of the Greeks to Greece. Nor is there any clear trace of the replacement of Ionians by Achaeans. This suggests that the evidence for these prehistoric Ionians needs to be carefully scrutinized. There is no doubt that the ancient authors described Ἴωνες as located in the Peloponnese; but it may be doubted whether these people can be identified with speakers of an Ionic dialect as defined by modern scholars. Obviously Herodotus could not have known the dialect spoken by prehistoric peoples.

Herodotus appears to use the term Ἴωνες in three distinct ways: (1) strictly, the Ionians of the Asiatic Dodecapolis (I, 146, 1); (2) more generally, ὅσοι ἀπ᾽ Ἀθηνέων γεγόνασι καὶ Ἀπατού-ρια ἄγουσι (I, 147, 2), 'those who trace their origin to Athens and keep the feast of Apaturia', thus including all whom we call in dialect terms Attic-Ionic; (3) in reference to prehistoric Greece, a people settled in various parts of the Peloponnese and central Greece (e.g. v, 58, 2, VII, 94, VIII, 44, 2; 73, 3, IX, 26, 3). In no case does Herodotus make the use of a common dialect his criterion, since at one point (I, 142, 4) he distinguishes four linguistic groups among the Ionian cities of Asia Minor, for it is scarcely possible that he means here to refer to the barbarian speech of the non-Greek inhabitants. The references to Ionians in early Greece must therefore not be interpreted as meaning that they were speakers of what we should now recognize as an Ionic dialect; it probably means little more than that the contemporary Ionians claimed them as ancestors.

At the same time the legends which told of Ionians in the Peloponnese must have some meaning. The statement that Argives and Athenians once spoke the same dialect (Pausanias II, 37, 3) need not be disputed; but it should not be claimed as evidence for Ionic speech in Argos. Rather it reflects, if true, the existence of a common Mycenaean idiom spoken all over southern Greece. We may start therefore by assuming that Ionian in this context means little more than non-Dorian.

Secondly, we may ask whether the theory of three waves of invaders receives any support from archaeology. Here too we must advance warily, for there is no direct connexion between the cultures distinguished by the archaeologist and the linguistic groups distinguished by the dialect-historian. There is for instance no archaeological feature which can be used as a certain test for Dorian occupation. None the less, the Dorian invasions can be correlated with the collapse of the Mycenaean civilization, whether or not we identify them as the efficient cause of the collapse. The great Mycenaean palaces were destroyed about the thirteenth to twelfth centuries and most of these cities were later occupied by Dorians.

The archaeologists divide the Greek Bronze Age into three main periods, Early, Middle and Late Helladic. But these are not absolute divisions, and recent work has shown that in the Argolid at least the principal break in culture is between Early Helladic II and III, not as is usually assumed between Early and Middle Helladic.[1] The archaeological evidence suggests that around 2100 B.C. a new people, with new techniques and habits, destroyed the principal inhabited sites in the Argolid and established themselves as rulers. The change may have come about later in other parts of Greece, but by the beginning of the Middle Helladic period, about 1900 B.C., this culture appears to be well diffused throughout mainland Greece.

Blegen and Haley[2] in 1928 showed that there was a significant correlation between certain non-Greek place names of Greece and sites showing the typical Early Helladic culture; and that no such correlation existed in other prehistoric periods. It follows that the people who named the sites were not Greeks, and these must be the peoples of Early Helladic I and II. Since we know that Greek was being spoken in Greece by the end of the fourteenth century B.C., if we accept the usual dating of the Linear B tablets of Cnossus, the language must have been introduced at some time during the previous seven centuries. But there is no archaeological evidence for the intrusion of a new culture until the end of the Late Helladic or Mycenaean Age, and this is rather a destruction of a highly organized society by one which had nothing to put in its place. The transition from Middle to Late Helladic shows no marks of violence, and there is nothing material to suggest that this is the date when the bearers of the dominant language entered Greece.[3] It has therefore been generally accepted that the first Greeks entered Greece about the twentieth century B.C., a date which may now need to be raised by as much as two centuries.

[1] §III, 4.          [2] §III, 8.          [3] §III, 24.

On the theory that the Greeks arrived in a series of waves, the violent change towards the end of the Early Helladic period might be equated with the arrival of the Ionians; the Late Helladic period might then mark the coming of the Achaeans; and the destruction of the Mycenaean culture would be associated with the Dorians. The alternative that, despite the archaeological evidence, the Ionians arrived only at the beginning of the Late Helladic period[1] involves the difficulty that there is then no archaeological event which can be associated with the Achaean dialect group.

This wave theory has held the field for half a century, but it is not entirely satisfactory. It involves supposing that the Greek language was formed outside Greece, and then imported by three successive waves of invaders. Yet if the division of the dialects had taken place before the Greeks invaded Greece, we might have expected the Greek peoples to have moved in different directions, and to have left traces, as did later the Gauls and the Goths, in widely scattered parts of the world. Even allowing that all the Greek peoples became superimposed on each other in one small geographical area, there is still the difficulty of the original home of the Greek language.

All Greek dialects share a number of words borrowed from unknown languages, and some of these show differing forms in the dialects which prove that the borrowing took place in prehistoric times. For instance, Attic (and presumably Boeotian) κυπάριττος, instead of κυπάρισσος found elsewhere, implies that this borrowing took place while the form was something like *κυπάριτσος, the group -τσ- being assimilated to -ττ- by Attic but to -σσ- by most other dialects. It is unlikely that Attic substituted -ττ- for -σσ- in a word borrowed after the development of these sounds, because the same suffix is found with the same treatment in prehellenic place names, and names like Ὑμηττός or Λυκαβηττός (parallel to Ἁλικαρν-ασσός) must have been attached to these places before the Greeks reached Attica. Many of these borrowed words are the names of plants and animals peculiar to the Mediterranean region, and are unlikely to have been brought to Greece by a people coming from the plains of Central Europe.

Thus to ask when the Greeks reached Greece may well be a meaningless question.[2] We have no evidence to prove that Greek existed as a separate language before its speakers were established in Greece, and some indications to the contrary. If we postulate a single invasion at the beginning of the Early Helladic III

---

[1] §III, 14, 96.     [2] §III, 9.

period bringing an Indo-European idiom which, after influence by the surviving indigenous peoples, emerged as Greek, we have a more economical hypothesis and one which fits better the facts as at present known. The development of the dialects will then have taken place inside the southern Balkan area, and after 2100 B.C.

The existence of two Greek dialects in the Late Helladic or Mycenaean period can be demonstrated beyond doubt. The group -τι is regularly changed to -σι by the East Greek dialects, including Mycenaean, but it is retained intact by West Greek. For example, the third person plural active of the thematic verb had the suffix -οντι (cf. Skt. *bhár-anti*, Lat. *ferunt* < *\*fer-onti*). This is preserved in West Greek (φέροντι, ἔχοντι etc.); all East Greek dialects have forms ending in -σι: Arcadian ἔχονσι, Lesbian ἔχοισι, Attic-Ionic ἔχουσι, Mycenaean *e-ko-si*, probably representing the same form as Arcadian. This innovation had therefore taken place by 1400 B.C., but the original form must have been preserved by the ancestral form of West Greek, since it survived into the classical period.

Another innovation of East Greek was the nominative plural masculine and feminine of the article. West Greek retains the original forms with initial τ-, τοί, ταί (cf. Skt. *té*, *táḥ*), which were replaced by οἰ, αἰ in East Greek on the analogy of the singular ὁ, ἁ (ἡ). The Mycenaean form is here unknown, since the article as such is absent from the texts, though its presence in all historical dialects suggests that its development from demonstrative to article may have at least begun.

An innovation by West Greek can be seen in the formation of the future of the verb. Most verbs originally formed the future in -σω, but stems ending in a liquid or nasal in *\*-έσω*, whence -έω. West Greek extended this type to all stems: e.g. δωσέω against East Greek δώσω (Myc. *do-se* = δώσει).

In other cases the distinction depends rather on different choices between possible forms.[1] The termination of the first person plural active of the verb seems to have been *\*-mes*, *\*-mos* (Lat. -*mus*, Skt. -*maḥ* in primary tenses) or *\*-men*, *\*-mṇ* (Skt. -*ma* in secondary tenses). West Greek generalized -μες, East Greek -μεν. The modal particle of West Greek is κα, East Greek κε or ἄν; an ingenious theory has derived all these forms from a common origin,[2] but whether this is accepted or not, the choice clearly goes back to an early dialect division. Similarly East Greek prefers the vowel ε in ἱερός, Ἄρτεμις, West Greek α:

[1] §III, 1, 27.        [2] §III, 7.

ἱαρός, Ἄρταμις. In both these words Mycenaean follows the East Greek pattern.

Thus the existence by 1400 B.C. of two Greek dialects is certain, and a period of separate development must have been required for this division to take place, but no reliable estimate can be made on linguistic grounds of the length of this period. But the traditional theory postulates the existence at this period of not two, but three dialects, one of which would be ancestral to Attic-Ionic.

Recent work, notably by W. Porzig[1] and E. Risch,[2] has severely weakened the case for this third dialect. It has been shown that the most characteristic features of Ionic, such as the shift of ā to η, are of relatively recent date. Although this shift is already present in the earliest Attic and Ionic inscriptions, there is evidence that in the seventh century Naxian still distinguished between original ē (noted E) and ē arising from ā (noted H). Moreover other changes, such as the loss of digamma, can be shown to be subsequent to the shift of ā to η; Attic κόρη, apparently in defiance of the rule that ā is protected by preceding ρ, is due to loss of digamma after κόρϝα had become *κόρϝη (Ionic κούρη). By deductions of this kind, many features of Ionic can be securely dated as post-Mycenaean, and it is therefore questionable whether Ionic was differentiated from the common Mycenaean dialect in Mycenaean times.

In particular, it has been remarked that in many ways Ionic agrees with Arcado-Cypriot, as might be expected if it were a descendant of Mycenaean. But in other ways it differs from Arcado-Cypriot, and agrees instead with West Greek. This is remarkable, for if it were really a totally separate dialect group we should expect it to show early characteristics which were not shared with other dialects. In fact, the development of Ionic can, at least partially, be explained as due to the fusion of West Greek elements with a dialect of Mycenaean type. At the very least we can be sure that, in the Mycenaean period, Ionic was not strongly differentiated from the dialects of the Peloponnese. Thus the theory of three basic dialect groups, justified as it is as a historical distribution, has no validity if projected backwards into the second millennium B.C.

It is in fact more likely that the Aeolic group was distinct in Mycenaean times. Certainly the Aeolic dialects show common features that are not shared by any other dialect; but here again the dating of innovations is difficult, and could still be just later

---

[1] §II, 4.      [2] §II, 5; §III, 15; §III, 16.

than the Mycenaean age. For instance, the replacement of the original perfect participle active termination *-ϝώς, gen. *-ϝόος, which is preserved in Mycenaean, was clearly motivated by the need to avoid vowel-contractions which would have produced an anomalous declension. West Greek, Arcadian and Attic-Ionic all solved this problem by generalizing in the declension the forms with medial -τ-; the Aeolic dialects all extended to the perfect the terminations of the present participle, -ων, -οντος. The existence of a number of features such as this, which are shared by all three Aeolic dialects, suggests that the Aeolians formed a separate linguistic group at some prehistoric period; this might have been located in Mycenaean Thessaly. But the unity of the dialects was later disturbed by the influence of other dialects, that of West Greek on the mainland dialects, and of Ionic on Lesbian.

To sum up, the certain facts are these. The Greek peoples were not indigenous, but the Greek language arose through the mixture of a group of Indo-European speakers with an earlier population, and this group penetrated Greece at some time during the Middle Helladic or Early Helladic III period. The Greek language was in existence and already divided into at least two dialects by the Late Helladic III period, and probably earlier. The unity of dialect in the Mycenaean kingdoms of southern Greece was broken by the Dorian invasions and the consequent relapse into near-barbarism, and it was during this little known period that the historical dialect groups became differentiated and emerged in their known positions.

The old theory of the irruption into Greece of three or more waves of Greek speakers is unnecessary, and the facts can be better explained by setting the genesis of the Greek language inside Greece (or at least the southern Balkan area) and later than 2100 B.C. At all events, those who speak of the coming of Greeks to Greece must define what they mean by 'Greeks' in this context. The development of separate dialects among the isolated tribes of the mountainous North-west and possibly among the more Mycenaeanized peoples of the North-east is to be expected; and the movements of population subsequent to the destruction of the Mycenaean kingdoms in the twelfth century spread these older dialects over new areas of Greece, and at the same time led to the formation of dialect differences among the former speakers of the general Mycenaean dialect. The pattern of distribution in historical times is complicated, and the events which led to it were doubtless more complex than we can hope to reconstruct.

# CHAPTER XXXIX(*b*)

## THE HOMERIC POEMS AS HISTORY

### I. INTRODUCTION

THE survival of some twenty-eight thousand lines of poetry almost contemporary with his period of study, and concerning one of its chief events, is a gift of which the historian can hardly complain. The Iliad and Odyssey provide a more graphic and more detailed account of life around the end of the Bronze Age than exists for any other period in Greece until the late fifth century B.C. There emerges from them a wonderful if rather indistinct picture of what it was like to be an Achaean nobleman on campaign, or traversing dangerous seas, or at home in his palace. They give a generous if blurred taste of a distant heroic age, its beliefs, customs and limitations. Yet the picture *is* indistinct, the taste blurred, and the historian must ruthlessly resist their vague and merely aesthetic blandishments. Not that the indistinct picture is entirely without historical value: in itself, indeed, it may contain more of history, in one real sense of the word, than bare archaeological facts devoid of human mediation and direct human reference. Nevertheless those bare facts are necessary as a framework, and without enough of them the literary and humane picture often becomes horribly misleading. Now some literary pictures contain, clearly visible, their own factual framework, and that at first sight may seem to be the case with the Homeric poems. Yet the truth is that they turn out on inspection to be fickle and treacherous in this respect. In the present context, therefore, it is more necessary to assess with unsentimental accuracy the nature of the Iliad and Odyssey as evidence than to expound their beauty or the detailed structure of their plot.

The historian must seek to identify and release the valid evidence of these poems—evidence, therefore, for nothing so vague as 'the early age of Greece' or 'the Heroic Age'. The factual framework needs to be more precisely fixed than that. The poems must be scrutinized for evidence applicable to three distinct periods: first, the late Bronze Age, the period of the Trojan war and the last generations of Mycenae's greatness; second, the

---

* An original version of this chapter was published as fascicle 22 in 1964; the present chapter includes revisions made in 1970.

early Iron Age, the so-called Dark Age of the eleventh and tenth centuries, the time of the Submycenaean and Protogeometric pottery styles; and third, the age of large-scale composition of the poems in Ionia, probably the eight century B.C.

The Iliad and Odyssey were created progressively, up to the point of large-scale composition itself, and each of the three periods contributed its share. The formal subject of the poems is the Achaean attack on Troy and its immediate aftermath, which we place late in the thirteenth century and close to the decline of Achaean culture as a whole. The monumental composition of the poems we know, or something like them, belongs half a millennium later. Stories about the Trojan subject-matter filtered down through the intervening centuries. Whether or not these stories originated as poetry, they must have been put into poetical form comparatively early, as we shall see, and they were then progressively expanded and elaborated. The consequence is that the Iliad and Odyssey may reflect events, objects, customs, beliefs and techniques from any or every period within this five-hundred-year range. In places they certainly exceed this range, either by the reminiscence of tales which originated before the latest part of the Achaean age, or conversely by additions made after the main act of composition had been achieved.

## II. THE ILIAD AND ODYSSEY AS TRADITIONAL ORAL POEMS

Two preliminary points must be made. First, writing probably disappeared from the Greek world from the end of the Bronze Age (the time of the last destruction of Mycenae, and the termination of any need for accounts in Linear B) until the introduction of the Phoenician alphabetic script not much before the eighth century B.C.[1] Second, oral tradition in an age of illiteracy is not confined to oral *poetical* tradition. The handing down of stories from generation to generation, not necessarily in the more or less formalized shape implied by saga, goes on all the time, whether or not accompanied by a developed poetical tradition. Thus the passage into the Homeric poems of traditional material derived from the Bronze Age does not of necessity mean that the tradition in or immediately after that age was a poetical one.

The illiteracy of the Homeric tradition can be shown by the characteristics of the poems themselves, as well as by the absence of physical evidence for literacy. So, too, can the fact that it

[1] G, 1, 68–71; §II, 5, 552 f.; §II, 6, 1–21.

really is a tradition—that the poems are based on materials which go back many generations beyond the time of main composition. The surest indication is the fixed or formular phraseology. The poetical language of Homer is composed not so much of separate, individual word-units as of formular phrase-units, which are rarely reduplicated or needlessly varied and are designed to fall easily into one or other of the four or five main divisions of the hexameter verse—especially into the main divisions of the second half of the line.[1] Such a complex system of ready-made and standard phraseology, with its high degree of functionalism, can only result (as the study of other oral heroic poetry confirms) from an oral and illiterate *tradition*, and a comparatively long one at that—from several generations, at least, of unlettered poets who sing narrative songs by ear, who learn from their elders a technique of reproduction and elaboration and a whole stock not only of phrases but also of themes, and who in favourable conditions can gradually extend and perfect the scope and economy of the formalized elements of their particular poetical inheritance.

This scope and economy of the formular language of Homer cannot be fortuitous, but must have been evolved deliberately. That is indicated by the utter pointlessness, for the literate, pen-and-paper kind of composer, of such a tortuous and, from his point of view, restrictive system. On the other hand the advantages of such a system for the illiterate and oral composer are shown by a glance at its detailed operation. The most striking kind of formula in Homer, and that in which the scope and economy of the system are most clearly seen, is the epithet-name group, of the type 'goodly Odysseus'.[2] That hero is called 'goodly Odysseus', 'many-counselled Odysseus' or 'much-enduring goodly Odysseus' (δῖος Ὀδυσσεύς, πολύμητις Ὀδυσσεύς, πολυτλὰς δῖος Ὀδυσσεύς) simply according as the last 2, $2\frac{1}{2}$ or $3\frac{1}{4}$ metrical feet of the verse require to be filled on any particular occasion. Odysseus nearly always has one of these standard descriptions, and virtually no other, in the latter part of the verse—and it is there that proper names often gravitate, leaving the opening portion free for object, verb, and other parts of the sentence. Between those three epithet-groups the choice is determined solely by metrical convenience, depending on the space needed for the rest of the clause or sentence. Moreover each main character, human or divine, and each main place, as well as many common objects, possess a more or less complete set of unvaried epithets to fill the main sections of the verse.[3] In

---

[1] §II, 11; G, 1, 59–68; G, 2, ch. 6.     [2] §II, 11, 47 ff.     [3] §II, 11, 50 f.

origin such descriptions were chosen for their appropriateness to their subject; but gradually alternatives must have been rejected and a type of natural selection took place, leaving a standard range which was made to serve on every occasion. Thus Troy is always 'steep', 'windy', or 'with good horses', Argos is 'horse-rearing' or 'with much wheat', Hector (in the nominative) is nearly always 'glorious' or 'with shining helmet'.[1] Things like ships, weapons or the sea acquired a particularized standard system of descriptive epithets, which were used repeatedly and from which selection was made according to practical and metrical needs.[2] If sense was slightly offended in a particular case, that was unimportant: hands are always 'thick', even when they happen to belong to Penelope. Other formulas were developed for common types of action ('he/she/they answered/ went away/threw a spear', and so on). The consequence was that thousands of different kinds of statement, covering a large variety of possible events and characters and many of the recurrent minor themes of heroic narrative, could be constructed out of these ready-made, interlocking and highly functional locutions.

Not only would the evolution of such a complex and extensive system be quite pointless for a poet who composes *de novo* with the help of writing materials and several different drafts: it would also be impossible for him to achieve, unless he set to work not as a poet but as a cryptographer or a kind of primitive Milman Parry. For the oral poet, on the other hand, such a system has the overwhelming advantage of enormously reducing the labour of composition, of putting words together so as to form meaningful, relevant and metrical statements. It does so because many of the major elements of his metrical phraseology, acquired at the time when he is learning songs from other singers, thereafter lie continuously available in his mind. Whatever the powers of memory and spontaneous elaboration of the illiterate singer—and they are staggering by literate standards—he cannot and does not create entirely *new* poetry, at any rate continuously and with tolerable fluency. What he does is to learn an accepted poetical phrase-language and use this, with or without personal elaboration, as the means of expressing traditional themes, sometimes in familiar combinations and sometimes in fresh ones.

Thus the formular system is, for the oral poet, completely functional. It is also one which must have been evolved over successive generations; and it is always to some extent in flux. Certain phrases would always be passing out of use, either because

---

[1] §II, 2; G, 2, 287.          [2] §II, 4.

the objects or customs they described were no longer common or interesting, or because some better description had been developed. Other phrases would continually be invented (though perhaps few in any one generation, and very few by any one poet) to describe new objects and fresh ideas. Neither economy nor scope was ever absolutely complete, even in the Homeric system, although each far exceeded what can be found among oral poems of other cultures. The result was a traditional language of great richness and almost impenetrable complexity.[1]

Much of all this has been discovered by analysing the phraseology of the Iliad and Odyssey; and important confirmation has been provided by the study of comparable phenomena in the surviving oral traditions of Russia, Cyprus, Crete, Ireland and Yugoslavia.[2] The last of these has given the best conditions for study, and there Milman Parry and his assistant A. B. Lord made extensive recordings of many different oral poets.[3] (Recently the tradition has seriously declined under the impact of literacy, politics and tourism.) As well as their songs, Parry recorded conversations with many of the best Yugoslav singers, in which they were questioned about their background, technique and poetical aims. The answers are often disappointing since most of these heroic singers are simple, unsophisticated and quite unused to abstract discussion. Yet it emerges clearly enough that they learn the technique of epic poetry and much of its formular phraseology when they are very young.[4] They linger in the coffee-houses or attach themselves to an older singer and simply absorb song after song, slowly learning to play an accompaniment on the *gusle* or single-stringed violin, and to reproduce, by a complex process in which a degree of improvisation is combined with literal memory, the substance and much of the traditional language of the songs they have heard from others—heard not once but, with some variation, time after time. In the rare cases where a singer learns to read after acquiring an oral repertoire, his poetical technique becomes laboured and he loses both range and spontaneity. Nevertheless a song-book version can be used as an aid for genuine oral elaboration, if it is read out by a literate accomplice; and the printed text of one version of 'The wedding of Smailagić Meho' was the ultimate basis of the lengthened and elaborated poem elicited by Parry from the outstanding singer Avdo Međedović—a poem of over twelve thousand (short) lines,

[1] G, I, 228 f., 333 f.    [2] §II, 1; §II, 3; §II, 10; G, I, 55–9.
[3] §II, 12; §II, 9, 3–138.    [4] §II, 9, ch. 2.

and thus possessing something of the massive scale of the Iliad or Odyssey.[1]

This modern comparative material is helpful, yet we must be careful not to use it too mechanically as a means of filling gaps in our knowledge of the techniques of ancient heroic poetry. There are important differences, as well as some essential similarities, between the modern and the ancient tradition.[2] For one thing, each appears to be differently placed on the path that leads from the first stages of an oral poetical movement to its ultimate decline. The leading Yugoslav singers are capable of elaboration and recombination along traditional lines. Yet there is little evidence that they often create substantially new verses and passages, or make a radically new treatment even of traditional themes. It seems reasonable to conjecture that the singers who composed the first monumental Iliad and Odyssey were capable of greater originality; that they invented many new passages and episodes, though always against a background of inherited themes and a rich traditional phraseology.

The distinction between creation and reproduction, though blurred in an oral system, retains some validity. Nearly all of the Yugoslav material seems to be directly drawn from a more fertile and creative phase in the untraceable past, and the recent singers studied by Lord and Parry are essentially reproductive—although it is important to emphasize once again that they do not simply learn by heart, simply memorize, but assimilate a technique and a mass of pre-existing material which they habitually rearrange according to their own tastes and needs and the demands of their particular audience. That is one way in which the *guslari* differ from the *aoidoi* or singers of the Homeric epos. Another is in the metrical rigour of the two traditions. The Greek hexameter verse is a far tighter and more demanding structure than the loose decasyllable of the South Slavic poetry, and must have exacted different procedures from its exponents. Similarly the formular phraseology of the newer tradition, though it may be said to exist, is much less highly developed in economy and scope than that of the Homeric system. The consequence of these differences is that we cannot always rely on direct inferences from details of the known habits and techniques of *guslari*, or other modern equivalents, to the methods that gave rise to the infinitely richer Homeric poems.

This limitation of the comparative method has perhaps been undervalued by those who conclude that the Homeric poems

[1] §II, 9, 78–81, 105–9.    [2] §II, 7; G, 1, 88–95.

must have been dictated to a literate accomplice by an illiterate composer, just as some of the long Yugoslav poems were sometimes dictated to Parry's Yugoslav assistant.[1] The conclusion is perhaps preferable to the assumption that 'Homer' himself must have been literate (which is not easily compatible with the detailed formular system); but it too depends on the further assumptions, first that oral poems are never sung twice in anything like the same form, and second that the Iliad and Odyssey survived more or less intact from the first moment of their monumental composition.[2] These two assumptions have been held to prove that the poems must have been immediately recorded in a fixed form, that is, in writing. Now it is true that the Yugoslav *guslari*, whatever their professions to the contrary, vary a song considerably each time they sing it; but it does not follow that the same must have been the case *to any similar degree* in the much fuller and more tightly organized Greek tradition. Its stricter and more crystallized language, and above all its rigid metrical framework, must have entailed greater accuracy and severity in transmission—and once a massive poem like the Iliad existed, its special position would in all probability assure for it a respect not earned by the more anonymous and commonplace materials of shorter heroic songs. In other words the building up for the first time of the massive epic may have given 'Homer' an authority quite unparalleled by any of his predecessors or any of the simpler South Slavic bards—an individual authority which would cause his themes, arrangement and language to be assimilated with unusual care. Even so, it is clear that the Homeric poems would not have passed from singer to singer in an exact and completely unchanging form.

Here the second assumption arises, that they must have survived virtually intact from the time of their first monumental appearance. Yet this we know to be untrue. Certain sizeable portions, notably the Dolon episode which forms the tenth book of the Iliad, and much of the eleventh and twenty-fourth books of the Odyssey, have been recognized from antiquity onwards as post-Homeric elaborations of the poems. In other ways, too, the Iliad and Odyssey were undoubtedly slightly altered after the eighth century B.C., and certain shorter interpolations can be recognized by changes of style and taste—above all, perhaps, by occasional drastic departures from the traditional epic language.[3] Thus the argument that the poems could not have been preserved verbatim by any other means than a written copy is simply

---

[1] §II, 8; §II, 9, ch. 6; §II, 7.    [2] A, 6, 181–201; A, 4, 169.    [3] G, 1, 204–8.

irrelevant, since they were not so preserved.  It seems at least as probable that they were maintained, with some fluctuation, at first by oral means and then with some support from written aids: initially by reproductive singers and subsequently by their post-oral descendant, a special Greek phenomenon, the unaccompanied reciter or rhapsode.  That is important for the historical validity of the poems; for, although there is no need to envisage extensive perversion, yet the fact remains that one cannot be sure of any long sequence in either poem that it represents precisely what the monumental composer sang in the eighth century B.C.

Thus the Iliad and Odyssey are to an important degree traditional poems, which probably did not reach any definitely fixed form until some time after their date of monumental composition. It follows, first, that no secure *terminus ante quem* can necessarily be assumed for any part of them (even though first monumental composition and most of the contents can fairly be placed before 700 or at the very latest 675 B.C.),[1] and second that no *terminus post quem*, either, can be assumed, except in the case of a very few linguistic characteristics and some equally rare cultural and historical phenomena to which we think we can assign a definite date of origin.  Even where a linguistic usage or the description of a particular datable object seems in itself to be old, it is impossible to be sure that its particular use in a particular Homeric context is not due to unconscious conservatism or conscious archaism.  In any case it cannot be held to date its wider context unless it can be shown to be inextricably associated with that context, and this is nearly always difficult or impossible to do.

Nor can early and late portions of the Iliad and Odyssey be recognized through so-called Analytical arguments about the gradual development of the poems in terms of an Ur-Ilias, redactors and so on.[2]  All that has been made largely obsolete by the comparative study of oral poetry, in particular of the way in which themes are varied and interwoven in the Yugoslav epic songs. The Analysts' conception of a substantial original core being then expanded by a single redactor, or possibly in two distinct editorial stages, is hopelessly over-simplified; and the whole concept of the 'editor' or 'redactor', with its implications of written literature and indeed the scholar's study, seriously misrepresents the complex and continuous process of informal adaptation and elaboration by generations of singers in an oral tradition.  Nor, indeed, does it at all adequately represent the activities of the monumental singer himself. The oral epic develops

---

[1] G, 1, 282–7          [2] E.g. §11, 12.

gradually and almost imperceptibly from one performance to another, from one singer to the next, from generation to generation. Themes become inextricably interwoven, so much so that it becomes impossible for the hearer (or even, after a time, the singer himself) to determine the origin of any particular element. The history of the Iliad or the Odyssey should be viewed not in terms of two, three or four main contributors, but of one main contributor in each case—I mean the monumental composer—and scores or even hundreds of preceding subsidiary singers (not to speak of those involved in immediate post-monumental transmission), whose specific contributions cannot now, and probably could not in the ninth or eighth centuries B.C., be properly disentangled.

## III. THE LANGUAGE OF THE POEMS

The evidence of language takes on a new importance against this background of archaism and innovation.[1] In brief, the Homeric language is an artificial amalgam, in which a predominantly Ionic dialect is interspersed with Arcado-Cypriot, Aeolic, and even a few Attic forms. These last were presumably caused by agglomeration and surface distortion during the era of post-Homeric transmission.[2] The Arcado-Cypriot forms, on the other hand, were old ones going back ultimately to the Mycenaean dialect, of which historical Arcadian and Cypriot were later conservative descendants. True Aeolic forms (that is, those which could not be explained as relics, perhaps, of North Mycenaean) are not very numerous, and are more difficult to account for; they probably represent the influence of a non-Ionic epic tradition which originated in the Aeolic-speaking parts of the mainland, and later established itself in the Aeolic colonization-area of the Asia Minor coast.[3] The artificiality of the Homeric language goes even beyond this mixture of dialects, and extends to the creation, usually by analogy, of new forms, inflexions, and compounds, as well as to the almost arbitrary lengthening of certain syllables to meet metrical difficulties.[4]

There are different linguistic stages, as well as different regional dialects, represented in the language of Homer. Yet because of the lack of fixed points in the early history of the dialects on the one hand, and the effects of archaizing or poetical

---

[1] See above, ch. xxxix (a).
[2] §iii, 1, vol. i, 513; §iii, 7.                        [3] G, i, 150–6.
[4] §iii, 1, vol. i, ch. 7; §iii, 2, 171 ff.; G, i, 194 f.

artificiality on the other, it is usually difficult or impossible to assign specific *termini* to different linguistic phenomena. So far as the dialects are concerned, it may be accepted that the Atticisms —about the extent of which, however, there is disagreement— are unlikely to have entered the tradition before the time of probable monumental composition; while the Mycenaean forms must for the most part have entered relatively early, within two or three generations after the collapse of the Bronze Age world. The rest belong somewhere within the half-millennium, more or less, that separates the ostensible subject-matter of the poems from the time of their large-scale composition.

There are, admittedly, certain usages and syntactical forms which stand out as rare, exceptional, and different from the common epic practice. Thus ὁ, ἡ, τό, usually demonstrative, is sometimes used as a true definite article, and that is a development which was completed in classical Greek.[1] Such phenomena obviously belong late rather than early within our four or five hundred year span. Yet there is no justification for declaring them, with many experts, to be 'post-Homeric', and therefore for treating them as indicators of addition or interpolation.[2] We simply do not know when such developments began to affect the epic singers; and their introduction into the language of poetry may have depended not so much on the date of invention of a linguistic form as on the individuality of a particular singer—or, to put it another way, on his *in*discipline with respect to the traditional forms of poetical speech. The use of a true definite article *might* have been spreading as early as 900 B.C., in theory (for there is no known practice to contravert the assumption); if so, it was probably kept out of the conservative and traditional language of poetry until laxer or less hide-bound poets, encouraged by ambiguous attributive uses, introduced it at some uncertain date. Yet again it is probable that the actual date came later rather than earlier in the tradition, since untraditional features seem to have become progressively more common. So too the developed similes, which seem to have been composed relatively late in the tradition,[3] often describe practices like riding or fishing which did not belong to the conventional picture of heroic life.

Two linguistic tendencies do, however, notwithstanding what has been said, seem to have an objective *terminus post quem*. The first is the contraction or blending together of adjacent vowel-sounds; the second the abolition of the semi-vowel digamma,

---

[1] §III, I, vol. II, 158 ff.; §III, 2, ch. 7; §III, 3, 136–8.
[2] G, I, 200 f.        [3] §III, 5, chs. 2 and 3.

something like our $w$.[1] Contraction is not found in the Linear B
tablets, and it was probably also unknown, or at least not prominent, in the speech of late Bronze Age Greece.[2] Indeed it
seems to have arisen for the most part after the beginning of the
Aeolic and Ionic migrations to Asia Minor, since εο, for instance,
is contracted to ου in Attic speech but remains uncontracted, or is
eventually represented as ευ, in eastern Ionic.[3] This shows that
the tendency to merge these sounds had not been completed—
had perhaps hardly begun—when the settlers left Attica about
1050 B.C. The disappearance of digamma from Ionic speech (it
was retained in Aeolic down into the archaic period) was perhaps
roughly contemporary with the tendency towards contraction.
It came after the Ionian conversion of $\bar{a}$ to η had been completed,
since for example καλϝός gave rise to κᾱλός not κηλός; and that
conversion was in progress when the settlers first heard of the
Mada—since they called them Μῆδοι not Μᾶδοι—surely not
before $c.$1000 B.C. and perhaps later.[4] It is quite possible (though
far from certain, for the above arguments are not watertight)
that both these tendencies developed in the course of the tenth
century B.C.; and highly probable that they did not develop
much before the start of that century. This is important, because
if true it means that no Homeric verse or formula which essentially depends on either tendency can have been composed before
that time.

The probable consequence is that a very widespread and basic
formula like ἔπεα πτερόεντα προσηύδα, which occurs over a hundred
times in the Iliad and Odyssey together, was developed in its
present form after the beginning of the Ionic and Aeolic migrations—for (unless it preserves a lost Aeolic form *ā(t)) it contains
the metrically essential contraction -ηύδᾱ. More certainly, phrases
which ignore digamma, and where the consonantal effect of the
letter cannot reasonably be restored by emendation, cannot have
been developed earlier than the early Iron Age and the period of
migrations. Thus ὄφρ' (ϝ)εἴπω (5 times in each poem) or ἦμᾰρ
(ϝ)ιδέσθαι (3 times Od.), cannot by any means be of Bronze Age
or even Submycenaean origin. Nor can θυμὸς (-ὸν) (ϝ)εκάστου (12
times), which in addition contains an essential contraction in its
last syllable. The same is the case with many other lines which
must always have ended in forms like μηροῦ or αὐτοῦ, with the
contracted form of the genitive singular.

---

[1] §III, 1, vol. 1, ch. 3; G, 1, 196–9.
[2] §III, 6, 78.
[3] §III, 4.                                   [4] §III, 4, 65, 68.

## IV. THE EXTENT AND IMPLICATION OF
## BRONZE AGE SURVIVALS

It is essential to emphasize the many post-Mycenaean features in the formular language, because in recent years, and especially since the decipherment of the Linear B script, there has been growing optimism about the amount of Bronze Age poetical phraseology and accurate Bronze Age information to be found in the Homeric poems. Yet the many examples of essential contraction and ignored digamma provide something approaching proof that much of the formular system which survives in our texts was developed at least two or three hundred years after the fall of Troy. Many students of Homer might feel that no such proof is needed—that most of the poetical language was *obviously* developed within the Ionian environment itself. Yet that, in its turn, is not so certain as it may once have seemed. It is important, in fact, not to emphasize either the Achaean or the Ionian element at the expense of the other.

There may well have been a good deal of heroic poetry on the mainland before the migrations began, and it could have been from there, rather than from Aeolis at a later date, that the Aeolic forms entered the poetical vocabulary. At the same time the poems as we have them are Ionian products, and their language is largely Ionic. It would be absurd to argue that the development in Ionia was not profound; and the extensive penetration of contraction and ignored digamma, even into a fundamentally conservative poetical speech, supports this presumption. Yet the degree of detailed Bronze Age knowledge preserved in the poems—and seen most notably in the political geography of the Achaean Catalogue in the second book of the Iliad, on which see §v—while it certainly does not necessarily suggest the survival of an extensive *poetical* account from the time of the Trojan war itself, does suggest that heroic poetry on this subject must have established itself at least within some two or three generations of the final Mycenaean cataclysm around 1125 B.C. For that length of time an ordinary prose tradition could preserve a knowledge of the greater past without too much distortion. Most children know a good deal about their grandfathers, almost nothing about their great-grandfathers. If certain details of the Achaean Catalogue were to survive, as they did, for longer, they had to be crystallized in a medium more fixed than ordinary informal tradition or even prose saga. That means crystallization in poetry, the only fixed medium for the preservation of details in an illiterate age. Thus it is likely that poetry about the Trojan war existed by the period of the migrations, and that the relatively new poetical tradition was carried to Asia Minor by the migrants.

Oral poetry may, indeed, have existed in the Greek Bronze Age itself. In fact it is more probable than not that it did, in the Achaean palace-states as in certain parallel cultures of the second-millennium Near East.[1] Whether it was heroic poetry, and hexameter poetry, and in particular how far any of it concerned the Trojan war and its aftermath, is harder to conjecture. Homeric reminiscences of events before the Trojan war, notably of the greatness and overthrow of Thebes, are hardly specific enough to entail a definitely poetical tradition. Even the knowledge of Greece at the time of the attack on Troy, except for the Achaean Catalogue, is fairly general, and the evidence for its survival as poetry must be primarily linguistic. Now there are a number of words of Mycenaean colouring in the Homeric vocabulary; but it must be remembered that they could and would have been retained for some time in ordinary speech even after the Achaean collapse, and could have entered the poetical vocabulary even as late as 1000 B.C. For example, ἄναξ is a word used in Mycenaean Greek, and one which after the end of the Bronze Age, and the disappearance of the overlords whom the word denoted, fell out of all save ritual use in Greece itself—except in the Homeric poems, where it is most conspicuously enshrined in the common name-epithet formula ἄναξ ἀνδρῶν Ἀγαμέμνων. Are we to conclude that this formula *must* have been invented within the Bronze Age? I think not, because the term must have been remembered and sometimes used for two or three generations into the Dark Age, and could have been picked up and incorporated in poetry, as an appropriate title for Agamemnon, at any time within that period. Of course, that does not prove that the formula was not of Bronze Age origin; it merely proves that it need not have been.

In order to show that Bronze Age heroic poetry, remnants of which came down into Homer, is anything more than an interesting possibility, its supporters must rely not on single words but on conglomerations of Mycenaean forms, Mycenaean formulas in fact. There may be several of these lurking unrecognized in the Iliad and Odyssey, but at present not even φάσγανον ἀργυρόηλον, 'sword silver-studded', appears to meet the case. Two of its three components occur in Mycenaean Greek (and ἧλος looks Mycenaean too), but that is not enough, since ἄργυρος

[1] G, 2, ch. 6; G, 1, ch. 5; §IV, 4, ch. 3.

at least, not to mention ἦλος, was used in later Greek also. However, archaeology suggests that swords with silver-riveted (as distinct from gold- or bronze-riveted) pommels were made in Greece down to about 1400 B.C. and no later (though they are also found in Cyprus c. 800).[1] If so, then the formula might derive not only from the Bronze Age but also from well within that age. Now admittedly one assured Mycenaean dactylic formula concerned with armature is enough to suggest that there *was* contemporary poetry about war, and possibly the great Trojan war; and it may well be that 'sword silver-studded' almost meets the conditions. Yet the lack of stronger or even similar cases suggests that very little of the poetical language of that early heroic tradition survived unchanged down into the Ionian period of the epic.

It may be that phrases such as αἴσιμον ἦμαρ are also Mycenaean, and the metrical pattern of, for example, φίλε ἑκυρέ or ἀπὸ ἕο, with their apparent memory of a reduplicated initial digamma representing IE *sw-*, could well be old.[2] ἐυκνήμιδες Ἀχαιοί, 'well-greaved Achaeans', could be Mycenaean, too, not because of recognizable and specific Mycenaean language, but because distinctive metal greaves have been found from the last centuries of the Bronze Age but are then lacking in Greece until c. 700 B.C.[3] But here, as in the case of silver-studded swords, the number of archaeological finds is too small to provide a firm statistical basis, and it is possible that early Iron Age metallic greaves may turn up to confound theories, just as the discovery of an L.H. IIb/IIIa bronze plate-corslet at Dendra has confounded much speculation about the lateness of passages mentioning corslets in the Iliad.[4]

## V. CONTINUITY OF TRADITION FROM THE BRONZE AGE DOWN TO HOMER

Ultimately the decision whether the poetical tradition stretched back continuously and actively into the Bronze Age itself will depend on how much detailed and accurate information about that age is preserved in the monumental poems. If there is much information of that kind, then it could only have survived in a continuous and systematic poetical tradition. If on the other hand the information is scarce, vague, and patchy, then it is more probable that for a time it was passed down and dissipated by ordinary word of mouth, to be erratically recorded in poetry after not more than two or three generations. The present section

[1] §IV, 3, 273; §v, 4, 14; G, 1, 114 f.; G, 2, 278.     [2] §III, 1, 146 f.
[3] §IV, 1.                                                [4] §IV, 2, 9 f.; A, 7, 171–4.

considers the positive side, the detailed information which does survive (or, more strictly, can be identified); while section VI will consider the negative factors, the evidence of broken continuity and in particular the evident Bronze Age characteristics which are either misrepresented in the poems or not represented at all.

The poems indicate that there was a united Achaean attack on the powerful fortress of Troy, which was inhabited by a prosperous horse-breeding people surprisingly like the Achaeans in most of their customs; that Agamemnon, lord of Mycenae, was recognized as over-all leader of the Achaean contingents, each of which was led by its own king or kings; that eventually Troy was captured by means of the wooden horse, whatever that was; that some of the Achaean leaders were killed, others met difficulties on their way home; that they were conspicuous for their greaves and their hair-style; that men of that age used long thrusting-spears and war-chariots; that bronze and not iron was the normal metal for swords, knives, daggers and cutting-tools; that different kinds of helmet were worn, and that a few heroes carried tower-like shields. All this the Iliad and Odyssey tell us, together with a certain amount about the physical appearance and organization of the palaces in which the Achaean kings lived. In addition there are some not very specific reminiscences of certain earlier ventures, especially the expedition of the Seven against Thebes.

Now certain of these pieces of information, as the results of excavation show, apply distinctively to the Bronze Age—a few, like conspicuous greaves and thrusting-spears, recur in the late eighth century, for example, but must be earlier than that in the poems because of the developed formular language used to describe them. All this suggests that a distinct memory survived of the great war against Troy, and of some of the martial practices and some of the social organization of the Achaeans who took part in it. There is, too, a great deal of genealogical information— who was king of what place and who was his brother and his father and his father's father and where they originally came from. The historical accuracy of that information cannot be checked, since later Greek references to it are heavily infected by Homer. By internal evidence it is often inconsistent and confused, though perhaps not so confused as would be likely if it were entirely fictitious. One may suspect that many of the main characters were descended from historical personages of the late Bronze Age, though not all of these would belong to the generation of the Trojan war. One may suspect too, that a number of well-defined pieces of information about such characters came down from the distant past—that Achilles was killed before Troy, that Troy fell to a ruse devised by Odysseus, that Philoctetes was abandoned in Lemnos, that Agamemnon was murdered on his return home. Unfortunately there is no way of positively confirming these suspicions. Yet in any case this kind of information is fairly simple; it can be reduced to a comparatively small number of very brief propositions; and these could have been passed down in informal local traditions, not poetical in character: in ordinary nostalgic story-telling, in fact.

More favourable to the idea of a continuous poetical tradition stretching back into the Bronze Age itself are the detailed descriptions in the Iliad and Odyssey of particular objects or practices which seem to have been familiar in the Bronze Age and not later. The silver-studded sword has already been mentioned, and to it may be added the vast body-shield used mainly by Ajax, in the Iliad, and the boar's-tusk helmet carefully described at Il. x. 261 ff.—a definitely Bronze Age object embedded in an equally definitely appended episode, composed at or near the end of the oral period. Yet the equipment and usages of warfare tend to be remembered for a surprisingly long time even in a fluid, uncrystallized, unpoetical tradition, because warfare is the very stuff of heroic life and post-heroic nostalgia. As an indication of *poetical* tradition it would be better to consider non-martial Bronze Age phenomena in the poems. Their number, however, seems much smaller than it used to seem.[1] Nestor's cup (Il. xi. 632 ff.) probably belongs to the Bronze Age (though of course it is not exactly like Schliemann's cup from the fourth shaft grave at Mycenae), and so do the silver, wheeled work-basket at Od. iv. 131 f. and the practice of metal inlay described in a confused way in the making of Achilles's shield in the eighteenth book of the Iliad.[2] The design of Odysseus's palace as described in the second half of the Odyssey has many Mycenaean features, too, but again it seems to be incomplete and not fully understood by the singer who compounded the passages that we actually have in our poem.[3] In these last two cases, then, it may be unlikely that Bronze Age poetical descriptions came down in the tradition: the mixture of truth and confusion is more what we should expect from a loose prose tradition *later* incorporated in poetry. As for the work-basket, the cup, and of course the body-shield and boar's-tusk helmet from the martial category, the possibility of the survival of occasional actual examples or at least representa-

[1] G, 1, 110–12.          [2] Inlay: §v, 4, 3 f.          [3] Though cf. §v, 5, 10–12.

tions cannot be discounted, but neither can that of the survival of detailed, poetical descriptions from the Bronze Age itself. Again, however, as with 'sword silver-studded', it is fair to observe how very scarce these possible cases of identifiable poetical survival appear to be.

Some of these isolated, striking and simple facts about the more heroic past would be of curious interest in an age of dissolution and decline, and not hard to remember in themselves. Another and more complex type of reminiscence about Bronze Age conditions may entail a different hypothesis. That is the kind of minute information about the distribution of Achaean cities which is given in the catalogue of the Achaean army (the Achaean Catalogue or 'Catalogue of Ships') in the second book of the Iliad.[1] This survey of Greece and the islands names many places, like Eutresis, Dorium, and Pylus, which were abandoned during the Dorian migrations and could not be precisely located when men began to interest themselves in Homeric details from the fifth century B.C. onwards. At least half of the hundred and seventy or so places mentioned in the list have so far been identified as Achaean sites, and it looks as though there is a solid core of information, in this section of the Iliad, about the political centres of late Bronze Age Greece. Indeed it has been argued that the unusual and specific epithets attached to many of these places, like *many-vined* Arne, *many-doved* Messe, *flowery* Pyrasus, presuppose specific local knowledge of them while they still flourished.[2] If so, these name-epithet groups go back into Bronze Age poetry. That might be so, but again it might not. Many of the epithets which appear specific could apply to many or most towns in different general regions: settlements in the hills or on rocky coasts were likely to be steep or windy or to have many doves, those in the plains to have many vines or flowers or sheep. At the same time these epithets are not the usual Homeric ones for places, and they undoubtedly emphasize the difference of the Catalogue from the rest of the Iliad in style and content.

Of the towns themselves we must ask whether all or most of them were really completely abandoned at the end of the Bronze Age—so much so that the memory of their past importance would have utterly disappeared from the ordinary non-poetical tradition of men. The answer, on reflexion, is negative. Athens and Iolcus were not abandoned at all;[3] and in many other places, as in Asine and Mycenae itself, a nucleus of survivors

---

[1] G, 2, ch. 4; §v, 2; A, 3, 153 ff.          [2] G, 2, 123 f.
[3] §v, 1; §v, 7.

lived on after the Dorian occupation,[1] in a rebuilt settlement which was perhaps only a hamlet, to preserve, it may be, the memory of past glories and ancestors of more noble dimensions. Even apart from these instances of continuity or resettlement, in many places which were completely abandoned there would have been ruins of stone-built palaces and walls, as well as conspicuous tholos-tombs, to keep alive some kind of regional tradition for at least the gap of two or three generations with which we are primarily concerned.

Neither the general outlines nor most of the details of the Homeric picture of the Trojan war need have descended by a continuous poetical tradition. The Catalogue presents us with a possible exception, just as it is quite exceptional in its relation to the other Homeric poetry. In spite of the reservations mentioned above, its size and thoroughness are impressive: it cannot be just an archaizing construction. Not only is the Peloponnese covered in detail, but there is a surprisingly large list of places in the north mainland, from Boeotia to Thessaly and Epirus. Some of this list, admittedly, seems muddled and exaggerated (though fresh Bronze Age sites are being discovered in Thessaly in considerable numbers), and the prominence of the Boeotian contingent must be due to special factors. It is still safest, at present, to concentrate attention on the Peloponnesian information; and here it does seem probable that a nucleus was formed in the late Bronze Age itself. Probably this nucleus extended to Aetolia, at least, and the islands; but much remains uncertain. 'Fine-walled Gortyn' in Crete, for example, reminds us to be cautious even about the most plausible-looking phrases, since the first prominent walls at Gortyn may turn out to date from the last Bronze Age generation or from the Submycenaean period itself.[2] At all events the Achaean Catalogue (which is quite different in its degree of detail from the Trojan) certainly seems to fulfil, in some of its parts, the condition of complex, specific and accurate information which suggests transmission in poetical form from a very early date—a date at which the political geography of Achaean lands was still keenly remembered, whether within the Bronze Age itself or in the broad Submycenaean period down into the eleventh century B.C.

---

[1] §v, 3, 297.   [2] §v, 6; A, 1, 182 f., 235; A, 3, 111 f.

## VI. DISCONTINUITY OF TRADITION FROM THE BRONZE AGE DOWN TO HOMER

Why, when there is some evidence, slight though it is, for survivals of late Bronze Age or at least Submycenaean poetry in Homer, refuse to admit that there must be a great deal of the Achaean epic scattered about the poems, including old specific formulas like 'well-greaved Achaeans', 'Priam of the good ash-spear', 'gleaming-helmeted Hector', 'windy Ilios', 'lord of men Agamemnon', and archaic ones like 'along the bridges of war' or 'at the milking-time of night'? Why emphasize that nearly all such cases could be derived, in their poetical form, from the full Dark Age rather than the late Bronze Age? The reason is partly the wish to be accurate about the exact implications of the evidence, and the desire not to distort the probable cultural status either of the Mycenaean period or of the often misrepresented Dark Age; but partly it is more concrete, that apart from elements of dubious poetical continuity there seems in certain respects to be a strong *dis*continuity between the poetry of Homer and the historical realities of the period it purports to describe. At least there is evidence for a distortion of the factual tradition sufficient to suggest that very little poetical material had descended directly from the Achaean age itself. This reflects significantly on the historical value of the poems as detailed evidence for the late Bronze Age.

Certain military details, like body-shields, thrusting-spears, and boar's-tusk helmets, undoubtedly derive from the Mycenaean period;[1] yet such details are often misunderstood in the poems, and combined nonsensically (from the historical, not the literary, point of view) with different information stemming from the later practice of post-Mycenaean Greece. For example evidence for the use in warfare of a pair of light throwing-spears, as opposed to the single heavy thrusting-spear, is archaeologically equivocal for the Bronze Age, and the practice seems to have become common much later.[2] In both poems the picture is confused, and a single description may veer between one type of spear and the other: Paris and Menelaus in their duel in book III of the Iliad first have two spears each, then are felt to have had only one, then have two again.[3] Thus any image of contemporary fighting which descended from the time of the Trojan war cannot have been precise and detailed enough to preclude the imposition of later prac-

[1] See Plate 124(c).    [2] §IV, 3, 256–8; A, 7, 115 f., 136–9.
[3] Il. III. 18, 345, 355–61, 380.

tices. Admittedly oral poets, whether in Greece or Yugoslavia, tend to modernize, and it is well known that historical events and personalities can be confused, conflated, and transposed from one century to another. Yet the basic misunderstanding of the very stuff of heroic poetry—that is, of the detailed description of warfare—is improbable in itself, at least on any extensive scale, and is hard to parallel in any tradition that is both poetical and continuous. In most important respects, indeed, the Homeric description of warfare seems reasonably accurate.[1] The inaccuracies over weapons are minor ones. Only the use of chariots raises a serious problem.

In the Iliad nearly all the main heroes have their chariot and pair, whose function is to carry them into the very midst of the fighting or from one part of the battle to another, and to withdraw them when they are tired, wounded or isolated. Yet in Bronze Age warfare the actual, historical use of the chariot seems to have been different: the chariot was a fighting machine, used for massed charges, and the warrior fought with spear or arrows from his chariot. So it was with the Egyptians, and so it was with the Hittites themselves, from whom the Greeks seem first to have learned about chariots.[2] This use—which is remembered in a small minority of Homeric instances, and is once identified by Nestor (at Il. IV. 308) as a specifically archaic custom—makes sense, even though it might have had to be modified for the rougher terrain of Greece. The use described so fully in the Iliad does not. Now this is a drastic assertion, on which a good deal may depend, and its justification must be based on a practical estimate of the probable consequences of a battle conducted on Homeric lines. Would real live warriors have put up with chariots and pairs trotting or galloping about the line of fighting, easy targets for even an indifferent spear-cast or a random arrow-shot? Even a slightly wounded horse becomes utterly intractable, and the whole chariot-apparatus is immediately put out of action— and we know from Homer, confirmed by excavation and the tablets, that the Achaean horses were not armoured. Such embarrassments and the casualties they involved might be worth risking, but only if the chariot itself were a valuable tactical instrument. Used in the mass, on the right ground, as a swiftly mobile platform for archer or spearsman, it can be so. Even when the ground is not right, it may be conceded that chariots might be useful for transport behind the lines; sometimes they would bring fighters from the camp up to the rear lines. They

[1] A, 8, 93 ff.          [2] §IV, 3, 321 ff.; cf. C.A.H. II³, pt. I, pp. 494 f.

might even on occasion carry warriors close to the fighting itself. But even that is quite different from the common situation of the Iliad, where the heroes bring their chariots into the thick of the mêlée, and often, having dismounted, keep them there with the horses breathing consolingly down their necks.[1] That picture in my submission, is a fairy-tale, the result of a progressive and radical misunderstanding of a vague and undetailed tradition about the organized warfare of the past. The singer of the Dark Age, living in times when chariots (always an expensive item) must have been almost unknown, knew by tradition that chariots were used in the great days of his Achaean ancestors—that ownership of a chariot, and its use in war, was one of the marks of the nobleman. Traditions of the Trojan war may have told of chariots operating before Troy, and probably did so; but could they have been detailed traditions, such as even oral poetry supplies, if they were to give rise to the curious hybrid picture, the equine taxi-service, of the Iliad? Achaean poetical descriptions of the attack on Troy would surely, if they had survived in any substantial form, have made this misconception impossible. The conclusion is that they probably did not survive, if they existed at all, or survived in the merest fragments.

Another subject which is extensively treated in the poems (this time primarily in the Odyssey), but which does not tally with the detailed realities of the late Bronze Age, is social organization and the administration of the great Achaean palaces.[2] The lesson of other oral traditions is that many details of social structure persist through centuries of poetry, even though personalities and events may get hopelessly confused. Now it is true that the structure of Homeric society is basically Achaean. Substantial palaces, as described for Nestor, Menelaus, and even Odysseus, in the Odyssey, and as assumed for Agamemnon and others in the Iliad, ceased to exist after the end of the Bronze Age; and in the subsequent period of poverty and disruption the life of most Achaean survivors in Greece was almost certainly organized on what we might loosely describe as a village basis—even where, as apparently at Iolcus, the town-settlement as distinct from the palace continued to be inhabited.[3] Gradually there grew up a notably different social order, one into which the monumental composers were themselves born: the primarily aristocratic order, though with an

---

[1] The British *esseda* described by Julius Caesar (*B.G.* iv, 33, cited by J. K. Anderson, *A.J.A.* 69 (1965), 349 f.) were used differently; they were driven among enemy *cavalry*.

[2] G, 1, ch. 2; G, 2, ch. 5; §vi, 1; A, 2, 81–9.          [3] §v, 7.

upsurging mercantile *demos*, which was exemplified in the small towns of eighth-century Ionia. Yet, if the general outline of the social organization described in the Homeric poems reflects the Bronze Age rather than any later period, in detail the picture is strangely defective. We now possess an important external control in the form of the Linear B tablets; and there are serious discrepancies between the picture presented by the tablets and that given by Homer. First, the terminology for the officers of state is significantly changed. Many terms of social or administrative status found in the tablets are entirely absent from Homer, and some of Homer's terms are missing from the tablets.[1] Those that are common to both sources, with the possible exception of *wa-na-ka/anax* in its application to the king of Pylus or to Agamemnon, seem to have different meanings—for example *pa₂-si-re-u* (*basileus*) in the tablets describes a kind of mayor or overseer, while in Homer the word means either 'king' or at least one of the chief noblemen who act as the king's advisers.

The common facts of social and economic life present similar discrepancies. The singers who left their mark on the Homeric poems were almost ignorant, so it seems, of some of the most conspicuous and indeed startling aspects of life in an Achaean palace-state like Pylus or Mycenae. The extreme specialization of labour revealed by the tablets, and broadly paralleled in other Near Eastern palace-cultures of the Bronze Age, and the complex centralized economy in which every single act of agriculture, manufacture, or distribution of goods was directed and controlled by the multitudinous palace bureaucracy, are more or less unknown, or at the very least gravely underestimated, in the Iliad and Odyssey. It is true that there is little occasion in the Iliad for this kind of information; but in the Odyssey, with its descriptions of the palaces at Pylus, Lacedaemon, Ithaca and Scherië, the occasions are manifold. Certain specialists there of course are—metalsmiths and carpenters, goatherds, swineherds, cowmen and shepherds—but these are separate occupations in almost any ancient society. The fifty female servants in Scherië are evidently an exceptional number, and they are divided simply into grinders of corn and spinners and weavers (Od. VII. 103–5). Odysseus's palace in Ithaca may be relatively small, remote, and disrupted by unusual circumstances, so that one might not expect to find the full organization of detailed accounting and distribution; but even so one would expect to find more than the Odyssey's one old woman in charge of the palace storeroom. Moreover this

---

[1] §VI, I, 140–4; A, 2, 83.

limitation does not apply to the descriptions of Pylus, Lace-daemon and Scherië.

If there were narrative poetry in the historical palaces, could it exclude frequent mention of the extraordinary economic conditions in which it must have flourished? Would it have omitted all reference to scribes and writing, so marked a characteristic of contemporary civilization? I believe not; and, if so, the conclusion is that in this respect, as in the case of chariot warfare, there was a break in any *detailed, poetical* tradition from the Bronze Age onwards. The tradition survived for the most part in vague, general outlines, for a time at least in the ordinary processes of informal prose reminiscence.

## VII. THE DARK AGE AND AFTER

With the burning of Mycenae about 1125 B.C. the Achaean culture of the late Bronze Age finally collapsed.[1] Weakened, probably, by economic crisis and internal feuds, the palaces had been gradually finished off, presumably by—or under the impulse of—the intruding Dorians.[2] Many Achaean survivors took refuge overseas, or in remote and hilly regions where the new tribes left them undisturbed. A few Achaean pockets continued even in the plains, at Amyclae[3] for example and round Pylus itself;[4] while Athens, having resisted and then been by-passed by the new tribes, remained as the chief surviving urban centre. Through Greece as a whole there was a serious and rapid decline in culture. Stone buildings, writing and luxury articles like jewellery virtually disappear; the art of decorated pottery sinks to a low level, though poorish relics of the old patterns are found, notably in Attica, Salamis and the Argolid. By 1050 B.C., however, the promising Protogeometric style begins to spread from Athens, and at the same time the migrations to the eastern shores of the Aegean mark the beginning of a steady resurgence—and, with the integration of the Dorians in the Peloponnese, the first foundations of classical Greek culture.

That is the general background against which we must estimate the early development of the Homeric poems. Little is known about it in detail; the 'Dark Age' proper, in the sense of an age of drastic decline, extends only from about 1125 to about 1050, but the lack of information which is also implied by 'dark' extends far longer. The Homeric poems themselves supply little definite information, again in part because of the difficulty of

---

[1] See above, p. 668.    [2] A, 1, ch. x.    [3] §VII, 6.    [4] §VII, 5.

precisely dating references in an archaizing tradition. Yet it cannot be doubted that the eleventh century B.C. made important contributions to our poems: first because detailed traditions about the Achaeans had to be put into poetry by that time, if they were to survive as they did; and second because, in a persistent oral tradition, transmission entails constant poetical activity and development. Thus the very existence of the Homeric poems in their present form gives one vital piece of information about the Dark Age, to add to the implication of pottery which was at least often decorated: that social conditions then were not, as most modern accounts seem to imply, utterly chaotic, so completely disintegrated that no shred of 'culture' of any kind remained. On the contrary, the growth or at least the continuation of an oral poetical tradition reminds us clearly that in villages and hamlets, as well as in still-inhabited urban quarters and the unique centre of Athens, life continued and men carried on their social amusements, not entirely cut off from the cultural inheritance of the past.[1]

It is maddening that we cannot properly isolate the early Iron Age contributions to the often composite picture given in the poems. Much may be suspected but almost nothing can be proved. In language, as has been seen, the practice of vowel-contraction and the gradual disappearance of digamma are post-Mycenaean, but are probably to be dated not much earlier than 1000 B.C.—and many extant manifestations are obviously later in origin. It is quite probable that infinitives in -μεν (and also τοί, ταί[2] and the perfect participle in -ων, -οντος) are mainland Aeolic contributions made before and during the migrations to Aeolis and Ionia—but they could possibly be North Mycenaean survivals which were retained in mainland Aeolic speech and not elsewhere. Even if some linguistic elements *could* be tied down to the first post-Mycenaean generations, it is still doubtful whether they could be firmly associated with other types of cultural phenomenon—objects, customs, beliefs or historical events. These must be studied in themselves, as described in the poems.

One of the most remarkable pieces of archaization is the almost total exclusion of reference to the Dorians, who are specifically mentioned only among different inhabitants of Crete at Od. xix. 177. Yet one or two stories about Heracles, the adopted hero of the Dorians, are probably to be associated with them, and may have entered the poems at a time when details of the migrations were still fresh. Thus in the Achaean Catalogue at Il. ii. 653–70

[1] G, 1, ch. 6, esp. pp. 135–8.          [2] See above, p. 817.

Rhodes is colonized by Tlepolemus, son of Heracles and of Astyocheia from Ephyra in Epirus, the region from which the Dorians started their movement down into Greece. The Heraclid-Dorian reference is confirmed by the description of the Rhodians as dwelling 'in three divisions, by tribes' (τριχθὰ δὲ ᾤκηθεν καταφυλαδόν, 668)—an almost certain allusion to the three Dorian tribes.[1] Soon afterwards, at Il. II. 676–80, the contingents of other nearby islands are led by two sons of the Heraclid Thessalus, eponymous ancestor of a people directly involved in the Dorian movements. This part of the Catalogue, at least, probably reflects the Dorian immigration at the end of the Bronze Age;[2] but it must also be later than the Dorian occupation of the south-eastern islands, which the archaeological evidence so far, diverging here from the literary tradition, places little before the late tenth century B.C.[3]

Nestor's Pylian reminiscences are fascinating and peculiar, but no less precarious as evidence. They seem to represent part of a Pylian epos or cycle, which may have been carried to Athens by Neleid refugees and subsequently incorporated with the Trojan material in Ionia. The significant reminiscences are at Il. VII. 132 ff. and XI. 670 ff., concerning wars between the men of Pylus and the Arcadians and Epeians respectively. Fighting between Pylians and *Arcadians* is at least as likely to have occurred after c. 1200 B.C., and the burning of the great palace at Ano Englianos, as before—that is, if Achaean refugees thronged into the Arcadian uplands. In the *Epeian* war the men of Pylus were weakened through an earlier attack by Heracles, who had slain the best of them including Nestor's eleven brothers (Il. XI. 689 ff.). This tradition can hardly reflect the expansive palatial period at Pylus, roughly from 1300 to 1200 B.C. It may stem from the era before 1300, and correspond with certain fire-damage to the South-western Building which seems to have occurred earlier than the building of the great palace;[4] but the possibility cannot be excluded that it may reflect, with some chronological displacement, the last disastrous attack of about 1200. Once again Heracles may imply the Dorians; admittedly many of his feats, devoid of Dorian association, were located in the central Peloponnese,[5] but the Pylus reference seems distinct.

At all events the Epeians being called by the almost certainly post-Bronze Age name 'Eleans' at Il. XI. 671, together with the

---

[1] See above, p. 689.
[2] For a different view see above, p. 689 and *C.A.H.* II³, pt. 1, pp. 644 f. and 654.
[3] See above, pp. 667 and 674 f.    [4] §VII, 2.    [5] *C.A.H.* II³, pt. 1, pp. 652 f.

mention of inter-state horse-races in Elis and the implied reference to an early form of the Olympic games, suggests a relatively late origin for this particular Pylian tradition. Moreover the geography of these reminiscences is seriously confused. More than once Nestor's Pylus is implied to be, not in Messenia (where it belongs in the Iliadic tradition as a whole, and where the tablets and the ruins at Epáno Englíanos would place it), but on the borders of Elis; and there seems little doubt that after the Bronze Age the Messenian Pylus was confused with the much smaller remains of Triphylian Pylus at the modern Kakovatos.[1]

References to iron as still rare and expensive, but yet as already used for cutting tools, presumably come from the early Iron Age; the clearest case is the lump of iron given as a prize by Achilles in the funeral games (Il. xxiii. 826–35). Other supposed Dark Age phenomena are fallacious. Twin throwing-spears, already mentioned, become common in the Iron Age, but no earlier than about 900 B.C.;[2] cremation, assumed at Od. xi. 128 to be the normal peacetime practice, was introduced in eastern Attica, at least, as early as the twelfth century B.C.;[3] references to separate temples are probably no earlier, again, than c. 900.[4] And that is almost all, except for unprofitable speculations about the exceptional power wielded among the Phaeacians by the queen (and probable heiress) Arete. The conclusion must be that, in the present state of the evidence, little further progress can be made with the identification of cultural or historical elements introduced into the poems between the end of the Bronze Age and the developed Ionian period.

## VIII. THE ORAL TRADITION IN IONIA, AND LATER TRANSMISSION

The third important contribution to the Homeric tradition, after the Bronze Age and the early Iron Age contributions, was the Ionian. The predominantly Ionic dialect of the poems shows how significant the Ionian stage was. It was significant, above all, because it included the monumental composition of each poem; but beyond that the heroic tradition must have flourished for at least several generations in Ionia, and many of the extensive poetical materials used by the main composers must have been

---

[1] A, 3, 82. For a different view see *C.A.H.* II³, pt. I, p. 647.

[2] §IV, 3, 256–8; §VII, 1; A, 7, 115 f., 136–9.          [3] §VII, 3; cf. A, 1, 71.

[4] §VII, 4, 194. The extension of the Minoan-type shrine at Keos does not really alter this, *contra* A, 3, 2.

developed by specifically Ionian predecessors. The Ionian colouring of the poems, especially in the dialect—which is fundamentally and not merely superficially Ionic—is strongly marked and pervasive. The poems are in a real sense Ionian poems, even though many of their materials had come down in a tradition which first developed, probably, on the mainland. The most likely assumption, indeed, is that stories of the Trojan campaign were first sung among returning Achaean warriors in the Bronze Age itself, and were then developed during the Dark Age; the nascent tradition was carried overseas with the Aeolic and Ionian migrants, and took on new strength in the Ionian towns as they gradually became more settled in the ninth and eighth centuries. The development for the first time of a unified poem of colossal length was probably caused not by the particular demands of palace or festival audiences, but primarily by the imagination of a particularly gifted and ambitious singer with a large repertory of songs based on the Trojan war.[1]

There is little reason to doubt the broad outlines of the tradition which placed Homer (as the first monumental poet) in Smyrna or Chios, even though the details of his life are largely fictitious. It was in Chios that the Homeridae or 'descendants of Homer', who claimed special rights and special knowledge in the recitation of the poems, were later established.[2] Apart from dialect, there are secondary indications of the intensive Ionian penetration of our poems. References to Ionia, or at least to the Asia Minor littoral, are relatively common: to the birds near the mouth of the Cayster, to a storm in the Icarian sea, to north-west winds blowing down from Thrace, to the supposed figure of Niobe on Mount Sipylus, to the altar of Apollo at the Ionian centre of Delos.[3] Theoretically most of these could be derived from the time of the Trojan war itself, and so could the comparatively detailed knowledge of the Troad. Yet those references which are not directly linked with Troy come mainly in similes, which in their developed and particularly Homeric form are marked by their language as belonging relatively late in the epic tradition.[4] They suggest the experience of Ionian singers, who frequently introduced the sights and sounds of their own times into their elaborate comparisons, rather than that of the Achaeans before Troy or their descendants who settled in places like Mile-

---

[1] G, 1, 280 f.
[2] For example, §viii, 6, 398–402; §viii, 5, 258 ff.
[3] Il. ii. 459 ff., 144–6; ix. 5; xxiv. 614 ff.; Od. vi. 162 f.
[4] §iii, 5, chs. 2 and 3; G, 1, 201–3.

tus—descendants who seem to have had comparatively little effect on the development of the poetical tradition.

It must be clearly acknowledged that much of this certainly Ionian information is geographical, and tells us almost nothing about the history or customs of the Ionian Greeks. There is another class of evidence which is possibly or probably Ionian in colouring, and which may reveal more; but once again it is ambiguous. The Odyssean descriptions of Alcinous's Scherië or of the Cyclopes' island are thought by many, with reason, to reflect the outlook of early colonists, eastern as much as western. The position of the kings in Scherië, who form an aristocratic council, and the nature of the references to the *demos* there, suggest that the monarchical system of the late Bronze Age is being conflated with later political developments.[1] There is no necessary restriction of locality, but it is plausible to think of the Ionian towns as providing the model. At the same time there may be some western, as well as Cretan, influences on the poems, and not everything that appears to be later than the Bronze and Dark Ages is necessarily Ionian in inspiration. The Odyssey is sporadically interested in Sicily, and the choice of a hero from Ithaca may mean that western poetical traditions were used—though the vagueness over the very position of Ithaca suggests that there was no extensive poetical borrowing.[2]

Subjects in the poems which can be objectively dated within the tenth, ninth or eighth centuries are much fewer than was assumed a generation ago.[3] Phoenician trading in Greek waters is something which might have been underestimated, had it not been for the Iliad and Odyssey; but it now seems as though they exaggerate Phoenician penetration, and in any case the date of trade contacts is probably little earlier than 900 B.C.[4] Only two subjects are definitely as late as the eighth century (apart from the probably Attic funeral practice mentioned at Il. VII. 334 f., which is later): the use of hoplite tactics, which are probably but not certainly envisaged in three or four Iliadic contexts,[5] and the Gorgon-head as a decorative motif, which becomes common in the 'orientalizing' period of the seventh century but was probably coming in from the Near East in the eighth.[6] There must be numerous other references in the poems which were due to Ionian singers, especially to the monumental composers themselves,

[1] §IV, 4, 157.    [2] §VIII, 7, 398 ff.
[3] §VII, 4, 193–5.    [4] §IV, 3, 65 ff.
[5] Especially Il. XIII. 130–5, 145–52; XVI. 211–17. See G, 1, 186–8.
[6] Il. v. 741; VIII. 348; XI. 36; Od. XI. 634. See §VIII, 3, 63.

and which reflect the customs, objects and beliefs of their own period rather than any previous one. Many such references are to be seen in the similes, but again there is no absolute certainty in any particular case. Yet the similes, and the simile-like descriptions of the Shield of Achilles, give some insight into a non-heroic experience which must have been primarily Ionian. The interest in dancing, whether or not accompanied by song, and in the observation of animal and human behaviour, could be Ionian or earlier; but the sophisticated tastes for which the urbanized Ionians were later famous probably show up in Demodocus's frank and witty song about the love of Ares and Aphrodite in the eighth book of the Odyssey. Other passages of lyricism and fantasy or of mild eroticism, like Poseidon's journey at the beginning of the thirteenth book of the Iliad or the love-making of Zeus and Hera in the fourteenth, probably reveal the same Ionian influences.

The subsequent history of the monumental poems throws no direct light on the history of the late Bronze and early Iron Ages, but is highly relevant to the documentary value of the poems. The alphabet was being used for informal purposes in Greece by 725 B.C.,[1] and, although literacy and the making of a rigidly formular poem do not go well together, it is arguable that Homer could have dictated the Iliad to a literate accomplice (see pp. 825–7 above). It may be found more probable that the poems were transmitted orally—and, because of their special size and prestige, with unusual accuracy—for two or three generations before being taken up by the rhapsodes, who were reciters, not singers, and who may have used written aids. The rhapsodes must have been capable of considerable verbal accuracy, but their virtuoso aims probably caused them to concentrate more and more on the most dramatic passages; so that when the Panathenaic festival gained lustre in the sixth century B.C. it became necessary to decree that the Homeric poems should be recited without gaps.[2] To this end, and to exercise control over the rhapsodic contests, an official text of some kind seems to have been established in Athens. There was some superficial Atticizing at this point; but it is more serious that the written texts which were produced in numbers in the fifth and fourth centuries can be seen by the evidence of quotations to be still rather fluid.[3] With the age of scholarship in Alexandria a new effort at stabilization was made, most successfully by Aristarchus of Samothrace.[4]

[1] G, 1, 68–71; §11, 5, 554.     [2] G, 1, 301–3, 306–12; §VIII, 5, 269 ff.
[3] §VIII, 4.     [4] §VIII, 2; §VIII, 1, 223 ff.

His attempts at re-establishing an 'authentic' text of Homer extruded a number of palpable additions and largely prevented further deviation, and in the course of subsequent transmission down to the present day the shape of the poems has changed very little. Many technical problems remain, but from the historical point of view it may be accepted that our texts are reasonably close (and certainly as close as we are likely to get) to the Panathenaic version; and that this, though it must have differed in many minor respects and by one or two major additions, was not too far distant from what the monumental composers sang in the eighth century B.C.

## IX. CONCLUSION

The Iliad and Odyssey are traditional poems which incorporate elements from the Bronze Age background of their formal subjects, from the Ionian environment of the singers to whom the poems in their developed form belonged, and from the whole intervening period. The broad picture of the Trojan expedition and its aftermath belongs to the Bronze Age, and the similes and much of the detailed non-heroic observation belong primarily to the Ionian period; but otherwise only a small part of the contents of the poems can be attached to one stage in their development rather than another. Admittedly it is possible to work out a *terminus post quem* for certain components, including a few linguistic phenomena; but, because of the conservative and archaistic nature of such a tradition, it is illegitimate to assume that extant uses derive from a period close to their theoretical *terminus*. This and other characteristics of an oral tradition severely limit the use of the poems as an exact historical source. The mixture of different elements, which in most cases cannot be separated out because of the almost infinite complexity of the process of oral transmission and elaboration, added to the dubious chronological status of many of the elements themselves, makes the attempt to unearth new historical detail in the poems extremely precarious; their chief use in this respect must be to lend support to what is conjectured on other grounds. And yet they *do* provide a wonderful picture, erratic and confused admittedly, but full of colour and vitality, of a Greek Heroic Age—an age that we should otherwise have barely guessed at; an age seen, as most such ages are, through the flattering vision of a diminished posterity, but one which did have existence of some kind, and which the historian, however imprecise his evidence, must try to understand and assess.

On the Iliad and Odyssey as poetry nothing has here been said. From most points of view that is an utterly repellent way of treating them; but it does have advantages in the present context and in the light of their recurrent historical misuse. And yet in another way *poetry* is one of the most certainly proved historical facts which the poems reveal. The survival of a heroic tradition from the late Bronze Age onwards, detailed enough to require the fixity of poetry for most though perhaps not all of its length, is proved by the very existence of our poems—and that survival means that singing and listening to narrative poetry, and the conscious re-creation of a heroic past, were carried on in Greece even through parts of the loosely-termed Dark Age, then borne overseas to strengthen the common ties between the mainland and the new foundations in Asia Minor. Indeed, the poems provided one of the most important elements of a common culture for the whole of the Greek world. That is obvious enough for the classical period; yet it may now be seen that the singing and elaboration of heroic songs, and the crystallization of a greater and more unified past, were a widespread cultural influence on Greeks of many different periods, regions and occupations. How important such an influence was likely to be may be estimated by comparison with the place of heroic poetry in the life of the South Slavic peoples down to the last war.

Thus the historian is reminded, finally, that he cannot neglect the poems as literature—that the cultural life and therefore the history of every generation from the end of the Bronze Age to the time of the rhapsodes was directly affected by the contemporary state of oral song and the strength of the heroic poetical tradition.

# CHAPTER XL

## THE RELIGION AND MYTHOLOGY
## OF THE GREEKS

### I. THE FORMATION OF GREEK RELIGION

THERE is something anomalous in writing of Greek religion down to the time of Homer. The Homeric poems are the earliest literary documents of Greece which we possess, and more fitted for a starting-point than a conclusion. Many of the characteristic features of Greek religion belong to a later age, and to discuss, for example, Athena without the background of Athenian democracy, the Parthenon and the Panathenaea may seem a curious proceeding. The limitations of this chapter make it inappropriate to begin, as would otherwise be natural in writing an account of the religion of a particular people, by noting some of its general features, the typical marks by which it is distinguished from the religions of other peoples and periods, before going on to fill in the details of the picture. We are indeed scarcely concerned with Greek religion as we ordinarily and rightly regard it, but only with an early stage in its formation. This must not of course be exaggerated. Homer represents one of the finest achievements of the distinctively Greek genius. Yet in the religion of the classical period Homer, though still a dominant influence, was only one element out of many. By dividing up Greek religion as the plan of this work demands, we are confined to a very strict interpretation of the historical method.

It is usual to start a historic account of Greek religion from the undoubted fact that the Greeks were immigrants to Greece, speaking an Indo-European tongue, who entered the peninsula and the adjacent islands in a series of waves, mainly between about 2000 and 1000 B.C. The people who inhabited the country before their arrival had already a religion, and there is plenty of evidence that the Greek instinct was not to wipe out, but rather to fear and respect the gods of any land to which they came. Moreover in the course of an infiltration extending perhaps over a millennium the Indo-European tribes must, though retaining

* An original version of this chapter was published as fascicle 2 in 1961; the present chapter includes revisions made in 1971.

their language, have become inextricably mingled racially with their predecessors. Consequently the religion of the Greeks in historical times must have been in its broadest lines an amalgam of the forms of worship indigenous to the Aegean basin with the cults and beliefs which they brought with them. The first problem encountered in any historical study of Greek religion which seeks to go back to its beginnings is to determine how far it is right to try to identify and separate these two broad divisions, and whether such a separation, if possible, will throw light on Greek religion in historical times.

The problem teems with obvious difficulties. It would be absurd to expect a clear-cut division in historical Greece between two contrasting types of religion. Religion does not develop like that. Nor should we assume that the historical Greeks were composed of two, and only two, sharply contrasted racial elements, still less claim that we are in a position to say when, how and where the Greek invaders imposed themselves successively upon the earlier (and assuredly already complex) population of the area. Nevertheless to shrink from the question as insoluble would be to give up all hope of understanding the early stages of the development of religion in Greece, and an attempt must be made.

Before going on to discuss the evidence in succeeding sections, we may permit ourselves to look ahead for a moment to ask a question highly relevant to the present chapter. Do we find in the religion of later Greece any trace of a dual character which might indicate that the double tradition existed and had not entirely vanished? We shall not, if we have rightly understood the prevailing character of the Greeks, ask or expect to find them divided into two sharply defined and mutually exclusive sects. Given two sets of gods, they would happily worship both, and even unite representatives of both under the same name, marking the difference by a change of epithet at most. Given contrasting rites which seem to us to call for a different approach and a different conception of the relations between heaven and earth, the same man, if he is a Greek, will enter with equal zest into both. All the more remarkable will it be if there is still any disparity left to be detected. And undoubtedly there is. The difference between Olympian (or Uranian) and chthonian cults is one which strikes any student of Greek religion and was recognized by Greek authorities themselves.[1] Moreover the one derives obviously from Homer, and seems especially suited to a race of roving warriors, the other, having its roots in the fecundity of

[1] Cf., e.g., Plato, *Laws* 728c.

animals and plants, finds a more natural origin in a settled and humble people who wrested their livelihood from the land by hunting, stock-raising or agriculture. The Homeric Olympian religion shows us a society of gods with clear-cut characters and strong personalities, gods with whom man's relations are purely external, maintained by sacrifice and prayer in a spirit of bargaining or seeking for favours. They differ from men in being more powerful and exempt from death. Men are weak and mortal, and must know their place, since such gods are highly jealous of any trespass on their prerogatives and it is useless to challenge their overwhelming might. In the chthonian cults the religious atmosphere is entirely different. They are mystical, exciting, intoxicating, and their avowed aim is to lift man out of himself and unite his nature, be it only for a fleeting moment, with that of the divinity he worships. They teach that man can become filled with god, and they contain, either latent or expressed, the promise of immortality.

To mention this now is to expose oneself to the risk of serious misunderstanding unless the necessary precautions are added and emphasized. We clearly cannot simply label Homeric religion Greek, and all chthonian manifestations Pelasgian or Minoan, or whatever name we choose to give to the pre-Greek inhabitants of Greece and the Aegean islands. Classical Greek religion was a highly complex phenomenon. Its chthonian and mystical side was enriched by newcomers from the east or north, like Dionysus (pp. 881 f. below), and by the teaching of men like Pythagoras and Empedocles in the west. Moreover we must admit that we know little of the history of the lengthy process whereby the land was overrun by a succession of Indo-European-speaking tribes. Homer's Achaeans, though their identity is hard to decide, were presumably not the first to come, and the people whom they found and subjected in Greece doubtless spoke already a form of their own language. Yet even if they were predominantly of the same race, these earlier comers may have been largely assimilated, in religious customs and even in physical type, to the original inhabitants of the country. Feudal England exhibits a similar class of warriors living on the labour of the conquered people of the land. Yet if we knew as little of the serf and villein classes as we do of their counterparts in Homeric Greece, we should have little chance of making a correct guess at the various elements— Briton, Celtic, Saxon, Danish—of which they were composed.

All this, and much more, must be taken into account. Yet the two contrasting elements remain, seeming to form as it were the

warp and woof of the fabric upon which, in later centuries, was
embroidered the intricate and many-coloured pattern of Greek
religion. Dionysus was identified with the ancient god of Crete,
whose rites were similarly orgiastic and to whom on account of his
primeval greatness the Greeks had already, however incon-
gruously, given the name of the Indo-European God 'Zeus'. The
remarkable religious movement which appears to have started in
the late archaic period, and taught that the soul of man was a
fallen god or daemon impatient of its imprisonment in an alien
body, that movement associated with the names of Orpheus,
Pythagoras and Empedocles cannot of course claim to be a part
of the Greek inheritance from their Mediterranean predecessors;
but it is at least arguable that the response which it aroused was
due to a reawakening of ideas from the distant past of that people
with whom the Greeks were now inextricably mingled. Besides
the chthonian worship of the Cretan Zeus, we may point to the
fact that the Eleusinian cult can be traced back to a pre-Greek
origin, and the probability that both the name and the conception
of Elysium are pre-Greek. Our first task must be to say what can
be said (and it is little enough, if we confine ourselves to certain-
ties or near-certainties) about these two foundations of Greek
religion, the religion of the invading tribes and that of the peoples
in whose land they settled, and their intermingling.

In the Bronze Age the Aegean area was the seat of a highly
developed civilization, with its centre in Crete, where material
prosperity and artistic achievement were at their height during
the first half of the second millennium B.C., the so-called Middle
Minoan period. A parallel but less brilliant culture developed
on the smaller islands of the Aegean and is known as the Cycladic.
The mainland (Helladic) peoples were more independent, until,
about 1600 B.C., they were much influenced by Cretan culture
and produced a new and splendid efflorescence, particularly in
the Peloponnese and Boeotia. This is the civilization named after
Mycenae, the memory of whose strength and wealth was preserved in Homer and later Greek poets, to whom she remained
'the city of much gold'. Although impregnated with Cretan
culture, this mainland civilization was not without its original
features. At its height, moreover, it attained such power (reflected
in the Greek stories of Agamemnon's empire, and confirmed by
archaeology) that it in turn became a centre from which strong
influence radiated all round the islands, including Cyprus, and
the coasts of Syria and Palestine down to Egypt. Its most
prosperous period was from about 1400 to 1150 B.C., thus in-

cluding the traditional date of Agamemnon's expedition to Troy
and continuing to the end of the Bronze Age.

The Cretan civilization had its own religion, which influenced
that of later Greece through its offspring, the Mycenaean age.
So much is clear, but when we go on to ask what races were
involved at different stages of this evolution, the problem becomes highly complicated and in parts at least insoluble. We may
take it, however, that the creators of the magnificent Minoan
civilization were not Greek, and very possibly not Indo-European.
The evidence of place-names and of certain foreign words in
Greek suggests that from the beginning of the Bronze Age until
the coming of the first Greeks, not only Crete, but Greece itself,
the islands, and the south-western fringe of Anatolia were inhabited by speakers of several languages, whose origins are
disputed.

The first Greek-speaking tribes seem to have made their appearance first perhaps at Lerna in E.H. III and generally on the
mainland of Greece during the Middle Bronze Age (c. 2000–
1600 B.C.).[1] The view has also been maintained that they did not
come until about 1600. On the latter supposition the first waves
of Greek immigrants will have come almost immediately into
contact with the contemporary civilization of Crete, on the former
they will have been settled in the land for several centuries before
making this momentous contact. For the history of Greek religion,
the point is of minor importance. Where these people came from
is not certain. The old idea of them as Northerners has been
shaken by more recent archaeological discoveries, which suggest
affinities with north-west Anatolia. Doubtless not all the tribes
came by the same route, and there may have been static periods
during their wanderings sufficiently long for some assimilation of
culture, and even mixture of blood, to have taken place. The
present-day rejection of all talk of 'fair-haired Northerners' seems
sometimes tinged with a natural reaction against its emotional
championship by certain German scholars, and may have gone
too far. Achilles, Menelaus and Odysseus as described by Homer
were certainly not black-haired.

Thus the Mycenaeans will have been a blend (to look no
further back) of the neolithic inhabitants of Greece (who had
nothing in common with their Cretan contemporaries), the Early
Bronze Age folk who inhabited the mainland and Crete alike,
and the Indo-European invaders of the Middle Bronze Age and
later. Tradition and archaeology unite to make us believe that

[1] See *C.A.H.* ii³, pt. 1, pp. 139 f.

Homer's Achaeans, whose greatest representative was Agamemnon, king of Mycenae, were not the earliest of these invaders but that it was they who raised Mycenae to its highest glory from 1400 B.C. onwards and spread its influence over the whole Aegean world, to Cyprus, the coasts of Palestine and Syria, Egypt and Western Anatolia including the Troad. Now and even earlier pottery travelled westward as far as South Italy, Sicily, the Lipari islands and Ischia.[1] This people must have been, as Homer describes them, a hardy and enterprising race of seafarers, fighters and traders.

We can say little of the religion of the Indo-European immigrants before they came in contact with the world of the Aegean. Much in later Greek religion may indeed be derived from this source, but little can be attributed to it with certainty. Religion corresponds to the needs of a people, and therefore to their circumstances and surroundings, but unfortunately our ignorance concerning the former home of the earliest Hellenes is such as to preclude us from drawing any inferences from it. More illuminating is likely to be the fact that by the time they reached Greece they were both a wandering and a fighting people, and their religion must have reflected these conditions. One central religious name and conception we can say with certainty they brought from the original Indo-European stock: Zeus in the capacity of Father and supreme god, and at the same time god of the weather—Cloud-gatherer, Thunderer, Rain-bringer. This twofold character, as patriarchal protector of the household, and controller of the weather, was retained by Zeus not only in the Homeric poems but throughout the pagan history of Greece.

In order to complete our prolegomena to historical Greek religion, it remains to indicate what is known of the religion of the Minoan and Mycenaean peoples, and attempt an estimate of how far the religion of these times survived in the Homeric poems and in later Greece.


## II. MINOAN AND MYCENAEAN RELIGION

The decipherment of the Linear B tablets of the Mycenaean age, with its proof that they are written in Greek, may be accepted as in principle accomplished, though the unsuitability of their syllabary to represent some sounds of the Greek language leaves reading and meaning in many cases doubtful. Thus the history of Minoan

---

[1] This trade began in the Late Helladic I and II periods; Lipari indeed seems to have received no L.H. III pottery.

and Mycenaean religion is no longer entirely 'a picture-book without text'. Nevertheless, in spite of the array of divine names which they now attest for this earlier period, the nature of the records precludes them from giving more than a momentary glimpse of the externals of religious life. The absence of literary documents remains a serious handicap, and to marry the monuments to our scanty and dubious epigraphical texts is not easy. One may well imagine how far astray an interpreter of Christianity or any other religion might go, if he had nothing but artistic representations and a few brief inscriptions to guide him. In many cases there is no objective criterion by which to decide in the first place whether a particular object is a religious document or purely secular in its use and significance; and even to divide representations more or less successfully into 'religious' and 'secular' is to give a falsely black-and-white appearance to a phenomenon whose truth lies in a delicate series of greys. Our imaginary archaeologist of the future would rightly identify the cross as a religious symbol among the Christians. But what would he know of its significance as worn on the breast of an educated Catholic priest, a superstitious peasant, a Protestant bishop, or a young woman at a society dinner-party?

In Crete, caves, used as dwelling-places by the Stone Age inhabitants and burial-places in the Early Minoan period (third millennium B.C.), seem to have become sacred, that is, regarded as the dwelling-place of some deity, in Middle Minoan times. Votive offerings and remains of animal sacrifices testify to this, and the sacredness of Cretan caves is borne out by Greek myths of the birthplace and burial-place of Zeus. The title Dictaean, commemorating the birth of Zeus in a cave on the Cretan Mount Dicte, occurs already on a tablet from Cnossus of Mycenaean date,[1] and on another, Eileithyia is connected with Amnisus, where Homer tells us she had her cave.[2] The sanctity of caves is of course by no means peculiar to Crete, nor is Cretan religion likely to be particularized until we reach a more sophisticated period and social level. Also from the beginning of the Middle Minoan period, if not earlier, dates the custom of building sanctuaries at or near the tops of mountains, as on Mount Juktas south of Cnossus, Petsophas above Palaikastro, and elsewhere. The northern summit of Juktas is surrounded by a massive wall, perhaps to protect a population of refugees in time of trouble, within which, near the western edge of the summit, are the remains of a building and a deposit of votive vases and figurines in

[1] KN Fp. 1.      [2] KN Gg 705.

a layer of ash. Some half-dozen similarly situated sanctuaries have been identified, and it is of interest to learn that the worship of deities of the mountain-top, familiar in Asia Minor and on the mainland of Greece, was practised at this early date in Crete, even though the finds tell us nothing about the deities concerned. The presence among the votive objects of many detached human limbs and sections of the body has naturally led some to think of the cult of a divinity of healing. On the other hand the aspect of the remains at Petsophas suggested to their discoverers that a bonfire had been repeatedly lit on the spot, into which the little figures had been thrown. The finds on Juktas are susceptible of the same interpretation. This is reminiscent of the annual fire-festivals known in Greece, at which representations of human beings, animals and other objects, as well as live animals, were thrown into the flames of a bonfire kindled for preference on the top of a hill. These festivals occurred, though not exclusively, in the cult of Artemis the 'Mistress of Animals', a goddess whose counterpart was, as we shall see, widely worshipped in Crete. Yet we cannot even be certain whether the worship on the Cretan mountains was directed to a goddess of this type (though it is very probable) or to a male weather-god.

As Minoan civilization progressed, and the great palaces began to be built, we note that, in marked contrast to the practice of classical Greece, there are no great temples for the housing and worship of the gods of a whole community. The cult-places found are domestic, mostly integral parts of kings' palaces or wealthy private houses. Some of the rooms in which sacred objects have been found show no signs of having been more than places of deposit for safe keeping. Others, with their raised plat-form across one end on which images and other cult objects were displayed, are more obviously actual chapels. This preference for domestic shrines may be textually reflected on a tablet from Cnossus in the title 'Lady (*Potnia*) of the Labyrinth',[1] if the labyrinth was within the royal palace, and possibly in other titles of the 'Potnia'.

The original appearance of Minoan shrines may be inferred not only from the ruins of actual examples but also from repre-sentations on frescoes or gems and models in the round. Most prominent among the sacred furniture, and frequently represented in decoration—on walls, altars, vases, sarcophagi—are the horns of consecration, so called because they seem to be the recognized location for a sacred object or cult-implement rather than objects

[1] KN Gg 702.

of cult themselves. Vessels, boughs and double axes are all shown set on the base between a pair of these upward-curving horns (Fig. 3).[1] Their original significance is uncertain (though Evans's interpretation of them as conventionalized *bucrania* remains probable),[2] but there is no doubt of their use and importance in cult. One engraved gem actually shows a young god himself standing between the horns, attended by two animal daemons one of which carries a libation-jug (Fig. 4). These horns often appear on altars, which were naturally in use in Minoan as in other cults. That shown in front of the standing hero on the Hagia Triada sarcophagus is stepped.[3] Others were rectangular in shape capped with a slab which projected all round (in fact very similar to Greek altars), and covered with elaborately painted stucco. There was also a round portable type with incurving sides, resembling the object used in the game of diabolo. On all these altars sacred objects were placed and, it would seem, libations poured, but scenes of animal sacrifice represent the victim as lying bound on a table of quite different design, with separate legs (Fig. 5).

Related in function to the altars, assuming that their sacral purpose is undoubted, will have been the so-called tables of offering or libation: short-legged tripods of plaster or clay with shallow depressions in their round tops. One of many examples was found in the Late Minoan 'Shrine of the Double Axes' at Cnossus, its feet imbedded in the centre of the raised floor in front of the ledge on which stood the images and other sacred objects. Its situation must indicate a religious use, though in shape and size it would be well suited to serve as a charcoal brazier and some may have been used for this purpose. One in fact had charcoal on it when discovered, but this specimen was in a tomb. In the Middle Minoan shrine at Phaestus was a receptacle of a similar kind, also imbedded in the floor, a legless rectangular tray with raised and ornamented rim and a circular basin hollowed out near the centre.[4]

More or less distantly reminiscent of these are a large number of stone receptacles of various shapes and sizes, solidly made with the round basin hollowed out of the top, not all of which need have had a religious use. Some have two, three or four depressions,[5] or a whole ring of them round the edge, which leads naturally to a consideration of a class of composite vessels interesting for their possible connexion with the cult-implements of later

---

[1] All figures in this chapter are taken from M. P. Nilsson, *Geschichte der griechische Religion*, vol. 1 (Munich, 1941).     [2] Cf. also §11, 14, 162.
[3] See Plate 121.          [4] See Plate 178 (*c*).          [5] See Plate 178 (*b*).

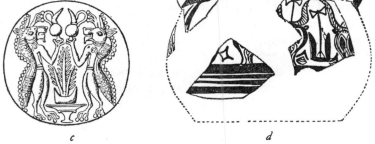

Fig. *3a*. Sacrificial jug between horns of consecration; gem in the British Museum (Nilsson pl. 2. 2). *3b*. Woman blowing a shell trumpet; gem from the Idaean Cave (Nilsson pl. 7. 3). *3c*. Daemons watering sacred branches between horns of consecration; gem from Vaphio (Nilsson pl. 7. 4). *3d*. Double axes between horns of consecration; vase from Salamis in Cyprus (Nilsson pl. 8. 2).

Fig. 4                                    Fig. 5

Fig. 4. Male figure standing between horns, and attended by daemons; gem from Kydonia (Nilsson pl. 19. 4).

Fig. 5. Bull lying on an altar; gem from Candia (Nilsson pl. 19. 2).

Greece. Those made of clay all consist of a number of small cups attached to some common support, which may be a tray, a post round which they cluster, or a flat ring (Fig. 6). Designs vary widely, but in one form these vessels tally remarkably with descriptions of the *kernos* as used in Greek mystery-cults and found at Eleusis.

Libations were poured from jugs, with round belly, tall neck, long upward-sloping lip and high handle. The formal method of carrying these—one hand on the handle, the other beneath the base—is shown in processional and other scenes on gems and seals (Fig. 7). It is possible that the occasion of one of these processions is described on a tablet from Pylus which mentions offerings of gold vessels to the gods and men and women who may have been their bearers.[1] Another kind of vessel testifies to the Minoan cult of snakes by the modelled snakes which twine around them. They are of curious shapes, including a bottomless tube into which we may suppose libations were poured to soak into the earth and be received by chthonian powers, whether the spirits of the dead or others (Fig. 8). Many were found in buildings identified from other evidence as shrines, but none in tombs.

The commonest and most certainly attested religious symbol is the double axe. It was of course in actual use as a tool, but specimens exist in miniature or other unsuitable sizes, in ornamental shapes, and in materials such as gold, silver, lead and stone which exclude the idea of any practical purpose. They occur earlier than any other certainly religious object, being found in cave-sanctuaries of the middle of the Early Minoan period. In art they are ubiquitous, and there is a possible reference to a 'lord of the axe' on a Pylian tablet.[2] They may appear set upright on pillars or bases, or between horns. Their precise significance is disputed. It is natural to connect them with the double axe in the cults of better known regions and periods of the Near East, where it commonly represents the thunderbolt wielded by the hand of a weather-god, though occurring also as a separate symbol without the anthropomorphic representation. To this it has been objected that it never appears in the hands of a male deity in Crete, where in fact the male deity appears to have played a subordinate part. This is not perhaps final, and the evidence of analogy from neighbouring lands is strong. Alternatively it has been thought that the axe acquired its sanctity in the eyes of these people from its use in killing the sacrificial animal, shown more than once as a bull. It is set not only between the conventional 'horns of

---

[1] PY Tn 316.          [2] PY Va 15.

Fig. 6a. 'Kernos' from Pyrgos (Nilsson pl. 5. 2). 6b. 'Kernos' from Melos
(Nilsson pl. 5. 3). 6c. 'Kernos' from Kumasa (Nilsson pl. 5. 4).

Fig. 7                                        Fig. 8

Fig. 7. Daemons worshipping a goddess; gold ring from Tiryns (Nilsson pl. 16. 4).
Fig. 8. Libation vessel; from Gournia (Nilsson pl. 1).

Fig. 9*a*. Tree shrine with a god descending in front of it; gold ring from Cnossus (Nilsson pl. 13. 4). 9*b*. Tree cult scene; gold ring from Mycenae (Nilsson pl. 13. 5).

consecration', whose derivation from bulls' horns is disputed, but also on top of actual *bucrania*.[1] Nevertheless elaborate scenes of ritual like that performed before the double axes on their tree columns on the Hagia Triada sarcophagus[2] make this simple supposition improbable. It seems extremely likely that some of the miniature examples were used as charms, perhaps (if the connexion with the weather is not excluded) rain-charms or at least charms to further some agricultural purpose.

There is good evidence for the religious significance in Crete, as in the Anatolian, Semitic and later Greek cults of neighbouring lands, of both pillar-shaped stones and wrought pillars. In the cave of Eileithyia at Amnisus a stalagmite was found to be surrounded by an enclosure built up of stones in which was set, in front of the stalagmite, a quadrangular stone which may have served as an altar. In scenes depicted on rings single free-standing columns, both with and without capitals, appear in shrine-like aediculae in the presence of worshippers (Fig. 9). The

[1] See Plate 178 (*d*).          [2] See Plate 121.

Fig. 10*a*. Pillar flanked by sphinxes; gem from Mycenae (Nilsson pl. 12. 3).
10*b*. Goddess flanked by lions; gem from Mycenae (Nilsson pl. 20. 6).

columns which are such a prominent feature of artistic representations of shrines, though clearly performing a structural function, are made to appear standing between 'horns of consecration' (Fig. 15*a*). A frequent design on engraved Cretan gems is of the type made famous by the Lion Gate at Mycenae, a single upright pillar flanked by a pair of guardian animals (Fig. 10*a*). Sometimes the same arrangement is preserved, but the anthropomorphic figure of a god or goddess takes the place of the pillar (Fig. 10*b*), which may therefore have been believed to contain the power of the deity. Certain rectangular piers in rooms of Minoan palaces and houses have the double axe incised on their blocks[1] and have on this account been thought to have had some sacred character. They were an integral part of the structure, and the axes may have been no more than masons' marks or at the most intended to put the building under divine protection. Since many if not all of the piers were covered with stucco, they were evidently not intended to be seen, though for all we know they may have been repeated on the decoration of the stucco. The degree and kind of sanctity attributed to these things cannot be determined in the absence of literary evidence. At one extreme the stone or pillar may be regarded as the actual image of the god; at the other, the attachment of religious emblems to the pillars of a house may imply only some form of dedication for the purpose of securing divine protection against the ever-present dangers of earthquake or fire. Both extremes, as well as intermediate stages, could be paralleled from Greek religion. Particularly interesting is the

[1] See Plate 178(*e*).

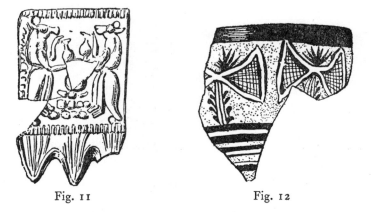

Fig. 11                    Fig. 12

Fig. 11. Daemons bring libations to a cairn; glass plaque from Mycenae (Nilsson pl. 22. 5).

Fig. 12. Double axes with sprouting leaves; fragment of a vase from Gournia (Nilsson pl. 9. 4).

representation, as early as the Middle Minoan period, of cairns or heaps of stones in an apparently religious setting, for example, accompanied by wild goats or lions 'heraldically' arranged with their forefeet on the cairn. At Mycenae animal-daemons of Minoan type bring libations to such a cairn with what looks like a large rough stone set upon it (Fig. 11). The parallel with the Greek *herma* or *hermaion* is striking.

In passing to the Minoan cult of trees and vegetation, we may note that the columns and the double axe are connected with it in such a way as to make it probable that all alike reflected a single complex of religious ideas. In the ritual scenes on the sarcophagus from Hagia Triada, libations are being poured into a crater set between the bases of two tall columns on which are large double axe-heads with birds perching on them. The columns however, if that is the right word for them, are covered with green, pointed projections, and either represent the trunks of date-palms (which they closely resemble except for their tapering shape) or are thickly covered with leaves. One is inevitably reminded of the Dionysus-columns of classical Greece, with the mask of the god hanging on them and foliage not only twined round them but growing out of their sides. On Late Minoan vases, axes are shown with leaves apparently sprouting from their handles (Fig. 12). On another sarcophagus appear what would seem to be three lilies growing from a single root. The middle 'flower' is however a double axe

Fig. 13. Tree cult scene; gold ring from Mycenae (Nilsson pl. 13. 1).

set on a base between horns, and its 'stem' a thin pillar with base and capital. The two lilies on either side have stamen-tips shaped like axe-blades. On a jar from the islet of Pseira, the hafts of double axes have lily-heads.

These examples put trees and plants in a religious setting, and their actual cult is attested in more than one way. We see boughs set up between 'horns of consecration', and animal-daemons watering them with libation-jugs. Other scenes show trees protected by small, carefully built enclosures, in front of which men or women either stand in devout attitudes (Fig. 13), or more remarkable, grasp the tree and pull it towards them, sometimes with the most ardent gestures, at the same time falling forward on one knee. Other figures meanwhile engage in ecstatic dancing. We seem to have here a type of rustic vegetation-worship such as commonly meets us in primitive religion and modern folklore.

So far we have spoken of cult-objects of various sorts without saying anything about the gods or goddesses whom the Minoans may be supposed to have worshipped. The difficulty of deciding whether a particular figure in an artistic representation is human or divine is almost insuperable. Actual images should be easier to classify, but even when found in undoubtedly religious surroundings may sometimes be either divine idols or votive offerings in human form.[1] One type which must be a goddess is the small semi-anthropomorphic image whose lower half consists of a plain cylinder (the so-called bell-shaped idol).[2] Its divinity is indicated by its position on the raised platforms of shrines and by the attributes of bird or snake which occasionally appear on it. Birds are frequent in religious scenes, and it is doubtless right to regard them as divine epiphanies. The snake-goddess occurs not only in this crude form but also among the finest works of art of the

[1] A, 10, 146 f.
[2] See Plate 179 (a).

Middle Minoan period, for to this period belongs the splendid faience figure from the 'palace sanctuary' of Cnossus, dressed in the sumptuous female fashion of the period, with a high tiara on her head and three snakes coiled around her, one with its head resting in her hand. Another image of her, grasping a snake in either hand, is in ivory and gold.[1] Religious conservatism venerated the primitive, less-than-human idol alongside of the beautifully executed statuette, as in many places did the Greek contemporaries of Pheidias or Praxiteles. Recent discoveries at Mycenae, of which only preliminary reports have been made,[2] have revealed a cult-room with raised platforms, clay figures nearly all female, and coiled snakes of clay. The room and the objects seem to belong to the late fourteenth and early thirteenth centuries, and they indicate the strength of the Minoan tradition in Mycenaean religion.

The snake-goddess evidently belonged to household shrines. She is not shown on engraved rings or gems, though one seal of doubtful significance from Zakro may depict a tiny 'bell-shaped idol'.[3] On this small scale however the lower half may be intended for a proper skirt. In general the scenes on rings and gems show worship in the open air, especially tree-cult. One in which a man is falling on his knees as he drags towards him a young tree in a shrine, while on the other side of the picture a woman bends with head in arms over a low structure in an attitude of mourning (Fig. 9 b), has been thought to represent ceremonies connected with various phases of the vegetation-cycle. Between them stands a woman in flounced skirt with hands at hips, probably dancing. Here as elsewhere the decision whether or not we are in the presence of a goddess is largely at the mercy of subjective impressions based on attitudes and positions as seen, very often, upon much-enlarged line-drawings of tiny objects in various states of preservation. Those which show a figure much smaller than the rest high up in the field may in fact portray, as is commonly thought, a divinity 'hovering in' or 'descending through the air'; but even here one must not forget the limitations of cramped space on bezel or gem, and the difficulty of rendering distance in actual space. One such epiphany, on a gold ring from Cnossus, shows a male deity, spear or staff in hand, descending in front of a tall pillar behind which is a shrine containing short

[1] See Plate 179 (b).

[2] See *Archaeological Reports for 1968–69*, 11 f. and *for 1969–70*, 12; and A, 14.

[3] See Plate 179 (a). Persson, in §11, 14, sees 'bell-shaped idols' on his rings nos. 8 (p. 49) and 26 (p. 82), though both have flounced skirt and leg.

Fig. 14*a*. God between two lions; gem from Cydonia (Nilsson pl. 20. 4).
14*b*. Daemon between two lions; gem from Mycenae (Nilsson pl. 20. 7).

free-standing column (or altar) and tree. In front of him stands a woman with forearms raised in obvious adoration (Fig. 9 *a*).[1]

Since we have introduced the subject of male deities, we may add that nude male figures are also occasionally found among the sacred objects of the house-shrines, and a god, beardless and youthful in appearance, is depicted on a number of gems and seals. We have seen him already standing between horns of consecration attended by monsters who are his frequent companions. They put his divinity beyond doubt, and also their own nature as subordinate supernatural beings, serving the god as the goatish Satyrs serve Dionysus. They commonly carry libation-jugs, and we see the god with his hands laid imperiously on their heads (Fig. 14 *a*), or even holding them by their tongues. They wear curious 'tail-coats' of skin, of one piece with their animal-heads, which would suggest men masquerading as beasts, were it not that legs and feet are as bestial as the rest. If the god was served, like many other gods, by priests in animal disguise, it is perhaps not unlikely that they would be shown in art as being more fully that which they strove to be but could not be completely in nature. But indeed, Greek descriptions of the Curetes and similar beings are sufficient to show that in such circumstances no clear distinction would be evident to the worshippers between priests and the legendary figures whom they impersonate. The monsters in their turn have power over the animals, placing their hands on the heads of lions as the god does on theirs (Fig. 14 *b*); and the god

[1] The genuineness of this ring has however been doubted. On this and the general question of 'hovering' deities see §11, 3, 147.

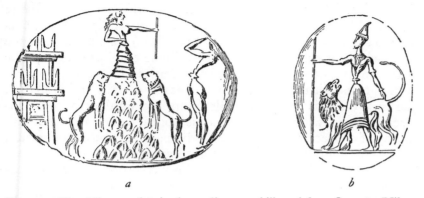

Fig. 15*a*. The Mistress of Animals standing on a hill; seal from Cnossus (Nilsson pl. 18. 1). 15*b*. The Mistress of Animals walking with a lion; seal from Cnossus (Nilsson pl. 18. 4).

who is their master may truly be described as the 'Master of Animals'. He also is shown with his hands on the heads of lions, and on a ring from Mycenae grasps one lion by the throat and another by the hind leg. The beard with which he is here provided, in contrast to all Cretan examples, is probably an innovation of the Greek immigrants.

More frequently it is a goddess who stretches her hands over the beasts, or in other ways shows her power over them. The Mistress of Animals is best known from the famous seal from Cnossus on which she stands in triumphant attitude on the top of a hill or large cairn holding out her staff or spear. On each side a lion rests its forepaws on the cairn, behind her is a shrine with horns of consecration, and in front a male figure with hands to head in apparent veneration (Fig. 15*a*). On another seal a similar figure strides along with shorter skirt and peaked cap, spear in hand, while a lion walks beside her and looks up into her face. She too must be the divine Mistress of Animals (Fig. 15*b*),[1] since human beings do not go out for walks in daily life accompanied by lions. This Minoan goddess is justly famous for her resemblance to her counterparts elsewhere in the Aegean, Cybele who yoked the lions to her car and was a goddess of the mountain, and above all the Artemis who is described as the Mistress of Wild Animals by Homer himself.

Much discussion has been devoted to the question of the functions and number of Minoan deities. It will be convenient to sum up the archaeological evidence here, and discuss later, under

[1] Unless the figure is masculine, as Deubner suspects (§II, 3, 148).

the head of Mycenaean religion, the light thrown by the divine names which occur on the Greek tablets. Attributes or symbols help to some extent, but one cannot pin down, say, the axe, or the birds which often seem to indicate a divine epiphany, to any one of the anthropomorphically depicted deities. The snake-goddess of the house-shrines seems to possess a certain individuality, marking off this domestic cult from the outdoor vegetation-ceremonies in which also a goddess appears. Yet a shrine with 'horns of consecration', thought to be peculiar to the house-cult, appears in conjunction with the outdoor goddess on the mountain, the Mistress of Animals; and the sacred boughs of the tree-cult are set between the horns of the domestic shrine.

Multiplicity of deities may mean one of two quite different things. The same people may believe in several goddesses because they conceive of each as having a different character and presiding over a different function, as in Greek polytheism Hera is wife of Zeus and goddess of marriage, Artemis huntress, Athena patron of wisdom, art and war, Aphrodite of love. Alternatively, different communities may, when communications are rudimentary, worship goddesses essentially identical, but with different names because of their isolation. Such would appear to be Dictynna and Britomartis, goddesses of Crete whom the Greeks of later times knew and identified with Artemis. It is unprofitable to discuss the question of Cretan polytheism without distinguishing these two kinds. Since Crete is a mountainous island about 156 miles long, it is improbable that even with the achievement of political unity in the Late Minoan period, the whole island with its 'ninety cities' ever worshipped a single goddess and god in the second, or local and nominal sense. As to the first, it is a matter of temperament rather than evidence whether a scholar supposes that the Minoans worshipped separate goddesses of the house, the fields, the mountains and wild animals, the sea, and war (the last two functions, like the others, are suggested by ring- and seal-engravings), or one great goddess who combined these aspects and was worshipped primarily as Our Lady of this or that according to the needs of different classes.[1] The clear-cut polytheism of Greece owes much to the Greek poetic imagination. The art of the Minoans is not lacking in imagination, but on the whole they do not seem to have brought

---

[1] Cf. Marinatos, in *Eph. Arch.* (1927), 26. There is great probability in Persson's view that the Greeks, with their leanings towards personification and the concrete, made separate deities out of what to the Minoans had been invocatory epithets. See below, p. 883.

it to bear on their religion, and it is unlikely that they evolved anything similar. The opinion may be ventured that a single goddess, essentially of the Mountain Mother type and of universal appeal, was, if not unique, at least predominant. She would be primarily a nature-goddess, fostering and controlling the animal and vegetable life of the earth, and regarded, at least among the more backward sections of the population, as Mother Earth personified. As such she would care, like the Greek Demeter, both for the fruits of her fields and the souls of the dead who are buried within her.[1] The chthonic character of the household- or palace-goddess is attested by the bottomless tube-shaped vessels found in her shrines, which on the most probable explanation (supported by Greek analogy) were intended for libations to the *chthonioi*. These in the palaces may have been thought of as dead ancestors, but cults of the dead and of spirits of fertility are normally allied. The domestic goddess has also her snakes, which have been said to be no more than friendly household genii. There are good parallels for this, but the snake is also a chthonian creature. It is probably a mistake to suppose that the minds of these people kept rigidly apart a set of ideas which are commonly related and associated with the same material symbol.

This characterization of the chief Minoan goddess, if not proved by the monuments, is strongly suggested by them, and supported by the analogy of neighbouring cults. If it is the true one, she will have had a youthful consort. Here again the monuments show nothing against the supposition, and something in its favour. They give us at least a young god, Master of Animals, who could have filled the role like the young hunters Adonis and Attis, the lovers of Aphrodite and Cybele.

On the important subject of the Minoan attitude to death and the after-life, there is not much that can be inferred with certainty from the archaeological remains. Burial, not cremation, was the rule, and the body was often deposited within the house, even just under the floor of the living room, which would seem to argue affection rather than fear. A frequent method of disposal was in large *pithoi*, a practice widespread in the Aegean area and in Asia Minor.[2] Objects of daily use buried with the dead imply the common belief in the continuance of a life similar to this one. It would be surprising if there were no actual tendance of the

---

[1] So formerly Evans, and now Persson in §11, 14, 121 ff. and elsewhere, and Marinatos, *Eph. Arch.* (1937), 290; (1927), 26. Nilsson still disagrees. See §11, 9, ch. 12, and Guthrie, *Cl. Rev.* 65 (1951), 106 f.

[2] §11, 14, 13–15.

dead, but opinions differ as to the actual amount of evidence for it which the remains afford. The bottomless, tube-shaped vessels have already been mentioned. If they were used to convey libations to the dead beneath the ground, this Minoan custom survived or was renewed at a later period in Greece. Three objects found in or hard by the necropolis at Khrysolakkos near Mallia have been thought significant in this connexion. Just outside the enclosure was lying a 'table of offering', that is, a stone block with a circular cavity in the top surrounded by two rings of small cup-shaped depressions. It resembles one found in the court of the palace of Mallia itself, and the cupules are supposed to have held a *panspermia*, an offering of various fruits of the earth to the great goddess. The connexion with the dead appears to be assumed from the position of the find. Secondly, in a room within the enclosure was a low circular 'table of offering' again with circular central cavity. This was covered in yellowish-white stucco, bearing black and reddish marks suggestive of the action of fire. The French excavators suppose this to have contained either an oil-light or some aromatic substance burned in honour of the dead. A bench in this room might have held cult-accessories or served as a seat for participants in the cult. The third object is a curiously shaped hollow block in one of the rectangular rooms fitted in between the eastern wall of the enclosure itself and the broad outer wall which runs parallel to it. Its shape may be described as a circle inscribed in a square with broken angles, the oblique sides of the resulting octagon being zigzagged into a series of toothlike projections. The hollow interior was filled with loose rubble which the excavators removed to a depth of 15 cm. below the surrounding floor, and there seems no doubt that it was open to the earth beneath. Comparing the hollow altar or *bothros* built above the fourth shaft-grave at Mycenae, the excavators have concluded that this served the same purpose, namely to receive libations for the dead. In the stucco of the floor beside the altar is again found a series of cupules, and arguing from the assumption that these are to be referred to the cult of the great goddess, and the presence of similar cupules in the palace, the French authorities have concluded that the worship of the goddess and the cult of the dead are connected. The principal Cretan deity, the mistress of life, was also mistress of souls after death. The occasional presence of female idols in tombs may point to the same conclusion, but this is disputed.

The most elaborate and important monument in this context is the painted sarcophagus of L.M. II or early L.M. III from

Hagia Triada.[1] Unfortunately the complex nature of the several scenes depicted on it has put interpreters in a dilemma. Being on a sarcophagus, they presumably have some reference to the dead man. Yet though the animal-sacrifices and libations shown might be offered to the dead (as among the Greeks by Odysseus in the Homeric *Nekyia*), there are many symbols of divinity difficult to relate to a cult of the dead or picture of the after-life. The figure standing at the end of one side, with arms concealed in a long robe, is without much doubt the dead man in front of his tomb. He faces three men who bring him offerings: animals and a model boat. The boat is probably a symbol of the belief that the journey between this world and the next was a sea-voyage. This may be only a slight adaptation of Egyptian ideas, and it survived in later Greece in the idea of the Islands of the Blest, to which—for it is by no means the destiny of the ordinary mortal—Menelaus is told that he will go by virtue of his kinship with the gods. The same fate awaits the race of demi-gods or heroes according to Hesiod. Characteristically perhaps, the Homeric Greeks regarded this translation not as following upon death, but as an alternative to it. The limitation to a privileged class, and the connexion with apotheosis, may already have been present in Crete. Nilsson saw in the combination of funerary and divine cult the actual apotheosis of a dead king. This depended partly on assuming that one of two figures in a chariot drawn by griffins was the dead man, whereas further cleaning has revealed that both are women. F. Matz[2] now divides the scenes into two series, one of divine cult and the other concerned with the dead man. Both, he argues, are invocations. Like the goddesses, who are approaching in their griffin-car, the dead man is also being summoned from the other world, whether for propitiation or to obtain his aid and advice. The deities are invoked with sacrifice and prayer to ensure his reappearance and be present at it. This implies that he dwells with them, and probably had divine status, but it is not his apotheosis that is represented. Deification of the dead has also been argued from the so-called 'temple-tomb' at Cnossus, where a cult-place has been built above the tomb-chamber. It forms a remarkable parallel to the two-storied tomb which, according to Diodorus (IV, 79), the exiled Cretans built for Minos in Sicily; but in this case at least the shrine above the tomb was devoted to 'Aphrodite', doubtless a name for the divine protectress of the Minoan kings.

A few words are necessary on the question of bull-cult, which

---

[1] See Plate 179(*c*).          [2] §II, 6, 18–27.

would almost certainly be taken for granted as a feature of the Minoan religion were it not for the determined opposition of an authority so universally acknowledged as M. P. Nilsson. In view of the prevalence of cults of bull-gods and cow-goddesses, and of myths reflecting them, in Egypt, Western Asia and Greece, it would be surprising to find it absent from an island lying in the centre of this area. Many of the Greek myths involving bull or cow relate specifically to Crete—the stories of Europa and the bull-Zeus, of Pasiphaë, of the Minotaur—and both the Cretan Zeus and Dionysus were worshipped by the Greeks in bull-form. Bull-worship seems to have gone naturally with fertility-religion, the lusty animal being considered, like the goat, as the embodiment of reproductive power. Taking this into account, it seems justifiable to attach weight even to slight indications in the fragmentary archaeological material to which we are deliberately confining ourselves at the moment.

The most striking appearances of the bull in Minoan art are of course in the representations of *Corridas*, the main excitement of which lay in the hazardous leaps over the animal's back, though the killing of it seems also to have entered in. Most scholars agree with Evans's view that these performances were not mere sport but had religious significance. Persson regarded them as intimately associated with the vegetation-cult and constituting in fact 'the great official spring festival'. As indications of this on the actual monuments, he points to the facts that the bull in scenes of bull-leaping is ithyphallic, and that in a representation of the grasping or shaking of sacred trees a man and a woman engaged in this act are both dressed for the bull-ring. The girl, as Nilsson had already pointed out, wears the loin-cloth which is properly the costume of female toreadors. Elsewhere female worshippers in scenes of tree-cult wear the long flounced dress. Persson drew the conclusion that both are 'drawing strength for the great and difficult task before them by grasping or shaking the holy tree', and that in consequence the bull-game must be admitted as part of the cult's practices. This of course is curious logic. From the fact that a soldier before a battle enters a church in uniform and prays for strength, there is no need to infer that the battle is part of a religious performance.

No positive conclusion can be drawn from the representation on seals of bull-headed human figures, or Minotaurs. In the first place the man-bull is only one of a series of Minoan monsters which includes men and women with the heads or other parts of goats, stags and birds as well as bulls. Secondly, these composite

creatures seem to play only a subordinate role as servants, attendants, libation-bearers. Undoubtedly they have daemonic powers
(above, p. 868), but they can hardly be called gods. On the other
hand the obvious consecrating power of the sacral horns (which
are not stags' or goats' horns) suggests that they were believed to
impart the *numen* of, and hence to symbolize, a deity who must therefore, one would have thought, have been imagined in bull-form.

Our conclusion must be that there is evidence, slight in respect
of the archaeological remains but overwhelmingly strong, even
if it must be called circumstantial, in Greek mythology[1] and the
religion of other neighbouring lands, for the existence of bull-
worship in Crete; and that the counter-arguments of Nilsson are
not conclusive. That the bull was sacrificed, as appears from the
Hagia Triada sarcophagus and elsewhere, is of course no argument against its divinity. The sacrifice of the animal embodying
the god, often followed by a sacramental meal in which by eating
its body the worshippers draw on the strength and power of
divinity, is established practice. Thus even if the *bucrania* which
appear frequently in Minoan art, sometimes with a double axe
between them, represent as Nilsson thinks no more than the heads
of sacrificed animals, this need not rob them of their right to be
considered at the same time as symbols of the god.

In trying to sum up a people's religion, especially where the
evidence is so plainly insufficient, we must take into account what is
known of their general outlook. The Minoans appear to have been
a peaceful people, who built a maritime empire on trade rather
than war, but hardy enough to be enthusiastic about such sports
as boxing and bull-leaping. In spite of their foreign contacts, they
had a markedly independent genius. Their character has been
described as 'a curious mixture of religious formalism and a real
*joie de vivre* of a somewhat heartless and childlike nature' by an
authority who relates these traits to the influence of the palace
worship.[2] The civilization was urban, gay and worldly, and to this
atmosphere the predominantly domestic religious cults were
doubtless no exception. As always, it is the rich and powerful
who have left the most telling memorials of their life. Even
among them, a worship of chthonic spirits and of the powers of
nature, especially, as so often, in the person of a great goddess,
appears widespread, and must have been even more widespread
among the humbler people of the countryside. The animal-headed
nature-daemons on which the gem-cutter rejoiced to exercise his art
were doubtless more real to those who 'have left no memorial'.

---

[1] To be considered more fully later.      [2] §II, 13, 275.

Besides the contemporary and local evidence of the finds, one can of course make more or less probable inferences about Minoan religion from Greek sources. These may come later. We shall conclude this section with some remarks on the religion of the Mycenaean Greeks.

In the sixteenth century B.C. Cretan influences on the mainland of Greece became very strong. Cretan works of art were imported, and native art was Cretan in style. Gradually the native element reasserted itself, and from the fourteenth century down to the final destruction wrought by the Dorian invasions towards the end of the twelfth century, it is possible to speak of a new age, the Mycenaean, preserving many Cretan features but stamped with the individuality of a different people, whom we now know to have been Greek-speaking. The centre of power is Mycenae itself, where the palace and citadel, rebuilt on a magnificent scale at the beginning of the fourteenth century, display such un-Cretan features as the large *megaron* with its fixed hearth and the massive fortification-walls with the carefully squared stonework of their bastions and gate-ways. At Tiryns, in the Argolid, and in Boeotia the pattern is repeated. The magnificent architecture of the tholos-tombs is developed at the same time, and pottery of new, mainland design is actually imported into Crete and influences the Cretan craftsmen in its turn. The energetic character of the new masters of Greece is strikingly shown by the archaeological evidence of their progress to the south and east, spreading their influence to Rhodes, Cyprus, Syria and Egypt. Nor did they come as peaceful traders only, but in contrast to their Minoan predecessors seem to have delighted in warlike adventure. This taste for fighting, not only in foreign expeditions but also perhaps between the princes on the Greek mainland itself, is also suggested by the tremendous fortifications which surround their palaces. In spite of many external resemblances, due to the lingering influence of the earlier centre of Aegean civilization, we are clearly confronted with a different outlook and a different spirit from that which animated the Minoans. If we wish to find out something of the religion of Mycenaean Greece, it will not be wise to forget either that we are dealing with a new people or on the other hand that this people had been deeply impregnated with Minoan culture over a long period of time.

A survey of the monuments suggests that in broad outline, though with one or two significant exceptions, the Mycenaeans had adopted the beliefs and customs of Crete. Yet one must always bear in mind Nilsson's caveat that the same artistic representations may conceal religious ideas of a very different order. He aptly cites the paintings of Orpheus playing to the animals which decorate the Christian catacombs.

We note first the rarity of large temples[1] and the use of palace- or house-sanctuaries as in Crete. These have been discovered at Mycenae itself, where the shrine-room containing three-legged stuccoed 'tables of offering' like that in the Shrine of the Double Axes at Cnossus has been largely overlaid by the later classical temple; at Berbati not far off, at Malthi (Dorium) in Messenia and at Asine. At Asine the cult was carried on not in a small room but in the corner of a large *megaron*. The large Mycenaean *megaron* was a feature lacking in Minoan Crete. Its association with an invading race rests perhaps on slenderer foundations than is generally supposed, and the fixed hearth found in it is more likely to have been a natural, and therefore old, product of the need of the mainland for domestic heating during a longer part of the year, at least at any distance from the sea. At any rate the hearth was a mainland feature, and one worth mentioning because it may well have been connected with new cult-practices. It was of great religious importance in later Greece, and there could have been no cult of Hestia where, as in Minoan Crete, the hearth was lacking. We also find the characteristic form of small shrine with three lower compartments and a higher structure on top of the centre one. These appear on a wall-painting from Cnossus, and traces of a similar façade were recognized by Evans on one side of the central court of the Palace. Models of them appear again on the mainland in gold leaf, from the shaft graves at Mycenae and from Volo. Those from Mycenae have birds as *acroteria* on each side and a double pair of horns of consecration in the centre.[2]

The horns of consecration, again, are common. We see them on a columnar structure approached by women, or crowning a column with birds and animals arranged heraldically on either side and another bird perched between them.[3] Altars have the same 'diabolo' shape. Ring-shaped *kernoi*, with cups set on the ring at intervals, have been found, and the jugs used in scenes of libation are of the same type as in Crete. Underneath the *adyton* of the temple of Apollo at Delphi was an animal-headed *rhyton* of Cretan type which must have been an implement of cult. The

---

[1] Two small buildings excavated on Delos may have been temples, and another on Ceos appears to have been one, to judge from cult-statues found in it. A megaron at Eleusis is claimed to be the original temple of Demeter. See H. G. de Santerre, *Délos primitive et archaïque* (Paris, 1958), 89 ff.; *Archaeological Reports for 1961–2*, 20; A, 10, ch. 6; A, 18, 34 ff.      [2] See Plate 180(*b*).      [3] See Plate 180(*a*).

double axe also appears, though not nearly so frequently in
Mycenaean Greece as in Crete. One may mention the sealstone
from Mycenae which shows it on the head of a goddess flanked
by lions and wearing the Cretan flounced skirt.[1] Several stepped
bases, some with a hole in the top, have been recognized from
Cretan parallels as supports for double axes, and they occur
occasionally on vases. A double axe-head was found in the house-
shrine at Malthi. Sacred pillars or baetyls are seen in little shrines
with trees, and the character of the pillar as emblem of divinity is
strikingly demonstrated by representations such as that on the
Lion-Gate at Mycenae, where lions flank a column with their
forefeet on its base. The arrangement is repeated on gems where
the animals are sometimes lions, sometimes others such as
griffins or goats, and are shown in varying attitudes. On a seal
already mentioned, the column is crowned with horns of consecration between which is a bird, and the sacredness of columns
is also shown by the way in which they seem to replace a deity.
A precisely similar arrangement is repeated with 'Mistress of
Animals' or daemon in the central position between the animals,
as on the famous 'Mountain Mother' seal from Cnossus. Glass
plaques from Mycenae show also the bringing of libations by
animal-daemons to what appears to be a sacred stone set on a
cairn, a prototype of the Greek *hermaion*.[2]

The last-named form a convenient transition to the vegetation-
cult, for on the same page of Nilsson's *Minoan–Mycenaean
Religion* may be seen another scene of libation-pouring by animal-
daemons, similar to that already mentioned save that in this case
the object of their attention is some leafy boughs set between a
pair of horns. Of this cult it need only be said that, whereas we
have spoken of its presence in Crete, some of the most striking
evidence for it comes from Mycenae, notably the scene in which
a goddess is seated beneath a tree holding poppy-heads in her
hand like the Greek Demeter and approached by worshippers
who bring her flowers or ears of corn (Fig. 16). Scenes of men and
women grasping in apparent ecstasy the trunks of trees set in
built enclosures are repeated in the Peloponnese as in Crete.

Here, as in Crete, worship is directed primarily to a goddess
(or goddesses) of nature who takes both animal and vegetable life
for her province. But it is in this question of the types of anthropomorphic deities involved that we seem to detect the influx of
new blood and a new way of life. The shield-goddess who appears
on a painted limestone tablet from Mycenae[3] (and perhaps also

[1] See Plate 180(c).     [2] See above, p. 865.     [3] See Plate 180(d).

Fig. 16. Goddess sitting under a tree, approached by worshippers; gold ring
from Mycenae (Nilsson pl. 17. 1).

in the little figure covered with a shield on a gold ring from the
same place), in whom Nilsson and others have seen the prototype
of Athena, is a war-goddess more suited to the martial Mycenaean kings than to those of Crete. The male deity appears
rather more prominently, and for the first time is bearded, as on
a 'Master of Animals' ring from Mycenae. The Cretans were
always clean-shaven, but the beard was a Mycenaean fashion, and
we cannot help remembering that the Greek Zeus was bearded.
In this connexion much has been made of a head which was found
with vessels and some small female figurines on and below the
ledge of the *megaron* sanctuary at Asine. Drawing attention to
a stone axehead found among these objects, Nilsson has claimed
this head as the first authentic representation of Zeus.[1]

A grouping unique among Minoan–Mycenaean religious
remains is furnished by the beautiful ivory found at Mycenae
representing two women seated on the ground with a small boy

---

[1] G, 13, 321 f. Miss Lorimer (§v, 12, 434) thought that 'the male head
represents certainly the principal, possibly the only deity; whether the female figures
are goddesses, divine attendants, or human worshippers, there is no doubt of their
subordination'. Unfortunately the sex of this head has been doubted. Its discoverer
Persson, who was at first inclined to interpret it as Poseidon, has since retracted,
denied that it is bearded, and called it female, on the grounds (*a*) of the traces of
white paint as well as red, (*b*) of its similarity to the head of a sub-Minoan goddess
found at Gazi in Crete (§11, 14, 100). Nilsson disagrees with (*a*) (§11, 9, 114, n. 5).
I would allow myself two comments: (1) the two heads can be conveniently seen
from the same angle, both in profile, by comparing O. Frodin and A. W. Persson, *Asine*
(Stockholm, 1938), 307, with *Eph. Arch.* (1934), pl. 2. 1. They are not very similar,
and in particular the shape of the chin is different, suggesting that one is intended to be
bearded and the other not. (2) I sought out the head itself in the Nauplia museum in
1951, and felt no doubt at all that it was bearded. Of other authorities, A. J. Evans
(*The Palace of Minos*, IV (London, 1935), 756) thought it beardless and female,
and Picard (§1, 3, 250) says rather oddly that it 'doit avoir été féminine'.

standing between and leaning over the knees of one of them.[1]
Wace thought it probable that it came from the shrine of the
palace which was just above. It has a small hole in the centre of
the base, possibly for mounting 'as the head of a ceremonial staff
or sceptre' (Wace). The possibility cannot perhaps be excluded
that it has no religious significance, but all things considered this
is unlikely, and if it has, then the suggestion of the two goddesses
Demeter and Kore with the divine child Plutus, as known later
from the Eleusinian cult, is remarkable. Moreover a series of
Mycenaean inscriptions,[2] though their precise significance is disputed, probably refers to 'the two queens', who must, one would
think, be the Mother-goddess and her daughter. The cult at
Eleusis is known to go back to Mycenaean times and earlier, and
the Cretan connexions of Demeter are strong.

Thanks to the decipherment of the Linear B script, we now
know that a number of Greek deities were already worshipped
under their familiar names in the Mycenaean age. We have seen
that the monuments depict three main types of goddess: goddess
of vegetation, Mistress of Animals, and household goddess. The
first suggests Demeter, whose name, according to the most likely
interpretation, appears on a Pylus tablet.[3] It may be used there to
mean 'land', but if so one would conclude from the form that
the earth was personified and called Mother, as universally in
later Greece. Artemis is the Mistress of Animals in Homer
(p. 902 below), and the phrase 'slave of Artemis' occurs on a
Mycenaean inscription.[4] The Mistress of Animals in Cretan art
is doubtless either Artemis or a Cretan goddess identified with
her by the Greeks. The snake-goddess of Cretan household
shrines, appearing also as a bird, is generally thought to be
identical with the shield-goddess of the Mycenaean limestone
tablet: the king's personal protector turned warrior by the needs
of warlike Mycenaean princes. She had been rightly thought of
as Athena, or a forerunner of Athena, who later lived with her
snake, bird, shield and tree in the house of Erechtheus. The name
'Athana Potnia' has now turned up at Cnossus.[5] 'Potnia Athenaie'
is one of her titles in Homer, but Potnia appears so often on the
tablets with a dependent genitive that on this one too the phrase
may mean 'Lady of Athana', Athana being a place-name. Even
so, we have probably here the origin of the name Athena, goddess
called after cult-place.

We have seen grounds for believing that before the coming of

[1] See Plate 143 (a).     [2] PY Fr 1222, Fr 1227, Fr 1228, etc.
[3] PY En 609.     [4] PY Es 650.          [5] KN V 52.

the Greeks a single great goddess, personifying the earth, mother of all life, was worshipped in Crete under different aspects. It was probably the Greeks, with their more concrete imagination, who divided these aspects among different personalities, creating names out of what they had taken over as epithets (pp. 870 above and 884 below). If this is true, the Mycenaean tablets are interesting evidence that the process of individuation was already well advanced by the thirteenth century. However, the predominance of the title of Potnia ('Our Lady') suggests a transitional stage. It appears alone, with a dependent genitive, and with epithet. She was probably the earth in all its aspects, the universal Mother-goddess: mother of fruits (Demeter is Potnia in Homer, and Earth in Aeschylus), giver of grain (on a tablet at Mycenae),[1] mother and mistress of animals (as Artemis is Potnia of animals in Homer) and having the king and his palace under her especial protection (Lady of the Labyrinth and later Potnia Athena). The 'Divine Mother' to whom oil is offered on another Pylian tablet will be the same figure.[2]

The name of Zeus occurs once at Pylus, more frequently in Crete.[3] Its comparative rarity is no doubt accidental, and no evidence that the sky-god Zeus was not already supreme among the Hellenic tribes when they entered Greece. Names derived from his also occur, applied to a month,[4] a goddess (Diuia),[5] and perhaps a shrine.[6] His identification with the youthful god of Crete, in Greek the *Kouros*, will be discussed later.

The name Dionysus is found on two fragments of tablets[7] devoid of context. If, as is most likely, it is the name of the god, it gives the important information that Dionysus was already in Greece in Mycenaean times. This has caused much speculation, but it is not surprising in view of the casual references in Homer (who was not interested in popular religion) to the persecution of the god, his maenads, and the myth of Ariadne. The new knowledge challenges the priority of Apollo at Delphi, but in spite of the myth of Ariadne, the balance of the evidence is still in favour of his having come to Greece from Phrygia and (as Bacchus) Lydia; probably also by another route from Thrace, whence Phrygia had been populated. Undoubtedly the young Cretan god, with his power over animals, bears a strong resemblance to Dionysus, and was worshipped in the same orgiastic way; but the Greeks at their first contact named him Zeus, doubtless

---

[1] MY Oi 701.    [2] PY Fr 1202.    [3] PY Tn 316; KN Fp1, F51.
[4] KN Fp 5.    [5] PY Cn 1287, Tn 316.
[6] PY Fr 1230.    [7] PY Xa 102, 1419.

because he was the supreme male deity of the land (p. 899 below). The resemblance between the cults is probably due to an initial, prehistoric identity, if the Cretans were originally of south-west Anatolian stock. The type is characteristically Western Anatolian.

Poseidon's name appears at Cnossus and several times at Pylus, where he seems to have had a certain precedence, a state of affairs remembered by Homer (*Od.* iii, *init.*). Among other divine names identified in the records of Mycenaean Greek are Enyalius, Paian (though not so far Apollo), Eileithyia, Hera, Hermes and perhaps Ares.

The inscriptions show Mycenaean Pylus to have been organized as a palace bureaucracy like that of some more familiar societies in the Near East. It has been suggested that, as in some of them, the ruler (*Wanax*) was worshipped as divine. He may have been the earthly representative of a god who himself was known as *Wanax* (Lord) in addition to any more specific name, but there is no inscriptional evidence that he was deified during his lifetime, and the palace-shrines rather suggest that he was a mortal who needed his divine protectress. Among Greece's near neighbours the Hittites, kings were not believed divine, nor offered cult, during their lifetime, but only after death.

The contribution of Mycenaean epigraphy to our knowledge of Greek religion is still under lively discussion, and many ideas are being produced and criticized which may well prove fruitful, but as yet are not sufficiently well established to find their place in a general history. It is however probable that further work will show the religion of the early Greeks to have been basically a worship of the powers of fertility conforming in general pattern to the cults of their Near Eastern neighbours. This is in keeping with the increasing evidence from archaeology and comparative mythology in favour of contact and cultural exchange between the peoples of all these Mediterranean lands.

Inhumation of the dead continued to be the regular custom in the Mycenaean as in the Minoan civilization, in contrast to the practice of cremation depicted in Homer. Cremation begins sporadically in the sub-Mycenaean and becomes common in the proto-geometric period. In some Mycenaean graves offerings to the dead have been burned, though not, as in Homer, with the corpse itself. This was once explained as the relic of an original Greek custom of burning the dead, abandoned as they became 'Minoized' and later resumed, but our wider knowledge of Early and Middle Helladic burials lends no support to this view. It may be that (as Mylonas thinks) the objects were burned to propitiate the inhabitant of a tomb, and persuade him to stay there, if it was reopened for another burial before the body had completely decayed and so released the spirit to the underworld, though this does not seem a full explanation of the act of burning. Whatever the reason for this peculiar feature, the change from inhumation to cremation need not imply any fundamental change of belief regarding the life after death. Objects of use, and offerings of food and drink, continue to be given to the dead even in classical Greece, when cremation is the regular practice. The chorus in the *Choephoroe* say, when Agamemnon's children supplicate him with libations at his tomb: 'The raging jaw of the fire quells not the mind of the dead man.'

The food and drink, clothing and utensils buried with a dead man show that he was believed to survive and have needs in the tomb. On the other hand, except at the royal shaft-graves at Mycenae,[1] there is no evidence of a continuation of regular cult after the actual burial. On the contrary, tombs seem to have been revisited only for the purpose of interring another body, and the unceremonious way in which the bones of previous occupants were then swept aside shows a remarkable lack of respect or fear for their spirits. The explanation may be that the spirit was believed to haunt the grave so long as the flesh remained on the bones, but that when a body had completely decomposed it fled, like the Homeric *psyche*, to the world of shades, and had no longer any interest in the actions of the living. The unmistakable evidence of regular cult over the royal graves at Mycenae would then be evidence that kings were thought of as superhuman, god-born as in Homer, and therefore exempt from the common lot of mortals. 'But for thee it is not fated, god-nurtured Menelaus, to die and meet thy fate in horse-rearing Argos...because thou hast Helen for wife and in the eyes of the gods art son-in-law of Zeus' (*Od.* iv, 561). It is doubtful, however, whether the archaeological evidence has finally solved the problem of the Mycenaean attitude to the dead.

Representations of the bull-games occur on fragments of fresco from Mycenae and Tiryns, on a sarcophagus from Thebes and on two rings from Asine. The frescoes are Minoan in subject and may have been executed by Cretan workmen. Of the extent to which the games themselves were introduced on the mainland it would be hard to speak.

[1] G. E. Mylonas now doubts even this. See his *Ancient Mycenae* (1957), 111 ff.

## III. THE DEBT OF
## GREEK RELIGION AND MYTHOLOGY TO THEIR
## MINOAN–MYCENAEAN PREDECESSORS

It cannot be doubted that Greek religion of the historic period owed an immense amount to that of Minoan Crete and the Mycenaean mainland; but to prove this in detail is naturally difficult in view of the ambiguity of much of the evidence for Minoan-Mycenaean religion itself. Representations of Greek myth and belief have been eagerly sought in Minoan–Mycenaean art, but amount to little more than a probable Europa on the bull (Fig. 17) and a possible Zeus with the scales of destiny.[1] On the other hand the mythological links connecting Greece with Crete are many and important. The whole Minotaur complex, beginning with the love of Pasiphaë, wife of Minos, for a bull, and including the labyrinth (a non-Greek word) and the story of the tribute of Athenian youths and maidens, of Theseus and Ariadne, is a notable example linking Crete and Cretan customs with Mycenaean Athens. Daedalus does the same. Glaucus, who is found in many parts of the Greek world, was said to be a son of Minos, and there seem to be some grounds for connecting certain elements in his story, especially the manner of his death by falling into a large jar full of honey, with pre-Greek customs of the Aegean area.[2] The names of the Cretan heroines or nymphs Pasiphaë ('all-shining'), Ariadne ('very holy' or 'very visible'), Phaedra ('bright'), Dictynna ('she of Mount Dicte'), Britomartis (not Greek, but said by Greek grammarians to mean 'good' or 'sweet maiden' in the Cretan tongue), like that of Glaucus ('grey-green'), are all *adjectives*, and suggest that the Greeks, with their genius for concreteness and personification, may have made separate personalities out of invocations to a single great Cretan goddess or god in different capacities. Some they translated, to others they attached a fanciful Greek etymology (e.g. *diktys* = a net, for Dictynna, itself the genesis of a new myth).[3] There is other evidence that Pasiphaë, Ariadne and Helen herself were Cretan goddesses, or aspects of a goddess, connected with moon-worship or tree-cult. Britomartis and Dictynna became for the Greeks nymphs attendant on Artemis, herself the Greek successor of the Cretan Mistress of Animals.

---

[1] See Plate 181. Discussion in §II, 9, 34 ff. Nilsson is convinced of the scales of destiny, but cf. §I, 3, 290, and §II, 3, 146.

[2] §II, 14, ch. I.          [3] Cf. §II, 14, ch. V.

Fig. 17. Europa on the bull; glass plaque, from Midea
(Nilsson pl. 16. 7).

As Nilsson has pointed out, the heroic sagas of Greece are almost all tied to places now known to have been the seats of powerful Mycenaean rulers: Agamemnon was lord of Mycenae, Heracles of Tiryns, the Thebes of Oedipus had a Mycenaean palace, the Argonauts were Minyans from Mycenaean Orchomenus, Athens itself was a Mycenaean site.

If the myths suggest an origin in the Mycenaean age, so does the cult, for often the same places retained an unbroken sanctity from Mycenaean to historic times.[1] At Mycenae and Tiryns, Athens and Eleusis, the site chosen for later Greek temples or other religious buildings was that of the palace of the Mycenaean prince itself. Delphi, holiest of all places to the historic Greeks, was holy already to their Mycenaean forebears. The mysteries at Eleusis are a subject for a later volume, but their origin can be traced back to Mycenaean times, and the Mother Goddess Demeter is connected with Crete by Hesiod and in the great Homeric Hymn which describes the aetiology of the rites. The Eleusinian triad, as we have seen (p. 880 above), is probably represented on a Mycenaean ivory. The historic claim of Crete to have been the original home of what the Greeks called *mysteria* was probably well founded. (There is a possible mention of initiation on a Mycenaean tablet from Pylus.)[2] Zeus himself, as we shall see later, took on under Cretan influence some incongruous characteristics more suited to an Aegean vegetation-spirit and to a mystery-religion than to the august Father whom the Greeks brought with them into Greece.

[1] For a more sceptical view, see §II, 3, 149 f., quoting G, 19, 1, 117–18; A, 7.
[2] PY Un 2.

The building of temples by the Greeks over the remains of Mycenaean palaces reminds us that to Minoan and Mycenaean rulers cult was primarily domestic, and the sanctuary of the deity a part of the house. In a remarkable passage of the *Odyssey* (VII, 80–1), Athena after her visit to Scherië to assure Odysseus's welfare is said to have left the island and returned to her own city, Athens (here called simply Athene like the goddess), where she entered the strong house of Erechtheus. Erechtheus was a legendary king of Athens, and under the later temple known as the Erechtheum and the old temple of Athena herself have been found the remains of a Mycenaean palace. Originally the goddess had no special temple, but shared the house of the king, whose patron she was, and we see how in Homer she and other goddesses still play the role of personal protector to a hero.[1]

Further details on this subject will be more in place when we come to discuss the separate members of the Olympian pantheon. It may be added however that the Oriental flavour in certain Greek myths, which has only recently begun to be justly appraised, may perhaps owe something to the eastward trend of the Mycenaeans. The Phoenician origin of Europa and Cadmus, the oriental character of Aphrodite, the parallels between the cosmogonic myths of Hesiod and those of the Babylonians, Canaanites and Hittites—these and similar features may reflect the contacts made by this adventurous people, which planted settlements in Cyprus and on the coasts of Anatolia and Syria, and had relations with the Egyptian and Hittite empires. Yet in view of the possibility that the first Greeks, and even earlier peoples, came into Greece rather from the east than from the north, these affinities may have older roots. Much research remains to be done before such problems can be settled.

The question of the possible Mycenaean connexions of Greek hero-cult was touched on at the end of the previous section. In the matter of the after-life, the tension which we find in Greek religion between two contrasting conceptions is most convincingly interpreted as a tension between original Greek and Minoan beliefs. In Homer the regular picture of Hades is one of unrelieved gloom, in which the dead exist as bodiless, and therefore unhappy and strengthless shadows of their former selves. In contrast to this is the promise made to Menelaus that by reason of his relationship to Zeus he will escape death and be sent instead to Elysium on the farthest bounds of the earth, where life is easy for men and 'falls not rain nor hail nor any snow'. The same

---

[1] On *Od.* VII, 80–1 see especially §v, 12, 436, and cf. §v, 13, 365.

place is called the Islands of the Blest by Hesiod. Thus the idea of a blessed immortality was introduced, and once the heroic insistence on the possession of a living body as a condition of happiness had faded with the rest of the heroic age, the belief returned to what had doubtless been its original form: that is, a belief in a better life *after* death, not in substitution for death. This was the belief behind the Eleusinian mysteries in later times, and the teaching of the Orphics.

Now it seems certain, after the work of Nilsson, Malten and others, that the notion of an Elysium (or Islands of the Blest) is Minoan.[1] In the passage of Homer it is described as the dwelling of Rhadamanthys, brother of Minos, whose name is un-Greek and who is especially associated with the neighbourhood of Phaestus. The Egyptianizing scenes on the Hagia Triada sarcophagus suggest similar beliefs, which accord well with the rest of our scanty knowledge of Minoan religion. It appears primarily as a religion of fertility, with an element of ecstatic dancing and a paramount goddess who was mistress of animal and plant life and doubtless therefore a Great Mother like her Near Eastern relations. Fertility-cult and concern with life after death are always found together, as at Eleusis where the Great Mother and her daughter the Corn-Maiden, with a young male spirit of fertility, preside over the mysteries which will assure to the initiates a better life after death. We are brought back to the Cretan claim to have given the mysteries to Greece.

A final word of caution. The Greeks had their full share of the religious conservatism which is common to all mankind. Side by side with higher forms, we find more than hints of primitive phenomena like stone-worship and aniconic cult in general, taboos, purification-rites, the worship of deities in animal form by priests or devotees in animal guise, and so forth, which are met with in all parts of the world, and which therefore there is no strong reason to connect with any particular branch of the Greek ancestry.

## IV. EARLY COSMOGONICAL AND THEOGONICAL MYTHS

Homer was not interested in the origin of things. He accepted the world as he found it, and his poems show only faint and occasional traces of a knowledge that it was not always so. In this

---

[1] Despite the feeling of Deubner that there are 'no really decisive arguments' (§II, 3, 150).

the heroic epics are peculiar, for a consuming interest in beginnings is a characteristic of the Greeks. Hesiod, though probably writing at a slightly later date than that of the composition of the *Iliad* and *Odyssey*, has with his peasant outlook collected and systematized myths on this subject which are far older and therefore may properly be considered here. Hesiod has indeed a particular interest as pointing both backwards and forwards. Together with stories of a primitive crudity, he gives an account of the origin of the world which, in spite of its outwardly mythical form, foreshadows the framework adopted by the rationalistic Ionian philosophers of the sixth and later centuries.

The essence of the mythical element consists in the explanation of things by birth and begetting in a series of genealogies. This applies alike to personal gods, natural phenomena and abstract qualities. Of these latter, some, like Justice, were probably familiar personifications in the peasant society to which the poet belonged, whereas others will have owed their origin to his own imagination. Thus Earth bears the mountains and the sea; Night bears, besides the Hesperides, such abstractions as Death, Sleep, Woe, Deceit, Old Age, Strife. Strife has a similarly abstract, and appropriate, progeny. The Nereids include, among many whose names suggest actual sea and seafaring, also Victory, First Counsellor, Fair Speaking, Public Speaking and one or two other political and mental virtues.

It seems to have been a common feature of early Greek cosmogonical beliefs, which they share with those of the Near East and elsewhere, that in the beginning all was fused together in an undifferentiated mass. The initial act, whether imagined as creative or evolutionary, was a separation. In the Hebrew creation-myth recounted in Genesis 'God *divided* the light from the darkness...and divided the waters which were under the firmament from the waters which were above the firmament' and so on. Diodorus begins his account of the origin of the world, which appears to go back to a fifth-century original, by saying that in the beginning heaven and earth had a single form because their nature was mingled, and quotes a line of Euripides to the same effect. The same idea appears in the monism of the early Ionian philosophers, and Anaxagoras declares that 'all things were together' until Mind imposed order upon them. The theogonies attributed to Orpheus and Musaeus expressed it like the monist philosophers by saying that 'all things came to be from one', and embodied it in a myth of their own.

The ubiquity of this conception in Greek thought justifies us in taking literally the opening words of Hesiod's account: 'First of all the Gap (*Chaos*) came into being.'[1] The first act of world-genesis must be the separation of elements blent in a primeval fusion, in which earth and heaven particularly were one. This early part of the Theogony, though retaining the image of birth, is well on the road from myth to philosophy. Once the Gap has come into being, Earth appears, and with her Eros, for so long as the idea of procreation is retained, the power of sexual love must be there from the beginning. He is usually imagined as having his abode between earth and heaven, as in Plato's *Symposium* and in a version of the Orphic Theogony in which he appears from an egg, of which the two halves, splitting apart, form earth and heaven respectively. When myth comes to be thought too crude a vehicle for the conveyance of truth (a stage which is not far ahead of these early lines of Hesiod), this mediating power is easily rationalized, as the rain which falls from heaven and fertilizes the earth or the more general 'moist element' in which philosophers saw the origin of life.

From the Gap come Darkness and Night (a male and female pair), and from Night, naturally enough, Light (*Aither*, masc.) and Day (fem.). Earth brings forth the starry heaven, the mountains and the sea. At this point we seem to slip back from the threshold of rational cosmogony to an earlier world of popular mythology in which Gaia and Uranus are not simply, as their names indicate, the earth and the sky, but the anthropomorphic ancestors of that marvellous race of gods and goddesses, daemons and nymphs, with which the universe was populated by the fertile Greek imagination. That we have here not simply a continuation but an older stratum of myth is suggested by the traces of a second and much cruder account of the separation of heaven and earth, necessitating their portrayal as fully anthropomorphic figures.

Gaia lay with Uranus and bore Oceanus, the Titans (among whom was Cronus), the Cyclopes and the three hundred-armed and fifty-headed monsters Kottos, Briareos and Gyes. Uranus hated his children, and thrust them back into the darkness of Gaia's womb. In her distress she appealed to her children, of whom only one, Cronus, was bold enough to attack their father. Taking an iron sickle which Gaia had fashioned, he cut off the genitals of Uranus as he lay outstretched on the body of Gaia. Hesiod goes no further with this part of the tale, using it only to continue his complicated genealogies by telling of the creatures that were born from the genitals of the mutilated Sky-father.

[1] Not 'was': *Chaos* was the space between heaven and earth; cf. Arist. *Birds*, 192.

Drops were received by Gaia, who bore the Furies, the Giants and certain nymphs, and from other parts, which fell into the sea, sprang Aphrodite, child of a popular etymology (*aphros*—foam). But scholars from Andrew Lang onwards have perceived in the exploit of Cronus an example of the violent separation of earth and sky which appears in the myths of many other peoples besides the Greeks.[1]

We may pass over the intricate and not always consistent genealogies whereby Hesiod tries to make a connected pantheon out of a host of supernatural beings diverse in their origin and nature. From this welter there stand out two of the Titans, Cronus and Rhea, well known to every Greek as the parents of the all-powerful ruler of the present order, Zeus. With them the theme of the father's hostility to his children is repeated. Cronus swallowed them as soon as they were born, lest any should usurp the royal power which he himself had attained. Now for the first time Zeus enters on the scene, and we are approaching the second element in Hesiod's Theogony, which presents a double aspect,[2] as first a genealogical account of the origin of the gods from the beginning of the world, and secondly a hymn to the glory of Zeus and the other gods of the present Olympian generation, who have overcome the earlier powers, the Titans and the dragon Typhoeus.

In her predicament Rhea consulted her parents Gaia and Uranus, who sent her to Crete. Here she bore Zeus, and Gaia, who herself took over the nurture of the infant god, hid him in a cave. Gaia also dealt with Cronus, by giving him a stone wrapped in swaddling-clothes which he swallowed in mistake for the babe. Later Cronus disgorged the stone, and with it the elder brothers and sisters of Zeus.

On the advice of Gaia, Zeus when he grew up released the three hundred-armed monsters whom their father Uranus had imprisoned beneath the earth, and these in gratitude gave him the thunderbolt which became his characteristic weapon, and to which he owes his position as supreme lord of the world. The battle of the Olympians with the older generation was now on. After ten years the Titans were beaten by the new weapon and the active assistance of the Hundred-armed, and hurled into Tartarus beneath the earth.

Zeus's rule, however, was not yet secured. When he had driven the Titans from heaven, Earth and Tartarus together brought

---

[1] §IV, 3, 103,

[2] A point made by Kern, G, 10, 264, and developed by Cornford, G, 2, chs. XI and XII.

forth Typhoeus, a monster with a hundred serpents' heads growing from his shoulders, and roaring terribly with the voices of all sorts of creatures. Had Zeus not been quick to attack him, he would not have been ruler of mortals and immortals. After a struggle involving convulsions on a cosmic scale, he too was defeated, maimed with the thunderbolts and imprisoned in Tartarus. From him come the storm-winds.

Zeus is now undisputed master, and urged by the other Olympian gods he assumes the royal power to rule by the counsels of Gaia, and distributes to the others their appropriate honours and functions. This important act of Zeus after his victory is referred to also near the beginning of the Theogony, in the description of the Muses as hymning the praises of the Father. 'For he reigns in heaven, grasping the thunder and the flaming thunderbolt, having mightily overcome his father Cronus; and to the immortals he distributed all things aright and determined their honours. These things the Muses sang.' The effect of this orderly distribution is seen in Homer, where Poseidon relates how the main divisions of the world were given in a threefold allotment to the three great sons of Cronus, and each received his allotted honour: Poseidon the sea, Hades the underworld, while Zeus himself retained the heaven. The earth's surface and Mount Olympus are shared by all in common.

The victory and settlement are followed by the marriage of the new king. Once again he is counselled by Gaia and Uranus, and to escape the fate of his father he swallows his wife Metis lest she bear an heir stronger than himself. There follow the birth of Athena from his head and further unions and begettings of Zeus.

A noteworthy feature of the whole account is the abiding influence of Gaia, the Earth, from the earliest generation to the latest, not as supreme ruler herself, but as the universally acknowledged power behind the throne. She gave Cronus the iron sickle and was responsible for his rise to kingship. Again, by her counsel and action Zeus was saved and shown how to usurp the throne. By her counsel he rules, and by it he has been saved from overthrow himself. These things are described as being fated, but Gaia has both foreknowledge of what is to be and power to be herself the instrument of fate. All this reflects a genuine religious fact. Throughout the religious changes which took place in Greece, culminating in the vivid anthropomorphism of the Olympian religion which the classical Greeks inherited from Homer, the awe inspired by the Earth-Mother never failed, though she was recognized to be, as indeed she was, a far older power in the land than the Olympians. Nor were her prophetic powers forgotten. At Delphi itself she was acknowledged as the original tenant of the oracle now presided over by Apollo on behalf of Zeus.

These myths, so conscientiously collected and systematized by Hesiod, reveal a primitive mentality which was beneath the notice of the courtly poet of the *Iliad* and *Odyssey*. However they may have reached the Boeotian writer, they have their origin in lands to the east, in the religious literature of Babylonians, Hurrians and Hittites. The Babylonian story of Marduk and the Hittite of Kumarbi (the latter taken over from Hurrian sources) both tell of a conflict of successive generations of gods, of the forcible separation of heaven and earth, of castration. Marduk, before becoming king of the gods, must fight a dragon whose body he splits in two to make of its upper half the sky. The Kumarbi story shows even more striking resemblances to Hesiod's Theogony: earth is fertilized by the seed of the castrated god, Kumarbi declares his intention of eating his children, and is put off with a stone. It has been suggested[1] that an opportunity for the transference of these stories to Greece may have been provided in the Late Bronze Age when Mycenaean traders possessed a regular station at Ugarit on the north coast of Syria, where they would meet Hurrian and other oriental people, or later when Greeks and Phoenicians were in contact at al-Mina. On the other hand if it is right to consider the Greek tribes themselves as having come originally from eastern rather than from northern lands,[2] these motifs may also have been dimly lodged in their own folk-memory.

These oriental parallels to the conflict of generations among the gods may seem to cast discredit on a theory which has commanded considerable support, namely that the overthrow by Zeus of the Titans has a historical explanation, embodying a memory of the fruitless opposition offered by the older religion of Greece to the Olympian religion introduced by invading Greek tribes. The question cannot be decided yet. The Greeks were adept at giving their own, Hellenic twist to older or borrowed mythological material, and these tales learned from the Orient may only be the mould of expression into which they cast memories of their own composite history. If they were borrowed, we have at least to seek a reason for the borrowing. In Syria or Babylonia they formed the basis of an elaborate ritual for which there is no evidence that they were used among the Greeks.

[1] §IV, 2, 100 f.; §IV, 3, ch. XVI.     [2] Cf. §I, 3, 225, 231.

Hesiod's is the only theogonical work which is preserved entire, but—apart from the scanty theogonical references in Homer—others are referred to or quoted by ancient writers. Foremost of these is that attributed to Orpheus and believed by the Greeks to be of venerable antiquity. Others are attributed to Pherecydes, Epimenides, and Acusilaus. They illustrate the facility with which a Greek would use traditional material to teach a new religious lesson by some change of emphasis or order. All depend to some extent on Hesiod, and where they introduce different elements one may be sure that these are not invented by the writer.

The one cosmogonical idea preserved by Homer is that of the origin of all things from water. This is expressed mythologically by calling Oceanus, the river which encircled the earth's disc, the origin of all things (*Il.* xiv, 246), or saying that the gods owe their origin to Oceanus, and that Tethys his wife is their mother (*ibid.* 201). It is probably an Ionian idea, since it reappears in Ionian philosophy and in the eastern peoples to whose influence early Ionia lay particularly open. The only other point of interest which Homer furnishes in this connexion is the isolated statement of Hypnos in the same book (*Il.* xiv, 259 ff.) that Night is a great power, 'subduer of gods and men', before whose displeasure even Zeus himself must quail. This is strikingly parallel to the position of Night in the so-called 'Rhapsodic Theogony' attributed to Orpheus in Graeco-Roman sources. There Night is one of the oldest powers, mother of Uranus, but retains her dominating influence down to the time of Zeus, whom she counsels as she did his predecessors. She seems in fact to occupy the same position of permanent dignity as does Gaia in Hesiod. That her cosmic importance is a feature of the Orphic tradition seems to be confirmed by the cosmogony of Aristophanes' *Birds*, in which she is said to have laid the world-egg. Epimenides perhaps stands here in the same tradition (cf. fr. 5 Diels-Kranz), of whose existence we have further evidence in Aristotle's general reference to 'those *theologoi* who make Night the origin of things' (*Metaph.* 1071 b 27). Pherecydes, more philosopher than mythographer, seems to have been original in placing Zeus, together with Time and Earth, at the very beginning of creation, thus abandoning the evolutionary scheme according to which the present ruler of the universe comes at the end of a line of forebears going back to pre-anthropomorphic cosmic powers. Zeus in fact is the creator, though in deference to the tradition of sexual generation he is said to have changed himself into Eros for the purpose.

### V. HOMERIC RELIGION

Only the most general characteristics of Homeric religion can be described here. Its gods are the most fully anthropomorphic that have ever been known. This may suggest that the poems reflect a very naïve and undeveloped state of religious beliefs. Yet it exhibits its own form of rationalism, and is a great advance both on earlier popular notions of vague, uncanny power of the 'mana' type (which certainly preceded it and have left unmistakable traces) and on the monstrous forms which still haunt the *Theogony* of Hesiod. The uncanny and the magical are reduced to a minimum, and for this circumstance later Greek religion is greatly in Homer's debt. The conception of gods as superior human beings, powerful and immortal but liable to human passions and failings, is not a very lofty one. But at least they were civilized human beings, with whom reasonable relations were possible.

The struggle for power belongs to the past, Zeus holds universal sway as leader of a large family of gods whose portions are assigned and known. Nor is there any hint that the present order can be other than permanent. The family on Olympus, over which Zeus presides as father and ruler, is often quarrelsome. The other gods may object to the decisions of Zeus, even disobey or temporarily outwit him. Nor is he so absolute a ruler that it would be wise for him to ignore completely the will of the others. When Sarpedon is about to be killed by Patroclus, Zeus is in two minds whether to save him from what is regarded by the gods as his fate, or allotted portion (*moira*). Evidently this would not be beyond his power. However, 'Do so', says Hera, 'but do not expect the approval of all of us. You are not the only god to have a mortal son in the fighting. How would it be if we all took this line?' Zeus listens, and gives way. This however is because he values a peaceful life. It is made quite clear that once he has made up his mind, none of the other gods could withstand him, and the penalties for attempting to do so would be fearful.

The superiority of the gods to mortals lies in physical power and in immortality. Zeus controls the weather and his weapon is the thunderbolt. Poseidon can cause storm and shipwreck. Any god or goddess can appear in whatever form he or she chooses, or remain invisible to mortals, can traverse distances in a moment of time, drain a man of his strength or his wits and invest another temporarily with superhuman strength or beauty, snatch a favourite from the battle or conceal him from view. Here folk-tale and religion meet. Above all they are immortal, and so closely linked in the Greek mind, from Homer onwards, is man's helplessness before the gods with his ephemeral nature that 'mortals' and 'immortals' are for them interchangeable terms with 'men' and 'gods'. When, after the passing of the heroic age, the longing for immortality again began to be felt, it had to reckon with this conviction that for man to claim immortality was to put himself on a level with the gods.

Homer's society was the warlike aristocracy of a heroic age, in which a god-descended king or chieftain holds absolute sway, though not beyond the criticism of others of the same class, his peers. These high-born warriors regarded their gods as very like themselves, a higher aristocracy still, and projected their own morality upon them. They certainly stand for the beginnings of a moral code, such as would appeal to an age of chivalry. Zeus disapproves of injustice and oppression. He is the protector of the stranger and the suppliant, and upholds the sanctity of the oath. Yet there is an arbitrariness in the dealings of gods with men which may be resented but must be borne, just as it is the right of the human king to deal arbitrarily with his own subjects. They take sides in human quarrels, and have their own particular favourites, which Penelope says in the *Odyssey* is the mark or right of 'godlike kings'. This right depends on no standard of abstract justice, but on the fact of power. Shame (*aidos*) inhibits the performance of actions which contravene the notion that *noblesse oblige*; therefore petty deceit or other undignified behaviour is avoided on the whole by gods and kings alike. Yet fraud is by no means alien to the divine nature. There is no stain involved when a god takes a mortal woman, for the kings too were accustomed to take whom they pleased from the lower orders.

All this makes for an external, rather than an internal or spiritual relationship between men and gods. Prophecy is of the 'sane' or technical kind, working by the rational interpretation of signs or omens, rather than the inspired or mantic sort, and sacrifice is usually offered in a bargaining spirit, to secure favours or avert displeasure. It is however a pleasant feature of Homeric life that every meal was also a sacrifice, in which the meat was dedicated to the gods with prayer and the ritual sprinkling of barley.

The favouritism of the gods has a historical explanation. The tendency of the Homeric poems is towards universality, and Zeus is already a universal god. But others had been cult-gods of certain localities, as Hera of Argos, or Athena of Athens, and this was not entirely forgotten. Each city and each prince had a divine protector, a reflection of the fact that in the Mycenaean age the goddess was a household goddess with her shrine in the palace of the prince whose patron she was.

The element of miraculous intervention by a god is even more prominent in the *Odyssey*, which is essentially a glorified folk-tale, than in the *Iliad*. Athena as the guardian deity of Odysseus is with him at every turn, and the two plot and plan together like a pair of conspirators. But the gods fulfil also a second purpose, and in conformity with the greater seriousness of the *Iliad*, this is more noticeable there. To have a guardian angel in battle was an obvious and pressing need for the Homeric hero. There was also another, arising out of the emotional and mental instability of these men, to which Nilsson has rightly drawn attention. They wept freely, were seized with unaccountable panic, suffered hallucinations, or gave way to blind fury. When they came to themselves, they would see they had committed an irreparable mistake or done some other action which they had no wish to do and every reason to wish undone. Obviously, as it seemed to the hero, he had not himself done this. Some god had taken his wits away, and the unaccountable action was the work of heaven. So the shade of Elpenor explains the fact that in Circe's house he got drunk and fell from the roof to his death. If second thoughts come in time to check the hasty action, then some watchful god has intervened. In his quarrel with Agamemnon, Achilles' mounting fury nearly gets the better of him, and he is actually drawing his sword from its scabbard to strike him down, but with an effort of self-control he checks himself. So we might express it, remembering, as he would himself, what fearful consequences would follow from the murder of the supreme commander of all the Achaean forces. But in Homer the incident is described in terms of one of the most vivid and personal encounters between a man and a goddess. It was Athena who, sent by Hera, persuaded him, in courteous terms and with promise of rich compensation, to stay his hand. This notion that the gods were responsible for much in human action, especially where the passions were involved, plays an important part in the evolution of Greek religious ideas, and was an obvious target for rationalist criticism, like that of Xenophanes. The critical spirit is already abroad in the *Odyssey*, where Zeus is made to say: 'How shameful, the way mortals lay blame upon the gods. They say that evils come from us, but it is they themselves who through the blindness of their own hearts have sorrows beyond their proper share.' Zeus is referring to Aegisthus, who went beyond his due, or allotted portion, in murdering Agamemnon and taking his wife. The commonest words for fate in Homer have, like the Moslem *kismet*, this root meaning of fair share or allotted portion. Where mortals are concerned, it may be possible to exceed this limit, as Aegisthus did, but it can only lead to misery. On other occasions, as with the 'portion' of death, man's destiny is fixed and will happen when the gods have decreed it. It is sometimes suggested that fate is a power superior to the gods themselves, but it seems rather to be the portion that they themselves have decreed as right. The passage about Sarpedon already quoted implies only that it would be unwise of Zeus to go back on a decision already made. Like other no less abstract notions, fate too was made by the Greeks into a divinity or divinities, and Moira, the Moirai, or Aisa could be spoken of either personally or otherwise. A considerable degree of fatalism concerning human affairs is common among people in whose lives war plays a large part. It can never be linked quite consistently with other notions to which the human mind is equally prone, and so it was in the Homeric epics.

The prevailing Homeric idea about the fate of the dead is based on the assumption, natural in a society given over to fighting, sport, and good living, that flesh and blood are the source of all good in life. Death is the separation of man's *psyche*, or life, from his body. Consequently, though it does not mean extinction, it leads to a feeble and colourless existence regarded with horror by the living. The *psyche* is strengthless and witless, it is compared to a bat, to smoke, to a dream, to a shadow or a phantom. It flits twittering to the dank, dark realm of Hades. If the due funeral rites, including the burning of the body, are neglected, it hovers even more unhappily between the two realms, importuning its relatives for the last rites and possibly even becoming malignant (as any spirit might be according to the older and more popular beliefs which those of the Achaean aristocracy have here temporarily overlaid). 'Leave me not unwept and unburied, lest I become for you a god-sent curse', says the shade of Elpenor to Odysseus, and the shade of Patroclus pleads pathetically with Achilles for the same privilege. Now he is barred from the realm of souls, but once his body is burned he will return no more.

In later Greek religion we often find the dead regarded as beings of great power for good or evil. Their wrath must be propitiated, and their aid or counsel may be invoked. From such belief arises the characteristic Greek practice of hero-worship. The dwelling of the dead is localized, each continuing to inhabit his tomb, where weapons and other necessities are buried for his use (as in Mycenaean graves) and liquid offerings are made which will reach him as they penetrate through the funnel-like vessels into which they are poured. These are widespread and primitive conceptions which are likely to have existed in an age far earlier than Homer's. They reappear with the passing of the somewhat artificial Homeric society, and traces of them survive in the epics themselves. In the *Odyssey* the spirit of the seer Tiresias is described as alone retaining the power of reason, by special grace of Persephone. Yet the detailed description of the rites of his invocation show knowledge of what must have been a well-established practice of necromancy. Again, the elaborate and costly rites performed at the funeral of Patroclus suggest a different belief about the soul from that which prevails in Homer, nor does the poet seem to understand or approve them. The mound heaped over the bones after cremation is intended as a memorial only, not a means of serving and nourishing the spirit with future offerings and rites. With the passing of the heroic age came the return of other, more universally human religious ideas, yet so great was the later influence of the prevailing Homeric view that the Greek always wished his natural beliefs to be reconciled with it as far as possible. So for example he dealt with the conception of Elysium or the Islands of the Blest, a pre-Homeric idea of posthumous bliss which the poet of the heroic age had modified into a continuation of bodily existence reserved for a few human relatives of the immortal gods (cf. p. 886 above).

## VI. THE OLYMPIAN GODS

The character of Zeus in Homer has already been briefly described. He is the august father of gods and men, whose word is law. His name, derived from an Indo-European root meaning to shine, connects him with the sky, though not only with the bright sky, and his powers as the weather-god are much in evidence. Being supreme, he tended to embrace an even wider sphere of influence, and his name might be attached to sea-god or underworld god, in spite of the original division of the universe between the three brothers. He presided over political and social institutions, and was guardian of such morality as his subjects observed, as is indicated by the epithets which they heaped upon him: Zeus of Fathers, of the Home, of the Storehouse, of Suppliants, of

Strangers, of the Oath, of the City, of the Brotherhood and so forth. In Homer the way is already prepared for the Zeus of Aeschylus and even of the Stoics.

To the Greeks, however, Zeus was not only the Indo-European sky-god of Homer, even when one has added to this figure all the attributes which sovereignty brought. The Homeric chieftains did not think of the immortal Father of all as ever having been a baby, yet not only was the birth of Zeus, as we have seen, a part of his mythology, but even his death. The tomb of Zeus, like his birth-place, was claimed by the Cretans, a claim which, in Greek eyes, gave colour to their traditional reputation for untruthfulness. The great god of the Greeks had come to a land which already possessed its own forms of worship and belief, connected not, like those of the invaders, with battle, honour, pride of birth and all the needs and standards of a society of knightly warriors, but rather with the problems of wresting a daily living from the soil and its products. The objects of this worship were in many places dis-possessed by Zeus, though this might only mean that the indi-genous spirit took the name of the conqueror but absorbed him without changing its own essential nature. Evidently the greatest of these Mediterranean cults was that of the ancient Cretan civilization, and the assimilation of Zeus to their god was the most thorough and the most universally recognized. As a fertility spirit he is imagined, after the story of his birth and miraculous nurture, chiefly as a youth (*kouros, koures*). So Zeus is invoked in Crete, and we see traces of the mystical element which is a natural accompaniment of fertility cults in the fact that a dance is per-formed by young men calling themselves *Kouroi* or *Kouretes* even while they summon Zeus as 'Greatest Kouros'. Worshippers and deity are assimilated just as in the mystic fertility-cult of Dionysus god and worshippers alike are *Bacchoi*. Stories of Zeus meta-morphosed into a bull also lead back to Crete and emphasize his character there as a god of fertility.

The youthfulness of the Cretan Zeus makes likely what analogy would in any case suggest, that this fertility-spirit was originally, like Attis or Adonis, the subordinate consort of a great nature-goddess. The evidence for the supremacy of such a goddess in prehistoric Crete we have already seen. Here as in other parts of Greece and the Near East she must have had her youthful and obsequious companion. The coming of the Greeks with their supreme male deity transformed this relationship into a solemn union of two great figures in which the male predominates, as Zeus over his official spouse, the goddess Hera of Argos, and others. In Crete, the home of mysteries, the older ideas resisted with more tenacity than elsewhere.

Hera to the Greeks was the one legitimate consort of Zeus, and the patron and guardian of marriage. She also presided over the life of women at its crises, which gave her a natural interest in fecundity. Nor was this interest confined to the fecundity of the human race, a limitation which would seem arbitrary and unnatural to the Greeks. Together with her patronage of childbearing and fertility, we may notice her passionate attachment to a particular locality. From the *Iliad* onwards she is 'Argive Hera' who loves above all cities the three in the Peloponnese, Argos, Mycenae and Sparta. Her famous cult on Samos was believed to have been founded from Argos. We cannot go far wrong in supposing her to have been originally a local form of the Earth-mother, though for the historical Greeks she was the Olympian wife of Zeus, and her chthonian associations had sunk into the background.

Poseidon, brother of Zeus, was to the historical Greeks god of the sea and of earthquakes, and has a connexion with horses exemplified by the title *Hippios*. There are various theories as to his origin, but he was most probably a deity introduced into Greece by the Greeks, with a Greek name meaning 'Husband (or Lord) of Earth'. If he was brought by immigrant speakers of Greek, it is unlikely that his character as a sea-god is original, since it was only after their settlement around the Aegean that the sea acquired the importance in their lives which the position of Poseidon suggests. If 'Husband of Earth' was his original name then he was a male fertility-spirit belonging not, like those whom we generally meet with in Greece, to the Mediterranean precursors of the Greeks, but to Indo-European lore. It is no wonder if his original nature was forgotten in the conditions under which the Hellenic tribes lived during and after their migrations.[1] His connexion with horses, and actual appearance in the form of a horse, could be part of a general character as fertility-spirit. The Arcadian story of his pursuit of Demeter in the form of a stallion points to this, and there is analogy outside Greece for the conception of river-spirits as horses. Perhaps however, as has been suggested, his equine nature goes back to a pastoral stage of the Greeks' existence, and his title belongs only to the time of the migrations, when the Greeks first encountered the Aegean earth-goddess and married Poseidon to her as they did Zeus.

[1] The name may however be a translation from some Near Eastern language: 'The Lord' was the common title for the consort of the Great Mother throughout Western Asia and the East Mediterranean littoral.

Apollo, son of Zeus and Leto, one of the 'younger gods', is a complex character, reflecting no doubt a complex origin. The multiplicity of suggested etymologies probably indicates that his name is not Greek, and in Homer he is on the side of the Trojans. There has been much dispute whether he came to the Greeks from the north or the east, but though in becoming a great and Panhellenic deity he seems to have absorbed, by historical times, other deities or religious elements of different origins, it is most likely that the Greeks first met him in Anatolia and that he had come there from more northerly parts of Asia. The mysterious Hyperboreans, with whom legend connects him so emphatically, have been traced with more likelihood to Northern Asia than to Northern Europe, and the Apolline type of prophecy, together with the character and magical journeys of his legendary followers like Aristeas and Abaris, strongly recall the shamanism of Siberia. The prominence of women in his cult, as priests and prophets, is a particular mark of Anatolian religion, and his epithet Lycius is most plausibly interpreted as 'Lycian'. The female element links him with Dionysus or Bacchus, god of Phrygia and Lydia, who shared his central shrine of Delphi and with whom he seems to have been on paradoxical terms of brotherhood and tension.

Pytho (Delphi) is mentioned but once in the *Iliad* as Apollo's shrine, and once in the *Odyssey* as the seat of his oracle. In Homer he is the archer-god, to whose shafts are attributed pestilence and death among men and beasts. There is a strangeness, or foreignness, about him, and an indefinable atmosphere of dread which sets him a little apart from the all-too-human company of Olympus. He is already Phoebus, the shining one, but this does not mean an identification with the sun, nor is it likely that the idea of Apollo as a solar deity, so firmly implanted in Greek mythology, is an old one.

His character in the eyes of the historic Greeks may be briefly described. They regarded him first and foremost as the embodiment of the Hellenic spirit. Though perhaps especially the god of the Dorians, his influence was Panhellenic and a powerful force for unity in Greece. All that marked off Greeks from barbarians —art, music, poetry, sanity and moderation, obedience to law— were summed up in Apollo, and he was the especial patron of youth. From Delphi he laid down, or ratified, the constitutions of cities, and advised on the foundation of colonies. Through the institution of *exegetai*, Delphic officials who resided in the various cities of which they were citizens, his oracle exercised considerable influence over the internal affairs of city-states, and like the oracle itself the *exegetai* could also advise in private matters.

In the sphere of law he dealt above all with cases of murder or homicide, and this was closely connected with the fact that he was the god of purification, who could rid a killer of the religious *miasma* in which his act had automatically involved him. Its removal necessitated the appeasement of the nether powers, carried out for example by the sacrifice of a pig, the animal peculiarly dedicated to the spirits of the underworld, and Apollo's authority in these matters links him to the chthonians and helps to explain his position as a bridge between them and the Olympian world. These underworld spirits, whether regarded as gods of fertility or the souls of dead heroes, contribute to Greek religion the elements of mystery and dread, of ecstasy and communion, which were lacking to the aristocratic gods of Homer. They were certainly older, and the tension between the two types of worship in the religion of post-Homeric Greece accounts for much of its peculiar character. Other features of Apolline religion to remind us of its non-Olympian side are the ecstatic or 'possessed' character of his prophecy, the literal *ekstasis* or separation of soul from body attributed to his legendary servants like Aristeas and Hermotimus, and the transmigration of souls, implied in the story of Aristeas who took the body of a raven, and prominent in the teaching of Pythagoras and his school whose god Apollo was. All this is by no means inconsistent with the evidence for his having been, in primitive times, a rural god of hunters, shepherds and farmers, interested in the growth of vegetation and having his own sacred trees.

Artemis, sister of Apollo, is in Homer an archer like her brother, patron of huntsmen, goddess of all wild things, the 'mistress of animals' who ranges the mountains with her nymphs 'rejoicing in boars and swift deer'. Her shafts, which bring death to women, are yet described as 'gentle', and sometimes prayed for. Her cult shows that the description 'mistress of animals' indicates her true character as goddess of all wild nature, of forests and lakes and the creatures in them, and with her un-Greek name she is clearly an example of the great nature-goddess who meets us all over the Aegean from prehistoric times. A characteristic of this goddess was her fertile motherhood, and in the cult of the many-breasted Artemis of Ephesus we see her original form. Such a figure was unsympathetic to the masculine and rational Greeks, and under their transforming genius Artemis actually became the embodiment of chastity. There are other signs, however, that the Huntress was not originally virgin. She had her young male attendant, as in the story of Hippolytus, and the Greeks seemed to see nothing improper in her, the devotee of chastity who punished with death any breach of it among her followers, being the assister of women in childbirth. Some of her nymphs, like Callisto in Arcadia, who had amorous adventures and became mothers, were originally the goddess herself, or related nature-goddesses whom she had supplanted. We have already noticed Dictynna and Britomartis of Crete in this connexion (pp. 870 f. above).

Athena, goddess of disciplined war and of wisdom, was born of Zeus without a mother, and was always, as Aeschylus makes her say, 'very much her father's daughter'. In the *Iliad* she is among the Olympians the most powerful champion of the Greeks. Her connexion with her own city of Athens is of immemorial antiquity. Her oldest temple was built over the palace of its Mycenaean ruler, and in Homer too she dwells in the house of its king, Erechtheus. Her sacred olive-tree and snake seem to take us back to the religion of Minoan Crete. The legend of Erichthonius, the early king sometimes identified with Erechtheus, tells how he was born not from a mortal mother but direct from Mother Earth, who gave him into Athena's keeping. Thus she was first and foremost Polias, the keeper of the citadel, not only at Athens but in other *poleis* too, whither her worship spread and where she ousted local divine protectors and took their names, or the names of their cities, as epithets: Alalcomeneis, Alea, or Itonia. From Homer onwards she was the patron of skilled handicrafts, of potters, weavers and metal-workers, and as her own city developed into the School of Hellas she became the representative of *sophia*—philosophy and science—in general.

Hermes occupies a minor position on Olympus, as servant and messenger of Zeus, but to men he is all the more approachable for that, and has indeed a curiously likeable and friendly nature. He is never violent, but will appear unobtrusively to help the wayfarer and advise the simple, for his strong point is his cleverness. He was indeed, from the day of his birth which he marked by inventing the lyre and stealing Apollo's cattle, a clever rogue and the patron of thieves, but there is no malice in him. A piece of luck was a gift from Hermes. He is god of shepherds, but equally of the market place. The derivation of his name from *herma* (a cairn), deemed 'transparent' by Nilsson, seems discredited by the absence of digamma in Homer and early Greek Cretan inscriptions, and also on the Mycenaean tablets if his name there has been correctly identified.[1] Yet his connexion with the cairns, supporting an upright stone, which served the Greeks as guide-post, boundary mark or wayside grave, is strong. He preserved throughout historic times his aniconic or semi-human shape, a simple pillar called by his name with no more than head and phallus to suggest the god. Such Herms were set up outside houses to protect property. His function of conducting souls on their last journey probably arose out of his general character as guide.

Ares, though recognized as a member of the Olympic circle and indeed the son of Zeus and Hera, appears in Homer as an unsympathetic figure, disliked by his father, which, in conjunction with his constant association with Thrace, may indicate a foreign origin. Enyalius, a second name for him from Homer onwards, occurs on a Mycenaean tablet.[2] Unlike Athena, who represents a different aspect of war, he is blustering, brutal and even cowardly. In later times he has little importance either in myth or cult. The story of his intrigue with Aphrodite, though there is evidence of a cult-connexion between them, is used by Homer simply as the vehicle for a burst of Homeric laughter.

Aphrodite has been made by Homer into all that one would desire a goddess of love to be. She is of unmatched beauty, golden, laughter-loving, giver of beauty and desirability to mortals. He knows nothing of Hesiod's barbarous tale of her birth from the severed genitals of Uranus, but calls her daughter of Zeus by Dione. This Dione was a somewhat shadowy consort worshipped with Zeus at his ancient sanctuary of Dodona. Her name is simply a feminine doublet of Zeus-Dios itself, and though she probably ousted a pre-Greek earth-goddess at Dodona, she became completely overshadowed by Hera. By this adoption Aphrodite, the mistress of the Syrian Adonis, who owes most of her character to oriental sources, was given the Greek pedigree fitting for one whom the poet thought worthy of inclusion among the Olympian family. Her ancient cult on Cyprus, which gave her her second title, was certainly not Greek, and the Greeks evidently adopted and adapted in her one of the mother-goddesses worshipped under different names all over the nearer parts of Asia. Like Ares and even Artemis, she seems to stand on a lower plane of dignity than the greatest Olympians, an indication, perhaps, that none of them really 'belong'. Like them also she favours the Trojan side in the war.

[1] §II, 16, 126 and 288.    [2] KN V 52.

Hephaestus, god of fire, is god also of all the advances in material civilization which the use of fire made possible. He is the divine smith, mighty of arm but lame of leg, who at his forge on Olympus fashions miraculous as well as more ordinary objects: statues and tripods which move about of themselves, armour which no weapon can pierce. At Athens, where his cult was an ancient one, he was naturally associated with Athena, goddess of handicraft, and worshipped assiduously by the large manufacturing population. In Homer he is the legitimate husband of Aphrodite, and the relations of this ill-assorted pair form the climax of that comic relief which the poet provides, with no apparent sense of incongruity, from the divine rather than the human element in his story. He is a minor figure in Greek religion, probably another foreigner from the east, whose cult spread westwards from Lycia, thence to the islands and in particular to Lemnos. Homer tells the story of how this unfortunate divinity landed on Lemnos at the end of a whole day's fall, when Zeus had thrown him from Olympus for interfering in a quarrel between himself and Hera.

From this brief sketch of the most important of the Olympian gods of Homer we may see what an extraordinary feat the epic tradition accomplished in welding into a single family of deities, with clear-cut human characters, a strange collection of divine beings of widely diverse origins and nature. The achievement may appear to be poetic and literary rather than religious, and if the Homeric poems stood by themselves it might be possible so to characterize it. Its religious aspect was, however, taken with great seriousness by the later Greeks, and for that reason the religion of Homer must be regarded as, for good or ill, one of the most influential elements in Greek religion as a whole.

# BIBLIOGRAPHY

## ABBREVIATIONS

*Abh. Berlin (München etc.).*   *Abhandlungen der Preussischen (Bayerischen etc.) Akademie der Wissenschaften, Phil.-hist. Klasse*

*Abh. D.O.G.*   *Abhandlungen der Deutschen Orient-Gesellschaft*

*A.Bo.T.*   *Ankara Arkeoloji Müzesinde bulunan Boğazköy Tabletleri*

*Acta Arch.*   *Acta Archaeologica*

*Acta Or.*   *Acta Orientalia*

*Ägyptol. Abh.*   *Ägyptologische Abhandlung*

*Ägyptol. Forsch.*   *Ägyptologische Forschungen*

*A.I.A.R.S.*   *Acta Instituti Atheniensis Regni Sueciae*

*A.I.R.R.S.*   *Acta Instituti Romani Regni Sueciae*

*A.J.*   *Antiquaries Journal*

*A.J.A.*   *American Journal of Archaeology*

*A.J.Ph.*   *American Journal of Philology*

*A.J.S.L.*   *American Journal of Semitic Languages and Literatures*

*Alte Or.*   *Der Alte Orient*

*Altor. Forsch.*   *Altorientalische Forschungen*

*A.M.*   *Annales du Midi*

*A.M.I.*   *Archäologische Mitteilungen aus Iran*

*An. Or.*   *Analecta Orientalia*

*A.N.E.T.*   *Ancient Near Eastern Texts relating to the Old Testament*

*Ann. Arch. Anthr.*   *Annals of Archaeology and Anthropology* (Liverpool)

*Ann. Arch. de Syrie.*   *Annales Archéologiques de Syrie*

*Ann. A.S.O.R.*   *Annual of the American Schools of Oriental Research*

*Ann. Inst. philol. hist. or.* (et slaves).   *Annuaire de l'Institut de philologie et d'histoire orientales (et slaves)*

*Ann. Mus. Guimet.*   *Annales du Musée Guimet*

*Ann. Serv.*   *Annales du Service des Antiquités de l'Égypte*

*Ann. Univ. Ferrara.*   *Annali della Università di Ferrara*

*Antiq.*   *Antiquity*

*A.O.B.*   *Altorientalische Bibliothek*

*A.O.S.*   *American Oriental Series/Society*

*Arch. Anz.*   *Archaeologischer Anzeiger.* Beiblatt zum *Jahrbuch des deutschen archäologischen Instituts*

*Arch. de l'Institut de Pal. hum.*   *Archives de l'Institut de Paléontologie humaine*

*Arch. Delt.*   Ἀρχαιολογικὸν Δελτίον

*Arch. Eph.* (Ἀρχ. Ἐφ.).   Ἀρχαιολογικὴ Ἐφημερίς

*Arch. f. Keil.*   *Archiv für Keilschriftforschung*

*Arch. f. Or.*   *Archiv für Orientforschung*

*Arch. f. Rel.*   *Archiv für Religionswissenschaft*

*Arch. Orient.*   *Archiv Orientální*

*Arh. Radovi i Rasprave.*   *Arheologiski radovi i rasprave*

*Arkæol. Kunsthist. Medd. Dan. Vid. Selsk.*   *Kongelige Danske Videnskabernes Selskab, Arkæologisk-kunsthistoriske Meddelelser*

*A.R.M.T.*   *Archives royales de Mari* (translation vols.)

*A.S.A.A.* *Annuario della Scuola archeologica di Atene e delle Missioni italiane in Oriente*

*A. St.* *Anatolian Studies*

*Ath. Mitt.* *Athenische Mitteilungen, Mitteilungen des deutschen archäologischen Instituts, Athenische Abteilung*

*Atti Accad. Lincei.* *Atti della Accademia nazionale dei Lincei*

*Austr. Bibl. Rev.* *Australian Biblical Review*

*B.A.* *Beiträge zur Assyriologie*

*B.C.H.* *Bulletin de correspondance hellénique*

*B.E.* *Babylonian Expedition of the University of Pennsylvania*

*Beitr. z. Hist. Theol.* *Beiträge zur historischen Theologie*

*Beitr. zur Wiss. vom A. (u. N.) T.* *Beiträge zur Wissenschaft vom Alten (und Neuen) Testament*

*Bi. Ar.* *Biblical Archaeologist*

*Bib.* *Biblica*

*Bibl. Aeg.* *Bibliotheca Aegyptiaca*

*Bibl. arch. et hist.* *Bibliothèque archéologique et historique*

*B.I.C.S.* *Bulletin of the Institute of Classical Studies of the University of London*

*Bi. Or.* *Bibliotheca Orientalis*

*Bol. de la Soc. Esp. de Excursiones.* *Boletín de la Sociedad Española de Excursiones*

*Boll. d'Arte.* *Bollettino d'Arte*

*Boll. della Soc. Geog. Ital.* *Bollettino della Società Geografica Italiana*

*Boll. di Paletn. Ital.* *Bollettino di Paletnologia Italiana*

*Bo. Stu.* *Boghazköi-Studien*

*Brooklyn Mus. Annual* *Brooklyn Museum Annual*

*B.S.A.* *Annual of the British School of Archaeology at Athens*

*Bull. Amer. Inst. for Persian Art and Arch.* *Bulletin of the American Institute for Persian Art and Archaeology*

*Bull. A.S.O.R.* *Bulletin of the American Schools of Oriental Research*

*Bull. Hist. Med.* *Bulletin of the History of Medicine*

*Bull. Inst. Archaeol. London.* *Bulletin of the Institute of Archaeology, University of London*

*Bull. Inst. d'Ég.* *Bulletin de l'Institut d'Égypte*

*Bull. M.M.A.* *Bulletin of the Metropolitan Museum of Art* (New York)

*Bull. Ryl. Libr.* *Bulletin of the John Rylands Library* (Manchester)

*Bull. S.A.J.* *British School of Archaeology in Jerusalem. Bulletin*

*Bull. S.O.A.S.* *Bulletin of the School of Oriental and African Studies*

*Bull. Soc. fr. Égyptol.* *Bulletin de la Société française d'Égyptologie*

*Bull. Soc. Ling.* *Bulletin de la Société de linguistique de Paris*

*Bull. Soc. préh. fr.* *Bulletin de la Société préhistorique française*

*Bull. Univ. Mus. Penna.* *Bulletin of the University Museum, University of Pennsylvania*

*C.A.H.* *Cambridge Ancient History*

*Cah. Ar. B.* *Cahiers d'archéologie biblique*

*Cah. H.M.* *Cahiers d'histoire mondiale* (cf. *J.W.H.*)

*Cath. Bibl. Quart.* *Catholic Biblical Quarterly*

*C.C.G.* *Cairo Museum, Catalogue général des antiquités égyptiennes*

*Chron. d'Ég.* *Chronique d'Égypte*

*Cl. Phil.* *Classical Philology*

*Cl. Quart.* *Classical Quarterly*

*Cl. Rev.* *Classical Review*

*C.-R. Ac. Inscr. B.-L.*   *Comptes-Rendus de l'Académie des Inscriptions et Belles-Lettres*

*Denk. k. Akad. Wiss. Wien.*   *Denkschriften des kaiserlichen Akademie der Wissenschaften in Wien*

*D.L.Z.*   *Deutsche Literaturzeitung*

*Eph. Arch.*   'Εφημερὶς 'Αρχαιολογική

*E.E.S.*   *Egypt Exploration Society*

*Flles Inst. fr. Caire.*   *Fouilles de l'Institut français du Caire*

*Forsch. Rel. Lit.*   *Forschungen zur Religion und Literatur des Alten und Neuen Testaments*

*Forsch. u. Fortschr.*   *Forschungen und Fortschritte*

*G.J.*   *Geographical Journal*

*G.R.B.S.*   *Greek, Roman and Byzantine Studies, Duke University, Durham, N.C.*

*Harv. Stud. Class. Phil.*   *Harvard Studies in Classical Philology*

*H.U.C.A.*   *Hebrew Union College Annual*

*I.E.J.*   *Israel Exploration Journal*

*Ill. Ldn News.*   *Illustrated London News*

*Indogerm. Forsch.*   *Indogermanische Forschungen*

*Ist. Mitt.*   *Istanbuler Mitteilungen, Deutsches archäologisches Institut, Abteilung Istanbul*

*J.A.*   *Journal asiatique*

*Jahrb. f. Cl. Ph.*   *Jahrbuch für classische Philologie*

*J.A.O.S.*   *Journal of the American Oriental Society*

*J.A.R.C.E.*   *Journal of the American Research Center in Egypt*

*J. Bibl. Lit.*   *Journal of Biblical Literature and Exegesis*

*J.C.S.*   *Journal of Cuneiform Studies*

*J.D.A.I.*   *Jahrbuch des deutschen archäologischen Instituts*

*J.E.A.*   *Journal of Egyptian Archaeology*

*J.E.O.L.*   *Jaarbericht van het Vooraziatisch-Egyptisch Genootschap, 'Ex Oriente Lux'*

*J.E.S.H.O.*   *Journal of the Economic and Social History of the Orient*

*J.H.S.*   *Journal of Hellenic Studies*

*J.K.F.*   *Jahrbuch für Kleinasiatische Forschung*

*J.K.P.K.*   *Jahrbuch der königlich-preussischen Kunstammlungen*

*J.N.E.S.*   *Journal of Near Eastern Studies*

*J.P.O.S.*   *Journal of the Palestine Oriental Society*

*J.R.A.S.*   *Journal of the Royal Asiatic Society*

*J.S.S.*   *Journal of Semitic Studies*

*J.T.S.*   *Journal of Theological Studies*

*J.W.H.*   *Journal of World History* (cf. *Cah. H.M.*)

*K. Bo.*   *Keilschrifttexte aus Boghazköi*

*K.F.*   *Kleinasiatische Forschungen*

*K.U.B.*   *Keilschrifturkunden aus Boghazköi*

*M.A.O.G.*   *Mitteilungen der Altorientalischen Gesellschaft*

*M.D.O.G.*   *Mitteilungen der Deutschen Orient-Gesellschaft*

*Mél. Bibl. A. Robert.*   *Mélanges bibliques rédigés en honneur de A. Robert*

*Mél. Dussaud.*   *Mélanges Syriens offerts à M. R. Dussaud*

*Mél. Maspero.*   *Mélanges Maspero* (Mem. Inst. fr. Caire 66–8)

*Mém. Ac. Inscr. B.-L.*   *Mémoires de l'Académie des Inscriptions et Belles-Lettres*

*Mém. D.P.*   *Mémoires de la Délégation en Perse*

*Mém. Inst. fr. Caire.*   *Mémoires publiés par les membres de l'Institut français d'archéologie orientale du Caire*

*Mém. Miss. fr. Caire.* *Mémoires publiés par les membres de la Mission archéologique française au Caire*

*Mem. Mus. Civ. St. Nat. Ven. Trident.* *Memorie del Museo di Storia Naturale della Venezia Tridentina*

*Misc. Ac. Berolinensia.* *Miscellanea Academica Berolinensia*

*Mitt. deutsch. Inst. Kairo.* *Mitteilungen des deutschen Instituts für ägyptische Altertumskunde in Kairo*

*Mitt. Inst. Or.* *Mitteilungen des Instituts für Orientforschung*

*M.M.A.* *Metropolitan Museum of Art* (New York)

*Mus. Helv.* *Museum Helveticum*

*M.U.S.J.* *Mélanges de l'Université St-Joseph, Beyrouth*

*M.V.Ae.G.* *Mitteilungen der vorderasiatisch-ägyptischen Gesellschaft*

*Nachr. Göttingen.* *Nachrichten von der Gesellschaft der Wissenschaften zu Göttingen, Phil.-hist. Klasse*

*N.C.* *La Nouvelle Clio*

*Nederl. Theol. Tijdschrift.* *Nederlands Theologisch Tijdschrift*

*Num. Chron.* *Numismatic Chronicle*

*O.I.C.* *Oriental Institute Communications*

*O.I.P.* *Oriental Institute Publications*

*Ö.J.H.* *Österreichische Jahreshefte*

*O.L.Z.* *Orientalistische Literaturzeitung*

*Op. Arch.* *Opuscula Archaeologica, Acta Instituti Romani Regni Sueciae*

*Op. Ath.* *Opuscula Atheniensia, Acta Instituti Atheniensis Regni Sueciae*

*Or.* *Orientalia*

*Or. antiq.* *Oriens antiquus*

*Or. Suecana.* *Orientalia Suecana*

*P.A.E.* Πρακτικὰ τῆς Ἀρχαιολογικῆς Ἑταιρείας

*P.B.S.* *Publications of the Babylonian Section, The University Museum, University of Pennsylvania*

*P.E.F.* *Quarterly Statement of the Palestine Exploration Fund*

*P.E.Q.* *Palestine Exploration Quarterly*

*P.J.B.* *Palästina Jahrbuch*

*P.P.S.* *Proceedings of the Prehistoric Society*

*Prähist. Zeitschr.* *Prähistorische Zeitschrift*

*Proc. Amer. Philos. Soc.* *Proceedings of the American Philosophical Society*

*Proc. Brit. Acad.* *Proceedings of the British Academy*

*Proc. Camb. Philol. Soc.* *Proceedings of the Cambridge Philological Society*

*P.W.* *Pauly-Wissowa-Kroll-Mittelhaus, Real-Encyclopädie der classischen Altertumswissenschaft*

*Q.D.A.P.* *Quarterly of the Department of Antiquities of Palestine*

*R.A.* *Revue d'assyriologie et d'archéologie orientale*

*R.D.A.C.* *Report of the Department of Antiquities, Cyprus*

*Rec. trav.* *Recueil de travaux relatifs à la philologie et à l'archéologie égyptiennes et assyriennes*

*Rend. Acc. Napoli* *Rendiconti Accademia Napoli*

*Rev. anth.* *Revue anthropologique*

*Rev. arch.* *Revue archéologique*

*Rev. bibl.* *Revue biblique*

*Rev. de Guimarães.* *Revista de Guimarães*

*Rev. d'égyptol.* *Revue d'égyptologie*

*Rev. des Arts.* *Revue des Arts*

*Rev. d'hist. et philos. relig.* *Revue d'histoire et de philosophie religieuses*

*Rev. ét. anc.*    *Revue des études anciennes*

*Rev. ét. lig.*    *Revue des études ligures*

*Rev. hist.*    *Revue historique*

*Rev. hist. rel.*    *Revue de l'histoire des religions*

*Revue arch. de l'Est et du Centre-Est.*    *Revue archéologique de l'Est et du Centre-Est*

*R.H.A.*    *Revue hittite et asianique*

*Riv. Arch. Comense.*    *Rivista archeologica dell'antica provincia e diocesi di Como*

*Riv. di Scienze Preistoriche.*    *Rivista di Scienze Preistoriche*

*Riv. stud. or.*    *Rivista degli studi orientali*

*R.L.A.*    *Reallexikon der Assyriologie*

*S.A.O.C.*    *Studies in Ancient Oriental Civilization, Oriental Institute of the University of Chicago*

*Sitzungsb. Berlin (München etc.).*    *Sitzungsberichte der Preussischen (Bayerischen etc.) Akademie der Wissenschaften*

*Theol. Rundschau.*    *Theologische Rundschau*

*Theol. St. Kr.*    *Theologische Studien und Kritiken*

*Theol. Stud.*    *Theological Studies*

*Theol. Zeitschr.*    *Theologische Zeitschrift*

*T.L.Z.*    *Theologische Literaturzeitung*

*Trans. Amer. Philos. Soc.*    *Transactions of the American Philosophical Society*

*Türk. Hist. Gesell. Veröff.*    *Veröffentlichungen der Türkischen Historischen Gesellschaft*

*U.E.*    *Ur Excavations*

*U.E.T.*    *Ur Excavations: Texts*

*Unters.*    *Untersuchungen zur Geschichte und Altertumskunde Ägyptens*

*Urk.*    *Urkunden des ägyptischen Altertums*

*V.A.B.*    *Vorderasiatische Bibliothek*

*V.T.*    *Vetus Testamentum*

*We. Or.*    *Die Welt des Orients*

*Westminster Theol. Journ.*    *Westminster Theological Journal*

*Wien. St.*    *Wiener Studien*

*Wiss. Zeitschr. Halle.*    *Wissenschaftliche Zeitschrift der Martin-Luther-Universität, Halle-Wittenberg*

*W.V.D.O.G.*    *Wissenschaftliche Veröffentlichungen der Deutschen Orient-Gesellschaft*

*W.Z.K.M.*    *Wiener Zeitschrift für die Kunde des Morgenlandes*

*Y.O.S.*    *Yale Oriental Series*

*Z.A.*    *Zeitschrift für Assyriologie und vorderasiatische Archäologie*

*Z.Ä.S.*    *Zeitschrift für ägyptische Sprache und Altertumskunde*

*Z.A.W.*    *Zeitschrift für alttestamentliche Wissenschaft*

*Z.D.M.G.*    *Zeitschrift der Deutschen Morgenländischen Gesellschaft*

*Z.D.P.V.*    *Zeitschrift des Deutschen Palästina-Vereins*

*Z.E.*    *Zeitschrift für Ethnologie*

*Z. f. Kirchl. Wiss. u. Kirchl. Leben.*    *Zeitschrift für Kirchliche Wissenschaft und Kirchliches Leben*

*Z. f. Theol u. Kirche.*    *Zeitschrift für Theologie und Kirche*

# BIBLIOGRAPHY

## CHAPTER XVII

### G. GENERAL

#### *Texts*

1. Berlin, Staatliche Museen, Vorderasiatische Abteilung. *Keilschrifturkunden aus Boghazköi* (*K.U.B.*), I–XXXII. Berlin, 1921–42.
2. British Museum. *Hittite Texts in the Cuneiform Character from Tablets in the British Museum* (*H.T.*). London, 1920.
3. Deutsche Akademie der Wissenschaften zu Berlin, Institut für Orientforschung. *Keilschrifturkunden aus Boghazköi* (*K.U.B.*), XXXV–XXXVII, XXXIX. Berlin, 1953–55, 1963.
4. Deutsche Orient-Gesellschaft. *Keilschrifttexte aus Boghazköi* (*K.Bo.*): I–IV = *Wissenschaftliche Veröffentlichung* 30. Leipzig, 1916–23; V–VI = idem 36, Leipzig, 1921; VII–XII, XIV = idem 68–70, 72, 73, 77, 79, Berlin, 1954–63.
5. Deutsche Orient-Gesellschaft zu Berlin. *Keilschrifturkunden aus Boghazköi* (*K.U.B.*), XXXIII–XXXIV. Berlin, 1943–4.
6. Götze, A. *Verstreute Boghazköi-Texte* (*V.Bo.T.*). Marburg/Lahn, 1930.
7. Laroche, E. 'Fragments Hittites de Genève' (F.H.G.). In *R.A.* 45 (1951), 131 ff.; 184 ff.; *R.A.* 46 (1952), 42 ff.
8. T(ürk) C(umhuriyet) Maarif Vekilliği. Antikite ve Müzeler Müdürlüğü Yayınlarından Seri III Sayı 1. *Istanbul Arkeoloji Müzelerinde Bulunan Boğazköy Tabletlerinden Seçme Metinler* (*I.Bo.T.* 1). Istanbul, 1944.
9. T(ürk) C(umhuriyet) Milli Eğitim Bakanlığı, Eski Eserler ve Müzeler Genel Müdürlüğü Yayınlarından Seri III Sayı 2: *Istanbul Arkeoloji Müzelerinde Bulunan Boğazköy Tabletleri* II (*Boğazköy-Tafeln im Archäologischen Museum zu Istanbul*, II) (*I.Bo.T.* II). Istanbul, 1947.
10. T(ürk) C(umhuriyet) Maarif Vekâleti, Eski Eserler ve Müzeler Genel Müdürlüğü Yayınlarından Seri III Sayı 5: *Istanbul Arkeoloji Müzelerinde Bulunan Boğazköy Tabletleri*, III (*Boğazköy-Tafeln im Archäologischen Museum zu Istanbul*, III) (*I.Bo.T.* III). Istanbul, 1954.
11. T(ürk) C(umhuriyet) Milli Eğitim Bakanlığı. Eski Eserler ve Müzeler Genel Müdürlüğü Yayınlarından Seri III Sayı 3: *Ankara Arkeoloji Müzesinde Bulunan Boğazköy Tabletleri* (*Boğazköy-Tafeln im Archäologischen Museum zu Ankara*) (*A.Bo.T.*). Istanbul, 1948.
12. Knudtzon, J. A. *Die El-Amarna-Tafeln* (*Vorderasiatische Bibliothek*, 2). 2 vols. Leipzig, 1915.
13. Mercer, S. A. B. *The Tell El-Amarna Tablets*. 2 vols. Toronto, 1939.
14. Thureau-Dangin, F. 'Nouvelles lettres d'El-Amarna.' In *R.A.* 19 (1921), 91 ff.
15. Nougayrol, J. *Textes accadiens des Archives Sud* (*Le palais royal d'Ugarit*, IV = *Mission de Ras Shamra*, IX). Paris, 1956.
16. Schaeffer, C. F. A. (and others). *Ugaritica*, III (*Mission de Ras Shamra*, VIII). Paris, 1956.
17. Breasted, J. A. *Ancient Records of Egypt*. 5 vols. Chicago, 1906.
18. Pritchard, J. B. (ed.). *Ancient Near Eastern Texts Relating to the Old Testament*. Ed. 2. Princeton, 1955.

### History

19. Bilabel, F. *Geschichte Vorderasiens und Ägyptens.* I. Band: *16.–11. Jahrh. v. Chr.* Heidelberg, 1927.
20. Cavaignac, E. *Histoire général de l'antiquité.* Paris, 1946.
21. Götze, A. *Das Hethiter-Reich* (*Alte Or.* 27/2). Leipzig, 1928.
22. Goetze, A. *Kleinasien* (*Kulturgeschichte des Alten Orients*, III, 1, im *Handbuch der Altertumswissenschaft*). 2. Auflage. München, 1957.
23. Goetze, A. 'On the Chronology of the Second Millennium B.C.' In *J.C.S.* 11 (1957), 53 ff., 63 ff.
24. Gurney, O. R. *The Hittites* (Pelican Book A259). Ed. 2. Harmondsworth, 1962.
25. Helck, W. *Die Beziehungen Ägyptens zu Vorderasien im 3. und 2. Jahrtausend v. Chr.* (*Ägyptol. Abh.*, 5). Wiesbaden, 1962.
26. Liverani, M. *Storia di Ugarit nell'età degli archivi politici* (*Studi Semitici*, 6). Roma, 1962.
27. Scharff, A. and Moortgat, A. *Ägypten und Vorderasien im Altertum.* 2. Auflage, München, 1959.
28. Schmökel, a. *Geschichte des Alten Vorderasien* (*Handbuch der Orientalistik*, II, 3). Leiden, 1957.

### I. MITANNIANS AND HITTITES—TUSHRATTA AND SHUPPILULIUMASH

1. Cavaignac, E. *Subbiluliuma et son temps.* Paris, 1932.
2. Cavaignac, E. 'L'Égypte et les Hittites de 1370 à 1345.' In *Syria*, 33 (1956), 42 ff.
3. Götze, A. 'Die historische Einleitung des Aleppo-Vertrages (*K.Bo.* I, 6).' In *M.A.O.G.* IV (Meissner Festschrift) (1928), 59 ff.
4. Goetze, A. *Kizzuwatna and the Problem of Hittite Geography* (*Y.O.S.* Researches, vol. 22). New Haven, Conn., 1940.
5. Kitchen, K. A. *Suppiluliuma and the Amarna Pharaohs* (*Liverpool Monographs in Archaeology and Oriental Studies*). Liverpool, 1962.
6. Klengel, H. 'Der Schiedsspruch des Muršili II. hinsichtlich Barga und seine Übereinkunft mit Duppi-Tešup von Amurru (*K.Bo.* III, 3).' In *Or.* n.s. 32 (1963), 32 ff.
7. Klengel, H. 'Aziru of Amurru and his Position in the History of the Amārna Age.' In *Mitt. Inst. Or.* 10 (1964), 57 ff.
8. Weidner, E. F. *Politische Dokumente aus Kleinasien* (*Bo.Stu.* 8/9). Leipzig, 1923.
9. Wiseman, D. J. *The Alalakh Tablets* (*Occasional Publications of the British Institute of Archaeology at Ankara*, 2). London, 1953.

### II. FIRST SYRIAN WAR OF SHUPPILULIUMASH

1. Forrer, E. 'The Hittites in Palestine.' In *P.E.Q.* 68 (1936), 190 ff.; 69 (1937), 100 ff.
2. Freydank, H. 'Eine hethitische Fassung des Vertrags zwischen dem Hethiterkönig Šuppiluliuma und Aziru von Amurru.' In *Mitt. Inst. Or.* 7 (1960), 356 ff.
3. Friedrich, J. *Staatsverträge des Ḫatti-Reiches in hethitischer Sprache.* 2 vols. (*M.V.Ae.G.* 31 and 34/1). Leipzig, 1926 and 1930.
4. Götze, A. 'Šuppiluliumas syrische Feldzüge.' In *Klio*, 19 (1924), 347 ff.

5. Götze, A. 'Die Pestgebete des Muršiliš.' In *K.F.* 1 (1929), 161 ff.
6. Güterbock, H. G. *Siegel aus Boğazköy* (*Arch. f. Or.*, Beihefte 5 and 7). Berlin, 1940 and 1942.
7. Güterbock, H. G. 'The Deeds of Suppiluliuma as told by his Son, Mursili II.' In *J.C.S.* 10 (1956), 41 ff., 107 ff.
8. Güterbock, H. G. 'Mursili's Accounts of Suppiluliuma's dealings with Egypt.' In *R.H.A.*, 18 (fasc. 66–67) (1960), 57 ff.
9. Houwink ten Cate, Ph. 'The Date of the Kurustama Treaty.' In *Bi. Or.* 20 (1963), 274.
10. Malamat, A. 'Doctrines of Causality....' In *V.T.* 5 (1955), 1 ff.
11. Virolleaud, Ch. 'Niqmad et Suppiluliuma.' In *Syria*, 21 (1940), 260 ff.

### III. SECOND SYRIAN WAR OF SHUPPILULIUMASH

1. Eissfeldt, O. 'Zu den Urkunden über den Tribut Niqmad's, Königs von Ugarit, an den hethitischen Grosskönig Schuppiluluma.' In *Festschrift Bertholet* (1950), 147 ff.
2. Friedrich, J. 'Šuppiluluma von Ḫatti und Nqmd von Ugarit.' In *Z.D.M.G.* 96 (1942), 471 ff.
3. Sturm, J. 'Zur Datierung der El-Amarna-Briefe.' In *Klio*, 26 (1932), 1 ff.

### IV. THE HURRIAN WAR OF SHUPPILULIUMASH

1. Cavaignac, E. 'La lettre 101 de Tell el-Amarna.' In *J.A.* 243 (1955), 135 ff.
2. Edel, E. 'Neue keilschriftliche Umschreibungen ägyptischer Namen aus den Boğazköy-Texten.' In *J.N.E.S.* 7 (1948), 11 ff.
3. Federn, W. 'Daḫamunzu KBo V 6 iii 8.' In *J.C.S.* 14 (1960), 33.
4. Forrer, E. *Forschungen.* 1/1, 1/2, 11/1. Erkner bei Berlin, 1926–9.
5. Friedrich, J. 'Ein Bruchstück des Vertrages Mattiwaza-Šuppiluluma in hethitischer Sprache.' In *Arch. f. Keil.* 2 (1924/5), 119 ff.
6. Smith, Sidney. 'Amarna Letter 170 and Chronology.' In *Halil Edhem Hâtira Kitabi* (1947), 33 ff.
7. Sturm, J. 'Wer ist Pipḫururiaš?' In *R.H.A.* 4 (fasc. 13) (1933), 161 ff.
8. Vergote, J. *Toutankhamon dans les archives hittites* (*Uitgaven van het Nederlands Hist.-Arch. Instituut te Istanbul*, XII, 1961).

## CHAPTER XVIII

### G. GENERAL

1. Balkan, K. *Kassitenstudien I: Die Sprache der Kassiten.* New Haven, 1945.
2. Bilabel, F. *Geschichte Vorderasiens und Ägyptens vom 16–11 Jahrhundert v. Chr.* Heidelberg, 1927.
3. Borger, R. *Einleitung in die assyrischen Königsinschriften: Erster Teil, Das zweite Jahrtausend v. Chr.* Leiden/Köln, 1961.
4. Budge, E. A. W. and King, L. W. *Annals of the Kings of Assyria*, vol. 1. London, 1902.
5. *C.A.D. The Assyrian Dictionary.* Chicago, 1956–.
6. Contenau, G. *Manuel d'Archéologie Orientale.* Paris, 1927–47.
7. *C.T. Cuneiform Texts . . . in the British Museum.* London, 1896–.

8. Ebeling, E., Meissner, B. and Weidner, E. F. *Die Inschriften der altassyrischen Könige*. Leipzig, 1926.
9. Ebeling, E., Meissner, B. and Weidner, E. F. (eds.). *Reallexikon der Assyriologie*, I–III–. Berlin and Leipzig, 1932–.
10. El-Wailly, F. 'Synopsis of Royal Sources of the Kassite Period.' In *Sumer*, 10 (1954), 43 ff.
11. Frankfort, H. *Cylinder Seals*. London, 1939.
12. Frankfort, H. *The Art and Architecture of the Ancient Orient*. Harmondsworth, 1954.
13. Gadd, C. J. and Legrain, L. *Royal Inscriptions* (*U.E.T.* 1). London and Philadelphia, 1928.
14. Gelb, I. J. *Hurrians and Subarians* (*S.A.O.C.* 22). Chicago, 1944.
15. Gelb, I. J. 'New light on Hurrians and Subarians.' In *Studi orientalistici in onore di Giorgio Levi della Vida*, 1 (Rome, 1956), 378 ff.
16. Gelb, I. J. *Old Akkadian Writing and Grammar*, Ed. 2. Chicago, 1961.
17. Jordan, J., Lenzen, H. and others. *Vorläufige Berichte über die . . . in Uruk-Warka . . . Ausgrabungen*, I–XX. In *Abh. Berlin*, 1930–40; *Abh. D.O.G.* 1956–60; *Deutsches Archäologisches Institut: Abteil. Baghdad*, 1962–64.
18. King, L. W. *Chronicles concerning Early Babylonian Kings*, 2 vols. London, 1907.
19. King, L. W. *History of Babylon*. London, 1915.
20. Knudtzon, J. A. *Die el-Amarna Tafeln*. Leipzig, 1915.
21. Kramer, S. N. *The Sumerians; Their History, Culture, and Character*. Chicago, 1963.
22. Luckenbill, D. D. *Ancient Records of Assyria and Babylonia*, 2 vols. Chicago, 1926–7.
23. Messerschmidt, L. and Schroeder, O. *Keilschrifttexte aus Assur historischen Inhalts* (*W.V.D.O.G.* 16 and 37). Leipzig, 1911, 1922.
24. Olmstead, A. T. *History of Assyria*. London, 1923.
25. Pallis, S. A. *The Antiquity of Iraq*. Copenhagen, 1956.
26. Poebel, A. 'The Assyrian King-list from Khorsabad.' In *J.N.E.S.* 1 (1942), 247 ff., 460 ff.; 2 (1943), 56 ff.
27. Pritchard, J. B. (ed.). *Ancient Near-Eastern Texts relating to the Old Testament*, Ed. 2. Princeton, 1955.
28. Smith, S. *Early History of Assyria*. London, 1928.
29. Thureau-Dangin, F. *Die sumerischen und akkadischen Königsinschriften*. Leipzig, 1907.

I. RECOVERY IN WESTERN ASIA

1. Dougherty, R. P. *The Sealand of Ancient Arabia* (*Y.O.S.* 9). New Haven, 1932.
2. Edel, E. 'Neue keilschriftliche Umschreibungen ägyptischer Namen aus den Boğazköytexte.' In *J.N.E.S.* 7 (1948), 11 ff.
3. Fine, H. A. *Studies in Middle-Assyrian Chronology and Religion*. Cincinnati, 1955.
4. Gelb, I. J., Purves, P. M. and MacRae, A. A. *Nuzi Personal Names* (*O.I.P.* 57). Chicago, 1943.
5. Goetze, A. 'Some observations on Nuzu Akkadian.' In *Language*, 14 (1938), 134 ff.
6. Goetze, A. Review of Gelb, I. J. *Hurrians and Subarians*. In *J.N.E.S.* 5 (1946), 165 ff.

7. Gordon, C. A. 'The dialect of the Nuzu tablets.' In *Or.* n.s. 7(1938), 215 ff.
8. Hrouda, B. 'Waššukanni, Urkiš, Šubat-Enlil.' In *M.D.O.G.* 90(1958), 22 ff.
9. Jaritz, K. 'Quellen zur Geschichte der Kaššû-Dynastie.' In *Mitt. Inst. Or.* 6(1958), 187 ff.
10. Koschaker, P. *Neue keilschriftliche Rechtsurkunden aus der el-Amarna Zeit* (*Abh. Leipzig*, 39, no. 5, 1928).
11. Lacheman, E. R. 'Nuzi geographical names I: names of countries.' In *Bull. A.S.O.R.* 78(1940), 18 ff.
12. Lewy, H. 'The *titennûtu*-texts from Nuzi.' In *Or.* n.s. 10(1941), 313 ff.
13. Lewy, H. 'The Nuzian feudal system.' In *Or.* n.s. 11(1942), 1 ff., 209 ff. 297 ff.
14. Lewy, H. 'Miscellanea Nuziana.' In *Or.* n.s. 28(1959), 1 ff., 113 ff.
15. Lewy, H. 'Notes on the political organization of Asia Minor at the time of the Old Assyrian Texts.' In *Or.* n.s. 33(1964), 181 ff.
16. O'Callaghan, R. T. *Aram-Naharaim* (*An. Or.* 26). Rome, 1948.
17. Oppenheim, A. L. 'Étude sur la topographie de Nuzi.' In *R.A.* 35(1938), 136 ff.
18. Oppenheim, A. L. 'Zur Landessprache von Arrapḫa-Nuzi.' In *Arch. f. Or.* 11(1936–7), 56 ff.
19. Oppenheim, A. L. 'Les rapports entre les noms de personnes des textes cappadociens et des textes de Nuzi.' In *R.H.A.* fasc 33(1938), 7 ff.
20. Pfeiffer, R. H. 'Nuzi and the Hurrians.' In *Smithsonian Report* for 1935 (Washington, 1936), 535 ff.
21. Pfeiffer R. H. and Speiser, E. A. *One hundred new selected Nuzi texts* (*Ann. A.S.O.R.* 16). New Haven, 1936.
22. Poebel, A. *Miscellaneous Studies* (*Assyriological Studies* 14). Chicago, 1947.
23. Speiser, E. A. *Introduction to Hurrian* (*Ann. A.S.O.R.* 20). New Haven, 1940.
24. Speiser, E. A. 'Hurrians and Subarians.' In *J.A.O.S.* 68(1948), 1 ff.
25. Weidner, E. F. *Politische Dokumente aus Kleinasien*, I, II (*Bo. Stu.* 8, 9). Leipzig, 1923.
26. Weidner, E. F. 'Die Kämpfe Adadnarâris I gegen Ḫanigalbat.' In *Arch. f. Or.* 5(1928–9), 89 ff.

### II. EXTERNAL RELATIONS

1. Campbell, E. F. *The Chronology of the Amarna Letters*. Baltimore, 1964.
2. Dupont-Sommer, A. and Starcky, J. *Les Inscriptions araméennes de Sfiré* (*Mém. Ac. Inscr. B.-L.* tome 15(1960), 1ère partie, 197 ff.).
3. Edzard, D. O. 'Die Beziehungen Babyloniens und Ägyptens in der mittelbabylonischen Zeit und das Gold.' In *J.E.S.H.O.* 3(1960), 38 ff.
4. Friedrich, J. 'Ein Bruchstück des Vertrages Mattiwaza-Suppiluliuma in hethitischer Sprache.' In *Arch. f. Keil.* 2(1924), 119 ff.
5. Gadd, C. J. 'Tablets from Chagar-Bazar and Tall Brak.' In *Iraq*, 7(1940), 22 ff.
6. Güterbock, H. G. 'The deeds of Suppiluliuma as told by his son Mursili II.' In *J.C.S.* 10(1956), 41 ff., 75 ff., 107 ff.

### III. THE ASSYRIANS IN BABYLONIA

1. Delitzsch, F. *Die babylonische Chronik* (Anhang: Synchronistische Geschichte P, 43 ff.). Leipzig, 1906.
2. Ebeling, E. *Bruchstücke eines politischen Propaganda-gedichtes aus einer assyrischen Kanzlei* (*M.A.O.G.* 12, Heft 2). Leipzig, 1938.

3. Frankena, R. 'Het Epos van de Pestgod Irra.' In *J.E.O.L.* 15(1957–8), 160 ff.
4. Gössman, P. F. *Das Era-Epos.* Würzburg, 1956.
5. Gurney, O. R. 'Texts from Dur-Kurigalzu.' In *Iraq*, 11(1949), 131 ff.
6. Lambert, W. G. Review of Gössman, P. F. *Das Era-Epos.* In *Arch. f. Or.* 18(1957–8), 393 ff.
7. Lambert, W. G. 'Three unpublished fragments of the Tukulti-Ninurta Epic.' In *Arch. f. Or.* 18(1957–8), 38 f.
8. Weidner, E. F. *Die Inschriften Tukulti-Ninurtas I und seiner Nachfolger* (*Arch. f. Or.* Beiheft 12). Graz, 1959.
9. Weidner, E. F. 'Assyrische Epen über die Kassiten-Kämpfe.' In *Arch. f. Or.* 20(1963), 113 ff.

IV. ENLIL-NĪRĀRI AND ARIK-DĒN-ILI

1. *A.R.M.T. Archives royales de Mari* (texts in transliteration and translation, vols. I–XIII; vol. XV, répertoire analytique des tomes I–IX). Paris, 1950–64.
2. Böhl, F. M. Th. de Liagre. 'Ein Brief des Königs Samsu-Iluna von Babylon.' In *Bi. Or.* 8(1951), 50 ff.
3. Læssøe, J. *The Shemshāra Tablets.* (*Arkæol. Kunsthist. Medd. Dan. Vid. Selsk.* 4, no. 3 (1959).

V. SOCIETY IN THE MIDDLE KASSITE PERIOD

1. Aro, J. *Glossar zu den mittelbabylonischen Briefen* (*Studia Orientalia*, 22). Helsinki, 1957.
2. Böhl, F. M. Th. 'Die fünfzig Namen des Marduk.' In *Arch. f. Or.* 11(1936–7), 191 ff.
3. Boyer, G. 'ṣupur x kima kunukkišu.' In *Symbolae ... Paulo Koschaker dedicatae* (Leiden, 1939), 208 ff.
4. Brinkman, J. A. 'Provincial administration in Babylonia under the Second Dynasty of Isin.' In *J.E.S.H.O.* 6(1963), 233 ff.
5. Brinkman, J. A. 'Merodach-baladan II.' In *Studies presented to A. Leo Oppenheim* (Chicago, 1964), 6 ff.
6. Clay, A. T. *Documents from the Temple Archives of Nippur, dated in the reigns of Cassite rulers* (*B. E.* XIV, XV, and *P.B.S.* II, no. 2). Philadelphia, 1906, 1912.
7. Cross, D. *Movable Property in the Nuzi Documents* (*A.O.S.* 10). New Haven, 1937.
8. David, M. 'Zwei Bestimmungen über die Binnenschiffahrt in mittelassyrischer Zeit.' In *J.E.O.L.* 6(1939), 135 ff.
9. David, M. 'Zur Verfügung eines Nichtberechtigten nach den mittelassyrischen "Gesetzesfragmenten".' In *Symbolae.... Paulo Koschaker dedicatae* (Leiden, 1939), 121 ff.
10. Diakonoff, I. M. 'Sale of land in pre-Sargonic Sumer.' In *Papers presented by the Soviet Delegation at the XXIII International Congress of Orientalists*, Moscow, 1954.
11. Diakonoff, I. M. *Sumer: society and state in Ancient Mesopotamia* (in Russian, with English résumé). Moscow, 1959.
12. Driver, G. R. and Miles, J. C. *The Assyrian Laws.* Oxford, 1935.
13. Ebeling, E. *Keilschrifttexte aus Assur juristischen Inhalts* (*W.V.D.O.G.* 50). Leipzig, 1927.
14. Ebeling, E. 'Urkunden des Archivs von Assur aus mittelassyrischer Zeit.' In *M.A.O.G.* 7(1933), 1 ff.

15. Ebeling, E. 'Die Eigennamen der mittelassyrischen Rechts- und Geschäfts-
    urkunden.' In *M.Á.O.G.* 13(1939), 1 ff.
16. Falkenstein, A. 'Zur Chronologie der sumerischen Literatur.' In *M.D.O.G.*
    85(1953), 1 ff.
17. Fine, H. A. 'Two middle-Assyrian adoption documents.' In *R.A.* 46(1952),
    205 ff.
18. Gadd, C. J. 'Tablets from Kirkuk.' In *R.A.* 23(1926), 49 ff.
19. Gadd, C. J. *Teachers and Students in the Oldest Schools.* London, 1956.
20. Gadd, C. J. 'Fragments of Assyrian scholastic literature.' In *Bull. S.O.A.S.*
    20(1957), 255 ff.
21. Hallo, W. W. 'New viewpoints on cuneiform literature.' In *I.E.J.* 12(1962),
    13 ff.
22. Hallo, W. W. 'On the antiquity of Sumerian literature.' In *J.A.O.S.*
    83(1963), 167 ff.
23. Heidel, A. *The Babylonian Genesis* (Ed. 2). Chicago, 1951.
24. Hincke, W. J. *A new boundary-stone of Nebuchadrezzar I from Nippur.*
    Philadelphia, 1907.
25. Hinz, W. *Das Reich Elam.* Stuttgart, 1964.
26. Hirsch, H. 'Die Inschriften der Könige von Agade.' In *Arch. f. Or.* 20(1963),
    1 ff.
27. King, L. W. *Babylonian Boundary-stones and Memorial Tablets in the British
    Museum.* London, 1912.
28. Klíma, J. 'Le droit élamite au IIme millénaire av. n. è. et sa position envers le
    droit babylonien.' In *An. Or.* 31(1963), 287 ff.
29. Korošec, V. 'Die Ususehe nach assyrischem Recht.' In *Or.* n.s. 6(1937), 1 ff.
30. Labat, R. *Le Poème babylonien de la Création.* Paris, 1935.
31. Lambert, W. G. 'A catalogue of texts and authors.' In *J.C.S.* 16(1962), 59 ff.
32. Landsberger, B. 'Assyrische Königsliste und "dunkles Zeitalter".' In *J.C.S.*
    8(1954), 31 ff., 47 ff., 106 ff.
33. Leemans, W. F. '*kidinnu*: un symbole de droit divin babylonien.' In *Festschr.
    J. Ch. Van Oven* (Leiden, 1946), 36 ff.
34. Lutz, H. F. *Selected Sumerian and Babylonian Texts* (*P.B.S.* 1, no. 2).
    Philadelphia, 1919.
35. Oppenheim, A. L. 'Ein Beitrag zum Kassitenproblem.' In *Miscellanea
    Orientalia . . . dedicata Antonio Deimel* (*An. Or.* 12), 266 ff. Rome, 1935.
36. Radau, H. *Letters to Cassite Kings* (*B.E.* xvii, pt 1). Philadelphia, 1908.
37. Saggs, H. W. F. 'Assyrian Warfare in the Sargonid period.' In *Iraq*, 25(1963),
    145 ff.
38. Schmökel, H. 'Ḫammurabi und Marduk.' In *R.A.* 53(1959), 183 ff.
39. Schott, A. 'Die Anfänge Marduks als eines assyrischen Gottes.' In *Z.A.*
    43(1936), 318 ff.
40  Schuler, Einar von *Hethitische Dienstanweisungen für höhere Hof- und Staats-
    beamte.* (*Arch. f. Or.* Beiheft 10). Graz, 1957.
41. Smith, S. 'The king's share.' In *J.R.A.S.* 1926, 436 ff.
42. Soden, W. von 'Das Problem der zeitlichen Anordnung akkadischer Literatur-
    werke.' In *M.D.O.G.* 85 (1953), 14 ff.
43. Soden, W. von 'Drei mittelassyrische Briefe aus Nippur.' In *Arch. f. Or.* 18
    (1957–8), 368 ff.
44. Steinmetzer, F. X. *Die babylonische* kudurru (*Grenzsteine*) *als Urkundenform.*
    Paderborn, 1922.
45. Ungnad, A. 'Gab es eine sumerische Fassung der Siebenten Tafel des Welt-
    schöpfungsgedichtes?' In *Z.A.* 31 (1917–18), 153 ff.

46. Waschow, H. *Babylonische Briefe aus der Kassitenzeit* (*M.A.O.G.* x, Heft 1). Leipzig, 1936.
47. Weidner, E. F. 'Das Alter der mittelassyrischen Gesetzestexte.' In *Arch. f. Or.* 12 (1937–9), 46 ff.
48. Weidner, E. F. 'Hof- und Harems-Erlasse assyrischer Könige aus dem 2 Jahrtausend v. Chr.' In *Arch. f. Or.* 17 (1956), 257 ff.
49. Weidner, E. F. 'Eine Erbteilung in mittelassyrischer Zeit.' In *Arch. f. Or.* 20 (1963), 121 ff.


VI. NEW INFLUENCES IN ART

1. Andrae, W. *Das Gotteshaus und die Urformen des Bauens im Alten Orient.* Berlin, 1930.
2. Baqir, Ṭaha. 'Iraq Government excavations at 'Aqar Qūf' (1st–3rd interim reports). In *Iraq*, supplements 1 and 2 (1944, 1945) and 8 (1946), 73 ff.
3. Batault, H. 'Un sceau-cylindre cassite du Musée d'Art et d'Histoire de Genève.' In *Genava*, n.s. 6 (1958), 217 ff.
4. Beran, T. 'Assyrische Glyptik des 14 Jahrhunderts.' In *Z.A.* 52 (1957), 141 ff.
5. Beran, T. 'Die babylonische Glyptik der Kassitenzeit.' In *Arch. f. Or.* 18 (1958), 257 ff.
6. Buchanan, B. 'On the seal-impressions on some Old Babylonian tablets.' In *J.C.S.* 11 (1957), 45 ff.
7. Busink, Th. A. *Sumerische en babylonische Tempelbouw.* Batavia, 1940.
8. Delougaz, P. and Lloyd, Seton. *Pre-Sargonid Temples in the Diyala Region* (*O.I.P.* 58). Chicago, 1942.
9. Dossin, G. 'L'inscription du sceau-cylindre cassite MAH.19356.' In *Genava*, n.s. 6 (1958), 223 ff.
10. Goff, B. L. 'Cylinder-seals as amulets.' In *Journ. Warburg Inst.* 19, 23 ff.
11. Hüsing, G. *Die einheimischen Quellen zur Geschichte Elams.* Leipzig, 1916.
12. Jaritz, K. 'Mesopotamische Megara als kassitischer Import.' In *Z.E.* 83 (1958), 110 ff.
13. Kent, R. G. *Old Persian: Grammar, Texts, Lexicon* (*A.O.S.* 33). New Haven, 1950.
14. Langdon, S. H. 'Inscriptions on Kassite seals.' In *R.A.* 16 (1919), 69 ff.
15. Lucas, A. *Ancient Egyptian Materials and Industries* (Ed. 4, revised by J. R. Harris). London, 1962.
16. Martiny, G. *Die Kultrichtung in Mesopotamien.* Berlin, 1932.
17. Martiny, G. 'Archaeologica zur assyrisch-babylonischen Tempel-orientation.' In *Act. XXe Congr. Int. Orient.* (Louvain, 1940), 108 f
18. Moortgat, A. 'Assyrische Glyptik des 13 Jahrhunderts.' In *Z.A.* 47 (1942), 50 ff.
19. Nagel, W. 'Datierte Glyptik aus Altvorderasien.' In *Arch. f. Or.* 20 (1963), 125 ff.
20. Neugebauer, P. V. and Schott, A. Review of Martiny, G. *Die Kultrichtung in Mesopotamien.* In *Z.A.* 42 (1934), 198 ff.
21. Parrot, A. *Ziggurats et Tour de Babel.* Paris, 1949.
22. Porada, E. *Seal-impressions of Nuzi* (*Ann. A.S.O.R.* 24). New Haven, 1947.
23. Porada, E. and Buchanan, B. *Corpus of Ancient Near Eastern Seals in North American Collections: Collection of the Pierpont Morgan Library*, vols. 1 and 11. Washington, 1948.
24. Pritchard, J. B. *The Ancient Near East in Pictures.* Princeton, 1954.

25. Unvala, J. M. 'Three panels from Susa.' In *R.A.* 25 (1928), 179 ff.
26. Van Buren, E. D. *The Flowing Vase and the God with Streams.* Berlin, 1933.
27. Van Buren, E. D. 'The esoteric significance of Kassite glyptic art.' In *Or.* n.s. 23 (1954), 1 ff.
28. Van Buren, E. D. 'Representations of fertility divinities in glyptic art.' In *Or.* n.s. 24 (1955), 345 ff.
29. Woolley, Sir Leonard. *The Kassite Period and the Period of the Assyrian Kings* (*U.E.* 8). London and Philadelphia, 1965.

## CHAPTER XIX

### G. GENERAL

1. Breasted, J. H. *Ancient Records of Egypt: Historical Documents* (*Ancient Records, 2nd Series*), 2: *The Eighteenth Dynasty.* 3: *The Nineteenth Dynasty.* Chicago, 1906.
2. Breasted, J. H. *A History of Egypt from the Earliest Times to the Persian Conquest.* Ed. 2. London, 1948.
3. Černý, J. *Ancient Egyptian Religion.* London, 1952.
4. Drioton, É. and Vandier, J. *L'Égypte* (Clio: *Les peuples de l'Orient méditerranéen*, 2). Ed. 4. Paris, 1962, pp. 343–55, 367–9, 373–5, 384–6, 414–18, 446–7.
5. Gardiner, A. H. *Ancient Egyptian Onomastica.* 3 vols. Oxford, 1947.
6. Gardiner, A. H. *Egypt of the Pharaohs.* Oxford, 1961.
7. Hayes, W. C. *The Scepter of Egypt.* Part 2. New York, 1959.
8. Kees, H. *Ancient Egypt, A Cultural Topography.* Ed. T. G. H. James. London, 1961.
9. Lacau, P. *Stèles du Nouvel Empire* (*C.C.G.* nos. 34001–189). Cairo, 1909–57.
10. Petrie, W. M. F. *A History of Egypt,* II. *The XVIIth and XVIIIth Dynasties.* Ed. 7. London, 1924.
11. Porter, B. and Moss, R. L. B. *Topographical Bibliography of Ancient Egyptian Hieroglyphic Texts, Reliefs and Paintings.* 7 vols. Oxford, 1927–64.
12. Säve-Söderbergh, T. *Ägypten und Nubien. Ein Beitrag zur Geschichte altägyptischer Aussenpolitik.* Lund, 1941.
13. Sethe, K. and Helck, H.-W. *Urkunden der 18 Dynastie* (*Urk. IV*). Hefte 1–22. Leipzig and Berlin, 1906–58.
14. Smith, G. E. *The Royal Mummies* (*C.C.G.* nos. 61051–100). Cairo, 1912.
15. Thomas, E. *The Royal Necropoleis of Thebes.* Princeton, 1966.
16. Waddell, W. G. *Manetho, with an English Translation* (The Loeb Classical Library). London and Cambridge (Mass.), 1940.

### I. THE PROBLEM OF A CO-REGENCY BETWEEN AMENOPHIS III AND AKHENATEN

1. Aldred, C. 'Year Twelve at El-'Amārna.' In *J.E.A.* 43 (1957), 30 ff.
2. Aldred, C. 'Two Theban Notables during the Later Reign of Amenophis III.' In *J.N.E.S.* 18 (1959), 113 ff.
3. Aldred, C. 'The Beginning of the El-'Amārna Period.' In *J.E.A.* 45 (1959), 19 ff.
4. Aldred, C. *Akhenaten, Pharaoh of Egypt: A New Study,* Chapters VI, VII and XI. London, 1968.

5. Campbell, E. F. *The Chronology of the Amarna Letters*, Chapter 11. Baltimore, 1964.
6. Drioton, É. and Vandier, J. *L'Égypte* (Clio: *Les peuples de l'Orient méditerranéen*, 2). Ed. 4. Paris, 1962. Pp. 384–6, 631, 658–61.
7. Engelbach, R. 'Material for a Revision of the History of the Heresy Period of the XVIIIth Dynasty.' In *Ann. Serv.* 40 (1940), 134 ff.
8. Fairman, H. W. 'A Block of Amenophis IV from Athribis.' In *J.E.A.* 46 (1960), 80 ff.
9. Gardiner, A. H. 'The So-called Tomb of Queen Tiye.' In *J.E.A.* 43 (1957), 10 ff.
10. Hayes, W. C. 'Inscriptions from the Palace of Amenophis III.' In *J.N.E.S.* 10 (1951).
11. Helck, H.-W. 'Die Sinai-Inschrift des Amenmose.' In *Mitt. Inst. Or.* 2 (1954), 189 ff.
12. Hornung, E. *Untersuchungen zur Chronologie und Geschichte des Neuen Reiches*, Chapter x. Wiesbaden, 1964.
13. Kitchen, K. A. 'On the Chronology and History of the New Kingdom.' In *Chron. d'Ég.* 40 (1965), 310 ff.
14. Kitchen, K. A. Review of E. F. Campbell, *The Chronology of the Amarna Letters*. In *J.E.A.* 53 (1967), 178 ff.
15. Kitchen, K. A. 'Further Notes on New Kingdom Chronology and History. In *Chron. d'Ég.* 43 (1968), 313 ff.
16. Pendlebury. J. D. S. *Tell el-Amarna*. London, 1935.
17. Pendlebury, J. D. S. 'Summary Report on Excavations at Tell el-'Amārnah, 1935–6.' In *J.E.A.* 22 (1936), 197–8.
18. Pendlebury, J. D. S. *et al. The City of Akhenaten*, Part III (E.E.S. 44th Memoir). 2 vols. London, 1951.
19. Redford, D. B. *History and Chronology of the Eighteenth Dynasty of Egypt: Seven Studies*, Chapter 5. Toronto, 1967.
20. Smith, W. S. *The Art and Architecture of Ancient Egypt*. Harmondsworth, 1958.
21. Wente, E. F. Review of D. B. Redford, *History and Chronology of the Eighteenth Dynasty*. In *J.N.E.S.* 28 (1969), 273 ff.

## II. THE CHARACTER OF THE AMARNA 'REVOLUTION'

1. Aldred, C. 'The Beginning of the El-'Amārna Period.' In *J.E.A.* 45 (1959), 19 ff.
2. Aldred, C. *Akhenaten, Pharaoh of Egypt: A New Study*. London, 1968.
3. Bothmer, B. V. 'A New Fragment of an Old Palette.' In *J.A.R.C.E.* 8 (1969), 1–4.
4. Breasted, J. H. *A History of Egypt from the Earliest Times to the Persian Conquest*. Ed. 2. London, 1948.
5. Cottevieille-Giraudet, R. *Rapport sur les fouilles de Médamoud, 1932. Les reliefs d'Amenophis IV Akhenaten* (Flles. Inst. fr. Caire, 13). Cairo, 1936.
6. Davis, T. M., Maspero, G. *et al. Tomb of Iouiya and Touiyou*. London, 1907.
7. Edgerton, W. F. 'The Government and the Governed in the Egyptian Empire.' In *J.N.E.S.* 6 (1947), 152 ff.
8. Fakhry, A. 'A Note on the Tomb of Kheruef at Thebes.' In *Ann. Serv.* 42 (1943), 447 ff.
9. Gardiner, A. H. *The Wilbour Papyrus*. 3 vols. Oxford, 1941–8. Vol. IV, Indices, by R. O. Faulkner. Oxford, 1952.

10. Gardiner, A. H. 'Ramesside Texts Relating to the Transport and Taxation of Corn.' In *J.E.A.* 27 (1941), 19 ff.

11. Petrie, W. M. F. *Royal Tombs of the Earliest Dynasties.* Part II (E.E.S. 21st Memoir). London, 1901.

12. Stewart, H. M. 'Some Pre-ʿAmārneh Sun-Hymns.' In *J.E.A.* 46 (1960), 83 ff.

13. Wilson, J. A. *The Burden of Egypt: An Interpretation of Ancient Egyptian Culture.* Chicago, 1951.

### III. THE REIGN OF AKHENATEN

1. Aldred, C. 'The Gayer Anderson Jubilee Relief of Amenophis IV.' In *J.E.A.* 45 (1959), 104.

2. Aldred, C. and Sandison, A. T. 'The Tomb of Akhenaten at Thebes.' In *J.E.A.* 47 (1961), 41 ff.

3. Aldred, C. and Sandison, A. T. 'The Pharaoh Akhenaten: A Problem in Egyptology and Pathology.' In *Bull. Hist. Med.* 36 (1962), 293 ff.

4. Anthes, R. 'Die Maat des Echnaton von Amarna.' In *J.A.O.S.* 14 (Supplement) 1952, 1–36.

5. Badawy, A. 'Maru-Aten: Pleasure Resort or Temple.' In *J.E.A.* 42 (1956), 58 ff.

6. Bennett, J. 'Notes on the "aten".' In *J.E.A.* 51 (1965), 207 ff.

7. Bissing, F. W. von, *et al. Das Re-Heiligtum des Königs Ne-Woser-Re (Rathures).* 3 vols. Berlin and Leipzig, 1905–28.

8. Borchardt, L. 'Ausgrabungen in Tell el-Amarna.' In *M.D.O.G.* nos. 34, 46, 50, 52, 55 (1907–14).

9. Bouriant, U. *et al. Monuments pour servir à l'étude du culte d'Atonou en Égypte.* I. *Les tombes de Khouitatonou (Mém. Inst. fr. Caire,* 8). Cairo, 1903.

10. Bouriant, U. *Deux jours de fouilles à Tell el-Amarna (Mém. Miss. fr. Caire,* I, 1). Paris, 1884.

11. Brunner, H. 'Eine Neue Amarna-Prinzessin.' In *Z.Ä.S.* 74 (1938), 104 ff.

12. Chevrier, H. 'Rapport(s) sur les travaux de Karnak.' In *Ann. Serv.* 26–39 (1926–9) and 46–53 (1947–55) *passim.*

13. Davies, Norman de G. *The Rock Tombs of El Amarna.* 6 vols. London, 1903–8.

14. Davies, Norman de G. 'Akhenaten at Thebes.' In *J.E.A.* 9 (1923), 132 ff.

15. Davies, Norman de G. *The Tomb of the Vizier Ramose* (Mond Excavations at Thebes I). London, 1941.

16. Doresse, M. 'Les Temples Atoniens de la région thébaine.' In *Orientalia,* 24 (1955), 113 ff.

17. Fairman, H. W. 'Town Planning in Pharaonic Egypt.' In *Town Planning Review,* 20 (1949), 32 ff.

18. Fairman, H. W. 'The supposed Year 21 of Akhenaten.' In *J.E.A.* 46 (1960), 108 ff.

19. Frankfort, H., Pendlebury, J. D. S., *et al. The City of Akhenaten,* Part II (E.E.S. 40th Memoir). London, 1933.

20. Gardiner, A. H. 'Four Papyri of the 18th Dynasty from Kahun.' In *Z.Ä.S.* 43 (1906), 27 ff.

21. Gauthier, H. *Le Livre des rois d'Égypte,* II (*Mém. Inst. fr. Caire,* 18). Cairo, 1912.

22. Ghalioungui, P. 'A Medical Study of Akhenaten.' In *Ann. Serv.* 47 (1947), 29 ff.

23. Griffith, F. Ll. 'The Jubilee of the Aten.' In *J.E.A.* 5 (1918), 61 ff. Also *ibid.* 8 (1922), 199 ff.

24. Gunn, B. 'Notes on the Aten and his Names.' In *J.E.A.* 9 (1923), 168 ff.

25. Habachi, L. 'Varia from the Reign of King Akhenaten.' In *Mitt. deutsch. Inst. Kairo*, 20 (1965), 70 ff.

26. Hamza, M. 'The Alabaster Canopic Box of Akhenaten, and the Royal Alabaster Canopic Boxes of the XVIIIth Dynasty.' In *Ann. Serv.* 40 (1941), 537 ff.

27. Harrison, R. G. 'An Anatomical Examination of the Pharaonic Remains Purported to be Akhenaten.' In *J.E.A.* 52 (1966), 95 ff.

28. Kamal, M. 'Fouilles du Service des Antiquités à Tell el-Amarna.' In *Ann. Serv.* 35 (1935), 193 ff., and *ibid.* 39 (1939), 381 ff.

29. Lange, K. *König Echnaton und die Amarna-Zeit*. Munich, 1951.

30. Legrain, G. 'Notes d'Inspection: 1. Les stèles d'Aménôthès IV à Zernik et à Gebel Silsileh.' In *Ann. Serv.* 3 (1902), 259 ff.

31. Monnet, J. 'Remarques sur la famille et les successeurs de Ramsès III.' In *Bull. Inst. fr. Caire*, 63 (1965), 209 ff.

32. Peet, T. E., Woolley, C. L., *et al. The City of Akhenaten*. Part 1 (E.E.S. 38th Memoir). London, 1923.

33. Pendlebury, J. D. S. 'Report on the clearance of the Royal Tomb at El-'Amârna.' In *Ann. Serv.* 21 (1931), 123–5.

34. Pendlebury, J. D. S. 'Preliminary Report[s] of Excavations at Tell el-'Amarnah 1930–33.' In *J.E.A.* 17 (1931), 233 ff.; 18 (1932), 143 ff.; 19 (1933), 113 ff.

35. Petrie, W. M. F. *Tell el-Amarna*. London, 1894.

36. Reymond, E. A. E. *The Mythical Origin of the Egyptian Temple*. Manchester, 1969.

37. Roeder, G. *Ein Jahrzehnt deutscher Ausgrabungen in einer ägyptischen Stadtruine*. Hildesheim, 1951.

38. Schäfer, H. 'Altes und Neues zur Kunst und Religion von Tell el-Amarna.' In *Z.Ä.S.* 55 (1918), 1 ff.

39. Schäfer, H. 'Das Wesen der "Amarnakunst".' In *M.D.O.G.* 64 (1926), 54–61.

40. Sethe, K. *Beiträge zur Geschichte Amenophis' IV*. (*Nachr. Göttingen*, Phil.-hist. Klasse, 1921). Berlin, 1921.

41. Smith, R. W. 'The Akhenaten Temple Project.' In *Expedition* (*Bull. Univ. Mus. Penna.*), 10, No. 1 (1967), 24–32.

42. Uphill, E. 'The Sed-Festivals of Akhenaten.' In *J.N.E.S.* 22 (1963), 123 ff.

### IV. THE IMMEDIATE SUCCESSORS OF AKHENATEN

1. Aldred, C. 'The Harold Jones Collection.' In *J.E.A.* 48 (1962), 160–2.

2. Bennett, J. 'The Restoration Inscription of Tut'ankhamūn.' In *J.E.A.* 25 (1939), 8 ff.

3. Blackman, A. M. 'The Haggard Collection.' In *J.E.A.* 4 (1917), 43 ff.

4. Bosse-Griffiths, K. 'Finds from "the Tomb of Queen Tiye" in the Swansea Museum.' In *J.E.A.* 47 (1961), 66 ff.

5. Carter, H., *et al. The Tomb of Tut.Ankh.Amen*. 3 vols. London, 1923–33.

6. Černý, J. *Hieratic Inscriptions from the Tomb of Tut'ankhamūn*. Oxford, 1965.

7. Černý, J. 'Three Regnal Dates of the Eighteenth Dynasty.' In *J.E.A.* 50 (1964), 37 ff.

8. Daressy, G. 'Le Cercueil de Khu-n-Aten.' In *Bull. Inst. fr. Caire*, 12 (1916), 145 ff.
9. Davies, Nina de G. and Gardiner, A. H. *The Tomb of Huy, Viceroy of Nubia in the Reign of Tut'ankhamun.* London, 1926.
10. Davies, Norman de G. *The Tomb of Nefer-Ḥotep at Thebes.* 2 vols. New York, 1933.
11. Davis, T. M., Maspero, G., *et al. The Tomb of Queen Tîyi.* London, 1910.
12. Derry, D. 'Note on the Skeleton hitherto believed to be that of King Akhenaten.' In *Ann. Serv.* 31 (1931), 115 ff.
13. Desroches-Noblecourt, C. 'La Cueillette du Raisin à la Fin de l'Époque amarnienne.' In *J.E.A.* 54 (1968), 82 ff.
14. Drioton, É., and Vigneau, A. *Encyclopédie Photographique de l'Art: Le Musée du Caire.* Editions 'Tel'. Paris, 1949.
15. Edwards, I. E. S. 'The Prudhoe Lions.' In *Ann. Arch. Anthr.* 26 (1939), 3 ff.
16. Engelbach, R. 'The So-called Coffin of Akhenaten.' In *Ann. Serv.* 31 (1931), 98 ff.
17. Fairman, H. W. 'Once again the So-called Coffin of Akhenaten.' In *J.E.A.* 47 (1961), 25 ff.
18. Gardiner, A. H. 'The Graffito in the Tomb of Pere.' In *J.E.A.* 14 (1928), 10–11.
19. Gardiner, A. H. 'Regnal Years and the Civil Calendar in Pharaonic Egypt.' In *J.E.A.* 31 (1945), 11 ff.
20. Gardiner, A. H. 'The So-called Tomb of Queen Tiye.' In *J.E.A.* 43 (1957), 10 ff.
21. Hall, H. R. 'Objects of Tut'ankhamūn in the British Museum.' In *J.E.A.* 14 (1928), 74 ff.
22. Lucas, A. 'The Canopic Vases from the "Tomb of Queen Tîyi".' In *Ann. Serv.* 31 (1931), 120 ff.
23. Newberry, P. E. 'Akhenaten's Eldest Son-in-Law.' In *J.E.A.* 14 (1928), 3 ff.
24. Newberry, P. E. 'King Ay, the Successor of Tut'ankhamūn.' In *J.E.A.* 18 (1932), 50 ff.
25. Piankoff, A. 'Les Peintures dans la Tombe du roi Ai.' In *Mitt. deutsch. Inst. Kairo*, 16 (1958), 247 ff.
26. Piankoff, A. *The Shrines of Tut-Ankh-Amon.* New York, 1962.
27. Roeder, G. 'Thronfolger und König Smench-ka-Rê.' In *Z.Ä.S.* 83 (1958), 43 ff.
28. Seele, K. C. 'King Ay and the Close of the Amarna Age.' In *J.N.E.S.* 14 (1955), 168 ff.
29. Steindorff, G. 'Die Grabkammer des Tutanchamun.' In *Ann. Serv.* 38 (1938), 641 ff.
30. Vilimkova, M. and Abdu-Rahman, M. H. *Egyptian Jewellery.* London, 1969. Pls. 32–67.
31. Weigall, A. 'The Mummy of Akhenaten.' In *J.E.A.* 8 (1922), 193 ff.

### V. THE REIGN OF HOREMHEB

1. Aldred, C. 'Two Monuments of the Reign of Ḥaremḥab.' In *J.E.A.* 54 (1968), 100 ff.
2. Breasted, J. H. 'King Harmhab and his Sakkara Tomb.' In *Z.Ä.S.* 38 (1900), 47 ff.
3. Capart, J. 'The Memphite Tomb of King Ḥaremḥab.' In *J.E.A.* 7 (1921), 31 ff.

4. Carter, H. and Newberry, P. E. *The Tomb of Thoutmôsis IV (C.C.G. nos. 46001–529)*. London, 1904.

5. Cooney, J. D. 'A Relief from the Tomb of Ḥaremḥab.' In *J.E.A.* 30 (1944), 2–4.

6. Davis, T. M., Maspero, G. *et al. The Tombs of Harmhabi and Touatânkhamanou*. London, 1912.

7. Erman, A. 'Aus dem Grabe eines Hohenpriesters von Memphis.' In *Z.Ä.S.* 33 (1895), 18 ff.

8. Gardiner, A. H. *The Inscription of Mes. A Contribution to the Study of Egyptian Judicial Procedure. (Unters., IV, 3.)* Leipzig, 1905.

9. Gardiner, A. H. 'The Memphite Tomb of the General Ḥaremḥab.' In *J.E.A.* 39 (1953), 3 ff.

10. Gardiner, A. H. 'The Coronation of King Ḥaremḥab.' In *J.E.A.* 39 (1953), 13 ff.

11. Goedicke, H. 'Some Remarks on the 400-Year Stela.' In *Chron. d'Ég.* 41 (1966), 23 ff.

12. Hari, R. *Horemheb et la Reine Moutnedjemet, ou la Fin d'une Dynastie*. Geneva, 1965.

13. Harris, J. R. 'How long was the Reign of Ḥoremḥeb?' In *J.E.A.* 54 (1968), 95 ff.

14. Helck, H.-W. 'Das Dekret des Königs Ḥaremḥab.' In *Z.Ä.S.* 80 (1955), 109 ff.

15. Hölscher, U. and Anthes, R. *The Temples of the Eighteenth Dynasty. The Excavations of Medinet Habu II*. Chicago, 1939.

16. Pflüger, K. *Haremhab und die Amarnazeit. Teildruck: Haremhabs Laufbahn bis zur Thronbesteigung*. Zwickau, 1936.

17. Pflüger, K. 'The Edict of King Haremhab.' In *J.N.E.S.* 5 (1946), 260 ff.

18. Piankoff, A. and Hornung, E. 'Das Grab Amenophis III.' In *Mitt. deutsch. Inst. Kairo*, 17 (1961), 111 ff.

19. Schulman, A. R. 'The Berlin "Trauerrelief" (No. 12411) and some Officials of Tut'ankhamūn and Ay.' In *J.A.R.C.E.* 4 (1965), 55 ff.

20. Seele, K. C. *The Coregency of Ramses II with Seti I and the Date of the Great Hypostyle Hall at Karnak*. Chicago, 1940.

21. Spiegelberg, W. 'Die Datierung des Berliner Trauerreliefs.' In *Z.Ä.S.* 60 (1925), 56 ff.

22. Walle, B. van de and Pflüger, K. 'Le Décret d'Horemheb.' In *Chron. d'Ég.* 22 (1947), 230 ff.

23. Winlock, H. E. 'A Statue of Ḥoremḥab before his Accession.' In *J.E.A.* 10 (1924), 1–5.

## VI. THE ROYAL FAMILY AT THE END OF THE EIGHTEENTH DYNASTY

1. Aldred, C. 'The End of the El-'Amārna Period.' In *J.E.A.* 43 (1957), 30 ff.

2. Blankenburg-Van Delden, C. *Large Commemorative Scarabs of Amenophis III*. London, 1969.

3. Gardiner, A. H. 'Tuthmosis III Returns Thanks to Amūn.' In *J.E.A.* 38 (1952), 6 ff.

4. Helck, H.-W. *Der Einfluss der Militärführer in der 18 ägyptischen Dynastie*. Leipzig, 1939.

5. Helck, H.-W. *Zur Verwaltung des mittleren und neuen Reichs*. Leiden–Cologne, 1958.

6. Helck, H.-W. 'Die Tochterheirat ägyptischer Könige.' In *Chron. d'Ég.* 44 (1969), 22 ff.

7. Helck, H.-W. 'Amarna Probleme.' In *Chron. d'Ég.* 44 (1969), 200ff.
8. Munro, P. 'Die Namen Semenech-ka-Re's.' In *Z.Ä.S.* 95 (1969), 108 ff.
9. Quibell, J. E. *Tomb of Yuaa and Thuiu (C.C.G. nos. 51001–191).* Cairo, 1908.
10. Sauneron, S. 'Quelques Monuments de Soumenou au Musée de Brooklyn.' In *Kemi*, 18 (1968), 66ff.
11. Schiaparelli, E. *Relazione sui lavori della Missione Archeologica Italiana in Egitto*, 1903–20, I. Turin, n.d.
12. Walle, B. van de. 'La Princesse Isis, fille et épouse d'Amenophis III.' In *Chron. d'Ég.* 43 (1968), 36ff.
13. Yoyotte, J. 'Le bassin de Djâroukha.' In *Kemi*, 15 (1959), 23ff.

### VII. FOREIGN AFFAIRS

1. Albright, W. F. 'The Egyptian Correspondence of Abimilki, Prince of Tyre.' In *J.E.A.* 23 (1937), 190ff.
2. Albright, W. F. 'Cuneiform Material for Egyptian Prosopography.' In *J.N.E.S.* 5 (1946), 7ff.
3. Aldred, C. 'The Foreign Gifts Offered to Pharaoh.' In *J.E.A.* 56 (1970), 105ff.
4. Kitchen, K. A. *Suppiluliuma and the Amarna Pharaohs: A Study in Relative Chronology.* Liverpool, 1962.
5. Knudtzon, J. A. *et al. Die El-Amarna-Tafeln.* 2 vols. Leipzig, 1908, 1915.
6. Langdon, S. and Gardiner, A. H. 'The Treaty of Alliance between Hattušili, King of the Hittites, and the Pharaoh Ramesses II of Egypt.' In *J.E.A.* 6 (1920), 179ff.
7. Mercer, S. A. B. *The Tell el-Amarna Tablets.* 2 vols. Toronto, 1939.
8. Schulman, A. R. 'Some Remarks on the Military Background of the Amarna Period.' In *J.A.R.C.E.* 3 (1964), 51ff.
9. Winlock, H. E. *The Treasure of Three Egyptian Princesses.* New York, 1948.

### VIII. RELIGION, LITERATURE AND ART

1. Aldred, C. 'Hair Styles and History.' In *Bull. M.M.A.* n.s. 15 (1957), 141ff.
2. Aldred, C. *New Kingdom Art in Ancient Egypt during the Eighteenth Dynasty.* Ed. 2. London, 1961.
3. Aldred, C. 'The "New Year" Gifts to the Pharaoh.' In *J.E.A.* 55 (1969), 73ff.
4. Anthes, R. *The Head of Queen Nofretete.* Berlin, 1968.
5. Borchardt, L. *Porträts der Königin Nofret-ete aus den Grabungen 1912–13.* In *Tell Amarna.* Leipzig, 1923.
6. Bothmer, B. V. 'Private Sculpture of Dynasty XVIII in Brooklyn.' In *Brooklyn Mus. Annual*, 8 (1966–7), 79–89.
7. Brooklyn Museum: 'Additions to the Museum's Collections: Department of Ancient Art.' In *Brooklyn Mus. Annual*, 10 (1968–9), 167 (No. 69·45).
8. Budge, E. A. W. *Tutānkhamen, Amenism, Atenism and Egyptian Monotheism.* London, 1923.
9. Caminos, R. A. *Literary Fragments in the Hieratic Script.* Oxford, 1956.
10. Cooney, J. D. and Simpson, W. K. 'An Architectural Fragment from Amarna.' In *Bull. Brooklyn Mus.* 12, 4 (1951), 1–12.
11. Cooney, J. D. *Amarna Reliefs from Hermopolis in American Collections.* Brooklyn Museum, 1965.

12. Davies, Nina de G. *Ancient Egyptian Paintings.* 3 vols. Chicago, 1936.
13. Desroches-Noblecourt, C. *L'Ancienne Égypte: L'extraordinaire aventure amarnienne.* Paris, 1960.
14. Desroches-Noblecourt, C. *Tutankhamen: Life and death of a pharaoh.* London, 1963.
15. Doresse, M. and J. 'Le Culte d'Aton sous la XVIIIe dynastie avant le schisme amarnien.' In *J.A.,* 233 (1941–2), 181 ff.
16. Drioton, É. 'Trois Documents d'Époque Amarnienne.' In *Ann. Serv.* 43 (1944), 15 ff.
17. Erman, A. *The Literature of the Ancient Egyptians, translated from the German by A. M. Blackman.* London, 1927.
18. Erman, A. *Die Religion der Ägypter.* Berlin and Leipzig, 1934.
19. Fecht, G. 'Amarna-Probleme (1–2).' In *Z.Ä.S.* 85 (1960), 83 ff.
20. Fox, P. *Tutankhamun's Treasure.* London, 1951.
21. Frankfort, H. *et al. The Mural Painting of El-'Amarneh (E.E.S.* II F. G. *Newton Memorial Volume).* London, 1929.
22. Gardiner, A. H. and Nina de G. Davies. *The Tomb of Amenemhet (No. 82).* London, 1915.
23. Gardiner, A. H. 'A Stele in the Macgregor Collection.' In *J.E.A.* 4 (1917), 188 ff.
24. Gardiner, A. H. 'The Astarte Papyrus.' In *Studies Presented to F. Ll. Griffith.* London, 1932. pp. 74 ff.
25. Glanville, S. R. K. 'Some Notes on Material for the Reign of Amenophis III.' In *J.E.A.* 15 (1929), 2 ff.
26. Gunn, B. 'The Religion of the Poor in Ancient Egypt.' In *J.E.A.* 3 (1916), 87 ff.
27. Hassan, S. 'A Representation of the Solar Disk with Human Hands....' In *Ann. Serv.* 38 (1938), 53 ff.
28. Lange, K. and Hirmer, M. *Egypt: Architecture, Sculpture and Painting.* London, 1956.
29. Piankoff, A. 'Les tombeaux de la Vallée des Rois avant et après l'hérésie amarnienne.' In *Bull. Soc. fr. Égyptol.* Nos. 28–9 (1959), 7 ff.
30. Piankoff, A. 'Les compositions théologiques du nouvel empire égyptien.' In *Bull. Inst. fr. Caire,* 62 (1964), 121 ff.
31. Piankoff, A. 'Les grandes compositions religieuses du nouvel empire et la réforme d'Amarna.' In *Bull. Inst. fr. Caire,* 62 (1964), 207 ff.
32. Posener, G. 'La légende égyptienne de la mer insatiable.' In *Ann. Inst. philol. hist. orient. et slaves,* 13 (1953), 461 ff.
33. Posener, G. 'L'exorde de l'instruction éducative d'Amennakhte.' In *Rev. d'Égypt.* 10 (1955), 61 ff.
34. Pritchard, J. B. ed. *Ancient Near Eastern Texts relating to the Old Testament.* Ed. 2. Princeton, 1955.
35. Ranke, H. *Masterpieces of Egyptian Art.* London, 1951.
36. Roeder, G. 'Lebensgrosse Tonmodelle aus einer Altägyptischen Bildhauer Werkstatt.' In *Jahrb. Preuss. Kunstsam.* 62 (1941), 145 ff.
37. Roeder, G. 'Amarna-Blöcke aus Hermopolis.' In *Mitt. deutsch. Inst. Kairo,* 14 (1956), 160 ff.
38. Säve-Söderbergh, T. *Four Eighteenth Dynasty Tombs (Private Tombs at Thebes,* 1). Oxford, 1957.
39. Schäfer, H. *Kunstwerke aus El-Amarna (Meisterwerke in Berlin),* 2 vols. Berlin, n.d.
40. Schäfer, H. *Amarna in Religion und Kunst.* Leipzig, 1931.

41. Stewart, H. M. 'Traditional Egyptian Sun Hymns of the New Kingdom.' In *Bull. Inst. Archaeol. London*, 6 (1967), 29 ff.

42. Stewart, H. M. 'A Monument with Amarna Traits.' In *Bull. Inst. Archaeol. London*, 7 (1968), 85 ff.

43. Walle, B. van de, *La transmission des textes littéraires égyptiens* (avec une annexe de G. Posener). Brussels, 1948.

44. Williams, C. R. 'Wall Decorations of the Main Temple of the Sun at el-'Amarneh.' In *M.M.A. Studies*, 2 (1930), 135 ff.

45. Witt, C. de. *La Statuaire de Tell el-Amarna*. Antwerp, 1950.

46. Wolf, W. 'Vorläufer der Reformation Echnatons.' In *Z.Ä.S.* 59 (1924), 109 ff.

47. Wolf, W. *Das schöne Fest von Opet; die Festzugdarstellung im grossen Säulengange des Temples von Luksor*. Leipzig, 1931.

48. Wolf, W. *Die Kunst Aegyptens: Gestalt und Geschichte*. Stuttgart, 1957.

### A. ADDENDA

1. Aldred, C. *Akhenaten and Nefertiti: Art from the Age of the Sun King*. New York, 1973.

2. Edwards, I. E. S. *Treasures of Tutankhamun* (Catalogue of the Tutankhamun Exhibition held in the British Museum). London, 1972.

3. Fairman, H. W. 'Tutankhamun and the End of the 18th Dynasty.' In *Antiq.* 46 (1972), 15 ff.

4. Harrison, R. G. and Abdalla, A. B. 'The Remains of Tutankhamun.' In *Antiq.* 46 (1972), 8 ff.

5. Hornung, E. *Das Grab des Haremhab im Tal der Könige*. Bern, 1971.

6. Martin, G. T. *The Rock Tombs of El Amarna*, Part VII—*The Royal Tomb at El-Amarna*, Vol. 1: *The Objects*. London, 1974.

7. Redford, D. 'A Report on the Work of the Akhenaten Temple Project of the University Museum, University of Pennsylvania.' In *J.A.R.C.E.* 11.

8. Roeder, G. *Amarna-Reliefs aus Hermopolis*. Hildesheim, 1969.

9. Saad, R. 'Les travaux d'Aménophis IV au IIIe pylône du temple d'Amon Re à Karnak.' In *Kemi*, 20 (1970), 187 ff.

10. Samson, J. *Amarna, City of Akhenaten and Nefertiti*. London, 1972.

11. Sauneron, S. and Saad, R. 'Le démontage et l'étude du IXe pylône à Karnak.' In *Kemi*, 19 (1969), 137 ff.

## CHAPTER XX

### I. THE TABLETS AND THEIR CHRONOLOGY

1. Albright, W. F. 'Canaanite *ḥofši*, "free", in the Amarna Tablets.' In *J.P.O.S.* 4 (1924), 169 ff.

2. Albright, W. F. 'The town of Selle (Zaru) in the 'Amarnah Tablets.' In *J.E.A.* 10 (1924), 6 ff.

3. Albright, W. F. 'The Jordan Valley in the Bronze Age.' In *Ann. A.S.O.R.* 6 (1924–5), 13 ff.

4. Albright, W. F. 'A teacher to a man of Shechem about 1400 B.C.' In *Bull. A.S.O.R.* 86 (1942), 28 ff.

5. Albright, W. F. 'A case of Lèse-Majesté in Pre-Israelite Lachish, with some remarks on the Israelite Conquest.' In *Bull. A.S.O.R.* 87 (1942), 32 ff.

6. Albright, W. F. 'Two little-understood letters from the Middle Jordan Valley.' In *Bull. A.S.O.R.* 89 (1943), 7 ff.
7. Albright, W. F. 'An archaic Hebrew proverb in an Amarna Letter from Central Palestine.' In *Bull. A.S.O.R.* 89 (1943), 29 ff.
8. Albright, W. F. 'A tablet of the Amarna Age from Gezer.' In *Bull. A.S.O.R.* 92 (1943), 28 ff.
9. Albright, W. F. 'A Prince of Taanach in the Fifteenth Century, B.C.' In *Bull. A.S.O.R.* 94 (1944), 12 ff.
10. Albright, W. F. and Moran, W. L. 'A re-interpretation of an Amarna Letter from Byblos (EA 82).' In *J.C.S.* 2 (1948), 239 ff.
11. Albright, W. F. and Moran, W. L. 'Rib-Adda of Byblos and the Affairs of Tyre (EA 98).' In *J.C.S.* 4 (1950), 163 ff.
12. Alt, A. 'Neues über Palästina aus dem Archiv Amenophis IV.' In *P.J.B.* 20 (1924), 22 ff.
13. Bezold, C. and Budge, E. A. W. (eds.). *The Tell el-Amarna Tablets in the British Museum*. London, 1892.
14. Böhl, F.-M. Th. *Die Sprache der Amarnabriefe*. Leipzig, 1909.
15. Böhl, F.-M. Th. 'Die bei den Ausgrabungen von Sichem gefundenen Keilschrifttafeln.' In *Z.D.P.V.* 49 (1926), 321 ff.
16. Bottéro, J. *Le Problème des Ḫabiru (Cahiers de la Société Asiatique, 12)*. Paris, 1954.
17. Campbell, E. F. 'The Amarna Letters and the Amarna Period.' In *Bi. Ar.* 23 (1960), 2 ff.
18. Campbell, E. F. *The Chronology of the Amarna Letters*. Baltimore, 1963.
19. De Koning, J. *Studiën over de El-Amarnabrieven en het Oude-Testament inzonderheid uit historisch Oogpunt*. Delft, 1940.
20. Dhorme, P. 'Amarna (Lettres d'el-Amarna).' In *Dictionnaire de la Bible: Supplément*. Paris, 1928.
21. Dhorme, P. 'Les Ḫabiru et les Hébreux.' In *J.P.O.S.* 4 (1924), 162 ff.
22. Dhorme, P. 'La langue de Canaan.' In *Rev. bibl.* n.s. 10 (1913), 369 ff.
23. Dhorme, P. 'La langue de Canaan.' In *Rev. bibl.* n.s. 11 (1914), 37 ff. and 344 ff.
24. Dhorme, P. 'Les nouvelles tablettes d'El-Amarna.' In *Rev. bibl.* 33 (1924), 5 ff.
25. Dossin, G. 'Une nouvelle lettre d'El-Amarna.' In *R.A.* 31 (1934), 125 ff.
26. Ebeling, E. *Das Verbum der El-Amarna-Briefe*. Leipzig, 1910.
27. Edel, E. 'Neue keilschriftliche Umschreibungen ägyptischer Namen aus den Boğazköytexten.' In *J.N.E.S.* 7 (1948), 11 ff.
28. Gadd, C. J. 'The Tell el-Amarna Tablets.' (Review of Mercer, S. A. B., *The Tell el-Amarna Tablets*.) In *P.E.Q.* 72 (1940), 116 ff.
29. Gardiner, A. H. 'The so-called Tomb of Queen Tiye.' In *J.E.A.* 43 (1957–8), 10 ff.
30. Goetze, A. and Levy, S. 'Fragment of the Gilgamesh Epic from Megiddo.' In *'Atiqot*, 2 (1959), 121 ff.
31. Gordon, C. H. 'The new Amarna Tablets.' In *Or.* n.s. 16 (1947), 1 ff.
32. Greenberg, M. *The Ḫab/piru (A.O.S. 39)*. New Haven, 1955.
33. Helck, H. W. *Die Beziehungen Ägyptens zu Vorderasien im 3. und 2. Jahrtausend v. Chr. (Ägyptologische Abhandlungen, Band 5)*. Wiesbaden, 1962.
34. Kitchen, K. A. *Suppiluliuma and the Amarna Pharaohs: A Study in Relative Chronology (Liverpool Monographs in Archaeology and Oriental Studies, ed. H. W. Fairman)*. Liverpool, 1962.
35. Knudtzon, J. A. *Die El-Amarna-Tafeln (Vorderasiatische Bibliothek, 2)*. Leipzig, 1915.

36. Landsberger, B. 'Assyrische Königsliste und "Dunkles Zeitalter".' In *J.C.S.* 8 (1954), 31 ff.
37. Lewy, J. '*Ḫabirū* and Hebrews.' In *H.U.C.A.* 14 (1939), 587 ff.
38. Lewy, J. 'A New Parallel between *Ḫabirū* and Hebrews.' In *H.U.C.A.* 15 (1940), 47 ff.
39. Maisler (Mazar), B. 'Canaan and the Canaanites.' In *Bull. A.S.O.R.* 102 (1946), 7 ff.
40. Mendelsohn, I. 'The Canaanite Term for "Free Proletarian".' In *Bull. A.S.O.R.* 83 (1941), 36 ff.
41. Mendelsohn, I. 'New Light on the *Ḫupšu*.' In *Bull. A.S.O.R.* 139 (1955), 9 ff.
42. Mercer, S. A. B. *The Tell el-Amarna Tablets.* Toronto, 1939.
43. O'Callaghan, R. T. *Aram Naharaim (An. Or. 26).* Rome, 1948.
44. Pritchard, J. B. (ed.). *Ancient Near-Eastern Texts relating to the Old Testament.* Ed. 2. Princeton, 1955.
45. Sachs, A. J. 'Two Notes on the Taanach and Amarna Letters.' In *Arch. f. Or.* 12 (1937–39), 371 ff.
46. Schroeder, O. *Die Tontafeln von El-Amarna (Vorderasiatische Schriftdenkmäler der königlichen Museen zu Berlin,* 11–12). Leipzig, 1914–15.
47. Sellin, E. and Hrozný, F. *Tell Taʿannek (Denk. K. Akad. Wiss. Wien,* Phil.-hist. Klasse, 50), 113 ff. Vienna, 1904.
48. Sellin, E. and Hrozný, F. *Eine Nachlese auf dem Tell Taʿannek in Palästina (Denk. K. Akad. Wiss. Wien,* Phil.-hist. Klasse, 52), 36 ff. Vienna, 1906.
49. Smith, S. Contribution to Garstang, J. 'Jericho; city and necropolis, fourth report.' In *Ann. Arch. Anthr.* 21 (1934), 116 f.
50. Thureau-Dangin, F. 'Nouvelles lettres d'El Amarna.' In *R.A.* 19 (1921), 91 ff.
51. Winckler, H. *Der Thontafelfund von El-Amarna,* I–III. (*Mittheilungen aus den orientalischen Sammlungen der königlichen Museen zu Berlin,* 1–3). Berlin, 1889–90.
52. Wright, G. E. *Shechem.* New York, 1965.
53. Youngblood, R. 'Amorite Influence in a Canaanite Amarna Letter.' In *Bull. A.S.O.R.* 168 (1962), 24 ff.

### II. POLITICAL ORGANIZATION OF PALESTINE IN THE AMARNA AGE

1. Albright, W. F. 'Cuneiform material for Egyptian Prosopography, 1500–1200 B.C.' In *J.N.E.S.* 5 (1946), 7 ff.
2. Helck, H. W. *Der Einfluss der Militärführer in der 18. ägyptischen Dynastie (Untersuchungen zur Geschichte und Altertumskunde Aegyptens,* 14). Leipzig, 1939.
3. Newberry, P. E. *Scarabs.* London, 1908.
4. Pflüger, K. 'The Edict of King Haremhab.' In *J.N.E.S.* 5 (1946), 260 ff.
5. Sethe, K. and Helck, H. W. *Urkunden der 18. Dynastie.* Leipzig and Berlin, 1906–.

### III. PALESTINE: DEMOGRAPHY AND SOCIETY

1. Albright, W. F. 'The Egyptian correspondence of Abimilki, Prince of Tyre.' In *J.E.A.* 23 (1937), 190 ff.
2. Albright, W. F. 'Abram the Hebrew; a new archaeological Interpretation.' In *Bull. A.S.O.R.* 163 (1961), 36 ff.
3. Albright, W. F. *The Biblical Period, from Abraham to Ezra.* New York, 1964.

4. Borger, R. 'Das Problem der 'Apīru ("Ḫabiru").' In *Z.D.P.V.* 74 (1958), 131.
5. *C.A.D. The Assyrian Dictionary.* Chicago, 1956–.
6. Dhorme, E. 'Les Habirou et les Hébreux.' In *Rev. hist.* 211 (1954), 256 ff.
7. Dothan, T. 'Spinning Bowls.' In *I.E.J.* 13 (1963), 97 ff.
8. Falkenstein, A. Review of Kupper, J. R. *Les Nomades en Mésopotamie.* In *Z.A.* 53 (1959), 280 ff.
9. Kramer, S. N. *The Sumerians: their History, Culture, and Character.* Chicago, 1963.
10. Nougayrol, J. *Le Palais Royal d'Ugarit IV: Textes accadiens des Archives Sud (Mission de Ras Shamra,* tome IX). Paris, 1956.
11. Otten, H. 'Zwei althethitische Belege zu den Ḫapiru (SA. GAZ).' In *Z.A.* 52 (1957), 216 ff.
12. Säve-Söderbergh, T. 'The *'prw* as vintagers in Egypt.' In *Or. Suecana,* 1 (1952), 5 ff.
13. Soden, W. von. *Assyrisches Handwörterbuch.* Wiesbaden, 1959–.
14. Steele, F. R. 'An additional fragment of the Lipit-Ishtar Code tablet from Nippur.' In *Arch. Orient.* 18, nos. 1–2 (1950), 489 ff.

## CHAPTER XXI(*a*)

### G. GENERAL

1. Berlin, Staatliche Museen, Vorderasiatische Abteilung. *Keilschrifturkunden aus Boghazköi* (*K.U.B.*), I–XXXII. Berlin, 1921–42.
2. Deutsche Orient-Gesellschaft. *Keilschrifttexte aus Boghazköi* (*K.Bo.*): I–IV = *Wissenschaftliche Veröffentlichung* 30. Leipzig, 1916–23; V–VI = idem 36, Leipzig, 1921; VII–XII, XIV = idem 68–70, 72, 73, 77, 79, Berlin, 1954–63.
3. Götze, A. *Verstreute Boghazköi-Texte* (*V.Bo.T.*). Marburg/Lahn, 1930.
4. Knudtzon, J. A. *Die El-Amarna Tafeln* (*V.A.B.* 2). 2 vols. Leipzig, 1915.
5. Messerschmidt, L. and Schroeder, O. *Keilschrifttexte aus Assur historischen Inhalts.* 2 vols. Leipzig, 1911–22.
6. Pritchard, J. B. (ed.). *Ancient Near Eastern Texts Relating to the Old Testament* (Ed. 2). Princeton, 1955.

### I. THE RESTORATION OF HITTITE POWER

1. Friedrich, J. *Staatsverträge des Ḫatti-Reiches in hethitischer Sprache.* 2 vols. (*M.V.Ae.G.* 31 and 34/1). Leipzig, 1926 and 1930.
2. Goetze, A. *Kizzuwatna and the Problem of Hittite Geography* (*Y.O.S.* Researches, vol. 22). New Haven, Conn., 1940.
3. Gurney, O. R. 'Hittite Prayers of Mursili II.' In *Ann. Arch. Anthr.* 27 (1940).
4. Güterbock, H. G. 'The Deeds of Suppiluliuma as told by his son, Mursili II.' In *J.C.S.* 10 (1956), 41 ff., 107 ff.
5. Rost, L. 'Die ausserhalb von Boğazköy gefundenen hethitischen Briefe.' In *Mitt. Inst. Or.* 4 (1956), 328 ff.

## II. THE HITTITE EMPIRE UNDER MURSHILISH

1. Cavaignac, E. 'L'affaire de Iaruvatta.' In *R.H.A.* fasc. 6 (1932), 189 ff.
2. Ebeling, E., Meissner, B. and Weidner, E. F. *Die Inschriften der altassyrischen Könige (Altorientalische Bibliothek*, 1). Leipzig, 1926.
3. Forrer, E. *Forschungen* 1/1, 1/2, 11/1. Erkner bei Berlin, 1926–9.
4. Friedrich, J. *Aus dem hethitischen Schrifttum*, 1 (*Alte Or.* 24/3). Leipzig, 1925.
5. Götze, A. *Die Annalen des Muršiliš* (*M.V.Ae.G.* 38). Leipzig, 1933.
6. Güterbock, H. G. *Siegel aus Boğazköy*, 1, 11. *Arch.f. Or.* Beihefte 5 (1940) and 7 (1942).
7. Klengel, H. 'Der Schiedsspruch des Muršili II. hinsichtlich Barga....' In *Or.* n.s. 32 (1963), 32 ff.
8. Laroche, E. 'Documents hiéroglyphiques hittites provenants du palais d'Ugarit.' In *Ugaritica*, 111 ( = *Mission de Ras Shamra*, VIII) (1956), 97 ff.
9. Nougayrol, J. *Textes accadiens des Archives sud* (*Le palais royal d'Ugarit*, IV = *Mission de Ras Shamra*, IX). Paris, 1956.
10. Schuler, E. von. *Hethitische Dienstanweisungen für höhere Hof- und Staatsbeamte. Arch.f. Or.* Beiheft 10 (1957).
11. Weidner, E. F. *Politische Dokumente aus Kleinasien* (*Bo. Stu.*, 8). Leipzig, 1923.

## III. ASIA MINOR UNDER MUWATALLISH

1. Götze, A. *Ḫattušiliš. Der Bericht über seine Thronbesteigung nebst den Paralleltexten* (*M.V.Ae.G.* 1924/3). Leipzig, 1925.
2. Götze, A. *Neue Bruchstücke zum Grossen Text des Ḫattušiliš und den Paralleltexten* (*M.V.Ae.G.* 1929/2). Leipzig, 1930.
3. Szemerényi, O. 'Vertrag des Hethiterkönigs Tudḫalija IV mit Ištarmuwa von Amurru (*K.U.B.* XXIII, 1).' In *Acta Soc. Hungaricae Orientalis*, 9 (1945), 113 ff.

## APPENDIX: THE AHHIYAWA PROBLEM

(see above, p. 119, n. 5)

1. Forrer, E. 'Die Griechen in den Boghazköi-Texten.' In *O.L.Z.* 1924, 113 ff.
2. Forrer, E. 'Vorhomerische Griechen in den Keilschrifttexten von Boghazköy.' In *M.D.O.G.* 63 (1924), 1 ff.
3. Friedrich, J. 'Werden in den hethitischen Keilschrifttexten die Griechen erwähnt?' In *K.F.* 1 (1927), 87 ff.
4. Forrer, E. 'Für die Griechen in den Boghazköi-Inschriften.' In *K.F.* 1 (1929), 252 ff.
5. Sommer, F. *Die Aḫḫijavā-Urkunden* (*Abh. München*, n.F. 6). München, 1932.
6. Sommer, F. *Aḫḫijavāfrage und Sprachwissenschaft* (*Abh. München*, n.F. 9). München, 1934.
7. Götze, A. Review of Sommer, *Die Aḫḫijavā-Urkunden.* In *Gnomon*, 10 (1934), 177 ff.
8. Schachermeyer, F. *Hethiter und Achäer* (*M.A.O.G.* IX, 1/2). Leipzig, 1935.
9. Güterbock, H. G. 'Neue Aḫḫijavā-Texte.' In *Z.A.* 43 (1936), 321 ff.
10. Sommer, F. 'Aḫḫijavā und kein Ende.' In *Indogerm. Forsch.* 55 (1937), 169 ff.
11. Cavaignac, E. 'La question hittite-achéenne d'après les dernières publications.' In *B.C.H.* 70 (1946), 58 ff.

12. Völkl, K. 'Achchijawa.' In *N.C.* 4 (1952), 329 ff.
13. Dussaud, R. *Prélydiens, Hittites et Achéens.* Paris, 1953.
14. Schachermeyr, F. 'Zur Frage der Lokalisierung von Achiawa.' In *Minoica—Festschrift Sundwall* (1958), 365 ff.
15. Garstang, John and Gurney, O. R. *The Geography of the Hittite Empire.* Occasional Publications of the British Institute of Archaeology at Ankara, no. 5. London, 1959.
16. Huxley, G. *Achaeans and Hittites.* Oxford, 1960.
17. Page, D. L. *History and the Homeric Iliad.* Berkeley, 1959; Cambridge, 1963.

## CHAPTER XXI(*b*)

### IV. UGARIT IN THE FOURTEENTH AND THIRTEENTH CENTURIES B.C.

1. Albright, W. F. 'The Egyptian Correspondence of Abimilki Prince of Tyre.' In *J.E.A.* 23 (1937), 190 ff.
2. Albright, W. F. 'Recent Progress in North Canaanite Research.' In *Bull. A.S.O.R.* 70 (1938), 18 ff.
3. Albright, W. F. 'An unrecognised Amarna Letter from Ugarit.' In *Bull. A.S.O.R.* 95 (1944), 30 ff.
4. Albright, W. F. and Moran, W. L. 'Ribaddu of Byblos and the affairs of Tyre.' In *J.C.S.* 4 (1950), 163 ff.
5. Astour, M. C. 'Les étrangers à Ugarit et le status juridique des Ḫabiru.' In *R.A.* 53 (1959), 70 ff.
6. Astour, M. C. *Hellenosemitica. An ethnic and cultural study in West Semitic impact on Mycenaean Greece.* Leiden, 1965.
7. Astour, M. C. 'New Evidence on the Last Days of Ugarit.' In *A.J.A.* 69 (1965), 253 ff.
8. Cavaignac, E. 'L'Egypte et les Hittites de 1370 à 1345.' In *Syria,* 33 (1956), 42 ff.
9. Cazelles, H. 'Hébreux, Ubru et Hapiru.' In *Syria,* 35 (1958), 198 ff.
10. Courtois, J.-C. 'Deux villes du royaume d'Ugarit dans la vallée du Nahr-el-Kebir en Syrie du Nord.' In *Syria,* 40 (1963), 261 ff.
11. Dussaud, R. *Les découvertes de Ras Shamra (Ugarit) et l'Ancien Testament.* Paris, 1941.
12. *EA.* The Amarna Letters, as numbered in G, 4.
13. Edel, E. 'Die Abfassungszeit des Briefes KBo 1 10 (Ḫattušil-Kadašman-Ellil) und seine Bedeutung für die Chronologie Ramses' 11.' In *J.C.S.* 12 (1958), 130 ff.
14. Eissfeldt, O. *Kleine Schriften.* 4 vols. Tübingen, 1962–.
15. Freydank, H. 'Eine hethitische Fassung des Vertrages zwischen dem Hethiterkönig Šuppiluliuma und Aziru von Amurru.' In *Mitt. Inst. Or.* 7 (1960), 356 ff.
16. Goetze, A. 'Hittite Courtiers and their Titles.' In *R.H.A.* 12, 54 (1952), 1 ff.
17. Gordon, C. H. 'Observations on the Akkadian Texts from Ugarit.' In *R.A.* 50 (1956), 127 ff.
18. Gordon, C. H. *Ugaritic Handbook (An. Or.* 25). Rome, 1947.
19. Gurney, O. *The Hittites.* Ed. 2 revised. Harmondsworth, 1966.
20. Kapelrud, A. S. *The Ras Shamra Discoveries and the Old Testament.* Oxford, 1965.

21. Kitchen, K. A. *Suppiluliuma and the Amarna Pharaohs.* Liverpool, 1962.
22. Klengel, H. Review of M. Liverani, *Storia di Ugarit*, in *O.L.Z.* 57 (1962), 453 ff.
23. Korošec, V. 'Les Hittites et leurs vassaux syriens à la lumière de nouveaux textes d'Ugarit (*PRU*, iv).' In *R.H.A.* 66 (1960), 65 ff.
24. Laroche, E. 'Études sur les hiéroglyphes hittites: 6. Adana et Danouniens.' In *Syria*, 35 (1958), 263 ff.
25. Liverani, M. 'Karkemiš nei testi di Ugarit.' In *Riv. stud. or.* 35 (1960), 135 ff.
26. Liverani, M. *Storia di Ugarit nell' età degli archivi politici* (Studi Semitici 6). Rome, 1962.
27. Moran, W. L. 'The scandal of the "Great Sin" at Ugarit.' In *J.N.E.S.* 18 (1959), 280 f.
28. Nougayrol, J. 'Guerre et paix à Ugarit.' In *Iraq*, 25 (1963), 110 ff.
29. Otten, H. 'Neue Quellen zum Ausklang des Hethitischen Reiches.' In *M.D.O.G.* 94 (1963), 1 ff.
30. *Le Palais Royal d'Ugarit.* 4 vols. (*Mission de Ras Shamra*, ed. C. F. A. Schaeffer, vii, vi, ix, xi). Paris, 1955–65.
31. Rainey, A. F. 'The Kingdom of Ugarit.' In *Bi. Ar.* 28 (1965), 102 ff.
32. Revere, R. B. 'No Man's Coast; Ports of Trade in the Eastern Mediterranean.' In *Trade and Market in the Early Empires.* Eds. K. Polyani, C. M. Arensburg and H. W. Pearson (Glencoe, Ill., 1957). Pp. 38 ff.
33. Riis, P. J. 'Excavations in Phoenicia.' In *Archaeology*, 14 (1961), 214 ff.
34. Schaeffer, C. F. A. 'A Bronze Sword from Ugarit with Cartouche of Mineptah.' In *Antiq.* 29 (1955), 226 ff.
35. Schaeffer, C. F. A. *The Cuneiform Texts of Ras Shamra-Ugarit* (Schweich Lectures for 1936). Oxford, 1939.
36. Schaeffer, C. F. A. 'Les fouilles de Minet el-Beida et de Ras Shamra, deuxième campagne (printemps 1930).' In *Syria*, 12 (1931), 1 ff.
37. Schaeffer, C. F. A. 'Les fouilles de Ras Shamra-Ugarit. Dix-septième campagne de fouilles.' In *Ann. Arch. de Syrie*, 3 (1953), 117 ff.
38. Schaeffer, C. F. A. 'Les fouilles de Ras Shamra-Ugarit. Quinzième, seizième et dix-septième campagnes (1951, 1952, et 1953).' In *Syria*, 31 (1954), 14 ff.
39. Schaeffer, C. F. A. 'Nouvelles découvertes à Ras Shamra-Ugarit.' In *C.-R. Ac. Inscr. B.-L.* (1961), 232 ff.
40 Schaeffer, C. F. A. 'Nouvelles fouilles de la mission archéologique de Ras Shamra dans le palais d'Ugarit (campagne 1951).' In *Ann. Arch. de Syrie*, 2 (1952), 3 ff.
41. Schaeffer, C. F. A. 'Nouvelles fouilles et découvertes à Ras Shamra-Ugarit, XXVe campagne, automne 1961.' In *C.-R. Ac. Inscr. B.-L.* (1962), 198 ff.
42. Schaeffer, C. F. A. 'Reprise de recherches archéologiques à Ras Shamra-Ugarit. Sondages de 1948 et 1949, et campagne de 1950.' In *Syria*, 28 (1951), 1 ff.
43. Schaeffer, C. F. A. *Stratigraphie comparée et chronologie de l'Asie Occidentale.* London, 1948.
44. Schaeffer, C. F. A. *Ugaritica* (*Mission de Ras Shamra*, iii, v, viii, ix, xvi, xvii). 6 vols. Paris, 1939–69.
45. Schmidtke, F. 'Das Ende der antiken Siedlung von Ras Schamra.' In *Atti del XIX Congresso Internazionale degli Orientalisti* (Rome, 1938), 434 ff.
46. Schmökel, H. *Keilschriftforschung und alte Geschichte Vorderasiens* (*Handbuch der Orientalistik*, ed. B. Spüler, Bd. ii, 3. Abschnitt). Leiden, 1957.

47. Simons, J. *Handbook for the Study of Egyptian Topographical Lists.* Leiden, 1937.
48. Sommer, F. *Die Aḫḫijavā-Urkunden (Abh. München, n.F. 6).* Munich, 1932.
49. Thureau-Dangin, F. 'Une lettre assyrienne de Ras Shamra.' In *Syria,* 16 (1935), 188 ff.
50. Thureau-Dangin, F. 'Vocabulaires de Ras-Shamra.' In *Syria,* 12 (1931), 225 ff.
51. Tsevat, M. 'Marriage and monarchical legitimacy in Ugarit and Israel.' In *J.S.S.* 3 (1958), 237 ff.
52. van Buren, E. D. 'Homage to a deified king.' In *Z.A.* 50 (1952), 92 ff.
53. Virolleaud, Ch. 'Lettres et documents administratifs provenant des archives d'Ugarit.' In *Syria,* 21 (1940), 247 ff.
54. Virolleaud, Ch. 'Les nouveaux textes alphabétiques de Ras-Shamra.' In *C.-R. Ac. Inscr. B.-L.* (1962), 92 ff.
55. Woolley, Sir Leonard. *Alalakh: An Account of the Excavations at Tell Atchana.* Oxford, 1955.
56. Woolley, Sir Leonard. *A Forgotten Kingdom.* Harmondsworth, 1955.
57. Yaron, R. 'A royal divorce at Ugarit.' In *Or.* n.s. 32 (1963), 21 ff.

## V. CANAANITE RELIGION AND LITERATURE

1. Aistleitner, J. *Wörterbuch der ugaritischen Sprache. Verhandl. Leipzig,* phil.-hist. Klasse 106, 3.) Ed. 3. Berlin, 1967.
2. Albright, W. F. *Archaeology and the Religion of Israel.* Ed. 3. Baltimore, 1953.
3. Albright, W. F. 'Astarte plaques and figurines from Tell Beit Mirsim.' In *Mél. Dussaud,* 1 (Paris, 1939), 107 ff.
4. Albright, W. F. 'The Canaanite God Ḥaurôn (Ḥôrôn).' In *A.J.S.L.* 53 (1936), 1 ff.
5. Albright, W. F. *From the Stone Age to Christianity.* Ed. 2. Baltimore, 1957.
6. Albright, W. F. 'The High Place in Ancient Palestine.' In *V.T.* Suppl. 4 (1957), 242 ff.
7. Albright, W. F. 'The Song of Deborah in the Light of Archaeology.' In *Bull. A.S.O.R.* 62 (1936), 26 ff.
8. Albright, W. F. 'Zabûl Yam and Thâpit Nahar in the Combat between Baal and the Sea.' In *J.P.O.S.* 16 (1936), 17 ff.
9. Astour, M. C. 'Some new divine names from Ugarit.' In *J.A.O.S.* 86 (1966), 277 ff.
10. Barrelet, M.-T. 'Deux déesses syro-phéniciennes sur un bronze du Louvre.' In *Syria,* 35 (1958), 27 ff.
11. Barrois, A. G. *Manuel d'archéologie biblique.* 2 vols. Paris, 1939, 1953.
12. Bonnet, H. *Reallexikon der aegyptischen Religionsgeschichte.* Berlin, 1952.
13. Bowra, C. M. *Homer and his Forerunners.* Edinburgh, 1955.
14. Bowra, C. M. *Tradition and Design in the Iliad.* Oxford, 1930.
15. Caquot, A. 'Le dieu 'Athtar et les textes de Ras Shamra.' In *Syria,* 35 (1958), 45 ff.
16. Caquot, A. 'La divinité solaire ougaritique.' In *Syria,* 36 (1959), 90 ff.
17. Cassuto, U. *The Goddess Anath.* Jerusalem, 1965.
18. Cazelles, H. 'L'hymne ugaritique à Anath.' In *Syria,* 33 (1956), 49 ff.
19. Clemen, C. *Die phönikische Religion nach Philo von Byblos (M.V.A.G.* Bd. 42, 3. Heft). Leipzig, 1939.

20. Cory, Isaac P. *Ancient Fragments of the Phoenician, Chaldaean, Egyptian, Tyrian and other writers.* Ed. 2. London, 1832.
21. Dahood, M. H. 'Ancient Semitic Deities in Syria and Palestine.' In *Le antiche divinità semitiche (Studi Semitici,* 1), ed. S. Moscati, pp. 65 ff. Rome, 1958.
22. Dhorme, É. 'Le Dieu Baal et le Dieu Moloch dans la Tradition biblique.' In *A. St.* 6 (1956), 57 ff.
23. Dhorme, É. *Recueil Édouard Dhorme: Études bibliques et orientales.* Paris, 1951.
24. Dunand, M. *Les fouilles de Byblos.* 2 vols. Paris, 1939, 1954.
25. Driver, G. R. *Canaanite Myths and Legends (Old Testament Studies,* 3). Edinburgh, 1967.
26. Dussaud, R. *Les origines cananéennes du sacrifice israëlite.* Ed. 2. Paris, 1941.
27. Dussaud, R. *Les Religions des Hittites et des Hourrites, des Phéniciens et des Syriens (Mana,* 1, 11, 2). Paris, 1945.
28. Eissfeldt, O. *Baal Zaphon, Zeus Kasios und der Durchgang der Israeliten durchs Meer (Beiträge zur Religionsgeschichte des Altertums,* 1). Halle (Saale), 1932.
29. Eissfeldt, O. *Einleitung in das Alte Testament.* 3 Aufl. Tübingen, 1964.
30. Eissfeldt, O. 'Kanaanäische-Ugaritische Religion.' In *Handbuch der Orientalistik,* 1 Abt., Bd. viii, Lief. 1, pp. 76 ff. Leiden 1964.
31. Eissfeldt, O. *Molk als Opferbegriff im Punischen und Hebräischen und das Ende des Gottes Moloch (Beiträge zur Religionsgeschichte des Altertums,* 3). Halle (Saale), 1935.
32. Eissfeldt, O. *Ras Shamra und Sanchuniaton (Beiträge zur Religionsgeschichte des Altertums,* 4). Halle, 1939.
33. Eissfeldt, O. *Sanchunjaton von Berut und Ilumilku von Ugarit (Beiträge zur Religionsgeschichte des Altertums,* 5). Halle, 1952.
34. Eusebius of Pamphylia. *Evangelicae Praeparationis Libri XV,* ed. E. H. Gifford. 4 vols. Oxford, 1903.
35. Gaster, T. H. 'A Canaanite Magical Text.' In *Or.* n.s. 11 (1942), 41 ff.
36. Gaster, T. H. 'A Canaanite Ritual Drama.' In *J.A.O.S.* 66 (1946), 49 ff.
37. Gaster, T. H. 'The "Graces" in Semitic Folklore: A Wedding Song from Ras Shamra.' In *J.R.A.S.* 65 (1938), 37 ff.
38. Gaster, T. H. *Thespis: Myth, Ritual and Drama in the Ancient Near East.* New York, 1950.
39. Ginsberg, H. L. *The Legend of King Keret (Bull. A.S.O.R. Supplementary Studies,* 2–3). Baltimore, 1946.
40. Ginsberg, H. L. 'Two Religious Borrowings in Ugaritic Literature: 1. A Hurrian Myth in Semitic Dress.' In *Or.* n.s. 8 (1939), 317 ff.
41. Ginsberg, H. L. 'Ugaritic Myths, Epics and Legends.' In *Ancient Near Eastern Texts relating to the Old Testament.* Ed. James B. Pritchard. Princeton, 1955, 129 ff.
42. Gordon, C. H. 'Homer and Bible: the Origin and Character of East Mediterranean Literature.' *H.U.C.A.* 26 (1955), 43 ff.
43. Gordon, C. H. *Ugaritic Literature.* Rome, 1949.
44. Gray, J. *The Canaanites (Ancient People and Places,* 38). London, 1964.
45. Gray, J. '*Dt'n* and *Rp'um* in Ancient Ugarit.' In *P.E.Q.* 84 (1952), 39 ff.
46. Gray, J. *The KRT text in the literature of Ras Shamra. A social myth of ancient Canaan,* ed. 2 (*Documenta et Monumenta Orientis Antiqui,* v). Leiden, 1964.
47. Gray, J. *The Legacy of Canaan. The Ras Shamra Texts and their relevance to the Old Testament.* Ed. 2 (*V.T.* Suppl. 5). Leiden, 1965.
48. Hooke, S. H. *The Canaanite Origins of Early Semitic Ritual* (Schweich Lectures for 1935). London, 1938.

49. Jack, J. W. *The Ras Shamra Tablets and their bearing upon the Old Testament* (O.T. Studies 1). Edinburgh, 1935.

50. Kapelrud, A. S. *Baal in the Ras Shamra Texts.* Copenhagen, 1952.

51. Langhe, R. de. *Les textes de Ras Shamra-Ugarit et leurs rapports avec le milieu biblique de l'Ancien Testament.* 2 vols. (*Universitas Catholica Lovaniensis,* diss. sér. 2, tom. 35.) Paris, 1945.

52. Langhe, R. de 'Myth, Ritual and Kingship in the Ras Shamra Tablets.' In *Myth, Ritual and Kingship,* ed. S. H. Hooke (Oxford, 1958), 122 ff.

53. Lucian of Samosata. *Lucian,* with an English translation by A. M. Harmon and K. K. Kilburn. 8 vols. (*Loeb Classical Library*). Cambridge, Mass., 1913–61.

54. Matthiae, P. 'Note sul dio siriano Rešef.' In *Or. Antiq.* 2 (1963), 27 ff.

55. Nougayrol, J. 'Nouveaux textes accadiens de Ras-Shamra.' In *C.-R. Ac. Inscr. B.-L.* (1963), 163 ff.

56. Nougayrol, J. 'Nouveaux textes d'Ugarit en cunéiformes babyloniens (20e campagne, 1956).' In *C.-R. Ac. Inscr. B.-L.* (1957), 77 f.

57. Nougayrol, J. 'Nouveaux textes d'Ugarit en cunéiformes babyloniens.' In *Ann. Arch. de Syrie,* 14 (1964), 39 ff.

58. Obermann, J. *Ugaritic Mythology.* New Haven, 1948.

59. Patai, R. 'The Goddess Asherah.' In *J.N.E.S.* 24 (1965), 37 ff.

60. Pope, M. R. *El in the Ugaritic Texts* (*V.T.* Suppl. 2). Leiden, 1955.

61. Pritchard, J. B. *Palestinian figurines in relation to certain goddesses known through literature.* A.O.S. Publns. 24. New Haven, 1943.

62. Rowe, A. *The four Canaanite Temples at Beth Shan.* I. *The Temples and Cult Cult Objects* (*Publns. of the Palestinian Section of the University Museum, University of Pennsylvania,* 2). Philadelphia, 1940.

63. Schaeffer, C. F. A. 'La XVIIIe campagne de fouilles à Ras Shamra-Ugarit, (1954).' In *C.-R. Ac. Inscr. B.-L.* (1955), 249 ff.

64. Schaeffer, C. F. A. 'Les fouilles de Ras-Shamra (Ugarit). Sixième campagne (printemps 1934). Rapport sommaire.' In *Syria,* 16 (1935), 141 ff.

65. Schaeffer, C. F. A. 'Neue Entdeckungen in Ugarit.' In *Arch. f. Or.* 20 (1963), 206 ff.

66. Schaeffer, C. F. A. 'Résumé des résultats de la XIXe campagne de fouilles à Ras Shamra–Ugarit, 1955.' In *Ann. Arch. de Syrie,* 7 (1957), 35 ff.

67. Schaeffer, C. F. A. 'Les fouilles de Ras Shamra-Ugarit, dixième et onzième campagnes (automne et hiver 1938–39).' In *Syria,* 20 (1939), 277 ff.

68. Seton-Williams, M. V. 'Palestinian Temples.' In *Iraq,* 9 (1949), 77 ff.

69. Virolleaud, Ch. 'États nominatifs et pièces comptables provenant de Ras-Shamra.' In *Syria,* 18 (1937), 159 ff.

70. Virolleaud, Ch. *La légende de Kéret, Roi des Sidoniens* (*Mission de Ras-Shamra,* II). Paris, 1936.

71. Virolleaud, Ch. 'La légende du roi Kéret d'après de nouveaux documents.' In *Mél. Dussaud,* 2 (1939), 755 ff.

72. Virolleaud, Ch. *La légende phénicienne de Danel* (*Mission de Ras-Shamra,* 1). Paris, 1936.

73. Virolleaud, Ch. 'Les noms propres de personne à Ras-Shamra.' In *Groupe linguistique d'Études Chamito-Sémitiques,* 7 (1957), 108 ff.

74. Virolleaud, Ch. 'Un nouvel épisode du mythe ugaritique de Baal.' In *C.-R. Ac. Inscr. B.-L.* (1960), 180 ff.

75. Virolleaud, Ch. 'Les nouvelles tablettes alphabétiques de Ras-Shamra (XIXe campagne).' In *C.-R. Ac. Inscr. B.-L.* (1956), 60 ff.

76. Virolleaud, Ch. 'Les nouvelles tablettes de Ras Shamra (1948–1949).' In *Syria,* 28 (1951), 22 ff.

77. Virolleaud, Ch. 'Les nouveaux textes alphabétiques de Ras-Shamra (XVIe campagne, 1952).' In *Syria*, 30 (1953), 187 ff.
78. Virolleaud, Ch. 'Les nouveaux textes mythologiques de Ras-Shamra.' In *C.-R. Ac. Inscr. B.-L.* (1962), 105 ff.
79. Virolleaud, Ch. 'Les villes et corporations du royaume d'Ugarit.' In *Syria*, 21 (1940), 123 ff.
80. Webster, T. B. L. *From Mycenae to Homer.* London, 1958.
81. Weidner, E. 'Das Pantheon von Ugarit.' In *Arch. f. Or.* 18 (1957–8), 167 ff.
82. Wiseman, D. M. *The Alalakh Tablets* (British Institute of Archaeology in Ankara: Occasional Publications, 2). London, 1953.
83. Yadin, Y. and others. *Hazor. The James A. Rothschild Expedition at Hazor.* 4 vols. Jerusalem, 1958–65.

A. ADDENDA

1. Aartun, Kjell. 'Beiträge zum ugaritischen Lexikon.' In *Welt des Or.* 4 (1967–8), 278 ff.
2. Aistleitner, J. *Die mythologischen und kultischen Texte aus Ras Schamra.* Ed. 2. Budapest, 1964.
3. Albright, W. F. *Yahweh and the Gods of Canaan.* London, 1967.
4. Astour, M. C. 'The Partition of the Confederacy of Mukiš-Nuḫašše-Nii by Šuppiluliuma.' In *Or.* 38 (1969), 381 ff.
5. Astour, M. 'Some New Divine Names from Ugarit.' In *J.A.O.S.* 86 (1966), 277 ff.
6. Astour, Michael C. 'Two Ugaritic Serpent Charms.' In *J.N.E.S.* 27 (1968), 13 ff.
7. Bronner, Leah. *The Stories of Elijah and Elisha as Polemics against Baal Worship.* Pretoria Oriental Series VI. Leiden, 1968.
8. Campbell, A. F. 'Homer and Ugaritic Literature.' In *Abr. Naharain*, 5 (1964–5) 1966, 29 ff.
9. Cassuto, U. and Abrahams, L. *The Goddess Anath; Canaanite Epics of the Patriarchal Age.* Jerusalem, 1970.
10. Dietrich, M. and Loretz, O. 'Die soziale Struktur von Alalaḫ und Ugarit I.' In *We. Or.* 3 (1966), 188 ff.
11. Dietrich, M. and Loretz, O. 'Der Vertrag zwischen Šuppiluliuma und Niqmandu.' In *We. Or.* 3 (1966), 206 ff.
12. Du Mesnil du Buisson, Robert. *Études sur les dieux phéniciens hérités par l'Empire romain* (Études préliminaires aux religions orientales dans l'Empire romain, 14). Leiden, 1970.
13. Fisher, Loren R. and Knutson, F. B. 'An enthronement ritual at Ugarit.' In *J.N.E.S.* 28 (1969), 157 ff.
14. Gordon, C. H. *Ugarit and Minoan Crete. The Bearing of the Tablets on the Origins of Western Culture.* New York, 1966.
15. Gordon, C. H. *An Ugaritic Textbook* (Analecta Orientalia 38). Rome, 1965.
16. Gröndahl, F. *Die Personennamen der Texte von Ugarit* (Studia Pohl 1). Rome 1967.
17. Güterbock, H. G. 'The Hittite Conquest of Cyprus Reconsidered.' In *J.N.E.S.* 26 (1967), 73 ff.
18. Hammershaib, E. 'History and Cult in the Old Testament.' In *Near Eastern Studies in Honor of William Foxwell Albright*, ed. H. Goedicke (Baltimore & London, 1971), pp. 269 ff.

19. Herdner, A. *Corpus des Tablettes en cunéiformes alphabétiques découvertes à Ras Shamra-Ugarit de 1929 à 1939* (Mission de Ras Shamra x). Paris, 1963.

20. Klengel, H. *Geschichte Syriens im 2. Jahrtausend v. u. Z.* 3 vols. (Deutsche Akad. d. Wissenschaften zu Berlin, Institut für Orientforschung, Veröff. 40, 70, 40). Berlin, 1965–70.

21. Malamat, A. 'The Egyptian Decline in Canaan and the Sea-Peoples.' In *Judges* (World History of the Jewish People, Series 1, vol. iii, ed. B. Mazar), pp. 23 ff. Tel Aviv, 1971.

22. Muntingh, L. M. 'The Social and Legal Status of the free Ugaritic female.' In *J.N.E.S.* 26 (1967), 102 ff.

23. Neiman, D. 'The Supercaelian Sea.' In *J.N.E.S.* 28 (1969), 243 ff.

24. Oldenburg, Ulf. *The Conflict between El and Ba'al in Canaanite Religion* (Suppl. *Numen*, dissertationes vol. iii). Leiden, 1969.

25. Otten, H. 'Ein hethitischer Vertrag aus dem 15/14 Jhr. v. Chr.' In *Ist. Mitt.* 17 (1967), 55 ff.

26. Pope, Marvin H. 'The scene on the Drinking Mug from Ugarit.' In *Near Eastern Studies in honor of William Foxwell Albright*, ed. H. Goedicke (Baltimore & London, 1971), pp. 393 ff.

27. Riis, P. J. *Sukas I. The North-east Sanctuary and the first settling of Greeks in Syria and Palestine* (Publns of the Carlsberg Expedn to Phoenicia 1). Copenhagen, 1970.

28. Sasson, Jack M. 'Canaanite Maritime Involvement in the second millennium B.C.' In *J.A.O.S.* 86 (1966), 126 ff.

29. Schaeffer, C. F. A. 'Le culte d'El à Ras Shamra-Ugarit et le veau d'or.' In *C.R.A.I.B.L.* (1966), pp. 327 ff.

30. Schaeffer, Claude. 'Lettre relative à la campagne de fouilles à Ras Shamra-Ugarit.' In *C.R.A.I.B.L.* (1969), pp. 524 f.

31. Schaeffer, C. F. A. 'Nouveaux témoignages du culte de El et de Baal à Ras Shamra–Ugarit et ailleurs en Syrie–Palestine.' In *Syria* 43 (1966), 1 ff.

32. Vanel, A. *L'iconographie du dieu de l'orage dans le Proche-Orient jusqu'au VIIe siècle avant Jesus-Christ.* Paris, 1965.

33. Watson, Paul L. 'The Death of "Death" in the Ugaritic Texts.' In *J.A.O.S.* 92 (1972), 60 ff.

34. Zaccagnini, C. 'Note sulle terminologia metallurgica di Ugarit.' In *Or. Antiq.*, 9 (1970), 313 ff.

## CHAPTER XXI(*c*)

1. Blegen, C. W., Boulter, C. G., Caskey, J. L., Rawson, M., and Sperling, J. *Troy: Excavations Conducted by the University of Cincinnati, 1932–1938.* 4 vols. Princeton, 1950–8.

2. Dörpfeld, W. *Bericht über die im Jahre 1893 in Troja veranstalteten Ausgrabungen.* Leipzig, 1894.

3. Dörpfeld, W. *Troja und Ilion.* Athens, 1902.

4. Leaf, W. *Troy. A Study in Homeric Geography.* London, 1912.

5. Leaf, W. *Strabo on the Troad.* Cambridge, 1923.

6. Leake, W. M. *Journal of a Tour in Asia Minor.* London, 1824.

7. Lechevalier, J. F. *Voyage de la Troade.* Paris, 1802.

8. Maclaren, C. *Dissertation on the Topography of the Plain of Troy.* Edinburgh, 1822.

9. Matz, F. *Kreta, Mykene, Troja, die minoische und die homerische Welt.* Ed. 2. Stuttgart, 1956.
10. Meyer, E. *Briefe von Heinrich Schliemann*, 1936.
11. Meyer, E. *Heinrich Schliemanns Briefwechsel*, I (1953), II (1958).
12. Page, D. L. *History and the Homeric Iliad.* California University Press, 1959.
13. Schachermeyr, F. *Die ältesten Kulturen Griechenlands.* Stuttgart, 1955.
14. Schachermeyr, F. *Prähistorische Kulturen Griechenlands* (Pauly–Wissowa–Kroll, Bd. 22). Stuttgart, 1954.
15. Schliemann, H. *Ithaka, der Peloponnes und Troja.* Leipzig, 1869.
16. Schliemann, H. *Troy and its Remains.* London, 1875.
17. Schliemann, H. *Ilios, the City and Country of the Trojans.* London, 1880.
18. Schliemann, H. *Troja: Results of the Latest Researches and Discoveries on the Site of Homer's Troy.* London, 1884.
19. Schliemann, H. *Bericht über die Ausgrabungen in Troja im Jahre 1890.* Leipzig, 1891.
20. Schmidt, H. *Heinrich Schliemann's Sammlung Trojanischer Altertümer.* Berlin, 1902.
21. Schuchhardt, C. *Schliemann's Excavations* (English trans. E. Sellers). London, 1892.

## CHAPTER XXII(a)

### I. THE ECLIPSE OF THEBES

1. Ålin, P. *Das Ende der mykenischen Fundstätten auf dem griechischen Festland* (*Studies in Mediterranean Archaeology*, vol. 1). Lund, 1962.
2. Blegen, C. W. [Reports on excavations at Pylus.] In *A.J.A.* 57 (1953) to 67 (1963).
3. Keramopoullos, A. D. Ἀνασκαφὴ τοῦ ἀνακτόρου τοῦ Κάδμου ἐν Θήβαις. In *P.A.E.* 1927, 32 ff.
4. Keramopoullos, A. D. Ἡ οἰκία τοῦ Κάδμου. In Ἀρχ. Ἐφ. 1909, 57–122.
5. Staΐs, V. [Report on excavations at Thoricus.] In Πρακτικὰ τῆς Ἀρχαιολ. Ἑταιρείας, 1893, 12 ff.
6. Stubbings, F. H. 'The Mycenaean Pottery of Attica.' In *B.S.A.* 42 (1947), 1–75.

### III. THE MATERIAL EVIDENCE

1. Blegen, C. W. *A Guide to the Palace of Nestor.* Cincinnati, 1962.
2. Blegen, C. W. [Reports on excavations of the 'Palace of Nestor' at Pylus.] In *A.J.A.* 57 (1953) to 67 (1963).
3. Blegen, C. W. *Prosymna.* Cambridge, 1937.
4. Catling, H. W. 'A Bronze Greave from a 13th Century Tomb at Enkomi.' In *A.I.A.R.S.* 4° ser. 3 (1955) (= *Opuscula Atheniensia*, II), 21 ff.
5. Fimmen, D. *Die Kretisch-mykenische Kultur.* Leipzig and Berlin, 1921.
6. Furumark, A. *The Chronology of Mycenaean Pottery.* Stockholm, 1941.
7. Furumark, A. *The Mycenaean Pottery.* Stockholm, 1941.
8. Holland, L. B. 'The Strong House of Erechtheus.' In *A.J.A.* 28 (1924), 142–69.
9. Hood, M. S. F. 'Archaeology in Greece, 1960–1.' In *Archaeological Reports*, 1960–1.
10. Karo, G. 'Die Perseia von Mykenai.' In *A.J.A.* 38 (1934), 123 ff.

11. Karo, G. *Führer durch Tiryns.* Athens, 1934.
12. Kelso, J. L. and Thorley, J. P. 'The Potter's Technique at Tell Beit Mirsim....' In *Ann. A.S.O.R.* xxi–xxii (1941–3), 86–142.
13. Lolling, H. *et al. Das Kuppelgrab bei Menidi.* Athens, 1880.
14. Marinatos, S. and Hirmer, M. *Crete and Mycenae.* London, 1960.
15. Matz, F. *Crete and Early Greece. The Prelude to Greek Art* (Art of the World, vol. v). London, 1962.
16. Montélius, O. *La Grèce préclassique*, part 1. Stockholm, 1924.
17. Müller, K. 'Die Architektur der Burg und des Palastes.' In *Tiryns*, vol. III (ed. G. Karo). Augsburg, 1930.
18. Mylonas, G. E. Ἡ ἀκρόπολις τῶν Μυκηνῶν. In Ἀρχ. Ἐφ. 1958, 153 ff.
19. Mylonas, G. E. *Ancient Mycenae.* London, 1957.
20. Nylander, C. 'Die sog. mykenischen Säulenbasen auf der Akropolis in Athen.' In *A.I.A.R.S.* 4° ser. viii ( = *Opuscula Atheniensia IV*), 31–77. Lund, 1963.
21. Orlandos, A. K. (ed.). Τὸ ἔργον τῆς Ἀρχαιολογικῆς Ἑταιρείας. (Athens, 1954– , annual publication.)
22. Papadimitriou, J. and Petsas, P. Ἀνασκαφαὶ ἐν Μυκήναις. In Πρακτικὰ τῆς Ἀρχαιολ. Ἑταιρείας, 1951, 192–6.
23. Persson, A. W. *New Tombs at Dendra near Midea.* Lund, 1942. ( = *Acta Reg. Soc. Human. Litt. Lundensis,* 34.)
24. Persson, A. W. *The Royal Tombs at Dendra near Midea.* Lund, 1931.
25. Rodenwaldt, G. *Der Fries des Megarons von Mykenai.* Halle, 1921.
26. Rodenwaldt, G. 'Die Fresken des Palastes.' In *Tiryns*, vol. II (ed. G. Karo). Athens, 1912.
27. Schliemann, H. *Mycenae.* New York, 1880.
28. Schliemann, H. *Tiryns.* London, 1886.
29. Shear, T. L. [Excavations in the Athenian Agora.] 'The Campaign of 1939.' In *Hesperia*, 9 (1940), 261–307.
30. Stubbings, F. H. 'A Bronze Founder's Hoard [at Mycenae].' In *B.S.A.* 49 (1954), 292 ff.
31. Stubbings, F. H. 'The Mycenaean Pottery of Attica.' In *B.S.A.* 42 (1947), 1–75.
32. Theochares, D. R. 'Iolkos.' In *Archaeology*, 11 (1958), 13–18.
33. Verdelis, N. M. 'Tiryns' Water-supply.' In *Archaeology*, 16 (1963), 120–30.
34. Wace, A. J. B. *et al.* 'Mycenae.' In *B.S.A.* 24 (1919–21), 185–209.
35. Wace, A. J. B. *et al.* 'Excavations at Mycenae.' In *B.S.A.* 25 (1921–3).
36. Wace, A. J. B. *Chamber Tombs at Mycenae.* London, 1932. ( = *Archaeologia,* 82.)
37. Wace, A. J. B. *Mycenae, an Archaeological History and Guide.* Princeton, 1949.
38. Wace, A. J. B. [Reports on excavations of houses at Mycenae.] In *B.S.A.* 48 (1953), 9 ff.; 49 (1954), 233 ff.; 50 (1955), 180 ff.; 51 (1956), 107 ff.; 52 (1957), 193 ff.
39. Wace, A. J. B. and Stubbings, F. H. (eds.). *A Companion to Homer.* London, 1962.
40. Wace, H. *Ivories from Mycenae, No. 1, The Ivory Trio.* 1961.
41. Wace, H. and Williams, C. *Mycenae Guide*, 3rd ed. 1963.

IV. MYCENAEAN SOCIETY

1. Bennett, Emmett L. 'The Mycenae Tablets.' In *Proc. Amer. Philos. Soc.* 97 (1953), 42 ff.
2. Bennett, Emmett L. (ed.). 'The Mycenae Tablets II.' In *Trans. Amer. Philos. Soc.* 48 (1958), part 1.

3. Bennett, Emmett L. *The Pylos Tablets: Texts of the Inscriptions found 1939–54*. Princeton, 1955.
4. Chadwick, J. *The Decipherment of Linear B*. Cambridge, 1958.
5. Chadwick, J. (ed). 'The Mycenae Tablets III.' In *Trans. Amer. Philos. Soc.* 52 (1962), part 7.
6. Hope-Simpson, R. 'Mycenaean Highways.' Summary of paper in Univ. of London Inst. of Class. Stud. Minutes of Mycenaean Seminar, 31 Jan. 1962.
7. Ventris, M. G. F. and Chadwick, J. *Documents in Mycenaean Greek*. Cambridge, 1956.

V. OVERSEAS CONTACTS

1. Barnett, R. D. 'Early Greek and Oriental Ivories.' In *J.H.S.* 68 (1948), 1ff.
2. Barnett, R. D. 'Phoenician and Syrian Ivory Carving.' In *P.E.F.* (1939), 4–19.
3. Bass, G. F. and Throckmorton, P. 'Excavating a Bronze Age Shipwreck.' In *Archaeology*, 14 (1961), 78–87.
4. Blegen, C. W. *et al. Troy*. 4 vols. Princeton, 1950–8.
5. Buchholz, H. G. 'Der Kupferhandel des zweiten vorchristlichen Jahrtausends....' In *Minoika, Festschrift zum 80. Geburtstag von Johannes Sundwall* (ed. E. Grumach). Berlin, 1958.
6. Catling, H. W. 'Patterns of Settlement in Bronze Age Cyprus.' In *A.I.A.R.S.* 4° ser. VIII (1963) ( = *Opuscula Atheniensia*, IV), 129 ff.
7. Grace, V. R. 'The Canaanite Jar.' In *The Aegean and the Near East: Studies presented to Hetty Goldman...*' (ed. S. Weinberg). Locust Valley, N.Y., 1956.
8. Gurney, O. R. *The Hittites*. London, 1952.
9. Holland, L. B. 'Colophon.' In *Hesperia*, 13 (1944), 91 ff.
10. Huxley, G. L. *Achaeans and Hittites*. Oxford, 1960.
11. Page, D. L. *History and the Homeric Iliad*. Berkeley and Los Angeles, 1959.
12. Seton-Williams, M. V. 'Cilician Survey.' In *Anatolian Studies*, 4 (1954), 121–74.
13. Sjöqvist, E. *Problems of the Late Cypriot Bronze Age*. Stockholm, 1940.
14. Sommer, F. *Die Aḫḫijavā-Urkunden. Abh. d. Bayer. Akad. d. Wissenschaften*, phil.-hist. Abt., N.F. 6 (1932), 1–469.
15. Stubbings, F. H. *Mycenaean Pottery from the Levant*. Cambridge, 1951.
16. Taylour, Lord W. D. *Mycenaean Pottery in Italy and Adjacent Areas*. Cambridge, 1958.
17. Weickert, C. 'Die Ausgrabung beim Athena-Tempel in Milet.' In *Ist. Mitt.* (a) 7 (1957), 102, 32; (b) 9/10 (1959/60), 1–96.
18. Weickert, C. 'Neue Ausgrabungen in Milet.' In *Neue deutsche Ausgrabungen im Mittelmeergebiet u. im vorderen Orient*, ed. by E. Boehringer, Berlin, 1959.

A. ADDENDA

1. Bass, G. F. 'Cape Gelidonya: a Bronze Age shipwreck.' In *Trans. Amer. Philos. Soc.* n.s. 57 (1967), part 8.
2. Blegen, C. W. and Rawson, M. *The Palace of Nestor at Pylos in Western Messenia*. Vol. I, *The Buildings and their Contents*. Princeton, 1966.
3. Catling, H. W. *et al.* 'Correlations between composition and provenance of Mycenaean and Minoan pottery.' In *B.S.A.* 58 (1963), 94–115.
4. Catling, H. W. *Cypriot Bronzework in the Mycenaean World*. Oxford, 1964.
5. Catling, H. W. 'Minoan and Mycenaean pottery: composition and provenance.' In *Archaeometry*, 6 (1963), 1–9.

6. Catling, H. W. and Millett, A. 'A study of composition patterns of Mycenaean pictorial pottery from Cyprus.' In *B.S.A.* 60 (1965), 212–24.

7. Catling, H. W. and Millett, A. 'A study of the inscribed stirrup-jars from Thebes.' In *Archaeometry*, 8 (1965), 1–85.

8. Hankey, V. M. 'Mycenaean pottery in the Middle East: notes on finds since 1951.' In *B.S.A.* 62 (1967), 107–47.

9. Lang, M. L. *The Palace of Nestor at Pylos in Western Messenia.* Vol. II, *The Frescoes.* Princeton, 1969.

10. Lejeune, M. 'Les forgerons de Pylos.' In *Historia*, 10 (1961), 409–34.

11. Lejeune, M. 'Textes mycéniens relatifs aux esclaves.' In *Historia*, 8 (1959), 129–44.

12. McDonald, W. A. 'Overland communications in Greece during L.H. III, with special reference to south-west Peloponnese.' In *Mycenaean Studies: Proc. of the 3rd Internat. Colloquium for Mycenaean Studies...1961* (ed. Bennett, E. L.). Madison, 1964.

13. Mylonas, G. E. *Mycenae and the Mycenaean Age.* Princeton, 1966.

14. Mylonas, G. E. *Mycenae's last century of greatness.* (Myer Foundation Lecture 1968.) Sydney and London, 1969.

15. Palmer, L. R. *The Interpretation of Mycenaean Greek Texts.* Oxford, 1963.

16. Platon, N. and Touloupa, E. 'Oriental seals from the Palace of Cadmus.' In *Ill. Ldn News*, 28 Nov. 1964, 859–61.

17. Platon, N. and Touloupa, E. 'Ivories and Linear B from Thebes.' In *Ill. Ldn News*, 5 Dec. 1964, 896 f.

18. Porada, E. 'Cylinder seals from Thebes; a preliminary report.' [Summary of a paper.] In *A.J.A.* 69 (1965), 173.

19. Porada, E. 'Further notes on the cylinders from Thebes.' [Summary of a paper.] In *A.J.A.* 70 (1966), 194.

20. Touloupa, E. *et al.* [Reports of excavations at Thebes] in *Arch. Delt.* (*a*) 19 (1964) B2, 192–7; (*b*) 20 (1965) B2, 230–5; (*c*) 21 (1966) B2, 177–91.

## CHAPTER XXII(*b*)

### G. GENERAL

1. Casson, S. *Ancient Cyprus.* London, 1937.

2. Daniel, J. F. Review of S. Casson, *Ancient Cyprus.* In *A.J.A.* 43 (1939), 354–7.

3. Daniel, J. F. Review of E. Sjöqvist, *Problems of the Late Cypriote Bronze Age.* In *A.J.A.* 46 (1942), 286–93.

4. Gjerstad, E. and others. *The Swedish Cyprus Expedition. Finds and results of the excavations in Cyprus, 1927–1931*, I, II and III. Stockholm, 1934–7.

5. Helbaek, H. 'Late Cypriote Vegetable Diet at Apliki,' In *Op. Ath.* IV (1963), 171–86.

6. Hill, Sir George F. *A History of Cyprus*, I. Cambridge, 1940.

7. Karageorghis, V. 'Ten Years of Archaeology in Cyprus, 1953–1962.' In *Arch. Anz.* (1963), 498–600.

8. Karageorghis, V. 'Chronique des fouilles et découvertes archéologiques à Chypre. In *B.C.H.* 83 (1959), 336–61; 84 (1960), 242–99; 85 (1961), 256–315'; 86 (1962), 327–414; 87 (1963), 325–87; 88 (1964), 289–379.

9. Karageorghis, V. *Treasures in the Cyprus Museum.* Nicosia, 1962.

10. Murray, A. S., Smith, A. H. and Walters, H. B. *Excavations in Cyprus.* London, 1900.
11. Myres, J. L. and Ohnefalsch-Richter, M. A. *Catalogue of the Cyprus Museum.* Oxford, 1899.
12. Schaeffer, C. F. A. *Missions en Chypre, 1932–1935.* Paris, 1936.

### VI. THE PATTERN OF LATE CYPRIOT SETTLEMENT

1. Catling, H. W. 'Patterns of Settlement in Bronze Age Cyprus.' In *Op. Ath.* IV (1963), 129–69.
2. Hennessy, J. B. *Stephania: A Middle and Late Bronze Age Cemetery in Cyprus.* London, n.d.
3. Nikolaou, K. Κίτιον Ἑλληνίς. In Κυπριακαὶ Σπουδαί, xxv (1961), 21–39.

### VII. EVENTS IN CYPRUS BEFORE THE AEGEAN CONNEXION

1. Benson, J. L. 'The White Slip Sequence at Bamboula, Kourion.' In *P.E.Q.* (1961), 61–9.
2. Heurtley, W. A. 'A Palestinian Vase Painter of the Sixteenth Century B.C.' In *Q.D.A.P.* VIII, 21–34.
3. Merrillees, R. S. 'Opium Trade in the Bronze Age Levant.' In *Antiquity,* XXXVI (1962), 287–92.
4. Merrillees, R. S. 'Bronze Age Spindle Bottles from the Levant.' In *Op. Ath.* IV (1963), 187–96.
5. Popham, M. R. 'The Proto-White Slip Pottery of Cyprus.' In *Op. Ath.* IV (1963), 277–97.
6. Porada, E. 'The Cylinder seals of the Late Cypriote Bronze Age.' In *A.J.A.* 52 (1948), 178–98.
7. Schaeffer, C. F. A. 'Enkomi.' In *A.J.A.* 52 (1948), 165–77.
8. Schaeffer, C. F. A. *Enkomi-Alasia.* Paris, 1952.
9. Sjöqvist, E. *Problems of the Late Cypriote Bronze Age.* Stockholm, 1940.
10. Stewart, J. R. 'When did Base-Ring ware first occur in Palestine?' *Bull. A.S.O.R.* 138, 47–9.
11. Westholm, A. 'Some Late Cypriote tombs at Milia.' In *Q.D.A.P.* VIII (1939), 1–20.
12. Westholm, A. 'Built tombs in Cyprus.' In *Op. Arch.* II (1941), 29–58.

### VIII. CYPRUS AND THE AEGEAN AREA

1. Åkerström, A. 'Das mykenische Töpferviertel in Berbati in der Argolis.' In *Bericht über den VI. internationalen Kongress für Archäologie* (Berlin, 1940), pp. 296–8.
2. Benson, J. L. 'Aegean and Near Eastern seal impressions from Cyprus.' In *The Aegean and the Near East* (New York, 1956), pp. 59–77.
3. Benson, J. L. 'Coarse Ware Stirrup Jars of the Aegean.' In *Berytus,* XIV (1961), 37–51.
4. Benson, J. L. 'Observations on Mycenaean vase-painters.' In *A.J.A.* 65 (1961), 337–47.
5. Catling, H. W., Richards, E. E. and Blin-Stoyle, A. E. 'Correlations between Composition and Provenance of Mycenaean and Minoan Pottery.' In *B.S.A.* 58 (1963), 94–115.
6. Catling, H. W. *Cypriot Bronzework and the Mycenaean World.* Oxford, 1964.

7. Coche de la Ferté, É. *Essai de classification de la céramique mycénienne d'Enkomi.* Paris, 1951.
8. Furumark, A. *The Mycenaean Pottery.* Stockholm, 1941.
9. Furumark, A. *The Chronology of Mycenaean Pottery.* Stockholm, 1941.
10. Furumark, A. 'The Settlement at Ialysos and Aegean History.' In *Op. Arch.* VI (1950), 150–271.
11. Furumark, A. 'A Scarab from Cyprus.' In *Op. Ath.* I (1953), 47–65.
12. Immerwahr, S. A. 'Three Mycenaean vases from Cyprus in the Metropolitan Museum of Art.' In *A.J.A.* 49 (1945), 534–56.
13. Immerwahr, S. A. 'Mycenaean Trade and Colonization.' In *Archaeology*, 13 (1960), 4–13.
14. Kantor, H. J. 'The Aegean and the Orient in the second millennium B.C.' In *A.J.A.* 51 (1947), 1–103.
15. Kantor, H. J. 'Ivory Carving in the Mycenaean Period.' In *Archaeology*, 13 (1960), 14–25.
16. Karageorghis, V. 'Un cylindre de Chypre.' In *Syria*, XXXVI (1959), 111–18.
17. Karageorghis, V. Αἱ σχέσεις Κύπρου καὶ Κρήτης κατὰ τοὺς προϊστορικοὺς χρόνους. In Κυπριακαὶ Σπουδαί, XXIII (1959), 3–10.
18. Karageorghis, V. 'Supplementary notes on the Mycenaean vases from the Swedish Tombs at Enkomi.' In *Op. Ath.* III (1960), 135–53.
19. Karageorghis, V. Μυκηναϊκὴ τέχνη ἐν Κύπρῳ. In Κυπριακαὶ Σπουδαί, XXV (1961), 7–17.
20. Karageorghis, V. 'Le cratère Mycénien aux taureaux des Musées de Berlin.' In *B.C.H.* 86 (1962), 11–17.
21. Karageorghis, V. *Corpus Vasorum Antiquorum: Cyprus Fascicule*, I. Nicosia, 1963.
22. Karageorghis, V. 'A Late Cypriote tomb at Angastina.' In *R.D.A.C.* 1964 (Nicosia, 1964), 1–26.
23. Marshall, F. H. *Catalogue of the Jewellery, Greek, Roman and Etruscan in the Department of Antiquities, British Museum.* London, 1911.
24. Nikolaou, K. 'Mycenaean Terracotta Figurines in the Cyprus Museum.' In *Op. Ath.* V (1965), 47–57.
25. Stubbings, F. H. *Mycenaean Pottery from the Levant.* Cambridge, 1951.

### IX. THE IDENTIFICATION OF CYPRUS WITH ALASHIYA

1. Åström, P. 'A Handle Stamped with the Cartouche of Seti I from Hala Sultan Tekke in Cyprus.' In *Op. Ath.* V (1965), 115–21.
2. Helck, W. *Die Beziehungen Ägyptens zu Vorderasien im 3. und 2. Jahrtausend v. Chr.* Wiesbaden, 1962.
3. Huxley, G. L. *Achaeans and Hittites.* Oxford, 1960.
4. Knudtzon, J. A. *Die el-Amarna-Tafeln mit Einleitung und Erläuterungen*, 1–2. Leipzig, 1915.
5. Marinatos, S. Ἀλάσια-Ἀλασυὴς καὶ ὁ Ἑλληνικὸς ἀποικισμὸς τῆς Κύπρου, Πρακτικὰ τῆς Ἀκαδημίας Ἀθηνῶν, 36 (1961), 5–15.
6. Nougayrol, J. 'Nouveaux textes accadiens du Palais d'Ugarit (Campagne 1954).' *C.-R. Ac. Inscr. B.-L.* (1955), pp. 141–5.
7. Nougayrol, J. *Le Palais Royal d'Ugarit IV: Textes Accadiens des Archives Sud.* Paris, 1956.
8. Nougayrol, J. 'Nouveaux textes accadiens de Ras Shamra.' In *C.-R. Ac. Inscr. B.-L.* (1960), pp. 163–71.

9. Otten, H. 'Neue Quellen zum Ausklang des hethitischen Reiches.' In *M.D.O.G.* 94 (1963), 1–23.
10. Page, D. L. *History and the Homeric Iliad.* Berkeley, 1959.
11. Schachermayr, F. 'Zum ältesten Namen von Kypros.' In *Klio*, xvii (1921), 230–9.
12. Schaeffer, C. F. A. and Masson, O. 'Matériaux pour l'étude des relations entre Ugarit et Chypre.' In *Ugaritica* iii (Paris, 1956), ch. iii, 227–50.
13. Steiner, G. 'Neue Alašija-Texte.' In *Kadmos*, i (1962), 130–8.
14. Wainwright, G. A. 'Alashia = Alasa; and Asy.' In *Klio*, xiv (1915), 1–36.
15. Wiseman, D. J. *The Alalakh Tablets.* London, 1953.

### X. LITERACY IN THE LATE CYPRIOT PERIOD

1. Benson, J. L. and Masson, O. 'Cypro-Minoan Inscriptions from Bamboula, Kourion; General Remarks and New Documents.' In *A.J.A.* 64 (1960), 145–51.
2. Daniel, J. F. 'The Inscribed Pithoi from Kourion.' In *A.J.A.* 43 (1939), 102–3.
3. Daniel, J. F. 'Prologemena to the Cypro-Minoan Script.' In *A.J.A.* 45 (1941), 249–82.
4. Dikaios, P. 'An Inscribed Tablet from Enkomi, Cyprus.' In *Antiquity*, xxvii (1953), 103–5.
5. Dikaios, P. 'A Second Inscribed Clay Tablet from Enkomi.' In *Antiquity*, xxvii (1953), 233–7.
6. Dikaios, P. 'A New Inscribed Tablet from Enkomi.' In *Antiquity*, xxx (1956), 40–2.
7. Dikaios, P. 'The Context of the Enkomi Tablets.' In *Kadmos*, ii (1963), 39–52.
8. Karageorghis, Mme. J. V. 'Quelques observations sur l'origine du syllabaire chypro-minoen.' In *R.A.* (1958), ii, 1–19.
9. Karageorghis, Mme. J. V. 'Histoire de l'écriture Chypriote.' In Κυπριακαὶ Σπουδαί, xxv (1961), 43–60.
10. Masson, O. 'Cylindres et cachets Chypriotes portant des caractères Chypro-Minoens.' In *B.C.H.* 81 (1957), 6–37.
11. Masson, O. 'Répertoire des inscriptions Chypro-Minoennes.' In *Minos*, v (1957), 9–27.
12. Masson, O. *Les inscriptions Chypriotes syllabiques. Recueil critique et commenté.* Paris, 1961.
13. Meriggi, P. and Masson, O. 'Relations entre les Linéaires A, B et le Chypro-Minoen; rapport.' *Études mycéniennes* (Paris), 1956, pp. 269–71.
14. Mitford, T. B. 'The Status of Cypriot Epigraphy; Cypriot Writing, Minoan to Byzantine.' In *Archaeology*, 5 (1952), 151–6.
15. Persson, A. 'Some Inscribed Terracotta Balls from Enkomi.' In *Symbolae philologicae O.A. Davidson octogenario dedicatae.* Uppsala, 1932, pp. 269–73.
16. Pope, M. *Aegean Writing and Linear A* (Studies in Mediterranean Archaeology. viii). Lund, 1964.
17. Schaeffer, C. F. A. 'More Tablets from Syria and Cyprus.' In *Antiquity*, xxviii (1954), 38–9.
18. Ventris, M. and Chadwick, J. *Documents in Mycenaean Greek.* Cambridge, 1956.

### XI. THE ACHAEAN COLONIZATION OF CYPRUS

1. Catling, H. W. 'A Bronze Greave from a 13th-century B.C. tomb at Enkomi.' In *Op. Ath.* II (1955), 21–36.
2. Catling, H. W. 'A New Bronze Sword from Cyprus.' In *Antiquity*, XXXV (1961), 115–22.
3. Courtois, J.-C. 'Un nouveau sanctuaire de la fin de l'âge du bronze et du début de l'âge du fer à Enkomi dans l'île de Chypre.' In *C.-R. Ac. Inscr. B.-L.* (1963), pp. 155–61.
4. Desborough, V. R. d'A. *The last Mycenaeans and their Successors.* Oxford, 1964.
5. Furumark, A. 'The Mycenaean IIIC Pottery and its Relation to Cypriote Fabrics.' In *Op. Arch.* III (1944), 194–265.
6. Furumark, A. 'Utgrävningarna vid Sinda. Några historiska resultat.' In *Arkeologiska forskningar och fynd* (Stockholm, 1952), 59–69.
7. Iliffe, J. H. and Mitford, T. B. 'An Ivory Masterpiece and Treasures of Gold and Silver from the Cyprus of 3000 Years Ago: Remarkable Finds from a Bronze Age Cemetery near Old Paphos.' In *Ill. Ldn News*, 2 May 1953, 710–11.
8. Karageorghis, V. 'Fouilles de Kition, 1959.' In *B.C.H.* 84 (1960), 504–88.
9. Karageorghis, V. 'Recent Archaeological Investigations at Kition.' In Κυπριακαὶ Σπουδαὶ, XXVI (1962), 167–71.
10. Karageorghis, V. 'Excavations at Kition, 1963.' In *R.D.A.C.* (1963), 3–15.
11. Masson, O. 'Remarques sur les rapports entre la Crète et Chypre à la fin de l'âge du Bronze.' In *Kretika Chronika* (1963), 156–61.
12. Picard, C. 'Les origines achéennes de Kition (Chypre).' In *R.A.* (1959), II, 111–12.

### XII. THE END OF THE BRONZE AGE IN CYPRUS

1. Benson, J. L. 'Bronze Tripods from Kourion.' In *G.R.B.S.* III (1960), 7–16.
2. Daniel, J. F. 'Two Late Cypriote III Tombs from Kourion.' In *A.J.A.* 41 (1937), 56–85.
3. Daniel, J. F. 'Excavations at Kourion; the Late Bronze Age Settlement— Provisional Report.' In *A.J.A.* 42 (1938), 261–75.
4. Daniel, J. F. 'Kourion, the Late Bronze Age Settlement.' In *Bulletin of the University Museum of Pennsylvania*, 7, no. 3, April 1939, 14–21.
5. Dikaios, P. 'The Bronze Statue of a Horned God from Enkomi.' In *Arch. Anz.* (1962), 1–40.
6. Gjerstad, E. 'Initial Date of the Cypriote Iron Age.' In *Op. Arch.* III (1944), 73–106.
7. Gjerstad, E. *The Swedish Cyprus Expedition*, IV, part 2. The Cypro-Geometric, Cypro-Archaic and Cypro-Classical periods. Stockholm, 1948.
8. McFadden, G. H. 'A Late Cypriote III Tomb from Kourion: Kaloriziki No. 40.' In *A.J.A.* 58 (1954), 131–42.
9. Picard, C. 'El, Kinyras ou quelque guerrier Chypriot?' In *R.A.* XLV (1955), 48–9.
10. du Plat Taylor, J. 'A Late Bronze Age Settlement at Apliki, Cyprus.' In *A.J.* XXXII, 133–67.
11. du Plat Taylor, J. 'Late Cypriot III in the Light of Recent Excavations.' In *P.E.Q.* (1956), 22–37.
12. du Plat Taylor, J. and others. *Myrtou-Pigadhes: a Late Bronze Age Sanctuary in Cyprus.* Oxford, 1957.
13. Riis, P. J. 'Rod-tripods.' In *Acta Arch.* X (1939), 1–30.

### XIII. CYPRUS AND COPPER IN THE LATE BRONZE AGE

1. Bass, G. 'The Cape Gelidonya Wreck: Preliminary Report.' In *A.J.A.* 65 (1961), 267–76.
2. Buchholz, H.-G. 'Der Kupferhandel des zweiten vorchristlichen Jahrtausends im Spiegel der Schriftforschung.' In *Minoica* (Festschrift Sundwall). Berlin, 1958.
3. Buchholz, H.-G. 'Keftiubarren und Erzhandel im zweiten vorchristlichen Jahrtausend.' In *Prähist. Zeitschr.* XXXVII (1959), 1–40.
4. Cullis, C. G. and Edge, A. B. *Report on the Cupriferous deposits of Cyprus.* London (Crown Agents), 1927.
5. Davies, O. 'The Copper Mines of Cyprus.' In *B.S.A.* 30 (1932), 74–85.
6. Deshayes, J. *Les outils de bronze de l'Indus au Danube.* Paris, 1960.

### XIV. THE LATE CYPRIOT PERIOD AND THE FOUNDATION LEGENDS

1. Deshayes, J. *La Nécropole de Ktima: Mission Jean Bérard 1953–5.* Paris, 1963.
2. Gjerstad, E. 'The Colonization of Cyprus in Greek Legend.' In *Op. Arch.* III (1944), 107–23.
3. Wainwright, G. A. 'A Teucrian at Salamis in Cyprus.' In *J.H.S.* LXXXIII (1963), 146–51.

## CHAPTER XXIII

### G. GENERAL

1. Breasted, J. H. *Ancient Records of Egypt.* 7 vols. Chicago, 1906.
2. Breasted, J. H. *History of Egypt.* Ed. 2. London, 1948.
3. Gardiner, A. H. *Ancient Egyptian Onomastica.* 3 vols. Oxford, 1947.
4. Gardiner, A. H. *Egypt of the Pharaohs.* Oxford, 1961.
5. Gardiner, A. H. and Peet, T. E. *The Inscriptions of Sinai.* Ed. 2, revised by J. Černý. 2 vols. London, 1952.
6. Hall, H. R. *The Ancient History of the Near East.* Ed. 11. London, 1950.
7. Petrie, W. M. F. *History of Egypt*, vol. III. Ed. 3. London, 1925.
8. Porter, B. and Moss, R. L. B. *Topographical Bibliography of Ancient Egyptian Hieroglyphic Texts, Reliefs and Paintings.* 7 vols. Oxford, 1927–51.
9. Wreszinski, W. *Atlas zur altaegyptischen Kulturgeschichte.* Teil II. Leipzig, 1935.

### I. THE RISE OF THE NINETEENTH DYNASTY

1. Černý, J. 'Note on the supposed beginning of a Sothis period under Sethos I.' In *J.E.A.* 47 (1961), 150 ff.
2. Legrain, G. 'Les statues de Paramessou.' In *Ann. Serv.* 14 (1914), 29 ff.
3. Piankoff, A. 'La tombe de Ramsès Ier.' In *Bull. Inst. fr. Caire*, 56 (1957). 189 ff.
4. Schott, S. *Der Denkstein Sethos' I für die Kapelle Ramses' I in Abydos (Nachr. Göttingen*, 1964, No. 1).

## II. THE FOREIGN WARS OF SETHOS I

1. Faulkner, R. O. 'The Wars of Sethos I'. In *J.E.A.* 33 (1947), 34 ff.
2. Gardiner, A. H. *Egyptian Hieratic Texts.* Series 1, Part 1. *The Papyrus Anastasi I and the Papyrus Koller.* Leipzig, 1911.
3. Gardiner, A. H. 'The Ancient Military Road between Egypt and Palestine.' In *J.E.A.* 6 (1920), 99 ff.
4. Grdseloff, B. *Une stèle scythopolitaine du roi Séthos Ier.* Cairo, 1949.
5. Müller, W. M. 'The Egyptian Monument of Tell esh-Shihab.' In *P.E.F.* (1904), 78 ff.
6. Rowe, A. *The Topography and History of Beth-Shan.* Philadelphia, 1930.

## III. INTERNAL AFFAIRS UNDER SETHOS I

1. British Museum. *A Guide to the Egyptian Galleries (Sculpture).* London, 1909.
2. Brugsch, E. 'On et Onion.' In *Rec. trav.* 8 (1886), 1 ff.
3. Calverley, A. M. and Broome, M. F. *The Temple of King Sethos I at Abydos.* 4 vols. London and Chicago, 1933–58.
4. Frankfort, H. *The Cenotaph of Seti I at Abydos.* 2 vols. London, 1933.
5. Gardiner, A. H. 'Some Reflections on the Nauri Decree.' In *J.E.A.* 38 (1952), 24 ff.
6. Gardiner, A. H. *The Royal Canon of Turin.* Oxford, 1959.
7. Griffith, F. Ll. 'The Abydos Decree of Seti I at Nauri.' In *J.E.A.* 13 (1927), 193 ff.
8. Hamza, M. 'Excavations of the Department of Antiquities at Qantir.' In *Ann. Serv.* 30 (1929), 31 ff.
9. Lefébure, E. *Le tombeau de Séti Ier (Ann. Mus. Guimet,* vol. IX). Paris, 1885.
10. Meyer, E. *Aegyptische Chronologie (Abh. Berlin,* 1904). Berlin, 1904.
11. Winlock, H. E. *The Temple of Ramesses I at Abydos.* New York, 1937.

## IV. SINAI, THE EASTERN DESERT AND NUBIA UNDER SETHOS I

1. Gunn, B. and Gardiner, A. H. 'New Renderings of Egyptian Texts. I. The Temple of the Wâdy Abbâd.' In *J.E.A.* 4 (1917), 241 ff.
2. Hintze, F. 'Die Felsenstele Sethos I bei Qasr Ibrim.' In *Z.Ä.S.* 87 (1962), 31 ff.
3. Reisner, G. A. and Reisner, M. B. 'Inscribed Monuments from Gebel Barkal. Part 3. The Stela of Sety I.' In *Z.Ä.S.* 69 (1933), 73 ff.
4. Säve-Söderbergh, T. *Ägypten und Nubien.* Lund, 1941.
5. Schott, S. *Kanais, der Tempel Sethos I im Wadi Mia (Nachr. Göttingen,* 1961, no. 6).

## V. THE FIRST YEARS OF RAMESSES II

1. Caminos, R. A. *Late Egyptian Miscellanies.* Oxford, 1954.
2. Habachi, L. 'Khatâ'na-Qantîr'. In *Ann. Serv.* 52 (1954), 443 ff.
3. Pritchard, J. B. (ed.). *Ancient Near Eastern Texts relating to the Old Testament.* Princeton, 1950.
4. Seele, K. C. *The Coregency of Ramses II with Seti I.* Chicago, 1940.
5. Sethe, K. 'Die Berufung eines Hohenpriesters des Amon unter Ramses II.' In *Z.Ä.S.* 44 (1907–8), 30 ff.
6. Yoyotte, J. 'Les stèles de Ramses II à Tanis.' In *Kémi,* 10 (1949), 58 ff.

## VI. THE STRUGGLE WITH THE HITTITES

For the Bibliography of the battle of Qadesh
see below, p. 952.

1. Edel, E. 'Der geplante Besuch Ḥattušilis III in Äegypten.' In *M.D.O.G.* 92 (1960), 15 ff.
2. Kuentz, C. 'La stèle de mariage de Ramses II.' In *Ann. Serv.* 25 (1925), 181 ff.
3. Langdon, S. and Gardiner, A. H. 'The Treaty of Alliance between Ḥattušili, King of the Hittites, and the Pharaoh Ramesses II of Egypt.' In *J.E.A.* 6 (1920), 179 ff.
4. Rowton, M. B. 'The Background of the Treaty between Ramesses II of Egypt and Hattušiliš III.' In *J.C.S.* 13 (1959), 1 ff.

## VII. THE OTHER WARS OF RAMESSES II

1. *Bull. Soc. fr. Égyptol.* no. 6 (1951), pl. 1.
2. Hölscher, W. *Libyer und Ägypter.* Glückstadt, 1937.
3. Kitchen, K. A. 'Some New Light on the Asiatic Wars of Ramesses II.' In *J.E.A.* 50 (1964), 47 ff.
4. Rowe, A. *A History of Ancient Cyrenaica (Ann. Serv. Suppl.* Cahier 12). Cairo, 1958.
5. Wainwright, G. A. 'The Meshwesh.' In *J.E.A.* 48 (1962), 89 ff.

## VIII. THE KINGDOM UNDER RAMESSES II

1. Davies, Nina M. *Ancient Egyptian Paintings*, vol. II. Chicago, 1936.
2. Fairman, H. W. 'Preliminary Report on the Excavations at 'Amāra West, Anglo-Egyptian Sudan, 1938–9.' In *J.E.A.* 25 (1939), 139 ff. *Idem*, 1947–8. In *J.E.A.* 34 (1948), 3 ff.
3. Gardiner, A. H. *The Inscription of Mes (Unters.* 4, 3). Leipzig, 1905.
4. Lefebvre, C. *Histoire des grands prêtres d'Amon de Karnak.* Paris, 1929.
5. Mond, R. and Myers, O. H., *Temples of Armant.* London, 1940.
6. Montet, P. *Tanis.* Paris, 1942.

## IX. MERNEPTAH: EGYPT ON THE DEFENSIVE

1. Maspero, G. 'Notes sur quelques points de grammaire et d'histoire.' In *Z.Ä.S.* 21 (1883), 65 ff., §xxxv.
2. Müller, W. M. *Egyptological Researches*, vol. 1. Washington, 1906.
3. Roeder, G. 'Die Weihinschrift des Königs Mer-en-Ptah.' In *Ann. Serv.* 52 (1954), 319 ff.
4. Spiegelberg, W. 'Der Siegeshymnus des Merneptah auf der Flinders-Petrie Stela.' In *Z.Ä.S.* 34 (1896), 1 ff.
5. Wainwright, G. A. 'Some Sea-peoples and others in the Hittite Archives.' In *J.E.A.* 25 (1939), 148 ff.
6. Wainwright, G. A. 'Merneptah's Aid to the Hittites.' In *J.E.A.* 46 (1960), 24 ff.

## X. THE END OF THE NINETEENTH DYNASTY

1. Aldred, C. 'The Parentage of King Siptah.' In *J.E.A.* 49 (1963), 41 ff.
2. Aldred, C. 'Valley Tomb No. 56 at Thebes.' In *J.E.A.* 49 (1963), 176 ff.

3. Beckerath, J. von. 'Die Reihenfolge der letzten Könige der 19. Dynastie.' In
   *Z.D.M.G.* 106 (1956), 241 ff.
4. Beckerath, J. von. 'Queen Twosre as Guardian of Siptah.' In *J.E.A.* 48
   (1962), 70 ff.
5. Caminos, R. A. 'Two Stelae in the Kurnah Temple of Sethos I.' In O.
   Firchow, *Ägyptol. Studien Hermann Grapow...gewidmet.* Berlin, 1955.
6. Černý, J. *Ostraca hiératiques (C.C.G.).* Cairo, 1935.
7. Černý, J. 'Papyrus Salt 124 (Brit. Mus. 10055).' In *J.E.A.* 15 (1929),
   243 ff.
8. Chevrier, H. *Le Temple reposoir de Seti II.* Cairo, 1940.
9. Gardiner, A. H. 'The Delta Residence of the Ramessides,' part III. In *J.E.A.*
   5 (1918), 179 ff.
10. Gardiner, A. H. 'The Tomb of Queen Twosre.' In *J.E.A.* 40 (1954),
    40 ff.
11. Gardiner, A. H. 'Only one King Siptah and Twosre not his Wife.' In *J.E.A.*
    44 (1958), 12 ff.
12. Helck, W. 'Zur Geschichte der 19. und 20. Dynastie.' In *Z.D.M.G.* 105
    (1955), 27 ff.

### XI. THE RISE OF THE TWENTIETH DYNASTY: SETHNAKHTE

1. Černý, J. 'Queen Ēse of the Twentieth Dynasty and her Mother.' In *J.E.A.*
   44 (1958), 31 ff.
2. Erichsen, W. *Papyrus Harris I (Bibl. Aeg. v).* Brussels, 1933.

### XII. THE WARS OF RAMESSES III

1. Chicago University, Oriental Institute. *Medinet Habu.* 4 vols. Chicago,
   1932–40.
2. Edgerton, W. and Wilson, J. A. *Historical Records of Ramses III.* Chicago,
   1936.

### XIII. THE KINGDOM UNDER RAMESSES III

1. Buck, A. de. 'The Judicial Papyrus of Turin.' In *J.E.A.* 23 (1927), 152 ff.
2. Černý, J. 'Datum des Todes Ramses' III und die Thronbesteigung Ramses'
   IV.' In *Z.Ä.S.* 72 (1936), 109 ff.
3. Chicago University, Oriental Institute. *Reliefs and Inscriptions at Karnak.*
   2 vols. Chicago, 1936.
4. Edgerton, W. F. 'The Strikes in Ramses III's Twenty-ninth Year.' In
   *J.N.E.S.* 10 (1951), 137 ff.
5. Edgerton, W. F. and Wilson, J. A. *Historical Records of Ramses III.* Chicago,
   1936.
6. Goedicke, H. 'Was Magic used in the Harem Conspiracy against Ramesses
   III?' In *J.E.A.* 49 (1963), 175 ff.
7. Schulman, A. R. 'A Cult of Ramesses III at Memphis.' In *J.N.E.S.* 22
   (1963), 177 ff.
8. Seele, K. C. 'Some Remarks on the Family of Ramesses III.' In O. Firchow,
   *Ägyptol. Studien Hermann Grapow...gewidmet.* Berlin, 1955.
9. Wente, E. F. 'A Letter of Complaint to the Vizier To.' In *J.N.E.S.* 20 (1961),
   252 ff.
10. Yoyotte, J. 'The Tomb of a Prince Ramesses in the Valley of the Queens
    (No. 53).' In *J.E.A.* 44 (1958), 31 ff.

### XIV. RELIGION, ART AND LITERATURE UNDER THE RAMESSIDES

1. Blackman, A. M. 'Oracles in Ancient Egypt.' In *J.E.A.* 11 (1925), 249 ff.; 12 (1926), 176 ff.
2. Bonomi, J. and Sharpe, S. *The Alabaster Sarcophagus of Oimenepthah I, King of Egypt*. London, 1864.
3. British Museum. *Hieratic Papyri in the British Museum. Third Series. Chester Beatty Gift*. Ed. A. H. Gardiner, London, 1935.
4 Černý, J. *Ancient Egyptian Religion*. London, 1952.
5. Erman, A. *Die Religion der Ägypter*. Berlin and Leipzig, 1934.
6. Erman, A. *The Literature of the Ancient Egyptians*, translated from the German by A. M. Blackman. London, 1927.
7. Gardiner, A. H. *The Chester Beatty Papyri, No. I*. London, 1931.
8. Gunn, B. 'The Religion of the Poor in Ancient Egypt.' In *J.E.A.* 3 (1916), 81 ff.
9. Gunn, B. and Gardiner, A. H. 'New Renderings of Egyptian Texts. II. The expulsion of the Hyksos.' In *J.E.A.* 5 (1918), 36 ff.
10. Jéquier, G. *Le livre de ce qu'il y a dans l'Hadès (Bibliothèque de l'École des Hautes Études*, fasc. 97). Paris, 1894.
11. Mekhitarian, A. *Egyptian Painting*. Editions d'Art Albert Skira. Geneva, 1954.
12. Müller, W. M. *Die Liebespoesie der alten Äegypter*. Leipzig, 1899.
13. Neugebauer, O. and Parker, R. A. *Egyptian Astronomical Texts. I. The Early Decans (Brown Egyptological Studies*, vol. III). London, 1960.
14. Peet, T. E. 'The Legend of the Capture of Joppa and the Story of the Fore-doomed Prince.' In *J.E.A.* 11 (1925), 225 ff.
15. Piankoff, A. *The Tomb of Ramesses VI (Bollingen Series*, vol. XL). New York, 1954.
16. Roeder, G. 'Ramses II. als Gott.' In *Z.Ä.S.* 61 (1926), 57 ff.
17. Wente, E. F. 'Two Ramesside Stelas pertaining to the Cult of Amenophis I.' In *J.N.E.S.* 22 (1962), 31 ff.

## CHAPTER XXIV

### G. GENERAL

1. *Ankara Arkeoloji Müzesinde bulunan Boğazköy Tabletleri*. Istanbul, 1948.
2. Borger, R. *Einleitung in die assyrischen Königsinschriften (Handbuch der Orientalistik*. 1. Abt., Ergänzungsband 5). Leiden and Köln, 1961.
3. Breasted, J. H. *Ancient Records of Egypt*. 5 vols. Chicago, 1906.
4. Ebeling, E., Meissner, B. and Weidner, E. F. *Die Inschriften der altassyrischen Könige (Altorientalische Bibliothek*, 1). Leipzig, 1926.
5. *Keilschrifttexte aus Boghazköi*, 1–XIV. Leipzig and Berlin, 1916–63.
6. *Keilschrifturkunden aus Boghazköi*, 1–XXXIX. Berlin, 1921–63.
7. Nougayrol, J. *Textes accadiens des Archives sud (Le palais royal d'Ugarit*, IV = *Mission de Ras Shamra*, IX). Paris, 1956.
8. Pritchard, J. B. (ed.). *Ancient Near Eastern Texts Relating to the Old Testament*. Ed. 2. Princeton, 1955.

9. Weissbach, F. H. *Die Denkmäler und Inschriften an der Mündung des Nahr el-Kelb* (*Wiss. Veröff. des Deutsch-Türkischen Denkmalschutz-Kommandos*, 6). Berlin and Leipzig, 1922.
10. Wreszinski, W. *Atlas zur altägyptischen Kulturgeschichte*, 11. Leipzig, 1935.

### I. THE LATER REIGN OF MUWATALLISH

1. Alt, A. 'Zur Topographie der Schlacht bei Kades.' In *Z.D.P.V.* 55 (1932), 1 ff.
2. Alt, A. 'Noch einmal zur Schlacht bei Kades.' In *Z.D.P.V.* 66 (1943), 1 ff.
3. Bérard, J. 'Vérité et fiction dans le poème de Pentaour.' In *Rev. ét. anc.* 49 (1947), 217 ff.
4. Botterweck, J. G. 'Der sogennante hattische Bericht über die Schlacht bei Qadesch, ein verkannter Brief Ramses' II.' In *Bonner Biblische Beiträge*, 1 (1950), 26 ff.
5. Breasted, J. H. *The Battle of Kadesh* (*Univ. of Chicago, Decennial Publ.* 1/5). Chicago, 1904.
6. Edel, E. 'KBo I 15+19, ein Brief Ramses' II. mit einer Schilderung der Kadešschlacht.' In *Z.A.* 49 (1950), 195 ff.
7. Edel, E. 'Zur historischen Geographie der Gegend von Kadeš.' In *Z.A.* 50 (1953), 253 ff.
8. Faulkner, R. O. 'The Wars of Sethos I.' In *J.E.A.* 33 (1947), 34 ff.
9. Faulkner, R. O. 'The Battle of Kadesh.' In *Mitt. deutsch. Inst. Kairo*, 16 (1958), 93 ff.
10. Friedrich, J. *Staatsverträge des Ḫatti-Reiches in hethitischer Sprache.* 2 vols. (*M.V.Ae.G.* 31 and 34/1). Leipzig, 1926 and 1930.
11. Gardiner, A. *The Ḳadesh Inscriptions of Ramesses II.* Oxford, 1960.
12. Götze, A. *Ḫattušiliš* (*M.V.Ae.G.* 29/3). Leipzig, 1925.
13. Götze, A. *Neue Bruchstücke zum Grossen Text des Ḫattušiliš und den Parallel-texten* (*M.V.Ae.G.* 34/2). Leipzig, 1930.
14. Götze, A. 'Zur Schlacht von Qadesch.' In *O.L.Z.* 32 (1929), 832 ff.
15. Helck, W. *Die Beziehungen Ägyptens zu Vorderasien im 3. und 2. Jahrtausend v. Chr.* (*Ägyptol. Abh.* 5). Wiesbaden, 1962.
16. Korošec, V. 'Les Hittites et leurs vassaux syriens à la lumière des nouveaux textes d'Ugarit (PRU IV).' In *R.H.A.* 18, fasc. 66 (1960), 65 ff.
17. Kuentz, Ch. *La bataille de Qadech* (*Mem. Inst. fr. Caire*, 55). Cairo, 1928.
18. Montet, P. 'De Tjarou à Qadech avec Ramesès II.' In *R.H.A.* 18, fasc. 67 (1960), 109 ff.
19. Noth, M. 'Ramses II. in Syrien.' In *Z.D.P.V.* 64 (1941), 39 ff.
20. Pézard, M. *Qadesh, Mission arch. à Tell Nebi Mend 1921–1922* (*Bibl. arch. et hist.* 15). Paris, 1931.
21. Selim Hassan. *Le poème dit de Pentaour et le rapport officiel sur la bataille de Qadesh.* Cairo, 1928.
22. Sturm, J. *Der Hettiterkrieg Ramses II.* (*W.Z.K.M.*, Beiheft 4). Wien, 1939.
23. Weidner, E. F. *Politische Dokumente aus Kleinasien* (*Bo. Stu.* 8). Leipzig, 1923.
24. Weidner, E. F. 'Die Kämpfe Adadnāraris I gegen Ḫanigalbat.' In *Arch. f. Or.* 5 (1928–9), 89 ff.
25. Weidner, E. F. 'Wasašatta, König von Ḫanigalbat.' In *Arch. f. Or.* 6 (1930–1), 21 f.
26. Wilson, J. A. 'The texts of the Battle of Kadesh.' In *A.J.S.L.* 43 (1927), 266 ff.

## II. URKHI-TESHUB AND KHATTUSHILISH

1. Güterbock, H. G. 'L'inscription hiéroglyphique Hittite sur la matrice du sceau de Muršili II provenant de Ras Shamra.' In Schaeffer, Cl. F. A., *Ugaritica*, III (1956), 161 ff.
2. Helck, W. 'Urḫi-Tešup in Ägypten.' In *J.C.S.* 17 (1963), 87 ff.
3. Schaeffer, Cl. F. A. 'La matrice d'un sceau du roi hittite Mursil II retirée des cendres du palais royal d'Ugarit.' In *Ugaritica*, III (1956), 87 ff.


## III. KHATTUSHILISH AS GREAT KING

1. Cavaignac, E. 'La lettre de Ramses II au roi de Mira.' In *R.H.A.* 3, fasc. 18 (1955), 25 ff.
2. Edel, E. 'Die Rolle der Königinnen in der ägyptisch-hethitischen Korrespondenz von Boğazköy.' In *Indogerm. Forsch.* 60 (1950), 72 ff.
3. Edel, E. 'KUB III 63, ein Brief aus der Heiratskorrespondenz Ramses' II.' In *Jahrb. für kleinasiatische Forschung*, 2 (1953), 262 ff.
4. Edel, E. 'Weitere Briefe aus der Heiratskorrespondenz Ramses' II.' In *Festschrift A. Alt* (1953), 29 ff.
5. Edel, E. 'Die Abfassungszeit des Briefes KBo I 10 und seine Bedeutung für die Chronologie Ramses' II.' In *J.C.S.* 12 (1958), 130 ff.
6. Edel, E. 'Der geplante Besuch Ḫattušilis III. in Ägypten.' In *M.D.O.G.* 92 (1960), 15 ff.
7. Forrer, E. *Forschungen*, I/1, 1/2, II/1. Erkner bei Berlin, 1926–9.
8. Friedrich, J. *Aus dem hethitischen Schrifttum*, 1 (*Alte Or.* 24/3). Leipzig, 1925.
9. Goetze, A. 'A New Letter from Ramesses to Ḫattušiliš.' In *J.C.S.* 1 (1948), 244 ff.
10. Korošec, V. 'Podelitev hetitske pokrajine Dattašše Ulmi-Tešupu (= *K. Bo.* IV 10).' In *Akad. znanosti in umetnosti v Ljubljani*, pravni razred, 1943, 53 ff.
11. Kuentz, Ch. 'La stèle de mariage de Ramsès II.' In *Ann. Serv.* 25 (1925), 181 ff.
12. Meissner, B. 'Die Beziehungen Ägyptens zum Ḫattireiche nach ḫattischen Quellen.' In *Z.D.M.G.* 72 (1918), 32 ff.
13. Müller, W. M. *Der Bündnisvertrag Ramses' II. und des Chetiterkönigs* (*M.V.Ae.G.* 7/5). Leipzig, 1902.
14. Ranoschek, R. *Ein Brief des Königs Ḫattušil von Ḫatti an den König Kadašman-Enlil von Babylon*. Diss. Breslau, 1922.
15. Rowton, M. B. 'The Background of the Treaty between Ramesses II and Hattušiliš III.' In *J.C.S.* 13 (1959), 1 ff.
16. Sethe, K. 'Neue Forschungen zu den Beziehungen zwischen Ägypten und dem Chattireiche auf Grund ägyptischer Quellen.' In *D.L.Z.* n.F. 3 (1926), 1873 ff.


## IV. THE LAST KINGS OF THE KHATTI LAND

1. Bossert, H. Th. *Asia*. Istanbul, 1946.
2. Götze, A. *Madduwattaš* (*M.V.Ae.G.* 32). Leipzig, 1928.
3. Laroche, E. 'Šuppiluliuma II.' In *R.A.* 47 (1953), 70 ff.
4. Laroche, E. 'Documents hiéroglyphiques hittites provenant du palais d'Ugarit.' In Schaeffer, Cl. F. A., *Ugaritica*, III (1956), 97 ff.
5. Liverani, M. 'Karkemiš nei testi di Ugarit.' In *Riv. stud. or.* 35 (1960), 135 ff.
6. Moran, W. L. 'The Scandal of the "Great Sin" at Ugarit.' In *J.N.E.S.* 18 (1959), 282 f.

7. Nougayrol, J. 'Nouveaux textes accadiens de Ras-Shamra.' In *Mém. Ac. Inscr. B.-L.* Comptes Rendus, 1960, 163 ff.

8. Otten, H. 'Keilschrifttexte [der Grabung 1957].' In *M.D.O.G.* 91 (1958), 73 ff.

9. Otten, H. 'Korrespondenz mit Tukulti-Ninurta aus Boğazköy.' In Weidner, E., *Die Inschriften Tukulti-Ninurtas I* (*Arch. f. Or.* Beiheft 12, 1959), 64 ff.

10. Otten, H. 'Neue Quellen zum Ausklang des Hethitischen Reiches.' In *M.D.O.G.* 94 (1963), 1 ff.

11. Ranoszek, R. 'Kronika króla hetyckiego Tuthaljasa (IV).' In *Rocznik Orjentalistyczny*, 9 (1934), 43 ff.

12. Sommer, F. Die Aḫḫijavā-Urkunden (*Abh. München*, n.F. 6, 1932).

13. Szemerényi, O. 'Vertrag des Hethiterkönigs Tudḫalija IV. mit Ištarmuwa von Amurru (*K.U.B.* xxiii 1).' In *Acta Soc. Hungaricae Orientalis*, 9 (1945), 113 ff.

14. Weidner, E. *Die Inschriften Tukulti-Ninurtas I. und seiner Nachfolger* (*Arch. f. Or.* Beiheft 12). Graz, 1959.

15. Yaron, R. 'A Royal divorce at Ugarit.' In *Or.* n.s. 32 (1963), 21 ff.

### V. HITTITE CIVILIZATION IN THE EMPIRE PERIOD

1. Akurgal, Ekrem and Hirmer, M. *Die Kunst der Hethiter.* München, 1961.

2. Akurgal, Ekrem. 'Die Kunst der Hethiter.' In *Historia*, Sonderheft 'Hethiter' (1964), 37 ff.

3. Bittel, K. 'Nur hethitische oder auch hurritische Kunst.' In *Z.A.* 49 (1950), 256 ff.

4. Goetze, A. *Kleinasien* (*Kulturgeschichte des Alten Orients*, iii, 1, im *Handbuch der Altertumswissenschaft*). 2. Auflage. München, 1957.

5. Goetze, A. 'Warfare in Asia Minor.' In *Iraq*, 25 (1963), 124 ff.

6. Goetze, A. 'State and Society of the Hittites.' In *Historia*, Sonderheft 'Hethiter' (1964), 25 ff.

7. Güterbock, H. G. *Siegel aus Boğazköy.* 2 vols. (*Arch. f. Or.* Beihefte 5 and 7). Berlin, 1940 and 1942.

8. Güterbock, H. G. 'The Hurrian Element in the Hittite Empire.' In *J.W.H.* 2 (1954), 383 ff.

9. Güterbock, H. G. 'Toward a Definition of the term Hittite.' In *Oriens*, 10 (1957), 233 ff.

10. Güterbock, H. G. 'Religion und Kultus der Hethiter.' In *Historia*, Sonderheft 'Hethiter' (1964), 1 ff.

11. Laroche, E. 'Le panthéon de Yazilikaya.' In *J.C.S.* 6 (1952), 115 ff.

12. Laroche, E. 'Documents hiéroglyphiques hittites provenant du palais d'Ugarit.' In Schaeffer, Cl. F.A. (and others), *Ugaritica*, iii (*Mission de Ras Shamra*, 8). Paris, 1956.

13. Laroche, E. *Les hiéroglyphiques hittites.* Paris, 1960.

14. Meriggi, P. *Hieroglyphisch-hethitisches Glossar.* 2. Auflage. Wiesbaden, 1962.

15. Moortgat, A. *Die bildende Kunst des alten Orients und die Bergvölker.* Berlin, 1932.

16. Naumann, R. *Architektur Kleinasiens.* Tübingen, 1955.

17. Otten, H. 'Schrift, Sprache und Literatur der Hethiter.' In *Historia*, Sonderheft 'Hethiter' (1964), 78 ff.

18. Schuler, E. von. 'Staatsverträge und Dokumente hethitischen Rechts.' In *Historia*, Sonderheft 'Hethiter' (1964), 92 ff.

## CHAPTER XXV

### G. GENERAL

1. Delitzsch, F. *Die Babylonische Chronik.* Leipzig, 1906.
2. Ebeling, E., Meissner, B. and Weidner, E. *Die Inschriften der altassyrischen Könige (A.O.B.* I). Leipzig, 1926.
3. Ebeling, E., *Keilschrifttexte aus Assur juristischen Inhalts (W.V.D.O.G.* 50). Leipzig, 1927.
4. El-Wailly, F. J. 'Synopsis of Royal Sources of the Kassite Period.' In *Sumer,* 10 (1954), 43 ff.
5. Fine, H. A. *Studies in Middle-Assyrian Chronology and Religion.* Cincinnati, 1955.
6. Forrer, E. 'Assyrien.' In *R.L.A.* 1 (1932), 228 ff.
7. Jaritz, K. 'Quellen zur Geschichte der Kaššû-Dynastie.' In *Mitt. Inst. Or.* 6 (1958), 187 ff.
8. *Keilschrifttexte aus Boghazköi,* Heft 1–xiv. Leipzig and Berlin, 1916–63.
9. *Keilschrifturkunden aus Boghazköi,* Heft 1–xxxix. Berlin, 1921–63.
10. Laroche, E. 'Catalogue des textes hittites, 11.' In *R.H.A.* 14, fasc. 59 (1956), 75 ff.
11. Luckenbill, D. D. *Ancient Records of Assyria and Babylonia,* 1. Chicago, 1926.
12. Messerschmidt, L. (vol. 1) and Schroeder, O. (vol. 2). *Keilschrifttexte aus Assur historischen Inhalts (W.V.D.O.G.* 16 and 37). Leipzig, 1911, 1922.
13. Schroeder, O. *Keilschrifttexte aus Assur verschiedenen Inhalts (W.V.D.O.G.* 35). Leipzig, 1920.
14. Weidner, E. 'Studien zur assyrisch-babylonischen Chronologie und Geschichte auf Grund neuer Funde.' In *M.V.A.G.* 20/4 (1915).
15. Weidner, E. 'Die neue Königsliste aus Assur.' In *Arch. f. Or.* 4 (1927), 11 ff.
16. Winckler, H. *Altorientalische Forschungen.* Leipzig, 1893–1901.

### I. THE CAMPAIGNS OF ADAD-NIRARI I

1. Dossin, G. 'Le site de la ville de Kaḫat.' In *Compte-rendu de l'onzième Rencontre Assyriologique internationale.* Leiden, 1964, 4 f.
2. Edel, E. 'Die Abfassungszeit des Briefes KBo 1 10 (Hattušil-Kadašman-Ellil) und seine Bedeutung für die Chronologie Ramses' II.' In *J.C.S.* 12 (1958), 130 ff.
3. Falkner, M. 'Studien zur Geographie des alten Mesopotamien.' In *Arch. f. Or.* 18 (1957–58), 1 ff.
4. Friedrich, J. 'Aus dem hethitischen Schrifttum.' In *Alte Or.* 24/3 (1925), 24 ff.
5. Friedrich, J. 'Staatsverträge des Ḫatti-Reiches in hethitischer Sprache, 2.' In *M.V.A.G.* 34/1 (1930), 1 ff.
6. Gelb, I. J. *Hurrians and Subarians (S.A.O.C.* 22). Chicago, 1944.
7. Goetze, A. *Kizzuwatna and the Problem of Hittite Geography (Y.O.S. Researches,* 22). New Haven, 1940.
8. Goetze, A. Review of Gelb, I. J., *Hurrians and Subarians.* In *J.N.E.S.* 5 (1946), 165 ff.
9. Goetze, A. 'An Old Babylonian Itinerary.' In *J.C.S.* 7 (1953), 51 ff.
10. Rowton, M. B. 'The Background of the Treaty between Ramesses II and Ḫattušiliš III.' In *J.C.S.* 13 (1959), 1 ff.
11. Rowton, M. B. 'Comparative Chronology at the Time of Dynasty XIX.' In *J.N.E.S.* 19 (1960), 15 ff.

12. Ungnad, A. *Subartu: Beiträge zur Kulturgeschichte und Völkerkunde Vorderasiens*. Berlin and Leipzig, 1936.
13. Weidner, E. 'Aus den hethitischen Urkunden von Boghazköi.' In *M.D.O.G.* 58 (1917), 53 ff.
14. Weidner, E. 'Die Kämpfe Adad-narâris I gegen Ḫanigalbat.' In *Arch. f. Or.* 5 (1928–29), 89 ff.
15. Weidner, E. 'Wasašatta, König von Ḫanigalbat.' In *Arch. f. Or.* 6 (1930–31), 21 f.
16. Weidner, E. 'Eine neue Inschrift Adad-narâris I.' In *Arch. f. Or.* 19 (1959–60), 104.
17. Winckler, H. 'Vorläufige Nachrichten über die Ausgrabungen in Boghaz-köi im Sommer 1907.' In *M.D.O.G.* 35 (1907), 1 ff.

II. SHALMANESER I AND THE CONQUEST OF KHANIGALBAT

1. Burney, C. A. 'Urartian Fortresses and Towns in the Van Region.' In *A.St.* 7 (1957), 37 ff.
2. Diakonoff, I. M. 'A Comparative Study of the Hurrian and Urartean Languages.' In Diakonoff, I. M. and Shereteli, G. V. (eds.), *Peredneaziatskii Sbornik Voprosy Khettologii i Khurritologii*. English summary, 598 ff. Moscow, 1961.
3. Ebeling, E. *Bruchstücke einer mittelassyrischen Vorschriftensammlung für die Akklimatisierung und Trainierung von Wagenpferden*. Berlin, 1951.
4. Finkelstein, J. J. 'Cuneiform Tablets from Tell Billa.' In *J.C.S.* 7 (1953), 111 ff.
5. Ghirshman, R. French summary of §11, 9. In *Iranica Antiqua*, 3 (1963), 60 ff.
6. Goetze, A. *Kleinasien*. (Kulturgeschichte des alten Orients, Abschnitt III, 1.) Ed. 2. Munich, 1957.
7. Klengel, H. 'Zum Brief eines Königs von Ḫanigalbat (*I.Bo.T.* 1 34).' In *Or.* n.s. 32 (1963), 280 ff.
8. Melikishvili, G. A. *Nairi-Urartu*. Tiflis, 1954.
9. Piotrovsky, B. B. *Vanskoye Tsarstvo (Urartu)*. Moscow, 1959.
10. Streck, M. 'Das Gebiet der heutigen Landschaften Armenien, Kurdistan und Westpersien nach den babylonisch-assyrischen Keilinschriften.' In *Z.A.* 13 (1898), 57 ff.

III. TUKULTI-NINURTA I AND THE CONQUEST OF BABYLONIA

1. Dossin, G. 'Bronzes inscrits du Luristan de la collection Foroughi.' In *Iranica Antiqua*, 2 (1962), 149 ff.
2. Ebeling, E. 'Urkunden des Archivs von Assur aus mittelassyrischen Zeit: aus dem Briefwechsel eines assyrischen Kanzlers.' In *M.A.O.G.* 7 (1933), 3 ff.
3. Klengel, H. 'Tukulti-Ninurta I, König von Assyrien.' In *Das Altertum*, 7 (1961), 67 ff.
4. Nougayrol, J. *Textes accadiens des archives sud (archives internationales)*. (Mission de Ras Shamra, 9. *Le Palais royal d'Ugarit*, 4.) Paris, 1956.
5. Otten, H. 'Ein Brief aus Hattuša an Babu-aḫu-iddina.' In *Arch. f. Or.* 19 (1959–60), 39 ff.
6. Otten, H. 'Neue Quellen zum Ausklang des hethitischen Reiches.' In *M.D.O.G.* 94 (1963), 1 ff.
7. Schnabel, P. 'Studien zur babylonisch-assyrischen Chronologie.' In *M.V.A.G.* 13 (1908), 1 ff.

8. Smith, S. *Early History of Assyria*. London, 1928.

9. Sommer, F. *Die Aḫḫijavā-Urkunden (Abh. München, n.F. 6)*. München, 1932.

10. Weidner, E. 'Studien zur Zeitgeschichte Tukulti-Ninurtas I.' In *Arch. f. Or.* 13 (1939–40), 109 ff.

11. Weidner, E. 'Das Reich Sargons von Akkad.' In *Arch. f. Or.* 16 (1952–53), 1 ff.

12. Weidner, E. *Die Inschriften Tukulti-Ninurtas I und seiner Nachfolger (Arch. f. Or.* Beiheft 12). Graz, 1959.

13. Weidner, E. 'Der Kanzler Salmanassars I.' In *Arch. f. Or.* 19 (1959–60), 33 ff.

IV. LITERATURE

1. Baumgartner, W. 'Zur Form des assyrischen Königsinschriften.' In *O.L.Z.* 27 (1924), 313 ff.

2. Borger, R. *Einleitung in die assyrischen Königsinschriften. I. Das zweite Jahrtausend vor Chr.* (Handbuch der Orientalistik, Abt. I: Der nahe und der mittlere Osten, Ergänzungsband 5.) Leiden and Cologne, 1961.

3. Dossin, G. 'L'inscription de fondation de Iaḫdun-Lim, roi de Mari.' In *Syria*, 32 (1955), 1 ff.

4. Ebeling, E. 'Aus den Keilschrifttexten aus Assur religiösen Inhalts.' In *M.D.O.G.* 58 (1917), 22 ff.

5. Ebeling, E. 'Bruchstücke eines politischen Propagandagedichtes aus einer assyrischen Kanzlei.' In *M.A.O.G.* 12/2 (1938), 1 ff.

6. Labat, R. 'Résumé des cours de 1955–1956: Assyriologie.' In *Annuaire du Collège de France*, 56 année (1956), 252 ff.

7. Lambert, W. G. 'Three Unpublished Fragments of the Tukulti-Ninurta Epic.' In *Arch. f. Or.* 18 (1957–58), 38 ff.

8. Mowinckel, S. 'Die vorderasiatischen Königs- und Fürsteninschriften. Eine stilistische Studie.' In *Festschrift Gunkel*. Göttingen, 1923.

9. Olmstead, A. T. 'Assyrian Historiography: a Source Study.' In *University of Missouri Studies, Social Science Series*, 3/1 (1916), 1 ff.

10. Reiner, E. Review of Weidner, E., *Die Inschriften Tukulti-Ninurtas I*. In *Bi. Or.* 19 (1962), 158 f.

11. Scheil, V. 'Fragment des "Annales" de Pudi-ili, roi d'Assyrie.' In *O.L.Z.* 7 (1904), 216 f.

12. Speiser, E. A. 'Ancient Mesopotamia.' In Dentan, R. C. (ed.), *The Idea of History in the Ancient Near East*. Yale U.P. 1955, 37 ff.

13. Tadmor, H. 'The Campaigns of Sargon II of Assur: a Chronological-historical Study.' In *J.C.S.* 12 (1958), 22, 77.

14. Tadmor, H. 'Historical Implications of the Correct Reading of Akkadian *dâku*.' In *J.N.E.S.* 17 (1958), 129 ff.

15. Thompson, R. C. and Hutchinson, R. W. 'Excavations on the Temple of Nabu at Nineveh.' In *Archaeologia*, 79 (1929), 103 ff.

16. Thompson, R. C. 'The British Museum Excavations at Nineveh, 1931–32.' In *Ann. Arch. Anthr.* 20 (1933), 71 ff.

17. Weidner, E. Review of Thompson, R. W. and Hutchinson, R. W., 'Excavations on the Temple of Nabu at Nineveh'. *Archaeologia*, 79. In *Arch. f. Or.* 7 (1931–32), 280.

18. Weidner, E. 'Die Bibliothek Tiglatpilesers I.' In *Arch. f. Or.* 16 (1952–53), 197 ff.

19. Weidner, E. Note in *Arch. f. Or.* 17 (1954–56), 384 f.

20. Weidner, E. 'Assyrische Epen über die Kassiten-Kämpfe.' In *Arch. f. Or.* 20 (1963–64), 113 ff.

V. ARCHITECTURE AND THE ARTS

1. Andrae, W. *Die Festungswerke von Assur* (*W.V.D.O.G.* 23). Leipzig, 1913.
2. Andrae, W. *Coloured Ceramics from Ashur*. London, 1925.
3. Andrae, W. *Kultrelief aus dem Brunnen des Assurtempels zu Assur* (*W.V.D.O.G.* 53). Leipzig, 1931.
4. Andrae, W. *Die jüngeren Ischtar-Tempel in Assur* (*W.V.D.O.G.* 58). Leipzig, 1935.
5. Andrae, W. *Das wiedererstandene Assur*. Leipzig, 1938.
6. Beran, T. 'Assyrische Glyptik des 14. Jahrhunderts.' In *Z.A.* 52 (1957), 141 ff.
7. Beran, T. 'Die babylonische Glyptik der Kassitenzeit.' In *Arch. f. Or.* 18 (1957–58), 256 ff.
8. Frankfort, H. *Cylinder Seals, a Documentary Essay on the Art and Religion of the Ancient Near East*. London, 1939.
9. Frankfort, H. *The Art and Architecture of the Ancient Orient*. Harmondsworth, 1954.
10. Haller, A. *Die Gräber und Grüfte von Assur* (*W.V.D.O.G.* 65). Berlin, 1954.
11. Haller, A. *Die Heiligtümer des Gottes Assur und der Sin-Šamaš-Tempel in Assur* (*W.V.D.O.G.* 67). Berlin, 1955.
12. Köcher, F. 'Ein Inventartext aus Kār-Tukulti-Ninurta.' In *Arch. f. Or.* 18 (1957–58), 300 ff.
13. Maxwell-Hyslop, K. R. 'The Ur Jewellery.' In *Iraq*, 22 (1960), 105 ff.
14. McEwan, C. W. (ed.). *Soundings at Tell Fakhariyah* (*O.I.P.* 79). Chicago, 1958.
15. Moortgat, A. 'Assyrische Glyptik des 13. Jahrhunderts.' In *Z.A.* 47 (1942), 50 ff.
16. Opitz, D. 'Ein Altar des Königs Tukulti-Ninurta I von Assyrien.' In *Arch. f. Or.* 7 (1931–32), 83 ff.
17. Oppenheim, L. 'Die akkadischen Personennamen der "Kassitenzeit".' In *Anthropos*, 31 (1936), 470 ff.
18. Parrot, A. 'Les fouilles de Mari.' In *Syria*, 18 (1937), 54 ff.
19. Parrot, A. 'Les fouilles de Mari.' In *Syria*, 29 (1952), 183 ff.
20. Parrot, A. *Nineveh and Babylon*. London, 1961.
21. Porada, E. *Corpus of Ancient Near Eastern Seals in North American Collections*, I. Washington, 1948.
22. Preusser, C. *Die Wohnhäuser in Assur* (*W.V.D.O.G.* 64). Berlin, 1954.
23. Preusser, C. *Die Paläste in Assur* (*W.V.D.O.G.* 66). Berlin, 1955.
24. Smith, S. 'A Pre-Greek Coinage in the Near East?' In *Num. Chron.*, 5th series, vol. 2 (1922), 176 ff.
25. Starr, R. F. S. *Nuzi. Report on the Excavations at Yorghan Tepe near Kirkuk, Iraq. 1927–1931*, II. Cambridge, Mass., 1937–39.
26. Weidner, E. Review of Andrae, W., *Das wiedererstandene Assur*. In *Arch. f. Or.* 13 (1939–40), 157 ff.
27. Weidner, E. 'Säulen aus Naḫur.' In *Arch. f. Or.* 17 (1954–56), 145 f.


A. ADDENDA

1. Bibby, G. *Looking for Dilmun*. Pelican ed. Harmondsworth, 1964.
2. Brinkman, J. A. *A Political History of Post-Kassite Babylonia, 1158–722 B.C.* (*An. Or.* 43.) Rome, 1968.
3. Brinkman, J. A. 'The Names of the Last Eight Kings of the Kassite Dynasty.' In *Z.A.* 59 (1969), 231 ff.

4. Brinkman, J. A. 'Ur: the Kassite period and the Period of the Assyrian kings.' In *Or.* n.s. 38 (1969), 310 ff.
5. Brinkman, J. A. 'Notes on Mesopotamian History in the Thirteenth Century B.C.' In *Bi. Or.* 27 (1970), 301 ff.
6. Carter, T. H. 'Early Assyrians in the Sinjar.' In *Expedition*, 7 (1964), 34 ff.
7. Carter, T. H. 'Excavations at Tell al-Rimah, 1964. Preliminary Report.' In *B.A.S.O.R.* 78 (1965), 49 ff.
8. Cassin, E. 'Tecniche della guerra e strutture sociali in Mesopotamia nella Seconda Metà del II Millennio.' *In Rivista Storica Italiana*, 77 (1965), 445 ff.
9. Cornwall, P. B. 'Two Letters from Dilmun.' In *J.C.S.* 6 (1952), 136 ff.
10. Edzard, D. O. 'A New inscription of Adad-narari I.' In *Sumer*, 20 (1964), 49 ff.
11. Fischer Weltgeschichte, vol. 3. *Die altorientalischen Reiche II. Das Ende des 2. Jahrtausends.* Frankfurt-am-Main, 1966.
12. Freydank, H. 'Anmerkungen zu Mittelassyrischen Texte.' In *O.L.Z.* 66 (1971), 534 f.
13. Köcher, F. 'Ein mittelassyrisches Ritualfragment zum Neujahrsfest.' In *Z.A.* 50 (1952), 192 ff.
14. Oates, D. 'The Excavations at Tell al Rimah, 1964.' In *Iraq*, 27 (1965), 40 ff.
15. Oates, D. 'The Excavations at Tell al Rimah, 1965.' In *Iraq*, 28 (1966), 122 ff.
16. Oates, D. 'The excavations at Tell al Rimah, 1966.' In *Iraq*, 29 (1967), 70 ff.
17. Oates, D. 'The Excavations at Tell al Rimah, 1967.' In *Iraq*, 30 (1968), 115 ff.
18. Oates, D. 'The Excavations at Tell al Rimah, 1968.' In *Iraq*, 32 (1970), 1 ff.
19. Oates, D. 'The Excavations at Tell al Rimah, 1971.' In *Iraq*, 34 (1972), 77 ff.
20. Oppenheim, A. L. *Letters from Mesopotamia*. Chicago, 1967.
21. Saggs, H. W. F. 'The Tell al-Rimah Tablets.' In *Iraq*, 30 (1968), 154 ff.
22. Salvini, M. *Nairi e Ur(u)aṭri*. Rome, 1967.
23. Saporetti, C. Review of *C.A.H.* II², ch. xxv. In *Or.* n.s. 37 (1968), 482 f.
24. Seux, M. J. *Épithètes royales akkadiennes et sumériennes*. Paris, 1967.
25. Van Driesl, G. *The Cult of Aššur*. Assen, 1969.
26. Weidner, E. 'Assyrien und Ḫanigalbat.' In *Ugaritica*, 6 (1969), 519 ff.
27. Wiseman, D. J. 'The Tell al Rimah Tablets, 1966.' In *Iraq*, 30 (1968), 175 ff.

# CHAPTER XXVI

## (a) THE EXODUS AND WANDERINGS

### G. GENERAL

1. Albright, W. F. *From the Stone Age to Christianity*, Ed. 2. Baltimore, 1946.
2. Albright, W. F. 'Syrien, Phönizien und Palästina.' In *Historia mundi*, II, 331 ff., 629. Munich, 1953.
3. Auerbach, E. *Wüste und Gelobtes Land*, I. Ed. 2. Berlin, 1938.
4. Bright, J. *A History of Israel*. Philadelphia, 1959.
5. Gordon, C. H. *Introduction to Old Testament Times*. Ventnor, 1953.
6. Gordon, C. H. *The World of the Old Testament*. New York, 1958.
7. Gordon, C. H. *Before the Bible*. London, 1962.
8. Grollenberg, L. H. *Atlas of the Bible*. Translated by Reid, Joyce M. H. and Rowley, H. H. London, 1956.

9. Herrmann, S. 'Das Werden Israels.' In *T.L.Z.* 87 (1962), 561 ff.
10. Kittel, R. *Geschichte des Volkes Israel*, 1. Eds. 5 and 6. Gotha, 1923.
11. Kraeling, Emil G. *Bible Atlas*. Chicago, 1956.
12. Kraus, H.-J. 'Israel.' In *Propyläen-Weltgeschichte*, 11, 237 ff. Berlin, 1962.
13. Lods, A. *Israël. Des origines au milieu du VIII<sup>e</sup> siècle*. Paris, 1930. Translated by S. H. Hooke. London, 1932.
14. May, Herbert G. *Oxford Bible Atlas*. London, 1962.
15. Meek, T. J. *Hebrew Origins*, Rev. ed. New York, 1950.
16. Meyer, Eduard. *Die Israeliten und ihre Nachbarstämme*. Halle, 1906.
17. Noth, M. *The History of Israel*. Ed. 2. London, 1960.
18. Noth, M. *Geschichte Israels*. Ed. 5. Göttingen, 1961.
19. Noth, M. *Die Welt des Alten Testaments*. Ed. 4. Berlin, 1962.
20. Oesterley, W. O. E. and Robinson, Th. H. *A History of Israel*, 1 and 11. Oxford, 1932.
21. Olmstead, A. T. *History of Palestine and Syria to the Macedonian Conquest*. New York, 1931.
22. Pritchard, J. B. (ed.). *Ancient Near-Eastern Texts relating to the Old Testament*. Ed. 2. Princeton, 1955.
23. Renckens, H. *De Godsdienst van Israël (De Godsdiensten der Mensheid* 14). Roermond en Maaseik, 1962.
24. Rowley, H. H. *From Joseph to Joshua*. London, 1950.
25. Smend, R. *Jahwekrieg und Stämmebund. Erwägungen zur ältesten Geschichte Israels (Forsch. Rel. Lit.* 84). Göttingen, 1963.
26. Stade, B. *Geschichte des Volkes Israel*, 1. Ed. 2. Berlin, 1889.
27. Wellhausen, J. *Israelitische und jüdische Geschichte*. Ed. 9. Berlin, 1958.
28. Wright, G. E. and Filson, F. V. *The Westminster Historical Atlas to the Bible*. London, 1946.

### I. THE LITERARY CHARACTER OF THE PENTATEUCH

1. Bentzen, A. *Introduction to the Old Testament*. Ed. 2. Copenhagen, 1952.
2. Eissfeldt, O. *Hexateuch-Synopse*. Ed. 2. Darmstadt, 1962.
3. Eissfeldt, O. *Die ältesten Traditionen Israels. Ein kritischer Bericht über C. A. Simpson's 'The Early Traditions of Israel'*. (*Z.A.W.* Beiheft 71). Berlin, 1950.
4. Eissfeldt, O. *Die Genesis der Genesis*. Ed. 2. Tübingen, 1961.
5. Eissfeldt, O. *Einleitung in das Alte Testament*. Ed. 3. Tübingen, 1964.
6. Gottwald, Norman K. *A Light to the Nations*. New York, 1959.
7. Hölscher, G. *Geschichtsschreibung in Israel. Untersuchungen zum Jahvisten und Elohisten (Acta Soc. Hum. Litt. Lundensis*, 1). Lund, 1952.
8. Lods, A. *Histoire de la littérature hébraïque et juive*. Paris, 1950.
9. Noth, M. *Überlieferungsgeschichte des Pentateuch*. Ed. 2. Stuttgart, 1960.
10. Noth, M. *Überlieferungsgeschichtliche Studien*, 1. Ed. 2. Stuttgart, 1957.
11. Oesterley, W. O. E. and Robinson, Th. H. *Introduction to the Books of the Old Testament*. London, 1934.
12. Pfeiffer, R. H. *Introduction to the Old Testament*. Ed. 2. New York, 1948.
13. Procksch, O. *Das nordhebräische Sagenbuch. Die Elohimquelle*. Leipzig, 1906.
14. Rad, G. von. 'Das formgeschichtliche Problem des Hexateuch'. In *Gesammelte Studien zum Alten Testament*, 9 ff. Munich, 1958.
15. Robert, A. and Feuillet, A. *Introduction à la Bible*. Ed. 2. Tournai, 1959.
16. Simpson, C. A. *The Early Traditions of Israel*. Oxford, 1948.
17. Simpson, C. A. *Composition of the Book of Judges*. Oxford, 1957.

18. Smend, R. *Die Erzählung des Hexateuch auf ihre Quellen untersucht.* Berlin, 1912.
19. Weiser, A. *Introduction to the Old Testament.* Transl. by D. M. Barton. London, 1961.
20. Wellhausen, J. *Die Composition des Hexateuchs und der historischen Bücher des Alten Testaments.* Ed. 3. Berlin, 1899.

## II. THE TRADITIONS OF THE PATRIARCHS AND MODERN CRITICISM

1. Albright, W. F. 'A millennium of Biblical History in the Light of Recent Excavations.' In *Proc. Am. Philos. Soc.* 69 (1930), 441 ff., 446 ff.
2. Albright, W. F. *Recent Discoveries in Bible Lands.* New York, 1955.
3. Albright, W. F. *Die Bibel im Lichte der Altertumsforschung.* Ed. 2. Stuttgart, 1959.
4. Alt, A. 'Die Landnahme der Israeliten in Palästina.' In *Kleine Schriften*, I. Ed. 2, 89 ff. Munich, 1959.
5. Alt, A. 'Der Gott der Väter. Ein Beitrag zur Vorgeschichte der israelitischen Religion.' In *Kleine Schriften*, I. Ed. 2, 1 ff. Munich, 1959.
6. Alt, A. 'Erwägungen über die Landnahme der Israeliten in Palästina.' In *Kleine Schriften*, I. Ed. 2, 126 ff. Munich, 1959.
7. Alt, A. 'Die Herkunft der Hyksos in neuer Sicht.' In *Kleine Schriften*, III, 72 ff. Munich, 1959.
8. Bauer, Th. *Die Ostkanaanäer.* Leipzig, 1926.
9. Bea, A. 'La Palestina Preisraelitica.' In *Bib.* 24 (1943), 231 ff.
10. Böhl, Franz M. Th. 'Die Könige von Gen. 14.' In *Z.A.W.* 36 (1916), 65 ff.
11. Böhl, Franz M. Th. 'Tud'alia I, Zeitgenosse Abrahams um 1650 v. Chr.' In *Z.A.W.* 42 (1924), 148 ff.
12. Böhl, F. M. Th. 'Das Zeitalter Abrahams.' In *Opera Minora.* Groningen, 1953.
13. Borger, R. 'Das Problem der 'apiru ("Ḫabiru").' In *Z.D.P.V.* 74 (1958), 121 ff.
14. Bottéro, J. *Le problème des Ḫabiru (Cahiers de la Société Asiatique*, 12). Paris, 1954.
15. Brentjes, B. 'Das Kamel im Alten Orient.' In *Klio*, 38 (1960), 23 ff.
16. Campbell, Edward F. jr. 'The Amarna-Letters and the Amarna Period.' In *Bi. Ar.* 23 (1960), 2 ff.
17. Dahood, M. J. 'Ancient Semitic Deities in Syria and Palestine.' In *Studi Semitici*, 1 (1958), 65 ff.
18. Dhorme, Éd. 'Les pays bibliques au temps d'el Amarna d'après la nouvelle publication des Lettres.' In *Rev. bibl.* 5 (1908), 500 ff.; 6 (1909), 50 ff. and 368 ff.
19. Dhorme, Éd. 'Les Amorrhéens. À propos d'un livre récent.' In *Recueil Édouard Dhorme*, 81 ff. Paris, 1951.
20. Dhorme, Éd. 'Abraham dans le cadre de l'histoire.' In *Recueil Édouard Dhorme*, 191 ff. Paris, 1951.
21. Dhorme, Éd. *La religion des Hébreux nomades.* Bruxelles, 1937.
22. Dossin, G. 'Benjaminites dans les textes de Mari.' In *Mél. Dussaud*, 981 ff. Paris, 1939.
23. Eissfeldt, O. 'Stammessage und Novelle in den Geschichten von Jakob und von seinen Söhnen.' In *Kleine Schriften*, I, 84 ff. Tübingen, 1962.
24. Eissfeldt, O. ''El and Yahweh.' In *J.S.S.* 1 (1956), 25 ff.
25. Eissfeldt, O. 'Jahwes Verhältnis zu 'Eljon und Schaddaj nach Psalm 91.' In *We. Or.* 2 (1954), 343 ff.

26. Eissfeldt, O. *Der Beutel der Lebendigen. Alttestamentliche Erzählungs- und Dichtungsmotive im Lichte neuer Nuzi-Texte (Sitzungsb. Leipzig,* 105, 6). Berlin, 1960.

27. Gelb, I. J. 'La lingua degli Amoriti.' In *Atti Accad. Lincei.* Rendic. Ser. VIII, 13 (1958), 143 ff.

28. Gelb, I. J. *Hurrians and Subarians (S.A.O.C.* 22). Chicago, 1944.

29. Glueck, N. 'Exploring Southern Palestine.' In *Bi. Ar.* 22 (1959), 82 ff.

30. Gordon, C. H. 'Biblical Customs and the Nuzu Tablets.' In *Bi. Ar.* 3 (1942), 1 ff.

31. Gordon, C. H. 'The Patriarchal Age.' In *J. Bibl. Lit.* 21 (1953), 238 ff.

32. Gordon, C. H. 'Abraham and the Merchants of Ur.' In *J.N.E.S.* 17 (1958), 28 ff.

33. Greenberg, M. *The Ḫab/piru.* New Haven, 1955.

34. Gressmann, H. 'Sage und Geschichte in den Patriarchenerzählungen.' In *Z.A.W.* 30 (1910), 1 ff.

35. Guillaume, A. 'The Habiru, the Hebrews, and the Arabs.' In *P.E.Q.* 78 (1946), 65 ff.

36. Hayes, William C. 'Egypt: From the Death of Ammenemes III to Seqenenre II.' In *C.A.H.* II³, pt. 1, ch. II. Cambridge, 1973.

37. Jean, Ch.-F. 'Les noms propres de personnes dans les lettres de Mari.' In *Studia Mariana,* 63 ff. Leiden, 1950.

38. Kaiser, O. 'Stammesgeschichtliche Hintergründe der Josephsgeschichte.' In *V.T.* 10 (1960), 1 ff.

39. Klengel, H. 'Zu einigen Problemen des altvorderasiatischen Nomadentums.' In *Arch. Orient.* 30 (1962), 585 ff.

40. Kline, M. G. 'The Ḫa-BI-ru—Kin or Foe of Israel?' In *Westminster Theol. Journ.* 19 (1956), 1 ff. and 170 ff.; 20 (1957/58), 46 ff.

41. Kraeling, E. G. 'The Origin of the Name Hebrews.' In *A.J.S.L.* 58 (1941), 237 ff.

42. Kupper, J.-R. *Les nomades en Mésopotamie au temps des rois de Mari.* Paris, 1957.

43. Kupper, J.-R. 'Northern Mesopotamia and Syria.' In *C.A.H.* II³, pt. 1, ch. 1. Cambridge, 1973.

44. Lambert, W. G. 'The Domesticated Camel in the Second Millennium—Evidence from Alalakh and Ugarit.' In *Bull. A.S.O.R.* 160 (1960), 42 ff.

45. Lanczkowski, G. 'Zur Herkunft der Hyksos.' In *O.L.Z.* 51 (1956), 389 ff.

46. Maag, V. 'Jakob–Esau–Edom.' In *Theol. Zeitschr.* 13 (1957), 418 ff.

47. Malamat, A. 'Mari and the Bible: Some Patterns of Tribal Organizations and Institutions.' In *J.A.O.S.* 82 (1962), 143 ff.

48. Noth, M. 'Das alttestamentliche Bundesschließen im Lichte eines Mari-Textes.' In *Gesammelte Studien z. A.T.* 142 ff. München, 1960.

49. Noth, M. *Die Ursprünge des alten Israel im Lichte neuer Quellen (Veröffentl. d. Arbeitsgemeinschaft f. Forschung d. Landes Nordrhein-Westfalen,* 94). Köln, Opladen, 1961.

50. Parrot, A. *Abraham et son temps (Cah. Ar. B.,* no. 14). Neuchâtel, 1962.

51. Rowley, H. H. 'Recent Discovery and the Patriarchal Age.' In *Bull. Ryl. Libr.* 32 (1949/50), 3 ff.

52. Rowley, H. H. 'Melchizedek and Zadok.' In *Bertholet-Festschrift.* Tübingen, 1950, 461 ff.

53. Säve-Söderbergh, T. 'The Hyksos Rule in Egypt.' In *J.E.A.* 37 (1951), 53 ff.

54. Saggs, H. W. F. 'Ur of the Chaldees. A Problem of Identification.' In *Iraq,* 22 (1960), 200 ff.

55. Speiser, E. A. 'The Hurrian Participation in the Civilisation of Mesopotamia, Syria and Palestine.' In *Cah. H.M.* 1, 2 (1933), 311 ff.
56. Vaux, R. de. 'Les patriarches hébreux et les découvertes modernes.' In *Rev. bibl.* 53 (1946), 321 ff.; 55 (1948), 321 ff.; 56 (1949), 5 ff.
57. Vaux, R. de. *Die hebräischen Patriarchen und die modernen Entdeckungen.* Düsseldorf, 1961.
58. Walz, R. 'Gab es ein Esel-Nomadentum im Alten Orient?' In *Akten des XXIV. Internat. Or.-Kongr. München*, 150 ff. Wiesbaden, 1959.

III. THE ISRAELITE SETTLEMENTS BEFORE THE DESCENT INTO EGYPT

1. Alt, A. 'Neues über Palästina aus dem Archiv Amenophis' IV.' In *Kleine Schriften*, III, 158 ff. Munich, 1959.
2. Astour, M. 'Benê-Iamina et Jéricho.' In *Semitica*, 9 (1959), 5 ff.
3. Eissfeldt, O. 'Der geschichtliche Hintergrund der Erzählung von Gibeas Schandtat (Richter 19–21).' In *Kleine Schriften*, II, 64 ff. Tübingen, 1963.
4. Harrelson, W., Anderson, B. W. and Wright, G. E. 'Shechem, "Navel of the Land".' In *Bi. Ar.* 20 (1957), 2 ff.
5. Mowinckel, S. '"Rahelstämme" und "Leastämme".' In *Z.A.W.* Beiheft, 77 (1958), 129 ff.
6. Muilenburg, J. 'The Birth of Benjamin.' In *J. Bibl. Lit.* 75 (1956), 194 ff.
7. Nielsen, E. *Shechem. A Traditio-Historical Investigation.* Copenhagen, 1945.
8. Noth, M. *Das System der zwölf Stämme Israels.* Stuttgart, 1930.
9. Noth, M. 'Eine siedlungsgeographische Liste in 1. Chron. 2 und 4.' In *Z.D.P.V.* 55 (1932), 97 ff.
10. Noth, M. 'Die Ansiedlung des Stammes Juda auf dem Boden Palästinas.' In *P.J.B.* 30 (1934), 31 ff.
11. Vincent, A. 'Jericho. Une hypothèse.' In *M.U.S.J.* 37 (1960/61), 79 ff.

IV. THE NATURE OF THE DESCENT INTO EGYPT

1. Gressmann, H. 'Ursprung und Entwicklung der Joseph-Sage.' In *Forsch. Rel. Lit.* 36, 1, 1 ff. Göttingen, 1923.
2. Gunkel, H. 'Die Komposition der Joseph-Geschichten.' In *Z.D.M.G.* 76 (1922), 55 ff.
3. Janssen, J. M. A. 'Egyptological Remarks on the Story of Joseph in Genesis.' In *J.E.O.L.* 14 (1955/56), 63 ff.
4. Kaiser, O. 'Stammesgeschichtliche Hintergründe der Josephsgeschichte.' In *V.T.* 10 (1960), 1 ff.
5. Montet, P. *L'Égypte et la Bible* (*Cah. Ar. B.*, no. 11). Neuchâtel, 1959.
6. Vergote, J. *Joseph en Égypte. Genèse chap. 37–50 à la lumière des études égyptologiques récentes.* Louvain, 1959.

V. THE HISTORICAL EVIDENCE FOR THE EXODUS

1. Albright, W. F. 'Baal-Zephon.' In *Bertholet-Festschr.* 1 ff. Tübingen, 1950.
2. Auerbach, E. *Moses.* Amsterdam, 1953.
3. Couroyer, B. 'La résidence Ramesside du Delta et la Ramsès Biblique.' In *Rev. bibl.* 53 (1946), 75 ff.
4. Drioton, E. 'La date de l'Exode.' In *Rev. d'hist. et philos. relig.* 35 (1955), 36 ff.

5. Eissfeldt, O. *Baal Zaphon, Zeus Kasios und der Durchzug der Israeliten durchs Meer.* Halle/Saale, 1932.
6. Gressmann, H. *Mose und seine Zeit.* Göttingen, 1913.
7. Griffith, J. Gwyn. 'The Egyptian Derivation of the Name Moses.' In *J.N.E.S.* 12 (1953), 225 ff.
8. Lucas, A. 'The Date of the Exodus.' In *P.E.Q.* 73 (1941), 110 ff.
9. Meek, T. J. 'Moses and the Levites.' In *A.J.S.L.* 56 (1939), 113 ff.
10. Noth, M. 'Der Schauplatz des Meerwunders.' In *Eissfeldt-Festschr.* 181 ff. Halle/Saale, 1947.
11. Rowley, H. H. 'Israel's Sojourn in Egypt.' In *Bull. Ryl. Libr.* 22 (1938), 3 ff.
12. Rowley, H. H. 'The Date of the Exodus.' In *P.E.Q.* 73 (1941), 152 ff.
13. Winnett, F. V. *The Mosaic Tradition.* Toronto, 1949.

VI. THE WANDERINGS

1. Aharoni, Y. 'Results of the Archaeological Investigations [in the Sinai Peninsula].' In *Antiquity and Survival*, 2 (1957), 287 ff.
2. Albright, W. F. 'Exploring in Sinai with the University of California Expedition.' In *Bull. A.S.O.R.* 109 (1948), 5 ff.
3. Alt, A. 'Emiter und Moabiter.' In *Kleine Schriften*, I. Ed. 2, 203 ff. Munich, 1959.
4. Arnold, W. R. *Ephod and Ark.* Cambridge, 1917.
5. Beyerlin, W. *Herkunft und Geschichte der ältesten Sinaitraditionen.* Tübingen, 1961.
6. Eissfeldt, O. 'Lade und Stierbild.' In *Kleine Schriften*, II, 282 ff. Tübingen, 1963,
7. Eissfeldt, O. 'Sinai-Erzählung und Bileam-Sprüche.' In *H.U.C.A.* 32 (1961), 179 ff.
8. Eissfeldt, O. 'Die älteste Erzählung vom Sinaibund.' In *Z.A.W.* 73 (1961), 137 ff.
9. Glueck, N. 'Explorations in Eastern Palestine.' In *Ann. A.S.O.R.* 14 (1933); 15 (1935); 18–19 (1939); 25–28 (1951).
10. Glueck, N. 'Kenites and Kenizzites.' In *P.E.Q.* 72 (1940), 22 ff.
11. Gressmann, H. 'Der Sinaikult in heidnischer Zeit.' In *T.L.Z.* 42 (1917), 153 ff.
12. Harding, G. L. *The Antiquities of Jordan.* London, 1959.
13. Hartmann, R. 'Zelt und Lade.' In *Z.A.W.* 37 (1918), 209 ff.
14. Hölscher, G. 'Sinai und Choreb.' In *Bultmann-Festschr.* 127 ff. Stuttgart, 1949.
15. Kirk, G. E. 'The Negev or Southern Desert of Palestine.' In *P.E.Q.* 73 (1941), 57 ff.
16. Kirk, G. E. 'An Outline of the Ancient Cultural History of Transjordan.' In *P.E.Q.* 76 (1944), 180 ff.
17. Kirk, G. E. 'Two Connected Problems relating to the Israelite Settlement in Transjordan.' In *P.E.2.* 79 (1947), 87 ff.
18. Lammens, H. 'Le culte des Bétyles et les processions religieuses chez les Arabes préislamites.' In Lammens, H. *L'Arabie occidentale avant l'Hégire*, 101 ff. Beyrouth, 1928.
19. Mendenhall, G. E. 'Covenant Forms in Israelitic Tradition.' In *Bi. Ar.* 17 (1954), 49 ff.
20. Morgenstern, J. *The Ark, the Ephod, and the "Tent of Meeting".* Cincinnati, 1945.

21. Moritz, B. *Der Sinaikult in heidnischer Zeit* (*Abh. Göttingen*, 16, 2). Göttingen, 1916.
22. Mowinckel, S. 'Kadesj, Sinai og Jahwe.' In *Norsk Geografisk Tidsskrift*, 9 (1942), 1 ff.
23. Noth, M. 'Der Wallfahrtsweg zum Sinai.' In *P.J.B.* 36 (1940), 5 ff.
24. Noth, M. 'Num. 21 als Glied der "Hexateuch"-Erzählung.' In *Z.A.W.* 58 (1940/41), 161 ff.
25. Noth, M. 'Beiträge zur Geschichte des Ostjordanlandes. I.' In *P.J.B.* 37 (1941), 50 ff.; II, in *Z.A.W.* 60 (1944), 11 ff.; III, in *Z.D.P.V.* 68 (1951), 1 ff.
26. Philby, H. St John. *The Land of Midian*. London, 1957.
27. Phythian-Adams, W. J. T. 'The Mount of God.' In *P.E.F.* 1930, 135 ff. and 192 ff.
28. Phythian-Adams, W. J. T. 'The Volcanic Phenomena of the Exodus.' In *J.P.O.S.* 12 (1932), 86 ff.
29. Rad, G. von. 'Zelt und Lade.' In *Gesammelte Studien z. Alten Testament*, 109 ff. München, 1958.
30. Vaux, R. de et Savaignac, R. 'Nouvelles recherches dans la région de Cadès.' In *Rev. bibl.* 47 (1938), 89 ff., pls. VIIIf.

## (*b*) THE ARCHAEOLOGICAL EVIDENCE

### VII. PROBLEMS: THE NATURE OF THE EVIDENCE

1. Aharoni, Y. 'Problems of the Israelite conquest in the light of archaeological discoveries.' In *Antiquity and Survival* (ed. W. A. Ruysch), II (1957), 131 ff.
2. Aharoni, Y. *The Land of the Bible; a historical geography*. London, 1966.
3. Albright, W. F. *The Archaeology of Palestine*. London, 1949.
4. Albright, W. F. Review of G. M. Shipton, *Notes on the Megiddo pottery of Strata VI–XX*. In *A.J.A.* 44 (1940), 546 ff.
5 Dothan, T. 'Archaeological reflections on the Philistine problem.' In *Antiquity and Survival* (ed. W. A. Ruysch), II (1957), 151 ff.
6. Eggers, H. J. *Einführung in die Vorgeschichte*, ch. v. Munich, 1959.
7. Franken, H. J. 'Tell es-Sultan and Old Testament Jericho.' In *Oudtestamentische Studiën*, deel XIV. Leiden, 1965.
8. Kenyon, K. M. *Jericho I*. London, 1960.
9. Kenyon, K. M. *Jericho II*. London, 1965.
10 Kenyon, K. M. *Archaeology in the Holy Land*. London, 1964.
11. Kenyon, K. M. 'Tombs of the Intermediate Early-Bronze–Middle-Bronze Age at Tell Ajjul.' In *Ann. of the Department of Antiquities, Jordan*, III (1956), 41 ff.
12. Sinclair, L. A. 'An archaeological study of Gibeah, Tell el-Fûl.' In *Ann. A.S.O.R.* 34 (1960), 5 ff.

### VIII. RESULTS

1. Albright, W. F. 'The excavation of Tell Beit Mirsim, vol. I.' In *Ann. A.S.O.R.* 12 (1932).
2. Albright, W. F. 'The Israelite conquest of Canaan in the light of archaeology.' In *Bull. A.S.O.R.* 74 (1939), 11 ff.
3. Albright, W. F. 'The first month of excavation at Bethel.' In *Bull. A.S.O.R.* 55 (1934), 23 ff.

4. Albright, W. F. 'The Kyle Memorial excavation at Bethel.' In *Bull. A.S.O.R.* 56 (1934), 11 ff.
5. Crowfoot, J. W., Crowfoot, G. M. and Kenyon, K. M. *Samaria-Sebaste*, vol. III, London, 1957.
6. Dothan, M. 'The excavations at 'Afula.' In *'Atiqot*, 1 (1955), 19 ff.
7. Franken, H. J. Review of A. H. Van Zyl, *The Moabites*. In *V.T.* 11 (1961), 100 f.
8. Franken, H. J. Review of *Ann. A.S.O.R.* 34, 35 (1960). In *V.T.* 11 (1961), 471 ff.
9. Franken, H. J. and Kalsbeek, J. *Deir 'Alla*, vol. 1. Leiden, 1968.
10. Glueck, N., 'Explorations in Eastern Palestine, I–IV.' In *Ann. A.S.O.R.* 14 (1934), 15 (1935), 18–19 (1939), 25–28 (1951).
11. Gray, J. 'Hazor.' In *V.T.* 16 (1966), 26 ff.
12. Hennessy, J. B. 'Excavation of a Bronze Age temple at Amman'. In *P.E.Q.* (1966), 155 ff.
13. Horn, S. H. 'Shechem.' In *J.E.O.L.* 18 (1964), 284 ff.
14. Kenyon, K. M. *Digging up Jericho*. London, 1957.
15. Marquet, Y. *Les Fouilles de 'Ai*. Beyrouth, 1949.
16. Matson, F. R. *Ceramics and Man*. London, 1965.
17. Noth, M. *Überlieferungsgeschichte des Pentateuch*. Stuttgart, 1948.
18. Rothenberg, B. *God's Wilderness*. London, 1961.
19. Rothenberg, B. 'Excavations at Timna.' In *Bulletin*, 7, Museum Ha'aretz, Tel Aviv, 1965.
20. Rowley, H. H. *From Joseph to Joshua*. London, 1950.
21. Tufnell, O. *Lachish*, vol. III. London, 1953.
22. Winton Thomas, D. (ed.). *Archaeology and Old Testament Study*. Oxford, 1967.
23. Wolf, C. Umhau. 'Khirbet en-Nitla not the Byzantine Gilgal.' In *Ann. A.S.O.R.* 29–30 (1955), 57 ff.
24. Wright, G. E. *Shechem*. New York, 1965.

## CHAPTER XXVII

### I. DISTURBANCES IN THE EASTERN MEDITERRANEAN

1. Breasted, J. H. *Ancient Records of Egypt* (5 vols.). Chicago, 1906.
2. Desborough, V. R. D. *The last Mycenaeans and their Successors*. Oxford, 1964.
3. Goetze, A. 'Hethitische Texte. 3. Madduwattaš.' In *Mitt. d. Vorderasiatisch-Aegyptischen Gesellschaft*, 32 (1927), 1.
4. Gurney, O. R. *The Hittites*. London, 1952.
5. Huxley, G. L. *Achaeans and Hittites*. Oxford, 1960.
6. Page, D. L. *History and the Homeric Iliad*. Berkeley and Los Angeles, 1959.
7. Sommer, F. *Die Aḫḫijavā-Urkunden*. (*Abh. München*, Phil.-hist. Klasse, N.F. 6 (1932), 1–469.)
8. Stubbings, F. H. *Mycenaean Pottery from the Levant*. Cambridge, 1951.
9. Weickert, C. 'Die Ausgrabung beim Athena-Tempel in Milet.' In *Ist. Mitt.*, (a) 7 (1957), 102–32; (b) 9/10 (1959/60), 1–96.
10. Weickert, C. 'Neue Ausgrabungen in Milet.' In *Neue deutsche Ausgrabungen im Mittelmeergebiet u. im vorderen Orient*, ed. by E. Boehringer. Berlin, 1959.
11. Woolley, Sir Leonard. *A Forgotten Kingdom*. London, 1953.

## II. THE TROJAN WAR

1. Allen, T. W. *The Homeric Catalogue of Ships*. Oxford, 1921.
2. Burr, V. Νεῶν κατάλογος. In *Klio*, Beiheft IXL (=XLIX) (N.F. Heft 36). Leipzig, 1944.
3. Forsdyke, J. *Greece before Homer*. London, 1956.
4. Hammond, N. G. L. *A History of Greece*. Ed. 2. Oxford, 1967.
5. Huxley, G. L. *Achaeans and Hittites*. Oxford, 1960.
6. Lamb, W. *Excavations at Thermi in Lesbos*. Cambridge, 1936.
7. Page, D. L. *History and the Homeric Iliad*. Berkeley and Los Angeles, 1959.
8. Ventris, M. J. F. and Chadwick, J. *Documents in Mycenaean Greek*. Cambridge, 1956.
9. Wace, A. J. B. and Stubbings, F. H. *A Companion to Homer*. London, 1962.

See also *C.A.H.* I³, pt. 1, pp. 649 f.

## III. DISTURBANCES WITHIN GREECE: INVASION AND EMIGRATION

1. Ålin, P. *Das Ende der myken. Fundstätten auf dem griechischen Festland* (*Studies in Mediterranean Archaeology*, vol. 1). Lund, 1962.
2. Barnett, R. D. 'Mopsos.' In *J.H.S.* 73 (1953), 140–3.
3. Bérard, J. *La colonisation grecque de l'Italie méridionale et de la Sicile dans l'antiquité*. Paris, 1957.
4. Blegen, C. W. [Reports on excavation of the 'Palace of Nestor' at Pylus.] In *A.J.A.* 57 (1953) to 67 (1963).
5. Blegen, C. W. *Zygouries*. Cambridge, Mass., 1928.
6. Broneer, O. 'A Mycenaean fountain on the Athenian Acropolis.' In *Hesperia*, 8 (1939), 317–433.
7. Broneer, O. 'Excavations at Isthmia.' In *Hesperia*, 28 (1959), 298 ff.
8. Broneer, O. 'Excavations on the north slope of the Acropolis in Athens.' In *Hesperia*, 2 (1933), 350–72.
9. Broneer, O. 'The Corinthian isthmus and the Isthmian sanctuary.' In *Antiq.* 32 (1958), 80 ff.
10. French, E. B. 'Pottery groups from Mycenae.' In *B.S.A.* 58 (1963), 44 ff.
11. Gjerstad, E. 'The colonization of Cyprus in Greek legend.' In *A.I.R.R.S.* X (= *Opuscula Archaeologica*, III) (1944), 107–23.
12. Hood, M. S. F. 'Archaeology in Greece 1959.' In *Archaeological Reports*, 1959–60, 9.
13. Jannoray, J. and van Effenterre, H. 'Fouilles de Krisa.' In *B.C.H.* 61 (1937), 299–326.
14. Luria, S. J. 'Burgfrieden in Sillyon.' In *Klio*, 37 (1959), 7–20.
15. Mylonas, G. E. Ἡ ἀκρόπολις τῶν Μυκηνῶν. In Ἀρχ. Ἐφ. (1961), 153–207.
16. Orlandos, A. K. (ed.). Τὸ ἔργον τῆς Ἀρχαιολογικῆς Ἑταιρείας (Athens, 1954– annual publication).
17. Seton Williams, M. V. 'Cilician Survey.' In *Anatolian Studies*, IV (1954), 121–74.
18. Taylour, Lord William D. *Mycenaean Pottery in Italy and Adjacent Areas*. Cambridge, 1958.
19. Verdelis, N. M. Ἀνασκαφὴ μυκηναϊκῆς ἐπιχώσεως ἐν Τίρυνθι. In Ἀρχ. Ἐφ. (1956), suppl., 5 ff.
20. [Verdelis, N. M.] 'Tiryns' Water-supply.' In *Archaeology*, 16 (1963), 129–30.

21. Wace, A. J. B. [Reports on excavation of houses at Mycenae.] In *B.S.A.* 48 (1953), 9 ff.; 49 (1954), 233 ff.; 50 (1955), 180 ff.; 51 (1956), 107 ff.; 52 (1957), 193ff.
22. Waterhouse, H., and Hope-Simpson, R. 'Prehistoric Laconia, Part I.' In *B.S.A.* 55 (1960), 67–107.

A. ADDENDA

1. Blegen, C. W. and Rawson, M. *The Palace of Nestor at Pylos in Western Messenia*. Vol. I, *The Buildings and their Contents*. Princeton, 1966.
2. Mylonas, G. E. *Mycenae and the Mycenaean Age*. Princeton, 1966.
3. Taylour, W. D. T. 'A note on the recent excavations at Mycenae, and the scheme proposed for their publication.' In *B.S.A.* 64 (1969), 259–60.

CHAPTER XXVIII

I. THE SEA PEOPLES

1. Albright, W. F. 'Dunand's New Byblos Volume: A Lycian at the Byblian Court.' In *Bull.A.S.O.R.* 155 (1959), 31 ff.
2. Astour, M. C. *Hellenosemitica*. Leiden, 1965.
3. Astour, M. C. 'New Evidence on the Last Days of Ugarit.' In *A.J.A.* 69 (1965), 253 ff.
4. Breasted, J. H. *Ancient Records of Egypt*, III–IV. Chicago, 1906.
5. Carpenter, R. *Discontinuity in Greek Civilization*. Cambridge, 1966.
6. Gardiner, Sir A. *Ancient Egyptian Onomastica*, I (200–5, The Battle of Kadesh). Oxford, 1947.
7. Gardiner, Sir A. *The Kadesh Inscriptions of Ramesses II*. Oxford, 1960.
8. Hall, H. R. 'The Peoples of the Sea.' In *Recueil d'études égyptologiques dédiées à ... Champollion*, 297 ff. Paris, 1922.
9. Helck, H. W. *Die Beziehungen Ägyptens zu Vorderasien im 3. und 2. Jahrtausend v. Chr*. Wiesbaden, 1962.
10. Knudtzon, J. A. *Die El-Amarna Tafeln*. Leipzig, 1915.
11. Kuentz, C. *La Bataille de Qadech (Mém. Inst. fr. Caire, 55)*. Cairo, 1928.
12. Nougayrol, J. *Le Palais Royal d'Ugarit*, III, IV. Paris, 1955–6.
13. Pritchard, J. B. *Ancient Near Eastern Texts Relating to the Old Testament*. Princeton, 1954.
14. Pritchard, J. B. *The Ancient Near East in Pictures relating to the Old Testament*. Princeton, 1954.
15. Riis, P. J. 'L'Activité de la Mission Archéologique Danoise sur la Côte Phénicienne.' In *Ann. Arch. de Syrie*, 8–9 (1954–9) and 10 (1960).
16. Riis, P. J. *Hama*, III, 3. *Les Cimetières à Crémation*. Copenhagen, 1948.
17. Vercoutter, J. *L'Égypte et le Monde Égéen Préhellénique (Inst. fr. Caire, Bibliothèque d'Études, 22)*. Cairo, 1956.
18. Woolley, C. L. *Alalakh. An Account of the Excavations at Tell Atchana in the Hatay, 1937–1949*. Oxford, 1955.
19. Wreszinski, W. *Atlas zur Altägyptischen Kulturgeschichte*, Part II. Leipzig, 1935.
20. Yadin, Y. *The Art of Warfare in Biblical Lands*. 2 vols. New York, 1963.

II. SHERDEN, SARDINIA

1. Guido, M. *Sardinia*. London, 1963.
2. Grosjean, R. 'Recent Work in Corsica.' In *Antiq.* 40 (1966), 190 ff. and pls. XXIX–XXXI.

III. SHEKLESH

1. Brea, L. B. *Sicily before the Greeks*. London, 1957.
2. Wainwright, G. A. 'Sheklesh or Shasu?' In *J.E.A.* 50 (1964), 40 ff.
3. Wainwright, G. A. 'Some Sea-Peoples.' In *J.E.A.* 47 (1961), 71 ff.

IV. ANATOLIA, DANAOI, DNNYM

1. Barnett, R. D. 'Mopsos.' In *J.H.S.* 73 (1953), 140 ff.
2. Bossert, H. T. *Asia*. Istanbul, 1946.
3. Bossert, H. T. *Ein Hethitisches Königssiegel*. Istanbuler Forschungen 17, Berlin 1944.
4. Bossert, H. T. 'Die phönizisch-hethitischen Bilinguen I.' In *Oriens*, I (1948), 163 ff.; II in *Arch. Orient.* 3 (1950), 10 ff.; III in *J.K.F.* I (1951), 265 ff.; 4 in *J.K.F.* 2 (1952–3), 167 ff. and 293 ff.
5. Dupont-Sommer, A. 'Étude du texte phénicien des inscriptions de Karatepe.' In *Oriens*, I (1948), 193 ff.; *Arch. Orient.* 18 (1950), 43 ff.; *J.K.F.* 2 (1951–3), 189 ff.
6. Eilers, W. 'Das Volk der Karkā in den Achämenideninschriften.' In *O.L.Z.* 38 (1935), 201 ff.
7. Garstang, J. *Prehistoric Mersin*. Oxford, 1953.
8. Garstang, J. and Gurney, O. R. *The Geography of the Hittite Empire*. London, 1959.
9. Götze, A. *Madduwattaš (M.V.Ae.G.* 32). Leipzig, 1928.
10. Goldman, H. *Excavations at Gözlu Küle, Tarsus*, II and III. Princeton, 1956 and 1963.
11. Holland, L. B. 'The Danaoi.' In *Harv. Stud. Class. Phil.* 39 (1928), 59 ff.
12. Houwink ten Cate, Ph. H. J. *The Luwian Population Groups of Lycia and Cilicia Aspera during the Hellenistic Period (Documenta et Monumenta Orientis Antiqui*, 10). Leiden, 1961.
13. Kretschmer, P. 'Die Hypachäer.' In *Glotta*, 21 (1932), 213 ff.
14. Kretschmer, P. 'Nochmals die Hypachäer und Alaksanduš.' In *Glotta* 24 (1936), 203 ff.
15. Landsberger, B. *Sam'al, Studien zur Entdeckung der Ruinenstätte Karatepe*. Erste Lieferung. (*Türk. Hist. Gesell. Veröff.* 7, 16). Ankara, 1948.
16. Malamat, A. 'Western Asia Minor in the Time of the Sea Peoples.' In *Yediot Bahaqirat Eretz Israel Weatiqoteha*, 30 (1966), 195 ff. (in Hebrew).
17. Mellink, M. J. 'Report on the First Campaign of Excavations at Karataş-Semayük.' In *Türk. Arkeoloji Dergisi*, 13 (1964), 97 ff.
18. Otten, H. 'Neue Quellen zum Ausklang des hethitischen Reiches.' In *M.D.O.G.* 94 (1963), 1 ff.
19. Wainwright, G. A. 'Caphtor, Cappadocia.' In *V.T.* 6, 2 (1956), 200 ff.
20. Wainwright, G. A. 'Caphtor, Keftiu and Cappadocia.' In *P.E.F.* (1931), 203 ff.
21. Wainwright, G. A. 'Keftiu.' In *J.E.A.* 17 (1931), 26 ff.
22. Wainwright, G. A. 'Keftiu and Karamania (Asia Minor).' In *A. St.* 4 (1954), 38 ff.

23. Wainwright, G. A. 'Keftiu: Crete or Cilicia?' In *J.H.S.* 57 (1931), 1 ff.
24. Wainwright, G. A. 'The Keftiu People of the Egyptian Monuments.' In *Ann. Arch. Anthr.* 6 (1913), 24 ff.
25. Xanthus. *Fragmenta Historicorum Graecorum* (ed. C. and Th. Müller), 1. Paris, 1841.

#### V.  AHHIYAWA

1. Carruba, O. 'Wo lag Ahhiyawa?' In *Compte-rendu du XIème Rencontre Ass.* (Leiden, 1964).
2. Desborough, V. R. d'A. *The Last Myceneans and their Successors.* Oxford, 1964.
3. Huxley, G. L. *Achaeans and Hittites.* Oxford, 1960.
4. Sommer, F. *Die Aḫḫijavā–Urkunden* (*Abh. München*, n.F. 6, 1932).
5. Steiner, G. 'Die Ahhiyawa Frage heute.' In *Saeculum*, 15 (1964), 365 ff.
6. Ventris, M. G. F. and Chadwick, J. *Documents in Mycenaean Greek.* Cambridge, 1956.
7. Vermeule, E. *Greece in the Bronze Age.* Chicago, 1964.

#### VI.  CYPRUS

1. Dikaios, P. 'The Bronze Statue of a Horned god from Enkomi.' In *J.D.A.I.* Heft 1 (1962), 1 ff.
2. Dikaios, P. 'Excavations and Historical Background: Enkomi in Cyprus.' *Journal of Historical Studies*, Autumn, 1967.
3. Karageorghis, V. 'Recent Archaeological Investigations at Kition.' In Κυπριακαὶ Σπουδαί (Nicosia, 1962).
4. Schaeffer, C. F. A. *Enkomi-Alasia* I. Paris, 1952.
5. Schaeffer, C. F. A. 'Götter der Nord und Inselvölker in Zypern.' In *Arch. f. Or.* 21 (1966), 59 ff.
6. Schaeffer, C. F. A. *Ugaritica* V. Paris, 1949.
7. Sjøqvist, E. *Problems of the Late Cypriot Bronze Age.* Stockholm, 1940.
8. Wainwright, G. A. 'A Teucrian at Salamis in Cyprus.' In *J.H.S.* 83 (1963), 146 ff.

#### VII.  THE PHILISTINES

1. Aharoni, Y. *The Land of the Bible: a Historical Geography.* London, 1967.
2. Albright, W. F. 'Some Oriental Glosses on the Homeric Problem.' In *A.J.A.* 54 (1950), 162 ff.
3. Bonfante, G. 'Who were the Philistines?' In *A.J.A.* 50 (1946), 251 ff.
4. Dothan, M. and Friedman, D. N. *Ashdod I. The First Season of Excavations, 2* ('*Atiqot* VII). Jerusalem, 1967.
5. Dothan, T. 'Archaeological Reflections on the Philistine Problem.' In *The Holy Land* (*Antiquity and Survival* (ed. W. A. Ruysch) II, 2/3, 151 ff.). The Hague and Jerusalem, 1957.
6. Dothan, T. *Ha-pelishtim ve-tarbutam ha-ḥomrit.* [*The Philistines and their Material Culture.*] Jerusalem, 1967. (In Hebrew, with English summary.)
7. Eissfeldt, O. 'Philister.' In *P.W.* 38 (1938), 2301 ff.
8. Eissfeldt, O. 'Philister und Phönizier.' In *Alte Or.* 34 (1936).
9. Erlenmeyer, M. L. and H. 'Über Philister und Kreter, I.' In *Or.* n.s. 29 (1960), 121 ff.; 241 ff.; 30 (1961), 269 ff.
10. Evans, Sir A. *Scripta Minoa*, I. Oxford, 1909.
11. Franken, H. J. 'The Stratigraphic Context of the Clay Tablets found at Deir 'Alla.' In *P.E.Q.* 22 (1964), 79 ff.

12. Gordon, C. H. 'The Rôle of the Philistines.' In *Antiq.* 30 (1956), 22 ff.
13. Greenfield, J. C. 'Philistines.' In *Interpreter's Dictionary of the Bible, III, K-C*, 791 ff. New York, 1962.
14. Hempel, J. 'Westliche Kultureinflüsse auf das alttestamentliche Palästina.' In *P.J.B.* 23 (1927), 52 ff.
15. Heurtley, W. A. 'The Relationship between "Philistine" and Mycenean Pottery.' In *Q.D.A.P.* 5 (1936), 90 ff.
16. Hrouda, B. 'Die Einwanderung der Philister in Palästina.' In *Vorderasiatische Archäologie: Studien und Aufsätze: Festschrift Moortgat* (1965), 126 ff.
17. Macalister, R. A. S. *The Philistines, their History and Civilization.* London, 1913.
18. Macalister, R. A. S. *The Philistines, their History and Civilisation* (reprint of 17 with an introduction by Dr Abraham Silverstein). Chicago, 1965.
19. Mazar, B. 'The Sanctuary of Arad and the Family of Hobab the Kenite.' In *J.N.E.S.* 24 (1965), 297 ff.
20. Mazar, B. 'The Philistines and the Rise of Israel and Tyre.' In *The Israel Academy of Sciences and Humanities, Proceedings*, 1, no. 7 (1964), 1 ff.
21. Mitchell, T. C. 'Philistia.' In D. Winton Thomas (ed.), *Archaeology and Old Testament Study.* Oxford, 1967.
22. Müller, M. 'Die Urheimat der Philister.' In 'Studien zur Vorderasiatischen Geschichte', *M.V.A.G.* 1 (1900), 1 ff.
23. Oppenheim, M. von. *Der Tell Halaf.* Leipzig, 1931.
24. Petrie, W. M. F. *Beth-pelet I (Tell Fara).* London, 1930.
25. Phythian-Adams, W. J. 'Philistine Origins in the Light of Palestinian Archaeology.' In *Bull. S.A.J.* 3 (1923), 20 ff.
26. Wright, G. E. 'Philistine Coffins and Mercenaries.' In *Bi. Or.* 22 (1959), 54 ff.
27. Waldbaum, J. 'Philistine Tombs at Tell Fara and their Aegean Prototypes.' In *A.J.A.* 70 (1966), 331 ff.

### A. ADDENDA

1. Dikaios, P. *Excavations at Enkomi (1948–1958).* Mainz (1969).
2. Dothan, M. 'Excavations at Ashdod II and III.' In *I.E.J.* 18 (1968), 253–4.
3. Dothan, M. 'Ashdod II and III, 2nd and 3rd Seasons of Excavation, 1963, 1965: Soundings in 1967.' In *'Atiqot* IX–X (1971).
4. Dothan, M., Perlman, I. and Asaro, F. 'An introductory study of Mycenaean III c I ware from Tel Ashdod.' In *Archaeometry* 13 (1971), 169 ff.
5. Dothan, T. 'Anthropoid Clay Coffins from a Late Bronze Age Cemetery near Deir-el-Balah: Preliminary Report I.' In *I.E.J.* 22 (1972), 65 ff.
6. Dothan, T. *Idem*, Preliminary Report II. In *I.E.J.* 23 (1973.), 129 ff.
7. Hestrin, R. *The Philistines and the other Sea Peoples.* (The Israel Museum, Jerusalem, 1970: Cat. no. 68.)
8. James, F. W. *The Iron Age at Beth Shan. A Study of Levels VI–IV* (University of Pennsylvania, Museum Monographs). Philadelphia, 1960.
9. Karageorghis, V. 'The Mycenaeans at Kition: a preliminary survey.' In *Studi Ciprioti e Rapporti di Scavo*, 1, (1971), 217 ff. 495 ff.
10. Malamat, A. 'The Egyptian Decline in Canaan and the Sea Peoples.' In *The World History of the Jewish People* (ed. B. Mazar), ch. 11. First Series: Ancient Times, Vol. III. Tel Aviv (1971).
11. Mellink, M. 'Excavations at Karataş-Semayük in Lycia.' In *A.J.A.* 23 (1969), 320 ff.

12. Otten, H. *Sprachliche Stellung und Datierung der Madduwatta-Textes.* Studien zu den Bogazköy-Texten, Heft 11. Wiesbaden, 1969.
13. Vaux, R. de 'La Phénicie et les peuples de la mer.' In *Melanges de l'Université St. Joseph,* 45 (1969), 481 ff.


CHAPTER XXIX

GENERAL

1. Bork, F., Hüsing, G. and König, F. W. *Corpus Inscriptionum Elamicarum.* Hannover, 1926.
2. Cameron, G. G. *History of Early Iran.* Chicago, 1936.
3. Delaporte, L. *L'Iran antique.* Paris, 1943.
4. Dhorme, E. 'Élam, Élamites.' In *Dictionnaire de la Bible,* Supplément II, 920 ff. Paris, 1934.
5. König, F. W. 'Geschichte Elams.' In *Alte Or.* 29, 4 (Leipzig, 1931).
6. König, F. W. 'Elam.' In *R.L.A.* 2 (1938).
7. *Mémoires de la Délégation en Perse.* Paris, 1900–
8. Pézard, M. *Les Antiquités de la Susiane.* Paris, Musée du Louvre, 1913.


I. REIGNS AND EVENTS

1. Gelb, I. J. *Hurrians and Subarians.* Chicago, 1944.
2. Gelb, I. J. 'Hurrians at Nippur in the Sargonic Period.' In *Festschrift Johannes Friedrich* (Heidelberg, 1959), 187 ff.
3. Hilprecht, H. V. *Old Babylonian Inscriptions* (*B.E.* series A, 1). Philadelphia, 1893.
4. Hüsing, G. *Die einheimischen Quellen zur Geschichte Elams.* Leipzig, 1916.
5. King, L. W. *Chronicles concerning Early Babylonian Kings.* London, 1907.
6. König, F. W. 'Drei altelamische Stelen.' In *M.V.A.G.* 30 (1925).
7. König, F. W. 'Pinikir.' In *Arch. f. Or.* 5 (1928–9), 101 ff.
8. Ungnad, A. 'Urkunden aus Dilbat.' In *B.A.* 6, 5 (1909).
9. Weidner, E. F. 'Die Inschriften Tukulti-Ninurtas I.' In *Arch. f. Or.* Beiheft 12 (1959).


II. ARCHITECTURE AND THE ARTS

1. Ghirshman, R. Principal articles describing the excavations at Choga-Zanbil in *Ill. Ldn News,* 5229 (1952), 954 ff.; 5964 (1953), 226 f.; 6011 (1954), 13 ff.; 6062 (1955), 1140 f.; 6118 (1956), 387 ff.; 6162 (1957), 76 ff.; 6262 (1959), 1025 ff.; 6269 (1959), 319. In *C.-R. Ac. Inscr. B.-L.* 1954, 233 ff.; 1955, 112, 322 ff.; 1957, 231 ff. In *Rev. Arch.* 42 (1953), 1 ff.; 44 (1954), 1 ff.; 46 (1955), 63 ff.; 49 (1957), 1 ff. In *Rev. des Arts,* 4 (1954), 169 f. In *Arts Asiatiques,* 1 (1954), 83 ff.; 2 (1955), 163 ff.; 3 (1956), 163 ff.; 4 (1957), 113 ff. In *Ars Orientalis,* 1 (1954), 173 ff. In *Archaeology,* 8 (1955), 260 ff. In *Les Cahiers techniques de l'Art* (Strasbourg), 3 (1956), 31 ff. In *Rev. de l'Enseignement supérieur,* 3 (1959), 101 ff.
2. Le Breton, L. 'The Early Period at Susa: Mesopotamian Relations.' In *Iraq,* 19 (1957), 79 ff.
3. Parrot, A. *Ziggourats et 'Tour de Babel'.* Paris, 1949.

### III. RELIGION

1. Amiet, P. 'Représentations antiques de constructions susiennes.' In *R.A.* 53 (1959), 39 ff.
2. Contenau, G. *Manuel d'Archéologie Orientale*, i–iv. Paris, 1927–47.
3. Delaporte, L. *Catalogue des Cylindres, etc., Musée du Louvre.* Paris, 1920–3.
4. King, L. W. *Babylonian Boundary Stones...in the British Museum.* London, 1912.
5. Moortgat, A. *Vorderasiatische Rollsiegel.* Berlin, 1940.
6. Van Buren, E. D. *The Flowing Vase and the God with Streams.* Berlin, 1933.
7. Van Buren, E. D. 'Entwined Serpents.' In *Arch. f. Or.* 10 (1935–6), 53 ff.
8. Van Buren, E. D. 'Religious Rites and Ritual in the time of Uruk IV–III.' In *Arch. f. Or.* 13 (1939–40), 32 ff.

## CHAPTER XXX

#### G. GENERAL

1. Bittel, K. *Grundzüge der Vor- und Frühgeschichte Kleinasiens.* Ed. 2, esp. ch. ii–v. Tübingen, 1963.
2. Bittel, K. *Kleinasiatische Studien; Kimmerier, Phryger und Skythen in Kleinasien* (*Ist. Mitt.*, Heft 5). Istanbul, 1942.
3. Goetze, A. *Kleinasien* (*Kulturgeschichte des alten Orients*, iii, 1, in *Handbuch der Altertumswissenschaft*). Ed. 2. München, 1957.
4. Melikishvili, G. A. *Nairi-Urartu* (*Akademia Nauk Gruzinskoi SSR*). Tiflis, 1954.
5. Mellink, M. (ed.). *Dark Ages and Nomads c. 1000 B.C.* (*Uitgaven van het Historisch-Archaeologisch Instituut te Istanbul*, xviii). Istanbul, 1964.
6. Mellink, M., 'Mita, Mushki and the Phrygians.' In *Anadolu Araştirmalari* (H. T. Bossert memorial volume). Istanbul, 1965.
7. Ruge, W. and Friedrich, J. 'Phrygia' (Topographie, Sprache, Geschichte). In *P.W.* 39, 781 ff. Stuttgart, 1941.

#### I. GEOGRAPHY

1. Alkım, U. B. 'Ein altes Wegenetz im südwestlichen Antitaurus-Gebiet.' In *Anadolu Araştirmalari*, i. 2 (1959), 207 ff. (formerly *J.K.F.*, iii). Also published in Turkish with an English summary in *Belleten* 89 (1959), 59 ff.
2. Birmingham, J. M. 'The overland route across Anatolia in the eighth and seventh centuries B.C.' In *A. St.* 11 (1961), 185 ff.
3. Bossert, H. *Asia.* Istanbul, 1946.
4. Garstang, J. 'The Location of Pakhuwa.' In *Ann. Arch. Anthr.* 28 (1948), 48 ff.
5. Gurney, O. R. 'Mita of Paḫḫuwa.' In *Ann. Arch. Anthr.* 28 (1948), 32 ff.
6. Jones, A. H. M. *Cities of the East Roman Provinces.* Oxford, 1937.
7. Ramsay, Sir W. M. *Historical geography of Asia Minor* (*Royal Geographical Society Supplementary Papers*, vol. 4). London, 1890, reprinted 1962.
8. Ramsay, Sir W. M. *Cities and Bishoprics of Phrygia.* London, 1895–7.
9. Ramsay, Sir W. M. *Historical commentary on Galatians.* London, 1899.
10. Young, R. 'Gordion of the Royal Road.' In *P.A.P.S.* 107 (1963), 362 ff.

## II. THE NEWCOMERS AND THE CLASH WITH ASSYRIA

1. Adontz, N. *Histoire d'Arménie. Les Origines – du Xe Siècle au VIe (av. J.-C.)*. Paris, 1946.
2. Barnett, R. D. and Falkner, M. *The Sculptures of Tiglath-pileser III*. London, 1962.
3. Luckenbill, D. D. *Ancient Records of Assyria and Babylonia, Historical Records of Assyria*, vols. 1 and 2. Chicago, 1926, 1927.
4. König, F. W. *Handbuch der chaldischen Inschriften (Arch. f. Or.*, Beiheft 8, 1). Graz, 1955.
5. Naster, P. *L'Asie Mineure et l'Assyrie aux VIIIe et VIIe siècles av. J.-C.* Louvain, 1938.
6. Thureau-Dangin, F. *Une relation de la huitième campagne de Sargon*. Paris, 1912.
7. Thureau-Dangin, F. and Dunand, M. *Tel Ahmar – Til Barsip*. Paris, 1936.
8. Tadmor, H. 'Azriyau of Yaudi.' In *Scripta Hierosolymitana*, 8 (1962), 232 ff.
9. Young, R. 'The Nomadic Impact: Gordion.' In M. Mellink (ed.), *Dark Ages and Nomads c. 1000 B.C.* Istanbul, 1964.


## III. PHRYGIAN ART AND ARCHAEOLOGY

1. Akok, M. and Özgüç, T. 'Die Ausgrabungen an zwei Tumuli auf dem Mausoleumshügel bei Ankara.' In *Belleten*, 11 (1947), 57 ff.
2. Akurgal, E. *Die Kunst Anatoliens von Homer bis Alexander*. Berlin, 1961.
3. Arik, R. O. *Les Fouilles d'Alaca Höyük (TTK Yayınlarından, v/1)*. Ankara, 1937.
4. Barnett, R. D. 'The Phrygian Rock Façades and the Hittite Monuments.' In *Bi. Or.* 10 (1953), 77 ff.
5. Bellinger, L. 'Textiles from Gordion.' In *Bulletin of the Needle and Bobbin Club*, 46 (1962), 5 ff.
6. Bittel, K. and Güterbock, H. G. *Boğazköy: Neue Untersuchungen in der Hethitischen Hauptstadt*. Berlin, 1935.
7. Bittel, K. and Naumann, R. *Boğazköy-Hattuša: Ergebnisse der Ausgrabungen 1931–1939 (W.V.D.O.G. 63)*. Stuttgart, 1952.
8. Bittel, K., Naumann, R. *et al. Boğazköy III: Funde aus den Grabungen 1952–1955*. Berlin, 1957.
9. Blegen, C., Boulter, C. G., Caskey, L. Rawson, M. *Troy IV: Settlement VIIIa, VIIb and VIII*, parts 1 and 2. Princeton, 1958.
10. Bossert, H. *Altanatolien*. Berlin, 1932.
11. Bossert, H., Cambel, H. and Alkim, U. B. *Karatepe: First and Second Preliminary Reports*. Istanbul, 1946, 1947.
12. Delaporte, L. *Malatya-Arslantepe I: La Porte des Lions*. Paris, 1940.
13. Gabriel, A. *Phrygie* II: *La Cité de Midas. Topographie: Le Site et les Fouilles*. Paris, 1952.
14. Haspels, E. *Phrygie* III: *La Cité de Midas. Céramique et Trouvailles diverses*. Paris, 1951.
15. Hogarth, D. G., Woolley, C. L., Lawrence, T. E., Guy, P. L. O., Barnett, R. D. *Carchemish: Excavations of the British Museum*, parts I–III. London, 1914–1952.
16. Kohler, E. L. 'Phrygian Animal Style and Nomadic Art' In M. Mellink (ed.), *Dark Ages and Nomads c. 1000 B.C.* Istanbul, 1964.
17. Körte, G. and Körte; A. 'Gordion: Ergebnisse der Ausgrabung im Jahre 1900.' In *J.D.A.I.*, Ergänzungsheft 5 (1904), 1 ff.

18. Koşay, H. Z. *Alaca Höyük Hafriyati*. (*TKK Yayınlarından*, v/2). Ankara, 1938.
19. Koşay, H. Z. *Les Fouilles de Pazarlı*. (*TKK Yayınlarından*, v/4). Ankara, 1941.
20. Lloyd, S. H. F. 'Beycesultan Excavations.' In *A. St.* 8 (1958), 93 ff.
21. Mellink, M. *A Hittite Cemetery at Gordion* (*Museum Monographs*). Philadelphia, 1956.
22. Mellink, M. 'Postcript on Nomadic Art.' In *Dark Ages and Nomads c. 1000 B.C.* Istanbul, 1964.
23. Muscarella, O. 'Oriental Origins of Siren Cauldron Attachments.' In *Hesperia* 31 (1962), 317 ff.
24. Osten, H. H. von der, *The Alishar Hüyük*: *Seasons of 1930–1932*, part III (*Researches in Anatolia* 8). Chicago, 1937.
25. Özgüç, T. 'Excavations at Kültepe.' In *A. St.* 7 (1957), 19 ff.
26. Özgüç, T. 'Excavations at Altıntepe.' In *Belleten*, 25 (1961), 253 ff.
27. Perrot, G. and Chipiez, C. *Histoire de l'Art dans l'Antiquité*, vol. 5. (English translation). London, 1892.
28. Young, R. Reports on 'Excavations at Gordion.' In *A.J.A.* 59 (1955), 1 ff.; 60 (1956), 249 ff.; 61 (1957), 319 ff.; 62 (1958), 148 ff.; 64 (1960), 227 ff.; 66 (1962), 154 ff. In *Archaeology*, 3 (1950) 197 ff.; 6 (1953), 159 ff.; 9 (1956), 263 ff.; 10 (1957), 217 ff.; 11 (1958), 227 ff.; 12 (1959), 286 ff.

### IV. PHRYGIAN LIFE AND CULTURE

1. Akurgal, E. *Phrygische Kunst*. Ankara, 1955.
2. Botta, E. *Monument de Ninive*. 5 vols. Paris, 1849–1850.
3. Bittel, K. 'Phrygische Kunstbild aus Boğazköy.' In *Antike Plastik*, Lieferung 2. Berlin, 1965.
4. Brandenburg, E. 'Neue Untersuchungen im Gebiet der phrygischen Felsfassaden.' In *Abh. München* 23 (1900), 633 ff.
5. Dunbabin, T. J. *The Greeks and their Eastern Neighbours*. London, 1957.
6. Garstang, J. and Gurney, O. R. *Geography of the Hittite Empire*. London, 1959.
7. Luschan, F. von. *Ausgrabungen in Sendschirli*, vols. 1–5. Berlin, 1893–1943.
8. Mellaart, J. 'Iron Age Pottery from Southern Anatolia.' In *Belleten*, 19 (1955), 74 ff.
9. Mellink, M. 'The City of Midas.' In *Scientific American*, 201 (1959), 100 ff.
10. Muscarella, O. 'Ancient Safety Pins.' In *Expedition*, 6 (1964), 34 ff.
11. Osten, H. von der, *Explorations in Hittite Asia Minor* (*O.I.C.* 6). Chicago, 1929.
12. Parrot, A. *Nineveh and Babylon*. London, 1961.
13. Payne, H. and Dunbabin, T. J. *Perachora*, vols 1, 2. Oxford, 1940, 1962.
14. Reber, F. von. *Die phrygischen Felsdenkmäler*. Munich, 1897.
15. Temizer, R. 'Ankara'da bulunan Kybele Kabartması.' In *Anatolia*, 4 (1959) (Un Bas-Relief de Cybèle découvert à Ankara), 179 ff.
16. Young, R. 'Phrygian Construction and Architecture', part 1. In *Expedition*, 2 (1960), 2 ff.; part 2 in *Expedition*, 4 (1962), 2 ff.
17. Young, R. 'Bronzes from Gordion's Royal Tombs.' In *Archaeology*, 11 (1958), 227 ff.

### V. THE PHRYGIAN LANGUAGE

1. Calder, Sir W. (ed.). *Monumenta Asiae Minoris Antiqua VII: Monuments from Eastern Phyrygia*. Manchester, 1956.
2. Diakonov, I. M. 'Phrygians, Hittites and Armenians.' In *Problems of Hittitology and Hurrology*. (*Peredneaziatskiy Zbornik*), 333 ff.; 594 ff. Moscow, 1961.

3. Friedrich, J. *Kleinasiatische Sprachdenkmäler.* Berlin, 1932.
4. Friedrich, J. 'Phrygia' (Sprache). In *P.W.* 39, 868 ff. Stuttgart, 1941.
5. Gusmani, R. 'Il frigio e le altre lingue indeuropee.' In *Rendiconti dell'Istituto Lombardo,* 93 (1959), 17 ff.
6. Gusmani, R. 'Relazioni linguistiche tra frigio e licio.' In *Archivio Glottologico Italiano,* 44 (1959), 9 ff.
7. Gusmani, R. 'Studi sull'antico frigio. La popolazione, le glosse frige presso gli Antichi.' In *Rendiconti dell' Istituto Lombardo,* 92 (1958), 835 ff.
8. Gusmani, R. 'Le iscrizioni dell'antico frigio.' *Ibid.* 870 ff.
9. Gusmani, R. 'Monumenti frigi minori e onomastica. Tipi di iscrizioni neo-frige diversi da quello deprecatorio.' *Ibid.* 904 ff.
10. Haas, O. 'Zur Deutung der phrygischen Inschriften.' In *R.H.A.* 11, fasc. 53 (1951), 1 ff.
11. Haas, O. 'Die sprachgeschichtliche Stellung des Phrygischen.' In *Studia linguistica in honorem acad. Stéphanie Mladenov,* 451 ff. Sofia, 1957.
12. Haas, O. 'Neue spätphrygische Texte.' In *Sprache,* 6 (1960), 9 ff.
13. Heubeck, A. 'Bemerkungen zu den neuphrygischen Fluchformeln.' In *Indogerm. Forsch.* Heft 1 (1958), 13 ff.
14. Masson, O. 'Epigraphie asianique.' In *Or.* n.s. 23 (1954), 441 ff.

### VI. PHRYGIAN RELIGION

1. Barnett, R. D. 'Some contacts between Greek and Oriental Religions.' In *Éléments orientaux dans la religion grecque ancienne. Colloque de Strasbourg 1958,* 143 ff. Paris, 1960.
2. Frazer, Sir J. G. 'Adonis', 'Attis', 'Osiris'. In *The Golden Bough,* vol. 1. London, 1890.
3. Güterbock, H. G. 'The Song of Ullikummi: Revised Text of the Hittite Version of a Hurrian Myth.' In *J.C.S.* 5 (1951), 135 ff.; 6 (1952), 8 ff.
4. Graillot, H. 'Le culte de Cybèle, Mère des Dieux, à Rome et dans l'Empire romain.' In *Bibl. des Ecoles françaises d'Athènes et de Rome,* 10 (1912).
5. Hepding, H. *Attis: seine Mythen und sein Kult.* Giessen, 1903.
6. Kronasser, H. *Die Umsiedelung der schwarzen Gottheit (Sitzungsber. Wien 241, Bd. 3).* Wien, 1963.
7. Laroche, E. 'Koubaba, déesse anatolienne, et le problème des origines de Cybèle.' In *Éléments orientaux dans la religion grecque ancienne. Colloque de Strasbourg 1958,* 113 ff. Paris, 1960.
8. Mellaart, J. 'Excavations at Hacılar.' In *A. St.* 11 (1961), 39 ff.
9. Roscher, W. and Rapp, A. Articles 'Agdistis', 'Attis', 'Kybele'. In *Lexikon der griechische und römische Mythologie,* ed. Roscher, W. Leipzig, 1884–1894.
10. Rose, H. J. *A Handbook of Greek Mythology,* ed. 3. London, 1945.

### VII. THE NEIGHBOURS OF THE PHRYGIANS

1. Akurgal. E. *Späthethitische Bildkunst.* Ankara, 1949.
2. Barnett, R. D. 'Early Greek and Oriental Ivories.' In *J.H.S.* 68 (1948), 1 ff.
3. Barnett, R. D. 'Mopsus.' In *J.H.S.* 73 (1953), 140 ff.
4. Barnett, R. D. 'Ancient Oriental Influences on Archaic Greece.' In *Studies presented to Hetty Goldman,* 212 ff. New York, 1956.
5. Barnett, R. D. 'Karatepe: The key to the Hittite hieroglyphs.' In *A. St.* 3 (1953), 53 ff.

6. Bossert, H. 'Zur Geschichte von Karkamis.' In *Studi Classici ed Orientali*, I (1951), 35 ff.

7. Bossert, H. 'Die Felsinschrift von Şirzi.' In *Arch. f. Or.* 17 (1954), 56 ff.

8. Buckler, W. H. *The Lydian Inscriptions* (*Publications of the American Society for the Excavation of Sardis*, VI/2). Leyden, 1924.

9. Bürchner, —. Articles 'Karer' and Karia'. In *P.W.* 20, 1940 ff. Stuttgart, 1919.

10. Bürchner, —. Deeters, G., Keil, J. and Stein, —, Article 'Lydia'. In *P.W.* 26, 2122 ff. Stuttgart 1927.

11. Butler, H. C. *The Sardis Excavations* (*Publications of the American Society for the Excavation of Sardis*, I/1). Leyden, 1922.

12. Deeters, G. and Ruge, W. Article 'Lykia'. In *P.W.* 26, 2270 ff. Stuttgart, 1927.

13. Friedrich, J. *Kleinasiatische Sprachdenkmäler*. Berlin, 1932.

14. Goetze, A. *Madduwattaš* (*M.V.Ae.G.* 32/1 (1927)). Leipzig, 1928.

15. Gurney, O. R. *The Hittites*. Harmondsworth, 1961.

16. Hanfmann, G. M. A. 'Excavations at Sardis: 1st–3rd Campaigns.' In *Bull. A.S.O.R.* 154 (1959); '4th Campaign', 162 (1961); 166 (1962); also in *A.J.A.* 49 (1945), 570 ff.; 52 (1948), 135 ff.; 63 (1959), 151 ff.

17. Hanfmann, G. M. A. *Lydiaka* (*Harv. Stud. Class. Phil.* 63). Cambridge (Mass.), 1958.

18. Heubeck, A. *Lydiaka* (*Erlanger Forschungen*, A/9). Erlangen, 1959.

19. Houwink ten Cate, Ph. H. J. *The Luwian Population Groups of Lycia and Cilicia Aspera during the Hellenistic Period*. Leiden, 1961.

20. Kaletsch, H. 'Zur lydischen Chronologie.' In *Historia*, 7 (1958), 1 ff.

21. Kalinka, E. and Heberdey, R. *Tituli Lyciae* (*Tituli Asiae Minoris*, 1). Vienna, 1901.

22. Keil, J. 'Die Kulte Lydiens.' In *Studies presented to Sir William Ramsay*, 239 ff. Manchester, 1923.

23. Kluge, Th. *Die Lykier, ihre Geschichte und ihre Inschriften* (*Alte Or.* 11/2). Leipzig, 1910.

24. Laroche, E. *Les Hiéroglyphes hittites*, 1. Paris, 1960.

25. Landsberger, B. *Sam'al* (*TTK Yayınlarından*, VII/16). Ankara, 1948.

26. Littmann, E. *Lydian Inscriptions* (*Publications of the American Society for the Excavation of Sardis*, VI/1). Leyden, 1916.

27. Meriggi, P. 'Der indogermanische Charakter des Lydischen.' In *Festschrift für H. Hirt*, 2 (1936), 283 ff.

28. Neumann, G. *Untersuchungen zum Weiterleben hethitischen und luwischen Sprachgutes in hellenistischer und römischer Zeit*. Wiesbaden, 1961.

29. Pedersen, H. *Lykisch und Hittitisch* (*Det Kgl. Danske Videnskabernes Selskab: hist.-fil. meddelelser* 30, 4). Copenhagen, 1945.

30. Radet, G. *La Lydie et le Monde Grec au Temps des Mermnades*. Paris, 1893.

31. Sundwall, J. *Die einheimischen Namen der Lykier*. Leipzig, 1913.

32. Tritsch, F. J. 'Lycian, Luwian and Hittite.' In *Arch. Orient.* 18, 1/2 (1950), 494 ff.

33. Vermeule, E. 'The Early Bronze Age in Caria.' In *Archaeology*, 17 (1964), 244.

#### A. ADDENDA

1. Beran, T. 'Eine Kultstätte Phrygischer Zeit in Boghazköy.' In *M.D.O.G.* 94 (1963), 33 ff.

2. Carruba, O. 'Lydisch und Lyder.' In *Mitt. Inst. Or.* 8 (1963), 383 ff.

3. Haas, O. *Die phrygischen Sprachdenkmäler* (Ling. Balkan 10). Sofia, 1966.

4. Hanfmann, G. M. A. and Waldbaum, J. G. 'New Excavations at Sardis and some problems of Western Anatolian Archaeology.' In *Near Eastern Archaeology in the Twentieth Century* (*Essays in Honor of Nelson Glueck*), ed. James A. Sanders, 307 ff. New York, 1970.

5. Hawkins, D. 'Building Inscriptions of Carchemish.' In *Anatolian Studies*, 22 (1972), 87 ff.

6. Houwink ten Cate, Ph. J. 'Kleinasien zwischen Hethitern und Persern.' In *Die Altorientalischen Reiche* III (*Die erste Hälfte des Ersten Jahrtausend*). Fischer Weltgeschichte, Bd. 4. Frankfurt am Main & Hamburg, 1967.

7. Masson, O. 'Liste chronologique des travaux concernant l'écriture et la langue des Cariens (1932–1972).' *Bull. Soc. Ling.* 25 (1973).

8. Neumann, G. *Lykisch*. In no. 12, below.

9. Orthmann, W. *Untersuchungen zur späthethitischen Kunst*. Bonn, 1971.

10. Postgate, N. 'Assyrian Texts and Fragments.' In *Iraq*, 25 (1973), 13 ff.

11. Ševoroskin, V. V. 'On Carian.' In *R.H.A.* 22 (1964), 55 ff.

12. Spüler, B. *Handbuch der Orientalistik*, Erste Abtlg., Band 2, *Keilschriftforschung und alte Geschichte Vorderasiens*, Lieferung 2, *Altkleinasiatische Sprachen*. Leiden, 1969.

13. Ussishkin, D. 'On the Dating of some Groups of Reliefs from Carchemish and Til Barsip.' In *A. St.* 17 (1967), 181 ff.

14. Werner, R. 'Die Phryger und ihre Sprache.' In *Bi. Or.* 26 (1969), 177 ff.

15. Young, R. S. 'Old Phrygian Inscriptions from Gordion: Towards a History of the Phrygian alphabet.' In *Hesperia*, 33 (1969), 255 ff. and pls. 67 ff.

## CHAPTER XXXI

### G. GENERAL

1. Borger, R. *Einleitung in die assyrischen Königsinschriften* (*Erster Teil*); *Das Zweite Jahrtausend vor Chr.* Leiden, 1961.

2. Brinkman, J. A. *A Political History of Post-Kassite Babylonia* (unpubl. dissertation, University of Chicago, 1962). See below, A, 3.

3. Brinkman, J. A. 'A Preliminary Catalogue of Written Sources for a Political History of Babylonia: 1160–722 B.C.' In *J.C.S.* 16 (1962), 83 ff.

4. Budge, E. A. W. and King, L. W. *Annals of the Kings of Assyria*, I. London, 1902.

5. Cornelius, F. 'Die Chronologie des vorderen Orients im 2 Jahrtausend v. Chr.' In *Arch. f. Or.* 17 (1956), 294 ff.

6. Delitzsch, F. *Die babylonische Chronik*. Leipzig, 1906.

7. Ebeling, E., Meissner, B. and Weidner, E. F. *Die Inschriften der altassyrischen Könige*. Leipzig, 1926.

8. Ebeling, E., Meissner, B. and Weidner, E. F. (eds.). *Reallexikon der Assyriologie*, I–III. Berlin and Leipzig, 1932–.

9. Fine, H. A. *Studies in Middle-Assyrian Chronology and Religion*. Cincinnati, 1955.

10. Gelb, I. J. 'Two Assyrian King Lists.' In *J.N.E.S.* 13 (1954), 209 ff.

11. King, L. W. *A History of Babylon*. London, 1919.

12. King, L. W. *Babylonian Boundary-Stones and Memorial-Tablets in the British Museum*. London, 1912.

13. King, L. W. *Chronicles concerning Early Babylonian Kings*. London, 1907.

14. Luckenbill, D. D. *Ancient Records: Assyria.* Chicago, 1926.
15. *Mémoires de la Délégation en Perse.* Paris, 1900–.
16. Messerschmidt, L. and Schroeder, O. *Keilschrifttexte aus Assur historischen Inhalts.* Leipzig, 1911, 1922.
17. Nassouhi, E. 'Grande liste des rois d'Assyrie.' In *Arch. f. Or.* 4 (1927), 1 ff.
18. Oppenheim, A. L. 'Babylonian and Assyrian Historical Texts.' In *A.N.E.T.* (1955), 265 ff.
19. Poebel, A. 'The Assyrian King-List from Khorsabad.' In *J.N.E.S.* 1 (1942), 247 ff., 460 ff., and 2 (1943), 56 ff.
20. Smith, S. *Early History of Assyria to 1000 B.C.* London, 1928.
21. Weidner, E. F. 'Die grosse Königsliste aus Assur.' In *Arch. f. Or.* 3 (1926), 66 ff.
22. Weidner, E. F. *Die Inschriften Tukulti-Ninurtas I. und seiner Nachfolger* (*Arch. f. Or.* Beiheft 12), Graz, 1959.
23. Weidner, E. F. 'Die Königsliste aus Chorsābād.' In *Arch. f. Or.* 14 (1944), 362 ff.
24. Weidner, E. F. 'Die neue Königsliste aus Assur.' In *Arch. f. Or.* 4 (1927), 11 ff.

I. THE END OF THE KASSITE DOMINATION

1. Balkan, K. *Kassitenstudien.* 1. *Die Sprache der Kassiten.* New Haven, 1945.
2. Baqir, T. 'Iraq Government Excavations at 'Aqar Qūf; 1942–1943.' In *Iraq*, Supplement (1944), 1 ff.
3. Baqir, T. 'Iraq Government Excavations at 'Aqar Qūf; Second Interim Report, 1943–44.' In *Iraq*, Supplement (1945), 1 ff.
4. Baqir, T. 'Iraq Government Excavations at 'Aqar Qūf; Third Interim Report, 1944–45.' In *Iraq*, 8 (1946), 73 ff.
5. El-Wailly, F. 'Synopsis of Royal Sources of the Kassite Period.' In *Sumer* 10 (1954), 43 ff.
6. Gurney, O. R. 'Texts from Dur-Kurigalzu.' In *Iraq*, 11 (1949), 131 ff.
7. Hilprecht, H. V. *Old Babylonian Inscriptions chiefly from Nippur* (*B.E.* 1, pt 1). Philadelphia, 1893.
8. Hincke, W. J. *Selected Babylonian Kudurru Inscriptions* (*Semitic Study Series*, 14). Leiden, 1911.
9. Jaritz, K. 'Quellen zur Geschichte der Kaššû-Dynastie.' In *Mitt. Inst. Or.* 6 (1958), 187 ff.
10. King, L. W. *Records of the Reign of Tukulti-Ninib I.* London, 1904.
11. Steinmetzer, F. X. *Die babylonischen Kudurru (Grenzsteine) als Urkundenform.* Paderborn, 1922.
12. Tadmor, H. 'Historical Implications of the Correct Rendering of Akkadian *dâku.*' In *J.N.E.S.* 17 (1958), 129 ff.
13. Weidner, E. F. 'Aus den Tagen eines assyrischen Schattenkönigs.' In *Arch. f. Or.* 10 (1935), 1 ff.
14. Weidner, E. F. 'Studien zur Zeitgeschichte Tukulti-Ninurtas I.' In *Arch. f. Or.* 13 (1940), 109 ff.
15. Winckler, H. *Untersuchungen zur altorientalischen Geschichte.* Leipzig, 1886.

II. THE SECOND ISIN DYNASTY

1. Böhl, F. M. de L. 'Fünf Urkunden aus der Zeit des Königs Itti-Marduk-balaṭu.' In *Arch. f. Keil.* 2 (1924), 49 ff.
2. Dossin, G. 'Bronzes inscrits du Luristan de la collection Foroughi.' In *Iranica Antiqua*, 2 (1962), 149 ff.

3. Edzard, D. O. Review of § 11, 6. In *Z.A.* 53 (1959), 308 f.
4. Landsberger, B. 'Studien zu den Urkunden aus der Zeit des Ninurta-tukul-Aššur.' In *Arch. f. Or.* 10 (1935), 140 ff.
5. Nagel, W. 'Die Königsdolche der Zweiten Dynastie von Isin.' In *Arch. f. Or.* 19 (1961), 95 ff.
6. Poebel, A. *The Second Dynasty of Isin according to a New King-List Tablet* (*Assyriological Studies*, 15). Chicago, 1955.
7. Ungnad, A. 'Zur Geschichte und Chronologie des Zweiten Reiches von Isin.' In *Or.* n.s. 13 (1944), 73 ff.
8. Weidner, E. F. Review of § 11, 6. In *Arch. f. Or.* 17(1956), 383 f.

### III. DYNASTIC TROUBLES IN ASSYRIA

1. Andrae, W. *Die Stelenreihen in Assur* (*W.V.D.O.G.* 24). Leipzig, 1913.
2. Falkner, M. 'Studien zur Geographie des alten Mesopotamien.' In *Arch. f. Or.* 18 (1957), 1 ff.
3. Landsberger, B. 'Assyrische Königsliste und Dunkles Zeitalter.' In *J.C.S.* 8 (1954), 31 ff., 47 ff., 106 ff.
4. Landsberger, B. 'Jahreszeiten im Sumerisch-Akkadischen.' In *J.N.E.S.* 8 (1949), 248 ff.
5. Ledrain, E. 'Une statuette de bronze avec le nom d'Ašur-dan.' In *R.A.* 2 (1892), 91 ff.
6. Lloyd, H. S. 'Some ancient sites in the Sinjar District.' In *Iraq*, 5 (1938), 123 ff.
7. Smith, S. Review of A. T. Olmstead, *History of Assyria*. In *J.E.A.* 10 (1924), 70 ff.
8. Soden, W. von. 'Die Assyrer und der Krieg.' In *Iraq*, 25 (1963), 131 ff.
9. Stephens, F. J. *Votive and Historical Texts from Babylonia* (*Y.O.S.* 9). New Haven, 1937.
10. Thompson, R. C. 'A New Record of an Assyrian Earthquake.' In *Iraq*, 4 (1937), 186 ff.
11. Thompson, R. C. 'The Buildings on Quyunjiq, the larger mound of Nineveh.' In *Iraq*, 1 (1934), 95 ff.
12. Thompson, R. C. and Hamilton, R. W. 'The British Museum Excavations on the Temple of Ishtar at Nineveh, 1930–31.' In *Ann. Arch. Anthr.* 19 (1932), 55 ff.
13. Thompson, R. C. and Hutchinson, R. W. 'The Site of the Palace of Ashurnasirpal at Nineveh, excavated in 1929–30 on behalf of the British Museum.' In *Ann. Arch. Anthr.* 18 (1931), 79 ff.
14. Thompson, R. C. and Mallowan, M. E. L. 'The British Museum Excavations at Nineveh, 1931–32.' In *Ann. Arch. Anthr.* 20 (1933), 71 ff.
15. Thureau-Dangin, F. 'Inscriptions diverses du Louvre.' In *R.A.* 6 (1907), 133 ff.
16. Weidner, E. F. 'Aššurdân I.' In *R.L.A.* 1 (1932), 208 f.
17. Weidner, E. F. 'Eine Bauinschrift des Königs Aššurnadinapli von Assyria.' In *Arch. f. Or.* 6 (1930), 11 ff.
18. Winckler, H. 'Die Bronze Aššur-dans.' In *Z.A.* 6 (1891), 326 f.

### IV. NEBUCHADREZZAR I

1. Böhl, F. M. de L. 'Eine zweisprachige Weihinschrift Nebukadnezars I.' In *Bi. Or.* 7 (1950), 42 ff.
2. Clay, A. T. *Miscellaneous Inscriptions in the Yale Babylonian Collection* (*Y.O.S.* Bab. Texts 1). New Haven, 1915.
3. Figulla, H. *Business Documents of the New-Babylonian Period* (*U.E.T.* 4), London, 1949.
4. Hehn, J. 'Hymnen und Gebete an Marduk.' In *B.A.* 5 (1906), 279 ff.
5. Hincke, W. J. *A New Boundary Stone of Nebuchadrezzar I from Nippur.* Philadelphia, 1907.
6. Meek, T. J. 'Some bilingual Religious Texts.' In *A.J.S.L.* 35 (1919), 134 ff.
7. Pinches, T. G. 'A New Historical Fragment from Nineveh.' In *J.R.A.S.* (1904), 407 ff.
8. Winckler, H. 'Bruchstücke von Keilschrifttexten.' In *Altor. Forsch.* Reihe I, VI (1897), 516 ff.

### V. TIGLATH-PILESER I

1. Gelb, I. J. 'Studies in the Topography of Western Asia.' In *A.J.S.L.* 55 (1938), 66 ff.
2. Melikishvili, G. A. 'Assyria and the Nairi-lands at the turn of the XII-XI centuries B.C.' (In Russian.) In *Vestnik Drevney Istorii*, 84 (1963), 115 ff.
3. Melikishvili, G. A. *Nairi-Urartu.* (In Russian.) Tiflis, 1954.
4. Soden, W. von. *Der Aufstieg des Assyrerreichs als geschichtliches Problem* (*Alte Or.* no. 37, Heft 1/2). Leipzig, 1937.
5. Thompson, R. C. 'The Excavations on the Temple of Nabû at Nineveh.' In *Archaeologia*, 79 (1929), 103 ff.
6. Weidner, E. F. 'Die Annalen des Königs Aššurbêlkala von Assyrien.' In *Arch. f. Or.* 6 (1930), 75 ff.
7. Weidner, E. F. 'Die Bauten Tiglathpilesers I in Nineve.' In *Arch. f. Or.* 19 (1959), 141 ff.
8. Weidner, E. F. 'Die Bibliothek Tiglathpilesers I.' In *Arch. f. Or.* 16 (1953), 197 ff.
9. Weidner, E. F. 'Die Eponymen der Zeit Tiglathpilesers I.' In *Arch. f. Or.* 16 (1953), 283 f.
10. Weidner, E. F. 'Die Feldzüge und Bauten Tiglathpilesers I.' In *Arch. f. Or.* 18 (1958), 342 ff.
11. Weidner, E. F. 'Samarra in der Synchronistischen Geschichte?' In *Arch. f. Or.* 17 (1956), 309.
12. Weidner, E. F. 'Šilkan(ḫe)ni, König von Muṣri, ein Zeitgenosse Sargons II.' In *Arch. f. Or.* 14 (1941), 40 ff.

### VI. PRESSURES FROM THE WEST

1. Forrer, E. *Die Provinzeinteilung des assyrischen Reiches.* Leipzig, 1921.
2. Gadd, C. J. 'On Two Babylonian Kings.' In *Studia Orientalia*, 1 (1925), 25 ff.
3. Gadd, C. J. and Legrain, L. *Royal Inscriptions* (*U.E.T.* 1). London and Philadelphia, 1928.
4. Haller, A. *Die Gräber und Grüfte von Assur* (*W.V.D.O.G.* 65). Berlin, 1954.
5. Jaritz, K. 'The Problem of the "Broken Obelisk".' In *J.S.S.* 4 (1959), 204 ff.

6. Lambert, W. G. Review of F. Gössmann, *Das Era-Epos*. In *Arch. f. Or.* 18 (1958), 395 ff.
7. Langdon, S. *Excavations at Kish I*. Paris, 1924.
8. Lewy, J. 'The Middle Assyrian Votive Bead found at Tanis.' In *Ignaz Goldziher Memorial Volume*, 1 (1948), 313 ff.
9. Luckenbill, D. D. *The Annals of Sennacherib* (*O.I.P.* 11). Chicago, 1924.
10. Meek, T. J. 'Bronze Swords from Luristan.' In *Bull. A.S.O.R.* 74 (1939), 7 ff.
11. Olmstead, A. T. *History of Assyria*. London, 1923.
12. Place, V. *Ninive et l'Assyrie*, 1–111. Paris, 1867–70.
13. Poebel, A. 'Kein neuer Vater Adad-apla-iddinas!' In *Arch. f. Or.* 5 (1928–9), 103 f.
14. Rowton, M. B. 'Comparative Chronology at the Time of Dynasty XIX.' In *J.N.E.S.* 19 (1960), 15 ff.
15. Schroeder, O. *Keilschrifttexte aus Assur verschiedenen Inhalts*. Leipzig, 1920.
16. Sollberger, E. *Royal Inscriptions* (*U.E.T.* viii). London and Philadelphia, 1965.
17. Weidner, E. F. 'Aššurbêlkala.' In *R.L.A.* 1 (1932), 207 ff.
18. Weidner, E. F. 'Aššurnaṣirapli I.' In *R.L.A.* 1 (1932), 213 ff.

### VII. THE SECOND SEALAND AND BAZI DYNASTIES

1. Conteneau, G. 'Pointe de flèche au nom d'É-Ulmaš-šâkin-šumi?' In *R.A.* 29 (1932), 29 f.
2. Dougherty, R. P. *The Sealand of Ancient Arabia* (*Y.O.S.* 9). New Haven, 1932.
3. Millard, A. R. 'Another Babylonian Chronicle Text.' In *Iraq*, 26 (1964), 14 ff.
4. Rowton, M. B. 'Mesopotamian Chronology and the Era of Menophres.' In *Iraq*, 8 (1946), 94 ff.

### VIII. LAW AND ADMINISTRATION

1. Brinkman, J. A. 'Provincial Administration in Babylonia under the Second Dynasty of Isin.' In *J.E.S.H.O.* 6 (1963), 233 ff.
2. Driver, G. R. and Miles, J. C. *The Assyrian Laws*. Oxford, 1935.
3. Ebeling, E. 'Die Eigennamen der mittelassyrischen Rechts- und Geschäftsurkunden.' In *M.A.O.G.* 13 (1939), 1 ff.
4. Ebeling, E. 'Urkunden des Archivs von Assur aus mittelassyrischer Zeit.' In *M.A.O.G.* 7 (1933), 1 ff.
5. Ebeling, E. *Keilschrifttexte aus Assur juristischen Inhalts*. Leipzig, 1927.
6. Kraus, F. R. *Ein Edikt des Königs Ammiṣaduqa von Babylon*. Leiden, 1958.
7. Lewy, H. 'The Assyrian Calendar.' In *Arch. f. Or.* 11 (1939), 35 ff.
8. Olmstead, A. T. 'Tiglath-Pileser I and his Wars.' In *J.A.O.S.* 37 (1917), 169 ff.
9. Reiner, E. Review of E. F. Weidner, *Die Inschriften Tukulti-Ninurtas I, und seiner Nachfolger*. In *Bi. Or.* 19 (1962), 158 f.
10. Smith, S. 'A Pre-Greek Coinage in the Near East?' In *Num. Chron.* (5th series), 2 (1922), 2 ff.
11. Ungnad, A. 'Eponymen.' In *R.L.A.* 2 (1938), 412 ff.
12. Weidner, E. F. 'Die assyrischen Eponymen.' In *Arch. f. Or.* 13 (1940), 308 ff.

13. Weidner, E. F. 'Eine Erbteilung in mittelassyrischer Zeit.' In *Arch. f. Or.* 20 (1963), 121 ff.
14. Weidner, E. F. 'Hof- und Harems-Erlasse assyrischer Könige aus dem 2 Jahrtausend v. Chr.' In *Arch. f. Or.* 17 (1956), 257 ff.

IX. LITERATURE, RELIGION AND THE ARTS

1. Andrae, W. *Der Anu-Adad-Tempel in Assur* (*W.V.D.O.G.* 10). Leipzig, 1909.
2. Andrae, W. *Die Festungswerke von Assur* (*W.V.D.O.G.* 23). Leipzig, 1913.
3. Andrae, W. *Das wiedererstandene Assur.* Leipzig, 1938.
4. Aro, J. *Glossar zu den mittelbabylonischen Briefen* (*Studia Orientalia,* 22). Helsinki, 1957.
5. Aro, J. *Studien zur mittelbabylonischen Grammatik* (*Studia Orientalia,* 20). Helsinki, 1955.
6. Beran, T. 'Assyrische Glyptik des 14 Jahrhunderts.' In *Z.A.* 52 (1957), 141 ff.
7. Ebeling, E. *Keilschrifttexte aus Assur religiösen Inhalts.* Leipzig, 1919–1923.
8. Ebeling, E. 'Kultische Texte aus Assur.' In *Or.* n.s. 20 (1951), 399 ff.; 21 (1952), 129 ff.; 22 (1953), 25 ff.; 23 (1954), 114 ff.; 24 (1955), 1 ff.
9. Frankfort, H. H. *Cylinder Seals, A Documentary Essay on the Art and Religion of the Ancient Near East.* London, 1939.
10. Frankfort, H. H. *The Art and Architecture of the Ancient Orient.* Harmondsworth, 1954.
11. Gadd, C. J. *The Stones of Assyria.* London, 1936.
12. Hallo, W. W. 'Royal Hymns and Mesopotamian Unity.' In *J.C.S.* 17 (1963), 112 ff.
13. Köcher, F. 'Ein mittelassyrisches Ritualfragment zum Neujahrsfest.' In *Z.A.* 50 (1952), 192 ff.
14. Lambert, W. G. 'Ancestors, Authors and Canonicity.' In *J.C.S.* 11 (1957), 1 ff.
15. Lambert, W. G. 'A Catalogue of Texts and Authors.' In *J.C.S.* 16 (1962), 59 ff.
16. Lambert, W. G. *Babylonian Wisdom Literature.* Oxford, 1960.
17. Lambert, W. G. 'The Reign of Nebuchadnezzar I: A Turning Point in the History of Ancient Mesopotamian Religion.' In McCullough, W. S. (ed.), *The Seed of Wisdom,* 3 ff. Toronto, 1964.
18. Moortgat, A. 'Assyrische Glyptik des 13. Jahrhunderts.' In *Z.A.* 47 (1943), 50 ff.
19. Moortgat, A. 'Assyrische Glyptik des 12. Jahrhunderts.' In *Z.A.* 48 (1944), 23 ff.
20. Müller, K. F. 'Das assyrische Ritual. Teil 1. Texte zum assyrischen Königsritual.' In *M.V.Ae.G.* 41 (1937), Heft 3.
21. Opitz, D. 'Die Siegel Ninurta-tukul-Aššurs und seiner Frau Rimeni.' In *Arch. f. Or.* 10 (1935), 48 ff.
22. Porada, E. *Corpus of Ancient Near Eastern Seals in North American Collections,* I. Washington, 1948.

A. ADDENDA

1. Biggs, R. D. 'More Babylonian Prophecies.' In *Iraq,* 29 (1967), 117 ff.
2. Birot, M. 'Découvertes épigraphiques à Larsa (Campagne 1967).' In *Syria,* 45 (1968), 242 ff.

3. Brinkman, J. A. *A Political History of Post-Kassite Babylonia, 1158–722 B.C.* (Analecta Orientalia, 43). Rome, 1968. See above, G, 2.

4. Brinkman, J. A. 'The Names of the Last Eight Kings of the Kassite Dynasty.' In *Z.A.* 59 (1969), 231 ff.

5. Brinkman, J. A. 'Ur: The Kassite Period and the Period of the Assyrian Kings.' In *Or.* 38 (1969), 310 ff.

6. Buccellati, G. and Biggs, R. D. *Cuneiform Texts from Nippur, Eighth and Ninth Seasons* (Assyriological Studies, 17). Chicago, 1969.

7. Goetze, A. 'An Inscription of Simbar-šīḫu.' In *J.C.S.* 19 (1965), 121 ff.

8. Grayson, A. K. and Lambert, W. G. 'Akkadian Prophecies.' In *J.C.S.* 18 (1964), 9 ff.

9. Hallo, W. W. 'Akkadian Apocalypses.' In *I.E.J.* 16 (1966), 231 ff.

10. Klengel, H. 'Lullubum. Ein Beitrag zur Geschichte der altvorderasiatischen Gebirgsvölker.' In *Mitt. Inst. Or.* 11 (1966), 349 ff.

11. Millard, A. R. 'Fragments of Historical Texts from Nineveh: Middle Assyrian and Later Kings.' In *Iraq* 32 (1970), 167 ff.

12. Oates, D. 'The Excavations at Tell Al Rimah, 1966.' In *Iraq*, 29 (1967), 70 ff.

13. Oates, D. 'The Excavations at Tell Al Rimah, 1968.' In *Iraq*, 32 (1970), 1 ff.

14. Röllig, W. 'Die Glaubwürdigkeit der Chronik P.' In *Heidelberger Studien*, 1 (1967), 173 ff.

15. Saggs, H. W. F. 'The Tell Al Rimah Tablets, 1965.' In *Iraq*, 30 (1968), 154 ff.

16. Tadmor, H. 'Que and Muṣri.' In *I.E.J.* 11 (1961), 143 ff.

17. Wiseman, D. J. 'The Tell Al Rimah Tablets, 1966.' In *Iraq*, 30 (1968), 175 ff.

## CHAPTER XXXII

### G. GENERAL

1. Bork, F., Hüsing, G. and König, F. W. *Corpus Inscriptionum Elamicarum.* Hanover, 1926.

2. Cameron, G. G. *History of Early Iran.* Chicago, 1936.

3. Delaporte, L. and Huart, C. *L'Iran antique et la civilisation iranienne.* Paris, 1943.

4. Dhorme, E. 'Élam, Élamites.' In *Dictionnaire de la Bible, Supplément* II (Paris, 1934), 929 ff.

5. Ebeling, E., Meissner B. and Weidner, E. F. (eds.). *Reallexikon der Assyriologie*, II. Berlin and Leipzig, 1938.

6. Gadd, C. J. and Legrain, L. *Ur Excavations. Texts* I: *Royal Inscriptions.* London, 1928.

7. Ghirshman, R. *L'Iran des origines à l'Islam.* Paris, 1951.

8. Hüsing, G. *Die einheimischen Quellen zur Geschichte Elams.* Leipzig, 1916.

9. König, F. W. and Christian, V. 'Elam.' In *R.L.A.* II (1938), 324 ff.

10. König, F. W. *Geschichte Elams (Alte Or.* no. 29, Heft 4). Leipzig, 1931.

11. Lambert, M. 'Littérature élamite.' In *L'histoire générale des littératures.* Paris, 1961.

12. Luckenbill, D. D. *Ancient Records of Assyria and Babylonia.* Chicago, 1926–7.

13. Mayer, R. 'Die Bedeutung Elams in der Geschichte des alten Orients.' In *Saeculum*, 7 (1956), 198 ff.

14. *Mém. D.P.* (*Mémoires de la Délégation en Perse.*) Paris, 1900–. Numbers of the volumes are quoted in the footnotes.

15. Olmstead, A. T. *History of Assyria.* New York, 1923.

16. Smith, S. *Early History of Assyria*. London, 1928.
17. Weissbach, F. H. *Anzanische Inschriften und Vorarbeiten zu ihrer Entzifferung*. Leipzig, 1891.
18. Weissbach, F. H. 'Kossaioi.' In *P.W.*, Band 11 (1922), 1499 ff.

### I. SHUTRUK-NAHHUNTE AND KUTIR-NAHHUNTE

1. Jordan, J. 'Erster vorläufiger Bericht über die...in Uruk-Warka...Ausgrabungen.' In *Abh. Berlin*, 1929, no. 7.
2. König, F. W. 'Die Berliner elamischen Texte VA 3397–3402.' In *W.Z.K.M.* 32 (1925), 212 ff.
3. Parrot, A. (ed.). *Studia Mariana, publiées sous la direction de André Parrot*. Leiden, 1950.
4. Scheil, V. 'Textes élamites-anzanites.' In *Mém. D.P.* 3 (1901); 5 (1904).
5. Scheil, V. 'Légendes de Shutruk-Nahhunte sur cuves de pierre.' In *R.A.* 16 (1919), 195 ff.
6. Scheil, V. 'Kutir-Nahhunte I.' In *R.A.* 29 (1932), 67 ff.
7. Tadmor, H. 'Historical Implications of the Correct Rendering of Akkadian *dâku*.' In *J.N.E.S.* 17 (1958), 129 ff.
8. Unvala, J. M. 'Three Panels from Susa.' In *R.A.* 25 (1928), 179 ff.

### II. SHILKHAK-IN-SHUSHINAK

1. Cameron, G. G. *Persepolis Treasury Tablets* (*O.I.P.* 65). Chicago, 1948.
2. Debevoise, N. C. 'The Rock Reliefs of Ancient Iran.' In *J.N.E.S.* 1 (1942), 78 ff.
3. Herzfeld, E. 'Zarathustra, 1: Der geschichtliche Vistāspa.' In *A.M.I.* 1 (1929), 77 ff.
4. Herzfeld, E. 'Drei Inschriften aus persischem Gebiet.' In *M.A.O.G.* 4 (1928), 82 ff.
5. König, F. W. 'Drei altelamische Stelen.' In *M.V.Ae.G.* 30 (1925). Leipzig, 1925.
6. Scheil, V. 'Inscriptions de Shilkhak-In-Shushinak.' In *Mém. D.P.* 5 (1904), 11 (1911).
7. Weidner, E. F. 'Aus den Tagen eines assyrischen Schattenkönigs.' In *Arch. f. Or.* 10 (1935), 1 ff.

### III. ELAMITE CIVILIZATION C. 1125 B.C.

1. Cruveilhier, P. *Les principaux résultats des nouvelles fouilles de Suse*. Paris, 1921.
2. Gautier, J. E. 'Le sit-shamshi de Shilkhak-In-Shushinak.' In *Mém. D.P.* 12 (1911), 143 ff.
3. Morgan, J. de. 'Table de bronze: bas-relief de bronze.' In *Mém. D.P.* 1 (1900), 161 ff.
4. Scheil, V. 'Bronze aux guerriers.' In *Mém. D.P.* 11 (1911).
5. Vincent, L.-H. *Canaan d'après l'exploration récente*. Paris, 1907.

### IV. THE TOPOGRAPHY OF SUSA

1. Böhl, F. M. Th. 'Die Tochter des Königs Nabonid.' In *Symbolae...Paulo Koschaker dedicatae* (Leiden, 1939), 151 ff.
2. Harper, R. F. *Assyrian and Babylonian Letters*. London, 1892–1902.

3. Mecquenem, R. de 'Constructions élamites sur l'Acropole de Suse.' In *Mém. D.P.* 12 (1911), 65 ff.
4. Morgan, J. de 'Ruines de Suse: constructions élamites.' In *Mém. D.P.* 1 (1900), 50 ff., 196 ff.

V. KHUTELUTUSH-IN-SHUSHINAK

1. Hüsing, G. 'Lakti-Šipak von Bît-Karziaš-ku.' In *O.L.Z.* 17 (1914), 156 f.
2. Jequier, G. 'Fouilles de Suse de 1899 à 1902.' In *Mém. D.P.* 7 (1905), 9 ff.
3. King, L. W. *Babylonian Boundary Stones...in the British Museum.* London, 1912.
4. König, F. W. 'Mutterrecht und Thronfolge im alten Orient.' In *Festschrift der Nationalbibliothek* (Wien, 1926), 529 ff.
5. Koschaker, P. 'Fratriarchat, Hausgemeinschaft und Mutterrecht in Keilschriftrechten, III. Elam.' In *Z.A.* 41 (1933), 46 ff.
6. Olmstead, A. T. 'Kashshites, Assyrians and the Balance of Power.' In *A.J.S.L.* 36 (1920), 120 ff.
7. Smith, S. 'An Egyptian in Babylonia.' In *J.E.A.* 18 (1932), 28 ff.
8. Thompson, R. C. *Reports of the Astrologers of Nineveh and Babylon.* London, 1900.
9. Thureau-Dangin, F. 'Un Synchronisme entre la Babylonie et l'Élam.' In *R.A.* 10 (1913), 97 ff.
10. Weidner, E. F. 'Die astrologische Serie Enûma Anu Enlil.' In *Arch.f. Or.* 14 (1941–4), 172 ff.
11. Winckler, H. *Altorientalische Forschungen*, Reihe 1. Leipzig, 1893.

VI. THE POLITICAL GEOGRAPHY OF WESTERN PERSIA

1. *Archives royales de Mari* (*A.R.M.T.* texts in transliteration and translation), I–IX. Paris, 1950–60.
2. Balkan, K. *Kassitenstudien*: 1. *Die Sprache der Kassiten.* New Haven, 1954.
3. Billerbeck, A. *Das Sandschak Suleimania und dessen persische Nachbarlandschaften zur babylonischen und assyrischen Zeit.* Leipzig, 1898.
4. Boudou, R. P. 'Liste de noms géographiques.' In *Or.* 36–8 (1929).
5. Childe, G. *New Light on the Most Ancient East.* London, 1934.
6. Edmonds, C. J. 'Two Ancient Monuments in Southern Kurdistan.' In *G.J.* 55 (1925), 63 ff.
7. Edmonds, C. J. *Kurds, Turks and Arabs.* London, 1957.
8. Falkner, M. 'Iran.' In *Arch.f. Or.* 18 (1957), 184 ff.
9. Falkner, M. 'Hasanlu.' In *Arch.f. Or.* 20 (1963), 232 ff.
10. Forrer, E. *Die Provinzeinteilung des assyrischen Reiches.* Leipzig, 1920.
11. Gelb, I. J. *Hurrians and Subarians* (*S.A.O.C.* 22). Chicago, 1944.
12. Gelb, I. J. 'New Light on Hurrians and Subarians.' In *Studi orientalistici in onore di G. Levi della Vida*, I, 378 ff.
13. Ghirshman, R. *Fouilles de Sialk près de Kashan, 1933, 1934, 1937.* Paris, 1938–9.
14. Ghirshman, R. *7000 ans d'art en Iran* (Catalogue de l'Exposition). Paris, 1961.
15. Goetze, A. *Hethiter, Churriter, und Assyrer.* Oslo, 1936.
16. Goetze, A. *Kleinasien* (2nd ed.). München, 1957.
17. Gutschmid, A. von. *Geschichte Irans und seine Nachbarländer.* Tübingen, 1888.

18. Herzfeld, E. *Archaeological History of Iran*. London, 1935.
19. Herzfeld, E. 'Die Kunst des zweiten Jahrtausends in Vorderasien.' In *A.M.I.* 8, no. 3 (1937).
20. Herzfeld, E. *Iran in the Ancient East*. Oxford, 1941.
21. Hüsing, G. *Der Zagros und seine Völker* (*Alte Or.* 9, Heft 3/4). Leipzig, 1908.
22. Kupper, J.-R. *Les Nomades en Mesopotamie au temps des rois de Mari*. Paris, 1957.
23. Læssøe, J. *The Shemshāra Tablets*. Copenhagen, 1959.
24. Minorski, V. 'Les études historiques et géographiques sur la Perse depuis 1900.' In *Acta Or.* 10 (1932), 278 ff.
25. Mironov, N. P. 'Aryan Vestiges in the Near East of the Second millennary B.C.' In *Acta Or.* 11 (1932), 140 ff.
26. Olmstead, A. T. *History of the Persian Empire*. Chicago, 1948.
27. Poebel, A. 'Eine sumerische Inschrift Samsuilunas über die Erbauung der Festung Dur-Samsuiluna.' In *Arch. f. Or.* 9 (1933–4), 241 ff.
28. Rawlinson, H. C. *The Cuneiform Inscriptions of Western Asia*, v. London, 1884.
29. Rogers, R. W. *A History of Ancient Persia*. New York, 1929.
30. Sarre, F. *L'art de la Perse ancienne*. Paris, 1921.
31. Schmidt, E. F. *Excavations at Tepe Hissar Damghan*. Philadelphia, 1937.
32. Speiser, E. A. *Southern Kurdistan in the Annals of Ashurnasirpal and To-day* (*Ann. A.S.O.R.* 8, 1926–7). New Haven, 1928.
33. Speiser, E. A. 'Hurrians and Subarians.' In *J.A.O.S.* 68 (1948), 1 f.
34. Streck, M. 'Armenien, Kurdistan, und Westpersien nach den babylonisch-assyrischen Keilinschriften.' In *Z.A.* 13 (1898), 57 ff.; 14 (1899), 103 ff.; 15 (1900), 257 ff.
35. Thureau-Dangin, F. 'La fin de la domination gutienne.' In *R.A.* 9 (1912), 111 ff.
36. Thureau-Dangin, F. 'Un double de l'inscription d'Utuhegal.' In *R.A.* 10 (1913), 98 ff.
37. Thureau-Dangin, F. *Une relation de la huitième campagne de Sargon*. Paris, 1912.
38. Ungnad, A. *Subartu*. Berlin, 1936.
39. Vanden Berghe, L. 'Iran. De stand van de archaeologische onderzoekingen in Iran.' In *J.E.O.L.* 13 (1953–4), 347 ff.
40. Vanden Berghe, L. *Archéologie de l'Iran ancien*. Leyden, 1959.
41. Von der Osten, H. *Die Welt der Perser*. Stuttgart, 1956.
42. Wilkinson, Ch. K. 'Two Ancient Silver Vessels.' In *Bull. M.M.A.* 15 (1956–7), 9 ff.
43. Witzel, P. Maurus. 'Bemerkungen zu der Siegesinschrift Utuhegals von Uruk.' In *Babyloniaca*, 7 (1913–23), 51 ff.
44. Wulsin, F. R. *Excavations at Turang-Tepe, near Asterabad* (*Bull. Amer. Inst for Persian Art and Arch.* Suppl., 1932).

## CHAPTER XXXIII

### G. GENERAL

1. Albright, W. F. 'Syrien, Phönizien und Palästina.' In *Historia Mundi*, II, 331 ff. Berne, 1953.
2. Albright, W. F. *The Biblical Period from Abraham to Ezra*. New York, 1963.

3. Bilabel, F. *Geschichte Vorderasiens und Ägyptens vom 16–11 Jahrhundert v. Chr.* Heidelberg, 1927.
4. Breasted, J. H. *Ancient Records of Egypt*, i–v. Chicago, 1906.
5. Erman, A. und Grapow, H. *Wörterbuch der ägyptischen Sprache*, 5 vols. Leipzig, 1928–31.
6. Friedrich, J. *Phönizisch-punische Grammatik.* Rome, 1951.
7. Gordon, C. H. *Before the Bible.* New York, 1962.
8. Harris, Z. S. *A Grammar of the Phoenician Language.* New Haven, 1937.
9. *Interpreter's Dictionary of the Bible* (ed. G. A. Buttrick). Nashville, Tennessee, 1962.
10. Luckenbill, D. D. *Ancient Records of Assyria and Babylonia: Historical Records of Assyria*, i–ii. Chicago, 1926–7.
11. Meyer, E. *Geschichte des Altertums*, ii, 1, 2. Stuttgart and Berlin, 1928, 1931.
12. Olmstead, A. T. *History of Palestine and Syria.* New York, 1941.

### I. THE SEA PEOPLES IN PALESTINE

1. Albright, W. F. 'A Colony of Cretan Mercenaries on the Coast of the Negeb.' In *J.P.O.S.* 1 (1921), 187 ff.
2. Albright, W. F. 'Egypt and the Early History of the Negeb.' In *J.P.O.S.* 4 (1924), 131 ff.
3. Albright, W. F. In *Ann. A.S.O.R.* 12 (1932), 53 ff.
4. Albright, W. F. *The Vocalization of the Egyptian Syllabic Orthography* (*Amer. Orient. Ser.* 5). New Haven, 1934.
5. Albright, W. F. 'Some Oriental Glosses on the Homeric Problem.' In *A.J.A.* 54 (1950), 162 ff.
6. Albright, W. F. 'The Eastern Mediterranean about 1060 B.C.' In *Studies Presented to David Moore Robinson.* St Louis, 1951.
7. Albright, W. F. *The Archaeology of Palestine* (*Pelican Archaeology Series*). London, 1949–63, esp. 1954 edition.
8. Bossert, H. Th. *Altkreta.* Berlin, 1923.
9. Burn, A. R. *Minoans, Philistines, and Greeks.* London, 1930.
10. Carruba, O. 'Lydisch und Lyder.' In *Mitt. Inst. Or.* 8 (1963), 383 ff.
11. Desborough, V. R. d'A. *The Last Mycenaeans and Their Successors.* Oxford, 1964.
12. Dothan, T. 'Philistine Civilization in the Light of Archaeological Finds in Palestine and Egypt.' In *Eretz-Israel*, 5 (1958), 55 ff. (in Hebrew).
13. Dothan, T. 'Archaeological Reflections on the Philistine Problem.' In *The Holy Land* (*Antiquity and Survival*, ii, 2/3, 151 ff.). The Hague and Jerusalem, 1957.
14. Edgerton, W. F. and Wilson, J. A. *Historical Records of Ramses III. The Texts in Medinet Habu*, i–ii. Chicago, 1936.
15. Eissfeldt, O. 'Philister.' In *P.W.* 19 (1938), cols. 2390–2402.
16. Erlenmeyer, M. L. and Erlenmeyer, H. 'Über Philister und Kreter. i.' In *Or.* n.s. 29 (1960), 121 ff.
17. Erlenmeyer, M. L. and Erlenmeyer, H. 'Über Philister und Kreter. ii.' In *Or.* n.s. 29 (1960), 241 ff.
18. Erlenmeyer, M. L. and Erlenmeyer, H. 'Über Philister und Kreter. iii.' In *Or.* n.s. 30 (1961), 269 ff.
19. Erlenmeyer, M. L. and Erlenmeyer, H. 'Über Philister und Kreter. iv.' In *Or.* n.s. 33 (1964), 199 ff.
20. Goetze, A. 'Cilicians.' In *J.C.S.* 16 (1962), 48 ff.

21. Grant, E. and Wright, G. E. *Ain Shems Excavations*, v. Haverford (Penna.), 1939.
22. Hall, H. R. 'The Peoples of the Sea.' In *Mélanges Champollion*, 297 ff. Paris, 1922.
23. Helck, W. *Die Beziehungen Ägyptens zu Vorderasien im 3. und 2. Jahrtausend v. Chr. (Ägyptologische Abhandlungen*, 5). Wiesbaden, 1962.
24. Heurtley, W. A. 'The Relationship between "Philistine" and Mycenaean Pottery.' In *Q.D.A.P.* 5 (1936), 90 ff.
25. Landes, G. M. 'The Material Civilization of the Ammonites.' In *Bi. Ar.* 24 (1961), 66 ff.
26. Macalister, R. A. S. *The Philistines*. London, 1913.
27. Mazar, B. 'The Philistines and the Rise of Israel and Tyre.' In *The Israel Academy of Sciences and Humanities, Proceedings*, 1, 7 (1964), 1 ff.
28. Naveh, J. 'Khirbat al-Muqannaʿ-Ekron: an archaeological survey.' In *I.E.J.* 8 (1958), 87 ff. and 165 ff.
29. Nelson, H. H. *Medinet Habu, 1924–28 (O.I.C.* 5). Chicago, 1929.
30. Nelson, H. H. and others. *Medinet Habu*, I–II (*O.I.P.* 8–9). Chicago, 1930–32.
31. Petrie, W. M. F. *Gerar*. London, 1928.
32. Petrie, W. M. F. *Beth-pelet I*. London, 1930.
33. Phythian-Adams, W. J. 'Philistine Origins in the Light of Palestinian Archaeology.' In *Bull. B.S.A.J.* 3 (1923), 20 ff.
34. Saussey, E. 'La céramique philistine.' In *Syria*, 5 (1924), 169 ff.
35. Stähelin, F. *Die Philister*. Basel, 1918.
36. Starkey, J. L. and Harding, L. *Beth-pelet II*. London, 1932.
37. Ten Cate, Ph. H. J. H. *The Luwian Population Groups of Lycia and Cilicia Aspera During the Hellenistic Period (Documenta et Monumenta Orientis Antiqui*, 10). Leiden, 1961.
38. Watzinger, C. *Denkmäler Palästinas*, 1. Leipzig, 1933, 77 ff.
39. Wilson, J. A. *Medinet Habu 1928–1929: the language of the historical texts commemorating Ramses III.* (*O.I.C.* 7.) Chicago, 1930.
40. Wright, G. E. 'Iron: the Date of Its Introduction into Common Use in Palestine.' In *A.J.A.* 43 (1939), 458 ff.
41. Wright, G. E. *Biblical Archaeology*. Philadelphia and London, 1957.
42. Wright, G. E. 'Philistine Coffins and Mercenaries.' In *Bi. Ar.* 22 (1959), 54 ff.
43. Yoyotte, J. 'Un souvenir du "Pharaon" Taousert en Jordanie.' In *V.T.* 12 (1962), 464 ff.

## II. THE CANAANITE REVIVAL IN PHOENICIA

1. Albright, W. F. 'New Light on the Early History of Phoenician Colonization.' In *Bull. A.S.O.R.* 83 (1941), 14 ff.
2. Albright, W. F. 'The Phoenician Inscriptions of the Tenth Century B.C. from Byblos.' In *J.A.O.S.* 67 (1947), 153 ff.
3. Albright, W. F. *Archaeology and the Religion of Israel* (3rd ed.). Baltimore, 1953.
4. Albright, W. F. 'Was the Age of Solomon without Monumental Art?' In *Eretz-Israel*, 5 (1958), 1 ff.
5. Albright, W. F. 'The Role of the Canaanites in the History of Civilization.' In *The Bible and the Ancient Near East* (ed. G. E. Wright), 328 ff. New York, 1961.

6. Barnett, R. D. 'The Nimrud Ivories and the Art of the Phoenicians.' In *Iraq*, 2 (1935), 179 ff.
7. Barnett, R. D. *A Catalogue of the Nimrud Ivories in the British Museum*. London, 1957.
8. Bass, G. F. 'A Bronze Age Shipwreck.' In *Expedition* (Philadelphia), 3 (1961), 2 ff.
9. Bonsor, J. E. *Early Engraved Ivories*. New York, 1928.
10. Bosch-Gimpera, P. 'Fragen der Chronologie der phönizischen Kolonisation in Spanien.' In *Klio*, 1928, 345 ff.
11. Černý, J. *ap*. Posener, G. 'Les richesses inconnues de la littérature égyptienne.' In *Rev. égyptol.* 6 (1949), 41.
12. Černý, J. *Paper and Books in Ancient Egypt*. London, 1952.
13. Chiappisi, S. *Il Melqart di Sciacca e la Questione fenicia in Sicilia*, Rome, 1961.
14. Contenau, G. *La Civilisation phénicienne*. Paris, 1939.
15. Covey-Crump, W. W. 'The Situation of Tarshish.' In *J.T.S.* 17 (1916), 280 ff.
16. Dawkins, R. M. *The Sanctuary of Artemis Orthia at Sparta*. London, 1929.
17. Dunand, M. *Fouilles de Byblos*, 1. Paris, 1939.
18. Dunand, M. *Byblia Grammata*. Beyrouth, 1945.
19. Dunand, M. 'Phénicie.' In *Supplément au Dictionnaire de la Bible*. Paris, 1961.
20. Dussaud, R. 'Les inscriptions phéniciennes du tombeau d'Ahiram, roi de Byblos.' In *Syria*, 5 (1924), 135 ff.
21. Dussaud, R. 'Dédicace d'une statue d'Osorkon I<sup>er</sup> par Elibaal, roi de Byblos.' In *Syria*, 6 (1925), 101 ff.
22. Eissfeldt, O. 'Philister und Phönizier.' In *Alte Or.* 34 (1936).
23. Eissfeldt, O. 'Phoiniker, Phoinikia.' In *P.W.* 20 (1941), cols. 350–380.
24. Garbini, G. 'L'espansione fenicia nel mediterraneo.' In *Cultura e scuola*, 7 (1963), 92 ff.
25. Glueck, N. *The Other Side of the Jordan*. New Haven, 1940.
26. Harden, D. B. *The Phoenicians*. London, 1962.
27. Hennequin, L. 'Fouilles en Phénicie.' In *Supplément au Dictionnaire de la Bible*, III. cols. 436–470. Paris, 1936.
28. Loud, G. *The Megiddo Ivories* (*O.I.P.* 52). Chicago, 1939.
29. Maisler, B. 'The Phoenician Inscriptions from Gebal and the Evolution of the Phoenico-Hebrew Alphabetic Script.' In *Leshonenu*, 14 (1936), 166 ff. (in Hebrew).
30. Mertzenfeld, C. de. 'Les ivoires de Megiddo.' In *Syria*, 19 (1938), 345 ff.
31. Montet, P. *Byblos et l'Egypte*. Paris, 1928.
32. Moscati, S. 'La Questione Fenicia.' In *Accademia Nazionale dei Lincei*, serie 8, vol. 8 (1963), 483 ff.
33. Pietschmann, R. *Geschichte der Phönizier*. Berlin, 1889.
34. Poulsen, F. *Der Orient und die frühgriechische Kunst*. Leipzig, 1912.
35. Prakken, D. W. *Studies in Greek Genealogical Chronology*. Lancaster (Penna.), 1943.
36 Thomsen, P. Articles in Ebert, M. *Reallexikon der Vorgeschichte*: 'Byblos', II (1926), 246 ff.; 'Sidon', XII (1928), 77 ff.; 'Tyrus', XIII (1929), 516 ff.
37. Vincent, L. H. 'Les fouilles de Byblos.' In *Rev. bibl.* 34 (1925), 161 ff.
38. Watzinger, C. 'Phönikien und Palästina: Blütezeit.' In Otto, W. *Handbuch der Archäologie*, 1, 805 ff. Munich, 1939.

### III. THE SYRO-HITTITE STATES

1. Akurgal, E. *Remarques stylistiques sur les reliefs de Malatya*. Istanbul, 1946.
2. Albright, W. F. 'Northeast-Mediterranean Dark Ages and the Early Iron Age Art of Syria.' In *The Aegean and the Near East: Studies presented to Hetty Goldman*, 144 ff. New York, 1956.
3. Albright, W. F. 'The date of the Kapara Period at Gozan (Tell Halaf).' In *A.St.* 6 (1956), 75 ff.
4. Albright, W. F. 'The Biblical tribe of Massa and some Congeners.' In *Studi Orientalistici...Giorgio Levi Della Vida* (Rome, 1956), 1 ff.
5. Austin, W. M. 'Is Armenian an Anatolian Language?' In *Language*, 18 (1942), 22 ff.
6. Bérard, J. 'Philistins et Préhellènes.' In *Rev. arch.* série 6, 37 (1951), 129 ff.
7. Bossert, H. Th. *Altanatolien*. Berlin, 1942.
8. Bossert, H. Th. *Karatepe*. Istanbul, 1946.
9. Bossert, H. Th. 'Zur Chronologie der Skulpturen von Malatya.' In *Felsefe Arkivi*, 2 (1947), 85 ff.
10. Bossert, H. Th. 'Zur Geschichte von Karkamis.' In *Studi Classici e Orientali*, 1 (1951), 35 ff.
11. Bossert, H. Th. *Altsyrien*. Tübingen, 1951.
12. Bowman, R. A. 'The Old Canaanite Alphabet at Tell Halaf: the Date of the Altar Inscription.' In *A.J.S.L.* 58 (1941), 359 ff.
13. Christian, V. 'Untersuchungen zur nordsyrisch-"hettitischen" Kunst.' In *Arch. f. Or.* 9 (1933–4), 1 ff.
14. Contenau, G. *La civilisation des Hittites et des Mitanniens*. Paris, 1934.
15. Dupont-Sommer, A. *Les Araméens*. Paris, 1949.
16. Février, J. G. 'L'ancienne marine phénicienne.' In *N.C.* 1/2 (1950), 128 ff.
17. Forrer, E. Article, 'Aramu'. In *R.L.A.* 1 (1929), 131 ff.
18. Forrer, E. Article, 'Assyrien'. In *R.L.A.* 1 (1930), 282 ff.
19. Franken, H. J. 'Deir 'Alla 14–4–1964.' In *V.T.* 14 (1964), 377 ff.
20. Frankfort, H. *The Art and Architecture of the Ancient Orient (The Pelican History of Art)*. Baltimore, 1955.
21. Garstang, J. *The Hittite Empire*. London, 1929.
22. Gelb, I. *Hittite Hieroglyphs*, I–III. Chicago, 1931–42.
23. Güterbock, H. G. and Özgüç, N. *Guide to the Hittite Museum in the Bedestan at Ankara*. Istanbul, 1946.
24. Hogarth, D. G. and Woolley, C. L. *Carchemish*, I–II. London, 1914–21.
25. Hrozný, B. *Les inscriptions hittites-hiéroglyphiques*, I–III. Praha, 1933–7.
26. Kraeling, E. G. H. *Aram and Israel*. New York, 1918.
27. Laroche, E. 'Études sur les hiéroglyphes hittites.' In *Syria*, 35, 252 ff.
28. Laroche, E. 'Les hiéroglyphes Hittites.' In *L'écriture*, 35 (1960), 1 ff.
29. Luschan, F. von and others. *Ausgraben in Sendschirli*, I–V. Berlin, 1893–1943.
30. Malamat, A. *The Aramaeans in Aram Naharaim and the Rise of their States* (in Hebrew). Jerusalem, 1952.
31. Malamat, A. 'The Kingdom of David and Solomon in its contact with Aram Naharaim.' In *Bi. Ar.* 21 (1958), 96 ff.
32. Mazar, B. 'The Aramaean Empire and its relations with Israel.' In *Bi. Ar.* 25 (1962), 98 ff.
33. Meissner, B. 'Die Keilschrifttexte auf den steinernen Orthostaten und Statuen aus dem Tell Halaf.' In *Festschrift Max Freiherrn von Oppenheim*, 71 ff. Berlin, 1933.

34. Meriggi, P. 'Die längsten Bauinschriften in "hethitischen" Hieroglyphen nebst Glossar zu sämtlichen Texten.' In *M.V.A.G.* 39 (1934).
35. Meriggi, P. *Hieroglyphisch-Hethitisches Glossar* (2. Aufl.). Wiesbaden, 1962.
36. Moortgat, A. *Die bildende Kunst des alten Orients und die Bergvölker*. Berlin, 1932.
37. Moritz, B. 'Die Nationalität der Arumu-Stämme in Südost-Babylonien.' In *Paul Haupt Anniversary Volume* (Leipzig, 1926), 184 ff.
38. Oppenheim, Max von. *Der Tell Halaf*. Leipzig, 1931.
39. Pottier, E. *L'art hittite*, 1. Paris, 1920.
40. Schiffer, S. *Die Aramäer*. Leipzig, 1911.
41. Streck, M. 'Über die älteste Geschichte der Aramäer.' In *Klio*, 6 (1906), 185 ff.
42. Unger, Merrill F. *Israel and the Aramaeans of Damascus*. Grand Rapids, Michigan, 1957.
43. Weidner, E. F. 'Die Annalen des Königs Aššurbêlkala von Assyrien.' In *Arch. f. Or.* 6 (1930–1), 75 ff.
44. Woolley, L. and Barnett, R. D. *Carchemish*, III. London, 1952.

## CHAPTER XXXIV

### GENERAL

1. Albright, W. F. *From the Stone Age to Christianity*. Ed. 2. Baltimore, 1946.
2. Albright, W. F. 'Syrien, Phönizien und Palästina.' In *Historia Mundi*, vol. 2, 331 ff. München, 1953.
3. Albright, W. F. *Archaeology and the Religion of Israel*. Ed. 3. Baltimore, 1953.
4. Albright, W. F. *Recent Discoveries in Bible Lands*. Ed. 2. New York, 1955.
5. Albright, W. F. *The Archaeology of Palestine*. Revised and reprinted. Harmondsworth, 1960.
6. Albright, W. F. *The Biblical Period from Abraham to Ezra*. New York, Evanston, 1963.
7. Auerbach, E. *Wüste und Gelobtes Land*. Berlin, 1932.
8. Bright, J. *A History of Israel*. Philadelphia, 1959.
9. Burrows, M. *What mean these Stones?* New Haven, 1941.
10. Freedman, D. N. and Campbell, E. F. 'The Chronology of Israel and the Ancient Near East.' In *Essays W. F. Albright*, 203 ff. London, 1961.
11. Galling, K. *Biblisches Reallexikon*. Tübingen, 1937.
12. Gordon, C. H. *The World of the Old Testament*. New York, 1958.
13. Gordon, C. H. *Before the Bible*. London, 1962.
14. Gray, J. *Archaeology and the Old Testament World*. London, 1962.
15. Gressmann, H. *Altorientalische Texte zum Alten Testament*. Ed. 2. Berlin and Leipzig, 1926.
16. Gressmann, H. *Altorientalische Bilder zum Alten Testament*. Ed. 2. Berlin and Leipzig, 1927.
17. Grollenberg. L. H. *Atlas of the Bible*. London, 1956.
18. Herrmann, S. 'Das Werden Israels.' In *T.L.Z.* 87 (1962), 561 ff.
19. Kittel, R. *Geschichte des Volkes Israel*. Vol. 1, eds. 5–6. Gotha, 1923.
20. Kraeling, E. G. *Bible Atlas*. New York, 1961.
21. Kraus, H.-J. 'Israel.' In *Propyläen-Weltgeschichte* (eds. G. Mann and A. Heuss). Vol. 2, 237 ff. Berlin, 1962.

22. Lods, A. *Israel from its Beginnings to the Middle of the Eighth Century* (tr. S. H. Hooke). London, 1932.
23. May, H. G. *Oxford Bible Atlas*. London, 1962.
24. Meek, T. J. *Hebrew Origins*. Rev. ed. New York, 1950.
25. Meyer, Ed. *Die Israeliten und ihre Nachbarstämme*. Halle, 1906.
26. Neher, André and René. *Histoire biblique du peuple Israël*, I, II. Paris, 1962.
27. Noth, M. *The History of Israel*. Ed. 2, transl. revised by P. R. Ackroyd. London, 1961.
28. Noth, M. *Die Welt des Alten Testaments*. Ed. 4. Berlin, 1962.
29. Pritchard, J. B. *Ancient Near Eastern Texts relating to the Old Testament*. Ed. 2. Princeton, 1955.
30. Pritchard, J. B. *The Ancient Near East in Pictures relating to the Old Testament*. Princeton, 1954.
31. Pritchard, J. B. *Archaeology and the Old Testament*. Princeton, 1959.
32. Renckens, D. H. *De Godsdienst van Israël*. Roermond en Maaseik, 1962.
33. Robinson, Th. H. *A History of Israel*. I. *From the Exodus to the Fall of Jerusalem 586 B.C.* Oxford, 1932.
34. Rowley, H. H. *From Joseph to Joshua. Biblical Traditions in the Light of Archaeology*. London, 1950.
35. Stade, B. *Geschichte des Volkes Israel*, I. Giessen, 1887.
36. Thomas, D. Winton. *Documents from Old Testament Times*. Ed. 2. New York, 1961.
37. Vaux, R. de. *Ancient Israel* (tr. J. McHugh). London, 1961.
38. Watzinger, C. *Denkmäler Palästinas*. Leipzig, I, 1933; II, 1935.
39. Wellhausen, J. *Prolegomena zur Geschichte Israels*. Ed. 6. Berlin, 1905.
40. Wellhausen, J. *Israelitische und jüdische Geschichte*. Ed. 7. Berlin, 1914.
41. Wright, G. E. and Filson, F. V. *The Westminster Historical Atlas to the Bible*. Philadelphia, 1956.
42. Wright, G. E. *Biblical Archaeology*. Ed. 2. Philadelphia and London, 1962.
43. Pritchard, J. B. *The Ancient Near East: Supplementary Texts and Pictures relating to the Old Testament*. Princeton, 1955.
44. Ricciotti, G. *The History of Israel*. Transl. by C. della Petra and R. T. Murphy. 2 vols. Milwaukee, 1955.

I. THE LITERARY CHARACTER OF THE OLD TESTAMENT HISTORICAL BOOKS

1. Albers, E. *Die Quellenberichte in Josua i–xii. Beitrag zur Quellenkritik des Hexateuchs*. Bonn, 1891.
2. Benzinger, I. *Jahwist und Elohist in den Königsbüchern* (*Beitr. zur Wiss. vom A.T.* II, 2). Berlin, Leipzig and Stuttgart, 1921.
3. Budde, K. *Die Bücher Richter und Samuel. Ihre Quellen und ihr Aufbau*. Giessen, 1890.
4. Cornill, C. H. 'Zur Quellenkritik der Bücher Samuelis.' In *Königsberger Studien*, I (1887), 65–89.
5. Eissfeldt, O. *Die Quellen des Richterbuches*. Leipzig, 1925.
6. Eissfeldt, O. *Die Komposition der Samuelisbücher*. Leipzig, 1931.
7. Gurewicz, S. B. 'The Bearing of Judges i–ii. 5 on the Authorship of the Book of Judges.' In *Austral. Bibl. Rev.* 7 (1959), 37 ff.
8. Hölscher, G. 'Das Buch der Könige, seine Quellen und seine Redaktion.' In *Forsch. Rel. Lit.* 36, 1, 158 ff. Göttingen, 1923.
9. Jenni, E. 'Zwei Jahrzehnte Forschung an den Büchern Josua bis Könige.' In *Theol. Rundschau*, 27 (1961), 1 ff., 97 ff.

10. Jepsen, A. *Die Quellen des Königsbuches.* Ed. 2. Halle, 1956.
11. Kittel, R. 'Die pentateuchischen Urkunden in den Büchern Richter und Samuel.' In *Theol. St. Kr.* 65 (1892), 44 ff.
12. MacLaurin, E. C. B. *The Hebrew Theocracy in the Tenth to the Sixth Centuries. An Analysis of the Books of Judges, Samuel and Kings.* Sydney, 1953.
13. Mowinckel, S. *Zur Frage nach dokumentarischen Quellen in Josua 13–19* (*Avhandlinger Norske Videnskaps-Akad.* II, *Hist. Filos. Klasse.* 1946. No. 1). Oslo, 1946.
14. Noth, M. *Überlieferungsgeschichtliche Studien,* 1. *Die sammelnden und bearbeitenden Geschichtswerke.* Ed. 2. Stuttgart, 1960.
15. Noth, M. 'Überlieferungsgeschichtliches zur zweiten Hälfte des Josuabuches.' In *Nötscher-Festschrift,* 152 ff. Bonn, 1950.
16. Simpson, C. A. *Composition of the Book of Judges.* Oxford, 1957.
17. Smend, R. 'JE in den geschichtlichen Büchern des Alten Testaments.' In *Z.A.W.* 39 (1921), 181 ff.
18. Vriezen, Th. C. 'De Compositie van de Samuël-Boeken.' In *Orientalia Neerlandica* (1948), 167 ff.
19. Wallis, G. 'Die Anfänge des Königtums in Israel.' In *Wiss. Zeitschr. Halle,* 12 (1963), 239 ff.
20. Wiener, H. M. *The Composition of Judges i. 11 to I Kings ii. 46.* Leipzig, 1929.
21. Wiese, K. *Zur Literarkritik des Buches der Richter.* In Sprank, S. und Wiese, K., *Studien zu Ezechiel und dem Buch der Richter* (*Beitr. zur Wiss. vom. A. u. N.T.* III, 4). Stuttgart, 1926.
22. Winckler, H. 'Beiträge zur Quellenscheidung der Königsbücher.' In *Alttestamentliche Untersuchungen,* 1 ff. Leipzig, 1892.
23. Wright, G. E. 'The Literary and Historical Problem of Joshua 10 and Judges 1.' In *J.N.E.S.* 5 (1946), 105 ff.

## II. THE TRADITIONAL HISTORY AND MODERN CRITICISM

1. Auerbach, E. 'Untersuchungen zum Richterbuch.' In *Z.A.W.* 48 (1930), 286 ff.; 51 (1933), 47 ff.
2. Eissfeldt, O. *Geschichtsschreibung im Alten Testament. Ein kritischer Bericht über die neueste Literatur.* Berlin, 1948.
3. Hölscher, G. *Die Anfänge der hebräischen Geschichtsschreibung* (*Sitzungsb. Heidelberg,* 18, 2). Heidelberg, 1942.
4. Montgomery, J. A. 'Archival Data in the Book of Kings.' In *J. Bibl. Lit.* 53 (1934), 46 ff.
5. Rost, L. *Die Überlieferung von der Thronnachfolge Davids* (*Beitr. zur Wiss. vom A. u. N.T.* III, 6). Stuttgart, 1926.

## III. THE LAND SETTLEMENT

1. Aharoni, Y. 'Problems of the Israelite Conquest in the Light of Archaeological Discoveries.' In *Antiquity and Survival,* II, 2/3 (1957), 131 ff.
2. Albright, W. F. and others. 'Reports on Excavations at Bethel.' In *Bull. A.S.O.R.* 55 (1934); 56 (1934); 137 (1955); 151 (1958); 163 (1961); 164 (1962).
3. Alt, A. *Die Landnahme der Israeliten in Palästina.* In *Kleine Schriften,* I, 89 ff. München, 1953.
4. Alt, A. 'Josua.' In *Kleine Schriften,* I, 176 ff.. München, 1953.

5. Astour, M. 'Benê-Iamina et Jéricho.' In *Semitica*, 9 (1959), 5 ff.
6. Eissfeldt, O. 'Der geschichtliche Hintergrund der Erzählung von Gibeas Schandtat (Richter 19–21).' In *Kleine Schriften*, II, 64 ff. Tübingen, 1963.
7. Eissfeldt, O. 'Jahwe Zebaoth.' In *Misc. Ac. Berolinensia*, II, 2 (1950), 128 ff.
8. Eissfeldt, O. 'Lade und Stierbild.' In *Kleine Schriften*, II, 282 ff. Tübingen, 1963.
9. Eissfeldt, O. 'Jahwe, der Gott der Väter.' In *T.L.Z.* 88 (1963), 481 ff.
10. Eissfeldt, O. 'Jakobs Begegnung mit El und Moses Begegnung mit Jahwe.' In *O.L.Z.* 58 (1963), 325 ff.
11. Garstang, J. and J. B. E. *The Story of Jericho*. Ed. 2. London, 1948.
12. Grintz, Y. ' 'Ai which is beside Beth-Aven. A Re-examination of Identity of 'Ai.' In *Bib.* 42 (1961), 201 ff.
13. Hartmann, R. 'Zelt und Lade.' In *Z.A.W.* 37 (1917/18), 209 ff.
14. Kaufmann, Y. *The Biblical Account of the Conquest of Palestine*. Transl. from the Hebrew by H. Dagut. Jerusalem, 1953; on this Alt, A. 'Utopien.' In *T.L.Z.* 81 (1956), 521 ff.; Eissfeldt, O. 'Die Eroberung Palästinas durch Altisrael.' In *We. Or.* II, 2 (1955), 158 ff.
15. Kaufmann, Y. 'Traditions concerning Early Israelite History in Canaan.' In *Scripta Hieros.* VIII (1961), 302 ff.
16. Kelso, J. L. 'Excavations at Bethel.' In *Bi. Ar.* 19 (1956), 36 ff.
17. Kenyon, Kathleen M. 'Excavations at Jericho 1957–58.' In *P.E.Q.* 92 (1960), 86 ff., pls. VI–XII.
18. Lods, A. 'Les fouilles d'Aï et l'époque de l'entrée des Israëlites en Palestine.' In *Ann. Inst. phil. hist. or.* 4 (1936), 847 ff.
19. Maass, F. 'Hazor und das Problem der Landnahme.' In *Z.A.W.* Beiheft 77 (1958), 105 ff.
20. Malamat, A. 'Doctrines of Causality in Hittite and Biblical Historiography.' In *V.T.* 5 (1955), 1 ff.
21. Marquet-Krause, J. *Les fouilles de 'Ay (Et-Tell, 1933–35) (Bibl. arch. et hist.* XLV). Beyrouth and Paris, 1949.
22. Mendenhall, G. E. 'The Hebrew Conquest of Palestine.' In *Bi. Ar.* 25 (1962), 66 ff.
23. Möhlenbrink, K. 'Die Landnahmesage des Buches Josua.' In *Z.A.W.* 56 (1938), 238 ff.
24. Noth, M. 'Bethel und 'Ai.' In *P.J.B.* 31 (1935), 7 ff.
25. Noth, M. 'Beiträge zur Geschichte des Ostjordanlandes.' In *P.J.B.* 37 (1941), 50 ff.; *Z.A.W.* 60 (1944), 11 ff.; *Z.D.P.V.* 68 (1951), 1 ff.
26. Noth, M. 'Gilead und Gad.' In *Z.D.P.V.* 75 (1959), 14 ff.
27. Noth, M. 'Der Beitrag der Archäologie zur Geschichte Israels.' In *Suppl. to V.T.* VII (1960), 262 ff.
28. Pritchard, J. B. *Gibeon, Where the Sun Stood Still*. Princeton, 1962.
29. Pritchard, J. B. *The Bronze Age Cemetery at Gibeon* (Museum Monographs). Philadelphia, 1963.
30. Schmidt, H. 'Kerubenthron und Lade.' In *Forsch. Rel. Lit.* 36, 1 (1923), 120 f.
31. Schmidtke, J. *Die Einwanderung Israels in Kanaan*. Breslau, 1933.
32. Schunck, K.-D. *Benjamin. Untersuchungen zur Entstehung und Geschichte eines israelitischen Stammes (Z.A.W.* Beiheft 86). Berlin, 1963.
33. Schunck, K.-D. 'Erwägungen zur Geschichte und Bedeutung von Mahanaim.' In *Z.D.M.G.* 113 (1963), 34 ff.
34. Simons, J. 'Een opmerking over het 'Aj-problem.' In *J.E.O.L.* 9 (1940), 26 ff.
35. Soggin, J. A. 'Ancient Biblical Traditions and Modern Archaeological Discoveries.' In *Bi. Ar.* 23 (1960), 95 ff.

36. Soggin, J. A. 'La conquista israelitica della Palestina nei sec. XIII e XII e le scoperte archeologiche.' In *Protestantesimo*, 17 (1962), 193 ff.
37. Steuernagel, C. *Die Einwanderung der israelitischen Stämme in Kanaan*. Berlin, 1901.
38. Vaux, R. de. 'Exploration de la Région de Salṭ.' In *Rev. bibl.* 47 (1938), 398 ff., pls. XVII–XXIII.
39. Vincent, A. 'Jericho: une hypothèse.' In *M.U.S.J.* 37 (1957/58), 81 ff.
40. Wambacq, B. N. *L'épithète divine Jahvé Ṣᵉba'ôt*. Paris, 1947.
41. Wright, G. E. 'Epic of Conquest.' In *Bi. Ar.* 3 (1940), 26 ff.
42. Yadin, Y. 'Excavations at Hazor.' In *Bi. Ar.* 19 (1956), 2 ff.
43. Yadin, Y. 'Further Light on Biblical Hazor.' In *Bi. Ar.* 20 (1957), 34 ff.
44. Yadin, Y. *Hazor I. An Account of the First Season of Excavation, 1955*. Jerusalem, 1958.
45. Yadin, Y. *Hazor II. An Account of the Second Season of Excavations, 1956*. Jerusalem, 1960.

IV. THE TWELVE TRIBES

1. Alt, A. 'Die Staatenbildung der Israeliten in Palästina.' In *Kleine Schriften*, II, 1 ff. München, 1953.
2. Eissfeldt, O. '"Gut Glück!" in semitischer Namengebung.' In *J. Bibl. Lit.* 82 (1963), 195 ff.
3. Hoftijzer, J. 'Enige opmerkingen rond het israëlitische 12-stammensysteem.' In *Nederl. Theol. Tijdschrift*, 14 (1959/60), 241 ff.
4. Köhler, L. *Die hebräische Rechtsgemeinde*. Zürich, 1931.
5. Mowinckel, S. '"Rahelstämme" und "Leastämme".' In *Z.A.W.* Beiheft 77 (1958), 129 ff.
6. Noth, M. *Das System der zwölf Stämme Israels (Beitr. zur Wiss. vom A.u.N.T. 52)*. Stuttgart, 1930.
7. Orlinsky, H. M. 'The Tribal System of Israel and Related Groups in the Period of Judges.' In *Or. antiq.* 1 (1962), 11 ff.
8. Smend, R. *Jahwekrieg und Stämmebund (Forsch. Rel. Lit. 84)*. Göttingen, 1963.

V. THE PERIOD OF THE JUDGES

1. Albright, W. F. 'Historical Geography of Palestine.' In *Ann. A.S.O.R.* II/III (1923), 1 ff.
2. Albright, W. F. 'The Song of Deborah in the Light of Archaeology.' In *Bull. A.S.O.R.* 62 (1936), 265 ff.
3. Alt, A. 'Beth Anath.' In *P.J.B.* 22 (1926), 55 ff.
4. Alt, A. 'Die Ursprünge des israelitischen Rechts.' In *Kleine Schriften*, I, 278 ff. München, 1953.
5. Alt, A. 'Meros.' In *Z.A.W.* 58 (1940/41), 240 ff.
6. Alt, A. 'Megiddo im Übergang vom kanaanäischen zum israelitischen Zeitalter.' In *Z.A.W.* 60 (1944), 67 ff.
7. †Alt, A. (Bach, R.). 'Israel. 1. Geschichte.' In *Religion in Geschichte und Gegenwart*, III. Ed. 3, 936 ff. Tübingen, 1959.
8. Davies, H. G. 'Judges viii. 22–23.' In *V.T.* 13 (1963), 151 ff.
9. Dus, J. 'Die "Sufeten Israels".' In *Arch. Orient.* 31 (1963), 444 ff.
10. Fensham, F. C. 'The Judges and Ancient Israelite Jurisprudence.' In *Die Ou Testamentiese Werkgemeenskap Pretoria*, 1959, 15 ff. Pretoria, 1960.
11. Grether, O. 'Die Bezeichnung "Richter" für die charismatischen Helden der vorstaatlichen Zeit.' In *Z.A.W.* 57 (1939), 110 ff.

12. Grether, O. *Das Deboralied*. Gütersloh, 1941.

13. Hertzberg, H. W. 'Die kleinen Richter.' In *T.L.Z.* 79 (1954), 285 ff.

14. Kraus, H. J. *Die prophetische Verkündigung des Rechtes in Israel (Theol. Stud.*, 51). Basel, 1957.

15. Kraus, H. J. *Gottesdienst in Israel* (Sachregister Zwölfstämmeverband). Ed. 2. München, 1962.

16. Malamat, A. 'Cushan Rishathaim and the Decline of the Near East around 1200 B.C.' In *J.N.E.S.* 13 (1954), 231 ff.

17. Nielsen, E. 'La guerre considerée comme une religion et la religion comme une guerre. Du chant de Deborah au rouleau de la guerre de Qoumran.' In *Studia Theologica*, 15 (1961), 93 ff.

18. Noth, M. 'Das Amt des "Richters Israels".' In *Festschrift Bertholet*, 404 ff. Tübingen, 1950.

19. Rowton, M. B. 'The Early Period of the Judges in Israel.' In *Chronology (C.A.H.* 1², ch. VI, sect. 11). Cambridge, 1963.

20. Sellin, E. 'Das Deboralied.' In *Procksch-Festschrift*, 149 ff. Leipzig, 1941.

21. van Selms, A. 'The Title "Judge".' In *OuTestamentiese Werkgemeenskap*, Pretoria, 1959, 41 ff. Pretoria, 1960.

22. Täubler, E. 'Cushan-Rishataim.' In *H.U.C.A.* 20 (1942), 137 ff.

23. Täubler, E. *Biblische Studien. Die Epoche der Richter*. Tübingen, 1958.

24. Vollborn, W. 'Der Richter Israels.' In *Rendtorff-Festschrift*, 21 ff. Berlin, 1958.

25. Vollborn, W. 'Die Chronologie des Richterbuches.' In *Baumgärtel-Festschrift*, 192 ff. Erlangen, 1959.

26. Walz, R. 'Neue Untersuchungen zum Domestikationsproblem der altweltlichen Cameliden.' In *Z.D.M.G.* 104 (1954), 45 ff.

27. Weiser, A. 'Das Deboralied. Eine gattungs- und traditionsgeschichtliche Studie.' In *Z.A.W.* 71 (1959), 67 ff.

28. Wright, G. E. 'Archaeological Observations on the Period of the Judges and the Early Monarchy.' In *J. Bibl. Lit.* 60 (1941), 27 ff.

29. Yeivin, S. 'Topographic and Ethnic Notes. II E. The Five Cushite Clans in Canaan.' In *'Atiqot*, 3 (1961), 176 ff.

## VI. CANAAN AND ISRAEL

1. Albright, W. F. 'The Babylonian Matter in the pre-Deuteronomic Primeval History (JE) in Gen. i–xi.' In *J. Bibl. Lit.* 58 (1939), 91 ff.

2. Albright, W. F. 'The Role of the Canaanites in the History of Civilization.' In *Essays W. F. Albright*, 328 ff. London, 1961.

3. Albright, W. F. 'An Archaic Hebrew Proverb in an Amarna Letter from Central Palestine.' In *Bull. A. S.O.R.* 89 (1943), 29 ff.

4. Albright, W. F. 'The Old Testament and Canaanite Language and Literature.' In *Cath. Bibl. Quart.* 7 (1945), 5 ff.

5. Albright, W. F. 'The Early Alphabetic Inscriptions from Sinai and their Decipherment.' In *Bull. A.S.O.R.* 110 (1948), 6 ff.

6. Albright, W. F. 'Some Canaanite-Phoenician Sources of Hebrew Wisdom.' Suppl. to *V.T.* III (1955), 1 ff.

7. Albright, W. F. 'Archaic Survivals in the Text of Canticles.' In *Studies G. R. Driver*, 1 ff. Oxford, 1963.

8. Alt, A. 'Die Weisheit Salomos.' In *Kleine Schriften*, II, 90 ff. München, 1953.

9. Amiet, P. *La Glyptique mésopotamienne archaïque*. Paris, 1961.

10. Amiet, P. 'La Glyptique syrienne archaïque. Notes sur la diffusion de la civilisation mésopotamienne en Syrie du Nord.' In *Syria*, 40 (1963), 57 ff. Pls. V–VI.

11. Barnett, R. D. *A Catalogue of the Nimrud Ivories with Other Examples of Ancient Near Eastern Ivories in the British Museum*. London, 1957.

12. Bauer, H. and Leander, P. *Historische Grammatik der Hebräischen Sprache des Alten Testaments*. Halle, 1922. (Hildesheim, 1962 : Reprograf. Nachdruck.)

13. Baumgartner, W. *Israelitische und altorientalische Weisheit*. Tübingen, 1933.

14. Baumgartner, W. 'Was wir heute von der hebräischen Sprache und ihrer Geschichte wissen.' In *Zum A.T. und seiner Umwelt*, 208 ff. Leiden, 1959.

15. Böhl, F. M. Th. *Die Sprache der Amarna-Briefe*. Leipzig, 1909.

16. Böhl, F. M. Th. *Kanaanäer und Hebräer (Beitr. zur Wiss. vom A.T. 9)*. Leipzig, 1911.

17. Brongers, H. A. *Oud-Oosters en Bijbels Recht*. Nijkerk, 1960.

18. Cross, F. M. 'The Evolution of the Proto-Canaanite Alphabet.' In *Bull. A.S.O.R.* 134 (1954), 15 ff.

19. Cross, F. M. 'A Ugaritic Abecedary and the origins of the Proto-Canaanite Alphabet.' In *Bull. A.S.O.R.* 160 (1960), 21 ff.

20. Crowfoot, J. W. and G. *Early Ivories from Samaria*. London, 1938.

21. Dahood, M. J. *Proverbs and Northwest Semitic Philology*. Roma, 1963.

22. Descamps de Merzenfeld, C. *Inventaire commenté des ivoires phéniciens et apparentés découvertes dans le Proche-Orient*. Texte et Album. Paris, 1954.

23. Dhorme, É. 'La langue de Canaan.' In *Recueil É. Dhorme*, 405 ff. and 766. Paris, 1951.

24. Diringer, D. 'Early Hebrew Writing.' In *Bi. Ar.* 13 (1950), 74 ff.

25. Diringer, D. *Writing*. London, 1962.

26. Driver, G. R. *Semitic Writing, from Pictograph to Alphabet (The Schweich Lectures of the British Academy, 1944)*. Rev. ed. London, 1954.

27. Dussaud, R. *Les origines cananéennes du sacrifice israélite* Ed. 2. Paris, 1941.

28. Dussaud, R. *Les découvertes de Ras Shamra et l'Ancien Testament*. Ed. 2. Paris, 1941.

29. Dussaud, R. *L'art Phénicien du IIe millenaire*. Paris, 1949.

30. Ebeling, E. *Das Verbum der el-Amarna-Briefe (B.A. VIII, 2)*. Leipzig, 1910.

31. Eissfeldt, O. 'Gabelhürden im Ostjordanland.' In *Forsch u. Fortschr.* 25 (1949), 9 ff.

32. Eissfeldt, O. 'Zur Deutung von Motiven auf den 1937 gefundenen phönikischen Elfenbeinarbeiten von Megiddo.' In *Forsch. u. Fortschr.* 26 (1950), 1 ff.

33. Fichtner, J. *Die altorientalische Weisheit in ihrer israelitisch-jüdischen Ausprägung (Z.A.W. Beiheft 62)*. Giessen, 1933.

34. Finet, A. *L'Accadien des lettres de Mari (Ac. R. de Belgique, 2e serie, Tome LI, 1, 1956)*.

35. Gardiner, A. H. *The Library of A. Chester Beatty. Description of a Hieratic Papyrus with a Mythological Story, Love Songs, and other Miscellaneous Texts (The Chester Beatty Papyri, 1, no. 1)*. London, 1931.

36. Gordon, C. H. *Ugaritic Handbook*. Roma, 1947.

37. Gray, J. *The Legacy of Canaan. The Ras Shamra Texts and their Relevance to the O.T.* (Suppl. to *V.T.* v). Leiden, 1957.

38. Guillaume, A. *Prophecy and Divination among the Hebrews and other Semites*. London, 1938.

39. Haldar, A. *Association of the Cult Prophets among the Ancient Semites*. Uppsala, 1945.

40. Harris, Z. S. *Development of the Canaanite Dialects (American Oriental Series, vol. 16)*. New Haven, 1939.

41. Hölscher, G. *Die Profeten*. Leipzig, 1914.

42. Horst, F. 'Recht und Religion im Bereich des Alten Testaments.' In *Gottes Recht*, 260 ff. München, 1961.
43. Hyatt, J. Ph. 'The Writing of an Old Testament Book.' In *Bi. Ar.* 6 (1943), 71 ff.
44. Jacob, E. *Ras Shamra et l'Ancient Testament (Cahiers d'Archéologie Biblique*, no. 12). Neuchâtel, 1960.
45. Jepsen, A. 'Die Hebräer und ihr Recht.' In *Arch. f. Or.* 15 (1945/51), 55 ff.
46. Jepsen, A. 'Kanaanäisch und Hebräisch.' In *XXV Int. Congr. Or.* 1, 316 ff. Moskau, 1962.
47. Jirku, A. *Altorientalischer Kommentar zum Alten Testament*. Leipzig und Erlangen, 1923.
48. Johnson, A. R. *The Cultic Prophet in Ancient Israel*. Ed. 2. Cardiff, 1962.
49. Kjaer, H. 'The Excavation of Shilo.' In *J.P.O.S.* 10 (1930), 87 ff.
50. Kjaer, H. *I det hellige Land. De danske Udgravinger i Shilo*. København, 1931.
51. Knight, H. *The Hebrew Prophetic Consciousness*. London, 1948.
52. Lindblom, J. 'Zur Frage des kanaanäischen Ursprungs des altorientalischen Prophetismus.' In *Z.A.W.* Beiheft 77 (1958), 89 ff.
53. Loud, G. *The Megiddo Ivories (O.I.P.* LII). Chicago, 1939.
54. Loundine, A. 'Sur le titre *mlk* "roi" en Arabie du sud vers le milieu du premier millénaire avant notre ère' (Russian with French summary). In *Instituta Naradov Asii*, 46 (1962), 220ff.
55. Malamat, A. '"Prophecy" in the Mari Documents' (Hebrew with English summary). In *Eretz-Israel*, 4 (1956), 74 ff. and 81 ff.
56. Malamat, A. 'History and Prophetic Vision in a Mari Letter' (Hebrew with English summary). In *Eretz-Israel*, 5 (1958), 67 ff. and 86*–87*.
57. Marty, J. 'Contribution à l'étude de fragments épistolaires antiques, conservés principalement dans la Bible Hébraïque. Les formules de salutation.' In *Mél. Dussaud*, II, 845 ff. Paris, 1939.
58. Matthiae, P. *Ars Syra. Arte figurativa siriana nelle età del Medio et Tardo Bronzo*. Roma, 1962.
59. Mendenhall, G. E. *Law and Covenant in Israel and the Ancient Near East*. Pittsburgh, 1955.
60. Moscati, S. *L'epigrafia ebraica antica 1935–1950*. Roma, 1952.
61. Moscati, S. *Stato e problemi dell'epigrafia ebraica antica (Atti dell'Accad. Fiorentina di Scienze Morali*, 1952).
62. Mowinckel, S. *Psalmenstudien III. Kultprophetie und prophetische Psalmen*. Kristiania, 1923, 1961.
63. Mowinckel, S. 'General Oriental and Specific Israelite Elements in the Israelite Conception of the Sacral Kingdom.' In Suppl. to *Numen*, IV (1959), 283 ff.
64. Mowinckel, S. *The Psalms in Israel's Worship*, II. Oxford, 1962.
65. Müller, W. M. (ed.). *Die Liebespoesie der alten Ägypter*. Leipzig, 1899.
66. Noth, M. 'Gott, König und Volk im Alten Testament.' In *Gesammelte Studien zum A.T.*, ed. 2, 188 ff. München, 1960.
67. Noth, M. 'Mari und Israel. Eine Personennamenstudie.' In *Beitr. z. Hist. Theol.* 16 (1953), 127 ff.
68. Noth, M. *Die Ursprünge des alten Israel im Lichte neuer Quellen (Veröffentl. d. Arbeitsgemeinschaft f. Forschung d. Landes Nordrhein-Westfalen*, 94). Köln, Opladen, 1961.
69. O'Callaghan, R. T. 'Echoes of Canaanite Literature in the Psalms.' In *V.T.* 4 (1954), 164 ff.
70. Oesterley, W. O. E. and Robinson, Th. H. *Hebrew Religion*. London, 1930.
71. Paterson, J. *The Wisdom of Israel*. London, 1960.
72. Patton, J. H. *Canaanite Parallels in the Book of Psalms*. Baltimore, 1944.

73. Puukko, A. F. Die altassyrischen und hethitischen Gesetze und das Alte Testament.' In *Studia Orientalia*, 1 (1925), 125 ff.
74. Rhodokanakis, N. 'Das öffentliche Leben in den alten südarabischen Staaten.' In *Handbuch der altarabischen Altertumskunde*, hrsg. von D. Nielsen, 1, 109 ff. Leipzig, 1927.
75. Ridderbos, N. H. *Israels Profetie en 'Profetie' buiten Israel.* Delft, 1955.
76. Ryckmans, G. 'Rites et Croyances pré-islamiques.' In *Muséon*, 55 (1942), 165 ff.
77. Schott, S. *Altägyptische Liebeslieder.* Zürich, 1950.
78. Sellers, O. R. 'Musical Instruments of Israel.' In *Bi. Ar.* 4 (1941), 33 ff.
79. Smith, J. P. M. *The Origin and History of Hebrew Law.* Chicago, 1960.
80. Story, C. J. K. 'The Book of Proverbs and North-West Semitic Literature.' In *J. Bibl. Lit.* 64 (1949), 319 ff.
81. Thomas, D. W. 'The Language of the Old Testament.' In *Record and Revelation*, 1938, 324 ff.
82. Ullendorff, E. 'Ugaritic Studies within their Semitic and Eastern Mediterranean Setting.' In *Bull. Ryl. Libr.* 46 (1963/64), 236 ff.

VII. WARS WITH THE PHILISTINES AND CHOICE OF A KING

1. Albright, W. F. 'Historical Adjustments in the Concept of Sovereignty in the Near East.' In *Approaches to World Peace*, 1 ff. New York, 1944.
2. Alt, A. 'Gibeon und Beeroth.' In *P.J.B.* 22 (1926), 11 ff.
3. Alt, A. 'Zur Geschichte von Beth-Sean, 1500–1000 v. Chr.' In *Kleine Schriften*, 1, 246 ff. München, 1953.
4. Alt, A. 'Gitthaim.' In *P.J.B.* 35 (1939), 100 ff.
5. Alt, A. 'Ägyptische Tempel in Palästina und die Landnahme der Philister.' In *Kleine Schriften*, 1, 216 ff. München, 1953.
6. Ap-Thomas, D. R. 'Saul's "Uncle".' In *V.T.* 11 (1961), 241 ff.
7. Buccellati, G. 'Da Saul a David. Le origini della monarchia israelitica alla luce della storiografia contemporanea.' In *Bibbia e Oriente*, 1 (1959), 99 ff.
8. Cornill, C. H. 'Ein elohistischer Bericht über die Entstehung des israelitischen Königtums in I Samuelis 1–15 aufgezeigt.' In *Z. f. Kirchl. Wiss. u. Kirchl. Leben*, 6 (1885), 113 ff.
9. Cornill, C. H. 'Noch einmal Sauls Königswahl und Verwerfung.' In *Z.A.W.* 10 (1890), 96 ff.
10. Dothan, T. 'Archaeological Reflections on the Philistine Problem.' In *Antiquity and Survival*, 11, 2/3 (1957), 151 ff.
11. Dupont-Sommer, A. *Les Araméens.* Paris, 1949.
12. Eissfeldt, O. 'Israelitisch-philistäische Grenzverschiebungen von David bis auf die Assyrerzeit.' In *Kleine Schriften*, 11, 453 ff. Tübingen, 1963.
13. Eissfeldt, O. *Das Lied Moses Deuteronomium 32, 1–43 und das Lehrgedicht Asaphs Psalm 78 samt einer Analyse der Umgebung des Mose-Liedes (Berichte der Akademie Leipzig, 104, 5).* Berlin, 1958.
14. Engnell, I. *Studies in Divine Kingship in the Ancient Near East.* Uppsala, 1943.
15. Forrer, E. 'Aramu.' In *R.L.A.* 1 (1932), 131 ff.
16. Frankfort, H. *Kingship and the Gods. A Study of Near Eastern Religion as the Integration of Society and Nation.* Chicago, 1948.
17. Gadd, C. J. *Ideas of Divine Rule in the Ancient East.* London, 1948.
18. Galling, K. *Die israelitische Staatsverfassung in ihrer vorderorientalischen Umwelt (Alte Or. 28, 3/4).* Leipzig, 1929.
19. Irwin, W. A. 'Samuel and the Rise of Monarchy.' In *A.J.S.L.* 58 (1941), 113 ff.

20. Junge, E. *Der Wiederaufbau des Heerwesens des Reiches Juda unter Josia* (*Beitr. zur Wiss. vom A. u. N.T.* 75). Stuttgart, 1937.

21. Malamat, A. 'The Kingdom of David and Solomon in its Contacts with Egypt and Aram Naharaim.' In *Bi. Ar.* 21 (1958), 96 ff.

22. Mazar, B. 'The Aramean Empire and its Relations with Israel.' In *Bi. Ar.* 25 (1962), 98 ff.

23. Möhlenbrink, K. 'Sauls Ammoniterfeldzug und Samuels Beitrag zum Königtum des Saul.' In *Z.A.W.* 58 (1940/41), 57 ff.

24. Noth, M. 'Das Reich von Hamath als Grenznachbar des Reiches Israel.' In *P.J.B.* 33 (1937), 36 ff.

25. O'Callaghan, R. T. *Aram Naharaim. A Contribution to the History of Upper Mesopotamia in the Second Millennium B.C.* Roma, 1948.

26. Rowe, A. *The Topography and History of Beth-Shan* (*Publications of the Palestine Section of the Museum of the University of Pennsylvania*, 1). Philadelphia, 1930.

27. Ryckmans, G. 'Le *qayl* en Arabie méridionale préislamique.' In *Studies G. R. Driver*, 144 ff. Oxford, 1963.

28. Weiser, A. *Samuel. Seine geschichtliche Aufgabe und religiöse Bedeutung* (*Forsch. Rel. Lit.* 81). Göttingen, 1962.

29. Wildberger, H. 'Samuel und die Entstehung des israelitischen Königtums.' In *Theol. Zeitschr.* 13 (1957), 442 ff.

30. Willesen, F. 'The Philistine Corps of the Scimitar from Gath.' In *J.S.S.* 3 (1958), 327 ff.

31. Wright, G. E. 'I Samuel 13: 19–22.' In *Bi. Ar.* 6 (1943), 33 ff.

32. Wright, G. E. 'Philistine Coffins and Mercenaries.' In *Bi. Ar.* 22 (1959), 54 ff.

VIII. DAVID

1. Alt, A. 'Jerusalems Aufstieg.' In *Kleine Schriften*, III, 243 ff. München, 1959.

2. Alt, A. 'Das Gottesurteil auf dem Karmel.' In *Kleine Schriften*, II, 135 ff. München, 1953.

3. Ap-Thomas, D. R. 'Excavations in Jerusalem (Jordan).' In *Z.A.W.* 74 (1962), 321 f.

4. Begrich, J. 'Sofēr und Mazkīr.' In *Z.A.W.* 58 (1940/41), 1 ff.

5. Caquot, A. 'La prophetie de Nathan et ses échos lyriques.' In Suppls. to *V.T.* IX (1963), 210 ff.

6. Crowfoot, J. W. and FitzGerald, G. M. *Excavations in the Tyropoion Valley* (*P.E.F. Annual*, v). London, 1929.

7. Donner, H. 'Der "Freund des Königs".' In *Z.A.W.* 73 (1961), 269 ff.

8. Eissfeldt, O. 'Ein gescheiterter Versuch der Wiedervereinigung Israels (2 Sam. 2, 12–3, 1).' In *N.C.* 3 (1951), 110 ff.

9. Eissfeldt, O. 'Noch einmal: Ein gescheiterter Versuch der Wiedervereinigung Israels.' In *N.C.* 4 (1952), 55 ff.

10. Glueck, N. *The Other Side of the Jordan.* New Haven, 1940.

11. Gressmann, H. *Der Messias* (*Forsch. Rel. Lit.* 43). Göttingen, 1929, 1 ff.

12. Gunkel, H. and Begrich, J. *Einleitung in die Psalmen.* Göttingen, 1933.

13. Jepsen, A. 'Israel und Damaskus.' In *Arch. f. Or.* 14 (1941/44), 153 ff.

14. Kenyon, K. M. 'Excavations in Jerusalem, 1961.' In *P.E.Q.* 94 (1962), 72 ff., pls. XVII–XXV.

15. Kenyon, K. M. 'Excavations in Jerusalem, 1962.' In *P.E.Q.* 95 (1963), 7 ff., pls. I–X.

16. Krauss, S. 'Moriah-Ariel.' In *P.E.Q.* 79 (1947), 45 ff. and 102 ff.
17. Kutsch, E. 'Die Dynastie von Gottes Gnaden.' In *Z. f. Theol. u. Kirche*, 58 (1961), 137 ff.
18. Macalister, R. A. S. and Duncan, J. G. *Excavations on the Hill of Ophel* (*P.E.F. Annual*, iv). London, 1926.
19. McKenzie, J. L. 'The Dynastic Oracle: II Sam. 7.' In *Theol. Stud.* 8 (1947), 187 ff.
20. Malamat, A. 'Aspects of the Foreign Policies of David and Solomon.' In *J.N.E.S.* 22 (1963), 1 ff.
21. Mazar, B. 'David's Reign in Hebron and the Conquest of Jerusalem.' In *Essays H. Silver*, 235 ff. New York and London, 1963.
22. Mendelsohn, I. 'State Slavery in Ancient Palestine.' In *Bull. A.S.O.R.* 85 (1942), 14 ff.
23. Mendelsohn, I. *Slavery in the Ancient Near East.* New York, 1949.
24. Morgenstern, J. 'Amos Studies, III.' In *H.U.C.A.* 15 (1940), 59 ff.
25. Noth, M. 'David und Israel in 2 Samuel 7.' In *Gesammelte Studien zum A.T.* Ed. 2, 334 ff. München, 1960.
26. Reventlow, H. 'Das Amt des Mazkir.' In *Theol. Zeitschr.* 15 (1959), 161 ff.
27. Ryckmans, J. *L'institution monarchique en Arabie méridionale avant l'Islam* (Ma'în et Saba). Louvain, 1951.
28. Stoebe, H. J. 'Die Einnahme Jerusalems und der Ṣinnor.' In *Z.D.P.V.* 73 (1957), 73 ff.
29. Vaux, R. de. 'Titres et fonctionnaires égyptiens à la cour de David et de Salomon.' In *Rev. bibl.* 48 (1939), 394 ff.
30. Weill, R. *La Cité de David: Compte rendu des fouilles exécutées à Jérusalem, sur le site de la ville primitive. Campagne de 1913–1914.* Paris, 1920.
31. Weill, R. *La Cité de David, etc. Campagne de 1923–1924* (*Bibl. arch. et hist.*, tome 44). Paris, 1947.
32. Yeivin, S. 'The Sepulchres of the Kings of the House of David.' In *J.N.E.S.* 7 (1948), 30 ff.

IX. SOLOMON

1. Aharoni, Y. 'Recent Discoveries in the Sinai Peninsula. A Preliminary Note: I. Results of the Archaeological Investigations.' In *Antiquity and Survival*, ii, 2/3 (1957), 287 ff.
2. Albright, W. F. 'The Administrative Divisions of Israel and Judah.' In *J.P.O.S.* 5 (1925), 25 ff.
3. Albright, W. F. 'Two Cressets from Marisa and the Pillars of Jachin and Boaz.' In *Bull. A.S.O.R.* 85 (1942), 18 ff.
4. Alt, A. 'Israels Gaue unter Salomo.' In *Kleine Schriften*, ii, 76 ff. München, 1953.
5. Alt, A. 'Judas Gaue unter Josia.' In *Kleine Schriften*, ii, 276 ff. München, 1953.
6. Alt, A. 'Verbreitung und Herkunft des syrischen Tempeltypus.' In *Kleine Schriften*, ii, 100 ff. München, 1953.
7. Auerbach, E. 'Die Herkunft der Ṣadoḳiden.' In *Z.A.W.* 49 (1931), 327 ff.
8. van Beek, G. W. 'South Arabian History and Archaeology.' In *Essays W. F. Albright*, 229 ff. London, 1961.
9. Bentzen, A. *Studier over det Zadokidiske Praesterskabs Historie.* København, 1931.
10. Bentzen, A. 'Zur Geschichte der Ṣadoḳiden.' In *Z.A.W.* 51 (1933), 173 ff.
11. Chastel, A. 'La Légende de la Reine de Saba.' In *Rev. hist. rel.* 119 (1939), 204 ff.; 120 (1939), 27 ff., 160 ff.
12. Dunand, M. et Duru, R. *'Oumm el-'Amed. Texte et Atlas.* Paris, 1962.

13. Eissfeldt, O. *Tempel und Kulte syrischer Städte in hellenistisch-römischer Zeit.* Leipzig, 1941.
14. Eissfeldt, O. 'Silo und Jerusalem.' In Suppl. to *V.T.* IV (1960), 138 ff.
15. Garber, P. L. 'Reconstructing Solomon's Temple.' In *Bi. Ar.* 14 (1951), 2 ff.
16. Garber, P. L. 'Reconsidering the Reconstruction of Solomon's Temple.' In *J. Bibl. Lit.* 77 (1958), 123 ff.
17. Hauer, C. E. 'Who was Zadok?' In *J. Bibl. Lit.* 82 (1963), 89 ff.
18. Heathcote, A. W. *Israel to the Time of Solomon.* London, 1960.
19. Herbig, R. 'Das archäologische Bild des Puniertums.' In *Rom und Karthago,* hrsg. von J. Vogt, 139 ff. Leipzig, 1943.
20. Liver, J. 'The Chronology of Tyre at the Beginning of the First Millennium B.C.' In *I.E.J.* 3 (1953), 113 ff.
21. Macalister, R. A. S. *The Excavations of Gezer, 1902–5 and 1907–9,* 3 vols. London, 1912.
22. McEwan, C. W. 'The Syrian Expedition of the Oriental Institute.' In *A.J.A.* (1937), 8 ff.
23. Maisler, B. 'Two Hebrew Ostraca from Tell Qasîle.' In *J.N.E.S.* 10 (1951), 265 ff., pls. XI f.
24. Mashal, Z. 'A Casemate Wall at Ezion-Geber' [Hebrew with English summary]. In *Bull. I.E.S.* 25 (1961), 157 ff. and III.
25. May, H. G. 'The Two Pillars before the Temple of Solomon.' In *Bull. A.S.O.R.* 88 (1942), 19 ff.
26. Möhlenbrink, K. *Der Tempel Salomos (Beitr. zur Wiss. vom A. u. N.T.* 59). Stuttgart, 1932.
27. Myres, J. L. 'King Solomon's Temple and Other Buildings and Works of Art.' In *P.E.Q.* 80 (1948), 14 ff.
28. Parrot, A. *Le Temple de Jérusalem.* Neuchâtel and Paris, 1954.
29. Perowne, S. 'Note on I Kings X.1–13.' In *P.E.Q.* 71 (1939), 199 ff.
30. Pirenne, J. *Le Royaume Sud-Arabe de Qatabân et sa Datation d'après l'Archéologie et les Sources Classiques jusqu'au Périple de la Mer Erythrée (Bibl. du Muséon,* 48). Louvain, 1961.
31. Rothenberg, B. '"Cadès Barné".' In *Bible et Terre Sainte,* 32 (1960), 4 ff.
32. Rothenberg, B. 'Ancient Copper Industries in the Western Arabah. An Archaeological Survey of the Arabah, Part I. Appendix I by Y. Aharoni, Appendix II by B. H. McLeod.' In *P.E.Q.* 94 (1962), 5 ff., pls. I–XVI.
33. Rowley, H. H. 'Zadok and Nehushtan.' In *J. Bibl. Lit.* 68 (1939), 113 ff.
34. Rowley, H. H. 'Melchizedek and Zadok (Gen. 14 and Psalm 110).' In *Bertholet-Festschrift,* 461 ff. Tübingen, 1950.
35. Ryckmans, J. 'Petites royaumes sud-arabes d'après les auteurs classiques.' In *Muséon,* 70 (1957), 75 ff.
36. Schmidt, H. *Der heilige Fels in Jerusalem.* Tübingen, 1933.
37. Schreiden, K. 'Les enterprises navales du roi Salomon.' In *Ann. Inst. phil. hist. or.* 13 (1955), 587 ff.
38. Scott, R. B. Y. 'The Pillars Jachin and Boaz.' In *J. Bibl. Lit.* 68 (1939), 143 ff.
39. Smith, Sidney. 'Timber and Brick or Masonry Construction.' In *P.E.Q.* 83 (1941), 5 ff.
40. Tadmor, H. 'Que and Muṣri.' In *I.E.J.* 11 (1961), 143 ff.
41. Thieberger, F. *Le roi Salomon et son temps. Un des carrefours de l'histoire.* Paris, 1957.
42. Ullendorff, E. 'The Queen of Sheba.' In *Bull. Ryl. Libr.* 45 (1962/63), 486 ff.
43. Vaux, R. de. 'Nouvelles recherches dans la région de Cadès I–IV.' In *Rev. bibl.* 47 (1938), 89 ff., pl. VIII.

44. Vincent, H. *Jérusalem de l'Ancien Testament*, II, III. Paris, 1956.
45. Vincent, H. 'Le caractère du temple Salomonien.' In *Mél. Bibl. A. Robert*, 137 ff. Paris, 1957.
46. Williams, M. V. S. 'Palestinian Temples.' In *Iraq*, 11 (1949), 77 ff., pl. XXXIII.
47. Wright, G. E. 'Solomon's Temple resurrected.' In *Bi. Ar.* 4 (1941), 17 ff.
48. Wright, G. E. 'A Solomonic City Gate at Gezer.' In *Bi. Ar.* 21 (1958), 103 f.
49. Wright, G. E. 'More on King Solomon's Mines.' In *Bi. Ar.* 24 (1961), 59 ff.
50. Yadin, Y. 'Solomon's City Wall and Gate at Gezer.' In *I.E.J.* 8 (1958), 80 ff.
51. Yadin, Y. 'New Light on Solomon's Megiddo.' In *Bi. Ar.* 23 (1960), 62 ff.
52. Yeivin, S. 'Jachin and Boaz.' In *P.E.Q.* 91 (1959), 6 ff.

## CHAPTER XXXV

### I. THE LAST RAMESSIDES

1. Beckerath, J. von. *Tanis und Theben* (*Ägyptol. Forsch.* 16). Glückstadt–Hamburg–New York, 1951.
2. Botti, G. and Peet, T. E. *Il giornale della necropoli di Tebe*. Turin, 1928.
3. Breasted, J. H. *Ancient Records of Egypt, Historical Documents* (*Ancient Records*, 2nd Series), 4: *The Twentieth to the Twenty-sixth Dynasties*. Chicago, 1906.
4. Lord Carnarvon and Carter, H. *Five Years' Exploration at Thebes*. London, 1912.
5. Carter, H. and Gardiner, A. H. 'The Tomb of Ramesses IV and the Turin Plan of a Royal Tomb.' In *J.E.A.* 4 (1917), 130–58.
6. Černý, J. *Catalogue des ostraca hiératiques non littéraires de Deir el Médineh* ( = *Documents de fouilles Inst. fr. Caire*, 3, 4, 5, 6, 7), 5 vols. Cairo, 1935–51.
7. Černý, J. 'Datum des Todes Ramses' III. und der Thronbesteigung Ramses' IV.' In *Z.Ä.S.* 72 (1936), 109–18.
8. Černý, J. *Ostraca hiératiques* (*C.C.G.* nos. 25501–832), 2 vols. Cairo, 1935.
9. Černý, J. 'Queen Ese of the Twentieth Dynasty and her Mother.' In *J.E.A.* 44 (1958), 31–7.
10. Černý, J. and Gardiner, A. H. *Hieratic Ostraca*, 1. Oxford, 1957.
11. Couyat, J. and Montet, P. *Les inscriptions hiéroglyphiques et hiératiques du Ouâdi Hammâmât* ( = *Mém. Inst. fr. Caire*, 34). Cairo, 1912.
12. Christophe, L. 'Quatre enquêtes ramessides.' In *Bull. Inst. d'Ég.* 37 (1956), 5–37.
13. Christophe, L. 'Ramsès IV et le musée du Caire.' In *Cahiers d'histoire égyptienne*, series III (Cairo, 1950), 47 ff.
14. Christophe, L. 'La stèle de l'an III de Ramsès IV au Ouâdi Hammâmât (No. 12).' In *Bull. Inst. fr. Caire*, 48 (1949), 1–38.
15. Christophe, L. 'Sur deux textes de Ramsès IV, Inscription No. 86 du Ouâdi Hammâmât.' In *Ann. Serv.* 48 (1948), 151–4.
16. Daressy, G. *Ostraca* (*C.C.G.* nos. 25001–385). Cairo, 1901.
17. Daressy, G. 'Remarques et notes.' In *Rec. trav.* 11 (1889), 79–95.
18. Dévéria, Th. *Le papyrus judiciaire de Turin et les papyrus Lee et Rollin*. Paris, 1868.
19. Erichsen, W. *Papyrus Harris I, Hieroglyphische Transkription* ( = *Bibliotheca Aegyptiaca*, v). Brussels, 1933.
20. Gardiner, Sir Alan. *Egypt of the Pharaohs*. Oxford, 1961.
21. Gardiner, Sir Alan. *Ramesside Administrative Documents*. London, 1948.

22. Gardiner, A. H. 'The House of Life.' In *J.E.A.* 24 (1938), 157–79.
23. Gardiner, A. H. *The Wilbour Papyrus*, 3 vols. Oxford, 1941–8. Vol. IV, *Indices*, by R. O. Faulkner. Oxford, 1952.
24. Gardiner, A. H., Peet, T. E. and Černý, J. *The Inscriptions of Sinai*, 2 vols. London, 1952, 1955.
25. Gauthier, H. *Le livre des rois d'Égypte*, III ( = *Mém. Inst. fr. Caire*, 19). Cairo, 1914.
26. Goyon, G. *Nouvelles inscriptions rupestres du Wadi Hammamat*. Paris, 1957.
27. Goyon, G. 'Le papyrus de Turin dit "des mines d'or" et le Wadi Hammamat.' In *Ann. Serv.* 49 (1949), 337–92.
28. Harris, J. R. *Lexicographical Studies in Ancient Egyptian Minerals*. Berlin, 1961.
29. Hayes, W. C. *The Scepter of Egypt*, 2 parts. New York, 1953, 1959.
30. Helck, W. 'Zur Geschichte der 19. und 20. Dynastie.' In *Z.D.M.G.* 105 (1955), 27–52.
31. Helck, W. *Zur Verwaltung des Mittleren und Neuen Reiches* ( = *Probleme der Ägyptologie*, edited by H. Kees, III). Leiden–Cologne, 1958.
32. Lansing, A. 'The Museum's Excavations at Thebes.' In *The Metropolitan Museum of Art, The Egyptian Expedition 1934–1935* (New York, 1935), 4–16.
33. Lansing, A. 'The Egyptian Expedition 1915–1916.' In *Bull. M.M.A.* 12 (1917), *Supplement*, 7–26.
34. Lepsius, R. *Denkmäler aus Ägypten und Äthiopien, Text*, 5 vols. Leipzig, 1897–1913.
35. Mariette, A. *Abydos*, 2 vols. Paris, 1869–80.
36. *Medinet Habu*, V. University of Chicago Press, 1957.
37. Montet, P. 'L'effectif d'une expédition à la montagne de Bekhen en l'an III de Ramsès IV.' In *Kêmi*, 13 (1954), 59–62.
38. Otto, E. *Topographie des thebanischen Gaues*. Berlin, 1952.
39. Parker, R. A. 'The Length of the Reign of Ramses X.' In *Rev. d'égyptol.* 11 (1957), 163–4.
40. Peet, T. E. 'The Chronological Problems of the Twentieth Dynasty.' In *J.E.A.* 14 (1928), 52–73.
41. Peet, T. E. *The Great Tomb-robberies of the Twentieth Egyptian Dynasty*, 2 vols. Oxford, 1930.
42. Peet, T. E. 'A Historical Document of Ramesside Age.' In *J.E.A.* 10 (1924), 116–27.
43. Peet, T. E. 'A Possible Year Date of King Ramesses VII.' In *J.E.A.* 11 (1925), 72–5.
44. Pleyte, W. and Rossi, F. *Papyrus de Turin*, 2 vols. Leiden, 1869–76.
45. Porter, B. and Moss, R. L. B. *Topographical Bibliography of Ancient Egyptian Hieroglyphic Texts, Reliefs and Paintings*, 7 vols. Oxford, 1927–51.
46. Robichon, C. and Varille, A. 'Fouilles des temples funéraires thébains (1937).' In *Rev. d'égyptol.* 3 (1938), 99–102.
47. Schädel, H. D. 'Der Regierungsantritt Ramses IV.' In *Z.Ä.S.* 74 (1938), 96–104.
48. Seele, K. C. 'Ramesses VI and the Medinet Habu Procession of the Princess.' In *J.N.E.S.* 19 (1960), 184–204.
49. Smith, G. E. *The Royal Mummies* (*C.C.G.*, nos. 61051–100). Cairo, 1912.
50. Spiegelberg, W. *Zwei Beiträge zur Geschichte der thebanischen Nekropolis*. Strassburg, 1898.
51. Vandier d'Abbadie, J. 'Un monument inédit de Ramsès VII au Musée du Louvre.' In *J.N.E.S.* 9 (1950), 134–6.

52. Varille, A. *Karnak*, 1 ( = *Flles Inst. fr. Caire*, 19). Cairo, 1943.
53. Waddell, W. G. *Manetho with an English Translation* (*The Loeb Classical Library*). London and Cambridge, Mass., 1940.
54. Winlock, H. E. *Excavations at Deir el Baḥri 1911–1931*. New York, 1942.
55. Yoyotte, J. 'A propos des scarabées attribués à Ramsès VIII.' In *Kêmi*, 10 (1949), 86–9.

II. THE INVASIONS OF THE LIBYANS AND THEIR SETTLEMENT IN EGYPT

1. Černý, J. *Late Ramesside Letters* ( = *Bibliotheca Aegyptiaca*, IX). Brussels, 1939.
2. Gardiner, A. H. *Ancient Egyptian Onomastica*, 3 vols. Oxford, 1947.
3. Maspero, G. *Mémoire sur quelques papyrus du Louvre*. Paris, 1875.
4. Peet, T. E. *The Mayer Papyri A and B*. London, 1920.
5. Peet, T. E. 'The Supposed Revolution of the High-priest Amenḥotpe.' In *J.E.A.* 12 (1926), 254–9.
6. Yoyotte, J. 'Les principautés du Delta au temps de l'anarchie libyenne.' In *Mél. Maspero*, 1, 4e fasc. ( = *Mém. Inst. fr. Caire*, LXVI), 121–81.

III. WORKMEN OF THE KING'S TOMB

1. Bruyère, B. *Rapport sur les fouilles de Deir el Médineh* (*Flles Inst. fr. Caire*), 16 vols. Cairo, 1924–53.
2. Černý, J. 'Le culte d'Aménophis Ier chez les ouvriers de la nécropole thébaine.' In *Bull. Inst. fr. Caire*, 27 (1927), 159–203.
3. Černý, J. 'Egyptian Oracles' ( = chapter IV in Parker, R. A., *A Saite Oracle Papyrus from Thebes*. Providence, R.I., 1962).
4. Černý, J. 'Une famille de scribes de la nécropole royale de Thèbes.' In *Chron. d'Ég.* no. 22 (July 1936), 247–50.
5. Černý, J. 'Prices and Wages in Egypt in the Ramesside Period.' In *Cahiers d'histoire universelle*, 1 (1954), 903–21.
6. Daressy, G. 'Un plan égyptien d'une tombe royale.' In *Rev. arch.* 3e série, 32 (1898), 235–40.
7. Gardiner, A. H. 'Ramesside Texts Relating to the Taxation and Transport of Corn.' In *J.E.A.* 27 (1941), 19–73.
8. Sauneron, S. *Catalogue des ostraca hiératiques non littéraires de Deir el Médineh* (*Documents de fouilles Inst. fr. Caire*, 13). Cairo, 1959.
9. Žába, Z. 'La date de la première entrée du recto du papyrus de Turin No. 1880.' In *Arch. Orient.* 20 (1952), 642–5.

IV. HIGH PRIESTS OF AMUN AND VICEROYS OF NUBIA

1. Capart, J. and Gardiner, A. H. *Le papyrus Léopold II...et le papyrus Amherst*. Brussels, 1939.
2. Černý, J. 'Two King's Sons of Kush of the Twentieth Dynasty.' In *Kush*, 7 (1959), 71–5.
3. Gardiner, A. H. 'A Lawsuit arising from the Purchase of Two Slaves.' In *J.E.A.* 21 (1935), 140–6.
4. Kees, H. *Das Priestertum im ägyptischen Staat vom Neuen Reich bis zur Spätzeit* ( = *Probleme der Ägyptologie*, 1), 2 vols. Leiden–Cologne, 1953, 1958.
5. Lefèbvre, G. *Histoire des grands prêtres d'Amon de Karnak jusqu'à la XXIe dynastie*. Paris, 1929.

6. Lefèbvre, G. *Inscriptions concernant les grands prêtres d'Amon Rômê-Roy et Amenhotep.* Paris, 1929.

7. Lepsius, R. *Denkmäler aus Ägypten und Äthiopien,* 6 parts. Berlin, 1849–59.

8. Reisner, G. A. 'The Viceroys of Ethiopia.' In *J.E.A.* 6 (1920), 28–55 and 73–88.

9. Schädel, H. D. *Die Listen des grossen Papyrus Harris, ihre wirtschaftliche und politische Ausdeutung (Leipziger Ägyptol. St.* 6). Glückstadt–Hamburg–New York, 1936.

10. Sethe, K. 'Die angebliche Rebellion des Hohenpriesters Amenḥotep unter Ramses IX.' In *Z.Ä.S.* 59 (1924), 60–1.

11. Sethe, K. 'Die Berufung eines Hohenpriesters des Amon unter Ramses II.' In *Z.Ä.S.* 49 (1907–8), 30–5.


**V. HRIHOR AND RAMESSES XI**

1. Boeser, P. A. A. *Beschreibung der ägyptischen Sammlung des niederländischen Reichsmuseum der Altertümer,* vol. VI. The Hague, 1913.

2. Budge, E. A. W. *The Book of the Dead. Facsimiles of the Papyri Hunefer, Anhai, Kerasher and Netchemet.* London, 1899.

3. Drioton, É. and Vandier, J. *L'Égypte* (in *Clio*), 4th ed. Paris, 1962.

4. Erman, A. and Grapow, H. *Wörterbuch der ägyptischen Sprache,* 5 vols. Leipzig, 1926–31.

5. Gardiner, A. H. *Late-Egyptian Stories* ( = *Bibl. Aeg.* I). Brussels, 1932.

6. Kees, H. 'Herihor und die Aufrichtung des thebanischen Gottesstaates.' In *Nachr. Göttingen,* 1936, no. I.

7. Korostovcev, A. *Puteŝestvie Un-amuna v Bibl.* Moscow, 1960.

8. Maspero, G. *Les momies royales de Deir el-Baharî (Mém. Miss. fr. Caire.* I, 511–789). Paris, 1889.

9. Meyer, E. 'Gottesstaat, Militärherrschaft und Standwesen in Ägypten.' In *Sitzungsb. Berlin,* 1928, 495–532.

10. Naville, É. 'Trois reines de la XXIe dynastie.' In *Z.Ä.S.* 16 (1878), 29–32.

11. Nims, C. F. 'An Oracle dated in the Repeating of Births.' In *J.N.E.S.* 7 (1948), 157–62.

12. Piehl, K. *Inscriptions hiéroglyphiques recueillies en Europe et en Égypte,* 3 series. Leipzig, 1886–93.

13. Pierret, P. *Recueil d'inscriptions inédites du Musée égyptien du Louvre,* 2 vols. Paris, 1874–8.

14. Shorter, A. W. *Catalogue of Egyptian Religious Papyri in the British Museum.* London, 1938.

15. Steindorff, G. *Aniba,* 2 vols. Glückstadt, 1935–7.

16. Weigall, A. *Report on the Antiquities of Lower Nubia.* Oxford, 1907.

17. Wiedemann, A. *Ägyptische Geschichte.* Gotha, 1884. *Supplement.* Gotha, 1888.


**VI. THE TWENTY-FIRST DYNASTY**

1. Borchardt, L. *Die Mittel zur zeitlichen Festlegung von Punkten der ägyptischen Geschichte und ihre Anwendung* ( = *Quellen und Untersuchungen zur Zeitbestimmung ägyptischer Geschichte,* 2). Cairo, 1935.

2. Bouriant, U. 'Notes de voyage.' In *Rec. trav.* 11 (1889), 131–59.

3. Brugsch, H. *Recueil de monuments égyptiens,* 2 parts. Leipzig, 1862–3.

4. Brugsch, H. *Reise nach der Grossen Oase El Khargeh.* Leipzig, 1878.

5. Černý, J. 'Studies in the Chronology of the Twenty-first Dynasty.' In *J.E.A.* 32 (1946), 24–30.

6. Chaban, M. 'Fouilles à Achmounéin.' In *Ann. Serv.* 8 (1907), 210–23.

7. Champollion, J. F. *Monuments de l'Égypte, Notices descriptives*, 2 vols. Paris, 1844 ff.

8. Daressy, G. 'Les carrières de Gebelein et le roi Smendès.' In *Rec. trav.* 10 (1888), 133–8.

9. Daressy, G. 'Les cercueils des prêtres d'Ammon.' In *Ann. Serv.* 8 (1907), 3–38.

10. Daressy, G. *Cercueils des cachettes royales (C.C.G.* nos. 61001–44). Cairo, 1909.

11. Daressy, G. Contribution à l'étude de la XXIe dynastie égyptienne.' In *Rev. arch.*, 3e série, 28 (1896), 1, 72–90.

12. Daressy, G. 'Le décret d'Amon en faveur du grand prêtre Pinozem.' In *Rec. trav.* 32 (1910), 175–86.

13. Daressy, G. 'Exploration archéologique de la montagne d'Abydos.' In *Bulletin de l'Institut égyptien*, 3e série, no. 9 (1898), 279–88.

14. Daressy, G. In Pillet, M., 'Fouilles de l'angle nord-ouest de l'enceinte du grand temple d'Amon à Karnak.' In *Ann. Serv.* 22 (1922), 60–4.

15. Daressy, G. 'Notes et remarques.' In *Rec. trav.* 14 (1893), 20–38.

16. Daressy, G. 'Les rois Psousennès.' In *Rec. trav.* 21 (1899), 9–12.

17. Daressy, G. 'Le scarabée du cœur de la grande prêtresse Asi-m-kheb.' In *Ann. Serv.* 20 (1920), 17–18.

18. Derry, D. E. 'Report on Skeleton of King Amenemōpet.' In *Ann. Serv.* 41 (1942), 140.

19. Gardiner, A. H. 'The Dakhleh Stela.' In *J.E.A.* 19 (1933), 19–30.

20. Gardiner, A. H. 'Davies's Copy of the Great Speos Artemidos Inscription.' In *J.E.A.* 32 (1946), 43–56.

21. Gardiner, Sir Alan, 'The Gods of Thebes as Guarantors of Personal Property.' In *J.E.A.* 48 (1962), 57–69.

22. Gauthier, H. 'A travers la Basse-Égypte.' In *Ann. Serv.* 22 (1922), 199–208.

23. Grdseloff, B. 'En marge des récentes recherches sur Tanis.' In *Ann. Serv.* 47 (1947), 203–16.

24. Hayes, W. C. 'A Canopic Jar of King Nesu-ba-neb-dēdet of Tanis.' In *Bull. M.M.A.* 5 (June 1947), 261–3.

25. Hayes, W. C. 'Writing Palette of the High Priest of Amūn Smendes.' In *J.E.A.* 34 (1948), 47–50.

26. Legrain, G. 'Notes prises à Karnak.' In *Rec. trav.* 22 (1900), 51–65.

27. Legrain, G. *Statues et statuettes des rois et particuliers (C.C.G.* nos. 42001–250), 3 vols. Cairo, 1906–14.

28. Legrain G. 'Le temple et les chapelles d'Osiris à Karnak.' In *Rec. trav.* 24 (1902) 208–14.

29. Lepsius, R. *Auswahl der wichtigsten Urkunden des ägyptischen Altertums.* Leipzig, 1842.

30. Mariette, A. *Karnak*, 2 vols. Paris 1875.

31. Mariette, A. *Les papyrus égyptiens du Musée de Boulaq*, 3 vols. Paris, 1871–6.

32. Mariette, A. *Le Sérapéum de Memphis*, III. Paris, 1857.

33. Maspero, G. 'Notes sur quelques points de grammaire et d'histoire.' In *Z.Ä.S.* 20 (1882), 120–35.

34. Montet, P. *Le drame d'Avaris: Essai sur la pénétration des Sémites en Égypte.* Paris, 1940.

35. Montet, P. *Les énigmes de Tanis.* Paris, 1952.

36. Montet, P. 'La nécropole des rois tanites.' In *Kêmi*, 9 (1942), 1–96.
37. Montet, P. *La nécropole de Tanis, II: Les constructions et le tombeau de Psousennès à Tanis*. Paris, 1951.
38. Murray, M. A. *The Osireion at Abydos*. London, 1904.
39. Naville, E. *Inscription historique de Pinodjem III*. Paris, 1883.
40. Naville, E. *Papyrus funéraires de la XXIe dynastie*, 2 vols. Paris, 1912, 1914.
41. Peet, T. E. *Egypt and the Old Testament*. Liverpool and London, 1922.
42. Prisse d'Avennes, A. *Monuments égyptiens*. Paris, 1847.
43. Ransom Williams, C. 'The Egyptian Collection in the Museum of Art at Cleveland, Ohio.' In *J.E.A.* 5 (1918), 272–85.
44. Sander-Hansen, C. E. *Das Gottesweib des Amun* (*Det Kongelige Danske Videnskabernes Selskab, Hist.-fil. Skrifter*, I, 1). Copenhagen, 1940.
45. Spiegelberg, W. 'Briefe der 21. Dynastie aus El-Hibe.' In *Z.Ä.S.* 53 (1917), 1–30.
46. Wainwright, G. A. 'El-Hibeh and Esh Shurafa and their Connection with Herakleopolis and Cusae.' In *Ann. Serv.* 27 (1927), 76–104.

A. ADDENDA

1. Beckerath, J. von. 'Ein Denkmal zur Genealogie der XX. Dynastie.' In *Z.Ä.S.* 97 (1971), 7–12.
2. Helck, W. 'Feiertage und Arbeitstage in der Ramessidenzeit.' In *J.E.S.H.O.* 7 (1964), Part 2, 136–66.
3. Hornung, E. *Untersuchungen zur Chronologie und Geschichte des Neuen Reiches*. Wiesbaden, 1964.
4. Kees, H. *Die Hohenpriester des Amun von Karnak von Herihor bis zum Ende der Äthiopienzeit* (*Probleme der Ägyptologie*, xx, 4). Leiden, 1964.
5. Kitchen, K. A. *The Third Intermediate Period in Egypt (1100–650 B.C.)*. Warminster, 1973.
6. Wenig, S. 'Einige Bemerkungen zur Chronologie der frühen 21. Dynastie.' In *Z.Ä.S.* 94 (1967), 134–9.
7. Wente, E. F. 'The Suppression of the High-Priest Amenhotep.' In *J.N.E.S.* 25 (1966), 73–87.
8. Wente, E. F. 'On the Chronology of the Twenty-first Dynasty.' In *J.N.E.S.* 26 (1967), 155–76.
9. Young E. 'Some Notes on the Chronology and Genealogy of the Twenty-first Dynasty.' In *J.A.R.C.E.* 2 (1963), 99–132.

CHAPTER XXXVI

(*a*) THE ARCHAEOLOGICAL BACKGROUND

GENERAL

1. Desborough, V. R. d'A. *Protogeometric Pottery*. Oxford, 1952.
2. Furumark, A. *The Mycenaean Pottery: Analysis and Classification*. Stockholm, 1941.
3. Furumark, A. *The Chronology of Mycenaean Pottery*. Stockholm, 1941.
4. Furumark, A. 'The Mycenaean IIIC Pottery and its Relation to Cypriote Fabrics.' In *Opuscula Archaeologica* (1944), 194 ff.
5. Karo, G. H. 'Mykenische Kultur.' In *Pauly–Wissowa–Kroll*, Suppl. Bd. VI (1935), 584 ff.

6. Lorimer, H. *Homer and the Monuments*. London, 1950.
7. Matz, F. 'Die Ägäis.' In *Handbuch der Archäologie*, 2, 1 (1950), Textband 2, 179 ff. Tafelband 2, pls. 13–40.
8. Pendlebury, J. D. S. *The Archaeology of Crete*. London, 1939.

I. THE END OF THE MYCENAEAN WORLD

1. Albright, W. F. *The Archaeology of Palestine*. London, 1954.
2. Andronikos, M. 'An Early Iron Age Cemetery at Vergina, near Beroea.' In *Balkan Studies*, 2 (1961), 85 ff.
3. Benton, S. 'Excavations in Ithaca, III.' In *B.S.A.* 39 (1938–9), 1 ff.
4. Benton, S. 'Second Thoughts on "Mycenaean" Pottery in Ithaca.' In *B.S.A.* 44 (1949), 307 ff.
5. Blegen, C. W. *Zygouries*. Cambridge, Mass., 1928.
6. Blegen, C. W. 'Excavations at Pylos.' In *A.J.A.* 43 (1939) and *A.J.A.* 57 (1953) ff.
7. Breasted, J. H. *Ancient Records of Egypt*, vol. IV. Chicago, 1906.
8. Broneer, O. 'A Mycenaean Fountain on the Athenian Acropolis.' In *Hesperia*, 8 (1939), 317 ff.
9. Broneer, O. 'The Corinthian Isthmus and the Isthmian Sanctuary.' In *Antiquity*, 32 (1958), 80 ff.
10. Catling, H. W. 'Bronze Cut-and-Thrust Swords in the Eastern Mediterranean.' In *P.P.S.* 22 (1956), 102 ff.
11. Catling, H. W. 'A New Bronze Sword from Cyprus.' In *Antiquity*, 35 (1961), 115 ff.
12. Chadwick, J. and Ventris, M. *Documents in Mycenaean Greek*. Cambridge, 1956.
13. Charitonides, S. Report on excavation at Argos. In *Praktika*, 1952, 425.
14. Condoleon, N. M. ''Ανασκαφὴ ἐν Νάξῳ.' In *Praktika*, 1949–51.
15. Condoleon, N. M. Reports on excavations in Naxos. In *Ergon* for 1958, 1959 and 1960.
16. Courbin, P. Reports on excavations at Argos. In *B.C.H.* 80 (1956), 81 (1957) and 83 (1959).
17. Dakares, S. Report on tombs at Kalbaki. In *Arch. Eph.* 1956, 115 ff.
18. Dawkins, R. M. 'The Mycenaean City near the Menelaion.' In *B.S.A.* 16 (1909–10), 4 ff.
19. Dawkins, R. M. and Droop, J. P. Report on excavations at Phylakopi. In *B.S.A.* 17 (1910–11), 1 ff.
20. Deshayes, J. Reports on excavations at Argos. In *B.C.H.* 79 (1955), 80 (1956) and 83 (1959).
21. Dikaios, P. Report on excavations at Enkomi. In Κυπριακὰ Γράμματα, 21 (1956), 25 ff.
22. Frödin, O. (with Persson, A. W.). *Asine*. Stockholm, 1938.
23. Gallet de Santerre, H. *Délos Primitive et Archaïque*. Paris, 1958.
24. Gjerstad, E. *The Swedish Cyprus Expedition*, vol. IV, 2. Stockholm, 1948.
25. Goldman, H. *Excavations at Gözlü Kule, Tarsus*, vol. II. Princeton, 1956.
26. Heurtley, W. A. *Prehistoric Macedonia*. Cambridge, 1939.
27. Heurtley, W. A. 'Excavations in Ithaca, IV.' In *B.S.A.* 40 (1939–40), 1 ff.
28. Hogarth, D. G. and others. *Excavations at Phylakopi in Melos*. London, 1904.
29. Huxley, G. L. *Achaeans and Hittites*. Oxford, 1960.
30. Iakovides, S. Reports on excavations at Perati. In *Praktika*, 1953 ff., and *Ergon* for 1954 ff.

31. Jacopi, G. 'Nuovi scavi nella necropoli micenea di Jalisso.' In *A.S.A.A.* 13–14 (1930–31), 253 ff.
32. Keramopoullos, A. D. 'Excavations at Thebes.' In *Deltion*, 3 (1917), 123 ff.
33. Kourouniotes, K. (with Blegen, C. W.). 'Excavations at Pylos.' In *A.J.A.* 43 (1939).
34. Kraiker, W. and Kübler, K. *Kerameikos: Ergebnisse der Ausgrabungen*, Bd. 1. Berlin, 1939.
35. Kyparisses, N. Reports on excavations in Achaea. In *Praktika*, 1925–40.
36. Lerat, L. Report on excavations at Delphi. In *B.C.H.* 81 (1957), 708 ff.
37. Lerat, L. Report on excavations at Crisa. In *B.C.H.* 61 (1937), 299 ff.
38. Maiuri, A. 'Jalisos: La necropoli micenea.' In *A.S.A.A.* 6–7 (1923–4), 83 ff.
39. Marinatos, S. 'Αἱ ἀνασκαφαὶ Goekoop ἐν Κεφαλληνίᾳ.' In *Arch. Eph.* 1932, 1 ff. and 1933, 68 ff.
40. McDonald, W. A. (with Hope-Simpson, R.). 'Prehistoric Habitation in South-western Peloponnese.' In *A.J.A.* 65 (1961), 221 ff.
41. Morricone, L. 'Scavi e ricerche a Coo.' In *Boll. d'Arte*, 1950, 323 ff.
42. Mylonas, G. E. 'Eleusiniaca.' In *A.J.A.* 40 (1936), 415 ff.
43. Mylonas, G. E. Report on excavation at Mycenae. In *Ergon* for 1959, 93 ff.
44. Papademetriou, J. Report on excavation at the Sanctuary of Apollo Maleatas. In *Praktika*, 1950, 194 ff.
45. Schaeffer, C. F. A. *Enkomi-Alasia*. Paris, 1952.
46. Schaeffer, C. F. A. 'Les Fouilles de Ras Shamra-Ugarit.' In *Syria*, 31 (1954), 14 ff. and elsewhere.
47. Skeat, T. C. *The Dorians in Archaeology*. London, 1934.
48. Sommer, F. Die Aḫḫiava-Urkunden. In *Abh. München*, N.F. 6 (1932).
49. Stubbings, F. H. *Mycenaean Pottery from the Levant*. Cambridge, 1951.
50. Taylour, Lord William (with Papademetriou, J.). 'The Last Days of Mycenae.' In *I.L.N.* 23 Sept. 1961, 490 ff.
51. Theochares, D. Reports on excavations at Iolcus. In *Archaeology*, 11 (1958), 13 ff. and in *Ergon* for 1956 and 1960.
52. Threpsiades, J. Reports on excavations at Gla. In *Ergon* for 1955–1960.
53. Verdhelis, N. M. Ὁ Πρωτογεωμετρικὸς Ῥυθμὸς τῆς Θεσσαλίας. Athens, 1958.
54. Verdhelis, N. M. Report on excavation at Tiryns. In *Arch. Eph.* 1956, suppl. 5 ff. Cf. *B.C.H.* 82 (1958), 706 f.
55. Vermeule, E. T. 'The Mycenaeans in Achaia.' In *A.J.A.* 64 (1960), 1 ff.
56. von Massow, W. Report on excavations at Amyclae. In *A.M.* 52 (1927), 24 ff.
57. Wace, A. J. B. *Mycenae*. Princeton, 1949.
58. Wace, A. J. B. 'Excavations at Mycenae.' In *B.S.A.* 25 (1921–3).
59. Wace, A. J. B. Reports on further excavations at Mycenae. In *B.S.A.* 48–52 (1953–7).
60. Waterhouse, H. (with Hope-Simpson, R.). 'Prehistoric Laconia, part 1.' In *B.S.A.* 55 (1960), 67 ff.
61. Weickert, C. Reports on excavations at Miletus. In *Ist. Mitt.* 7 (1956) and 9–10 (1959–60).
62. Weinberg, S. *Corinth*, vol. VII, part 1. Cambridge, Mass., 1943.
63. Wide, S. 'Account of excavations on Salamis.' In *A.M.* 35 (1910), 17 ff.
64. Woolley, Sir Leonard. *Alalakh*. Oxford, 1955.
65. Zapheiropoulos, N. Report of excavations on Naxos. In *Ergon* for 1960, 189 ff.

## II. THE PROTOGEOMETRIC PERIOD

1. Andronikos, M. 'An Early Iron Age Cemetery at Vergina.' In *Balkan Studies*, 2 (1961), 85 ff.
2. Benton, S. 'Excavations in Ithaca, II.' In *B.S.A.* 39 (1938–9), 1 ff.
3. Cook, J. M. 'Old Smyrna, 1948–1951.' In *B.S.A.* 53–4 (1958–9), 1–34.
4. Cook, J. M. 'Greek Archaeology in Western Asia Minor.' In *Archaeological Reports for 1959–60*, 27 ff.
5. Evangelides, D. Report on excavations on Scyros. In *Arch. Delt.* 4 (1918), παρ. 41 ff.
6. Heurtley, W. A. *Prehistoric Macedonia*. Cambridge, 1939.
7. Heurtley, W. A. and Skeat, T. C. Report on the cemetery at Marmariani. In *B.S.A.* 31 (1930–31), 1 ff.
8. Kraiker, W. and Kübler, K. *Kerameikos: Ergebnisse der Ausgrabungen*, Bd. 1. Berlin, 1939.
9. Kraiker, W. *Aigina: die Vasen des 10. bis 7. Jahrhunderts v. Chr.* Berlin, 1951.
10. Kübler, K. *Kerameikos: Ergebnisse der Ausgrabungen*, Bd. IV. Berlin, 1943.
11. Levi, D. Report on excavations on Tenos. In *A.S.A.A.* 8–9 (1925–6), 203 ff.
12. Morricone, L. Report on Excavations on Cos. In *Boll. d'Arte* (1950), 320 ff.
13. Paton, W. R. Report on excavations at Assarlık. In *J.H.S.* 8 (1887), 64 ff.
14. Papademetriou, J. Report on excavation on Scyros. In *Arch. Anz.* 1936, 228 ff.
15. Robertson, C. M. 'The Excavations at Al Mina, Soueidia, IV. The Early Greek Vases.' In *J.H.S.* 60 (1940), 2 ff.
16. Sauciuc, T. Report on tombs on Andros. In *Sonderschriften d. Öst. arch. Inst.* VIII, 46 ff.
17. Skeat, T. C. *The Dorians in Archaeology*. London, 1934.
18. Soteriades, G. Report on excavations at Vranesi. In *A.M.* 30 (1905), 132 f.
19. Theochares, D. Report on excavations at Iolcus. In *Ergon* for 1960.
20. von Massow, W. Report on excavations at Amyclae. In *A.M.* 52 (1927), 46 ff.
21. Wace, A. J. B. and Thompson, M. S. *Prehistoric Thessaly*. Cambridge, 1912.
22. Wace, A. J. B. and Thompson, M. S. Report on tombs at Halos. In *B.S.A.* 18 (1917–18), 1 ff.
23. Weickert, C. Report on excavations at Miletus. In *Istanbuler Mitteilungen*, 9–10 (1959–60), 1 ff.
24. Weinberg, S. *Corinth*, vol. VII, part 1, 3 ff. Cambridge, Mass., 1943.
25. Yaloures, N. In *B.C.H.* 85 (1961), 682 and 697.
26. Zapheiropoulas, N. In *Praktika*, 1954, 400 ff.

## III. CRETE

1. Boardman, J. *The Cretan Collection in Oxford*. Oxford, 1961.
2. Brock, J. K. *Fortetsa*. Cambridge, 1957.
3. Deshayes, J. and Dessenne, A. *Mallia:* Maisons II (1960).
4. Hall, E. H. 'Excavations in Eastern Crete, Vrokastro.' In *Univ. of Pennsylvania Anthropological Publications*, vol. III, 3 (1914).
5. Hood, M. S. F., Huxley, G. and Sandars, N. 'A Minoan Cemetery on Upper Gypsades.' In *B.S.A.* 53–4 (1958–9), 194 ff.
6. Levi, D. Report on excavations at Gortyn. In *A.S.A.A.* (N.S.) 17–18 (1955–6), 216 f.
7. Levi, D. Report on excavations at Phaestus. In *A.S.A.A.* (N.S.) 19–20 (1957–8), 255 ff.

8. Pendlebury, J. D. S. 'Excavations in the plain of Lasithi, III: Karphi.' In *B.S.A.* 38 (1937–8), 57 ff.
9. Platon, N. Report on excavations at Kefala. In *Ergon* for 1957, 1958, 1959 and 1960.
10. Platon, N. Report on excavations at Modi. In *Kretika Chronika*, 1953, 485 f.
11. Seiradaki, M. 'Pottery from Karphi.' In *B.S.A.* 55 (1960), 1 ff.
12. Xanthoudides, S. Account of tombs at Mouliana. In *Arch. Eph.* 1904, 21 ff.

### A. ADDENDA

1. Ålin, P. *Das Ende der Mykenischen Fundstätten auf dem Griechischen Festland.* Lund, 1962.
2. Andronikos, M. Βεργίνα I. Athens, 1969.
3. Bass, G. F. 'Mycenaean and Protogeometric Tombs in the Halicarnassus Peninsula.' In *A.J.A.* 71 (1967), 353 ff.
4. Benson, J. 'Bronze Tripods from Kourion.' In *G.R.B.S.* 3 (1960), 7 ff.
5. Bingen, J. Report on silver-extraction at Thorikos. In *Thorikos*, 2 (1964), 25 ff.
6. Blegen, C. W. and Rawson, M. *The Palace of Nestor*, vol. I. Princeton, 1966.
7. Bouzek, J. *Homerisches Griechenland.* Prague, 1969.
8. Carpenter, Rhys. *Discontinuity in Greek Civilisation.* Cambridge, 1968.
9. Caskey, J. L. Reports on excavations on Ceos. In *Hesperia*, 31 (1962), 33 (1964), 35 (1966).
10. Catling, H. W. *Cypriot Bronzework in the Mycenaean World.* Oxford, 1964.
11. Choremis, A. Report on excavation at Karpophora. In *Athens Annals of Archaeology*, 1 (1968), 205 ff.
12. Coldstream, J. N. *Greek Geometric Pottery.* London, 1968.
13. Condoleon, N. M. Reports on excavations in Naxos. In *Praktika* for 1960, 1963, 1965 and 1967.
14. Courbin, P. 'Stratigraphie et Stratigraphie.' In *Études Archéologiques* 1963.
15. Daux, G. Reports on excavations at Argos. In *B.C.H.* 77 (1953) ff. (Chronique des Fouilles.)
16. Desborough, V. R. d'A. 'A Group of Vases from Amathus.' In *J.H.S.* 77 (1957), 212 ff.
17. Desborough, V. R. d'A. *The Last Mycenaeans and their Successors.* Oxford, 1964.
18. Desborough, V. R. d'A. 'The Greek Mainland, c. 1150–c. 1000 B.C.' In *P.P.S.* 31 (1965), 213 ff.
19. Deshayes, J. *Argos: les Fouilles de la Deiras.* Paris, 1966.
20. Dikaios, P. *Enkomi*, vols. I and III. Mainz, 1969 and 1971.
21. Dothan, T. *The Philistines and their Material Culture.* Jerusalem, 1967.
22. Furumark, A. 'The Excavations at Sinda.' In *Op. Ath.* 6 (1965), 99 ff.
23. Gjerstad, E. 'The initial date of the Cypriote Iron Age.' In *Op. Ath.* 3 (1944), 73 ff.
24. Hutchinson, R. W. *Prehistoric Crete.* London, 1962.
25. Iakovides, Sp. *Perati*, vols. I–III. Athens, 1969–70.
26. Karageorghis, V. Reports on excavations at Kition. In *B.C.H.* 84 (1960) ff.
27. Karageorghis, V. 'Αἱ σχέσεις μεταξὺ Κύπρου καὶ Κρήτης κατὰ τὸν 11ον αἰ. π. Χ.' In *Proceedings of the 2nd International Cretological Congress*, vol. I, 180 ff. Athens, 1967.
28. Leon, V. 'Zweiter vorläufiger Bericht über die Ausgrabungen in Alt-Elis.' In *Ö.J.H.* 46 (1961–3) Beiblatt, 33 ff.

29. Mastrokostas, E. Reports on excavations at Teichos Dymaion. In *Praktika* for 1962–5.
30. Mastrokostas, E. Reports on excavations in Aetolia. In *Arch. Delt.* 17, ii (1961–2), 183 and *Arch. Delt.* 22, iii (1967), 320.
31. Matz, F. and Buchholz, H.-G. (edd.). *Archaeologia Homerica*. Göttingen, 1967– .
32. McDonald, W. A. and Hope Simpson, R. 'Further explorations in south-western Peloponnese.' In *A.J.A.* 73 (1969), 123 ff.
33. Morricone, L. 'Eleone e Langada, Sepolcreti della tarda Età del Bronzo a Coo.' In *A.S.A.A.* 43–4 (1965–6), 5 ff.
34. Müller-Karpe, H. 'Die Metallbeigaben der früheisenzeitlichen Kerameikos-Gräber.' In *J.D.A.I.* 77 (1962), 59 ff.
35. Kylonas, G. E. *Mycenae and the Mycenaean Age*. Princeton, 1966.
36. Ohly, D. 'Frühe Tonfiguren aus dem Heraion von Samos I.' In *A.M.* 65 (1940), 57 ff.
37. Petsas, Ph. Report on excavations at Vergina. In *Arch. Delt.* 17, i (1961–2), 218 ff.
38. Popham, M. R. 'Some Late Minoan III pottery from Crete.' In *B.S.A.* 60 (1965), 316 ff.
39. Popham, M. R. and Sackett, L. H. *Excavations at Lefkandi, Euboea, 1964–66*. London, 1968.
40. Rizza, G. and Santa Maria Scrinari, V. *Il Santuario sull'Acropoli di Gortina*, 1. Rome, 1968.
41. Sackett, L. H. and Popham, M. R. 'Excavations at Palaikastro VI.' In *B.S.A.* 60 (1965), 248 ff.
42. Schaeffer, C. F. A. and others. *Ugaritica*, v. Paris, 1968.
43. Smithson, E. L. 'The Protogeometric Cemetery at Nea Ionia.' In *Hesperia*, 30 (1961), 147 ff.
44. Styrenius, C.-G. *Submycenaean Studies*. Lund, 1967.
45. Themelis, P. G. Reports on finds in Messenia. In *Arch. Delt.* 20, ii (1965), 207 f.
46. Theocharis, D. Reports on excavations at Iolcus. In *Praktika* for 1960 and 1961.
47. Theocharis, D. Report on excavations at Hexalophos. In *Arch. Delt.* 23, iii (1968), 263 ff., and *Athens Annals of Archaeology*, 1 (1968), 289 ff.
48. Tzedakis, I. G. 'Céramique Postpalatiale à Kydonia.' In *B.C.H.* 93 (1969), 396 ff.
49. Vatin, C. *Médéon de Phocide*. Paris, 1969.
50. Verdhelis, N. M. 'Neue Geometrischer Gräber in Tiryns.' In *A.M.* 78 (1963), 1 ff.
51. Vermeule, E. T. *Greece in the Bronze Age*. Chicago, 1964.
52. Walter, H. *Samos V: Frühe Samische Gefässe*. Bonn, 1968.
53. Yalouris, N. Report on excavations at Ancient Elis. In *Arch. Delt.* 17, ii (1961–2), 125 f. and *Arch. Delt.* 19, ii (1964), 181.
54. Zapheiropoulos, N. Report on excavations on Naxos. In *Praktika* for 1960.

## (b) THE LITERARY TRADITION

References to ancient authorities are given in the text.
Use is made also of the bibliography for part (a) of this chapter.

### GENERAL

1. Barnett, R. D. 'Mopsos.' In *J.H.S.* 73 (1953), 140–3.
2. Bury, J. B. 'The Achaeans and the Trojan War.' In *C.A.H.* II (1926), 473–97.
3. Daniel, J. F., Broneer, O. and Wade-Gery, H. T. 'The Dorian Invasion.' In *A.J.A.* 52 (1948), 107–118.
4. Dow, S. 'The Greeks in the Bronze Age.' In Reports of the *XIe Congrès international des sciences historiques* at Stockholm, 1960, 1–34.
5. Hammond, N. G. L. 'Prehistoric Epirus and the Dorian Invasion.' In *B.S.A.* 32 (1931–2), 131–79.
6. Hammond, N. G. L. *A History of Greece to 322 B.C.* Ed. 2. Oxford, 1967.
7. Hanell, K. *Megarische Studien.* Lund, 1934.
8. Heurtley, W. A. 'A Western Macedonian Site and the Dorian Invasion.' In *B.S.A.* 28 (1926), 159–94.
9. Huxley, G. L. 'Mycenaean Decline and the Homeric Catalogue of Ships.' In *Institute of Classical Studies Bulletin,* 3 (1956), 19–31, of the University of London.
10. Matz, F. 'Die Katastrophe der mykenischen Kultur im Lichte der neuesten Forschung.' In *Archeologia Classica,* 1 (1961), 197–209.
11. Milojčić, V. 'Die dorische Wanderung im Lichte der vorgeschichtlichen Funde.' In *Arch. Anz.* 1948, coll. 12–36.
12. Miltner, F. 'Die dorische Wanderung.' In *Klio,* 27 (1934), 54–68.
13. Müller, K. O. *Die Dorier,* I–II. Ed. 20. Breslau, 1844.
14. Schmid, P. B. *Studien zu griechischen Ktisissagen.* Freiburg, 1947.
15. Vitalis, G. *Die Entwickelung der Sage von der Rückkehr der Herakliden.* Greifswald, 1930.
16. Wade-Gery, H. T. 'The Dorians.' In *C.A.H.* II (1926), 518–41.
17. Will, E. *Doriens et Ioniens.* Paris, 1956.

### A. ADDENDA

1. Broneer, O. 'The Cyclopean Wall on the Isthmus of Corinth.' In *Hesperia,* 35 (1966), 355 ff.
2. Dakares, S. I. 'A Mycenaean III B dagger from the palaeolithic site of Kastritsa in Epirus.' In *P.P.S.* 33 (1967), 30 ff.
3. Evangelides, D. Report on researches in Epirus. In *Epeirotika Chronika* (1935), 192 ff.
4. Hammond, N. G. L. *Epirus.* Oxford, 1967.
5. Hammond, N. G. L. 'Tumulus Burial in Albania etc.' In *B.S.A.* 62 (1967), 77 ff.
6. Hope Simpson, R. and Lazenby, J. F. *The Catalogue of the Ships in Homer's Iliad.* Oxford, 1970.
7. Kitanovski, B. 'Deux tombes appartenant à l'âge du fer ancien près de Prilep.' In *Starinar,* 11 (1960), 209 ff.
8. Islami, S. and Ceka, H. In *Studia Albanica* (1964), 1.
9. Islami, S., Ceka, H., Prendi, F. and Anamali, S. 'Zbulime të kulturës ilire në luginën e Matit.' In *Buletin për shkencat shoqërore* (1955), 1.

10. Korkuti, M. 'Qeramika e pikturuar e kohës së vone te bronxit dhe e kohës së hershme të hekurit dhe karakteri ilir i bartësve të saj. In *Studime Historike* (1969), 3, 159 ff.
11. Mačkić, P., Simaska, D. and Trbuhović. 'Une nécropole appartenant à l'Hallstatt ancien dans la localité de Saraj près de Brod.' In *Starinar*, 11 (1960), 199 ff.
12. Rebani, B. 'Keramika ilire e qytezës së Gajtanit.' In *Studime Historike* (1966), 1, 41 ff.
13. Schárnil, J. *Die Vorgeschichte Böhmens und Mährens*. Berlin, 1928.
14. Vokotopoulou, I. P. 'Report on tombs at Elaphotopos and Mazaraki.' In *Arch. Eph.* (1969), 179 ff.
15. Vučković-Todorović, D. 'Demir Kapija dans l'antiquité.' In *Starinar*, 12 (1961), 229 ff.

## CHAPTER XXXVII

### G. GENERAL

1. Bérard, G. *Bibliographie topographique des principales cités grecques...* Paris, 1941.
2. Bernabò Brea, L. 'Studies of the Spread of Cardial Wares.' In *Rev. ét. lig.* (1949), 21; (1950), 24.
3. Boardman, J. *The Greeks Overseas*. London, 1964.
4. Breuil, H. *Four Hundred Centuries of Cave Art*. Montignac, 1952.
5. Cann, J. R. and Renfrew, C. 'The Characterisation of Obsidian and its Application to the Mediterranean Region.' In *P.P.S.* 30 (1964), 111–33.
6. Cary, M. *The Geographic Background to Greek and Roman History*. Oxford, 1949.
7. Clark, J. G. D. 'Radiocarbon dates and the spread of farming economy.' In *Antiq.* 39 (1965), 47; 'Radiocarbon Dating and the Expansion of Farming Culture from the Near East over Europe.' In *P.P.S.* 31 (1965), 58–73.
8. Cornaggia Castiglione, O., Fussi, F. and d'Agnolo, M. 'Indagni sulla provenienza dell'ossidiana in uso nelle industrie italiane.' I e II *Atti della Società Italiana di Scienze Naturali e del Museo Civico di Storia Naturale di Milano*, 9 (1962, 1963).
9. Daniel, G. E. *The Megalith-builders of Western Europe*. London, 1958.
10. Dunbabin, T. J. *The Western Greeks*. Oxford, 1948.
11. Graziosi, P. *L'Arte dell'Antica Età della Pietra*. Florence, 1957.
12. Harden, D. *The Phoenicians*. London, 1962.
13. Houston, J. M. *The Western Mediterranean World*. London, 1964.
14. *Radiocarbon* (*Am. Journ. Science*), New Haven, Conn. 1959, and annually.
15. Sangmeister, E. 'La Civilisation du vase campaniforme.' In *Les Civilisations Atlantiques du Néolithique à l'Age du Fer* (Brest, 1963), 25–55.
16. M. Sauter. *Préhistoire de la Méditerranée*. Paris, 1948.
17. Semple, E. C. *The Geography of the Mediterranean region: its relation to ancient history*. London, 1932.
18. Shackleton, M. R. *Europe, A Regional Geography*, 6th ed. London, 1958.
19. Woodhead, A. G. *The Greeks in the West*. London, 1962.

## I. ITALY

1. Anati, E. *Camonica Valley*. New York, 1960.
2. Batović, Š. 'Neolitsko naselje u Smilčiću.' In *Diadora*, 1 (1959), 5–26; 2 (1960–1), 31–116.
3. Battaglia, R. 'Sulla distribuzione geografica delle statue-menhirs.' In *Studi Etruschi*, 7 (1933), 11–37.
4. Battaglia, R. 'La palafitta del Lago di Ledro nel Trentino.' In *Mem. Mus. Civ. St. Nat. Ven. Trident.* 7 (1943), 3–63.
5. Bella, F. Blanc, A. C. and Cortesi, C. 'Une prima datazione con il carbonio-14 della formazione pleistocenica di Grotta Romanelli (Terra d'Otranto).' In *Quaternaria*, 5 (1958–61), 87–94.
6. Benac, A. 'Črvena Stijena–1955.' In *Glasnik Zemalskog Muzeja u Sarajevu* (1957), 19–50.
7. Benac, A. and Brodar, M. 'Črvena Stijena–1956.' In *Glasnik Zemalskog Museja u Sarajevu* (1958), 20–64.
8. Bernabò Brea, L. *Gli Scavi nella Caverna delle Arene Candide (Finale Ligure)*, parts I and II. Bordighera, 1946, 1956.
9. Bicknell, C. *A Guide to the Prehistoric Rock Engravings in the Italian Maritime Alps*. Bordighera, 1913.
10. Blanc, A. C. 'Grotta Romanelli, I, II.' In *Archivo di Antropologia ed Etnologia*, 50 (1920); 53 (1928).
11. Blanc, A. C. 'Nuove manifestazioni di arte paleolitica superiore nella Grotta Romanelli in Terra d'Otranto.' In *Rendiconti dell'Accademia Italiana*, 1940.
12. Blanc, A. C. 'I Paleoantropi di Saccopastore e del Circeo.' In *Quartär*, 4 (1942), 1–32.
13. Blanc, A. C. 'Torre in Pietra, Saccopastore e Monte Circeo. La cronologia dei giacimenti e la paleogeografia quaternaria del Lazio.' *Boll. della Soc. Geog. Ital.* 54 (1958).
14. Bradford, J. '"Buried Landscapes" in Southern Italy.' In *Antiq.* 23 (1949), 58–72.
15. Bradford, J. 'The Apulia Expedition; an interim report.' In *Antiq.* 24 (1950), 84–94.
16. Bradford, J. and Williams Hunt, P. R. 'Siticulosa Apulia.' In *Antiq.* 20 (1946), 191–200.
17. Buchner, G. 'Nota preliminare sulle ricerche preistoriche nell'isola d'Ischia.' In *Boll. di Paletn. Ital.* n.s. 1 (1936–7), 78.
18. Calzoni, U. 'Un fondo di capanna scoperto presso Norcia.' In *Boll. di Paletn. Ital.* n.s. 3 (1939), 37–50.
19. Cambi, L. 'I metalli dei cimeli della grotta tombale di Monte Bradoni (Volterra).' In *Boll. di Paletn. Ital.* n.s. 12 (1958–9), 137–45.
20. Childe, V. G. 'The Italian Axe-Mould from Mycenae.' In *Civiltà del Ferro* (Bologna, 1959), 575–8.
21. Cornaggia Castiglione, O. 'Nuove ricerche nella stazione palafitticola della Lagozza di Besnate.' In *Sibrium*, 2 (1955), 93–104.
22. Dumitrescu, V. *L'Età del Ferro nel Piceno*. Bucarest, 1929.
23. Emiliani, C., Cardini, L., Mayeda, T., MacBurney, C. B. M. and Tongiorgi, E. Palaeotemperature Analysis of Fossil Shells of Marine Molluscs (Food Refuse) from the Arene Candide Cave, Italy, and the Haua Fteah Cave, Cyrenaica. In *Isotopic and Cosmic Chemistry* (ed. H. Craig), North Holland Publishing Co., 1964, 133–56.

24. Gervasio, M. *I Dolmen e la civiltà del Bronzo nelle Puglie*, Bari, 1913.
25. Graziosi, P. 'I Balzi Rossi.' In *Istituto Internazionale di Studi Liguri* (1959).
26. Kaschnitz-Weinberg, G. von. 'Italien mit Sardinien.' In *Handbuch der Archäologie*, ed. Otto and Herbig, vol. 2, Erste Lieferung, 311–402.
27. Korošec, J. *Neolititska naseobina u Danilu Bitinju*. Zagreb, 1959.
28. Laviosa Zambotti, P. 'La ceramica de la Lagozza e la civiltà palafitticola italiana nei suoi rapporti con le civiltà mediterranee ed europee.' In *Boll. di Paletn. Ital.* n.s. 3 (1939), 62–112; 4 (1940), 83–164.
29. Laviosa Zambotti, P. 'Sulla costituzione dell'eneolitico italiano.' In *Studi Etruschi*, 13 (1939), 11–83.
30. Laviosa Zambotti P. 'Civiltà palafitticola lombarde e Civiltà di Golasecca.' In *Riv. Arch. Comense* (1939).
31. Leonardi, P. 'Témoignages de l'Homme de Néanderthal dans l'Italie du Nord.' In *Hundert Jahre Neanderthaler*, ed. G. H. R. von Koenigswald (1958), 231–52.
32. MacIver, D. Randall, *Villanovans and Early Etruscans*, Oxford, 1924.
33. MacIver, D. Randall. *The Iron Age in Italy*. Oxford, 1927.
34. Malvolti, F. *Appunti per una cronologia relativa del neoeneolitico emiliano*. Modena, 1953.
35. Mayer, M. *Apulien*. Berlin, 1914.
36. Mercando, L. *Le incisione rupestri di Monte Bego alla luce degli ultimi studi*. Turin, 1957.
37. Merhart, G. von. 'Donauländische Beziehungen der Früheisenzeitlichen Kulturen Mittelitaliens.' In *Bonner Jahrbücher* (1945), 1–90.
38. Müller-Karpe, G. *Beiträge zur Chronologie der Urnenfelderzeit nordlich und sudlich der Alpen*. Berlin, 1959.
39. Müller-Karpe, G. 'Sulla cronologia della tarda età del bronze e della prima età del ferro in Italia, nella zona alpina e nella Germania Meridionale.' In *Civiltà del Ferro* (Bologna, 1959), 447–60.
40. Müller-Karpe, G. *Zur Stadtwerdung Roms*, Heidelberg, 1962.
41. Novak, G. 'Markova spilja na Otoku Hvaru.' In *Arh. Radovi i rasprave*, I (1959), 5–60; II (1962), 91–102.
42. Onorato, G. O. *La ricerca archeologica in Irpinia*, 1960, 29.
43. Ornella Acanfora, M. 'Fontanella Mantovana e la cultura di Remedello.' In *Boll. di Paletn. Ital.* n.s. 10 (1956), 321–85.
44. Ornella Acanfora, M. Le Statue antropomorfe dell'Alto Adige. In *Cultura atesina*, VI (1952), 5–47.
45. Pallottino, M., 'Sulle facies culturale archaiche dell'Etruria.' In *Studi Etruschi* 13 (1939), 85–129.
46. Peroni, R. 'Dati di scavo sul sepolcreto di Pianello di Genga.' In *Arch. Anz.* (1963), cols. 363–403.
47. Ponzetti, F. M. and Biancofiore, F. 'Tomba di tipo siculo con nuovo osso a globuli nel territorio di Altamura (Bari).' In *Boll. di Paletn. Ital.* n.s. 11 (1957), 5–40.
48. Puglisi, S. M. 'Industria microlitica nei livelli a ceramica impressa di Coppa Nevigata.' In *Riv. di Scienze Preistoriche*, 10 (1955), 19–37.
49. Puglisi, S. M. *La civiltà apenninica*, Florence, 1959.
50. Radmilli, A. M. 'Considerazioni sul Mesolitico Italiano.' In *Ann. Univ. Ferrara* (1960).
51. Radmilli, A. M. (ed.) *Piccola Guida della preistoria Italiana*. Florence, 1962.
52. Rellini, U. *La più antica ceramica dipinta in Italia*. Rome, 1934.
53. Ritattore, F. 'La necropoli di Canegrate.' In *Sibrium*, I (1953–54), 7–48.

54. Säflund, G. *Le Terremare*. Lund, 1939.
55. Sestieri, P. C. 'Primi resultati dello scavo della necropoli preistorica di Paestum.' In *Rend. Acc. Napoli* (1947–8); also *Riv. di Scienze Preistoriche*, 1 (1946), 245–66, 11 (1947), 283–90.
56. Stevenson, R. B. K. 'The Neolithic Cultures of South-east Italy.' In *P.P.S.* 13 (1947), 85–100.
57. Taylour, Lord William, *Mycenaean Pottery in Italy and Adjacent Areas*. Cambridge, 1958.
58. Trump, D. H. 'The Apennine Culture of Italy.' In *P.P.S.* 24 (1958), 165–200.
59. Trump, D. H. 'Excavations at La Starza, Ariano Irpino.' In *Papers of the British School at Rome*, 31, n.s. 18 (1963).
60. Vaufrey, R. 'Le Paléolithique Italien.' In *Arch. de l'Institut de Pal. Hum.* Mém. 3 (Paris, 1928).
61. Verneau, R. Villeneuve, L. de, Boule, M. and Cartailhac, E. *Les Grottes de Grimaldi*. Monaco, 1906–19.
62. Walker, D. S. *A Geography of Italy*. London, 1958.
63. Zorzi, F. 'Le palafitte o terremare del Basso Veronese e il problema dei palafitticole in genere.' In *Sibrium*, 2 (1955), 157–73.

II. SICILY AND MALTA

1. Arias, P. E. 'La Stazione preistorica di Serraferlicchio presso Agrigento.' In *Mon. Ant.* 36 (1938), 693–838.
2. Baldacchino, J. G. and Evans, J. D. 'Prehistoric Tombs near Zebbuġ, Malta.' In *Papers of the British School at Rome*, 22 (1954), 1–21.
3. Bernabò Brea, L. 'Cueva Coruggi en el territorio de Pachino.' In *Ampurias*, 11 (1949), 1–23.
4. Bernabò Brea, L. 'Yacimientos paleolíticos del sudeste de Sicilia.' In *Ampurias*, 12 (1950), 135.
5. Bernabò Brea, L. 'Villaggio dell'Età del Bronzo nell'isola di Panarea.' In *Boll. d'Arte* (1951), 31–9.
6. Bernabò Brea, L. 'Segni grafici e contrasegni sulle ceramiche dell'Età del Bronzo delle Isole Eolie.' In *Minos*, 2 (1952), 5–28.
7. Bernabò Brea, L. *La Sicilia prehistórica y sus relaciones con Oriente*. Madrid, 1954.
8. Bernabò Brea, L. *Sicily before the Greeks*. London, 1957.
9. Bernabò Brea, L. 'Necropoli a incinerazione della Sicilia protostorica.' In *Civiltà del Ferro* (Bologna, 1960), 194–164.
10. Bernabò Brea, L. and Cavalier, M. 'Civiltà preistoriche delle Isole Eolie e del territorio di Milazzo.' In *Boll. di Paletn. Ital.* n.s. 10 (1956), 3–95.
11. Bernabò Brea, L. and Cavalier, M. 'Stazioni preistoriche delle Isole Eolie.' In *Boll. di Paletn. Ital.* n.s. 11 (1957).
12. Bernabò Brea, L. and Cavalier, M. *Meligunis Lipara*, 1. Palermo, 1960.
13. Cavalier, M. 'Salina: a Prehistoric Village in the Aeolian Islands.' In *Antiq.* 31 (1957), 9–14.
14. Cavalier, M. 'Les Cultures préhistoriques des îles éoliennes et leur rapport avec le monde égéen.' In *Bull. de Corr. Hell.* 84 (1960–1), 319–346.
15. Evans, J. D. 'The Prehistoric Culture-Sequence in the Maltese Archipelago.' In *P.P.S.* 19 (1953), 41–94.
16. Evans, J. D. 'Bossed Bone Plaques of the Second Millennium B.C.' In *Antiq.*, 30 (1956), 80–93.

17. Evans, J. D. 'The "Dolmens" of Malta and the Tarxien Cemetery Culture.' In *P.P.S.* 22, (1956), 85–101.
18. Evans, J. D. *Malta*. London, 1959.
19. Graziosi, P. 'Le Pitture e i graffiti preistorici dell'isola di Levanzo nel-l'Arcipelago della Egadi (Sicilia).' In *Riv. di Scienze Preistoriche*, 5 (1950), 1–43.
20. Graziosi, P. 'Nuovi graffiti della Grotta di Levanzo (Egadi).' In *Riv. di Scienze Preistoriche*, 8 (1953), 123–237; 10 (1954), 79–88.
21. Marconi Bovio, I. 'La cultura dipo Conca d'Oro della Sicilia Nord-Occidentale.' In *Mon. Ant.* 15 (1944).
22. Marconi Bovio, I. 'Incisioni rupestre all'Addaura (Palermo).' In *Boll. di Paletn. Ital.* n.s. 7 (1953), 5–22.
23. Marconi Bovio, I. 'Interpretazione dell'Arte parietale dell'Addaura.' In *Boll. d'Arte*, 36 (1953), 61–8.
24. Orsi, P. 'Stazione neolitica di Stentinello.' In *Boll. di Paletn. Ital.* 16 (1890), 177–200.
25. Orsi, P. 'Megara Hyblaea: Villaggio neolitico e tempio greco e di taluni singo-larissimi vasi di Paterno.' In *Mon. Ant.* 27 (1921), 109–80.
26. Peet, T. E. 'Contributions to the Study of the Prehistoric Period in Malta.' In *Papers of the British School at Rome*, 5 (1910), 141–63.
27. Time, S. 'Età del Rame in Sicilia e "Cultura tipo Conca d'Oro".' In *Boll. di Paletn. Ital.* n.s. 13 (1960–1), 113–51.
28. Trump, D. H. 'Note on new work at Ta Ħaġrat, Mġarr, 1961.' *Museum Dept. Annual Report* 1961 (Malta, 1962), 4–5.
29. Trump, D. H. 'Skorba, Malta and the Mediterranean.' In *Antiq.* 35 (1961), 300–3.
30. Trump, D. H. 'The Later Prehistory of Malta.' In *P.P.S.* 27 (1961), 253–62.
31. Trump, D. H. 'Progress reports on Skorba excavations.' In *Ill. Ldn. News*, 12 August 1961, 30 December 1961, 11 August 1962, 23 March 1963, 14 September 1963.
32. Trump, D. H. 'Carbon, Malta and the Mediterranean.' In *Antiq.* 37 (1963), 302–3.
33. Trump, D. H. *Skorba: Excavations carried out on behalf of the National Museum of Malta*, 1962–64. Soc. of Antiquaries Research Report no. xxii, Oxford, 1966.
34. Vaufrey, R. 'Les éléphants nains des îles méditerranéennes.' In *Arch. de l'Inst. de Paléont. hum.*, Mém. 6 (1929).

III. SARDINIA AND CORSICA

1. Audibert, J. 'Préhistoire de la Sardaigne: Résultats de Mission archéologique. In *Bull. Mus. d'Anth. Préh. de Monaco*, 5 (1958).
2. Bass, G. F. 'The Cape Gelidonya Wreck.' In *A.J.A.* (1961), 271.
3. Bass, G. F. and Throckmorton, P. 'Excavating a Bronze Age Shipwreck.' In *Archaeology*, 14 (1961), 78.
4. Bonfante, G. 'Who were the Philistines?' In *A.J.A.* (1946), 251.
5. Bray, W. *Aspects of the Early Metal Age in Sardinia* (Ph.D. dissertation no. 4177). Cambridge, 1962.
6. Bray, W. 'The Ozieri Culture of Sardinia.' In *Riv. di Scienze Preistoriche* (1963), 155.
7. Daniel, G. E. 'The Dual Nature of the Megalithic Colonisation of Prehistoric Europe.' In *P.P.S.* (1941), 1.

8. Grosjean, R. 'Les Statues-Menhirs de la Corse, I.' In *Etudes Corses*, 7 (1955), 1; 'Les Statues-Menhirs de la Corse, II.' In *Etudes Corses*, 12 (1956), 1.

9. Grosjean, R. 'Filitosa et son contexte archéologique.' In *Monuments et Mémoires Fondation Eugène Piot*, vol. 52, fasc. 1 (1961).

10. Grosjean, R. 'Recent Research in Corsica.' In *Antiq.* 40 (1966), 86.

11. Grosjean, R. *Filitosa et les monuments protohistoriques de la vallée du Taravo.* Paris, 1960.

12. Grosjean, R. 'Les Armes portées par les Statues-Menhirs de Corse.' In *Rev. Arch.* (July/Sept. 1962).

13. Grosjean, R. 'Die Megalithkultur von Korsika.' In *Die Umschau in Wissenschaft und Technik*, 13 (1964), 403.

14. Guido, M. *Sardinia.* London, 1963.

15. Lilliu, G. *La Civiltà dei Sardi dal neolitico all'età dei nuraghi.* Turin, 1963.

16. Lilliu, G. *I Nuraghi—torri preistoriche della Sardegna nuragica.* Rome, 1950.

17. Lilliu, G. 'The Nuraghi of Sardinia.' In *Antiq.* 33 (1959), 32.

18. Lilliu, G. *Scultura della Sardegna Nuragica.* Cagliari, 1956.

19. Mackenzie, D. 'Le Tombe dei Giganti nelle loro relazioni dei nuraghi della Sardegna.' In *Ausonia* (1908) 18; 'The tombs of the Giants and the Nuraghi of Sardinia in their West-European relations.' In *Memnon* (1908), 280.

20. Mackenzie, D. 'The Dolmens, Tombs of the Giants and Nuraghi of Sardinia.' In *Papers of the British School at Rome*, 5 (1910), 89; 'Dolmens and Nuraghi of Sardinia,' *ibid.* 6 (1913), 127.

21. Mortillet, A. de. 'Rapport sur les Monuments Mégalithiques de la Corse.' In *Nouvelles archives des Missions scientifiques et littéraires* (1893), 1.

22. Pallottino, M. *The Etruscans.* London, 1955.

23. Pallottino, M. *La Sardegna nuragica.* Rome, 1950.

24. Pesce, G. *Nora: guida degli scavi.* Cagliari, 1957.

25. Pesce, G. *Sardegna Punica.* Cagliari, 1957.

26. Piggott, S. *The Neolithic Culture of the British Isles.* Cambridge, 1954.

27. Sandars, N. K. 'The Last Mycenaeans and the European Late Bronze Age.' In *Antiq.* 38 (1964), 258.

28. Schaeffer, C. F. A. *Enkomi-Alasia.* Paris, 1952, p. 28.

29. Wainwright, G. A. 'The Teresh, the Etruscans and Asia Minor.' In *A. St.* 9 (1959), 197.

30. Wainwright, G. A. 'Some Sea Peoples.' In *J.E.A.* 47 (1961), 71.

31. Walker, W. G. (ed.). *Sardinian Studies.* London, 1938.

32. Zervos, C. *La Civilisation de la Sardaigne du début de l'Enéolithique à la fin de la Période Nouragique.* Paris, 1954.

#### IV. SOUTHERN FRANCE

1. Arnal, J. *Les Dolmens du Département de l'Hérault.* 1963. (Being vol. 15 of *Préhistoire.*)

2. Arnal, J. 'La Grotte de la Madeleine.' In *Zephyrus* (1956), 33.

3. Arnal, J. *Bull. Soc. préh. fr.* (1961), 571; Arnal, J., Martin-Granel, H. and Sangmeister, E. *Germania*, 41 (1963), 229, and *Antiq.* (1964), 191.

4. Arnal, J. Quoted in *Antiq.* 38 (1964), 246, and 39 (1965), 2.

5. Arnal, J. and Prades, H. 'El Neolítico y Calcolítico Franceses.' In *Ampurias*, 21 (1959), 69.

6. Bailloud, G. and Mieg de Boofzheim, P. *Les Civilisations Néolithiques de la France dans leur Contexte Européen.* Paris, 1955.

7. Benoit, F. *Entremont, capitale celto-ligure des Salyens de Provence.* Aix, 1957.

8. Benoit, F. 'Relations de Marseille Grecque avec le Monde Occidental.' In *Riv. Studi Liguri* (1956), 1–32.
9. Bérard, G. *Bull. Soc. préh. fr.* (1954), 281; (1955), 666.
10. Bernabò Brea, L. 'Le culture preistoriche della Francia Meridionale.' In *Riv. Studi Liguri* (1949) 45.
11. Briard, J. *L'Age de Bronze*. Paris, 1959.
12. Burnez, C. In *Bull. Soc. préh. fr.* (1957), 535.
13. Burnez, C. quoted in Coursaget, J., Giot, P. R. and Le Run, J. 'C-14 Neolithic Dates from France.' In *Antiq.* 34 (1960), 148.
14. Constantin, E. 'Mobilier funéraire des Dolmens de la Région des "Grands Causses".' In *Genava* (1953), 85.
15. Crawford, O. G. S. *Antiq.* 1 (1927), 100, 259, 387; (1928), 4; (1929), 353; (1930), 362.
16. Daniel, G. E. 'The Chronology of French Megalithic Tombs.' In *P.P.S.* (1958), 1.
17. Daniel, G. E. *The Prehistoric Chamber Tombs of France*. London, 1960.
18. Déchelette, J. *Manuel d'Archéologie Préhistorique, Celtique, et Gallo-Romaine. I. Archéologie Préhistorique*. Paris, 1908.
19. Escalon de Fonton, M. 'Préhistoire de la Basse Provence.' In *Préhistoire* (1950), 1.
20. Hatt, J.-J. *Histoire de la Gaule Romaine*, 120 B.C. *to* 451 A.D. Paris, 1959.
21. Hemp, W. J. *A.J.* (1933), 33; *P.P.S.* (1935), 108.
22. Hencken, H. O'N. *The Archaeology of Cornwall and Scilly*. London, 1932.
23. Hodson, F. R. 'Some Aspects of the Celto-Ligurians in Southern France between the Foundation of Marseille (600 B.C.) and the Roman Occupation (123 B.C.)' (Ph.D. dissertation 3315). Cambridge, 1958.
24. Jacobsthal, P. *Early Celtic Art*. Oxford, 1949.
25. Jacobsthal, P. and Neuffer, E. 'Gallia Graeca: Recherches sur l'Hellénisation de la Provence.' In *Préhistoire* (1933).
26. Joffroy, R. *L'Oppidum de Vix et la Civilisation Hallstattienne Finale dans l'Est de la France*. Paris, 1960.
27. Kimmig, W. *Revue arch. de l'Est et du Centre-Est* (1952), 7 and 137; (1954), 7.
28. Kimmig, W. 'Zur Urnenfelderkultur in Westeuropa.' In *Festschrift für Peter Goessler* (1954), 41.
29. Lantier, R. and Hubert, J. *Les Origines de l'Art Français*. Paris, 1947.
30. Leroi-Gourhan, A., Hatt, J.-J. and Duval, P.-M. *Les Celtes*, no. 147 in *La Documentation photographique*. Paris, 1955.
31. Louis, M. 'Le Néolithique dans le Gard.' In *Cahiers d'histoire et d'archéologie* (1933), 1.
32. Louis, M. *Préhistoire du Languedoc méditerranéen et du Roussillon*. Nîmes, 1948.
33. Louis, M., Taffanel, O. and Taffanel, J. *Le Premier Age du Fer Languedocien*. Bordighera–Montpellier, 1955.
34. Mortillet, G. de. *Le Préhistorique*. Paris, 1883.
35. Mortillet, G. de. *Formation de la Nation Française*. Paris, 1897.
36. Mortillet, G. and Mortillet A. de. *Musée Préhistorique*. Paris, 1881.
37. Navarro, J. M. de. 'Massilia and Early Celtic Culture.' In *Antiq.* 2 (1928), 423.
38. Niederlender, A., Lacam, R. and Arnal, J. In *Bull. Soc. préh. fr.* 49 (1952), 477; 50 (1953), 241 and 515.
39. Niederlender, A. Quoted in Coursaget, J., Giot, P.-R. and Le Run, J. 'C-14 Neolithic Dates from France.' In *Antiq.* 34 (1960), 147.

40. Octobon, E. 'Statues-menhirs, stèles gravées, dalles sculptées.' In *Rev. anth.* (1931), 299.

41. Piggott, S. 'Le néolithique occidental et le chalcolithique en France: esquisse préliminaire.' In *Anth.* (1953), 401; (1954), 1.

42. Pradenne, V. de. 'The Glozel Forgeries.' In *Antiq.* 4 (1930), 201.

43. Sandars, N. K. *Bronze Age Cultures in France: the later phases from the thirteenth to the seventh century, B.C.* Cambridge, 1957.

44. Savory, H. N. 'The "Sword-bearers". A reinterpretation.' In *P.P.S.* (1948), 155.

45. Smith, M. A. 'The Mesolithic in the South of France.' In *P.P.S.* (1952), 103.

46. Varagnac, A. and Fabre, G. *L'Art gaulois.* 1956.

### V. SPAIN AND PORTUGAL

1. Almagro, M. 'El depósito de la ria de Huelva y el final de la Edad del Bronce en el Occidente de Europa.' In *Ampurias*, 2 (1940), 85–143.

2. Almagro, M. In *Historia de España*, ed. R. Menéndez Pidal, vol. 1, part 1 (Madrid, 1946), 443–85.

3. Almagro, M. In *Historia de España*, ed. R. Menéndez Pidal, vol. 1, part 2 (Madrid, 1952), 141–241.

4. Almagro, M. *Origen y formación del Pueblo Hispano.* Barcelona, 1958.

5. Almagro, M. 'La Primera Fecha absoluta para la cultura de Los Millares a base del Carbono 14.' In *Ampurias*, 21 (1959), 249–51.

6. Almagro, M. *Manual de Historia Universal. Vol.* 1. *Prehistoria*, ch. VIII. Madrid, 1960.

7. Almagro, M. 'El poblado de Almizaraque de Herrerías (Almería).' In *Atti del VI Congresso Internazionale delle Scienze Preistoriche e Protostoriche, Roma, 1962, II*, Communicazioni 1–IV (1965), 378.

8. Almagro, M. 'El problema de la revisión de la Cronología del Arte Rupeste Quaternario.' In *Miscelania en Homenaje al Abate Henri Breuil* (Barcelona, 1964), 87–100.

9. Almagro, M. and Arribas, A. *El Poblado y la Necrópolis Megalíticos de Los Millares (Sante Fe de Mondújar, Almería)* Madrid, 1963.

10. Arambourg, C. 'Une Découverte récente en Paléontologie Humaine, *l'Atlanthropus* de Ternifine (Algérie).' In *Quaternaria*, 2 (1954–5), 5–13.

11. Arribas, A. 'El urbanismo durante el bronce primitivo.' In *Zephyrus*, 10 (1959), 81–128.

12. Arribas, A. *The Iberians.* London, 1963.

13. Athayde, A. and Texeira, C. 'A necropole e o esqueleto de S. Paio de Antas e o problema dos vasos de largo bordo horizontal.' *Communicações apresentados ao I° Congresso do Mundo Português*, 1940.

14. Blance, B. 'Early Bronze Age Colonists in Iberia.' In *Antiq.* 35 (1961) 192–202.

15. Blance, B. 'The Argaric Bronze Age in Iberia.' In *Rev. de Guimarães*, 74 (1964), 129–42.

16. Bosch Gimpera, P. *Etnologia de la Península Ibérica.* Barcelona, 1930.

17. Bosch Gimpera, P. 'Two Celtic Waves in Spain.' In *Proc. Brit. Acad.* 26 (1939), 7–126.

18. Evans, J. D. 'Two Phases of Prehistoric Settlement in the Western Mediterranean.' In *Bull Inst. Archaeol. London*, 1 (1955–6), 16–22.

19. Gimenez Reyna, S. 'Alcaide.' In *Noticiario Arqueológico Hispánico*, 1 (1952), 47–57.

20. Gossé, G. 'Aljoroque, estación neolítica inícial de la provincia de Almería.' In *Ampurias*, 3 (1941), 63–84.
21. Hawkes, C. F. C. 'Las relaciones entre la Península Ibérica y las Islas Británicas.' In *Ampurias*, 14 (1952), 81–119.
22. Hencken, H. 'Carp's Tongue Swords in Spain, France and Italy.' In *Zephyrus*, 7, 125–78.
23. Jordá Cerdá, F. *El Solutrense en España*. Oviedo, 1955.
24. Junghans, S., Sangmeister, E. and Schroeder, M. *Metallanalysen Kupferzeitlicher und frühbronzezeitlicher Bodenfunde aus Europa*. Berlin, 1960.
25. Leisner, G. and Leisner, V. *Die Megalithgraber des Iberischen Halbinsel, Der Süden* (Berlin, 1943); *Der Westen*, I–III (Berlin, 1956, 1959, 1960).
26. Leisner, G. and Leisner, V. *Antas do Concelho de Reguengos de Monsaraz*. Lisbon, 1951.
27. Leisner, G., Leisner, V. and Cerdán Márquez, C. *Los Sepulcros Megalíticos de Huelva*. Madrid, 1952.
28. Leisner, V. and Veiga Ferreira, O da. 'Primeiras datas de radiocarbono 14 para a cultura megalitica portuguesa.' In *Rev. de Guimarães*, 13 (1963), 359–66.
29. MacWhite, E. *Estudios sobre las relaciones Atlánticas de la Península Hispánica en la Edad del Bronce*. Madrid, 1951.
30. Maluquer de Motes, J. In *Historia de España*, ed. R. Menéndez Pidal, vol. 1, part 1 (1946), 717–51.
31. Maluquer de Motes, J. *La Cueva de Toralla*. Zaragoza, 1949.
32. Maluquer de Motes, J. *El Yacimiento de Cortes de Navarra, Estudio Crítico*, I, II, Pamplona, 1954, 1958.
33. Maluquer de Motes, J. *Nuevas Orientaciones en el Problema de Tartessos*. Primer Symposium de Prehistoria Peninsular, 273–97. Pamplona, 1960.
34. Maluquer de Motes, J. and Taracena, B. In *Historia de España*, ed. R. Menéndez Pidal, vol. 1, part 3 (1954), 5–299.
35. Mata Carriazos, J. de. 'Gold of Tarshish.' In *Ill. Ldn News*, 31 January 1959.
36. Maxwell Hyslop, R. 'Notes on some distinctive kinds of bronzes from Populonia, Etruria.' In *P.P.S.* 22 (1956), 126–42.
37. Mélida, Tesoro de la Aliseda. *Bol. de la Soc. Esp. de Excursiones*, 2 (1921), 96–128; 'Der Schatz von Aliseda.' In *Arch. Anz.* (1928), 497–510.
38. Menéndez Pidal, R. (ed.). *Historia de España*, vol. 1, parts 1–3. Madrid, 1946–54.
39. Paço, A. do and Sangmeister, E. 'Vila Nova de San Pedro, eine befestigte Siedlung der Kupferzeit in Portugal.' In *Germania*, 34 (1956), 223.
40. Pericot, L. *La Cueva de Parpalló, Gandia*. Madrid, 1942.
41. Pericot, L. 'La Cueva de la Cocina.' In *Archivo de Prehist. Levant.* 2 (1945), 8–12.
42. Pericot, L. *Los Sepulcros Megalíticos Catalanes y la Cultura Pirinaica*, 2nd ed. Barcelona, 1950.
43. Pericot, L. *Historia de España*, vol. 1 (2nd ed.). Barcelona, 1958.
44. Pericot, L. (ed.) *Corpus de Sepulcros Megalíticos*, fascs. 1 and 2, Barcelona, 1961; fasc. 3, Gerona, 1964. In progress.
45. Pierson Dixon, L. *The Iberians of Spain*. Oxford, 1940.
46. Ramón, J. and Oxea, F. *Lápidas sepulcrales de la Edad del Bronce en Extremadura*. Madrid, 1951.
47. Renfrew, A. C. 'The Neolithic and Early Bronze Age Cultures of the Cyclades and their External Relations' (Ph.D. dissertation). Cambridge, 1965.

48. Santa Olalla, J. M. 'Cereales y plantas de la cultura Ibero-Sahariana en Almizaraque (Almería). In *Cuadernos de Historia Primitiva*, 1 (1946), 35–45.
49. San Valero Aparisi, J. 'El Neolítico Europeo y sus Raices,' In *Cuadernos de de Historia Primitiva*, 9–10 (1954–55).
50. Savory, H. N. 'The Atlantic Bronze Age in South-West Europe.' In *P.P.S.* 15 (1949), 128–55.
51. Schubart, H. 'Zum Beginn der El Argar-Kultur.' In *Atti del VI Congresso Internazionale delle Scienze Preistoriche e Protostoriche, Roma, 1962, II,* Communicazioni I–IV, (1965), 415.
52. Schule, W. 'Problem der Eisenzeit auf der Iberischen Halbinsel.' In *Jahrbuch des Römisch-Germanischen Zentralmuseums Mainz,* 7. Jahrgang (1960), 59–125.
53. Serra y Ráfols, J. de C. 'La Exploración de la Necrópolis Neolítica de la Bóvila Madurell en Sant Quirze de Galliners.' In *Museo de la Ciudad de Sabadell,* 3 (1947), 57–79.
54. Siret, H. and Siret, L. *Les Premiers Ages du Métal dans le Sud-est de l'Espagne.* Brussels, 1887.
55. Taradell, M. 'Die Ausgrabung von Ghar Cahal ("Schwarze Höhle") in Spanisch Morokko.' In *Germania,* 33 (1955).
56. Taramelli, *Il ripostiglio di bronzi nuraghici di Monte Sa Idda, Cagliari.* In *Mon. Ant.* 27 (1921), 5–98.

### VI. NORTH AFRICA

1. Alimen, H. *The Prehistory of Africa.* London, 1957.
2. Balout, L. *Préhistoire de l'Afrique du Nord.* Paris, 1955.
3. Breuil, H. *L'Afrique Préhistorique.* Paris, 1940.
4. Cornevin, R. and Cornevin, M. *Histoire de l'Afrique des origines à nos jours.* Paris, 1964.
5. Ford Johnston, J. L. *Neolithic cultures of North Africa.* Liverpool, 1959.
6. Gautier, E. F. *Le passé de l'Afrique du Nord.* Paris, 1937; *Les siècles obscures du Maghreb.* Paris, 1942.
7. Gsell, S. *Histoire ancienne de l'Afrique du Nord.* Paris, 1913–27.
8. Julien, C. A. *Histoire de l'Afrique du Nord des origines à la conquête arabe* (revised by C. Courtois). Paris, 1951.
9. Leakey, L. S. B. *Stone Age Africa; an Outline of Prehistory in Africa.* Oxford, 1936.
10. Lhote, H. *A la découverte des fresques de Tassili.* Paris, 1959.
11. MacBurney, C. B. M. *The Stone Age of Northern Africa.* London, 1960.
12. MacBurney, C. B. M. *Haua Fteah.* Cambridge (forthcoming).
13. Pedrals, D. P. de. *Archéologie de l'Afrique Noire.* Paris, 1950.
14. Reygasse, M. *Monuments funéraires préhistoriques de l'Afrique du Nord.* Algiers, 1950.
15. Ruhlmann, A. *Le Marve Préhistorique.* Algiers, 1948.
16. Vaufrey, R. 'L'Art Rupestre Nord-Africain.' In *Inst. de. Paléont. Humaine,* Mém. 20 (1939).
17. Vaufrey, R. *Préhistoire de l'Afrique. I. Le Maghreb.* Paris, 1950.
18. Wulsin, F. R. 'The Prehistoric Archaeology of North-West Africa.' In *Papers of the Peabody Museum,* XIX, no. 1 (1941).

## CHAPTER XXXVIII

References have been given in the text for the most important passages in ancient authors which concern the Dark Age migrations to the Eastern Aegean.

### I. AEOLIC SETTLEMENT IN LESBOS AND THE ADJACENT COASTLANDS
#### General

1. Koldewey, R. *Die antiken Baureste der Insel Lesbos*. Berlin, 1890.
2. Mantzouranes, D. Οἱ πρῶτες ἐγκαταστάσεις τῶν ῾Ελλήνων στὴ Λέσβο. Mytilene, 1949.
3. Bérard, J. 'La migration éolienne.' In *Rev. arch.* 1959, t. I, 1–28.

#### Excavations

4. Lamb, W. *Excavations at Thermi in Lesbos*. Cambridge, 1936.
5. Lamb, W. 'Antissa.' In *B.S.A.* 31 (1930–1), 166–78; 32 (1931–2), 41–6.

#### Topography and sites

6. Blegen, C. W., Boulter, Cedric G., Caskey, John L. and Rawson, Marion. *Troy*, IV. Princeton, 1958.
7. Cook, J. M. 'Greek Archaeology in Western Asia Minor.' In *Archaeological Reports for 1959–60*. London, 1960.
8. Leaf, W. *Strabo on the Troad*. Cambridge, 1923.

### II. THE IONIC MIGRATIONS
#### General

1. Cassola, F. *La Ionia nel Mondo Miceneo*. Naples, 1957.
2. Cook, J. M. *Greek Archaeology in Western Asia Minor*.
3. Sakellariou, M. P. *La migration grecque en Ionie*. Athens, 1958.

#### Excavations

4. Cook, J. M. 'Old Smyrna, 1948–1951.' In *B.S.A.* 53–4 (1958–9), 1–34.
5. Gerkan, A. von. *Milet*, I, 8 (*Kalabaktepe, Athenatempel und Umgebung*). Berlin, 1925. Weickert, C., reports in *Ist. Mitt.* 7 (1956), and later issues.
6. For other sites, references to recent work will be found in M. J. Mellink's annual reports in *A.J.A.* 59 (1955), and later issues; and in Cook, J. M., *Greek Archaeology in Western Asia Minor*.

#### Topography and sites

7. Keil, J. 'Zur Topographie von der ionischen Küste südlich von Ephesos.' In *Ö.J.H.* 11 (1908), Beiblatt, 135–68; 'Forschungen in der Erythraea, I.' In *Ö.J.H.* 13 (1910), Beiblatt, 5–74; and 'Forschungen in der Erythraea, II.' In *Ö.J.H.* 15 (1912), Beiblatt, 49–76. Cook, J. M., *Greek Archaeology in Western Asia Minor*.

### III. THE TRIOPIAN DORIANS AND THE CARIAN COAST
#### Evidence of pottery

1. Desborough, V. R. d'A. *Protogeometric Pottery*. Oxford, 1952.
2. Stubbings, F. H. *Mycenaean Pottery from the Levant*. Cambridge, 1951.

## Topography, sites and cults

3. Bean, G. E. and Cook, J. M. 'The Cnidia.' In *B.S.A.* 47 (1952), 171–212.
4. Bean, G. E. and Cook, J. M. 'The Carian Coast, III.' In *B.S.A.* 52 (1957), 58–146.
5. Fraser, P. M. and Bean, G. E. *The Rhodian Peraea and Islands.* Oxford, 1954. Cook, J. M. 'Cnidian Chersonese and Rhodian Peraea.' In *J.H.S.* 81 (1961).
6. Laumonier, A. *Les cultes indigènes en Carie.* Paris, 1958.
7. Strabo XIII, 611. Paton, W. R. and Myres, J. L., 'Karian Sites and Inscriptions.' In *J.H.S.* 16 (1896), 188–271. Bean, G. E. and Cook, J. M., 'The Halicarnassus Peninsula.' In *B.S.A.* 50 (1955), 85–171.

### IV. THE IONIC CITIES IN THE DARK AGE

#### General

1. Cook, R. M. 'Ionia and Greece in the Eighth and Seventh Centuries, B.C.' In *J.H.S.* 66 (1946), 67–98.
2. Roebuck, C. *Ionian Trade and Colonization.* New York, 1959.

#### Excavations

3. Buschor, E. and others on Samos in *Ath. Mitt.* 58 (1933), and later issues.
4. Cook, J. M., 'Old Smyrna, 1948–1951', and Nicholls, R. V., 'Old Smyrna: the Iron Age Fortifications and associated Remains in the City Perimeter.' In *B.S.A.* 53–4 (1958–9), 1–137.
5. Keil, J. 'XII. Vorläufiger Bericht über die Ausgrabungen in Ephesos.' In *Ö.J.H.* 23 (1926), Beiblatt, 247 ff.
6. Kleiner, G. 'Entdeckung und Ausgrabung des Panionion.' In *Neue deutsche Ausgrabungen im Mittelmeergebiet und im vorderen Orient.* Berlin, 1959.
7. Current reports on Phrygia and Lydia by R. S. Young and G. R. Edwards (Gordium) and by G. M. A. Hanfmann and A. H. Detweiler (Sardis) in recent issues of *A.J.A.* For Phrygian art, E. Akurgal, *Phrygische Kunst,* Ankara, 1955. For Greece and the East, T. J. Dunbabin, *The Greeks and their Eastern Neighbours.* London, 1957.

#### Panionic League

8. Wilamowitz-Moellendorff, U. von. 'Panionion.' In *Sitzungsb. Berlin* (1906), 38–57 (*Kleine Schriften*, v, 1, 128 ff.). Roebuck, C. 'The Early Ionian League.' In *Cl. Phil.* 50 (1955), 26–40.

### A. ADDENDA

#### General

1. Akurgal, Ekrem. *Die Kunst Anatoliens von Homer bis Alexander.* Berlin, 1961.
2. Cook, J. M. *The Greeks in Ionia and the East.* London, 1962.
3. Cook, J. M. and Blackman, D. J. 'Greek Archaeology in Western Asia Minor.' In *Archaeological Reports for 1964–65.* London, 1965.
4. Bean, G. E. *Aegean Turkey.* London, 1966.

I

5. Lesbian amphictyony: for other possible situations of the 'common' sanctuary see J. D. Quin, *A.J.A.* 65 (1961), 391–3, and M. Paraskevaidis, *P.W.* 24 (1963), 1419–20 (s.v. 'Pyrrha').

II–III

6. For Mycenaean finds in western Asia Minor add V. R. d'A. Desborough, *The Last Mycenaeans and their Successors* (Oxford, 1964), 158–65; J. M. Cook and D. J. Blackman, *Greek Archaeology in Western Asia Minor* (1965), 43–4; Yusuf Boysal, 'Müzkebi Kazısı 1963 Kısa Raporu', *Belleten*, xxxi, no. 121 (1967), 67–76, *id.* 'New Excavations in Caria', *Anadolu*, 11 (1967), 32–56; G. M. A. Hanfmann and Jane C. Waldbaum, 'Two Submycenaean Vases and a Tablet from Stratonikeia in Caria', *A.J.A.* 72 (1968), 51–3.
7. Reports on excavations at Iasos, Dr Levi in *A.S.A.A.* 39–40 (1961–62) and later issues.

IV

8. Kleiner, G. *Alt-Milet*, Wiesbaden 1966, *id. Die Ruinen von Milet.* Berlin 1968 (with references to recent reports on discoveries at Miletus, pp. 158–9).
9. Boardman, John. *Excavations in Chios 1952–1955, Greek Emporio.* London, 1967.
10. Kleiner, G., Hommel, P., Müller-Wiener, W. *Panionion und Melie.* Berlin, 1967.
11. Huxley, G. L. *The Early Ionians.* London, 1966.
12. Roebuck, C. 'Tribal Organization in Ionia.' In *Trans. Amer. Philos. Soc.* 92 (1961), 495–507.

## CHAPTER XXXIX(*a*)

### I. THE IDENTIFICATION OF GREEK

1. Hoffmann, O. and Debrunner, A. *Geschichte der griechischen Sprache.* 2 vols. Berlin, 1953–4.
2. Lejeune, M. *Traité de phonétique grecque.* Ed. 2. Paris, 1955.
3. Meillet, A. *Aperçu d'une histoire de la langue grecque.* Ed. 6. Paris, 1948.
4. Myres, J. L. *Who were the Greeks?* Berkeley, 1930.
5. Schwyzer, E. *Griechische Grammatik.* 2 vols. Munich, 1938 (2nd impression 1953); 1950.

### II. THE CLASSIFICATION OF THE DIALECTS

1. Bechtel, F. *Die griechischen Dialekte.* 3 vols. Berlin, 1921–4.
2. Buck, C. D. *The Greek Dialects.* Revised ed. Chicago, 1955.
3. Palmer, L. R. 'The Language of Homer.' In Wace, A. J. B. and Stubbings, F. H., *A Companion to Homer.* London, 1962.
4. Porzig, W. 'Sprachgeographische Untersuchungen zu den altgriechischen Dialekten.' In *Indogerm. Forsch.* 61 (1954), 147 ff.

5. Risch, E. 'Die Gliederung der griechischen Dialekte in neuer Sicht.' In *Mus. Helv.* 12 (1955), 61 ff.
6. Thumb, A. and Scherer, A. *Handbuch der griechischen Dialekte.* Part 2. Heidelberg, 1959.

### III. HISTORICAL RECONSTRUCTION

1. Adrados, F. R. *La dialectologia griega como fuente para el estudio de las migraciones indoeuropeas en Grecia.* Salamanca, 1952.
2. Adrados, F. R. 'Achäisch, Jonisch und Mykenisch.' In *Indogerm. Forsch.* 62 (1955), 240 ff.
3. Buck, C. D. 'The Language Situation in and about Greece in the Second Millennium B.C.' In *Cl. Phil.* 21 (1926), 1 ff.
4. Caskey, J. L. 'The Early Helladic Period in the Argolid.' In *Hesperia*, 29 (1960), 285 ff.
5. Chadwick, J. 'The Greek Dialects and Greek Pre-history.' In *Greece and Rome*, 2nd series, 3 (1956), 38 ff.
6. Dow, S. 'The Greeks in the Bronze Age.' In *Rapports du XIe Congrès international des sciences historiques.* Stockholm, 1960.
7. Forbes, K. 'The Relations of the Particle ἄν with κε(ν) κα καν.' In *Glotta*, 37 (1958), 179 ff.
8. Haley, J. B. and Blegen, C. W. 'The Coming of the Greeks.' In *A.J.A.* 32 (1928), 141 ff.
9. Hampl, F. 'Die Chronologie der Einwanderung der griechischen Stämme.' In *Museum Helveticum*, 17 (1960), 57 ff.
10. Heubeck, A. 'Linear B und das ägäische Substrat.' In *Minos*, 5 (1957), 149 ff.
11. Kretschmer, P. 'Zur Geschichte der griechischen Dialekte.' In Gercke–Norden, *Einleitung.* Göttingen, 1896. Pp. 70 ff.
12. Lejeune, M. *Mémoires de philologie mycénienne.* Ière série. Paris, 1958.
13. Palmer, L. R. *Achaeans and Indoeuropeans.* Oxford, 1955.
14. Palmer, L. R. 'Luvian and Linear A.' In *Transactions of the Philological Society*, 1958, 75 ff.
15. Risch, E. 'La position du dialecte mycénien.' In *Études Mycéniennes.* Paris, 1956.
16. Risch, E. 'Frühgeschichte der griechischen Sprache.' In *Museum Helveticum*, 16 (1959), 215 ff.
17. Ruijgh, C. J. 'Le traitement des sonantes voyelles dans les dialectes grecs et la position du mycénien.' In *Mnemosyne*, series 4, 14 (1961), 193 ff.
18. Schachermeyr, F. 'Prähistorische Kulturen Griechenlands.' In *P.W.* 22, 2, cols. 1352 ff.
19. Schachermeyr, F. *Die ältesten Kulturen Griechenlands.* Stuttgart, 1955.
20. Tovar, A. 'Primitiva extensión geográphica del Jonio.' In *Emerita*, 12 (1944), 253 ff.
21. Tovar, A. 'Nochmals Ionier und Achäer im Lichte der Linear-B-Tafeln.' In Μνήμης Χάριν, Vienna, 1957. Vol. 2, pp. 188 ff.
22. Ventris, M. and Chadwick, J. *Documents in Mycenaean Greek.* Cambridge, 1956.
23. Vilborg, E. *A Tentative Grammar of Mycenaean Greek.* Göteborg, 1960.
24. Wace, A. J. B. 'Aegean Prehistory.' In *Antiq.* 32 (1958), 30 ff.

## CHAPTER XXXIX(*b*)

### G. GENERAL

1. Kirk, G. S. *The Songs of Homer*. Cambridge, 1962.
2. Page, D. L. *History and the Homeric Iliad*. Berkeley, 1959; Cambridge, 1963.

### II. THE ILIAD AND ODYSSEY AS TRADITIONAL ORAL POEMS

1. Bowra, Sir C. M. *Heroic Poetry*. London, 1952.
2. Bowra, Sir C. M. 'Homeric Epithets for Troy.' In *J.H.S.* 80 (1960), 16 ff.
3. Chadwick, H. M. and N. K. *The Growth of Literature*. 3 vols. Cambridge, 1932–40.
4. Gray, D. H. F. 'Homeric Epithets for Things.' In *Cl. Quart.* 61 (1947), 109 ff.; reprinted at A, 5, 55 ff.
5. Jeffery, L. H. 'Writing.' In Wace, A. J. B. and Stubbings, F. H. *A Companion to Homer*. London, 1962.
6. Jeffery, L. H. *The Local Scripts of Archaic Greece*. Oxford, 1961.
7. Kirk, G. S. 'Homer and Modern Oral Poetry: Some Confusions.' In *Cl. Quart*, n.s. 10 (1960), 371 ff.; reprinted at A, 5, 79 ff.
8. Lord, A. B. 'Homer's Originality: Oral Dictated Texts.' In *Trans. Amer. Philos. Soc.* 84 (1953), 124 ff.; reprinted at A, 5, 68 ff.
9. Lord, A. B. *The Singer of Tales*. Cambridge, Mass., 1960.
10. Notopoulos, J. A. 'Homer and Cretan Heroic Poetry.' In *A.J.Ph.* 73 (1952), 225 ff.
11. Parry, M. *L'Epithète traditionnelle dans Homère*. Paris, 1928. See below, A, 8.
12. Parry, M. and Lord, A. B. *Serbocroatian Heroic Songs*, 1. Cambridge, Mass., 1954.
13. Von der Mühll, P. 'Odyssee.' In *P.W.* Supplb. VII. Stuttgart, 1940, pp. 696 ff.

### III. THE LANGUAGE OF THE POEMS

1. Chantraine, P. *Grammaire homérique*. Paris, 1953–8.
2. Meillet, A. *Aperçu d'une histoire de la langue grecque*. Paris, 1930.
3. Palmer, L. R. 'The Language of Homer.' In Wace, A. J. B. and Stubbings, F. H., *A Companion to Homer*. London, 1962.
4. Risch, E. 'Die Gliederung der griechischen Dialekte in neuer Sicht.' In *Museum Helveticum*, 12 (1955), 61 ff.; reprinted at A, 5, 90 ff.
5. Shipp, G. P. *Studies in the Language of Homer*. Cambridge, 1953.
6. Ventris, M. and Chadwick, J. *Documents in Mycenaean Greek*. Cambridge, 1956.
7. Wackernagel, J. *Sprachliche Untersuchungen zu Homer*. Göttingen, 1916.

### IV. THE EXTENT AND IMPLICATION OF BRONZE AGE SURVIVALS

1. Bowra, Sir C. M. ''ΕΥΚΝΗΜΙΔΕΣ 'ΑΧΑΙΟΙ.' In *Mnemosyne* 14 (1961), 97 ff.
2. Hood, M. S. F. 'Archaeology in Greece, 1960–1.' In *Archaeological Reports for 1960–61*, 9 f.
3. Lorimer, H. L. *Homer and the Monuments*. Oxford, 1950.
4. Webster, T. B. L. *From Mycenae to Homer*. London, 1958.

V. CONTINUITY OF TRADITION FROM THE BRONZE AGE DOWN TO HOMER

1. Broneer, O. 'What Happened at Athens.' *A.J.A.* 52 (1948), 111 ff.
2. Burr, V. 'ΝΕΩΝ ΚΑΤΑΛΟΓΟΣ.' *Klio*, Beiheft 49 (1944).
3. Desborough, V. R. d'A. *Protogeometric Pottery.* Oxford, 1952.
4. Gray, D. H. F. 'Metal-working in Homer.' In *J.H.S.* 74 (1954), 1 ff.
5. Gray, D. H. F. 'Houses in the *Odyssey*.' In *Cl. Quart.* n.s. 5 (1955), 1 ff.
6. Levi, D. Report on excavation at Gortyn. In *A.S.A.A.* n.s. 33/4 (1955/6), 298 ff.
7. Orlandos, A. K. (ed.) Report on excavation at Iolcus. In *To Ergon* for 1961 (Athens, 1962), 51 ff., esp. 58 f.

VI. DISCONTINUITY OF TRADITION FROM THE BRONZE AGE
DOWN TO HOMER

1. Finley, M. I. 'Homer and Mycenae: Property and Tenure.' In *Historia*, 6 (1957), 133 ff.; reprinted at A, 5, 191 ff.

VII. THE DARK AGE AND AFTER

1. Blegen, C. W. 'Two Athenian Grave-groups of about 900 B.C.' In *Hesperia*, 21 (1952), 286 f.
2. Blegen, C. W. 'The Palace of Nestor Excavations of 1956.' In *A.J.A.* 61 (1957), 129–31.
3. Iakovides, S. Report on excavation at Perati. In *Praktika* for 1953 (Athens, 1956), 88 ff., esp. 100 f.
4. Kirk, G. S. 'Objective Dating Criteria in Homer.' In *Mus. Helv.* 17 (1960), 189 ff.; reprinted at A, 5, 174 ff.
5. Kourouniotes, K. Report on excavation at Traghanes. In 'Αρχ. 'Εφ. 1914, 99 ff., esp. 116 f.
6. von Massow, W. Report on excavation at Amyclae. In *Ath. Mitt.* 52 (1927), 24 ff.

VIII. THE ORAL TRADITION IN IONIA, AND LATER TRANSMISSION

1. Davison, J. A. 'The Transmission of the Text.' In Wace, A. J. B. and Stubbings, F. H., *A Companion to Homer.* London, 1962.
2. Erbse, H. 'Über Aristarchs Iliasausgaben.' In *Hermes*, 87 (1959), 275 ff.
3. Hampe, R. *Frühe griechische Sagenbilder.* Athens, 1936.
4. Labarbe, J. *L'Homère de Platon.* Liège, 1949.
5. Mazon, P. *Introduction à l'Iliade.* Paris, 1948.
6. Monro, D. B. *Homer's Odyssey, books XIII–XXIV.* Oxford, 1891.
7. Stubbings, F. H. 'Ithaca.' In Wace, A. J. B. and Stubbings, F. H., *A Companion to Homer.* London, 1962.

A. ADDENDA

1. Desborough, V. R. d'A. *The Last Mycenaeans and their Successors.* Oxford, 1964.
2. Finley, M. I. *Early Greece: the Bronze and Archaic Ages.* London, 1970.
3. Hainsworth, J. B. *The Flexibility of the Homeric Formula.* Oxford, 1968.

4. Hope Simpson, R. and Lazenby, J. F. *The Catalogue of the Ships in Homer's Iliad*. Oxford, 1970.
5. Kirk, G. S. 'Homer's *Iliad* and Ours.' In *Proc. Camb. Philol. Soc.*, n.s. (1970), 48 ff.
6. Kirk, G. S., ed. *Language and Background of Homer*. Heffer, Cambridge, 1964.
7. Parry, A. 'Have we Homer's *Iliad*?' *Yale Classical Studies*, 20 (1966), 175 ff.
8. Parry, A., ed. *The Making of Homeric Verse*: the collected papers of Milman Parry. Oxford, 1971. (Includes §11, 11.)
9. Snodgrass, A. *Early Greek Armour and Weapons*. Edinburgh, 1964.
10. Vernant, J.-P., ed. *Problèmes de la guerre en grèce ancienne*. Paris, 1968.

## CHAPTER XL

### GENERAL

1. Cook, A. B. *Zeus: A Study in Ancient Religion*. 3 vols. in 5. Cambridge, 1914–40.
2. Cornford, F. M. *Principium Sapientiae*. Cambridge, 1952.
3. Dodds, E. R. *The Greeks and the Irrational*. California University Press, 1951.
4. Farnell, L. R. *The Cults of the Greek States*. 3 vols. Oxford, 1896–1909.
5. Farnell, L. R. *Greek Hero Cults and Ideas of Immortality*. Oxford, 1921.
6. Gruppe, O. *Griechische Mythologie und Religionsgeschichte* (*Müllers Handbuch*, v, 2, 1 and 2). 2 vols. Munich, 1906.
7. Guthrie, W. K. C. *The Greeks and their Gods*. London, 1950.
8. Harrison, J. E. *Prolegomena to the Study of Greek Religion*. Ed. 3. Cambridge, 1922.
9. Harrison, J. E. *Themis: a Study of the Social Origins of Greek Religion*. Cambridge, 1912.
10. Kern, O. *Die Religion der Griechen*, I. Berlin, 1926.
11. Moulinier, L. *Le Pur et l'Impur dans la Pensée des Grecs*. Paris, 1952. Ch. 1: 'Les Origines'.
12. Nilsson, M. P. *A History of Greek Religion*. Ed. 2. Oxford, 1949.
13. Nilsson, M. P. *Geschichte der griechischen Religion*, I. Ed. 3. Munich, 1967.
14. Onians, R. B. *Origins of European Thought*. Ed. 2. Cambridge, 1954.
15. Rohde, E. *Psyche: the Cult of Souls and Belief in Immortality among the Greeks*. English translation. Ed. 2. New York, 1966.
16. Rose, H. J. *A Handbook of Greek Mythology*. Ed. 6. London, 1964.
17. Rose, H. J. *Ancient Greek Religion*. London, n.d. (1948).
18. Stengel, P. *Die griechischen Kultusaltertümer* (*Müllers Handbuch*, v, 3).
19. Wilamowitz, U. von. *Der Glaube der Hellenen*. 2 vols. Berlin, 1931–2.

### I. THE FORMATION OF GREEK RELIGION

1. Nilsson, M. P. *Geschichte der griechischen Religion*, I. Ed. 3. Munich, 1967. Introduction and sections I and II.
2. Pettazzoni, R. 'Les deux sources de la religion grecque.' In *Mnemosyne* ser. 3, vol. 4 (1951), 1–8.
3. Picard, C. *Les religions préhelléniques*. Paris, 1948.
4. Rose, H. J. *Modern Methods in Classical Mythology*. St Andrews, 1930.

## II. MINOAN AND MYCENAEAN RELIGION

1. Bennett, E. L., jnr. 'The Olive-Oil Tablets of Pylos.' In *Minos*, suppl. 2 (Salamanca, 1958). See also review of this by L. R. Palmer in *Gnomon*, 32 (1960), 193 ff.
2. Bohme, R. *Orpheus: das Alter der Kitharoden.* Berlin, 1953. App. IV: 'Zum grossen Goldring von Mykenä'.
3. Deubner, O. Review of M. P. Nilsson, 'The Minoan–Mycenaean Religion and its Survival in Greek Religion'. In *Gnomon*, 25 (1953), 145 ff.
4. Guthrie, W. K. C. 'Early Greek Religion in the Light of the Decipherment of Linear B.' In *B.I.C.S.* no. 6 (1959), 35 ff.
5. Herkenrath, E. 'Mykenische Kultszenen.' In *A.J.A.* 41 (1937), 411 ff.
6. Matz, F. *Göttererscheinung und Kultbild im minoischen Kreta.* Mainz Ak. d. Wiss. u. Litt., Wiesbaden, 1958.
7. Mylonas, G. E. 'Homeric and Mycenaean Burial Customs.' In *A.J.A.* (1958), 56 ff.
8. Mylonas, G. E. 'The Cult of the Dead in Helladic Times.' In *Studies... D. M. Robinson*, I, 1958, 64 ff.
9. Nilsson, M. P. *The Minoan–Mycenaean Religion and its Survival in Greek Religion.* Ed. 2. Lund, 1950.
10. Nilsson, M. P. *Homer and Mycenae.* London, 1933. Especially ch. VII.
11. Nilsson, M. P. *Geschichte der griechischen Religion*, I. Ed. 3. Munich, 1967. Section II.
12. Nock, A. D. Review of A. W. Persson, *The Religion of Greece in Prehistoric Times.* In *A.J.A.* 47 (1943), 492 ff.
13. Pendlebury, J. D. S. *The Archaeology of Crete.* London, 1939.
14. Persson, A. W. *The Religion of Greece in Prehistoric Times.* California and Cambridge, 1952.
15. Picard, C. *Les religions préhelléniques.* Paris, 1948. Chs. II–IV.
16. Ventris, M. and Chadwick, J. *Documents in Mycenaean Greek.* Cambridge, 1956.
17. Vallois, R. Review of M. P. Nilsson, *The Minoan–Mycenaean Religion and its Survival in Greek Religion.* In *Rev. ét. anc.* 32 (1930), 47 ff.

## III. GREEK RELIGION AND MYTHOLOGY

1. Nilsson, M. P. *The Minoan–Mycenaean Religion and its Survival in Greek Religion.* Ed. 2. Lund, 1950. Appendix, 34–40.
2. Nilsson M. P. *The Mycenaean Origin of Greek Mythology.* California and Cambridge, 1942.
3. Nilsson M. P. 'Mycenaean and Homeric Religion' (Lecture delivered at Cambridge and Manchester). In *Arch. f. Rel.* 33 (1936), 84 ff. (= M. P. Nilsson, *Opuscula Selecta*, II, Lund, 1952, 683 ff.).
4. Nilsson M. P. *Geschichte der griechischen Religion*, I. Ed. 3. Munich, 1967. Section II.
5. Persson, A. W. *The Religion of Greece in Prehistoric Times.* California and Cambridge, 1952. Ch. v.
6. Wust, E. 'Die Seelenwagung in Ägypten und Griechenland.' In *Arch. f. Rel.* 36 (1939), 162 ff.

### IV. EARLY COSMOGONICAL AND THEOGONICAL MYTHS

1. Baccou, R. *Histoire de la science grecque de Thalès à Socrate.* Paris, 1951. Ch. II: 'Période Homérique et Hésiodique.'
2. Barnett, R. D. 'The Epic of Kumarbi and the Theogony of Hesiod.' In *J.H.S.* 65 (1945), 100 f.
3. Cornford, F. M. 'A Ritual Basis for Hesiod's Theogony'. In *The Unwritten Philosophy.* Cambridge, 1950, 95 ff.
4. Cornford, F. M. *Principium Sapientiae.* Cambridge, 1952. Chs. XII–XVI.
5. Diels, H. and Kranz, W. *Die Fragmente der Vorsokratiker*, I. Ed. 6. Berlin, 1951–2, A I: 'Kosmologische Dichtung der Frühzeit'.
6. Dussaud, R. *Les antécédents orientaux de la Théogonie d'Hésiode.* Brussels, 1949.
7. Gaster, T. *Thespis.* Revised ed. New York, 1961.
8. Gomperz, H. 'Zur Theogonie des Pherekydes.' In *Wien. St.* 47 (1929), 14 ff.
9. Gruppe, O. *Die griechischen Culte und Mythen in ihren Beziehungen zu den orientalischen Religionen*, I. Leipzig, 1887.
10. Gruppe, O. *Die rhapsodische Theogonie und ihre Bedeutung innerhalb der orphischen Litteratur* (XVII. Supplementband des *Jahrb. f. Cl. Ph.*, 1890).
11. Hesiod. *Theogony* (ed. P. Mazon, with introduction). Paris, 1928.
12. Kern, O. *Orphicorum Fragmenta.* Ed. 2. Berlin, 1963.
13. Kern. O. *Die Religion der Griechen*, I. Berlin, 1926. Ch. XI: 'Hesiodos von Askra'.
14. Kern, O. *De Orphei Epimenidis Pherecydis theogoniis quaestiones criticae.* Berlin, 1888.
15. Kirk, G. S. and Raven, J. E. *The Presocratic Philosophers.* Cambridge, 1957. Ch. I: 'The Forerunners of Philosophical Cosmogony.'
16. Lesky, A. 'Zum hethitischen und griechischen Mythos.' In *Eranos*, 52 (1954), 9 ff.
17. Lukas, F. *Die Grundbegriffe in den Kosmogonien der alten Völker.* Leipzig, 1893. Ch. V: 'Die Kosmogonien der Griechen'.
18. Schwenn, F. *Die Theogonie des Hesiodos.* Heidelberg, 1934.
19. Walcot, P. 'The Text of Hesiod's Theogony and the Hittite Epic of Kumarbi.' In *Cl. Quart.* 49 (1956). P. 199, n. 3, for bibliography on Hittite and Greek mythology.

### V. HOMERIC RELIGION

1. Calhoun, G. M. 'Zeus the Father in Homer.' In *Trans. Amer. Philos. Soc.* 66 (1935), 1 ff.
2. Calhoun, G. M. 'Homer's Gods: Prolegomena.' In *Trans. Amer. Philos. Soc.* 68 (1937), 11 ff.
3. Calhoun, G. M. 'The Higher Criticism on Olympus'. In *A.J.Ph.* 58 (1938), 257 ff.
4. Duffy, J. M. *A Comparative Study of the Religion of the Iliad and the Odyssey.* Chicago, 1937.
5. Ehnmark, E. *The Idea of God in Homer.* Uppsala, 1935.
6. Ehnmark, E. *Anthropomorphism and Miracle.* Uppsala, 1939.
7. Greene, W. C. *Moira: Fate, Good and Evil in Greek Thought.* Harvard, 1944.
8. Grube, G. M. A. 'The Gods of Homer.' In *The Phoenix*, 5 (1951), 62 ff.
9. Heden, E. *Homerische Götterstudien.* Uppsala, 1912.
10. Krause, W. 'Zeus und Moira bei Homer.' In *Wien. St.* 64 (1949), 10 ff.
11. Kullmann, W. *Das Wirken der Götter in der Ilias.* Berlin, 1956.
12. Lorimer, H. L. *Homer and the Monuments.* London, 1950.

13. Nilsson, M. P. 'Götter und Psychologie bei Homer.' In *Arch. f. Rel.* 22 (1923–4) (= M. P. Nilsson, *Opuscula Selecta*, 1 (Lund, 1951), 355 ff.).
14. Robert, F. *Homère*. Paris, 1950.

### VI. THE OLYMPIAN GODS

1. Guthrie, W. K. C. *The Greeks and their Gods*. London, 1950. Ch. II.
2. Nilsson, M. P. *Geschichte der griechischen Religion*, I. Ed. 3. Munich, 1967. Section III.
3. Schachermeyr, F. *Poseidon und die Entstehung des griechischen Götterglaubens*. Bern, 1950.

#### A. ADDENDA

##### General

1. Kirk, G. S. *Myth: its Meaning and Functions in Ancient and Other Cultures*. California and Cambridge, 1970.
2. Willetts, R. F. *Cretan Cults and Festivals*. London, 1962.

##### §II

3. Branigan, K. *The Foundations of Palatial Crete*, chs. 5 and 8.
4. Dietrich, B. C. 'Some light from the East on Cretan cult practice.' In *Historia*, 16 (1967), 387 ff.
5. Furumark, A. 'Gods of ancient Crete.' In *Op. Ath.* 6 (1965), 85 ff.
6. Gill, M. A. V. 'The Minoan "Genius".' In *Ath. Mitt.* 79 (1964), 1 ff.
7. Hägg, R. 'Mykenische Kultstätten im archäologischen Material.' In *Op. Ath.* 8 (1968), 39 ff.
8. Hood, S. *The Minoans: Crete in the Bronze Age*, ch. x. London, 1971.
9. Hutchinson, R. W. *Prehistoric Crete*, ch. 8. Harmondsworth, 1962.
10. Mylonas, G. E. *Mycenae and the Mycenaean Age*, chs. VI and VII. Princeton, 1966.
11. Mylonas, G. E. "Ο Ϝάναξ τῶν πινακίδων.' In *Arch. Eph.* (1966), 127 ff.
12. Palmer, L. R. *The Interpretation of Mycenaean Greek Texts*, ch. VI. Oxford, 1963.
13. Schachermeyr, F. *Die minoische Kultur des alten Kreta*, ch. 17. Stuttgart, 1964.
14. Taylour, Lord Wm. 'New Light on Mycenaean Religion.' In *Antiquity*, 44 (1970), 270 ff.

##### §III

15. Brandon, S. G. F. *The Judgment of the Dead: An Historical and Comparative Study of the Idea of a Post-Mortem Judgment in the Major Religions*. London, 1967.
16. Dietrich, B. C. 'Prolegomena to the study of Greek cult continuity.' In *Acta Classica* (Cape Town), 11 (1968), 153 ff.
17. Kerényi, C. *Eleusis: Archetypal Image of Mother and Daughter*. London, 1967.
18. Mylonas, G. E. *Eleusis and the Eleusinian Mysteries*. Princeton, 1962.
19. Puhvel, J. 'Eleuthḗr and Oinoâtis: Dionysiac Data from Mycenaean Greece.' In *Mycenaean Studies*, ed. E. L. Bennett, 161 ff. Madison, 1964.
20. Willetts, R. F. *Ancient Crete: a Social History*. London, 1965.
21. Willetts, R. F. *Cretan Cults and Festivals*. London, 1962.

§IV

22. Hesiod, *Theogony* (ed. M. L. West, with prolegomena and commentary). Oxford, 1966. (Bibliography on Near Eastern Mythology, pp. 106–7.)
23. Walcot, P. *Hesiod and the Near East.* Cardiff, 1966.
24. Adkins, A. W. H. *From the Many to the One,* chs. 2 and 3. London, 1970.
25. Adkins, A. W. H. *Merit and Responsibility: a Study in Greek Values.* Oxford, 1960.
26. Dietrich, B. C. *Death, Fate and the Gods: the Development of a Religious Idea in Greek Popular Belief and in Homer.* London, 1965.
27. Lesky, A. *Göttliche und Menschliche Motivation im homerischen Epos* (Sitzb. Heidelb. Akad., philos.-hist. Klasse, Jg. 1961). Heidelberg, 1961.


§VI

28. Kardara, C. "Ὑπαίθριοι στῦλοι καὶ δένδρα, ὡς μέσα ἐπιφανείας τοῦ θεοῦ τοῦ κερκυνοῦ.' In *Arch. Eph.* (1966), 149 ff.
29. Severyns, A. *Les dieux d'Homère.* Paris, 1966.
30. Wiesner, J. 'Der Künstlergott Hephaistos und seine aussergriechischen Beziehungen in kretisch-mykenischer Zeit.' In *Arch. Anz.* (1968), 167 ff.

# CHRONOLOGICAL TABLES

# (A) EGYPT

## Kings from the Eighteenth to the Twenty-first Dynasties

### EIGHTEENTH DYNASTY: 1570–1320 B.C.

| | |
|---|---|
| Nebpehtyre Amosis | 1570–1546 B.C. |
| Djeserkare Amenophis I | 1546–1526 B.C. |
| Akheperkare Tuthmosis I | 1525–*c.* 1512 B.C. |
| Akheperenre Tuthmosis II | *c.* 1512–1504 B.C. |
| Makare Hatshepsut | 1503–1482 B.C. |
| Menkheperre Tuthmosis III (21)* | 1504–1450 B.C. |
| Akheprure Amenophis II | 1450–1425 B.C. |
| Menkheprure Tuthmosis IV | 1425–1417 B.C. |
| Nebmare Amenophis III | 1417–1379 B.C. |
| Neferkheprure Amenophis IV (Akhenaten) | 1379–1362 B.C. |
| (Ankhkheprure) Smenkhkare (3)* | 1364–1361 B.C. |
| Nebkheprure Tutankhamun | 1361–1352 B.C. |
| Kheperkheprure Ay | 1352–1348 B.C. |
| Djeserkheprure Horemheb | 1348–1320 B.C. |

### NINETEENTH DYNASTY: 1320–1200 B.C.

| | |
|---|---|
| Menpehtyre Ramesses I | 1320–1318 B.C. |
| Menmare Sethos I | 1318–1304 B.C. |
| Usermare Ramesses II | 1304–1237 B.C. |
| Baenre Merneptah | 1236–1223 B.C. |
| Menmare Amenmesses† | 1222–1217 B.C. (?) |
| Userkheprure Sethos II | 1216–1210 B.C. (?) |
| Akhenre-setepenre Merneptah Siptah‡ ⎫ | |
| Sitre-meryetamun Tewosret ⎭ | 1209–1200 B.C. (?) |

### TWENTIETH DYNASTY: 1200–1085 B.C.

| | |
|---|---|
| Userkhaure Sethnakhte | 1200–1198 B.C. |
| Usermare-meryamun Ramesses III | 1198–1166 B.C. |
| Usermare-setepenamun§ Ramesses IV | 1166–1160 B.C. |
| Usermare-sekheperenre Ramesses V | 1160–1156 B.C. |
| Nebmare-meryamun Ramesses VI | 1156–1148 B.C. |
| Usermare-meryamun-setepenre Ramesses VII | 1148–1147 B.C. |
| Usermare-akhenamun Ramesses VIII | 1147–1140 B.C. |
| Neferkare-setepenre Ramesses IX | 1140–1121 B.C. |
| Khepermare-setepenre Ramesses X | 1121–1113 B.C. |
| Menmare-setepenptah Ramesses XI | 1113–1085 B.C. |

\* Years of co-regency with his predecessor.     † Position in Dynasty uncertain.
‡ Also named Sekhaenre Ramesses Siptah.
§ Later named Hikmare-setepenamun.

TWENTY-FIRST DYNASTY: 1085–945 B.C.

Highest recorded year

| | |
|---|---|
| Hedjkheperre-setepenre Smendes | — |
| Neferkare-hikwast Amenemnisu | — |
| Akheperre-setepenamun Psusennes I | 19 |
| Usermare-setepenamun Amenemope | 49 |
| Nutekheperre-setepenamun Siamun | 17 |
| Titkheprure-setepenamun Psusennes II | — |

HIGH PRIESTS OF AMUN AT THEBES FROM RAMESSES XI TO PSUSENNES II

Hrihor
Piankh
Pinudjem I
Masahert
Menkheperre
Nesbenebded
Pinudjem II

## (B) WESTERN ASIA, FOURTEENTH TO TENTH CENTURIES B.C.

| DATE | ISRAEL | KHATTI | AMURRU | CARCHEMISH | UGARIT | MITANNI | ELAM | ASSYRIA | BABYLONIA | DATE |
|---|---|---|---|---|---|---|---|---|---|---|
| 1390 | | Tudkhaliash III (son of Khattushilish II) | 'Abdi-Ashirta | | Ammistamru I | Tushratta (brother of Artashshumara) c. 1385– | | Eriba-Adad I (27) 1392–1366 | Kadashman-Enlil I (son of Kurigalzu I?) | 1390 |
| 1350 | | Shuppiluliumash I (son) | Aziru | Piyashilish | Niqmaddu II (son) | Shuttarna III | | Ashur-uballit I (36) 1365–1330 | Burnaburiash II (29) c. 1375–1347 | 1350 |
| | | Arnuwandash II (son) | | Sharre-Kushukh | Ar-Khalbu (son) | Kurtiwaza (son of Tushratta) | | | Karakhardash | |
| | | Murshilish II (brother) | | | | | | | Nazibugash | |
| | | | DU-Teshub | …-Sharruma | Niqmepa (brother) | | Khurpatila | Enlil-nirari (10) 1329–1320 | Kurigalzu II (22) 1345–1324 | |
| | | | Tuppi-Teshub | Shakhurunuwash | | | Pakhir-ishshan | Arik-den-ili (12) 1319–1308 | Nazimaruttash (26) 1323–1298 | |
| | | Muwatallish (son) | | | | | | | | |
| 1300 | Captivity in Egypt | | | | | Shattuara I | | Adad-nirari I (33) 1307–1275 | | 1300 |
| | | Urkhi-Teshub (son) | Bente-shina | | | Wasashatta (son) | Attar-kittakh (brother) | | Kadashman-Turgu (18) 1297–1280 | |
| | | Khattushilish III (son of Murshilish II) | Shapilish | | | | Khumban-numena | | Kadashman-Enlil II (15) 1279–1265 | |
| | | | Bente-shina | Ini-Teshub | Ammistamru II (son) | Shattuara II | | Shalmaneser I (30) 1274–1245 | Kudur-Enlil (9) 1264–1256 | |
| | | | | | | | Untash-dGAL (son) | | | |
| | | | | | | | | | Shagarakti-Shuriash (13) 1255–1243 | |
| 1250 | Exodus | Tudkhaliash IV (son) | Shaushga-muwash | | | | Unpatar-dGAL c. 1245– | Tukulti-Ninurta I (37) 1244–1208 | Kashtiliash IV (8) 1242–1235 | 1250 |

1234–1228

Enlil-nādin-shumi (3)

(brother)

Kadashman-Kharbe
1227–1225

Adad-shuma-iddina (6)
1224–1219

Adad-shuma-uṣur (30)
1218–1189

Arnuwandash III
(son)

Ibiranu (son)

Ashur-nādin-apli
(4)
1207–1204

Ashur-nīrāri III (6)
1203–1198

Khallutush-In-
Shushinak

Niqmaddu III
(son)
'Ammurapi

Shuppiluliumash II
(brother)

*First settlement in
Canaan, c. 1230*

1200

Enlil-kudurri-uṣur
(5)
1197–1193

Ninurta-apil-Ekur
(13)
1192–1180

Talmi-Teshub

*Judges*
*c. 1200–1020*

*End of Khatti*
*c. 1200*

1200

Meli-Shikhu (15)
1188–1174

Shutruk-Nahhunte
(son)

Marduk-apla-iddina
(13)
1173–1161

Ashur-dan I

Zababa-shuma-iddina
(1)
1160

(+6)

Kutir-Nahhunte

Enlil-nādin-akhi (3)
1159–1157

Ninurta-
tukulti-
Ashur

1150

Marduk-kabit-ahhēshu
(18)
1156–1139

Shilkhak-In-
Shushinak
(brother)

Mutakkil-
Nusku
1179–1134

Itti-Marduk-balāṭu (8)
1138–1131

1150

| DATE | ISRAEL | KHATTI | AMURRU | CARCHEMISH | UGARIT | MITANNI | ELAM | ASSYRIA | BABYLONIA | DATE |
|---|---|---|---|---|---|---|---|---|---|---|
| 1100 | | | | | | | Khutelutush-In-Shushinak | Ashur-rēsha-ishi I (18) 1133–1116 | Ninurta-nādin-shumi (6) 1130–1125 | |
| | | | | | | | | Tiglath-pileser I (39) 1115–1077 | Nebuchadrezzar I (22) 1124–1103 | 1100 |
| | | | | | | | Silkhina-khamru-Lakamar (brother) | | Enlil-nādin-apli (4) 1102–1099 | |
| | | | | | | | | | Marduk-nādin-ahhē (18) 1098–1081 | |
| 1050 | | | | | | | | Ashared-apil-Ekur (2) 1076–1075 | Marduk-shāpik-zēri (13) 1080–1068 | |
| | | | | | | | | Ashur-bēl-kala (18) 1074–1057 | Adad-apla-iddina (22) 1067–1046 | |
| | | | | | | | | Eriba-Adad II (2) 1056–1055 | | 1050 |
| | | | | | | | | Shamshi-Adad IV (4) 1054–1051 | | |
| | | | | | | | | Ashurnasirpal I (19) 1050–1032 | Marduk-ahhē-eriba (1) 1045 | |

| | | |
|---|---|---|
| | | 1000 |
| | | Saul c. 1020–1000 |
| | | David c. 1000–960 |
| | | Solomon c. 960–930 |

| | | |
|---|---|---|
| Marduk-zēr-[x] (12) 1044–1033 | Shalmaneser II (12) 1031–1020 | |
| Nabu-shumu-libur (8) 1032–1025 | Ashur-nirari IV (6) 1019–1014 | |
| Simbar-Shikhu (18) 1024–1007 | Ashur-rabi II (41) 1013–973 | |
| Ea-mukin-zēri (5 mos.) 1007 | | |
| Kashshu-nādin-akhi (3) 1006–1004 | | |
| E-ulmash-shakin-shumi (7) 1003–987 | | |
| 1000 Ninurta-kudurri-usur (3) 986–984 | Ashur-rēsha-ishi II (5) 972–968 | |
| Shirikti-Shuqamuna (3 mos.) 984 | Tigleth-pileser II (33) 967–935 | |
| Mar-biti-apla-usur (6) 983–978 | | |

# (C) CRETE, THE AEGEAN ISLANDS
# AND MAINLAND GREECE

(Note: Items in *italics* refer to legendary events. Datings are given by
centuries and are not to be regarded as precise. F.H.S.)

| B.C. | CRETE | AEGEAN ISLANDS | MAINLAND GREECE |
|---|---|---|---|
| 1300 | | | LATE HELLADIC IIIb begins<br>Myc. trading settlements in Cyprus and ? Syria (Ras Shamra) |
| | LATE MINOAN IIIb | Aḫḫiava (? of Rhodes) in conflict with Hittites in S.W. Asia Minor & Eastern Mediterranean | Mycenaean trade with Tell Abu Hawam near Haifa; but trade with Cyprus declines |
| | | Miletus (Millawanda) destroyed and re-fortified (? against Ahhiyawa) | |
| 1200 | | | TROJAN WAR<br>Wall at Isthmus built<br>*First attempted return of Heraclidae*<br>Destruction at Mycenae, Zygouries, etc., etc.<br>Athenian acropolis strengthened<br>Sack of Pylus |
| ?1180 | Some revival of intercourse with Mainland Greece (apparent in pottery style) | Rhodes trading with Attica & S. Italy | LATE HELLADIC IIIc begins<br>Increased Myc. settlement in Achaea and Cephallenia<br>'Close Style' pottery<br>Myc. IIIc pottery appears in Cyprus and at Tarsus<br>*Teucer founds Salamis (Cyprus)*<br>*Amphilochus and Mopsus in Cilicia* |

| B.C. | CRETE | AEGEAN ISLANDS | MAINLAND GREECE |
|---|---|---|---|
| ?1180 (*cont.*) | | | LATE HELLADIC IIIC begins |
| | | | Dorian incursions |
| | | | (*Return of Heraclidae*) |
| | | | 'Granary class' pottery |
| | | | ? Further Myc. migration to Cyprus |
| | | Destruction of walls at Miletus | Destruction of Iolcus |
| 1100 | | | Final sack of Mycenae |

# INDEX TO MAPS

*The Arabic definite article (Al-, El-, etc.) has been disregarded as an element in the alphabetical arrangement of place-names. For example, El-Amarna is to be found under 'A'.*

# GENERAL INDEX

*The Arabic definite article (Al-, El- etc.) has been disregarded as an element in the alphabetical arrangement of place-names. For example, El-Amarna is to be found under 'A'.*

*Apart from the above, the order of main headings is strictly alphabetical by letters, e.g. Tanis, Tan-Uli, Tan Ware.*

*Bold figures indicate main references; italic figures indicate illustrations, plans and diagrams.*

*All dates are B.C. unless otherwise indicated.*

Aakhitek (district of Elam), 383, 384
'Abdi-Ashirta of Amurru, 9–11 *passim*, 83, 84, 100
'Abdi-Kheba of Jerusalem, 105, 110, 114; letter of, *quoted*, 116 & n (5)
Abiba'al of Byblos, 521, 525
Āb-i Diz river, in Elam, 393, 408
Abiezer (clan/family of Manasseh tribe), 554–7 *passim*
Abimelech (son of Gideon), 554, 557, 570
Abimelech of Gerar and Shechem, 115, 310, 315
Abi-milki of Tyre, 15, 101–2, 104, 508
ablution rites, Elamite, 411–12, 497
Abner (King Saul's cousin and commander of levies), 573, 577, 579, 584
Abraham (patriarch), 113, 308–15 *passim*, 320, 531
Absalom (son of David), 586
Abu Ghurāb, sanctuary of Re, 58
Abu Ḥabbah (Sippar), 462, 471
Abuli of Uqumeni, 284
Abu Simbel, in Nubia, 230–2 *passim*, 238, 249
Abydos, in Upper Egypt, 52, 222–5, 226, 230–1, 249, 610, 646
Acarnanes, 701
Acarnania, 347, 700
Accho (Acre, *q.v.*, Map 11), princes of, 110, 114
Achaea (Maps, 3, 12), 166, 207, 659–67 *passim*, 671, 700, 702, 703
Achaea: colonization of Cyprus, **207–9**, 211; cemeteries, 665; Catalogue (*see also* Catalogue of Ships), 687, 700, 701, 831, 832, 836, 837, 843–4; kingdoms, 787; palace-states, 841; culture of Late Bronze Age, 842
Achaeans (*Achaioi*), 119, 339, 347, 348, 365, 370, 686, 694, 702–5 *passim*, 853, 896, 897; capture and destroy Troy, 163; 'sub-Achaeans' of Cilicia, 365; and Akawasha, *q.v.*, 367; and Rhodes, 371; Dorian victory over, 694, 695; in

Asia Minor, 788; in Rhodes and Cos, 790–1; and Mycenae, 856
Achaemenids (Iranian dynasty), 422, 437, 699
Achan, stoning of, 546
Achilles, 347, 687, 688, 801, 855, 896, 897; his shield (in Homer), 848
Achish of Gath, 552, 578
Achor, valley of, 546
Achshaph, princes of, 110, 114
Acre (Accho, *q.v.*, Map 11): Bay of, 182; plain of, 110, 114, 511, 512; port of, 220
Adad (Assyrian and Babylonian god), 386, 403, 405, 409–10, 458, 479; his pseudonyms, 409; and Shala, 409–10 *passim*, 461 & n (5), 464; shrine in Babylon, 457; in Elam, 392, 396
Adad-apla-iddina of Babylonia, 42, 448, 466–7, 469, 478, 533
Adad-nīrāri I of Assyria (r. 1307–1275, son of Arik-dēn-ili), 30, 31, 255, 258, 282, 291, 299; claims title of 'Great King', 258; and Khattushilish III of Khatti, 258, 277, 278–9; his campaigns, **274–9**; and Khanigalbat, 276–8, 296, 299; and Shattuara I, 255, 276–8 *passim*; and Urkhi-Teshub and Muwatallish, 277; his inscriptions, 296, 297; and Nazimaruttash, 275 & n, 298; his riverine works, 299, 468
Adad-nīrāri II of Assyria (r. 911–891, son of Ashur-dan II), 470, 535
Adad-nīrāri Epic, 275 & n, 298
Adad-shuma-iddina of Babylonia (r. 1224–1219), 288–90 *passim*, 300, 388, 443–5 *passim*; 'founder of cities', 300
Adad-shuma-usur of Babylonia (r. 1218–1189, a son of Kashtiliash IV), 288–9, 388, 443–5 *passim*, 450, 479, 483
Adana (city), 365 & n (6), 442, 680
Addaura, in Sicily (Map 14), 723–4
administration and law in Assyria and Babylonia, **474–7**

366 n (4), 664, 671, 672–3, 882–3, 898;
Philistine, 334, 374; in Sardinia,
736–42 passim; in Sicily, 729, 732,
734; see also cremation, graves, inhumation and tombs
Burnaburiash II, Kassite king of Babylon,
13, 16, 34, 38; his letters to the ruler
of Egypt, 24–6, 29; and Syrian menace,
26; and Assyrians, 26, 28–31
Bushire, 'island' of, 405, 485, 493
Buṣruna, in Bashan, prince of, 104
Büyükkale, in Anatolia, see Boğazköy
Byblians (of Byblos), 518
Byblos (Gubla, q.v., Maps 1, 4), 83, 131,
137, 182, 235, 362, 461, 517, 642, 643,
656; correspondence, 101, 110; princes
of, 108, 515 (see also Rib-Adda); king
of, 134, 519; Egyptian troops at, 137,
252; temple, 148, 149; Tjekker at, 376;
accepts Egyptian suzerainty, 521; and
Sidon, 521, 522; and Tyre, 522;
Wenamun at, 642–3

Cabul, in Galilee (Map 11), 587
Cáceres, in Spain, 524, 525
Cadmea (palace-citadel of Thebes (Greece)),
169
Cadmeïs (later Boeotia, q.v.), 686, 688,
690
Cadmus (god or hero), 166–7, 886; House
of, 169
Cain (Israelite tribe, Kenites, q.v.), 327,
552
cairns (heaps of stones), 903–4; sacred, 865,
869, 878, 904
Cairo Museum, 98, 237, 247, 655
Calabria, in southern Italy, 714, 716, 721,
723
Calchas (prophet, seer), 355, 364, 679
Caldare, in Sicily (Map 14), 734
Caleb the Kenizzite, 328; tribe or clan of,
328
calendar, Assyrian and Babylonian, 476–7
Callinus of Ephesus (epic poet), 355, 679
Callisto (a nymph) in Arcadia, 903
Calydnae (island, Map 10), 681, 689
Calydon (Maps 3, 8), 167; siege of, 347
Calymnos, Calymnus (island, Maps 3, 12,
16), 667
camels, 310, 314, 515, 532, 536, 770; riding
(dromedaries), 310, 536, 553
Camirus, in Rhodes (Maps 10, 16), 792
Cammania, 701
Campania, in southern Italy (Map 5), 356,
357, 715, 717, 722
Camp de Chassey, in southern France, 746,
751

Camp de Peu-Richard, in southern France,
747
Canaan (son of Noah), 316
'Canaan', derivation of the name, 520
Canaan, land of, 234, 316, 318; and
Ugarit, 141; gods of, called 'Ba'al',
153; the patriarchs in, 307–9, 314–19,
541; decisive invasion of, by Israel,
310; and the 'promised land', 314;
conquest of, and final settlement in, by
Israelites, 315, 316, 325, 541–8
Canaanite: amphorae, 184; bronzes, 561;
cult practices, institutions and music,
565; culture, 334; deities, 151–8;
extension of the term, 130 n; festivals
(agricultural), 564; gems, 561; ivories,
305, 561; language(s) and idiom(s),
109, 115, 136, 565–9 passim: North
(Ugaritic, q.v.), 136, 530; South
(Phoenician, q.v.), 530); laws and
regulations, 563–4, 569; literature,
152–60 passim, 566, 567, 568; merchants, 111; military organization;
575; morale, 105; pantheon, 309, 310;
princes (called 'kings'), 104, 115;
religion (and literature), 130, 148–58;
revival in Phoenicia, 516–26; school of
art, 305; scribes, 99, 104, 115; seals,
561; temples (Late Bronze Age), 149;
towns destroyed, 514; word for
'peasant' or 'serf', 110; writing, 569
Canaanites, 25, 81, 99, 101, 102, 104, 111,
112, 134; and Babylon, 25; of Gibeon,
110; and Hittites, 143–4; and divination, 151; Eastern 312; and Hebrews
in Palestine, 331–7, 545–8 passim;
and Israelites, 149–50, 311, 328, 517,
553, 554, 559–60, 560–9, 576–7, 585,
591
cannibalism in Babylonia (due to famine),
465
Cantabria, in Spain, 757–9 passim
Cap d'Agde, shipwreck off, 752
Caphtor (son of Miṣraim (Egypt)), 374
Caphtor (Crete or Cilicia, see also Kaphtor),
158, 375
Capo Graziano culture and ware, in Lipari
(Map 5), 731–3 passim
Cappadocia and Cappadocians, 421, 422
Capri (island, Map 14), 716
caravaneers, donkey, 114, 532
caravan routes (trade routes, see also communications), 131, 182, 582–3, 587,
592, 593
caravans, 113–14, 532; between Babylon
and Egypt, 25, 131; of 20th and 19th
centuries B.C., 113; donkey, 113, 114

233, 242, 243; against Peoples of the Sea, *q.v.*, 242–3, 372; Libyans in, 618 & n, 619 (*see also above and* Libyans)

Demeter, Eleusinian (goddess of vegetation), 784, 871, 877 n, 878, 880–1 *passim*, 900

Demir Kapu (Map 13), 708

demons and demonesses, 413; on seals, 303, 304 (*see also* daemons)

Dendra, near Midea (Map 3), 175–8 *passim*

Denyen, 242, 339–40, 371, 377, 508; *see also* Danuna

deportation and replacement of defeated peoples, 451, 462

deposition ceremony, Assyrian, 300

Dēr, in Babylonia (*modern* Badrah), 290, 388, 444, 455, 467, 502

Ed-Derr, in Nubia, 230

desert-dwellers, invading Egypt (*see also* Libyans), 617–18

destruction of ancient towns, possible causes of, 333

Deuteronomist schools, 537

Deuteronomium, 537

devotees (of gods and goddesses), 151

Dew (Canaanite goddess, daughter of Ba'al), 153, 158

Dhali (Maps 6, 7; *formerly* Idalium, *q.v.*), 193

Dhavlos, in Cyprus (Map 7), 189

Dhenia, in Cyprus (Maps 6, 7), 189

Dhikomo, in Cyprus (Maps 6, 7), 196

Diana culture and pottery (Bellavista), 716–17, 725–7 *passim*, 731

Ed-Dibābīya, in Egypt, 645

Dictynna (goddess), 870, 884, 903

Dinah, story of (Genesis XXXIV), 116

Dinītu (Ishtar, *q.v.*, Assyrian goddess), 299

Dīn-sharri (city), in Elam, 502

Diodorus Siculus, 108, 522, 680, 791, 873, 888

Diomede, 343, 346, 356

Dione ('shadowy' consort of Zeus), 904; of Dodona, 700

Dionysus (god of wine, son of Zeus Sabazius and Semele; *see also* Bacchus), 437, 439, 779, 789, 853, 854, 874, 881; columns, 865; and satyrs, 868; his origins, 881; fertility cult of, 899

Dionysus Omestes, 779

Dirmil, on Halicarnassian peninsula, 440, 674

diseases: and their treatment, 40; incantations against, 151

Disk, the Great, *see* Sun-disk

disputes between kingdoms, 143

divination, 151, 251; Babylonian, 43; at Clarus, 364; Hittite, 270; in Malta, 730

divine wrath against offenders, invocation of, 35

divinity of kings, *see* kings

divorces, royal, 142, 145, 262

Diyala (Turnat) river, plain and area, 388, 444, 446, 451, 485, 490, 504; Lower, 486; Upper, 447, 461, 489, 491, 492

Diyarbakr district, 285, 459

Dodecanese islands (Map 12), 663, 666, 673–7 *passim*, 689; Dorians in, 696

Dodona, in southern Epirus (Maps 8, 13), 687–8 *passim*, 690, 699, 708, 710, 904; plains of, 685, 687; and Thebes, 688; shrine of Zeus, 699, 904

Dog River (Nahr el-Kalb, *q.v.*), 255

dogs, 178

dolmens, 733, 740–1, 743, 751, 760

Dolopes, 691, 693

*domus di gianas* (witches' houses), in Sardinia, 737, 742

Domuz Tepe, in Asia Minor, 442

donkey-: caravans, 113, 114 & n (2), 532; nomads, 111

donkeys, 113, 114 n (2), 623

Dor, south of Carmel (Map 11, *modern* El-Burj), 243, 376, 377, 512, 514, 558

Dorian: colonies, 698, 699; games, 792; institutions, 696–9; invaders of Greece (*c.* 1120 B.C.), **681–702**, 703–5 *passim*, 710, 712, 812–13, 815, 816, 819, 842; kingdoms, 697–9 *passim*; kingship, 702; tribal state (Dōrikon), 697, 698, 702; tribes, 697–8 *passim*, 701

Dorians (*general*, Map 13; *see also next below*), 171, 691; invasion of Mycenaean Greece, 343, 354, 357, 358, 660, 685 (reasons for, 693); origins and wanderings of, 681–7, 701; their way of life, 685; and the Heracleidae, 685, 689, 696–8; origin of the name, 688–9; three tribes of (*named*, 689), 697–8; in Crete, 689, 705; in Dodecanese, 696; in Rhodes, 689; their route to the Peloponnese, 691–3; and Arcadia, 691–2; and the Argolid, 692, 702; illiterate, 692; sea-power of, 692–3 *passim*, 695; overseas settlements of, 696; their special gods (*see also* Apollo *and* Zeus), 699; and other invaders (relationships), 700–2; and Ionians, *compared*, 802; in Homer, 843–4

Dorians: before the Trojan War, **681–9**; between the Trojan War and their entry into the Peloponnese, **690–4**; their conquest of the Peloponnese, **694–6**, 842; their institutions, **696–9**;